# America
# Reads

*Projection in Literature*

*Counterpoint in Literature*

*Outlooks through Literature*

*Exploring Life through Literature*

*The United States in Literature*
All My Sons edition

*The United States in Literature*
The Glass Menagerie edition

*England in Literature*
Macbeth edition

*England in Literature*
The Taming of the Shrew edition

**Edmund James Farrell** *Assistant Executive Secretary, National Council of Teachers of English. Formerly Supervisor of Secondary English, University of California, Berkeley; formerly English Department Chairman, James Lick High School, San Jose, California.*

**Mabel H. Pittman** *Instructor of English, Jackson State College, Jackson, Mississippi. Formerly teacher of English, Lanier High School, Jackson, Mississippi; formerly Vice Chairman, English Department, Jackson Public Schools.*

**James L. Pierce** *Teacher of English, Redwood High School, Larkspur, California. Formerly Coordinator of Student Teaching, English Department, University of Illinois, Chicago Circle. Formerly Supervisor of English, Tamalpais Union High-School District, Larkspur, California.*

**Jesse Hilton Stuart** *Author of over forty volumes: novels, biography, autobiography, poetry, and short story collections. Lecturer at the Jesse Stuart Writer's Workshop, Murray State University, Murray, Kentucky. Formerly Lecture Specialist for the U.S. State Department to students and educators throughout the world; formerly high-school English teacher and one-room rural teacher in Kentucky and Ohio public schools.*

# Outlooks
## through
## Literature

**Scott, Foresman and Company** • Glenview, Illinois

Dallas, Tex. • Oakland, N.J. • Palo Alto, Cal. • Tucker, Ga. • Brighton, England

Edmund James Farrell
James L. Pierce
Mabel H. Pittman
Jesse Hilton Stuart

ISBN: 0-673-10209-2

5678910-VHJ-8584838281807978

# Contents

**1**

1–143  **The Short Story**

**4**

**Romeo and Juliet**  282–363

**2**

144–211  **Nonfiction**

**5**

**Classical Heritage**  364–439

**3**

212–281  **Poetry**

**6**

**At Random**  440–540

Composition Guides  541

Handbook of Literary Terms  559

Glossary  594

Index of Titles and Authors  621

Credits  623

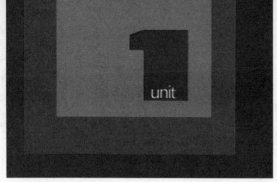

unit 1

# The Short Story

2 **Peter Two**
*Irwin Shaw*

9 **The Most Dangerous Game**
*Richard Connell*

23 **Claudine's Book**
*Harvey Swados*

37 **Luther**
*Jay Neugeboren*

47 **Bargain**
*A. B. Guthrie*

55 **The Endless Streetcar Ride into the Night, and the Tinfoil Noose**
*Jean Shepherd*

61 **The Sky Is Gray**
*Ernest Gaines*

78 **The Lottery Ticket**
*Anton Chekhov*

**The Idealist** 82
*Frank O'Connor*

**Rain on Tanyard Hollow** 89
*Jesse Stuart*

**A Reading Problem** 97
*Jean Stafford*

**The Scarlet Ibis** 111
*James Hurst*

**To Da-duh, in Memoriam** 120
*Paule Marshall*

**The Fifty-first Dragon** 128
*Heywood Broun*

**By the Waters of Babylon** 134
*Stephen Vincent Benét*

unit

# Nonfiction

## Autobiography

146    from *Portrait of Myself*
    Margaret Bourke-White

from *Narrative of the Life of*
161    *Frederick Douglass*
    Frederick Douglass

168    from *Black Elk Speaks*
    John G. Neihardt

## Article and Essay

The Rose-Beetle Man    179
Gerald Durrell

My Planet 'Tis of Thee    186
Isaac Asimov

The Dog That Bit People    194
James Thurber

The Risk Takers    198
Robert Daley

unit **3**

# Poetry

### Responses

214    **Dust of Snow**
*Robert Frost*

215    **Earth Dweller**
*William Stafford*

216    **Song of the Sky Loom**
*Tewa Indian*

217    **Lots of Lakes**
*Ron Loewinsohn*

218    **Aphrodite Metropolis**
*Kenneth Fearing*

219    **Fog**
*Carl Sandburg*

220    **By Morning**
*May Swenson*

221    **The Manoeuvre**
*William Carlos Williams*

### Battlegrounds

**Here Dead Lie We**    226
*A. E. Housman*

**Conscientious Objector**    227
*Edna St. Vincent Millay*

**The Conquerors**    228
*Phyllis McGinley*

**The Mother**    230
*Padraic Pearse*

**My Enemy Was Dreaming**    231
*Norman Russell*

**Grass**    232
*Carl Sandburg*

**There Will Come Soft Rains**    233
*Sara Teasdale*

### Curses

222    **Traveller's Curse After Misdirection**
*Robert Graves*

223    **May He Lose His Way**
*Archilochos*
(Translated by Guy Davenport)

224    **Nine Charms Against the Hunter**
*David Wagoner*

225    **At the Theatre**
To the Lady Behind Me
*Sir A. P. Herbert*

### Portraits

**The Courage That My Mother Had**    234
*Edna St. Vincent Millay*

**Miss Rosie**    235
*Lucille Clifton*

**Melora Vilas**    236
*Stephen Vincent Benét*

**The Bean Eaters**    238
*Gwendolyn Brooks*

**Portrait of a Certain Gentleman**    239
*Sara Henderson Hay*

## Blues

240 **Trouble in Mind**
*Richard M. Jones*

241 **I Used to Be Fairly Poor**
*Han-shan*
**(Translated by Burton Watson)**

242 **The Housewife's Lament**
*Anonymous*

243 **The Whipping**
*Robert Hayden*

244 **Yonder See the Morning Blink**
*A. E. Housman*

245 **Insomniac**
*Patricia Y. Ikeda*

247 **Birthday in the House of the Poor**
*Jeannette Nichols*

## Destinations

248 **Lessons**
*Gerald Jonas*

250 **The Most Perilous Moment in Life**
*César Vallejo*
**(Translated by Clayton Eshleman)**

251 **El Momento más Grave de la Vida**
*César Vallejo*

**How Everything Happens** 252
(Based on a Study of the Wave)
*May Swenson*

**Item** 253
*Howard Nemerov*

**Ka'Ba** 255
*LeRoi Jones (Imamu Amiri Baraka)*

## Phantoms 256

**Haunted** 256
*Amy Lowell*

**The Witch** 257
*Sara Henderson Hay*

**The Skater of Ghost Lake** 258
*William Rose Benét*

**Thirteen O'Clock** 260
*Kenneth Fearing*

**Exposure** 261
*John Updike*

**The Rime of the Ancient Mariner** 262
*Samuel Taylor Coleridge*

unit 4

# Romeo and Juliet

**Act One**

| 287 | scene one |
| 293 | scene two |
| 295 | scene three |
| 297 | scene four |
| 300 | scene five |

**Act Two**

| 306 | scene one |
| 307 | scene two |
| 311 | scene three |
| 314 | scene four |
| 317 | scene five |
| 319 | scene six |

**Act Three**

| 321 | scene one |
| 326 | scene two |
| 329 | scene three |
| 333 | scene four |
| 333 | scene five |

**Act Four**

| 340 | scene one |
| 343 | scene two |
| 344 | scene three |
| 347 | scene four |
| 348 | scene five |

**Act Five**

| 350 | scene one |
| 352 | scene two |
| 353 | scene three |

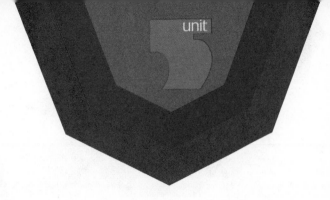

unit 5

# Classical Heritage

## Myth

369 **The Story of Daedalus and Icarus**
*Ovid*
(Translated by Rolfe Humphries)

371 **The Story of Cadmus**
*Ovid*
(Translated by Rolfe Humphries)

## Epic

376 **The Surprise**
*John Masefield*

381 **The Flight of Aeneas**
*Virgil*
(Translated by C. D. Lewis)

389 **Odysseus in Ithaca**
(Retold from the ancient authors by Roger Lancelyn Green)

## Philosophers and Poets

394 **The Prophecy of Socrates**
*Plato*
(Translated by Benjamin Jowett)

396 **The Death of Socrates**
*Plato*

(Greek and Latin Poems translated by Dudley Fitts, Richmond Lattimore, Guy Davenport, and C. H. Sisson)

398 **Dedication of a Mirror**
*Plato*

398 **Inscription for the Tomb of Timon**
*Ptolemaios the Astrologer*

398 **Hesiod, Fortunate Deliverance From**
*Marcus Argentarius*

398 **Epitaph for Slain Spartans**
*Simonides of Ceos*

**On a Fortune-Teller** 399
*Lucilius*

**The Warrior of the Past** 399
*Mimnermus of Colophon*

**On Mauros the Rhetor** 399
*Palladas*

**I Do Despise a Tall General** 400
*Archilochos*

**Some Saian Mountaineer** 400
*Archilochos*

**The Fox and the Hedgehog** 400
*Archilochos*

**The Good-Natured** 401
*Archilochos*

**There's Nothing Now** 401
*Archilochos*

**When You Upbraid Me** 401
*Archilochos*

**Suffenus, Varus, Whom You Know So Well** 402
*Catullus*

**Lesbia Is Always Talking Scandal About Me** 402
*Catullus*

**My Woman Says There Is No One She Would Rather Marry** 402
*Catullus*

**Living, Dear Lesbia, Is Useless Without Loving** 402
*Catullus*

## Drama

**Antigone** 406
*Sophocles*
(Translated by E. F. Watling)

Unit

# At Random

## Short Story

442    **The Highland Boy**
*Leslie Norris*

449    **Forbidden Fries**
*Giovanni Guareschi*
(Translated by Gordon Sager)

454    **Between the Dark and the Daylight**
*Nancy Hale*

## Poetry

458    **Running**
*Richard Wilbur*

459    **Daybreak in Alabama**
*Langston Hughes*

460    **freddy the rat perishes**
*Don Marquis*

461    **dying is fine)but Death**
*E. E. Cummings*

463    ***Vale* from Carthage**
*Peter Viereck*

464    **Wild Grapes**
*Robert Frost*

## Autobiography

**from *Barrio Boy***    468
*Ernesto Galarza*

## Article and Essay

**Vulture Country**    483
*John D. Stewart*

**Outwitting the Lightning**    489
*Wolcott Gibbs*

**Fire Walking in Ceylon**    492
*Leonard Feinberg*

## Drama

**Visit to a Small Planet**    498
*Gore Vidal*

**The Mother**    516
*Paddy Chayefsky*

# Composition Guides

*Introduction* 541
**Lesson One:** *Explanation* 542
**Lesson Two:** *Opinions* 542
**Lesson Three:** *Character Sketch* 543
**Lesson Four:** *Explanation* 543
**Lesson Five:** *Description* 544
**Lesson Six:** *Opinions* 545
**Lesson Seven:** *Criticism* 545
**Lesson Eight:** *Evaluation* 545
**Lesson Nine:** *Persuasion* 546
**Lesson Ten:** *Personal Experience* 546
**Lesson Eleven:** *Opinions* 547
**Lesson Twelve:** *Description* 547
**Lesson Thirteen:** *Opinions* 548
**Lesson Fourteen:** *Comparison And Contrast* 548
**Lesson Fifteen:** *Character Sketch* 549

**Lesson Sixteen:** *Interpretation* 549
**Lesson Seventeen:** *Interpretation* 549
**Lesson Eighteen:** *Personal Experience* 550
**Lesson Nineteen:** *Interpretation* 550
**Lesson Twenty:** *Analysis of Character* 551
**Lesson Twenty-one:** *Dialogue* 552
**Lesson Twenty-two:** *Interpretation* 552
**Lesson Twenty-three:** *Myths* 553
**Lesson Twenty-four:** *Explanation* 554
**Lesson Twenty-five:** *Persuasion* 554
**Lesson Twenty-six:** *Persuasion* 555
**Lesson Twenty-seven:** *Script Writing* 555
**Lesson Twenty-eight:** *Description* 555
**Lesson Twenty-nine:** *Character Sketch* 556
**Lesson Thirty:** *Explanation* 556

# Supplementary Articles

Of Beginnings . . . 35
. . . and Endings 77
Everybody Talks About the Weather . . . 96
Symbolism in "The Scarlet Ibis" 119
Dragons 133
Biblical Allusions 142
Reading Poetry Aloud 259
A Little Stage History . . . and Film History 362
From Greek and Latin into English 438

# Handbook of Literary Terms

Atmosphere 559
Autobiography and Biography 560
Characterization 562
Dialogue 565
Fantasy 566
Figurative Language 568
Foreshadowing 570
Imagery 571
Inference 572
Irony 574
Plot 576
Point of View 579
Rhyme and Sound Devices 582
Rhythm 583
Satire 584
Setting 585
Soliloquy 586
Symbol 588
Theme 590
Tone 591

# 1

## The
## Short
## Story

# Peter Two

*Irwin Shaw*

**He was alone, and it was late. He wasn't sure where the screams were coming from until he turned off the television. Then he knew.**

IT was Saturday night and people were killing each other by the hour on the small screen. Policemen were shot in the line of duty, gangsters were thrown off roofs, and an elderly lady was slowly poisoned for her pearls, and her murderer brought to justice by a cigarette company after a long series of discussions in the office of a private detective. Brave, unarmed actors leaped at villains holding forty-fives, and ingénues were saved from death by the knife by the quick thinking of various handsome and intrepid young men.

Peter sat in the big chair in front of the screen, his feet up over the arm, eating grapes. His mother wasn't home, so he ate the seeds and all as he stared critically at the violence before him. When his mother was around, the fear of appendicitis hung in the air and she watched

carefully to see that each seed was neatly extracted and placed in an ashtray. Too, if she were home, there would be irritated little lectures on the quality of television entertainment for the young, and quick-tempered fiddling with the dials to find something that was vaguely defined as educational. Alone, daringly awake at eleven o'clock, Peter ground the seeds between his teeth, enjoying the impolite noise and the solitude and freedom of the empty house. During the television commercials Peter closed his eyes and imagined himself hurling bottles at large unshaven men with pistols and walking slowly up dark stairways toward the door behind which everyone knew the Boss was waiting, the bulge of his shoulder holster unmistakable under the cloth of his pencil-striped flannel jacket.

Peter was thirteen years old. In his class there were three other boys with the same given name, and the history teacher, who thought he was a funny man, called them Peter One, Peter Two (now eating grapes, seeds and all), Peter

Three, and Peter the Great.[1] Peter the Great was, of course, the smallest boy in the class. He weighed only sixty-two pounds, and he wore glasses, and in games he was always the last one to be chosen. The class always laughed when the history teacher called out "Peter the Great," and Peter Two laughed with them, but he didn't think it was so awfully funny.

He had done something pretty good for Peter the Great two weeks ago, and now they were what you might call friends. All the Peters were what you might call friends, on account of that comedian of a history teacher. They weren't *real* friends, but they had something together, something the other boys didn't have. They didn't like it, but they had it, and it made them responsible for each other. So two weeks ago, when Charley Blaisdell, who weighed a hundred and twenty, took Peter the Great's cap at recess and started horsing around with it, and

Peter the Great looked as if he was going to cry, he, Peter Two, grabbed the cap and gave it back and faced Blaisdell. Of course, there was a fight, and Peter thought it was going to be his third defeat of the term, but a wonderful thing happened. In the middle of the fight, just when Peter was hoping one of the teachers would show up (they sure showed up plenty of times when you didn't need them), Blaisdell let a hard one go. Peter ducked and Blaisdell hit him on the top of the head and broke his arm. You could tell right off he broke his arm, because he fell to the ground yelling, and his arm just hung like a piece of string. Walters, the gym teacher, finally showed up and carried Blaisdell off, yelling all the time, and Peter the Great came up and said admiringly, "Boy, one thing you have to admit, you sure have a hard head."

Blaisdell was out of class two days, and he still had his arm in the sling, and every time he was excused from writing on the blackboard because he had a broken arm, Peter got a nice warm feeling all over. Peter the Great hung

---

1. *Peter One. . . . Peter the Great.* Peter I (also called Peter the Great), Peter II, and Peter III were emperors of Russia in the seventeenth and eighteenth centuries.

around him all the time, doing things for him and buying him sodas, because Peter the Great's parents were divorced and gave him all the money he wanted, to make up to him. And that was O.K.

But the best thing was the feeling he'd had since the fight. It was like what the people on the television must feel after they'd gone into a room full of enemies and come out with the girl or with the papers or with the suspect, leaving corpses and desolation behind them. Blaisdell weighed a hundred and twenty pounds but that hadn't stopped Peter any more than the fact that the spies all had two guns apiece ever stopped the F.B.I. men on the screen. They saw what they had to do and they went in and did it, that was all. Peter couldn't phrase it for himself, but for the first time in his life he had a conscious feeling of confidence and pride in himself.

"Let them come," he muttered obscurely, munching grape seeds and watching the television set through narrowed eyes, "just let them come."

He was going to be a dangerous man, he felt, when he grew up, but one to whom the weak and the unjustly hunted could safely turn. He was sure he was going to be six feet tall, because his father was six feet tall, and all his uncles, and that would help. But he would have to develop his arms. They were just too thin. After all, you couldn't depend on people breaking their bones on your head every time. He had been doing pushups each morning and night for the past month. He could only do five and a half at a time so far, but he was going to keep at it until he had arms like steel bars. Arms like that really could mean the difference between life and death later on, when you had to dive under the gun and disarm somebody. You had to have quick reflexes, too, of course, and be able to feint to one side with your eyes before the crucial moment. And, most important of all, no matter what the odds, you had to be fearless. One moment of hesitation and it was a case for the morgue. But now, after the battle of Peter the Great's cap, he didn't worry about that part of it, the fearless part. From now on, it would just be a question of technique.

Comedians began to appear all over the dial,

laughing with a lot of teeth, and Peter went into the kitchen and got another bunch of grapes and two tangerines from the refrigerator. He didn't put on the light in the kitchen and it was funny how mysterious a kitchen could be near midnight when nobody else was home, and there was only the beam of the light from the open refrigerator, casting shadows from the milk bottles onto the linoleum. Until recently he hadn't liked the dark too much and he always turned on lights wherever he went, but you had to practice being fearless, just like anything else.

He ate the two tangerines standing in the dark in the kitchen, just for practice. He ate the seeds, too, to show his mother. Then he went back into the living room, carrying the grapes.

The comedians were still on and still laughing. He fiddled with the dial, but they were wearing funny hats and laughing and telling jokes about the income tax on all the channels. If his mother hadn't made him promise to go to sleep by ten o'clock, he'd have turned off the set and gone to bed. He decided not to waste his time and got down on the floor and began to do pushups, trying to be sure to keep his knees straight. He was up to four and slowing down when he heard the scream. He stopped in the middle of a pushup and waited, just to make sure. The scream came again. It was a woman and it was real loud. He looked up at the television set. There was a man there talking about floor wax, a man with a mustache and a lot of teeth, and it was a cinch *he* wasn't doing any screaming.

The next time the scream came there was moaning and talking at the end of it, and the sound of fists beating on the front door. Peter got up and turned off the television, just to be sure the sounds he was hearing weren't somehow being broadcast.

The beating on the door began again and a woman's voice cried "Please, please, *please. . .*" and there was no doubt about it any more.

Peter looked around him at the empty room. Three lamps were lit and the room was nice and bright and the light was reflected off the grapes and off the glass of the picture of the boats on Cape Cod that his Aunt Martha painted the year

she was up there. The television set stood in the corner, like a big blind eye now that the light was out. The cushions of the soft chair he had been sitting in to watch the programs were pushed in and he knew his mother would come and plump them out before she went to sleep, and the whole room looked like a place in which it was impossible to hear a woman screaming at midnight and beating on the door with her fists and yelling, "Please, please, *please. . . .*"

The woman at the door yelled "Murder, murder, he's killing me!" and for the first time Peter was sorry his parents had gone out that night.

"Open the door!" the woman yelled. "Please, *please* open the door!" You could tell she wasn't saying please just to be polite by now.

Peter looked nervously around him. The room, with all its lights, seemed strange, and there were shadows behind everything. Then the woman yelled again, just noise this time. Either a person is fearless, Peter thought coldly,

or he isn't fearless. He started walking slowly toward the front door. There was a long mirror in the foyer and he got a good look at himself. His arms looked very thin.

The woman began hammering once more on the front door and Peter looked at it closely. It was a big steel door, but it was shaking minutely, as though somebody with a machine was working on it. For the first time he heard another voice. It was a man's voice, only it didn't sound quite like a man's voice. It sounded like an animal in a cave, growling and deciding to do something unreasonable. In all the scenes of threat and violence on the television set, Peter had never heard anything at all like it. He moved slowly toward the door, feeling the way he had felt when he had the flu, remembering how thin his arms looked in the mirror, regretting that he had decided to be fearless.

"Oh, God!" the woman yelled, "Oh, God, don't do it!"

Then there was some more hammering and

the low, animal sound of the beast in the cave that you never heard over the air, and he threw the door open.

Mrs. Chalmers was there in the vestibule, on her knees, facing him, and behind her Mr. Chalmers was standing, leaning against the wall, with the door to his own apartment open behind him. Mr. Chalmers was making that funny sound and he had a gun in his hand and he was pointing it at Mrs. Chalmers.

The vestibule was small and it had what Peter's mother called Early American wallpaper and a brass light fixture. There were only the two doors opening on the vestibule, and the Chalmerses had a mat in front of theirs with "Welcome" written on it. The Chalmerses were in their mid-thirties, and Peter's mother always said about them, "One thing about our neighbors, they *are* quiet." She also said that Mrs. Chalmers put a lot of money on her back.

Mrs. Chalmers was kind of fat and her hair was pretty blond and her complexion was soft and pink and she always looked as though she had been in the beauty parlor all afternoon. She always said "My, you're getting to be a big boy" to Peter when she met him in the elevator, in a soft voice, as though she was just about to laugh. She must have said that fifty times by now. She had a good, strong smell of perfume on her all the time, too.

Mr. Chalmers wore pince-nez glasses most of the time and he was getting bald and he worked late at his office a good many evenings of the week. When he met Peter in the elevator he would say, "It's getting colder," or "It's getting warmer," and that was all, so Peter had no opinion about him, except that he looked like the principal of a school.

But now Mrs. Chalmers was on her knees in the vestibule and her dress was torn and she was crying and there were black streaks on her cheeks and she didn't look as though she'd just come from the beauty parlor. And Mr. Chalmers wasn't wearing a jacket and he didn't have his glasses on and what hair he had was mussed all over his head and he was leaning against the Early American wallpaper making this animal noise, and he had a big, heavy pistol in his hand and he was pointing it right at Mrs. Chalmers.

"Let me in!" Mrs. Chalmers yelled, still on her knees. "You've got to let me in. He's going to kill me. *Please!*"

"Mrs. Chalmers. . ." Peter began. His voice sounded as though he were trying to talk under water, and it was very hard to say the "s" at the end of her name. He put out his hands uncertainly in front of him, as though he expected somebody to throw him something.

"Get inside, you," Mr. Chalmers said.

Peter looked at Mr. Chalmers. He was only five feet away and without his glasses he was squinting. Peter feinted with his eyes, or at least later in his life he thought he had feinted with his eyes. Mr. Chalmers didn't do anything. He just stood there, with the pistol pointed, somehow, it seemed to Peter, at both Mrs. Chalmers and himself at the same time. Five feet was a long distance, a long, long distance.

"Good night," Peter said, and he closed the door.

There was a single sob on the other side of the door and that was all.

Peter went in and put the uneaten grapes back in the refrigerator, flicking on the light as he went into the kitchen and leaving it on when he went out. Then he went back to the living room and got the stems from the first bunch of grapes and threw them into the fireplace, because otherwise his mother would notice and look for the seeds and not see them and give him four tablespoons of milk of magnesia the next day.

Then, leaving the lights on in the living room, although he knew what his mother would say about that when she got home, he went into his room and quickly got into bed. He waited for the sound of shots. There were two or three noises that might have been shots, but in the city it was hard to tell.

He was still awake when his parents came home. He heard his mother's voice, and he knew from the sound she was complaining about the lights in the living room and kitchen, but he pretended to be sleeping when she came into his room to look at him. He didn't want to start in with his mother about the Chalmerses, because then she'd ask when it had happened and she'd want to know what he was doing up at twelve o'clock.

He kept listening for shots for a long time,

and he got hot and damp under the covers and then freezing cold. He heard several sharp, ambiguous noises in the quiet night, but nothing that you could be sure about, and after a while he fell asleep.

In the morning, Peter got out of bed early, dressed quickly, and went silently out of the apartment without waking his parents. The vestibule looked just the way it always did, with the brass lamp and the flowered wallpaper and the Chalmerses' doormat with "Welcome" on it. There were no bodies and no blood. Sometimes when Mrs. Chalmers had been standing there waiting for the elevator, you could smell her perfume for a long time after. But now there was no smell of perfume, just the dusty, apartment-house usual smell. Peter stared at the Chalmerses' door nervously while waiting for the elevator to come up, but it didn't open and no sound came from within.

Sam, the man who ran the elevator and who didn't like him, anyway, only grunted when Peter got into the elevator, and Peter decided not to ask him any questions. He went out into the chilly, bright Sunday-morning street, half expecting to see the morgue wagon in front of the door, or at least two or three prowl cars. But there was only a sleepy woman in slacks airing a boxer and a man with his collar turned up hurrying up from the corner with the newspapers under his arm.

Peter went across the street and looked up to the sixth floor, at the windows of the Chalmerses' apartment. The Venetian blinds were pulled shut in every room and all the windows were closed.

A policeman walked down the other side of the street, heavy, blue, and purposeful, and for a moment Peter felt close to arrest. But the policeman continued on toward the avenue and turned the corner and disappeared and Peter said to himself, They never know anything.

He walked up and down the street, first on one side, then on the other, waiting, although it was hard to know what he was waiting for. He saw a hand come out through the blinds in his parents' room and slam the window shut, and he knew he ought to get upstairs quickly with a good excuse for being out, but he couldn't face

them this morning, and he would invent an excuse later. Maybe he would even say he had gone to the museum, although he doubted that his mother would swallow that. Some excuse. Later.

Then, after he had been patrolling the street for almost two hours, and just as he was coming up to the entrance of his building, the door opened and Mr. and Mrs. Chalmers came out. He had on his pince-nez and a dark-gray hat, and Mrs. Chalmers had on her fur coat and a red hat with feathers on it. Mr. Chalmers was holding the door open politely for his wife, and she looked, as she came out the door, as though she had just come from the beauty parlor.

It was too late to turn back or avoid them, and Peter just stood still, five feet from the entrance.

"Good morning," Mr. Chalmers said as he took his wife's arm and they started walking past Peter.

"Good morning, Peter," said Mrs. Chalmers in her soft voice, smiling at him. "Isn't it a nice day today?"

"Good morning," Peter said, and he was surprised that it came out and sounded like good morning.

The Chalmerses walked down the street toward Madison Avenue, two married people, arm in arm, going to church or to a big hotel for Sunday breakfast. Peter watched them, ashamed. He was ashamed of Mrs. Chalmers for looking the way she did the night before, down on her knees, and yelling like that and being so afraid. He was ashamed of Mr. Chalmers for making the noise that was not like the noise of a human being, and for threatening to shoot Mrs. Chalmers and not doing it. And he was ashamed of himself because he had been fearless when he opened the door, but had not been fearless ten seconds later, with Mr. Chalmers five feet away with the gun. He was ashamed of himself for not taking Mrs. Chalmers into the apartment, ashamed because he was not lying now with a bullet in his heart. But most of all he was ashamed because they had all said good morning to each other and the Chalmerses were walking quietly together, arm in arm, in the windy sunlight, toward Madison Avenue.

It was nearly eleven o'clock when Peter got back to the apartment, but his parents had gone back to sleep. There was a pretty good program on at eleven, about counterspies in Asia, and he turned it on automatically, while eating an orange. It was pretty exciting, but then there was a part in which an Oriental held a ticking bomb in his hand in a roomful of Americans, and Peter could tell what was coming. The hero, who was fearless and who came from California, was beginning to feint with his eyes,

and Peter reached over and turned the set off. It closed down with a shivering, collapsing pattern. Blinking a little, Peter watched the blind screen for a moment.

Ah, he thought in sudden, permanent disbelief, after the night in which he had faced the incomprehensible, shameless, weaponed grown-up world and had failed to disarm it, ah, they can have that, that's for kids.

---

## DISCUSSION

1. In the course of the story, Peter shows himself to have a complex personality. Find incidents that suggest that Peter is (a) a dreamer; (b) rebellious; (c) courageous; (d) frightened; (e) realistic. (See the Handbook entry for *inference*.)

2. (a) What information does the author give us about Mrs. Chalmers? Mr. Chalmers? (b) What might his purpose be in not supplying us with more information?

3. What has Peter learned about heroes and villains, adults, and himself?

4. Peter "was ashamed because they had all said good morning to each other and the Chalmers were walking quietly together, arm in arm" on the morning after their violent behavior at the door of his apartment. Why was their morning behavior shameful?

## WORD STUDY

There are three aids which can help you understand words you don't know:

*Context*—the setting in which the word appears; that is, other words or ideas in the sentence, paragraph, or selection.

*Structure*—the arrangement and meaning of parts of words.

*Dictionary*

How does context help? Read the sentences below:

1. "Peter *feinted* with his eyes, or at least later in life he thought he had *feinted* with his eyes."

2. "The hero, who was fearless and who came from California, was beginning to *feint* with his eyes. . . ."

3. "You had to have quick reflexes, too, of course, and to be able to *feint* to one side with your eyes before the crucial moment."

Which sentence contains the most clues to the meaning of *feint*? What happens to one's eyes if one *feints* to one side? What is the purpose of *feinting* with one's eyes?

Many words have more than one meaning. Context can help you tell which meaning is intended:

1. Jenny ate the oranges, *pips* and all.

2. The tiny *pips* on the radar screen indicated the presence of ships.

Context can also alert you to an unfamiliar meaning of a familiar word:

1. Her dress was made of cotton *piqué*.

2. The dancers practiced the *piqué*, a difficult step, until they were ready to drop.

Using context as an aid, select from the definitions given after each of the following sentences the appropriate definition for the italicized word. If no context clues are given, write "n.c."

1. Laura seems much too old and worldly to play the *ingénue*, but her director must feel otherwise. (a) nursemaid; (b) young, innocent girl; (c) lead role; (d) heroine.

2. After the fire, in the *foyer* of the building there were about one hundred people in various stages of night clothing. (a) elevator; (b) lobby; (c) office; (d) stairway.

3. George has a reputation for being *intrepid*, although those who know him best might dispute that. (a) bashful; (b) fearless; (c) generous; (d) slow-witted.

4. Four out of five of the algebra problems were *incomprehensible*, so Angela failed the test. (a) not understandable; (b) easy; (c) not audible; (d) of no consequence.

# The Most Dangerous Game

*Richard Connell*

"OFF there to the right—somewhere—is a large island," said Whitney. "It's rather a mystery——"

"What island is it?" Rainsford asked.

"The old charts call it 'Ship-Trap Island,'" Whitney replied. "A suggestive name, isn't it? Sailors have a curious dread of the place. I don't know why. Some superstition——"

"Can't see it," remarked Rainsford, trying to peer through the dank tropical night that was palpable as it pressed its thick, warm blackness in upon the yacht.

"You have good eyes," said Whitney, with a laugh, "and I've seen you pick off a moose moving in the brown fall bush at four hundred yards; but even you can't see four miles or so through a moonless Caribbean night."

"Nor four yards," admitted Rainsford. "Ugh! It's like moist black velvet."

"It will be light enough in Rio," promised Whitney. "We should make it in a few days. I hope the jaguar guns have come. We'll have some good hunting up the Amazon. Great sport, hunting."

"The best sport in the world," agreed Rainsford.

"For the hunter," amended Whitney. "Not for the jaguar."

"Don't talk rot, Whitney," said Rainsford. "You're a big-game hunter, not a philosopher. Who cares how a jaguar feels?"

"Perhaps the jaguar does," observed Whitney.

"Bah! They've no understanding."

"Even so, I rather think they understand one thing—fear. The fear of pain and the fear of death."

"Nonsense," laughed Rainsford. "This hot weather is making you soft, Whitney. Be a realist. The world is made up of two classes—the hunters and the hunted. Luckily, you and I are hunters. Do you think we've passed that island yet?"

"I can't tell in the dark. I hope so."

"Why?" asked Rainsford.

"The place has a reputation—a bad one. It's gotten into sailor lore, somehow. Didn't you notice that the crew's nerves seemed a bit jumpy today?"

"They were a bit strange, now you mention it. Even Captain Nielsen——"

"Yes, even that tough-minded old Swede, who'd go up to the devil himself and ask him for a light. All I could get out of him was: 'This place has an evil name among seafaring men, sir.' Then he said to me, very gravely: 'Don't you feel anything?'—as if the air about us was actually poisonous. Now, you mustn't laugh when I tell you this—I did feel something like a sudden chill.

"There was no breeze. The sea was as flat as a plate-glass window. We were drawing near the island then. What I felt was a—a mental chill; a sort of sudden dread."

"Pure imagination," said Rainsford. "One superstitious sailor can taint the whole ship's company with his fear."

"Maybe. But sometimes I think sailors have an extra sense that tells them when they are in danger. Sometimes I think evil is a tangible thing—with wave lengths, just as sound and light have. An evil place can, so to speak, broadcast vibrations of evil. Anyhow, I'm glad we're getting out of this zone. Well, I think I'll turn in now, Rainsford."

"I'm not sleepy," said Rainsford. "I'm going to smoke another pipe up on the afterdeck."

"Good night, then, Rainsford. See you at breakfast."

"Right. Good night, Whitney."

Rainsford, reclining in a steamer chair, indolently puffed on his favorite brier. The sensuous drowsiness of the night was on him. "It's so dark," he thought, "that I could sleep without closing my eyes; the night would be my eyelids——"

An abrupt sound startled him. Off to the right he had heard it, and his ears, expert in such matters, could not be mistaken. Again he heard the sound, and again. Somewhere, off in the blackness, someone had fired a gun three times.

Rainsford sprang up and moved quickly to the rail, mystified. He strained his eyes in the direction from which the reports had come, but it was like trying to see through a blanket. He leaped upon the rail and balanced himself there, to get greater elevation; his pipe, striking a rope, was knocked from his mouth. He lunged for it; a short, hoarse cry came from his lips as he realized he had reached too far and had lost his balance. The cry was pinched off short as the blood-warm waters of the Caribbean Sea closed over his head.

He struggled up to the surface and tried to cry out, but the wash from the speeding yacht made him gag and strangle. Desperately he struck out with strong strokes after the receding lights of the yacht, but he stopped before he had swum fifty feet. A certain cool-headedness had come to him; it was not the first time he had been in a tight place. There was a chance that his cries could be heard by someone aboard the yacht, but that chance was slender, and grew more slender as the yacht raced on. He wrestled himself out of some of his clothes, and shouted with all his power. The lights of the yacht became faint and ever-vanishing fireflies; then they were blotted out entirely by the night.

Rainsford remembered that the shots had come from the right; and doggedly he swam in that direction, swimming with slow, deliberate strokes, conserving his strength. For a seemingly endless time he fought the sea. He began to count his strokes; he could do possibly a hundred more and then——

Rainsford heard a sound. It came out of the darkness, a high, screaming sound, the sound of an animal in an extremity of anguish and terror.

He did not recognize the animal that made the sound; he did not try to; with fresh vitality he swam toward the sound. He heard it again; then it was cut short by another noise, crisp, staccato.

"Pistol shot," muttered Rainsford, swimming on.

Ten minutes of determined effort brought another sound to his ears—the most welcome he had ever heard—the muttering and growling of the sea breaking on a rocky shore. He was almost on the rocks before he saw them. With his remaining strength he dragged himself from the swirling waters. Jagged crags appeared to jut up into the opaqueness; he forced himself upward, hand over hand. Gasping, his hands raw, he reached a flat place at the top. Dense jungle came down to the very edge of the cliffs. What perils that tangle of trees and underbrush might hold for him did not concern Rainsford just then. All he knew was that he was safe from the sea, and that utter weariness was on him. He flung himself down and tumbled headlong into the deepest sleep of his life.

When he opened his eyes, he knew from the position of the sun that it was late in the afternoon. Sleep had given him new vigor; a sharp hunger was picking at him. He looked about him, almost cheerfully.

"Where there are pistol shots, there are men. Where there are men, there is food," he thought. But what kind of men, he wondered, in so forbidding a place? An unbroken front of snarled and ragged jungle fringed the shore. He saw no sign of a trail through the closely knit web of weeds and trees; it was easier to go along the shore, and he floundered along by the water. Not far from where he had landed, he stopped.

Some wounded thing, by the evidence a large animal, had thrashed about in the underbrush; the jungle weeds were crushed down and the moss was lacerated; one patch of weeds was stained crimson. A small, glittering object not far away caught Rainsford's eye and he picked it up. It was an empty cartridge.

"A twenty-two," he remarked. "That's odd. It must have been a fairly large animal, too. The hunter had his nerve with him to tackle it with a light gun. It's clear that the brute put up a fight. I suppose the first three shots I heard was when the hunter flushed his quarry[1] and wounded it. The last shot was when he trailed it here and finished it."

He examined the ground closely and found what he had hoped to find—the print of hunting boots. They pointed along the cliff in the direction he had been going. Eagerly he hurried along, now slipping on a rotten log or a loose stone, but making headway; night was beginning to settle down.

Bleak darkness was blacking out the sea and jungle when Rainsford sighted the lights. He came upon them as he turned a crook in the coastline, and his first thought was that he had come upon a village, for there were many lights. But as he forged along he saw to his great astonishment that all the lights were in one enormous building—a lofty structure with pointed towers plunging upward into the gloom. His eyes made out the shadowy outlines of a palatial château; it was set on a high bluff, and on three sides of it cliffs dived down to where the sea licked greedy lips in the shadows.

"Mirage," thought Rainsford. But it was no

---

1. *flushed his quarry*, drove the pursued animal out of its hiding place.

mirage, he found, when he opened the tall spiked iron gate. The stone steps were real enough; the massive door with a leering gargoyle for a knocker was real enough; yet about it all hung an air of unreality.

He lifted the knocker; and it creaked up stiffly, as if it had never before been used. He let it fall, and it startled him with its booming loudness. He thought he heard steps within; the door remained closed. Again Rainsford lifted the heavy knocker, and let it fall. The door opened suddenly, and Rainsford stood blinking in the river of glaring gold light that poured out. The first thing his eyes discerned was the largest man he had ever seen—a gigantic creature, solidly made and black-bearded almost to the waist. In his hand the man held a long-barreled revolver, and he was pointing it straight at Rainsford's heart. Out of the snarl of beard two small eyes regarded Rainsford.

"Don't be alarmed," said Rainsford with a smile which he hoped was disarming. "I'm no robber. I fell off a yacht. My name is Sanger Rainsford of New York City."

The menacing look in the eyes did not change. The revolver pointed as rigidly as if the giant were a statue. He gave no sign that he understood Rainsford's words, or that he had even heard them. He was dressed in uniform, a black uniform trimmed with gray astrakhan.

"I'm Sanger Rainsford of New York," Rainsford began again. "I fell off a yacht. I am hungry."

The man's only answer was to raise with his thumb the hammer of his revolver. Then Rainsford saw the man's free hand go to his forehead in a military salute, and he saw him click his heels together and stand at attention. Another man was coming down the broad marble steps, an erect, slender man in evening clothes. He advanced to Rainsford and held out his hand.

In a cultivated voice marked by a slight accent that gave it added precision and deliberateness, he said: "It is a very great pleasure and honor to welcome Mr. Sanger Rainsford, the celebrated hunter, to my home."

Automatically Rainsford shook the man's hand.

"I've read your book about hunting snow leopards in Tibet, you see," explained the man. "I am General Zaroff."

Rainsford's first impression was that the man was singularly handsome; his second was that there was an original, almost bizarre quality about the general's face. He was a tall man past middle age, for his hair was a vivid white; but his thick eyebrows and pointed military mustache were as black as the night from which Rainsford had come. His eyes, too, were black and very bright. He had high cheekbones, a sharp-cut nose, a spare, dark face, the face of a man used to giving orders, the face of an aristocrat. Turning to the giant in uniform, the general made a sign. The giant put away his pistol, saluted, withdrew.

"Ivan is an incredibly strong fellow," remarked the general, "but he has the misfortune to be deaf and dumb. A simple fellow, but, I'm afraid, like all his race, a bit of a savage."

"Is he Russian?"

"He is a Cossack,"[2] said the general, and his smile showed red lips and pointed teeth. "So am I."

"Come," he said, "we shouldn't be chatting here. We can talk later. Now you want clothes, food, rest. You shall have them. This is a most restful spot."

Ivan had reappeared, and the general spoke to him with lips that moved but gave forth no sound.

"Follow Ivan, if you please, Mr. Rainsford," said the general. "I was about to have my dinner. I'll wait for you. You'll find that my clothes will fit you, I think."

It was to a huge, beam-ceilinged bedroom with a canopied bed big enough for six men that Rainsford followed the silent giant. Ivan laid out an evening suit, and Rainsford, as he put it on, noticed that it came from a London tailor who ordinarily cut and sewed for none below the rank of duke.

The dining room to which Ivan conducted him was in many ways remarkable. There was a medieval magnificence about it; it suggested a baronial hall of feudal times with its oaken

---

2. *He is a Cossack* (kos′ak). The Cossacks, who lived in southern Russia, were noted for their love of fighting and their excellent horsemanship.

panels, its high ceiling, its vast refectory table where twoscore men could sit down to eat. About the hall were mounted heads of many animals—lions, tigers, elephants, moose, bears; larger or more perfect specimens Rainsford had never seen. At the great table the general was sitting alone.

"You'll have a cocktail, Mr. Rainsford," he suggested. The cocktail was surpassingly good; and, Rainsford noted, the table appointments were of the finest—the linen, the crystal, the silver, the china.

They were eating borsch.[3] Half apologetically General Zaroff said: "We do our best to preserve the amenities of civilization here. Please forgive any lapses. We are well off the beaten track, you know."

Rainsford was finding the general a most thoughtful and affable host, a true cosmopolite. But there was one small trait of the general's that made Rainsford uncomfortable. Whenever he looked up from his plate he found the general studying him, appraising him narrowly.

"Perhaps," said General Zaroff, "you were surprised that I recognized your name. You see, I read all books on hunting published in English, French, and Russian. I have but one passion in my life, Mr. Rainsford, and that is the hunt."

"You have some wonderful heads here," said Rainsford as he ate a particularly well-cooked filet mignon. "That Cape buffalo is the largest I ever saw."

"Oh, that fellow. Yes, he was a monster."

"Did he charge you?"

"Hurled me against a tree," said the general. "Fractured my skull. But I got the brute."

"I've always thought," said Rainsford, "that the Cape buffalo is the most dangerous of all big game."

For a moment the general did not reply; he was smiling his curious red-lipped smile. Then he said slowly: "No. You are wrong, sir. The Cape buffalo is not the most dangerous big game." He sipped his wine. "Here in my preserve on this island," he said in the same slow tone, "I hunt more dangerous game."

Rainsford expressed his surprise. "Is there big game on this island?"

The general nodded. "The biggest."

"Really?"

"Oh, it isn't here naturally, of course. I have to stock the island."

"What have you imported, general?" Rainsford asked. "Tigers?"

The general smiled. "No," he said. "Hunting tigers ceased to interest me some years ago. I exhausted their possibilities, you see. No thrill left in tigers, no real danger. I live for danger, Mr. Rainsford."

The general took from his pocket a gold cigarette case and offered his guest a long black cigarette with a silver tip; it was perfumed and gave off a smell like incense.

"We will have some capital hunting, you and I," said the general. "I shall be most glad to have your society."

"But what game——" began Rainsford.

"I'll tell you," said the general. "You will be amused, I know. I think I may say, in all modesty, that I have done a rare thing. I have invented a new sensation. May I pour you another glass of port, Mr. Rainsford?"

"Thank you, general."

The general filled both glasses, and said: "God makes some men poets. Some He makes kings, some beggars. Me He made a hunter. My hand was made for the trigger, my father said. He was a very rich man with a quarter of a million acres in the Crimea,[4] and he was an ardent sportsman. When I was only five years old, he gave me a little gun to shoot sparrows with. When I shot some of his prize turkeys with it, he did not punish me; he complimented me on my marksmanship. I killed my first bear when I was ten. My whole life has been one prolonged hunt. I went into the army—it was expected of noblemen's sons—and for a time commanded a division of Cossack cavalry, but my real interest was always the hunt. I have hunted every kind of game in every land. It would be impossible for me to tell you how many animals I have killed."

The general puffed at his cigarette.

---

3. *borsch* (bôrsh), a rich red soup, colored with beet juice and served with sour cream.

4. *the Crimea* (krī mē ə *or* kri mē ə), a peninsula in southwestern Russia, jutting down into the Black Sea.

"After the debacle in Russia[5] I left the country, for it was imprudent for an officer of the Czar to stay there. Many noble Russians lost everything. I, luckily, had invested heavily in American securities. Naturally, I continued to hunt—grizzlies in your Rockies, crocodiles in the Ganges,[6] rhinoceroses in East Africa. It was in Africa that the Cape buffalo hit me and laid me up for six months. As soon as I recovered I started for the Amazon to hunt jaguars, for I had heard they were unusually cunning. They weren't." The Cossack sighed. "I was bitterly disappointed. I was lying in my tent with a splitting headache one night when a terrible thought pushed its way into my mind. Hunting was beginning to bore me! And hunting, remember, had been my life. I have heard that in America businessmen often go to pieces when they give up the business that has been their life."

"Yes, that's so," said Rainsford.

The general smiled. "I had no wish to go to pieces," he said. "I must do something. Now, mine is an analytical mind, Mr. Rainsford. Doubtless that is why I enjoy the problems of the chase."

"No doubt, General Zaroff."

"So," continued the general, "I asked myself why the hunt no longer fascinated me. You are much younger than I am, Mr. Rainsford, and have not hunted as much; but perhaps you can guess the answer."

"What was it?"

"Simply this: hunting had ceased to be what you call 'a sporting proposition.' It had become too easy. I always got my quarry. Always. There is no greater bore than perfection."

The general lit a fresh cigarette.

"No animal had a chance with me any more. That is no boast; it is a mathematical certainty. The animal had nothing but his legs and his instinct. Instinct is no match for reason. When I thought of this it was a tragic moment for me, I can tell you."

Rainsford leaned across the table, absorbed in what his host was saying.

"It came to me as an inspiration what I must do," the general went on.

"And that was?"

The general smiled the quiet smile of one who has faced an obstacle and surmounted it with success. "I had to invent a new animal to hunt," he said.

"A new animal? You're joking."

"Not at all," said the general. "I never joke about hunting. I needed a new animal. I found one. So I bought this island, built this house, and here I do my hunting. The island is perfect for my purposes—there are jungles with a maze of trails in them, hills, swamps——"

"But the animal, General Zaroff?"

"Oh," said the general, "it supplies me with the most exciting hunting in the world. No other hunting compares with it for an instant. Every day I hunt, and I never grow bored now, for I have a quarry with which I can match my wits."

Rainsford's bewilderment showed in his face.

"I wanted the ideal animal to hunt," explained the general. "So I said: 'What are the attributes of an ideal quarry?' And the answer was, of course: 'It must have courage, cunning, and, above all, it must be able to reason.'"

"But no animal can reason," objected Rainsford.

"My dear fellow," said the general, "there is one that can."

"But you can't mean——" gasped Rainsford.

"And why not?"

"I can't believe you are serious, General Zaroff. This is a grisly joke."

"Why should I not be serious? I am speaking of hunting."

"Hunting? Good God, General Zaroff, what you speak of is murder."

The general laughed with entire good nature. He regarded Rainsford quizzically. "I refuse to believe that so modern and civilized a young man as you seem to be harbors romantic ideas about the value of human life. Surely your experiences in the recent war——"

"Did not make me condone cold-blooded murder," finished Rainsford stiffly.

Laughter shook the general. "How extraor-

---

5. *the debacle* (dā bä′kəl *or* di bak′əl) *in Russia.* In the Russian Revolution of 1917 the government of the Czar was overthrown, the property of the nobles confiscated, and most of the nobility driven into exile.

6. *Ganges* (gan′jēz), a river in India regarded by the Hindus as being sacred.

dinarily droll you are!" he said. "One does not expect nowadays to find a young man of the educated class, even in America, with such a naive, and, if I may say so, mid-Victorian point of view. Ah, well, I'll wager you'll forget your notions when you go hunting with me. You've a genuine new thrill in store for you, Mr. Rainsford."

"Thank you, I'm a hunter, not a murderer."

"Dear me," said the general, quite unruffled, "again that unpleasant word. But I think I can show you that your scruples are quite ill-founded."

"Yes?"

"Life is for the strong, to be lived by the strong, and, if needs be, taken by the strong. The weak of the world were put here to give the strong pleasure. I am strong. Why should I not use my gift? If I wish to hunt, why should I not? I hunt the scum of the earth—sailors from tramp ships—lascars,[7] blacks, Chinese, whites, mongrels—a thoroughbred horse or hound is worth more than a score of them."

"But they are men," said Rainsford hotly.

"Precisely," said the general. "That is why I use them. It gives me pleasure. They can reason, after a fashion. So they are dangerous."

"But where do you get them?"

The general's left eyelid fluttered down in a wink. "This island is called Ship-Trap," he answered. "Sometimes an angry god of the high seas sends them to me. Sometimes, when Providence is not so kind, I help Providence a bit. Come to the window with me."

Rainsford went to the window and looked out toward the sea.

"Watch! Out there!" exclaimed the general, pointing into the night. Rainsford's eyes saw only blackness, and then, as the general pressed a button, far out to sea Rainsford saw the flash of lights.

The general chuckled. "They indicate a channel," he said, "where there's none: giant rocks with razor edges crouch like a sea monster with wide-open jaws. They can crush a ship as easily as I crush this nut." He dropped a walnut on the hardwood floor and brought his heel grinding down on it. "Oh, yes," he said,

casually, as if in answer to a question, "I have electricity. We try to be civilized here."

"Civilized? And you shoot down men?"

A trace of anger was in the general's black eyes, but it was there for only a second; then he said, in his most pleasant manner: "Dear me, what a righteous young man you are! I assure you I do not do the thing you suggest. That would be barbarous. I treat these visitors with every consideration. They get plenty of good food and exercise. They get into splendid physical condition. You shall see for yourself tomorrow."

"What do you mean?"

"We shall visit my training school," smiled the general. "It's in the cellar. I have about a dozen pupils down there now. They're from the Spanish bark *San Lucar* that had the bad luck to go on the rocks out there. A very inferior lot, I regret to say. Poor specimens and more accustomed to the deck than to the jungle."

He raised his hand, and Ivan brought thick Turkish coffee. Rainsford, with an effort, held his tongue in check.

"It's a game, you see," pursued the general blandly. "I suggest to one of them that we go hunting. I give him a supply of food and an excellent hunting knife. I give him three hours' start. I am to follow, armed only with a pistol of the smallest caliber and range. If my quarry eludes me for three whole days, he wins the game. If I find him"—the general smiled—"he loses."

"Suppose he refuses to be hunted?"

"Oh," said the general, "I give him his option, of course. He need not play that game if he doesn't wish to. If he does not wish to hunt, I turn him over to Ivan. Ivan once had the honor of serving as official knouter to the Great White Czar,[8] and he has his own ideas of sport. Invariably, Mr. Rainsford, invariably they choose the hunt."

"And if they win?"

The smile on the general's face widened. "To date I have not lost," he said.

---

7. *lascars* (las′kərz), East Indian sailors.

8. *Ivan . . . knouter* (nout′ər) *to the Great White Czar* (zär). During the reign of Alexander III (1881–1894), Ivan was the official flogger of those doomed to be lashed with a knout, a terrible whip made of plaited leather thongs and wire.

Then he added, hastily: "I don't wish you to think me a braggart, Mr. Rainsford. Many of them afford only the most elementary sort of problem. Occasionally I strike a tartar.[9] One almost did win. I eventually had to use the dogs."

"The dogs?"

"This way, please. I'll show you."

The general steered Rainsford to a window. The lights from the windows sent a flickering illumination that made grotesque patterns on the courtyard below, and Rainsford could see moving about there a dozen or so huge black shapes; as they turned toward him, their eyes glittered greenly.

"A rather good lot, I think," observed the general. "They are let out at seven every night. If anyone should try to get into my house—or out of it—something extremely regrettable would occur to him." He hummed a snatch of a gay French song.

"And now," said the general, "I want to show you my new collection of heads. Will you come with me to the library?"

"I hope," said Rainsford, "that you will excuse me tonight, General Zaroff. I'm really not feeling at all well."

"Ah, indeed?" the general inquired solicitously. "Well, I suppose that's only natural after your long swim. You need a good, restful night's sleep. Tomorrow you'll feel like a new man, I'll wager. Then we'll hunt, eh? I've one rather promising prospect——"

Rainsford was hurrying from the room.

"Sorry you can't go with me tonight," called the general. "I expect rather fair sport—a big, strong black. He looks resourceful——Well, good night, Mr. Rainsford; I hope you have a good night's rest."

The bed was good, and the pajamas of the softest silk, and he was tired in every fiber of his being; nevertheless Rainsford could not quiet his brain with the opiate of sleep. He lay, eyes wide open. Once he thought he heard stealthy steps in the corridor outside his room. He sought to throw open the door; it would not open. He went to the window and looked out. His room was high up in one of the towers.

The lights of the château were out now, and it was dark and silent, but there was a fragment of sallow moon, and by its wan light he could see, dimly, the courtyard; there, weaving in and out in the pattern of shadow, were black, noiseless forms; the hounds heard him at the window and looked up, expectantly, with their green eyes. Rainsford went back to the bed and lay down. By many methods he tried to put himself to sleep. He had achieved a doze when, just as morning began to come, he heard, far off in the jungle, the faint report of a pistol.

General Zaroff did not appear until luncheon. He was dressed faultlessly in the tweeds of a country squire. He was solicitous about the state of Rainsford's health.

"As for me," sighed the general, "I do not feel so well. I am worried, Mr. Rainsford. Last night I detected traces of my old complaint."

To Rainsford's questioning glance the general said: "Ennui. Boredom."

Then, taking a second helping of crêpes suzette,[10] the general explained: "The hunting was not good last night. The fellow lost his head. He made a straight trail that offered no problems at all. That's the trouble with these sailors; they have dull brains to begin with, and they do not know how to get about in the woods. They do excessively stupid and obvious things. It's most annoying. Will you have another glass of wine, Mr. Rainsford?"

"General," said Rainsford firmly, "I wish to leave this island at once."

The general raised his eyebrows; he seemed hurt. "But, my dear fellow," he protested, "you've only just come. You've had no hunting——"

"I wish to go today," said Rainsford. He saw the dead black eyes of the general on him, studying him. General Zaroff's face suddenly brightened.

He filled Rainsford's glass from a dusty bottle.

"Tonight," said the general, "we will hunt—you and I."

Rainsford shook his head. "No, general," he said. "I will not hunt."

The general shrugged his shoulders and delicately ate a hothouse grape. "As you wish, my

9. *strike a tartar.* The General means that sometimes he encounters a man who isn't easily manageable.

10. *crêpes suzette*, thin dessert pancakes, usually rolled, sometimes served with a flaming brandy sauce.

friend," he said. "The choice rests entirely with you. But may I not venture to suggest that you will find my idea of sport more diverting than Ivan's?"

He nodded toward the corner to where the giant stood, scowling, his thick arms crossed on his hogshead of a chest.

"You don't mean——" cried Rainsford.

"My dear fellow," said the general, "have I not told you I always mean what I say about hunting? This is really an inspiration. I drink to a foeman worthy of my steel—at last."

The general raised his glass, but Rainsford sat staring at him.

"You'll find this game worth playing," the general said enthusiastically. "Your brain against mine. Your woodcraft against mine. Your strength and stamina against mine. Outdoor chess! And the stake is not without value, eh?"

"And if I win——" began Rainsford huskily.

"I'll cheerfully acknowledge myself defeated if I do not find you by midnight of the third day," said General Zaroff. "My sloop will place you on the mainland near a town."

The general read what Rainsford was thinking.

"Oh, you can trust me," said the Cossack. "I will give you my word as a gentleman and a sportsman. Of course, you in turn must agree to say nothing of your visit here."

"I'll agree to nothing of the kind," said Rainsford.

"Oh," said the general, "in that case—but why discuss that now? Three days hence we can discuss it over a bottle of wine, unless——"

The general sipped his port.

Then a businesslike air animated him. "Ivan," he said to Rainsford, "will supply you with hunting clothes, food, a knife. I suggest you wear moccasins; they leave a poorer trail. I suggest, too, that you avoid the big swamp in the southeast corner of the island. We call it Death Swamp. There's quicksand there. One foolish fellow tried it. The deplorable part of it was that Lazarus followed him. You can imagine my feelings, Mr. Rainsford. I loved Lazarus; he was the finest hound in my pack. Well, I must beg you to excuse me now. I always take a siesta after lunch. You'll hardly have time for

a nap, I fear. You'll want to start, no doubt. I shall not follow till dusk. Hunting at night is so much more exciting, don't you think? *Au revoir*,[11] Mr. Rainsford, *au revoir*."

General Zaroff, with a deep, courtly bow, strolled from the room. From another door came Ivan. Under one arm he carried khaki hunting clothes, a haversack of food, a leather sheath containing a long-bladed hunting knife; his right hand rested on a cocked revolver thrust in the crimson sash about his waist. . . .

Rainsford had fought his way through the bush for two hours. "I must keep my nerve. I must keep my nerve," he said through tight teeth.

He had not been entirely clear-headed when the château gates snapped shut behind him. His whole idea at first was to put distance between himself and General Zaroff; and, to this end, he had plunged along, spurred on by something very much like panic. Now he had got a grip on himself, had stopped, and was taking stock of himself and the situation.

He saw that straight flight was futile; inevitably it would bring him face to face with the sea. He was in a picture with a frame of water, and his operations, clearly, must take place within that frame.

"I'll give him a trail to follow," muttered Rainsford, and he struck off from the rude path he had been following into the trackless wilderness. He executed a series of intricate loops; he doubled on his trail again and again, recalling all the lore of the fox hunt, and all the dodges of the fox. Night found him leg-weary, with hands and face lashed by the branches, on a thickly wooded ridge. He knew it would be insane to blunder on through the dark, even if he had the strength. His need for rest was imperative and he thought: "I have played the fox, now I must play the cat of the fable."[12] A big tree with a thick trunk and outspread branches was nearby, and, taking care to leave not the slightest mark, he climbed up, and stretching out on one of the broad limbs,

---

11. *Au revoir* (ō rə vwär′), good-by; till I see you again. [*French*]
12. *I have played the fox . . . cat of the fable.* Rainsford means that he has used craft; now he must, like a cat at a mousehole, employ watchful waiting.

after a fashion, rested. Rest brought him new confidence and almost a feeling of security. Even so zealous a hunter as General Zaroff could not trace him there, he told himself; only the devil himself could follow that complicated trail through the jungle after dark. But, perhaps, the general was a devil——

An apprehensive night crawled slowly by like a wounded snake, and sleep did not visit Rainsford, although the silence of a dead world was on the jungle. Toward morning when a dingy gray was varnishing the sky, the cry of some startled bird focused Rainsford's attention in that direction. Something was coming through the bush, coming slowly, carefully, coming by the same winding way Rainsford had come. He flattened himself down on the limb, and through a screen of leaves almost as thick as tapestry, he watched. The thing that was approaching was a man.

It was General Zaroff. He made his way along with his eyes fixed in utmost concentration on the ground before him. He paused, almost beneath the tree, dropped to his knees and studied the ground. Rainsford's impulse was to hurl himself down like a panther, but he saw that the general's right hand held something metallic—a small automatic pistol.

The hunter shook his head several times, as if he were puzzled. Then he straightened up and took from his case one of his black cigarettes; its incense-like smoke floated up to Rainsford's nostrils.

Rainsford held his breath. The general's eyes had left the ground and were traveling inch by inch up the tree. Rainsford froze there, every muscle tensed for a spring. But the sharp eyes of the hunter stopped before they reached the limb where Rainsford lay; a smile spread over his brown face. Very deliberately he blew a smoke ring into the air; then he turned his back on the tree and walked carelessly away, back along the trail he had come. The swish of the underbrush against his hunting boots grew fainter and fainter.

The pent-up air burst hotly from Rainsford's lungs. His first thought made him feel sick and numb. The general could follow a trail through the woods at night; he could follow an extremely difficult trail; he must have un-canny powers; only by the merest chance had the Cossack failed to see his quarry.

Rainsford's second thought was even more terrible. It sent a shudder of cold horror through his whole being. Why had the general smiled? Why had he turned back?

Rainsford did not want to believe what his reason told him was true, but the truth was as evident as the sun that by now had pushed through the morning mists. The general was playing with him! The general was saving him for another day's sport! The Cossack was the cat; *he* was the mouse. Then it was that Rainsford knew the full meaning of terror.

"I will not lose my nerve. I will not."

He slid down from the tree, and struck off again into the woods. His face was set and he forced the machinery of his mind to function. Three hundred yards from his hiding place he stopped where a huge dead tree leaned precariously on a smaller, living one. Throwing off his sack of food, Rainsford took his knife from its sheath and began to work with all his energy.

The job was finished at last, and he threw himself down behind a fallen log a hundred feet away. He did not have to wait long. The cat was coming again to play with the mouse.

Following the trail with the sureness of a bloodhound, came General Zaroff. Nothing escaped those searching black eyes, no crushed blade of grass, no bent twig, no mark, no matter how faint, in the moss. So intent was the Cossack on his stalking that he was upon the thing Rainsford had made before he saw it. His foot touched the protruding bough that was the trigger. Even as he touched it, the general sensed his danger and leaped back with the agility of an ape. But he was not quite quick enough; the dead tree, delicately adjusted to rest on the cut living one, crashed down and struck the general a glancing blow on the shoulder as it fell; but for his alertness, he must have been smashed beneath it. He staggered, but he did not fall; nor did he drop his revolver. He stood there, rubbing his injured shoulder; and Rainsford, with fear again gripping his heart, heard the general's mocking laugh ring through the jungle.

"Rainsford," called the general, "if you are

within sound of my voice, as I suppose you are, let me congratulate you. Not many men know how to make a Malay man-catcher. Luckily for me I, too, have hunted in Malacca.[13] You are proving interesting, Mr. Rainsford. I am going now to have my wound dressed; it's only a slight one. But I shall be back. I shall be back."

When the general had gone, Rainsford took up his flight again. It was flight now, a desperate, hopeless flight that carried him on for some hours. Dusk came, then darkness, and still he pressed on. The ground grew softer under his moccasins; the vegetation grew ranker, denser; insects bit him savagely. Then, as he stepped forward, his foot sank into the ooze. He tried to wrench it back, but the muck sucked viciously at his foot as if it were a giant leech. With a violent effort, he tore his foot loose. He knew where he was now. Death Swamp and its quicksand.

His hands were tight closed as if his nerve were something tangible that someone in the darkness was trying to tear from his grip. The softness of the earth had given him an idea. He stepped back from the quicksand a dozen feet or so and, like some huge prehistoric beaver, he began to dig.

Rainsford had dug himself in in France when a second's delay meant death. That had been a pleasant pastime compared to his digging now. The pit grew deeper; when it was above his shoulders, he climbed out and from some hard saplings cut stakes and sharpened them to a fine point. These stakes he planted in the bottom of the pit with the points sticking up. With flying fingers he wove a rough carpet of weeds and branches, and with it he covered the mouth of the pit. Then, wet with sweat and aching with tiredness, he crouched behind the stump of a lightning-charred tree.

He knew his pursuer was coming; he heard the padding sound of feet on the soft earth, and the night breeze brought him the perfume of the general's cigarette. It seemed to Rainsford that the general was coming with unusual swiftness; he was not feeling his way along, foot by foot. Rainsford, crouching there, could not

see the general, nor could he see the pit. He lived a year in a minute. Then he felt an impulse to cry aloud with joy, for he heard the sharp crackle of the breaking branches as the cover of the pit gave way; he heard the sharp scream of pain as the pointed stakes found their mark. He leaped up from his place of concealment. Then he cowered back. Three feet from the pit a man was standing, with an electric torch in his hand.

"You've done well, Rainsford," the voice of the general called. "Your Burmese tiger pit[14] has claimed one of my best dogs. Again you score. I think, Mr. Rainsford, I'll see what you can do against my whole pack. I'm going home for a rest now. Thank you for a most amusing evening."

At daybreak Rainsford, lying near the swamp, was awakened by a sound that made him know that he had new things to learn about fear. It was a distant sound, faint and wavering; but he knew it. It was the baying of a pack of hounds.

Rainsford knew he could do one of two things. He could stay where he was and wait. That was suicide. He could flee. That was postponing the inevitable. For a moment he stood there, thinking. An idea that held a wild chance came to him, and, tightening his belt, he headed away from the swamp. The baying of the hounds drew nearer, then still nearer, nearer, ever nearer. On a ridge Rainsford climbed a tree. Down a watercourse, not a quarter of a mile away, he could see the bush moving. Straining his eyes, he saw the lean figure of General Zaroff; just ahead of him Rainsford made out another figure whose wide shoulders surged through the tall jungle weeds; it was the giant Ivan, and he seemed pulled forward by some unseen force; Rainsford knew that Ivan must be holding the pack in leash.

They would be on him any minute now. His mind worked frantically. He thought of a native trick he had learned in Uganda.[15] He slid down the tree. He caught hold of a springy young sapling and to it he fastened his hunting knife, with the blade pointing down the trail;

---

13. *Malacca* (mə lak′ə), an area in the southwestern part of the Malay Peninsula.

14. *Burmese* (bèr′mēz) *tiger pit*, a deep pit covered by brush for trapping tigers in Burma.

15. *Uganda* (yü gan′də *or* ü gän′dä), formerly a British protectorate in eastern Africa, now an independent state.

with a bit of wild grapevine he tied back the sapling. Then he ran for his life. The hounds raised their voices as they hit the fresh scent. Rainsford knew now how an animal at bay feels.

He had to stop to get his breath. The baying of the hounds stopped abruptly; and Rainsford's heart stopped, too. They must have reached the knife.

He shinned excitedly up a tree and looked back. His pursuers had stopped. But the hope that was in Rainsford's brain when he had climbed died, for he saw in the shallow valley that General Zaroff was still on his feet. But Ivan was not. The knife, driven by the recoil of the springing tree, had not wholly failed.

Rainsford had hardly tumbled to the ground when the pack took up the cry again.

"Nerve, nerve, nerve!" he panted, as he dashed along. A blue gap showed between the trees dead ahead. Ever nearer drew the hounds. Rainsford forced himself on toward that gap. He reached for it. It was the shore of the sea. Across a cove he could see the gloomy gray stone of the château. Twenty feet below him the sea rumbled and hissed. Rainsford hesitated. He heard the hounds. Then he leaped far out into the sea.

When the general and his pack reached the place by the sea, the Cossack stopped. For some minutes he stood regarding the blue-green expanse of water. He shrugged his shoulders. Then he sat down, took a drink of brandy from a silver flask, lit a perfumed cigarette, and hummed a bit from *Madame Butterfly*.[16]

General Zaroff had an exceedingly good dinner in his great paneled dining hall that evening. With it he had a bottle of his rarest wine. Two slight annoyances kept him from perfect enjoyment. One was the thought that it would be difficult to replace Ivan; the other was that his quarry had escaped him; of course the American hadn't played the game—so thought the general as he tasted his after-dinner liqueur. In his library he read, to soothe himself, from the works of Marcus Aurelius.[17] At ten he went up to his bedroom. He was deliciously tired, he said to himself, as he locked himself in. There was a little moonlight; so, before turning on his light, he went to the window and looked down at the courtyard. He could see the great hounds, and he called: "Better luck another time," to them. Then he switched on the light.

A man, who had been hiding in the curtains of the bed, was standing there.

"Rainsford!" screamed the general. "How did you get here?"

"Swam," said Rainsford. "I found it quicker than walking through the jungle."

The general sucked in his breath and smiled. "I congratulate you," he said. "You have won the game."

Rainsford did not smile. "I am still a beast at bay," he said, in a low, hoarse voice. "Get ready, General Zaroff."

The general made one of his deepest bows. "I see," he said. "Splendid! One of us is to furnish a repast for the hounds. The other will sleep in this very excellent bed. On guard, Rainsford."

He had never slept in a better bed, Rainsford decided.

---

**16.** *Madam Butterfly*, a tragic opera by Puccini (pü chē′ni).

**17.** *Marcus Aurelius* (mär′kəs ô rē′li əs), a Roman emperor (161 – 180 A.D.) and famous philosopher.

## DISCUSSION

1. What do you think is the main purpose of the shipboard conversation between Rainsford and Whitney? (See the Handbook entry for *dialogue*.)

2. How does "taking sides" with Rainsford against Zaroff increase suspense for the reader?

3. (a) In the dinner conversation between Rainsford and General Zaroff, the latter comments, "We do our best to preserve the amenities of civilization here." Why is this ironical? (b) What is the irony of Rainsford's situation? (See the Handbook entry for *irony*.)

4. To enjoy fully a story of suspense, we must feel that the actions and characters are believable. (a) Do you think the general is a believable character? (b) Could anyone actually have his philosophy of hunting? Defend your answer.

5. Could this story have taken place in any other setting? Explain.

6. (a) Do you think Rainsford's point of view at the beginning of the story changes because of his experience? (b) What do you think his future ideas on hunting will be?

## WORD STUDY

When you read this story, you were probably aware that the author used words and phrases intended to help the reader feel the suspense and terror of the situation. One of the two sentences in each group below contains words or phrases taken from the story. Number your paper from one to ten and next to each number write the letter of that sentence and also the words or phrases which you think he used to accomplish his purpose. Do you think he succeeded in all cases? Explain.

1. (a) The night was like moist black velvet.
   (b) It was a dark night.
2. (a) Sailors have a curious dread of the place.
   (b) Sailors are extremely frightened of the place.
3. (a) The cry stopped short as the lukewarm waters closed over his head.
   (b) The cry was pinched off as the blood-warm waters closed over his head.
4. (a) Dense jungle came down to the very edge of the cliffs.
   (b) Many plants and bushes grew on the edge of the cliffs.
5. (a) Bleak darkness was blacking out the sea and jungle when Rainsford sighted the lights.
   (b) It was almost dark when Rainsford saw the lights.
6. (a) The menacing look in the eyes did not change.
   (b) The odd expression in the eyes did not change.
7. (a) Giant rocks with razor edges crouch like a sea monster with wide-open jaws.
   (b) Giant rocks with sharp edges lie like an animal with wide-open jaws.
8. (a) The muck held tightly to his foot as if it were a giant leech.
   (b) The muck sucked viciously at his foot as if it were a giant leech.

## RICHARD CONNELL

The popularity of "The Most Dangerous Game" has not diminished with time. Since its publication in 1924, it has been included in dozens of anthologies. Of the more than three hundred stories Richard Connell wrote, it clearly remains the most popular.

Born in 1893, Connell began his writing career on the daily newspaper his father edited in Poughkeepsie. He later worked as an advertising copywriter, novelist, and short-story writer. During World War I, he enlisted in the army and edited *Gas Attack*, the weekly newspaper of his division.

He and his wife Louise Fox lived for many years in California, where he wrote screenplays. He died in 1949.

# Claudine's Book

*Harvey Swados*

*When Claudine finished her diaries she almost forgot about them, but then Aunt Lily found them. . . .*

NOT so long ago, in the town of Phoenix, a shopping center for upstate New York and western Vermont farmers since the days of the American Revolution, there lived a very bright young girl named Claudine.

Claudine's father, Fred Crouse, was a widower. He had brought his unmarried sister Lily over from Loudonville to cook and keep house for them, which she did very well, except that she was high-strung and got to feeling that she was wasting her life away in an old eleven-room house with no closets but a cupola big enough for a fancy-dress party. As soon as Claudine was old enough for school Lily got a part-time job, working at the local library four afternoons a week. It kept Lily in touch with the higher things and made her feel more worthwhile, but it meant that Claudine was left alone a lot.

Claudine didn't mind. She liked best hanging around her father's Mobilgas station on the state highway, but he didn't want her making all those crossings between school and the station; besides, the language of the truckers was apt to be kind of vulgar for a little girl's ears. Claudine didn't bother to tell her father, who worked thirteen hours a day and was harried with many worries, that she knew all those expressions already. Nothing ever happened in Phoenix was the main trouble. In fact, nothing ever had, not since Joseph Walker, whose widowed mother drank and took in sewing, got drafted and was captured in Korea and then wouldn't come back when the war was over. A turncoat, Aunt Lily called him, and said that when it was in *Life* magazine about his refusing to come home from China, two New York reporters had interviewed his mother, his school

friends and the librarian. But all that was before Claudine was born. Nothing else had happened since Joseph Walker had come back, which he finally did one day, to dig footings for contractors when he felt like working, and looking like the most ordinary man in the world.

But then Claudine looked like the most ordinary girl in the world. At least, you wouldn't have guessed from her appearance that extraordinary things were going to happen to her. Lily always said that Claudine's eyes were her best feature, which is what you always say about a girl who isn't pretty. She was long-legged and short-waisted, so that she seemed always to be groping up through the tops of her jumpers, like a giraffe reaching out over the fence; her nose was long, with widespread nostrils, like her father's, and had a tendency to run with the first frost. What was more, her short upper lip (Aunt Lily said that she had been a thumb-sucker) made her teeth seem unusually long, like Bugs Bunny's. Over all, she looked woebegone—although she rarely felt that way.

Claudine had only one friend. The other children at the consolidated school thought she was stuck-up, or funny-looking, or even dumb. When they caught her making faces at herself in the mirror of the girls' room—even though they did it sometimes themselves— they decided that Claudine was queer and left her to herself.

There was Robin Wales, though. He found none of these aspects of Claudine annoying, maybe because he had his own problems. First

---

lorraine fox

of all there was his name: it did him no good to bring up Robin Hood or even the great pitcher, Robin Roberts, because he didn't even try to hide from his tormentors the fact that he despised baseball. "It's boring and stupid," he said, and that finished him off in Phoenix, which prided itself on fielding a good Little League team.

Besides, Robin had no use for people who tried to push him around or play rough. "I'm not afraid of those guys, Eddie and Walter and the others," he told Claudine, and she knew that this was true, that he simply preferred going his own way, doing what she liked to do too.

In addition to his being more intelligent than any other sixth-grader, Claudine thought that Robin was quite handsome, despite his ears, which looked like the handles of a cream pitcher, and his mouth, in which there glittered a fat silver brace. The only thing about Robin that really bothered her—aside from his constantly trying to boss her, simply because he was a boy—was his transistor radio, which he wore suspended from his braided Indian belt that had his name spelled out defiantly and which he never turned off. All his allowance went for batteries, because he loved to surround himself with sound (just as Claudine, when she was not playing with him, loved to surround herself with silence).

"Weather in a word," he would shout when they met after school, "sultry!" But at least he knew what the word meant, and what the pollen count was, and underground testing, and Cambodia, as well as every rock-and-roll hit on the Top Ten from week to week and the Bargain of the Day at Giveaway Gordie's Used Carnival.

Much more important than his ordering her around when no one else even tried to, or constantly banging things in time to the noise that came from his beltline, was his ingenuity in figuring out new places to build huts. Neither could remember when they had started, for it seemed to them that they had been building huts forever. It was Robin's scheme to make a tree-house in the fork of the old hickory above the roof of the Crouses' barn and to make a lookout lodge out of Claudine's cupola where nobody ever went, not even Aunt Lily to store

winter stuff. And to build a hut in the back of the abandoned diner off Main Street, using some of the things that Robin's Uncle Burgie, who sold second-hand stoves, sinks, iceboxes, sump pumps, and hockey skates, couldn't get rid of, after they'd been standing outdoors for a season or two.

Like many married couples, Claudine and Robin derived separate benefits from their joint household arrangements. What was unusual was that Robin's pleasures were those you would commonly associate with a wife (although there was nothing sissyish about him), while Claudine's were of the kind ordinarily thought of as a husband's (although again she was no tomboy but an almost fragile girl, with those large, wondering, rather bulbous blue eyes). That is, what Robin enjoyed was the planning involved in making each place livable: finding scraps of carpeting, making pictures to hang on the walls, gluing up chairs out of abandoned camp stools, even rigging up hammocks for their sleeping bags, and then decorating with the boat paints and lacquers he grubbed from his father's garage.

But Claudine, although she cooperated willingly enough, was at bottom attached to the huts as sanctuaries. Just as a man will come home from a hard day in the world of affairs in search not of distractions but of a quiet zone for reflection and refreshment, so Claudine looked forward to her hours alone, when she had no obligations at home and Robin was busy feeding his hamsters or taking his accordion lessons.

It was from Robin's Uncle Burgie that Claudine got the big stack of old business diaries. They had some whitish mold on the binding part, and they dated back to 1926, but as Claudine pointed out to Robin, the inside pages were absolutely clean even if the days of the week didn't correspond, and lots of them were personalized with initials and enhanced with fascinating facts, like: Blériot Crossed the Channel This Day,[1] or Hebrew Feast of Pentecost[2]

---

1. *Blériot . . . Day.* On July 25, 1909, the French aviator Louis Blériot (blā′ryō′) made the first overseas flight in a heavier-than-air craft when he piloted a small monoplane across the English Channel.
2. *Hebrew Feast of Pentecost*, the Jewish festival of Shavuoth (shä vü′ōth), which is celebrated on the fiftieth day after Passover.

Begins This Day. Robin wasn't interested in these facts, however, or even in doing much with the diaries.

"Don't you want to find out who Blériot was? Or what the Hebrew Pentecost is? If you came to Feb twenty-two and it said G. Washington Born This Day and you were a foreigner, wouldn't it arouse your curiosity?"

"Everybody knows Washington. Even foreigners. Besides, I'm not a foreigner. The reason I got the diaries, they'll look good on the shelf."

"What shelf?"

"I know where to get the shelving. If you help me cover it, I'll put it up for you."

In return for her cooperating, Robin turned the diaries over to her. Standing there in rows, they posed a challenge beyond looking up Charles G. Dawes[3] and Gertrude Ederle:[4] all those blank pages cried out to be filled, while she was alone, quiet and sheltered, in one of the huts through which they had scattered the shelving and the diaries like so many branch libraries.

At first Claudine simply copied into them things that she liked. Sometimes it would be a special story out of the newspaper, like the one about the eleven-year-old girl who got up every morning at five o-clock to practice figure skating for two and a half hours before school so she could try out for the Olympics. Then, increasingly, it would be a poem or a stanza from a poem in one of the books that Aunt Lily was always bringing back from the library: live ones like Richard Eberhart[5] and Horace Gregory,[6] dead ones like Mallarmé[7] (because his name sounded like marmalade) and Keats[8] (because his mask was cool and his poems were not). She liked to copy down parts she didn't understand, because often they sounded the best. Sometimes she would look up the words in the dictionary; so she got to know

not only Blériot and Dawes but "sacrosanct" and "hyperbolic."

It took a good three or four months, and a couple of diaries all filled, before Claudine got up the nerve to put her own stuff in them. She started with what she called Wondering. "I wonder," she wrote, "why that girl Nanette got up every morning at five o'clock to go ice skating. Did she set the alarm herself? Did she make her own breakfast? Did she want to show her father she could be the greatest skater in the world? Why didn't the newspaper article tell all the things you would want to know?" Or: "I wonder what made Horace Gregory write that poem about the girl sitting at the piano. Was it just because he saw her once, in his own house? Maybe he made it all up. If I knew where to write to him, would he tell me, or would he think I was crazy?"

When she saw that Robin was really not interested in using the diaries, or even in looking at them, Claudine began to make up things out of her head for them.

"Sayings All My Own" was what she called them at first, and they fitted nicely into the one-day space of one diary, if she didn't write too small. If she was feeling businesslike, she would note that "The weather this day continues brillig and fine for Father's business. It makes people restless, so they get out on the road." Or, if she was moody and somewhat ingrown from having been left alone by her father, Aunt Lily, and Robin Wales, she would allow herself to become abstract and general: "Grownups believe that grownup is a babyish word. They prefer to call themselves adults. They don't think of children at all. They worry about them and they yell at them, but they don't think of them. It's more like putting them out of their minds. PS: Where does the expression come from, putting somebody out of his misery? Ask Robin."

But then when Robin asked her one day, "Say, Claudie, are you using those diaries?" she was almost ashamed to reply, "Yes, I put sayings into them."

Robin didn't seem to think there was anything odd about that, though. Claudine became all the more eager to fill the diaries, for now that they had become hers alone, she felt a

---

3. *Charles G. Dawes*, U.S. Vice-President (1925–1929). In 1925 he received a Nobel Peace Prize.
4. *Gertrude Ederle* (ā′dər lē), first woman to swim the English Channel.
5. *Richard Eberhart*, American poet.
6. *Horace Gregory*, American poet.
7. *Mallarmé*, Stéphane Mallarmé (stā′fän′ mä′lär′mā′), French poet.
8. *Keats*, John Keats, English poet.

funny responsibility to fill those hundreds of empty pages with her own words. Copying or pasting would be cheating.

She decided to make up a story with all kinds of things in it, descriptions of herself and her daily life, Robin and his radio, their mutual enemies, so that when she got to the end the diaries would have everything in them, like a good long novel.

"Today begins my life story," she wrote on New Year's Day. "My father was a very brave soldier, wounded during the Battle of the Bulge.[9] Now he is the prop. of a very big service station, the biggest Mobilgas station within a radius of 30 mi. He is 53, the oldest father I know of. My mother was a beautiful French girl named Adrienne who came to live in Phoenix with my father but could not have any children until I was born after 9 yrs of married life. She named me Claudine after her dead sister and then died herself before leaving the hospital. It was a tragedy of life for my father. I never knew her but Aunt Lily has lived with us ever since and is like a mother to me. Everyone says so. She is 48. Cont. tomorrow."

Next day, alone up in the cupola, Claudine curled her feet beneath her and began to write. "What do I look like? I am four foot nine inches tall and weigh 87 lbs. Aunt Lily says that if I hold up my chin and straighten my shoulders some day I will be a distinguished-looking woman. But right now I am homely, and I bet anything I am always going to be homely."

She paused to reach for a hand mirror that Robin had gotten from his Uncle Burgie. It had a fancy curved plastic handle, but the back had fallen off and a piece of the silver foil had peeled loose, so that when you looked at yourself in it there was a little hole smack in the middle of your forehead. You could squint through the hole clear to the tree outside the window, so that instead of seeing the skin on your forehead there would be a chickadee sitting freezing on the bare branch. "It goes to show," she wrote, "that once you can see not only the outside but the inside of your head, what you will find is a bird sitting on a branch

where your brains are supposed to be." And while she was at it, she made up a poem about the mirror with the hole in it that showed you the world as well as your face.

Not long after this, Claudine brought a newspaper clipping up to the cupola and stuck it in the diary with LePage's paste. It read: MODERN KIDS KNOW TOO MUCH, STATE PROF CLAIMS. Underneath the headline she wrote, "Why is he so sure. If he went to my school he'd claim just the opposite. Those kids don't know anything except the Top Ten." She hesitated, and then crossed out the last four words out of loyalty to Robin. "The real trouble is, they see more and more on TV, but they know less and less. They act wise but they think stupid."

When there was nothing special in the newspapers, Claudine wrote about her teachers ("Miss Bidwell wears stretch support stockings but she makes fun of other people"), her father ("I wish he didn't have to work such long hours, but what would he do at home? He never knows what to talk about to me or Aunt Lily"), and how she was changing so much every day it made her dizzy, even though when she looked in the mirror there she was, with the same popeyes and the same hole in the middle of her forehead. The only person she didn't describe, for reasons that weren't quite clear to her, was her Aunt Lily, who had to be in there when she wanted to write about food or clothes or books.

In about six months the diaries in the cupola were all written in. Claudine had to bring in the ones from the hut behind the diner and those Robin had wrapped in a poncho for her in the treehouse hut, and before she knew it they were filled up. Spring had come, and Claudine had been keenly aware of it, deserting the diaries for days on end to go fence walking and bike riding with Robin; but always she returned, when she was alone, to the diaries. It was almost as if without them she would have no excuse for being alone—or even for being.

And indeed it was strange that, once she had finished writing in the last of the diaries and brought her story up to date, putting on paper practically everything she had ever wanted to say, Claudine fell ill.

---

9. *Battle of the Bulge,* the last major battle between the Germans and the Americans in World War II.

It was a tremendous worry to Mr. Crouse, who couldn't cope with sickness, especially when the doctor wouldn't put an exact name to it. Despite everything his sister did, from making broths and compresses to reading to Claudine by the hour, her fever did not abate and at last she had to be taken to the hospital. There her weakened condition and lassitude were labeled as probable infectious mononucleosis, a very popular disease with children, but nobody would commit himself for sure. All they knew was that it seemed likely to be a long, slow business.

For Lily Crouse the house was now unbearably quiet, even though Claudine usually kept to herself when she was home. Just the idea that Claudine was up there in the cupola, doing Lord knew what with the Wales boy or even all by herself, had been comforting; but to come home from the library to that huge, ugly house and find it absolutely empty was almost more than Lily could stand. She would even have welcomed Robin's noisy presence, his piercing whistle and jangling transistor, but he never came by now—she was more likely to bump into him in the corridors of the hospital, where he came regularly to bring Claudine the gossip about Eddie, Walter, Miss Bidwell, and others.

One day, driven by uneasiness and loneliness, although she tried to tell herself that it was simply a desire to track down a lost library book (Gavin Maxwell's book on otters, actually, which Claudine had loved), Lily climbed the steep steps to the cupola. She had never once gone there during all the time that Claudine and Robin had been using it as a hideaway. Maybe Claudine had actually asked her not to, and she had promised—she couldn't quite remember. In any case the funny room looked absolutely unfamiliar; the kids had festooned the place with political posters and crepe paper left over from old birthday parties. A tatty, grease-stained straw mat lay on the floor and, against the wall, a lopsided bookcase was propped at one corner with broken ends of brick. In the bookcase were three rows of old diary volumes. Lily pulled one out and began to riffle its pages idly.

Several hours later, Lily crept down the stairs, her legs aching from having squatted for so long in one position. She went directly to her room and sat down at the desk where she kept the household accounts and mailed out statements to Fred's customers. Now she addressed an envelope to Josephine Schaefer, a classmate who had been working in New York for some years as a secretary in a large and aggressively successful publishing house.

*Dear Jo,* she wrote, *Under separate cover I am mailing you a carton of diaries which I have just found. As you will see, they are numbered in consecutive order with little pieces of adhesive tape. They are the work of Claudie, who has apparently been doing this writing on the sly for quite some time. I don't exactly know what to make of them—which is why I am taking the liberty of imposing on you. Is there someone in your office whom you could show them to?*

Lily gnawed at the corner of her mouth, and then added: *The thing is, Claudie has been in the hospital for some time (that's why I haven't been able to get down to the city) with an undiagnosed illness from which she is recuperating very slowly. I have a feeling now that it is all mixed up with what she's been writing, but anyway I don't want her to know I've been reading her private diaries—much less that I shipped them out of the house for anyone else's eyes. I'm sure you understand. Forgive me for not writing sooner, but as you can imagine things have been difficult here, what with Fred having to have a quick dinner and then scoot off to the hospital. Say hello to Janie—yours ever—Lily.*

It seemed to her only days later that the phone was ringing, wildly and demandingly, as Lily entered the empty echoing house. She hastened anxiously to the telephone, reaching out for it as she ran.

"Lily, it's me—Jo. Mr. Knowles says he sat up half the night with Claudine's diaries, and he wants to talk to you about them. All right?"

"Why, yes," she said uncertainly, "I suppose so."

In a moment a man's voice was saying, "Miss Crouse, I am grateful to you for sending us your niece's diaries. I would like very much to publish them, exactly as they are, and I think the firm will agree with me. They're a find. They're brilliant, they're unspoiled, there isn't a false note. Still, I have to ask you something."

Lily wanted very much to speak, but no words would come out. She moistened her lips, but it was no good.

Fortunately Mr. Knowles did not seem to expect a formal reply. "Miss Schaefer tells me that you're a librarian, Miss Crouse, and that Claudine is a small-town child, never been to New York more than once or twice, to Radio City Music Hall and the Metropolitan Museum. Can you assure me that you haven't had anything to do with her manuscript—I mean in the way of suggesting things to her to include or to leave out, or to change in any way?"

"Mr. Knowles," Lily said heatedly, "I never even knew those diaries existed until a few days ago. I never changed one word before I mailed them in to Jo. And if you don't believe me——"

"Your word is more than enough. I would like to take a run up to visit you, though, if I may. And Claudine, of course. When would it be most convenient, Miss Crouse?"

All she could think of to say was "Claudie is a very sick girl."

"Then we'll be in touch. Perhaps when she's well enough to travel, you can both come down here, as guests of the firm?"

That was the way it stood when Lily made her next visit to the hospital—she tried to space her visits between those of Fred and of Robin Wales. Claudine was propped up on two of those long, flat, slablike institutional pillows, her head so small and unsubstantial that it looked like some doll's carelessly placed in the middle of the bed. The pallor of her lengthy confinement accentuated the glitter of those pale prominent eyes, grown even more bulbous during the illness. Her forehead, too, jutted more sharply than ever (I'll have to make her bangs, Lily thought; surely that will help), while her body seemed scarcely to exist beneath the hospital blanket. She had been reading *A Tale of Two Cities*, which lay beside her on the coverlet.

"I like this," she said, pointing to it but scarcely opening her eyes. "Can you bring me some more Dickens books?"

"Listen, Claudie," Lily said determinedly, "I found your diaries."

Claudine gazed at her blankly. "They weren't lost."

"I mean, I read them." More unnerved by Claudine's silence than she had been by Mr. Knowles's talk, Lily added lamely, "It wasn't that I meant to pry. I was looking for a library book, and I just wondered what was in those old diaries, and then when I did open them. . . ."

Claudine stared at her, expressionless. She did not protest, or indicate that she had any intentions of interrupting. Finally Lily added, "Well, I thought they were just fascinating. Claudie, I do hope you're not angry."

"Why should I care?" Claudine gazed at her in puzzlement. "Listen, no fooling, can you bring me some more Dickens books? Like *Nicholas Nickleby*? I hear that's real good."

Lily stood helplessly at the bedside. It would be better to have Fred there, she guessed, before trying to explain about the publisher; and the doctor too—maybe she oughtn't to reveal anything more without consulting him. "Of course," she said. "I would have brought them with me now, except that I was a little, well, flustered."

Claudine could not have said why, but this announcement of Lily's, which only a month or two ago would have made her so angry that she would have been tempted to throw a babyish tantrum, now gave her a comfortable and comforting sense of relief. Is it like a secret that you don't want to tell but are sick of keeping and are glad when someone else finds it out and relieves you of the responsibility? It was almost better, she thought sleepily, snuggling down into the blankets, than the pills that the nurse gave her to swallow every evening and that made her drift off to sleep as though someone were paddling her off into the darkness on a Venetian gondola. As she heard Aunt Lily's footsteps fading away down the corridor, Claudine found herself thinking dreamily, It's over, it's over, and I'll get well now.

As soon as she awoke, refreshed and clearheaded, Claudine remembered those drowsy speculations. She had been right—it was all over—and she was restlessly eager to get out of the hospital. But the funny thing was, she observed in the next few days as she became more aware of others around her, that now Aunt Lily seemed to be suffering from the same symptoms that had afflicted her.

"I hope Aunt Lily didn't catch that bug from me," she said to her father when they were alone at home together, with Lily off to the library once again.

"Tootsie, what are you talking about?" Mr. Crouse demanded. "She's not sick or feverish. In fact she's back at work."

"Yes, but she's acting far away, like I was when it was first coming on. In fact . . . so are you."

And her father refused to look her in the eye. What was it, then? He was stubborn, like all adults, and there was no point in pressing him any further.

But Claudine knew she was right, and her suspicions were confirmed that Friday when she found her aunt furiously cleaning the house, as it had never been cleaned for as long as she could remember. What was more, Aunt Lily had made her a new corduroy jumper and bought her a blouse to go with it. Both had to be worn on Saturday morning, when Aunt Lily herself came out of her room with a brand-new outfit and two bright red spots on her cheekbones that might have been rouge but more likely were just plain excitement.

"What is this, the Fourth of July?" Claudine asked and was immediately sorry, for her aunt looked stricken.

"You know my friend Jo," Aunt Lily said, all in a rush. "Well, she is going to stop by for a bite of lunch with her boss, Mr. Knowles. He looks forward to meeting you."

"Me?" The whole thing sounded fishy. But it wasn't; it was all just as Aunt Lily had said. When it was over with, when Jo and Mr. Knowles had driven off in his little white sports car, Claudine couldn't even wait to wave goodby to them before she was off to explain everything to Robin, who had been forbidden access to the house, much less to the cupola, for the entire day.

"He's a great big stoop-shouldered man with the most beautiful shoes you ever saw," she explained to Robin when she found him at last,

up in the treehouse. "They look like they're handmade out of that cloth they use to put over loud-speakers—you know, with the little nubs in it."

"What's so great about that?"

"He wants to publish my book."

"What book?"

Claudine had to tell him the whole business of the diaries, which in fact she had almost forgotten about until Mr. Knowles brought up the subject.

"Wait a minute," Robin said wisely. "Wait a minute. You mean that guy came all the way up here from New York City just to see those old books I gave you? Just because you wrote some stuff in them?"

"He read it already. He wants to call it *Claudine's Book*. He says it's one of the best books he's read in a long time, and anyway I'm the youngest person he ever heard of to write a whole book."

"Are you going to get money for it?"

"I don't know. We didn't talk about that. Anyway my father would keep it for me, like he does my birthday money. Mr. Knowles was more interested in how I wrote the book, and where I wrote it, and all that. He made me take him up to the cupola and show him just how it was."

Robin was eying her somewhat suspiciously. "Did you tell him all about our huts?"

"Only what I had to. I mean, about your giving me the diaries and things like that. He didn't care about the huts, he just wanted to make sure I wrote it all myself."

"Who did he think wrote it? Me?"

Claudine shrugged. "What's the difference? I told him you were my very best friend, and that was why you gave me the diaries, and he said if I wanted to I could dedicate the book to you, instead of to Daddy or Aunt Lily."

But Robin had already lost interest, which was all right as far as Claudine was concerned, because in her heart she was even more surprised than he that anyone else, particularly a grownup, should be all that interested in what they had been doing. Robin had a pretty grandiose plan for a dam that would convert the little creek behind the Wales house into a fish hatchery.

They put a good part of the summer into the dam, with very few arguments except when Robin insisted on being insufferably bossy, and Claudine felt no great need to be off by herself, clipping newspapers and writing thoughts down—the way it was last winter, she reflected, when I was younger. They never did exactly finish the hatchery, because school started before they had collected all the stuff for the dam. And then, a couple of months after school had begun, Claudine's book arrived.

On the front of it was a great big picture of her with a dopey expression and her hair pulled back with a ribbon, and underneath in big letters, *Today begins my life story. . . .*

"Gee, I look awful," she said to her aunt.

Lily stared at her, astonished. "Aren't you excited? Aren't you proud?"

"I guess."

"Wait till the other children see the book. And your teachers! Then you won't be such a cool one."

It was true: the fuss was really something when the books turned up all over Phoenix. Kids that had ignored her for years wanted her to sit with them in the cafeteria. She was elected vice-president of her home room and made playground monitor. And Miss Bidwell—the old faker!—acted like she and Claudine had always been dear friends, and even asked her to sign her autograph on the title page of the book.

"But you know something?" she said to Robin as they pushed through the piles of heaped-up leaves on Genesee Street on their way home. "I think the whole thing is a pain in the neck."

"This is only the beginning, folks!" Robin shouted at her. "You ain't seen nothin' yet!"

"I'd rather be left alone."

"Then you shouldn't have written all that. Who forced you to do it? Nobody twisted your arm. When you make your bed you have to lie in it."

"That's a cliché. You don't even know what a cliché *is.*"

But it did make her uneasy in the days that followed, being stopped at her father's service station or in front of Dohrmeyer's Meat Market by total strangers who wanted her to pose with them for pictures, or sign things, or tell them what she would be when she grew up: was it really all her fault for writing in Robin's diaries? Claudine became more irritable as the demands on her got worse, and finally she took it out on Robin, mainly because instead of sympathizing he kept giving her more clichés.

"If it hadn't been for you and your Uncle Burgie and all those old diaries, I never would have gotten into all this trouble."

Robin was very hurt. He said she was ungrateful and bratty, and he wasn't going to play with her any more. In fact he wasn't even going to talk to her. She could hang out with her new fair-weather friends instead.

In the middle of all this a group of strangers checked in the Al-Rae Motel up the street from Mr. Crouse's Mobil station and fanned out from there like a bunch of G-men after a kidnaper—as if everyone in Phoenix didn't know what they were up to even before they had unpacked their bags. There were four of them, three men and a young woman researcher. They were all employed by a big picture magazine—the bearded Hungarian, weighted down with leather tote bags, was a photographer, the cynical young man with pockmarks was a writer, and the man who spoke in a whisper (as though, Claudine thought, he was ashamed of his own voice) was a consulting child psychologist.

The girl researcher, who was pretty, with a big wide mouth and an Irish grin, turned up everyplace you could think of, the photographer trotting along after, muttering in Hungarian and measuring the air with his light meter. They walked right into the school as if they owned it—you could see them through the seventh-grade window—and took millions of pictures. Then they went off in their rented Ford to the F. Crouse Mobil station, and the next day, which was Saturday, they were prowling around Robin's huts, even trying to climb into his treehouse. Claudine was afraid that Robin would think she had tipped them off (actually, they must have studied up on the huts in her book) and would get twice as sore. But he was keeping to his promise not to talk to her.

The other two, the pock-marked writer always grinning skeptically, as though he didn't even believe that the world was round, and the whispering psychologist, were much less in evidence. For a while Claudine didn't even know where they were, and it wasn't until they came to her house and sat down in the parlor with Aunt Lily that she got wind of what they were up to.

Aunt Lily thought Claudine had gone to the movies with Robin to see a Charlton Heston movie about God, so it was easy to sneak in through the kitchen pantry and listen. The child psychologist was doing most of the talking, in his tiny baby voice, and Aunt Lily, all dolled up with coral earrings and toilet water and her silk scarf, was sitting on the edge of her chair ready to fall off, listening so hard her earrings were practically standing on end.

"Surely it is obvious to a woman of your intelligence, Miss Crouse," the child psychologist was whispering, "that you have been responsible for the upbringing of one of the most remarkable children of modern times. That is, assuming that Claudine did all of the writing of the book herself."

"Why did you add that?"

From her vantage post Claudine could not see the psychologist, but she was in line with Aunt Lily's bust, rising and falling very fast, and with the pock-marked writer, grinning like an absolute fiend.

"Because in all of my years of experience, both in the clinic and in the field, I have never encountered such a combination of insight and steadfastness in one so young."

"You have to remember, Dr. Fibbage (that was what the name sounded like to Claudine), she has been very ingrown. She's had only one real friend, and no one but me to turn to for books and ideas."

The writer broke in, "Miss Crouse, I must say that it is your ideas and your sensitivity that I find in *Claudine's Book.*"

Claudine was fascinated by the expression that stole over her aunt's face. It was exactly like that of Aunt Lily's fat friend Marie Klemfuss when someone tried to tempt her off her crash diet with a slice of angel-food cake—a mixture of fear, greed, and calculation.

"Well," her aunt said slowly, "if Mr. Knowles believed me when he first decided to publish it, I don't see why I should have to explain any further."

"Mr. Knowles couldn't have known you as we do."

Aunt Lily turned red, and the writer, Mr. Craft, added hastily, "I'm not suggesting that you would ever deceive anyone. But in addition to being an intellectual, you are a very modest person. Obviously you would be reluctant to confirm the extent of your influence on little Claudine."

Little Claudine! All of a sudden she felt like throwing up. She tiptoed backward, pulled open the screen door soundlessly, and bolted off down the street. When she got to the Waleses she went right on into the kitchen without knocking and almost bumped into Robin, who was running his thumb around the inside edge of a jar of Skippy peanut butter.

"Don't tell me you're not going to speak to me," Claudine said breathlessly, taking advantage of the fact that Robin's mouth was stuck with peanut butter. "If you heard what I just did, you'd want advice, too."

He listened quite impassively to her description of Aunt Lily and the two visitors, and even turned down the volume of his transistor. But when she reached the part where Aunt Lily got the hungry look in her eye, Robin held up his hand.

"Just a sec." He twisted the dial to a roar. "And now the one you've asked for, the Madmen singing the number-one hit of the week, 'Weeping and Wailing.'"

Robin turned off the radio and said, very practically, "It's all clear to me. Those people are out to make trouble for you. They'll hound you worse than the Beatles."

"Don't you think I know that?"

"They're just zeroing in on you now—I heard all about the technique on Long John's program. First they interview your friends, then your enemies, and then your family. By the time they get to you, they know all about you and you feel like they've been reading your mail or listening to you talk in your sleep. Well, that's the way the ball bounces, Claudie."

"You and your expressions. They'll be after you too, watch and see."

"They were already. Where do you think they came before they got to your house?"

Claudine stared. "What did you tell them?"

"Nothing special." Robin was very casual. "I told them I got the diaries from Uncle Burgie for decoration for the huts. I told them I never knew what you did with them. I told them you had a good imagination, almost as good as mine."

"Thanks."

"They asked me about your aunt. I said she was the smartest lady in Phoenix, smarter than all our teachers put together, starting with Miss Bidwell."

"That wouldn't take much." Claudine thought for a moment. "Got any crackers?"

"Just Ritz."

"I like them." She dug deep into the box he offered her. "I can tell you've got an idea."

Robin nodded. "As long as everybody thinks you did the book all by yourself, they'll be after you. People like that Mr. Fibbage——"

"Dr. Fibbage."

"What's the diff? He'll hang around studying you like you were in a bottle. And they'll keep on pointing at you wherever you go. When you get to high school all the teachers will say, Well, Miss Crouse, I should think anyone who could write a whole book could do better than eighty-two on a simple test. And if you want to go to college——"

Claudine shuddered. "I could change my name, though."

"They're on to you. You think Jackie Kennedy could change her name?"

Claudine listened intently. Robin had a crazy imagination, but he was very smart when it came to practical matters. Smarter, in fact, than her own father, the only other person in the world with whom she might have consulted about this thing. Her father would be of no help at all. He meant well, when he was around, but he had never been able to bring himself to say anything to her about the book (as if it was dirty), so this was a decision she would have to make by herself. Ever since the business about the book had come out, Mr. Crouse had taken to looking at his daughter peculiarly; and now that it had gotten out of hand, he seemed positively frightened of her, as though he had fathered a witch.

Claudine walked home slowly. By the time she got there, the pock-marked writer and Dr.

Fibbage were standing on the porch saying good-by to Aunt Lily, who was clenching her hands tightly together, as if she held something between them, like a little bird, that she was afraid would fly away.

"Well, well, well," whispered Dr. Fibbage, "and here is Claudine. Just the very person I'd like to see."

"Would you like to see *us*, Claudine?" asked Mr. Craft, grinning at her as if he were about to eat her. The way he put it, she would be chicken if she said no. "I'll buy you a soda downtown if it's all right with your aunt."

"If Claudine would like to go. . . ." Aunt Lily said faintly.

"Sure I would." Before anyone could say another word, she was leading the way to their shiny rented car. "I'll be back soon, Aunt Lily."

"We won't keep her long."

"A very unusual woman, your aunt," the psychologist whispered to her from the back seat, and peered at her intently.

"That's for sure," Claudine said.

"You're not so very usual yourself," Mr. Craft remarked as he headed the car down to Main Street. "Muscling in on my racket like that. I got enough trouble with the competition without having to fend off eleven-year-old kids."

"I'm almost twelve."

"Big deal."

"Say, Mr. Craft," she asked, "do you like writing?"

"It beats working, I'll tell you that. But then I'm not famous. Just well known. How about you?"

"Oh, I got bored with it by the time I finished up the diaries. I don't think I'll do anymore."

"What makes you say that?" the doctor demanded eagerly.

"I just told you. It's boring. Besides, I got sick of my aunt nagging at me to fill up all those diaries."

"You what?" All of a sudden Dr. Fibbage was panting like a dog in the summer sun. "You mean your aunt knew about the book while you were writing it?"

"Hey," Claudine said to Mr. Craft, "stop here, at O'Molony's Pharmacy. They've got the best ice cream, with the little chunks in it, not the Softi-Freeze stuff."

"Wait a minute," Dr. Fibbage whispered at the top of his lungs as they stood in front of the drugstore. "You haven't answered my question yet."

"Can I have my sundae? Then we can talk some more."

In the booth, after she had ordered a Phoenix Monster Sundae, Claudine said to Dr. Fibbage, "Why did you get so shook up when I told you my aunt knew about the book?"

"Because it was supposed to have been as much of a surprise to her as it was to the rest of us, later on."

"Oh, she's just modest. You said yourself she's very unusual. The fact is, she thought up the whole thing, practically. Mr. Craft, be careful, you're spilling coffee on your tie."

"My hands are shaky. That's what too much writing does," the writer said to her. "I thought I heard you say the book was your aunt's and not yours. Isn't that silly of me?"

"Well, if you'll promise not to tell anybody . . . I mean, I promised my aunt I wouldn't tell anybody. But I don't think it's fair for me to keep getting all the credit and have people buying me sundaes and taking my picture and everything, when actually most of the good stuff in the book is Aunt Lily's. She loves to make believe. It was her idea right from the start, except she was afraid people would make fun of her, so she decided to put everything in my name."

She looked across the table at the child psy-chologist. "Dr. Fibbage," she said, "you look like you just saw a ghost. Did I say something wrong?"

He reached out uneasily to pat her hand. "I'm unused to such honesty from someone so young."

"Claudine is a red-blooded American girl, that's why," Mr. Craft said heartily. "Here you thought you could watch Emily Dickinson grow up under your microscope, Fibbage, and instead you found yourself buying Monster Sundaes for a healthy, normal seventh-grader. Am I right or wrong, Claudine?"

"You couldn't be more right, Mr. Craft," Claudine replied after she had licked off her spoon. "You know something? You talk very sensibly, for a writer. I told my friend Robin Wales that writers could be as sensible as archi-tects—that's what he's going to be. I'm begin-ning to think maybe some day I'll be a writer after all—I mean a real one, not an imitation. Well," she said, rising, "good-by now, and thanks a lot for the sundae. I promised Robin I'd play with him if all the reporters and pho-tographers would leave us alone. And I guess now they will, won't they?"

At the front of the drugstore, Claudine turned to look back at the two men who stood at the cashier's counter, their feet nailed to the floor, staring after her. She waved farewell to them and, whistling the "Marseillaise,"[10] ran off down the street in search of Robin.

---

**10.** *"Marseillaise"* (mär/se/yez/), the national anthem of France, composed during the French Revolution.

---

## DISCUSSION

1. Before Claudine begins to fill up her diary, what information does the author provide about her background, family, and habits?

2. (a) Why does Claudine begin writing? (b) What kinds of information does she record in her diaries?

3. Describe Claudine's re-lationship with her Aunt Lily, with her father, and with Robin.

4. How does Claudine become famous?

5. (a) How does Aunt Lily respond to Claudine's fame? Why? (b) How does Claudine, herself, respond?

6. How does Claudine regain her privacy?

7. Were you disappointed or satisfied with the ending? Why?

## WORD STUDY

Recognizing the arrangement and meaning of parts of words—the *structure* of words—is a help in understanding and pronouncing unfamiliar words.

Words that are composed of two or more words that combine their meaning to make a new word are called compound words. Words like *horse opera, oven-*

wood, penny pincher, and turncoat are colorful, easy words if you think about the parts that make up the compounds.

Some words are made up of a root word plus prefixes or suffixes (affixes).

| prefix | root | suffix |
|--------|------|--------|
| un | bear | able |

Many words have roots which come from Latin or Greek words. To help you review, look at the roots and affixes at the end of this word study. Then on your paper complete each sentence with a word that is made up of two or more of these word parts. In each case some part of the word is given.

1. Claudine spent a lot of time writing her *auto*_____.

2. Aunt Lily mailed Claudine's *manu*_____ off to New York.

3. There is an *in*_____ etched on the front of the tombstone.

4. Are you going to ask the author to _____*graph* a copy of her book?

5. If she writes a few sentences, we will hire a *graph* _____ to study her handwriting.

6. Do you think she'll be a geologist, a *bio*_____, or a novelist some day?

auto *self*
script *written*
-logy *study, science*
in-
graph (y) *write, draw*
-ist
manu *by hand*
bio *life*
-tion

## Of Beginnings . . .

The author of "Peter Two" makes a simple opening statement which sets the mood and establishes the setting for the rest of the story: "It was Saturday night and people were killing each other by the hour on the small screen."

Richard Connell begins with Whitney's foreshadowing remark about a mysterious island in "The Most Dangerous Game." In "Claudine's Book," Swados establishes setting and immediately introduces his main character.

Influenced by the literary fashions of the time in which they live or motivated solely by their own individual talents, writers have devised a number of ways of getting into their stories.

Perhaps one of the most intriguing beginnings is the first sentence of *Treasure Island* by Robert Louis Stevenson: "Squire Trelawney, Dr. Livesy, and the rest of these gentlemen having asked me to write down the whole particulars about Treasure Island, from the beginning to the end, keeping nothing back but the bearings of the island, and that only because there is still treasure not yet lifted, I take up my pen in the year of grace 17___, and go back to the time when my father kept the 'Admiral Benbow' Inn, and the brown old seaman, with the sabre cut, first took up his lodging under our roof."

This old-fashioned beginning courses along like a ship in full sail, providing new interest at every dip and plunge. Treasure not lifted? Brown old seaman with a sabre cut? This type of opening delights some and exasperates those who prefer something plainer, such as Dickens's no-nonsense opening to *A Christmas Carol*: "Marley was dead, to begin with."

Many authors prefer to make a general observation before acquainting us with the setting or characters: "It is a truth universally acknowledged, that a single man in possession of a good fortune must be in want of a wife." Do you detect a tinge of irony in this opening sentence from *Pride and Prejudice* by Jane Austen?

Description of the weather is a commonplace way of beginning (and ending) a story; that the technique still works well is illustrated by the opening sentence of "The Scarlet Ibis" in this unit: "It was in the clove of seasons, summer was dead but autumn had not yet been born, that the ibis lit in the bleeding tree."

One of the better opening sentences was written by Ernest Hemingway in "The Short Happy Life of Francis Macomber": "It was now lunch time and they were sitting under the double green fly of the dining tent pretending that nothing had happened." Of course, something *has* happened in this rather exotic setting, and only the most jaded reader could fail to want to read on.

The next supplementary article will examine some of the ways authors get themselves out of their stories—often a much more difficult task.

# LUTHER

*Jay Neugeboren*

LUTHER arrived at Booker T. Washington Junior High School (Columbus Avenue and 107th Street, Manhattan) in September of 1955, six months before I did. I met him at the end of February, the third week I taught there, when one of the assistant principals asked me to cover the cafeteria during fifth period for a teacher who had to be at a conference. "Good luck with the animals," I remember him saying.

I was on my guard when I entered the cafeteria; perhaps even a trifle scared. The stories I had been hearing in the teachers' lounge had prepared me to expect anything. During the winter months the students were not allowed to leave the lunchroom and the results of keeping them penned in—the fights, the food throwing, the high-pitched incessant chattering in Spanish, the way the Negro and Puerto Rican boys and girls chased each other around the tables—such things did, I had to admit, give the room a zoo-like quality.

The day I was assigned, however, was a Catholic holy day and many of the students were absent. Those who remained filled a little less than half of the large room and though they were noisy it was relatively easy to keep them in order. Luther sat at a table by himself, near the exit to the food line. Occasionally, I noticed, a few boys would come and sit next to him. The third time I patrolled his area, however, his table was empty and he stopped me.

"Hey, man," he said, poking me in the arm to get my attention, "you new here?"

He had a stack of about ten cookies in his other hand and he put one into his mouth as he waited for an answer. When I told him that I was not new, he nodded and looked at me. "You have any trouble yet?"

"No," I said, as sternly as possible. Despite my feelings of sympathy for the students, I knew that if I ever hoped to get anywhere with them I had to appear tough and confident. "No," I repeated, almost, I recall, as if I were challenging him. "I haven't."

Luther cocked his head to one side then and smiled slowly. "You will," he said, and went back to his cookies.

In the teachers' lounge, the first time I told the story, somebody asked if the boy who had stopped me was a little Negro kid, very black, with a slight hunchback. I said he was. The teachers laughed. "That's Luther," one of them said.

"He's batty," said another. "Just leave him be."

I repeated the story endlessly. It was the first anecdote of my teaching experience that excited admiration and some sort of reaction from those I told it to, and this was important to me then. I had no more direct encounters with Luther that term, though I did see him in the halls, between classes. I always smiled at him and he would smile back—or at least I thought he did. I could never be sure. This

Reprinted with the permission of Farrar, Straus & Giroux, Inc. and Victor Gollancz Ltd. from *Corky's Brother* by Jay Neugeboren, copyright © 1966, 1969 by Jay Neugeboren.

bothered me, especially the first time it happened. Through my retelling of the story, I realized, he had become so real to me, so much a part of my life that I think I took it for granted that our encounter had assumed equal significance in his life. The possibility that he had not even repeated the story to a single one of his friends disturbed me.

Once or twice during the term I spotted him wandering around the halls while classes were in session, slouching down a corridor, his body pressed against the tile walls. When I asked the other teachers if he was known for cutting classes, they told me again to just leave him be —that the guidance counselor had suggested the teachers let him do what he wanted to. He was harmless, they said, *if* you left him alone. Those teachers who had him in their classes agreed with the guidance counselor. Left alone, he didn't annoy them. When he wanted to, he worked feverishly—and did competent work; but when he didn't want to work he would either sit and stare or just get up, walk out of the room, and wander around the building. He was, they concluded, a mental case.

I returned to Booker T. Washington Junior High School the following September, and Luther turned up in one of my English classes. He had changed. He was no longer small, having grown a good five inches over the summer, and he was no longer quiet. When classwork bored him now, he would stand up and, instead of leaving the room, would begin telling stories. Just like that. He had his favorite topics, too—his cousin Henry who had epilepsy, Willie Mays, what was on sale at the supermarket, the football team he played on, the stories in the latest *Blackhawk* comic book. When he ran out of stories, he would pull *The National Enquirer* out of his back pocket and begin reading from it, always starting with an item in the "Personals" columns that had caught his eye. I never knew what to do. When I would yell at him to sit down and be quiet, he would wave his hand at me impatiently and continue. Moreover, no expression on his face, nothing he ever said, indicated that he thought he was doing anything wrong. An hour after disrupting a class, if I would see him in the corridor, he would give me a big smile and a hello. After a

while, of course, I gave up even trying to interrupt him. I listened with the other students —laughing, fascinated, amazed.

I tried to remember some of his stories, but when I retold them they never seemed interesting, and so I purposely gave Luther's class a lot of composition work, trying to make the topics as imaginative as possible—with the hope, of course, that he would use one of them to let loose. But all the topics, he declared, were "stupid" and he refused to write on any of them. Then, when I least expected it, when I assigned the class a "How to—" composition, he handed one in. It was typewritten on a piece of lined notebook paper, single-spaced, beginning at the very top of the page and ending just at the first ruled line. It was titled "How to Steal Some Fruits."

How to Steal Some Fruits, by Luther
Go to a fruit store and when the fruitman isn't looking take some fruits. Then run. When the fruitman yells "Hey you stop taking those fruits" run harder. That is how to steal some fruits.

The next day he sat quietly in class. When I looked at him, he looked down at his desk. When I called on him to answer a question, he shrugged and looked away. At three o'clock, however, no more than five seconds after I had returned from escorting my official class downstairs, he bounded into my room, full of life, and propped himself up on the edge of my desk.

"Hey, man," he said. "How'd you like my composition? It was deep, wasn't it?"

"Deep?"

"Deep, swift, *cool*—you know."

"I liked it fine," I said, laughing.

"Ah, don't put me on, man—how *was* it?"

"I liked it," I repeated, my hands clasped in front of me on the desk. "I mean it."

His face lit up. "You mean it? I worked hard on it, Mr. Carter. I swear to God I did." It was the first time, I remember, that he had ever addressed me by my name. He stopped and wiped his mouth. "How'd you like the typing? Pretty good, huh?"

"It was fine."

"Man," he said, stepping down from my desk and moving to the blackboard. He picked up a piece of chalk and wrote his name, printing it in capital letters. "How come you so tight? Why don't you loosen up? I ain't gonna do nothing. I just want to know about my composition. That's all."

I felt I could reach him, talk to him. I wanted to—had wanted to for some time, I realized —but he was right. I was tight, uncomfortable, embarrassed. "Where'd you get a typewriter?" I offered.

He smiled. "Where I get fruits," he replied, then laughed and clapped his hands. I must have appeared shocked, for before I could say anything he was shaking his head back and forth. "Oh man," he said. "You are really deep. I swear. You really are." He climbed onto my desk again. "You mind talking?"

"No," I said.

"Good. Let me ask you something—you married?"

"No," I said. "Do you think I should be married?"

"It beats stealing fruits," he said, and laughed again. His laugh was loud and harsh and at first it annoyed me, but then his body began rocking back and forth as if his comment had set off a chain of jokes that he was telling himself silently, and before I knew it I was laughing with him.

"I really liked the composition," I said. "In fact, I hope you don't mind, but I've already read it to some of the other teachers."

"Yeah?"

"They thought it was superb."

"It's superb," he said, shaking his head in agreement. "Oh, it's superb, man," he said, getting up again and walking away. His arms and legs moved in different directions and he seemed so loose that when he turned his back to me and I noticed the way his dirty flannel shirt was stretched tightly over his misshapen back, I was surprised—as if I'd noticed it for the first time. He walked around the room, muttering to himself, tapping on desks with his fingertips, and then he headed for the door. "I'm superb," he said. "So I be rolling on my superb way home——"

"Stay," I said.

He threw his arms apart. "You win!" he declared. "I'll stay." He came back to my desk, looked at me directly, then rolled his eyes and smiled. "People been telling stories to you about me?"

"No."

"None?" he questioned, coming closer.

"All right," I said. "Some——"

"That's all right," he said, shrugging it off. He played with the binding of a book that was on my desk. Then he reached across and took my grade book. I snatched it away from him and he laughed again. "Oh, man," he exclaimed. "I am just so restless!—You know what I mean?"

He didn't wait for an answer but started around the room again. The pockets of his pants were stuffed and bulging, the cuffs frayed. The corner of a red and white workman's handkerchief hung out of a back pocket. He stopped in the back of the room, gazed into the glass bookcase, and then turned to me and leaned back. "You said to stay—what you got to say?"

The question was in my mind, and impulsively I asked it: "Just curious—do you remember me from last year?"

"Sure," he said, and turned his back to me again. He looked in the bookcase, whirled around, and walked to the side of the room, opening a window. He leaned out and just as I was about to say something to him about it, he closed it and came back to the front of the room. "Man," he exclaimed, sitting on my desk again. "Were you ever scared that day! If I'd set off a cherry bomb, you'd have gone through the fan." He put his face closer to mine. "Man, you were scared green!"

"Was I scared of you, Luther?" I asked, looking straight into his eyes.

"Me? Nah. Nothing to be scared of." He hopped off the desk and wiped his name off the blackboard with the palm of his hand; then he started laughing to himself. He looked at me, over his shoulder. "Bet I know what you're thinking now," he said.

"Go ahead——"

"You're thinking you'd like to *help* a boy like me. Right? You're getting this big speech ready in your head about——"

"No," I interrupted. "I wasn't."

He eyed me suspiciously. "You sure?"

"I'm sure."

"Not even with compositions? Oh, man, if you'd help me with compositions, before we'd be through with me, I'd be typing like a whiz." He banged on a desk with his palms, and then his fingers danced furiously on the wood as he made clicking noises inside his mouth. "Ding!" he said, swinging the carriage across. "Ain't it fun to type!"

"Okay," I said. "Okay. Maybe I was thinking that I would like to help you."

"I knew it, man," he said to himself. "I just knew it."

"You have a good mind, Luther—much better than you let on."

"I do, I do," he muttered, chuckling. I stood up and went to the closet to get my coat. "Okay. What do I get if I work for you?" he asked.

I shrugged. "Nothing, maybe. I can't promise anything."

"I *like* that, man," he said.

"Could you call me Mr. Carter?" I asked somewhat irritably. "I don't call you, 'Hey, you' —— "

"Okay, Mr. Carter," he said. He took my coat sleeve. "Let me help you on with your coat, Mr. Carter."

We walked out of the room and I locked the door. "You ain't a *real* social worker like the others," he commented as we started down the stairs. He held the door open for me. "I do like that."

I nodded.

"Playing it close to the vest again, huh? Tight-mouthed."

"Just thinking," I said.

When we were outside, he asked me what he had to do.

"For what?" I asked.

"To get you to help me to be somebody, to educate myself—all that stuff."

"Do what you want to do," I said. "Though you might start by doing your homework. Then we'll see —— "

"I know," he said, cocking his head to one side again. "If I play ball with you, you'll play ball with me. Right? Okay, okay. I know."

Then he was gone, running down the street, his arms spread wide as if he were an airplane, a loud siren-like noise rising and falling from him as he disappeared from view.

The next few months were without doubt the most satisfying to me of any during the eight years I've been a teacher. Luther worked like a fiend. He was bright, learned quickly, and was not really that far behind. He did his homework, he paid attention in class, he studied for tests, and he read books. That was most important. On every book he read I asked him to write a book report: setting, plot, theme, characters, his opinion of the book—and once a week, on Thursday afternoons, we would get together in my room for a discussion. During the remainder of the term he must have gone through at least forty to fifty books. Most of them had to do with sports, airplanes, and insects. For some reason he loved books about insects. All the reports came to me typed, and on some he drew pictures—"illustrations" he called them, which, he claimed, would be a help to me in case I had not read the book.

When we would finish talking about books, I would help him with his other subjects, and his improvement was spectacular. I looked forward to my sessions with him, to his reports, to just seeing him—yet from day to day, from moment to moment, I always expected him to bolt from me, and this pleased me. Every time he came to me for a talk I was truly surprised.

When the term ended, he asked if I would continue to help him. I said I would. He was not programed for any of my English classes during the spring term, but we kept up with our weekly discussions. As the weather improved, however, he read less and less; I didn't want him to feel that he *had* to come see me every Thursday, and so, about a week before the opening of the baseball season, I told him I thought he had reached the point where he could go it alone. "When you feel like talking, just come knocking," I said. "We don't need a schedule." He seemed relieved, I thought, and I was proud that I had had the sense to release him from any obligation he might have felt.

Then, suddenly, I didn't see him anywhere for three weeks. I asked his homeroom teacher about him and she said she hadn't seen him either; she had sent him a few postcards but had received no reply. That very night—it was almost as if he had been there listening, I thought—he telephoned me at home.

"Is this Mr. Carter? This is Luther here."

"Hi, Luther," I said.

"I looked you up in the telephone book. You mind me calling you at home?"

"No, no. I don't mind."

"Okay," he said, breathing hard. "I just wanted to let you know not to worry about me because I'm not in school. Okay?"

"Sure," I said. "Sure."

"I had some things to take care of—you know?"

"Sure," I said.

"Man, you *know* you're itching to ask me *what?*" He laughed. "You are deep. I'll be back Monday."

That was all. On Monday, as he'd promised, he returned to school and came to visit me in my room at three o'clock. We talked for a while about the way the pennant race was going, and then he said, "Okay, let's cut the jazz, man. I got something to say to you." He seemed very intense about it and I told him that I was listening carefully. He pointed a finger at me. "Now, we stopped our sessions, right?"

"Right," I said.

"And the day after we stopped, I began to play the hook for three straight weeks, right?"

"Right."

"Okay. Now you can tell me it ain't so, but I'll bet you'll be thinking it was your fault. It ain't. If you want the truth, I ain't done a stick of work all term for *any* teacher—so don't go thinking that I stopped being a good student cause we stopped our meetings." He let out a long breath.

"I'm glad you told me," I said.

"Man," he said, getting up and going to the door. "Don't *say* anything, huh? Why you got to *say* something all the time?" He came toward me. "*Why?*" He was almost screaming and I slid my chair back from the desk. He shook his head frantically. "Why, man?" he said. He reached into his side pocket and I started to stand up. Abruptly, he broke into laughter. "Oh man, you are deep! You are just so deep!" He clapped his hands and laughed

at me some more. "Ra-ta-tat-tat!" he said as he banged on a desk. "You're real sweet, man! Just so sweet! Ra-ta-tat-tat! Comin' down the street!" He sat down in one of the seats. "But don't you worry none. I got seven liberry cards now and books growing out the ceiling. I got a liberry card for Luther King and one for Luther Queen and one for Luther Prince and one for Luther Jones and one for Luther Smith and one for Luther Mays and one for Luther B. Carter." He banged on the top of the desk with his fist, then drummed with his fingers again. "But don't you worry none—ra-ta-tat-tat—just don't you worry——"

"I'm not," I said.

"That's all," he said, and dashed out of the room.

He attended classes regularly for about two weeks and then disappeared again for a week. He returned for a few days, stayed away, returned. The pattern continued. In the halls when we saw each other he would always smile and ask if I was worrying and I would tell him I wasn't. Once or twice, when he was absent, he telephoned me at home and asked me what was new at school. He got a big charge out of this. Then another time, I remember, he came riding through the schoolyard on a bicycle during sixth period, when I was on patrol. "Don't report me, man!" he yelled, and rode right back out, waving and shouting something in Spanish that made everybody laugh.

Near the end of May, the assistant principal in charge of the eighth grade called me into his office. He knew I was friendly with Luther, he said, and he thought that I might talk to the boy. For the past six or seven months, he told me, Luther had been in and out of juvenile court. "Petty thefts," the assistant principal explained. I wasn't surprised; Luther had hinted at this many times. I'd never pressed him about it, however, not wanting to destroy our relationship by lecturing him. The assistant principal said he didn't care whether I said anything to Luther or not. In fact, he added, he would have been just as happy to get rid of him—but before he was shipped off to a 600 school[1] or put away somewhere else, he wanted to give me an

---

1. *600 school,* a school for emotionally disturbed and disruptive students.

opportunity to do what I could. More for me, he said, than for Luther.

About a week after this, on a Friday, Luther telephoned me.

"How've you been?" I asked.

"Superb, man," he said. "Hey, listen—we ain't been seeing much of each other lately, have we?"

"No——"

"No. Okay. Listen—I got two tickets to see the Giants play tomorrow. You want to come?" I didn't answer immediately. "Come on—yes or no—tickets are going fast——"

"I'd like to," I said. "Yes. Only—only I was wondering where you got the money for the tickets." I breathed out, glad I had said it.

Luther just laughed. "Oh man, you're not gonna be like that, are you? You been listening to too many stories again. That judge from the court must of been gassing with you. Tell you what—you come to the game and I'll tell you where I got the tickets. A deal?"

"A deal."

"Meet you in front of the school at eleven o'clock—I like to get there early to see Willie go through batting practice. Batting practice— that's more fun than the game sometimes. You know?"

He was waiting for me when I got there a few minutes before eleven the following day. "Let's go," he said, flourishing the tickets. "But don't ask me now, man—let's enjoy the game first. Okay?"

I did enjoy the game. The Giants were playing the Cardinals and to Luther's delight Willie Mays had one of his better days, going three-for-four at bat, and making several brilliant plays in the field. For most of the game I was truly relaxed. Along about the eighth inning, however, I began to think about the question again —to wonder when would be the best time to ask it. Luther, it seemed, had forgotten all about it. The Giants were winning 5–2.

"Oh man," he said. "If only that Musial don't do something, we're home free. Look at Willie!" he exclaimed. "Ain't he the greatest that ever lived. He is just so graceful! You know? How you like to see a team of Willie Mayses out there? Wow!" Wes Westrum, the Giant catcher, grounded out, short to first, and the eighth

inning was over. "One to go, one to go," Luther said. Then he jabbed me in the arm with his finger. "Hey, listen—I been thinking. Instead of an All-Star game every year between the leagues, what they ought to do one year is have the white guys against our guys. What you think?"

I shrugged. "I don't know," I said.

"Sure," he said. "Listen—we got Willie in center. Then we put Aaron in right and Doby in left. He's got the raw power. Some outfield, huh? Then we got Campy catching and Newcombe pitching. You can't beat that. That Newcombe—he's a mean one, but he throws. Okay. I been thinking about this a long time—" He used his fingers to enumerate. He was excited, happy. "At first base we put Luke Easter, at second Junior Gilliam, at short Ernie Banks, and at third base we bring in old Jackie Robinson, just to give the team a little class—you know what I mean? Man, what a line-up! Who could you match it with?"

When I said I didn't know, Luther eyed me suspiciously. "C'mon—Musial, Mantle, Williams, Spahn—you name 'em and I'll match 'em, man for man, your guys against ours." He stopped and cheered as a Cardinal popped out to Whitey Lockman at first. "What's the matter—don't you like the idea? Ha! Face it, man, we'd wipe up the field with you. Swish! Swish!" He laughed and slapped me on the knee. "Hey, I know what's bugging you, I bet——" He leaned toward me, cupping his hand over his mouth, and whispered in my ear. "Tell the truth now, would you have ever offered to help me if I wasn't colored?"

"Would I——?" I stopped. "Sure," I said. "Of course I would. Of course——"

Luther smiled, triumphantly, dubiously.

"Look," I said. "As long as we're asking questions, let me ask you something."

"About the tickets, right?"

"No," I said. "Forget the tickets. No long lectures, either. Just a question. Just one: how come you steal?"

"Oh man," he said, laughing. "That's an easy one! Because I'm not getting what I want and when you don't get what you want, man, you got to take. Don't you know that?"

I stared at him, not sure I had heard right. He

winked at me. "Enjoy the ball game, man! Say hey, Willie!" he shouted as Mays caught a fly ball, bread-basket style, for the second out. "Ain't he the sweetest!"

A minute later the game was over and the players were racing across the field toward the clubhouse in center field, trying to escape the fans who scrambled after them. "They won't get Willie," Luther said. "He's too swift, too swift."

When we were outside, I thanked Luther and told him how much I'd enjoyed the game. "How about a Coke or something?" I offered.

"Nah," he said. "I got things to do." He extended his hand quickly and I shook it, the first time we had ever done that. "Okay. You go get spiffed up and get a wife. Time you were married." He tossed his head back and laughed. "Ain't you married yet? No, no. *Smile*, man— how you gonna get a wife, never smiling." He started away, through the crowd. "Stay loose," he called back. "Don't steal no fruits."

I never questioned him again about stealing, but even if I'd wanted to, I wouldn't have had much opportunity. He didn't come to see me very often the rest of that year. When he returned to school in September of 1958 for his last year of junior high school, he had grown again. But not up. He never did go higher than the five-five or five-six he had reached by that time. He had taken up weightlifting over the summer, however, and his chest, his neck, his arms—they had all broadened incredibly. Instead of the dirty cotton and flannel shirts he had worn the two previous years, he now walked through the halls in laundry-white T-shirts, the sleeves rolled up to the shoulder, his powerful muscles exposed. There were always a half-dozen Negro boys following him around and they all dressed the way he did —white T-shirts, black chino pants, leather wrist straps, and—hanging from their necks on pieces of string—miniature black skulls.

The guidance counselor for the ninth grade came to me one day early in the term and asked me if I could give him any evidence against Luther. He claimed that Luther and his gang were going around the school, beating and torturing those students who refused to "loan" them money. All of the students, he said, were afraid to name Luther. "The kid's a born sadist," he added. I told him I didn't know anything.

The term progressed and the stories and rumors increased. I was told that the police in Luther's neighborhood were convinced that he and his gang were responsible for a series of muggings. I tried not to believe it, but Luther all but gave me conclusive proof one afternoon right before Christmas. He came into my room at three o'clock, alone, and said he had something for me. He said he trusted me not to tell anybody about it or show it to anyone. I said I wouldn't.

"Okay, man—here it is——" His eyes leapt around the room, frenzied, delirious. He took a little card from his wallet. "You might need this sometime—but don't ask me no questions. Ha! And don't you worry none. I'm doing okay. Expanding all the time. Don't you worry." I took the card from him. "See you now, Mr. Carter. See you, see you."

He left and I looked at the card. Across the top was printed THE BLACK AVENGERS, and below it was written: "Don't touch this white man. He's okay." It was signed by Luther and under his name he had drawn a skull and crossbones. I put the card in my wallet.

In January, to no one's great surprise, Luther was sent away to reform school in upstate New York. I was never exactly clear about the precise event that had led to it—the policeman assigned to our school said it had to do with brutally beating an old man; Luther's friends said it had to do with getting caught in a gang war. They claimed the fight was clean but that the cops had framed Luther. There was nothing in the papers, Luther had not contacted me, and I did not find out about it all until he'd already been shipped off.

I received a postcard from him that summer. It was brief.

I hate it here. I can't say anymore or they'll beat me up. I hate it. I'm reading some. I'll visit you when I get out and we'll have a session.

I answered the card with a letter. I told him I was sorry about where he was and that I'd be glad to talk to him whenever he wanted. I gave him some news of the school and included some current baseball clippings. I asked him if there was anything he needed and if there was anybody in his family he wanted me to get in touch with. I told him that in return for the time he'd taken me to the baseball game I had ordered a subscription to *Sport* magazine for him.

He replied with another postcard.

Visiting day this summer is August 21. I'd like for you to come.

When I arrived, he seemed glad to see me, but I remember that he was more polite than he had ever been before—and more subdued. I wondered, at the time, if they were giving him tranquilizers. I was only allowed an hour with him and we spent most of that time just walking around the grounds—the school was a work-farm reformatory—not saying anything.

The visit, I could tell, was a disappointment to him. I don't know what he expected of me, but whatever it was, I didn't provide it. I wrote him a letter when I got home, telling him I had enjoyed seeing him and that I'd be glad to come again if he wanted me to. He didn't answer it, and I heard no more from him for over a year and a half.

Then one day in the spring of 1961—just about the time of the Bay of Pigs invasion of Cuba, I remember—he popped into my room at school. He looked horrible. His face was unshaven, his clothes were filthy and ragged, his eyes were glazed. Underneath his clothes, his body had become flabby and he bent over noticeably when he walked. At first I didn't recognize him.

When I did, I was so glad to see him I didn't know what to do. "Luther—for crying out loud!" I said, standing up and shaking his hand. "How are you?"

He smiled at me. "I'm superb, man—can't you tell from looking at me?" He laughed then, and I laughed with him.

"You've gotten older," I said.

"Past sixteen," he said. "That means I don't got to go to school no more——"

He waited, but I didn't offer an opinion. "How about going down with me and having a cup of coffee? I'm finished here for the day —just getting through with midterms."

"Nah," he said, looking down and playing with his hands. "I gotta meet somebody. I'm late already. But I was in the neighborhood, so I thought I'd come let you know I was still alive." He came to my desk and looked down. He shook his head as if something were wrong.

"What's the matter?" I asked.

"Don't see no wedding ring on your finger yet." He looked straight into my face. "Hey, man—you dig girls, don't you?"

"Yes," I said, laughing.

He laughed, his mouth opening wide. "Okay. That's all the gas for today. I'll see you, man."

During the next few months he visited me several times. Sometimes he looked good, sometimes bad—but I never could find out what he was doing with his days. He never gave a straight answer to my questions. More and more, I felt that he was asking me for some kind of help, but when I would touch on anything personal or even hint that I wanted to do something for him, with him, he would become defensive.

I didn't see him over the summer, but the following fall he came by periodically. He seemed to be getting a hold on himself and sometimes he would talk about going to night school. Nothing came of the talk, though. In November he was arrested and sent to Riker's Island—to P.S. 616, the combination prison-school for boys between the ages of sixteen and twenty. His sentence was for eighteen months and during the first three months I visited him twice. Both times all he wanted to do was talk about the English class we had had and the stories and compositions he had made up. He said he was trying to remember some of them for the English teacher he had there, but couldn't do it all the time. He seemed to be in terrible shape, and I didn't have much hope for him.

So I was surprised when I began getting postcards from him again. "I am studying hard," the first one said. "There is a Negro who comes here to help me. I like him. I will be a new man when I come out. Yours sincerely, Luther." It was neatly and carefully written. The ones that followed were the same and they came at regular intervals of about five weeks. He told me about books he was reading, most of them having to do with Negro history, and about how he was changing. "Improving" was the word he used most.

I answered his cards as best I could and offered to come see him again, but he never took up any of my offers. When his eighteen months were up, I expected a visit from him. He never came. Sometimes I wondered what had become of him, but after the first few months passed and I didn't hear from him, I thought about him less and less. A year passed —two since we had last seen each other at Riker's Island—and then we met again.

I spotted him first. It was a beautiful summer night and I had gone up to Lewisohn Stadium for a concert. It had been good, I was relaxed and happy as I walked out of the stadium. Luther was standing at the corner of Amsterdam Avenue and 138th Street. He was wearing a dark blue suit, a white shirt, and a tie. He was clean-shaven, his hair was cut short, and he looked healthy and bright. He was stopping people and trying to sell them newspapers.

"How are you, Mr. Carter?" he asked when I walked up to him. His eyes were clear and he seemed very happy to see me. "Interested in buying a newspaper to help the colored people? Only a dime——"

"No, thanks," I said. The paper he was selling, as I'd expected, was *Muhammad Speaks*, the newspaper of the Black Muslims.[2] "You look fine," I added.

"Thanks. Excuse me a second." He turned and sold a copy to somebody. People snubbed him but this didn't stop him from smiling or trying. I waited. When the crowd had gone, he asked me where I was going. "Home," I said. "Cup of coffee first?"

"No, thanks," he said. "Thanks, but no thanks."

"When did all this start?" I asked, motioning to the newspapers.

"At Riker's Island," he said. He put up a hand, as if to stop my thoughts from becoming

---

2. *Black Muslims,* an organization advocating the separation of races and the religious and ethical teachings of Islam, particularly with regard to temperance in living habits.

words. "I know what you're thinking, what you hear on TV and read in the newspapers about us—but don't believe everything. We're essentially a religious organization, as you may or may not know."

"I know," I said.

"And it's meant a lot to me—I couldn't have made it without their help. They—they taught me to *believe* in myself." His eyes glowed as he twisted his body toward me. "Can you understand that?" It seemed very important to him that I believe him. "*Can* you?" He relaxed momentarily and shrugged. "I don't believe everything they teach, of course, but I follow their precepts: I don't smoke, I don't drink, I don't curse, I don't go out with women who aren't Muslims—I feel good *inside*, Mr. Carter. Things are straightening themselves out." He paused. "It hasn't been easy."

"I know," I said, and smiled.

He nodded, embarrassed, I thought. "I'm going back to school also——"

"I'm glad."

"Even my body feels good! I'm lifting weights again," he said. Then he laughed and the sound tore through the warm night. His eyes were flashing with delight. "Oh man—some day I'll be the head of a whole army! Me and my old hunchback." He laughed again, pleased with himself. His laughter subsided and he patted me on the shoulder. "Oh man, you are still so deep, so deep. Don't worry none, Mr. Carter. I don't go around advocating no violence." He chuckled. "I've got to go," he said, extending a hand. "It's been good seeing you again. Sure you don't want to buy a copy?"

"I'm sure," I said, shaking his hand. "Good luck to you, Luther. I'm glad to see you the way you are now——"

"Thanks." We looked at each other for a minute and he smiled warmly at me. Then I started toward the subway station. When I'd crossed the street, he called to me.

"Hey—Mr. Carter——"

I turned.

"Let me ask you something—do you still have that card I gave you?" He howled at this remark. "Oh man, I'd save that card if I were you! I'd do that. You never know when you might need it. You never know——"

I started back across the street, toward him. He tossed his head back and roared with laughter. "You never know, you never know," he repeated, and hurried away from me, laughing wildly. I stared at him until he disappeared in the darkness. Then I just stood there, dazed, unable to move—I don't know for how long. Finally I made myself turn around, and as I walked slowly toward the lights of Broadway all I could feel was the presence of his muscular body, powerful, gleaming, waiting under his white shirt, his clean suit.

---

## DISCUSSION

Below are ten statements about the story, "Luther." Number from 1 to 10 on a separate sheet of paper. After each number, write "a" if you *strongly agree* with a statement; "b" if you *agree;* "c" if you *have no opinion;* "d" if you *disagree;* "e" if you *strongly disagree.* Whenever possible, be prepared to support each of your opinions with evidence from the story.

1. Mr. Carter was interested in helping Luther principally because of his own pride.

2. The teachers were correct in believing Luther to be a mental case.

3. If Mr. Carter had been black, he would have found it easier to understand Luther and to help him.

4. With his background, Luther was bound to break laws and spend time in jail.

5. Luther lacked pride until he joined the Black Muslims.

6. Luther had a stronger influence on Mr. Carter than Mr. Carter had on him.

7. Luther's poverty and slightly deformed back were more responsible for his behavior than was his color.

8. Luther's personality traits would prevent him from ever succeeding in a white, middle-class society.

9. The events of this story, which took place from 1955 to 1964, could not happen today.

10. Because of its suggested violence between races and its depiction of Luther, this story should not have been printed in a high-school anthology.

### JAY NEUGEBOREN

Jay Neugeboren's work has appeared not only in several magazines, but in *Best American Short Stories* (1965) and *Prize Stories: The O. Henry Awards* (1968). He has taught at Stanford, in a private school, and at an experimental college. He has also worked for several civil rights and antiwar organizations.

*Parenthesis: An Autobiographical Journey* describes his change from non-involvement to political awareness.

# BARGAIN

A. B. Guthrie, Jr.

*A hundred and thirty-five pounds wasn't much to throw against two hundred. But Freighter Slade had a weakness, and Mr. Baumer knew what it was.*

MR. Baumer and I had closed the Moon Dance Mercantile Company and were walking to the post office, and he had a bunch of bills in his hand ready to mail. There wasn't anyone or anything much on the street because it was suppertime. A buckboard and a saddle horse were tied at Hirschs' rack, and a rancher in a wagon rattled for home ahead of us, the sound of his going fading out as he prodded his team. Freighter Slade stood alone in front of the Moon Dance Saloon, maybe wondering whether to have one more before going to supper. People said he could hold a lot without showing it except in being ornerier even than usual.

Mr. Baumer didn't see him until he was almost on him, and then he stopped and fingered through the bills until he found the right one. He stepped up to Slade and held it out.

Slade said, "What's this, Dutchie?"

Mr. Baumer had to tilt his head up to talk to him. "You know vat it is."

Slade just said, "Yeah?" You never could

"Bargain." Copyright 1952 by Esquire, Inc. From *The Big It and Other Stories* by A. B. Guthrie, Jr. Copyright 1948, 1949, 1952, © 1959 by Esquire, Inc. Copyright © 1960 by A. B. Guthrie, Jr. Reprinted by permission of Houghton Mifflin Company, A. M. Heath & Company Ltd. and Brandt & Brandt. (Originally published as "Bargain at Moon Dance" in *Esquire*, October 1952.)

tell from his face what went on inside his skull. He had dark skin and shallow cheeks and a thick-growing mustache that fell over the corners of his mouth.

"It is a bill," Mr. Baumer said. "I tell you before it is a bill. For twenty-vun dollars and fifty cents."

"You know what I do with bills, don't you, Dutchie?" Slade asked.

Mr. Baumer didn't answer the question. He said, "For merchandise."

Slade took the envelope from Mr. Baumer's hand and squeezed it up in his fist and let it drop on the plank sidewalk. Not saying anything, he reached down and took Mr. Baumer's nose between the knuckles of his fingers and twisted it up into his eyes. That was all. That was all at the time. Slade half turned and slouched to the door of the bar and let himself in. Some men were laughing in there.

Mr. Baumer stooped and picked up the bill and put it on top of the rest and smoothed it out for mailing. When he straightened up I could see tears in his eyes from having his nose screwed around.

He didn't say anything to me, and I didn't say anything to him, being so much younger and feeling embarrassed for him. He went into the post office and slipped the bills in the slot, and we walked on home together. At the last, at the crossing where I had to leave him, he remembered to say, "Better study, Al. Is good to know to read and write and figure." I guess he felt he had to push me a little, my father being dead.

I said, "Sure. See you after school tomorrow" —which he knew I would anyway. I had been working in the store for him during the summer and after classes ever since pneumonia took my dad off.

Three of us worked there regularly, Mr. Baumer, of course, and me and Colly Coleman, who knew enough to drive the delivery wagon but wasn't much help around the store except for carrying orders out to the rigs at the hitchpost and handling heavy things like the whisky barrel at the back of the store which Mr. Baumer sold quarts and gallons out of.

The store carried quite a bit of stuff—sugar and flour and dried fruits and canned goods and such on one side and yard goods and coats and caps and aprons and the like of that on the other, besides kerosene and bran and buckets and linoleum and pitchforks in the storehouse at the rear—but it wasn't a big store like Hirsch Brothers up the street. Never would be, people guessed, going on to say, with a sort of slow respect, that it would have gone under long ago if Mr. Baumer hadn't been half mule and half beaver. He had started the store just two years before and, the way things were, worked himself close to death.

He was at the high desk at the end of the grocery counter when I came in the next afternoon. He had an eyeshade on and black sateen protectors on his forearms, and his pencil was in his hand instead of behind his ear and his glasses were roosted on the nose that Slade had twisted. He didn't hear me open and close the door or hear my feet as I walked back to him, and I saw he wasn't doing anything with the pencil but holding it over paper. I stood and studied him for a minute, seeing a small, stooped man with a little paunch bulging through his unbuttoned vest. He was a man you wouldn't remember from meeting once. There was nothing in his looks to set itself in your mind unless maybe it was his chin, which was a small, pink hill in the gentle plain of his face.

While I watched him, he lifted his hand and felt carefully of his nose. Then he saw me. His eyes had that kind of mistiness that seems to go with age or illness, though he wasn't really old or sick, either. He brought his hand down quickly and picked up the pencil, but he saw I still was looking at the nose, and finally he sighed and said, "That Slade."

Just the sound of the name brought Slade to my eye. I saw him slouched in front of the bar, and I saw him and his string[1] coming down the grade from the buttes, the wheel horses held snug and the rest lined out pretty, and then the string leveling off and Slade's whip lifting hair from a horse that wasn't up in the collar. I had heard it said that Slade could make a horse scream with that whip. Slade's name wasn't Freighter, of course. Our town had

---

1.  *string*, a group of horses driven in single or double file.

nicknamed him that because that was what he was.

"I don't think it's any good to send him a bill, Mr. Baumer," I said. "He can't even read."

"He could pay yet."

"He don't pay anybody," I said.

"I think he hate me," Mr. Baumer went on. "That is the thing. He hate me for coming not from this country. I come here, sixteen years old, and learn to read and write, and I make a business, and so I think he hate me."

"He hates everybody."

Mr. Baumer shook his head. "But not to pinch the nose. Not to call Dutchie."

The side door squeaked open, but it was only Colly Coleman coming in from a trip so I said, "Excuse me, Mr. Baumer, but you shouldn't have trusted him in the first place."

"I know," he answered, looking at me with his misty eyes. "A man make mistakes. I think some do not trust him, so he will pay me because I do. And I do not know him well then. He only came back to town three-four months ago, from being away since before I go into business."

"People who knew him before could have told you," I said.

"A man make mistakes," he explained again.

"It's not my business, Mr. Baumer, but I would forget the bill."

His eyes rested on my face for a long minute, as if they didn't see me but the problem itself. He said, "It is not twenty-vun dollars and fifty cents now, Al. It is not that any more."

"What is it?"

He took a little time to answer. Then he brought his two hands up as if to help him shape the words. "It is the thing. You see, it is the thing."

I wasn't quite sure what he meant.

He took his pencil from behind the ear where he had put it and studied the point of it. "That Slade. He steal whisky and call it evaporation. He sneak things from his load. A thief, he is. And too big for me."

I said, "I got no time for him, Mr. Baumer, but I guess there never was a freighter didn't steal whisky. That's what I hear."

It was true, too. From the railroad to Moon Dance was fifty miles and a little better—a two-day haul in good weather, heck knew how long in bad. Any freight string bound home with a load had to lie out at least one night. When a freighter had his stock tended to and maybe a little fire going against the dark, he'd tackle a barrel of whisky or of grain alcohol[2] if he had one aboard, consigned to Hirsch Brothers or Mr. Baumer's or the Moon Dance Saloon or the Gold Leaf Bar. He'd drive a hoop out of place, bore a little hole with a nail or bit, and draw off what he wanted. Then he'd plug the hole with a whittled peg and pound the hoop back. That was evaporation. Nobody complained much. With freighters you generally took what they gave you, within reason.

"Moore steals it, too," I told Mr. Baumer. Moore was Mr. Baumer's freighter.

"Yah," he said, and that was all, but I stood there for a minute, thinking there might be something more. I could see thought swimming in his eyes, above that little hill of chin. Then a customer came in, and I had to go wait on him.

Nothing happened for a month, nothing between Mr. Baumer and Slade, that is, but fall drew on toward winter and the first flight of ducks headed south and Mr. Baumer hired Miss Lizzie Webb to help with the just-beginning Christmas trade, and here it was the first week in October, and he and I walked up the street again with the monthly bills. He always sent them out. I guess he had to. A bigger store, like Hirschs', would wait on the ranchers until their beef or wool went to market.

Up to a point things looked and happened almost the same as they had before, so much the same that I had the crazy feeling I was going through that time again. There was a wagon and a rig tied up at Hirschs' rack and a saddle horse standing hipshot[3] in front of the harness shop. A few more people were on the street now, not many, and lamps had been lit against the shortened day.

It was dark enough that I didn't make out Slade right away. He was just a figure that came out of the yellow wash of light from the

---

2. *grain alcohol*, a liquid made from grain and used in intoxicating beverages, medicine, etc.

3. *hipshot*, with one hip lower than the other.

Moon Dance Saloon and stood on the board walk and with his head made the little motion of spitting. Then I recognized the lean, raw shape of him and the muscles flowing down into the sloped shoulders, and in the settling darkness I filled the picture in—the dark skin and the flat cheeks and the peevish eyes and the mustache growing rank.

There was Slade and here was Mr. Baumer with his bills and here I was, just as before, just like in the second go-round of a bad dream. I felt like turning back, being embarrassed and half-scared by trouble even when it wasn't mine. Please, I said to myself, don't stop, Mr. Baumer! Don't bite off anything! Please, short-sighted the way you are, don't catch sight of him at all! I held up and stepped around behind Mr. Baumer and came up on the outside so as to be between him and Slade where maybe I'd cut off his view.

But it wasn't any use. All along I think I knew it was no use, not the praying or the walking between or anything. The act had to play itself out.

Mr. Baumer looked across the front of me and saw Slade and hesitated in his step and came to a stop. Then in his slow, business way, his chin held firm against his mouth, he began fingering through the bills, squinting to make out the names. Slade had turned and was watching him, munching on a cud of tobacco like a bull waiting.

"You look, Al," Mr. Baumer said without lifting his face from the bills. "I cannot see so good."

So I looked, and while I was looking Slade must have moved. The next I knew Mr. Baumer was staggering ahead, the envelopes spilling out of his hands. There had been a thump, the clap of a heavy hand swung hard on his back.

Slade said, "Haryu, Dutchie?"

Mr. Baumer caught his balance and turned around, the bills he had trampled shining white between them and, at Slade's feet, the hat that Mr. Baumer had stumbled out from under.

Slade picked up the hat and scuffed through the bills and held it out. "Cold to be goin' without a sky-piece," he said.

Mr. Baumer hadn't spoken a word. The lamp-shine from inside the bar caught his eyes, and in them it seemed to me a light came and went as anger and the uselessness of it took turns in his head.

Two men had come up on us and stood watching. One of them was Angus McDonald, who owned the Ranchers' Bank, and the other was Dr. King. He had his bag in his hand.

Two others were drifting up, but I didn't have time to tell who. The light came in Mr. Baumer's eyes, and he took a step ahead and swung. I could have hit harder myself. The first landed on Slade's cheek without hardly so much as jogging his head, but it let hell loose in the man. I didn't know he could move so fast. He slid in like a practiced fighter and let Mr. Baumer have it full in the face.

Mr. Baumer slammed over on his back, but he wasn't out. He started lifting himself. Slade leaped ahead and brought a boot heel down on the hand he was lifting himself by. I heard meat and bone under that heel and saw Mr. Baumer fall back and try to roll away.

Things had happened so fast that not until then did anyone have a chance to get between them. Now Mr. McDonald pushed at Slade's chest, saying, "That's enough, Freighter. That's enough now," and Dr. King lined up, too, and another man I didn't know, and I took a place, and we formed a kind of screen between them. Dr. King turned and bent to look at Mr. Baumer.

"Damn fool hit me first," Slade said.

"That's enough," Mr. McDonald told him again while Slade looked at all of us as if he'd spit on us for a nickel. Mr. McDonald went on, using a half-friendly tone, and I knew it was because he didn't want to take Slade on any more than the rest of us did. "You go on home and sleep it off, Freighter. That's the ticket."

Slade just snorted.

From behind us Dr. King said, "I think you've broken this man's hand."

"Lucky for him I didn't kill him," Slade answered. "Damn Dutch penny-pincher!" He fingered the chew out of his mouth. "Maybe he'll know enough to leave me alone now."

Dr. King had Mr. Baumer on his feet. "I'll take him to the office," he said.

Blood was draining from Mr. Baumer's nose and rounding the curve of his lip and dripping from the sides of his chin. He held his hurt right hand in the other. But a thing was that he didn't look beaten even then, not the way a man who has given up looks beaten. Maybe that was why Slade said, with a show of that fierce anger, "You stay away from me! Hear? Stay clear away, or you'll get more of the same!"

Dr. King led Mr. Baumer away, Slade went back into the bar, and the other men walked off, talking about the fight. I got down and picked up the bills, because I knew Mr. Baumer would want me to, and mailed them at the post office dirty as they were. It made me sorer, someway, that Slade's bill was one of the few that wasn't marked up. The cleanness of it seemed to say that there was no getting the best of him.

Mr. Baumer had his hand in a sling the next day and wasn't much good at waiting on the trade. I had to hustle all afternoon and so didn't have a chance to talk to him even if he had wanted to talk. Mostly he stood at his desk, and once, passing it, I saw he was practicing writing with his left hand. His nose and the edges of the cheeks around it were swollen some.

At closing time I said, "Look, Mr. Baumer, I can lay out of school a few days until you kind of get straightened out here."

"No," he answered as if to wave the subject away. "I get somebody else. You go to school. Is good to learn."

I had a half notion to say that learning hadn't helped him with Slade. Instead, I blurted out that I would have the law on Slade.

"The law?" he asked.

"The sheriff or somebody."

"No, Al," he said. "You would not."

I asked why.

"The law, it is not for plain fights," he said. "Shooting? Robbing? Yes, the law come quick. The plain fights, they are too many. They not count enough."

He was right. I said, "Well, I'd do something anyhow."

"Yes," he answered with a slow nod of his head. "Something you vould do, Al." He didn't tell me what.

Within a couple of days he got another man

to clerk for him—it was Ed Hempel, who was always finding and losing jobs—and we made out. Mr. Baumer took his hand from the sling in a couple or three weeks, but with the tape on it it still wasn't any use to him. From what you could see of the fingers below the tape it looked as if it never would be.

He spent most of his time at the high desk, sending me or Ed out on the errands he used to run, like posting and getting the mail. Sometimes I wondered if that was because he was afraid of meeting Slade. He could just as well have gone himself. He wasted a lot of hours just looking at nothing, though I will have to say he worked hard at learning to write left-handed.

Then, a month and a half before Christmas, he hired Slade to haul his freight for him.

Ed Hempel told me about the deal when I showed up for work. "Yessir," he said, resting his foot on a crate in the storeroom where we were supposed to be working. "I tell you he's throwed in with Slade. Told me this morning to go out and locate him if I could and bring him in. Slade was at the saloon, o' course, and says to hell with Dutchie, but I told him this was honest-to-God business, like Baumer had told me to, and there was a quart of whisky right there in the store for him if he'd come and get it. He was out of money, I reckon, because the quart fetched him."

"What'd they say?" I asked him.

"Search me. There was two or three people in the store and Baumer told me to wait on 'em, and he and Slade palavered back by the desk."

"How do you know they made a deal?"

Ed spread his hands out. "'Bout noon, Moore came in with his string, and I heard Baumer say he was makin' a change. Moore didn't like it too good, either."

It was a hard thing to believe, but there one day was Slade with a pile of stuff for the Moon Dance Mercantile Company, and that was proof enough with something left for boot.

Mr. Baumer never opened the subject up with me, though I gave him plenty of chances. And I didn't feel like asking. He didn't talk much these days but went around absent-minded, feeling now and then of the fingers that curled yellow and stiff out of the bandage

like the toes on the leg of a dead chicken. Even on our walks home he kept his thoughts to himself.

I felt different about him now, and was sore inside. Not that I blamed him exactly. A hundred and thirty-five pounds wasn't much to throw against two hundred. And who could tell what Slade would do on a bellyful of whisky? He had promised Mr. Baumer more of the same, hadn't he? But I didn't feel good. I couldn't look up to Mr. Baumer like I used to and still wanted to. I didn't have the beginning of an answer when men cracked jokes or shook their heads in sympathy with Mr. Baumer, saying Slade had made him come to time.

Slade hauled in a load for the store, and another, and Christmas time was drawing on and trade heavy, and the winter that had started early and then pulled back came on again. There was a blizzard and then a still cold and another blizzard and afterwards a sunshine that was ice-shine on the drifted snow. I was glad to be busy, selling overshoes and sheep-lined coats and mitts and socks as thick as saddle blankets and Christmas candy out of buckets and hickory nuts and the fresh oranges that the people in our town never saw except when Santa Claus was coming.

One afternoon when I lit out from class the thermometer on the school porch read 42° below. But you didn't have to look at it to know how cold the weather was. Your nose and fingers and toes and ears and the bones inside you told you. The snow cried when you stepped on it.

I got to the store and took my things off and scuffed my hands at the stove for a minute so's to get life enough in them to tie a parcel. Mr. Baumer—he was always polite to me—said, "Hello, Al. Not so much to do today. Too cold for customers." He shuddered a little, as if he hadn't got the chill off even yet, and rubbed his broken hand with the good one. "Ve need Christmas goods," he said, looking out the window to the furrows that wheels had made in the snow-banked street, and I knew he was thinking of Slade's string, inbound from the railroad, and the time it might take even Slade to travel those hard miles.

Slade never made it at all.

Less than an hour later our old freighter, Moore, came in, his beard white and stiff with frost. He didn't speak at first but looked around and clumped to the stove and took off his heavy mitts, holding his news inside him.

Then he said, not pleasantly, "Your new man's dead, Baumer."

"My new man?" Mr. Baumer said.

"Who the hell do you think? Slade. He's dead."

All Mr. Baumer could say was, "Dead!"

"Froze to death, I figger," Moore told him while Colly Coleman and Ed Hempel and Miss Lizzie and I and a couple of customers stepped closer.

"Not Slade," Mr. Baumer said. "He know too much to freeze."

"Maybe so, but he sure's God's froze now. I got him in the wagon."

We stood looking at one another and at Moore. Moore was enjoying his news, enjoying feeding it out bit by bit so's to hold the stage. "Heart might've given out for all I know."

The side door swung open, letting in a cloud of cold and three men who stood, like us, waiting on Moore. I moved a little and looked through the window and saw Slade's freight outfit tied outside with more men around it. Two of them were on a wheel of one of the wagons, looking inside.

"Had a extra man, so I brought your stuff in," Moore went on. "Figgered you'd be glad to pay for it."

"Not Slade," Mr. Baumer said again.

"You can take a look at him."

Mr. Baumer answered no.

"Someone's takin' word to Connor to bring his hearse. Anyhow I told 'em to. I carted old Slade this far. Connor can have him now."

Moore pulled on his mitts. "Found him there by the Deep Creek crossin', doubled up in the snow an' his fire out." He moved toward the door. "I'll see to the horses, but your stuff'll have to set there. I got more'n enough work to do at Hirschs'."

Mr. Baumer just nodded.

I put on my coat and went out and waited my turn and climbed on a wagon wheel and looked inside, and there was Slade piled on some bags of bran. Maybe because of being frozen, his face was whiter than I ever saw it, whiter and deader, too, though it never had been lively. Only the mustache seemed still alive, sprouting thick like greasewood from alkali. Slade was doubled up all right, as if he had died and stiffened leaning forward in a chair.

I got down from the wheel, and Colly and then Ed climbed up. Moore was unhitching, tossing off his pieces of information while he did so. Pretty soon Mr. Connor came up with his old hearse, and he and Moore tumbled Slade into it, and the team that was as old as the hearse made off, the tires squeaking in the snow. The people trailed on away with it, their breaths leaving little ribbons of mist in the air. It was beginning to get dark.

Mr. Baumer came out of the side door of the store, bundled up, and called to Colly and Ed and me. "We unload," he said. "Already is late. Al, better you get a couple lanterns now."

We did a fast job, setting the stuff out of the wagons on to the platform and then carrying it or rolling it on the one truck[4] that the store owned and stowing it inside according to where Mr. Baumer's good hand pointed.

A barrel was one of the last things to go in. I edged it up and Colly nosed the truck under it, and then I let it fall back. "Mr. Baumer," I said, "we'll never sell all this, will we?"

"Yah," he answered. "Sure we sell it. I get it cheap. A bargain, Al, so I buy it."

I looked at the barrel head again. There in big letters I saw "Wood Alcohol[5]—Deadly Poison."

"Hurry now," Mr. Baumer said. "Is late." For a flash and no longer I saw through the mist in his eyes, saw, you might say, that hilly chin repeated there. "Then ve go home, Al. Is good to know to read."

---

4. *truck*, a low platform or frame on wheels used for transporting heavy articles.
5. *Wood Alcohol*, like grain alcohol in many ways but made from wood, used often as fuel, and poisonous to drink.

## DISCUSSION

Before answering the first three questions below, you may find it helpful to review the entries in the Handbook for *characterization*, *plot*, and *setting*.

1. In the first paragraph of this story, the author gives us important information about the setting and characters. Turn back to this paragraph and find answers to the following questions: (a) In what occupation are Mr. Baumer and the narrator apparently engaged? (b) What time of day is it? (c) What section of the country is suggested in the description? (d) What period of time is suggested? (e) What two significant facts about Freighter Slade are given?

2. (a) If you were asked to outline the plot of this story, what would you list as the first step? (b) Where is the first instance of conflict?

3. What methods of characterization has Guthrie used to reveal the character of Mr. Baumer? Of Freighter Slade? Of Al, the narrator? Which character seems to you to be the most fully developed? Explain.

4. When do you think Mr. Baumer gets his idea for revenge —when the narrator first mentions the fact that Slade can't read, or later? Cite evidence for your answer.

5. (a) In what ways does Al, the narrator, try to justify Slade's actions? (b) What do you think is the narrator's purpose in doing this? (c) The author's purpose? (d) Why does this attempted justification have no effect on Mr. Baumer?

6. (a) How does Mr. Baumer interest Slade in working for him? (b) What does this tell you about Mr. Baumer's knowledge of human nature?

7. What is the significance of the title of this story?

8. What do the townspeople expect will be the result of the conflict between Baumer and Slade? In what ways, then, might the ending be regarded as ironic?

## A. B. GUTHRIE

Montana and its people have proved rich sources for the fiction of A. B. Guthrie. In his introduction to *The Big It*, which includes "Bargain," he notes, "I said that every story in the collection had some basis in fact.

'Bargain' was no exception. An illiterate freighter did die years ago some forty miles from my hometown because he could not read. He tapped a barrel plainly marked Wood Alcohol. The problem . . . was to put the incident into the frame of fiction."

His first recognized novel was *The Big Sky* and his second, *The Way West*, won a Pulitzer Prize. These books began a four-novel series completed with the recent *Arfive*, which depicts the changing West from the 1830's to the early 1900's.

# the endless streetcar ride into the night, and the tinfoil noose

### Jean Shepherd

*There are about four times in a man's life, or a woman's, too . . . when unexpectedly, from out of the darkness . . . the cosmic searchlight of Truth shines full upon them.*

Mewling, puking babes. That's the way we all start. Damply clinging to someone's shoulder, burping weakly, clawing our way into life. *All* of us. Then gradually, surely, we begin to divide into two streams, all marching together up that long yellow brick road of life, but on opposite sides of the street. One crowd goes on to become the Official people, peering out at us from television screens, magazine covers. They are forever appearing in newsreels, carrying attaché cases, surrounded by banks of microphones while the world waits for their decisions and statements. And the rest of us go on to become . . . just us.

They are the Prime Ministers, the Presidents, Cabinet members, Stars, dynamic molders of the Universe, while we remain forever the onlookers, the applauders of their real lives.

Forever down in the dark dungeons of our souls we ask ourselves:

"How did they get away from me? When did I make that first misstep that took me forever to the wrong side of the street, to become eternally part of the accursed, anonymous Audience?"

It seems like one minute we're all playing around back of the garage, kicking tin cans and yelling at girls, and the next instant you find yourself doomed to exist as an office boy in the Mail Room of Life, while another ex-mewling, puking babe sends down Dicta, says "No comment" to the Press, and lives a real, genuine *Life* on the screen of the world.

Countless sufferers at this hour are spending billions of dollars and endless man-hours lying on analysts' couches, trying to pinpoint the exact moment that they stepped off the track and into the bushes forever.

It all hinges on one sinister reality that is rarely mentioned, no doubt due to its implacable, irreversible inevitability. These decisions cannot be changed, no matter how many brightly cheerful, buoyantly optimistic books on HOW TO ACHIEVE A RICHER, FULLER, MORE BOUNTIFUL LIFE or SEVEN MAGIC GOLDEN KEYS TO INSTANT DYNAMIC SUCCESS or THE SECRET OF HOW TO BECOME A BILLIONAIRE we read, or how many classes are attended for instruction in handshaking, back-slapping, grinning, and making After-Dinner speeches. Joseph Stalin was not a Dale Carnegie graduate.[1] He went all the way. It is an unpleasant truth that is swallowed, if at all, like a rancid, bitter pill. A star is a star; a numberless cipher is a numberless cipher.

---

From *In God We Trust, All Others Pay Cash* by Jean Shepherd. Copyright © 1966 by Jean Shepherd. Reprinted by permission of Doubleday & Company, Inc.

**1.** *Joseph Stalin . . . graduate.* Stalin was the premier of the U.S.S.R. from 1941 to 1953. The Dale Carnegie course teaches the adoption of certain positive attitudes as aids to successful living.

Even more eerie a fact is that the Great Divide is rarely a matter of talent or personality. Or even luck. Adolf Hitler had a notoriously weak handshake. His smile was, if anything, a vapid mockery. But inevitably his star zoomed higher and higher. Cinema luminaries of the first order are rarely blessed with even the modicum of Talent, and often their physical beauty leaves much to be desired. What is the difference between Us and Them, We and They, the Big Ones and the great, teeming rabble?

There are about four times in a man's life, or a woman's, too, for that matter, when unexpectedly, from out of the darkness, the blazing carbon lamp, the cosmic searchlight of Truth shines full upon them. It is how we react to those moments that forever seals our fate. One crowd simply puts on its sunglasses, lights another cigar, and heads for the nearest plush French restaurant in the jazziest section of town, sits down and orders a drink, and ignores the whole thing. While we, the Doomed, caught in the brilliant glare of illumination, see ourselves inescapably for what we are, and from that day on skulk in the weeds, hoping no one else will spot us.

Those moments happen when we are least able to fend them off. I caught the first one full in the face when I was fourteen. The fourteenth summer is a magic one for all kids. You have just slid out of the pupa stage, leaving your old baby skin behind, and have not yet become a grizzled, hardened, tax-paying beetle. At fourteen you are made of cellophane. You curl easily and everyone can see through you.

When I was fourteen, Life was flowing through me in a deep, rich torrent of Castoria. How did I know that the first rocks were just ahead, and I was about to have my keel ripped out on the reef? Sometimes you feel as though you are alone in a rented rowboat, bailing like mad in the darkness with a leaky bailing can. It is important to know that there are at least two billion other ciphers in the same boat, bailing with the same leaky can. They all think they are alone and are crossed with an evil star. They are right.

I'm fourteen years old, in my sophomore year at high school. One day Schwartz, my purported best friend, sidled up to me edgily outside of school while we were waiting on the steps to come in after lunch. He proceeded to outline his plan:

"Helen's old man won't let me take her out on a date on Saturday night unless I get a date for her girlfriend. A double date. The old coot figures, I guess, that if there are four of us there won't be no monkey business. Well, how about it? Do you want to go on a blind date with this chick? I never seen her."

Well. For years I had this principle—absolutely *no* blind dates. I was a man of perception and taste, and life was short. But there is a time in your life when you have to stop taking and begin to give just a little. For the first time the warmth of sweet Human Charity brought the roses to my cheeks. After all, Schwartz was my friend. It was little enough to do, have a blind date with some no doubt skinny, pimply girl for your best friend. I would do it for Schwartz. He would do as much for me.

"Okay. Okay, Schwartz."

Then followed the usual ribald remarks, feckless boasting, and dirty jokes about dates in general and girls in particular. It was decided that next Saturday we would go all the way. I had a morning paper route at the time, and my life savings stood at about $1.80. I was all set to blow it on one big night.

I will never forget that particular Saturday as long as I live. The air was as soft as the finest of spun silk. The scent of lilacs hung heavy. The catalpa trees rustled in the early evening breeze from off the Lake. The inner Me itched in that nameless way, that indescribable way that only the fourteen-year-old Male fully knows.

All that afternoon I had carefully gone over my wardrobe to select the proper symphony of sartorial brilliance. That night I set out wearing my magnificent electric blue sport coat, whose shoulders were so wide that they hung out over my frame like vast, drooping eaves, so wide I had difficulty going through an ordinary door head-on. The electric blue sport coat that draped voluminously almost to my knees, its wide lapels flapping soundlessly in the slightest breeze. My pleated gray flannel slacks began just below my breastbone and indeed chafed my armpits. High-belted, cascading down finally to grasp my ankles in a vise-like grip.

My tie, indeed one of my most prized possessions, had been a gift from my Aunt Glenn upon
the state occasion of graduation from eighth
grade. It was of a beautiful silky fabric, silvery
pearly colored, four inches wide at the fulcrum,
and of such a length to endanger occasionally
my zipper in moments of haste. Hand-painted
upon it was a magnificent blood-red snail.

I had spent fully two hours carefully arranging and rearranging my great mop of wavy hair,
into which I had rubbed fully a pound and a half
of Greasy Kid Stuff.

Helen and Schwartz waited on the corner
under the streetlight at the streetcar stop near
Junie Jo's home. Her name was Junie Jo Prewitt.
I won't forget it quickly, although she has, no
doubt, forgotten mine. I walked down the dark
street alone, past houses set back off the street,
through the darkness, past privet hedges, under
elm trees, through air rich and ripe with promise. Her house stood back from the street even
farther than the others. It sort of crouched in the
darkness, looking out at me, kneeling. Pregnant
with Girldom. A real Girlfriend house.

The first faint touch of nervousness filtered
through the marrow of my skullbone as I
knocked on the door of the screen-enclosed
porch. No answer. I knocked again, louder.
Through the murky screens I could see faint
lights in the house itself. Still no answer. Then I
found a small doorbell button buried in the
sash. I pressed. From far off in the bowels of the
house I heard two chimes "Bong" politely.
It sure didn't sound like our doorbell. We had a
real ripper that went off like a broken buzz saw,
more of a BRRRAAAAKKK than a muffled Bong.
This was a rich people's doorbell.

The door opened and there stood a real,
genuine, gold-plated Father: potbelly, underwear shirt, suspenders, and all.

"Well?" he asked.

For one blinding moment of embarrassment
I couldn't remember her name. After all, she
was a blind date. I couldn't just say:

"I'm here to pick up some girl."

He turned back into the house and hollered:

"JUNIE JO! SOME KID'S HERE!"

"Heh, heh. . . ." I countered.

He led me into the living room. It was an
itchy house, sticky stucco walls of a dull orange
color, and all over the floor this Oriental rug
with the design crawling around, making loops
and sworls. I sat on an overstuffed chair covered
in stiff green mohair that scratched even through
my slacks. Little twisty bridge lamps stood
everywhere. I instantly began to sweat down the
back of my clean white shirt. Like I said, it was
a very itchy house. It had little lamps sticking
out of the walls that looked like phony candles,
with phony glass orange flames. The rug started
moaning to itself.

I sat on the edge of the chair and tried to talk
to this Father. He was a Cub fan. We struggled
under water for what seemed like an hour and a
half, when suddenly I heard someone coming
down the stairs. First the feet; then those legs,
and there she was. She was magnificent! The
greatest-looking girl I ever saw in my life! I
have hit the double jackpot! And on a blind
date! Great Scot!

My senses actually reeled as I clutched the
arm of that bilge-green chair for support. Junie
Jo Prewitt made Cleopatra look like a Girl
Scout!

Five minutes later we are sitting in the streetcar, heading toward the bowling alley. I am
sitting next to the most fantastic creation in
the Feminine department known to Western
man. There are the four of us in that long,
yellow-lit streetcar. No one else was aboard;
just us four. I, naturally, being a trained gentleman, sat on the aisle to protect her from
candy wrappers and cigar butts and such.
Directly ahead of me, also on the aisle, sat
Schwartz, his arm already flung affectionately
in a death grip around Helen's neck as we
boomed and rattled through the night.

I casually flung my right foot up onto my
left knee so that she could see my crepe-soled,
perforated, wing-toed, Scotch bluchers with
the two-toned laces. I started to work my famous charm on her. Casually, with my practiced offhand, cynical, cutting, sardonic humor
I told her about how my Old Man had cracked
the block in the Oldsmobile, how the White
Sox were going to have a good year this year,
how my kid brother wet his pants when he saw
a snake, how I figured it was going to rain, what
a great guy Schwartz was, what a good second
baseman I was, how I figured I might go out

for football. On and on I rolled, like Old Man River, pausing significantly for her to pick up the conversation. Nothing.

Ahead of us Schwartz and Helen were almost indistinguishable one from the other. They giggled, bit each other's ears, whispered, clasped hands, and in general made me itch even more.

From time to time Junie Jo would bend forward stiffly from the waist and say something I could never quite catch into Helen's right ear.

I told her my great story of the time that Uncle Carl lost his false teeth down the airshaft. Still nothing. Out of the corner of my eye I could see that she had her coat collar turned up, hiding most of her face as she sat silently, looking forward past Helen Weathers into nothingness.

I told her about this old lady on my paper route who chews tobacco and roller-skates in the backyard every morning. I still couldn't get through to her. Casually I inched my right arm up over the back of the seat behind her shoulders. The acid test. She leaned forward, avoiding my arm, and stayed that way.

"Heh, heh, heh. . . ."

As nonchalantly as I could, I retrieved it, battling a giant cramp in my right shoulder blade. I sat in silence for a few seconds, sweating heavily as ahead Schwartz and Helen are going at it hot and heavy.

It was then that I became aware of someone saying something to me. It was an empty car. There was no one else but us. I glanced around, and there it was. Above us a line of car cards looked down on the empty streetcar. One was speaking directly to me, to me alone.

**DO YOU OFFEND?**

Do I *offend?!*

With no warning, from up near the front of the car where the motorman is steering I see this thing coming down the aisle directly toward *me*. It's coming closer and closer. I can't escape it. It's this blinding, fantastic, brilliant, screaming blue light. I am spread-eagled in it. There's a pin sticking through my thorax. I see it all now.

*I* AM THE BLIND DATE!
*ME!!*
*I'M* the one they're being nice to!

I'm suddenly getting fatter, more itchy. My new shoes are like bowling balls with laces; thick, rubber-crepe bowling balls. My great tie that Aunt Glenn gave me is two feet wide, hanging down to the floor like some crinkly tinfoil noose. My beautiful hand-painted snail is seven feet high, sitting up on my shoulder, burping. Great Scot! It is all clear to me in the searing white light of Truth. My friend Schwartz, I can see him saying to Junie Jo:

"I got this crummy fat friend who never has a date. Let's give him a break and. . ."

*I* AM THE BLIND DATE!

They are being nice to *me!* She is the one who is out on a Blind Date. A Blind Date that didn't make it.

In the seat ahead, the merriment rose to a crescendo. Helen tittered; Schwartz cackled. The marble statue next to me stared gloomily out into the darkness as our streetcar rattled on. The ride went on and on.

*I* AM THE BLIND DATE!

I didn't say much the rest of the night. There wasn't much to be said.

## DISCUSSION

1. (a) Into what two divisions does the narrator place all people? (b) What determines the division a person is placed in?

2. Briefly describe the sequence of events which led the narrator to a "moment of truth."

3. From what the narrator tells us of himself, was Junie Jo's behavior toward him justified? Explain.

4. As the narrator tells the story, he reveals much of his personality to the reader. Into which of the two divisions of people would you place him? Why?

5. (a) The author uses hyperbole to heighten the humor of his story. Find at least five examples of hyperbole in the story. (To review *hyperbole*, see the entry for *figurative language* in the Handbook.) (b) Which of the examples chosen do you consider most effective? Explain.

## WORD STUDY

Jean Shepherd's stories are filled with fresh, original figurative language and unusual descriptions. When the narrator speaks of his tie as a tinfoil noose, his shoes as bowling balls with laces, and his girl friend's home as an "itchy house," we acutely feel his discomfort. Often one word makes the difference between a memorable sentence and a quickly forgotten one. From the words in parenthesis after each sentence, choose a word that seems to you to make each image as memorable and appropriate as possible or fill in the blank with a word of your own choosing.

1. Her face shone like _____ as she received the trophy. (a neon sign—a star)

2. His figure resembled _____ in a high wind. (a piece of string—a cattail)

3. His shoes were the color of _____ (coffee grounds—potato peelings) and his jacket had a _____ look about it. (tapioca—biscuit)

4. His grin was as wide as ____. (a tennis net—an ear of corn)

5. Extatic face cream will soften your face as water softens ____. (a prune—a sponge)

6. When he saw the dented fender, his expression was like _____ breaking in two. (dry sticks—a headache)

7. Her bracelets were _____, her earrings _____. (basketball hoops—snowshoes; hockey pucks—cymbals)

## JEAN SHEPHERD

Jean Shepherd's gifts as a humorist first reached a wide audience over New York's WOR radio in 1956. His nightly free-form ramblings, including nostalgic "Kid Stories," "Army Stories," and satirical observations about life in twentieth-century America, have since been heard in Boston, San Francisco, and other major cities.

As an actor and television performer, Shepherd has been seen on the New York stage and on the television series *Jean Shepherd's America*, which appeared on the Public Broadcasting Service.

Born in Chicago in 1923, Shepherd spent his boyhood in Hammond, Indiana, a boyhood he has chronicled in such books as *In God We Trust All Others Pay Cash* (1966), and *Wanda Hickey's Night of Golden Memories and Other Disasters* (1971). Although best known for his nostalgic, satirical stories of the struggle to grow up in midwestern America, Shepherd has also written plays and screenplays and is a contributing editor for *Playboy* magazine.

# The Sky Is Gray

*Ernest J. Gaines*

GO'N be coming in a few minutes. Coming 'round that bend down there full speed. And I'm go'n get out my hankercher and I'm go'n wave it down, and us go'n get on it and go.

I keep on looking for it, but Mama don't look that way no more. She looking down the road where us jest come from. It's a long old road, and far's you can see you don't see nothing but gravel. You got dry weeds on both sides, and you got trees on both sides, and fences on both sides, too. And you got cows in the pastures and they standing close together. And when us was coming out yer to catch the bus I seen the smoke coming out o' the cow's nose.

I look at my mama and I know what she thinking. I been with Mama so much, jest me and her, I know what she thinking all the time. Right now its home—Auntie and them. She thinking if they got 'nough wood—if she left 'nough there to keep 'em warm till us get back. She thinking if it go'n rain and if any of 'em go'n have to go out in the rain. She thinking 'bout the hog—if he go'n get out, and if Ty and Val be able to get him back in. She always worry like that when she leave the house. She don't worry too much if she leave me there with the smaller ones 'cause she know I'm go'n look after 'em and look after Auntie and everything else. I'm the oldest and she say I'm the man.

I look at my mama and I love my mama. She wearing that black coat and that black hat and she looking sad. I love my mama and I want put my arm 'round her and tell her. But I'm not s'pose to do that. She say that's weakness and that's cry-baby stuff, and she don't want no cry-baby 'round her. She don't want you to be scared neither. 'Cause Ty scared of ghosts and she always whipping him. I'm scared of the dark, too. But I make 'tend I ain't. I make 'tend I ain't 'cause I'm the oldest, and I got to set a good sample for the rest. I can't ever be scared and I can't ever cry. And that's the reason I didn't never say nothing 'bout my teef. It been hurting me and hurting me close to a month now. But I didn't say it. I didn't say it 'cause I didn't want act like no cry-baby, and 'cause I know us didn't have 'nough money to have it pulled. But, Lord, it been hurting me. And look like it won't start till at night when you trying to get little sleep. Then soon's you shet your eyes—umm-umm, Lord. Look like it go right down to your heart string.

"Hurting, hanh?" Ty'd say.

I'd shake my head, but I wouldn't open my mouth for nothing. You open your mouth and let that wind in, and it almost kill you.

---

I'd just lay there and listen to 'em snore. Ty, there, right 'side me, and Auntie and Val over by the fireplace. Val younger 'an me and Ty, and he sleep with Auntie. Mama sleep 'round the other side with Louis and Walker.

I'd just lay there and listen to 'em, and listen to that wind out there, and listen to that fire in the fireplace. Sometime it'd stop long enough to let me get little rest. Sometime it just hurt, hurt, hurt. Lord, have mercy.

II

Auntie knowed it was hurting me. I didn't tell nobody but Ty, 'cause us buddies and he ain't go'n tell nobody. But some kind o' way Auntie found out. When she asked me, I told her no, nothing was wrong. But she knowed it all the time. She told me to mash up a piece o' aspirin and wrap it in some cotton and jugg it down in that hole. I did it, but it didn't do

no good. It stopped for a little while, and started right back again. She wanted to tell Mama, but I told her Uh-uh. 'Cause I knowed it didn't have no money, and it jest was go'n make her mad again. So she told Monsieur Bayonne, and Monsieur Bayonne came to the house and told me to kneel down 'side him on the fireplace. He put his finger in his mouth and made the sign of the cross on my jaw. The tip of Monsieur Bayonne finger is some hard, 'cause he always playing on that guitar. If us sit outside at night us can always hear Monsieur Bayonne playing on his guitar. Sometime us leave him out there playing on the guitar.

He made the sign of the cross over and over on my jaw, but that didn't do no good. Even when he prayed and told me to pray some, too, that teef still hurt.

"How you feeling?" he say.

"Same," I say.

He kept on praying and making the sign of the cross and I kept on praying, too.

"Still hurting?" he say.

"Yes, sir."

Monsieur Bayonne mashed harder and harder on my jaw. He mashed so hard he almost pushed me on Ty. But then he stopped.

"What kind o' prayers you praying, boy?" he say.

"Baptist," I say.

"Well, I'll be—no wonder that teef still killing him. I'm going one way and he going the other. Boy, don't you know any Catholic prayers?"

"Hail Mary," I say.

"Then you better start saying it."

"Yes, sir."

He started mashing again, and I could hear him praying at the same time. And, sure 'nough, afterwhile it stopped.

Me and Ty went outside where Monsieur Bayonne two hounds was, and us started playing with 'em. "Let's go hunting," Ty say. "All right," I say; and us went on back in the pasture. Soon the hounds got on a trail, and me and Ty followed 'em all cross the pasture and then back in the woods, too. And then they cornered this little old rabbit and killed him, and me and Ty made 'em get back, and us picked up the rabbit and started on back home. But it had started hurting me again. It was hurting me plenty now, but I wouldn't tell Monsieur Bayonne. That night I didn't sleep a bit, and first thing in the morning Auntie told me go back and let Monsieur Bayonne pray over me some more. Monsieur Bayonne was in his kitchen making coffee when I got there. Soon's he seen me, he knowed what was wrong.

"All right, kneel down there 'side that stove," he say. "And this time pray Catholic. I don't know nothing 'bout Baptist, and don't want know nothing 'bout him."

### III

Last night Mama say: "Tomorrow us going to town."

"It ain't hurting me no more," I say. "I can eat anything on it."

"Tomorrow us going to town," she say.

And after she finished eating, she got up and went to bed. She always go to bed early now. 'Fore Daddy went in the Army, she used to stay up late. All o' us sitting out on the gallery or 'round the fire. But now, look like soon's she finish eating she go to bed.

This morning when I woke up, her and Auntie was standing 'fore the fireplace. She say: "'Nough to get there and back. Dollar and a half to have it pulled. Twenty-five for me to go, twenty-five for him. Twenty-five for me to come back, twenty-five for him. Fifty cents left. Guess I get a little piece o' salt meat with that."

"Sure can use a piece," Auntie say. "White beans and no salt meat ain't white beans."

"I do the best I can," Mama say.

They was quiet after that, and I made 'tend I was still sleep.

"James, hit the floor," Auntie say.

I still made 'tend I was sleep. I didn't want 'em to know I was listening.

"All right," Auntie say, shaking me by the shoulder. "Come on. Today's the day."

I pushed the cover down to get out, and Ty grabbed it and pulled it back.

"You, too, Ty," Auntie say.

"I ain't getting no teef pulled," Ty say.

"Don't mean it ain't time to get up," Auntie say. "Hit it, Ty."

Ty got up grumbling.

"James, you hurry up and get in your clothes and eat your food," Auntie say. "What time y'all coming back?" she say to Mama.

"That 'leven o'clock bus," Mama say. "Got to get back in that field this evening."

"Get a move on you, James," Auntie say.

I went in the kitchen and washed my face, then I ate my breakfast. I was having bread and syrup. The bread was warm and hard and tasted good. And I tried to make it last a long time.

Ty came back there, grumbling and mad at me.

"Got to get up," he say. "I ain't having no teef pulled. What I got to be getting up for."

Ty poured some syrup in his pan and got a piece of bread. He didn't wash his hands, neither his face, and I could see that white stuff in his eyes.

"You the one getting a teef pulled," he say. "What I got to get up for. I bet you if I was getting a teef pulled, you wouldn't be getting up. Shucks; syrup again. I'm getting tired of this old syrup. Syrup, syrup, syrup. I want me some bacon sometime."

"Go out in the field and work and you can have bacon," Auntie say. She stood in the middle door looking at Ty. "You better be glad you got syrup. Some people ain't got that—hard's time is."

"Shucks," Ty say. "How can I be strong."

"I don't know too much 'bout your strength," Auntie say; "but I know where you go'n be hot, you keep that grumbling up. James, get a move on you; your mama waiting."

I ate my last piece of bread and went in the front room. Mama was standing 'fore the fireplace warming her hands. I put on my coat and my cap, and us left the house.

### IV

I look down there again, but it still ain't coming. I almost say, "It ain't coming, yet," but I keep my mouth shet. 'Cause that's something else she don't like. She don't like for you to say something just for nothing. She can see it ain't coming, I can see it ain't coming, so why say it ain't coming. I don't say it, and I turn and look at the river that's back o' us. It so cold the smoke just raising up from the water. I see a bunch of pull-doos not too far out—jest on the other side the lilies. I'm wondering if you can eat pull-doos. I ain't too sure, 'cause I ain't never ate none. But I done ate owls and blackbirds, and I done ate redbirds, too. I didn't want kill the redbirds, but she made me kill 'em. They had two of 'em back there. One in my trap, one in Ty trap. Me and Ty was go'n play with 'em and let 'em go. But she made me kill 'em 'cause us needed the food.

"I can't," I say. "I can't."

"Here," she say. "Take it."

"I can't," I say. "I can't. I can't kill him, Mama. Please."

"Here," she say. "Take this fork, James."

"Please, Mama, I can't kill him," I say.

I could tell she was go'n hit me. And I jecked back, but I didn't jeck back soon enough.

"Take it," she say.

I took it and reached in for him, but he kept hopping to the back.

"I can't, Mama," I say. The water just kept running down my face. "I can't."

"Get him out o' there," she say.

I reached in for him and he kept hopping to the back. Then I reached in farther, and he pecked me on the hand.

"I can't, Mama," I say.

She slapped me again.

I reached in again, but he kept hopping out my way. Then he hopped to one side, and I reached there. The fork got him on the leg and I heard his leg pop. I pulled my hand out 'cause I had hurt him.

"Give it here," she say, and jecked the fork out my hand.

She reached and got the little bird right in the neck. I heard the fork go in his neck, and I heard it go in the ground. She brought him out and helt him right in front o' me.

"That's one," she say. She shook him off and gived me the fork. "Get the other one."

"I can't, Mama. I do anything. But I can't do that."

She went to the corner o' the fence and broke the biggest switch over there. I knelt 'side the trap crying.

"Get him out o' there," she say.

"I can't, Mama."

She started hitting me cross the back. I went down on the ground crying.

"Get him," she say.

"Octavia," Auntie say.

'Cause she had come out o' the house and she was standing by the tree looking at us.

"Get him out o' there," Mama say.

"Octavia," Auntie say; "explain to him. Explain to him. Jest don't beat him. Explain to him."

But she hit me and hit me and hit me.

I'm still young. I ain't no more'an eight. But I know now. I know why I had to. (They was so little, though. They was so little. I 'member how I picked the feathers off 'em and cleaned 'em and helt 'em over the fire. Then us all ate 'em. Ain't had but little bitty piece, but us all had little bitty piece, and ever'body jest looked at me, 'cause they was so proud.) S'pose she had to go away? That's why I had to do it. S'pose she had to go away like Daddy went away? Then who was go'n look after us? They had to be somebody left to carry on. I didn't know it then, but I know it now. Auntie and Monsieur Bayonne talked to me and made me see.

## V

Time I see it, I get out my hankercher and start waving. It still 'way down there, but I keep waving anyhow. Then it come closer and stop and me and Mama get on. Mama tell me go sit in the back while she pay. I do like she say, and the people look at me. When I pass the little sign that say White and Colored, I start looking for a seat. I jest see one of 'em back there, but I don't take it, 'cause I want my mama to sit down herself. She come in the back and sit down, and I lean on the seat. They got seats in the front, but I know I can't sit there, 'cause I have to sit back o' the sign. Anyhow, I don't want sit there if my mama go'n sit back here.

They got a lady sitting 'side my mama and she look at me and grin little bit. I grin back, but I don't open my mouth, 'cause the wind'll get in and make that teef hurt. The lady take out a pack o' gum and reach me a slice, but I shake my head. She reach Mama a slice, and Mama shake her head. The lady jest can't understand why a little boy'll turn down gum, and she reached me a slice again. This time I point to my jaw. The lady understand and grin little bit, and I grin little bit, but I don't open my mouth, though.

They got a girl sitting 'cross from me. She got on a red overcoat, and her hair plaited in one big plait. First, I make 'tend I don't even see her. But then I start looking at her little bit. She make 'tend she don't see me neither, but I catch her looking that way. She got a cold, and ever' now and then she hist that little hankercher to her nose. She ought to blow it, but she don't. Must think she too much a lady or something.

Ever' time she hist that little hankercher, the lady 'side her say something in her yer. She shake her head and lay her hands in her lap again. Then I catch her kind o' looking where I'm at. I grin at her. But think she'll grin back? No. She turn up her little old nose like I got some snot on my face or something. Well, I show her both o' us can turn us head. I turn mine, too, and look out at the river.

The river is gray. The sky is gray. They have pull-doos on the water. The water is wavy, and the pull-doos go up and down. The bus go 'round a turn, and you got plenty trees hiding the river. Then the bus go 'round another turn, and I can see the river again.

I look to the front where all the white people sitting. Then I look at that little old gal again. I don't look right at her, 'cause I don't want all them people to know I love her. I jest look at her little bit, like I'm looking out that window over there. But she know I'm looking that way, and she kind o' look at me, too. The lady sitting 'side her catch her this time, and she lean over and say something in her yer.

"I don't love him nothing," that little old gal say out loud.

Ever'body back there yer her mouth, and all of 'em look at us and laugh.

"I don't love you, neither," I say. "So you don't have to turn up your nose, Miss."

"You the one looking," she say.

"I wasn't looking at you," I say. "I was looking out that window, there."

"Out that window, my foot," she say. "I seen you. Ever' time I turn 'round you look at me."

"You must o' been looking yourself if you seen me all them times," I say.

"Shucks," she say. "I got me all kind o' boyfriends."

"I got girlfriends, too," I say.

"Well, I just don't want you to get your hopes up," she say.

I don't say no more to that little old gal, 'cause I don't want have to bust her in the mouth. I lean on the seat where Mama sitting, and I don't even look that way no more. When us get to Bayonne, she jugg her little old tongue out at me. I make 'tend I'm go'n hit her, and she duck down side her mama. And all the people laugh at us again.

## VI

Me and Mama get off and start walking in town. Bayonne is a little bitty town. Baton Rouge is a hundred times bigger 'an Bayonne. I went to Baton Rouge once—me, Ty, Mama, and Daddy. But that was 'way back yonder—'fore he went in the Army. I wonder when us go'n see him again. I wonder when. Look like he ain't ever coming home. . . . Even the pavement all cracked in Bayonne. Got grass shooting right out the sidewalk. Got weeds in the ditch, too; jest like they got home.

It some cold in Bayonne. Look like it colder 'an it is home. The wind blow in my face, and I feel that stuff running down my nose. I sniff. Mama say use that hankercher. I blow my nose and put it back.

Us pass a school and I see them white children playing in the yard. Big old red school, and them children jest running and playing. Then us pass a café, and I see a bunch of 'em in there eating. I wish I was in there 'cause I'm cold. Mama tell me keep my eyes in front where they blonks.

Us pass stores that got dummies, and us pass another café, and then us pass a shoe shop, and that baldhead man in there fixing on a shoe. I look at him and I butt into that white lady, and Mama jeck me in front and tell me stay there.

Us come to the courthouse, and I see the flag waving there. This one yer ain't like the one us got at school. This one yer ain't got but a handful of stars. One at school got a big pile of stars—one for ever' state. Us pass it and us turn and there it is—the dentist office. Me and Mama go in, and they got people sitting ever' where you look. They even got a little boy in there younger 'an me.

Me and Mama sit on that bench, and a white lady come in there and ask me what my name. Mama tell her, and the white lady go back. Then I yer somebody hollering in there. And soon's that little boy hear him hollering, he start hollering, too. His mama pat him and pat him, trying to make him hush up, but he ain't thinking 'bout her.

The man that was hollering in there come out holding his jaw.

"Got it, hanh?" another man say.

The man shake his head.

"Man, I thought they was killing you in there," the other man say. "Hollering like a pig under a gate."

The man don't say nothing. He jest head for the door, and the other man follow him.

"John Lee," the white lady say. "John Lee Williams."

The little boy jugg his head down in his mama lap and holler more now. His mama tell him go with the nurse, but he ain't thinking 'bout her. His mama tell him again, but he don't even yer. His mama pick him up and take him in there, and even when the white lady shet the door I can still hear him hollering.

"I often wonder why the Lord let a child like that suffer," a lady say to my mama. The lady's sitting right in front o' us on another bench. She got on a white dress and a black sweater. She must be a nurse or something herself, I reckoned.

"Not us to question," a man say.

"Sometimes I don't know if we shouldn't," the lady say.

"I know definitely we shouldn't," the man say. The man look like a preacher. He big and fat and he got on a black suit. He got a gold chain, too.

"Why?" the lady say.

"Why anything?" the preacher say.

"Yes," the lady say. "Why anything?"

"Not us to question," the preacher say.

The lady look at the preacher a little while and look at Mama again.

"And look like it's the poor who do most the suffering," she say. "I don't understand it."

"Best not to even try," the preacher say. "He works in mysterious ways. Wonders to perform."

Right then Little John Lee bust out hollering, and ever'body turn they head.

"He's not a good dentist," the lady say. "Dr. Robillard is much better. But more expensive. That's why most of the colored people come here. The white people go to Dr. Robillard. Y'all from Bayonne?"

"Down the river," my mama say. And that's all she go'n say, 'cause she don't talk much. But the lady keep on looking at her, and so she say: "Near Morgan."

"I see," the lady say.

## VII

"That's the trouble with the black people in this country today," somebody else say. This one yer sitting on the same side me and Mama sitting, and he kind o' sitting in front of that preacher. He look like a teacher or somebody that go to college. He got on a suit, and he got a book that he been reading. "We don't question is exactly the trouble," he say. "We should question and question and question. Question everything."

The preacher jest look at him a long time. He done put a toothpick or something in his mouth, and he jest keep turning it and turning it. You can see he don't like that boy with that book.

"Maybe you can explain what you mean," he say.

"I said what I meant," the boy say. "Question everything. Every stripe, every star, every word spoken. Everything."

"It 'pears to me this young lady and I was talking 'bout God, young man," the preacher say.

"Question Him, too," the boy say.

"Wait," the preacher say. "Wait now."

"You heard me right," the boy say. "His existence as well as everything else. Everything."

The preacher jest look cross the room at the boy. You can see he getting madder and madder. But mad or no mad, the boy ain't thinking 'bout him. He look at the preacher jest's hard's the preacher look at him.

"Is this what they coming to?" the preacher say. "Is this what we educating them for?"

"You're not educating me," the boy say. "I wash dishes at night to go to school in the day. So even the words you spoke need questioning."

The preacher jest look at him and shake his head.

"When I come in this room and seen you there with your book, I said to myself, There's an intelligent man. How wrong a person can be."

"Show me one reason to believe in the existence of a God," the boy say.

"My heart tell me," the preacher say.

"My heart tells me," the boy say. "My heart tells me. Sure, my heart tells me. And as long as you listen to what your heart tells you, you will have only what the white man gives you and nothing more. Me, I don't listen to my heart. The purpose of the heart is to pump blood throughout the body, and nothing else."

"Who's your paw, boy?" the preacher say.

"Why?"

"Who is he?"

"He's dead."

"And your mom?"

"She's in Charity Hospital with pneumonia. Half killed herself working for nothing."

"And 'cause he's dead and she sick, you mad at the world?"

"I'm not mad at the world. I'm questioning the world. I'm questioning it with cold logic, sir. What do words like Freedom, Liberty, God, White, Colored mean? I want to know. That's why *you* are sending us to school, to read and to ask questions. And because we ask these questions, you call us mad. No, sir, it is not us who are mad."

"You keep saying 'us'?"

" 'Us' . . . why not? I'm not alone."

The preacher jest shake his head. Then he look at ever'body in the room—ever'body. Some of the people look down at the floor, keep from looking at him. I kind o' look 'way myself, but soon's I know he done turn his head, I look that way again.

"I'm sorry for you," he say.

"Why?" the boy say. "Why not be sorry for yourself? Why are you so much better off than I am? Why aren't you sorry for these other people in here? Why not be sorry for the lady who had to drag her child into the dentist office? Why not be sorry for the lady sitting on that bench over there? Be sorry for them. Not for me. Some way or other I'm going to make it."

"No, I'm sorry for you," the preacher say.

"Of course. Of course," the boy say, shaking his head. "You're sorry for me because I rock that pillar you're leaning on."

"You can't ever rock the pillar I'm leaning on, young man. It's stronger than anything man can ever do."

"You believe in God because a man told you to believe in God. A white man told you to believe in God. And why? To keep you ignorant, so he can keep you under his feet."

"So now, we the ignorant?"

"Yes," the boy say. "Yes." And he open his book again.

The preacher jest look at him there. The boy done forgot all about him. Ever'body else make 'tend they done forgot 'bout the squabble, too.

Then I see that preacher getting up real slow. Preacher a great big old man, and he got to brace hisself to get up. He come 'cross the room where the boy is. He jest stand there looking at him, but the boy don't raise his head.

"Stand up, boy," preacher say.

The boy look up at him, then he shet his book real slow and stand up. Preacher jest draw back and hit him in the face. The boy fall 'gainst the wall, but he straighten hisself up and look right back at that preacher.

"You forgot the other cheek,"[1] he say.

The preacher hit him again on the other side. But this time the boy don't fall.

"That hasn't changed a thing," he say.

The preacher jest look at the boy. The preacher breathing real hard like he jest run up a hill. The boy sit down and open his book again.

"I feel sorry for you," the preacher say. "I never felt so sorry for a man before."

The boy make 'tend he don't even hear that preacher. He keep on reading his book. The preacher go back and get his hat off the chair.

"Excuse me," he say to us. "I'll come back some other time. Y'all, please excuse me."

And he look at the boy and go out the room. The boy hist his hand up to his mouth one time, to wipe 'way some blood. All the rest o' the time he keep on reading.

### VIII

The lady and her little boy come out the dentist, and the nurse call somebody else in. Then little bit later they come out, and the nurse call another name. But fast's she call somebody in there, somebody else come in the place where we at, and the room stay full.

The people coming in now, all of 'em wearing big coats. One of 'em say something 'bout sleeting, and another one say he hope not. Another one say he think it ain't nothing but rain. 'Cause, he say, rain can get awful cold this time o' year.

All 'cross the room they talking. Some of 'em talking to people right by 'em, some of 'em talking to people clare 'cross the room, some of 'em talking to anybody'll listen. It's a little bitty room, no bigger 'an us kitchen, and I can see ever'body in there. The little old room's full of

smoke, 'cause you got two old men smoking pipes. I think I feel my teef thumping me some, and I hold my breath and wait. I wait and wait, but it don't thump me no more. Thank God for that.

I feel like going to sleep, and I lean back 'gainst the wall. But I'm scared to go to sleep: Scared 'cause the nurse might call my name and I won't hear her. And Mama might go to sleep, too, and she be mad if neither us heard the nurse.

I look up at Mama. I love my mama. I love my mama. And when cotton come I'm go'n get her a newer coat. And I ain't go'n get a black one neither. I think I'm go'n get her a red one.

"They got some books over there," I say. "Want read one of 'em?"

Mama look at the books, but she don't answer me.

"You got yourself a little man there," the lady say.

Mama don't say nothing to the lady, but she must 'a' grin a little bit, 'cause I seen the lady grinning back. The lady look at me a little while, like she feeling sorry for me.

"You sure got that preacher out here in a hurry," she say to that other boy.

The boy look up at her and look in his book again. When I grow up I want be jest like him. I want clothes like that and I want keep a book with me, too.

"You really don't believe in God?" the lady say.

"No," he say.

"But why?" the lady say.

"Because the wind is pink," he say.

"What?" the lady say.

The boy don't answer her no more. He jest read in his book.

"Talking 'bout the wind is pink," that old lady say. She sitting on the same bench with the boy, and she trying to look in his face. The boy make 'tend the old lady ain't even there. He jest keep reading. "Wind is pink," she say again. "Eh, Lord, what children go'n be saying next?"

The lady 'cross from us bust out laughing.

"That's a good one," she say. "The wind is pink. Yes, sir, that's a good one."

"Don't you believe the wind is pink?" the

---

1. *You forgot . . . cheek*, an ironic reference to a passage in the Bible: ". . . whosoever shall smite thee on thy right cheek, turn to him the other also" (Matt. 5:39).

boy say. He keep his head down in the book.

"Course I believe it, Honey," the lady say. "Course I do." She look at us and wink her eye. "And what color is grass, Honey?"

"Grass? Grass is black."

She bust out laughing again. The boy look at her.

"Don't you believe grass is black?" he say.

The lady quit laughing and look at him. Ever'body else look at him now. The place quiet, quiet.

"Grass is green, Honey," the lady say. "It was green yesterday, it's green today, and it's go'n be green tomorrow."

"How do you know it's green?"

"I know because I know."

"You don't know it's green. You believe it's green because someone told you it was green. If someone had told you it was black you'd believe it was black."

"It's green," the lady say. "I know green when I see green."

"Prove it's green."

"Surely, now," the lady say. "Don't tell me it's coming to that?"

"It's coming to just that," the boy say. "Words mean nothing. One means no more than the other."

"That's what it all coming to?" that old lady say. That old lady got on a turban and she got on two sweaters. She got a green sweater under a black sweater. I can see the green sweater 'cause some of the buttons on the other sweater missing.

"Yes, ma'am," the boy say. "Words mean nothing. Action is the only thing. Doing. That's the only thing."

"Other words, you want the Lord to come down here and show Hisself to you?" she say.

"Exactly, ma'am."

"You don't mean that, I'm sure?"

"I do, ma'am."

"Done, Jesus," the old lady say, shaking her head.

"I didn't go 'long with that preacher at first," the other lady say; "but now—I don't know. When a person say the grass is black, he's either a lunatic or something wrong."

"Prove to me that it's green."

"It's green because the people say it's green."

"Those same people say we're citizens of the United States."

"I think I'm a citizen."

"Citizens have certain rights. Name me one right that you have. One right, granted by the Constitution, that you can exercise in Bayonne."

The lady don't answer him. She jest look at him like she don't know what he talking 'bout. I know I don't.

"Things changing," she say.

"Things are changing because some black men have begun to follow their brains instead of their hearts."

"You trying to say these people don't believe in God?"

"I'm sure some of them do. Maybe most of them do. But they don't believe that God is going to touch these white people's hearts and change them tomorrow. Things change through action. By no other way."

Ever'body sit quiet and look at the boy. Nobody say a thing. Then the lady 'cross from me and Mama jest shake her head.

"Let's hope that not all your generation feel the same way you do," she say.

"Think what you please, it doesn't matter," the boy say. "But it will be men who listen to their heads and not their hearts who will see that your children have a better chance than you had."

"Let's hope they ain't all like you, though," the old lady say. "Done forgot the heart absolutely."

"Yes, ma'am, I hope they aren't all like me," the boy say. "Unfortunately I was born too late to believe in your God. Let's hope that the ones who come after will have your faith—if not in your God, then in something else, something definitely that they can lean on. I haven't anything. For me, the wind is pink; the grass is black."

IX

The nurse come in the room where us all sitting and waiting and say the doctor won't take no more patients till one o'clock this evening. My mama jump up off the bench and go up to the white lady.

"Nurse, I have to go back in the field this evening," she say.

"The doctor is treating his last patient now," the nurse say. "One o'clock this evening."

"Can I at least speak to the doctor?" my mama say.

"I'm his nurse," the lady say.

"My little boy sick," my mama say. "Right now his teef almost killing him."

The nurse look at me. She trying to make up her mind if to let me come in. I look at her real pitiful. The teef ain't hurting me a tall, but Mama say it is, so I make 'tend for her sake.

"This evening," the nurse say, and go back in the office.

"Don't feel 'jected, Honey," the lady say to Mama. "I been 'round 'em a long time—they take you when they want to. If you was white, that's something else; but you the wrong shade."

Mama don't say nothing to the lady, and me and her go outside and stand 'gainst the wall. It's cold out there. I can feel that wind going through my coat. Some of the other people come out of the room and go up the street. Me and Mama stand there a little while and start to walking. I don't know where us going. When us come to the other street us jest stand there.

"You don't have to make water, do you?" Mama say.

"No, ma'am," I say.

Us go up the street. Walking real slow. I can tell Mama don't know where she going. When us come to a store us stand there and look at the dummies. I look at a little boy with a brown overcoat. He got on brown shoes, too. I look at my old shoes and look at his'n again. You wait till summer, I say.

Me and Mama walk away. Us come up to another store and us stop and look at them dummies, too. Then us go again. Us pass a café where the white people in there eating. Mama tell me keep my eyes in front where they blonks, but I can't help from seeing them people eat. My stomach start to growling 'cause I'm hungry. When I see people eating, I get hungry; when I see a coat, I get cold.

A man whistle at my mama when us go by a filling station. She make 'tend she don't even see him. I look back and I feel like hitting him in the mouth. If I was bigger, I say. If I was bigger, you see.

Us keep on going. I'm getting colder and colder, but I don't say nothing. I feel that stuff running down my nose and I sniff.

"That rag," she say.

I git it out and wipe my nose. I'm getting cold all over now—my face, my hands, my feet, ever'thing. Us pass another little café, but this'n for white people, too, and us can't go in there neither. So us jest walk. I'm so cold now, I'm 'bout ready to say it. If I knowed where us was going, I wouldn't be so cold, but I don't know where us going. Us go, us go, us go. Us walk clean out o' Bayonne. Then us cross the street and us come back. Same thing I seen when I got off the bus. Same old trees, same old walk, same old weeds, same old cracked pave—same old ever'thing.

I sniff again.

"That rag," she say.

I wipe my nose real fast and jugg that hankercher back in my pocket 'fore my hand get too cold. I raise my head and I can see David hardware store. When us come up to it, us go in. I don't know why, but I'm glad.

It warm in there. It so warm in there you don't want ever leave. I look for the heater, and I see it over by them ba'ls. Three white men standing 'round the heater talking in Creole. One of 'em come to see what Mama want.

"Got any ax handle?" she say.

Me, Mama, and the white man start to the back, but Mama stop me when us come to the heater. Her and the white man go on. I hold my hand over the heater and look at 'em. They go all the way in the back, and I see the white man point to the ax handle 'gainst the wall. Mama take one of 'em and shake it like she trying to figure how much it weigh. Then she rub her hand over it from one end to the other. She turn it over and look at the other side, then she shake it again, and shake her head and put it back. She get another one and she do it jest like she did the first one, then she shake her head. Then she get a brown one and do it that, too. But she don't like this one neither. Then she get another one, but 'fore she shake it or anything, she look at me. Look like she trying to say something to me, but I don't know what it is. All I know is I done got warm now and I'm feeling right smart better. Mama shake this ax handle jest like she done the others, and shake her head and say something to the white man. The white man jest look at his pile of ax handle, and when Mama pass by him to come to the front, the white man jest scratch his head and follow her. She tell me come on, and us go on out and start walking again.

Us walk and walk, and no time at all I'm cold again. Look like I'm colder now 'cause I can still remember how good it was back there. My stomach growl and I suck it in to keep Mama from yering it. She walking right 'side me, and it growl so loud you can yer it a mile. But Mama don't say a word.

### X

When us come up to the courthouse, I look at the clock. It got quarter to twelve. Mean us got another hour and a quarter to be out yer in the cold. Us go and stand side a building. Something hit my cap and I look up at the sky. Sleet falling.

I look at Mama standing there. I want stand close 'side her, but she don't like that. She say that's cry-baby stuff. She say you got to stand for yourself, by yourself.

"Let's go back to that office," she say.

Us cross the street. When us get to the dentist I try to open the door, but I can't. Mama push me on the side and she twist the knob. But she can't open it neither. She twist it some more, harder, but she can't open it. She turn 'way from the door. I look at her, but I don't move and I don't say nothing. I done seen her like this before and I'm scared.

"You hungry?" she say. She say it like she mad at me, like I'm the one cause of ever'thing.

"No, ma'am," I say.

"You want eat and walk back, or you rather don't eat and ride?"

"I ain't hungry," I say.

I ain't jest hungry, but I'm cold, too. I'm so hungry and I'm so cold I want cry. And look like I'm getting colder and colder. My feet done got numb. I try to work my toes, but I can't. Look like I'm go'n die. Look like I'm go'n stand right here and freeze to death. I think about home. I think about Val and Auntie and Ty and Louis and Walker. It 'bout twelve o'clock and I know they eating dinner. I can hear Ty making jokes. That's Ty. Always trying to make some

kind o' joke. I wish I was right there listening to him. Give anything in the world if I was home 'round the fire.

"Come on," Mama say.

Us start walking again. My feet so numb I can't hardly feel 'em. Us turn the corner and go back up the street. The clock start hitting for twelve.

The sleet's coming down plenty now. They hit the pave and bounce like rice. Oh, Lord; oh, Lord, I pray. Don't let me die. Don't let me die. Don't let me die, Lord.

### XI

Now I know where us going. Us going back o' town where the colored people eat. I don't care if I don't eat. I been hungry before. I can stand it. But I can't stand the cold.

I can see us go'n have a long walk. It 'bout a mile down there. But I don't mind. I know when I get there I'm go'n warm myself. I think I can hold out. My hands numb in my pockets and my feet numb, too, but if I keep moving I can hold out. Jest don't stop no more, that's all.

The sky's gray. The sleet keep falling. Falling like rain now—plenty, plenty. You can hear it hitting the pave. You can see it bouncing. Sometimes it bounce two times 'fore it settle.

Us keep going. Us don't say nothing. Us jest keep going, keep going.

I wonder what Mama thinking. I hope she ain't mad with me. When summer come I'm go'n pick plenty cotton and get her a coat. I'm go'n get her a red one.

I hope they make it summer all the time. I be glad if it was summer all the time—but it ain't. Us got to have winter, too. Lord, I hate the winter. I guess ever'body hate the winter.

I don't sniff this time. I get out my hankercher and wipe my nose. My hand so cold I can hardly hold the hankercher.

I think us getting close, but us ain't there yet. I wonder where ever'body is. Can't see nobody but us. Look like us the only two people moving 'round today. Must be too cold for the rest of the people to move 'round.

I can hear my teefes. I hope they don't knock together too hard and make that bad one hurt. Lord, that's all I need, for that bad one to start off.

I hear a church bell somewhere. But today ain't Sunday. They must be ringing for a funeral or something.

I wonder what they doing at home. They must be eating. Monsieur Bayonne might be there with his guitar. One day Ty played with Monsieur Bayonne guitar and broke one o' the string. Monsieur Bayonne got some mad with Ty. He say Ty ain't go'n never 'mount to nothing. Ty can go jest like him when he ain't there. Ty can make ever'body laugh mocking Monsieur Bayonne.

I used to like to be with Mama and Daddy. Us used to be happy. But they took him in the Army. Now, nobody happy no more. . . . I be glad when he come back.

Monsieur Bayonne say it wasn't fair for 'em to take Daddy and give Mama nothing and give us nothing. Auntie say, Shhh, Etienne. Don't let 'em yer you talk like that. Monsieur Bayonne say, It's God truth. What they giving his children? They have to walk three and a half mile to school hot or cold. That's anything to give for a paw? She's got to work in the field rain or shine jest to make ends meet. That's anything to give for a husband? Auntie say, Shhh, Etienne, shhh. Yes, you right, Monsieur Bayonne say. Best don't say it in front of 'em now. But one day they go'n find out. One day. Yes, s'pose so, Auntie say. Then what, Rose Mary? Monsieur Bayonne say. I don't know, Etienne, Auntie say. All us can do is us job, and leave ever'thing else in His hand. . . .

Us getting closer, now. Us getting closer. I can see the railroad tracks.

Us cross the tracks, and now I see the café. Jest to get in there, I say. Jest to get in there. Already I'm starting to feel little better.

### XII

Us go in. Ahh, it good. I look for the heater; there 'gainst the wall. One of them little brown ones. I jest stand there and hold my hand over it. I can't open my hands too wide 'cause they almost froze.

Mama standing right 'side me. She done unbuttoned her coat. Smoke rise out the coat, and the coat smell like a wet dog.

I move to the side so Mama can have more room. She open out her hands and rub 'em together. I rub mine together, too, 'cause this keeps 'em from hurting. If you let 'em warm too fast, they hurt you sure. But if you let 'em warm jest little bit at a time, and you keep rubbing 'em, they be all right ever' time.

They got jest two more people in the café. A lady back o' the counter, and a man on this side the counter. They been watching us ever since us come in.

Mama get out the hankercher and count the money. Both o' us know how much money she got there. Three dollars. No, she ain't got three dollars. 'Cause she had to pay us way up here. She ain't got but two dollars and a half left. Dollar and a half to get my teef pulled, and fifty cents for us to go back on, and fifty cents worse o' salt meat.

She stir the money 'round with her finger. Most o' the money is change 'cause I can hear it rubbing together. She stir it and stir it. Then she look at the door. It still sleeting. I can yer it hitting 'gainst the wall like rice.

"I ain't hungry, Mama," I say.

"Got to pay 'em something for they heat," she say.

She take a quarter out the hankercher and tie the hankercher up again. She look over her shoulder at the people, but she still don't move. I hope she don't spend the money. I don't want her spend it on me. I'm hungry, I'm almost starving I'm so hungry, but I don't want her spending the money on me.

She flip the quarter over like she thinking. She must be thinking 'bout us walking back home. Lord, I sure don't want walk home. If I thought it done any good to say something, I say it. But my mama make up her own mind.

She turn way from the heater right fast, like she better hurry up and do it 'fore she change her mind. I turn to look at her go to the counter. The man and the lady look at her, too. She tell the lady something and the lady walk away. The man keep on looking at her. Her back turn to the man, and Mama don't even know he standing there.

The lady put some cakes and a glass o' milk on the counter. Then she pour up a cup o' coffee and set it side the other stuff. Mama pay her for the things and come back where I'm at. She tell me sit down at that table 'gainst the wall.

The milk and the cakes for me. The coffee for my mama. I eat slow, and I look at her. She looking outside at the sleet. She looking real sad. I say to myself, I'm go'n make all this up one day. You see, one day, I'm go'n make all this up. I want to say it now. I want to tell how I feel right now. But Mama don't like for us to talk like that.

"I can't eat all this," I say.

They got just three little cakes there. And I'm so hungry right now, the Lord know I can eat a hundred times three. But I want her to have one.

She don't even look my way. She know I'm hungry. She know I want it. I let it stay there a while, then I get it and eat it. I eat jest on my front teefes, 'cause if it tech that back teef I know what'll happen. Thank God it ain't hurt me a tall today.

After I finish eating I see the man go to the juke box. He drop a nickel in it, then he jest stand there looking at the record. Mama tell me keep my eyes in front where they blonks. I turn my head like she say, but then I yer the man coming towards us.

"Dance, Pretty?" he say.

Mama get up to dance with him. But 'fore you know it, she done grabbed the little man and done throwed him 'side the wall. He hit the wall so hard he stop the juke box from playing.

"Some pimp," the lady back o' the counter say. "Some pimp."

The little man jump off the floor and start towards my mama. 'Fore you know it, Mama done sprung open her knife and she waiting for him.

"Come on," she say. "Come on. I'll cut you from your neighbo to your throat. Come on."

I go up to the little man to hit him, but Mama make me come and stand 'side her. The little man look at me and Mama and go back to the counter.

"Some pimp," the lady back o' the counter say. "Some pimp." She start laughing and pointing at the little man. "Yes, sir, you a pimp, all right. Yes, sir."

## XIII

"Fasten that coat. Let's go," Mama say.

"You don't have to leave," the lady say.

Mama don't answer the lady, and us right out in the cold again. I'm warm right now—my hands, my yers, my feet—but I know this ain't go'n last too long. It done sleet so much now you got ice ever'where.

Us cross the railroad tracks, and soon's us do, I get cold. That wind go through this little old coat like it ain't nothing. I got a shirt and a sweater under it, but that wind don't pay 'em no mind. I look up and I can see us got a long way to go. I wonder if us go'n make it 'fore I get too cold.

Us cross over to walk on the sidewalk. They got jest one sidewalk back here. It's over there.

After us go jest a little piece, I smell bread cooking. I look, then I see a baker shop. When us get closer, I can smell it more better. I shet my eyes and make 'tend I'm eating. But I keep 'em shet too long and I butt up 'gainst a telephone post. Mama grab me and see if I'm hurt. I ain't bleeding or nothing and she turn me loose.

I can feel I'm getting colder and colder, and I look up to see how far us still got to go. Uptown is 'way up yonder. A half mile, I reckoned. I try to think of something. They say think and you won't get cold. I think of that poem, "Annabel Lee." I ain't been to school in so long—this bad weather—I reckoned they done passed "Annabel Lee." But passed it or not, I'm sure Miss Walker go'n make me recite it when I get there. That woman don't never forget nothing. I ain't never seen nobody like that.

I'm still getting cold. "Annabel Lee" or no "Annabel Lee," I'm still getting cold. But I can see us getting closer. Us getting there gradually.

Soon's us turn the corner, I see a little old white lady up in front o' us. She the only lady on the street. She all in black and she got a long black rag over her head.

"Stop," she say.

Me and Mama stop and look at her. She must be crazy to be out in all this sleet. Ain't got but a few other people out there, and all of 'em men.

"Yall done ate?" she say.

"Jest finished," Mama say.

"Yall must be cold then?" she say.

"Us headed for the dentist," Mama say. "Us'll warm up when us get there."

"What dentist?" the old lady say. "Mr. Bassett?"

"Yes, ma'am," Mama say.

"Come on in," the old lady say. "I'll telephone him and tell him yall coming."

Me and Mama follow the old lady in the store. It's a little bitty store, and it don't have much in there. The old lady take off her head piece and fold it up.

"Helena?" somebody call from the back.

"Yes, Alnest?" the old lady say.

"Did you see them?"

"They're here. Standing beside me."

"Good. Now you can stay inside."

The old lady look at Mama. Mama waiting to hear what she brought us in here for. I'm waiting for that, too.

"I saw yall each time you went by," she say. "I came out to catch you, but you were gone."

"Us went back o' town," Mama say.

"Did you eat?"

"Yes, ma'am."

The old lady look at Mama a long time, like she thinking Mama might be jest saying that. Mama look right back at her. The old lady look at me to see what I got to say. I don't say nothing. I sure ain't going 'gainst my mama.

"There's food in the kitchen," she say to Mama. "I've been keeping it warm."

Mama turn right around and start for the door.

"Just a minute," the old lady say. Mama stop. "The boy'll have to work for it. It isn't free."

"Us don't take no handout," Mama say.

"I'm not handing out anything," the old lady say. "I need my garbage moved to the front. Ernest has a bad cold and can't go out there."

"James'll move it for you," Mama say.

"Not unless you eat," the old lady say. "I'm old, but I have my pride, too, you know."

Mama can see she ain't go'n beat this old lady down, so she jest shake her head.

"All right," the old lady say. "Come into the kitchen."

She lead the way with that rag in her hand. The kitchen is a little bitty thing, too. The table and the stove jest about fill it up. They got a little room to the side. Somebody in there laying cross the bed. Must be the person she was talking with: Alnest or Ernest—I forget what she call him.

"Sit down," the old lady say to Mama. "Not you," she say to me. "You have to move the cans."

"Helena?" somebody say in the other room.

"Yes, Alnest?" the old lady say.

"Are you going out there again?"

"I must show the boy where the garbage is," the old lady say.

"Keep that shawl over your head," the old man say.

"You don't have to remind me. Come boy," the old lady say.

Us go out in the yard. Little old back yard ain't no bigger 'an the store or the kitchen. But it can sleet here jest like it can sleet in any big back yard. And 'fore you know it I'm trembling.

"There," the old lady say, pointing to the cans. I pick up one of the cans. The can so light I put it back down to look inside o' it.

"Here," the old lady say. "Leave that cap alone."

I look at her in the door. She got that black rag wrapped 'round her shoulders, and she pointing one of her fingers at me.

"Pick it up and carry it to the front," she say. I go by her with the can. I'm sure the thing 's empty. She could 'a' carried the thing by herself, I'm sure. "Set it on the sidewalk by the door and come back for the other one," she say.

I go and come back, Mama look at me when I pass her. I get the other can and take it to the front. It don't feel no heavier 'an the other one. I tell myself to look inside and see just what I been hauling. First, I look up and down the street. Nobody coming. Then I look over my shoulder. Little old lady done slipped there jest 's quiet 's mouse, watching me. Look like she knowed I was go'n try that.

"Ehh, Lord," she say. "Children, children. Come in here, boy, and go wash your hands."

I follow her into the kitchen, and she point, and I go to the bathroom. When I come out, the old lady done dished up the food. Rice, gravy, meat, and she even got some lettuce and tomato in a saucer. She even got a glass o' milk and a piece o' cake there, too. It look so good. I almost start eating 'fore I say my blessing.

"Helena?" the old man say.

"Yes, Alnest?" she say.

"Are they eating?"

"Yes," she say.

"Good," he say. "Now you'll stay inside."

The old lady go in there where he is and I can hear 'em talking. I look at Mama. She eating slow like she thinking. I wonder what's the matter now. I reckoned she think 'bout home.

The old lady come back in the kitchen.

"I talked to Dr. Bassett's nurse," she say. "Dr. Bassett will take you as soon as you get there."

"Thank you, ma'am," Mama say.

"Perfectly all right," the old lady say. "Which one is it?"

Mama nod towards me. The old lady look at me real sad. I look sad, too.

"You're not afraid, are you?" she say.

"No'm," I say.

"That's a good boy," the old lady say. "Nothing to be afraid of."

When me and Mama get through eating, us thank the old lady again.

"Helena, are they leaving?" the old man say.

"Yes, Alnest."

"Tell them I say good-by."

"They can hear you, Alnest."

"Good-by both mother and son," the old man say. "And may God be with you."

Me and Mama tell the old man good-by, and us follow the old lady in the front. Mama open the door to go out, but she stop and come back in the store.

"You sell salt meat?" she say.

"Yes."

"Give me two bits worse."

"That isn't very much salt meat," the old lady say.

"That'll all I have," Mama say.

The old lady go back o' the counter and cut a big piece off the chunk. Then she wrap it and put it in a paper bag.

"Two bits," she say.

"That look like awful lot of meat for a quarter," Mama say.

"Two bits," the old lady say. "I've been selling salt meat behind this counter twenty-five years. I think I know what I'm doing."

"You got a scale there," Mama say.

"What?" the old lady say.

"Weigh it," Mama say.

"What?" the old lady say. "Are you telling me how to run my business?"

"Thanks very much for the food," Mama say.

"Just a minute," the old lady say.

"James," Mama say to me. I move towards the door.

"Just one minute, I said," the old lady say.

Me and Mama stop again and look at her. The old lady take the meat out the bag and unwrap it and cut 'bout half o' it off. Then she wrap it up again and jugg it back in the bag and give it to Mama. Mama lay the quarter on the counter.

"Your kindness will never be forgotten," she say. "James," she say to me.

Us go out, and the old lady come to the door to look at us. After us go a little piece I look back, and she still there watching us.

The sleet's coming down heavy, heavy now, and I turn up my collar to keep my neck warm. My mama tell me turn it right back down.

"You not a bum," she say. "You a man."

---

## DISCUSSION

1. (a) According to James, what are some of Mama's worries as they wait for the bus? (b) What events in the story can you cite as evidence of Mama's love for James? (c) When she meets Helena, the old white lady, in what ways does Mama reveal her pride?

2. How does James respond to the need for him to be a man?

3. (a) Events in this story take place before many civil rights reforms had been enacted. What evidence of discrimination do you find in the story? (b) Of this evidence, which might you still find today, and which would no longer exist?

4. (a) What is the basic difference in philosophy between the preacher and the young man with whom he argues in the dentist's office? (b) What does the young man mean by "the wind is pink," "the grass is black"? (c) This scene between the preacher and the young man does nothing to advance the action of the story. What, then, are some possible reasons for

including it? Do the ideas expressed here have anything to do with James or his Mama? If so, what?

5. Despite its general tone and its subject matter, this story has a number of humorous scenes. Which ones appealed to you and why?

6. What possible meanings might Ernest Gaines have had in mind in titling his story "The Sky Is Gray"?

## ERNEST J. GAINES

Ernest J. Gaines was born on a plantation near Oscar, Louisiana.

He worked in the fields as a boy and there came to know the rural people who are important figures in many of his stories.

After army service, Gaines earned a degree at San Francisco State College in 1957 and won a Wallace Stegner Creative Writing Fellowship for a year of study at Stanford.

His first published novel appeared in 1964, a second in 1967, and *Bloodline*, a collection of stories that includes "The Sky Is Gray," the following year.

His recent novel, *The Autobiography of Miss Jane Pittman*, is about a black woman who was

born a slave, freed at the end of the Civil War, and lived to be a participant in the second emancipation movement of the sixties.

---

## . . . and Endings

Longfellow said "Great is the art of beginning, but greater the art is of ending." More than one writer has wondered how to summarize his thoughts, extricate his characters from their troubles, tie up the plot, or otherwise gracefully end a story.

Some writers in moments of indecision have written alternative endings to their works. Dickens wrote two endings for *Great Expectations*. The original ending was an unhappy one—unusual for Dickens. He later changed the ending to a more hopeful one, probably at the urging of a friend.

In the previous supplementary article, the first sentence from *Treasure Island* was quoted. Below is the closing paragraph:

"The bar silver and the arms still lie, for all that I know, where Flint buried them; and certainly they shall lie there for me. Oxen and wain-ropes would not bring me back again to that accursed island;

and the worst dreams that ever I have are when I hear the surf booming about the coasts, or start upright in bed, with the sharp voice of Captain Flint still ringing in my ears: 'Pieces of eight! pieces of eight!'"

With this, the reader knows he has come full circle. The narrator has survived; the perils of his existence are over except in his dreams.

Some endings look backward, as does this one by Colette from *Claudine at School:* "Farewell to the classroom; farewell, Mademoiselle and her girl friend; farewell, feline little Luce and spiteful Anaïs! I am going to leave you to make my entry into the world; — I shall be very much astonished if I enjoy myself there as much as I have at school." We are at first prepared to look ahead to new occurrences when suddenly we are brought up short by the narrator's last few words. We cannot look beyond the story because the narrator herself does not do so.

Contrast this with the forward-looking ending of "Claudine's Book" or the purposeful ending of "The Sky Is Gray."

Some writers choose to close with a general statement about the human condition. Thackery did so in *Vanity Fair*, but he has disappointed some readers by seeming to imply that we are not to believe in his characters or their plight: "Ah *Vanitas Vanitatum!* Which of us is happy in this world? Which of us has his desire? or, having it, is satisfied?—Come, children, let us shut up the box and the puppets, for our play is played out."

The last three sentences of *Walden* by Henry David Thoreau have seemed to many to be a perfect ending, partly because it is appropriate to all that has gone before and partly because it is so characteristic of the man himself: "Only that day dawns to which we are awake. There is more day to dawn. The sun is but a morning star."

# The Lottery Ticket

*Anton Chekhov*

*"And if we have won," he said— "why, it will be a new life, it will be a transformation!" But the lottery ticket is not mine, he thought, it's hers.*

IVAN Dmitritch, a middle-class man who lived with his family on an income of twelve hundred a year and was very well satisfied with his lot, sat down on the sofa after supper and began reading the newspaper.

"I forgot to look at the newspaper today," his wife said to him as she cleared the table. "Look and see whether the list of drawings is there."

"Yes, it is," said Ivan Dmitritch; "but hasn't your ticket lapsed?"

"No; I took the interest on Tuesday."

"What is the number?"

"Series 9,499, number 26."

"All right . . . we will look . . . 9,499 and 26."

"The Lottery Ticket" from *The Wife and Other Stories* by Anton Chekhov, translated from the Russian by Constance Garnett. Copyright 1918 by The Macmillan Company, renewed 1946 by Constance Garnett. Reprinted by permission of The Macmillan Company and Chatto and Windus Ltd. for Mr. David Garnett.

Ivan Dmitritch had no faith in lottery luck, and would not, as a rule, have consented to look at the lists of winning numbers, but now, as he had nothing else to do and as the newspaper was before his eyes, he passed his finger downwards along the column of numbers. And immediately, as though in mockery of his scepticism, no further than the second line from the top, his eye was caught by the figure 9,499! Unable to believe his eyes, he hurriedly dropped the paper on his knees without looking to see the number of the ticket, and, just as though some one had given him a douche of cold water, he felt an agreeable chill in the pit of the stomach; tingling and terrible and sweet!

"Masha, 9,499 is there!" he said in a hollow voice.

His wife looked at his astonished and panic-stricken face, and realized that he was not joking.

"9,499?" she asked, turning pale and dropping the folded tablecloth on the table.

"Yes, yes . . . it really is there!"

"And the number of the ticket?"

"Oh, yes! There's the number of the ticket too. But stay . . . wait! No, I say! Anyway, the number of our series is there! Anyway, you understand. . . ."

Looking at his wife, Ivan Dmitritch gave a broad, senseless smile, like a baby when a bright object is shown it. His wife smiled too; it was as pleasant to her as to him that he only mentioned the series, and did not try to find out the number of the winning ticket. To torment and tantalize oneself with hopes of possible fortune is so sweet, so thrilling!

"It is our series," said Ivan Dmitritch, after a long silence. "So there is a probability that we have won. It's only a probability, but there it is!"

"Well, now look!"

"Wait a little. We have plenty of time to be disappointed. It's on the second line from the top, so the prize is seventy-five thousand. That's not money, but power, capital! And in a minute I shall look at the list, and there—26! Eh? I say, what if we really have won?"

The husband and wife began laughing and staring at one another in silence. The possibility of winning bewildered them; they could not have said, could not have dreamed, what they both needed that seventy-five thousand for, what they would buy, where they would go. They thought only of the figures 9,499 and 75,000 and pictured them in their imagination, while somehow they could not think of the happiness itself which was so possible.

Ivan Dmitritch, holding the paper in his hand, walked several times from corner to corner, and only when he had recovered from the first impression began dreaming a little.

"And if we have won," he said—"why, it will be a new life, it will be a transformation! The ticket is yours, but if it were mine I should, first of all, of course, spend twenty-five thousand on real property in the shape of an estate; ten thousand on immediate expenses, new furnishing . . . travelling . . . paying debts, and so on. . . . The other forty thousand I would put in the bank and get interest on it."

"Yes, an estate, that would be nice," said his wife, sitting down and dropping her hands in her lap.

"Somewhere in the Tula or Oryol provinces. . . . In the first place we shouldn't need a summer villa, and besides, it would always bring in an income."

And pictures came crowding on his imagination, each more gracious and poetical than the last. And in all these pictures he saw himself well fed, serene, healthy, felt warm, even hot! Here, after eating a summer soup, cold as ice, he lay on his back on the burning sand close to a stream or in the garden under a lime tree. . . . It is hot. . . . His little boy and girl are crawling about near him, digging in the sand or catching ladybirds in the grass. He dozes sweetly, thinking of nothing, and feeling all over that he need not go to the office today, tomorrow, or the day after. Or, tired of lying still, he goes to the hayfield, or to the forest for mushrooms, or watches the peasants catching fish with a net. When the sun sets he takes a towel and soap and saunters to the bathing shed, where he undresses at his leisure, slowly rubs his bare chest with his hands, and goes into the water. And in the water, near the opaque soapy circles, little fish flit to and fro and green water weeds nod their heads. After bathing there is tea with cream and milk rolls.

. . . In the evening a walk or *vint*[1] with the neighbours.

"Yes, it would be nice to buy an estate," said his wife, also dreaming, and from her face it was evident that she was enchanted by her thoughts.

Ivan Dmitritch pictured to himself autumn with its rains, its cold evenings, and its St. Martin's summer.[2] At that season he would have to take longer walks about the garden and beside the river, so as to get thoroughly chilled, and then drink a big glass of vodka and eat a salted mushroom or a soused cucumber, and then—drink another. . . . The children would come running from the kitchen garden, bringing a carrot and a radish smelling of fresh earth. . . . And then, he would lie stretched full length on the sofa, and in leisurely fashion turn over the pages of some illustrated magazine, or, covering his face with it and unbuttoning his waistcoat, give himself up to slumber.

The St. Martin's summer is followed by cloudy, gloomy weather. It rains day and night, the bare trees weep, the wind is damp and cold. The dogs, the horses, the fowls—all are wet, depressed, downcast. There is nowhere to walk; one can't go out for days together; one has to pace up and down the room, looking despondently at the grey window. It is dreary!

Ivan Dmitritch stopped and looked at his wife.

"I should go abroad, you know, Masha," he said.

And he began thinking how nice it would be in late autumn to go abroad somewhere to the South of France . . . to Italy . . . to India!

"I should certainly go abroad, too," his wife said. "But look at the number of the ticket!"

"Wait, wait! . . ."

He walked about the room and went on thinking. It occurred to him: what if his wife really did go abroad? It is pleasant to travel alone, or in the society of light, careless women who live in the present, and not such as think and talk all the journey about nothing but their children, sigh, and tremble with dismay over every farthing. Ivan Dmitritch imagined his wife in the train with a multitude of parcels, baskets, and bags; she would be sighing over something, complaining that the train made her head ache, that she had spent so much money. . . . At the stations he would continually be having to run for boiling water, bread and butter. . . . She wouldn't have dinner because of its being too dear. . . .

"She would begrudge me every farthing," he thought, with a glance at his wife. "The lottery ticket is hers, not mine! Besides, what is the use of her going abroad? What does she want there? She would shut herself up in the hotel, and not let me out of her sight. . . . I know!"

And for the first time in his life his mind dwelt on the fact that his wife had grown elderly and plain, and that she was saturated through and through with the smell of cooking, while he was still young, fresh, and healthy, and might well have got married again.

"Of course, all that is silly nonsense," he thought; "but . . . why should she go abroad? What would she make of it? And yet she would go, of course. . . . I can fancy. . . . In reality it is all one to her, whether it is Naples[3] or Klin.[4] She would only be in my way. I should be dependent upon her. I can fancy how, like a regular woman, she will lock the money up as soon as she gets it. . . . She will hide it from me. . . . She will look after her relations and grudge me every farthing."

Ivan Dmitritch thought of her relations. All those wretched brothers and sisters and aunts and uncles would come crawling about as soon as they heard of the winning ticket, would begin whining like beggars, and fawning upon them with oily, hypocritical smiles. Wretched, detestable people! If they were given anything, they would ask for more; while if they were refused, they would swear at them, slander them, and wish them every kind of misfortune.

Ivan Dmitritch remembered his own relations, and their faces, at which he had looked impartially in the past, struck him now as repulsive and hateful.

---

1. *vint*, a card game.
2. *St. Martin's summer*, Indian summer in November.

3. *Naples* (nā′plz), a seaport on the southwest coast of Italy.
4. *Klin* (klēn), a city fifty miles northwest of Moscow.

"They are such reptiles!" he thought.

And his wife's face, too, struck him as repulsive and hateful. Anger surged up in his heart against her, and he thought malignantly:

"She knows nothing about money, and so she is stingy. If she won it she would give me a hundred rubles, and put the rest away under lock and key."

And he looked at his wife, not with a smile now, but with hatred. She glanced at him, too, and also with hatred and anger. She had her own daydreams, her own plans, her own reflections; she understood perfectly well what her husband's dreams were. She knew who would be the first to try and grab her winnings.

"It's very nice making daydreams at other people's expense!" is what her eyes expressed. "No, don't you dare!"

Her husband understood her look; hatred began stirring again in his breast, and in order to annoy his wife he glanced quickly, to spite her, at the fourth page on the newspaper and read out triumphantly:

"Series 9,499, number 46! Not 26!"

Hatred and hope both disappeared at once, and it began immediately to seem to Ivan Dmitritch and his wife that their rooms were dark and small and low-pitched, that the supper they had been eating was not doing them good, but lying heavy on their stomachs, that the evenings were long and wearisome. . . .

"What the devil's the meaning of it?" said Ivan Dmitritch, beginning to be ill-humoured. "Wherever one steps there are bits of paper under one's feet, crumbs, husks. The rooms are never swept! One is simply forced to go out. Damnation take my soul entirely! I shall go and hang myself on the first aspen tree!"

---

## DISCUSSION

1. (a) What information about setting and the characters is provided in the first paragraph? (For review, see the entries for *setting* and *characterization* in your Handbook.) (b) Why is this information important in the light of the story's conclusion?

2. (a) What are Ivan and Masha's purposes in not looking immediately for the winning number? (b) What might the author's purposes be in not having his characters find the lucky number at once?

3. (a) Ivan daydreams of spending the money and his time in a variety of ways. What are they? (b) To what extent does Masha seem to share Ivan's daydreams? How might her daydreams, which are not specified, differ from his?

4. (a) What immediate effects does the possibility of winning a huge sum have on the relationship between Masha and Ivan? (b) Do you think these effects will be permanent? Explain.

5. What would you say is the theme of this story? (For review, see the entry for *theme* in your Handbook.)

## ANTON CHEKHOV

Fascinated by the theater when he was a teen-ager, Chekhov, along with his friends, became adept at disguising himself to outwit prowling school authorities who felt that the theater was a bad influence.

Chekhov was born into a poor Russian family in 1860 but managed with the help of a scholarship to receive a medical degree in 1884. By this time, he had already had several stories published. Spurred by this success, he continued to write and only infrequently practiced medicine. Chekhov is generally considered a pioneer in the making of the modern short story.

He wrote five serious plays, all still produced today. One of them, "The Cherry Orchard," was produced at the Moscow Art Theater in 1904, just a few months before he died of tuberculosis and only three years after his marriage to the actress Olga Knipper.

# THE IDEALIST

*Frank O'Connor*

I don't know how it is about education, but it never seemed to do anything for me but get me into trouble.

Adventure stories weren't so bad, but as a kid I was very serious and preferred realism to romance. School stories were what I liked best,

Copyright 1950 by Frank O'Connor. Reprinted from *Stories by Frank O'Connor* by permission of Alfred A. Knopf, Inc. and A. D. Peters and Company. Originally appeared in *The New Yorker*.

and, judged by our standards, these were romantic enough for anyone. The schools were English, so I suppose you couldn't expect anything else. They were always called "the venerable pile,"[1] and there was usually a ghost in them; they were built in a square that was called "the quad," and, according to the pictures, they were all clock-towers, spires, and pinnacles, like the lunatic asylum with us. The fellows in the stories were all good climbers, and got in and out of school at night on ropes made of knotted sheets. They dressed queerly; they wore long trousers, short black jackets, and top hats. Whenever they did anything wrong they were given "lines" in Latin. When it was a bad case, they were flogged and never showed any sign of pain; only the bad fellows, and they always said: "Ow! Ow!"

Most of them were grand chaps who always stuck together and were great at football and cricket. They never told lies and wouldn't talk to anyone who did. If they were caught out and asked a point-blank question, they always told the truth, unless someone else was with them, and then even if they were to be expelled for it they wouldn't give his name, even if he was a thief, which, as a matter of fact, he frequently was. It was surprising in such good schools, with fathers who never gave less than five quid, the number of thieves there were. The fellows in our school hardly ever stole, though they only got a penny a week, and sometimes not even that, as when their fathers were on the booze and their mothers had to go to the pawn.

I worked hard at the football and cricket, though of course we never had a proper football and the cricket we played was with a hurley stick against a wicket chalked on some wall. The officers in the barrack played proper cricket, and on summer evenings I used to go and watch them, like one of the souls in purgatory watching the joys of paradise.

Even so, I couldn't help being disgusted at the bad way things were run in our school. Our "venerable pile" was a red-brick building without tower or pinnacle a fellow could climb,

and no ghost at all: we had no team, so a fellow, no matter how hard he worked, could never play for the school, and, instead of giving you "lines," Latin or any other sort, Murderer Moloney either lifted you by the ears or bashed you with a cane. When he got tired of bashing you on the hands he bashed you on the legs.

But these were only superficial things. What was really wrong was ourselves. The fellows sucked up to the masters and told them all that went on. If they were caught out in anything they tried to put the blame on someone else, even if it meant telling lies. When they were caned they snivelled and said it wasn't fair; drew back their hands as if they were terrified, so that the cane caught only the tips of their fingers, and then screamed and stood on one leg, shaking out their fingers in the hope of getting it counted as one. Finally they roared that their wrist was broken and crawled back to their desks with their hands squeezed under their armpits, howling. I mean you couldn't help feeling ashamed, imagining what chaps from a decent school would think if they saw it.

My own way to school led me past the barrack gate. In those peaceful days sentries never minded you going past the guardroom to have a look at the chaps drilling in the barrack square; if you came at dinnertime they even called you in and gave you plumduff and tea. Naturally, with such temptations I was often late. The only excuse, short of a letter from your mother, was to say you were at early Mass. The Murderer would never know whether you were or not, and if he did anything to you you could easily get him into trouble with the parish priest. Even as kids we knew who the real boss of the school was.

But after I started reading those confounded school stories I was never happy about saying I had been to Mass. It was a lie, and I knew that the chaps in stories would have died sooner than tell it. They were all round me like invisible presences,[2] and I hated to do anything which I felt they might disapprove of.

One morning I came in very late and rather frightened.

"What kept you till this hour, Delaney?"

---

1. *the venerable pile,* a group of buildings respected or revered because of their age and historic associations. (The narrator, who attends an Irish school, is influenced by the stories he has read about the lives of boys in British schools.)

2. *presences,* spirits which are felt to be present.

Murderer Moloney asked, looking at the clock.

I wanted to say I had been at Mass, but I couldn't. The invisible presences were all about me.

"I was delayed at the barrack, sir," I replied in panic.

There was a faint titter from the class, and Moloney raised his brows in mild surprise. He was a big powerful man with fair hair and blue eyes and a manner that at times was deceptively mild.

"Oh, indeed," he said, politely enough. "And what delayed you?"

"I was watching the soldiers drilling, sir," I said.

The class tittered again. This was a new line entirely for them.

"Oh," Moloney said casually, "I never knew you were such a military man. Hold out your hand!"

Compared with the laughter the slaps were nothing, and besides, I had the example of the invisible presences to sustain me. I did not flinch. I returned to my desk slowly and quietly without snivelling or squeezing my hands, and the Murderer looked after me, raising his brows again as though to indicate that this was a new line for him, too. But the others gaped and whispered as if I were some strange animal. At playtime they gathered about me, full of curiosity and excitement.

"Delaney, why did you say that about the barrack?"

"Because 'twas true," I replied firmly. "I wasn't going to tell him a lie."

"What lie?"

"That I was at Mass."

"Then couldn't you say you had to go on a message?"

"That would be a lie too."

"Cripes, Delaney," they said, "you'd better mind yourself. The Murderer is in an awful wax. He'll massacre you."

I knew that. I knew only too well that the Murderer's professional pride had been deeply wounded, and for the rest of the day I was on my best behaviour. But my best wasn't enough, for I underrated the Murderer's guile. Though he pretended to be reading, he was watching me the whole time.

"Delaney," he said at last without raising his head from the book, "was that you talking?"

"'Twas, sir," I replied in consternation.

The whole class laughed. They couldn't believe but that I was deliberately trailing my coat,[3] and, of course, the laugh must have convinced him that I was. I suppose if people do tell you lies all day and every day, it soon becomes a sort of perquisite which you resent being deprived of.

"Oh," he said, throwing down his book, "we'll soon stop that."

This time it was a tougher job, because he was really on his mettle. But so was I. I knew this was the testing point for me, and if only I could keep my head I should provide a model for the whole class. When I had got through the ordeal without moving a muscle, and returned to my desk with my hands by my sides, the invisible presences gave me a great clap. But the visible ones were nearly as annoyed as the Murderer himself. After school half a dozen of them followed me down the school yard.

"Go on!" they shouted truculently. "Shaping as usual!"

"I was not shaping."

"You were shaping. You're always showing off. Trying to pretend he didn't hurt you—a blooming crybaby like you!"

"I wasn't trying to pretend," I shouted, even then resisting the temptation to nurse my bruised hands. "Only decent fellows don't cry over every little pain like kids."

"Go on!" they bawled after me. "You ould idiot!" And, as I went down the school lane, still trying to keep what the stories called "a stiff upper lip," and consoling myself with the thought that my torment was over until next morning, I heard their mocking voices after me.

"Loony Larry! Yah, Loony Larry!"

I realized that if I was to keep on terms with the invisible presences I should have to watch my step at school.

So I did, all through that year. But one day an awful thing happened. I was coming in from the yard, and in the porch outside our schoolroom I saw a fellow called Gorman taking something from a coat on the rack. I always

---

3. *trailing my coat,* trying to provoke or anger him.

described Gorman to myself as "the black sheep of the school." He was a fellow I disliked and feared; a handsome, sulky, spoiled, and sneering lout. I paid no attention to him because I had escaped for a few moments into my dream world in which fathers never gave less than fivers and the honour of the school was always saved by some quiet, unassuming fellow like myself—"a dark horse,"[4] as the stories called him.

"Who are you looking at?" Gorman asked threateningly.

"I wasn't looking at anyone," I replied with an indignant start.

"I was only getting a pencil out of my coat," he added, clenching his fists.

"Nobody said you weren't," I replied, thinking that this was a very queer subject to start a row about.

"You'd better not, either," he snarled. "You can mind your own business."

"You mind yours!" I retorted, purely for the purpose of saving face. "I never spoke to you at all."

And that, so far as I was concerned, was the end of it.

But after playtime the Murderer, looking exceptionally serious, stood before the class, balancing a pencil in both hands.

"Everyone who left the classroom this morning, stand out!" he called. Then he lowered his head and looked at us from under his brows. "Mind now, I said everyone!"

I stood out with the others, including Gorman. We were all very puzzled.

"Did you take anything from a coat on the rack this morning?" the Murderer asked, laying a heavy, hairy paw on Gorman's shoulder and staring menacingly into his eyes.

"Me, sir?" Gorman exclaimed innocently. "No, sir."

"Did you see anyone else doing it?"

"No, sir."

"You?" he asked another lad, but even before he reached me at all I realized why Gorman had told the lie and wondered frantically what I should do.

"You?" he asked me, and his big red face was

close to mine, his blue eyes were only a few inches away, and the smell of his toilet soap was in my nostrils. My panic made me say the wrong thing as though I had planned it.

"I didn't take anything, sir," I said in a low voice.

"Did you see someone else do it?" he asked, raising his brows and showing quite plainly that he had noticed my evasion. "Have you a tongue in your head?" he shouted suddenly, and the whole class, electrified, stared at me. "You?" he added curtly to the next boy as though he had lost interest in me.

"No, sir."

"Back to your desks, the rest of you!" he ordered. "Delaney, you stay here."

He waited till everyone was seated again before going on.

"Turn out your pockets."

I did, and a half-stifled giggle rose, which the Murderer quelled with a thunderous glance. Even for a small boy I had pockets that were museums in themselves: the purpose of half the things I brought to light I couldn't have explained myself. They were antiques, prehistoric and unlabelled. Among them was a school story borrowed the previous evening from a queer fellow who chewed paper as if it were gum. The Murderer reached out for it, and holding it at arm's length, shook it out with an expression of deepening disgust as he noticed the nibbled corners and margins.

"Oh," he said disdainfully, "so this is how you waste your time! What do you do with this rubbish—eat it?"

"'Tisn't mine, sir," I said against the laugh that sprang up. "I borrowed it."

"Is that what you did with the money?" he asked quickly, his fat head on one side.

"Money?" I repeated in confusion. "What money?"

"The shilling that was stolen from Flanagan's overcoat this morning."

(Flanagan was a little hunchback whose people coddled him; no one else in the school would have possessed that much money.)

"I never took Flanagan's shilling," I said, beginning to cry, "and you have no right to say I did."

"I have the right to say you're the most im-

4. *a dark horse*, a race horse, candidate, competitor, etc., about whom little is known or who unexpectedly wins.

pudent and defiant puppy in the school," he replied, his voice hoarse with rage, "and I wouldn't put it past you. What else can anyone expect and you reading this dirty, rotten, filthy rubbish?" And he tore my school story in halves and flung them to the furthest corner of the classroom. "Dirty, filthy, English rubbish! Now, hold out your hand."

This time the invisible presences deserted me. Hearing themselves described in these contemptuous terms, they fled. The Murderer went mad in the way people do whenever they're up against something they don't understand. Even the other fellows were shocked, and, heaven knows, they had little sympathy with me.

"You should put the police on him," they advised me later in the playground. "He lifted the cane over his shoulder. He could get the gaol[5] for that."

"But why didn't you say you didn't see anyone?" asked the eldest, a fellow called Spillane.

"Because I did," I said, beginning to sob all over again at the memory of my wrongs. "I saw Gorman."

"Gorman?" Spillane echoed incredulously. "Was it Gorman took Flanagan's money? And why didn't you say so?"

"Because it wouldn't be right," I sobbed.

"Why wouldn't it be right?"

"Because Gorman should have told the truth himself," I said. "And if this was a proper school he'd be sent to Coventry."[6]

"He'd be sent where?"

"Coventry. No one would ever speak to him again."

"But why would Gorman tell the truth if he took the money?" Spillane asked as you'd speak to a baby. "Jay, Delaney," he added pityingly, "you're getting madder and madder. Now, look at what you're after bringing on yourself!"

Suddenly Gorman came lumbering up, red and angry.

"Delaney," he shouted threateningly, "did you say I took Flanagan's money?"

Gorman, though I of course didn't realize it, was as much at sea as Moloney and the rest. Seeing me take all that punishment rather than

give him away, he concluded that I must be more afraid of him than of Moloney, and that the proper thing to do was to make me more so. He couldn't have come at a time when I cared less for him. I didn't even bother to reply but lashed out with all my strength at his brutal face. This was the last thing he expected. He screamed, and his hand came away from his face, all blood. Then he threw off his satchel and came at me, but at the same moment a door opened behind us and a lame teacher called Murphy emerged. We all ran like mad and the fight was forgotten.

It didn't remain forgotten, though. Next morning after prayers the Murderer scowled at me.

"Delaney, were you fighting in the yard after school yesterday?"

For a second or two I didn't reply. I couldn't help feeling that it wasn't worth it. But before the invisible presences fled forever, I made another effort.

"I was, sir," I said, and this time there wasn't even a titter. I was out of my mind. The whole class knew it and was awe-stricken.

"Who were you fighting?"

"I'd sooner not say, sir," I replied, hysteria beginning to well up in me. It was all very well for the invisible presences, but they hadn't to deal with the Murderer.

"Who was he fighting with?" he asked lightly, resting his hands on the desk and studying the ceiling.

"Gorman, sir," replied three or four voices—as easy as that!

"Did Gorman hit him first?"

"No, sir. He hit Gorman first."

"Stand out," he said, taking up the cane. "Now," he added, going up to Gorman, "you take this and hit him. And make sure you hit him hard," he went on, giving Gorman's arm an encouraging squeeze. "He thinks he's a great fellow. You show him now what we think of him."

Gorman came towards me with a broad grin. He thought it a great joke. The class thought it a great joke. They began to roar with laughter. Even the Murderer permitted himself a modest grin at his own cleverness.

"Hold out your hand," he said to me.

5. gaol (jāl), British spelling of jail.
6. sent to Coventry, made a social outcast.

I didn't. I began to feel trapped and a little crazy.

"Hold out your hand, I say," he shouted, beginning to lose his temper.

"I will not," I shouted back, losing all control of myself.

"You what?" he cried incredulously, dashing at me round the classroom with his hand raised as though to strike me. "What's that you said, you dirty little thief?"

"I'm not a thief, I'm not a thief," I screamed. "And if he comes near me I'll kick the shins off him. You have no right to give him that cane, and you have no right to call me a thief either. If you do it again, I'll go down to the police and then we'll see who the thief is."

"You refused to answer my questions," he roared, and if I had been in my right mind I should have known he had suddenly taken fright; probably the word "police" had frightened him.

"No," I said through my sobs, "and I won't answer them now either. I'm not a spy."

"Oh," he retorted with a sarcastic sniff, "so that's what you call a spy, Mr. Delaney?"

"Yes, and that's what they all are, all the fellows here—dirty spies!—but I'm not going to be a spy for you. You can do your own spying."

"That's enough now, that's enough!" he said, raising his fat hand almost beseechingly. "There's no need to lose control of yourself, my dear young fellow, and there's no need whatever to screech like that. 'Tis most unmanly. Go back to your seat now and I'll talk to you another time."

I obeyed, but I did no work. No one else did much either. The hysteria had spread to the class. I alternated between fits of exultation at my own successful defiance of the Murderer, and panic at the prospect of his revenge; and at each change of mood I put my face in my hands and sobbed again. The Murderer didn't even order me to stop. He didn't so much as look at me.

After that I was the hero of the school for the whole afternoon. Gorman tried to resume the fight, but Spillane ordered him away contemptuously—a fellow who had taken the master's cane to another had no status. But that wasn't the sort of hero I wanted to be. I preferred something less sensational.

Next morning I was in such a state of panic that I didn't know how I should face school at all. I dawdled, between two minds as to whether or not I should mitch. The silence of the school lane and yard awed me. I had made myself late as well.

"What kept you, Delaney?" the Murderer asked quietly.

I knew it was no good.

"I was at Mass, sir."

"All right. Take your seat."

He seemed a bit surprised. What I had not realized was the incidental advantage of our system over the English one. By this time half a dozen of his pets had brought the Murderer the true story of Flanagan's shilling, and if he didn't feel a monster he probably felt a fool.

But by that time I didn't care. In my school sack I had another story. Not a school story this time, though. School stories were a washout. "Bang! Bang!"—that was the only way to deal with men like the Murderer. "The only good teacher is a dead teacher."

---

## DISCUSSION

1. (a) What virtues of English schoolboys does the narrator admire? (b) What by contrast is the usual behavior of his schoolmates?

2. (a) What accounts for the narrator's being often late to school? (b) What excuse for his tardiness does he normally offer?

3. (a) How does Murderer Moloney respond when the narrator begins telling him the truth? (b) How do the other students react?

4. Over what incident does the narrator defy Moloney, and with what consequence?

5. What "incidental advantage of [his] system over the English one" does the narrator eventually discover?

6. At the conclusion of the

story, the narrator is no longer reading stories about English schoolboys. What kind of reading now interests him? Why?

7. Why does Delaney's attempt to live like the schoolboys he reads about fail?

8. If this story is humorous to you, what makes it so?

9. Mention idealists from history, from fiction, or currently in the news who (a) abandoned or modified their ideals to conform to those of their society or (b) maintained their ideals and changed society.

## WORD STUDY

The cricket we played was with a *hurley* stick.

What is a hurley stick? When neither context nor structure is a clue to the meaning of an unfamiliar word, you must use a dictionary.

Of course, dictionaries contain other information besides definitions. By answering the questions below with the help of your Glossary, you will see that a dictionary contains facts about language usage, geographical facts, biographical information, etymologies, and pronunciations.

1. In the sentence, "He was in an awful wax," is the use of *wax* chiefly Irish, Scottish, or British?

2. Does one *coddle* a child the same way one *coddles* an egg?

3. How do you pronounce *massacre*? (mas′ə kər *or* mas′ə-krē?)

4. According to the Glossary, are there plums in *plumduff*?

5. Under what entry word do you find the meaning of the expression "saving face"? What does it mean?

6. Where is Coventry?

7. How many men are on a cricket team?

8. Is *bash* considered slang, formal, or informal usage?

9. What language does *sulky* come from?

10. When was Frank O'Connor born?

## FRANK O'CONNOR

Attracted as a boy to roofs, bluffs, and fencetops, Frank O'Connor characterized the reading he loved as another and perhaps more dangerous form of height. Books transported him into imaginary worlds far from the slums of Cork (Ireland) where he was born.

He failed miserably at the first jobs he found but soon qualified as a teacher of Gaelic. O'Connor then became attracted to the Irish nationalists and their ideas and he participated briefly in the Irish struggle for independence. For this participation he was imprisoned. After his release in 1923 he worked as a librarian in county Cork and in Dublin.

He directed the national Abbey Theater for a time but finally dropped all public activities to write. His stories are characterized by humor and a compassionate familiarity with the Irish people he portrays.

O'Connor spent his later years in the United States and taught for a time at Stanford University. He died in 1966.

# RAIN ON TANYARD HOLLOW

*Jesse Stuart*

*"Let the Hollow grow dark. Let the chicken think that night has come and fly up in the apple trees to roost. Let the people think the end of time has come," Pappie prayed. I didn't wish him any bad luck, but I hoped he wouldn't get all he asked for.*

DON'T kill that snake, Sweeter," Mammie said. "Leave it alone among the strawberry vines and it'll ketch the ground moles that's eatin' the roots of the strawberry plants."

Mammie raised up from pickin' strawberries and stood with one hand in her apron pocket. Draps of sweat the size of white soup beans stood all over her sun-tanned face and shined like dewdrops on the sun. Mammie looked hard at Pappie but it didn't do any good.

"Kill that snake," Pappie shouted. "It must a thought my knuckle was a mole. It ain't goin' to rain nohow unless I kill a few more black snakes and hang 'em on the fence."

Pappie stood over the black snake. It was quiled and a-gettin' ready to strike at 'im again. It looked like the twisted root of a black-oak tree rolled up among the half-dead strawberry plants. It must a knowed Pappie was goin' to kill it the way it was fightin' him back. It kept drawin' its long black-oak-root body up tighter so it could strike harder at Pappie. It stuck its forked tongue out at him.

"You would fight me back," Pappie shouted as he raised a big flat rock above his head high as his arms would reach. "You would get me foul and bite me. That's just what you've done. Now I'm goin' to kill you and hang you on the fence and make it rain."

Pappie let the big rock fall on the black snake. The rock's sharp edge cut the snake in two in many places. Its tail quivered against the ground and rattled the dried-up leaves on the strawberry plants. Its red blood oozed out on the dry-as-gunpowder dust. Mammie stood and looked at the pieces of snake writhin' on the ground.

"Old Adam fit with rocks," Pappie said. "They air still good things to fight with."

Pappie stood with his big hands on his hips. He looked at the dyin' black snake and laughed.

"That black snake didn't hurt your hand when it bit you," Mammie said. "Sweeter, you air a hard-hearted man. You've kilt a lot of snakes and hung 'em on the fence to make it rain. They air still hangin' there. I ain't heard a rain-crow croakin' yet ner felt a drap of rain. The corn is burnt up. You know it has. The corn ain't goin' to git no taller. It's tasselin' and it's bumblebee corn. If you's to drap any ashes from

From *A Jesse Stuart Reader* by Jesse Stuart. Copyright © 1963 by McGraw-Hill, Inc. Used with permission of McGraw-Hill Book Company. First published in *Esquire* magazine 1941.

your cigar on this strawberry patch it would set the plants on fire. They look green but they air dry as powder. Where is your rain?''

"I don't know, Lizzie," Pappie said. "You tell me where the rain is."

"It's in the sky," Mammie said, "and you won't get it unless you pray fer it to fall. It's about too late fer prayer too. And the Lord wouldn't listen to a prayer from you."

When Mammie said this she looked hard at Pappie. Pappie stood there and looked at Mammie. What she said to him about the Lord not listenin' to his prayer made Pappie wilt. His blue eyes looked down at Mammie. The hot dry wind that moved across the strawberry patch and rustled the strawberry plants, moved the beard on Pappie's face as he stood in the strawberry patch with his big brogan shoes planted like two gray stumps. His long lean body looked like a dead snag where the birds come to light and the beard on his face and the long hair that stuck down below the rim of his gone-to-seed straw hat looked like sour-vines wrapped around the snag.

"Don't stand there, Sweeter, like a skeery-crow and look at me with your cold blue-water eyes," Mammie said. "You know you air a hard-hearted man and the Lord won't listen to your prayer. Look at the harmless black snakes you've kilt and have hangin' on the fence and you ain't got rain yet. Sweeter, I'm lettin' the rest of these strawberries dry on the stems. I'm leavin' the strawberry patch."

Mammie slammed her bucket against the ground. She pulled her pipe from her pocket. She dipped the light-burley terbacker crumbs from her apron pocket as she walked toward the ridgetop rustlin' the dyin' strawberry plants with her long peaked-toed shoes. By the time Mammie reached the dead white-oak snag that stood on the ridgetop and marked our strawberry patch for all the crows in the country, Mammie had her pipe lit and there was a cloud of smoke followin' her as she went over the hill toward the house.

"Tracey, your Mammie talked awful pert to me."

"Yep, she did, Pappie."

"She talked like the Lord couldn't hear my prayer."

When Pappie talked about what Mammie said about the Lord not payin' any attention to his prayers, his beardy lips quivered. I could tell Pappie didn't like it. He felt insulted. He thought if the Lord listened to prayers, he ought to listen to one of his prayers.

"I'm just hard on snakes, Tracey," Pappie said. "I don't like snakes. My knuckle burned like a hornet stung me when that dad-durned black snake hid among the strawberry plants and bit me. It didn't come out in the open and bite me. Your Mammie got mad because I kilt that snake. I know the baby-handed moles air bad to nose under the roots of the strawberry plants and eat their white-hair roots and the black snakes eat the moles. But that ain't no excuse fer a black snake's bitin' me on the knuckle."

"I don't blame you, Pappie," I said.

When I said this, Pappie looked at me and his face lost the cloud that was hangin' over it. The light on Pappie's face was like the mornin' sunshine on the land.

"It's a dry time, Tracey," Pappie said as he kicked the dry strawberry plants with his big brogan shoe. The leaves that looked green fell from the stems and broke into tiny pieces. Little clouds of dust rose from among the strawberry plants where Pappie kicked.

"We don't have half a strawberry crop," I said. "And if we don't get rain we won't have a third of a corn crop."

"You air right, Tracey," Pappie answered. "We'll get rain. If it takes prayers we'll get rain. Why won't the Lord listen to me same as he will listen to Lizzie? Why won't the Lord answer my prayer same as he will answer any other man's prayer in Tanyard Hollow?"

When Pappie said this he fell to his knees among the scorched strawberry plants. Pappie come down against the dry plants with his big fire-shovel hands and at the same time he turned his face toward the high heat-glimmerin' sky. Dust flew up in tiny clouds as Pappie beat the ground.

"Lord, will you listen to my prayer?" Pappie shouted. "I don't keer who hears me astin' you fer rain. We need it, Lord! The strawberries have shriveled on the vines and the corn is turnin' yaller. It's bumblebee corn, Lord. Give us rain,

Lord. I've kilt the black snakes and hung 'em on the fence and the rain don't fall. Never a croak from the rain-crow ner a drap of rain. The black snake on the fence is a false image, Lord."[1]

Pappie beat his hands harder on the ground. He jerked up strawberry plants with his hands and tossed them back on the ground. He dug up the hard dry ground and sifted it among the strawberry plants around him. He never looked at the ground. His face was turned toward the high clouds. The sun was beamin' down on Pappie and he couldn't look at the sun with his eyes open.

"Send rain, Lord, that will wash gully-ditches in this strawberry patch big enough to bury a mule in," Pappie shouted. "Let it fall in great sheets. Wash Tanyard Hollow clean."

I didn't bother with Pappie's prayer but I thought that was too much rain. Better to let the strawberry plants burn to death than to wash them out by the roots and take all the topsoil down Tanyard Hollow too. Can't grow strawberry in Tanyard Hollow unless you've got good topsoil of dead-leaf loam on the south hill slopes.

"Give us enough rain, Lord," Pappie shouted, "to make the weak have fears and the strong tremble. Wash rocks from these hillsides that four span of mules can't pull on a jolt-wagon. Wash trees out by the roots that five yoke of cattle can't pull. Skeer everybody nearly to death. Show them Your might, Lord. Put water up in the houses—a mighty river! Put a river of yaller water out'n Tanyard Hollow that is flowin' faster than a hound dog can run. Make the people take to the high hill slopes and let their feet sink into the mud instead of specklin' their shoes and bare feet with dust!"

Pappie prayed so hard that white foam fell from his lips. It was dry foam, the kind that comes from the work cattle mouths when I feed them corn nubbins. The big flakes of white foam fell upon the green-withered strawberry plants.

"Send the thunder rollin' like tater wagons across the sky over Tanyard Hollow," Pappie prayed. "Let the Hollow grow dark. Let the chicken think that night has come and fly up in the apple trees to roost. Let the people think the end of time has come. Make the Hollow so dark a body can't see his hand before him. Let long tongues of lightnin' cut through the darkness across the Hollow and split the biggest oaks in Tanyard Hollow from the tiptops to their butts like you'd split them with a big clapboard fro.[2] Let pieces of hail fall big enough if ten pieces hit a man on the head they'll knock 'im cuckoo. Let him be knocked cold in one of the biggest rains that Tanyard Hollow ever had. Let the rain wash the dead-leaf loam from around the roots of the trees and let the twisted black-oak roots lie like ten million black snakes quiled at the butts of the big oaks. Lord, give us a rain in Tanyard Hollow to end this drouth! Give us a rain that we'll long remember! I'm through with the brazen images of black snakes! Amen."

Pappie got up and wiped the dry foam from his lips with his big hand.

"I ast the Lord fer a lot," Pappie said. "I meant every word I prayed to Him. I want to see one of the awfulest storms hit Tanyard Hollow that ever hit it since the beginnin' of time. That goes way back yander. I ast fer an awful lot, and I hope by askin' fer a lot, I'll get a few things."

"Pappie, I don't want to wish you any bad luck," I said, "but I hope you won't get all you ast fer. If you get all you ast fer, there won't be anythin' left in Tanyard Hollow. We'll just haf to move out. The topsoil will all be washed away, the dirt washed from around the roots of the trees and they'll look like bundles of black snakes. The big oaks will split from their tiptops to their butts—right down through the hearts with forked tongues of lightnin'. Trees will be rooted up and rocks washed from the hillsides that a jolt-wagon can't hold up. There won't be any corn left on the hillsides and the strawberry patch will be ruint."

"Tracey, I've ast the Lord fer it," Pappie answered, "and if the Lord is good enough to give it to me, I'll abide by what He sends. I won't be low-lifed enough to grumble about somethin' I've prayed fer. I meant every word I said. I hope I can get part of all I ast fer."

---

1. *The black snake . . . false image, Lord.* Pappie thinks that he has violated the first of the Ten Commandments (which warns against worshipping a false image) by hanging a black snake on the fence to make it rain. Instead of depending on superstition, he turns to prayer.

2. *big clapboard fro,* a wedge-shaped tool for splitting boards used in covering the outer walls of buildings.

"It's time fer beans," I said. "I can step on the head of my shadder."[3]

Pappie left the strawberry patch. I followed him as he went down the hill. He pulled a cigar from his shirt pocket and took a match from his hatband where he kept his matches so he could keep them dry. He put the cigar in his mouth . . . struck a match on a big rock beside the path and lit his cigar.

"When I was prayin' fer the rain to wash the rocks from the hillsides," Pappie said, "this is one of the rocks I had in mind. It's allus been in my way when I plowed here."

"If we get a rain that will wash this rock from this hillside," I said, "there won't be any of us left and not much of Tanyard Hollow left."

"You'd be surprised at what can happen," Pappie said. "You can turn a double-barrel shotgun loose into a covey of quails and it's a sight at 'em that'll come out alive."

Sweat run off at the ends of Pappie's beard. It dripped on the dusty path. Sweat got in my eyes and dripped from my nose. It was so hot it just seemed that I was roastin' before a big wood fire. It looked like fall-time the way the grass was dyin'. Trees were dyin' in the woods. Oak leaves were turnin' brown.

Pappie took the lead down the hill. It was so steep that we had to hold to sassafras sprouts and let ourselves down the hill. The footpath wound down the hill like a long crooked snake crawlin' on the sand. When we got to the bottom of the hill, Pappie was wet with sweat as if he'd a swum the river. I was as wet as sweat could make me and my eyes were smartin' with sweat like I had a dozen sour-gnats in my eyes.

"Whooie," Pappie sighed as he reached the foot of the mountain and he rubbed his big hand over his beard and slung a stream of sweat on the sandy path. "It's too hot fer a body to want to live. I hope the Lord will answer my prayer."

"I hope Mammie has dinner ready."

Mammie didn't have dinner ready. She was cookin' over the hot kitchen stove. Aunt Rett and Aunt Beadie were helpin' Mammie.

"Lord, I hope we'll soon get rain," Mammie said to Aunt Rett. She stood beside the stove and slung sweat from her forehead with her index finger. Where Mammie slung the sweat in the floor was a long wet streak with little wet spots from the middle of the floor to the wall.

"It's goin' to rain," I said.

"Why is it goin' to rain?" Mammie ast.

"Because Pappie got down in the strawberry patch and prayed fer the Lord to send rain and wash this Hollow out," I said.

Mammie started laughin'. Aunt Rett and Aunt Beadie laughed. They stopped cookin' and all laughed together like three women standin' at the organ singin'.

"We'll get rain," Mammie said, "because Sweeter has prayed fer rain. We'll have a washout in Tanyard Hollow fer Sweeter prayed fer a washout in Tanyard Hollow. We'll get what Sweeter prayed fer."

They begin to sing, "We'll get rain in Tanyard Hollow fer Sweeter prayed fer it."

"Just about like his hangin' the snakes over the rail fence to get rain," Mammie cackled like a pullet. "That's the way we'll get rain."

Uncle Mort Shepherd and Uncle Luster Hix sat in the front room and laughed at Pappie's prayin' fer rain. They thought it was very funny. They'd come down out'n the mountains and were livin' with us until they could find farms to rent. Uncle Mort and Aunt Rett had seven children stayin' with us and Uncle Luster and Aunt Beadie had eight children. We had a big houseful. They's Mammie's people and they didn't think Pappie had any faith. They didn't think the Lord would answer his prayer. I felt like the Lord would answer his prayer, fer Pappie was a man of much misery. Seemed like all of Mammie's people worked against 'im. They'd sit in the house and eat at Pappie's table and talk about gettin' a house and movin' out but they never done it. They'd nearly et us out'n house and home. When they come to our house it was like locust year. Just so much noise when all their youngins got to fightin' you couldn't hear your ears pop.

"It's goin' to rain this afternoon," Pappie said. "There's comin' a cloudbust. If you ain't got the Faith you'd better get it."

Uncle Luster got up from the rockin' chear and went to the door. He looked at the yaller-of-

---

3. *It's time . . . shadder.* The narrator knows it is time for the midday meal because the sun is nearly overhead and he can step on the head of his shadow.

an-egg sun in the clear sky. Uncle Luster started laughin'. Uncle Mort got up from his chear and knocked out his pipe on the jam-rock. He looked at the sun in the clear sky and he started laughin'.

Uncle Mort and Uncle Luster hadn't more than got back to the two rockin' chears and started restin' easy until dinner was ready, when all at once there was a jar of thunder across the sky over Tanyard Hollow. It was like a big tater wagon rollin' across the sky. Mammie drapped her fork on the kitchen floor when she heard it. Aunt Rett nearly fell to her knees. Aunt Beadie set a skillet of fried taters back on the stove. Her face got white. She acted like she was skeered.

"Thunderin' when the sky is clear," Aunt Beadie said.

Then the thunder started. Pappie was pleased but his face got white. I could tell he was skeered. He thought he was goin' to get what he'd ast the Lord to send. The thunder got so loud and it was so close that it jarred the house. 'Peared like Tanyard Hollow was a big pocket filled with hot air down among the hills and the thunder started roarin' in this pocket. It started gettin' dark. Chickens flew up in the apple trees to roost.

When Mammie saw the chickens goin' to roost at noon, she fell to her knees on the hard kitchen floor and started prayin'. Mammie thought the end of time had come. The chickens hadn't more than got on the roost until the long tongues of lightnin' started lappin' across the Hollow. When the lightnin' started splittin' the giant oak trees from their tiptops to their butts it sounded louder than both barrels of a double-barreled shotgun.

"Just what I ast the Lord to send," Pappie shouted. Mammie jumped up and lit the lamps with a pine torch that she lit from the kitchen stove. I looked at Pappie's face. His eyes were big and they looked pleased. All Aunt Beadie's youngins were gathered around her and Uncle Luster. They were screamin'. They were screamin' louder than the chickens were cacklin' at the splittin' oak trees on the high hillsides. Uncle Mort and Aunt Rett got their youngins around them and Uncle Mort started to pray. All six of us got close to Mammie. I

didn't. I stuck to Pappie. I thought about how hard he'd prayed fer a good rain to break the long spring drouth. Now the rain would soon be delivered.

Mammie, Aunt Rett, and Aunt Beadie let the dinner burn on the stove. I was hungry and I could smell the bread burnin'. I didn't try to get to the kitchen. I saw the yaller water comin' from the kitchen to the front room. The front room was big and we had a big bed in each corner. When I looked through the winder and saw the big sycamores in the yard end up like you'd pull up horseweeds by the roots and throw 'em down, I turned around and saw Aunt Beadie and Uncle Luster make fer one of the beds in the corner of the room. Their youngins followed them. They were screamin' and prayin'. Uncle Mort and Aunt Rett and all their youngins made fer the bed in the other corner of the room. Mammie and my sisters and brothers made for the stairs. Mammie was prayin' as she run. I stayed at the foot of the stairs with Pappie. When he prayed in the strawberry patch, I thought he was astin' the Lord fer too much rain but I didn't say anythin'. I didn't interfere with his prayer.

The water got higher in our house. A rock too big fer a jolt-wagon to haul smashed through the door and rolled across the floor and stopped. If it had rolled another time it would have knocked the big log wall out'n our house. Uncle Mort waded the water from the bed to the stairs and carried Aunt Rett and their youngins to the stairs. When he turned one loose on the stairs he run up the stairs like a drowned chicken. Uncle Luster ferried Aunt Beadie and their youngins to the stairs and turned them loose. Pappie had to take to the stairs. I followed Pappie.

"If we get out'n this house alive," Uncle Mort prayed, "we'll stay out'n it, Lord."

Uncle Luster prayed a long prayer and ast the Lord to save his wife and family. He promised the Lord if He would save them that he would leave Tanyard forever. I never heard so much prayin' in a churchhouse at any of the big revivals at Plum Grove as I heard up our upstairs. Sometimes you couldn't hear the prayers fer the lightnin' strikin' the big oaks. You could hear trees fallin' every place.

"The Lord has answered my prayers," Pappie shouted.

"Pray for the cloudbust to stop," Mammie shouted. "Get down on your knees, Sweeter, and pray."

"Listen, Lizzie," Pappie shouted above the roar of the water and the thunder and the splittin' of the big oaks on the high slopes, "I ain't two-faced enough to ast the Lord fer somethin' like a lot of people and atter I git it—turn around and ast the Lord to take it away. You said the Lord wouldn't answer my prayer. You've been prayin'! Why ain't the Lord answered your prayers? You ain't got the Faith. You just think you have."

When the lightnin' flashed in at our upstairs scuttlehole we had fer a winder, I could see Uncle Mort huddled with his family and Uncle Luster holdin' his family in a little circle. Mammie had all of us, but Pappie and me, over in the upstairs corner. I looked out at the scuttlehole and saw the water surgin' down the Left Fork of Tanyard Hollow and down the Right Fork of Tanyard Hollow and meetin' right at our house. That's the only reason our house had stood. One swift river had kilt the other one when they met on this spot. I thought about what Pappie said.

I could see cornfields comin' off'n the slopes. I could see trees with limbs and roots on them bobbin' up and down and goin' down Tanyard Hollow faster than a hound dog could run. It was a sight to see. From my scuttlehole I told 'em what I saw until I saw a blue sky comin' over the high rim of rock cliffs in the head of Tanyard Hollow. That was the end of the storm. I never saw so many happy people when I told them about the patch of blue sky that I saw.

"This is like a dream," Uncle Mort said.

"It's more like a nightmare to me," Uncle Luster said.

"It's neither," Pappie said. "It's the fulfillment of a prayer."

"Why do you pray fer destruction, Sweeter?" Mammie ast.

"To show you the Lord will answer my prayer atter the way you talked to me in the strawberry patch," Pappie said. "And I want your brother Mort and your brother-in-law Luster to remember their promises to the Lord."

The storm was over. It was light again. The chickens flew down from the apple trees. The big yard sycamore shade trees went with the storm but the apple trees stood. There was mud two feet deep on our floor. It was all over the bedclothes. There were five big rocks on our house we couldn't move. We'd haf to take the floor up and dig holes and bury the rocks under the floor. Trees were split all over Tanyard Hollow hillside slopes. Great oak trees were splintered clean to the tops. Our corn had washed from the hill slopes. There wasn't much left but mud, washed-out trees, rocks, and waste. Roots of the black-oak trees where the dead-leaf loam had washed away looked like bundles of clean washed black snakes. The big rock upon the steep hillside that bothered Pappie when he was plowin' had washed in front of our door.

"I promised the Lord," Uncle Mort said, "if we got through this storm alive, I'd take my family and get out'n here and I meant it."

"Amen," Pappie shouted.

"Sorry we can't stay and hep you clean the place up," Uncle Luster said, "but I'm takin' my wife and youngins and gettin' out'n this Hollow."

They didn't stay and hep us bury the rocks under the floor. They got their belongin's and started wadin' the mud barefooted down Tanyard Hollow. They's glad to get goin'. Pappie looked pleased when he saw them pullin' their bare feet out'n the mud and puttin' 'em down again. Pappie didn't grumble about what he had lost. The fence where he had the black snakes hangin' washed down Tanyard Hollow. There wasn't a fence rail 'r a black snake left. The strawberry patch was gutted with gully-ditches big enough to bury a mule. Half of the plants had washed away.

"It wasn't the brazen images of snakes," Pappie said, "that done all of this. Tanyard Hollow is washed clean of most of its topsoil and lost a lot of its trees. But it got rid of a lot of its rubbish and it's a more fitten place to live."

## DISCUSSION

1. (a) What things do Mammie and Pappie argue about in the first part of the story? (b) What comment by Mammie offends Pappie? (c) How does he put her remark to the test?

2. (a) Locate in Pappie's prayer a number of phrases which vividly suggest the size of the rainstorm he asks for. (b) What is his intention in asking the lord "fer a lot"?

3. (a) At what point does it first seem apparent that his prayer is going to be answered? (b) How do his wife and relatives react before and after the first thunder?

4. How does Pappie reply to Mammie's request that he pray for the rain to stop?

5. (a) Briefly describe the damage done by the storm to Tanyard Hollow and to Pappie's home. (b) What kind of rubbish is Pappie referring to in the last line of the story?

6. How important is the setting to the development of this story? Explain.

## JESSE STUART

Jesse Stuart says that he has written as long as he can remember and that it delighted him when the themes he wrote in a one-room school in Kentucky made his classmates laugh.

Writing has excited him ever since, and he has had over three hundred stories published, in addition to poems and novels. Two of his best-known books are *The Thread That Runs So True*, the story of his experiences as a teacher and school superintendant, and *Man with a Bull-Tongue Plow*, a collection of poetry.

He was born in 1907 in W-Hollow, a valley in the Kentucky mountains. He and his wife Naomi still live there, despite their having traveled all over the world.

## "Everybody Talks About the Weather . . .

. . . but nobody does anything about it." That tired old observation may be true, but like Pappie, some people keep right on behaving as if their actions could influence the weather. When Pappie killed the black snake and hung it on the fence to make it rain, he was following a bit of local folklore. "Bury a snake, good weather to make; hanging it high brings storm clouds nigh."

Such beliefs are not restricted to the Kentucky hills. Because rain is essential to life, every society at some point in its history has developed magical or religious methods for producing it. In some societies rain was imitated by sprinkling water on a stone or sacred image. Sometimes the rain-maker imitated the sound of a storm by striking rocks together. In Java one rain-making custom required two men to thrash each other with sticks until the blood, representing rain, streamed down their backs.

Animals were often used as weather charms. Some societies sacrificed black fowls, black sheep, or black cattle at the graves of dead ancestors, and the rain-maker wore black clothes during the rainy season. Blackness was associated with a sky darkened by rain clouds.

An old Arabian rain charm in North Africa was to throw a holy man into a spring. An Armenian version of this charm called for throwing the wife of a holy man into the water.

The use of magic or prayer to influence the weather is not so common in modern societies, but predictions about the weather, many of them traceable back to rural American folklore, are still heard today. The farmer observed the behavior of plants, animals, and insects, watched the sky, sniffed the air, and forecast the weather:

"When the rooster crows at night, he tells you that a rain's in sight."/ "If turkey feathers are unusually thick by Thanksgiving, look for a hard winter."/"When the sheep collect and huddle, tomorrow will become a puddle."/"Flies bite more before a rain."

It has been said that the average American cannot begin a conversation without commenting about the weather, but most talk about the weather today is no more scientific than that of a rural old-timer like Pappie.

# A Reading Problem

*Jean Stafford*

**When Emily set out to read, she didn't want
to be bothered by the things of this world and
certainly not by those preaching the glories
of a world to come.**

ONE of the great hardships of my childhood—
and there were many, as many, I suppose, as
have ever plagued a living creature—was
that I could never find a decent place to read.
If I tried to read at home in the living room,
I was constantly pestered by someone saying,
"For goodness' sake, Emily, move where it's
light. You're going to ruin your eyes and no two
ways about it," or "You ought to be outdoors
with the other youngsters getting some roses
in your cheeks." Of course, I knew how to
reply to these kill-joy injunctions; to the first
I said, "They're *my* eyes," and to the second,
"Getting some brains in my head is more important than getting any so-called roses in
my cheeks." But even when I had settled the
hash of that Paul Pry[1]—mother, usually, but
sometimes a visiting aunt, or even a bossy
neighbor—I was cross and could no longer
concentrate. The bedroom I shared with my
sister Stella was even worse, because Stella
was always in it, making an inventory of her
free samples out loud, singing Camp Fire Girl
songs, practicing ballet steps and giggling
whenever she made a mistake; she was one of
the most vacant people I have ever known.

At one certain time of year, I could read up
in the mountains, in any number of clearings
and dingles and amphitheatres, and that was
in the fall. But in the winter it was too cold,
and in the spring there were wood ticks, and
in the summer there were snakes. I had tried
a pinewoods I was very fond of for several
weeks one summer, but it was no good, because at the end of every paragraph I had to
get up and stamp my feet and shout and describe an agitated circle on the ground with
a stick to warn the rattlers to stay away from
me.

The public library was better, but not much.
The librarian, Mrs. Looby, a fussbudgety old
thing in a yellow wig and a hat planted with
nasturtiums, was so strict about the silent rule

**1.** *Paul Pry*, an overly inquisitive individual, originally a character in a comedy by John Poole.

that she evicted children who popped their gum or cracked their knuckles, and I was a child who did both as a matter of course and constantly. Besides, she was forever coming into the children's section like a principal making rounds, and leaning over you to see what you were reading; half the time she disapproved and recommended something else, something either so dry you'd go to sleep reading it or so mushy you'd throw up. Moreover, our dog, Reddie, loved to follow me to the library, and quite often instead of waiting outside under the lilac bush, as he was supposed to do, he would manage to get in when someone opened the door. He didn't come to see me; he came to tease Mrs. Looby, who abominated anything that walked on four legs. He would sit on his haunches in front of her desk, wagging his tail and laughing, with his long pink tongue hanging out. "Shoo!" Mrs. Looby would scream, waving her hands at him. "Emily Vanderpool, you get this pesky dog of yours out of here this minute! The very idea! Quick, Emily, or I'll call the dogcatcher! I'll call the dogcatcher! I will positively call the dogcatcher if a dog ever comes into my library again." I had to give up the library altogether after one unlucky occasion when Reddie stood on his hind legs and put his paws on top of her high desk. She had had her back to him, and, thinking she heard a customer, she turned, saying in her library whisper, "Good afternoon, and what may I do for you this afternoon?" and faced the grinning countenance of my dog. That time, in her wrath and dismay, she clutched her head in her hands and dislodged her hat and then her wig, so that a wide expanse of baldness showed, and everyone in the children's section dived into the stacks and went all to pieces.

For a while after that, I tried the lobby of the downtown hotel, the Goldmoor, where the permanent residents, who were all old men, sat in long-waisted rocking chairs, rocking and spitting tobacco juice into embossed cuspidors and talking in high, offended, lonesome voices about their stomach aches and their insomnia and how the times had changed. All in the world the old duffers had left was time, which, hour after hour, they had to kill.

People like that, who are bored almost to extinction, think that everyone else is, too, and if they see someone reading a book, they say to themselves, "I declare, here's somebody worse off than I am. The poor soul's really hard up to have to depend on a book, and it's my bounden Christian duty to help him pass the time," and they start talking to you. If you want company on the streetcar or the bus or the interurban, open a book and you're all set. At first, the old men didn't spot me, because I always sat in one of the two bow windows in a chair that was half hidden by a potted sweet-potato plant, which, according to local legend, dated from the nineteenth century—and well it might have, since it was the size of a small-size tree. My chair was crowded in between this and a table on which was a clutter of seedy Western souvenirs—a rusted, beat-up placer pan with samples of ore in it, some fossils and some arrowheads, a tomahawk, a powder horn, and the shellacked tail of a beaver that was supposed to have been trapped by a desperado named Mountain Jim Nugent, who had lived in Estes Park[2] in the seventies. It was this tabletop historical museum that made me have to give up the hotel, for one day, when I was spang in the middle of *Hans Brinker*, two of the old men came over to it to have a whining, cantankerous argument about one of the rocks in the placer pan, which one maintained was pyrites and the other maintained was not. (That was about as interesting as their conversations ever got.) They were so angry that if they hadn't been so feeble, I think they would have thrown the rocks at each other. And then one of them caught sight of me and commenced to cackle. "Lookit what we got here," he said. "A little old kid in a middy reading windies[3] all by her lonesome." I had been taught to be courteous to my elders, so I looked up and gave the speaker a sickly smile and returned to my book, which now, of course, I could not follow. His disputant became his ally, and they carried on, laughing and teasing me as if I were a monkey that had

---

2. *Estes Park,* a small town in northern Colorado, the state in which this story is set. Other Colorado communities Miss Stafford mentions are Watkins, Adams, Mangol, and Niwot.
3. *windies,* a chiefly Western slang term meaning "tall tales."

suddenly entered their precincts for the sole purpose of amusing them. They asked me why I wasn't at the movies with my sweetheart, they asked me how I'd like to be paddled with the stiff old beaver tail of Mountain Jim's, and they asked me to sing them a song. All the other old men, delighted at this small interruption in their routine of spitting and complaining, started rubbernecking in my direction, grinning and chuckling, and a couple of them came shuffling over to watch the fun. I felt as if I had a fever of a hundred and five, because of the blush that spread over my entire person, including my insides. I was not only embarrassed, I was as mad as anything to be hemmed in by this phalanx of giggling old geezers who looked like a flock of turkey gobblers. "Maybe she ran away from home," said one of them. "Hasn't been any transients in this hotel since that last Watkins fella. Fella by the name of Fletcher. Is your name Fletcher, Missy?" Another said, "I think it's mighty nice of her to come and pay us a call instead of going to the show with her best beau," and when a third said, "I bet I know where there's a Hershey bar not a thousand miles from here," I got up and, in a panic, ducked through the lines and fled; taking candy from a strange old man was the quickest way to die like a dog from poison.

So the hotel after that was out. Then I tried the depot, but it was too dirty and noisy; a couple of times I went and sat in the back of the Catholic church, but it was dark there, and besides I didn't feel right about it, because I was a United Presbyterian in good standing. Once, I went into the women's smoking room in the library at the college, but it was full of worried-looking old-maid summer-school students who came back year after year to work on their Master's degrees in Education, and they asked me a lot of solemn questions, raising their voices as if I were deaf. Besides, it was embarrassing to watch them smoke; they were furtive and affected, and they coughed a good deal. I could smoke better than that and I was only ten; I mean the one time I had smoked I did it better—a friend and I each smoked a cubeb she had pinched from her tubercular father.

But at last I found a peachy place—the visitors' waiting room outside the jail in the basement of the courthouse. There were seldom any visitors, because there were seldom any prisoners, and when, on rare occasions, there were, the visitors were too edgy or too morose to pay any heed to me. The big, cool room had nothing in it but two long benches and a wicker table, on which was spread out free Christian Science literature. The sheriff, Mr. Starbird, was very sympathetic with me, for he liked to read himself and that's what he did most of the time (his job was a snap; Adams was, on the whole, a law-abiding town) in his office that adjoined the waiting room; he read and read, not lifting his eyes from Sax Rohmer[4] even when he was rolling a cigarette. Once, he said he wished his own daughters, Laverne, thirteen, and Ida, sixteen, would follow my example, instead of, as he put it, "rimfirin' around the county with paint on their faces and spikes on their heels and not caring two hoots for anything on God's green earth except what's got on pants." Mr. Starbird and I became good friends, although we did not talk much, since we were busy reading. One time, when we were both feeling restless, he locked me up in a cell so I could see how it felt; I kind of liked it. And another time he put handcuffs on me, but they were too big.

At the time I discovered the jail, in the first hot days in June, I was trying to memorize the books of the Bible. If I got them by heart and could name them off in proper order and without hesitating or mispronouncing, I would be eligible to receive an award of a New Testament at Sunday school, and if there was one thing I liked, it was prizes. So every day for several weeks I spent the whole afternoon more or less in jail, reading whatever fun thing I had brought along (*Rebecca of Sunnybrook Farm, Misunderstood Betsy, Trudy Goes to Boarding School*) and then working away at I Samuel, II Samuel, I Kings, II Kings, whispering so as not to disturb Mr. Starbird. Sometimes, on a

4. *Sax Rohmer*, pseudonym of Englishman Arthur Wade, creator of Dr. Fu Manchu, a diabolically ingenious Oriental villain, who was unsuccessfully pursued through dozens of books and several films by English hero Nayland Smith. The sheriff is an avid Fu Manchu fan.

really hot day, he would send out for two bottles of Dr. Pepper.

One blistering Saturday, when I was as limp as a rag after walking through the sun down the hill and into the hot valley where the courthouse was, I got to the stairs leading to the waiting room and was met by the most deafening din of men yelling and bars rattling and Mr. Starbird hollering "Quiet there!" at the top of his voice. I was shocked and scared but very curious, and I went on down the steps, hearing the vilest imaginable language spewing out from the direction of the cells. I had just sat down on the edge of one of the benches and was opening *Tom Sawyer Abroad* when Mr. Starbird, bright red in the face, came in, brushing his hands. Two sweating deputies followed him. "Not today, Emily," said Mr. Starbird when he saw me. "We got some tough customers today, worse luck. And me with a new Fu."

The prisoners were moonshiners, he told me as he led me by the arm to the stairs, whose still up in the mountains had been discovered, because they had drunk too much of their own rotgut and had got loose-tongued and had gone around bragging at the amusement park up at the head of the canyon. There were five of them, and they had had to be disarmed of sawed-off shot guns, although, as Mr. Starbird modestly pointed out, this wasn't much of a job, since they had been three sheets in the wind.[5] "Whew!" said the sheriff. "They got a breath on em like the whole shootin' match of St. Louis before the Volstead Act."[6] I told him I didn't mind (it would give me considerable prestige with my brother and my friends to be on hand if one of them should try to make a break, and I would undoubtedly get my name in the paper: "Emily Vanderpool, daughter of Mr. and Mrs. Peter Vanderpool, witnessed the attempted escape of the desperate criminals. Emily is to receive an award at the United Presbyterian Church on July 29th"), but Mr. Starbird told me, a little sharply, to go on now, and I had no choice but to go.

---

5. *three sheets in the wind*, drunk.
6. *Volstead Act*, a federal law passed in 1920 providing for enforcement of the Eighteenth Amendment, which prohibited the manufacture, sale, and transportation of intoxicating liquor.

Go where? I had exhausted every possibility in town. I thought of going to the Safeway, where my father was the manager, and asking him if I could read in his office, but I knew how that would go over on a busy Saturday when the farmers and the mountain people were in town buying potatoes and side meat; my father didn't have Mr. Starbird's temperament. Then, vaguely, I considered the front porch of a haunted house at the top of Carlyle Hill but rejected it when I remembered a recent rumor that there was a nest of bats under the eaves; I didn't want them in my hair, using my pigtails to swing on. I wasn't too sure I could read anyhow, because I was so excited over the prisoners, but it was far too hot to roller-skate, too hot to explore the dump—too hot, indeed, for anything but sitting quietly beside the lockup.

I started in the direction of home in a desultory way, stopping at every drinking fountain, window-shopping, going methodically through the ten-cent stores, looking for money in the gutters. I walked down the length of the main street, going toward the mountains, over whose summits hung a pale heat haze; the pavement was soft, and when it and the shimmering sidewalk ended, I had to walk in the red dirt road, which was so dusty that after a few steps my legs, above the tops of my socks, looked burned—not sunburned, *burned*.

At the outskirts of town, beside the creek, there was a tourist camp where funny-looking people pitched tents and filled up the wire trash baskets with tin cans; sometimes, on a still night, you could hear them singing state songs, and now and again there was the sound of an accordion or a harmonica playing a jig. Today there was only one tent up in the grounds, a sagging, ragged white one, and it looked forlorn, like something left behind. Nearby was parked a Model T, dark red with rust where its sky-blue paint had worn through, and to it was attached a trailer; I knew how hot the leather seat of that car would be and I could all but hear the sun beating on the top of it like hail-stones. There wasn't a soul in sight, and there wasn't a sound nearby except for a couple of magpies ranting at each other in the trees and the occasional digestive croak

of a bullfrog. Along the creek, there was a line of shady cottonwoods, and I decided to rest there for a while and cool off my feet in the water.

After I had washed as well as I could, I leaned back against the tree trunk, my feet still in the water, and opened the Bible to the table of contents, and then I closed my eyes so that I wouldn't cheat; I started reciting, softly and clearly and proud of myself. I had just got to Ezra,[7] having gone so far very fast and without a hitch, when a noise caused me to fling back my eyelids and to discover that a man's big foot in a high-buttoned shoe had materialized on the ground beside me. Startled, I looked up into the bearded face of a tall man in black clothes (black suit, black string tie,

black-rimmed eyeglasses, black hat—the hat was dented in such a way that it looked like a gravy boat) and into the small brown eyes of a girl about Stella's age, who wore a tennis visor and a long, dirty white thing that looked like her nightgown.

"Greetings, Christian soldier," said the man, in a deep, rich Southern accent, and he offered me a large, warty hand, "Evangelist Gerlash is the name, and this is my girl, Opal."

Opal put her hand on my head and said, "Peace."

"Same to you," I said awkwardly, and took my feet out of the water. "You can have this tree if you want. I was just leaving."

I started to get up, but Evangelist Gerlash motioned me to stay where I was, and he said, "It uplifts my heavy heart and it uplifts Opal's to find a believer in our wanderings through this godless world. All too seldom do we find

---

7. *Ezra*, the fifteenth Book in the King James Version of the Old Testament.

a person applying themself to the Book. Oh, sister, keep to this path your youthful feet have started on and shun the Sodoms *and* the Gomorrahs *and* the Babylons!"[8]

My youthful feet were so wet I was having a struggle to put on my socks, and I thought, Peace! That's all he knows about it. There's not an inch of peace or privacy in this whole town.

"Seek truth and *not* the fleshpots!" said the man. "Know light, *not* license! 'A little child shall lead them,' says the Book you hold in your small hands, as yet unused to woman's work. Perhaps *you* are that very child."

"Amen," said Opal, and with this they both sat down, tailor-fashion, on the bank of the stream. For some time, nothing more was said. The Gerlashes complacently scrutinized me, as if I were the very thing they had been looking for, and then they looked at each other in a congratulatory way, while I, breaking out in an itching rash of embarrassment, tried to think of an urgent bit of business that would excuse me from their company without being impolite. I could think only of the dentist or of a dancing class, but I was dressed for neither; some weeks before, my Uncle Will M'Kerrow, who lived in Ridley, Missouri, had gone to a sale at the Army and Navy store in St. Joe and had bought presents for me and my brother and my two sisters, and today I was wearing mine—khaki knickers and a khaki shirt and a cavalry hat. I had perked up the hat by twining a multi-colored shoelace around the band; the other shoelace I had cut in two to tie the ends of my pigtails; over my heart was sewn a red "C," a school letter that I had got in the spring for collateral reading. The dentist, Dr. Skeen, a humorist, would have died laughing if he had seen me in these A.E.F. regimentals,[9] and Miss Jorene Roy, the dancing teacher, would have had kittens. Although the Gerlashes had no way of knowing the personality of either of them, I was so

unskillful at useful lies, and believed so firmly that my mind could be read, that I did not dare pretend I was going to have a cavity filled or to assume the five ballet positions. I said nothing and waited for an inspiration to set me free. People who talked Bible talk like this made me ashamed for them.

Evangelist Gerlash was immensely tall, and his bones had only the barest wrapper of flesh; he made me think of a tree with the leaves off, he was so angular and gnarled, and even his skin was something like bark, rough and pitted and scarred. His wild beard was the color of a sorrel horse, but his long hair was black, and so were the whiskers on the backs of his hands that imperfectly concealed, on the right one, a tattoo of a peacock. His intense and watchful brown eyes were flecked with green, and so were Opal's. Opal's hair was the color of her father's beard and it fell ropily to her shoulders; it needed a good brushing, and probably a fine comb wouldn't have done it any harm.

Presently, the evangelist took his beard between his hands and squeezed as if he were strangling it, and he said, "We have had a weary journey, sister."

"You said a mouthful," said Opal, and hugely yawned.

"We come all the way from Arkansas this trip," said her father. "We been comin' since May."

"I liked it better last summer," said Opal, "up in Missouri and Iowa. I don't like this dry. Mountains give me the fantods."[10] She looked over her shoulder up at the heat-ridden range and shuddered violently.

"We been roving like gypsies of the Lord, warning the wicked and helping the sick," her father went on. "We are pleased to meet up with a person who goes to the source of goodness and spiritual health. In other words, we are glad to make the acquaintance of a *friend*." And, still wringing his beard, he gave me an alarming smile that showed a set of sharp, efficient teeth. "Yes, sir, it gladdens me right down to the marrowbone to see a little girl on a summer day reading the word of God instead of messing with the vanities of this

---

**8.** *the Sodoms and the Gomorrahs and the Babylons.* As recorded in the Book of Genesis, the Lord rained fire and brimstone upon the cities of Sodom and Gomorrah to punish them for their sinfulness. Babylon, a city noted for its wickedness, is mentioned many times in the Bible.

**9.** *A.E.F. regimentals*, American Expeditionary Force clothing, or, clothing worn by soldiers in World War I.

**10.** *give me the fantods*, make me restless, uneasy.

world *or* robbing the honest farmer of his watermelon *or* sassing her Christian mother."

"We stopped in nineteen towns and preached up a storm," said Opal. "You got any gum on you?"

Fascinated by the Gerlashes, although the piety the evangelist assigned to me discomfited me, since I was no more reading the Bible than your cat, I took a package of Beech-Nut out of the pocket of my knickers, and along with it came my hand-me-down Ingersoll that hadn't run for two years. Opal took a stick of gum, and her father, with his eye on my watch, said, "Don't mind if I do," and also took a stick. "That's a dandy timepiece you got there. Remember that nice old gold turnip I used to have, Opie?"

"Yeah," said Opal scornfully. "I remember you hocked that nice old gold turnip."

"Possessions are a woe and a heavy load of sin," said her father, and reached out for my watch. But after he had held it to his ear and fiddled with the stem for a while, he gave it back, saying *"Was* a dandy timepiece. Ain't nothing now but a piece of tin and isinglass." Then he returned to his thesis. "I reckon this is the one and only time I or Opal has come across a person, let alone a child, drinking at the wellspring of enlightenment." And he gave me his hand to shake again.

"Amen," said Opal.

There followed a drawling antiphonal recitative[11] that related the Gerlash situation. In the winter, they lived in a town called Hoxie, Arkansas, where Evangelist Gerlash clerked in the Buttorf drugstore and preached and baptized on the side. ("Hoxie may be only a wide space in the road," said Opal, "but she don't have any homely mountains.") Mrs. Gerlash, whom Abraham had untimely gathered to his bosom[12] the winter before, had been a hymn singer and an organ player and had done a little preaching herself. Opal, here, had got the word the day she was born, and by the time she was five and a half years old she could preach to a fare-thee-well against

the Catholics and the Wets.[13] She was also an A-1 dowser[14] and was renowned throughout the Wonder State.[15] In the summer, they took to the road as soon as Opal was out of school, and went camping and preaching and praying (and dowsing if there was a call for it) and spreading the truth all over the country. Last year, they had gone through the Middle West up as far as Chicago (here Opal, somewhat to her father's impatience, digressed to tell me the story of Mrs. O'Leary's cow),[16] and the year before they had gone through New England; on earlier trips they had covered Florida and Georgia. One of these days, they were going to set up shop in New York City, though they understood the tourist-camp situation there was poor. Sometimes they found hospitality and sometimes they didn't, depending on the heathens per capita. Sometimes, the Christian citizens lent them a hall, and they put up a sign on the front door saying, "The Bible Tabernacle"; often, in such a receptive community, they were invited to supper and given groceries by the believers. But sometimes they had to do their saving of souls in a public park or in a tourist camp. ("Not much business in this one," said Opal, gazing ruefully at their solitary tent.) Mr. Buttorf, the druggist in Hoxie, always said he wasn't going to keep Gerlash one more day if he didn't quit this traipsing around three months of the year, but the Lord saw to it that right after Labor Day Buttorf came to his senses and hired him again. They had arrived in Adams this morning, and if they found fertile ground, they meant to stay a week, sowing the seeds of righteousness. Evangelist Gerlash would be much obliged to learn from me what sort of town this was; he said he guessed nobody could give him the lay of the land—spiritually speaking—any better than a Bible-reading girl like me.

"But first," he said, "tell Opal and I a little

---

11. *antiphonal recitative.* Gerlash and Opal alternated speaking in a sort of chant.
12. *Abraham had untimely gathered to his bosom.* Abraham was the traditional founder of the ancient Hebrew nation. "In the bosom of Abraham" refers to heaven.
13. *Wets,* persons in favor of allowing the sale of alcoholic beverages.
14. *A-1 dowser,* an expert at finding water underground by holding a forked stick which is believed to pull downward over the water source.
15. *Wonder State,* since 1923, the official nickname of Arkansas.
16. *Mrs. O'Leary's cow.* According to legend, the Chicago fire of 1871 began when a cow belonging to one Mrs. O'Leary kicked over a lantern, setting the barn on fire.

something about yourself, sister." He took a black notebook out of the pocket of his black coat and took a stubby pencil out of his hatband, licked it, and began to ask me questions. All the time he was taking down my dossier, Opal rocked gently back and forth, hugging herself and humming "Holy, Holy, Holy." I was much impressed by her, because her jaws, as she diligently chewed her gum, were moving in the opposite direction to her trunk; I was sure she would be able to pat her head and rub her stomach at the same time.

It never occurred to me that I didn't have to answer questions put to me by adults (except for the old men in the Goldmoor, who were not serious)—even strange ones who had dropped out of nowhere. Besides, I was always as cooperative as possible with clergymen, not knowing when my number might come up. The evangelist's questions were harmless enough, but some of them were exceedingly strange. In between asking my name and my age and my father's occupation, he would say, "Which do you think is the Bible Sabbath—Saturday or Sunday?" and "Do you know if the Devil is a bachelor or is he a married man?" When to these hard, interesting questions I replied that I did not know, Opal left off her humming and said, "Amen."

When he had got from me all the data he wanted, he said "I bet you this here town is a candidate for brimstone. I bet you it's every bit as bad as that one out on the plains we were at for two weeks in a hall. Heathens they were, but *scared*, so they give us a hall. That Mangol."

"Mudhole is what I call it," said Opal.

Her father chuckled. "Opal makes jokes," he explained. Then he said, "That was the worst town we come across in all our travels, sister, and somewheres on me I've got a clipping from the Mangol daily showing what I told the folks down there. I wouldn't be surprised if the same situation was here in Adams, being in the same state with Mangol and not too far away from Mangol and having that college that is bound to sow free-thinking. Forewarned is forearmed is what I always say. I may have a good deal of hard work to do here." He began to fish things out of his pock-

ets, and you never saw such a mess—a knife, a plug of chewing tobacco, a thin bar of soap, envelopes with arithmetic on them, a handkerchief I am not going to describe, any number of small pamphlets and folded-up handbills. Finally, he handed me a clipping. It said,

### ANOTHER SOUR, GASSY STOMACH VICTIM SAYS GASTRO-PEP GAVE RELIEF

There was a picture of an indignant-looking man with a pointed head and beetling brows and a clenched jaw, who testified:

*"For 3 years I had been a Great Victim of stomach gas and indigestion," said Mr. Homer Wagman, prominent Oklahoma citizen of 238 Taos Street, Muskogee. "My liver was sluggish, I would get bloated up and painful and had that tired dragged out feeling all the time. Recently a friend told me about Gastro-Pep so I decided to give it a trial. After taking 3 bottles of this medicine my* WHOLE SYSTEM *has gone through such a change that I can hardly believe it! Now my gas and stomach discomfort are relieved and I can eat my meals without suffering. I sleep like a schoolboy." Advt.*

I did not know what I was reading, but I didn't like it anyway, since it had so nasty a sound; I didn't mind hearing about broken legs or diphtheria, but I hated any mention of anyone's insides. I started to read it for the second time, trying to think of something intelligent or complimentary to say to Evangelist Gerlash, and I must have made a face, because he leaned over me, adjusting his glasses, and said, "Oops! Hold on! Wrong write-up," and snatched the clipping out of my hand. I'm not absolutely sure, but I think Opal winked at me. Her father shuffled through his trash again and finally handed me another clipping, which, this time, was not an advertisement. The headline was:

## GERLASH LOCATES HELL IN
## HEART OF CITY OF MANGOL

and the story beneath it ran:

*"Hell is located right in the heart of the city of Mangol but will not be in operation until God sets up His Kingdom here in the earth," declared Evangelist Gerlash last night to another capacity crowd in the Bible Tabernacle.*

*"There are some very bad trouble spots in the city of Mangol that no doubt would be subjects of Hell right now," continued the evangelist and said, "but there are so many good people and places in this city that overshadow the bad that God has decided to postpone Hell in Mangol until the time of the harvest and the harvest, God says, 'is the end of the world' (Matthew 13:39).*

*"Hell, when started by God with eternal fire that comes from God out of Heaven and ignites the entire world, including this city will be an interesting place. It will be a real play of fireworks, so hot that all the elements of earth will melt; too hot all over to find a place for any human creature to live. God is not arranging this fireworks for any human creature and therefore, if you or I ever land in this place, it is because we choose to go there."*

*Evangelist Gerlash and his daughter, Opal Gerlash, 12, of Hoxie, Arkansas, have been preaching on alternate nights for the last week at the Bible Tabernacle, formerly the Alverez Feed and Grain Store at 1919 Prospect Street. Tonight Opal Gerlash will lecture on the subject, "Are You Born Again by Jumping, Rolling, Shouting, or Dancing?"*

I read this with a good deal more interest than I had read of Mr. Wagman's renascence, although as Evangelist Gerlash's qualifications multiplied, my emotion waned. I had assumed from the headline, which made the back of my neck prickle, that he had some hot tips on the iniquities of that flat, dull little prairie town of Mangol that now and again we drove through when we were taking a trip to the southwest; the only thing I had ever noticed about it was that I had to hold my nose as we went through it, because the smell of sugar beets was so powerfully putrid. The city of Mangol had a population of about six hundred.

Nevertheless, though the evangelist did not scare or awe me, I had to be polite, and so, handing back the clipping, I said, "When do you think the end of the world is apt to be?" Opal had stopped her humming and swaying, and both she and her father were staring at me with those fierce brown eyes.

"In the autumn of the world," said Evangelist Gerlash sepulchrally, and Opal said, as she could be counted on to do, "Amen."

"Yeah, I know," I said. "But what autumn? What year?" He and Opal simultaneously bowed their heads in silent prayer. Both of them thoughtfully chewed gum.

Then Opal made a speech. "The answer to this and many other questions will be found in Evangelist Gerlash's inspirational hundred-and-twelve-page book entitled *Gerlash on the Bible.* Each and every one of you will want to read about the seven great plagues to smite the people of the world just before the end. Upon who will they fall? Have they begun? What will it mean to the world? In this book, on sale for the nominal sum of fifty cents or a half dollar, Evangelist Gerlash lets the people in on the ground floor regarding the law of God." From one of the deep sleeves of her kimono—for that was what that grimy garment was—Opal withdrew a paper-bound book with a picture of her father on the front of it, pointing his finger at me.

"Fifty cents, a half dollar," said the author, "Which is to say virtually free, gratis, and for nothing."

Up the creek a way, a bullfrog made a noise that sounded distinctly like "Gerlash."

"What makes Mangol so much worse than anyplace else?" I asked, growing more and more suspicious now that the conversation had taken so mercantile a turn.

But the Gerlashes were not giving out information free. "You will find the answer to this and many other questions in the book," said Opal. "Such as 'Can Wall Street Run God's Business?'"

"Why does the Devil go on a sitdown strike for a thousand years?" said her father.

*"What?"* said I.

"Who will receive the mark of the beast?" said Opal.

"Repent!" commanded Evangelist Gerlash. "Watch! Hearken!"

"Ger-lash," went the bullfrog.

"Will Hell burn forever?" cried Opal. "Be saved from the boiling pits! Take out insurance against spending eternity on a griddle!"

"Thy days are numbered," declared her father.

Opal said, "Major Hagedorn, editor of the Markston *Standard,* in his editorial said, 'This man Gerlash is as smart as chain lightning and seems to know his Bible forwards and backwards.'" All this time, she was holding up the book, and her father, on the cover of it, was threatening to impale me on his accusing finger.

"Perhaps our sister doesn't have the where-withal to purchase this valuable book, or in other words the means to her salvation," he said, at last, and gave me a look of profound sadness, as if he had never been so sorry for anyone in his life. I said it was true I didn't have fifty cents (who ever heard of anyone ten years old going around with that kind of money?), and I offered to trade my Bible for *Gerlash on the Bible,* since I was interested in finding out whether the Devil was a bachelor or had a wife. But he shook his head. He began to throttle his beard again, and he said, "Does a dove need a kite? Does a giraffe need a neck? Does an Eskimo need a fur coat? Does Gerlash need a Bible?"

"Gerlash is a regular walking encyclopedia on the Bible," said Opal.

"One of the biggest trouble spots in the world is Mangol, Colorado," said Evangelist Gerlash. "No reason to think for a minute the contamination won't spread up here like a plague of locusts. Don't you think you had ought to be armed, Christian soldier?"

"Yes, I do," I said, for I had grown more and more curious. "But I don't have fifty cents."

"Considering that you are a Christian girl and a Bible reader," said the man, "I think we could make a special price for you. I reckon we could let you have it for twenty-five cents. O.K., Opal?"

Opal said rapidly, "Gastro-Pep contains over thirty ingredients. So it is like taking several medicines at once. And due to the immense volume in which it sells, the price of Gastro-Pep is reasonable, so get it now. Tonight!"

Evangelist Gerlash gave his daughter a sharp look. And, flustered, she stammered, "I mean, owing to the outstanding nature of Gerlash's information, the price of this *in*valuable book is a mere nothing. The truth in this book will stick and mark you forever."

"You want this book bad, don't you, sister Emily Vanderpool?" asked her father. "You are a good girl, and good girls are entitled to have this book, which is jam-packed with answers to the questions that have troubled you for years. You can't tell me your mammy and pappy are so mean that they wouldn't give their little girl a quarter for *Gerlash on the Bible.* Why don't you skedaddle over to home and get the small sum of twenty-five cents off your Christian ma?" He opened his notebook and checked my address. "Over to 125 Belleview Avenue."

"I'm hungry," said Opal. "I could eat me a horse."

"Never mind you being hungry," said her father, with a note of asperity in his mushy voice. "Don't you doubt me, sister Vander-pool," he went on, "when I tell you your innocent life is in danger. Looky here, when I got a call to go and enlighten the children of darkness in Mangol, just down the line from here, I got that call like a clap of thunder and I knew I couldn't waste no time. I went and I studied every den of vice in the city limits and some outside the city limits. It's bad, sister. For twenty-five cents, you and your folks can be prepared for when the Mangolites come a-swarming into this town." He glanced again at his notebook. "While you're getting the purchase price of my book, please ask your pure-hearted mother if I might have the loan of her garage to preach the word of God in. Are you folks centrally located?"

"My brother's got his skunk skins drying in it," I said. "You couldn't stand the smell."

"Rats!" said Evangelist Gerlash crossly, and then sternly he said, "You better shake a leg, sister. This book is offered for a limited time only."

"I can't get a quarter," I said. "I already owe her twenty cents."

"What're you going to have for supper?" asked Opal avidly. "I could eat a bushel of roasting ears.[17] We ain't had a meal in a dog's age—not since that old handout in Niwot."

"Alas, too true," said her father. "Do you hear that, my sister Emily? You look upon a hungry holy man of God and his girl who give to the poor and save no crust for himself. Fainting for the want of but a crumb from the rich man's groaning board, we drive ourself onwards, bringing light to where there is darkness and comfort to where there is woe. Perhaps your good Christian mother and father would give us an invite to their supper tonight, in exchange for which they and theirs would gladly be given this priceless book, free of charge, signed by hand."

"Well, gosh," I said, working my tennis shoes on over my wet socks, "I mean . . . Well, I mean I don't know."

"Don't know what?" said that great big man, glowering at me over the tops of his severe spectacles. "Don't you go and tell me that a good Bible-reading girl like you has got kin which are evolutionists and agnostics and infidels who would turn two needy ministers of God away from their door. To those who are nourished by the Law of the Lord, a crust now and then is sufficient to keep body and soul together. I don't suppose Opal and I have had hot victuals for a good ten days, two weeks." A piteous note crept into his versatile voice, and his brown eyes and his daughter's begot a film of tears. They did look awfully hungry, and I felt guilty the way I did when I was eating a sandwich and Reddie was looking up at me like a martyr of old.

"Didn't she say her daddy ran a grocery store?" asked Opal, and her father, consulting my vital statistics, smiled broadly.

"There's nothing the matter with *your* ears, Opie," he said. And then, to me, "How's about it, sister? How's about you going down to this Safeway store and getting Opal and I some bread and some pork chops and like that?"

"Roasting ears," said Opal. "And a mushmelon."

It had suddenly occurred to me that if I could just get up and run away, the incident would be finished, but Evangelist Gerlash was clairvoyant, and, putting two firmly restraining hands on my shoulders and glaring at me straight in the eye, he said, "We don't have a thing in the world tonight to do but show up at 125 Belleview Avenue round about suppertime."

"I'd rather cook out," said Opal. "I'd rather she brought the groceries."

Her father bent his head into his hands, and there was a great sob in his voice when he said, "I have suffered many a bitter disappointment in this vale of tears, but I suppose the bitterest is right now here in Adams, Colorado, where, thinking I had found a child of light, she turned out to be a mocker, grinding under her heel shod in gold the poor and the halt.[18] Oh, sister, may you be forgiven on the Day of Judgment!"

"Whyn't you go get us some eats?" said Opal, cajoling. "If you get us some eats, we won't come calling. If we come calling, like as not we'll spend the night."

"Haven't slept in a bed since May," said her father, snuffling.

"We don't shake easy," said Opal, with an absolutely shameless grin.

My mother had a heart made of butter, and our spare room was forever occupied by strays, causing my father to scold her to pieces after they'd gone, and I knew that if the Gerlashes showed up at our house (and plainly they would) with their hard-luck story and their hard-luck looks, and all their devices for saving souls, she would give them houseroom and urge them to stay as long as they liked, and my father would not simmer down for a month of Sundays.

So I got up and I said, "All right, I'll go get you a sack of groceries." I had a nebulous idea that my father might let me buy them on time or might give me a job as a delivery boy until I had paid for them.

To my distress, the Gerlashes got up, too,

---

17. *roasting ears,* sweet corn suitable for roasting.

18. *halt,* crippled, lame.

and the evangelist said, "We'll drive you down to Main Street, sister, and sit outside, so there won't be no slip-up."

"It's Saturday!" I cried. "You can't find a place to park."

"Then we'll just circle round and round the block."

"But I can't get into a car with strangers," I protested.

"Strangers!" exclaimed Evangelist Gerlash. "Why, sister, we're friends now. Don't you know all about Opal and I? Didn't we lay every last one of our cards on the table right off the bat?" He took my arm in his big, bony hand and started to propel me in the direction of the Ford, and just then, like the Mounties to the rescue, up came Mr. Starbird's official car, tearing into the camp-grounds and stopping, with a scream from the brakes, right in front of me and the Gerlashes. A man in a deputy's uniform was in the front seat beside him.

"Why, Emily," said Mr. Starbird as he got out of the car and pushed his hat back from his forehead. "I thought you went on home after that ruckus we had. You'll be glad to hear those scalawags are going off to the pen tomorrow, so you can come back to jail any time after 10 A.M."

Opal giggled, but her father shivered and looked as if a rabbit had just run over his grave. "We're getting outa here," he said to her under his breath, and started at a lope toward his car.

"That's them all right," said the man in the deputy's uniform. "They set up shop in the feed store, and when they wasn't passing out mumbo-jumbo about the world going up in firecrackers, they was selling that medicine. Medicine! Ninety per cent wood alcohol and ninety per cent fusel oil. Three cases of jake-leg[19] and God knows how many workers passed out in the fields."

Mr. Starbird and the deputy had closed in on the Gerlashes. Mr. Starbird said, "I don't want any trouble with you, Mister. I just want you to get out of Adams before I run you out on a rail. We got plenty of our own preachers and plenty of our own bootleggers, and we don't need any extra of either one. Just kindly

19. *jake-leg,* liquor that is sold illegally.

allow me to impound this so-called medicine and then you shove. What kind of a bill of goods were they trying to sell you, Emily, kid?"

The deputy said, "That's another of their lines. We checked on them after they left Mangol, checked all the way back to Arkansas. They get some sucker like a kid or an idiot and give them this spiel and promise they'll go to Heaven if they'll just get them some grub or some money or my Aunt Geraldine's diamond engagement ring or whatever."

I said nothing. I was thrilled, and at the same time I was mortally embarrassed for the Gerlashes. I was sorry for them, too, because, in spite of their predicament, they looked more hungry than anything else.

Opal said, "If we went to jail, we could eat," but her father gave her a whack on the seat and told her "Hush up, you," and the procession, including myself, clutching my Bible and *Tom Sawyer Abroad,* moved toward the tent and the Model T. The sheriff took two cases of medicine out of the tent and put them in his car, and then we stood there watching the Gerlashes strike camp and put all their bivouac gear into the trailer. They worked swiftly and competently, as if they were accustomed to sudden removals. When they were finished, Opal got into the front seat and started to cry. "Whyn't we ever have something to eat?" said the child preacher.

Mr. Starbird, abashed by the dirty girl's tears, took out his wallet and gave her a dollar. "Don't you spend a red cent of it in Adams," he said. "You go on and get out of town and then get some food."

Evangelist Gerlash, having cranked the car, making a noise like a collision, climbed into the driver's seat, and grinned at the sight of the dollar. "I have cast my bread upon the waters and I am repaid one hundredfold," he said. "And you, in casting your bread upon the waters, you, too, will be repaid one hundredfold."

"Amen," said Opal, herself again, no longer crying.

"Now beat it," said Mr. Starbird.

"And give Mangol a wide berth," said the deputy.

The car shook as if it were shaking itself to

death, and it coughed convulsively, and then it started up with a series of jerks and detonations, and disappeared in a screen of dust and black smoke.

Mr. Starbird offered to give me a lift home, and I got into the front seat beside him while the deputy from Mangol got in back. On the way up the hill, Mr. Starbird kept glancing at me and then smiling.

"I've never known a girl quite like you, Emily," he said. "Memorizing the books of the Bible in the hoosegow, wearing a buck-private hat."

I blushed darkly and felt like crying, but I was pleased when Mr. Starbird went on to say, "Yes, sir, Emily, you're going to go places. What was the book you were reading down at my place when you were wearing your father's Masonic fez?"[20] I grew prouder and prouder. "It isn't every girl of ten years of age who brushes up against some moonshiners with a record as long as your arm in the very same day that a couple of hillbilly fakers try to take her for a ride. Why, Emily, do you realize that if it hadn't of been for you, we might not have got rid of those birds till they'd set up shop and done a whole lot of mischief?"

"Really?" I said, not quite sure whether he was teasing me, and grinned, but did so looking out the window, so Mr. Starbird wouldn't see me.

Was I lucky that day! On the way home, I saw about ten people I knew, and waved and yelled at them, and when I was getting out in front of my house, Virgil Meade, with whom I had had an on-again off-again romance for some time and to whom I was not currently speaking, was passing by and he heard the sheriff say, "Come on down to jail tomorrow and we'll get some Dr. Pepper."

The sheriff's valedictory gave me a great prestige in the neighborhood, but it also put an end to my use of the jail as a library, because copycats began swarming to the courthouse and making so much racket in the waiting room that Mr. Starbird couldn't hear himself think, let alone follow Fu Manchu. And after a few weeks he had to post a notice forbidding anyone in the room except on business. Privately, he told me that he would just as lief let me read in one of the cells, but he was afraid word would leak out and it might be bad for my reputation. He was as sorry, he said, as he could be.

He wasn't half as sorry as I was. The snake season was still on in the mountains; Mrs. Looby hated me; Aunt Joey was visiting, and she and Mother were using the living room to cut out Butterick[21] patterns in; Stella had just got on to pig Latin and never shut her mouth for a minute. All the same, I memorized the books of the Bible, and I won the New Testament, and I'll tell you where I did my work—in the cemetery, under a shady tree, sitting beside the grave of an infant kinswoman of the sheriff, a late-nineteenth-century baby called Primrose Starbird.

---

**20.** *Masonic fez,* a red felt hat worn by members of the Freemasonry, an international secret society.

**21.** *Butterick,* brand name of a dress pattern.

# DISCUSSION

1. (a) What problems does Emily have to confront and what people must she battle whenever she tries to read? (b) Who is the one person who sympathizes with her? (c) Why does he do so, and how does he show his sympathy?

2. What chain of events on a hot Saturday leads Emily to her encounter with the Gerlashes?

3. (a) What picture of himself does Gerlash want to give? (b) How does he try to do this? (c) Show how his attempts are foiled, however inadvertently, by his daughter. (d) What does the contrast between Opal and Gerlash add to the story?

4. (a) In your opinion, what is funniest about "A Reading Problem"? (b) Does the humor in the story arise from an observation of life or from a distortion of it? Explain.

5. (a) Is this a purely humorous story, or are there undertones of sadness in it? (b) If the latter, from what does the sadness arise?

6. In this story—often in a single sentence—the narrator mixes a dignified vocabulary with a good many slang terms. For instance, in describing the li- brarian's reactions to finding a grinning Reddie at her desk, she says: "...in her wrath and dismay, she clutched her head in her hands and dislodged her hat and then her wig, so that a wide expanse of baldness showed, and everyone in the children's section dived into the stacks and went all to pieces." (a) Find other examples of such intermingling of formal and informal language. (b) Is the manner in which the narrator uses language appropriate to the nature of the story? Why or why not?

7. When the events described in the story took place, Emily was ten years old. How old does she seem to be when she is telling the story? In answering this question, consider the language she uses and the attitudes she displays toward Opal, Gerlash, and her younger self.

## JEAN STAFFORD

Jean Stafford was born in California in 1915 and raised in Colorado. After earning degrees at the University of Colorado, she

studied for a year at Heidelberg University in Germany. She later taught at Stephens College in Missouri and worked for a time for the *Southern Review* magazine.

In 1945 she won an award from the National Institute of Arts and Letters; in 1955 she won the O'Henry Memorial Award for the best short story of the year. Ten of her stories are collected in *Children Are Bored on Sunday.*

Miss Stafford writes frequently for *The New Yorker,* and her book reviews appear from time to time in the book sections of several newspapers.

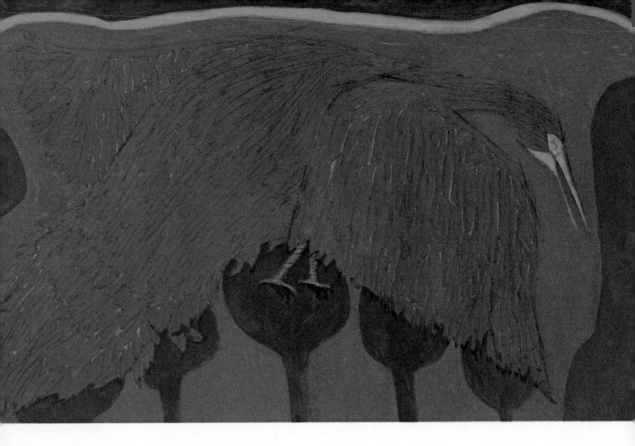

# The Scarlet Ibis

James Hurst

**How was he to know where love ended and cruelty began, or that pride is a seed bearing two vines, life and death?**

It was in the clove of seasons,[1] summer was dead but autumn had not yet been born, that the ibis lit in the bleeding tree. The flower garden was stained with rotting brown magnolia petals and ironweeds grew rank amid the purple phlox. The five o'clocks by the chimney still marked time, but the oriole nest in the elm was untenanted and rocked back and forth like an empty cradle. The last graveyard flowers were blooming, and their smell drifted across the cotton field and through every room of our house, speaking softly the names of our dead.

It's strange that all this is still so clear to me, now that that summer has long since fled and time has had its way. A grindstone stands where the bleeding tree stood, just outside the kitchen door, and now if an oriole sings in the elm, its song seems to die up in the leaves, a silvery dust. The flower garden is prim, the house a gleaming white, and the pale fence across the yard stands straight and spruce. But sometimes (like right now), as I sit in the cool, green-draped parlor, the grindstone

---

1. *clove of seasons,* the interval between two seasons.

begins to turn, and time with all its changes is ground away—and I remember Doodle.

Doodle was just about the craziest brother a boy ever had. Of course, he wasn't a crazy crazy like old Miss Leedie, who was in love with President Wilson and wrote him a letter every day, but was a nice crazy, like someone you meet in your dreams. He was born when I was six and was, from the outset, a disappointment. He seemed all head, with a tiny body which was red and shriveled like an old man's. Everybody thought he was going to die—everybody except Aunt Nicey, who had delivered him. She said he would live because he was born in a caul and cauls were made from Jesus' nightgown. Daddy had Mr. Heath, the carpenter, build a little mahogany coffin for him. But he didn't die, and when he was three months old Mama and Daddy decided they might as well name him. They named him William Armstrong, which was like tying a big tail on a small kite. Such a name sounds good only on a tombstone.

I thought myself pretty smart at many things, like holding my breath, running, jumping, or climbing the vines in Old Woman Swamp, and I wanted more than anything else someone to race to Horsehead Landing, someone to box with, and someone to perch with in the top fork of the great pine behind the barn, where across the fields and swamps you could see the sea. I wanted a brother. But Mama, crying, told me that even if William Armstrong lived, he would never do these things with me. He might not, she sobbed, even be "all there." He might, as long as he lived, lie on the rubber sheet in the center of the bed in the front bedroom where the white marquisette curtains billowed out in the afternoon sea breeze, rustling like palmetto fronds.

It was bad enough having an invalid brother, but having one who possibly was not all there was unbearable, so I began to make plans to kill him by smothering him with a pillow. However, one afternoon as I watched him, my head poked between the iron posts of the foot of the bed, he looked straight at me and grinned. I skipped through the rooms, down the echoing halls, shouting, "Mama, he smiled. He's all there! He's all there!" and he was.

When he was two, if you laid him on his stomach, he began to try to move himself, straining terribly. The doctor said that with his weak heart this strain would probably kill him, but it didn't. Trembling, he'd push himself up, turning first red, then a soft purple, and finally collapse back onto the bed like an old worn-out doll. I can still see Mama watching him, her hand pressed tight across her mouth, her eyes wide and unblinking. But he learned to crawl (it was his third winter), and we brought him out of the front bedroom, putting him on the rug before the fireplace. For the first time he became one of us.

As long as he lay all the time in bed, we called him William Armstrong, even though it was formal and sounded as if we were referring to one of our ancestors, but with his creeping around on the deerskin rug and beginning to talk, something had to be done about his name. It was I who renamed him. When he crawled, he crawled backwards, as if he were in reverse and couldn't change gears. If you called him, he'd turn around as if he were going in the other direction, then he'd back right up to you to be picked up. Crawling backward made him look like a doodlebug, so I began to call him Doodle, and in time even Mama and Daddy thought it was a better name than William Armstrong. Only Aunt Nicey disagreed. She said caul babies should be treated with special respect since they might turn out to be saints. Renaming my brother was perhaps the kindest thing I ever did for him, because nobody expects much from someone called Doodle.

Although Doodle learned to crawl, he showed no signs of walking, but he wasn't idle. He talked so much that we all quit listening to what he said. It was about this time that Daddy built him a go-cart and I had to pull him around. At first I just paraded him up and down the piazza, but then he started crying to be taken out into the yard and it ended up by my having to lug him wherever I went. If I so much as picked up my cap, he'd start crying to go with me and Mama would call from wherever she was, "Take Doodle with you."

He was a burden in many ways. The doctor

had said that he mustn't get too excited, too hot, too cold, or too tired and that he must always be treated gently. A long list of don'ts went with him, all of which I ignored once we got out of the house. To discourage his coming with me, I'd run with him across the ends of the cotton rows and careen him around corners on two wheels. Sometimes I accidentally turned him over, but he never told Mama. His skin was very sensitive, and he had to wear a big straw hat whenever he went out. When the going got rough and he had to cling to the sides of the go-cart, the hat slipped all the way down over his ears. He was a sight. Finally, I could see I was licked. Doodle was my brother and he was going to cling to me forever, no matter what I did, so I dragged him across the burning cotton field to share with him the only beauty I knew, Old Woman Swamp. I pulled the go-cart through the saw-tooth fern, down into the green dimness where the palmetto fronds whispered by the stream. I lifted him out and set him down in the soft rubber grass beside a tall pine. His eyes were round with wonder as he gazed about him, and his little hands began to stroke the rubber grass. Then he began to cry.

"For heaven's sake, what's the matter?" I asked, annoyed.

"It's so pretty," he said. "So pretty, pretty, pretty."

After that day Doodle and I often went down into Old Woman Swamp. I would gather wildflowers, wild violets, honeysuckle, yellow jasmine, snakeflowers, and water lilies, and with wire grass we'd weave them into necklaces and crowns. We'd bedeck ourselves with our handiwork and loll about thus beautified, beyond the touch of the everyday world. Then when the slanted rays of the sun burned orange in the tops of the pines, we'd drop our jewels into the stream and watch them float away toward the sea.

There is within me (and with sadness I have watched it in others) a knot of cruelty borne by the stream of love, much as our blood sometimes bears the seed of our destruction, and at times I was mean to Doodle. One day I took him up to the barn loft and showed him his casket, telling him how we all had believed he would die. It was covered with a film of Paris green[2] sprinkled to kill the rats, and screech owls had built a nest inside it.

Doodle studied the mahogany box for a long time, then said, "It's not mine."

"It is," I said. "And before I'll help you down from the loft, you're going to have to touch it."

"I won't touch it," he said sullenly.

"Then I'll leave you here by yourself," I threatened, and made as if I were going down.

Doodle was frightened of being left. "Don't go leave me, Brother," he cried, and he leaned toward the coffin. His hand, trembling, reached out, and when he touched the casket he screamed. A screech owl flapped out of the box into our faces, scaring us and covering us with Paris green. Doodle was paralyzed, so I put him on my shoulder and carried him down the ladder, and even when we were outside in the bright sunshine, he clung to me, crying, "Don't leave me. Don't leave me."

When Doodle was five years old, I was embarrassed at having a brother of that age who couldn't walk, so I set out to teach him. We were down in Old Woman Swamp and it was spring and the sick-sweet smell of bay flowers hung everywhere like a mournful song. "I'm going to teach you to walk, Doodle," I said.

He was sitting comfortably on the soft grass, leaning back against the pine. "Why?" he asked.

I hadn't expected such an answer. "So I won't have to haul you around all the time."

"I can't walk, Brother," he said.

"Who says so?" I demanded.

"Mama, the doctor—everybody."

"Oh, you can walk," I said, and I took him by the arms and stood him up. He collapsed onto the grass like a half-empty flour sack. It was as if he had no bones in his little legs.

"Don't hurt me, Brother," he warned.

"Shut up. I'm not going to hurt you. I'm going to teach you to walk." I heaved him up again, and again he collapsed.

This time he did not lift his face up out of the

2. *Paris green*, a poisonous emerald-green powder used to kill insects.

rubber grass. "I just can't do it. Let's make honeysuckle wreaths."

"Oh yes you can, Doodle," I said. "All you got to do is try. Now come on," and I hauled him up once more.

It seemed so hopeless from the beginning that it's a miracle I didn't give up. But all of us must have something or someone to be proud of, and Doodle had become mine. I did not know then that pride is a wonderful, terrible thing, a seed that bears two vines, life and death. Every day that summer we went to the pine beside the stream of Old Woman Swamp, and I put him on his feet at least a hundred times each afternoon. Occasionally I too became discouraged because it didn't seem as if he was trying, and I would say, "Doodle, don't you *want* to learn to walk?"

He'd nod his head, and I'd say, "Well, if you don't keep trying, you'll never learn." Then I'd paint for him a picture of us as old men, white-haired, him with a long white beard and me still pulling him around in the go-cart. This never failed to make him try again.

Finally one day, after many weeks of practicing, he stood alone for a few seconds. When he fell, I grabbed him in my arms and hugged him, our laughter pealing through the swamp like a ringing bell. Now we knew it could be done. Hope no longer hid in the dark palmetto thicket but perched like a cardinal in the lacy toothbrush tree, brilliantly visible. "Yes, yes," I cried, and he cried it too, and the grass beneath us was soft and the smell of the swamp was sweet.

With success so imminent, we decided not to tell anyone until he could actually walk. Each day, barring rain, we sneaked into Old Woman Swamp, and by cotton-picking time Doodle was ready to show what he could do. He still wasn't able to walk far, but we could wait no longer. Keeping a nice secret is very hard to do, like holding your breath. We chose to reveal all on October eighth, Doodle's sixth birthday, and for weeks ahead we mooned around the house, promising everybody a most spectacular surprise. Aunt Nicey said that, after so much talk, if we produced anything less tremendous than the Resurrection, she was going to be disappointed.

At breakfast on our chosen day, when Mama, Daddy, and Aunt Nicey were in the dining room, I brought Doodle to the door in the go-cart just as usual and had them turn their backs, making them cross their hearts and hope to die if they peeked. I helped Doodle up, and when he was standing alone I let them look. There wasn't a sound as Doodle walked slowly across the room and sat down at his place at the table. Then Mama began to cry and ran over to him, hugging him and kissing him. Daddy hugged him too, so I went to Aunt Nicey, who was thanks praying in the doorway, and began to waltz her around. We danced together quite well until she came down on my big toe with her brogans, hurting me so badly I thought I was crippled for life.

Doodle told them it was I who had taught him to walk, so everyone wanted to hug me, and I began to cry.

"What are you crying for?" asked Daddy, but I couldn't answer. They did not know that I did it for myself; that pride, whose slave I was, spoke to me louder than all their voices, and that Doodle walked only because I was ashamed of having a crippled brother.

Within a few months Doodle had learned to walk well and his go-cart was put up in the barn loft (it's still there) beside his little mahogany coffin. Now, when we roamed off together, resting often, we never turned back until our destination had been reached, and to help pass the time, we took up lying. From the beginning Doodle was a terrible liar and he got me in the habit. Had anyone stopped to listen to us, we would have been sent off to Dix Hill.

My lies were scary, involved, and usually pointless, but Doodle's were twice as crazy. People in his stories all had wings and flew wherever they wanted to go. His favorite lie was about a boy named Peter who had a pet peacock with a ten-foot tail. Peter wore a golden robe that glittered so brightly that when he walked through the sunflowers they turned away from the sun to face him. When Peter was ready to go to sleep, the peacock spread his magnificent tail, enfolding the boy gently like a closing go-to-sleep flower, burying him in the gloriously iridescent, rustling vortex.

Yes, I must admit it. Doodle could beat me lying.

Doodle and I spent lots of time thinking about our future. We decided that when we were grown we'd live in Old Woman Swamp and pick dog-tongue for a living. Beside the stream, he planned, we'd build us a house of whispering leaves and the swamp birds would be our chickens. All day long (when we weren't gathering dog-tongue) we'd swing through the cypresses on the rope vines, and if it rained we'd huddle beneath an umbrella tree and play stickfrog. Mama and Daddy could come and live with us if they wanted to. He even came up with the idea that he could marry Mama and I could marry Daddy. Of course, I was old enough to know this wouldn't work out, but the picture he painted was so beautiful and serene that all I could do was whisper Yes, yes.

Once I had succeeded in teaching Doodle to walk, I began to believe in my own infallibility and I prepared a terrific development program for him, unknown to Mama and Daddy, of course. I would teach him to run, to swim, to climb trees, and to fight. He, too, now believed in my infallibility, so we set the deadline for these accomplishments less than a year away, when, it had been decided, Doodle could start to school.

That winter we didn't make much progress, for I was in school and Doodle suffered from one bad cold after another. But when spring came, rich and warm, we raised our sights again. Success lay at the end of summer like a pot of gold, and our campaign got off to a good start. On hot days, Doodle and I went down to Horsehead Landing and I gave him swimming lessons or showed him how to row a boat. Sometimes we descended into the cool greenness of Old Woman Swamp and climbed the rope vines or boxed scientifically beneath the pine where he had learned to walk. Promise hung about us like the leaves, and wherever we looked, ferns unfurled and birds broke into song.

That summer, the summer of 1918, was blighted. In May and June there was no rain and the crops withered, curled up, then died under the thirsty sun. One morning in July a hurricane came out of the east, tipping over the oaks in the yard and splitting the limbs of the elm trees. That afternoon it roared back out of the west, blew the fallen oaks around, snapping their roots and tearing them out of the earth like a hawk at the entrails of a chicken. Cotton bolls were wrenched from the stalks and lay like green walnuts in the valleys between the rows, while the cornfield leaned over uniformly so that the tassels touched the ground. Doodle and I followed Daddy out into the cotton field, where he stood, shoulders sagging, surveying the ruin. When his chin sank down onto his chest, we were frightened, and Doodle slipped his hand into mine. Suddenly Daddy straightened his shoulders, raised a giant knuckly fist, and with a voice that seemed to rumble out of the earth itself began cursing heaven, hell, the weather, and the Republican Party. Doodle and I, prodding each other and giggling, went back to the house, knowing that everything would be all right.

And during that summer, strange names were heard through the house: Château-Thierry, Amiens, Soissons, and in her blessing at the supper table, Mama once said, "And bless the Pearsons, whose boy Joe was lost at Belleau Wood."[3]

So we came to that clove of seasons. School was only a few weeks away, and Doodle was far behind schedule. He could barely clear the ground when climbing up the rope vines and his swimming was certainly not passable. We decided to double our efforts, to make that last drive and reach our pot of gold. I made him swim until he turned blue and row until he couldn't lift an oar. Wherever we went, I purposely walked fast, and although he kept up, his face turned red and his eyes became glazed. Once, he could go no further, so he collapsed on the ground and began to cry.

"Aw, come on, Doodle," I urged. "You can do it. Do you want to be different from everybody else when you start school?"

"Does it make any difference?"

"It certainly does," I said. "Now, come on," and I helped him up.

---

3. *Château-Thierry* (sha tō′ tyär′i *or* shä tō′ tye rē′), *Amiens* (am′i ənz *or* ä myaɴ′), *Soissons* (swä sôɴ′), *Belleau* (bel ō′) *Wood*, French locations in or near which World War I battles were fought.

As we slipped through dog days, Doodle began to look feverish, and Mama felt his forehead, asking him if he felt ill. At night he didn't sleep well, and sometimes he had nightmares, crying out until I touched him and said, "Wake up, Doodle. Wake up."

It was Saturday noon, just a few days before school was to start. I should have already admitted defeat, but my pride wouldn't let me. The excitement of our program had now been gone for weeks, but still we kept on with a tired doggedness. It was too late to turn back, for we had both wandered too far into a net of expectations and had left no crumbs behind.

Daddy, Mama, Doodle, and I were seated at the dining-room table having lunch. It was a hot day, with all the windows and doors open in case a breeze should come. In the kitchen Aunt Nicey was humming softly. After a long silence, Daddy spoke. "It's so calm, I wouldn't be surprised if we had a storm this afternoon."

"I haven't heard a rain frog," said Mama, who believed in signs, as she served the bread around the table.

"I did," declared Doodle. "Down in the swamp."

"He didn't," I said contrarily.

"You did, eh?" said Daddy, ignoring my denial.

"I certainly did," Doodle reiterated, scowling at me over the top of his iced-tea glass, and we were quiet again.

Suddenly, from out in the yard, came a strange croaking noise. Doodle stopped eating, with a piece of bread poised ready for his mouth, his eyes popped round like two blue buttons. "What's that?" he whispered.

I jumped up, knocking over my chair, and had reached the door when Mama called, "Pick up the chair, sit down again, and say excuse me."

By the time I had done this, Doodle had excused himself and had slipped out into the yard. He was looking up into the bleeding tree. "It's a great big red bird!" he called.

The bird croaked loudly again, and Mama and Daddy came out into the yard. We shaded our eyes with our hands against the hazy glare of the sun and peered up through the still leaves. On the topmost branch a bird the size of a chicken, with scarlet feathers and long legs, was perched precariously. Its wings hung down loosely, and as we watched, a feather dropped away and floated slowly down through the green leaves.

"It's not even frightened of us," Mama said.

"It looks tired," Daddy added. "Or maybe sick."

Doodle's hands were clasped at his throat, and I had never seen him stand still so long. "What is it?" he asked.

Daddy shook his head. "I don't know, maybe it's——"

At that moment the bird began to flutter, but the wings were uncoordinated, and amid much flapping and a spray of flying feathers, it tumbled down, bumping through the limbs of the bleeding tree and landing at our feet with a thud. Its long, graceful neck jerked twice into an S, then straightened out, and the bird was still. A white veil came over the eyes and the long white beak unhinged. Its legs were crossed and its clawlike feet were delicately curved at rest. Even death did not mar its grace, for it lay on the earth like a broken vase of red flowers, and we stood around it, awed by its exotic beauty.

"It's dead," Mama said.

"What is it?" Doodle repeated.

"Go bring me the bird book," said Daddy.

I ran into the house and brought back the bird book. As we watched, Daddy thumbed through its pages. "It's a scarlet ibis," he said, pointing to a picture. "It lives in the tropics— South America to Florida. A storm must have brought it here."

Sadly, we all looked back at the bird. A scarlet ibis! How many miles it had traveled to die like this, in *our* yard, beneath the bleeding tree.

"Let's finish lunch," Mama said, nudging us back toward the dining room.

"I'm not hungry," said Doodle, and he knelt down beside the ibis.

"We've got peach cobbler for dessert," Mama tempted from the doorway.

Doodle remained kneeling. "I'm going to bury him."

"Don't you dare touch him," Mama warned.

"There's no telling what disease he might have had."

"All right," said Doodle. "I won't."

Daddy, Mama, and I went back to the dining-room table, but we watched Doodle through the open door. He took out a piece of string from his pocket and, without touching the ibis, looped one end around its neck. Slowly, while singing softly "Shall We Gather at the River,"[4] he carried the bird around to the front yard and dug a hole in the flower garden, next to the petunia bed. Now we were watching him through the front window, but he didn't know it. His awkwardness at digging the hole with a shovel whose handle was twice as long as he was made us laugh, and we covered our mouths with our hands so he wouldn't hear.

When Doodle came into the dining room, he found us seriously eating our cobbler. He was pale and lingered just inside the screen door. "Did you get the scarlet ibis buried?" asked Daddy.

Doodle didn't speak but nodded his head.

"Go wash your hands, and then you can have some peach cobbler," said Mama.

"I'm not hungry," he said.

"Dead birds is bad luck," said Aunt Nicey poking her head from the kitchen door. "Specially *red* dead birds!"

As soon as I had finished eating, Doodle and I hurried off to Horsehead Landing. Time was short, and Doodle still had a long way to go if he was going to keep up with the other boys when he started school. The sun, gilded with the yellow cast of autumn, still burned fiercely, but the dark green woods through which we passed were shady and cool. When we reached the landing, Doodle said he was too tired to swim, so we got into a skiff and floated down the creek with the tide. Far off in the marsh a rail was scolding, and over on the beach locusts were singing in the myrtle trees. Doodle did not speak and kept his head turned away, letting one hand trail limply in the water.

After we had drifted a long way, I put the oars in place and made Doodle row back against the tide. Black clouds began to gather

---

4. *"Shall We Gather at the River,"* a popular hymn sung in many churches a generation or so ago.

in the southwest, and he kept watching them, trying to pull the oars a little faster. When we reached Horsehead Landing, lightning was playing across half the sky and thunder roared out, hiding even the sound of the sea. The sun disappeared and darkness descended, almost like night. Flocks of marsh crows flew by, heading inland to their roosting trees, and two egrets, squawking, arose from the oyster-rock shallows and careened away.

Doodle was both tired and frightened, and when he stepped from the skiff he collapsed onto the mud, sending an armada of fiddler crabs rustling off into the marsh grass. I helped him up, and as he wiped the mud off his trousers, he smiled at me ashamedly. He had failed and we both knew it, so we started back home, racing the storm. We never spoke (What are the words that can solder cracked pride?), but I knew he was watching me, watching for a sign of mercy. The lightning was near now, and from fear he walked so close behind me he kept stepping on my heels. The faster I walked, the faster he walked, so I began to run. The rain was coming, roaring through the pines, and then like a bursting Roman candle, a gum tree ahead of us was shattered by a bolt of lightning. When the deafening peal of thunder had died, and in the moment before the rain arrived, I heard Doodle, who had fallen behind, cry out, "Brother, Brother, don't leave me! Don't leave me!"

The knowledge that Doodle's and my plans had come to naught was bitter, and that streak of cruelty within me awakened. I ran as fast as I could, leaving him far behind with a wall of rain dividing us. The drops stung my face like nettles, and the wind flared the wet glistening leaves of the bordering trees. Soon I could hear his voice no more.

I hadn't run too far before I became tired, and the flood of childish spite evanesced as well. I stopped and waited for Doodle. The sound of rain was everywhere, but the wind had died and it fell straight down in parallel paths like ropes hanging from the sky. As I waited, I peered through the downpour, but no one came. Finally I went back and found him huddled beneath a red nightshade bush beside the road. He was sitting on the ground, his face buried in his arms, which were resting on his drawn-up knees. "Let's go, Doodle," I said.

He didn't answer, so I placed my hand on his forehead and lifted his head. Limply, he fell backwards onto the earth. He had been bleeding from the mouth, and his neck and the front of his shirt were stained a brilliant red.

"Doodle! Doodle!" I cried, shaking him, but there was no answer but the ropy rain. He lay very awkwardly, with his head thrown far back, making his vermilion neck appear unusually long and slim. His little legs, bent sharply at the knees, had never before seemed so fragile, so thin.

I began to weep, and the tear-blurred vision in red before me looked very familiar. "Doodle!" I screamed above the pounding storm and threw my body to the earth above his. For a long long time, it seemed forever, I lay there crying, sheltering my fallen scarlet ibis from the heresy of rain.

---

## DISCUSSION

1. Explain why Doodle is different from other boys' brothers.

2. How do you feel about the narrator's attitude toward Doodle?

3. (a) Describe the progress that the narrator makes with Doodle. Is this really progress? Explain. (b) What motivated the narrator to teach his brother to walk?

4. (a) Outline the circumstances leading to the death of Doodle. (b) How much is the narrator to blame? Do you blame him or do you pity him? Explain your reactions.

---

### Symbolism in "The Scarlet Ibis"

Writers frequently use symbols for the presentation of ideas. James Hurst, for instance, provides some insight into the symbolism in his story:

"I wanted a bird," he said, "to represent Doodle—not Doodle's physical self, but his spirit. Certainly, Doodle inside had much more to admire than his outside. It was Doodle inside which was so rare, so courageous, so beautiful.

"This bird must be destined to die as Doodle was to die. A local bird, in order to die, would have to be sick. Was the ibis sick? Was Doodle inside sick? If the ibis had been back in a mangrove swamp, would it have died? Could not perhaps Doodle in another society have survived?

"The ancient Egyptians worshiped the ibis because, they said, it destroyed the crocodiles. In their liturgy, it took second place only to the phoenix. So I chose as my symbol a scarlet ibis, the most beautiful and rare member of the ibis family, exotic to the point of bizarrerie.

"To further my symbolism, Doodle unconsciously identifies himself with the scarlet ibis and at the very end his outside comes to resemble the bird when he dies in the same position the bird died, with the front of his shirt stained with blood."

From this explanation we can conclude that a literary symbol, not only represents what it is (the scarlet ibis is indeed a bird with a functional part in the story), but also means something more (the ibis represents Doodle's spirit as well).

Mr. Hurst also explains the implied meaning of the story's time setting:

"The story was set in 1918 so that World War I would loom in the background, amid the other misfortunes, i.e., the drouth and the storm. A major cause of wars is the desire to transform others into one's own image, and Doodle's and his brother's struggle resembles on a minute, personal scale, the great war."

Finally, what do you think *is* the meaning of the story? The author tells us that there are three sentences very important to the meaning:

There is within me (and with sadness I have watched it in others) a knot of cruelty borne by the stream of love, much as our blood sometimes bears the seed of our destruction.

Pride is a wonderful, terrible thing, a seed that bears two vines, life and death.

Brother, Brother, don't leave me. Don't leave me.

"This last sentence," the author continues, "could almost be called Doodle's theme and I hear it as the classic cry of all mankind wishing to belong and never to be lonely."

# To Da-duh, in Memoriam

*Paule Marshall*

*. . . Da-duh stared at me as if I were a creature from Mars, an emissary from some world she did not know which intrigued her and whose power she both felt and feared.*

". . . Oh Nana! all of you is not involved in this evil business
      Death,
Nor all of us in Life."
—From "At My Grandmother's Grave," by Lebert Bethune

I did not see her at first I remember. For not only was it dark inside the crowded disembarkation shed in spite of the daylight flooding in from outside, but standing there waiting for her with my mother and sister I was still somewhat blinded from the sheen of tropical sunlight on the water of the bay which we had just crossed in the landing boat, leaving behind us the ship that had brought us from New York lying in the offing. Besides, being only nine years of age at the time and knowing nothing of islands I was busy attending to the alien sights and sounds of Barbados,[1] the unfamiliar smells.

I did not see her, but I was alerted to her approach by my mother's hand which suddenly tightened around mine, and looking up I traced her gaze through the gloom in the shed until I finally made out the small, purposeful, painfully erect figure of the old woman headed our way.

"To Da-duh, In Memoriam" by Paule Marshall. Copyright © 1967 by Paule Marshall. Reprinted by permission of Cyrilly Abels, Literary Agent.
**1.** *Barbados* (bär bā′dōz), an island in the West Indies.

Her face was drowned in the shadow of an ugly, rolled-brim, brown felt hat, but the details of her slight body and of the struggle taking place within it were clear enough—an intense, unrelenting struggle between her back, which was beginning to bend ever so slightly under the weight of her eighty-odd years, and the rest of her, which sought to deny those years and hold that back straight, keep it in line. Moving swiftly toward us (so swiftly it seemed she did not intend stopping when she reached us but would sweep past us out the doorway which opened onto the sea and like Christ walk upon the water!), she was caught between the sunlight at her end of the building and the darkness inside—and for a moment she appeared to contain them both: the light in the long severe old-fashioned white dress she wore which brought the sense of a past that was still alive into our bustling present and in the snatch of white at her eye; the darkness in her black high-top shoes and in her face which was visible now that she was closer.

It was as stark and fleshless as a death mask, that face. The maggots might have already done their work, leaving only the framework of bone beneath the ruined skin and deep wells at the temple and jaw. But her eyes were alive, unnervingly so for one so old, with a sharp light that flicked out of the dim clouded depths like a lizard's tongue to snap up all in her view. Those eyes betrayed a child's curiosity about the world, and I wondered vaguely seeing them, and seeing the way the bodice of her ancient dress had collapsed in on her flat chest (what had happened to her breasts?), whether she might not be some kind of child at the same time that she was a woman, with fourteen children, my mother included, to prove it. Perhaps she was both, both child and woman, darkness and light, past and present, life and death—all the opposites contained and reconciled in her.

"My Da-duh," my mother said formally and stepped forward. The name sounded like thunder fading softly in the distance.

"Child," Da-duh said, and her tone, her quick scrutiny of my mother, the brief embrace in which they appeared to shy from each other rather than touch, wiped out the fifteen years my mother had been away and restored the old relationship. My mother, who was such a formidable figure in my eyes, had suddenly with a word been reduced to my status.

"Yes, God is good," Da-duh said with a nod that was like a tic. "He has spared me to see my child again."

We were led forward then, apologetically because not only did Da-duh prefer boys but she also liked her grandchildren to be "white," that is, fair-skinned; and we had, I was to discover, a number of cousins, the outside children of white estate managers and the like, who qualified. We, though, were as black as she.

My sister being the oldest was presented first. "This one takes after the father," my mother said and waited to be reproved.

Frowning, Da-duh tilted my sister's face toward the light. But her frown soon gave way to a grudging smile, for my sister, with her large mild eyes and little broad-winged nose, with our father's high-cheeked Barbadian cast to her face, was pretty.

"She's goin' be lucky," Da-duh said and patted her once on the cheek. "Any girl-child that takes after the father does be lucky."

She turned then to me. But oddly enough she did not touch me. Instead, leaning close, she peered hard at me, and then quickly drew back. I thought I saw her hand start up as though to shield her eyes. It was almost as if she saw not only me, a thin, truculent child who it was said took after no one but myself, but something in me which for some reason she found disturbing, even threatening. We looked silently at each other there in the noisy shed, our gaze locked. She was the first to look away.

"But Adry," she said to my mother, and her laugh was cracked, thin, apprehensive. "Where did you get this one here with this fierce look?"

"We don't know where she came out of, my Da-duh," my mother said, laughing also. Even I smiled to myself. After all, I had won the encounter. Da-duh had recognized my small strength—and this was all I ever asked of the adults in my life then.

"Come, soul," Da-duh said and took my hand. "You must be one of those New York terrors you hear so much about."

She led us, me at her side and my sister and

mother behind, out of the shed into the sunlight that was like a bright driving summer rain and over to a group of people clustered beside a decrepit lorry.[2] They were our relatives, most of them from St. Andrews although Da-duh herself lived in St. Thomas,[3] the women wearing bright print dresses, the colors vivid against their darkness, the men rusty black suits that encased them like strait jackets. Da-duh, holding fast to my hand, became my anchor as they circled round us like a nervous sea, exclaiming, touching us with their calloused hands, embracing us shyly. They laughed in awed bursts: "But look Adry got big-big children!"/ "And see the nice things they wearing, wrist watch and all!"/ "I tell you, Adry has done all right for sheself in New York. . . ."

Da-duh, ashamed at their wonder, embarrassed for them, admonished them the while. "But oh Christ," she said, "why you all got to get on like you never saw people from 'Away' before? You would think New York is the only place in the world to hear wunna. That's why I don't like to go anyplace with you St. Andrews people, you know. You all ain't been colonized."

We were in the back of the lorry finally, packed in among the barrels of ham, flour, cornmeal, and rice, and the trunks of clothes that my mother had brought as gifts. We made our way slowly through Bridgetown's clogged streets, part of a funereal procession of cars and open-sided buses, bicycles, and donkey carts. The dim little limestone shops and offices along the way marched with us, at the same mournful pace, toward the same grave ceremony—as did the people, the women balancing huge baskets on top their heads as if they were no more than hats they wore to shade them from the sun. Looking over the edge of the lorry I watched as their feet slurred the dust. I listened, and their voices, raw and loud and dissonant in the heat, seemed to be grappling with each other high overhead.

Da-duh sat on a trunk in our midst, a monarch amid her court. She still held my hand, but it was different now. I had suddenly become her anchor, for I felt her fear of the lorry with its

asthmatic motor (a fear and distrust, I later learned, she held of all machines) beating like a pulse in her rough palm.

As soon as we left Bridgetown behind though, she relaxed, and while the others around us talked, she gazed at the canes standing tall on either side of the winding marl road. "C'dear," she said softly to herself after a time. "The canes this side are pretty enough."

They were too much for me. I thought of them as giant weeds that had overrun the island, leaving scarcely any room for the small tottering houses of sun-bleached pine we passed or the people, dark streaks as our lorry hurtled by. I suddenly feared that we were journeying, unaware that we were, toward some dangerous place where the canes, grown as high and thick as a forest, would close in on us and run us through with their stiletto blades. I longed then for the familiar: for the street in Brooklyn where I lived, for my father who had refused to accompany us ("Blowing out good money on foolishness," he had said of the trip), for a game of tag with my friends under the chestnut tree outside our aging brownstone house.

"Yes, but wait till you see St. Thomas canes," Da-duh was saying to me. "They's canes' father, bo," she gave a proud arrogant nod. "Tomorrow, God willing, I goin' take you out in the ground and show them to you."

True to her word, Da-duh took me with her the following day out into the ground. It was a fairly large plot adjoining her weathered board and shingle house and consisting of a small orchard, a good-sized canepiece, and behind the canes, where the land sloped abruptly down, a gully. She had purchased it with Panama money sent her by her eldest son, my uncle Joseph, who had died working on the canal. We entered the ground along a trail no wider than her body and as devious and complex as her reasons for showing me her land. Da-duh strode briskly ahead, her slight form filled out this morning by the layers of sacking petticoats she wore under her working dress to protect her against the damp. A fresh white cloth, elaborately arranged around her head, added to her height, and lent her a vain, almost roguish air.

Her pace slowed once we reached the orchard, and glancing back at me occasionally

---

2. *lorry*, a large motor truck. [British]
3. *St. Andrews . . . St. Thomas*, parishes (districts) in Barbados.

over her shoulder, she pointed out the various trees.

"This here is a breadfruit," she said. "That one yonder is a papaw. Here's a guava. This is a mango. I know you don't have anything like these in New York. Here's a sugar apple (the fruit looked more like artichokes than apples to me). This one bears limes. . . ." She went on for some time, intoning the names of the trees as though they were those of her gods. Finally, turning to me, she said, "I know you don't have anything this nice where you come from." Then, as I hesitated: "I said I know you don't have anything this nice where you come from. . . ."

"No," I said and my world did seem suddenly lacking.

Da-duh nodded and passed on. The orchard ended and we were on the narrow cart road that led through the canepiece, the canes clashing like swords above my cowering head. Again she turned and her thin muscular arms spread wide, her dim gaze embracing the small field of canes, she said—and her voice almost broke under the weight of her pride, "Tell me, have you got anything like these in that place where you were born?"

"No."

"I din' think so. I bet you don't even know that these canes here and the sugar you eat is one and the same thing. That they does throw the canes into some damn machine at the factory and squeeze out all the little life in them to make sugar for you all so in New York to eat. I bet you don't know that."

"I've got two cavities and I'm not allowed to eat a lot of sugar."

But Da-duh didn't hear me. She had turned with an inexplicably angry motion and was making her way rapidly out of the canes and down the slope at the edge of the field which led to the gully below. Following her apprehensively down the incline amid a stand of banana plants whose leaves flapped like elephants' ears in the wind, I found myself in the middle of a small tropical wood—a place dense and damp and gloomy and tremulous with the fitful play of light and shadow as the leaves high above moved against the sun that was almost hidden from view. It was a violent place, the tangled foliage fighting each other for a chance at the sunlight, the branches of the trees locked in what seemed an immemorial struggle, one both necessary and inevitable. But despite the violence, it was pleasant, almost peaceful in the gully, and beneath the thick undergrowth the earth smelled like spring.

This time Da-duh didn't even bother to ask her usual question, but simply turned and waited for me to speak.

"No," I said, my head bowed. "We don't have anything like this in New York."

"Ah," she cried, her triumph complete. "I din' think so. Why, I've heard that's a place where you can walk till you near drop and never see a tree."

"We've got a chestnut tree in front of our house," I said.

"Does it bear?" She waited. "I ask you, does it bear?"

"Not anymore," I muttered. "It used to, but not anymore."

She gave the nod that was like a nervous twitch. "You see," she said. "Nothing can bear there." Then, secure behind her scorn, she added, "But tell me, what's this snow like that you hear so much about?"

Looking up, I studied her closely, sensing my chance, and then I told her, describing at length and with as much drama as I could summon, not only what snow in the city was like, but what it would be like here, in her perennial summer kingdom.

". . . And you see all these trees you got here," I said. "Well, they'd be bare. No leaves, no fruit, nothing. They'd be covered in snow. You see your canes. They'd be buried under tons of snow. The snow would be higher than your head, higher than your house, and you wouldn't be able to come down into this here gully because it would be snowed under. . . ."

She searched my face for the lie, still scornful but intrigued. "What a thing, huh?" she said finally, whispering it softly to herself.

"And when it snows you couldn't dress like you are now," I said. "Oh no, you'd freeze to death. You'd have to wear a hat and gloves and galoshes and ear muffs so your ears wouldn't freeze and drop off, and a heavy coat. I've got a

Shirley Temple coat with fur on the collar. I can dance. You wanna see?"

Before she could answer I began, with a dance called the Truck which was popular back then in the 1930's. My right forefinger waving, I trucked around the nearby trees and around Da-duh's awed and rigid form. After the Truck I did the Suzy-Q, my lean hips swishing, my sneakers sidling zigzag over the ground. "I can sing," I said and did so, starting with "I'm Gonna Sit Right Down and Write Myself a Letter," then without pausing, "Tea For Two," and ending with "I Found a Million Dollar Baby in a Five and Ten Cent Store."

For long moments afterwards Da-duh stared at me as if I were a creature from Mars, an emissary from some world she did not know but which intrigued her and whose power she both felt and feared. Yet something about my performance must have pleased her, because bending down she slowly lifted her long skirt and then, one by one, the layers of petticoats until she came to a drawstring purse dangling at the end of a long strip of cloth tied round her waist. Opening the purse she handed me a penny. "Here," she said, half-smiling against her will. "Take this to buy yourself a sweet at the shop up the road. There's nothing to be done with you, soul."

From then on, whenever I wasn't taken to visit relatives, I accompanied Da-duh out into the ground, and alone with her amid the canes or down in the gully I told her about New York. It always began with some slighting remark on her part: "I know they don't have anything this nice where you come from," or "Tell me, I hear those foolish people in New York does do such and such. . . ." But as I answered, recreating my towering world of steel and concrete and machines for her, building the city out of words, I would feel her give way. I came to know the signs of her surrender: the total stillness that would come over her little hard dry form, the probing gaze that like a surgeon's knife sought to cut through my skull to get at the images there, to see if I were lying; above all, her fear, a fear nameless and profound, the same one I had felt beating in the palm of her hand that day in the lorry.

Over the weeks I told her about refrigerators, radios, gas stoves, elevators, trolley cars, wringer washing machines, movies, airplanes, the cyclone at Coney Island, subways, toasters, electric lights: "At night, see, all you have to do is flip this little switch on the wall and all the lights in the house go on. Just like that. Like magic. It's like turning on the sun at night."

"But tell me," she said to me once with a faint, mocking smile, "do the white people have all these things too, or it's only the people looking like us?"

I laughed. "What d'ya mean," I said. "The white people have even better." Then: "I beat up a white girl in my class last term."

"Beating up white people!" Her tone was incredulous.

"How you mean!" I said, using an expression of hers. "She called me a name."

For some reason Da-duh could not quite get over this and repeated in the same hushed, shocked voice, "Beating up white people now! Oh, the lord, the world's changing up so I can scarce recognize it anymore."

One morning toward the end of our stay, Da-duh led me into a part of the gully that we had never visited before, an area darker and more thickly overgrown than the rest, almost impenetrable. There in a small clearing amid the dense bush, she stopped before an incredibly tall royal palm which rose cleanly out of the ground, and drawing the eye up with it, soared high above the trees around it into the sky. It appeared to be touching the blue dome of sky, to be flaunting its dark crown of fronds right in the blinding white face of the late morning sun.

Da-duh watched me a long time before she spoke, and then she said very quietly, "All right, now, tell me if you've got anything this tall in that place you're from."

I almost wished, seeing her face, that I could have said no. "Yes," I said. "We've got buildings hundreds of times this tall in New York. There's one called the Empire State Building that's the tallest in the world. My class visited it last year and I went all the way to the top. It's got over a hundred floors. I can't describe how tall it is. Wait a minute. What's the name of that hill I went to visit the other day, where they have the police station?"

"You mean Bissex?"

"Yes, Bissex. Well, the Empire State Building is way taller than that."

"You're lying now!" she shouted, trembling with rage. Her hand lifted to strike me.

"No, I'm not," I said. "It really is. If you don't believe me I'll send you a picture post card of it soon as I get back home so you can see for yourself. But it's way taller than Bissex."

All the fight went out of her at that. The hand poised to strike me fell limp to her side, and as she stared at me, seeing not me but the building that was taller than the highest hill she knew, the small stubborn light in her eyes (it was the same amber as the flame in the kerosene lamp she lit at dusk) began to fail. Finally, with a vague gesture that even in the midst of her defeat still tried to dismiss me and my world, she turned and started back through the gully, walking slowly, her steps groping and uncertain, as if she was suddenly no longer sure of the way, while I followed triumphant yet strangely saddened behind.

The next morning I found her dressed for our morning walk but stretched out on the Berbice chair in the tiny drawing room where she sometimes napped during the afternoon heat, her face turned to the window beside her. She appeared thinner and suddenly indescribably old.

"My Da-duh," I said.

"Yes, nuh," she said. Her voice was listless and the face she slowly turned my way was, now that I think back on it, like a Benin mask,[4] the features drawn and almost distorted by an ancient abstract sorrow.

"Don't you feel well?" I asked.

"Girl, I don't know."

"My Da-duh, I goin' boil you some bush tea," my aunt, Da-duh's youngest child, who lived with her, called from the shed roof kitchen.

"Who tell you I need bush tea?" she cried, her voice assuming for a moment its old authority. "You can't even rest nowadays without some malicious person looking for you to be dead. Come girl," she motioned me to a place beside her on the old-fashioned lounge chair, "give us a tune."

I sang for her until breakfast at eleven, all my brash, irreverent tin-pan-alley songs, and then just before noon we went out into the ground. But it was a short, dispirited walk. Da-duh didn't even notice that the mangoes were beginning to ripen and would have to be picked before the village boys got to them. And when she paused occasionally and looked out across the canes or up at her trees it wasn't as if she were seeing them but something else. Some huge, monolithic shape had imposed itself, it seemed, between her and the land, obstructing her vision. Returning to the house she slept the entire afternoon on the Berbice chair.

She remained like this until we left, languishing away the morning on the chair at the window, gazing out at the land as if it were already doomed; then, at noon, taking the brief stroll with me through the ground during which she seldom spoke, and afterwards returning home to sleep till almost dusk sometimes.

On the day of our departure she put on the austere, ankle-length white dress, the black shoes and brown felt hat (her town clothes she called them), but she did not go with us to town. She saw us off on the road outside her house and in the midst of my mother's tearful, protracted farewell, she leaned down and whispered in my ear, "Girl, you're not to forget now to send me the picture of that building, you hear."

By the time I mailed her the large colored picture post card of the Empire State Building she was dead. She died during the famous '37 strike[5] which began shortly after we left. On the day of her death England sent planes flying low over the island in a show of force— so low, according to my aunt's letter, that the downdraft from them shook the ripened mangoes from the trees in Da-duh's orchard. Frightened, everyone in the village fled into the canes. Except Da-duh. She remained in the house at the window so my aunt said, watching as the planes came swooping and screaming like monstrous birds down over the village, over her house, rattling her trees and

---

4. *Benin mask* (be nēn′), a mask sculpted by natives of Benin, formerly a kingdom in West Africa, now a district in Nigeria.

5. *the famous '37 strike.* In 1937 during the world wide depression, poor economic conditions in Barbados, then a British colony, led to strikes, riots, and other disorders, with the people demanding better living conditions and political rights.

flattening the young canes in her field. It must have seemed to her lying there that they did not intend pulling out of their dive, but like the hardback beetles which hurled themselves with suicidal force against the walls of the house at night, those menacing silver shapes would hurl themselves in an ecstasy of self-immolation onto the land, destroying it utterly.

When the planes finally left and the villagers returned, they found her dead on the Berbice chair at the window.

She died and I lived, but always, to this day even, within the shadow of her death. For a brief period after I was grown I went to live alone, like one doing penance, in a loft above a noisy factory in downtown New York and there painted seas of sugar cane and huge swirling Van Gogh suns[6] and palm trees striding like brightly-plumed Watusi[7] across a tropical landscape, while the thunderous tread of the machines downstairs jarred the floor beneath my easel, mocking my efforts.

---

6. *swirling Van Gogh suns*, suns painted in the style of the Dutch painter Vincent van Gogh (van gō′), probably with swirling brushstrokes of brilliant yellows and oranges.
7. *Watusi* (wä tü′ sē), a people in central Africa known especially for their exceptional height and slenderness (many are over six feet six inches tall).

---

## DISCUSSION

There follow a number of quotations, some of which come directly from "To Da-duh, in Memoriam," some of which are comments about the story. Try to explain in your own words the meaning of each passage as it relates to the story.

1. "Perhaps she was both, both child and woman, darkness and light, past and present, life and death—all the opposites contained and reconciled in her."

2. Throughout the story, one can sense a conflict between nature and technology, the familiar and the unknown, the traditional and the modern, the old and the young—a conflict represented by the relationship between Da-duh and her granddaughter.

3. She had pride—yes, much of that; and curiosity, almost to the very end. But the fear of having been passed by, of living in an old world when a new one had been built, that's what finally killed her.

4. It was only appropriate that she die on the day she did.

5. "For a brief period after I was grown I went to live alone like one doing penance, in a loft above a noisy factory in downtown New York and there painted seas of sugar cane and huge swirling Van Gogh suns and palm trees striding like brightly-plumed Watusi across a tropical landscape, while the thunderous tread of the machines downstairs jarred the floor beneath my easel, mocking my efforts."

## PAULE MARSHALL

Asphalt and canebrake, Brooklyn and Barbados are the elements that have influenced Paule Marshall's life and shaped her writing. She first encountered her West Indian heritage at nine on the trip remembered in "To Da-duh, in Memoriam." This visit inspired a notebook of poetry and the paintings mentioned in the story. With subsequent visits, she made West Indian life and people increasingly important in her stories.

Her first novel, *Brown Girl, Brownstones* portrays the experiences of a family which had, like hers, left Barbados for Brooklyn and found the transition difficult.

After graduating from Brooklyn College, Paule Marshall married, worked in several libraries, and wrote feature articles for *Our World* magazine. *Soul Clap Hands and Sing*, a collection of four novellas, was published in 1961. In 1969 she published *Chosen Place, the Timeless People*, a novel set in the West Indies.

# The Fifty-first Dragon

*Heywood Broun*

*"I've forgotten the magic word," stammered Gawaine.*
*"What a pity," said the dragon.*

OF all the pupils at the knight school Gawaine le Coeur-Hardy was among the least promising. He was tall and sturdy, but his instructors soon discovered that he lacked spirit. He would hide in the woods when the jousting[1] class was called, although his companions and members of the faculty sought to appeal to his better nature by shouting to him to come out and break his neck like a man. Even when they told him that the lances were padded, the horses no more than ponies and the field unusually soft for late autumn, Gawaine refused to grow enthusiastic. The Headmaster and the Assistant Professor of Pleasaunce were discussing the case one spring afternoon and the Assistant Professor could see no remedy but expulsion.

"No," said the Headmaster, as he looked out at the purple hills which ringed the school, "I think I'll train him to slay dragons."

"He might be killed," objected the Assistant Professor.

"So he might," replied the Headmaster brightly, but he added, more soberly, "we must consider the greater good. We are responsible for the formation of this lad's character."

"Are the dragons particularly bad this year?" interrupted the Assistant Professor. This was

1. *jousting*, fighting with lances on horseback.

characteristic. He always seemed restive when the head of the school began to talk ethics and the ideals of the institution.

"I've never known them worse," replied the Headmaster. "Up in the hills to the south last week they killed a number of peasants, two cows, and a prize pig. And if this dry spell holds there's no telling when they may start a forest fire simply by breathing around indiscriminately."

"Would any refund on the tuition fee be necessary in case of an accident to young Coeur-Hardy?"

"No," the principal answered, judicially, "that's all covered in the contract. But as a matter of fact he won't be killed. Before I send him up in the hills I'm going to give him a magic word."

"That's a good idea," said the Professor. "Sometimes they work wonders."

From that day on Gawaine specialized in dragons. His course included both theory and practice. In the morning there were long lectures on the history, anatomy, manners, and customs of dragons. Gawaine did not distinguish himself in these studies. He had a marvelously versatile gift for forgetting things. In the afternoon he showed to better advantage, for then he would go down to the South Meadow and practice with a battle-ax. In this exercise he was truly impressive, for he had enormous strength as well as speed and grace. He even developed a deceptive display of ferocity. Old alumni say that it was a thrilling sight to see Gawaine charging across the field toward the dummy paper dragon which had been set up for his practice. As he ran he would brandish his ax and shout, "A murrain on thee!"[2] or some other vivid bit of campus slang. It never took him more than one stroke to behead the dummy dragon.

Gradually his task was made more difficult. Paper gave way to papier-mâché[3] and finally to wood, but even the toughest of these dummy dragons had no terrors for Gawaine. One sweep of the ax always did the business. There

were those who said that when the practice was protracted until dusk and the dragons threw long, fantastic shadows across the meadow, Gawaine did not charge so impetuously nor shout so loudly. It is possible there was malice in this charge. At any rate, the Headmaster decided by the end of June that it was time for the test. Only the night before a dragon had come close to the school grounds and had eaten some of the lettuce from the garden. The faculty decided that Gawaine was ready. They gave him a diploma and a new battle-ax and the Headmaster summoned him to a private conference.

"Sit down," said the Headmaster. "Have a cigarette."

Gawaine hesitated.

"Oh, I know it's against the rules," said the Headmaster. "But after all, you have received your preliminary degree. You are no longer a boy. You are a man. Tomorrow you will go out into the world, the great world of achievement."

Gawaine took a cigarette. The Headmaster offered him a match, but he produced one of his own and began to puff away with a dexterity which quite amazed the principal.

"Here you have learned the theories of life," continued the Headmaster, resuming the thread of his discourse, "but after all, life is not a matter of theories. Life is a matter of facts. It calls on the young and the old alike to face these facts, even though they are hard and sometimes unpleasant. Your problem, for example, is to slay dragons."

"They say that those dragons down in the south wood are five hundred feet long," ventured Gawaine, timorously.

"Stuff and nonsense!" said the Headmaster. "The curate saw one last week from the top of Arthur's Hill. The dragon was sunning himself down in the valley. The curate didn't have an opportunity to look at him very long because he felt it was his duty to hurry back to make a report to me. He said the monster— or shall I say, the big lizard?—wasn't an inch over two hundred feet. But the size has nothing at all to do with it. You'll find the big ones even easier than the little ones. They're far slower on their feet and less aggressive, I'm

---

2. *A murrain* (mĕr′ən) *on thee!* A plague on you! An archaic expression.
3. *papier-mâché* (pā′pər mə shā′), a mixture of paper pulp and a stiffener. It can be molded when wet and becomes hard when dry.

told. Besides, before you go I'm going to equip you in such fashion that you need have no fear of all the dragons in the world."

"I'd like an enchanted cap," said Gawaine.

"What's that?" asked the Headmaster, testily.

"A cap to make me disappear," explained Gawaine.

The Headmaster laughed indulgently. "You mustn't believe all those old wives' stories," he said. "There isn't any such thing. A cap to make you disappear, indeed! What would you do with it? You haven't even appeared yet. Why, my boy, you could walk from here to London, and nobody would so much as look at you. You're nobody. You couldn't be more invisible than that."

Gawaine seemed dangerously close to a relapse into his old habit of whimpering. The Headmaster reassured him: "Don't worry; I'll give you something much better than an enchanted cap. I'm going to give you a magic word. All you have to do is to repeat this magic charm once and no dragon can possibly harm a hair of your head. You can cut off his head at your leisure."

He took a heavy book from the shelf behind his desk and began to run through it. "Sometimes," he said, "the charm is a whole phrase or even a sentence. I might, for instance, give you 'To make the'—no, that might not do. I think a single word would be best for dragons."

"A short word," suggested Gawaine.

"It can't be too short or it wouldn't be potent. There isn't so much hurry as all that. Here's a splendid magic word: 'Rumplesnitz.' Do you think you can learn that?"

Gawaine tried and in an hour or so he seemed to have the word well in hand. Again and again he interrupted the lesson to inquire, "And if I say 'Rumplesnitz' the dragon can't possibly hurt me?" And always the Headmaster replied, "If you only say 'Rumplesnitz,' you are perfectly safe."

Toward morning Gawaine seemed resigned to his career. At daybreak the Headmaster saw him to the edge of the forest and pointed him to the direction in which he should proceed. About a mile away to the southwest a cloud of steam hovered over an open meadow in the woods and the Headmaster assured Gawaine that under the steam he would find a dragon. Gawaine went forward slowly. He wondered whether it would be best to approach the dragon on the run as he did in his practice in the South Meadow or to walk slowly toward him, shouting "Rumplesnitz" all the way.

The problem was decided for him. No sooner had he come to the fringe of the meadow than the dragon spied him and began to charge. It was a large dragon and yet it seemed decidedly aggressive in spite of the Headmaster's statement to the contrary. As the dragon charged it released huge clouds of hissing steam through its nostrils. It was almost as if a gigantic teapot had gone mad. The dragon came forward so fast and Gawaine was so frightened that he had time to say "Rumplesnitz" only once. As he said it, he swung his battle-ax and off popped the head of the dragon. Gawaine had to admit that it was even easier to kill a real dragon than a wooden one if only you said "Rumplesnitz."

Gawaine brought the ears home and a small section of the tail. His schoolmates and the faculty made much of him, but the Headmaster wisely kept him from being spoiled by insisting that he go on with his work. Every clear day Gawaine rose at dawn and went out to kill dragons. The Headmaster kept him at home when it rained, because he said the woods were damp and unhealthy at such times and that he didn't want the boy to run needless risks. Few good days passed in which Gawaine failed to get a dragon. On one particularly fortunate day he killed three, a husband and wife and a visiting relative. Gradually he developed a technique. Pupils who sometimes watched him from the hilltops a long way off said that he often allowed the dragon to come within a few feet before he said "Rumplesnitz." He came to say it with a mocking sneer. Occasionally he did stunts. Once when an excursion party from London was watching him he went into action with his right hand tied behind his back. The dragon's head came off just as easily.

As Gawaine's record of killings mounted higher the Headmaster found it impossible to keep him completely in hand. He fell into the habit of stealing out at night and engaging in long drinking bouts at the village tavern. It was after such a debauch that he rose a little before dawn one fine August morning and started out after his fiftieth dragon. His head was heavy and his mind sluggish. He was heavy in other respects as well, for he had adopted the somewhat vulgar practice of wearing his medals, ribbons and all, when he went out dragon hunting. The decorations began on his chest and ran all the way down to his abdomen. They must have weighed at least eight pounds.

Gawaine found a dragon in the same meadow where he had killed the first one. It was a fair-sized dragon, but evidently an old one. Its face was wrinkled and Gawaine thought he had never seen so hideous a countenance. Much to the lad's disgust, the monster refused to charge and Gawaine was obliged to walk toward him. He whistled as he went. The dragon regarded him hopelessly, but craftily. Of course it had heard of Gawaine. Even when the lad raised his battle-ax the dragon made no move. It knew that there was no salvation in the quickest thrust of the head, for it had been informed that this hunter was protected by an enchantment. It merely waited, hoping something would turn up.

Gawaine raised the battle-ax and suddenly lowered it again. He had grown very pale and he trembled violently.

The dragon suspected a trick. "What's the matter?" it asked with false solicitude.

"I've forgotten the magic word," stammered Gawaine.

"What a pity," said the dragon. "So that was the secret. It doesn't seem quite sporting to me, all this magic stuff, you know. Not cricket, as we used to say when I was a little dragon; but after all, that's a matter of opinion."

Gawaine was so helpless with terror that the dragon's confidence rose immeasurably and it could not resist the temptation to show off a bit.

"Could I possibly be of any assistance?" it asked. "What's the first letter of the magic word?"

"It begins with an 'r,'" said Gawaine weakly.

"Let's see," mused the dragon, "that doesn't tell us much, does it? What sort of a word is this? Is it an epithet, do you think?"

Gawaine could do no more than nod.

"Why, of course," exclaimed the dragon, "reactionary Republican."

Gawaine shook his head.

"Well, then," said the dragon, "we'd better get down to business. Will you surrender?"

With the suggestion of a compromise Gawaine mustered up enough courage to speak.

"What will you do if I surrender?" he asked.

"Why, I'll eat you," said the dragon.

"And if I don't surrender?"

"I'll eat you just the same."

"Then it doesn't mean any difference, does it?" moaned Gawaine.

"It does to me," said the dragon with a smile. "I'd rather you didn't surrender. You'd taste much better if you didn't."

The dragon waited for a long time for Gawaine to ask "Why?" but the boy was too frightened to speak. At last the dragon had to give the explanation without his cue line. "You see," he said, "if you don't surrender you'll taste better because you'll die game."

This was an old and ancient trick of the dragon's. By means of some such quip he was accustomed to paralyze his victims with laughter and then to destroy them. Gawaine was sufficiently paralyzed as it was, but laughter had no part in his helplessness. With the last word of the joke the dragon drew back his head and struck. In that second there flashed into the mind of Gawaine the magic word "Rumplesnitz," but there was no time to say it. There was time only to strike and, without a word, Gawaine met the onrush of the dragon with a full swing. He put all his back and shoulders into it. The impact was terrific and the head of the dragon flew almost a hundred yards and landed in a thicket.

Gawaine did not remain frightened very long after the death of the dragon. His mood was one of wonder. He was enormously puzzled. He cut off the ears of the monster almost in a trance. Again and again he thought to himself, "I didn't say 'Rumplesnitz'!" He was sure of that and yet there was no question that he had killed the dragon. In fact, he had never killed one so utterly. Never before had he driven a head for anything like the same distance. Twenty-five yards was perhaps his best previous record. All the way back to the knight school he kept rumbling about in his mind seeking an explanation for what had occurred. He went to the Headmaster immediately and after closing the door told him what had happened. "I didn't say 'Rumplesnitz,'" he explained with great earnestness.

The Headmaster laughed. "I'm glad you've found out," he said. "It makes you ever so much more of a hero. Don't you see that? Now you know that it was you who killed all these dragons and not that foolish word 'Rumplesnitz.'"

Gawaine frowned. "Then it wasn't a magic word after all?" he asked.

"Of course not," said the Headmaster, "you ought to be too old for such foolishness. There isn't any such thing as a magic word."

"But you told me it was magic," protested Gawaine. "You said it was magic and now you say it isn't."

"It wasn't magic in a literal sense," answered the Headmaster, "but it was much more wonderful than that. The word gave you confidence. It took away your fears. If I hadn't told you that, you might have been killed the very first time. It was your battle-ax did the trick."

Gawaine surprised the Headmaster by his attitude. He was obviously distressed by the explanation. He interrupted a long philosophic and ethical discourse by the Headmaster with "If I hadn't of hit 'em all mighty hard and fast any one of 'em might have crushed me like a, like a——" He fumbled for a word.

"Egg shell," suggested the Headmaster.

"Like a egg shell," assented Gawaine, and he said it many times. All through the evening meal people who sat near him heard him muttering, "Like a egg shell, like a egg shell."

The next day was clear, but Gawaine did not get up at dawn. Indeed, it was almost noon when the Headmaster found him cowering in bed, with the clothes pulled over his head. The principal called the Assistant Professor of Pleasaunce, and together they dragged the boy toward the forest.

"He'll be all right as soon as he gets a couple more dragons under his belt," explained the Headmaster.

The Assistant Professor of Pleasaunce agreed. "It would be a shame to stop such a fine run," he said. "Why, counting that one yesterday, he's killed fifty dragons."

They pushed the boy into a thicket above which hung a meager cloud of steam. It was obviously quite a small dragon. But Gawaine did not come back that night or the next. In fact, he never came back. Some weeks afterward brave spirits from the school explored the thicket, but they could find nothing to remind them of Gawaine except the metal parts of his medals. Even the ribbons had been devoured.

The Headmaster and the Assistant Professor of Pleasaunce agreed that it would be just as well not to tell the school how Gawaine had achieved his record and still less how he came to die. They held that it might have a bad effect on school spirit. Accordingly, Gawaine has lived in the memory of the school as its greatest hero. No visitor succeeds in leaving the building today without seeing a great shield which hangs on the wall of the dining hall. Fifty pairs of dragons' ears are mounted upon the shield and underneath in gilt letters is "Gawaine le Coeur-Hardy," followed by the simple inscription, "He killed fifty dragons." The record has never been equaled.

## DISCUSSION

1. (a) What details read like ordinary events in a boys' school? (b) How does the author make the background seem real? (Review the Handbook entry for *fantasy*.

2. (a) What details seem to you to be unreal or unlikely? (b) Does the author treat these details seriously or does he make them appear ridiculous? Give some examples.

3. (a) What is the significance of the magic word given to Gawaine? (b) How does it affect his success? (c) What happens when he learns that the word is not magic? (d) When the Headmaster explains the purpose of the magic word, how does Gawaine react?

4. (a) This story is an *allegory*,

a story written to explain or teach something. What do you think the author is explaining? (b) How can this story be applied to everyone?

## WORD STUDY

Sometimes words which look and sound alike are easily confused. Look carefully at the words in parentheses, say them softly to yourself, and write on your paper the word which correctly completes the sentence.

1. The headmaster paused and then resumed the thread of his ___. (discourse—recourse)

2. The dragon displayed false _____. (solitude—solicitude)

3. The dragon tried to be helpful by thinking of an _____. (epitaph—epithet)

4. When he looked at the dragon, Gawaine thought he had never seen so hideous a _____. (countenance—continents)

5. Gawaine was pushed into a _____ and never returned. (thickness—thicket)

## HEYWOOD BROUN

Heywood Broun was a journalist and sportswriter and, during World War I, a war correspondent in France.

He was born in 1888 in Brooklyn. He attended Harvard University for four years, but he never received a degree because of his difficulties with elementary French.

His career as a sportswriter began in the sports department of the New York Morning *Telegraph*. In 1912 he went to work for the *Tribune*, where he began his column "It Seems to Me." This column ran in several newspapers for eighteen years.

Broun was married twice, the first time in 1917 to Ruth Hale. Their son, Heywood Hale Broun, is a sportswriter and sports announcer for radio and television.

Broun founded the American Newspaper Guild in 1933 and was for several years a member of the editorial board of the Book-of-the-Month Club. He died in 1939.

---

## Dragons

Several hundred years ago people thought dragons were real, and scientists included them in their classifications of animals of the world. The *draco* (a Latin word derived from the Greek *drakon*) was described in a twelfth-century book as the largest of all living

creatures, with a long coiled tail that could suffocate an elephant.

Dragons in Christian tradition became symbols of sin, with dragon slayers like St. Michael and St. George representing the triumph of good over evil. A Biblical description of a dragon appears in the New Testament: "And there appeared another wonder in heaven; and behold a great red dragon having seven heads and ten horns, and seven crowns upon his heads" (Rev. 12:3).

In the Far East, where dragons have a much better reputation, the dragon became the emblem of the emperor of Japan and the national symbol of China. Dragons in Taoist religion were lifegiving nature deities, quite different creatures from the evil monsters slain by Western knights like Gawaine.

# By the Waters of Babylon

*Stephen Vincent Benét*

*Babylon, an ancient city on the Euphrates River in southwest Asia, was the center of one of the great early civilizations. Old Testament prophets predicted that Babylon would be destroyed because its inhabitants were wicked. Thus, Babylon has come to symbolize any place of wickedness and excessive luxury.*

THE north and the west and the south are good hunting ground, but it is forbidden to go east. It is forbidden to go to any of the Dead Places except to search for metal and then he who touches the metal must be a priest or the son of a priest. Afterwards, both the man and the metal must be purified. These are the rules and the laws; they are well made. It is forbidden to cross the great river and look upon the place that was the Place of the Gods—this is most strictly forbidden. We do not even say its name though we know its name. It is there that spirits live, and demons—it is there that there are the ashes of the Great Burning. These things are forbidden—they have been forbidden since the beginning of time.

My father is a priest; I am the son of a priest. I have been in the Dead Places near us, with my father—at first, I was afraid. When my father went into the house to search for the metal, I stood by the door and my heart felt small and weak. It was a dead man's house, a spirit house. It did not have the smell of man, though there were old bones in a corner. But it is not fitting that a priest's son should show fear. I looked at the bones in the shadow and kept my voice still.

Then my father came out with the metal—a good, strong piece. He looked at me with both eyes but I had not run away. He gave me the metal to hold—I took it and did not die. So he knew that I was truly his son and would be a priest in my time. That was when I was very young—nevertheless, my brothers would not have done it, though they are good hunters. After that, they gave me the good piece of meat and the warm corner by the fire. My father watched over me—he was glad that I should be a priest. But when I boasted or wept without a reason, he punished me more strictly than my brothers. That was right.

After a time, I myself was allowed to go into the dead houses and search for metal. So I learned the ways of those houses—and if I saw bones, I was no longer afraid. The bones are light and old—sometimes they will fall into dust if you touch them. But that is a great sin.

I was taught the chants and the spells—I was taught how to stop the running of blood from a wound and many secrets. A priest must know many secrets—that was what my father said. If the hunters think we do all things by chants and spells, they may believe so—it does not hurt them. I was taught how to read in the old books and how to make the old writings—that was hard and took a long time. My knowledge made me happy—it was like a fire in my heart. Most of all, I liked to hear of the Old Days and the stories of the gods. I asked myself many questions that I could not answer, but it was good to ask them. At night, I would lie awake and listen to the wind—it seemed to me that it was the voice of the gods as they flew through the air.

We are not ignorant like the Forest People—our women spin wool on the wheel, our priests wear a white robe. We do not eat grubs from the tree, we have not forgotten the old writings, although they are hard to understand. Nevertheless, my knowledge and my lack of knowledge burned in me—I wished to know more. When I was a man at last, I came to my father and said, "It is time for me to go on my journey. Give me your leave."

He looked at me for a long time, stroking his beard, then he said at last, "Yes. It is time." That night, in the house of the priesthood, I asked for and received purification. My body hurt but my spirit was a cool stone. It was my father himself who questioned me about my dreams.

He bade me look into the smoke of the fire and see—I saw and told what I saw. It was what I have always seen—a river, and, beyond it, a great Dead Place and in it the gods walking. I have always thought about that. His eyes were stern when I told him—he was no longer my father but a priest. He said, "This is a strong dream."

"It is mine," I said, while the smoke waved and my head felt light. They were singing the Star song in the outer chamber and it was like the buzzing of bees in my head.

He asked me how the gods were dressed and I told him how they were dressed. We know how they were dressed from the book, but I saw them as if they were before me. When I had finished, he threw the sticks three times and studied them as they fell.

"This is a very strong dream," he said. "It may eat you up."

"I am not afraid," I said and looked at him with both eyes. My voice sounded thin in my ears but that was because of the smoke.

He touched me on the breast and the forehead. He gave me the bow and the three arrows.

"Take them," he said. "It is forbidden to travel east. It is forbidden to cross the river. It is forbidden to go to the Place of the Gods. All these things are forbidden."

"All these things are forbidden," I said, but it was my voice that spoke and not my spirit. He looked at me again.

"My son," he said. "Once I had young dreams. If your dreams do not eat you up, you may be a great priest. If they eat you, you are still my son. Now go on your journey."

I went fasting, as is the law. My body hurt but not my heart. When the dawn came, I was out of sight of the village. I prayed and purified myself, waiting for a sign. The sign was an eagle. It flew east.

Sometimes signs are sent by bad spirits. I waited again on the flat rock, fasting, taking no food. I was very still—I could feel the sky above me and the earth beneath. I waited till the sun was beginning to sink. The three deer passed in the valley, going east—they did not mind me or see me. There was a white fawn with them—a very great sign.

I followed them, at a distance, waiting for what would happen. My heart was troubled about going east, yet I knew that I must go. My head hummed with my fasting—I did not even see the panther spring upon the white fawn. But, before I knew it, the bow was in my hand. I shouted and the panther lifted his head from the fawn. It is not easy to kill a panther with one arrow but the arrow went through his eye and into his brain. He died as he tried to spring—he rolled over, tearing at the ground. Then I knew I was meant to go east—I knew that was my journey. When the night came, I made my fire and roasted meat.

It is eight suns' journey to the east and a man passes by many Dead Places. The Forest People are afraid of them but I am not. Once I made my fire on the edge of a Dead Place at night and, next morning, in the dead house, I found a good knife, little rusted. That was small to what came afterward but it made my heart feel big. Always when I looked for game, it was in front of my arrow, and twice I passed hunting parties of the Forest People without their knowing. So I knew my magic was strong and my journey clean, in spite of the law.

Toward the setting of the eighth sun, I came to the banks of the great river. It was half-a-day's journey after I had left the god-road—we do not use the god-roads now for they are falling apart into great blocks of stone, and the forest is safer going. A long way off, I had seen the water through trees but the trees were thick. At last, I came out upon an open place at the top of a cliff. There was the great river below, like a giant in the sun. It is very long, very wide. It could eat all the streams we know and still be thirsty. Its name is Ou-dis-sun, the Sacred, the Long. No man of my tribe had seen it, not even my father, the priest. It was magic and I prayed.

Then I raised my eyes and looked south. It was there, the Place of the Gods.

How can I tell what it was like—you do not know. It was there, in the red light, and they were too big to be houses. It was there with the red light upon it, mighty and ruined. I knew that in another moment the gods would see me. I covered my eyes with my hands and crept back into the forest.

Surely, that was enough to do, and live. Surely it was enough to spend the night upon the cliff. The Forest People themselves do not come near. Yet, all through the night, I knew that I should have to cross the river and walk in the places of the gods, although the gods ate me up. My magic did not help me at all and yet there was a fire in my bowels, a fire in my mind. When the sun rose, I thought, "My journey has been clean. Now I will go home from my journey." But, even as I thought so, I knew I could not. If I went to the Place of the Gods, I would surely die, but, if I did not go, I could never be at peace with my spirit again.

It is better to lose one's life than one's spirit, if one is a priest and the son of a priest.

Nevertheless, as I made the raft, the tears ran out of my eyes. The Forest People could have killed me without fight, if they had come upon me then, but they did not come. When the raft was made, I said the sayings for the dead and painted myself for death. My heart was cold as a frog and my knees like water, but the burning in my mind would not let me have peace. As I pushed the raft from the shore, I began my death song—I had the right. It was a fine song.

"I am John, son of John," I sang "My people
    are the Hill People. They are the men.
I go into the Dead Places but I am not slain.
I take the metal from the Dead Place but I am
    not blasted.
I travel upon the god-roads and am not afraid.
    E-yah! I have killed the panther, I have
    killed the fawn!
E-yah! I have come to the great river. No man
    has come there before.
It is forbidden to go east, but I have gone, for-
    bidden to go on the great river, but I am
    there.
Open your hearts, you spirits and hear my song.
    Now I go to the Place of the Gods, I shall
    not return.
My body is painted for death and my limbs
    weak, but my heart is big as I go to the
    Place of the Gods!"

All the same, when I came to the Place of the Gods, I was afraid, afraid. The current of the great river is very strong—it gripped my raft with its hands. That was magic, for the river itself is wide and calm. I could feel evil spirits about me, in the bright morning; I could feel their breath on my neck as I was swept down the stream. Never have I been so much alone— I tried to think of my knowledge, but it was a squirrel's heap of winter nuts. There was no strength in my knowledge any more and I felt small and naked as a new-hatched bird— alone upon the great river, the servant of the gods.

Yet, after a while, my eyes were opened and I saw. I saw both banks of the river—I saw that once there had been god-roads across it, though now they were broken and fallen like broken vines. Very great they were, and wonderful and broken—broken in the time of the Great Burning when the fire fell out of the sky. And always the current took me nearer to the Place of the Gods, and the huge ruins rose before my eyes.

I do not know the customs of rivers—we are the People of the Hills. I tried to guide my raft with the pole but it spun around. I thought the river meant to take me past the Place of the Gods and out into the Bitter Water of the legends. I grew angry then—my heart felt strong. I said aloud, "I am a priest and the son of a priest!" The gods heard me—they showed me how to paddle with the pole on one side of the raft. The current changed itself—I drew near to the Place of the Gods.

When I was very near, my raft struck and turned over. I can swim in our lakes—I swam to the shore. There was a great spike of rusted metal sticking out into the river—I hauled myself up upon it and sat there, panting. I had saved my bow and two arrows and the knife I found in the Dead Place but that was all. My raft went whirling downstream toward the Bitter Water. I looked after it, and thought if it had trod me under, at least I would be safely dead. Nevertheless, when I had dried my bowstring and restrung it, I walked forward to the Place of the Gods.

It felt like ground underfoot; it did not burn me. It is not true what some of the tales say, that the ground there burns forever, for I have been there. Here and there were the marks and stains of the Great Burning, on the ruins, that is true. But they were old marks and old stains. It is not true either, what some of our priests say, that it is an island covered with fogs and enchantments. It is not. It is a great Dead Place—greater than any Dead Place we know. Everywhere in it there are god-roads, though most are cracked and broken. Everywhere there are the ruins of the high towers of the gods.

How shall I tell what I saw? I went carefully, my strung bow in my hand, my skin ready for danger. There should have been the wailings of spirits and the shrieks of demons, but there were not. It was very silent and sunny where I had landed—the wind and the rain and the birds that drop seeds had done their work—the grass grew in the cracks of the broken stone. It is a fair island—no wonder the gods built there. If I had come there, a god, I also would have built.

How shall I tell what I saw? The towers are not all broken—here and there one still stands, like a great tree in a forest, and the birds nest high. But the towers themselves look blind, for the gods are gone. I saw a fish-hawk, catching fish in the river. I saw a little dance of white butterflies over a great heap of broken stones and columns. I went there and looked about me—there was a carved stone with cut-letters, broken in half. I can read letters but I could not understand these. They said UBTREAS. There was also the shattered image of a man or a god. It had been made of white stone and he wore his hair tied back like a woman's. His name was ASHING, as I read on the cracked half of a stone. I thought it wise to pray to ASHING, though I do not know that god.

How shall I tell what I saw? There was no smell of man left, on stone or metal. Nor were there many trees in that wilderness of stone. There are many pigeons, nesting and dropping in the towers—the gods must have loved them, or, perhaps, they used them for sacrifices. There are wild cats that roam the god-roads, green-eyed, unafraid of man. At night they wail like demons but they are not demons. The wild dogs are more dangerous, for they hunt in a pack, but them I did not meet till later. Everywhere there are the carved stones, carved with magical numbers or words.

I went North—I did not try to hide myself. When a god or a demon saw me, then I would die, but meanwhile I was no longer afraid. My hunger for knowledge burned in me—there was so much that I could not understand. After awhile, I knew that my belly was hungry. I could have hunted for my meat, but I did not hunt. It is known that the gods did not hunt as we do—they got their food from enchanted boxes and jars. Sometimes these are still found in the Dead Places—once, when I was a child and foolish, I opened such a jar and tasted it and found the food sweet. But my father found out and punished me for it strictly, for, often, that food is death. Now, though, I had long gone past what was forbidden, and I entered the likeliest towers, looking for the food of the gods.

I found it at last in the ruins of a great temple in the mid-city. A mighty temple it must have been, for the roof was painted like the sky at night with its stars—that much I could see, though the colors were faint and dim. It went down into great caves and tunnels—perhaps they kept their slaves there. But when I started to climb down, I heard the squeaking of rats, so I did not go—rats are unclean, and there must have been many tribes of them, from the squeaking. But near there, I found food, in the heart of a ruin, behind a door that still opened. I ate only the fruits from the jars—they had a very sweet taste. There was drink, too, in bottles of glass—the drink of the gods was strong and made my head swim. After I had eaten and drunk, I slept on the top of a stone, my bow at my side.

When I woke, the sun was low. Looking down from where I lay, I saw a dog sitting on his haunches. His tongue was hanging out of his mouth; he looked as if he were laughing. He was a big dog, with a gray-brown coat, as big as a wolf. I sprang up and shouted at him but he did not move—he just sat there as if he were laughing. I did not like that. When I reached for a stone to throw, he moved swiftly out of the way of the stone. He was not afraid of me; he looked at me as if I were meat. No doubt I could have killed him with an arrow, but I did not know if there were others. Moreover, night was falling.

I looked about me—not far away there was a great, broken god-road, leading North. The towers were high enough, but not so high, and while many of the dead-houses were wrecked, there were some that stood. I went toward this god-road, keeping to the heights of the ruins, while the dog followed. When I had reached the god-road, I saw that there were others behind him. If I had slept later, they would have come upon me asleep and torn out my throat. As it was, they were sure enough of me; they did not hurry. When I went into the dead-house, they kept watch at the entrance—doubtless they thought they would have a fine hunt. But a dog cannot open a door and I knew, from the books, that the gods did not like to live on the ground but on high.

I had just found a door I could open when the dogs decided to rush. Ha! They were surprised when I shut the door in their faces—it was a good door, of strong metal. I could hear their foolish baying beyond it but I did not stop to answer them. I was in darkness—I found stairs and climbed. There were many stairs, turning around till my head was dizzy. At the top was another chamber—on one side of it was a bronze door that could not be opened, for it had no handle. Perhaps there was a magic word to open it but I did not have the word. I turned to the door in the opposite side of the wall. The lock of it was broken and I opened it and went in.

Within, there was a place of great riches. The god who lived there must have been a powerful god. The first room was a small ante-room—I waited there for some time, telling the spirits of the place that I came in peace and not as a robber. When it seemed to me that they had had time to hear me, I went on. Ah, what riches! Few, even, of the windows had been broken—it was all as it had been. The great windows that looked over the city had not been broken at all though they were dusty and streaked with many years. There were coverings on the floors, the colors not greatly faded, and the chairs were soft and deep. There were pictures upon the walls, very strange, very wonderful—I remember one of a bunch of flowers in a jar—if you came close to it, you could see nothing but bits of color, but if you stood away from it, the flowers might have been picked yesterday. It made my heart feel strange to look at this picture—and to look at the figure of a bird, in some hard clay, on a table and see it so like our birds. Everywhere there were books and writings, many in tongues that I could not read. The god who lived there must have been a wise god and full of knowledge. I felt I had right there, as I sought knowledge also.

Nevertheless, it was strange. There was a washing-place but no water—perhaps the gods washed in air. There was a cooking-place but no wood, and though there was a machine to cook food, there was no place to put fire in it. Nor were there candles or lamps—there were things that looked like lamps but they had neither oil nor wick. All these things were magic, but I touched them and lived—the magic had gone out of them. Let me tell one thing to show. In the washing-place, a thing said "Hot" but it was not hot to the touch—another thing said "Cold" but it was not cold. This must have been a strong magic but the magic was gone. I do not understand—they had ways—I wish that I knew.

It was close and dry and dusty in their house of the gods. I have said the magic was gone but that is not true—it had gone from the magic things but it had not gone from the place. I felt the spirits about me, weighing upon me. Nor had I ever slept in a Dead Place before—and yet, tonight, I must sleep there. When I thought of it, my tongue felt dry in my throat, in spite of my wish for knowledge. Almost I would have gone down again and faced the dogs, but I did not.

I had not gone through all the rooms when the darkness fell. When it fell, I went back to the big room looking over the city and made fire. There was a place to make fire and a box with wood in it, though I do not think they cooked there. I wrapped myself in a floor-covering and slept in front of the fire—I was very tired.

Now I tell what is very strong magic. I woke in the midst of the night. When I woke, the fire had gone out and I was cold. It seemed to me that all around me there were whisperings and voices. I closed my eyes to shut them out. Some will say that I slept again, but I do not think that I slept. I could feel the spirits drawing my spirit out of my body as a fish is drawn on a line.

Why should I lie about it? I am a priest and the son of a priest. If there are spirits, as they say, in the small Dead Places near us, what spirits must there not be in that great Place of the Gods? And would not they wish to speak? After such long years? I know that I felt myself drawn as a fish is drawn on a line. I had stepped out of my body—I could see my body asleep in front of the cold fire, but it was not I. I was drawn to look out upon the city of the gods.

It should have been dark, for it was night, but it was not dark. Everywhere there were lights—lines of light—circles and blurs of light—ten thousand torches would not have been the same. The sky itself was alight—you could barely see the stars for the glow in the sky. I thought to myself "This is strong magic" and trembled. There was a roaring in my ears like the rushing of rivers. Then my eyes grew used to the light and my ears to the sound. I knew that I was seeing the city as it had been when the gods were alive.

That was a sight indeed—yes, that was a sight: I could not have seen it in the body— my body would have died. Everywhere went the gods, on foot and in chariots—there were gods beyond number and counting and their chariots blocked the streets. They had turned night to day for their pleasure—they did not sleep with the sun. The noise of their coming and going was the noise of many waters. It was magic what they could do—it was magic what they did.

I looked out of another window—the great vines of their bridges were mended and the god-roads went East and West. Restless, restless, were the gods and always in motion! They burrowed tunnels under rivers—they flew in the air. With unbelievable tools they did giant works—no part of the earth was safe from them, for, if they wished a thing, they summoned it from the other side of the world. And always, as they labored and rested, as they feasted and made love, there was a drum in their ears— the pulse of the giant city, beating and beating like a man's heart.

Were they happy? What is happiness to the gods? They were great, they were mighty, they were wonderful and terrible. As I looked upon them and their magic, I felt like a child— but a little more, it seemed to me, and they would pull down the moon from the sky. I saw them with wisdom beyond wisdom and knowledge beyond knowledge. And yet not all they did was well done—even I could see that— and yet their wisdom could not but grow until all was peace.

Then I saw their fate come upon them and that was terrible past speech. It came upon them as they walked the streets of their city. I have been in the fights with the Forest People —I have seen men die. But this was not like that. When gods war with gods, they use weapons we do not know. It was fire falling out of the sky and a mist that poisoned. It was the time of the Great Burning and the Destruction. They ran about like ants in the streets of their city—poor gods, poor gods! Then the towers began to fall. A few escaped—yes, a few. The legends tell it. But, even after the city had become a Dead Place, for many years the poison was still in the ground. I saw it happen. I saw the last of them die. It was darkness over the broken city and I wept.

All this, I saw. I saw it as I have told it, though not in the body. When I woke in the morning, I was hungry, but I did not think first of my hunger for my heart was perplexed and confused. I knew the reason for the Dead Places but I did not see why it had happened. It seemed to me it should not have happened, with all the magic they had. I went through the house looking for an answer. There was so much in the house I could not understand— and yet I am a priest and the son of a priest. It was like being on one side of the great river, at night, with no light to show the way.

Then I saw the dead god. He was sitting in his chair, by the window, in a room I had not entered before and, for the first moment, I thought that he was alive. Then I saw the skin on the back of his hand—it was like dry leather. The room was shut, hot and dry—no doubt that had kept him as he was. At first I was afraid to approach him—then the fear left me. He was sitting looking out over the city— he was dressed in the clothes of the gods. His age was neither young nor old—I could not tell his age. But there was wisdom in his face and great sadness. You could see that he would have not run away. He had sat at his window, watching his city die—then he himself had died. But it is better to lose one's life than one's spirit—and you could see from the face that his spirit had not been lost. I knew, that, if I touched him, he would fall into dust—and yet, there was something unconquered in the face.

That is all of my story, for then I knew he

was a man—I knew then that they had been men, neither gods nor demons. It is a great knowledge, hard to tell and believe. They were men—they went a dark road, but they were men. I had no fear after that—I had no fear going home, though twice I fought off the dogs and once I was hunted for two days by the Forest People. When I saw my father again, I prayed and was purified. He touched my lips and my breast, he said, "You went away a boy. You come back a man and a priest." I said, "Father, they were men! I have been in the Place of the Gods and seen it! Now slay me, if it is the law—but still I know they were men."

He looked at me out of both eyes. He said, "The law is not always the same shape—you have done what you have done. I could not have done it my time, but you came after me. Tell!"

I told and he listened. After that, I wished to tell all the people but he showed me otherwise. He said, "Truth is a hard deer to hunt. If you eat too much truth at once, you may die of the truth. It was not idly that our fathers forbade the Dead Places." He was right—it is better that the truth should come little by little. I have learned that, being a priest. Perhaps, in the old days, they ate knowledge too fast.

Nevertheless, we make a beginning. It is not for the metal alone we go to the Dead Places now—there are the books and the writings. They are hard to learn. And the magic tools are broken—but we can look at them and wonder. At least, we make a beginning. And, when I am chief priest we shall go beyond the great river. We shall go to the Place of the Gods—the place new-york—not one man but a company. We shall look for the images of the gods and find the god ASHING and the others —the gods Licoln and Biltmore and Moses. But they were men who built the city, not gods or demons. They were men. I remember the dead man's face. They were men who were here before us. We must build again.

---

## DISCUSSION

1. (a) As this story opens, you realize that the time is not the present. When did you get the first hint that the time is in the future? (b) By what facts and incidents is the time made clear?

2. (a) To what city of the past does the young priest go? (HINT: It is on an island.) (b) UBTREAS refers to the Subtreasury Building. Whom do you think ASHING refers to?

3. (a) Why do you suppose it is forbidden to go East? (b) What is meant by the "Dead Places"?

4. (a) Tell what the young priest finds in the Place of the Gods. (b) What conclusions does he draw? (c) What does he tell his father?

5. Why is the narrator so surprised to find that people, not gods, built the city?

6. This story has often been termed a modern parable—that is, a story which teaches some moral lesson or truth. What is the truth (or truths) that Benét conveys here?

## STEPHEN VINCENT BENÉT

"By the Waters of Babylon" was written a decade before Hiroshima introduced people to the possibility of a cataclysmic end to society. Benét's writing often revealed his intuitive sense of the future. For example, in *Western Star*, an unfinished narrative poem that won a Pulitzer Prize after his death in 1943, Benét describes the initial sea journey to America as a "five months' voyage to settle Mars."

The Civil War furnished the background for his long narrative poem, *John Brown's Body*, which was also a Pulitzer Prize winner. ("Melora Vilas" in the poetry unit of this book is an excerpt from this poem.) Legend, humor, and American history are mingled in "The Devil and Daniel Webster," one of Benét's most popular works.

## Biblical Allusions

Writers and speakers frequently make *allusions* to earlier people, periods, fictitious characters, or situations. Biblical allusions are common in literature. The Garden of Eden, Job, David, Goliath, Babylon, Lot's wife, Ruth, and Solomon are just a few Old Testament places or figures that have become symbols and thus common enough that most readers understand allusions made to them.

You may remember that in "A Reading Problem" Evangelist Gerlash speaks of his late wife as having been untimely gathered to the bosom of Abraham. Earlier, he has warned Emily to "shun the Sodoms *and* Gomorrahs *and* the Babylons."

The headnote for this story explains in part why Benét titled his story "By the Waters of Babylon." Other writers, too, have alluded to Babylon. F. Scott Fitzgerald wrote a short story titled "Babylon Revisited" in which the main character returns briefly to Paris and then recalls the abandoned sort of life he had led there earlier. A novel titled *Alas, Babylon* by Pat Frank is the story of massive destruction of the United States by an atomic war.

There is even a very old nursery rhyme which begins: "How many miles to Babylon?/ Three score miles and ten." Some scholars have suggested that "Babylon" here is a corruption of "Babyland," while others have held that it is likely to have meant a far away, luxurious city.

Cairo was called "Babylon" by the crusaders, the Puritans referred to Rome as "Babylon," and someone once labeled Hollywood a "celluloid Babylon."

Many writers besides Benét, Fitzgerald, and Frank have taken titles for their stories, plays, or novels directly from the Bible. *Lilies of the Field, Giants in the Earth*, "Pale Horse, Pale Rider," and *The Little Foxes* are only a few examples of modern Biblical allusions.

## UNIT 1 REVIEW

There follow 20 statements about the short stories in the unit you have just completed. Number from 1 to 20 on a separate sheet of paper. After each number, write "a" if you *strongly agree* with the statement that corresponds in number; "b" if you *agree;* "c" if you *have no opinion;* "d" if you *disagree;* "e" if you *strongly disagree* with the statement.

Whenever possible, be prepared to support each of your opinions with evidence from the stories. Before beginning the Unit Review, you may find it helpful first to review in your Handbook the following terms: *plot, character, setting, theme, point of view, symbolism, irony, figurative language.*

1. "Peter Two" would have been a more exciting story if the author had used a first person—rather than third person, limited intelligence—point of view.

2. Peter Two and Delaney, the narrator of "The Idealist," have much in common.

3. The theme of "Bargain" might be clearly stated as follows: "Being able to read well is more important than being able to fight well with one's fists."

4. Had they never checked the newspaper to find whether their ticket had won, the husband and wife in "The Lottery Ticket" would have remained happily married.

5. In "The Most Dangerous Game," setting and plot are more important than character.

6. If it were written from Mama's point of view, "The Sky Is Gray" would not be as effective a story.

7. At least three short stories in the unit make effective use of irony.

8. The word *Rumplesnitz* in "The Fifty-first Dragon" symbolizes Gawaine's failure to believe in himself rather than in word magic.

9. James, the narrator in "The Sky is Gray," and Luther, the boy in the story of the same name, have quite different values.

10. The author of "To Da-duh, in Memoriam" attempts to convince the reader that a modern technological society is superior to a primitive society.

11. It is almost impossible to imagine "Rain on Tanyard Hollow" taking place anywhere else with any other characters.

12. Without its figurative language, "The Endless Streetcar Ride into the Night and the Tinfoil Noose" would not be a humorous story.

13. In her own way, the narrator of "To Da-duh, in Memoriam" is as cruel to her grandmother as is the narrator of "The Scarlet Ibis" to his younger brother.

14. Luther, in the story of that name, and Gawaine of "The Fifty-first Dragon" have some of the same traits of personality.

15. If Pappie of "Rain on Tanyard Hollow" knew Evangelist Gerlash of "A Reading Problem," he would want him as a friend.

16. Over the years since its publication in 1937, the plot of "By the Waters of Babylon" has become increasingly far-fetched.

17. General Zaroff of "The Most Dangerous Game" is more like Mr. Chalmers of "Peter Two" than he is like Freighter Slade of "Bargain."

18. If only one story from this unit were to be read by the entire class, that story should be "The Scarlet Ibis."

19. Though her behavior might be understandable, Claudine was nevertheless cruel to her Aunt Lily at the conclusion of "Claudine's Book."

20. Without learning terms like *plot, character, setting, theme,* and *irony,* one could understand these stories just as well, and appreciate them more.

**Autobiography
Article and Essay**

# Nonfiction

FROM

# PORTRAIT OF MYSELF

*Margaret Bourke-White*

*For more than twenty-five years the pages of Life magazine contained the words and photographs of foreign correspondent Margaret Bourke-White. But in 1928 she was an inexperienced college student, photographing waterfalls through a cracked lens.*

IT was sheer luck that I still had an old second-hand camera when I returned to college for my senior year. My mother had bought it for me shortly after my father's death, when she could barely afford it. The camera was a 3¼-x-4¼ Ica Reflex, modeled like a Graflex. It cost twenty dollars and had a crack straight through the lens.

Counting night school and summer sessions, I had attended five colleges in the last four years. Now I was transferring once again. This time I enrolled at Cornell—because I had read there were waterfalls on the campus.

Arriving in Ithaca, I did what other college students do when they are broke: I tried to get a job as a waitress. Luckily for my photographic future the waitress jobs were all taken. By the time I got to the student library to apply for a tempting forty-cents-an-hour job there, that was snapped up, too.

I believe it was the drama of the waterfalls that first gave me the idea I should put that old cracked lens to work. Here I was on one of the most spectacular campus sites in America, with fine old ivy-covered architecture and Cayuga Lake on the horizon and those boiling columns of water thundering over the cliffs and down through the gorges. Surely there would be students who would buy photographs of scenes like these.

I knew so little about photography it seemed almost impudence to think about trying to take pictures to sell. All autumn went into making a collection of a mere eight or ten that I felt were worth presenting. Still, I was surprised at the growing feeling of rightness I had with a camera in my hands. I arranged with a commercial photographer in Ithaca to use his darkroom at night to work up sample enlargements of my pictures, which he would copy "in quantity" if we ever got orders "in quantity."

The pictures went like a blaze. I organized a staff of student salesmen on a commission basis to help me handle them, prevailed on the college co-op to carry them, and then made a mistake that nearly prejudiced me against photography forever. Not realizing that the demand was seasonal, I overstocked, and tied up my small capital in prints which remained unsold for months. I grew to hate the sight of those prints piled behind my cot in the dormitory.

Five dollars came in regularly from sales for covers to the *Alumni News*. Reassuring as this was to me, it was less important than another totally unexpected result. I began getting letters from architects who were alumni of Cornell, inquiring whether I intended to go into photography after I got out of school, and stating there were few good architectural photographers in the country. This opened a dazzling new vista. Never had I thought of becoming a professional photographer. Also it opened a new conflict. Should I drop my major in biology for a field for which I was so little trained? On the biology side I had something that looked pretty close to an offer from the American Museum of Natural History in New York. But to be a professional photographer—what a tantalizing possibility!

I decided I must get an unbiased opinion of my work. These architects were graduates of Cornell, after all, bound to be sentimental about pictures of their alma mater. I would go to New York during Easter vacation, walk in on some architect cold, and base my momentous decision on his opinion.

I don't recall who gave me the name of York & Sawyer, a large architectural firm—and suggested a Mr. Benjamin Moskowitz, one of its members, who as a non-Cornellian would qualify. Arriving, unwisely, late in the day, I went into the upper reaches of the midtown skyscraper where their office was located, entered a frighteningly spacious lobby and asked to see Mr. Moskowitz. The tall dark man who came out in response to this request was plainly a commuter on his way to a train. As I outlined my problem he unobtrusively though steadily edged his way toward the elevator. I did not realize he had not taken in a word until he pushed the down button. If the elevator had arrived on time, I am sure that the next morning would have found me on the doorstep of the Museum of Natural History. But as we waited, the silence became so embarrassing that I opened my big portfolio. Mr. Moskowitz glanced at the picture on top, a view of the library tower.

"Did you take this photograph yourself?"

"Yes, that's what I've been telling you."

"Let's go back and look at these," said Mr. Moskowitz.

He let his train go, stood up the photographs against the dark wood paneling of the conference room, called in the other members of the firm to look them over. At the conclusion of the kind of golden hour one remembers for a lifetime, I left with the assurance of Messrs. York, Sawyer, and associates that I could "walk into any architect's office in the country with that portfolio and get work."

Everything was touched with magic now. The Cornell pictures sold out in the commencement rush. College over, I took the Great Lakes night boat from Buffalo to Cleveland, which I had grown fond of during a year I had spent studying at Western Reserve University. Rising early, I stood on the deck to watch the city come into view. As the skyline took form in the morning mist, I felt I was coming to my promised land—columns of masonry gaining height as we drew toward the pier, derricks swinging like living creatures. Deep inside I knew these were my subjects.

In the mammoth backyard of Cleveland, stretching from the plateau of soaring office buildings to the swampy shore of Lake Erie, lies a sprawling, cluttered area known as the Flats. Slashed across by countless railroad tracks and channeled by the wandering Cuyahoga River, the Flats are astir with nervous life. Locomotives slap and shove reluctant coal cars, tugboats coax their bulging barges around the river bends. Overhead, traffic roars into the city on high-flung bridges. At the far edge of this clanging confusion, on the upper rim of the Flats, chimney stacks rise smoking over the blast furnaces, where ore meets coke and becomes steel.

To me, fresh from college with my camera over my shoulder, the Flats were a photographic paradise. The smokestacks ringing the horizon were the giants of an unexplored world, guarding the secrets of the steel mills. When, I wondered, would I get inside those huge slab-sided coffin-black buildings with their mysterious unpredictable flashes of light leaking out the edges? Cautious inquiries produced the discouraging information that women were unwelcome in steel mills, especially in these particular mills, where they had been prohibited ever since a visiting schoolteacher twenty years earlier had inconsiderately fainted from the heat and fumes.

To break down this imperious prohibition was one of my aims. Meanwhile I hoped to earn enough doing photographs for architects to pay for the experimental industrial photographs I wanted to take.

I began making daily rounds with my portfolio of pictures, building up a card file on the architects and landscape architects I had visited. My file included cross references recording what costume I had worn that day. Since my entire wardrobe consisted of a gray suit which I wore with red hat and red gloves or with blue hat and blue gloves, keeping track of my outfits placed a minimum amount of strain on my documentary abilities. But it was a great morale factor with me to know that any given prospect was going to see me on a follow-up visit in a fresh color scheme. Perhaps by the time I got to a third visit, there would be a job and a check behind me, and that would mean a third color.

On a red glove day I got my first job. This was to photograph a new school which had been designed by Pitkin & Mott, architects and Cornell alumni. Messrs. Pitkin & Mott were almost as new in their business as I was in mine, and therefore it meant a good deal to them to get their schoolhouse published in a national architectural magazine. The editors of *Architecture* had expressed an interest in the school if good pictures of it could be obtained, but those already submitted had been rejected as not up to publication standards. Did I want to take on the job? I did—with joy—at five dollars a photograph.

A visit to the school revealed why my predecessor had had difficulty with the pictures. The building stood in the midst of a wasteland, littered with unused lumber, gravel dug out of the foundations, and withering remnants of workmen's lunches. The solution was to photograph it in silhouette against a sunrise. For four successive mornings I arose before dawn, hurried to location and found the stubborn sun rising behind overcast. On the fifth morning the sunrise was everything a photographer could ask, but the whole idea proved fruitless because heaps of refuse in strategic places blotted out the best angles.

If only I could supply a few softening touches of landscaping! I ran to the nearest florist, invested in an armful of asters, carried them to the schoolhouse and stuck them in the muddy ground. Placing my camera low, I shot over the tops of the flowers, then moved my garden as I proceeded from one viewpoint to the next. By the time my asters had given up, exhausted, I had completed the photographs of the school from all points of view.

When I delivered the pictures (which of course I took care to do in blue gloves) I don't know who was the more amazed—Mr. Mott or Mr. Pitkin—at the miraculous appearance of landscaping. The editors of *Architecture* took it in stride, and publication of the pictures brought more work and a tinge of prestige to the Bourke-White Studio.

At this stage the Bourke-White Studio was only a name on a letterhead and a stack of developing trays in the kitchen sink. I did my processing in the kitchenette and the rinsing in the bathtub. The living room could double as reception room when the in-a-door bed was pushed out of the way. At that time, however, no one had yet come to be received. Still, my pavement-pounding was beginning to bring some results, mainly from landscape architects who ordered pictures of gardens or estates they had landscaped—and this meant sales to the estate owners also.

One day while doing the rounds with my portfolio, I was passing through the public square and saw an earnest Negro preacher standing on a soapbox and exhorting the air. No one in the square was paying the slightest attention to him, but soaring about his widespread eloquent arms and gathered in a bobbing congregation at his feet were flocks of pigeons. What a wonderful picture! But that day I had no camera.

Dashing to the nearest camera store, I begged to be allowed to rent or borrow a cam-era. The clerk eyed me curiously through his thick spectacles as I explained breathlessly about the preacher and the pigeons, but he reached below the counter and handed me a Graflex. I flew back to the square, pausing only to buy a bag of peanuts on the way, and found to my relief that the parson was still on his soapbox. His flock had begun to stray, but a few well-aimed peanuts brought them fluttering back.

It was only when I went back to return the camera to the clerk behind the counter that I noticed his remarkably astute and kindly expression. Everything about him seemed a step above the ordinary, as though intensified by some inner magnifying glass as strong as the spectacles he wore. When he moved, he swung strong arms from a powerful, barrel-shaped chest. When he spoke, the words streamed out all in capitals, underlined and sparked with exclamation points. Balding, short, enthusiastic and fiftyish, Alfred Hall Bemis was as eager to give photographic advice as I was to receive it. It was lunchtime, so naturally we went out to lunch. And naturally I told him how I felt about steel mills.

Perhaps if there had been no Mr. Bemis, others would have helped—for I believe a burning purpose attracts others who are drawn along with it and help fulfill it. But one would need ten others to replace a single Bemis.

"Beme," as I soon began to call my new friend, gave me badly needed technical pointers, but he never failed to recognize there was more to making pictures than technique. "Listen, child," he would say, "you can make a million technicians but not photographers, and that's the truth." Mr. Bemis took one look at my primitive darkroom facilities, salvaged an old chipped-up pair of condensers the store was throwing out, and built an enlarger in my breakfast room. "All we need is a little wood" (he found that free somewhere) "and a camera rack and bellows" (he tore these out of some discarded wreck of a camera). "Shove in a light—and you're on your way."

Fate was extraordinarily kind to me in those early Cleveland days. If the morning mail brought an overdraft of eight dollars, before the day was over I was sure to sell a print or two and get a check for ten dollars. Various small magazines in Cleveland began publishing my garden pictures. The Cleveland chamber of commerce used my Negro preacher on the cover of their monthly, *The Clevelander*, paid me ten dollars, and ordered more covers. These extras were helpful, for my hardest problem was to get enough rock-bottom work from the architects and garden owners to pay for the supplies I needed to keep shooting industrials in the Flats.

Autumn was advancing and the sky was full of luminous clouds. To this day it hurts me to waste good clouds, but then every moment I was not using this fine backdrop of a sky jabbed at me like a thorn. On brilliant days, as soon as I finished my regular architectural or garden work, and always on Sundays, I raced down to the Flats and photographed the industrial subjects I loved.

It never occurred to me that I could sell these pictures, nor that I was doing anything new. These were things I was impelled to take because they were close to my own heart, so close that for some little time I was too shy about the photographs even to show them.

Then, unexpectedly, I sold my first industrial picture. A friend urged me to take a portfolio to one of the banks. I could hardly imagine a bank buying a picture; however, the public relations officer of the Union Trust Company needed covers for the bank's monthly magazine *Trade Winds*. He turned rapidly through my photographs, picked a shot of the High Level Bridge, said, "Make us a glossy of this," and with magnificent fairness added, "Send us a bill for fifty dollars." This was five times the price I would have dared to ask. That picture paid for a lot of film. But I have always felt that the benefits went deeper than fifty dollars.

Each month I brought to the bank a portfolio of the industrial pictures I had taken and the public relations man went through them and picked a *Trade Winds* cover. No one gave me any directions. I was free to use my own imagination, develop my own style. I was away from the usual influences—the art director who hands you a tissue paper layout, the advertiser who wants a situation glamorized no matter how far it may be from real life. These would have been strongly operative if I had started in New York and been drawn into the advertising agency circuit, as I inevitably would have been. But here I was free to make my own experiments and my own mistakes during this formative period when I had so much to learn about photography. How much I had to learn I was soon to find out.

Now that I had the delightful certainty of fifty dollars a month, I made a down payment for a battered, third-hand, green Chevrolet coupe which I named Patrick. I added a third color to my wardrobe—purple—a dress which I made myself. I stitched up three new camera cloths, purple velvet to use with the purple dress, blue velvet for the blue outfit, and black velvet for the red. I felt very smart indeed taking photographs in my matching ensembles.

When my new client, the Union Trust, called me in to photograph a prize steer in their bank lobby, I chose the blue velvet cloth and matching ensemble as having just the right restraint and richness for a bank. The steer had been raised by schoolboys, and whether it was being exhibited to help induce the youth of Ohio to raise more steers or to raise more dollars to deposit in the Union Trust, I never found out. I took one look at that steer in his roped-in enclosure—pure jet lucifer with horns against dead white marble—and I decided it would take more than a blue camera cloth to photograph it properly. I fled to Mr. Bemis.

"You must have artificial light, child, a lot of it," he told me. I had never used artificial light in my life. "Do you know how to use flash-powder? I'll lend you the apparatus (we had no flashbulbs in those days), but I don't want you to blow a hand off."

A few minutes of instruction convinced Beme that not only would I endanger my own hand if I were turned loose with flash, but all the depositors in the Union Trust lobby would be placed in peril.

"Can't you wait until the lunch hour? I'll lend you Earl."

Earl Leiter was a wizard photofinisher who

worked in the spider-webby darkness of the fifth floor over the camera store. Among all the varied negatives that cross a photofinisher's table during a day, Earl, in an instant accurate analysis, could pick the right print timing, and come up with the winning number. Earl's trouble was that with horses, too, he hoped to come up with the winning number. He placed daily bets and lived for the moment in late afternoon when he could phone for news of the races. In all the time I knew him—and he came to work for me later when a studio in the Terminal Tower supplanted my kitchen sink— Earl made substantial winnings on a horse only once.

Like all good photofinishers Earl was a competent photographer, and when we reached the bank he took charge of everything. As soon as we climbed into the roped-in enclosure we drew interested attention both from the friendly noontime crowd and the distinctly hostile-looking steer. Earl helped me set up the camera Beme had lent me, got ready to shoot off his flashpan, looked to me to give me the cue, and saw from my look of stage fright that I had forgotten Beme's directions for the camera. Manipulating the shutter with his left hand, which was hidden under the blue cloth so it would look as though I were working the camera, Earl set off charges of flashpowder with his right. Billows of gray smoke rolled through the bank. Ashes showered down on the shoulders of the depositors, and my blue outfit and blue velvet camera cloth looked as though they had been dipped in a flour bin.

Back in Earl's bailiwick on the fifth floor, we rushed out a proof. The picture was no artistic masterpiece but it plainly showed a discontented steer standing sharp and clear against a vast, pillared bank lobby. The bank officials liked it well enough to order 485 copies, which they would get out to a lot of newspapers and schools next day. Could I deliver them tomorrow morning? Oh of course! Delighted, I ran back to Beme.

"Kiddo, it would take you a week to turn out 485 prints with that homemade enlarger of yours."

I could not speak for disappointment.

"I doubt if there's a commercial studio in

town would take on an order to make 485 enlargements overnight."

My expression must have shown that I didn't want to let the bank down.

"Come back at six o'clock when the store closes, child. Maybe we can think of something. It's glossy prints they wanted? I don't know whether there are enough ferrotype tins in the city. But come back when the store closes. We aren't licked yet."

At six o'clock Beme locked the store, we picked up Earl, went to Stouffer's restaurant and ordered thick steak. Feeling a little like conspirators, we crept back into the store, climbed those five flights of inky steps, and turned on the ruby lights in Earl's darkroom. We set up a conveyor-belt formation: Earl with his precision timing struck off the prints, I was permitted to shuffle them about in the rinse water—the spot where, I suppose, I could do the least damage—while Beme squeegeed them onto the many ferrotype tins, which he spread out against walls, over floors and tables, under the blast of the electric fans. Shortly before daylight the last black steer had been peeled off its shiny tin and the prints were trimmed and packaged.

After arranging with a trusted porter, whom I knew at the Hotel Cleveland, to deliver the precious package when the bank opened, I started home to get some sleep. I had been too busy to give a thought to the financial benefits of the night's work, but now it occurred to me that 485 enlargements at twenty-five cents an enlargement plus the fifty dollar fee for taking the shot equaled, according to my arithmetic, a Turner-Reich convertible lens and a Compur shutter with separate elements for the long-focus effects I loved so much. A lens worthy of any steel mill.

In an exalted mood, I drove the long way around so I could catch a glimpse of the steel mills on the way. Dawn was coming with a rush as I drove along the upper rim of the Flats. I parked Patrick on a high rise overhanging the Riverside Plant of Otis Steel. As though sealed away from the daylight, the steel mills lay in a fog-filled bowl, brooding, mysterious, their smokestacks rising high above them in ghostly fingers.

Suddenly the mist was warmed with flame as a line of slag thimbles shot out of the dark and, like a chain of blazing beads, rolled over the tracks to the edge of an embankment below where I stood. Car after car tipped their burning, bleeding loads down the slope, then rattled back to vanish into the murk again.

"And this is just the waste," I thought. "This is just what's left over! If the sweepings, the crumbs, can be so spectacular, what possibilities there must be inside, where those slag thimbles come from!" And I drove home in Patrick, wondering how I was going to get into that magic place.

"Beme, aren't the officers of the banks on the boards of directors of the industries, and vice versa?" We were eating goulash in Stouffer's restaurant. "Someone like the vice president of Union Trust, I mean."

"Listen, child, old John Sherwin is on the board of half the firms in town. More than half, maybe."

"And I photographed Mrs. John Sherwin's garden. Maybe he never saw the picture of the steer in his own bank; that's all public relations, but he must surely know the pictures of his own estate."

We both sat silent and smiling over our goulash, turning over the same thought. Then Beme said, "I'd rather do business with the head man any day than some whippersnapper down in the aisle."

"Yes," I said, "especially if it's the head of the bank that you get to introduce you to the president of the steel mills."

And so it turned out. John Sherwin, vice president of Union Trust, was puzzled that a "pretty young girl should want to take pictures in a dirty steel mill." But he was quite willing to send a letter of introduction to his friend, Elroy Kulas at Otis Steel.

Mr. Kulas was forceful, short of stature, able. In the twelve years since he had become president, his company's output of steel ingots had quadrupled.

This of course I did not know, but I knew very well why I wanted to photograph the making of those steel ingots, and Mr. Kulas eyed me kindly while I tried to explain.

I do not remember the words I used, but I do remember standing there by his massive carved desk trying to tell him of my belief that there is a power and vitality in industry that makes it a magnificent subject for photography. He must have been a little surprised at the intensity of this twenty-one-year-old girl, possessed of this strange desire to photograph a steel furnace. And I too was a little surprised to find myself talking so fearlessly to the first industrial magnate I had ever had to face.

But during my camera explorations down in the Flats, among the ore boats and bridges, I had done a good deal of thinking about these very things. To me these industrial forms were all the more beautiful because they were never designed to be beautiful. They had a simplicity of line that came from their direct application to a purpose. Industry, I felt, had evolved an unconscious beauty—often a hidden beauty that was waiting to be discovered. And recorded! That was where I came in.

As I struggled to express these ideas to Mr. Kulas, I remembered to tell him certain things I had decided in advance I must say—to assure him I was not trying to sell him something, that at this stage I wanted only permission to experiment. And he in turn expressed a polite interest in seeing and perhaps purchasing for the company some of the pictures if they turned out well. I said, "Wait till we see what I get first."

Mr. Kulas turned to the portfolio I had brought, looked at the pictures one by one, and stopped to study a photograph of the Sherwin rock garden. It showed little rills from a spring falling through moss-covered stones, with a little lead figure of a Cupid or nymph guarding each rill.

"Your pictures of flower gardens are very artistic," said Mr. Kulas looking up, "but how can you find anything artistic in my mill?"

"Please let me try."

And he did. He called in some vice presidents and gave the word that I was to be admitted whenever I came to the plant to take pictures. And then he did me the greatest favor of all. He went off to Europe for five months.

I did not know what a long-term task I had taken on, nor did Mr. Kulas, nor his vice presidents. I believe the Otis officials expected me to come down once or twice for a few snap-shots. I came nearly every night for a whole winter. If there had been someone, however kindly, asking how I was getting along—asking to see pictures (when for months there was nothing worth looking at) I could never have taken the time I needed to learn all the things I had to learn. The steel mills, with their extreme contrasts of both light and shade, make a difficult subject even today, with all our superior techniques and equipment. But then I had no technique, almost no experience. Also, my difficulties were more than technical. The theme itself was colossal. Despite my enthusiasm I needed orientation. I needed to go through a kind of digestive process before I could even choose viewpoints on my subjects.

The mill officials grew impatient. I was doubtless in the way. They were sure I was going to break a leg or fall into a ladle of molten metal. And a girl who came back night after night! What kind of a pest was that? But the president had given his word. No one could gainsay it. I had my five months.

The first night was sheer heaven. Beme talked about it when we met years later.

"We were standing up high some place and they pulled a furnace.[1] You were as delighted as a kid with a Fourth of July firecracker. You grabbed your camera and were off.

"You weren't exactly dressed for the occasion. You had on some kind of a flimsy skirt and velvet slippers. And there you were dancing on the edge of a fiery crater in your slippers, taking pictures like blazes and singing for joy."

My singing stopped when I saw the films. I could scarcely recognize anything on them. Nothing but a fifty-cent-sized disk marking the spot where the molten metal had churned up in the ladle.

I couldn't understand it. "We're woefully underexposed," explained Beme. "The light from the molten metal looks like it's illuminating the whole place, but it's all heat and no light. No actinic value."

So for weeks we struggled with actinic values, trying to balance up light and darkness in my pictures. We brought in some floodlights, we laid cables. But still our illumination was simply gobbled up in the vast, inky maw of the steel mill.

One tends to forget how quickly photography has developed as a science. Even with present-day equipment, steel mills still must be approached with respect, but then film and paper had little latitude, negative emulsions were very slow, there were no flashbulbs, no strobe; the miniature camera was not yet on the market. Stepped-up high-speed developers were unheard of.

Each night Beme borrowed some piece of equipment from the store and we tried it out. "There's no one camera will take every kind of picture," Beme said. "A guy goes out to shoot pictures like you do needs a whole potful of cameras." A lens came in which we thought remarkably "fast,"—f/3.5. It would seem quite average today. Beme lent it to me from the store till I saved enough to buy it. We still suffered, sometimes from underexposure, sometimes from overexposure. The faster lens helped, but not enough: our shadows were far too dim; our highlights, blurred paste. We heard of an exciting new development in film: infrared. I wired to get some, learned from the research department of Eastman Kodak it was made up only for motion picture film.

I tried closer viewpoints, hoping to get more help from the light of the molten steel. The men put up a metal sheet to protect me from the heat while I set my camera in place, slipping their shield away while I made my shots. The varnish on my camera rose up in blisters and I looked as though I had been under a tropical sun. I climbed up the hanging ladder into the overhead crane so I could shoot directly down into the molten steel during the pour.[2] During some of the shots, bursts of dense yellow smoke at the height of the pour blotted out everything in front of the lens; during others, the crane cab started trembling during the vital moments and my pictures were blurred.

By this time I was living entirely for the steel mills. The jobs I was able to keep going during the daytime just about paid for the films I shot up at night. And those same films, after ex-

1. *pulled a furnace*, released the molten steel from the furnace into a ladle from which it would be poured into molds.

2. *the pour*, the pouring of molten steel from a ladle into molds.

posure in the mills and processing in my kitchen sink, filled up my wastebasket—a gluey mass of sick, limping, unprintable negatives. At the end of a developing session Beme would light one of his endless cigarettes and start for the door saying, "I'm going home now to read the whole Book of Job. How Job sat in the ashes. Maybe it will do some good."

And apparently it did. Out of nowhere, new helpers materialized.

The first of these was H. F. Jackson, long-armed and long-legged, with a profile like Abraham Lincoln. Jack was traveling representative for the Meteor Company, which handled "photographic specialties." Beme called me excitedly when Jack came to town: "I haven't seen Jack since we were both sixteen-year-old kids, until he turns up all of a sudden with his case full of samples. I told him about your problem, how you couldn't get enough light. Oh, *he* could get enough light, he says, to light up a hole in Hades. And he drags out these big magnesium flares with wooden handles, like Roman candles. He's on his way to Hollywood to demonstrate them for the movies. I told him if he would come with us, he could see the steel mills—and he fell for it."

We had more than our usual red tape at the mill gate that night—a strange guard who didn't recognize our passes and then phoned endlessly until he could rouse some higher-up who would admit Jack with us. And while all this went on in the drafty guardhouse, a wet snow blew up. Through the storm we could watch the rising crescendo of rosy light glowing from the door of the open hearth, which showed us we were missing a "heat"[3] and would have to wait three hours for the next pour.

I know of no colder place than a steel mill in winter between "heats"—and no hotter place than a mill during the pour. During our three-hour wait we roamed the windy catwalks, climbed up and down ladders with the sleet driving through, and planned our shots. I was eager to work out a side lighting which would emphasize the great hulk and roundness of the ladles and molds and still not flatten

---

3. *a heat,* the melting of one furnace-load of scrap, pig iron, and iron ore to make steel.

and destroy the magic of the place. To do that properly would take two flares for each shot, Jack decided, used at each side and at varying distances from the camera.

At the end of the third hour, Jack made a heroic decision. In his sample case were one dozen flares with which he had set out to conquer Hollywood. He would save only one flare to demonstrate to the movie colony; eleven he would demonstrate in the steel mills.

Then, in a great rush, the pour began. With the snow at our backs and the heat in our faces we worked like creatures possessed. The life of each flare was half a minute. During those thirty seconds, I steadied my reflex camera on a cross rail, made exposures of eight seconds, four seconds, two seconds, dashed to a closer viewpoint, hand-held the camera for slow instantaneous shots until the flare died.

In the beginning, Beme stood at one end and Jack at the other, each holding one flare. Then, as the metal rose bubbling in the ladle, with great bursts of thick orange smoke shrouding the mill, Jack was afraid we were not getting enough fill-in light. So we took the great gamble: he and Beme held two flares each. The eleventh flare we saved for that last spectacular moment in the pouring of the ingot molds—that dramatic moment when the columns of tall tubular forms are full to bursting, each crowned with a fiery corona of sparks, and the cooling ladle in one last effort empties the final drops of its fiery load and turns away.

Next night we developed the films and there it all was, the noble shapes of ladles, giant hooks and cranes, the dim vast sweep of the mill. There was one moment of anxiety, when we developed the negative we had taken with the eleventh flare. It was filled with black curving lines, just as though someone had scratched it with his fingernails.

Beme couldn't make it out. "The film seems to be damaged in some manner."

"But the marks are so regular," I said, "like looped wire. Each one is a perfect curve."

And suddenly I knew. I had photographed the actual path of the sparks.

We reached our next roadblock after Jack had moved on to Hollywood (his company, I am glad to add, sent him another sample case from Chicago). We were printing up our results. "Beme," I said, "these enlargements look terrible. So dull and lifeless." I couldn't understand it.

"The paper doesn't have enough latitude," said Beme.

In this final crisis Beme triumphed again. He produced another salesman. Charlie Bolwell was as plump and pink-faced as Jack had been lean and gaunt. He was selling a new type of developing paper that offered a richer emulsion, heavier deposits of silver. It had what Charlie called "the long gray scale."

These were magic words. My heart beat faster and I could hear Beme's voice growing excited on the other end of the line. "I told Charlie, 'I know someone needs that long gray scale awful bad,' and Charlie said, 'Lead me to him.' I told him, 'It's a her.' I showed him some of the prints we'd made, and he's under the impression he can do better. We're perfectly willing to let him try, aren't we, Kiddo!"

Yes, we were willing. We would all have a steak that night and then come out to my kitchenette. In concluding these arrangements, Beme all but sang into the phone, "Best of all, Charlie has innumerable samples to donate to the cause."

Charlie Bolwell donated more than his paper samples to the cause. He taught me how to print. He showed me how much can be done with a hand gliding through the shaft of light that falls from enlarger to paper, how one moves the fingers to keep the "dodging" imperceptible, masking off thin portions, burning through the too-dense highlights. He showed me what the warmth of a palm in the developer will do, coaxing up a difficult area of the enlargement. From Charlie I received a new conception of darkroom work, as though your hands—working in the laboratory— have become an extension of the lens that took the picture, as though it were all one conscious stream of creation, from the judging of the light when the picture is taken to that final sparkle in the tray when your print is what you want it to be.

By the time Charlie Bolwell had rescued my pictures and was on his way with a lightened sample case to make other converts, Mr. Kulas was back from Europe and quite naturally expressed some curiosity to see what that girl had been doing for five months in his steel mill. I picked the twelve best shots, put them on fresh white mounts, made a new red dress for myself to give me confidence—and the dreaded, hoped-for appointment was made.

Beme drove to the mills with me and waited outside in my car. I got out and picked up my portfolio. Beme could see I was trembling. "Child, you've come through with the kind of pictures no one has ever seen until now. Now run along."

I walked over the long, long narrow wooden trestle that spanned the yard of the mill to the office building. I remember waiting inside Mr. Kulas' office, standing near the entrance and behind a screen while he finished with some other people. Then my turn came. I remember his surprise and pleasure in the pictures. He wanted to buy some of them. How much would they be? I had given this no end of thought.

I have always had the philosophy that either one does things free—for a gift, or when someone cannot afford to pay—or else charges what the work is worth. There is no middle ground. And I told Mr. Kulas this. I assured him I would give him the pictures gladly but, if he wished to pay, the price would be quite a lot. Because of the amount of time and supplies that had gone into the work, I had decided it should be $100 a picture.

"I don't think that's a lot," said Mr. Kulas, "and in any case I am glad to have the chance to encourage you in your pioneer work."

He picked out eight photographs, commissioned me to make eight more, started laying plans for a privately printed book (*The Story of Steel*), which would be sent to his stockholders and would contain my photographs.

I was back again on the wooden trestle. Beme says I came running like a mad woman to tell him the news. We tore into town and bought a bottle of champagne and raced up to the fifth floor over the camera store to tell Earl the news. I had never had champagne before, nor had Earl.

Beme pulled the cork and the champagne gushed to the ceiling and sprayed all of Earl's negatives hung up to dry.

The phone rang. Earl disappeared to answer it and came running back with a dazed expression. He had won eighty-four dollars on a horse named Heat Lightning.

A few months later, in the spring of 1929, I received a telegram from a man I had never met: HAVE JUST SEEN YOUR STEEL PHOTOGRAPHS. CAN YOU COME TO NEW YORK WITHIN WEEK AT OUR EXPENSE. It was signed: HENRY R. LUCE and under his name: TIME, THE WEEKLY NEWS-MAGAZINE. I very nearly did not go. For two days the telegram lay unanswered, and then the yeast of New York began to work.

When I arrived, the inevitable portfolio under my arm, Mr. Luce and his associates explained that they were planning to launch a new magazine of business and industry—*Fortune*, they planned to call it—and they hoped to illustrate it with the most dramatic photographs of industry that had ever been taken. Did I think this was a good idea, he wanted to know?

A good idea? This was the very role I believed photography should play. I said yes and went back to Cleveland to pick up my belongings. Before I left again for New York, I wrote my mother: "I feel as if the world has been opened up and I hold all the keys."

## DISCUSSION

1. What was it about the steel mills, the smokestacks, and the railroad tracks that excited Margaret Bourke-White?

2. What part did lucky breaks and chance happenings play in her success?

3. Which of her experiences in Cleveland might have influenced Margaret Bourke-White's belief that "a burning purpose attracts others who are drawn along with it and help fulfill it"?

4. From reading this selection, from looking at the photos, and from what you know about photography, what do you think distinguishes a superior photographer from a mediocre one?

5. Review the Handbook entry for *autobiography and biography*. What is the advantage to the reader of having Margaret Bourke-White tell her own story?

## WORD STUDY

The etymology, or history, of a word is found after the last definition in a dictionary entry and usually tells the language or lan-guages from which the word is derived.

**bail i wick** (bāl/ə wik), *n.* **1.** district over which a bailiff or bailie has authority. **2.** a person's field of knowledge, work or authority. [< *bailie* + *wick* office < OE *wice*]

If you then look up *bailie*, you see that a bailie is a municipal officer or magistrate in a Scottish town.

Read the six clues below. Then on your paper write the matching word from the list. You will probably have to read the etymology for each word first.

1. This person was a hang-man in England.

2. This means "star" in Greek.

3. This is the only word in the list which comes from the Italian language.

4. This is derived from the name of a hungry, thirsty, mytho-logical king.

5. This originally meant "herds-man's meat."

6. This comes from the Latin word for "plague."

| | |
|---|---|
| goulash | aster |
| pest | crescendo |
| tantalize | derrick |

## MARGARET BOURKE-WHITE

Margaret Bourke-White left Cleveland and spent from 1929 to 1935 with *Fortune* magazine.

During an assignment to cover the 1934 drought, she became more aware of people as subjects for her camera. This awareness, which was to distinguish her work, increased as she worked with author Erskine Caldwell, later her husband, on a book titled *You Have Seen Their Faces* (1937).

The photograph for the first cover of *Life* in 1936 was hers (see page 157), and she continued to work for *Life* throughout her career.

During World War II she became the first woman war photographer. She was in Moscow when it was bombed, her ship was torpedoed when she was covering the invasion of North Africa, and she was with General Patton's forces in Germany in 1945.

A victim of Parkinson's disease, she describes her determined fight against its encroachment in *Portrait of Myself*. She died in 1971.

Sharecroppers photographed for You Have Seen Their Faces (1937), for which Bourke-White did the photography and Erskine Caldwell wrote the text.

Fort Peck Dam in Montana—the cover of the first issue of Life magazine.

This photograph of a 200-ton ladle at the Otis Steel Company won the Cleveland Art Museum award and was used by Fortune magazine.

Margaret Bourke-White:
# A PORTFOLIO

*Above: Mahatma Gandhi, April 1946, with his spinning wheel, symbol of India's struggle for independence.*

*Below: Margaret Bourke-White on a rooftop, photographed by her friend Ralph Steiner.*

*Right: Gold miners in a mine two miles below Johannesburg, South Africa.*

FROM

# Narrative of the Life of
# **Frederick Douglass,**
## an American Slave

*Frederick Douglass*

*In 1845 when the Narrative of the Life of Frederick Douglass was published, Douglass was twenty-seven. He had been born into and lived in slavery for twenty years until his escape to the North in 1838. In the North he became a powerful speaker, drawing huge crowds to hear his recollections of life as a slave and his appeals for the abolition of slavery.*

*The following episode from the Narrative relates his experience at age seventeen with Edward Covey, a professional slave-breaker to whom he had been hired out for one year by his owner, Thomas Auld. Covey's farm was on the eastern shore of Maryland, seven miles from St. Michael's, the town where Douglass had worked for Auld.*

I left Master Thomas's house and went to live with Mr. Covey on the first of January, 1833. I was now, for the first time in my life, a field hand. In my new employment, I found myself even more awkward than a country boy appeared to be in a large city. I had been at my new home but one week before Mr. Covey gave me a very severe whipping, cutting my back, causing the blood to run, and raising ridges on my flesh as large as my little finger. The details of this affair are as follows: Mr.

Covey sent me, very early in the morning of one of our coldest days in the month of January, to the woods to get a load of wood. He gave me a team of unbroken oxen. He told me which was the in-hand ox, and which the off-hand one. He then tied the end of a large rope around the horns of the in-hand ox, and gave me the other end of it, and told me if the oxen started to run that I must hold on upon the rope. I had never driven oxen before, and of course I was very awkward. I, however, succeeded in getting to the edge of the woods with little difficulty; but I had got a very few rods into the woods when the oxen took fright and started full tilt, carrying the cart against trees and over stumps in the most frightful manner. I expected every moment that my brains would be dashed out against the trees. After running thus for a considerable distance, they finally upset the cart, dashing it with great force against a tree, and threw themselves into a dense thicket. How I escaped death, I do not know. There I was, entirely alone, in a thick wood, in a place new to me. My cart was upset and shattered, my oxen were entangled among the young trees, and there was none to help me. After a long spell of effort, I succeeded in getting my cart righted, my oxen disentangled and again yoked to the cart. I now proceeded with my team to the place where I had, the day before, been chopping wood, and loaded my cart pretty heavily, thinking in this way to tame my oxen. I then proceeded on my way home. I had now consumed one half of the day. I got out of the woods safely and now felt out of danger. I stopped my oxen to open the woods gate; and just as I did so, before I could get hold of my ox-rope, the oxen again started, rushed through the gate, catching it between the wheel and the body of the cart, tearing it to pieces, and coming within a few inches of crushing me against the gatepost. Thus twice, in one short day, I escaped death by the merest chance. On my return, I told Mr. Covey what had happened and how it happened. He ordered me to return to the woods again immediately. I did so, and he followed on after me. Just as I got into the woods, he came up and told me to stop my cart, and that he would teach me how to trifle away my time and break gates. He then went to a large gum tree, and with his axe cut three large switches, and, after trimming them up neatly with his pocketknife, he ordered me to take off my clothes. I made him no answer, but stood with my clothes on. He repeated his order. I still made him no answer, nor did I move to strip myself. Upon this he rushed at me with the fierceness of a tiger, tore off my clothes, and lashed me till he had worn out his switches, cutting me so savagely as to leave the marks visible for a long time after. This whipping was the first of a number just like it, and for similar offences.

I lived with Mr. Covey one year. During the first six months of that year, scarce a week passed without his whipping me. I was seldom free from a sore back. My awkwardness was almost always his excuse for whipping me. We were worked fully up to the point of endurance. Long before day we were up, our horses fed, and by the first approach of day we were off to the field with our hoes and ploughing teams. Mr. Covey gave us enough to eat, but scarce time to eat it. We were often less than five minutes taking our meals. We were often in the field from the first approach of day till its last lingering ray had left us; and at saving-fodder time, midnight often caught us in the field binding blades.[1]

Covey would be out with us. The way he used to stand it, was this. He would spend the most of his afternoons in bed. He would then come out fresh in the evening, ready to urge us on with his words, example, and frequently with the whip. Mr. Covey was one of the few slaveholders who could and did work with his hands. He was a hard-working man. He knew by himself just what a man or a boy could do. There was no deceiving him. His work went on in his absence almost as well as in his presence, and he had the faculty of making us feel that he was ever present with us. This he did by surprising us. He seldom approached the spot where we were at work openly, if he could do it secretly. He always aimed at taking us by surprise. Such was his cunning, that we used to call him, among ourselves, "the snake." When we were at work in the cornfield, he would sometimes crawl on his hands and knees to avoid detection, and all at once he would rise nearly in our midst, and scream out, "Ha, ha! Come, come! Dash on, dash on!" This being his mode of attack, it was never safe to stop a single minute. His comings were like a thief in the night. He appeared to us as being ever at hand. He was under every tree, behind every stump, in every bush, and at every window, on the plantation. He would sometimes mount his horse, as if bound to St. Michael's, a distance of seven miles, and in half an hour afterwards you would see him coiled up in the corner of the wood fence, watching every motion of the slaves. He would, for this purpose, leave his horse tied up in the woods. Again, he would sometimes walk up to us and give us orders as though he was upon the point of starting on a long journey, turn his back upon us, and make as though he was going to the house to get ready; and, before he would get halfway thither, he would turn short and crawl into a fence corner, or behind some tree, and there watch us till the going down of the sun.

Mr. Covey's forte[2] consisted in his power to deceive. His life was devoted to planning and perpetrating the grossest deceptions. Every thing he possessed in the shape of learning or religion, he made conform to his disposition to deceive. He seemed to think himself equal to deceiving the Almighty. He would make a short prayer in the morning and a long prayer

---

1. *binding blades,* tying together sheaves (bundles) of wheat.

2. *forte* (fôrt), something a person does very well; strong point.

at night; and, strange as it may seem, few men would at times appear more devotional than he. The exercises of his family devotions were always commenced with singing, and, as he was a very poor singer himself, the duty of raising the hymn generally came upon me. He would read his hymn and nod at me to commence. I would at times do so; at others, I would not. My noncompliance would almost always produce much confusion. To show himself independent of me, he would start and stagger through with his hymn in the most discordant manner. In this state of mind, he prayed with more than ordinary spirit. Poor man! such was his disposition and success at deceiving, I do verily believe that he sometimes deceived himself into the solemn belief that he was a sincere worshiper of the most high God. . . .

If at any one time of my life more than another, I was made to drink the bitterest dregs of slavery, that time was during the first six months of my stay with Mr. Covey. We were worked in all weathers. It was never too hot or too cold; it could never rain, blow, hail, or snow too hard for us to work in the field. Work, work, work was scarcely more the order of the day than of the night. The longest days were too short for him, and the shortest nights too long for him. I was somewhat unmanageable when I first went there, but a few months of this discipline tamed me. Mr. Covey succeeded in breaking me. I was broken in body, soul, and spirit. My natural elasticity was crushed, my intellect languished, the disposition to read departed, the cheerful spark that lingered about my eye died; the dark night of slavery closed in upon me; and behold a man transformed into a brute!

Sunday was my only leisure time. I spent this in a sort of beastlike stupor, between sleep and wake, under some large tree. At times I would rise up, a flash of energetic freedom would dart through my soul, accompanied with a faint beam of hope that flickered for a moment and then vanished. I sank down again, mourning over my wretched condition. I was sometimes prompted to take my life and that of Covey, but was prevented by a combination of hope and fear. My sufferings on this plantation seem now like a dream rather than a stern reality.

Our house stood within a few rods of the Chesapeake Bay, whose broad bosom was ever white with sails from every quarter of the habitable globe. Those beautiful vessels, robed in purest white, so delightful to the eye of freemen, were to me so many shrouded ghosts, to terrify and torment me with thoughts of my wretched condition. I have often, in the deep stillness of a summer's Sabbath, stood all alone upon the lofty banks of that noble bay, and traced, with saddened heart and tearful eye, the countless number of sails moving off to the mighty ocean. The sight of these always affected me powerfully. My thoughts would compel utterance; and there, with no audience but the Almighty, I would pour out my soul's complaint, in my rude way, with an apostrophe to the moving multitude of ships:

"You are loosed from your moorings and are free; I am fast in my chains and am a slave! You move merrily before the gentle gale, and I sadly before the bloody whip! You are freedom's swift-winged angels, that fly round the world; I am confined in bands of iron! O that I were free! O, that I were on one of your gallant decks and under your protecting wing! Alas! betwixt me and you, the turbid waters roll. Go on, go on. O that I could also go! Could I but swim! If I could fly! O, why was I born a man, of whom to make a brute! The glad ship is gone; she hides in the dim distance. I am left in the hottest hell of unending slavery. O God, save me! God, deliver me! Let me be free! Is there any God? Why am I a slave? I will run away. I will not stand it. Get caught, or get clear, I'll try it. I had as well die with ague as the fever. I have only one life to lose. I had as well be killed running as die standing. Only think of it; one hundred miles straight north, and I am free! Try it? Yes! God helping me, I will. It cannot be that I shall live and die a slave. I will take to the water. This very bay shall yet bear me into freedom. The steamboats steered in a northeast course from North Point. I will do the same; and when I get to the head of the bay, I will turn my canoe adrift and walk straight through Delaware into Pennsylvania. When I get there, I shall not be required to have a pass; I can travel without being disturbed. Let but the first opportunity offer, and, come what will,

I am off. Meanwhile, I will try to bear up under the yoke. I am not the only slave in the world. Why should I fret? I can bear as much as any of them. Besides, I am but a boy, and all boys are bound to someone. It may be that my misery in slavery will only increase my happiness when I get free. There is a better day coming."

Thus I used to think, and thus I used to speak to myself; goaded almost to madness at one moment, and at the next reconciling myself to my wretched lot.

I have already intimated that my condition was much worse during the first six months of my stay at Mr. Covey's than in the last six. The circumstances leading to the change in Mr. Covey's course toward me form an epoch in my humble history. You have seen how a man was made a slave; you shall see how a slave was made a man. On one of the hottest days of the month of August 1833, Bill Smith, William Hughes, a slave named Eli, and myself, were engaged in fanning wheat.[3] Hughes was clearing the fanned wheat from before the fan, Eli was turning, Smith was feeding, and I was carrying wheat to the fan. The work was simple, requiring strength rather than intellect; yet, to one entirely unused to such work, it came very hard. About three o'clock of that day, I broke down; my strength failed me; I was seized with a violent aching of the head, attended with extreme dizziness; I trembled in every limb. Finding what was coming, I nerved myself up, feeling it would never do to stop work. I stood as long as I could stagger to the hopper with grain. When I could stand no longer, I fell, and felt as if held down by an immense weight. The fan of course stopped; everyone had his own work to do, and no one could do the work of the other and have his own go on at the same time.

Mr. Covey was at the house, about one hundred yards from the treading yard where we were fanning. On hearing the fan stop, he left immediately and came to the spot where we were. He hastily inquired what the matter was. Bill answered that I was sick, and there was no one to bring wheat to the fan. I had by this time crawled away under the side of the post

3. *fanning wheat,* using a fan to blow the chaff (husks) of the wheat away from the grain.

and rail fence by which the yard was enclosed, hoping to find relief by getting out of the sun. He then asked where I was. He was told by one of the hands. He came to the spot, and, after looking at me awhile, asked me what was the matter. I told him as well as I could, for I scarce had strength to speak. He then gave me a savage kick in the side and told me to get up. I tried to do so, but fell back in the attempt. He gave me another kick and again told me to rise. I again tried and succeeded in gaining my feet; but, stooping to get the tub with which I was feeding the fan, I again staggered and fell. While down in this situation, Mr. Covey took up the hickory slat with which Hughes had been striking off the half-bushel measure, and with it gave me a heavy blow upon the head, making a large wound, and the blood ran freely; and with this again told me to get up. I made no effort to comply, having now made up my mind to let him do his worst. In a short time after receiving this blow, my head grew better. Mr. Covey had now left me to my fate. At this moment I resolved, for the first time, to go to my master, enter a complaint, and ask his protection. In order to [do] this, I must that afternoon walk seven miles; and this, under the circumstances, was truly a severe undertaking. I was exceedingly feeble, made so as much by the kicks and blows which I received as by the severe fit of sickness to which I had been subjected. I, however, watched my chance, while Covey was looking in an opposite direction, and started for St. Michael's. I succeeded in getting a considerable distance on my way to the woods when Covey discovered me and called after me to come back, threatening what he would do if I did not come. I disregarded both his calls and his threats and made my way to the woods as fast as my feeble state would allow; and, thinking I might be overhauled by him if I kept the road, I walked through the woods, keeping far enough from the road to avoid detection and near enough to prevent losing my way. I had not gone far before my little strength again failed me. I could go no farther. I fell down and lay for a considerable time. The blood was yet oozing from the wound on my head. For a time I thought I should bleed to death; and think now that I should have done so, but that the blood so matted my hair as to stop the wound. After lying there about three-quarters of an hour, I nerved myself up again and started on my way through bogs and briers, barefooted and bareheaded, tearing my feet sometimes at nearly every step; and after a journey of about seven miles, occupying some five hours to perform it, I arrived at master's store. I then presented an appearance enough to affect any but a heart of iron. From the crown of my head to my feet, I was covered with blood. My hair was all clotted with dust and blood; my shirt was stiff with blood. My legs and feet were torn in sundry places with briers and thorns and were also covered with blood. I suppose I looked like a man who had escaped a den of wild beasts, and barely escaped them. In this state I appeared before my master, humbly entreating him to interpose his authority for my protection. I told him all the circumstances as well as I could, and it seemed, as I spoke, at times to affect him. He would then walk the floor and seek to justify Covey by saying he expected I deserved it. He asked me what I wanted. I told him, to let me get a new home; that as sure as I lived with Mr. Covey again, I should live with but to die with him, that Covey would surely kill me; he was in a fair way for it. Master Thomas ridiculed the idea that there was any danger of Mr. Covey's killing me and said that he knew Mr. Covey; that he was a good man and that he could not think of taking me from him; that, should he do so, he would lose the whole year's wages; that I belonged to Mr. Covey for one year and that I must go back to him, come what might; and that I must not trouble him with any more stories, or that he would himself *get hold of me*. After threatening me thus, he gave me a very large dose of salts, telling me that I might remain in St. Michael's that night (it being quite late), but that I must be off back to Mr. Covey's early in the morning; and that if I did not, he would *get hold of me*, which meant that he would whip me. I remained all night, and, according to his orders, I started off to Covey's in the morning (Saturday morning), wearied in body and broken in spirit. I got no supper that night or breakfast that morning. I reached Covey's about nine

o'clock; and, just as I was getting over the fence that divided Mrs. Kemp's fields from ours, out ran Covey with his cowskin, to give me another whipping. Before he could reach me, I succeeded in getting to the cornfield; and as the corn was very high, it afforded me the means of hiding. He seemed very angry and searched for me a long time. My behavior was altogether unaccountable. He finally gave up the chase, thinking, I suppose, that I must come home for something to eat; he would give himself no further trouble in looking for me. I spent that day mostly in the woods, having the alternative before me—to go home and be whipped to death, or stay in the woods and be starved to death. That night, I fell in with Sandy Jenkins, a slave with whom I was somewhat acquainted. Sandy had a free wife who lived about four miles from Mr. Covey's; and, it being Saturday, he was on his way to see her. I told him my circumstances, and he very kindly invited me to go home with him. I went home with him, and talked this whole matter over and got his advice as to what course it was best for me to pursue. I found Sandy an old adviser. He told me, with great solemnity, I must go back to Covey; but that before I went, I must go with him into another part of the woods, where there was a certain root, which, if I would take some of it with me, carrying it *always on my right side*, would render it impossible for Mr. Covey, or any other white man, to whip me. He said he had carried it for years; and since he had done so, he had never received a blow, and never expected to while he carried it. I at first rejected the idea that the simple carrying of a root in my pocket would have any such effect as he had said and was not disposed to take it; but Sandy impressed the necessity with much earnestness, telling me it could do no harm, if it did no good. To please him, I at length took the root, and, according to his direction, carried it upon my right side. This was Sunday morning. I immediately started for home; and, upon entering the yard gate, out came Mr. Covey on his way to meeting. He spoke to me very kindly, made me drive the pigs from a lot near by, and passed on towards the church. Now, this singular conduct of Mr.

Covey really made me begin to think that there was something in the root which Sandy had given me; and had it been on any other day than Sunday, I could have attributed the conduct to no other cause than the influence of that root; and as it was, I was half inclined to think the root to be something more than I at first had taken it to be. All went well till Monday morning. On this morning the virtue of the root was fully tested. Long before daylight, I was called to go and rub, curry, and feed the horses. I obeyed and was glad to obey. But whilst thus engaged, whilst in the act of throwing down some blades from the loft, Mr. Covey entered the stable with a long rope; and just as I was half out of the loft, he caught hold of my legs and was about tying me. As soon as I found what he was up to, I gave a sudden spring, and as I did so, he holding to my legs, I was brought sprawling on the stable floor. Mr. Covey seemed now to think he had me and could do what he pleased; but at this moment—from whence came the spirit I don't know—I resolved to fight; and, suiting my action to the resolution, I seized Covey hard by the throat; and as I did so, I rose. He held on to me, and I to him. My resistance was so entirely unexpected that Covey seemed taken all aback. He trembled like a leaf. This gave me assurance, and I held him uneasy, causing the blood to run where I touched him with the ends of my fingers. Mr. Covey soon called out to Hughes for help. Hughes came, and, while Covey held me, attempted to tie my right hand. While he was in the act of doing so, I watched my chance, and gave him a heavy kick close under the ribs. This kick fairly sickened Hughes, so that he left me in the hands of Mr. Covey. This kick had the effect of not only weakening Hughes, but Covey also. When he saw Hughes bending over with pain, his courage quailed. He asked me if I meant to persist in my resistance. I told him I did, come what might; that he had used me like a brute for six months, and that I was determined to be used so no longer. With that, he strove to drag me to a stick that was lying just out of the stable door. He meant to knock me down. But just as he was leaning over to get the stick, I seized him with both hands by his collar, and brought him by a sudden snatch to the ground. By this time, Bill came. Covey called upon him for assistance. Bill wanted to know what he could do. Covey said, "Take hold of him, take hold of him!" Bill said his master hired him out to work, and not to help to whip me; so he left Covey and myself to fight our own battle out. We were at it for nearly two hours. Covey at length let me go, puffing and blowing at a great rate, saying that if I had not resisted, he would not have whipped me half so much. The truth was that he had not whipped me at all. I considered him as getting entirely the worst end of the bargain; for he had drawn no blood from me, but I had from him. The whole six months afterwards that I spent with Mr. Covey, he never laid the weight of his finger upon me in anger. He would occasionally say he didn't want to get hold of me again. "No," thought I, "you need not; for you will come off worse than you did before."

This battle with Mr. Covey was the turning point in my career as a slave. It rekindled the few expiring embers of freedom and revived within me a sense of my own manhood. It recalled the departed self-confidence, and inspired me again with a determination to be free. The gratification afforded by the triumph was a full compensation for whatever else might follow, even death itself. He only can understand the deep satisfaction which I experienced, who has himself repelled by force the bloody arm of slavery. I felt as I never felt before. It was a glorious resurrection, from the tomb of slavery, to the heaven of freedom. My long-crushed spirit rose, cowardice departed, bold defiance took its place; and I now resolved that, however long I might remain a slave in form, the day had passed forever when I could be a slave in fact. I did not hesitate to let it be known of me that the white man who expected to succeed in whipping must also succeed in killing me.

From this time I was never again what might be called fairly whipped, though I remained a slave four years afterwards. I had several fights, but was never whipped.

## DISCUSSION

1. Douglass says that Covey's strong point was his power to deceive. What deceptions by Covey are described in this episode?

2. The author writes that after a few months with Covey his "natural elasticity was crushed [and his] intellect languished." How had he changed and what had changed him?

3. What effect did the nearness of Chesapeake Bay have on Douglass's thoughts of freedom?

4. Douglass considered killing himself and Covey. What prevented him?

5. Because of his abilities as a public speaker, some northerners found it hard to believe that Douglass had really been a slave. He wrote the *Narrative* partly to prove that his descriptions of slavery were true, firsthand accounts. What specific details in this episode might have convinced a skeptic?

6. What does Douglass consider the turning point in his career as a slave?

7. How would you characterize the tone of the *Narrative: (a)* bitterly indignant, *(b)* lighthearted, *(c)* direct and straightforward, *(d)* self-pitying, *(e)* inflammatory? Explain.

## WORD STUDY

Frederick Douglass's narrative is written in a *formal* rather than an *informal* style. For instance, he writes, "scarce a week passed without his whipping me." The word "hardly" might be substituted for "scarce" in more informal writing. In most instances, Douglass's style is not difficult, even though it is that of the period in which he lived.

To show the differences between a formal and an informal style, reword the italicized formal words and phrases in the sentences below so that they become informal.

1. *Such was his cunning* that we used to call him "the snake."

2. He *appeared to us as being ever at hand.*

3. Mr. Covey's *forte consisted in his power to deceive.*

4. I *was seized with a violent aching of the head.*

5. After a journey of almost seven miles, *occupying some five hours to perform it,* I arrived at master's store.

6. I *was not disposed* to carry the root.

## FREDERICK DOUGLASS

The publication of the *Narrative of the Life of Frederick Douglass* in 1845 was a significant turning point in this escaped slave's life: he had committed himself— at the risk of a return to slavery— to the abolitionist cause. The initial edition of five thousand copies of the book was sold out in four months. By 1850 a total of thirty thousand copies had been published.

Douglass was born a slave in Maryland in 1817. When he was eight, he became a houseboy in Baltimore and there was taught to read. He was then sent to St. Michaels and shortly afterward hired out to Edward Covey. In 1838 he escaped to New Bedford, Massachusetts.

He then sent for and married Anna, a free black woman from Baltimore. He held assorted jobs until 1841, when he was asked to speak at an abolition meeting. Soon he became a full-time, persuasive lecturer for the abolitionist cause.

In 1847 he moved to Rochester, where he published a weekly antislavery paper, *The North Star.* He made his home one of the headquarters of the underground railroad and gave much from his lecture fees to aid runaway slaves. He worked to make slavery the issue of the Civil War, and after the war he pressed for voting rights for blacks.

From 1871 to 1891, he held several government posts. At his funeral in 1895, senators, officials of Howard University, and a justice of the Supreme Court were among those who paid their respects to this man who had spent his life urging the government to make good on its commitment to equality.

When Black Elk was nine years old, he had a great
holy vision in which many things were revealed to
him. Although he told no one of this vision, shortly
after it occurred, Whirlwind Chaser, a medicine man,
looked at Black Elk closely and then said to Black
Elk's father: "Your boy there is sitting in a sacred
manner. I do not know what it is, but there is something special for him to do, for just as I came in I
could see a power like a light all through his body."

After this time, and throughout his life, Black Elk
continued to have extraordinary visions. He was able
to predict certain happenings, to cure the sick, and to
instruct his people.

In 1930, John G. Neihardt, a poet seeking material
for a long narrative poem entitled Cycle of the West,
met Black Elk. During Neihardt's visit, Black Elk decided to let him record the story of his life so that
he could "save his Great Vision for men." Neihardt
returned in 1931 and, with Black Elk's son Ben acting
as interpreter, recorded the old man's story. In 1932
Neihardt published Black Elk Speaks, the autobiography from which the following excerpts were
taken.

FROM

# BLACK ELK SPEAKS

as told through
### John G. Neihardt
(Flaming Rainbow)

M Y friend, I am going to tell you the story of
my life, as you wish; and if it were only the
story of my life I think I would not tell it; for
what is one man that he should make much of
his winters, even when they bend him like a
heavy snow? So many other men have lived
and shall live that story, to be grass upon the
hills.

It is the story of all life that is holy and is good to tell, and of us two-leggeds sharing in it with the four-leggeds and the wings of the air and all green things; for these are children of one mother and their father is one Spirit.

This, then, is not the tale of a great hunter or of a great warrior, or of a great traveler, although I have made much meat in my time and fought for my people both as boy and man, and have gone far and seen strange lands and men. So also have many others done, and better than I. These things I shall remember by the way, and often they may seem to be the very tale itself, as when I was living them in happiness and sorrow. But now that I can see it all as from a lonely hilltop, I know it was the story of a mighty vision given to a man too weak to use it; of a holy tree that should have flourished in a people's heart with flowers and singing birds, and now is withered; and of a people's dream that died in bloody snow. . . .

## I. Early Boyhood

I am a Lakota of the Oglala band.[1] My father's name was Black Elk, and his father before him bore the name, and the father of his father, so that I am the fourth to bear it. He was a medicine man and so were several of his brothers. Also, he and the great Crazy Horse's father were cousins, having the same grandfather. My mother's name was White Cow Sees; her father was called Refuse-to-Go, and her mother, Plenty Eagle Feathers. I can remember my mother's mother and her father. My father's father was killed by the Pawnees when I was too little to know, and his mother, Red Eagle Woman, died soon after.

I was born in the Moon of the Popping Trees (December) on the Little Powder River in the Winter When the Four Crows Were Killed (1863), and I was three years old when my father's right leg was broken in the Battle of the Hundred Slain.[2] From that wound he limped until the day he died, which was about the time when Big Foot's band was butchered on Wounded Knee (1890). He is buried here in these hills.

I can remember that Winter of the Hundred Slain as a man may remember some bad dream he dreamed when he was little, but I can not tell just how much I heard when I was bigger and how much I understood when I was little. It is like some fearful thing in a fog, for it was a time when everything seemed troubled and afraid.

I had never seen a Wasichu[3] then, and did not know what one looked like; but everyone was saying that the Wasichus were coming and that they were going to take our country and rub us all out and that we should all have to die fighting. It was the Wasichus who got rubbed out in that battle, and all the people were talking about it for a long while; but a hundred Wasichus was not much if there were others and others without number where those came from.

I remember once that I asked my grandfather about this. I said: "When the scouts come back from seeing the prairie full of bison somewhere, the people say the Wasichus are coming; and when strange men are coming to kill us all, they say the Wasichus are coming. What does it mean?" And he said, "That they are many."

When I was older, I learned what the fighting was about that winter and the next summer. Up on the Madison Fork the Wasichus had found much of the yellow metal that they worship and that makes them crazy, and they wanted to have a road up through our country to the place where the yellow metal was; but my people did not want the road. It would scare the bison and make them go away, and also it would let the other Wasichus come in like a river. They told us that they wanted only to use a little land, as much as a wagon would take between the wheels; but our people knew better. And when you look about you now, you can see what it was they wanted.

Once we were happy in our own country and we were seldom hungry, for then the two-leggeds and the four-leggeds lived together

---

1. *a Lakota of the Oglala band.* The Indians that white men called Sioux called themselves Lakotas or Dakotas. The Oglala were a sub-tribe of the Lakotas.
2. *Battle of the Hundred Slain,* the Fetterman Fight, commonly described as a "massacre," in which Captain Fetterman and 81 men were killed on Peno Creek near Fort Phil Kearney, Nebraska, December 21, 1866.
3. *Wasichu,* a term used to designate the white man, but having no reference to the color of his skin.

like relatives, and there was plenty for them and for us. But the Wasichus came, and they have made little islands for us and other little islands for the four-leggeds, and always these islands are becoming smaller, for around them surges the gnawing flood of the Wasichu; and it is dirty with lies and greed.

A long time ago my father told me what his father told him, that there was once a Lakota holy man, called Drinks Water, who dreamed what was to be; and this was long before the coming of the Wasichus. He dreamed that the four-leggeds were going back into the earth and that a strange race had woven a spider's web all around the Lakotas. And he said: "When this happens, you shall live in square gray houses, in a barren land, and beside those square gray houses you shall starve." They say he went back to Mother Earth soon after he saw this vision, and it was sorrow that killed him. You can look about you now and see that he meant these dirt-roofed houses we are living in, and that all the rest was true. Sometimes dreams are wiser than waking. . . .

## II. Walking the Black Road

. . . Wherever we went, the soldiers came to kill us, and it was all our own country. It was ours already when the Wasichus made the treaty with Red Cloud that said it would be ours as long as grass should grow and water flow. That was only eight winters before, and they were chasing us now because we remembered and they forgot.

After that we started west again, and we were not happy anymore, because so many of our people had untied their horses' tails[4] and gone over to the Wasichus. We went back deep into our country, and most of the land was black from the fire, and the bison had gone away. We camped on the Tongue River where there was some cottonwood for the ponies, and a hard winter came on early. It snowed much; game was hard to find, and it was a hungry time for us. Ponies died, and we ate them. They died because the snow froze hard and they could not find the grass that was left in the valleys and there was not enough cottonwood to feed them

all. There had been thousands of us together that summer, but there were not two thousand now.

News came to us there in the Moon of the Falling Leaves (November) that the Black Hills had been sold to the Wasichus and also all the country west of the Hills—the country we were in then.[5] I learned when I was older that our people did not want to do this. The Wasichus went to some of the chiefs alone and got them to put their marks on the treaty. Maybe some of them did this when they were crazy from drinking the minne wakan (holy water, whiskey) the Wasichus gave them. I have heard this; I do not know. But only crazy or very foolish men would sell their Mother Earth. Sometimes I think it might have been better if we had stayed together and made them kill us all.

Dull Knife was camping with his band of Shyelas (Cheyennes) on Willow Creek in the edge of the Big Horn Mountains, and one morning very early near the end of the Moon of Falling Leaves the soldiers came there to kill them.[6] The people were all sleeping. The snow was deep and it was very cold. When the soldiers began shooting into the tepees, the people ran out into the snow, and most of them were naked from their sleeping robes. Men fought in the snow and cold with nothing on them but their cartridge belts, and it was a hard fight, because the warriors thought of the women and children freezing. They could not whip the soldiers, but those who were not killed and did not die from the cold, got away and came to our camp on the Tongue.

I can remember when Dull Knife came with what was left of his starving and freezing people. They had almost nothing, and some of them had died on the way. Many little babies died. We could give them clothing, but of food we could not give them much, for we were eating ponies when they died. And afterwhile they left us and started for the Soldiers' Town on White River to surrender to the Wasichus; and so we were all alone there in that country that was ours and had been stolen from us.

After that the people noticed that Crazy

---

4. *untied their horses' tails*, left the war-path.

5. *News . . . then.* The treaty was signed in October 1876.
6. *one morning . . . kill them.* Colonel Mackenzie attacked the Cheyenne village as stated on November 26, 1876.

Horse was queerer than ever. He hardly ever stayed in the camp. People would find him out alone in the cold, and they would ask him to come home with them. He would not come, but sometimes he would tell the people what to do. People wondered if he ate anything at all. Once my father found him out alone like that, and he said to my father: "Uncle, you have noticed me the way I act. But do not worry; there are caves and holes for me to live in, and out here the spirits may help me. I am making plans for the good of my people."

He was always a queer man, but that winter he was queerer than ever. Maybe he had seen that he would soon be dead and was thinking how to help us when he would not be with us any more.

It was a very bad winter for us and we were all sad. Then another trouble came. We had sent out scouts to learn where the soldiers were, and they were camping at the mouth of the Tongue. Early in the Moon of Frost in the Tepee (January), some of our scouts came in and said that the soldiers were coming up the Tongue to fight us, and that they had two wagon guns (cannon) with them.

There was no better place to go, so we got ready to fight them; and I was afraid, because my father told me we had not much ammunition left. We moved the village a little way off up stream, and our warriors were ready on a high bluff when the walking soldiers and their wagons came in the morning.[7] The soldiers built fires and ate their breakfast there in the valley while our people watched them and were hungry. Then they began shooting with the wagon guns that shot twice, because the iron balls went off after they fell. Some of them did not go off, and we boys ran after one of these and got it.

Then the walking soldiers started up the bluff, and it began to snow hard, and they fought in the blizzard. We could not stop the soldiers coming up because we had not much ammunition. The soldiers had everything. But our men used spears and guns for clubs when the soldiers got there, and they fought hand to hand awhile, holding the soldiers back until

7. *the walking soldiers . . . morning.* General Miles attacked the village of Crazy Horse on the Tongue River, January 8, 1876.

the women could break camp and get away with the children and ponies. We fled in the blizzard southward up the Tongue and over to the Little Powder River. The soldiers followed us awhile, and there was fighting in our rear. We got away, but we lost many things we needed, and when we camped on the Little Powder, we were almost as poor as Dull Knife's people were the day they came to us. It was so cold that the sun made himself fires, and we were eating our starving ponies.

Late in the Moon of the Dark Red Calf (February) or early in the Moon of the Snowblind (March), Spotted Tail, the Brulé, with some others, came to us. His sister was Crazy Horse's mother. He was a great chief and a great warrior before he went over to the Wasichus. I saw him and I did not like him. He was fat with Wasichu food and we were lean with famine. My father told me that he came to make his nephew surrender to the soldiers, because our own people had turned against us, and in the spring when the grass was high enough for the horses, many soldiers would come and fight us, and many Shoshones and Crows and even Lakotas and our old friends, the Shyelas (Cheyennes), would come against us with the Wasichus. I could not understand this, and I thought much about it. How could men get fat by being bad, and starve by being good? I thought and thought about my vision, and it made me very sad; for I wondered if maybe it was only a queer dream after all.

And then I heard that we would all go into the Soldiers' Town when the grass should appear, and that Crazy Horse had untied his pony's tail and would not fight again.

In the Moon of the Grass Appearing (April) our little band started for the Soldiers' Town ahead of the others, and it was early in the Moon When the Ponies Shed (May) that Crazy Horse came in with the rest of our people and the ponies that were only skin and bones. There were soldiers and Lakota policemen in lines all around him when he surrendered there at the Soldiers' Town. I saw him take off his war bonnet. I was not near enough to hear what he said. He did not talk loud and he said only a few words, and then he sat down.

I was fourteen years old. . . .

## III. The First Cure

After the heyoka ceremony,[8] I came to live here where I am now between Wounded Knee Creek and Grass Creek.[9] Others came too, and we made these little gray houses of logs that you see, and they are square. It is a bad way to live, for there can be no power in a square.

You have noticed that everything an Indian does is in a circle, and that is because the Power of the World always works in circles, and everything tries to be round. In the old days when we were a strong and happy people, all our power came to us from the sacred hoop of the nation, and so long as the hoop was unbroken, the people flourished. The flowering tree was the living center of the hoop, and the circle of the four quarters nourished it. The east gave peace and light, the south gave warmth, the west gave rain, and the north with its cold and mighty wind gave strength and endurance. This knowledge came to us from the outer world with our religion. Everything the Power of the World does is done in a circle. The sky is round, and I have heard that the earth is round like a ball, and so are all the stars. The wind, in its greatest power, whirls. Birds make their nests in circles, for theirs is the same religion as ours. The sun comes forth and goes down again in a circle. The moon does the same, and both are round. Even the seasons form a great circle in their changing and always come back again to where they were. The life of a man is a circle from childhood to childhood, and so it is in everything where power moves. Our tepees were round like the nests of birds, and these were always set in a circle, the nation's hoop, a nest of many nests, where the Great Spirit meant for us to hatch our children.

But the Wasichus have put us in these square boxes. Our power is gone and we are dying, for the power is not in us any more. You can look at our boys and see how it is with us. When we were living by the power of the circle in the way we should, boys were men at twelve or thirteen years of age. But now it takes them very much longer to mature.

Well, it is as it is. We are prisoners of war while we are waiting here. But there is another world.

It was in the Moon of Shedding Ponies (May) when we had the heyoka ceremony. One day in the Moon of Fatness (June), when everything was blooming, I invited One Side to come over and eat with me. I had been thinking about the four-rayed herb that I had now seen twice—the first time in the great vision when I was nine years old, and the second time when I was lamenting on the hill.[10] I knew that I must have this herb for curing, and I thought I could recognize the place where I had seen it growing that night when I lamented.

After One Side and I had eaten, I told him there was an herb I must find, and I wanted him to help me hunt for it. Of course I did not tell him I had seen it in a vision. He was willing to help, so we got on our horses and rode over to Grass Creek. Nobody was living over there. We came to the top of a high hill above the creek, and there we got off our horses and sat down, for I felt that we were close to where I saw the herb growing in my vision of the dog.

We sat there awhile singing together some heyoka songs. Then I began to sing alone a song I had heard in my first great vision:

"In a sacred manner they are sending voices."

After I had sung this song, I looked down toward the west, and yonder at a certain spot beside the creek were crows and magpies, chicken hawks and spotted eagles circling around and around.

Then I knew, and I said to One Side: "Friend, right there is where the herb is growing." He said: "We will go forth and see." So we got on our horses and rode down Grass Creek until we came to a dry gulch, and this we followed up.

---

8. *the heyoka ceremony*, a ceremony in which men called heyokas, who have had a sacred vision, share their sacred power with their people by dressing and painting themselves as clowns and performing tricks to make the people laugh. Black Elk had performed as a heyoka in a ceremony which dramatized one of his visions for his people.

9. *here . . . Grass Creek.* Black Elk's log cabin was about two miles west of Manderson Post Office, Pine Ridge Reservation, South Dakota.

10. *lamenting on the hill.* In 1881, when Black Elk was eighteen, he had fasted four days and then spent a night on a hilltop, lamenting and praying to the Great Spirit for understanding. During the night he had a vision in which he again saw the four-rayed herb he had seen in the earlier vision when he was nine.

As we neared the spot the birds all flew away, and it was a place where four or five dry gulches came together. There right on the side of the bank the herb was growing, and I knew it, although I had never seen one like it before, except in my vision.

It had a root about as long as to my elbow, and this was a little thicker than my thumb. It was flowering in four colors, blue, white, red, and yellow.

We got off our horses, and after I had offered red willow bark to the Six Powers, I made a prayer to the herb, and said to it: "Now we shall go forth to the two-leggeds, but only to the weakest ones, and there shall be happy days among the weak."

It was easy to dig the herb, because it was growing in the edge of the clay gulch. Then we started back with it. When we came to Grass Creek again, we wrapped it in some good sage that was growing there.

Something must have told me to find the herb just then, for the next evening I needed it and could have done nothing without it.

I was eating supper when a man by the name of Cuts-to-Pieces came in, and he was saying: "Hey, hey, hey!" for he was in trouble. I asked him what was the matter, and he said: "I have a boy of mine, and he is very sick and I am afraid he will die soon. He has been sick a long time. They say you have great power from the horse dance and the heyoka ceremony, so maybe you can save him for me. I think so much of him."

I told Cuts-to-Pieces that if he really wanted help, he should go home and bring me back a pipe with an eagle feather on it. While he was gone, I thought about what I had to do; and I was afraid, because I had never cured anybody yet with my power, and I was very sorry for Cuts-to-Pieces. I prayed hard for help. When Cuts-to-Pieces came back with the pipe, I told him to take it around to the left of me, leave it there, and pass out again to the right of me. When he had done this, I sent for One Side to come and help me. Then I took the pipe and went to where the sick little boy was. My father and my mother went with us, and my friend, Standing Bear, was already there.

I first offered the pipe to the Six Powers, then

I passed it, and we all smoked. After that I began making a rumbling thunder sound on the drum. You know, when the power of the west comes to the two-leggeds, it comes with rumbling, and when it has passed, everything lifts up its head and is glad and there is greenness. So I made this rumbling sound. Also, the voice of the drum is an offering to the Spirit of the World. Its sound arouses the mind and makes men feel the mystery and power of things.

The sick little boy was on the northeast side of the tepee, and when we entered at the south, we went around from left to right, stopping on the west side when we had made the circle.

You want to know why we always go from left to right like that. I can tell you something of the reason, but not all. Think of this: Is not the south the source of life, and does not the flowering stick truly come from there? And does not man advance from there toward the setting sun of his life? Then does he not approach the colder north where the white hairs are? And does he not then arrive, if he lives, at the source of light and understanding, which is the east? Then does he not return to where he began, to his second childhood, there to give back his life to all life, and his flesh to the earth whence it came? The more you think about this, the more meaning you will see in it.

As I said, we went into the tepee from left to right, and sat ourselves down on the west side. The sick little boy was on the northeast side, and he looked as though he were only skin and bones. I had the pipe, the drum, and the four-rayed herb already, so I asked for a wooden cup, full of water, and an eagle bone whistle, which was for the spotted eagle of my great vision. They placed the cup of water in front of me; and then I had to think awhile, because I had never done this before and I was in doubt.

I understood a little more now, so I gave the eagle bone whistle to One Side and told him how to use it in helping me. Then I filled the pipe with red willow bark, and gave it to the pretty young daughter of Cuts-to-Pieces, telling her to hold it, just as I had seen the virgin of the east holding it in my great vision.

Everything was ready now, so I made low thunder on the drum, keeping time as I sent forth a voice. Four times I cried "Hey-a-a-hey," drumming as I cried to the Spirit of the World, and while I was doing this I could feel the power coming through me from my feet up, and I knew that I could help the sick little boy.

I kept on sending a voice, while I made low thunder on the drum, saying: "My Grandfather, Great Spirit, you are the only one and to no other can any one send voices. You have made everything, they say, and you have made it good and beautiful. The four quarters and the two roads crossing each other, you have made. Also you have set a power where the sun goes down. The two-leggeds on earth are in despair. For them, my Grandfather, I send a voice to you. You have said this to me: The weak shall walk. In vision you have taken me to the center of the world and there you have shown me the power to make over. The water in the cup that you have given me, by its power shall the dying live. The herb that you have shown me, through its power shall the feeble walk upright. From where we are always facing (the south), behold, a virgin shall appear, walking the good red road, offering the pipe as she walks, and hers also is the power of the flowering tree. From where the Giant lives (the north), you have given me a sacred, cleansing wind, and where this wind passes the weak shall have strength. You have said this to me. To you and to all your powers and to Mother Earth I send a voice for help."

You see, I had never done this before, and I know now that only one power would have been enough. But I was so eager to help the sick little boy that I called on every power there is.

I had been facing the west, of course, while sending a voice. Now I walked to the north and to the east and to the south, stopping there where the source of all life is and where the good red road begins. Standing there I sang thus:

"In a sacred manner I have made them walk.
A sacred nation lies low.
In a sacred manner I have made them walk.
A sacred two-legged, he lies low.
In a sacred manner, he shall walk."

While I was singing this I could feel something queer all through my body, something that made me want to cry for all unhappy things, and there were tears on my face.

Now I walked to the quarter of the west, where I lit the pipe, offered it to the powers, and, after I had taken a whiff of smoke, I passed it around.

When I looked at the sick little boy again, he smiled at me, and I could feel that the power was getting stronger.

I next took the cup of water, drank a little of it, and went around to where the sick little boy was. Standing before him, I stamped the earth four times. Then, putting my mouth to the pit of his stomach, I drew through him the cleansing wind of the north. I next chewed some of the herb and put it in the water, afterward blowing some of it on the boy and to the four quarters. The cup with the rest of the water I gave to the virgin, who gave it to the sick little boy to drink. Then I told the virgin to help the boy stand up and to walk around the circle with him, beginning at the south, the source of life. He was very poor and weak, but with the virgin's help he did this.

Then I went away.

Next day Cuts-to-Pieces came and told me that his little boy was feeling better and was sitting up and could eat something again. In four days he could walk around. He got well and lived to be thirty years old.

Cuts-to-Pieces gave me a good horse for doing this; but of course I would have done it for nothing.

When the people heard about how the little boy was cured, many came to me for help, and I was busy most of the time.

This was in the summer of my nineteenth year (1882), in the Moon of Making Fat.

## IV.  Bad Trouble Coming

. . . It was now near the end of the Moon of Popping Trees, and I was twenty-seven years old (December 1890). We heard that Big Foot was coming down from the Badlands with nearly four hundred people. Some of these were from Sitting Bull's band. They had run away when Sitting Bull was killed and joined Big Foot on Good River. There were only about

a hundred warriors in this band, and all the others were women and children and some old men. They were all starving and freezing, and Big Foot was so sick that they had to bring him along in a pony drag. They had all run away to hide in the Badlands, and they were coming in now because they were starving and freezing. When they crossed Smoky Earth River, they followed up Medicine Root Creek to its head. Soldiers were over there looking for them. The soldiers had everything and were not freezing and starving. Near Porcupine Butte the soldiers came up to the Big Foots, and they surrendered and went along with the soldiers to Wounded Knee Creek where the Brenan store is now.

It was in the evening when we heard that the Big Foots were camped over there with the soldiers, about fifteen miles by the old road from where we were. It was the next morning (December 29, 1890) that something terrible happened.

## V.  The Butchering at Wounded Knee

That evening before it happened I went in to Pine Ridge and heard these things, and while I was there, soldiers started for where the Big Foots were. These made about five hundred soldiers that were there next morning. When I saw them starting I felt that something terrible was going to happen. That night I could hardly sleep at all. I walked around most of the night.

In the morning I went out after my horses, and while I was out I heard shooting off toward the east, and I knew from the sound that it must be wagon guns (cannon) going off. The sounds went right through my body, and I felt that something terrible would happen.

When I reached camp with the horses, a man rode up to me and said: "Hey-hey-hey! The people that are coming are fired on! I know it!"

I saddled up my buckskin and put on my sacred shirt. It was one I had made to be worn by no one but myself. It had a spotted eagle outstretched on the back of it, and the daybreak star was on the left shoulder, because when facing south that shoulder is toward the east. Across the breast, from the left shoulder to the right hip, was the flaming rainbow, and there was another rainbow around the neck, like a necklace, with a star at the bottom. At each shoulder, elbow, and wrist was an eagle feather; and over the whole shirt were red streaks of lightning. You will see that this was from my great vision, and you will know how it protected me that day.

I painted my face all red, and in my hair I put one eagle feather for the One Above.

It did not take me long to get ready, for I could still hear the shooting over there.

I started out alone on the old road that ran across the hills to Wounded Knee.[11] I had no gun. I carried only the sacred bow of the west that I had seen in my great vision. I had gone only a little way when a band of young men came galloping after me. The first two who came up were Loves War and Iron Wasichu. I asked what they were going to do, and they said they were just going to see where the shooting was. Then others were coming up and some older men.

We rode fast, and there were about twenty of us now. The shooting was getting louder. A horseback from over there came galloping very fast toward us, and he said: "Hey-hey-hey! They have murdered them!" Then he whipped his horse and rode away faster toward Pine Ridge.

In a little while we had come to the top of the ridge where, looking to the east, you can see for the first time the monument and the burying ground on the little hill where the church is. That is where the terrible thing started. Just south of the burying ground on the little hill a deep dry gulch runs about east and west, very crooked, and it rises westward to nearly the top of the ridge where we were. It had no name, but the Wasichus sometimes call it Battle Creek now. We stopped on the ridge not far from the head of the dry gulch. Wagon guns were still going off over there on the little hill, and they were going off again where they hit along the gulch. There was much shooting down yonder, and there were many cries, and we could see cavalrymen scattered over the hills ahead of us. Cavalrymen were riding along the gulch and shooting into it, where the women

and children were running away and trying to hide in the gullies and the stunted pines.

A little way ahead of us, just below the head of the dry gulch, there were some women and children who were huddled under a clay bank, and some cavalrymen were there pointing guns at them.

We stopped back behind the ridge, and I said to the others: "Take courage. These are our relatives. We will try to get them back." Then we all sang a song which went like this:

"A thunder being nation I am, I have said.
A thunder being nation I am, I have said.
You shall live.
You shall live.
You shall live.
You shall live."

Then I rode over the ridge and the others after me, and we were crying: "Take courage! It is time to fight!" The soldiers who were guarding our relatives shot at us and then ran away fast, and some more cavalrymen on the other side of the gulch did too. We got our relatives and sent them across the ridge to the northwest where they would be safe.

I had no gun, and when we were charging, I just held the sacred bow out in front of me with my right hand. The bullets did not hit us at all.

We found a little baby lying all alone near the head of the gulch. I could not pick her up just then, but I got her later and some of my people adopted her. I just wrapped her up tighter in a shawl that was around her and left her there. It was a safe place, and I had other work to do.

The soldiers had run eastward over the hills where there were some more soldiers, and they were off their horses and lying down. I told the others to stay back, and I charged upon them holding the sacred bow out toward them with my right hand. They all shot at me, and I could hear bullets all around me, but I ran my horse right close to them, and then swung around. Some soldiers across the gulch began shooting at me too, but I got back to the others and was not hurt at all.

By now many other Lakotas, who had heard

---

11. *Wounded Knee.* Wounded Knee Creek, near Pine Ridge, South Dakota, was the site of the last major battle of the Indian Wars. More than two hundred Sioux men, women, and children were shot down by units of the U.S. Seventh Cavalry.

the shooting, were coming up from Pine Ridge, and we all charged on the soldiers. They ran eastward toward where the trouble began. We followed down along the dry gulch, and what we saw was terrible. Dead and wounded women and children and little babies were scattered all along there where they had been trying to run away. The soldiers had followed along the gulch, as they ran, and murdered them in there. . . .

When we drove the soldiers back, they dug themselves in, and we were not enough people to drive them out from there. In the evening they marched off up Wounded Knee Creek, and then we saw all that they had done there.

Men and women and children were heaped and scattered all over the flat at the bottom of the little hill where the soldiers had their wagon guns, and westward up the dry gulch all the way to the high ridge, the dead women and children and babies were scattered.

When I saw this I wished that I had died too, but I was not sorry for the women and children. It was better for them to be happy in the other world, and I wanted to be there too. But before I went there I wanted to have revenge. I thought there might be a day, and we should have revenge.

After the soldiers marched away, I heard from my friend, Dog Chief, how the trouble started, and he was right there by Yellow Bird when it happened. This is the way it was:

In the morning the soldiers began to take all the guns away from the Big Foots, who were camped in the flat below the little hill where the monument and burying ground are now. The people had stacked most of their guns, and even their knives, by the tepee where Big Foot was lying sick. Soldiers were on the little hill and all around, and there were soldiers across the dry gulch to the south and over east along Wounded Knee Creek too. The people were nearly surrounded, and the wagon guns were pointing at them.

Some had not yet given up their guns, and so the soldiers were searching all the tepees, throwing things around and poking into everything. There was a man called Yellow Bird, and he and another man were standing in front of the tepee where Big Foot was lying sick. They had white sheets around and over them, with eyeholes to look through, and they had guns under these. An officer came to search them. He took the other man's gun, and then started to take Yellow Bird's. But Yellow Bird would not let go. He wrestled with the officer, and while they were wrestling, the gun went off and killed the officer. Wasichus and some others have said he meant to do this, but Dog Chief was standing right there, and he told me it was not so. As soon as the gun went off, Dog Chief told me, an officer shot and killed Big Foot who was lying sick inside the tepee.

Then suddenly nobody knew what was happening, except that the soldiers were all shooting and the wagon guns began going off right in among the people.

Many were shot down right there. The women and children ran into the gulch and up west, dropping all the time, for the soldiers shot them as they ran. There were only about a hundred warriors and there were nearly five hundred soldiers. The warriors rushed to where they had piled their guns and knives. They fought soldiers with only their hands until they got their guns.

Dog Chief saw Yellow Bird run into a tepee with his gun, and from there he killed soldiers until the tepee caught fire. Then he died full of bullets.

It was a good winter day when all this happened. The sun was shining. But after the soldiers marched away from their dirty work, a heavy snow began to fall. The wind came up in the night. There was a big blizzard, and it grew very cold. The snow drifted deep in the crooked gulch, and it was one long grave of butchered women and children and babies, who had never done any harm and were only trying to run away.

## VI.   The End of the Dream

. . . I did not know then how much was ended. When I look back now from this high hill of my old age, I can still see the butchered women and children lying heaped and scattered all along the crooked gulch as plain as when I saw them with eyes still young. And I can see that something else died there in the bloody mud, and was buried in the blizzard. A people's dream died there. It was a beautiful dream.

And I, to whom so great a vision was given in my youth—you see me now a pitiful old man who has done nothing, for the nation's hoop is broken and scattered. There is no center any longer, and the sacred tree is dead.

## DISCUSSION

1. What does Black Elk say is his purpose in telling his life story?

2. Black Elk says that the "Power of the World always works in circles." How does he illustrate this statement?

3. What events in Black Elk's life convinced him that he had extraordinary powers?

4. What do the Indian names for children, events, and seasons of the year reveal about Indian life?

5. In his account of the wars with the Wasichus, Black Elk speaks of the Wasichus' destructive influence on the power of Indian life. (a) How did these outsiders help destroy Indian life? (b) How did the Indians help destroy it? (c) In what way does Black Elk feel he failed?

6. How might the Wasichus' story of the battle at Wounded Knee have differed from Black Elk's?

7. What is the mood of this autobiographical selection?

## JOHN G. NEIHARDT

John G. Neihardt was born in 1881 in Illinois. He attended Nebraska Normal College and earned his degree at the age of sixteen. When his family moved to Bancroft, Nebraska, at the edge of the Omaha Indian Reservation, Neihardt came to know the Indians well, sharing their memories and learning to see and feel as one of them.

In 1908 he published a book of poetry and he married Mona Martinson, a sculptor. In 1911 he began to plan five book-length narrative poems, each dealing with a relatively short period of time and the last ending with the battle of Wounded Knee—the final Indian resistance on the plains. The *Cycle of the West* was completed in 1949. Over a quarter of a century in the writing, it had led him to Black Elk.

Black Elk had declined to tell his story to others, but his response to Neihardt's arrival was later recorded by Neihardt: "As I sit here, I can feel in this man beside me a strong desire to know of the things of the Other World. He has been sent to learn what I know, and I will teach him." The spring following their first meeting, Neihardt and his daughters (one of whom took shorthand notes) spent many days listening to Black Elk and his friends; the result was *Black Elk Speaks.*

Neihardt's honors included election to the National Institute of Arts and Letters and the title Poet Laureate of the state of Nebraska. He died in 1973.

# The Rose-Beetle Man

*Gerald Durrell*

**Between the ages of ten and fifteen, Gerald Durrell lived on the Greek island of Corfu with his widowed mother, his two older brothers Larry and Leslie, his sister Margo, his dog Roger, assorted birds, insects, and other creatures. During the family's five-year stay on the island, Durrell began the zoological studies that were later to lead to a career as a naturalist and collector of animals for British zoos. Durrell has recorded his memories of Corfu in two books,** My Family and Other Animals **and** Birds, Beasts, and Relatives. ***In the excerpt that follows, Durrell recalls a tortoise with a passion for strawberries, a musical pigeon, and the Rose-Beetle Man.*

P ERHAPS one of the most weird and fascinating characters I met during my travels was the Rose-Beetle Man. He had a fairy-tale air about him that was impossible to resist, and I used to look forward eagerly to my infrequent meetings with him. I first saw him on a high, lonely road leading to one of the remote mountain villages. I could hear him long before I could see him, for he was playing a rippling tune on a shepherd's pipe, breaking off now and then to sing a few words in a curious nasal voice. As he rounded the corner both Roger and I stopped and stared at him in amazement.

He had a sharp, foxlike face with large, slanting eyes of such a dark brown that they appeared black. They had a weird, vacant look about them, and a sort of bloom such as one finds on a plum, a pearly covering almost like a cataract. He was short and slight, with a thinness about his wrists and neck that argued a lack of food. His dress was fantastic, and on his head was a shapeless hat with a very wide, floppy brim. It had once been bottle green, but was now speckled and smeared with dust, wine stains, and cigarette burns. In the band were stuck a fluttering forest of feathers: cock feathers, hoopoe feathers, owl feathers, the wing of a kingfisher, the claw of a hawk, and a large dirty white feather that may have come from a swan. His shirt was worn and frayed, gray with sweat, and round the neck dangled an enormous cravat of the most startling blue satin. His coat was dark and shapeless, with patches of different hues here and there; on the sleeve a bit of white cloth with a design of rosebuds; on the shoulder a triangular patch of wine-red and white spots. The pockets of this garment bulged, the contents almost spilling out: combs, balloons, little highly colored pictures of the saints, olive-wood carvings of snakes, camels, dogs, and horses, cheap mirrors, a riot of handkerchiefs, and long twisted rolls of bread decorated with seeds. His trousers, patched like his coat, drooped over a pair of scarlet *charouhias*, leather shoes with upturned toes decorated with a large black-and-white pompon. This extraordinary character carried on his back bamboo cages full of pigeons and young chickens, several mysterious sacks, and a large bunch of fresh green leeks. With one hand he held his pipe to his mouth, and in the other a number of lengths of cotton, to each of which was tied an almond-size rose beetle, glittering golden green in the sun, all of them flying round his hat with desperate, deep buzzings, trying to escape from the threads tied firmly round their waists. Occasionally, tired of circling round and round without success, one of the beetles would settle for a moment on his hat, before launching itself off once more on its endless merry-go-round.

When he saw us the Rose-Beetle Man stopped, gave a very exaggerated start, doffed his ridiculous hat, and swept us a low bow. Roger was so overcome by this unlooked-for attention that he let out a volley of surprised barks. The man smiled at us, put on his hat again, raised his hands, and waggled his long, bony fingers at me. Amused and rather startled by this apparition, I politely bade him good day. He gave another courtly bow. I asked him if he had been to some fiesta. He nodded his head vigorously, raised his pipe to his lips and played a lilting little tune on it, pranced a few steps in the dust of the road, and then stopped and jerked his thumb over his shoulder, pointing back the way he had come. He smiled, patted his pockets, and rubbed his forefinger and thumb together in the Greek way of expressing money. I suddenly realized that he must be dumb. So, standing in the middle of the road, I carried on a conversation with him and he replied with a varied and very clever pantomime. I asked what the rose beetles were for, and why he had them tied with pieces of cotton. He held his hand out to denote small boys, took one of the lengths of cotton from which a beetle hung, and whirled it rapidly round his head. Immediately the insect came to life and started on its planet-like circling of his hat, and he beamed at me. Pointing up at the sky, he stretched his arms out and gave a deep nasal buzzing, while he banked and swooped across the road. Airplane, any fool could see that. Then he pointed to the beetles, held out his hand to denote children and whirled his stock of beetles round his head so that they all started to buzz peevishly.

Exhausted by his explanation, he sat down by the edge of the road, played a short tune on his flute, breaking off to sing in his curious nasal voice. They were not articulate words he used, but a series of strange gruntings and tenor squeaks, that appeared to be formed at the back of his throat and expelled through his nose. He produced them, however, with such verve and such wonderful facial expressions that you were convinced the curious sounds really meant something. Presently he stuffed his flute into his bulging pocket, gazed at me reflectively for a moment, and then swung a small sack off his shoulder, undid it, and, to my delight and astonishment, tumbled half a dozen tortoises into the dusty road. Their shells had been polished with oil until they shone, and by some means or other he had managed to decorate their front legs with little red bows. Slowly and ponderously they unpacked their heads and legs from their gleaming shells and set off down the road, doggedly and without enthusiasm. I watched them, fascinated; the one that particularly took my fancy was quite a small one with a shell about the size of a teacup. It seemed more sprightly than the others, and its shell was a paler color—chestnut, caramel, and amber. Its eyes were bright and its walk was as alert as any tortoise's could be. I sat contemplating it for a long time. I convinced myself that the family would greet its arrival at the villa with tremendous enthusiasm, even, perhaps, congratulating me on finding such an elegant specimen. The fact that I had no money on me did not worry me in the slightest, for I would simply tell the man to call at the villa for payment the next day. It never occurred to me that he might not trust me. The fact that I was English was sufficient, for the islanders had a love and respect for the Englishman out of all proportion to his worth. They would trust an Englishman where they would not trust each other. I asked the Rose-Beetle Man the price of the little tortoise. He held up both hands, fingers spread out. However, I hadn't watched the peasants transacting business for nothing. I shook my head firmly and held up two fingers,

unconsciously imitating the man. He closed his eyes in horror at the thought, and held up nine fingers; I held up three; he shook his head, and after some thought held up six fingers; I, in return, shook my head and held up five. The Rose-Beetle Man shook his head, and sighed deeply and sorrowfully, so we sat in silence and stared at the tortoises crawling heavily and uncertainly about the road, with the curious graceless determination of babies. Presently the Rose-Beetle Man indicated the little tortoise and held up six fingers again. I shook my head and held up five. Roger yawned loudly; he was thoroughly bored by this silent bargaining. The Rose-Beetle Man picked up the reptile and showed me in pantomime how smooth and lovely its shell was, how erect its head, how pointed its nails. I remained implacable. He shrugged, handed me the tortoise, and held up five fingers.

Then I told him I had no money, and that he would have to come the next day to the villa, and he nodded as if it were the most natural thing in the world. Excited by owning this new pet, I wanted to get back home as quickly as possible in order to show it to everyone, so I said good-by, thanked him, and hurried off along the road. When I reached the place where I had to cut down through the olive groves, I stopped and examined my acquisition carefully. He was undoubtedly the finest tortoise I had ever seen, and worth, in my opinion, at least twice what I had paid for him. I patted his scaly head with my finger and placed him carefully in my pocket. Before diving down the hillside I glanced back. The Rose-Beetle Man was still in the same place on the road, but he was doing a little jig, prancing and swaying, his flute warbling, while in the road at his feet the tortoises ambled to and fro, dimly and heavily.

The new arrival was duly christened Achilles,[1] and turned out to be a most intelligent and lovable beast, possessed of a peculiar sense of humor. At first he was tethered by a leg in the garden, but as he grew tamer we let him go where he pleased. He learned his name in a very short time, and we had only to call out once or twice and then wait patiently for a while and he would appear, lumbering along

the narrow cobbled paths on tiptoe, his head and neck stretched out eagerly. He loved being fed, and would squat regally in the sun while we held out bits of lettuce, dandelions, or grapes for him. He loved grapes as much as Roger did, so there was always great rivalry. Achilles would sit mumbling the grapes in his mouth, the juice running down his chin, and Roger would lie nearby, watching him with agonized eyes, his mouth drooling saliva. Roger always had his fair share of the fruit, but even so he seemed to think it a waste to give such delicacies to a tortoise. When the feeding was over, if I didn't keep an eye on him, Roger would creep up to Achilles and lick his front vigorously in an attempt to get the grape juice that the reptile had dribbled down himself. Achilles, affronted at such a liberty, would snap at Roger's nose, and then, when the licks became too overpowering and moist, he would retreat into his shell with an indignant wheeze, and refuse to come out until we had removed Roger from the scene.

But the fruit that Achilles liked best were wild strawberries. He would become positively hysterical at the mere sight of them, lumbering to and fro, craning his head to see if you were going to give him any, gazing at you pleadingly with his tiny shoe-button eyes. The very small strawberries he could devour at a gulp, for they were only the size of a fat pea. But if you gave him a big one, say the size of a hazel nut, he behaved in a way that I had never seen another tortoise emulate. He would grab the fruit and, holding it firmly in his mouth, would stumble off at top speed until he reached a safe and secluded spot among the flower beds, where he would drop the fruit and then eat it at leisure, returning for another one when he had finished.

As well as developing a passion for strawberries, Achilles also developed a passion for human company. Let anyone come into the garden to sit and sun-bathe, to read, or for any other reason, and before long there would be a rustling among the sweet williams, and Achilles's wrinkled and earnest face would be poked through. If you were sitting in a chair, he contented himself with getting as close to your feet as possible, and there he would sink into a

---

1. *Achilles* (ə kil′ēz), Greek hero of the Trojan War.

deep and peaceful sleep, his head drooping out of his shell, his nose resting on the ground. If, however, you were lying on a rug, sunbathing, Achilles would be convinced that you were lying on the ground simply in order to provide him with amusement. He would surge down the path and onto the rug with an expression of bemused good humor on his face. He would pause, survey you thoughtfully, and then choose a portion of your anatomy on which to practise mountaineering. Suddenly to have the sharp claws of a determined tortoise embedded in your thigh as he tries to lever himself up onto your stomach is not conducive to relaxation. If you shook him off and moved the rug it would only give you temporary respite, for Achilles would circle the garden grimly until he found you again. This habit became so tiresome that, after many complaints and threats from the family, I had to lock him up whenever we lay in the garden. Then one day the garden gate was left open and Achilles was nowhere to be found. Search parties were immediately organized, and the family, who up till then had spent most of their time openly making threats against the reptile's life, wandered about the olive groves, shouting, "Achilles . . . strawberries, Achilles . . . Achilles . . . strawberries . . ." At length we found him. Ambling along in his usual detached manner, he had fallen into a disused well, the wall of which had long since disintegrated, and the mouth of which was almost covered by ferns. He was, to our regret, quite dead. Even Leslie's attempts at artificial respiration and Margo's suggestion of forcing strawberries down his throat (to give him, as she explained, something to live for) failed to get any response. So, mournfully and solemnly, his corpse was buried in the garden under a small strawberry plant (Mother's suggestion). A short funeral address, written and read in a trembling voice by Larry, made the occasion a memorable one. It was only marred by Roger, who, in spite of all my protests, insisted on wagging his tail throughout the burial service.

Not long after Achilles had been taken from us I obtained another pet from the Rose-Beetle Man. This time it was a pigeon. He was still very young and had to be force-fed on bread-and-milk and soaked corn. He was the most revolting bird to look at, with his feathers pushing through the wrinkled scarlet skin, mixed with the horrible yellow down that covers baby pigeons and makes them look as though they have been peroxiding their hair. Owing to his repulsive and obese appearance, Larry suggested we call him Quasimodo,[2] and, liking the name without realizing the implications, I agreed. For a long time after he could feed himself, and when all his feathers had grown, Quasimodo retained a sprig of yellow down on his head which gave him the appearance of a rather pompous judge wearing a wig several sizes too small.

Owing to his unorthodox upbringing and the fact that he had no parents to teach him the facts of life, Quasimodo became convinced that he was not a bird at all, and refused to fly. Instead he walked everywhere. If he wanted to get onto a table or a chair, he stood below it, ducking his head and cooing in a rich contralto until someone lifted him up. He was always eager to join us in anything we did and would even try to come for walks with us. This, however, we had to stop, for either you carried him on your shoulder, which was risking an accident to your clothes, or else you let him walk behind. If you let him walk, then you had to slow down your own pace to suit his, for should you get too far ahead you would hear the most frantic and imploring coos and turn round to find Quasimodo running desperately after you, his tail wagging seductively, his iridescent chest pouted out with indignation at your cruelty.

Quasimodo insisted on sleeping in the house; no amount of coaxing or scolding would get him to inhabit the pigeon loft I had constructed for him. He preferred to sleep on the end of Margo's bed. Eventually, however, he was banished to the drawing-room sofa, for if Margo turned over in bed at night Quasimodo would wake, hobble up the bed, and perch on her face, cooing loudly and lovingly.

It was Larry who discovered that Quasimodo

2. *Quasimodo* (kwä′sə mō′dō), the bell-ringer of Notre Dame Cathedral in Victor Hugo's novel *The Hunchback of Notre Dame*. Quasimodo was ridiculed because of his hunchbacked, bowlegged appearance.

was a musical pigeon. Not only did he like music, but he actually seemed to recognize two different varieties, the waltz and the military march. For ordinary music he would waddle as close to the gramophone as possible and sit there with pouting chest, eyes half closed, purring softly to himself. But if the tune was a waltz he would move round and round the machine, bowing, twisting, and cooing tremulously. For a march, on the other hand— Sousa for preference—he drew himself up to his full height, inflated his chest, and stamped up and down the room, while his coo became so rich and throaty that he seemed in danger of strangling himself. He never attempted to perform these actions for any other kind of music than marches and waltzes. Occasionally, however, if he had not heard any music for some time, he would (in his enthusiasm at hearing the gramophone) do a march for a waltz, or vice versa, but he invariably stopped and corrected himself halfway through.

One sad day we found, on waking Quasimodo, that he had duped us all, for there among the cushions lay a glossy white egg. He never quite recovered from this. He became embittered, sullen, and started to peck irritably if you attempted to pick him up. Then he laid another egg, and his nature changed completely. He, or rather she, became wilder and wilder, treating us as though we were her worst enemies, slinking up to the kitchen door for food as if she feared for her life. Not even the gramophone would tempt her back into the house. The last time I saw her she was

sitting in an olive tree, cooing in the most pretentious and coy manner, while further along the branch a large and very masculine-looking pigeon twisted and cooed in a perfect ecstasy of admiration.

For some time the Rose-Beetle Man would turn up at the villa fairly regularly with some new addition to my menagerie: a frog, perhaps, or a sparrow with a broken wing. One afternoon Mother and I, in a fit of extravagant sentimentalism, bought up his entire stock of rose beetles and, when he had left, let them all go in the garden. For days the villa was full of rose beetles, crawling on the beds, lurking in the bathroom, banging against the lights at night, and falling like emeralds into our laps.

The last time I saw the Rose-Beetle Man was one evening when I was sitting on a hilltop overlooking the road. He had obviously been to some fiesta and had been plied with much wine, for he swayed to and fro across the road, piping a melancholy tune on his flute. I shouted a greeting, and he waved extravagantly without looking back. As he rounded the corner he was silhouetted for a moment against the pale lavender evening sky. I could see his battered hat with the fluttering feathers, the bulging pockets of his coat, the bamboo cages full of sleepy pigeons on his back, and above his head, circling drowsily round and round, I could see the dim specks that were the rose beetles. Then he rounded the curve of the road and there was only the pale sky with a new moon floating in it like a silver feather, and the soft twittering of his flute dying away in the dusk.

## DISCUSSION

1. Durrell states in the first sentence that the Rose-Beetle Man was "weird" and "fascinating." How does his description support this opinion?

2. How does Durrell distinguish Achilles and Quasimodo from all other tortoises and pigeons?

3. Select one passage that you consider particularly clear and descriptive. Point out details that make it so.

## WORD STUDY

Professional writers spend a great deal of time searching for just the right word—the precise word that

works where no other word is appropriate.

In the previous selection, Durrell does not say that Achilles was a brown turtle; he says that its shell was chestnut, caramel, and amber. With these words he produces a sharp, clear image.

Study Durrell's use of words and then on your paper, complete each of the following sentences with the most specific word found within parentheses. Always choose the word which evokes the clearest image.

1. Each rose beetle was (small —almond-sized).

2. He played a short tune on his (flute—musical instrument).

3. When Achilles's name was called, he would come (walking— lumbering) along the garden path.

4. If you sat in the garden, there would soon be a (rustling— noise) in the (flowers—sweet williams), and Achilles would appear.

5. Quasimodo cooed in a rich (voice—contralto).

6. To have the claws of a tortoise (touching—embedded in) your thigh is not pleasant.

## GERALD DURRELL

Gerald Durrell was born in 1925 in India, where his father was an engineer. The youngest of three brothers and a sister, Gerald was educated by private tutors in France, Italy, Switzerland, and Greece. Five years were spent with his family (his mother was then widowed) on the island of Corfu; the family's adventures there are recorded in the two books mentioned in the headnote.

According to Durrell, the books were begun as natural history; he made the mistake, however, of introducing family members who "proceeded to establish themselves and invite various friends to share the chapters."

To hold the boy's attention, Durrell's tutor on Corfu combined zoology with other subjects whenever possible. Durrell recalls being told that Columbus's first words upon landing in America were "Great heavens, look . . . a jaguar."

After serving as a student keeper at the Whipsnade Zoo in London from 1945 to 1946, Durrell took

up collecting in 1947. He and his wife Jacqueline, also a writer, presently have in the Channel Islands a zoo which is devoted to the preservation of endangered species. He has been the leader of zoological collecting expeditions and has made filming expeditions for BBC's series "Two in the Bush."

# MY PLANET 'TIS OF THEE

*Isaac Asimov*

I love people, I really do, and yet, in viewing the future, I am forced to be guided by a certain cynicism because so many people, however lovable, seem immune to reason.

Several years ago, for instance, at some gathering, a Jewish woman argued, with considerable emotion, that she could never feel real confidence in the good will of Gentiles because they had stood aside and allowed Nazi Germany to torture and kill Jews by the millions without ever really doing anything about it.

I could appreciate her feelings, being Jewish myself, but didn't share them. To make my point, I asked her quietly, "What are you doing about Negro civil rights?"

And she answered sharply (and rather as I expected), "Let's solve our own problems before we take on those of other people."

But I had not made my point after all for—would you believe it—there turned out to be no way in which I could convince her of the inconsistency in her position.

But we have to take people as they are; complete with their aversion to the rational; and face, in these last decades of the twentieth century, the most crucial problem mankind has ever had to deal with. It is the question of sheer survival; not for this sect or that, this nation or that, this political or economic doctrine or that—but, quite simply, for civilization generally.

And maybe even for mankind generally.

And maybe even for multicellular life generally.

The prime problem is that of increasing population. Even if, right now as of this minute, the population of Earth levels off, we still face an overwhelming problem. The population of Earth is *already* too high for survival, for we grow in other ways than mere numbers.

You see, it is an article of faith with us that we must live in a "growing economy," that we must "progress" and "advance"; that we must have it ever better. Arguing against all that is like arguing against kindness and mercy and love, but I have to. Growing and advancing and having it better have a price tag. To have a still more affluent society inevitably means the utilization of Earth's resources at a still greater rate and, in particular, the consumption of energy at a still greater rate.

As it is, the utilization of irreplaceable resources and the consumption of energy have been increasing faster than the population for many decades, and I have seen it stated that by the time the United States has doubled its population, say by 2020, it will have increased its energy consumption sevenfold.

I strongly suspect that the rate of pollution of the environment is roughly proportional to the rate of energy consumption and that, barring strenuous action to prevent it, a sevenfold increase in the latter means a sevenfold increase in the former. And in only fifty years.

Look at it another way.

As it happens, the United States is currently consuming somewhat over half the irreplaceable resources produced on Earth—the metals,

fossil fuels and so on—despite the fact that it only has one-sixteenth the population of the Earth.

The rest of the world would, of course, like to attain our level of affluence, and it is hard to argue that they have no right to try to do so. But suppose they succeed and all Earth lives on the American living standard. The remaining fifteen-sixteenths of the Earth's population would then be using fifteen times as much of Earth's resources as our one-sixteenth does, and will produce fifteen times as much pollution.

The rate of coal and oil production then, of metal and mineral production, of paper, plastics, of automobiles and everything else would have to be something like eight times what it is now to keep all of Earth at American-like affluence even if the population increases no higher than it is right now. And eight times as much pollution.

Can we afford this?

And if population continues to increase at its present rate and world affluence is *still* expected, then in fifty years, with a sevenfold increase in energy consumption expected, the rate of rifling of Earth's resources must be over *fifty* times what it now is.

It can't be done. The resources simply don't exist for the rifling. The capacity for the absorption of a fiftyfold increase in pollution just isn't there.

The fact of the matter is that we can no longer proceed along the lines that have served us in the past. We can't imagine that we can continue to increase our rate of production just as fast as we can manage, that unlimited growth is possible (let alone desirable) and that good old Earth will give us all we need, however much that is, and take all the dregs we hand back, however much that is.

We are *not* in an infinite world any longer; we are (and have been for some time now) in a terribly *finite* world; and we must either adjust to that or die.

We can measure the finiteness of a world by its interdependence, and we can trace the growth of interdependence by a rough estimate of the value of distance at various times in history. Thus, as long as the Earth was essentially infinite, it was possible for particular portions to be far enough apart to ignore each other; and the greater the distance required for such ignoring the closer the approach of finiteness.

Just to take a few examples——

In 1650 B.C., it did not concern the Greeks that the Egyptian Middle Kingdom (five hundred miles away) had fallen to the Hyksos invaders. In 525 B.C., however, the fall of Egypt to Persia clearly heightened the dangers besetting Greece.

In 215 B.C., the deadly duel between Rome and Carthage raised no echo in the hearts of Britons on their tight little isle, one thousand miles away. By A.D. 400, however, the state of Italy with respect to Germanic invaders was of intense interest to Britain, for Alaric's presence in northern Italy cost Britain its Roman army—and its civilization.

By A.D. 1935, most Americans could still live as though it didn't matter what happened in Europe, three thousand miles away, but after less than another generation, they would be told, and believe, that what happened in Saigon, ten thousand miles away, was of such vital importance to Keokuk that tens of thousands of Americans must die.

If one wanted to take the trouble, one could extend this thing backward in time and fill in the chinks and work out a graph representing the change in minimum distance of separation required for isolation, with time. The line would not be straight but I think we can all see that it would rise more or less steadily; quite slowly at first; quite rapidly later on.

And now we've run out of distance. The maximum distance of separation of Earth's surface is 12,500 miles, and that is not far enough any longer to be safe. Oh, people might want to be isolated and might stubbornly insist they don't care what happens 12,500 miles away or even 500 miles away, but when they say that, they are simply closing their eyes at noon and insisting that the sun has set.

The interdependence is not just political and military, of course, but economic, social, cultural, and everything else. Nothing of significance (and hardly anything any longer is of insignificance) that happens anywhere can fail to affect everywhere. Because four rock singers in Liverpool decided a few years ago that it was a drag to go to the barber, I now wear sideburns.

But never mind the trivial. Let's go right to the top and make one thing clear. It is no longer possible to solve the real problems of our planet by working on the assumption that the world is infinite. Whatever the problem is, whether it is overpopulation, dwindling resources, multiplying pollution, or intensifying social unrest, no minor part of the planet can solve it without regard for, or attention to, the rest of Earth.

Since no single nation controls an effective majority of Earth's population, area, resources, or power, each nation comes under the heading of "minor part of the planet." It follows, in my opinion, that no nation can solve its own major problems alone.

Paraguay cannot solve its major problems in isolation, and neither can the United States, and for the same reason. Both Paraguay and the United States deal with too small a part of the problem, and anything either does, can and will be negated if the rest of the planet does not choose to go along.

Suppose the United States did decide to enforce a policy of strict population control and established a firm population plateau at two hundred million. Can this possibly solve our problems under any conditions, if the rest of the world continued to breed itself upward like rabbits?

One might, for the sake of argument, maintain that with a stable population and our superb technology, we could easily defend ourselves against the rest of the world, especially if the rest of the world sinks into starvation and disaster through overcrowding.

But some of them out there have nuclear weapons that can do us tremendous damage while we're wiping them out; and all of them have resources that we have to collect. We can harden our hearts to the famines they will undergo but can we harden our immunity to the plagues that will sweep them on the way to us?

And what if the rest of the world manages to achieve population stability also and continues to drive hard for greater economic affluence, each nation in a mad scramble for it without regard to the others? Can we tell them that half the resources they control belong to us and that they'd better not use those resources recklessly because we don't intend to give up our affluence for their sake? Our record in Vietnam doesn't fill me with confidence in our power to impose our will on the world.

And if they improve their lot somehow without disimproving ours and begin to pollute at the rate one would expect of affluence, what then?

If we in the United States cleaned up our rivers and unclogged our lakes and de-stinked our atmosphere, what super-Canute[1] is going to say to the air and water of the Earth generally: Cross not our borders for you are unclean?

In short, our problems are now planetary, and our solutions will have to be planetary too.

What this means is that the various nations have to come to some sort of agreement in order to find and implement planetary solutions.

As a barest minimum, the United States and the Soviet Union will have to work together. Not only is war between them unthinkable, but disagreement, short of war, out of national stubbornness and suspicion, that will prevent common action on these problems will only mean a somewhat slower and perhaps, in the long run, more agonizing death than war could bring.

Pride and patriotism aren't going to work on a national basis. It is utterly irrelevant that we think the Russians are a bunch of Commies or that they think we are a bunch of Imperialists. Whether they're right, or we're right, or both of us are right, or neither, makes no difference. We would still have to work together, agree on a common policy, and stay agreed on it, or all go under.

Even the United States and the Soviet Union together might not swing it. It might require the whole-hearted cooperation of Western Europe, China (Communist China, not Formosa), and India as well, to set up the minimum requirements for planetary solutions. The rest of the world could then follow voluntarily or reluctantly or even under the lash—but follow.

Don't get me wrong. I don't enjoy the thought of the powerful nations of the world getting together to force the rest of the planet into line. I would love to see a democratic world government with a strong, freely elected executive with limited tenure, a representative legislature, respected world courts, and a firm agreement on the part of all peoples to abide by majority decisions. The only trouble is I don't think we have the faintest chance of swinging it in thirty years, and thirty years are all the time we have in my opinion.

In the short run, therefore, we must settle for something less.

The trouble is that our society, our culture, our every way of thinking is built around the assumption of an infinite world. It is the very essence of my lady friend of the introduction and her: "Let's solve our own problems before we take on those of other people" that she doesn't see that there are no longer such things as my problems and your problems—but only problems.

It is not inconceivable, therefore, that under the dark glimmering of outmoded ways of thought, we will all sink to death rather than cooperate, for we will feel that *those* bad guys may use that cooperation to take advantage of *us* good guys. (And those guys would be saying exactly the same thing with the pronouns reversing referents.)

With this possibility horribly easy to see coming to pass and with an ideal world government almost certainly far in the future, I will be ecstatically happy to see cooperation on any terms. Let every nation desperately pretend it is retaining its sovereignty; let it bellow its resentment and hatred for the others; as long as each nation cooperates (even sneakily and sullenly) in measures that are even half-good and manage to keep us drifting along with our nostrils above water until such time as the real world government can be developed.

There is a historical analogy I would like to offer. It is imperfect and inadequate, as all historical analogies are, but here it is anyway.

In 1776, the rebelling British colonies on

---

1. *Canute* (kə nüt′) (994?–1035), Danish king of England, Denmark, and Norway, who is said to have commanded (in vain) the tide to recede in order to prove to his subjects, who had an exaggerated opinion of his power, that he was not all-powerful.

the North American east-central coast declared themselves "free and independent states" and were recognized as such by Great Britain in 1783.

Through long habit we think of states as parts of a nation, marked off for administrative purposes and possessing no true independence, but if so we are deluding ourselves. The word "state" refers to a self-contained political entity, entirely self-governing. The thirteen states, free and independent, were filled with the mutual suspicions you would expect of any neighboring governments. For several years after 1783, the United States were states that were united only in their title. They fought with each other propagandistically, economically, and, very nearly, militarily.

The tighter union, under the Constitution (prepared in 1787, adopted in 1789—with Rhode Island holding out till 1791), was by no means an enthusiastically accepted situation. It was forced upon the mutually hostile states, to their reluctance and chagrin, by the existence of Continental problems that required Continental solutions, failing which, European overlordship would surely have been reimposed.

Nor was the Constitution more than jerry-built at first. It was the states that were "sovereign," their acceptance of Union was thought to be voluntary, and at different times various states (suffering under a feeling of being abused) played with the notion of withdrawing that acceptance and leaving the Union.

Finally, in 1860 and 1861, such withdrawal was actually attempted by eleven states of the South, and it took four years of bloody warfare to point out the fallacy of their reasoning.

The situation of 1787 is being repeated now on a planetary scale in area and population, and considering the size of the first and the heterogeneity of the second, we might consider a happy ending this time as beyond hope, but I wonder——

In some ways difficulty has lessened. Advances in transportation and communication have made the entire planet a far smaller place in every way than the eastern seaboard of the United States was in 1787. And the heterogeneity of the world's population is less than

one might think. Tokyo and Cairo look more like Chicago in 1970, than Charleston looked like Boston in 1787. Of course, there are differences and great ones, but the ruling classes in all nations live more and more as part of the same (largely Americanized) culture.

So planetary union by paste and piano wire, while the pretense of national sovereignty is maintained, can come. But will it last?

How long did the American Constitution serve to hold the American states together? Seventy years.

Then came the bitterest and most stubbornly contested civil war in Western history, and it would not have taken much for it to end the other way, with the Union destroyed.

Fortunately for us, the world had not yet become finite in the nineteenth century. The United States could fight a civil war and survive.

But over a century has passed since then and we can no longer take such risks. Suppose a working planetary government is set up, conceived in expediency and dedicated to the proposition that mankind must somehow survive.

If, then, seventy years later, there is a planetary civil war, do you suppose we will have to see which side wins in order to find out whether any planetary government so conceived and so dedicated can long endure? Of course not; the mere fact that there is civil war at all would settle the matter. The government, civilization, mankind would not endure.

So in the decades that follow the beginnings of foot-dragging cooperation, we must go on to establish greater sympathy among peoples and steadily diminish idiotic national prejudices— and do so without a single false step. That is the price of finitude.

It won't be easy, but it's got to be done.

Well, how?

Shall we try another imperfect historical analogy?

It is my feeling that what did most to break down the sharp feeling of statism within the United States was the westward migration. The opening of the Western frontier was the common task of the settled states of the East. The West was not parceled out, area by area, for this state and that, so that each of the older states might increase its pride in its specialness and work up further ground for hatred against the rest. All the West was open to all Americans.

Men from the various states mixed freely and no significant portion of the task of "the winning of the West" could be attributed to anything smaller than the United States in general.

Sure, regional pride continued and will always continue, but it was defused to the point where members of one state do not feel they have a God-given right to kill members of another state.

And what is the equivalent of the westward migration on a planetary scale?

How about the space effort?

It is getting hard to say this. The entire program has been so nationalized by the traumatic effect of the Soviet Union having been the first nation to place a satellite in orbit that it has become the darling of the conservatives. It has been militarized, it has been draped with the flag, it has been permeated by an aura of *Reader's Digest* and Billy Graham.

So it has become an object of suspicion to the liberals.

To many of the latter it now seems like an opiate, designed to keep the eyes of the American people fixed on the Moon while on Earth the cities decay and people fester. Over and over again they tell us the choice is Moon or Earth, space or cities, rockets or people.

If that were really the choice, I would choose Earth, cities and people myself, but it isn't. The real problem is that almost every nation on Earth spends most of its money and effort on preparing for war (or actually fighting one). The choice is not Moon or Earth at all. The choice is war or Earth, soldiers or cities, missiles or people, and every nation chooses war, soldiers, and missiles.

Achieve a world government of any kind, however rickety, and let military expenditures die down and there will at once be enough muscle and brain extant to make possible both space and cities, both Earth and Moon, both people and rockets.

But why bother? What's the good of a man on the Moon?

I have argued in other places about the ma-

terial good that might come of it; of knowledge to be gained that will increase our understanding of Earth's geology, of the solar system's origin, even of the workings of life. I have spoken of the new technology that might become possible based on the abundance of vacuum, hard radiation, and low temperature on the Moon.

I have even argued in favor of the establishment of an ecologically independent colony on the Moon; one that (after its initial start with Earth capital) can continue on its own through the careful utilization of resources available from the Moon's crust—pointing out that such a Moon colony can offer Earth an abstract service far beyond any concrete advantage it might bring.

The reason for that is that the Moon is so obviously a finite world. Its lack of surface air and water means that any colonists on the Moon must cycle their resources with infinite care, for they will be living in a society that will leave almost no margin for error.

Assuming that the colony survives and functions, then it will serve us both as an inspiration and as an example. It will show us how human beings can live with finiteness, and it may even help teach us how.

But forget all that. Let us suppose that a real Moon colony turns out to be impossible; that the material benefits of space turn out to be an illusion; that the knowledge gained by scientists is of use to theoreticians only and remains worthless to the common man. Let us suppose that the space effort, both now and in the future, is simply a vastly expensive boondoggle, a mere climbing of super-Everests.

It would even so, *still* be infinitely worthwhile.

As it stands, the space effort has grown too expensive for any single nation—even for the United States or the Soviet Union—that insists on spending most of its effort on the sterility of armaments and war.

Once the more powerful nations, at least, are forced by dreadful circumstance into cooperation and the makeshift planetary government starts, the space effort will, almost inevitably, in my opinion, become a multinational effort.

And there lies my greatest hope for the survival of mankind.

Why should not all nations find a common ground in the assault on space? The only enemy there is the dark of the unknown and surely that is an enemy all mankind can fight with equal enthusiasm. The exploration of space can call upon us all alike to defeat ignorance, to open new horizons, and it will present mankind with a kind of accomplishment so large as by its very size to shrivel nations to insignificance and leave room in the mind for nothing smaller than planetary man.

Even now there is a glimpse of the supranational attraction of space accomplishment. The successful placing of a man on the Moon was, admittedly, a strictly American achievement, full of American flags stuck into lunar soil, and American Presidents hastening to the Pacific Ocean with their benediction, and American vice-presidents handing out bits of Moon rock to everyone in Asia—and *still* the accomplishment touched everyone, even the Russians. For it was Homo sapiens that was making footprints on the Moon and it was all of us without exception that those footprints stood for.

Let us have the space effort become multinational in the future, let there be a planetary flag thrust into the soil of Mars, let men of all parts of the world work on the vast project for the conquest and taming of the solar system, and surely the consciousness of our union-as-a-species will have a chance to grow.

Again regional rivalries will remain, always, but overriding them (just possibly) may be the sense of common accomplishment that will slowly but surely break down the disunion of men and leave them with just enough resigned endurance of one another (in the absence of love, resigned endurance will be enough) to turn a makeshift world government into a real one.

(It may not happen, to be sure, for the exploration of the New World in the sixteenth century did not bring the European nations together but exacerbated their rivalry—but then they never made it a multinational project.)

If it does happen, however, the space effort, whatever its cost, short of planetary bankruptcy, will have been worthwhile even if it brings us nothing else.

Also, if that happens, the twenty-first century will see mankind making the painful transition from the childhood of a pseudo-infinite world of subplanetary societies, through the adolescence of a cooperative national society and into the adulthood of a planetary government ruling over a finite world.

The chances for all of this are, I repeat, not large, for time is short and folly long, the need is great and vision small, the pressing problems enormously complex and the ruling minds dishearteningly mediocre.

But I must hope.

## DISCUSSION

1. (a) What opinion does Asimov express in the first paragraph of the essay? (b) How does he use this opinion to open the main discussion of the essay?

2. (a) According to Asimov, what is the most important problem facing humankind? (b) Explain how this problem creates other problems.

3. From Asimov's point of view, how would a dangerous situation be created if the remaining population of the earth were to live at the American level of affluence?

4. (a) How does Asimov explain the difference between a finite and an infinite world? (b) In which does he say we live?

5. (a) Why does Asimov consider interdependence a solution to our dilemma? (b) Do you agree with him? Explain. (c) How does the idea of interdependence relate to the title of the essay?

6. (a) What are some of the arguments against national support of space exploration? (b) How does Asimov think the ex-

ploration of space will help solve the problems of earth?

7. Asimov's method of developing his essay is to present a rather general idea which he follows with a specific example to illustrate his point. Cite several instances in which he does this.

8. In your opinion, what dangers might result from a planetary government? What benefits?

## WORD STUDY

Sometimes you must make use of both context and structure clues in figuring out the meaning of a word.

The use of such *irreplaceable* resources as coal and gas has been increasing.

In this sentence, context gives you a slight clue to the meaning of the italicized word, but your best clue is the structure of the word.

| ir | replace | able |
|----|---------|------|
| not | put back | capable of being |

Read the sentences below and on your paper write the meaning of the italicized word. After the meaning, write whether you used context or structure clues or both in figuring out the meaning. You may use a dictionary if neither context nor structure clues help.

1. The problem is whether *multicellular* life will survive.

2. The *interdependence* of the world's nations is not just political.

3. We might have a world government with an executive elected for limited *tenure*—say, four years.

4. The space effort may become a *multinational* effort.

5. It is possible that because of *outmoded* ways of thought, the nations of the world will not cooperate.

6. We are *deluding* ourselves if we think earth will support all nations at a high standard of living.

7. The *heterogeneity* of the world's population is lessening; Tokyo, Cairo, and Rio look a lot like Chicago and New York.

8. Instead of bringing European nations together, exploration of the New World *exacerbated* their rivalry.

## ISAAC ASIMOV

Isaac Asimov began reading science fiction at the age of nine, and at eleven he wrote a novel, *The Greenville Chums at College.*

Asimov, an excellent student, graduated from high school at fifteen. He received his bachelor's degree from Columbia in 1939, his master's in 1941, and, after serving at a naval experimental station and with the army during World War II, his doctor's degree in 1948.

In 1938 he submitted his first short story to *Astounding Science Fiction.* The editor rejected the story but encouraged Asimov. The story was accepted later that year;

thereafter in the next two decades, his stories appeared in almost every science-fiction magazine.

Since the publication of his first novel, *Pebble in the Sky,* in 1950, he has published over one hundred books. The following titles demonstrate his versatility: *The Martian Way, and Other Stories; Inside the Atom; Words from the Myths; The Genetic Code; Quick and Easy Math;* and *Nine Tomorrows: Tales of the Near Future.*

He teaches part time at Boston University School of Medicine, where he holds the rank of associate professor and where he was once involved in nucleic acid research.

Because, he says, writing is for him somewhat compulsive, he works at his craft many hours a day in his home in West Newton, Massachusetts.

# The DOG That Bit People

*James Thurber*

**Nobody knew exactly what was the matter with him.**

PROBABLY no one man should have as many dogs in his life as I have had, but there was more pleasure than distress in them for me except in the case of an Airedale named Muggs. He gave me more trouble than all the other fifty-four or -five put together, although my moment of keenest embarrassment was the time a Scotch terrier named Jeannie, who had just had six puppies in the clothes closet of a fourth floor apartment in New York, had the unexpected seventh and last at the corner of Eleventh Street and Fifth Avenue during a walk she had insisted on taking. Then, too, there was the prize-winning French poodle, a great big black poodle—none of your little, untroublesome white miniatures—who got sick riding in the rumble seat of a car with me on her way to the Greenwich Dog Show. She had a red rubber bib tucked around her throat and, since a rain storm came up when we were halfway through the Bronx, I had to hold over her a small green umbrella, really more of a parasol. The rain beat down fearfully, and suddenly the driver of the car drove into a big garage, filled with mechanics. It happened so quickly that I forgot to put the umbrella down and I will always remember, with sickening distress, the look of incredulity mixed with hatred that came over the face of the particular hardened garage man that came over to see what we wanted, when he took a look at me and the poodle. All garage men, and people of that intolerant stripe, hate poodles with their curious haircut, especially the pompoms that you got to leave on their hips if you expect the dogs to win a prize.

But the Airedale, as I have said, was the worst of all my dogs. He really wasn't my dog, as a matter of fact: I came home from a vacation one summer to find that my brother Roy had bought him while I was away. A big, burly, choleric dog, he always acted as if he thought I wasn't one of the family. There was a slight advantage in being one of the family, for he didn't bite the family as often as he bit strangers. Still, in the years that we had him he bit everybody but mother, and he made a pass at her once but missed. That was during the month when we suddenly had mice, and Muggs refused to do anything about them. Nobody ever had mice exactly like the mice we had that month. They acted like pet mice, almost like mice somebody had trained. They were so friendly that one night when mother entertained at dinner the Friraliras, a club she and my father had belonged to for twenty years, she put down a lot of little dishes with food in them on the pantry floor so that the mice would be satisfied with that and wouldn't come into the dining room. Muggs stayed out in the pantry with the mice, lying on the floor, growling to himself—not at the mice, but about all the people in the next room that he would have liked to get at. Mother slipped out into the pantry once to see how everything was going. Everything was going fine. It made her so mad to see Muggs lying there, oblivious of the mice—they came running up to her—that she slapped him and he slashed at her, but didn't make it. He was sorry immediately, mother said. He was always sorry, she said, after he bit someone, but we could not understand how she figured this out. He didn't act sorry.

Mother used to send a box of candy every Christmas to the people the Airedale bit. The list finally contained forty or more names. Nobody could understand why we didn't get rid of the dog. I didn't understand it very well myself, but we didn't get rid of him. I think that one or two people tried to poison Muggs—he acted poisoned once in a while—and old Major Moberly fired at him once with his service revolver near the Seneca Hotel in East Broad Street—but Muggs lived to be almost eleven years old and even when he could hardly get around he bit a Congressman who had called to see my father on business. My mother had never liked the Congressman—she said the signs of his horoscope showed he couldn't be trusted (he was Saturn with the moon in Virgo)—but she sent him a box of candy that Christmas. He sent it right back, probably because he suspected it was trick candy. Mother persuaded herself it was all for the best that the dog had bitten him, even though father lost an important business association because of it. "I wouldn't be associated with such a man," mother said. "Muggs could read him like a book."

We used to take turns feeding Muggs to be on his good side, but that didn't always work. He was never in a very good humor, even after a meal. Nobody knew exactly what was the matter with him, but whatever it was it made him irascible, especially in the mornings. Roy never felt very well in the morning, either, especially before breakfast, and once when he came downstairs and found that Muggs had moodily chewed up the morning paper he hit him in the face with a grapefruit and then jumped up on the dining-room table, scattering dishes and silverware and spilling the coffee. Muggs' first free leap carried him all the way across the table and into a brass fire screen in front of the gas grate but he was back on his feet in a moment and in the end he got Roy and gave him a pretty vicious bite in the leg. Then he was all over it; he never bit anyone more than once at a time. Mother always mentioned that as an argument in his favor; she said he had a quick temper but that he didn't hold a grudge. She was forever defending him. I think she liked him because he wasn't well. "He's not strong," she would say, pityingly, but that was inaccurate; he may not have been well but he was terribly strong.

One time my mother went to the Chittendon Hotel to call on a woman mental healer who was lecturing in Columbus on the subject of "Harmonious Vibrations." She wanted to find out if it was possible to get harmonious vibrations into a dog. "He's a large tan-colored Airedale," mother explained. The woman said that she had never treated a dog but she advised my mother to hold the thought that he did not bite and would not bite. Mother was holding the thought the very next morning when Muggs got the iceman, but she blamed that slip-up on the iceman. "If you didn't think he would bite you, he wouldn't," mother told him. He stomped out of the house in a terrible jangle of vibrations.

One morning when Muggs bit me slightly, more or less in passing, I reached down and grabbed his short stumpy tail and hoisted him into the air. It was a foolhardy thing to do and the last time I saw my mother, about six months ago, she said she didn't know what possessed me. I don't either, except that I was pretty mad. As long as I held the dog off the floor by his tail he couldn't get at me, but he twisted and jerked so, snarling all the time, that I realized I couldn't hold him that way very long. I carried him to the kitchen and flung him onto the floor and shut the door on him just as he crashed against it. But I forgot about the backstairs. Muggs went up the backstairs and down the frontstairs and had me cornered in the living room. I managed to get up onto the mantelpiece above the fireplace, but it gave way and came down with a tremendous crash throwing a large marble clock, several vases, and myself heavily to the floor. Muggs was so alarmed by the racket that when I picked myself up he had disappeared. We couldn't find him anywhere, although we whistled and shouted, until old Mrs. Detweiler called after dinner that night. Muggs had bitten her once, in the leg, and she came into the living room only after we assured her that Muggs had run away. She had just seated herself when, with a great growling and scratching of claws, Muggs emerged from under a davenport where he had been quietly hiding all the time and bit her again. Mother examined the bite and put arnica on it and told Mrs. Detweiler that it was only a bruise. "He just bumped you," she said. But Mrs. Detweiler left the house in a nasty state of mind.

Lots of people reported our Airedale to the police but my father held a municipal office at the time and was on friendly terms with the police. Even so, the cops had been out a couple times—once when Muggs bit Mrs. Rufus Sturtevant and again when he bit Lieutenant-Governor Malloy—but mother told them that it hadn't been Muggs's fault but the fault of the people who were bitten. "When he starts for them, they scream," she explained, "and that excites him." The cops suggested that it might be a good idea to tie the dog up, but mother said that it mortified him to be tied up and that he wouldn't eat when he was tied up.

Muggs at his meals was an unusual sight. Because of the fact that if you reached toward the floor he would bite you, we usually put his food plate on top of an old kitchen table with a bench alongside the table. Muggs would stand on the bench and eat. I remember that my mother's Uncle Horatio, who boasted that he was the third man up Missionary Ridge,[1] was splutteringly indignant when he found out that we fed the dog on a table because we were afraid to put his plate on the floor. He said he wasn't afraid of any dog that ever lived and that he would put the dog's plate on the floor

Lots of people reported our dog to the police.

if we would give it to him. Roy said that if Uncle Horatio had fed Muggs on the ground just before the battle he would have been the first man up Missionary Ridge. Uncle Horatio was furious. "Bring him in! Bring him in now!" he shouted. "I'll feed the _____ on the floor!" Roy was all for giving him a chance, but my father wouldn't hear of it. He said that Muggs had already been fed. "I'll feed him again!" bawled Uncle Horatio. We had quite a time quieting him.

In his last year Muggs used to spend practically all of his time outdoors. He didn't like to stay in the house for some reason or other—perhaps it held too many unpleasant memories for him. Anyway, it was hard to get him to come in and as a result the garbage man, the iceman, and the laundryman wouldn't come near the house. We had to haul the garbage down to the corner, take the laundry out

1. *Missionary Ridge,* site of a Civil War battle.

and bring it back, and meet the iceman a block from home. After this had gone on for some time we hit on an ingenious arrangement for getting the dog in the house so that we could lock him up while the gas meter was read, and so on. Muggs was afraid of only one thing, an electrical storm. Thunder and lightning frightened him out of his senses (I think he thought a storm had broken the day the mantel-piece fell). He would rush into the house and

*Muggs at his meals was an unusual sight.*

hide under a bed or in a clothes closet. So we fixed up a thunder machine out of a long narrow piece of sheet iron with a wooden han-dle on one end. Mother would shake this vigorously when she wanted to get Muggs

into the house. It made an excellent imitation of thunder, but I suppose it was the most roundabout system for running a household that was ever devised. It took a lot out of mother.

A few months before Muggs died, he got to "seeing things." He would rise slowly from the floor, growling low, and stalk stiff-legged and menacing toward nothing at all. Sometimes the Thing would be just a little to the right or left of a visitor. Once a Fuller Brush salesman got hysterics. Muggs came wandering into the room like Hamlet following his father's ghost. His eyes were fixed on a spot just to the left of the Fuller Brush man, who stood it until Muggs was about three slow, creeping paces from him. Then he shouted. Muggs wavered on past him into the hallway grum-bling to himself but the Fuller man went on shouting. I think mother had to throw a pan of cold water on him before he stopped. That was the way she used to stop us boys when we got into fights.

Muggs died quite suddenly one night. Mother wanted to bury him in the family lot under a marble stone with some such inscription as "Flights of angels sing thee to thy rest" but we persuaded her it was against the law. In the end we just put up a smooth board above his grave along a lonely road. On the board I wrote with an indelible pencil "Cave Ca-nem."[2] Mother was quite pleased with the simple classic dignity of the old Latin epitaph.

2. *"Cave Canem"* (kā/vē kā/nem). "Beware of the dog."

---

**DISCUSSION**

1. Why did the garage man look at Thurber and his poodle with a mixture of incredulity and hate?

2. (a) Why did the Thurbers keep Muggs? (b) Would you keep him if he belonged to you? Why or why not?

3. What were the symptoms of Muggs's final illness?

4. (a) What excuses does Thur-ber's mother offer for Muggs's be-havior? (b) How is her attitude toward Muggs like the attitude some parents have toward their children?

5. Thurber creates humor in a number of ways. Select a passage

or an episode that you find amus-ing. (a) Is the situation exag-gerated? (b) Is it presented in a matter-of-fact, understated way? (c) Is it ironic (the opposite of what one would expect)? (d) Does the situation contain incongruous elements (for instance a dog rid-ing in a rumble seat with a parasol over him)?

# The Risk Takers

### Robert Daley

WATCH the death-defying high-diving daredevil clinging to his tiny platform near the ceiling of the arena. His toes grip the edge. Drums roll. He dives into the void. The mob gasps.

He plunges five stories before the rope around his ankle stops him short and yanks him back part of the way he has come. Upside down, he swings back and forth, his head only eight feet from the ground. He then unhitches himself, stands, and accepts the crowd's tumultuous applause. He is a grinning twenty-four-year-old Pole named Sitkiewicz, and he is the featured aerialist with this year's Ringling Bros. and Barnum & Bailey Circus. He is a very amiable chap, always laughing. He says good morning to people, even at night. He speaks no language anyone else around speaks, the last word in alienated man. By learning one trick no one else will try, he has set himself apart from the rest of the world; and for performing this trick thirteen times a week, he earns something over two hundred dollars. The elephants are not the only circus performers who work for peanuts. Sitkiewicz's career is good for about ten years, if the rope doesn't break. After ten years, if he wants to stay employed, he had better find a new and more dangerous trick.

Watch the death-defying, snake-wrestling daredevil. His name is Kurt Severin. He calls himself "author . . . world traveler . . . photo journalist . . . adventurer." His specialty is snakes. In the past, it has also been sharks, crocodiles, and the puberty rites of Latin-American jungle tribes. Today, wading through the Amazon jungle, he comes upon an anaconda thicker through the middle than a man's thigh. About eighteen feet long, the anaconda dangles from a tree. Severin decides to grab it by the head while his guide photographs him and it, both grinning.

An instant later, the huge constrictor has flung Severin to the ground and is coiled around him, crushing the life out of him.

"Keep snapping," gasps Severin, who sees a great series of photos in this.

He has the anaconda by the throat with both hands, but the anaconda has him by the throat, too. Its tail is wrapped around Severin's windpipe and is sliding around in a second loop. Severin, contemplating how long the series of photos should be, fights for time. But soon his face goes red. He can't breathe or talk. He manages to pry the anaconda loose enough so that he can say, "Remove the necklace."

Three men, struggling, at last get the snake off Severin.

"Did you get a lot of photos?" gasps Severin, fingering his swollen throat.

Yes.

Severin is happy. "I've had much closer calls than that with cobras," he says.

Watch the death-defying daredevil José Meiffret pedaling a special bike in a wind-break behind a racing car at speeds of over 108 miles per hour, the former world record, which was set in 1941. In the sixties, Meiffret first raised the record to 109.6, then to 115.9. These are records no one cares about. They are worth absolutely nothing commercially. Each attempt costs Meiffret—a short, bald, fiftyish gardener with a concave dent in his skull from an earlier crash—thousands of dollars of his own money.

Now watch Meiffret on an autobahn[1] in Germany leaning forward over the handlebars, straining to make the oversize sprocket go around. Somewhere close to 60 miles an hour, he ducks in behind the windbreak jutting upward from the rear of the racing car. The mob tensely leans forward along both sides of the measured kilometer. The spectators stare down from the overpasses. Now the racing car, with Meiffret tucked into the windbreak, is speeding along at 100 miles per hour . . . 115 . . . 125. Inside the windbreak, Meiffret is straining to keep his front wheel one inch from a roller bar. If he touches the roller bar, he knows it won't roll, it will fling him off his bike and kill him. If he drops back out of the windbreak through loss of a pedal, or fatigue, or a heart spasm, the wind will throw him off the bike and kill him. If he hits a crack in the road, or a pebble, he is a dead man.

Out of the measured kilometer rockets the racing car. José Meiffret is still in the windbreak, upright, alive. Ladies and gentlemen, a new absolute speed record for miles per hour pedaled in a windbreak behind a racing car: 127.98 mph, by the death-defying José Meiffret, daredevil of international cycling!

This article is concerned with death and with those who risk it deliberately, gratuitously, and perhaps compulsively.

But that's not fair, you say. Each of the three men mentioned so far sounds like some kind of nut. The Pole is in a circus, exactly where he

belongs, indistinguishable from the other freaks there. Severin has gone to the Far East to see some snakes. Good, because we don't want him around here. Meiffret is frantically and unsuccessfully trying to find backers for a new record attempt, for he has no money left to pay for it himself. Glad to hear it. We are not interested in crackpots acting out death wishes.

But wait. I have some more daredevils for you. The boundary line gets fuzzy.

Watch the war photographer at Khesanh. His name is David Douglas Duncan and he is famous for photographing the art treasures of the Kremlin and Picasso's secret hoard of his own work. Duncan does not have to go to war. He is over fifty years old and he has been to too many wars already: World War II, Palestine, Greece, Korea, Indochina. But he recently went into the Marine outpost at Con Thien, got his photos, and came out alive. Now he flies into Khesanh, runs from the plane, which is being bombarded on the landing strip, and begins snapping a grim record of everyday terror and death. A C-130, machine-gunned while landing, skids the length of the runway and blows up. Duncan, running, braves the heat, the recurring explosions, and photographs live Marines pulling charred dead ones out of the blaze. A direct hit blows up part of the main ammo dump, leaving hundreds of scorched but unexploded artillery shells to be disposed of. Duncan photographs Marines gingerly handing scores of live, damaged shells down into a hole to be buried. An enemy rocket explodes fuel hoses that lead like fuses to the main gasoline dump. Marines fight the blaze; Duncan's cameras click. A single stray spark and they will

1. *autobahn,* German superhighway.

all be instantly immolated. Duncan, at his age, knows the danger better than they do.

After nine days, Duncan flies out of Khesanh. In New York, he shepherds his pictures into *Life* magazine and onto ABC television. Then he turns around and flies back to Vietnam, back into the middle of bursting shells, terror, and death. He might be photographing artsy scenery for *McCall's*, which once paid him fifty thousand dollars for some shots of Paris. But he chooses to go back into combat. Why?

"Death wish?" snorts Duncan. "I have no death wish. I have too much going for me. But it's the most important story of our time, perhaps in the entire history of our country."

Watch the ironworker fastening ribs to the skeleton of a skyscraper thirty or more stories above the street. His name is Edward Iannielli, Jr. Watch him, if you can stand to watch him, scamper across the void on an eight-inch beam, to get to a cup of coffee someone has sent up on an exposed dumbwaiter. Watch him scamper back across the eight-inch beam while studying the coffee carefully so as not to spill it. Listen to Eddie Iannielli talk.

"You're more of a crazy man up there at first, then it gets to be habit. You only focus on your feet, never on the ground. You have to have a sense of speed. You always start out on a beam at the same speed you're gonna finish. You can't change speeds in the middle. Of course, big beams you can walk out on with your eyes closed. You never start out on a beam unless you inwardly have said to yourself you can make it."

The son of an ironworker, Eddie once visited his father on a job, saw a ladder and climbed it, higher and higher: "Finally, I'm on the top, standing on this steel beam way up there, and I'm all alone and looking all around up there, looking out and seeing very far, and it was exciting; and as I stood there, all of a sudden I am thinking to myself, 'This is what I want to do!'" Eddie was then thirteen or fourteen.

When he was an apprentice, climbing a ladder while balancing about twenty cups of coffee for the men, he fell backward two flights, landed on some canvas and got scalded and nearly drowned by the coffee. Working on the First National City Bank Building in New York,

he fell into the void but landed on a beam three stories down and, though hurt, held on. The older workers told him he'd never live to see thirty.

Working on the Verrazano-Narrows bridge approach, he got one finger crushed and another amputated—the surgeon removed the crushed finger but sewed the amputated one back on in a crooked position, so Eddie could use it to hold onto beams. One day, high on the bridge, he turned to find a buddy clinging to a wire, feet dangling into emptiness, voice pleading, "Help me, Eddie."

Eddie had a grip on the man's clothes but couldn't hold him. The man fell three hundred fifty feet to his death. Eddie watched him fall, naked back showing as the shirt flapped in the wind.

"I nearly got killed three times since the bridge," says Eddie. "Sure, I've been thinking about it. But I couldn't quit. I love it too much. I wake up thinking today might be my last day. But that doesn't mean I'm going to stay in bed."

Watch the diver 140 miles east of Miami—and 432 feet below the surface of the sea. His name is Robert Stenuit. Inside the capsule that has taken him to the bottom, he takes a deep breath of pressurized gas, holds it, and swims down into the water. Across from him in the gloom is the rubber house in which he will live for two days. Above him is 432 feet of water. Wearing only a swimsuit, holding his breath, he pauses to look straight up toward the sun he cannot see and to realize that, at that depth, if anything goes wrong, he will have no chance of reaching the surface—none.

So he swims over to the rubber house and climbs in. The gas in there tastes to him as fresh as mountain air. "What calm in this other world," he thinks. "What silence. What peace."

He hurries to connect the gear. His colleague, Jon Lindbergh, swims in. They find that their dehumidifying apparatus doesn't work. Their lights implode, spraying slivers of glass into the rubber walls. In dark and cold, they wrestle into place the four-foot aluminum cylinders that will purify their rubber house of the rapidly accumulating carbon dioxide. But one cylinder is flooded and the other has the wrong cover on it and is useless. They are panting from exertion and the carbon dioxide level in the rubber house is already dangerous.

So they wait while a new cylinder is sent down. When it comes, they wrestle it into the rubber house. They work frantically. At last they hear it working—gas rushes in the way it is supposed to. They are, momentarily, safe. That night, on the bottom of the sea, they eat corned beef, drink canned water and carrot juice. In the morning, they work outside on the bottom.

After forty-nine hours on the bottom—the longest deep dive ever—and four days decompressing, they come out into the sunlight again.

"Our successors," exults Stenuit, "will stay in the depths that long or longer. They will colonize the sea floor, cultivating its resources instead of pillaging them."

You are against nuts, you say, but you tend to be for war photographers, ironworkers, and divers, if they don't take too many chances. You are for bravery, where it seems to pay off, though you are not entirely clear on what bravery is or how much payoff is necessary. Maybe you would like to believe that the daredevils you approve of display a higher quality of bravery than the ones you don't, or that you can measure the meaning of risk in terms of the good it may do—for someone else. You are against the death wish, whatever that is. You think nobody has a right to risk his life very much. We have a lot of laws against suicide and that kind of thing.

So let us see what you think about certain athletes.

Watch the daredevil bullfighter, El Cordobés, in Madrid. His first bull of the day gores him three inches deep under the arm. He springs up, ignores both his own wound and the bull's horns, and plays and kills it so skillfully that, in the general delirium, he is awarded both ears.[2]

Ducking into the infirmary, he allows his armpit to be sewed up without any anesthetic, then hurries outside to face his second bull. This one hooks him at once. He springs to his feet, runs back to it, and it spears him again, throws him, wheels, and is on top of him. Its horn rips

part of his costume off; he lies with his back bloody and exposed and the horn digs for him. His men drag him free and try to carry him off, but he breaks loose, scoops up his bloody cloth and gives the bull a hair-raising series of molinetes,[3] passing the animal behind his back. His costume is half gone, he is covered with blood, his eyes are as glazed as a fanatic's, and he is passing the bull again and again behind him.

People are screaming, "No, no, no!" A man near me is shouting, "Get him out of there. He doesn't know what he's doing." El Cordobés is being paid over sixteen thousand dollars today to give us thrills, but such insane bravery as this is not pretty to watch. "Get him out of there," we scream.

At last the fearful passes end. He kills the bull with a stroke. Now we cheer ourselves hoarse for him and award him an ear. Men jump down to parade him out the main gate on their shoulders.

Watch the daredevil racing driver, Jackie Stewart, on the fourteen-mile, 175-curve Nürburgring.[4] Listen to his reaction to the Fuchsröhre, a windy downhill plunge into a dip, then a steep uphill climb into a sharp left-hand turn, followed by a right, a left and another right.

Stewart says: "The first time you go down that hill, you're in fourth gear, and you decide you should be able to make it in sixth gear flat out. So the next time around, that's what you try; you go downhill in sixth gear at 163 miles an hour, switching back and forth from one side of the road to the other, the trees and hedges going by. You can't see anything but greenery and you think: '. . . I'm going too fast. It's bloody terrifying.' You think: 'I'm not going to have enough time to do everything.' In the dip at the bottom of the hill, the g forces are tremendous; you're squashed down in your seat, the suspension isn't working, and you realize you can't control the car anymore. You think: 'It is going to take its own line up the hill, whatever that line may be.' You can't get your foot off the accelerator onto the brake accurately—you

---

**2.** *both ears.* If a matador's performance has been exceptional, he is awarded one of the bull's ears after a bullfight. If his performance is extraordinary, he is awarded both ears.

**3.** *molinete* (mō lə nā′tā), a pass with the matador's cape.
**4.** *Nürburgring,* racing circuit near Cologne, Germany, in the Eifel Mountains. Site of the German Grand Prix.

only get a corner of it, and the car is going up the hill like on tram tracks. You're struggling to steer it and, at the same time, you're trying to come down two gears and get it slowed enough for the left-hander, and then there is a right, left, right coming—I tell you, it's bloody terrifying.

"But the second time you do it, your mind and body are synchronized to the elements you're competing against, and it is all clear to you, like in slow motion.

"It won't terrify you again until next year, when there will have been some improvements to the car and tires, and you go down there a little bit faster."

Or watch the daredevil mountain climber, Walter Bonatti, the Superman of the Alps, whose specialty is climbing sheer north faces in winter—alone. See him on the north face of the Matterhorn, climbing without gloves for a better grip, while the helicopters and light planes buzz about him all day. Every year or so up to now, he has made one of these fantastic climbs, selling his story and photos in advance to various European magazines. Every climb is much the same. Leaving his seventy pounds of gear behind, he climbs a little way up some sheer rock wall, hammering in pitons. Then he climbs down to get his gear and climbs up again, removing the pitons as he goes, for he will need the same pitons again higher up.

Each night, he hooks his sleeping sack to pitons planted more or less solidly in a fissure in the rock, curls himself into it in a fetal position, lights his spirit heater on his knees and cooks himself some bouillon or tea out of chunks of ice broken off the wall. He eats some dried chamois meat and some nougat candy. Then he hangs there all night, trying to sleep but kept awake, usually, by cold and terror.

Meanwhile, back in their warm, safe homes, Europeans watch that day's part of the climb on television, thank God they are not Walter Bonatti, and ask themselves what the hell he is doing up there alone.

He has been up there as long as seven days in the past. The Matterhorn climb takes only four. There is a huge cross atop the Matterhorn, raised there long ago by climbers who came up the easy way; and on the final afternoon, Bonatti at last spies the cross, with a halo of setting sun

behind it. The cross seems incandescent and miraculous all at once, and Bonatti feels blinded. He climbs the final meters between himself and safety and approaches the cross with open arms. When he feels it against his chest, he embraces it, falls on his knees, and begins to weep.

Do these people have a vision of life that is denied to most of us? Or are they all crazy? And what about the lives of spectators killed by stray racing cars or rescuers killed trying to get climbers off mountain walls? We also don't want to pay for any of the risk-taking via tax dollars. When a guy puts to sea in a ten-foot canoe, we don't want the Coast Guard going after him on our money. Should they be stopped? I don't know how you can stop most of them; you can't put police lines around every mountain or every sea. But would you want to stop them, if you could?

And let's look at this so-called death wish. Is there such a thing and, if so, is it everywhere and always deplorable? Or do we merely paste an easy label (because we do not understand) on what is really something else: courage, ambition, and technique of such awesome perfection that it removes most of the danger we, from a distance, think is there? Is it possible, most of the time, that most of these people are safer than you and I are walking to work? Is it further possible that they have a perfect right, regardless of society's approval or disapproval, to risk their lives as much as they please? Is it also possible that you and I have an absolute need of such men around us, the useless as much as the useful, those who get away with it as much as those who, misjudging the length of the rope, regale us with brains upon the floor?

Let us look more closely.

You ask what kind of men are these who regularly choose to risk their lives. A few of the ones I have known appear to be what the world calls weirdos. I think José Meiffret, the speed cyclist, is a bit strange, and I think this principally because his insanely dangerous record attempts are worth nothing to anyone else and nothing to him commercially. He does it strictly for glory: "At such speeds, I belong no longer to the earth and not yet to death. At such speeds I am—me!" Meiffret, small, poor, stepped on all his life, suddenly found a way to make people take notice. In the windbreak, crossing into the measured kilometer at 127 miles per hour, he says his head was filled with only one thought: "Twenty seconds more and the record is mine anew. The record will be my revenge on life, revenge on the misery I have suffered." To get to that moment, he practiced strict chastity, slept on a board, ate only health foods. He had written hundreds of letters, trying to line up backers and cooperation and he had spent every sou he owned. His life was not important to him, compared with the record.

I think Donald Campbell, the former land- and water-speed record holder, was a bit strange. Campbell had all sorts of fetishes and superstitions and also believed he could communicate with the dead. Just before setting his final record, as he sat in his cockpit quivering with fear, his face suddenly went calm, and in a moment, he rocketed safely down the run at 403 miles per hour. He explained that his dead father's face had appeared to him, reflected in the windscreen, his dead father's voice had assured him he would be safe.

Other racing drivers claimed Campbell reeked of death. Stirling Moss once told me he was absolutely certain Campbell would shortly kill himself. Moss was right. Campbell's boat blew up as he tried for the water-speed record.

And talking to Florida-based Kurt Severin about snakes and about fear is certainly an unsettling experience. "I don't know fear," he says. "It is one thing I am not acquainted with. I get an uncomfortable feeling at times, but it is not fear." Was he not frightened with the anaconda coiled around him? "No. There were three people around to get it off me. I only wanted to have a picture of myself with the anaconda to send to my wife."

Severin has been in the water with sharks and with crocodiles. He has been in three wars and about twenty revolutions. He claims to have been the first parachutist to photograph himself in flight. He did that in 1934.

But I do not know if I believe him about lack of fear. To get a photo of a cobra striking, he decided, he would have to give it something to strike. Why not himself? Why not, indeed. He built a plastic shield around his camera, pro-

voked the cobra, and it came right through the shield and hit his hand, missing a grip on the hand but pumping out enough venom to kill approximately twenty-two people. Severin dropped the camera, which broke open, spoiling the film. Another, stronger shield was built, and this time, Severin got the shot he wanted.

"I'm not afraid of snakes or sharks or animals. I'm afraid of bugs, though. I'm afraid of disease. I once slept in the bed of a guy who had just died of yellow fever. I didn't know it at the time, of course. Later, I was scared for eight days. It is not a funny feeling to think something might be encroaching on you."

Severin speaks five languages, plays the violin, and is interested in painting, ballet, and classical music. When he talks, he makes excellent sense; it is only when you mull over, later, what he has said that you become awed, or appalled.

"Fear of snakes is all in the mind," he says. "Snakes are not slimy. As a matter of fact, they have a very pleasant touch. It's like plastic. It's really quite nice."

Whatever Severin may think about fear, most other habitual risk takers are often terrified, and they admit it. In fact, what most separates them from the rest of us is not that they risk death but that they subject themselves to frequent terror, an emotion most of us struggle to avoid at all costs.

Every racing driver, every time he loses control of a car and waits for it to hit whatever it is going to hit, is terrified. Every matador, when he is down and the bull is on him, is terrified. El Cordobés, gored by the first bull he ever faced in Madrid, lay on the sand with the horn rooting about in his intestines: "It wasn't the pain I was worried about, it was the fear. When I felt the horn inside me, I was so scared I thought my heart would stop and I would die of the fear."

José Meiffret on his record bike is scared—he carries his last will and testament in his jersey pocket. The ironworker, Eddie Iannielli, is scared by every accident: "When something happens, all your fear comes back, but you suppress it. You just put it out of your mind." He talks about his most recent accident. He was sitting on top of a beam about two stories up, and the bolts at the base of the uprights broke or pulled out and the whole thing fell over sideways. Eddie suffered a back injury that kept him out of work for many weeks. "No matter how much you're prepared for something like that to happen, it happens so fast you're not prepared for it. A lot of guys get killed, and I'm still alive and I'm very grateful."

The climber, Bonatti, has known as much terror as any man alive, perhaps more. Climbing K2 in the Himalayas, he was unable to find two other climbers higher up, as night fell. At 27,000 feet, unable in the darkness to go up or down, without any food, heat or shelter of any kind, he was forced to spend the night in the open on an ice shelf, beating himself with his arms all night to keep himself awake and alive. That was prolonged terror.

Innumerable times, Bonatti has found himself clinging to some sheer wall, certain (for the moment) there was no possible way to go either up or down. On the Lavaredo in Italy, he had to inch across a fragile ledge of snow. On the Dru in France, he had to lasso a jutting projection and swing across the void like Tarzan, while wondering if the rope would slip off or the projection snap. Once, he was caught in a storm with six other men on a narrow ledge on Mont Blanc. Lightning was attracted by the group's sack of pitons, ice axes, and such. Bolt after bolt blasted and crackled around the group. The air was saturated with electricity. They could not get rid of the cursed sacks of steel—without them, they could get neither up nor down the mountain. They simply had to huddle there, terrified, waiting to be fried or blasted off the ledge. Again and again, lightning crashed about them. Bonatti found himself screaming.

I have known a good many people who habitually take risks, and although I have heard a number of them say they enjoy the danger, I have never heard one say he enjoyed the terror.

Habitual risk takers are able to do what they do, first because they suppress (or, in some cases, eliminate) certain fears that are normal in all of us: fear of height, fear of the depths of the sea, fear of excessive speed, fear of bullets and bombs, fear of wild beasts, fear of snakes. All of these fears, in them as in us, are basically fear of the unknown. Once all the facts and details are known, the fears become much less fearsome and a reasonable man is often able to ignore them. As Severin says, snakes are not slimy, and once you know that, there is no reason to be afraid. In fact, he says, almost all feared creatures "will scram out of there at the approach of man. If sharks were as dangerous as written, most of our beaches would be unsafe."

In other words, at least part of Severin's bravery is only knowledge. Similarly, the bullfighter is not normally afraid of the bull, because he has spent years learning how to handle bulls, just as the racing driver has spent years learning how to control speed that would frighten most of us. The mountaineer knows rocks, knows which fissures will hold a piton and which won't; and he also knows that once anchored to a piton, he is absolutely safe, no matter what the height. David Douglas Duncan goes in to photograph wars knowing in advance approximately what he will find there—he was once a U.S. Marine trained for combat. He knows he won't be surprised by anything, he knows he won't panic, and he knows instinctively now how to recognize places and moments that he judges overly dangerous; these he avoids. In other words, he knows when to stick his head up and when not to; he obeys certain rules, and these rules keep him alive. Occasionally, he will expose himself to get a picture; but by moving fast, he cuts the risk to a minimum. He is, of course, a brave man, but he is not a foolish one, and he accepts risk only when certain he understands it exactly and has put all odds in his favor. I once heard him tell Guy Lombardo that he would never drive one of Lombardo's speedboats: "I would be terrified. I'm not trained for that. I don't know anything about it." In combat, Duncan is obviously as vulnerable as each GI to some stray shell; but while in combat he runs no risk of being sideswiped by a taxicab, or mugged in the park, or hit on the head by a suicide on his way down from the roof. The odds can be said to come out almost the same, once you realize, as Duncan does, that life is not very safe.

In addition to possessing knowledge and technique, most of these risk takers approach each dangerous place only after having taken every possible precaution in advance. Bullfighters always have a surgeon present in the arena infirmary (indeed, surgeons are required by law in Spain) and the richer bullfighters often travel with their own personal horn-wound specialists—just in case. Sitkiewicz hangs around for an hour after his act; then, when the show ends and the audience empties out, he goes up and rerigs his rope himself for his next dive. No one else is allowed to touch it.

The racing driver, Jackie Stewart, feels that the modern, monocoque Grand Prix car[5] is so strong that the driver can survive almost any crash. The only danger then is fire—so Stewart wears fireproof long underwear, fireproof coveralls, fireproof gloves, socks and shoes, and a fireproof bandanna covering all his face except his eyes. Inside all this in a three-hour race he nearly suffocates, but he wears it. "I'm very safety conscious, as perhaps you've noticed," he told me once. "But in a fire, a man ought to be safe for thirty seconds, dressed that way; and by that time, somebody ought to be able to get him out. Thirty seconds is quite a long time, actually." That was the day of the 1966 Belgian Grand Prix. Stewart crashed in a rainstorm and the car crumpled around him so tight it was fifteen minutes before they got him out. The fire suit wouldn't have saved him. The next year, he turned up for the same race wearing, in addition to his fire suit, a patch over his breast, giving any eventual surgeons his blood type. Precautions, Stewart feels—all risk takers feel—are important.

Why do men such as these seem to search out danger?

Psychologists will tell you that each of them first selects a difficult profession in order to separate himself from the mass of men. Later, each raises his stake up to and beyond the danger line, in order to separate himself further from other men within the same profession. Psychologists will give you many such explanations, overlooking what are, in most cases, the two basic ones: Most men who search out danger do it for money and for the pure pleasure of it. For the standouts, the money comes only

one way: big. The pleasure usually comes big, too, sometimes even orgiastic, stupendous.

Start with money, the simplest of all human motives. Car racers and, even more so, bullfighters earn fantastic sums. Sitkiewicz may earn only a bit over two hundred dollars a week, but what else could he do, in Poland, to earn so much? Some photographers earn good pay also, but David Douglas Duncan, having taken the precaution (that word again) of selling his photos in advance to both *Life* and ABC television, will earn ten times as much by going into sticky combat zones most others want no part of.

By working high up on narrow beams where not many other men will go, Eddie Iannielli earns (counting bonuses and extra vacation time) roughly $20,000 a year, almost twice what laborers like himself earn below. He risks a quick death, yes, but his special skill is so rare that he never risks being out of work, a possibility that haunts—and terrifies—much of mankind all the time.

There is money in most danger and sometimes, paradoxically, even a little security. And there are pleasures, many pleasures. Start with the simplest of these.

To control anything—anything at all—delights man. He is delighted to control the way a plant grows or the shape of a bush or a dart thrown at a dartboard, or a car driven fast and well. So do not be surprised to hear that there is pleasure in controlling a very hot car, indeed, or a raging bull or one's feet on a beam. The controlled forces are tremendous, unpredictable, and therefore the pleasure of control is that much greater. A man thinks: "Look at me, fragile and puny human being that I am! Look what I am controlling!" This is never said aloud, because the fragile and puny human being in question would much rather have you believe him a hero. But this is the way he feels. He gets a kick out of controlling something hardly anybody else can control. It's nice that you down there are watching him and cheering his control, but he would feel pleasure whether you were there or not, for the principal applause he is listening to is his own.

There is pleasure in accepting challenge. At a world convention held in London, on under-

5. *monocoque Grand Prix car.* A Grand Prix (grän prē´) is any of a number of international automobile races. A monocoque body is similar to "unibody" construction—that is, the body is made essentially of one piece.

sea activities, the inventor Edwin Link spoke of sending a man to live at a depth of four hundred feet. Listen to the diver Robert Stenuit: "All heads turned to me. Four hundred feet! The very idea made my insides itch. Did I really want to descend to that awful depth, to shiver night and day and perhaps to furnish headlines for the journals that specialize in catastrophe?

"I really did. Always I have found joy in danger lucidly accepted and prudently overcome. And when a reporter put the question to me, I heard myself answer: 'Of course. Yes.'

"To me, it was the most extraordinary adventure of which a diver might dream."

There is pleasure in provoking terror in others, too. The gasp Sitkiewicz hears when he dives from the roof is pure pleasure to him. Most of the risk takers I have known delight in talking about danger, delight in mentioning death casually, delight in watching listeners' eyes go wide. Eddie Iannielli says: "Windy days, of course, are the hardest. Like, you're walking across an eight-inch beam, balancing yourself in the wind, and then, all of a sudden, the wind stops—and you temporarily lose your balance. It's some feeling when that happens." Eddie always enjoys the admiration, the near worship, when he talks like this. All of these men are aware from such reactions, from the questions they are constantly asked ("But why do you do it, why?"), and from the hypothesizing psychologists in the background that so-called normal people don't understand who they are or how they can accept such risk, and this is very pleasant. It is nice to feel so singular. The desire to feel singular is basic to the human personality; but the timid clerk at his desk may have to do without fulfilling this basic need every day of his long, safe life, subsisting on his Mittyesque[6] fantasies.

There is also the simple pleasure of physical activity. All of the risk takers are easily bored. They go crazy in static situations and normally they go on taking risks however long they may live. Duncan and Meiffret are over fifty. Kurt Severin is over sixty-five and on Medicare, and on a trip, as has been said, to the Far East to see

more snakes: "I have always had an urge to do things, to be in all sorts of funny situations. It's curiosity, it's—I don't know. I want to see things others haven't seen, and that involves danger, because one goes into the unknown. I'm a senior citizen. People tell me I should sit . . . and digest what I have seen and not expose myself anymore. But I can't do it. I have to go out."

There is pleasure as well in the belief of most risk takers that they are contributing to the world by doing something dangerous that has to be done. Stenuit believes one day men will colonize the continental shelf, thanks to his pioneering dives. If he is wrong, he may be accused of having risked his life for nothing. Nonetheless, at the time, he believed he was contributing his best and most important talent to the world. So does Duncan believe he is contributing by bringing back photos that may throw some light on the awful struggle in Vietnam. So does Walter Bonatti believe that he and all mountaineers contribute: "We demonstrate in the most stunning way of all—at the risk of our lives—that there is no limit to the effort man can demand of himself."

Now we come to pleasures that are not so simple and, therefore, not so easy to describe.

"I think we appreciate life better, because we live closer to death," the late Marquis de Portago once wrote of racing drivers. Does this make any sense to you? Danger heightens all the senses. A man feels extraordinarily alert and alive. Up to a certain point, alcohol does this, too, and I suppose drugs do, although I do not know this personally. But I firmly believe that nothing stimulates a man as much as danger does, and it doesn't even have to be very much danger.

One extremely hot day last January, I was hunting quail on the King Ranch in south Texas. There were other shooters, most of whom I did not know, and I was worried about possibly getting my head blown off by accident, or blowing off someone else's, and this made me alert. I was watching everybody very carefully, and then the girl nearest me jumped back and blasted a rattlesnake.

She stood there trembling, unable to move. The rattler, tail buzzing, writhed brokenly near

---

6. *Mittyesque,* made-up word from the name of James Thurber's fictitious character Walter Mitty, who daydreams to escape his humdrum life.

her feet, and I ran over and shot its head off.

At lunchtime, we gathered in a grove of oaks and dined on a stew made from kid goat and on broiled baby lamb chops and drank cold Rhine wine and talked of rattlesnakes. There were nine of us shooters in all, hunting in groups, and the total score in rattlesnakes so far was four. Much of the King Ranch was still under water from the fall hurricanes and the rattlers seemed to have come up onto the higher ground from all over; the sun had brought them out of their holes and it was plainly very dangerous to continue shooting. But nobody wanted to go home yet. Our excitement was too high.

In the afternoon, hunting through a grove of mesquite trees, I did not see what turned out to be the biggest rattler of the day, a six-footer, until I was within a stride of it. The diamondback rattler in that kind of country is almost impossible to see.

I gave it both barrels. This disturbance set off a bevy of quail, which flew all about me. People were shouting "Shoot!" but I was quivering too much even to reload.

But this emotion passed and we went on hunting, often through high, hummocky grass. "Some chance of seeing a rattler in here," I thought, but I plowed through it, anyway, eyeballs working over every blade, every shadow. I have never felt so alert in my life, presumably because my life depended on my alertness. I also have never felt so keenly aware of the sun on my back, or the smell of gunpowder, or the color of birds, or the buzzing of insects. I felt hungry and thirsty and tired in a very pleasant way, enjoying food and drink and rest in advance, while still slogging through fields, trying to flush quail.

When night fell, the groups came together at a dirt crossroads in the dark and drank gin and tonic mixed out of the trunks of the shooting cars. The total score was seven rattlers. We all agreed it was madness to have hunted in there that day. We were all glad we had done it. Ice tinkled in glasses. They were the best gin and tonics I have ever tasted. I was excited, alert, aware of all of the sights, sounds, and smells of the night. This lasted until I fell asleep later back at the ranch, and even until the next

morning, when I lay awake in bed, listening to the dew drip off the roof and feeling good all over.

This is one level of the excitement that exists in danger. There is another that is perhaps impossible to describe to someone who hasn't experienced it.

Years ago, in the streets of Jerusalem, Jewish terrorists waved David Duncan to take cover, then mowed down the three Arabs he was with. Duncan raced after the terrorists' car, photographing the whole show as police and bullets came from all directions. Later, Duncan cabled *Life:* "What a beautiful day to be still alive."

Now, some will assert that danger is a drug, that a man gets so he can't leave it alone; and this is true, though not in the way the speaker usually means. I have never heard a habitual risk taker articulate what the "drug" is, or what the sensation feels like; but to me, it is purely and simply the extraordinary exhilaration a man feels to find the danger gone and himself still alive. I have felt this exhilaration.

For many years, I have gone to the fiesta at Pamplona[7] each July and run in the streets with the bulls most mornings, and this is not particularly dangerous. There are many tricks for keeping well clear of the horns, and normally the bulls, obeying their strong herd instinct run flank to flank and ignore the runners completely. The only real danger is a bull separated from the herd. A bull alone will gore anything it sees.

There was one morning I ran in front of the bulls and, when they were close, I leaped high up onto a window grating, hoisting my derrière out of danger. When the herd had gone by, I dropped down into the street again and sauntered between the barriers toward the arena into which the herd had disappeared. There were other men in the street with me and mobs of people crowding the barriers along both sides of the ramp that goes down to the tunnel under the stands.

Suddenly, the men on the fences started shouting: "Falta uno!"[8] There was one bull still loose in the street.

The men in the street scattered and there I

---

7. *Pamplona,* city in Spain.
8. *Falta uno!* One missing! [*Spanish*]

stood, face to face with the bull, who for a moment, could not decide what to do.

I searched for an empty spot on the fence. There was none. What to do? Where to run? I remember thinking: Be calm. Think it out carefully. If you panic, you are lost. I saw I was the only man in the street. The bull was ten yards away. In the other direction was the ramp under the stands and the arena floor beyond. I thought: Can I beat the bull into the arena? If I could get into the arena, I could perhaps hurdle the *barrera* to safety. But I saw that the bull would catch me in the tunnel or before. I thought: It's the only chance you have; start running.

I ran.

The tunnel was twenty yards away . . . ten. I could hear the bull.

Suddenly, I spied a gap atop the fence. I leaped up there. The bull rushed by under my feet. A moment later, the wooden door slammed behind it. I was safe.

I felt none of the quivering one feels after losing control of a car or nearly stepping on a rattlesnake. Instead, I felt a flood of exhilaration. I did it! Look at me. I'm still alive!

It was one of the most stupendous feelings of my life. . . . So this is what all the talk has been about.

It wasn't a feeling of relief or of gratitude. It was exhilaration. I had faced real danger and got out of it on my own two feet and I was still alive and I felt great, absolutely great.

Then I thought: This must be the drug they speak of. It is a sensation I could get to love entirely too much; and the next day, I was afraid to run with the bulls (though I have run many times since), fearing that I might go for that extraordinary exhilaration again and this time, possibly, do something really stupid.

And so some of the habitual risk takers go for this feeling sometimes and some of them find it occasionally, but it must be rare. A feeling as glorious as that can't be common, and I

suppose you can call it a drug if you want to.

On a more practical level, you can't have a safe world *and* a progressive one. (Probably you can't have a safe world under any circumstances, so you might as well try for the progress, whatever the cost.) And you must admit that most progress comes from risk. This has always been the case. Five hundred years ago, Columbus risked his life and his ships and crews to discover a new world he didn't know was there, and that's why all of us are where we are today. The men of his time later called Columbus a hero. But there must have been a hundred other captains who never found the new world, because they looked in the wrong place; and some of them didn't come back, and no doubt "normal" people of the time called such men daredevils obeying some stupid death wish.

Or think of Edison fooling around with high voltage he didn't understand, high voltage that had killed several men before him and would kill many after him. Edison was obviously a daredevil. Was he acting out a death wish as well?

All of progress comes from pushing a little closer to the edge than the guy before you, and this involves risk. The world *needs* risk takers, needs an oversupply of them, and the spillover become the circus performers and daredevil athletes, all of whom have the same temperaments, basically, as all explorers and most inventors.

Cut off the right to risk one's life, and progress would end and society would atrophy and die. The right to *watch* men risk their lives on mountains, in car races, bullfights, and circuses is equally important. We need to know where death is, if only to avoid it; and such men show us that and much more. Often accused of having a death wish, they make careers out of staying alive. And that is the simplest, most singular thing about them. It should not be overlooked.

## DISCUSSION

1. According to Daley, how do habitual risk takers differ from the ordinary person? Use specific examples to support your answer.
2. What reasons does Daley give for persons risking their lives?
3. What attitude does he believe people have toward those who regularly risk their lives?
4. Which of the people mentioned in the article and listed below would you classify as "weirdos" and which as "normal, but unusually brave"? Why?

| | |
|---|---|
| Sitkiewicz | Stenuit |
| Severin | El Cordobés |
| Meiffret | Stewart |
| Duncan | Bonatti |
| Iannielli | Campbell |

5. (a) One of the points made by those interested in women's rights is that we use such terms as *man* and *mankind* when what we mean is *people* or *humankind*. Find examples of such terms in "The Risk Takers." Do you agree with the opinion that the use of such terms as *man* for *people* and *mankind* for *humankind* has the effect of overlooking or excluding women? If so, with what consequences? (b) The article does not mention the names of any women risk takers. Are there any women in the same occupations Daley mentions? Can you name any women in these or other dangerous occupations? If so, who?

## WORD STUDY

There are many compound words in the selection you just read— words such as *daredevil, windbreak,* and *bullfighter.* With the help of the article and your own imagination, see how many compounds you can make from the words below. You should be able to write at least fifteen compound words.

| | |
|---|---|
| pass | worker |
| fire | cab |
| cover | proof |
| all | rattle |
| snake | sky |
| taxi | iron |
| scraper | port |
| over | smoke |
| hole | turn |
| screen | man |

## ROBERT DALEY

Risk and the exhilaration of successful escape have long intrigued Robert Daley. While working as a sportswriter, he observed many risk takers, some of whom he featured in his books: *The Swords of Spain* examines the people, pageantry, and drama of the bullfight, while *The Cruel Sport* became the basis for the movie *Grand Prix.*

Born in New York in 1930, Daley graduated from Fordham University in 1951, served with the Air Force in Korea, and from 1953 to 1958 was publicity director for a New York football team.

During his six years based in Paris and Nice as European sports correspondent for the *New York Times,* Daley's realistic stories were widely read by sports fans. After returning to the United States, he left the newspaper to devote his time to writing novels.

As Deputy Police Commissioner of New York City (a position to which he was appointed in 1971) Daley, who has received several death threats, has himself become a risk taker.

---

## UNIT 2 REVIEW

1. (a) What does the excerpt from *Black Elk Speaks* have in common with the excerpt from *Narrative of the Life of Frederick Douglass* in content, in tone, and in purpose? (b) What characteristics did the two men have in common?
2. What passages from the autobiographical excerpts would you cite in a defense of the importance of freedom?
3. What do Asimov and Daley say or imply about freedom?
4. If you were the host of a TV talk show, what three questions would you ask (a) Black Elk, (b) Frederick Douglass, (c) Margaret Bourke-White, (d) Isaac Asimov, (e) Robert Daley? Be prepared to explain why.
5. Imagine for the moment that Black Elk and Isaac Asimov meet and speak to each other through an interpreter. Might they discover they have any interests or viewpoints in common? If so, what would they be?
6. (a) If you were a television or motion-picture producer sifting through the contents of this unit for material for a television show or a movie, what might you select? Why? (b) Who would you cast in your production? Would it be a drama, musical comedy, documentary? In short, describe your plans as if you were a producer trying to persuade someone to finance your production.

# Poetry

# Responses

**Dust of Snow**

*Robert Frost*

The way a crow
Shook down on me
The dust of snow
From a hemlock tree

Has given my heart
A change of mood
And saved some part
Of a day I had rued.

---

## DISCUSSION

1. (a) In what way was the poet's mood changed by having snow shaken down on him? (b) What context clues give you some idea of the meaning of "rued"?

2. Why might having snow shaken on you change your mood?

---

### Earth Dweller

*William Stafford*

It was all the clods at once become
precious; it was the barn, and the shed,
and the windmill, my hands, the crack
Arlie made in the axehandle: oh, let me stay
5  here humbly, forgotten, to rejoice in it all;
let the sun casually rise and set.
If I have not found the right place,
teach me, for, somewhere inside, the clods are
vaulted mansions, lines through the barn sing
10  for the saints forever, the shed and windmill
rear so glorious the sun shudders like a gong.

Now I know why people worship, carry around
magic emblems, wake up talking dreams
they teach to their children: the world speaks.
15  The world speaks everything to us.
It is our only friend.

---

## DISCUSSION

1. How does the speaker feel about the chunks of earth (clods) around him? Has he always felt this way?

2. (a) Reread the poem to the first colon. What else does the speaker feel is precious? (b) How do the last two details in the list (lines 2–4) differ from the others?

3. What desire does the speaker reveal in lines 4–5?

4. In the images in lines 8–11, ordinary things are transformed. How do these images contribute to the general mood of the poem?

5. What realization does the speaker come to as a consequence of his experience?

6. Why is the world called "our only friend"? Relate this idea to the title of the poem.

## WILLIAM STAFFORD

The influence of William Stafford's early years in small Kansas towns can be seen in the rural images of farm and prairie that appear in many of his poems. Born in Hutchinson, Kansas, in 1914, he graduated from the University of Kansas and earned his Ph.D at the University of Iowa.

During World War II he was a conscientious objector and active in pacifist organizations. *Down in My Heart* (1947) is an account of these wartime experiences.

Stafford has taught literature at Manchester College in Indiana, at San Jose State College, and at Lewis and Clark College in Portland, Oregon. *Traveling Through the Dark*, one of Stafford's several volumes of verse, won a National Book Award.

## Song of the Sky Loom

*Tewa Indian*

Oh our Mother the Earth oh our Father the Sky
Your children are we
   with tired backs we bring you the gifts you love

So weave for us a garment of brightness

May the warp be the white light of morning
May the weft be the red light of evening
May the fringes be the falling rain
May the border be the standing rainbow

Weave for us this bright garment
that we may walk where birds sing
   where grass is green

Oh our Mother the Earth oh our Father the Sky

---

## DISCUSSION

1. Indian songs usually serve a purpose—often that of communicating between a man and the life-giving forces that he believes govern his world. To whom is this song addressed? What would be the tone of the singer?

2. What would be woven into the garment of brightness? What desire does the garment represent?

3. The Tewa are a group of Indians who speak the Tewa language and live in the dry Southwest. How does knowing this help explain the choice of details used in the poem?

Slightly revised from Herbert J. Spinden, *Songs of the Tewa*, New York, 1933. Reprinted by permission of Ailes Spinden.

## Lots of Lakes

*Ron Loewinsohn*

The weather clear, late June afternoon,
  the evening seeming to hold back
for us, coming out of the Adirondacks
  in that failing light we saw
5  down in the valley a lake, in a lake's
  shape, so still grey water in what
light there was, down there among the trees.
  As we approach it its perfection grows, its
shape stated so precisely, in there among the trees,
10  its surface, so.

        But closer, we notice
it doesn't behave like a lake, & closer yet,
  it's not; it's a parking lot.
Some institution is off in the woods, & when
15  the people go there, drifting off over the paths
in among the trees, this is where they park
  their cars, to get hot under the June sun.
& when it snows they drive their white
  cars away, & there are all these car-sized spots
20  where the snow hasn't fallen.

        So we saw a lake
that was actually a lot.—& I don't know whether
  that was a good thing, or it was not.

---

## DISCUSSION

1. (a) What visual error does the speaker in the poem make? (b) What part do his assumptions or expectations about the setting (a wooded valley) play in his mistaken perception?

2. Is he disappointed that what he thought was a lake turns out to be a parking lot? What lines reveal his response?

3. The poet speculates on the appearance of the parking lot in winter. (a) Is the scene he describes ugly? Beautiful? Both? Neither? (b) Which do people more commonly praise, the beauties of nature or the beauties of man-made objects? (c) Turn back to the photograph of a dam that appeared on a *Life* magazine cover, page 157. Is there beauty in that structure? In a car? A building? A gun? Explain.

## RON LOEWINSOHN

Ron Loewinsohn came to the United States in 1945 from the Philippines, where he was born in 1937. After graduation from high school, he traveled around the United States, working on a variety of printing jobs.

Educated further at San Francisco State College and the University of California, Loewinsohn went on to earn a master's degree from Harvard.

He has taught in poetry workshops, as a teaching fellow in American literature at Harvard, and as a member of the English faculty of the University of California at Berkeley. He and his wife have two sons.

## Aphrodite[1] Metropolis

*Kenneth Fearing*

    "Myrtle loves Harry"—It is sometimes hard to remember a thing like that,
    Hard to think about it, and no one knows what to do with it when he has it,
    So write it out on a billboard that stands under the yellow light of an "L" platform
           among popcorn wrappers and crushed cigars,
    A poster that says "Mama I Love Crispy Wafers So."
5  Leave it on a placard where somebody else gave the blonde lady a pencil moustache,
           and another perplexed citizen deposited:
    "Jesus Saves. Jesus Saves."
    One can lay this bundle down there with the others,
    And never lose it, or forget it, or want it.
    "Myrtle loves Harry."
10  They live somewhere.

**1.** *Aphrodite* (af′rə dī′tē), the Greek goddess of love and beauty.

## Fog

*Carl Sandburg*

The fog comes
on little cat feet.

It sits looking
over harbor and city
on silent haunches
and then moves on.

---

## DISCUSSION

*Aphrodite Metropolis*

1. (a) If this were an older, romanticized poem on love, what images might be expected in place of the "yellow light of the 'L'," and the surrounding "popcorn wrappers and crushed cigars"? Where might "Myrtle loves Harry" be inscribed? (b) What is the effect of the names Myrtle and Harry? Would the tone of the poem be changed if the names were Gwendolyn and Sebastian? Explain.

2. (a) Compare and contrast the two messages which include the word "love." (b) What other communications are mentioned in the poem? How are they like or different from "Myrtle loves Harry"?

3. Throughout the poem, the pronoun "it" has referred to the phrase "Myrtle loves Harry." How is your perception of Myrtle and Harry changed by the last line, which begins with the pronoun "they"?

4. What is the speaker's attitude toward Myrtle's love for Harry? What lines tell you?

5. What is the effect of the use of the name of the Greek goddess of love in the title?

*Fog*

1. Point out words or phrases that indicate three distinct steps in the movement of the fog.

2. This poem contains an *extended metaphor*. You may remember that a metaphor is an implied comparison. What is the meaning of *extended metaphor*?

3. Is the comparison of fog and a cat a good one? Explain.

## By Morning

*May Swenson*

Some for everyone
  plenty

and more coming

Fresh    dainty    airily arriving
5  everywhere at once

Transparent at first
  each faint slice
  slow    soundlessly tumbling

then quickly thickly a gracious fleece
10  will spread like youth    like wheat
  over the city

Each building will be    a hill
  all sharps made round

dark worn noisy narrows made still
15  wide    flat    clean    spaces

Streets will be    fields
  cars be    fumbling sheep

A deep bright harvest will be seeded
  in a night

20 By morning we'll be    children
  feeding on manna[1]

a new loaf on every doorsill

"By Morning" (Copyright 1954 May Swenson) which first appeared in *The New Yorker*, is reprinted by permission of Charles Scribner's Sons from *To Mix with Time* by May Swenson.
1. *manna,* any needed substance that seems miraculously supplied.

## The Manoeuvre

*William Carlos Williams*

I saw the two starlings
coming in toward the wires.
But at the last,
just before alighting, they

turned in the air together
and landed backwards!
that's what got me—to
face into the wind's teeth.

---

## DISCUSSION

### By Morning

1. (a) This poem appears in a collection entitled *Poems to Solve*. To solve each poem, you must guess what it describes. What does this one describe? (b) What clues led you to the solution?

2. (a) To what sense or senses does the imagery in the poem appeal? (b) Point out several

figurative expressions that you feel are particularly effective.

3. (a) How will the city be changed? (b) How will the city's inhabitants be affected by the change? Cite lines from the poem to support your answer.

4. Is "manna" an appropriate word to describe what is found on every doorsill? Explain.

5. What devices instead of punctuation does the poet use to help you read the poem?

### The Manoeuvre

1. What in particular about the two starlings' actions affects the speaker? How is he affected?

2. How is the poem like and unlike Frost's "Dust of Snow"?

## WILLIAM CARLOS WILLIAMS

William Carlos Williams was born in Rutherford, New Jersey, in 1883. After schooling in Switzerland, Williams attended the University of Pennsylvania and received a medical degree in 1906.

He spent his adult life as a pediatrician in New Jersey, writing poetry, novels, short stories, plays, and an autobiography during the hours when he wasn't caring for patients. Williams championed the development of a distinctly American idiom in poetry—the unadorned language of natural speech.

He died in 1963.

# Curses

**Traveller's Curse After Misdirection**
*(from the Welsh)*

*Robert Graves*

May they stumble, stage by stage
On an endless pilgrimage,
Dawn and dusk, mile after mile,
At each and every step, a stile;[1]
5 At each and every step withal
May they catch their feet and fall;
At each and every fall they take
May a bone within them break;
And may the bone that breaks within
10 Not be, for variation's sake,
Now rib, now thigh, now arm, now shin,
But always, without fail THE NECK.

**1.** *stile*, a set of steps or rungs that allows people to pass over a fence or wall that contains animals.

*The Greek poet and soldier Archilochos (är kil′ ō kəs)
in the seventh century B.C. contracted marriage
with Neobulé, daughter of Lykambes, but Lykambes
broke his word and the marriage never took place.
This curse expresses Archilochos' bitter hatred for
Lykambes.*

## May He Lose His Way

*Archilochos*
*Translated from the Greek by Guy Davenport*

May he lose his way on the cold sea
And swim to the heathen Salmydessos,[1]
May the ungodly Thracians with their hair
Done up in a fright on the top of their heads
5  Grab him, that he know what it is to be alone
Without friend or family. May he eat slave's bread
And suffer the plague and freeze naked,
Laced about with the nasty trash of the sea.
May his teeth knock the top on the bottom
10  As he lies on his face, spitting brine,
At the edge of the cold sea, like a dog.
And all this it would be a privilege to watch,
Giving me great satisfaction as it would,
For he took back the word he gave in honor,
15  Over the salt and table[2] at a friendly meal.

---

## DISCUSSION

### Traveller's Curse

1. (a) Why are "they" being cursed by the traveller? (b) What makes the curse suitable as revenge?

2. (a) Note that "step" appears in line 4 and is repeated in line 5, "fall" appears in 6 and 7, and "bone" and "break" in lines 8 and 9. How does the curse change with each repetition of one of these words? (b) What impression does the changing curse give of the misdirected man's mood? Explain.

3. How would you change the poem so it would be appropriate to the driver of a car who has misdirected someone?

### May He Lose His Way

1. If Archilochos were cursing someone today, in what modern place might he wish for that person to "lose his way" (line 1)? What would that person be forced to eat instead of "slave's bread" (line 6)? From what disease might Archilochos wish him to "suffer" (line 7)?

2. Reread the last two lines. What quality of character was important to Archilochos?

3. To what senses does the poet appeal to help the reader (and Lykambes) realize what it would be like to suffer under this curse?

From *Carmina Archilochi: The Fragments of Archilochi*, translated from the Greek by Guy Davenport. Originally published by the University of California Press: reprinted by permission of The Regents of the University of California.

1. *Salmydessos* (säl mē des′ əs), a town on the coast of Thrace, which bordered the Black Sea.
2. *salt and table*. Salt, extremely valuable in ancient times, has throughout history been associated with friendship. Salt at the meal had by custom bound Lykambes and Archilochos and sanctioned the marriage contract.

## Nine Charms Against the Hunter

*David Wagoner*

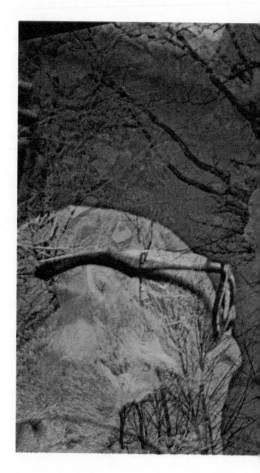

In the last bar on the way to your wild game,
May the last beer tilt you over among friends
And keep you there till sundown—failing that,
A breakdown on the road, ditching you gently
5  Where you may hunt for lights and a telephone.
Or may your smell go everywhere through the brush,
Upwind or crosswind. May your feet come down
Invariably crunching loudly on dry sticks.
Or may whatever crosses your hairlines[1]—
10  The flank of elk or moose, the scut of a deer,
The blurring haunch of a bear, or another hunter
Gaping along his sights at the likes of you—
May they catch you napping or freeze you with buck fever.
Or if you fire, may the stock butting your shoulder
15  Knock you awake around your bones as you miss,
Or then and there, may the noise pour through your mind
Imaginary deaths to redden your daydreams:
Dazed animals sprawling forward on dead leaves,
Thrashing and kicking, spilling themselves as long
20  As you could wish, as hard, as game,
And then, if you need it, imaginary skinning,
Plucking of liver and lights, unraveling guts,
Beheading trophies to your heart's content.
Or if these charms have failed and the death is real,
25  May it fatten you, hour by hour, for the trapped hunter
Whose dull knife beats the inside of your chest.

---

## DISCUSSION

1. One meaning of the word *charm*, is a thing, act, or saying believed to have power to ward off evil. What is the evil that the speaker wishes to ward off?

2. At what points, and how, during the hunting trip, does the speaker try to stop the hunter?

3. (a) What can you infer about the poet's opinion of hunters? (b) What images in the poem create sympathy for the "hunted"?

4. (a) What is the final charm against the hunter if all others fail? (b) Who or what is the "trapped hunter" (line 25), and what is his "dull knife" (line 26)?

## DAVID WAGONER

Poet and novelist David Wagoner

1. *hairlines,* usually, "cross hairs," two fine, crossed lines in a telescopic gun sight used for sighting.

was born in Massilon, Ohio, in 1926. Educated at Pennsylvania State and Indiana Universities, he has taught English at DePauw and Pennsylvania State, and since 1954 has been professor of English at the University of Washington in Seattle. There he has also been editor of *Poetry Northwest* magazine.

He has earned Guggenheim and Ford Foundation Fellowships and his work has won, among other honors, a National Institute of Arts and Letters Award.

## At the Theatre
To the Lady Behind Me

*Sir A. P. Herbert*

Dear Madam, you have seen this play;
I never saw it till today.
You know the details of the plot,
But, let me tell you, I do not.
5 The author seeks to keep from me
The murderer's identity,
And you are not a friend of his
If you keep shouting who it is.
The Actors in their funny way
10 Have several funny things to say,
But they do not amuse me more
If you have said them just before;
The merit of the drama lies,
I understand, in some surprise;
15 But the surprise must now be small
Since you have just foretold it all.
The lady you have brought with you
Is, I infer, a half-wit too,
But I can understand the piece
20 Without assistance from your niece.
In short, foul woman, it would suit
Me just as well if you were mute;
In fact, to make my meaning plain,
I trust you will not speak again.
25 And—may I add one human touch?—
Don't breathe upon my neck so much.

---

### DISCUSSION

1. What are the lady's specific offenses? Whom has she offended?
2. What punishment would the speaker like to impose on this woman?
3. What other situations might offer material for a similar poem, for instance, "To the Student in Front of Me in the Lunch Line"?
4. How would you describe the tone of voice in which this poem should be read?

### A. P. HERBERT

A lawyer who never practiced law, A. P. Herbert is probably best known for his contributions to *Punch*, the British humor magazine. Born in London in 1890, he served in the Royal Navy in World War I and was wounded in France. *Secret Battle* (1920) was based on his wartime experiences.

From 1935 to 1950 Herbert was a Member of Parliament. There he led a successful fight against the imposition of a wartime tax of twelve percent on the sale of books and aided in the passage of the Matrimonial Causes Bill, which modified the stringent British divorce laws.

Herbert's works include novels, plays, poetry, satirical essays, and librettos for several comic operas. He died in 1971.

# Battlegrounds

### Here Dead Lie We

*A. E. Housman*

Here dead lie we because we did not choose
   To live and shame the land from which we sprung.
Life, to be sure, is nothing much to lose,
   But young men think it is, and we were young.

## Conscientious Objector

*Edna St. Vincent Millay*

I shall die, but that is all that I shall do for Death.

I hear him leading his horse out of the stall; I hear the clatter on
    the barn-floor.
He is in haste; he has business in Cuba, business in the Balkans,
    many calls to make this morning.
But I will not hold the bridle while he cinches the girth.
5 And he may mount by himself: I will not give him a leg up.

Though he flick my shoulders with his whip, I will not tell him
    which way the fox ran.
With his hoof on my breast, I will not tell him where the black
    boy hides in the swamp.
I shall die, but that is all that I shall do for Death; I am not on
    his pay-roll.

I will not tell him the whereabouts of my friends nor of my
    enemies either.
10 Though he promise me much, I will not map him the route to
    any man's door.

Am I a spy in the land of the living, that I should deliver men
    to Death?
Brother, the password and the plans of our city are safe with me;
    never through me
Shall you be overcome.

---

## DISCUSSION

*Here Dead Lie We*

1. Who speaks in the poem?
2. (a) What choice did these young men have? (b) Would young men today feel the same way? Comment.
3. What statement is made in the poem about the value of life? Do you agree?

*Conscientious Objector*

1. What human attributes is death given in this poem?

From *Collected Poems*, Harper & Row. Copyright 1934, 1962 by Edna St. Vincent Millay and Norma Millay Ellis.

2. What is death's "business"? What geographical names could be substituted for Cuba and the Balkans today?
3. Throughout the poem, what role does the conscientious objector refuse to take in relation to death?
4. Would the poem be more effective or less effective if death were not personified? Explain.
5. A conscientious objector is often defined as one who refuses to serve in the armed forces or to bear arms because these actions would be against his moral or religious principles. In this poem, are the conscientious objector's principles applied only during wartime? Only to men? What lines support your answer?

## EDNA ST. VINCENT MILLAY

Born in 1892 in Rockland, Maine, and educated at Vassar, Edna St. Vincent Millay published her first major poem, "Renascence," when she was only nineteen.

In the 1920's her life and her poetry established her as an emancipated woman who gave voice to the thoughts and feelings of rebellious youth. Until her death in 1950, she wrote many volumes of poetry and several verse plays. *The Harp-Weaver and Other Poems*, won the 1923 Pulitzer Prize for poetry.

## The Conquerors

*Phyllis McGinley*

It seems vainglorious and proud
Of Atom-man to boast aloud
   His prowess homicidal
When one remembers how for years,
5  With their rude stones and humble spears,
Our sires, at wiping out their peers,
   Were almost never idle.

Despite his under-fissioned art
The Hittite[1] made a splendid start
10   Toward smiting lesser nations;
While Tamerlane,[2] it's widely known,
Without a bomb to call his own
   Destroyed whole populations.

Nor did the ancient Persian need
15 Uranium to kill his Mede,
   The Viking earl, his foeman.

The Greeks got excellent results
With swords and engined catapults.
   A chariot served the Roman.

20 Mere cannon garnered quite a yield
On Waterloo's tempestuous field.
   At Hastings and at Flodden
Stout countrymen, with just a bow
And arrow, laid their thousands low.
25   And Gettysburg was sodden.

Though doubtless now our shrewd machines
Can blow the world to smithereens
   More tidily and so on,
Let's give our ancestors their due.
30 Their ways were coarse, their weapons few.
But ah! how wondrously they slew
   With what they had to go on.

---

## DISCUSSION

1. Who is "Atom-man" and why should he not be "vainglorious" and "proud"?

2. What other individuals or groups are praised for their "prowess homicidal"?

3. How would our present world differ if the only weapons available were bows and arrows?

4. Is the language of the poem formal, informal, or mixed? Point out words or phrases in the poem to support your answer.

5. Which of the following words describe the tone of the poem? (More than one may apply): (a) inspirational, (b) sarcastic, (c) solemn, (d) comic, (e) sincerely patriotic, (f) ironic, (g) laudatory, (h) mocking. (You may wish to review the Handbook entry on *tone* before answering this question.)

**1.** *Hittite* (hit'īt), member of an ancient people in Asia Minor and Syria.
**2.** *Tamerlane* (tam' ər lān) 1333?–1405, Mongol conqueror of most of south and west Asia.

## PHYLLIS MCGINLEY

Phyllis McGinley was born in rural Oregon in 1905. Educated at the University of Utah and the University of California, she began to publish her poetry in national publications while still in college. After a year teaching in Utah, she moved to New York, where she worked for an advertising agency and wrote at night.

Growing acceptance of her poetry enabled her to write full time, and she has published over ten volumes of verse, several children's stories, and collected light essays on suburban life. Her *Times Three: Selected Verse* won a Pulitzer Prize in 1961.

# WAR POSTERS

Painting from the early 1800's and (below)
World War I poster urging civilians to plant gardens
to aid in the war effort.

Civil War recruiting poster.

World War II flags of the Allies poster.

## The Mother

*Padraic Pearse*

I do not grudge them; Lord, I do not grudge
My two strong sons that I have seen go out
To break their strength and die, they and a few,
In bloody protest for a glorious thing.
5  They shall be spoken of among their people,
The generations shall remember them,
And call them blessed;
But I will speak their names to my own heart
In the long nights;
10  The little names that were familiar once
Round my dead hearth.
Lord, thou art hard on mothers:
We suffer in their coming and their going;
And tho' I grudge them not, I weary, weary
15  Of the long sorrow—And yet I have my joy:
My sons were faithful, and they fought.

---

## DISCUSSION

1. Describe the mother's attitude toward the conflict in which her sons have died. How does this attitude affect her feelings about their deaths?

2. Twice the mother mentions the · "speaking" of her sons' names. Who will speak them and on what occasions?

3. (a) Suppose the mother were American, Vietnamese, Israeli, or Arabian and had lost her sons re-cently. How might her feelings be similar or different? (b) Can you think of a conflict—past, present, or future—in which you might feel much like this mother about the death of a friend or relative?

## PADRAIC PEARSE

"The Mother" expresses poet and revolutionary Padraic Henry Pearse's conviction that the sacrifice of dedicated lives was nec-essary to free Ireland from British rule. A leader in the Irish Republi-can forces, Pearse wrote articles, poems, and pamphlets designed to rouse citizens to rebellion.

Born in Dublin in 1879, he studied Gaelic from the age of twelve and became editor of a weekly publication of the na-tionalistic Gaelic League. Later he helped found a bilingual prep-aratory school for boys in Dublin.

Commander-in-chief of the Irish Republican forces in the Dublin Easter Rising, Pearse pro-claimed the formation of the pro-visional government of the Irish Republic from the steps of the Dublin General Post Office, which had been seized and used as the group's headquarters. Forced to surrender, Pearse was executed by a British firing squad May 3, 1916.

"The Mother" by Padraic Pearse from *1000 Years of Irish Poetry*, edited by Kathleen Hoagland. Published by the Devin-Adair Company.

## my enemy was dreaming

*Norman Russell*

when i found my enemy sleeping
i stood over him and as still
as the owl at night
as the heron waiting fish
5  i raised my knife to kill him

then i saw my enemy was dreaming
his mouth made a little smile
his legs trembled
he made small sleep sounds
10  a happy dream was in his mind

only i will have this memory
i will show the others
only the horse of my enemy
i will not tell the others
15  i left my enemy dreaming his dream.

---

## DISCUSSION

1. Are the owl and the heron appropriate images for the speaker poised above his enemy? Explain.

2. What changes the speaker's intentions toward his enemy?

3. What lines reveal that the speaker has done something different from what is expected of him?

4. What can you infer from the poem about the speaker's age, education, culture, attitudes, and personality?

## NORMAN H. RUSSELL

Although Norman Russell is part Cherokee, he has said that was not his real motivation for writing his Indian poems. Instead, he felt that "there was much we might learn today from a re-examination of the Indian's respect for his environment."

A professional botanist and professor of biology, Russell has spent much of his life studying the natural habitats of North American wildlife and until recently he wrote and published only in scientific fields.

Russell now resides in Edmond, Oklahoma, where he teaches biology at Central State College.

"My Enemy Was Dreaming" by Norman H. Russell from *The Dekalb Literary Arts Review* (Fall/Winter, 1969). Reprinted by permission.

## Grass

*Carl Sandburg*

Pile the bodies high at Austerlitz[1] and Waterloo.
Shovel them under and let me work—
               I am the grass; I cover all.

And pile them high at Gettysburg
5  And pile them high at Ypres and Verdun.
Shovel them under and let me work.
Two years, ten years, and passengers ask the conductor:
               What place is this?
               Where are we now?

10             I am the grass.
               Let me work.

## DISCUSSION

1. Who speaks in the poem? What attitude does the speaker have toward the war dead?

2. The poem pictures nature as able to erase in time much of the evidence of man's destructiveness. Would a poem written today be as likely to include this idea?

3. At the dedication of Gettysburg National Cemetery in 1863, Abraham Lincoln said: "The world will little note nor long remember what we say here, but it can never forget what they did here." In the light of history, which has proved to be more accurate: Lincoln's beliefs or the attitudes implied in this poem about Gettysburg? Explain.

## CARL SANDBURG

Born in Galesburg, Illinois, in 1878, the son of an immigrant blacksmith, Carl Sandburg left school at thirteen to work at a variety of jobs including barbershop porter, theater scene shifter, house painter, hotel dishwasher, and harvest hand. He served in the Spanish-American War and then returned to Galesburg to attend Lombard College.

Until his mid-thirties Sandburg was unknown to the literary world, but after the publication of *Chicago Poems* in 1916 his reputation grew and many honors followed, including two Pulitzer Prizes. His works include children's books, biography, autobiography, and a folk song collection. He often toured the country with his guitar or banjo, singing folk songs and reading his poetry.

Sandburg died in 1967.

1. *Austerlitz*. Austerlitz, Waterloo, Ypres (ē′pr), and Verdun (vĕr dun′) are sites of fierce European battles. Gettysburg is the scene of a bloody Civil War battle in Pennsylvania.

### There Will Come Soft Rains
(War Time)

*Sara Teasdale*

There will come soft rains and the smell of the ground,
And swallows circling with their shimmering sound;

And frogs in the pools singing at night,
And wild plum-trees in tremulous white.

5 Robins will wear their feathery fire
Whistling their whims on a low fence-wire;

And not one will know of the war, not one
Will care at last when it is done.

Not one would mind, neither bird nor tree,
10 If mankind perished utterly;

And Spring herself, when she woke at dawn,
Would scarcely know that we were gone.

---

## DISCUSSION

1. In what ways might rain be an appropriate image to signify the end of human beings and the world being returned to nature? Would sunshine, or snow, or nightfall serve just as well? Explain.

2. According to the poem, what will the natural world be like without man?

3. What is the speaker's attitude toward human beings' place in the universe?

4. Compare and contrast the style and the ideas of this poem with Carl Sandburg's "Grass."

Reprinted with permission of the Macmillan Company from *Collected Poems* by Sara Teasdale. Copyright 1920 by The Macmillan Company, renewed 1948 by Mamie T. Wheless.

## SARA TEASDALE

Sara Teasdale was born in St. Louis in 1884. After leaving school she traveled in Europe and the Near East. In 1914, following her rejection of a marriage proposal from poet Vachel Lindsay, she married a businessman, but the marriage ended in divorce.

*Love Songs*, published in 1917, won for her a special Pulitzer award, but that success failed to bring her happiness. She spent the rest of her life in New York, writing poetry in near seclusion, often suffering from ill health. In 1933 she was found drowned in the bath of her apartment.

# Portraits

## The Courage That My Mother Had

*Edna St. Vincent Millay*

The courage that my mother had
Went with her, and is with her still:
Rock from New England quarried;
Now granite in a granite hill.

5　The golden brooch my mother wore
She left behind for me to wear;
I have no thing I treasure more:
Yet, it is something I could spare.

Oh, if instead she'd left to me
10　The thing she took into the grave!—
That courage like a rock, which she
Has no more need of, and I have.

## DISCUSSION

1. Which two of her mother's possessions does the speaker mention? What value does she place on each?

2. Why might the poet have chosen rock, and particularly "granite," as a suitable substance with which to compare the mother's courage? Would wood have done as well? Water? Why or why not?

**Miss Rosie**

*Lucille Clifton*

When I watch you
wrapped up like garbage
sitting, surrounded by the smell
of too old potato peels
5 or
when I watch you
in your old man's shoes
with the little toe cut out
sitting, waiting for your mind
10 like next week's grocery
I say
when I watch you
you wet brown bag of a woman
who used to be the best looking gal in Georgia
15 used to be called the Georgia Rose
I stand up
through your destruction
I stand up

---

**DISCUSSION**

1. (a) Why might the poet have selected garbage as an image to describe Miss Rosie at this time in her life? (b) What does it mean to wait for your mind? Why is this like waiting for "next week's grocery"?

2. (a) What points in Miss Rosie's life do the "wet brown bag of a woman" and "the Georgia Rose" represent? What can the reader infer about the years between? (b) One can stand up *to* something or someone, stand up out of honor or respect, stand up *for* something, and stand up simply to get on with something. In what sense do you think the speaker "stands up" through Miss Rosie's destruction?

**LUCILLE CLIFTON**

Resilience in the face of life's troubles is a persistent theme in the poems of Lucille Clifton's first collection *Good Times* (1969). Her poems are straightforward and pared to essential thoughts; many exhibit her vigorous, sometimes mocking humor.

Her second collection *Good News About the Earth* (1972) continues the affirmation of black life and vitality.

Lucille Clifton was born in Depew, New York, in 1936 and attended Howard University and Fredonia State Teachers College. In addition to her poetry, she has written three books for children.

She lives in Baltimore with her husband and their six children.

### Melora Vilas

*Stephen Vincent Benét*

Melora Vilas, rising by candlelight,
Looked at herself in the bottom of the tin basin
And wished that she had a mirror.
                                 Now Spring was here,
She could kneel above the well of a forest pool
5 And see the shadow hidden under the water,
The intent brown eyes, the small face cut like a heart.
She looked at the eyes and the eyes looked back at her,
But just when it seemed they could start to talk to each other—
"What are you like? Who are you?"—
                               a ripple flawed
10 The deep glass and the shadow trembled away.

If she only had a mirror, maybe she'd know
Something, she didn't know what, but something important,
Something like knowing your skin and you were alive
On a good day, something as drenched as sleep,
15 As wise as sleep, as piercing as the bee's dagger.
But she'd never know it unless she could get a mirror
And they'd never get a mirror while they were hiders.
They were bound to be hiders as long as the war kept on.
Pop was that way. She remembered roads and places.
20 She was seventeen. She had seen a lot of places,
A lot of roads. Pop was always moving along.
Everybody she'd ever known was moving along.
—Dusty wagons full of chickens and children,
Full of tools and quilts, Rising Sun and Roses of Sharon,[1]
25 Mahogany dressers out of Grandmother's house,
Tin plates, cracked china, a couple of silver spoons,
Moving from State to State behind tired, scuffed horses
Because the land was always better elsewhere.

Next time they'd quit. Next stop they'd settle right down.
30 Next year they'd have time to rub up the mahogany dresser.
Next place, Mom could raise the flowers she wanted to raise.
But it never began. They were always moving along.

She liked Kansas best. She wished they'd go back to Kansas.
She liked the smell of the wind there.
35 But Pop hadn't wanted to join with the Free-Soilers[2]
And then the slavery men had shot up the town
And killed the best horse they had. That had settled Pop.

---

1. *Rising Sun and Roses of Sharon,* traditional quilt designs.
2. *Free-Soilers,* members of the Free-Soil party, a U.S. political
party that was opposed to extending slavery into territories not yet
admitted as states. It existed from 1848 to 1856.

He said something about a plague on both of your houses
And moved along. So now they were hiders here
40 And whenever you wanted to ask Pop about the war
All he said was that same old thing about the plague.
She mustn't call him Pop—that was movers'-talk.
She must call him Father, the way Mom, Mother wanted.
But it was hard to remember. Mom talked a lot
45 About old times back in the East and Grandmother's house.
She couldn't remember an East. The East wasn't real.
There was only the dusty road and moving along.
Although she knew that Mom had worn a silk dress
And gone to a ball, once. There was a picture of Pop
50 And Mom, looking Eastern, in queer old Eastern clothes.
They weren't white trash. She knew how to read and figure.
She'd read *Macbeth* and *Beulah* and *Oliver Twist*.
She liked *Beulah* best but *Macbeth* would have suited Pop.
Sometimes she wondered what had happened to them,
55 When Mother used to live in Grandmother's house
And wear silk dresses, and Father used to read Latin—
When had they started to go just moving along,
And how would it feel to live in Grandmother's house?

But it was so long ago, so hard to work out
60 And she liked it this way—she even liked being hiders.
It was exciting, especially when the guns
Coughed in the sky as they had all yesterday,
When Bent hid out in the woods to keep from recruiters,
And you knew there were armies stumbling all around you,
65 Big, blundering cows of armies, snuffling and tramping
The whole scuffed world with their muddy, lumbering hoofs,
Except the little lost brushpile where you were safe.
There were guns in the sky again today. Big armies.
An army must be fine to look at.
                                        But Pop
70 Would never let her do it or understand.

An army or a mirror. She didn't know
Which she'd rather find, but whenever she thought of it
The mirror generally won. You could keep a mirror yourself.

---

## DISCUSSION

1. (a) Why does Melora Vilas want a mirror? What does she

"Melora Vilas" from *John Brown's Body* by Stephen Vincent Benét (Holt, Rinehart and Winston, Inc.). Copyright 1927, 1928 by Stephen Vincent Benét. Copyright renewed 1955, 1956 by Rosemary Carr Benét. Reprinted by permission of Brandt & Brandt, New York.

expect it to tell her? (b) What do her subsitute mirrors reveal about her life?

2. (a) What made Melora's family "hiders"? Would they have settled down if they had not needed to hide? Explain. (b) What do the details in lines 23–27 reveal about such families?

3. Line 38 contains a well-

known quotation from Shakespeare. To whom does Pop refer in the words "both your houses"?

4. What is the background of the Vilas family? Why is the past important to Melora?

5. What is your impression of Melora Vilas? Is she mature or immature? Educated or uneducated? Content or restless?

### The Bean Eaters

*Gwendolyn Brooks*

They eat beans mostly, this old yellow pair.
Dinner is a casual affair.
Plain chipware on a plain and creaking wood,
Tin flatware.

5 Two who are Mostly Good.
Two who have lived their day,
But keep on putting on their clothes
And putting things away.

And remembering . . .
10 Remembering, with twinklings and twinges,
As they lean over the beans in their rented back room that
is full of beads and receipts and dolls and cloths,
tobacco crumbs, vases and fringes.

## DISCUSSION

1. What do the following details add—through what they picture and what the words suggest—to this portrait of two lives: (a) "they eat beans mostly"; (b) creaking wood, tin flatware; (c) rented back room; (d) receipts; (e) dolls; (f) tobacco crumbs?

2. (a) How might the reader's feelings toward these two have been affected if line 5 had described them as "Always Good"? (b) What kinds of memories does the phrase "twinklings and twinges" suggest?

3. In a painting to illustrate "The Bean Eaters" what would you suggest about the colors to be used, facial expressions, and details to be included in the setting?

## GWENDOLYN BROOKS

Though born in Topeka, Kansas, in 1917, Gwendolyn Brooks grew up in Chicago. At the age of thirteen, one of her poems was accepted by *American Childhood* magazine and her career began. At seventeen, her poems were appearing in a newspaper, the *Chicago Defender*.

From 1943–1945 she won four first prizes in the poetry division of the Midwestern Writers Conference and in 1945 published her first collection of poems, *A Street in Bronzeville*. In addition to a novel, *Maud Martha*, she has written several volumes of poetry, one of which, *Annie Allen*, earned a 1950 Pulitzer Prize.

Other honors include Guggenheim Fellowships, honorary doctorates, and an award from the American Institute of Arts and Letters. She annually awards two literary prizes to young black writers. In 1968 Gwendolyn Brooks became Poet Laureate of Illinois.

## Portrait of a Certain Gentleman

*Sara Henderson Hay*

This man's uncertain; he's afraid
To make a choice which, being made,
He must abide by, bad or good.
So he'd avoid it, if he could.

5 He'd like to hide away, to run
Out of reality's broad sun
Into a cave, a hole, a crack
In earth's kind substance; he'd go back

To what he fancies was secure,
10 The state of childhood, which was sure,
Since he was told what he should do.
That world's grown up, the man has, too.

Poor child, poor man, there's no escape
From what is termed your adult shape,
15 This form which you attain at last
Through such betrayals in the past.

Nor God nor man will tell you, now,
What you must do, or when, or how.
There's no retreat that may be won to,
20 No one except your self to run to.

---

## DISCUSSION

1. What is the man afraid of? Why?

2. What would he like to go back to? Why?

3. Why is the man addressed as both "Poor child" and "poor man"?

4. What does the speaker say goes with the man's "adult shape"?

5. To pun is to use a word humorously or ironically where it can have more than one meaning. Explain the pun in the title of the poem.

From *A Footing on This Earth*, by Sara Henderson Hay. Copyright 1942 by the New York Times Company. Reprinted by permission of Doubleday and Company, Inc.

## SARA HENDERSON HAY

The daily event, the small illumination within the context of the familiar, often provide subjects for Sara Henderson Hay's poetry.

In one volume, *Story Hour*, she reconsiders fairy tales and legends as if their events and characters were real. In a poem about "Jack in the Beanstalk," for example, she asks why no one questions Jack's means of success—"Guile, trespass, robbery, and homicide."

Born in 1906 in Pittsburgh, Sara Henderson Hay attended Brenau College and Columbia University. In 1951 she married a composer and professor of music at Carnegie Institute of Technology.

# Blues

## Trouble in Mind

*Richard M. Jones*

Trouble in mind, I'm blue,
But I won't be blue always,
'Cause the sun's gonna shine
In my back door some day.

5 I'm all alone at midnight
And my lamp is burnin' low,
Never had so much trouble
In my life before.

I'm gonna lay my head
10 On that lonesome railroad line,
Let the Two Nineteen
Pacify my mind.

You've been a hard-hearted mama
And you sure treat me unkind.
15 I'll be a hard-hearted daddy,
I swear I'll make you lose your mind.

Trouble in mind, I'm blue,
But I won't be blue always,
'Cause the sun's gonna shine
20 In my back door some day.

---

## DISCUSSION

1. Some of the most common themes of traditional blues lyrics are confusion or disappointment in love, the discomfort and loneliness of traveling and separation, the troubles and worries of working and surviving in a hostile world. (a) Which of these themes are touched on in "Trouble in Mind"? (Refer to specific lines in the song.) (b) What lyrics can you recall from modern songs that deal with these themes?

2. "Got the blues, but I'm just too mean to cry," declares a line from one old blues song. Many blues lyrics express that kind of ironic humor. (a) Is there any humor in "Trouble in Mind"? Explain. (b) Is any optimism expressed? Explain.

## RICHARD M. JONES

Richard M. Jones came from a musical family. He was born in Donaldsville, Louisiana, in 1889. By the age of thirteen he was play-ing alto horn in a brass band and by the age of twenty he was working on Basin Street in New Orleans primarily as a solo pianist. He worked in several bands, his own and others, with many famous New Orleans musicians, including King Oliver.

After moving to Chicago, Jones joined the staff of the Clarence Williams Publishing Company. Later he was a recording director for Okeh Records and Decca. He was active in Chicago as a composer, arranger, and conductor until his death in 1945. His compositions include "Riverside Blues," "Remember Me?", and "Ball o' Fire."

## I Used to Be Fairly Poor

*Han-shan*
*Translated from the Chinese by Burton Watson*

I used to be fairly poor, as poor goes;
Today I hit the bottom of poverty and cold.
Nothing I do seems to come out right;
Wherever I go I get pushed around.
I walk the muddy road and my footsteps falter;
I sit with the other villagers and my stomach
      aches with hunger.
Since I lost the brindle cat,
The rats come right up and peer into the pot.

---

### DISCUSSION

1. What similarities do you find between this poem and the blues song on the facing page (a) in content and theme (b) in tone?

2. The first six lines of the poem are general complaints about hunger and cold and mistreatment. The last two lines are more specific. What is the effect of the image in those last two lines?

"I Used to Be Fairly Poor," from *Cold Mountain: 100 Poems by the T'ang Poet Han-shan,* translated by Burton Watson. Copyright © 1962 by Burton Watson. Copyright © 1970 by Columbia University Press. Reprinted by permission of Columbia University Press and Jonathan Cape Ltd.

### HAN-SHAN

Because information about the life of Han-shan is so incomplete, we cannot even be certain when he lived. A date somewhere around the late eighth and early ninth centuries is most widely accepted.

It is generally believed that Han-shan was a gentleman farmer or a minor government official, troubled by poverty and/or family discord, who left his home and retired to a place called Cold Mountain in the T'ien-t'ai Mountains, a range along the seacoast in the northeastern corner of Chekiang Province in China.

On Cold Mountain Han-shan sought spiritual enlightenment through Zen Buddhism, but he remained poor, and many of his poems are laments about the hardships of life. Others are joyful descriptions of the wild scenery of Cold Mountain. The language of Han-shan's poems is simple, even slangy, although translators wrestling with the difficulties of rendering thousand-year-old colloquial Chinese into twentieth-century English have sometimes found that simplicity difficult to recreate.

## The Housewife's Lament

*Anonymous*

1  One day I was walking, I heard a complaining,
   And saw an old woman the picture of gloom.
   She gazed at the mud on her doorstep ('twas
         raining)
   And this was her song as she wielded her broom.

*Chorus:*
   Oh, life is a toil and love is a trouble,
   Beauty will fade and riches will flee,
   Pleasures they dwindle and prices they double,
   And nothing is as I would wish it to be.

2  There's too much of worriment goes to a bonnet,
   There's too much of ironing goes to a shirt,
   There's nothing that pays for the time you waste
         on it,
   There's nothing that lasts us but trouble and dirt.

3  In March it is mud, it is slush in December,
   The midsummer breezes are loaded with dust,

In fall the leaves litter, in muddy September
The wallpaper rots and the candlesticks rust.

4  There are worms on the cherries and slugs on the
         roses,
   And ants in the sugar and mice in the pies,
   The rubbish of spiders no mortal supposes
   And ravaging roaches and damaging flies.

5  With grease and with grime from corner to center,
   Forever at war and forever alert,
   No rest for a day lest the enemy enter,
   I spend my whole life in a struggle with dirt.

6  Last night in my dreams I was stationed forever
   On a far little rock in the midst of the sea,
   My one chance of life was a ceaseless endeavor
   To sweep off the waves as they swept over me.

7  Alas! 'Twas no dream; ahead I behold it,
   I see I am helpless my fate to avert. —
   She lay down her broom, her apron she folded,
   She lay down and died and was buried in dirt.

---

## DISCUSSION

1. Describe the housewife's attitude toward life.

Reprinted from *Sing Out!* Used with permission.

2. What are her opponents in life? What are her weapons?
3. What is ironic about the housewife's fate?
4. What details might be included in "The Student's Lament"? "The Father-of-a-Teenager's Lament"?

5. Suppose that you were assigned to write a lament using the same rhythm as is used here. By emphasizing the stressed syllables as you read the verses aloud, determine the rhythm you would use. (Review the Handbook entry on *rhythm*.)

## The Whipping

*Robert Hayden*

The old woman across the way
  is whipping the boy again
and shouting to the neighborhood
  her goodness and his wrongs.

5 Wildly he crashes through elephant ears,[1]
  pleads in dusty zinnias,
while she in spite of crippling fat
  pursues and corners him.

She strikes and strikes the shrilly circling
10   boy till the stick breaks
in her hand. His tears are rainy weather
  to woundlike memories:

My head gripped in bony vise
  of knees, the writhing struggle
15 to wrench free, the blows, the fear
  worse than blows that hateful

Words could bring, the face that I
  no longer knew or loved . . .
Well, it is over now, it is over,
20   and the boy sobs in his room,

And the woman leans muttering against
  a tree, exhausted, purged—
avenged in part for lifelong hidings
  she has had to bear.

---

## DISCUSSION

1. What scene does the speaker in the poem observe that stirs up personal memories?

2. (a) What sentence introduces the speaker's recollections? What does he remember? (b) Was it physical pain that made the speaker's memories "woundlike"? Explain.

3. (a) Why do you think the speaker gives no clue as to what the boy has done wrong? (b) For what, at least in part, does the speaker suggest the boy is being whipped? (c) Of what is the woman purged?

4. State the theme of this poem in your own words. (Review the Handbook entry on *theme*.)

5. From what the poem reveals about the speaker, can you infer the kind of parent he would be? Explain.

## ROBERT HAYDEN

Born in 1913 in Detroit, Robert

Hayden attended Wayne State University and the University of Michigan. He has taught English at Fisk University in Tennessee, the University of Louisville, the University of Washington, and the University of Michigan.

Hayden, who has been publishing poetry since 1940, was awarded the Grand Prize for English language poetry at the World Festival of Negro Arts at Dakar, Senegal in 1966. Other honors include the Hopwood Award in 1938 and 1942, a Rosenwald Fellowship, and a Ford Foundation Fellowship.

"The Whipping" by Robert Hayden from *Selected Poems*. Copyright © 1966 by Robert Hayden. Reprinted by permission of October House, Inc.

1. *elephant ears*, plant which produces large, heart-shaped leaves.

## Yonder See the Morning Blink

*A. E. Housman*

Yonder see the morning blink:
  The sun is up, and up must I,
To wash and dress and eat and drink
And look at things and talk and think
5    And work, and God knows why.

Oh often have I washed and dressed
  And what's to show for all my pain?
Let me lie abed and rest:
Ten thousand times I've done my best
10   And all's to do again.

## DISCUSSION

1. (a) What aspect of life troubles the speaker most? (b) What similar attitudes do you find in this poem and "The Housewife's Lament"?

2. The speaker expresses great weariness with his world. If he were a friend of yours, what would you recommend that he do to restore a zest for life?

## A. E. HOUSMAN

The oldest of a family of seven, Alfred Edward Housman was born in Worcestershire, England.

He began to write poetry while he was a student in classical studies at Oxford, where he failed his final exams. For ten years he was a clerk in the British Patent Office. Later, his published studies of Latin poets led to a teaching position. He became Latin Professor at University College in London and then at Cambridge University.

When his first successful volume of poems, *A Shropshire Lad*, was published, it received critical praise but sold slowly until World War I re-emphasized the relevance of its themes. *Last Poems* appeared in 1922 and *More Poems* and *Collected Poems* were published after his death in 1936.

Housman has said of poetry that he could "no more define it than a terrier [could] . . . a rat," but that both could recognize "the object by the symptoms" it provoked in them.

## Insomniac

*Patricia Y. Ikeda*

Sometimes when the moon
Looks like a slice of orange impaled on a tree fork
And the air is heavy with heat,
I die over and over in my bed
5  And think of that time when I will not rise,
Or whisper names into the shrill din
Of cricket voices that invades my room,
Or write poetry that must be destroyed
Because it is infected with night madness.

10  When summer is ripe and rank
With wet grass odors and berry smells,
I lie awake in the hot darkness,
The shadows sliding over my bedspread
Making dark patterns, like blood.
15  I raise my hands to my eyes.

When it is too hot to sleep
And my sheets will not lie unwrinkled
Under my restless body,
I sing muffled songs under the covers,
20  Or turn on my bed light and read
Until it is morning and my eyes burn,
Or walk in the still dark house
With the puzzled dog one clicking step behind.
We share our insomnia like a secret pact
25  And do not tell the others at breakfast.

### DISCUSSION

1. (a) What is the atmosphere of this poem? (b) What details contribute to this atmosphere?
2. What can you infer from these details about the age, sex, environment, and personality of the speaker?
3. What gives the dog a "clicking step"?
4. Why do you think the speaker does not wish to "tell the others at breakfast"?

### PATRICIA Y. IKEDA

When Patricia Ikeda wrote this poem she was a student at Green High School in Greensburg, Ohio, where her major interests were writing poetry and playing piano and clarinet.

Her poems have appeared in school literary magazines, in *typog*, a national magazine of high-school arts, and in *Literary Cavalcade*.

In 1971 Scholastic Magazines awarded her a college scholarship which they give annually to a high-school senior who shows a combination of outstanding creative ability and high academic standing.

"Insomniac" by Patricia Y. Ikeda. From *typog*, Fall, 1971. Copyright © 1971 by Scott, Foresman and Company.

## Birthday in the House of the Poor

*Jeannette Nichols*

This is the house
of the poor.
                    Today
I am come to 90 years
5  like a doorstep.
                    There is
no hope on the hall table.
                    The State
is my father, my mother
10  is the cook here
And never gives me enough.
                    When are you
coming, I mean I couldn't bear
to see you even then
15                              but when?
This is my home in this house
of the poor, and this

is my window.
                    I own all outside it
20  as far as the peach tree which
no longer bears. We are
sisters.
                    When you don't come
I will write again, when you don't write
25  I will say the $2 you didn't send
got lost.
                    How is your rich house
and how are your young hopes?
                                        Please write,
30  send money, and come
                              though I don't
want you to see me here, though
this poor house could never be home
even if I had money
35                              or even if you'd come.

---

## DISCUSSION

1. (a) Why would the speaker have these thoughts especially on her birthday? (b) What is the "Birthday in the House of the Poor" by Jeannette Nichols from *Atlantic Monthly* (March 1967). Copyright © 1967, by The Atlantic Monthly Company, Boston, Massachusetts. Reprinted with permission. "hope" that might have been on the hall table?

2. The woman sees many things in terms of "family." Explain her comments about the State, the cook, and the peach tree.

3. What are the woman's feelings toward her real family? Quote from the poem to support your answer.

4. The speaker says, "This is my home in this house of the poor," but later that "this poor house could never be home." How can both statements be true?

5. What clues about the state of the speaker's mind do the spacing of lines and the punctuation, or lack of it, suggest? Explain.

# Destinations

### Lessons

*Gerald Jonas*

"No one is ever ready!"
My father barks the time,
and the clocks race on
as I re-tie my laces
5 for the third time
and my brother hunts
for his belt in a drawerful
of underwear and frayed shirts
and my mother is undoing
10 the catch of a dress
too formal or not formal
enough for such an occasion,
and my father is still waiting
and letting us know it
15 as the laces snap
in my hands where
I knotted a new break
only yesterday, and my brother's
drawer gets stuck half-open
20 with his best belt
just out of reach,
and my mother's perfume-bomb
won't spray, and all of a sudden

it's *so late*
25  we have to rush
out of the house
without finishing any-
thing, and somehow or other
my brother has got hold of a belt
30  (if not his best) and
my laces will hold (just barely)
for a few more hours, and my mother
looks great in the mirror
and smells like herself up close,
35  and my father jams the key
in the ignition and *we're off*
for some life-or-death destination

No one is ever ready
is what I learned
40  on those breathless childhood nights,
before I learned that ends
and means may coincide, in time,
and destinations lose their meaning.
I am still waiting; I have arrived;
45  I will never be ready.

## DISCUSSION

1. Who says "no one is ever ready"?

2. Why do the family members become anxious as the "clocks race on"?

3. Which of the following events for which one "gets ready" would you consider life or death "destinations"? Why? (a) meeting someone you will love, (b) having a job interview, (c) having a baby, (d) attending a funeral, (e) going to the movies, (f) buying a house, (g) going to jail, (h) getting a college degree, (i) having an appendectomy, (j) becoming a conscientious objector.

4. (a) Have you ever been disappointed by happenings you had greatly anticipated? How does that experience help explain the phrases "I have arrived" and "destinations lose their meaning"?

(b) What is the speaker "still waiting" for?

5. When the speaker says in the last line, "I will never be ready," what do you think he means? (a) My shoelaces still break at the wrong times; (b) I dread the future; (c) I am never wholly prepared for the important things in life; (d) I will always be getting ready for another happening. Explain your choice or choices.

### The Most Perilous Moment in Life

*César Vallejo (Translated by Clayton Eshleman)*

A man said:

—The most perilous moment in my life was in the battle of
the Marne when I was struck in the chest.

Another man said:

5    —The most perilous moment in my life occurred during
a Yokohama seaquake, from which I was miraculously saved,
sheltered under the eaves of a lacquer shop.

And another man said:

—The most perilous moment in my life happens when I
10 sleep during the day.

And another said:

—The most perilous moment in my life has been in my
greatest loneliness.

And another said:

15    —The most perilous moment in my life was my imprisonment
in a Peruvian jail.

And another said:

—The most perilous moment in my life is the having surprised
my father in profile.

20    And the last man said:

—The most perilous moment in my life is yet to come.

---

## DISCUSSION

1. Which of the "perilous moments" involve physical danger?
2. What situations, feelings, and
after-effects might make sleeping
during the day seem perilous?

3. What is perilous about loneliness?

4. One student commented
after reading lines 18–19 that
usually when she was with her
father, he faced her and spoke to
her in his role as father. What in-
sights might "surprising" him in
profile offer?

5. What thoughts might be behind the last man's statement?

6. The Spanish word *grave* is
translated here as "perilous." It
might have been translated as
"difficult," "serious," "trouble-
some," or "momentous." Why do
you think the translator chose
"perilous"?

7. What would you describe as
your most perilous moment?

"El Momento más Grave de la Vida" (The
Most Perilous Moment in Life) by César
Vallejo, translated by Clayton Eshleman.
Copyright © 1968 by Grove Press, Inc.
Reprinted by permission of Grove Press,
Inc., and Jonathan Cape Ltd.

### El Momento más Grave de la Vida

*César Vallejo*

Un hombre dijo:

—El momento más grave de mi vida estuvo en la batalla del Marne, cuando fuí herido en el pecho.

Otro hombre dijo:

5    —El momento más grave de mi vida, ocurrió en un maremoto de Yokohama, del cual salvé milagrosamente, refugiado bajo el alero de una tienda de lacas.

Y otro hombre dijo:

—El momento más grave de mi vida acontece cuando
10 duermo de día.

Y otro dijo:

—El momento más grave de mi vida ha estado en mi mayor soledad.

Y otro dijo:

15    —El momento más grave de mi vida fue mi prisión en una cárcel del Perú.

Y otro dijo:

—El momento más grave de mi vida es el haber sorprendido de perfil a mi padre.

20    Y el último hombre dijo:

El momento más grave de mi vida no ha llegado todavía.

---

## CÉSAR VALLEJO

César Vallejo (sā'sär bä yā'hō) had a difficult, short career. He was only forty-six when he died in Paris in 1938. Illness and poverty haunted much of his life which began in 1892 in an isolated village in Peru. He was the youngest of eleven children.

His first volume of poetry was published in 1918 after several years spent studying, tutoring, and teaching school. He lived and worked as a journalist in Paris for many years.

The poetry collection *Poemas Humanos* is perhaps his best-known work.

**How Everything Happens (Based on a Study of the Wave)**

*May Swenson*

                                                              happen.
                                                          to
                                                      up
                                              stacking
                                          is
                                something
When nothing is happening

When it happens
                          something
                                  pulls
                                      back
                                          not
                                              to
                                                  happen.

When                                          has happened.
    `    pulling back          stacking up
                        happens

          has happened                                  stacks up.
When it              something              nothing
                            pulls back while

Then nothing is happening.

                                              happens.
                                          and
                              forward
                      pushes
                  up
              stacks
          something
Then

---

## Item

*Howard Nemerov*

I heard this morning on the news
They plan to colonize the moon
With senior citizens (or olds)

The less the pull of gravity
(the scientific theory goes)
The less the strain upon the heart

One adds: the less the atmosphere
(We know the moon has none at all)
The less the strain upon the nose

---

## DISCUSSION

### How Everything Happens

1. Describe how waves "stack up" and "pull back" on a beach.
2. Why are the words arranged on the page as they are? Is the arrangement effective? Explain.
3. Is this really how "everything" happens? Explain.

"Item" by Howard Nemerov first appeared in *Poetry*, © 1970 by the Modern Poetry Association, and is reprinted by permission of the Editor of *Poetry*, and Margot Johnson Agency.

### *Item*

1. Stanzas two and three seem to express concern for senior citizens. Is less strain upon the nose the most notable effect of a lack of atmosphere? Comment.
2. How would you headline this "item" if you as an editor wanted readers to feel that this would be a positive solution to the problem of where to locate the "olds"? If you felt it were a scheme against them?
3. Would you say that the narrator's attitude toward scientific solutions to human problems is (a) optimistic, (b) skeptical, (c) trusting, or (d) pessimistic? Explain.

### MAY SWENSON

May Swenson was born in Logan, Utah, in 1919. Educated at Utah State University, she was a reporter for the Salt Lake *Deseret News* and later became an editor for the New Directions publishing house.

Among the honors she has received are a Guggenheim Fellowship in 1959 and a National Institute of Arts and Letters Award in 1960. She was Poet in Residence at Purdue University in 1966–67 and has taught poetry seminars elsewhere. She lives in New York City.

# Ka'Ba[1]

*LeRoi Jones (Imamu Amiri Baraka)*

A closed window looks down
on a dirty courtyard, and black people
call across or scream across or walk across
defying physics in the stream of their will

5 Our world is full of sound
Our world is more lovely than anyone's
tho we suffer, and kill each other
and sometimes fail to walk the air

We are beautiful people
10 with african imaginations
full of masks and dances and swelling chants
with african eyes, and noses, and arms,

though we sprawl in grey chains in a place
full of winters, when what we want is sun.

15 We have been captured,
brothers. And we labor
to make our getaway, into
the ancient image, into a new

correspondence with ourselves
20 and our black family. We need magic
now we need the spells, to raise up
return, destroy, and create. What will be

the sacred words?

---

## DISCUSSION

1. Defying physics (line 4) and walking the air (line 8) both involve defying reality. (a) Does the speaker expect black people to defy reality? Explain. (b) What images in the poem suggest the nature of their present reality?

2. (a) What can you infer about the "ancient image" into which the speaker would have black people make a "getaway"? (b) The speaker implies that, in the past, his people matched this "ancient image." What caused them to change? (c) How is the phrase "raise up/return, destroy, and create" related to the idea of this renewed image for black people?

3. Relate the title to the need expressed in lines 16–23.

From *Black Magic, Collected Poetry 1961–1967,* copyright © 1969, by LeRoi Jones, reprinted by permission of the publisher, The Bobbs-Merrill Company, Inc. and The Sterling Lord Agency.
**1.** *Ka'Ba* (kä′ba), small, cubical building in the courtyard of the Great Mosque at Mecca which contains a sacred stone, the objective of Muslim pilgrimages.

## LEROI JONES (IMAMU AMIRI BARAKA)

LeRoi Jones' prolific writing career began early. As a child in Newark, New Jersey, where he was born in 1934, he created his own comic strips and science-fiction stories. Graduating from high school two years earlier than other students his age, he was offered several college scholarships.

At Howard University he first considered majoring in religion, switched to premedical studies, and finally majored in English with a minor in philosophy.

Following two years in the Air Force as a weatherman and gunner, he lived in Greenwich Village, where he helped found the American Theater for Poets and edited several literary magazines, including *Floating Bear, Kulchur,* and *Yugen.* A noted jazz critic, he is the author of *Blues People: Negro Music in America.*

Increasingly involved in black political and cultural movements, he moved to Harlem, where he founded the Black Arts Repertory Theater, and then to Newark, where he established a black cultural workshop called Spirit House. In recent years he has become a Muslim of the Kawaida faith and is now known as Imamu Amiri Baraka. (*Imamu* is Swahili for "spiritual leader.") At Spirit House Baraka founded the Black Community Development and Defense Organization, a group of Muslims who wear traditional African dress and speak Swahili in addition to English.

Arrested and convicted in 1968 on a charge of carrying a concealed weapon, Baraka was later acquitted in a new trial. In 1972 he was one of three co-chairmen of the first National Black Political Convention, held in Gary, Indiana.

His work includes poetry, plays, essays, short stories, and a semiautobiographical novel, *The System of Dante's Hell* (1966). He received an Obie award for the off-Broadway production of *Dutchman,* and a World Festival of Negro Arts prize at Dakar, Senegal in 1966.

# Phantoms

### Haunted

*Amy Lowell*

See! He trails his toes
Through the long streaks of moonlight,
And the nails of his fingers glitter:
They claw and flash among the tree-tops.
5 His lips suck at my open window,
And his breath creeps about my body
And lies in pools under my knees.
I can see his mouth sway and wobble,
Sticking itself against the window-jambs,
10 But the moonlight is bright on the floor,
Without a shadow.
Hark! A hare is strangling in the forest,
And the wind tears a shutter from the wall.

''Haunted'' from *The Complete Poetical Works of Amy Lowell* published by Houghton Mifflin Company.

## The Witch

*Sara Henderson Hay*

It pleases me to give a man three wishes,
Then trick him into wasting every one.
To set the simpering goosegirl on the throne
While the true princess weeps among the ashes.
5 I like to come unbidden to the christening,
Cackling a curse on the young princeling's head,
To slip a toad into the maiden's bed,
To conjure up the briers, the glass slope glistening.

And I am near, oh nearer than you've known.
10 You cannot shut me in a fairy book.
It was my step you heard, mine and my creatures',
Soft at your heel. And if you lean and look
Long in your mirror, you will see my features
Inextricably mingled with your own.

---

## DISCUSSION

### Haunted

1. How do you know that the "he" in the poem is not a real person?
2. The poet mixes natural and supernatural characteristics in describing the "he" in the poem. For example, "he" has toes (natural), but he trails them through streaks of moonlight (supernatural). What other characteristics seem to be natural?

Supernatural? What is the effect of mixing the two?

3. Which of the following are possible interpretations for what the speaker in the poem is experiencing? (a) a nightmare, (b) a ghost, (c) a stormy night, (d) fearful imaginings, (e) a burglar. Comment.

### The Witch

1. Who speaks in the poem?
2. (a) To what is the speaker referring in the first eight lines? (b) What line in the poem makes this clear?
3. According to the poem, how near is the witch? Where can she be seen?

### AMY LOWELL

Amy Lowell was born in 1874 in Brookline, Massachusetts, into a wealthy, distinguished family. She was educated privately, and although she spent her life in the family home in Brookline, she traveled extensively abroad.

When she was twenty-eight she decided to become a poet, but because she was determined to learn her craft thoroughly, her first volume was not published until 1912. She published eleven volumes of verse thereafter and, just before her death in 1925, a biography of John Keats. She was posthumously awarded a Pulitzer Prize in 1926 for *What's O'Clock*.

# The Skater of Ghost Lake

*William Rose Benét*

Ghost Lake's a dark lake, a deep lake and cold:
Ice black as ebony, frostily scrolled;
Far in its shadows a faint sound whirrs;
Steep stand the sentineled deep, dark firs.

5 A brisk sound, a swift sound, a ring-tinkle-ring;
Flit-flit—a shadow, with a stoop and a swing,
Flies from a shadow through the crackling cold.
Ghost Lake's a deep lake, a dark lake and old!

Leaning and leaning, with a stride and a stride,
10 Hands locked behind him, scarf blowing wide,
Jeremy Randall skates, skates late,
Star for a candle, moon for a mate.

Black is the clear glass now that he glides,
Crisp is the whisper of long lean strides,
15 Swift is his swaying—but pricked ears hark.
None comes to Ghost Lake late after dark!

Cecily only—yes, it is she!
Stealing to Ghost Lake, tree after tree,
Kneeling in snow by the still lake side,
20 Rising with feet winged, gleaming, to glide.

Dust of the ice swirls. Here is his hand.
Brilliant his eyes burn. Now, as was planned,
Arm across arm twined, laced to his side,
Out on the dark lake lightly they glide.

25 Dance of the dim moon, a rhythmical reel,
A swaying, a swift tune—skurr of the steel;
Moon for a candle, maid for a mate,
Jeremy Randall skates, skates late.

Black as if lacquered the wide lake lies;
30 Breath is a frost-fume, eyes seek eyes;
Souls are a sword-edge tasting the cold.
Ghost Lake's a deep lake, a dark lake and old!

Far in the shadows hear faintly begin
Like a string pluck-plucked of a violin,
35 Muffled in mist on the lake's far bound,
Swifter and swifter, a low singing sound!

Far in the shadows and faint on the verge
Of blue cloudy moonlight, see it emerge,
Flit-flit—a phantom, with a stoop and a swing . . .
40 Ah, it's a night bird, burdened of wing!

Pressed close to Jeremy, laced to his side,
Cecily Culver, dizzy you glide.
Jeremy Randall sweepingly veers
Out on the dark ice far from the piers.

45 "Jeremy!" "Sweetheart?" "What do you fear?"
"Nothing, my darling—nothing is here!"
"Jeremy?" "Sweetheart?" "What do you flee?"
"Something—I know not; something I see!"

Swayed to a swift stride, brisker of pace,
50 Leaning and leaning, they race and they race;
Ever that whirring, that crisp sound thin
Like a string pluck-plucked of a violin;

Ever that swifter and low singing sound
Sweeping behind them, winding them round;
55 Gasp of their breath now that chill flakes fret:
Ice black as ebony—blacker—like jet!

Ice shooting fangs forth—sudden like spears;
Crackling of lightning—a roar in their ears!
Shadowy, a phantom swerves off from its prey . . .
60 No, it's a night bird flit-flits away!

Low-winging moth-owl, home to your sleep!
Ghost Lake's a still lake, a cold lake and deep.
Faint in its shadows a far sound whirrs.
Black stand the ranks of its sentinel firs.

## DISCUSSION

1. Point out some of the images Benét uses to give Ghost Lake its mood of mysterious danger.

2. Several interpretations of this poem are possible. What do you think actually happens at Ghost Lake on the night the poet describes? What evidence in the poem leads you to this belief?

3. Do you think Jeremy Randall and Cecily Culver are real people or supernatural beings? Cite passages from the poem that support your opinion.

4. Would the poem be difficult or relatively easy to present as a short·film? Would you recommend color or black and white, sound or silent film? Who would be your actor and actress? Explain your choices with specific references to the poem.

## Reading Poetry Aloud

Poetry is intended for the ear as well as for the eye. Ideally, you should read every poem aloud; even when you don't actually say the words, you should "hear" them inside your head. By punctuation, line breaks, spacing, phrasing, word choice, rhythms, and so on, the poet has suggested to some extent the way the poem should sound. But ultimately the poet must hope for a reader who pays attention to his signals and reads the poem so that its sound reinforces its meaning.

In "Birthday in the House of the Poor" (page 247) notice how often the sounds *ow* and *oh* are echoed. The speaker in the poem is a lonely old woman, hurt by separation from her family. *Ow* and *oh* in this poem are lonely sounds—they are, in fact, the sounds we sometimes utter when we experience pain. Those sounds in the poem reinforce the sense of the words and establish a mood.

In "Lessons" (page 249) notice that there are no periods in the first stanza. In fact, that entire stanza is a single non-stop sentence. If you trust the poet's signals, that first stanza asks to be read at breathless speed, with hasty pauses to gulp a little air before each *and*. That's how the words sound. What are the words about? They are about a family hurrying to get ready because they are late. The poet has arranged words about hurrying so that you hurry as you read them.

The relationship between sound and sense is not as apparent in all poems as it is in "Lessons," but if the poem is a good one, and if you have understood the sense of it, some ways of reading it will sound better than others. When you encounter a new poem, try reading it aloud several times, varying your speed, emphases, and pauses each time. Experiment until the sounds of the words as you hear them express the sense of the words as you understand them.

Try reading "The Skater of Ghost Lake" aloud. Let the rhythm carry you along, but don't let it push you into a sing-song reading. Pay attention to the punctuation and to repeated sounds. Try to picture the scene described and feel the mood created. Then suggest the poem's content and mood with your voice. Make the sound express the sense.

In contrast to the regular meter and rhyme in "The Skater of Ghost Lake," "Haunted" (page 256) is closer to the natural rhythms of speech. It is, however, a heightened form of speech because the speaker in the poem is not talking about everyday events. How does the speaker in the poem feel? How would someone who feels that way sound? Try "talking" the poem so that your voice conveys the feeling the speaker in the poem is expressing.

### Thirteen O'Clock

*Kenneth Fearing*

Why do they whistle so loud, when they walk past the grave-
      yard late at night?
Why do they look behind them when they reach the gates?
      Why do they have any gates? Why don't they go
      through the wall?
But why, O why do they make that horrible whistling sound?

GO AWAY, LIVE PEOPLE, STOP HAUNTING THE DEAD.

5 If they catch you, it is said, they make you rap, rap, rap on
      a table all night,
And blow through a trumpet and float around the room in
      long white veils,
While they ask you, and ask you: Can you hear us, Uncle Ted?
Are you happy, Uncle Ted? Should we buy or should we sell?
      Should we marry, Uncle Ted?
What became of Uncle Ned, Uncle Ted, and is he happy,
      and ask him if he knows what became of Uncle Fred?

10 KEEP AWAY, LIVE PEOPLE, KEEP FAR AWAY,
STAY IN THE WORLD'S OTHER WORLD WHERE YOU REALLY BELONG.
      YOU WILL PROBABLY BE MUCH HAPPIER THERE.

And who knows what they are hunting for, always looking,
      looking, looking with sharp bright eyes where they
      ought to have sockets?
Whoever saw them really grin with their teeth?
Who knows why they worry, or what they scheme, with a
      brain where there should be nothing but good, damp air?

15 STAY AWAY, LIVE PEOPLE, STAY AWAY, STAY AWAY,
YOU MEAN NO HARM, AND WE AREN'T AFRAID OF YOU, AND WE
      DON'T BELIEVE SUCH PEOPLE EXIST,
BUT WHAT ARE YOU LOOKING FOR? WHO DO YOU WANT?
WHO? WHO? WHO? O WHO?

## Exposure

*John Updike*

Please do not tell me there is no voodoo,
For, if so, how then do you
Explain that a photograph of a head
Always tells if the person is living or dead?

5  Always, I have never known it to fail.
There is something misted in the eyes, something pale,
If not in the lips, then in the hair—
It is hard to put your finger on, but there.

A kind of third dimension settles in:
10  A blur, a kiss of otherness, a milky film.
If, while you hold a snapshot of Aunt Flo,
Her real heart stops, you will know.

## DISCUSSION

*Thirteen O'Clock*

1. Where do you find the first clue as to the speaker in this poem?

2. (a) In what ways and for what purposes do the living haunt the dead? (b) Do the living measure up to the physical and emotional standards of the dead? Explain.

3. What is humorously ironic in the last stanza?

4. Is "thirteen o'clock" an appropriate time for these complaints to be voiced? Comment.

*Exposure*

1. Believers in voodoo think that it is possible to affect a real person by altering an image of that person. Sticking pins in a voodoo doll would be an example. How is this belief related to the poem?

2. If Aunt Flo's real heart stops while you hold a snapshot of her, how will you know she has died?

3. What is the tone of the poem? How does the rhyme "voodoo"— "do you," and the name "Aunt Flo" help establish the tone of the poem?

## JOHN UPDIKE

John Updike's work has won for him a National Institute of Arts and Letters Award, a National Book Award, and a Guggenheim Fellowship. A hard-working, prolific writer, he has produced novels, poetry, and short stories.

Updike was born in Shillington, Pennsylvania, in 1932 and attended public school. After graduation from Harvard, he studied at the Ruskin School of Drawing and Fine Arts in Oxford, England. He is married and lives in Massachusetts.

# THE RiME OF THE ANCiENT MARINER

*Samuel Taylor Coleridge*

## ARGUMENT[1]

**HOW A SHIP, HAVING PASSED THE LINE,[2] WAS DRIVEN BY STORMS TO THE COLD COUNTRY TOWARD THE SOUTH POLE; AND HOW FROM THENCE SHE MADE HER COURSE TO THE TROPICAL LATITUDE OF THE GREAT PACIFIC OCEAN; AND OF THE STRANGE THINGS THAT BEFELL; AND IN WHAT MANNER THE ANCIENT MARINER CAME BACK TO HIS OWN COUNTRY.**

## PART THE FIRST

AN ANCIENT MARINER MEETETH THREE GALLANTS BIDDEN TO A WEDDING FEAST, AND DETAINETH ONE.

It is an ancient Mariner,
  And he stoppeth one of three.
"By thy long gray beard and glittering eye,
  Now wherefore stopp'st thou me?

5  "The Bridegroom's doors are opened wide,
  And I am next of kin;
The guests are met, the feast is set—
  May'st hear the merry din."

He[3] holds him with his skinny hand;
10  "There was a ship," quoth he.
"Hold off! unhand me, graybeard loon!"
  Eftsoons[4] his hand dropt he.

THE WEDDING GUEST IS SPELLBOUND BY THE EYE OF THE OLD SEAFARING MAN, AND CONSTRAINED TO HEAR HIS TALE.

He holds him with his glittering eye;
  The Wedding Guest stood still,
15  And listens like a three years' child—
  The Mariner hath his will.

The Wedding Guest sat on a stone—
  He cannot choose but hear;
And thus spake on that ancient man,
20  The bright-eyed Mariner.

THE MARINER TELLS HOW THE SHIP SAILED SOUTHWARD WITH A GOOD WIND AND FAIR WEATHER TILL IT REACHED THE LINE.

"The ship was cheered, the harbor cleared;
  Merrily did we drop
Below the kirk,[5] below the hill,
  Below the lighthouse top.

25  "The Sun came up upon the left;
  Out of the sea came he!
And he shone bright, and on the right
  Went down into the sea.

**1. Argument,** meaning here "a summary." In 1798, when "The Rime of the Ancient Mariner" was first published in **Lyrical Ballads**, by Samuel Taylor Coleridge and William Wordsworth, the reader was given no reading helps except the Argument. In later editions, Coleridge added the "Gloss," or prose summary, which is printed alongside the poem.
**2. the Line,** the Equator.
**3. He,** the Mariner.
**4. Eftsoons** (eft sünz'), immediately. (Archaic)

**5. kirk,** church. (Scottish and North English)

"Higher and higher every day,
30     Till over the mast at noon—"
The Wedding Guest here beat his breast,
For he heard the loud bassoon.

THE WEDDING
GUEST HEARETH
THE BRIDAL
MUSIC; BUT THE
MARINER CON-
TINUETH HIS TALE.
The Bride hath paced into the hall;
    Red as a rose is she;
35 Nodding their heads before her goes
    The merry minstrelsy.[6]

6. *minstrelsy,* group of singers or musicians.

The Wedding Guest he beat his breast,
    Yet he cannot choose but hear;
And thus spake on that ancient man,
40     The bright-eyed Mariner.

THE SHIP DRAWN
BY STORM
TOWARD THE
SOUTH POLE.
"And now the Storm Blast came, and he
    Was tyrannous and strong;
He struck with his o'ertaking wings,
    And chased us south along.

45 "With sloping masts and dipping prow,
    As who pursued with yell and blow
Still treads the shadow of his foe,
    And forward bends his head,[7]
The ship drove fast, loud roared the blast,
50     And southward aye we fled.

7. *As who . . . head,* as a person, who, pursued so closely that he is running in his enemy's shadow, bends forward in an effort to attain greater speed.

"And now there came both mist and snow,
    And it grew wondrous cold;
And ice, mast-high, came floating by
    As green as emerald.

THE LAND OF ICE,
AND OF FEARFUL
SOUNDS, WHERE
NO LIVING THING
WAS TO BE SEEN;
55 "And through the drifts the snowy clifts[8]
    Did send a dismal sheen;
Nor shapes of men nor beasts we ken[9]—
    The ice was all between.

8. *snowy clifts,* towering icebergs.
9. *ken,* saw. (Archaic)

"The ice was here, the ice was there,
60     The ice was all around;
It cracked and growled, and roared and howled,
    Like noises in a swound![10]

10. *Like noises in a swound,* like the roaring that a fainting person hears in his ears.
11. *Thorough*    (thə'rō), through.

TILL A GREAT SEA
BIRD CALLED THE
ALBATROSS CAME
THROUGH THE
SNOW-FOG, AND
WAS RECEIVED
WITH GREAT JOY
AND HOSPITALITY.
"At length did cross an Albatross;
    Thorough[11] the fog it came;
65 As if it had been a Christian soul,
    We hailed it in God's name.

"It ate the food it ne'er had eat,
    And round and round it flew.
The ice did split with a thunder-fit;
70     The helmsman steered us through!

AND LO! THE
ALBATROSS
PROVETH A BIRD
OF GOOD OMEN,
AND FOLLOWETH
THE SHIP AS IT
RETURNED
NORTHWARD,
THROUGH FOG
AND FLOATING
ICE.

"And a good south wind sprung up behind;
  The Albatross did follow,
And every day, for food or play,
  Came to the mariners' hollo!

75 "In mist or cloud, on mast or shroud,[12]
  It perched for vespers nine;[13]
Whiles all the night, through fog-smoke white,
  Glimmered the white moonshine."

**12. shroud,** rope running from a mast to the side of the ship.

**13. for vespers nine,** for nine evenings.

"God save thee, ancient Mariner,
80  From the fiends that plague thee thus!—
Why look'st thou so?"—"With my crossbow
  I shot the Albatross."

## PART THE SECOND

"The Sun now rose upon the right;
  Out of the sea came he,
85 Still hid in mist, and on the left
  Went down into the sea.

"And the good south wind still blew behind,
  But no sweet bird did follow,
Nor any day, for food or play,
90  Came to the mariners' hollo!

HIS SHIPMATES
CRY OUT AGAINST
THE ANCIENT
MARINER FOR
KILLING THE BIRD
OF GOOD LUCK.

"And I had done a hellish thing,
   And it would work 'em woe;
For all averred I had killed the bird
   That made the breeze to blow.
95 'Ah, wretch!' said they, 'the bird to slay,
   That made the breeze to blow!'

BUT WHEN THE
FOG CLEARS OFF,
THEY JUSTIFY THE
SAME, AND THUS
MAKE THEMSELVES
ACCOMPLICES IN
THE CRIME.

"Nor dim nor red, like God's own head,
   The glorious Sun uprist;[14]
Then all averred I had killed the bird
100   That brought the fog and mist.
''Twas right,' said they, 'such birds to slay,
   That bring the fog and mist.'

**14. uprist,** uprose.

THE FAIR BREEZE
CONTINUES; THE
SHIP ENTERS THE
PACIFIC OCEAN
AND SAILS
NORTHWARD,
EVEN TILL IT
REACHES THE
LINE.

"The fair breeze blew, the white foam flew,
   The furrow followed free;
105 We were the first that ever burst
   Into that silent sea.

THE SHIP HATH
BEEN SUDDENLY
BECALMED.

"Down dropt the breeze, the sails dropt down;
   'Twas sad as sad could be;
And we did speak only to break
110   The silence of the sea!

"All in a hot and copper sky,
   The bloody Sun, at noon,
Right up above the mast did stand,
   No bigger than the Moon.

115 "Day after day, day after day,
   We stuck, nor breath nor motion;
As idle as a painted ship
   Upon a painted ocean.

AND THE
ALBATROSS
BEGINS TO BE
AVENGED.

"Water, water, everywhere,
120   And all the boards did shrink;
Water, water, everywhere,
   Nor any drop to drink.

"The very deep did rot—O Christ!
   That ever this should be!
125 Yea, slimy things did crawl with legs
   Upon the slimy sea.

"About, about, in reel and rout
   The death fires[15] danced at night;
The water, like a witch's oils,
130   Burnt green, and blue, and white.

**15. death fires,** luminous glow caused by discharges of atmospheric electricity and often seen on masts of sailing ships in stormy weather.

A SPIRIT HAD
FOLLOWED THEM;
ONE OF THE
INVISIBLE INHABIT-
ANTS OF
THIS PLANET,

NEITHER
DEPARTED SOULS
NOR ANGELS;
CONCERNING
WHOM THE
LEARNED JEW
JOSEPHUS AND
THE PLATONIC
CONSTANTINO-
POLITAN, MICHAEL
PSELLUS,[16] MAY
BE CONSULTED.
THEY ARE VERY
NUMEROUS, AND
THERE IS NO
CLIMATE OR
ELEMENT
WITHOUT ONE OR
MORE.

THE SHIPMATES IN
THEIR SORE
DISTRESS WOULD
FAIN THROW THE
WHOLE GUILT ON
THE ANCIENT
MARINER; IN SIGN
WHEREOF THEY
HANG THE DEAD
SEA BIRD ROUND
HIS NECK.

THE ANCIENT
MARINER
BEHOLDETH A
SIGN IN THE
ELEMENT AFAR
OFF.

"And some in dreams assurèd were
 Of the spirit that plagued us so;
Nine fathom deep he had followed us
 From the land of mist and snow.

135 "And every tongue, through utter drought,
 Was withered at the root;
We could not speak, no more than if
 We had been choked with soot.

"Ah! well-a-day!—what evil looks
140 Had I from old and young!
Instead of the cross, the Albatross
 About my neck was hung."

## PART THE THIRD

"There passed a weary time. Each throat
 Was parched, and glazed each eye.
145 A weary time! a weary time!
 How glazed each weary eye!
When, looking westward, I beheld
 A something in the sky.

"At first it seemed a little speck,
150 And then it seemed a mist;
It moved, and moved, and took at last
 A certain shape, I wist.[17]

**16. the learned Jew Josephus**
(jō sē'fəs) . . . *Michael Psellus*
(sel'es). Josephus (37-95) was
a historian. Psellus (1018-
1079) was a theologian, born
in Constantinople, who admired Plato, the famous
ancient Greek philosopher.

**17. wist,** knew or discovered. (Archaic)

"A speck, a mist, a shape, I wist!
And still it neared and neared;
155 As if it dodged a water sprite,
It plunged and tacked and veered.

AT ITS NEARER
APPROACH, IT
SEEMETH HIM TO
BE A SHIP; AND AT
A DEAR RANSOM
HE FREETH HIS
SPEECH FROM THE
BONDS OF THIRST.

"With throats unslaked, with black lips baked,
We could nor laugh nor wail;
Through utter drought all dumb we stood!
160 I bit my arm, I sucked the blood,
And cried, 'A sail! a sail!'

A FLASH OF JOY;

"With throats unslaked, with black lips baked,
Agape they heard me call;
Gramercy![18] they for joy did grin,
165 And all at once their breath drew in,
As they were drinking all.

**18. Gramercy** (grə mẽr′si),
many thanks. (Archaic)

AND HORROR
FOLLOWS. FOR
CAN IT BE A SHIP
THAT COMES
ONWARD
WITHOUT WIND
OR TIDE?

"'See! see!' I cried, 'she tacks no more!
Hither to work us weal;[19]
Without a breeze, without a tide,
170 She steadies with upright keel!'

**19. to work us weal** (wēl), to
bring us good.

"The western wave was all aflame,
The day was well-nigh done!
Almost upon the western wave
Rested the broad bright Sun;
175 When that strange shape drove suddenly
Betwixt us and the Sun.

IT SEEMETH HIM
BUT THE SKELETON
OF A SHIP.

"And straight the Sun was flecked with bars
(Heaven's Mother send us grace!),
As if through a dungeon grate he peered,
180 With broad and burning face.

"'Alas!' thought I, and my heart beat loud,
    'How fast she nears and nears!
Are those *her* sails that glance in the Sun,
    Like restless gossameres?

185 "'Are those *her* ribs through which the Sun
    Did peer, as through a grate?
And is that Woman all her crew?
Is that a Death?[20] and are there two?
    Is Death that Woman's mate?'

**20.** *a Death,* a skeleton.

190 "Her lips were red, her looks were free,[21]
    Her locks were yellow as gold;
Her skin was as white as leprosy;
The Nightmare Life-in-Death was she,
    Who thicks man's blood with cold.

**21.** *her looks were free.* The
Specter Woman's manner is
bold and brazen.

195 "The naked hulk alongside came,
    And the twain were casting dice;
'The game is done! I've won! I've won!'
    Quoth she, and whistles thrice.

"The Sun's rim dips; the stars rush out;
200    At one stride comes the dark;
With far-heard whisper, o'er the sea,
    Off shot the specter bark.

**22.** *the courts of the sun,*
those far northern lands
where the sun shines most of
the day and night.

"We listened and looked sideways up!
Fear at my heart, as at a cup,
205    My lifeblood seemed to sip!

"The stars were dim, and thick the night;
The steersman's face by his lamp gleamed
        white;
    From the sails the dew did drip—
Till clomb above the eastern bar
210 The hornèd Moon,[23] with one bright star
    Within the nether tip.

**23.** *Till clomb . . . Moon,*
until the crescent moon
climbed (clomb) high above
the eastern horizon (bar).

"One after one, by the star-dogged Moon,
    Too quick for groan or sigh,
Each turned his face with a ghastly pang,
215    And cursed me with his eye.

"Four times fifty living men
    (And I heard nor sigh nor groan),
With heavy thump, a lifeless lump,
    They dropped down one by one.

220 "The souls did from their bodies fly—
    They fled to bliss or woe!

And every soul, it passed me by,
　Like the whizz of my crossbow!"

## PART THE FOURTH

THE WEDDING
GUEST FEARETH
THAT A SPIRIT IS
TALKING TO HIM;

"I fear thee, ancient Mariner!
235 　I fear thy skinny hand!
And thou art long, and lank, and brown,
　As is the ribbed sea sand.

BUT THE ANCIENT
MARINER AS-
SURETH HIM OF
HIS BODILY LIFE,
AND PROCEEDETH
TO RELATE HIS
HORRIBLE
PENANCE.

"I fear thee and thy glittering eye
　And thy skinny hand, so brown."
230 "Fear not, fear not, thou Wedding Guest!
　This body dropt not down.

"Alone, alone, all, all alone,
　Alone on a wide, wide sea!
And never a saint took pity on
235 　My soul in agony.

HE DESPISETH THE
CREATURES OF
THE CALM,

"The many men, so beautiful!
　And they all dead did lie;
And a thousand thousand slimy things
　Lived on; and so did I.

AND ENVIETH
THAT THEY
SHOULD LIVE, AND
SO MANY LIE
DEAD,

240 "I looked upon the rotting sea,
　And drew my eyes away;
I looked upon the rotting deck,
　And there the dead men lay.

"I looked to Heaven, and tried to pray;
245    But or ever a prayer had gusht,
A wicked whisper came, and made
    My heart as dry as dust.

"I closed my lids, and kept them close,
    And the balls like pulses beat;
250 For the sky and the sea, and the sea and
        the sky
Lay like a load on my weary eye,
    And the dead were at my feet.

BUT THE CURSE
LIVETH FOR HIM
IN THE EYE OF THE
DEAD MEN.

"The cold sweat melted from their limbs;
    Nor rot nor reek did they;
255 The look with which they looked on me
    Had never passed away.

"An orphan's curse would drag to Hell
    A spirit from on high;
But oh! more horrible than that
260    Is a curse in a dead man's eye!
Seven days, seven nights, I saw that curse,
    And yet I could not die.

IN HIS LONELINESS
AND FIXEDNESS HE
YEARNETH
TOWARD THE
JOURNEYING
MOON, AND THE
STARS THAT STILL
SOJOURN, YET
STILL MOVE
ONWARD; AND
EVERYWHERE THE
BLUE SKY BELONGS
TO THEM, AND IS
THEIR APPOINTED
REST AND THEIR
NATIVE COUNTRY
AND THEIR OWN
NATURAL HOMES,
WHICH THEY
ENTER UNAN-
NOUNCED, AS
LORDS THAT ARE
CERTAINLY EX-
PECTED AND YET
THERE IS A SILENT
JOY AT THEIR
ARRIVAL.

"The moving Moon went up the sky,
    And nowhere did abide;
265 Softly she was going up,
    And a star or two beside—

"Her beams bemocked the sultry main,[24]
    Like April hoarfrost spread;
But where the ship's huge shadow lay,
270 The charmèd water burnt alway
    A still and awful red.

**24. Her beams . . . main.** The moonbeams looked cool in contrast to the fiery sea.

"Beyond the shadow of the ship,
    I watched the water snakes;
They moved in tracks of shining white,
275 And when they reared, the elfish light
    Fell off in hoary flakes.

BY THE LIGHT OF
THE MOON HE
BEHOLDETH GOD'S
CREATURES OF
THE GREAT CALM,

"Within the shadow of the ship
    I watched their rich attire;
Blue, glossy green, and velvet black,
280 They coiled and swam; and every track
    Was a flash of golden fire.

THEIR BEAUTY
AND THEIR
HAPPINESS.

"O happy living things! no tongue
    Their beauty might declare;
A spring of love gushed from my heart;

285    And I blessed them unaware!
      Sure my kind saint took pity on me,
      And I blessed them unaware.

    "The selfsame moment I could pray;
      And from my neck so free
290  The Albatross fell off, and sank
      Like lead into the sea."

## PART THE FIFTH

    "Oh, sleep! it is a gentle thing,
      Beloved from pole to pole!
    To Mary Queen the praise be given!
295  She sent the gentle sleep from Heaven,
      That slid into my soul.

BY THE GRACE OF
THE HOLY
MOTHER, THE
ANCIENT MARINER
IS REFRESHED
WITH RAIN.

    "The silly[25] buckets on the deck,
      That had so long remained,
    I dreamt that they were filled with dew;
300    And when I awoke, it rained.

**25. *silly*,** simple.

    "My lips were wet, my throat was cold,
      My garments all were dank,
    Sure I had drunken in my dreams,
      And still my body drank.

305  "I moved, and could not feel my limbs;
      I was so light—almost
    I thought that I had died in sleep,
      And was a blessed ghost.

HE HEARETH
SOUNDS AND
SEETH STRANGE
SIGHTS AND
COMMOTIONS IN
THE SKY AND THE
ELEMENT.

    "And soon I heard a roaring wind;
310    It did not come anear;
    But with its sound it shook the sails
      That were so thin and sere.

    "The upper air burst into life!
      And a hundred fire-flags sheen;[26]
315  To and fro they were hurried about;
    And to and fro, and in and out,
      The wan stars danced between.

**26. *fire-flags sheen*,** flashes of lightning shone bright.

    "And the coming wind did roar more loud,
      And the sails did sigh like sedge;[27]
320  And the rain poured down from one black
      cloud;
      The Moon was at its edge.

**27. *sedge*,** coarse grass that grows in wet ground.

    "The thick, black cloud was cleft, and still

The Moon was at its side;
Like waters shot from some high crag,
325 The lightning fell with never a jag,
A river steep and wide.

THE BODIES OF
THE SHIP'S CREW
ARE INSPIRED,
AND THE SHIP
MOVES ON;

"The loud wind never reached the ship,
Yet now the ship moved on!
Beneath the lightning and the Moon
330 The dead men gave a groan.

"They groaned, they stirred, they all uprose;
Nor spake, nor moved their eyes;
It had been strange, even in a dream,
To have seen those dead men rise.

335 "The helmsman steered, the ship moved on;
Yet never a breeze up-blew.
The mariners all 'gan work the ropes,
Where they were wont to do;
They raised their limbs like lifeless tools—
340 We were a ghastly crew.

"The body of my brother's son
Stood by me, knee to knee;
The body and I pulled at one rope,
But he said naught to me."

345 "I fear thee, ancient Mariner!"
"Be calm, thou Wedding Guest!
'Twas not those souls that fled in pain,
Which to their corses²⁸ came again,        *28. corses*, corpses.
But a troop of spirits blest;

BUT NOT BY THE
SOULS OF THE
MEN, NOR BY
DEMONS OF
EARTH OR MIDDLE
AIR, BUT BY A
BLESSED TROOP OF
ANGELIC SPIRITS,
SENT DOWN BY
THE INVOCATION
OF THE GUARDIAN
SAINT.

350 "For when it dawned—they dropped their arms
And clustered round the mast;
Sweet sounds rose slowly through their mouths;
And from their bodies passed.

"Around, around, flew each sweet sound,
355 They darted to the Sun;
Slowly the sounds came back again,
Now mixed, now one by one.

"Sometimes a-dropping from the sky
I heard the skylark sing;
360 Sometimes all little birds that are,
How they seemed to fill the sea and air
With their sweet jargoning!

"And now 'twas like all instruments,
Now like a lonely flute;

<sub>365</sub> And now it is an angel's song,
That makes the heavens be mute.

"It ceased; yet still the sails made on
A pleasant noise till noon,
A noise like of a hidden brook
<sub>370</sub>    In the leafy month of June,
That to the sleeping woods all night
Singeth a quiet tune.

"Till noon we quietly sailed on.
Yet never a breeze did breathe;
<sub>375</sub> Slowly and smoothly went the ship,
Moved onward from beneath.

"Under the keel nine fathom deep,
From the land of mist and snow,
The spirit slid; and it was he
<sub>380</sub>    That made the ship to go.
The sails at noon left off their tune,
And the ship stood still also.

"The Sun, right up above the mast,
Had fixed her to the ocean,
<sub>385</sub> But in a minute she 'gan stir,
With a short, uneasy motion—
Backwards and forwards half her length
With a short, uneasy motion.

"Then like a pawing horse let go,
<sub>390</sub>    She made a sudden bound;
It flung the blood into my head,
And I fell down in a swound.

"How long in that same fit I lay,
I have not to declare;
<sub>395</sub> But ere my living life returned
I heard and in my soul discerned
Two voices in the air.

"'Is it he?' quoth one, 'Is this the man?
By Him who died on cross,
<sub>400</sub> With his cruel bow he laid full low
The harmless Albatross.

"'The spirit who bideth by himself
In the land of mist and snow,
He loved the bird that loved the man
<sub>405</sub>    Who shot him with his bow.'

"The other was a softer voice,

As soft as honeydew;
Quoth he, 'The man hath penance done
And penance more will do.'"

## PART THE SIXTH

*First Voice*
410 "'But tell me, tell me! speak again,
Thy soft response renewing—
What makes that ship drive on so fast?
What is the Ocean doing?'

*Second Voice*
"'Still as a slave before his lord,
415 The Ocean hath no blast;
His great bright eye most silently
Up to the Moon is cast—

"'If he may know which way to go;
For she guides him smooth or grim.
420 See, brother, see! how graciously
She looketh down on him.'

THE MARINER
HATH BEEN CAST
INTO A TRANCE;
FOR THE ANGELIC
POWER CAUSETH
THE VESSEL TO
DRIVE NORTH-
WARD FASTER
THAN HUMAN LIFE
COULD ENDURE.

*First Voice*
"'But why drives on that ship so fast,
Without or [29] wave or wind?'

*29. or,* either.

*Second Voice*
"'The air is cut away before,
425 And closes from behind.

"'Fly, brother, fly! more high, more high,
Or we shall be belated;
For slow and slow that ship will go,
When the Mariner's trance is abated.'

THE
SUPERNATURAL
MOTION IS
RETARDED; THE
MARINER AWAKES,
AND HIS PENANCE
BEGINS ANEW.

430 "I woke, and we were sailing on
As in a gentle weather.
'Twas night, calm night, the Moon was high;
The dead men stood together.

"All stood together on the deck,
435 For a charnel dungeon [30] fitter;
All fixed on me their stony eyes
That in the Moon did glitter.

*30. charnel* (chär'nl) *dungeon,* burial vault.

"The pang, the curse, with which they died,
Had never passed away;
440 I could not draw my eyes from theirs,
Nor turn them up to pray.

"And now this spell was snapt; once more
   I viewed the ocean green,
And looked far forth, yet little saw
445   Of what had else been seen—

"Like one that on a lonesome road
   Doth walk in fear and dread,
And having once turned round, walks on,
   And turns no more his head,
450 Because he knows a frightful fiend
   Doth close behind him tread.

"But soon there breathed a wind on me,
   Nor sound nor motion made;
Its path was not upon the sea,
455   In ripple or in shade.

"It raised my hair, it fanned my cheek
   Like a meadow gale of spring—
It mingled strangely with my fears,
   Yet it felt like a welcoming.

460 "Swiftly, swiftly flew the ship,
   Yet she sailed softly, too;
Sweetly, sweetly blew the breeze—
   On me alone it blew.

"Oh! dream of joy! is this indeed
465   The lighthouse top I see?
Is this the hill? Is this the kirk?
   Is this mine own countree?

"We drifted o'er the harbor bar,
   And I with sobs did pray—
470 'O let me be awake, my God!
   Or let me sleep alway.'

"The harbor bay was clear as glass,
So smoothly it was strewn!
And on the bay the moonlight lay,
475 And the shadow of the Moon.

"The rock shone bright, the kirk no less,
That stands above the rock;
The moonlight steeped in silentness
The steady weathercock.

THE ANGELIC
SPIRITS LEAVE THE
DEAD BODIES,

480 And the bay was white with silent light,
Till rising from the same,
Full many shapes, that shadows were,
In crimson colors came.

AND APPEAR IN
THEIR OWN FORMS
OF LIGHT.

"A little distance from the prow
485 Those crimson shadows were;
I turned my eyes upon the deck—
Oh, Christ! what I saw there!

"Each corse lay flat, lifeless and flat,
And, by the holy rood!³¹
490 A man all light, a seraph ³² man,
On every corse there stood.

**31. the holy rood** (rüd), the cross of Christ.
**32. seraph** (ser′əf), one of the highest order of angels.

"This seraph band, each waved his hand—
It was a heavenly sight!
They stood as signals to the land,
495 Each one a lovely light;

"This seraph band, each waved his hand;
No voice did they impart—
No voice; but oh! the silence sank
Like music on my heart.

500 "But soon I heard the dash of oars,
I heard the Pilot's cheer;
My head was turned perforce away,
And I saw a boat appear.

"The Pilot, and the Pilot's boy,
505 I heard them coming fast;
Dear Lord in Heaven! it was a joy
The dead men could not blast.

"I saw a third—I heard his voice;
It is the Hermit good!
510 He singeth loud his godly hymns
That he makes in the wood.
He'll shrieve my soul,³³ he'll wash away
The Albatross's blood."

**33. He'll shrieve** (shrīv) **my soul.** The Hermit of the wood will hear the Ancient Mariner's confession and, after listening to the tale of his wrongdoings, will impose a penance upon him. When this penance is carried out, the Mariner will secure peace and forgiveness for his sins.

## PART THE SEVENTH

THE HERMIT OF
THE WOOD

"This hermit good lives in that wood
515   Which slopes down to the sea;
How loudly his sweet voice he rears!
He loves to talk with marineres
   That come from a far countree.

"He kneels at morn, and noon, and eve—
520   He hath a cushion plump;
It is the moss that wholly hides
   The rotted old oak stump.

"The skiff boat neared; I heard them talk:
   'Why, this is strange, I trow![34]
525 Where are those lights so many and fair
   That signal made but now?'

**34. I trow** (trō *or* trou), I think.

APPROACHETH
THE SHIP WITH
WONDER.

"'Strange, by my faith!' the Hermit said—
   'And they answered not our cheer!
The planks look warped! and see those sails
530   How thin they are and sere!
I never saw aught like to them,
   Unless perchance it were

"'Brown skeletons of leaves that lag
   My forest brook along;
535 When the ivy tod[35] is heavy with snow;
And the owlet whoops to the wolf below
   That eats the she-wolf's young.'

**35. the ivy tod,** a clump of ivy.

"'Dear Lord! it hath a fiendish look'—
   (The Pilot made reply)
540 'I am a-feared'—'Push on, push on!'
   Said the Hermit cheerily.

"The boat came closer to the ship,
   But I nor spake nor stirred;
The boat came close beneath the ship,
545   And straight a sound was heard.

THE SHIP
SUDDENLY
SINKETH.

"Under the water it rumbled on,
   Still louder and more dread;
It reached the ship, it split the bay;
   The ship went down like lead.

THE ANCIENT
MARINER IS SAVED
IN THE PILOT'S
BOAT.

550 "Stunned by that loud and dreadful sound,
   Which sky and ocean smote,
Like one that hath been seven days drowned
   My body lay afloat;

But swift as dreams, myself I found
555    Within the Pilot's boat.

"Upon the whirl, where sank the ship,
    The boat spun round and round;
And all was still, save that the hill
    Was telling of the sound.

560  "I moved my lips—the Pilot shrieked
    And fell down in a fit;
The holy Hermit raised his eyes
    And prayed where he did sit.

"I took the oars; the Pilot's boy,
565    Who now doth crazy go,
Laughed loud and long, and all the while
    His eyes went to and fro.
'Ha! ha!' quoth he, 'full plain I see,
    The Devil knows how to row.'

570  "And now, all in my own countree,
    I stood on the firm land!
The Hermit stepped forth from the boat,
    And scarcely he could stand.

"'O shrieve me, shrieve me, holy man!'
575    The Hermit crossed his brow.
'Say quick,' quoth he, 'I bid thee say—
    What manner of man art thou?'

THE ANCIENT
MARINER
EARNESTLY EN-
TREATETH THE
HERMIT TO
SHRIEVE HIM; AND
THE PENANCE OF
LIFE FALLS ON
HIM,

"Forthwith this frame of mine was wrenched
   With a woeful agony,
580 Which forced me to begin my tale;
   And then it left me free.

"Since then, at an uncertain hour,
   That agony returns;
And till my ghastly tale is told,
585   This heart within me burns.

"I pass, like night, from land to land;
   I have strange power of speech;
That moment that his face I see,
I know the man that must hear me—
590   To him my tale I teach.

"What loud uproar bursts from that door!
   The wedding guests are there;
But in the garden bower the bride
   And bridemaids singing are;
595 And hark the little vesper bell,
   Which biddeth me to prayer!

"O Wedding Guest! this soul hath been
   Alone on a wide, wide sea;
So lonely 'twas that God himself
600   Scarce seemèd there to be.

"O sweeter than the marriage feast,
   'Tis sweeter far to me,
To walk together to the kirk
   With a goodly company!—

605 "To walk together to the kirk,
   And all together pray,
While each to his great Father bends,
Old men, and babes, and loving friends,
   And youths, and maidens gay!

610 "Farewell, farewell! but this I tell
   To thee, thou Wedding Guest!
He prayeth well who loveth well
   Both man and bird and beast.

"He prayeth best who loveth best
615   All things both great and small;
For the dear God who loveth us,
   He made and loveth all."

The Mariner, whose eye is bright,

AND EVER AND
ANON
THROUGHOUT HIS
FUTURE LIFE AN
AGONY CON-
STRAINETH HIM
TO TRAVEL FROM
LAND TO LAND,

AND TO TEACH, BY
HIS OWN
EXAMPLE, LOVE
AND REVERENCE
TO ALL THINGS
THAT GOD MADE
AND LOVETH.

Whose beard with age is hoar,[36]
620 Is gone; and now the Wedding Guest
Turned from the Bridegroom's door.

He went like one that hath been stunned,
And is of sense forlorn;
A sadder and a wiser man,
625 He rose the morrow morn.

**36. hoar,** gray or white.

---

## DISCUSSION

1. The first five stanzas of the poem give the setting. In your own words explain what happens in these stanzas.

2. What briefly interrupts the Mariner's tale?

3. How does the arrival of the albatross affect the Mariner's shipmates?

4. Who is speaking in lines 79–80?

5. (a) Why do the sailors at first chastise the Ancient Mariner and then approve his killing the bird? (b) Why do they accuse him again? (c) How do the sailors punish him?

6. (a) In Part the Third, what supernatural turn of events does the Mariner describe? (b) What fear does this part of the Mariner's tale create in the Wedding Guest?

7. (a) Why does the Mariner bless the water snakes? (b) What happens as a result?

8. How does the ship eventually get underway again?

9. In what way does the mood of the poem change in lines 350–376?

10. How do the Pilot and the Pilot's boy react to the Mariner?

11. (a) How does the Mariner select his listeners? (b) What lesson does he feel compelled to teach them?

12. (a) By marking the stressed and unstressed syllables in one stanza of the poem, determine the rhythm pattern. (b) What is the rhyme scheme? Is it the same throughout the poem? (c) Are the rhythm and rhyme appropriate to the poem? Explain. (See the Handbook entries on *rhyme* and *rhythm*.)

### SAMUEL TAYLOR COLERIDGE

Born in 1772 in Derbyshire, England, Coleridge was a prominent lecturer and literary critic as well as a poet. His most successful publishing venture was *Lyrical Ballads* (1798), which contained "The Rime of the Ancient Mariner" and poems by his friend William Wordsworth.

In poor health for most of his life, and by 1810 estranged from his wife and family, Coleridge turned in his last years to opium. He was never entirely free of his dependency on the drug, and his health and his writing declined until his death in 1834.

---

## UNIT 3 REVIEW

1. Illustrate each of the following statements by giving two or more examples from poems in this unit.

a. The speaker in a poem is not always the poet.

b. Some poems rhyme.

c. Some poems do not rhyme.

d. Some poems have regular, recurring, formal rhythm patterns.

e. Some poems use the natural rhythms of speech.

f. The language of some poems is informal.

g. The language of some poems is formal.

h. The words of some poems are arranged on the page so that they look like what they are about.

i. Some poems sound like what they are about.

j. Some poems are satirical.

k. Some poems are narrative, that is, they tell a story.

l. Some poems are contemplative.

2. To check your knowledge of some terms commonly used when discussing poetry, find an example of each of the following in the poems in this unit:

a. simile
b. metaphor
c. personification
d. onomatopoeia
e. alliteration

(For review, see the Handbook entries for *figurative language* and *rhyme and sound devices*.)

# Romeo and Juliet

Only a few basic facts, derived from documents and records of the time, are known about William Shakespeare, the foremost dramatist of his own day and one of the greatest writers of all times. He was born in the town of Stratford, England, in April 1564, the son of a glove-maker. It is probable that he attended the town's free grammar school where, as was the custom, he studied the Greek and Latin classics. The next definite information we have about him is that, at the age of eighteen, he married Anne Hathaway.

Several years after his marriage, Shakespeare left Stratford and went to London where he soon made a name for himself as an actor and where he began writing plays. In 1594 he was listed as a member of the Lord Chamberlain's Company (after 1603 called the King's Men). Among the members of this troupe were some of the greatest actors of the time, and it is very likely that Shakespeare, in developing the characters of his plays, took into consideration the talents of the actors who were to portray them on the stage. By this time Shakespeare was well established as a playwright as well as an actor, and his plays apparently enjoyed tremendous popularity with the theater-going public. In 1598 he is cited by a critic as the best author of both tragedy and comedy for the stage.

The Lord Chamberlain's Company continued to prosper. In 1599 the group erected the famous Globe Theater, the theater in which Shakespeare's greatest plays were probably first produced, and in 1608 the company acquired control of the Blackfriars, the only theater of the time built within the city limits. Shakespeare was a stockholder in both these ventures, suggesting that he had a head for business as well as for acting and writing.

About 1612, having written thirty-seven plays and having become a wealthy man, Shakespeare retired to Stratford where he died on April 23, 1616. The poetic powers of William Shakespeare and the plight of young romantic lovers lost in a world which doesn't understand them, have been combined to create a play which has endured over three centuries, has been performed by the greatest actors of each generation, and receives as much acclaim as when it was first performed.

The plot of *Romeo and Juliet,* as were many of Shakespeare's plots, was borrowed from other sources. The basic theme appears as early as the fourth century B.C. in a tale by a Greek writer. The idea of ill-fated lovers was also immensely popular among Italian writers of the fifteenth and sixteenth centuries. But the direct source of *Romeo and Juliet* was a long narrative poem written in 1562 by an English writer, Arthur Brooke. Shakespeare rewrote the story, emphasizing certain events, eliminating others, and developing the characters in much greater detail. Brooke's original plot included lively action, social conflict, intense passion, and the clash between youth and age. All these, Shakespeare kept.

While it is important in reading *Romeo and Juliet* to appreciate the author's powers of poetic description and the intrigue of the plot, the most important idea to keep in mind is that *Romeo and Juliet* is neither a poem nor a story but a play. First and foremost Shakespeare was a dramatist. To enjoy the reading of *Romeo and Juliet* we must visualize it upon the stage with real actors interpreting real characters in real conflicts.

ESCALUS (es′kə ləs), *Prince of Verona.*

MONTAGUE (mon′tə gyü) ⎤
⎥ *heads of two feuding households.*
CAPULET (kap′yü let) ⎦

LADY MONTAGUE ⎤
⎥ *their wives.*
LADY CAPULET ⎦

ROMEO, *son of the Montagues.*

JULIET, *daughter of the Capulets.*

MERCUTIO (mėr kyü′shi ō), *kinsman of Prince Escalus and friend
of Romeo.*

BENVOLIO (ben vōl′i ō), *nephew of Montague and friend of
Romeo.*

TYBALT (tib′əlt), *nephew of Capulet's wife.*

PARIS, *kinsman of Prince Escalus and a suitor of Juliet.*

---

## Prologue

CHORUS *(spoken by a single actor).* Two households, both alike
    in dignity,
In fair Verona, where we lay our scene,
From ancient grudge break to new mutiny,[1]
Where civil blood makes civil hands unclean.[2]
5 From forth the fatal loins of these two foes
A pair of star-crossed[3] lovers take their life,
Whose misadventured piteous overthrows
Do with their death bury their parents' strife.
The fearful passage[4] of their death-marked love,
10 And the continuance of their parents' rage,
Which, but[5] their children's end, naught could remove,
Is now the two hours' traffic of our stage,
The which if you with patient ears attend,
What here shall miss, our toil shall strive to mend.

                              *(Exit.)*

1. *mutiny,* rioting.
2. *Where civil blood . . . unclean,*
where citizens' hands are soiled
with one another's blood.
3. *star-crossed,* ill-fated. In
Shakespeare's day it was commonly believed that the stars
controlled people's lives.
4. *fearful passage,* progress
that is full of fear.
5. *but,* except for.

FRIAR LAURENCE, *counselor of Romeo.*

FRIAR JOHN, *trusted messenger of Friar Laurence.*

NURSE, *servant and friend of Juliet.*

OLD MAN, *member of the Capulet family.*

BALTHASAR (bäl′thə zär′), *servant of Romeo.*

SAMPSON ⎱
　　　　　⎰ *servants of Capulet.*
GREGORY ⎰

ABRAHAM, *servant of Montague.*

PETER, *servant of Juliet's nurse.*

APOTHECARY

MASKERS, MUSICIANS, WATCHMEN, PAGES, OFFICERS, CITIZENS,
AND ATTENDANTS

---

# Act One

*Scene 1: A public square in Verona.*

> *Enter SAMPSON and GREGORY, servants of the house*
> *of CAPULET, armed with swords and bucklers.[1]*

SAMPSON. Gregory, on my word, we'll not carry coals.[2] I mean
an[3] we be in choler,[4] we'll draw.

GREGORY. Ay, while you live, draw your neck out o' the collar.[5]

SAMPSON *(with mock belligerence).* I strike quickly, being moved.

5　GREGORY. But thou art not quickly moved to strike.

SAMPSON. A dog of the house of Montague moves me.

GREGORY. To move is to stir; and to be valiant is to stand;
therefore, if thou art moved, thou runn'st away.

SAMPSON. A dog of that house shall move me to stand; I will
10　take the wall of[6] any man of Montague's.

GREGORY. The quarrel is between our masters and us their
men.

SAMPSON. 'Tis all one. I will show myself a tyrant.

GREGORY *(warningly).* Draw thy sword! Here comes two of
15　the house of the Montagues.

SAMPSON. My naked weapon is out; quarrel, I will back thee.

1. *bucklers,* small shields.
2. *carry coals,* endure insults.
3. *an,* if.
4. *in choler,* angry.
5. *collar,* a halter used by the hangman.

6. *take the wall of,* figurative for "get the better of."

GREGORY. How! Turn thy back and run?

SAMPSON. Fear me not.[7]

GREGORY. No, marry;[8] I fear thee!

20 SAMPSON. Let us take the law of our sides; let *them* begin.

GREGORY. I will frown as I pass by, and let them take it as they list.[9]

SAMPSON. Nay, as they dare. I will bite my thumb[10] at them; which is a disgrace to them if they bear it.

*Enter* ABRAHAM *and* BALTHASAR, *servants of the* MONTAGUES.

25 ABRAHAM. Do you bite your thumb at us, sir?

SAMPSON. I do bite my thumb, sir.

ABRAHAM. Do you bite your thumb at *us*, sir?

SAMPSON *(aside.to* GREGORY). Is the law of our side if I say "Ay"?

GREGORY. No.

30 SAMPSON *(to* ABRAHAM). No, sir, I do not bite my thumb at you, sir; but I bite my thumb, sir.

GREGORY *(to* ABRAHAM). Do you quarrel, sir?

ABRAHAM. Quarrel, sir? No, sir.

SAMPSON. If you do, sir, I am for you. I serve as good a man

35 as you.

ABRAHAM. No better.

SAMPSON. Well, sir.

*Enter* BENVOLIO, *a nephew of* MONTAGUE *and hence a first cousin of* ROMEO.

GREGORY *(aside to* SAMPSON). Say "better"; here comes one of my master's kinsmen.

40 SAMPSON. Yes, better, sir.

ABRAHAM. You lie.

SAMPSON. Draw, if you be men. Gregory, remember thy swashing[11] blow.

*(The four* SERVANTS *fight.)*

BENVOLIO. Part, fools! *(He beats down their swords.)*

*Enter* TYBALT, *a hot-headed youth, nephew of* LADY CAPULET *and first cousin of* JULIET.

45 TYBALT *(contemptuously)*. What, art thou drawn among these heartless hinds?[12]
Turn thee, Benvolio, look upon thy death.

BENVOLIO *(quietly)*. I do but keep the peace. Put up thy sword, Or manage it to part these men with me.

TYBALT *(scornfully)*. What, drawn, and talk of peace? I hate the word

50 As I hate hell, all Montagues, and thee.          *(They fight.)*
Have at thee,[13] coward!

*Enter several of both houses, who join the fray; then enter* CITIZENS *with clubs or other weapons.*

7. *Fear me not.* Don't mistrust me.

8. *marry,* by the Virgin Mary; a mild oath.

9. *list,* wish.

10. *bite my thumb,* an insulting gesture.

11. *swashing,* crushing.

12. *heartless hinds,* cowardly servants.

13. *Have at thee.* I shall attack you; be on your guard.

FIRST CITIZEN. Clubs, bills, and partisans![14] Strike! Beat them
    down!
    Down with the Capulets! Down with the Montagues!

*Enter* CAPULET *in his gown*[15] *and* LADY CAPULET.
CAPULET *(who cannot resist joining in the quarrel).* What noise
    is this? Give me my long sword, ho!
55 LADY CAPULET *(scornfully).* A crutch,[16] a crutch! Why call you for
    a sword?
CAPULET. My sword, I say! Old Montague is come,
    And flourishes his blade in spite[17] of me.

*Enter* MONTAGUE *and* LADY MONTAGUE.
MONTAGUE. Thou villain Capulet! Hold me not, let me go.
LADY MONTAGUE. Thou shalt not stir one foot to seek a foe.

*Enter* PRINCE ESCALUS, *head of*
*Verona's government, with* ATTENDANTS.
60 ESCALUS *(sternly).* Rebellious subjects, enemies to peace,
    Profaners of this neighbor-stainèd steel—
    Will you not hear? What, ho! You men, you beasts,
    That quench the fire of your pernicious rage
    With purple fountains issuing from your veins,
65    On pain of torture, from those bloody hands
    Throw your mistempered weapons to the ground,
    And hear the sentence of your movèd prince.
    Three civil brawls, bred of an airy word
    By thee, old Capulet, and Montague,
70    Have thrice disturbed the quiet of our streets.
    If ever you disturb our streets again,
    Your lives shall pay the forfeit of the peace.[18]
    For this time, all the rest depart away.
    You, Capulet, shall go along with me;
75    And, Montague, come you this afternoon
    To know our further pleasure in this case,
    To old Freetown, our common judgment place.
    Once more, on pain of death, all men depart.
                  *(Exeunt*[19] *all but* MONTAGUE,
                LADY MONTAGUE, *and* BENVOLIO.)
MONTAGUE. Who set this ancient quarrel new abroach?[20]
80    (*To* BENVOLIO.) Speak, nephew. Were you by when it began?
BENVOLIO. Here were the servants of your adversary,
    And yours, close fighting ere I did approach.
    I drew to part them; in the instant came
    The fiery Tybalt, with his sword prepared,
85    Which, as he breathed defiance to my ears,
    He swung about his head and cut the winds,
    Who, nothing hurt withal,[21] hissed him in scorn.
    While we were interchanging thrusts and blows,

14. *bills . . . partisans,* long-
handled spears with sharp
cutting blades.

15. *gown,* dressing gown.

16. *crutch.* Lady Capulet implies that
a crutch is better suited to her aged
husband than a sword.

17. *spite,* defiance.

18. *forfeit of the peace,* penalty for disturbing the peace.

19. *Exeunt,* the plural form of
exit.

20. *set . . . new abroach,*
reopened or started again this
old quarrel.

21. *Who . . . withal,* the
winds, hurt not at all by
Tybalt's swinging of his sword.

Came more and more and fought on part and part,
Till the prince came, who parted either part.
LADY MONTAGUE. O, where is Romeo? Saw you him today?
Right glad I am he was not at this fray.
BENVOLIO. Madam, an hour before the worshiped sun
Peered forth the golden window of the east,
A troubled mind drave me to walk abroad;
Where, underneath the grove of sycamore
That westward rooteth from the city's side,
So early walking did I see your son.
Towards him I made, but he was ware of me
And stole into the covert of the wood.
I, measuring his affections[22] by my own,
That most are busied when they're most alone,
Pursued my humor,[23] not pursuing his,
And gladly shunned who gladly fled from me.
MONTAGUE. Many a morning hath he there been seen,
With tears augmenting the fresh morning's dew,
Adding to clouds more clouds with his deep sighs.
But all so soon as the all-cheering sun
Should in the farthest east begin to draw
The shady curtains from Aurora's[24] bed,
Away from light steals home my heavy[25] son,
And private in his chamber pens himself,
Shuts up his windows, locks fair daylight out,
And makes himself an artificial night.
Black and portentous must this humor prove,
Unless good counsel may the cause remove.
BENVOLIO. My noble uncle, do you know the cause?
MONTAGUE. I neither know it nor can learn of him.
BENVOLIO. Have you importuned him by any means?
MONTAGUE. Both by myself and many other friends;
But he, his own affections' counselor,
Is to himself—I will not say how true—
But to himself so secret and so close,[26]
So far from sounding and discovery,[27]
As is the bud bit with an envious[28] worm,
Ere he can spread his sweet leaves[29] to the air,
Or dedicate his beauty to the sun.
Could we but learn from whence his sorrows grow,
We would as willingly give cure as know.

*Enter* ROMEO *absorbed in thought.*
BENVOLIO. See where he comes; so please you, step aside.
I'll know his grievance or be much denied.[30]
MONTAGUE. I would thou wert so happy by thy stay[31]
To hear true shrift.[32] Come, madam, let's away.
     (*Exeunt* MONTAGUE *and* LADY MONTAGUE.)
BENVOLIO. Good morrow, cousin.[33]
ROMEO.         Is the day so young?

22. *affections,* wishes, feelings.
23. *humor,* mood, whim.

24. *Aurora,* goddess of the dawn.
25. *heavy,* sad.

26. *close,* not inclined to talk.
27. *sounding and discovery,* responding to efforts to understand his views.
28. *envious,* malicious.
29. *Ere . . . leaves,* before the bud can open its sweet leaves.

30. *be much denied.* He will find it difficult to refuse me an answer.
31. *happy by thy stay,* fortunate in your waiting.
32. *To hear true shrift,* as to hear true confession.
33. *Good morrow, cousin.* Good morning, cousin (any relative).

135  BENVOLIO. But new struck nine.
ROMEO.                                    Ay me! Sad hours seem long.
       Was that my father that went hence so fast?
BENVOLIO. It was. What sadness lengthens Romeo's hours?
ROMEO. Not having that which, having, makes them short.
BENVOLIO. In love?
140  ROMEO. Out——
BENVOLIO. Of love?
ROMEO. Out of her favor where I am in love.
BENVOLIO. Alas, that Love, so gentle in his view,
       Should be so tyrannous and rough in proof!³⁴
145  ROMEO. Alas, that Love, whose view is muffled still,³⁵
       Should, without eyes, see pathways to his will!
       Where shall we dine? O me! What fray was here?
       Yet tell me not, for I have heard it all.
       Here's much to do with hate, but more with love.
150    Why, then, O brawling love! O loving hate!
       O heavy lightness, serious vanity;³⁶
       Misshapen chaos of well-seeming forms!
       Feather of lead, bright smoke, cold fire, sick health!
       Still-waking³⁷ sleep, that is not what it is!
155    This love feel I, that feel no love in this.³⁸
       Dost thou not laugh?
BENVOLIO.                          No, coz,³⁹ I rather weep.
ROMEO. Good heart, at what?
BENVOLIO.                          At thy good heart's oppression.
ROMEO. Why, such is love's transgression.
       Griefs of mine own lie heavy in my breast,
160    Which thou wilt propagate, to have it pressed⁴⁰
       With more of thine; this love that thou hast shown
       Doth add more grief to too much of mine own.
       Farewell, my coz.
BENVOLIO.             Soft! I will go along;
       An if you leave me so, you do me wrong.
165  ROMEO. Tut, I have lost myself; I am not here.
       This is not Romeo; he's some otherwhere.
BENVOLIO. Tell me in sadness,⁴¹ who is that you love.
ROMEO. In sadness, cousin, I do love a woman.
BENVOLIO (smiling). I aimed so near when I supposed you loved.
170  ROMEO. A right good mark-man! And she's fair I love.
BENVOLIO. A right fair mark, fair coz, is soonest hit.
ROMEO. Well, in that hit you miss. She'll not be hit
       With Cupid's arrow. She hath Dian's wit;⁴²
       From Love's weak childish bow she lives unharmed.
175    She will not stay the siege of loving terms,⁴³
       Nor bide the encounter of assailing eyes;
       O, she is rich in beauty, only poor
       That, when she dies, with beauty dies her store.⁴⁴
BENVOLIO. Then she hath sworn that she will still live chaste?

34. *proof,* experience.
35. *view . . . still,* sight is blindfolded always.

36. *vanity,* frivolity.

37. *Still-waking,* always awake.
38. *that feel . . . in this,* that cannot take any pleasure in this love.
39. *coz,* a short form of *cousin.*

40. *pressed,* oppressed.

41. *sadness,* seriousness.

42. *Dian's wit,* the wisdom of the goddess Diana.
43. *She will not . . . terms.* She will not listen to avowals of love.
44. *with beauty . . . store.* She will die without children, and therefore her beauty will die with her.

ROMEO. She hath, and in that sparing makes huge waste,
    For beauty starved with her severity
    Cuts beauty off from all posterity.
    She is too fair, too wise, wisely too fair,
    To merit bliss by making me despair.
    She hath forsworn to love, and in that vow
    Do I live dead that live to tell it now.
BENVOLIO. Be ruled by me: forget to think of her.
ROMEO. O, teach me how I should forget to think!
BENVOLIO. By giving liberty unto thine eyes;
    Examine other beauties.
ROMEO.                  'Tis the way
    To call hers exquisite, in question more.[45]
    These happy masks that kiss fair ladies' brows,
    Being black, put us in mind they hide the fair;[46]
    He that is strucken blind cannot forget
    The precious treasure of his eyesight lost.
    Farewell. Thou canst not teach me to forget.
BENVOLIO. I'll pay that doctrine,[47] or else die in debt.

                                  *(Exeunt.)*

**45.** *'Tis the way . . . more.* To make her beauty the subject of more discussion is only to make me more aware of how exquisite her beauty is.
**46.** *These happy masks . . . fair.* The black masks that women sometimes wear in public (a common practice in Shakespeare's time) remind us of the beauty they hide.
**47.** *pay that doctrine,* teach Romeo to forget.

## CONSIDERING THE PROLOGUE AND SCENE 1

**1. (a)** Name the heads of the two households, or families, mentioned in the first line of the Prologue. **(b)** Identify the following characters who appear in Scene 1: Tybalt, Benvolio, Romeo, Escalus.

**2. (a)** What atmosphere does the Prologue suggest will be most strongly stressed in the play? **(b)** Choose words, phrases, or sentences from the Prologue that most clearly indicate this atmosphere.

**3. (a)** What threat does Prince Escalus make against the "enemies of peace"? **(b)** Do you think this threat will or will not end the conflict between the feuding families? State your reasons.

**4. (a)** What is Romeo's mood in this first scene and what has caused it? **(b)** How, according to Benvolio, might Romeo alter that mood? **(c)** How does Romeo react to Benvolio's suggestion? Why?

*Scene 2: A street in Verona.*

                   *Enter* CAPULET, PARIS, *and* SERVANT.
CAPULET *(addressing* PARIS*)*. But Montague is bound[1] as well as I,
    In penalty alike; and 'tis not hard, I think,
    For men so old as we to keep the peace.
PARIS. Of honorable reckoning[2] are you both;
    And pity 'tis you lived at odds so long.
    But now, my lord, what say you to my suit?
CAPULET. But saying o'er what I have said before:
    My child is yet a stranger in the world;
    She hath not seen the change of fourteen years.

**1.** *bound,* obliged to keep the peace.

**2.** *reckoning,* reputation.

10 Let two more summers wither in their pride,
Ere we may think her ripe to be a bride.
The earth hath swallowed all my hopes but she;
She is the hopeful lady of my earth.[3]
But woo her, gentle Paris, get her heart;
15 My will to her consent is but a part.[4]
An she agree, within her scope of choice
Lies my consent and fair according voice.
This night I hold an old accustomed feast,
Whereto I have invited many a guest,
20 Such as I love, and you, among the store,
One more, most welcome, makes my number more.
At my poor house look to behold this night
Earth-treading stars that make dark heaven light:
Such comfort as do lusty young men feel
25 When well-appareled April on the heel
Of limping winter treads, even such delight
Among fresh female buds shall you this night
Inherit[5] at my house; hear all, all see,
And like her most whose merit most shall be.
30 Come, go with me. *(To* SERVANT, *giving him a paper.)* Go,
    sirrah,[6] trudge about
Through fair Verona; find those persons out
Whose names are written there, and to them say
My house and welcome on their pleasure stay.
                    *(Exeunt* CAPULET *and* PARIS.)
SERVANT *(peering at the paper).* I am sent to find those persons
35 whose names are here writ, and can never find what names
the writing person hath here writ. I must to the learned!

                    Enter BENVOLIO *and* ROMEO.
BENVOLIO. Tut, man, one fire burns out another's burning,
    One pain is lessened by another's anguish.
    Take thou some new infection to thy eye,
40 And the rank poison of the old will die.
ROMEO. Your plantain leaf[7] is excellent for that.
BENVOLIO. For what, I pray thee?
ROMEO.                    For your broken shin.
BENVOLIO. Why, Romeo, art thou mad?
ROMEO. Not mad, but bound more than a madman is;
45 Shut up in prison, kept without my food,
    Whipped and tormented and—God-den,[8] good fellow.
SERVANT. God gi' god-den. I pray, sir, can you read?
ROMEO. Ay, mine own fortune in my misery.
SERVANT. Perhaps you have learned it without book; but, I pray,
50 can you read anything you see?
ROMEO. Ay, if I know the letters and the language.
SERVANT. Ye say honestly; rest you merry![9]
                    *(He thinks* ROMEO *is not taking
                    him seriously, and starts to leave.)*

3. *hopeful lady of my earth,* center of my existence.

4. *My will . . . part.* My wishes are of secondary importance to her consent.

5. *Inherit,* enjoy.

6. *sirrah,* customary form of address to servants.

7. *plantain leaf,* used as a salve for bruises.

8. *God-den,* a greeting like "good evening"; literally, "God give you a good evening."

9. *rest you merry!* May you continue happy.

ROMEO. Stay, fellow; I can read. *(He reads the paper.)*
   "Signior Martino and his wife and daughters; County Anselme
   and his beauteous sisters; the lady widow of Vitruvio; Signior
   Placentio and his lovely nieces; Mercutio and his brother
   Valentine; mine uncle Capulet, his wife and daughters; my
   fair niece Rosaline; Livia; Signior Valentio and his cousin
   Tybalt; Lucio and the lively Helena."
                              *(He returns the paper to the* SERVANT.)
   A fair assembly; whither should they come?
SERVANT. Up.
ROMEO. Whither?
SERVANT. To supper; to our house.
ROMEO. Whose house?
SERVANT. My master's.
ROMEO. Indeed, I should have asked you that before.
SERVANT. Now I'll tell you without asking. My master is the great
   rich Capulet; and if you be not of the house of Montagues, I
   pray come and crush a cup[10] of wine. Rest you merry!
                                                       *(Exit.)*

BENVOLIO. At this same ancient[11] feast of Capulet's
   Sups the fair Rosaline whom thou so lovest,
   With all the admirèd beauties of Verona.
   Go thither, and, with unattainted[12] eye,
   Compare her face with some that I shall show,
   And I will make thee think thy swan a crow.
ROMEO. One fairer than my love! The all-seeing sun
   Ne'er saw her match since first the world begun.
BENVOLIO. Tut, you saw her fair, none else being by,
   But weigh your lady against some other maid
   That I will show you shining at this feast,
   And she shall scant show well that now shows best.
ROMEO. I'll go along, no such sight to be shown,
   But to rejoice in splendor of mine own.[13]
                                                    *(Exeunt.)*

10. *crush a cup*, have a drink; a slang term like "crack a bottle" today.

11. *ancient*, customary.

12. *unattainted*, unprejudiced, impartial.

13. *splendor of mine own*, the beauty of the lady I love.

## CONSIDERING ACT ONE, SCENE 2

1. (a) In his talk with Capulet, what proposal does Paris make?
(b) What is Capulet's reaction to that proposal?

2. What do you think Shakespeare's purpose was in having the
Capulets plan a party?

3. (a) Quote arguments used by Benvolio in attempting to persuade
Romeo to attend the party. (b) What reason does Romeo give for deciding to go to the party after all?

*Scene 3: A room in Capulet's house.*

                       *Enter* LADY CAPULET *and* NURSE.
LADY CAPULET. Nurse, where's my daughter? Call her forth to me.

NURSE. I'll bid her come. What, lamb! What, ladybird!
 God forbid! Where's this girl? What, Juliet!

*Enter* JULIET.

JULIET. How now! Who calls?
5 NURSE. Your mother.
JULIET. Madam, I am here. What is your will?
LADY CAPULET. This is the matter:—Nurse, give leave[1] awhile,
 We must talk in secret.—Nurse, come back again;
 I have remembered me, thou's[2] hear our counsel.
10 Thou know'st my daughter's of a pretty age.
NURSE. Faith, I can tell her age unto an hour.
LADY CAPULET. She's not fourteen.
NURSE.                    I'll lay fourteen of my teeth—
 And yet, to my teen[3] be it spoken, I have but four—
 She is not fourteen. How long is it now
15 To Lammastide?[4]
LADY CAPULET.       A fortnight and odd days.
NURSE. Even or odd, of all days in the year,
 Come Lammas Eve at night shall she be fourteen.
 Susan and she—God rest all Christian souls!—
 Were of an age. Well, Susan is with God;
20 She was too good for me. But, as I said,
 On Lammas Eve at night shall she be fourteen;
 That shall she, marry; I remember it well.
 'Tis since the earthquake[5] now eleven years;
 And she was weaned—I never shall forget it—
25 Of all the days of the year, upon that day.
 My lord and you were then at Mantua:—
 Nay, I do bear a brain;[6] but, as I said,
 Since that time it is eleven years;
 For then she could stand alone. Nay, by the rood,[7]
30 She could have run and waddled all about,
 For even the day before, she broke her brow.[8]
 And then my husband—God be with his soul!
 A'[9] was a merry man—took up the child.
 "Yea," quoth he, "dost thou fall upon thy face?
35 Thou wilt fall backward when thou hast more wit,
 Wilt thou not, Jule?" and, by my holidame,[10]
 The pretty wretch left crying and said "Ay."
 To see, now, how a jest shall come about!
 I warrant, an I should live a thousand years,
40 I never should forget it: "Wilt thou not, Jule?" quoth he;
 And, pretty fool, it stinted[11] and said "Ay."
LADY CAPULET. Enough of this; I pray thee, hold thy peace.
NURSE. Yes, madam; yet I cannot choose but laugh
 To think it should leave crying and say "Ay."
45 JULIET. And stint thou, too, I pray thee, Nurse, say I.
NURSE. Peace, I have done. God mark thee to His grace!
 Thou wast the prettiest babe that e'er I nursed;

1. *give leave,* leave us alone.

2. *thou's,* thou shalt.

3. *teen,* sorrow, grief.

4. *Lammastide,* August 1.

5. *earthquake,* possibly a reference to a famous earthquake in 1580— eleven years earlier than it is thought Shakespeare may have been writing the play (1591).
6. *bear a brain,* have a good brain or memory.
7. *rood,* Holy Cross.

8. *even . . . brow,* just the day before she cut her forehead.
9. *A',* he.

10. *by my holidame,* a mild oath.

11. *stinted,* stopped crying.

An I might live to see thee married once,
I have my wish.
LADY CAPULET. Marry, that "marry" is the very theme
I came to talk of. Tell me, daughter Juliet,
How stands your disposition to be married?
JULIET. It is an honor that I dream not of.
LADY CAPULET. Well, think of marriage now; by my count,
I was your mother much upon these years[12]
That you are now a maid. Thus, then, in brief:
The valiant Paris seeks you for his love.
NURSE. A man, young lady! Lady, such a man
As all the world—why, he's a man of wax.[13]
LADY CAPULET. Verona's summer hath not such a flower.
NURSE. Nay, he's a flower; in faith, a very flower.
LADY CAPULET (to JULIET). What say you? Can you love the
gentleman?
This night you shall behold him at our feast.
Read o'er the volume of young Paris' face
And find delight writ there with beauty's pen;
Speak briefly; can you like of Paris' love?
JULIET. I'll look to like, if looking liking move.[14]

*Enter a* SERVANT.

SERVANT. Madam, the guests are come, supper served up, you
called, my young lady asked for, the nurse cursed in the
pantry, and everything in extremity. I must hence to wait;
I beseech you, follow straight.[15]
LADY CAPULET. We follow thee. (*Exit* SERVANT.) Juliet, the county
stays.[16]
NURSE. Go girl, seek happy days.                    (*Exeunt.*)

12. *much upon these years,* almost at the same age.

13. *a man of wax,* as hand-some as if modeled in wax.

14. *I'll look . . . move.* I am ready to look on him favorably—if mere eyesight can inspire liking.

15. *straight,* immediately.

16. *the county stays.* Count Paris awaits you.

## CONSIDERING ACT ONE, SCENE 3

1. (a) What subject does Lady Capulet want to take up with Juliet?
(b) How is their conversation postponed for a considerable time?

2. Which of these terms accurately describe the nurse: *garrulous,
refined, reserved, ready to give advice*? Point out supporting evidence
for your choices.

3. What is Juliet's attitude toward marrying Paris?

*Scene 4: A street in Verona that same evening.*

*Enter* ROMEO, MERCUTIO, BENVOLIO, *with five or
six* MASKERS, TORCHBEARERS, *and* OTHERS.
ROMEO. What, shall we on without apology?
BENVOLIO. We'll measure them a measure,[1] and be gone.
ROMEO. Give me a torch; I am not for this ambling;[2]
Being but heavy, I will bear the light.

1. *measure . . . measure,* perform a dance.
2. *ambling,* dancing in an affected manner.

5 MERCUTIO. Nay, gentle Romeo, we must have you dance.
ROMEO. Not I, believe me. You have dancing shoes
   With nimble soles; I have a soul of lead
   So stakes me to the ground I cannot move.
MERCUTIO. You are a lover; borrow Cupid's wings,
10  And soar with them above a common bound.³   3. *bound,* leap.
ROMEO. I am too sore enpierced with his shaft
   To soar with his light feathers; and so bound,
   I cannot bound a pitch⁴ above dull woe.   4. *pitch,* any distance.
   Under love's heavy burden do I sink.
15 MERCUTIO. And, to sink in it, should you burden love—
   Too great oppression for a tender thing.
ROMEO *(sighing).* Is love a tender thing? It is too rough,
   Too rude, too boisterous, and it pricks like thorn.
MERCUTIO. If love be rough with you, be rough with love.
20  Give me a case⁵ to put my visage in:   5. *case,* mask.
   A visor for a visor!⁶ *(Puts on a mask.)* What care I   6. *A visor . . . visor,* a mask
   What curious eye doth quote⁷ deformities?   for an ugly, masklike face.
BENVOLIO. Come, knock and enter; and no sooner in   7. *quote,* take notice of.
   But every man betake him to his legs.
25 ROMEO. A torch for me. Let wantons light of heart
   Tickle the senseless rushes⁸ with their heels;   8. *senseless rushes,* unfeeling
   For I am proverbed with a grandsire phrase;⁹   fibers used as floor coverings.
   I'll be a candle-holder,¹⁰ and look on.   9. *proverbed . . . phrase,*
MERCUTIO. Come, we burn daylight,¹¹ ho!   taught by an old saying.
30 ROMEO. Nay, that's not so.   10. *candle-holder,* spectator.
MERCUTIO.               I mean, sir, in delay   11. *burn daylight,* to light a
   We waste our lights in vain, like lamps by day.   candle while the sun is shin-
ROMEO. We mean well in going to this mask, sir;   ing; that is, to waste
   But 'tis no wit to go.   time, as Mercutio explains.
MERCUTIO.            Why, may one ask?
ROMEO. I dreamed a dream tonight.¹²   12. *tonight,* last night.
MERCUTIO.                     And so did I.
35 ROMEO. Well, what was yours?
MERCUTIO.                  That dreamers often lie.
ROMEO. In bed asleep while they do dream things true.
MERCUTIO. O, then, I see Queen Mab¹³ hath been with you.   13. *Queen Mab,* the fairy
   She is the fairies' midwife, and she comes   queen.
   In shape no bigger than an agate stone
40  On the forefinger of an alderman,
   Drawn with a team of little atomies¹⁴   14. *atomies,* tiny creatures.
   Athwart men's noses as they lie asleep;
   Her wagon spokes made of long spinners'¹⁵ legs,   15. *spinners',* spiders'.
   The cover of the wings of grasshoppers,
45  The traces of the smallest spider's web,
   The collars of the moonshine's watery beams,   16. *film,* delicate, light thread.
   Her whip of cricket's bone, the lash of film,¹⁶   17. *wagoner,* coachman.
   Her wagoner¹⁷ a small gray-coated gnat,   18. *worm . . . maid.* It was
   Not half so big as a round little worm   popularly believed that worms
50  Pricked from the lazy finger of a maid.¹⁸   breed in the fingers of the idle.

Her chariot is an empty hazel nut
Made by the joiner squirrel or old grub,
Time out o' mind the fairies' coachmakers.
And in this state[19] she gallops night by night
55  Through lovers' brains, and then they dream of love;
O'er lawyers' fingers, who straight dream on fees;
O'er ladies' lips who straight on kisses dream,
Which oft the angry Mab with blisters plagues,
Because their breaths with sweetmeats tainted are.
60  Sometime she gallops o'er a courtier's nose,
And then dreams he of smelling out a suit;[20]
Sometime she driveth o'er a soldier's neck,
And then dreams he of cutting foreign throats,
Of breaches, ambuscadoes, Spanish blades,[21]
65  Of healths five-fathom deep; and then anon
Drums in his ear, at which he starts and wakes,
And being thus frighted swears a prayer or two
And sleeps again. This is that very Mab
That plaits the manes of horses in the night,
70  And bakes the elf locks in foul sluttish hairs,[22]
Which once untangled much misfortune bodes;
This is she——
ROMEO.           Peace, peace, Mercutio, peace!
Thou talk'st of nothing.
MERCUTIO.                  True, I talk of dreams,
Which are the children of an idle brain,
75  Begot of nothing but vain fantasy,
Which is as thin of substance as the air
And more inconstant than the wind, who woos
Even now the frozen bosom of the north,
And, being angered, puffs away from thence,
80  Turning his face to the dew-dropping south.
BENVOLIO. This wind you talk of blows us from ourselves;
Supper is done, and we shall come too late.
ROMEO. I fear, too early; for my mind misgives
Some consequence yet hanging in the stars[23]
85  Shall bitterly begin his fearful date[24]
With this night's revels and expire[25] the term
Of a despisèd life closed in my breast
By some vile forfeit of untimely death.
But He that hath the steerage of my course,
90  Direct my sail! On, lusty gentlemen.

                    (*Exeunt.*)

19. *state*, pomp, dignity.

20. *smelling out a suit*, seeing an opportunity to gain royal favor.
21. *ambuscadoes, Spanish blades*, surprise attacks with swords made of fine steel from Toledo, in Spain.

22. *bakes . . . hairs*, mats together and tangles the hair.

23. *misgives . . . stars*, forebodes some future misfortune not yet determined.
24. *his fearful date*, its dreaded time.
25. *expire*, bring to an end.

## CONSIDERING ACT ONE, SCENE 4

1. Although Mercutio and Romeo are close friends, they differ strongly in their attitudes toward life. How are their contrasting moods brought out in this scene?

**2. (a)** What does Mercutio's long Queen Mab speech tell about his character? **(b)** Does Mercutio believe that men rule their own destinies entirely?

*Scene 5: A spacious room in Capulet's house.*

MUSICIANS *waiting. Enter* CAPULET, LADY
CAPULET, *with* JULIET, *the* NURSE, TYBALT, *and
others of the* CAPULET *clan, mingling with,
and talking to, the* GUESTS *and the* MASKERS.
CAPULET. *(As he speaks, the conversation dies down.)* Welcome,
   gentlemen! Ladies that have their toes
Unplagued with corns will have a bout[1] with you.
Ah ha, my mistresses! Which of you all
Will now deny to dance? She that makes dainty,[2]
5   She, I'll swear, hath corns; am I come near ye now?[3]
Welcome, gentlemen! I have seen the day
That I have worn a visor and could tell
A whispering tale in a fair lady's ear,
Such as would please. 'Tis gone, 'tis gone, 'tis gone.
10   You are welcome, gentlemen! Come, musicians, play.
A hall, a hall![4] Give room, and foot it, girls.
               *(Music plays, and they dance.)*
*(To* SERVANTS.*)* More light, you knaves, and turn the tables up,[5]
And quench the fire, the room is grown too hot.
*(To an elderly kinsman.)* Nay, sit, nay, sit, good cousin Capulet,
15   For you and I are past our dancing days.
How long is 't now since last yourself and I
Were in a mask?
SECOND CAPULET.   By'r lady,[6] thirty years.
CAPULET. What, man! 'Tis not so much, 'tis not so much.
'Tis since the nuptial of Lucentio,
20   Come Pentecost as quickly as it will,
  Some five and twenty years, and then we masked.
SECOND CAPULET. 'Tis more, 'tis more, his son is elder, sir;
His son is thirty.
CAPULET.         Will you tell me that?
His son was but a ward two years ago.
      *(*ROMEO, *who has been trying to locate* ROSALINE,
        *catches a fleeting glimpse of* JULIET, *whose
      beauty dazzles him. He halts a passing* SERVANT.*)*
25 ROMEO. What lady is that, which doth enrich the hand
  Of yonder knight?
SERVANT. I know not, sir.[7]
ROMEO. O, she doth teach the torches to burn bright!
It seems she hangs upon the cheek of night
30   Like a rich jewel in an Ethiope's ear;
Beauty too rich for use, for earth too dear![8]
So shows a snowy dove trooping with crows,

1. *have a bout,* dance a turn.

2. *makes dainty,* affectedly hesitates to dance.

3. *am . . . now?* Have I hit home to the truth?

4. *A hall, a hall!* Make room!

5. *turn the tables up.* The tables were flat leaves hinged together and placed on trestles. When they were folded, they took little space.

6. *By'r lady,* by the Virgin Mary; a mild oath.

7. *I know not, sir.* The servant has been hired for the party and does not know Juliet.

8. *dear,* precious.

As yonder lady o'er her fellows shows.
The measure done, I'll watch her place of stand,
And, touching hers, make blessèd my rude hand.
Did my heart love till now? Forswear it, sight!
For I ne'er saw true beauty till this night.

TYBALT (*who has been standing near* ROMEO). This by his voice,
    should be a Montague.
Fetch me my rapier, boy. What, dares the slave
Come hither, covered with an antic face,
To fleer[9] and scorn at our solemnity?[10]
Now, by the stock and honor of my kin,
To strike him dead I hold it not a sin.

CAPULET (*overhearing* TYBALT). Why, how now, kinsman!
    Wherefore storm you so?

TYBALT. Uncle, this is a Montague, our foe,
A villain that is hither come in spite,
To scorn at our solemnity this night.

CAPULET. Young Romeo, is it?

TYBALT.              'Tis he, that villain Romeo.

CAPULET. Content thee, gentle coz, let him alone;
He bears him like a portly[11] gentleman;
And, to say truth, Verona brags of him
To be a virtuous and well-governed youth.
I would not for the wealth of all the town
Here in my house do him disparagement;
Therefore be patient, take no note of him.
It is my will, the which if thou respect,
Show a fair presence and put off these frowns,
An ill-beseeming semblance for a feast.

TYBALT. It fits when such a villain is a guest;
I'll not endure him.

CAPULET (*sternly*).     He shall be endured.
What, goodman boy![12] I say, he shall. Go to;[13]
Am I the master here, or you? Go to.
You'll not endure him! God shall mend my soul![14]
You'll make a mutiny among my guests!

TYBALT (*grumbling*). Why, Uncle, 'tis a shame.

CAPULET.                Go to, go to.
You are a saucy boy; is't so, indeed?
This trick may chance to scathe[15] you, I know what.
You must contrary me![16] Marry, 'tis time.
(*To* GUESTS.) Well said, my hearts![17] (*To* TYBALT.) You are a
    princox;[18] go.
Be quiet, or—— (*To* SERVANTS.) More light, more light!
    (*To* TYBALT.) For shame!
I'll make you quiet. (*To* GUESTS.) What, cheerly, my hearts!

TYBALT. Patience perforce[19] with willful choler meeting
Makes my flesh tremble in their different greeting.[20]
I will withdraw; but this intrusion shall,
Now seeming sweet, convert to bitter gall.     (*Exit.*)

9. *fleer*, sneer.
10. *solemnity*, celebration.

11. *portly*, with dignity.

12. *goodman boy*, a scornful term.
13. *Go to*, come now (a reproof).
14. *God . . . soul!* God save me!

15. *scathe*, injure.
16. *You must contrary me!* You insist on opposing my wishes!
17. *Well said, my hearts!* You have danced well, good fellows!
18. *princox*, a saucy young-ster.

19. *Patience perforce*, imposed patience or restraint.
20. *different greeting*, opposition.

ROMEO (*to* JULIET.) If I profane with my unworthiest hand
This holy shrine, the gentle fine[21] is this:
My lips, two blushing pilgrims, ready stand
To smooth that rough touch with a tender kiss.

80 JULIET. Good pilgrim,[22] you do wrong your hand too much,
Which mannerly devotion shows in this;
For saints have hands that pilgrims' hands do touch,
And palm to palm is holy palmers' kiss.

ROMEO. Have not saints lips, and holy palmers too?

85 JULIET. Ay, pilgrim, lips that they must use in prayer.

ROMEO. O, then, dear saint, let lips do what hands do;
They pray, grant thou, lest faith turn to despair.

JULIET. Saints do not move, though grant for prayers' sake.

ROMEO. Then move not, while my prayer's effect I take.

90 Thus from my lips, by yours, my sin is purged.

(*His lips touch hers.*)

JULIET. Then have my lips the sin that they have took.

ROMEO. Sin from my lips? O trespass sweetly urged!
Give me my sin again.

JULIET.                              You kiss by the book.[23]

NURSE (*who has made her way through the crowds to find*
JULIET). Madam, your mother craves a word with you.

95 ROMEO (*aside to the* NURSE). What is her mother?

NURSE (*aside to* ROMEO).                    Marry, bachelor,
Her mother is the lady of the house,
And a good lady, and a wise and virtuous.
I nursed her daughter, that you talked withal;[24]
I tell you, he that can lay hold of her
100 Shall have the chinks.[25]

ROMEO.                    Is she a Capulet?
O dear[26] account! My life is my foe's debt.[27]

BENVOLIO (*coming forward*). Away, be gone; the sport is at the
best.

ROMEO. Ay, so I fear; the more is my unrest.

CAPULET (*addressing the guests who are about to take their
leave*). Nay, gentlemen, prepare not to be gone;
105 We have a trifling foolish banquet towards.[28]
Is it e'en so? Why, then, I thank you all;
I thank you, honest gentlemen; good night.
(*To a* SERVANT.) More torches here! Come on, then, let's to bed.
Ah, sirrah, by my fay,[29] it waxes late;
110 I'll to my rest.

(BENVOLIO *and* ROMEO *join the departing
guests;* NURSE *stands near* JULIET.)

JULIET. Come hither, Nurse. What is yond gentleman?

NURSE. The son and heir of old Tiberio.

JULIET. What's he that now is going out of door?

NURSE. Marry, that, I think, be young Petrucio.

115 JULIET. What's he that follows there, that would not dance?

NURSE. I know not. (*The* NURSE *does know, but tries to keep* JULIET

21. *gentle fine*, mild penance.

22. *pilgrim*. Romeo was masquerading as a palmer— a pilgrim who had visited the Holy Land.

23. *by the book*, according to rule.

24. *withal*, with.

25. *chinks*, money (inherited by Juliet from her father).

26. *dear*, costly.

27. *my foe's debt*, a debt due my foe, which he may or may not take, as he wishes.

28. *foolish banquet towards*, a simple dessert about to be served.

29. *fay*, faith.

*from learning that the man is* ROMEO—*and a* MONTAGUE.)
JULIET. Go, ask his name. If he is married,
My grave is like to be my wedding bed.
NURSE (*seeing that it is useless to hide* ROMEO's *identity*).
His name is Romeo, and a Montague,
The only son of your great enemy.
JULIET. My only love sprung from my only hate!
Too early seen unknown, and known too late!
Prodigious[30] birth of love it is to me,
That I must love a loathèd enemy.
NURSE. What's this? What's this?
JULIET.                         A rhyme I learned even now
Of one I danced withal.

                    (*A call off-stage: "Juliet."*)

NURSE.                 Anon, anon!
Come, let's away; the strangers all are gone.

                              (*Exeunt.*)

**30.** *Prodigious*, suggesting bad luck.

## CONSIDERING ACT ONE, SCENE 5

1. (a) What is the general atmosphere as the scene opens? (b) How is that atmosphere affected by Tybalt's attitude toward Romeo? (c) What is the atmosphere as the scene ends?

2. In line 36, page 302, Romeo asks, "Did my heart love till now?" How would you answer his question? Give reasons for your answer.

3. Having fallen deeply in love, Romeo and Juliet kiss and part. Then each makes a surprising discovery. (a) What is that discovery? (b) How does the discovery affect both Romeo and Juliet?

## LOOKING BACK—AND AHEAD

1. Make a brief outline of the most important events that have taken place in Act One.

2. Before starting to read Act Two, list several things that you think may happen now.

# Act Two

*Scene 1: A lane outside the wall of Capulet's orchard.*

*Enter* ROMEO.

ROMEO. Can I go forward when my heart is here?
  Turn back, dull earth,[1] and find thy center[2] out.

  *(He climbs the wall and leaps down within it.)*

*Enter* BENVOLIO *and* MERCUTIO.

BENVOLIO *(calling to the hidden* ROMEO*).* Romeo! My cousin
    Romeo!
MERCUTIO.      He is wise,
  And, on my life, hath stolen him home to bed.
5 BENVOLIO. He ran this way, and leaped this orchard wall.
  Call, good Mercutio.
MERCUTIO *(jestingly).*   Nay, I'll conjure too.
  Romeo! Humors![3] Madman! Passion! Lover!
  Appear thou in the likeness of a sigh;
  Speak but one rhyme, and I am satisfied;
10 Cry but "Ay me"; pronounce but "love" and "dove."
  *(To* BENVOLIO.*)* He heareth not, he stirreth not, he moveth not;
  The ape[4] is dead, and I must conjure him.
  *(Calls jestingly to* ROMEO.*)* I conjure thee by Rosaline's bright
    eyes,
  By her high forehead and her scarlet lip,
15 That in thy likeness thou appear to us!
BENVOLIO. An if he hear thee, thou wilt anger him.
MERCUTIO. This cannot anger him; my invocation
  Is fair and honest,[5] and in his mistress' name
  I conjure only but to raise up him.
20 BENVOLIO. Come, he hath hid himself among these trees,
  To be consorted with the humorous night;[6]
  Blind is his love and best befits the dark.
MERCUTIO. If love be blind, love cannot hit the mark.
  Romeo, good night. I'll to my truckle bed;[7]
25 This field bed[8] is too cold for me to sleep.
  Come, shall we go?
BENVOLIO.            Go, then; for 'tis in vain
  To seek him here that means not to be found.

*(Exeunt.)*

---

1. *dull earth,* Romeo himself.
2. *thy center,* Juliet.

3. *Humors!* Romantic whims.

4. *ape,* used as a term of
endearment.

5. *honest,* honorable.

6. *consorted . . . night,* associated with the moist night.

7. *truckle bed,* a small bed
that can be run under a larger
one.

8. *field bed,* the ground.

---

## CONSIDERING ACT TWO, SCENE 1

**1.** Why does Romeo hide from Benvolio and Mercutio?

**2.** Do you think Benvolio and Mercutio realize that Romeo has
found a new love? Quote lines to support your answer.

*Scene 2: A beautiful orchard in the Capulets' grounds, with a balcony of the house prominently placed outside Juliet's bedroom.*

Enter ROMEO.

ROMEO. He jests at scars that never felt a wound.[1]
*(Catching sight of* JULIET *at her dimly lighted window.)*
But soft, what light through yonder window breaks?
It is the east, and Juliet is the sun.
Arise, fair sun, and kill the envious moon,
5  Who is already sick and pale with grief,
That thou her maid art far more fair than she.
Be not her maid, since she is envious.

JULIET steps out onto the balcony.

It is my lady. O, it is my love!
O, that she knew she were!
10  She speaks, yet she says nothing. What of that?
Her eye discourses; I will answer it.
I am too bold, 'tis not to me she speaks;
Two of the fairest stars in all the heaven,
Having some business, do entreat her eyes
15  To twinkle in their spheres[2] till they return.
What if her eyes were there, they in her head?
The brightness of her cheek would shame those stars
As daylight doth a lamp; her eyes in heaven
Would through the airy region stream so bright
20  That birds would sing and think it were not night.
See how she leans her cheek upon her hand!
O, that I were a glove upon that hand,
That I might touch that cheek!
JULIET. Ay me!
ROMEO. She speaks.
O, speak again, bright angel, for thou art
25  As glorious to this night, being o'er my head,
As is a wingèd messenger of heaven
Unto the white-upturnèd wondering eyes
Of mortals that fall back to gaze on him
When he bestrides the lazy-pacing clouds
30  And sails upon the bosom of the air.
JULIET *(unaware that she is being overheard).* O Romeo, Romeo,
    wherefore art thou Romeo?
Deny thy father and refuse thy name;
Or, if thou wilt not, be but sworn my love,
And I'll no longer be a Capulet.
35 ROMEO *(aside).* Shall I hear more, or shall I speak at this?
JULIET. 'Tis but thy name that is my enemy;
Thou art thyself, though not a Montague.[3]
What's Montague? It is nor hand nor foot,
Nor arm, nor face, nor any other part

**1.** *He jests . . . wound.* Romeo has overheard the jests made by Mercutio, who, Romeo says, has never known the pangs of love.

**2.** *spheres,* the hollow, transparent globes in which, it was believed, the stars and other planets were set.

**3.** *though . . . Montague,* even if you were not a Montague.

40  Belonging to a man. O, be some other name!
    What's in a name? That which we call a rose
    By any other name would smell as sweet;
    So Romeo would, were he not Romeo called,
    Retain that dear perfection which he owes[4]   **4.** *owes,* owns.
45  Without that title. Romeo, doff thy name,
    And for that name, which is no part of thee,
    Take all myself.
    ROMEO (*speaking loudly enough to be heard by* JULIET).
                    I take thee at thy word.
    Call me but love, and I'll be new baptized;
    Henceforth I never will be Romeo.
50  JULIET. What man art thou that thus bescreened in night
    So stumblest on my counsel?[5]   **5.** *counsel,* secret thoughts.
    ROMEO.                    By a name
    I know not how to tell thee who I am.
    My name, dear saint, is hateful to myself,
    Because it is an enemy to thee;
55  Had I it written, I would tear the word.
    JULIET. My ears have not yet drunk a hundred words
    Of thy tongue's utterance, yet I know the sound.
    Art thou not Romeo and a Montague?
    ROMEO. Neither, fair saint, if either thee dislike.
60  JULIET. How camest thou hither, tell me, and wherefore?
    The orchard walls are high and hard to climb,
    And the place death, considering who thou art,
    If any of my kinsmen find thee here.
    ROMEO. With love's light wings did I o'erperch[6] these walls;   **6.** *o'erperch,* fly over and perch beyond.
65  For stony limits cannot hold love out,
    And what love can do, that dares love attempt;
    Therefore thy kinsmen are no let[7] to me.   **7.** *let,* hindrance.
    JULIET. If they do see thee, they will murder thee.
    ROMEO. Alack, there lies more peril in thine eye
70  Than twenty of their swords; look thou but sweet,
    And I am proof[8] against their enmity.   **8.** *proof,* safeguarded by armor.
    JULIET. I would not for the world they saw thee here.
    ROMEO. I have night's cloak to hide me from their sight;
    And but thou love me,[9] let them find me here.   **9.** *but thou love me,* unless you love me.
75  My life were better ended by their hate
    Than death prorogued,[10] wanting of[11] thy love.   **10.** *prorogued,* postponed.
                                                          **11.** *wanting of,* lacking.
    JULIET. By whose direction found'st thou out this place?
    ROMEO. By love, who first did prompt me to inquire;
    He lent me counsel and I lent him eyes.
80  I am no pilot; yet, wert thou as far
    As that vast shore washed with the farthest sea,
    I would adventure for such merchandise.
    JULIET. Thou know'st the mask of night is on my face,
    Else would a maiden blush bepaint my cheek
85  For that which thou hast heard me speak tonight.   **12.** *Fain,* gladly.
    Fain[12] would I dwell on form,[13] fain, fain deny   **13.** *dwell on form,* stick to formalities.

What I have spoke; but farewell compliment![14]
Dost thou love me? I know thou will say "Ay,"
And I will take thy word. Yet, if thou swear'st,
90 Thou mayst prove false; at lovers' perjuries,
They say, Jove[15] laughs. O gentle Romeo,
If thou dost love, pronounce it faithfully;
Or if thou think'st I am too quickly won,
I'll frown and be perverse and say thee nay,
95 So thou wilt woo; but else, not for the world.
In truth, fair Montague, I am too fond,[16]
And therefore thou mayst think my 'havior light.
But trust me, gentleman, I'll prove more true
Than those that have more cunning to be strange.[17]
100 I should have been more strange, I must confess,
But that thou overheard'st, ere I was ware,
My true love's passion; therefore pardon me,
And not impute this yielding to light love,
Which the dark night hath so discovered.[18]
105 ROMEO. Lady, by yonder blessèd moon I swear
    That tips with silver all these fruit tree tops——
JULIET. O, swear not by the moon, the inconstant moon,
    That monthly changes in her circled orb,
    Lest that thy love prove likewise variable.
110 ROMEO. What shall I swear by?
JULIET.                          Do not swear at all;
    Or, if thou wilt, swear by thy gracious self,
    Which is the god of my idolatry,
    And I'll believe thee.
ROMEO.                 If my heart's dear love——
JULIET. Well, do not swear. Although I joy in thee,
115 I have no joy of this contract tonight;
    It is too rash, too unadvised,[19] too sudden,
    Too like the lightning, which doth cease to be
    Ere one can say "It lightens." Sweet, good night!
    This bud of love, by summer's ripening breath,
120 May prove a beauteous flower when next we meet.
    Good night, good night! As sweet repose and rest
    Come to thy heart as that within my breast.
ROMEO. O, wilt thou leave me so unsatisfied?
JULIET. What satisfaction canst thou have tonight?
125 ROMEO. The exchange of thy love's faithful vow for mine.
JULIET. I gave thee mine before thou didst request it,
    And yet I would it were to give again.
ROMEO. Wouldst thou withdraw it? For what purpose, love?
JULIET. But to be frank,[20] and give it thee again.
130 And yet I wish but for the thing I have.
    My bounty is as boundless as the sea,
    My love as deep; the more I give to thee,
    The more I have, for both are infinite.
              (NURSE calls "Juliet" from inside the bedroom.)

14. *compliment*, ceremony, formal manners.

15. *Jove*, ruler of the gods and men.

16. *fond*, foolish.

17. *strange*, reserved, distant.

18. *discovered*, revealed.

19. *unadvised*, heedless.

20. *frank*, generous.

I hear some noise within; dear love, adieu!
135 Anon, good Nurse! Sweet Montague, be true.
Stay but a little, I will come again.
                    (JULIET *goes into her bedroom.*)
ROMEO. O blessèd, blessèd night! I am afeard,
  Being in night, all this is but a dream,
  Too flattering-sweet to be substantial.


                    JULIET *returns to the balcony.*
140 JULIET. Three words, dear Romeo, and good night indeed.
  If that thy bent of love[21] be honorable,
  Thy purpose marriage, send me word tomorrow,
  By one that I'll procure to come to thee,
  Where and what time thou wilt perform the rite;
145 And all my fortunes at thy foot I'll lay
  And follow thee my lord throughout the world.
NURSE *(within the bedroom).* Madam!
JULIET. I come, anon.—But if thou meanest not well,
  I do beseech thee——
NURSE *(within and more persistently).* Madam!
JULIET.                        By and by[22] I come—
150 To cease thy suit, and leave me to my grief.
  Tomorrow will I send.
ROMEO.              So thrive my soul——
JULIET. A thousand times good night!
                    (JULIET *goes inside for a few moments.*)
ROMEO. A thousand times the worse, to want thy light.
  Love goes toward love as schoolboys from their books,
155 But love from love, toward school with heavy looks.


                    JULIET *reappears.*
JULIET. Hist! Romeo, hist! O, for a falconer's voice,
  To lure this tassel-gentle[23] back again!
  Bondage is hoarse, and may not speak aloud;[24]
  Else would I tear the cave where Echo[25] lies,
160 And make her airy tongue more hoarse than mine
  With repetition of my Romeo's name.
ROMEO. It is my soul that calls upon my name.
  How silver-sweet sound lovers' tongues by night,
  Like softest music to attending ears!
165 JULIET. Romeo!
ROMEO.        My dear?
JULIET.                        At what o'clock tomorrow
  Shall I send to thee?
ROMEO.                  At the hour of nine.
JULIET. I will not fail; 'tis twenty years till then.
  I have forgot why I did call thee back.
ROMEO. Let me stand here till thou remember it.
170 JULIET. I shall forget, to have thee still stand there,
  Remembering how I love thy company.

21. *thy bent of love,* the intentions of your love.

22. *By and by,* at once.

23. *tassel-gentle,* a male hawk.
24. *Bondage . . . speak aloud.* I am bound down by the necessity of not being overheard.

25. *Echo,* a nymph who pined away for a handsome youth until only her voice was left.

ROMEO. And I'll still stay, to have thee still forget,
  Forgetting any other home but this.
JULIET. 'Tis almost morning; I would have thee gone,
75  And yet no further than a wanton's bird,
  Who lets it hop a little from her hand,
  Like a poor prisoner in his twisted gyves,
  And with a silk thread plucks it back again,
  So loving-jealous of his liberty.
80 ROMEO. I would I were thy bird.
JULIET.                          Sweet, so would I;
  Yet I should kill thee with much cherishing.
  Good night, good night! Parting is such sweet sorrow
  That I shall say good night till it be morrow.
                              *(She goes into her room.)*
ROMEO. Sleep dwell upon thine eyes, peace in thy breast!
85  Would I were sleep and peace, so sweet to rest!
  Hence will I to my ghostly[26] father's cell,
  His help to crave, and my dear hap[27] to tell.          *(Exit.)*

26. *ghostly,* spiritual.
27. *dear hap,* good fortune.

## CONSIDERING ACT TWO, SCENE 2

**1.** How has Romeo's attitude toward life changed since he has met Juliet?

**2.** A collection of famous quotations includes lines from thirteen speeches in this scene alone. Choose several lines that you would include in your own collection of favorite quotations.

*Scene 3: Friar Laurence's cell.*

                    Enter FRIAR LAURENCE *with a basketful*
                    *of herbs believed to be health-giving.*
FRIAR LAURENCE. The gray-eyed morn smiles on the frowning night,
  Check'ring the eastern clouds with streaks of light,
  And fleckèd darkness like a drunkard reels
  From forth day's path and Titan's[1] fiery wheels.
5  Now, ere the sun advance his burning eye,
  The day to cheer and night's dank dew to dry,
  I must up-fill this osier cage[2] of ours
  With baleful weeds and precious-juicèd flowers,
  Many for many virtues excellent,
10  None but for some[3] and yet all different.
  O, mickle[4] is the powerful grace[5] that lies
  In herbs, plants, stones, and their true qualities;
  For naught so vile that on the earth doth live
  But to the earth some special good doth give,

1. *Titan's.* Titan, the sun god, was descended from a race of giants called Titans.

2. *osier cage,* willow basket.

3. *None but for some.* No plant entirely lacks value.

4. *mickle,* much.

5. *grace,* virtue, worth.

15 Nor aught so good but strained from that fair use
Revolts from true birth,[6] stumbling on abuse.
Virtue itself turns vice, being misapplied,
And vice sometime's by action dignified.

ROMEO *enters and stands by the door unseen.*

Within the infant rind of this small flower
20 Poison hath residence and medicine power;
For this, being smelt, with that part cheers each part,[7]
Being tasted, slays all senses with the heart.[8]
Two such opposèd kings encamp them still
In man as well as herbs—grace and rude will;[9]
25 And where the worser is predominant,
Full soon the canker[10] death eats up that plant.

(ROMEO *advances and speaks.*)

ROMEO. Good morrow, Father.

FRIAR LAURENCE.                     Benedicite![11]
What early tongue so sweet saluteth me?
Young son, it argues a distempered head
30 So soon to bid good morrow[12] to thy bed.
Care keeps his watch in every old man's eye,
And where care lodges, sleep will never lie;
But where unbruisèd youth with unstuffed brain[13]
Doth couch his limbs, there golden sleep doth reign.
35 Therefore thy earliness doth me assure
Thou art up-roused by some distemperature;
Or if not so, then here I hit it right—
Our Romeo hath not been in bed tonight.

ROMEO. That last is true; the sweeter rest was mine.

40 FRIAR LAURENCE. God pardon sin! Wast thou with Rosaline?

ROMEO. With Rosaline, my ghostly father? No;
I have forgot that name, and that name's woe.

FRIAR LAURENCE. That's my good son; but where hast thou been
then?

ROMEO. I'll tell thee, ere thou ask it me again.
45 I have been feasting with mine enemy,
Where on a sudden one hath wounded me,
That's by me wounded; both our remedies
Within thy help and holy physic[14] lies.
I bear no hatred, blessèd man, for, lo,
50 My intercession likewise steads[15] my foe.

FRIAR LAURENCE. Be plain, good son, and homely in thy drift;[16]
Riddling[17] confession finds but riddling shrift.[18]

ROMEO. Then plainly know my heart's dear love is set
On the fair daughter of rich Capulet.
55 As mine on hers, so hers is set on mine,
And all combined,[19] save what thou must combine
By holy marriage. When and where and how
We met, we wooed, and made exchange of vow,
I'll tell thee as we pass; but this I pray,
60 That thou consent to marry us today.

6. *Revolts . . . birth,* betrays its own special purpose.

7. *that part . . . part.* Its odor refreshes all parts of the body.

8. *with the heart,* by stopping the heart.

9. *rude will,* violent, lustful disposition.

10. *canker,* cankerworm, which destroys plants.

11. *Benedicite* (ben′ə dis′ə ti). God bless us.

12. *good morrow,* farewell.

13. *unstuffed brain,* mind unoccupied with busy thoughts and cares.

14. *physic,* medicine.

15. *steads,* helps.
16. *homely . . . drift,* simple and direct in your speech.
17. *Riddling,* like a riddle.
18. *shrift,* absolution.

19. *all combined,* the arrangement is complete.

FRIAR LAURENCE. Holy Saint Francis, what a change is here!
Is Rosaline, whom thou didst love so dear,
So soon forsaken? Young men's love then lies
Not truly in their hearts, but in their eyes.
65 Jesu Maria, what a deal of brine
Hath washed thy sallow cheeks for Rosaline!
How much salt water thrown away in waste,
To season love, that of it doth not taste!
The sun not yet thy sighs from heaven clears,
70 Thy old groans ring yet in my ancient ears;
Lo, here upon thy cheek the stain doth sit
Of an old tear that is not washed off yet:
If e'er thou wast thyself and these woes thine,
Thou and these woes were all for Rosaline.
75 And art thou changed? Pronounce this sentence then:
Women may fall when there's no strength in men.
ROMEO. Thou chid'st20 me oft for loving Rosaline.

20. *chid'st,* scolded.

FRIAR LAURENCE. For doting, not for loving, pupil mine.
ROMEO. And bad'st me bury love.
FRIAR LAURENCE.                  Not in a grave,
80 To lay one in, another out to have.
ROMEO. I pray thee, chide me not; she whom I love now
Doth grace for grace and love for love allow;
The other did not so.
FRIAR LAURENCE.          O, she knew well
Thy love did read by rote21 and could not spell.

21. *did read by rote,* merely repeated conventional expressions of love.

85 But come, young waverer, come, go with me,
In one respect I'll thy assistant be;
For this alliance may so happy prove
To turn your households' rancor to pure love.
ROMEO. O, let us hence; I stand on22 sudden haste.

22. *I stand on,* I am in a position demanding.

90 FRIAR LAURENCE. Wisely and slow; they stumble that run fast.
(ROMEO *and the* FRIAR *go out.*)

## CONSIDERING ACT TWO, SCENE 3

**1.** Think of several adjectives you might use in describing Friar Laurence. Justify each one.

**2. (a)** What proposal does Romeo make to the friar? **(b)** What doubts does the friar have about Romeo's proposal? **(c)** Why does Friar Laurence finally accept Romeo's proposal?

*Scene 4: A street in Verona on the morning after the ball.*

*Enter* MERCUTIO *and* BENVOLIO.
MERCUTIO. Where the devil should this Romeo be?
Came he not home tonight?¹

1. *tonight,* last night.

BENVOLIO. Not to his father's; I spoke with his man.

MERCUTIO. Ah, that same pale hard-hearted wench, that Rosaline,
  Torments him so that he will sure run mad.

BENVOLIO. Tybalt, the kinsman of old Capulet,
  Hath sent a letter to his father's house.

MERCUTIO. A challenge, on my life.

BENVOLIO. Romeo will answer it.

MERCUTIO. Any man that can write may answer a letter.

BENVOLIO. Nay, he will answer the letter's master, how he dares,
  being dared.

MERCUTIO. Alas, poor Romeo! He is already dead, stabbed with
  a white wench's black eye, shot through the ear with a love
  song; the very pin[2] of his heart cleft with the blind bow-boy's
  butt-shaft;[3] and is he a man to encounter Tybalt?

BENVOLIO. Why, what is Tybalt?

MERCUTIO. More than Prince of Cats,[4] I can tell you. O, he is the
  courageous captain of compliments.[5] He fights as you sing,
  keeps time, distance, and proportion;[6] rests me his minim
  rest,[7] one, two, and the third in your bosom; the very butcher
  of a silk button,[8] a duelist, a duelist; a gentleman of the very
  first house,[9] of the first and second cause.[10] Ah, the immortal
  passado![11] the punto reverso![12] the hai![13]

*Enter* ROMEO, *who shows no sign*
*of his former moodiness.*

BENVOLIO. Here comes Romeo, here comes Romeo!

MERCUTIO. Signior Romeo, bon jour![14] There's a French salutation to your French slop.[15] You gave us the counterfeit[16] fairly
  last night.

ROMEO. Good morrow to you both. What counterfeit did I give
  you?

MERCUTIO. The slip,[17] sir, the slip; can you not conceive?

ROMEO. Pardon, good Mercutio, my business was great; and in
  such a case as mine a man may strain courtesy.
  *(He laughs and claps* MERCUTIO *on the shoulder.)*

MERCUTIO. Why, is not this better now than groaning for love?
  Now art thou sociable, now art thou Romeo.

*Enter* NURSE *and* PETER, *her servant.*
*He is carrying a large fan.*

ROMEO. Here's goodly gear![18]

MERCUTIO. A sail, a sail!

BENVOLIO. Two, two; a shirt and a smock.[19]

NURSE. Peter!

PETER. Anon!

NURSE. My fan, Peter.

MERCUTIO. Good Peter, to hide her face, for her fan's the fairer
  face.

NURSE. God ye good morrow,[20] gentlemen.

MERCUTIO. God ye good den, fair gentlewoman.

2. *pin,* the center of a target.

3. *butt-shaft,* an unbarbed arrow.
Mercutio suggests that Cupid needed
only the least powerful weapon to
overcome Romeo.

4. *Prince of Cats,* a play on Tybalt's
name. In a collection of fables the
name of the Prince of Cats was Tibert
or Tibalt.

5. *captain of compliments,*
master of rules of ceremony
in dueling.

6. *time, distance, and proportion,* technical fencing terms.

7. *minim rest,* a half rest in music.

8. *butcher . . . button,* one
who can select and cut off
any button of his adversary.

9. *of the very first house,* of
first rank as a duelist.

10. *of the first . . . cause,* ready to
quarrel over anything—or nothing.

11. *passado* (pə sä′dō), a step
forward or aside in thrusting.

12. *punto reverso* (pun′tō
ri vėr′sō), a backhanded
thrust from the left side of the
body.

13. *hai* (hä), a thrust which strikes
the opposing duelist.

14. *Signior* (sē′nyôr) . . . *bon jour*
(bôn zhür′). Sir Romeo, good day.

15. *slop,* large breeches (a
French style).

16. *gave . . . counterfeit,*
played us a trick.

17. *slip,* a counterfeit coin.

18. *gear,* business.

19. *shirt . . . smock,* indicating a man and a woman.

20. *God . . . morrow.* God
give you a good morning.

NURSE. Gentlemen, can any of you tell me where I may find the young Romeo?

ROMEO. I can tell you; but young Romeo will be older when you have found him than he was when you sought him. I am
50 the youngest of that name, for fault[21] of a worse.

NURSE. If you be he, sir, I desire some confidence[22] with you.

BENVOLIO. She will indite[23] him to some supper.

MERCUTIO. Romeo, will you come to your father's? We'll to dinner thither.

55 ROMEO. I will follow you.

MERCUTIO. Farewell, ancient lady; farewell. *(Singing.)* "Lady, lady, lady."

*(Exeunt* MERCUTIO *and* BENVOLIO.*)*

NURSE. Marry, farewell! I pray you, sir, what saucy merchant[24] was this, that was so full of his ropery?[25]

60 ROMEO. A gentleman, Nurse, that loves to hear himself talk, and will speak more in a minute than he will stand to[26] in a month.

NURSE. An a' speak anything against me, I'll take him down, an a' were lustier than he is, and twenty such Jacks;[27] and if I cannot, I'll find those that shall. Scurvy knave! I am none
65 of his flirt-gills.[28] *(To* PETER.*)* And thou must stand by, too, and suffer every knave to abuse me at his pleasure?

PETER. I saw no man abuse you at his pleasure. If I had, my weapon should quickly have been out, I warrant you. I dare draw as soon as another man if I see occasion in a good
70 quarrel, and the law on my side.

NURSE. Now, afore God, I am so vexed that every part about me quivers. Scurvy knave! Pray you, sir, a word; and, as I told you, my young lady bade me inquire you out. What she bade me say, I will keep to myself; but first let me tell ye,
75 if ye should lead her into a fool's paradise, as they say, it were a very gross kind of behavior, as they say. For the gentlewoman is young; and, therefore, if you should deal double with her, truly it were an ill thing to be offered to any gentlewoman, and very weak dealing.

80 ROMEO. Nurse, commend me to thy lady and mistress. I protest[29] unto thee——

NURSE. Good heart, and, i' faith, I will tell her as much. Lord, Lord, she will be a joyful woman.

ROMEO. What wilt thou tell her, Nurse? Thou dost not mark me.[30]

85 NURSE. I will tell her, sir, that you do protest; which, as I take it, is a gentlemanlike offer.

ROMEO. Bid her devise
Some means to come to shrift this afternoon;
And there she shall at Friar Laurence' cell
90 Be shrived and married. Here *(offers money)* is for thy pains.

NURSE. No, truly, sir, not a penny.

ROMEO. Go to;[31] I say you shall.

NURSE *(taking the money and pocketing it).* This afternoon, sir? Well, she shall be there.

---

**21.** *fault,* lack.
**22.** *confidence,* the nurse's blunder for *conference.*
**23.** *indite.* Imitating the nurse, Benvolio jokingly misuses *indite* for *invite.*

**24.** *merchant,* fellow.
**25.** *ropery,* roguery.

**26.** *stand to,* maintain.

**27.** *Jacks,* rascals.

**28.** *flirt-gills,* flirtatious women.

**29.** *protest,* vow.

**30.** *mark me,* pay attention to what I say.

**31.** *Go to,* say nothing more.

---

95 ROMEO. And stay, good Nurse, behind the abbey wall.
Within this hour my man shall be with thee,
And bring thee cords made like a tackled stair;[32]
Which to the high topgallant[33] of my joy
Must be my convoy[34] in the secret night.
100 Farewell; be trusty, and I'll quit[35] thy pains.
Farewell; commend me to thy mistress.
NURSE. Now God in heaven bless thee! Hark you, sir.
ROMEO. What say'st thou, my dear Nurse?
NURSE. Is your man secret?[36] Did you ne'er hear say,
105 Two may keep counsel, putting one away?
ROMEO. I warrant thee, my man's as true as steel.
NURSE. Well, sir, my mistress is the sweetest lady—Lord, Lord,
when 'twas a little prating thing! O, there is a nobleman in
town, one Paris, that would fain lay knife aboard;[37] but she,
110 good soul, had as lief see a toad, a very toad, as see him. I
anger her sometimes and tell her that Paris is the properer[38]
man; but, I'll warrant you, when I say so, she looks as pale
as any clout[39] in the versal[40] world. Doth not rosemary and
Romeo begin both with a letter?[41]
115 ROMEO. Ay, Nurse; what of that? Both with an R.
NURSE. Ah, mocker! That's the dog's name;[42] R is for the—No;
I know it begins with some other letter; and she hath the
prettiest sententious[43] of it, of you and rosemary, that it
would do you good to hear it.
120 ROMEO. Commend me to thy lady.
NURSE. Ay, a thousand times. (Exit ROMEO.) Peter!
PETER. Anon!
NURSE. Peter, take my fan, and go before, and apace.
(Exeunt.)

32. tackled stair, rope ladder.
33. topgallant, summit, height.
34. convoy, means of
conducting me.
35. quit, reward.

36. secret, trustworthy.

37. fain . . . aboard, gladly
seize, in the manner of a
pirate, what he desires.
38. properer, handsomer.
39. clout, rag.
40. versal, universal.
41. a letter, the same letter.
42. the dog's name. The sound of
the letter R was thought to resemble
a dog's snarl.
43. sententious, the nurse's
error for sentences (clever sayings).

## CONSIDERING ACT TWO, SCENE 4

**1. (a)** What examples of humor can you point out in this scene?
**(b)** Everything seems to be going well—except for a certain threat.
What is that threat?

**2.** Outline the steps the nurse is to take in carrying out Romeo's
instructions.

**3.** Identify Paris, to whom the nurse refers in line 117. What have
we learned about him in earlier scenes?

*Scene 5: Capulet's orchard.*

*Enter* JULIET.

JULIET (*with ever rising anxiety*). The clock struck nine when I
did send the nurse;
In half an hour she promised to return.

Perchance she cannot meet him—that's not so.
O, she is lame! Love's heralds should be thoughts,
5  Which ten times faster glide than the sun's beams,
Driving back shadows over louring hills.
Therefore do nimble-pinioned doves draw love,[1]
And therefore hath the wind-swift Cupid wings.
Now is the sun upon the highmost hill
10  Of this day's journey, and from nine till twelve
Is three long hours, yet she is not come.
Had she affections and warm youthful blood,
She would be as swift in motion as a ball;
My words would bandy[2] her to my sweet love,
15  And his to me.
But old folks, many feign as they were dead—
Unwieldy, slow, heavy, and pale as lead.
O God, she comes!

*Enter* NURSE *and* PETER.

O honey Nurse, what news?
Hast thou met with him? Send thy man away.
20  NURSE. Peter, stay at the gate.

(*Exit* PETER.)

JULIET. Now, good, sweet Nurse,—O Lord, why look'st thou sad?
Though news be sad, yet tell them[3] merrily;
If good, thou shamest the music of sweet news
By playing it to me with so sour à face.
25  NURSE. I am aweary; give me leave awhile.
Fie, how my bones ache! What a jaunce[4] have I had!
JULIET. I would thou hadst my bones, and I thy news.
Nay, come, I pray thee, speak; good, good Nurse, speak.
NURSE. Jesu, what haste? Can you not stay awhile?
30  Do you not see that I am out of breath?
JULIET (*with exasperation*). How art thou out of breath when
    thou hast breath
To say to me that thou art out of breath?
The excuse that thou dost make in this delay
Is longer than the tale thou dost excuse.[5]
35  Is thy news good, or bad? Answer to that;
Say either, and I'll stay the circumstance.[6]
Let me be satisfied: is 't good or bad?
NURSE. Well, you have made a simple choice; you know not
how to choose a man. Romeo? No, not he; though his face
40  be better than any man's, yet his leg excels all men's; and
for a hand, and a foot, and a body, though they be not to be
talked on, yet they are past compare. He is not the flower of
courtesy, but, I'll warrant him, as gentle as a lamb. Go thy
ways, wench; serve God. What, have you dined at home?
45  JULIET. No, no. But all this did I know before.
What says he of our marriage? What of that?
NURSE. Lord, how my head aches! What a head have I!

1. *nimble-pinioned . . . love.*
Swift-winged doves drew the chariot of
Venus, goddess of love.

2. *bandy*, hurry.

3. *news . . . them. News* was
often used in the plural.

4. *jaunce*, rough jaunt.

5. *excuse*, put off by making
excuses.

6. *stay the circumstance*,
await details.

It beats as it would fall in twenty pieces.
My back—O my back, my back!

50 Beshrew[7] your heart for sending me about
To catch my death with jauncing up and down!
JULIET. I' faith, I am sorry that thou art not well.
(Beseechingly.) Sweet, sweet, sweet Nurse, tell me, what says
my love?
NURSE. Your love says, like an honest gentleman, and a cour-

55 teous, and a kind, and a handsome, and I warrant, a virtuous—
Where is your mother?
JULIET. Where is my mother! Why, she is within;
Where should she be? How oddly thou repliest!—
"Your love says, like an honest gentleman,

60 Where is your mother?"
NURSE.                    O God's lady dear!
Are you so hot? Marry, come up, I trow;[8]
Is this the poultice for my aching bones?
Henceforward do your messages yourself.
JULIET. Here's such a coil![9] Come, what says Romeo?

65 NURSE. Have you got leave to go to shrift today?
JULIET. I have.
NURSE. Then hie[10] you hence to Friar Laurence' cell;
There stays a husband to make you a wife.
Now comes the wanton blood up in your cheeks;

70 They'll be in scarlet straight at any news.
Hie you to church; I must another way
To fetch a ladder, by the which your love
Must climb a bird's nest soon when it is dark:
I am the drudge, and toil in your delight.

75 Go; I'll to dinner; hie you to the cell.
JULIET. Hie to high fortune! Honest Nurse, farewell.
                    (They go out in opposite directions.)


*Scene 6: Friar Laurence's cell.*

                    Enter FRIAR LAURENCE *and* ROMEO.
FRIAR LAURENCE. So smile the heavens upon this holy act
That after hours with sorrow chide us not!
ROMEO. Amen, amen! But come what sorrow can,
It cannot countervail[1] the exchange of joy

5 That one short minute gives me in her sight.
Do thou but close our hands with holy words,
Then love-devouring death do what he dare;
It is enough I may but call her mine.
FRIAR LAURENCE. These violent delights have violent ends

10 And in their triumph die, like fire and powder,
Which as they kiss consume.[2] The sweetest honey
Is loathsome in his own deliciousness
And in the taste confounds[3] the appetite.

7. *Beshrew,* ill luck to.

8. *Marry . . . I trow.* Come, now; you are too impatient, I declare.

9. *coil,* commotion.

10. *hie,* hasten.

1. *countervail,* balance, equal.

2. *These violent delights . . . consume.* In lines 9–11 Friar Laurence expresses a premonition of evil.

3. *confounds,* destroys.

Therefore love moderately; long love doth so;
15  Too swift arrives as tardy as too slow.

*Enter* JULIET.

Here comes the lady. O, so light a foot
Will ne'er wear out the everlasting flint.[4]
A lover may bestride the gossamer[5]
That idles in the wanton summer air,
20  And yet not fall; so light is vanity.[6]
JULIET. Good even[7] to my ghostly confessor.
FRIAR LAURENCE. Romeo shall thank thee, daughter, for us both.
JULIET. As much to him,[8] else is his thanks too much.
ROMEO. Ah, Juliet, if the measure of thy joy
25  Be heaped like mine, and that[9] thy skill be more
To blazon[10] it, then sweeten with thy breath
This neighbor air, and let rich music's tongue
Unfold the imagined happiness that both
Receive in either by this dear encounter.
30  JULIET. Conceit,[11] more rich in matter than in words,
Brags of his substance, not of ornament.
They are but beggars that can count their worth;
But my true love is grown to such excess
I cannot sum up sum of half my wealth.
35  FRIAR LAURENCE. Come, come with me, and we will make short
        work;
For, by your leaves, you shall not stay alone
Till holy church incorporate two in one.

*(Exeunt.)*

4. *wear out . . . flint.* The friar is suggesting the roughness of life's journey.

5. *gossamer,* cobweb.

6. *so light is vanity,* so unsubstantial are the illusions of love.

7. *even,* evening.

8. *As much to him,* the same greeting to him.

9. *that,* if.

10. *blazon,* proclaim.

11. *Conceit,* imagination, understanding.

## CONSIDERING ACT TWO, SCENES 5 AND 6

**1.** Quote lines from Scene 5 that bring out especially well Juliet's desperate effort to wring the news from the nurse.

**2.** In what ways are the nurse's speeches in Scene 5 consistent (or inconsistent) with the impressions you have gained of her in earlier scenes?

**3.** What is the attitude of Friar Laurence toward the lovers' insistence that he marry them without delay?

## LOOKING BACK—AND AHEAD

**1.** Write a brief outline of the events in Act Two.

**2.** All seems to be going smoothly with Romeo and Juliet. On the other hand, do you find suggestions in Scene 6 that indicate that their happiness may not continue? Cite specific lines to uphold your answer.

# Act Three

*Scene 1: A public place in Verona.*

         *Enter* MERCUTIO, BENVOLIO, PAGE, *and* SERVANTS.

BENVOLIO. I pray thee, good Mercutio, let's retire.
    The day is hot, the Capulets abroad,
    And, if we meet, we shall not 'scape a brawl;
    For now, these hot days, is the mad blood stirring.

5 MERCUTIO. Thou art like one of those fellows that when he enters
    the confines of a tavern claps his sword upon the table and
    says "God send me no need of thee!" and by the operation
    of the second cup[1] draws it on the drawer,[2] when indeed
    there is no need.

10 BENVOLIO. Am I like such a fellow?

MERCUTIO. Come, come, thou art as hot a Jack[3] in thy mood[4]
    as any in Italy, and as soon moved to be moody, and as soon
    moody to be moved.

BENVOLIO. And what to?[5]

15 MERCUTIO. Nay, an there were two such, we should have none
    shortly, for one would kill the other. Thou! Why, thou wilt
    quarrel with a man that hath a hair more, or a hair less, in
    his beard than thou hast. Thou wilt quarrel with a man for
    cracking nuts, having no other reason but because thou hast
20     hazel eyes. Thy head is as full of quarrels as an egg is full of
    meat. Thou hast quarreled with a man for coughing in the
    street, because he hath wakened thy dog that hath lain asleep
    in the sun. Didst thou not fall out with a tailor for wearing
    his new doublet before Easter? And yet thou wilt tutor me
25     from quarreling!

BENVOLIO. An I were so apt to quarrel as thou art, any man
    should buy the fee-simple[6] of my life for an hour and a quarter.

MERCUTIO. The fee-simple! O simple!

BENVOLIO. By my head, here come the Capulets.

30 MERCUTIO. By my heel, I care not.

         *Enter* TYBALT *and other* CAPULETS.

TYBALT. Follow me close, for I will speak to them.
    Gentlemen, good den; a word with one of you.

MERCUTIO. And but one word with one of us? Couple it with
    something; make it a word and a blow.

35 TYBALT. You shall find me apt enough to that, sir, an you will
    give me occasion.

MERCUTIO. Could you not take some occasion without giving?

TYBALT. Mercutio, thou consort'st with[7] Romeo——

MERCUTIO. Consort! 'Zounds,[8] consort!

40 BENVOLIO. We talk here in the public haunt of men.
    Either withdraw unto some private place,
    And reason coldly of your grievances,

**1.** *by . . . the second cup,* by the time the second cup of wine begins to affect him.
**2.** *drawer,* one who draws wine from its container.

**3.** *Jack,* fellow.
**4.** *mood,* ill humor.

**5.** *what to,* moved to what.

**6.** *fee-simple,* absolute ownership.

**7.** *consort'st with,* accompany or wait upon.
**8.** *'Zounds,* a form of the oath "by God's wounds."

Or else depart;[9] here all eyes gaze on us.

MERCUTIO. Men's eyes were made to look, and let them gaze;
45    I will not budge for no man's pleasure, I.

*Enter* ROMEO.

TYBALT *(to* BENVOLIO*).* Well, peace be with you, sir. Here comes
     my man.[10]

MERCUTIO. But I'll be hanged, sir, if he wear your livery.[11]
     Marry, go before to field, he'll be your follower;[12]
     Your worship in that sense may call him "man."
50  TYBALT. Romeo, the hate I bear thee can afford
     No better term than this—thou art a villain.

ROMEO. Tybalt, the reason that I have to love thee
     Doth much excuse the appertaining rage
     To such a greeting;[13] villain am I none.
55    Therefore, farewell; I see thou know'st me not.

TYBALT *(contemptuously).* Boy, this shall not excuse the injuries
     That thou hast done me; therefore turn and draw.

ROMEO. I do protest, I never injured thee,
     But love thee better than thou canst devise,
60    Till thou shalt know the reason of my love.
     And so, good Capulet—which name I tender[14]
     As dearly as my own—be satisfied.

MERCUTIO. O calm, dishonorable, vile submission!
                              *(He draws his sword.)*
     Tybalt, you rat catcher,[15] will you walk?[16]
65  TYBALT. What wouldst thou have with me?

MERCUTIO. Good King of Cats, nothing but one of your nine
     lives; that I mean to make bold withal,[17] and, as you shall
     use me hereafter, dry-beat the rest of the eight.[18] Will you
     pluck your sword out of his pilcher[19] by the ears? Make haste,
70    lest mine be about your ears ere it be out.

TYBALT *(drawing).* I am for you.

ROMEO. Gentle Mercutio, put thy rapier up.

MERCUTIO. Come, sir, your passado.
                         *(*TYBALT *and* MERCUTIO *fight.)*

ROMEO. Draw, Benvolio; beat down their weapons.
75    Gentlemen, for shame, forbear this outrage!
     Tybalt, Mercutio, the prince expressly hath
     Forbidden bandying in Verona streets.
     Hold, Tybalt! Good Mercutio!
                    *(*TYBALT, *reaching under* ROMEO's *arm, stabs*
                        MERCUTIO, *and flies with his followers.)*

MERCUTIO.                   I am hurt.
     A plague o' both your houses! I am sped.[20]
80  BENVOLIO. What, art thou hurt?

MERCUTIO. Ay, ay, a scratch, a scratch; marry, 'tis enough.
     Where is my page? Go, villain,[21] fetch a surgeon.
                                   *(Exit* PAGE.*)*

ROMEO. Courage, man; the hurt cannot be much.

---

**9.** *depart,* separate.

**10.** *my man.* Tybalt speaks insultingly of Romeo as though Romeo were his servant.

**11.** *if . . . livery,* if Romeo wears the uniform (livery) of Tybalt's servants.

**12.** *go . . . follower.* If you went to the field of encounter, Romeo would follow you quickly enough.

**13.** *appertaining rage . . . greeting,* rage suitable to such a greeting.

**14.** *tender,* cherish.

**15.** *rat catcher,* an allusion to Tybalt as Prince of Cats.

**16.** *walk,* step aside with me.

**17.** *that . . . withal.* That one life I intend to take at once.

**18.** *dry-beat . . . eight,* soundly beat your other eight lives.

**19.** *his pilcher,* its scabbard.

**20.** *sped,* done for.

**21.** *villain,* a form of address to a servant.

MERCUTIO. No, 'tis not so deep as a well, nor so wide as a church door; but 'tis enough, 'twill serve. Ask for me tomorrow, and you shall find me a grave man.[22] I am peppered,[23] I warrant, for this world. A plague o' both your houses! 'Zounds, a dog, a rat, a mouse, a cat, to scratch a man to death! A braggart, a rogue, a villain, that fights by the book of arithmetic![24] Why the devil came you between us? I was hurt under your arm.

ROMEO. I thought all for the best.

MERCUTIO. Help me into some house, Benvolio,
Or I shall faint. A plague o' both your houses!
They have made worms' meat of me; I have it,
And soundly too. Your houses!
(MERCUTIO *is helped off by* BENVOLIO *and some* SERVANTS.)

ROMEO. This gentleman, the prince's near ally,[25]
My very[26] friend, hath got his mortal hurt
In my behalf; my reputation stained
With Tybalt's slander—Tybalt, that an hour
Hath been my kinsman! O sweet Juliet,
Thy beauty hath made me effeminate
And in my temper softened valor's steel!

*Re-enter* BENVOLIO.

BENVOLIO. O Romeo, Romeo, brave Mercutio's dead!
That gallant spirit hath aspired[27] the clouds,
Which too untimely here did scorn the earth.

ROMEO. This day's black fate on moe[28] days doth depend;[29]
This but begins the woe others must end.

*Re-enter* TYBALT.

BENVOLIO. Here comes the furious Tybalt back again.

ROMEO. Alive, in triumph—and Mercutio slain!
Away to heaven, respective lenity,[30]
And fire-eyed fury be my conduct[31] now!
Now, Tybalt, take the villain back again
That late thou gavest me; for Mercutio's soul
Is but a little way above our heads,
Staying for thine to keep him company:
Either thou, or I, or both, must go with him.

TYBALT. Thou wretched boy, that didst consort him here,
Shalt with him hence.

ROMEO.                    This shall determine that.
(*They fight.* TYBALT *falls dead.*)

BENVOLIO. Romeo, away, be gone!
The citizens are up, and Tybalt slain.
Stand not amazed;[32] the prince will doom thee death
If thou art taken; hence, be gone, away!

ROMEO. O, I am fortune's fool![33]

BENVOLIO.                    Why dost thou stay?
(*Exit* ROMEO.)

22. *a grave man.* Thus Mercutio puns with his last breath.

23. *peppered.* Mercutio means that receiving the one wound is as serious as being peppered with many wounds.

24. *book of arithmetic,* a textbook on fencing.

25. *ally,* kinsman.
26. *very,* true.

27. *aspired,* soared to.

28. *moe,* more.
29. *depend,* hang over threateningly.

30. *respective lenity,* considerate mildness.
31. *conduct,* guide.

32. *amazed,* stupefied.

33. *fortune's fool,* the plaything or pawn of fate.

125 FIRST CITIZEN. Which way ran he that killed Mercutio?
Tybalt, that murderer, which way ran he?
BENVOLIO. There lies that Tybalt.
FIRST CITIZEN.                    Up, sir, go with me;
I charge thee in the prince's name, obey.

*Enter* PRINCE ESCALUS, *attended;* MONTAGUE,
CAPULET, THEIR WIVES, *and* OTHERS.
PRINCE. Where are the vile beginners of this fray?
130 BENVOLIO. O noble Prince, I can discover[34] all
The unlucky manage[35] of this fatal brawl.
There lies the man, slain by young Romeo,
That slew thy kinsman, brave Mercutio.
LADY CAPULET. Tybalt, my cousin! O my brother's child!
135 O Prince! O cousin! Husband! O, the blood is spilt
Of my dear kinsman! Prince, as thou art true,
For blood of ours shed blood of Montague.
O cousin, cousin!
PRINCE. Benvolio, who began this bloody fray?
140 BENVOLIO. Tybalt, here slain, whom Romeo's hand did slay;
Romeo that spoke him fair, bade him bethink
How nice[36] the quarrel was, and urged withal
Your high displeasure. All this, uttered
With gentle breath, calm look, knees humbly bowed,
145 Could not take truce[37] with the unruly spleen[38]
Of Tybalt deaf to peace, but that he tilts[39]
With piercing steel at bold Mercutio's breast,
Who, all as hot, turns deadly point to point,
And, with a martial scorn, with one hand beats
150 Cold death aside, and with the other sends
It back to Tybalt, whose dexterity
Retorts[40] it. Romeo he cries aloud,
"Hold, friends; friends, part," and, swifter than his tongue,
His agile arm beats down their fatal points,
155 And 'twixt them rushes; underneath whose arm
An envious thrust from Tybalt hit the life
Of stout[41] Mercutio, and then Tybalt fled;
But by and by comes back to Romeo,
Who had but newly entertained[42] revenge,
160 And to 't they go like lightning, for ere I
Could draw to part them, was stout Tybalt slain,
And, as he fell, did Romeo turn and fly.
This is the truth, or let Benvolio die.
LADY CAPULET. He is a kinsman to the Montague;
165 Affection makes him false; he speaks not true.
Some twenty of them fought in this black strife,
And all those twenty could but kill one life.
I beg for justice, which thou, Prince, must give.
Romeo slew Tybalt; Romeo must not live.

34. *discover,* reveal.
35. *manage,* conduct.

36. *nice,* trivial.

37. *take truce,* make peace.
38. *unruly spleen,* ungovernable rage.
39. *tilts,* strikes.

40. *Retorts,* returns.

41. *stout,* brave.

42. *entertained,* harbored thoughts of.

170 PRINCE. Romeo slew him, he slew Mercutio;
   Who now the price of his dear blood doth owe?
   MONTAGUE. Not Romeo, Prince; he was Mercutio's friend.
   His fault concludes but what the law should end—
   The life of Tybalt.
   PRINCE.                    And for that offense
175 Immediately we do exile him hence.
   I have an interest in your hate's proceeding,
   My blood[43] for your rude brawls doth lie a-bleeding;
   But I'll amerce[44] you with so strong a fine
   That you shall all repent the loss of mine.[45]
180 I will be deaf to pleading and excuses;
   Nor tears nor prayers shall purchase out abuses.[46]
   Therefore use none. Let Romeo hence in haste,
   Else, when he's found, that hour is his last.
   Bear hence this body and attend our will.
185 Mercy but murders, pardoning those that kill.          (Exeunt.)

**43.** *My blood*, the blood of my kin.

**44.** *amerce*, punish by fine.

**45.** *mine*, my blood.

**46.** *purchase out abuses*, exempt misdeeds from penalty.

## CONSIDERING ACT THREE, SCENE 1

**1. (a)** Who renews the quarreling and feuding between the Montagues and the Capulets? **(b)** Which character attempts to serve as peacemaker? Why is he unsuccessful? **(c)** Why does Romeo refuse Tybalt's first challenge to fight?

**2.** Why does Romeo finally assume personal responsibility for avenging Mercutio's death? In your opinion, is Romeo's decision justified—or should he have left Tybalt's punishment to Prince Escalus? Give reasons for your answer.


*Scene 2: Capulet's orchard.*

*Enter* JULIET.

JULIET. Gallop apace, you fiery-footed steeds,
   Toward Phoebus'[1] lodging; such a wagoner
   As Phaëthon[2] would whip you to the west,
   And bring in cloudy night immediately.
5 Come, night; come, Romeo; come, thou day in night,
   For thou wilt lie upon the wings of night
   Whiter than new snow on a raven's back.
   Come, gentle night, come, loving, black-browed night,
   Give me my Romeo, and, when he shall die,
10 Take him and cut him out in little stars,
   And he will make the face of heaven so fine
   That all the world will be in love with night
   And pay no worship to the garish sun.
   O, here comes my nurse,
15 And she brings news; and every tongue that speaks
   But Romeo's name speaks heavenly eloquence.

**1.** *Phoebus* (fē′bəs), the sun god.

**2.** *Phaëthon* (fā′ə thon). He was allowed to drive the chariot of the sun for a day. Too weak to control the horses, he nearly destroyed the universe.

*Enter* NURSE *with the rope-ladder that*
ROMEO *had directed her to make ready.*

Now, Nurse, what news? What, hast thou there the cords
That Romeo bid thee fetch?

NURSE.                  Ay, ay, the cords.
*(She throws down the ladder.)*

JULIET. Ay me! What news? Why dost thou wring thy hands?

20 NURSE. Ah, well-a-day![3] He's dead, he's dead, he's dead!
    We are undone, lady, we are undone!
    Alack the day! He's gone, he's killed, he's dead!

JULIET. Can heaven be so envious?

NURSE.                Romeo can,
    Though heaven cannot. O Romeo, Romeo!
25     Who ever would have thought it? Romeo!

JULIET. What devil art thou, that dost torment me thus?
    This torture should be roared in dismal hell.
    Hath Romeo slain himself? Say thou but "Ay"
    And that bare vowel "I" shall poison more
30     Than the death-darting eye of cockatrice.[4]
    I am not I, if there be such an I,
    Or those eyes shut that make thee answer "Ay."
    If he be slain, say "Ay"; or, if not, "No."
    Brief sounds determine of my weal or woe.[5]

35 NURSE. I saw the wound, I saw it with mine eyes—
    God save the mark![6]—here on his manly breast.
    A piteous corse,[7] a bloody piteous corse;
    Pale, pale as ashes, all bedaubed in blood,
    All in gore-blood;[8] I swounded[9] at the sight.

40 JULIET. O, break, my heart! Poor bankrupt, break at once!
    To prison, eyes; ne'er look on liberty!
    Vile earth, to earth resign;[10] end motion[11] here;
    And thou and Romeo press one heavy bier!

NURSE. O Tybalt, Tybalt, the best friend I had!
45     O courteous Tybalt; honest gentleman!
    That ever I should live to see thee dead!

JULIET. What storm is this that blows so contrary?
    Is Romeo slaughtered, and is Tybalt dead?
    My dear-loved cousin, and my dearer lord?
50     Then, dreadful trumpet,[12] sound the general doom!
    For who is living if those two are gone?

NURSE. Tybalt is gone, and Romeo banished;
    Romeo that killed him, he is banished.

JULIET. O God! Did Romeo's hand shed Tybalt's blood?

55 NURSE. It did, it did; alas the day, it did!

JULIET. O serpent heart, hid with a flowering face!
    Did ever dragon keep[13] so fair a cave?
    O nature, what hadst thou to do in hell,
    When thou didst bower[14] the spirit of a fiend
60     In mortal paradise of such sweet flesh?
    Was ever book containing such vile matter

3. *well-a-day,* alas.

4. *cockatrice,* a fabled serpent which could kill with its glance.

5. *determine . . . woe,* decide my well-being or my sorrow.

6. *God . . . mark.* God have mercy on us.

7. *corse,* corpse.

8. *gore-blood,* clotted blood.

9. *swounded,* swooned.

10. *Vile earth . . . resign.* Miserable body, resign yourself to death.

11. *motion,* human activity.

12. *dreadful trumpet,* the trumpet proclaiming doomsday, or the end of the world.

13. *keep,* guard.

14. *bower,* give lodging to.

So fairly bound? O, that deceit should dwell
In such a gorgeous palace!
NURSE.                                  There's no trust,
No faith, no honesty in men; all perjured,
65   All forsworn,[15] all naught, all dissemblers.
Ah, where's my man? Give me some aqua vitae;[16]
These griefs, these woes, these sorrows make me old.
Shame come to Romeo!
JULIET.                             Blistered be thy tongue
For such a wish! He was not born to shame.
70   Upon his brow shame is ashamed to sit;
For 'tis a throne where honor may be crowned
Sole monarch of the universal earth.
O, what a beast was I to chide at him!
NURSE. Will you speak well of him that killed your cousin?
75   JULIET. Shall I speak ill of him that is my husband?
Ah, poor my lord, what tongue shall smooth thy name,
When I, thy three-hours' wife, have mangled it?
But, wherefore, villain, didst thou kill my cousin?
That villain cousin would have killed my husband.
80   Back, foolish tears, back to your native spring,
Your tributary drops belong to woe,
Which you, mistaking, offer up to joy.
My husband lives, that Tybalt would have slain;
And Tybalt's dead, that would have slain my husband.
85   All this is comfort; wherefore weep I then?
Some word there was, worser than Tybalt's death,
That murdered me. I would forget it fain;[17]
But, O, it presses to my memory,
Like damnèd guilty deeds to sinners' minds:
90   "Tybalt is dead, and Romeo—banishèd";
That "banishèd," that one word "banishèd,"
Hath slain ten thousand Tybalts. Tybalt's death
Was woe enough, if it had ended there.
Or, if sour woe delights in fellowship,
95   And needly[18] will be ranked with other griefs,
Why followed not, when she said "Tybalt's dead,"
Thy father or thy mother, nay, or both,
Which modern lamentation[19] might have moved?
But with a rearward[20] following Tybalt's death,
100   "Romeo is banishèd—to speak that word
Is father, mother, Tybalt, Romeo, Juliet,
All slain, all dead. "Romeo is banishèd!"—
There is no end, no limit, measure, bound,
In that word's death; no words can that woe sound.
105   Where is my father, and my mother, Nurse?
NURSE. Weeping and wailing over Tybalt's corse.
Will you go to them? I will bring you thither.
JULIET. Wash they his wounds with tears? Mine shall be spent,
When theirs are dry, for Romeo's banishment.

15. *forsworn,* untrue to one's sworn oath.

16. *aqua vitae* (ak′wə vī′tē), spirits to restore calmness.

17. *fain,* gladly.

18. *needly,* of necessity.

19. *modern lamentation,* ordinary grief.

20. *rearward,* a guard following at the rear of a group.

Take up those cords. Poor ropes, you are beguiled,
Both you and I, for Romeo is exiled.
NURSE. Hie to your chamber. I'll find Romeo
To comfort you. I wot²¹ well where he is.
Hark ye, your Romeo will be here at night;
I'll to him. He is hid at Laurence' cell.
JULIET. O, find him! Give this ring to my true knight,
And bid him come to take his last farewell.          (*Exeunt.*)

Scene 3: *Friar Laurence's cell.*

*Enter* FRIAR LAURENCE.

FRIAR LAURENCE. Romeo, come forth; come forth, thou fearful¹
man.
Affliction is enamored of thy parts²
And thou art wedded to calamity.

*Enter* ROMEO.

ROMEO. Father, what news? What is the prince's doom?
What sorrow craves acquaintance at my hand,
That I yet know not?
FRIAR LAURENCE.          Too familiar
Is my dear son with such sour company.
I bring thee tidings of the prince's doom.
ROMEO. What less than doomsday is the prince's doom?
FRIAR LAURENCE. A gentler judgment vanished³ from his lips—
Not body's death, but body's banishment.
ROMEO. Ha, banishment! Be merciful, say "death";
For exile hath more terror in his look,
Much more than death. Do not say "banishment."
FRIAR LAURENCE. Hence from Verona art thou banishèd.
Be patient, for the world is broad and wide.
ROMEO. There is no world without Verona walls,
But purgatory, torture, hell itself.
Hence—banishèd is banished from the world,
And world's exile⁴ is death. Then banishèd
Is death mistermed. Calling death "banishment,"
Thou cut'st my head off with a golden ax
And smilest upon the stroke that murders me.
FRIAR LAURENCE. O deadly sin! O rude unthankfulness!
Thy fault our law calls death, but the kind prince,
Taking thy part, hath rushed aside⁵ the law,
And turned that black word death to banishment.
This is dear⁶ mercy, and thou seest it not.
ROMEO. 'Tis torture, and not mercy. Heaven is here,
Where Juliet lives; and every cat and dog
And little mouse, every unworthy thing,
Live here in heaven and may look on her,
But Romeo may not; he is banishèd.

21. *wot,* know.

1. *fearful,* full of fear.

2. *Affliction . . . parts.* Misfortune thrives on the qualities (parts) you are showing—self-pity and despair.

3. *vanished,* issued.

4. *world's exile,* exile from the world that is everything to me—the world where Juliet dwells.

5. *rushed aside,* thrust aside; dodged.

6. *dear,* rare, unusual.

Hadst thou no poison mixed, no sharp-ground knife,
35  No sudden mean[7] of death, though ne'er so mean,[8]
But "banishèd" to kill me?—"Banishèd"?
O Friar, the damnèd use that word in hell;
Howlings attend it. How hast thou the heart,
Being a divine, a ghostly confessor,
40  A sin-absolver, and my friend professed,
To mangle me with that word "banishèd"?
FRIAR LAURENCE. Thou fond[9] mad man, hear me but speak a word.
ROMEO. O, thou wilt speak again of banishment.
FRIAR LAURENCE. I'll give thee armor to keep off that word;
45  Adversity's sweet milk, philosophy,
To comfort thee, though thou art banishèd.
ROMEO. Yet "banishèd"? Hang up philosophy!
Unless philosophy can make a Juliet,
Displant a town, reverse a prince's doom,
50  It helps not, it prevails not. Talk no more.
FRIAR LAURENCE. O, then I see that madmen have no ears.
ROMEO. How should they, when that wise men have no eyes?
FRIAR LAURENCE. Let me dispute[10] with thee of thy estate.[11]
ROMEO. Thou canst not speak of that thou dost not feel.
55  Wert thou as young as I, Juliet thy love,
An hour but married, Tybalt murdered,
Doting like me and like me banishèd,
Then mightst thou speak, then mightst thou tear thy hair,
And *(flinging himself full length upon the floor and sobbing)*
fall upon the ground, as I do now,
60  Taking the measure of an unmade grave.
*(The* NURSE *knocks on the door.)*
FRIAR LAURENCE. Arise; one knocks. Good Romeo, hide thyself.
ROMEO. Not I; unless the breath of heart-sick groans,
Mistlike, infold me from the search of eyes.
*(The* NURSE *knocks again.)*
FRIAR LAURENCE. Hark, how they knock! Who's there? Romeo,
arise;
65  Thou wilt be taken.—Stay awhile! Stand up.
*(Louder knocking.)*
Run to my study.—By and by! God's will,
What simpleness is this!—I come, I come!
*(Knocking continues.)*
Who knocks so hard? Whence come you? What is your will?
NURSE *(speaking off-stage)*. Let me come in, and you shall know
my errand.
70  I come from Lady Juliet.
FRIAR LAURENCE.                    Welcome, then.

*Enter* NURSE.

NURSE. O holy Friar, O, tell me, holy Friar,
Where is my lady's lord, where's Romeo?
FRIAR LAURENCE. There on the ground, with his own tears made
drunk.

7. *mean*, means.
8. *mean*, base, vile.

9. *fond*, foolish.

10. *dispute*, reason, discuss.
11. *estate*, situation, condition.

NURSE. O, he is even in my mistress' case,[12]
75    Just in her case! O woeful sympathy![13]
      Piteous predicament! Even so lies she,
      Blubbering and weeping, weeping and blubbering.
      Stand up, stand up; stand, an you be a man.
      For Juliet's sake, for her sake, rise and stand.

                              (ROMEO *rises*.)

80  ROMEO. Nurse!
    NURSE. Ah sir! ah sir! Well, death's the end of all.
    ROMEO. Spakest thou of Juliet? How is it with her?
      Doth she not think me an old[14] murderer,
      Now I have stained the childhood of our joy
85    With blood removed but little from her own?
      Where is she? And how doth she? And what says
      My concealed lady[15] to our canceled love?
    NURSE. O, she says nothing, sir, but weeps and weeps,
      And now falls on her bed, and then starts up,
90    And Tybalt calls, and then on Romeo cries,
      And then down falls again.
    ROMEO.                        As if that name,
      Shot from the deadly level[16] of a gun,
      Did murder her; as that name's cursèd hand
      Murdered her kinsman. O, tell me, Friar, tell me,
95    In what vile part of this anatomy
      Doth my name lodge? Tell me that I may sack
      The hateful mansion.

                         (ROMEO *draws his sword*.)
    FRIAR LAURENCE.          Hold thy desperate hand.
      Art thou a man? Thy form cries out thou art;
      Thy tears are womanish; thy wild acts denote
00    The unreasonable fury of a beast—
      Unseemly woman in a seeming man,
      Or ill-beseeming[17] beast in seeming both!
      Thou hast amazed me. By my holy order,
      I thought thy disposition better tempered.
05    Hast thou slain Tybalt? Wilt thou slay thyself?
      And slay thy lady too that lives in thee,
      By doing damnèd hate upon thyself?
      Why rail'st thou on[18] thy birth, the heaven, and earth—
      Since birth, and heaven, and earth, all three do meet
10    In thee at once, which thou at once wouldst lose?
      What, rouse thee, man! Thy Juliet is alive,
      For whose dear sake thou wast but lately dead;
      There[19] art thou happy. Tybalt would kill thee,
      But thou slew'st Tybalt; there art thou happy too.
15    The law that threatened death becomes thy friend
      And turns it to exile; there art thou happy.
      But, like a misbehaved and sullen wench,
      Thou pouts upon thy fortune and thy love.
      Take heed, take heed, for such die miserable.

12. *O, he is . . . case.* Romeo is in the same state as Juliet.

13. *woeful sympathy*, sad agreement.

14. *an old*, a real or actual.

15. *concealed lady*, secretly married wife.

16. *level*, line of fire.

17. *ill-beseeming*, unsuitable, inappropriate.

18. *Why rail'st thou on*, why do you complain about.

19. *There*, in this respect.

120 Go, get thee to thy love, as was decreed,
Ascend her chamber, hence and comfort her.
But look thou stay not till the watch be set,[20]
For then thou canst not pass to Mantua,
Where thou shalt live till we can find a time
125 To blaze[21] your marriage, reconcile your friends,
Beg pardon of the prince, and call thee back
With twenty hundred thousand times more joy
Than thou went'st forth in lamentation.
Go before, Nurse. Commend me to thy lady,
130 And bid her hasten all the house to bed,
Which heavy sorrow makes them apt unto.[22]
Romeo is coming.
NURSE. O Lord, I could have stayed here all the night
To hear good counsel. O, what learning is!
135 My lord, I'll tell my lady you will come.
ROMEO. Do so, and bid my sweet prepare to chide.
NURSE. Here is a ring she bid me give you, sir.
Hie you, make haste, for it grows very late.

(*Exit* NURSE.)

ROMEO. How well my comfort is revived by this!
140 FRIAR LAURENCE. Go hence; good night; and here stands all your
state—[23]
Either be gone before the watch be set,
Or by the break of day disguised from hence.
Sojourn in Mantua; I'll find out your man,[24]
And he shall signify from time to time
145 Every good hap[25] to you that chances here.
Give me thy hand; 'tis late. Farewell; good night.
ROMEO. But that a joy past joy calls out on me,
It were a grief, so brief to part with thee.
Farewell.                                   (*Exeunt.*)

**20.** *watch be set,* watchmen have taken their stand at the gates of Verona.

**21.** *blaze,* announce.

**22.** *apt unto,* inclined to.

**23.** *here stands . . . state.* Your fortune depends on acting exactly as follows.

**24.** *your man,* Romeo's servant, Balthasar.

**25.** *hap,* occurrence.

## CONSIDERING ACT THREE, SCENES 2 AND 3

**1. (a)** What are Juliet's first reactions to the tragic news brought to her by the nurse? **(b)** How do we know that, despite everything, Juliet will remain true to Romeo?

**2.** Scene 2 has shown how Juliet reacts to misfortune; Scene 3 shows how Romeo reacts to misfortune. Which of them makes the more favorable impression on you? Why?

**3. (a)** What arguments does the friar use in attempting to convince Romeo that his despair is not justified? **(b)** According to the friar, what steps should now be taken to safeguard Romeo? What is Romeo's reaction to the friar's suggestions?

*Scene 4: A room in Capulet's house.*

Enter LORD *and* LADY CAPULET *and* PARIS.

CAPULET (*to* PARIS). Things have fallen out, sir, so unluckily
    That we have had no time to move our daughter.[1]
    Look you, she loved her kinsman Tybalt dearly,
    And so did I.—Well, we were born to die.
    'Tis very late, she'll not come down tonight;
    I promise you, but for your company,
    I would have been abed an hour ago.
PARIS. These times of woe afford no time to woo.
    Madam, good night; commend me to your daughter.
LADY CAPULET. I will, and know her mind early tomorrow;
    Tonight she is mewed up to her heaviness.[2]
CAPULET. Sir Paris, I will make a desperate tender[3]
    Of my child's love. I think she will be ruled
    In all respects by me; nay, more, I doubt it not.
    Wife, go you to her ere you go to bed;
    Acquaint her here of my son[4] Paris' love,
    And bid her, mark you me, on Wednesday next—
    But soft! What day is this?
PARIS.                Monday, my lord.
CAPULET. Monday? Ha, ha! Well, Wednesday is too soon.
    O' Thursday let it be; o' Thursday, tell her,
    She shall be married to this noble earl.
    Will you be ready? Do you like this haste?
    We'll keep no great ado—a friend or two;
    For, hark you, Tybalt being slain so late,[5]
    It may be thought we held him carelessly,[6]
    Being our kinsman, if we revel much.
    Therefore we'll have some half-a-dozen friends,
    And there an end. But what say you to Thursday?
PARIS. My lord, I would that Thursday were tomorrow.
CAPULET. Well, get you gone; o' Thursday be it, then.
    (*To* LADY CAPULET.) Go you to Juliet ere you go to bed,
    Prepare her, wife, against[7] this wedding day.
    Farewell, my lord. Light to my chamber, ho!
    Afore me,[8] it is so very very late
    That we may call it early by-and-by.
    Good night.                       (*Exeunt.*)

1. *move our daughter,* talk to Juliet about marrying you.

2. *mewed . . . heaviness,* confined in her room with her grief.
3. *desperate tender,* rash offer.

4. *son,* prospective son-in-law.

5. *late,* recently.
6. *held him carelessly,* regarded him too lightly.

7. *against,* for.

8. *Afore me,* by my life!

---

*Scene 5: Capulet's orchard.*

Enter ROMEO *and* JULIET,
*at the window of her bedroom.*

JULIET. Wilt thou be gone? It is not yet near day.
    It was the nightingale, and not the lark,[1]
    That pierced the fearful hollow of thine ear;

1. *nightingale . . . lark.* The nightingale's song is associated with the night, the lark's song with dawn.

Nightly she sings on yond pomegranate tree.
5  Believe me, love, it was the nightingale.
ROMEO. It was the lark, the herald of the morn,
   No nightingale. Look, love, what envious streaks
   Do lace[2] the severing[3] clouds in yonder east.
   Night's candles are burnt out, and jocund day
10  Stands tiptoe on the misty mountain tops.
   I must be gone and live, or stay and die.
JULIET. Yond light is not daylight, I know it, I;
   It is some meteor that the sun exhales,
   To be to thee this night a torchbearer
15  And light thee on thy way to Mantua.
   Therefore stay yet; thou need'st not to be gone.
ROMEO. Let me be ta'en, let me be put to death;
   I am content, so thou wilt have it so.
   I have more care[4] to stay than will to go.
20  Come, death, and welcome! Juliet wills it so.
   How is 't, my soul? Let's talk; it is not day.
JULIET. It is, it is; hie hence, be gone, away!
   It is the lark that sings so out of tune,
   Straining harsh discords and unpleasing sharps.[5]
25  O, now be gone; more light and light it grows.
ROMEO. More light and light; more dark and dark our woes!

*Enter the* NURSE, *to the bedchamber.*
NURSE *(urgently)*. Madam!
JULIET. Nurse?
NURSE. Your lady mother is coming to your chamber.
30  The day is broke; be wary, look about.        *(Exit.)*
JULIET. Then, window, let day in and let life out.
ROMEO. Farewell, farewell! One kiss, and I'll descend.
                  *(He starts down the ladder.)*
JULIET. Art thou gone so, love, lord, ay, husband, friend?[6]
   I must hear from thee every day in the hour,
35  For in a minute there are many days.
   O, by this count I shall be much in years
   Ere I again behold my Romeo!
ROMEO. Farewell!
   I will omit no opportunity
40  That may convey my greetings, love, to thee.
JULIET. O, think'st thou we shall ever meet again?
ROMEO. I doubt it not; and all these woes shall serve
   For sweet discourses in our time to come.
JULIET. O God, I have an ill-divining[7] soul!
45  Methinks I see thee, now thou art below,
   As one dead in the bottom of a tomb.
   Either my eyesight fails, or thou look'st pale.
ROMEO. And trust me, love, in my eye so do you.
   Dry sorrow drinks our blood.[8] Adieu, adieu!        *(Exit.)*
50 JULIET. O fortune, fortune! All men call thee fickle;

2. *lace*, stripe, streak.
3. *severing*, scattering.

4. *care*, concern, desire.

5. *sharps*, high notes.

6. *friend*, lover.

7. *ill-divining*, anticipating evil.

8. *Dry sorrow . . . blood.* It was believed that sorrow dried up the blood.

If thou art fickle, what dost thou with him
That is renowned for faith? Be fickle, fortune,
For then I hope thou wilt not keep him long,
But send him back.
LADY CAPULET (*off-stage*). Ho, daughter! Are you up?
55 JULIET. Who is 't that calls? Is it my lady mother?
Is she not down[9] so late, or up so early?
What unaccustomed cause procures her hither?[10]

Enter LADY CAPULET.

LADY CAPULET. Why, how now, Juliet!
JULIET.                                       Madam, I am not well.
LADY CAPULET. Evermore weeping for your cousin's death?
60   What, wilt thou wash him from his grave with tears?
An if thou couldst, thou couldst not make him live;
Therefore, have done. Some grief shows much of love,
But much of grief shows still some want of wit.
JULIET. Yet let me weep for such a feeling[11] loss.
65 LADY CAPULET. So shall you feel the loss, but not the friend
Which you weep for.
JULIET.                          Feeling so the loss,
I cannot choose but ever weep the friend.
LADY CAPULET. Well, girl, thou weep'st not so much for his death
As that the villain lives which slaughtered him.
70 JULIET. What villain, madam?
LADY CAPULET.                          That same villain Romeo.
JULIET (*aside*). Villain and he be many miles asunder.—
(*Aloud.*) God pardon him! I do, with all my heart;
And yet no man like[12] he doth grieve my heart.
LADY CAPULET. That is because the traitor murderer lives.
75 JULIET. Ay, madam, from the reach of these my hands.
Would none but I might venge[13] my cousin's death!
LADY CAPULET. We will have vengeance for it, fear thou not;
Then weep no more. I'll send to one in Mantua,
Where that same banished runagate doth live,
80   Shall give him such an unaccustomed dram
That he shall soon keep Tybalt company;
And then, I hope, thou wilt be satisfied.
JULIET. Indeed, I never shall be satisfied
With Romeo till I behold him—dead[14]—
85   Is my poor heart so for a kinsman vexed.
Madam, if you could find out but a man
To bear a poison, I would temper[15] it,
That Romeo should, upon receipt thereof,
Soon sleep in quiet. O, how my heart abhors
90   To hear him named, and cannot come to him,
To wreak the love I bore my cousin
Upon his body that hath slaughtered him!
LADY CAPULET. Find thou the means, and I'll find such a man.
But now I'll tell thee joyful tidings, girl.

9. *down*, in bed.
10. *procures her hither*, leads her to come this way.

11. *feeling*, deeply felt.

12. *like*, so much as.

13. *venge*, avenge.

14. *dead*. Juliet arranges her words in such a way that Lady Capulet will mistakenly think that Juliet wishes to see Romeo dead.
15. *temper*, mix. Juliet continues to speak in a way that misleads her mother.

JULIET. And joy comes well in such a needy time;
　What are they,[16] I beseech your ladyship?
LADY CAPULET. Well, well, thou hast a careful[17] father, child,
　One who, to put thee from thy heaviness,
　Hath sorted out[18] a sudden day of joy,
　That thou expect'st not nor I looked not for.
JULIET. Madam, in happy time, what day is that?
LADY CAPULET. Marry, my child, early next Thursday morn,
　The gallant, young, and noble gentleman,
　The County Paris, at Saint Peter's Church,
　Shall happily make thee there a joyful bride.
JULIET (with vigorous spirit). Now, by Saint Peter's Church and
　　Peter too,
　He shall *not* make me there a joyful bride.
　I wonder at this haste, that I must wed
　Ere he that should be husband comes to woo.
　I pray you, tell my lord and father, madam,
　I will not marry yet, and when I do, I swear
　It shall be Romeo, whom you know I hate,
　Rather than Paris. These are news indeed!
LADY CAPULET (angrily). Here comes your father, tell him so
　　yourself,
　And see how he will take it at your hands.

　　　　　　　　Enter CAPULET *and the* NURSE.
CAPULET. How now! A conduit,[19] girl? What, still in tears?
　Evermore showering? In one little body
　Thou counterfeit'st a bark, a sea, a wind;
　For still thy eyes, which I may call the sea,
　Do ebb and flow with tears; the bark thy body is,
　Sailing in this salt flood; the winds, thy sighs,
　Who, raging with thy tears, and they with them,
　Without a sudden calm, will overset
　Thy tempest-tossèd body. How now, wife!
　Have you delivered to her our decree?
LADY CAPULET. Ay, sir, but she will none,[20] she gives you thanks.
　I would the fool were married to her grave!
CAPULET. Soft! Take me with you,[21] take me with you, wife.
　How! Will she none? Doth she not give us thanks?
　Is she not proud? Doth she not count her blest,
　Unworthy as she is, that we have wrought
　So worthy a gentleman to be her bridegroom?
JULIET. Not proud you have, but thankful that you have.
　Proud can I never be of what I hate,
　But thankful even for hate that is meant love.
CAPULET. How now, how now, choplogic![22] What is this?
　"Proud," and "I thank you," and "I thank you not";
　And yet "not proud." Mistress minion,[23] you,
　Thank me no thankings, nor proud me no prouds,
　But fettle[24] your fine joints 'gainst[25] Thursday next,

16. *they*, the "joyful tidings," in line 94.
17. *careful*, taking care to ensure your well-being.
18. *sorted out*, chosen.

19. *conduit*, fountain.

20. *will none*, refuses "our decree," in the preceding line.
21. *Take me with you.* Let me understand you.

22. *choplogic*, quibbler, one who argues unfairly.
23. *minion*, darling, favored person.
24. *fettle*, make ready.
25. *'gainst*, in preparation for.

To go with Paris to Saint Peter's Church,
Or I will drag thee on a hurdle²⁶ thither.
Out, you green-sickness²⁷ carrion! Out, you baggage,²⁸
You tallow-face!

LADY CAPULET (to CAPULET). Fie, fie! What, art you mad?

145 JULIET (kneeling). Good father, I beseech you on my knees,
Hear me with patience but to speak a word.

CAPULET. Hang thee, young baggage, disobedient wretch!
I tell thee what: get thee to church o' Thursday
Or never after look me in the face.
150 Speak not, reply not, do not answer me;
My fingers itch.²⁹ Wife, we scarce thought us blest
That God had lent us but this only child;
But now I see this one is one too much,
And that we have a curse in having her.
155 Out on her, hilding!³⁰

NURSE.                    God in heaven, bless her!
You are to blame, my lord, to rate³¹ her so.

CAPULET. And why, my lady wisdom? Hold your tongue,
Good prudence;³² smatter³³ with your gossips, go.

NURSE. I speak no treason.

CAPULET.                    O, God ye god-den.

160 NURSE. May not one speak?

CAPULET.                    Peace, you mumbling fool!
Utter your gravity³⁴ o'er a gossip's bowl,
For here we need it not.

LADY CAPULET.                    You are too hot.

CAPULET. God's bread!³⁵ It makes me mad:
Day, night, hour, tide, time, work, play,
165 Alone, in company—still my care hath been
To have her matched; and having now provided
A gentleman of noble parentage,
Of fair demesnes, youthful, and nobly trained,
Stuffed, as they say, with honorable parts,³⁶
170 Proportioned as one's thought would wish a man—
And then to have a wretched puling fool,
A whining mammet,³⁷ in her fortune's tender,³⁸
To answer "I'll not wed; I cannot love,
I am too young; I pray you, pardon me."
175 But, an you will not wed, I'll pardon you;
Graze where you will, you shall not house with me.
Look to 't, think on 't; I do not use to jest.³⁹
Thursday is near; lay hand on heart, advise.⁴⁰
An you be mine, I'll give you to my friend;
180 An you be not, hang, beg, starve, die in the streets,
For, by my soul, I'll ne'er acknowledge thee,
Nor what is mine shall never do thee good.
Trust to 't, bethink you; I'll not be forsworn.

(Exit CAPULET.)

JULIET. Is there no pity sitting in the clouds,

26. *hurdle*, a conveyance for transporting criminals.
27. *green-sickness*, an anemic ailment of young women.
28. *baggage*, worthless woman.

29. *My fingers itch*, that is, to choke or strike you.

30. *hilding*, good-for-nothing.

31. *rate*, berate, scold.

32. *Good prudence*, my wise one. Capulet is speaking ironically.
33. *smatter*, chatter.

34. *gravity*, wisdom.

35. *God's bread*, by the sacrament; a mild oath.

36. *parts*, qualities, abilities.

37. *mammet*, doll.
38. *in . . . tender*, offer of good fortune.

39. *I do not . . . jest*. I am unaccustomed to jesting.
40. *advise*, consider carefully.

That sees into the bottom of my grief?
O sweet my mother, cast me not away!
Delay this marriage for a month, a week;
Or, if you do not, make the bridal bed
In that dim monument where Tybalt lies.

LADY CAPULET. Talk not to me, for I'll not speak a word.
Do as thou wilt, for I have done with thee.
                    *(Exit, leaving* JULIET *and the* NURSE *alone.)*

JULIET. O God!—O Nurse, how shall this be prevented?
My husband is on earth, my faith in heaven;[41]
How shall that faith return again to earth
Unless that husband send it me from heaven
By leaving earth? Comfort me, counsel me.
Alack, alack, that heaven should practice stratagems[42]
Upon so soft a subject as myself!
What say'st thou? Hast thou not a word of joy?
Some comfort, Nurse.

NURSE.                    Faith, here it is.
Romeo is banished; and all the world to nothing,[43]
That he dares ne'er come back to challenge[44] you;
Or, if he do, it needs must be by stealth.
Then, since the case so stands as now it doth,
I think it best you married with the County.
O, he's a lovely gentleman!
Romeo's a dishclout to him;[45] an eagle, madam,
Hath not so green,[46] so quick, so fair an eye
As Paris hath. Beshrew[47] my very heart,
I think you are happy in this second match,
For it excels your first; or, if it did not,
Your first is dead, or 'twere as good he were
As living here and you no use of him.

JULIET. Speakest thou from thy heart?

NURSE.                    And from my soul too;
Or else beshrew them both.

JULIET.                    Amen!

NURSE.                    What?

JULIET. Well, thou hast comforted me marvelous much.
Go in, and tell my lady I am gone,
Having displeased my father, to Laurence' cell,
To make confession and to be absolved.

NURSE. Marry, I will; and this is wisely done.          *(Exit.)*

JULIET. Ancient damnation![48] O most wicked fiend!
Is it more sin to wish me thus forsworn,
Or to dispraise my lord with that same tongue
Which she hath praised him with above compare
So many thousand times? Go, counselor;
Thou and my bosom[49] henceforth shall be twain.
I'll to the friar to know his remedy.
If all else fail, myself have power to die.          *(Exit.)*

41. *faith in heaven.* Juliet refers to her marriage vows.

42. *practice stratagems,* contrive dreadful deeds.

43. *all . . . nothing.* The odds are all the world to nothing.
44. *challenge,* lay claim to.

45. *to him,* compared to him.
46. *green.* Green eyes were much admired in Shakespeare's day.
47. *Beshrew,* curse.

48. *Ancient damnation,* wicked old devil.

49. *bosom,* confidence.

## CONSIDERING ACT THREE, SCENES 4 AND 5

**1. (a)** Point out evidence that Capulet has wrongly assumed that Juliet will be "ruled in all respects" by his wishes. **(b)** What is Capulet's reaction to Juliet's stand?

**2. (a)** What is the attitude of Lady Capulet toward Juliet's defiance? **(b)** What is the nurse's advice to Juliet, and what is Juliet's reaction to that advice?

**3.** What does Juliet plan to do now?

## LOOKING BACK—AND AHEAD

**1.** Continue your outline of the play, listing the most important events that take place in Act Three.

**2.** Shakespeare not only tells us what his characters do, he also makes clear why (wisely or unwisely) they act as they do. Complete each of the following statements based on Act Three: **(a)** Because Tybalt slays Mercutio, Romeo _____. **(b)** Because Romeo avenges Mercutio's death, the prince sentences him to _____. **(c)** Because Juliet is eager to learn what plans Romeo has made for their marriage, she _____. **(d)** Because the nurse is a great talker, Juliet finds it almost impossible to _____. **(e)** Because Romeo cannot reconcile himself to being separated from Juliet, he threatens to _____.

**3.** On what note of foreboding does Act Three end?


# Act Four

*Scene 1: Friar Laurence's cell.*

*Enter* FRIAR LAURENCE *and* PARIS.

FRIAR LAURENCE. On Thursday, sir? The time is very short.

PARIS. My father[1] Capulet will have it so,
And I am nothing slow to slack his haste.[2]

FRIAR LAURENCE. You say you do not know the lady's mind.
5    Uneven is the course; I like it not.

PARIS. Immoderately she weeps for Tybalt's death,
And therefore have I little talked of love;
For Venus smiles not in a house of tears.
Now, sir, her father counts it dangerous
10    That she doth give her sorrow so much sway,[3]
And in his wisdom hastes our marriage,
To stop the inundation of her tears;
Which, too much minded by herself alone,[4]
May be put from her by society.[5]
15    Now do you know the reason of this haste.

1. *My father,* my prospective father-in-law.
2. *nothing slow . . . haste,* anxious to do nothing that might slow him down in his plans to hasten the marriage.

3. *doth give . . . sway,* allows her sorrow (over Tybalt's death) to control her feelings.
4. *minded . . . alone,* dwelt on by her in privacy.
5. *May be . . . society,* may be remedied if she mingles with others.

FRIAR LAURENCE (*speaking aside*). I would I knew not why it
    should be slowed.
    Look, sir, here comes the lady toward my cell.

                                    *Enter* JULIET.

PARIS. Happily met, my lady and my wife!
JULIET. That may be, sir, when I may be a wife.
PARIS. That may be, must be, love, on Thursday next.
JULIET. What must be shall be.
FRIAR LAURENCE.               That's a certain text.
PARIS. Come you to make confession to this father?
JULIET. To answer that, I should confess to you.
PARIS. Do not deny to him that you love me.
JULIET. I will confess to you that I love him.
PARIS. So will ye, I am sure, that you love me.
JULIET. If I do so, it will be of more price,
    Being spoke behind your back, than to your face.
PARIS. Poor soul, thy face is much abused with tears.
JULIET. The tears have got small victory by that,
    For it was bad enough before their spite.
PARIS. Thou wrong'st it, more than tears, with that report.
JULIET. That is no slander, sir, which is a truth;
    And what I spake, I spake it to my face.
PARIS. Thy face is mine, and thou hast slandered it.
JULIET. It may be so, for it is not mine own.
    Are you at leisure, holy father, now,
    Or shall I come to you at evening mass?
FRIAR LAURENCE. My leisure serves me, pensive daughter, now.
    My lord, we must entreat the time alone.[6]
PARIS. God shield[7] I should disturb devotion!
    Juliet, on Thursday early will I rouse ye.
    Till then, adieu; and keep this holy kiss.        *(Exit.)*
JULIET. O, shut the door! And when thou hast done so,
    Come weep with me—past hope, past cure, past help!
FRIAR LAURENCE. Ah, Juliet, I already know thy grief;
    It strains me past the compass of my wits.[8]
    I hear thou must, and nothing may prorogue it,
    On Thursday next be married to this county.
JULIET. Tell me not, Friar, that thou hear'st of this,
    Unless thou tell me how I may prevent it.
    If, in thy wisdom, thou canst give no help,
    Do thou but call my resolution wise,
    And with this knife I'll help it presently.[9]
    God joined my heart and Romeo's, thou our hands;
    And ere this hand, by thee to Romeo sealed,
    Shall be the label[10] to another deed,
    Or my true heart with treacherous revolt
    Turn to another, this shall slay them both.
    Therefore, out of thy long-experienced time,
    Give me some present counsel, or, behold,
    'Twixt my extremes[11] and me this bloody knife

6. *entreat . . . alone,* request that you
leave Juliet and me alone.
7. *shield,* forbid, prevent.

8. *It strains . . . wits.* It ex-
ceeds the limits of my wisdom.

9. *presently,* at once.

10. *label,* the seal attached
to a deed (a legal document)
showing proof of ownership.

11. *extremes,* extreme difficulties.

Shall play the umpire, arbitrating that
Which the commission[12] of thy years and art
65 Could to no issue of true honor bring.
Be not so long to speak; I long to die,
If what thou speak'st speak not of remedy.
FRIAR LAURENCE. Hold, daughter. I do spy a kind of hope,
Which craves as desperate an execution[13]
70 As that is desperate which we would prevent.
If, rather than to marry County Paris,
Thou hast the strength of will to slay thyself,
Then is it likely thou wilt undertake
A thing like death to chide away this shame,
75 That copest with[14] death himself to 'scape from it;
And, if thou darest, I'll give thee remedy.
JULIET. O, bid me leap, rather than marry Paris,
From off the battlements of yonder tower,
Or walk in thievish ways;[15] or bid me lurk
80 Where serpents are; chain me with roaring bears;
Or shut me nightly in a charnel house,[16]
O'ercovered quite with dead men's rattling bones,
With reeky[17] shanks and yellow chapless[18] skulls;
Or bid me go into a new-made grave
85 And hide me with a dead man in his shroud—
Things that, to hear them told, have made me tremble—
And I will do it without fear or doubt,
To live an unstained wife to my sweet love.
FRIAR LAURENCE. Hold, then; go home, be merry, give consent
90 To marry Paris. Wednesday is tomorrow;
Tomorrow night look that thou lie alone;
Let not thy nurse lie with thee in thy chamber.
Take thou this vial, being then in bed,
And this distillèd liquor drink thou off;
95 When presently through all thy veins shall run
A cold and drowsy humor,[19] for no pulse
Shall keep his native progress, but surcease;[20]
No warmth, no breath, shall testify thou livest;
The roses in thy lips and cheeks shall fade
100 To paly ashes, thy eyes' windows fall
Like death when he shuts up the day of life.
Each part, deprived of supple government,[21]
Shall, stiff and stark and cold, appear like death,
And in this borrowed likeness of shrunk death
105 Thou shalt continue two and forty hours,
And then awake as from a pleasant sleep.
Now, when the bridegroom in the morning comes
To rouse thee from thy bed, there art thou dead;
Then, as a manner of our country is,
110 In thy best robes uncovered[22] on the bier
Thou shalt be borne to that same ancient vault
Where all the kindred of the Capulets lie.

12. *commission,* authority.

13. *execution,* carrying out.

14. *copest with,* bargains with.

15. *in thievish ways,* along highways where thieves hide out.
16. *charnel house,* a vault where the bodies of the dead were placed.
17. *reeky,* foul-smelling.
18. *chapless,* with the lower jaw missing.

19. *humor,* liquid.
20. *surcease,* cease.

21. *supple government,* control over the flexibility of the body.

22. *uncovered,* with your face uncovered.

In the meantime, against thou shalt awake,[23]
Shall Romeo by my letters know our drift,[24]
And hither shall he come, and he and I
Will watch thy waking, and that very night
Shall Romeo bear thee hence to Mantua.
And this shall free thee from this present shame,
If no inconstant toy,[25] nor womanish fear,
Abate thy valor in the acting it.
JULIET. Give me, give me! O, tell not me of fear!
FRIAR LAURENCE. Hold! Get you gone. Be strong and prosperous
In this resolve. I'll send a friar with speed
To Mantua, with my letters to thy lord.
JULIET. Love give me strength, and strength shall help afford.
Farewell, dear father!                    (*Exeunt.*)

23. *against . . . awake,* in preparation for your awakening.
24. *drift,* intentions.

25. *inconstant toy,* fickle, trifling fancy.

## CONSIDERING ACT FOUR, SCENE 1

**1. (a)** Why does Paris call on Friar Laurence? **(b)** What is Juliet's reason for visiting the friar?

**2. (a)** How does Juliet's brief conversation with Paris reveal her attitude toward him? **(b)** Point out some double, or hidden, meanings in Juliet's remarks to Paris.

**3. (a)** Quote lines that reveal Juliet's desperate hope that the friar can devise a plan that will prevent her marriage to Paris. **(b)** Outline, step by step, the friar's plan. What is Juliet's reaction to that plan?

*Scene 2: A hall in Capulet's house.*

*Enter* CAPULET, LADY CAPULET,
*the* NURSE, *and* SERVINGMEN.

CAPULET. So many guests invite as here are writ.
                    (*Exit* FIRST SERVANT.)
Sirrah, go hire me twenty cunning cooks.
SECOND SERVANT. You shall have none ill, sir; for I'll try if they can lick their fingers.
CAPULET. How canst thou try them so?
SECOND SERVANT. Marry, sir, 'tis an ill cook that cannot lick his own fingers; therefore he that cannot lick his fingers goes not with me.
CAPULET. Go, be gone.                    (*Exit* SECOND SERVANT.)
What, is my daughter gone to Friar Laurence?
NURSE. Ay, forsooth.
CAPULET. Well, he may chance to do some good on her.
NURSE. See where she comes from shrift with merry look.

*Enter* JULIET. *She is
apparently in good spirits.*
CAPULET. How now, my headstrong! Where have you been gadding?

15 JULIET. Where I have learned me to repent the sin
      Of disobedient opposition
      To you and your behests, and am enjoined
      By holy Laurence to fall prostrate here
      And beg your pardon. *(She kneels.)* Pardon, I beseech you!
20    Henceforward I am ever ruled by you.
   CAPULET. Send for the county; go tell him of this.
      I'll have this knot knit up tomorrow morning.
   JULIET. I met the youthful lord at Laurence' cell,
      And gave him what becomèd[1] love I might,                    **1.** *becomèd,* suitable.
25    Not stepping o'er the bounds of modesty.
   CAPULET. Why, I am glad on 't; this is well. Stand up.
      This is as 't should be. Let me see the county;
      Ay, marry, go, I say, and fetch him hither.
      Now, afore God, this reverend holy friar,
30    All our whole city is much bound[2] to him.                   **2.** *bound,* indebted.
   JULIET. Nurse, will you go with me into my closet,[3]            **3.** *closet,* private room.
      To help me sort such needful ornaments
      As you think fit to furnish me[4] tomorrow?                   **4.** *furnish me,* fit me out.
   LADY CAPULET. No, not till Thursday; there is time enough.
35 CAPULET. Go, Nurse, go with her. We'll to church tomorrow.
                                 *(Exeunt* JULIET *and* NURSE.*)*
   LADY CAPULET. We shall be short in our provision;
      'Tis now near night.
   CAPULET.                Tush, I will stir about,
      And all things shall be well, I warrant thee, wife.
      Go thou to Juliet, help to deck her up;
40    I'll not to bed tonight; let me alone;
      I'll play the housewife for this once. What, ho!
      They are all forth. Well, I will walk myself
      To County Paris to prepare him up
      Against tomorrow. My heart is wondrous light,
45    Since this same wayward girl is so reclaimed.
                                              *(Exeunt.)*

*Scene 3: Juliet's bedchamber.*

                           *Enter* JULIET *and the* NURSE.
   JULIET. Ay, those attires are best; but, gentle Nurse,
      I pray thee, leave me to myself tonight,
      For I have need of many orisons
      To move the heavens to smile upon my state,
5     Which, well thou know'st, is cross[1] and full of sin.        **1.** *cross,* contrary.

                            *Enter* LADY CAPULET.
   LADY CAPULET. What, are you busy, ho? Need you my help?
   JULIET. No, madam; we have culled such necessaries
      As are behoveful[2] for our state tomorrow.                  **2.** *behoveful,* needed.
      So please you, let me now be left alone,
10    And let the nurse this night sit up with you,

For I am sure you have your hands full all
In this so sudden business.

LADY CAPULET.                    Good night;
Get thee to bed, and rest, for thou hast need.

*(Exeunt* LADY CAPULET *and the* NURSE.*)*

JULIET. Farewell! God knows when we shall meet again.

15    I have a faint cold fear thrills through my veins,[3]
That almost freezes up the heat of life;
I'll call them back again to comfort me.
Nurse!—What should she do here?
My dismal scene I needs must act alone.
20    Come, vial.
What if this mixture do not work at all?
Shall I be married then tomorrow morning?
No, no; this shall forbid it. Lie thou there.

*(She lays down her dagger.)*

What if it be a poison which the friar
25    Subtly hath ministered[4] to have me dead,
Lest in this marriage he should be dishonored
Because he married me before to Romeo?
I fear it is, and yet methinks it should not,
For he hath still been tried[5] a holy man.
30    How if, when I am laid into the tomb,
I wake before the time that Romeo
Come to redeem me?—There's a fearful point!
Shall I not then be stifled in the vault,
To whose foul mouth no healthsome air breathes in,
35    And there die strangled ere my Romeo comes?
Or, if I live, is it not very like[6]
The horrible conceit[7] of death and night,
Together with the terror of the place—
As[8] in a vault, an ancient receptacle
40    Where, for these many hundred years, the bones
Of all my buried ancestors are packed;
Where bloody Tybalt, yet but green in earth,[9]
Lies festering in his shroud; where, as they say,
At some hours in the night spirits resort;—
45    Alack, alack, is it not like that I,
So early waking, what with loathsome smells,
And shrieks like mandrakes'[10] torn out of the earth,
That living mortals, hearing them, run mad:—
O, if I wake, shall I not be distraught,
50    Environed with all these hideous fears,[11]
And madly play with my forefathers' joints,
And pluck the mangled Tybalt from his shroud,
And, in this rage,[12] with some great kinsman's bone,
As with a club, dash out my desperate brains?
55    O, look! Methinks I see my cousin's ghost
Seeking out Romeo, that did spit his body
Upon a rapier's point.—Stay, Tybalt, stay!

**3.** *faint . . . veins,* a feeling of coldness and faintness that courses through my veins.

**4.** *ministered,* applied or administered (something).

**5.** *still been tried,* always been proved to be.

**6.** *like,* likely.

**7.** *conceit,* idea.

**8.** *As,* namely.

**9.** *green in earth,* newly buried.

**10.** *mandrakes,* plants that resemble the human form. The mandrake was fabled to shriek and to cause madness when torn from the ground.

**11.** *fears,* objects of fear.

**12.** *rage,* madness.

Romeo, I come! This do I drink to thee.
                    *(She drinks and falls upon her curtained bed.)*


**CONSIDERING ACT FOUR, SCENES 2 AND 3**

**1.** In carrying out the friar's instructions, how does Juliet resort to deceit? Do you think her deceit was justified? Why or why not?

**2. (a)** What questions and doubts come to Juliet's mind during the famous "potion" scene? **(b)** What are your feelings toward Juliet in this scene? Read lines that were especially effective in arousing those feelings.


*Scene 4: A hall in Capulet's house.*

                    *Enter* LADY CAPULET *and the* NURSE.
LADY CAPULET. Hold, take these keys, and fetch more spices,
      Nurse.
NURSE. They call for dates and quinces in the pastry.[1]

                    *Enter* CAPULET.
CAPULET. Come, stir, stir, stir! The second cock hath crowed,
      The curfew bell hath rung, 'tis three o'clock.
      Look to the bakèd meats,[2] good Angelica;
      Spare not for cost.
NURSE. Get you to bed; faith, you'll be sick tomorrow
      For this night's watching.[3]
CAPULET. No, not a whit. What! I have watched ere now
      All night for lesser cause, and ne'er been sick.
LADY CAPULET. Ay; but I'll watch you from such watching now.
                    *(Exeunt* LADY CAPULET *and* NURSE.)

                    *Enter* SERVANTS *carrying baskets of food.*
CAPULET. Now, fellow! What's there?
FIRST SERVANT. Things for the cook, sir, but I know not what.
CAPULET. Make haste, make haste.
                    *(Exit* FIRST SERVANT.)
      *(To* SECOND SERVANT.) Sirrah, fetch drier logs;
      Call Peter, he will show thee where they are.
SECOND SERVANT. I have a head, sir, that will find out logs,
      And never trouble Peter for the matter.          *(Exit.)*
CAPULET. Mass,[4] and well said! A merry fellow, ha!
      Thou shalt be loggerhead.[5] Good faith, 'tis day.
      The county will be here with music straight,
      For so he said he would. I hear him near.
                    *(Music sounds off-stage.)*
      Nurse! Wife! What, ho! What, Nurse, I say!

                    *Enter* NURSE.

1. *pastry,* room in which pastry was made.

2. *bakèd meats,* pies, pastries.

3. *For . . . watching,* because of lying awake tonight.

4. *Mass,* by the Mass.
5. *loggerhead,* blockhead.

Go waken Juliet; go and trim her up.
I'll go and chat with Paris. Hie, make haste,
25 Make haste; the bridegroom he is come already;
Make haste, I say. *(Exeunt.)*


*Scene 5: Juliet's bedchamber. The curtains are drawn around Juliet's bed.*

*Enter the* NURSE.

NURSE *(urgently)*. Mistress! What, mistress! Juliet! Fast,[1] I
warrant her.
Why, lamb; why, lady! Fie, you slugabed!
Why, love, I say! *(She undraws the curtains around the bed.)*
Madam! Sweetheart! Why, bride!
What, not a word? How sound is she asleep!
5 I must needs wake her. Madam, madam, madam!
What, dressed, and in your clothes, and down again!
I must needs wake you. Lady! lady! lady!
Alas, alas! Help, help! My lady's dead!
O well-a-day, that ever I was born!
10 Some aqua vitae, ho! My lord! My lady!

*Enter* LADY CAPULET.

LADY CAPULET. What noise is here?
NURSE.                    O lamentable day!
LADY CAPULET. What is the matter?
NURSE.                    Look, look! O heavy day!
LADY CAPULET. O me, O me! My child, my only life,
Revive, look up, or I will die with thee!
15 Help, help! Call help!

*Enter* CAPULET.

CAPULET. For shame, bring Juliet forth; her lord is come.
NURSE. She's dead, deceased, she's dead; alack the day!
LADY CAPULET. Alack the day, she's dead, she's dead, she's dead!
CAPULET. Ha! Let me see her. Out, alas![2] She's cold;
20 Her blood is settled,[3] and her joints are stiff.
Life and these lips have long been separated.
Death lies on her like an untimely frost
Upon the sweetest flower of all the field.

*Enter* FRIAR LAURENCE *and* PARIS.

FRIAR LAURENCE. Come, is the bride ready to go to church?
25 CAPULET. Ready to go, but never to return.
Death is my son-in-law, Death is my heir;
My daughter he hath wedded. I will die
And leave him all. Life, living, all is Death's.
PARIS. Have I thought long to see this morning's face,[4]
30 And doth it give me such a sight as this?

1. *Fast,* fast asleep.

2. *Out, alas,* an exclamation of grief.

3. *settled,* thickened.

4. *thought long . . . face,* long looked forward to the dawn of this, my wedding day.

LADY CAPULET. Accursed, unhappy, wretched, hateful day!
  Most miserable hour that e'er time saw.
  But one thing to rejoice and solace in,
  And cruel Death hath catched it from my sight!
35 NURSE. O woe! O woeful, woeful, woeful day!
  Most lamentable day, most woeful day,
  That ever, ever, I did yet behold!
PARIS. Beguiled, divorced, wronged, spited, slain!
  Most detestable Death, by thee beguiled,
40  By cruel cruel thee quite overthrown!
  O love! O life; not life, but love in death!
CAPULET. O child! O child! My soul, and not my child!
  Dead art thou, dead! Alack, my child is dead,
  And with my child my joys are buried.
45 FRIAR LAURENCE. Peace, ho, for shame! Confusion's[5] cure lives not
  In these confusions. Heaven and yourself
  Had part in this fair maid; now heaven hath all,
  And all the better is it for the maid.
  Your part in her you could not keep from death,
50  But heaven keeps his part in eternal life.
  The most you sought was her promotion;
  For 'twas your heaven she should be advanced;[6]
  And weep ye now, seeing she is advanced
  Above the clouds, as high as heaven itself?
55  Dry up your tears, and stick your rosemary[7]
  On this fair corse; and, as the custom is,
  In all her best array bear her to church.
CAPULET. All things that we ordained festival,[8]
  Turn from their office to black funeral—
60  Our instruments to melancholy bells,
  Our wedding cheer to a sad burial feast,
  Our solemn hymns to sullen[9] dirges change;
  Our bridal flowers serve for a buried corse,
  And all things change them to the contrary.
65 FRIAR LAURENCE. Sir, go you in; and, madam, go with him;
  And go, Sir Paris; everyone prepare
  To follow this fair corse unto her grave.
  The heavens do lour upon you for some ill;[10]
  Move them no more by crossing their high will.
          (*Exeunt* CAPULET, LADY CAPULET, PARIS, *and* FRIAR.)

5. *Confusion's,* destruction's.

6. *advanced,* lifted up, promoted.

7. *rosemary,* symbol of immortality and enduring love; therefore, used at both funerals and weddings.

8. *ordained festival,* intended to be gay and festive.

9. *sullen,* mournful.

10. *ill,* sin committed by you.

## CONSIDERING ACT FOUR, SCENES 4 AND 5

1. Why may the hustle and bustle of preparation for the wedding feast be described as *ironical?*

2. How does Scene 5 indicate that an important step in the friar's plan has worked out just as he had hoped it would?

3. (a) What are your feelings toward Lord and Lady Capulet as they lament the "death" of their daughter? Explain why you feel as you do.

**(b)** Why had Juliet not taken the nurse into her confidence concerning the friar's plan?

## LOOKING BACK—AND AHEAD

**1.** Add your outline of the important events in Act Four to your previous outlines.

**2.** Point out ways in which Juliet has shown strength and courage in Act Four.

**3.** Do you think that Friar Laurence's plan will continue to work out well? Why or why not?

# Act Five

*Scene 1: A street in Mantua, where Romeo is living.*

ROMEO *enters.*

ROMEO. If I may trust the flattering truth of sleep,[1]
  My dreams presage some joyful news at hand.
  My bosom's lord[2] sits lightly in his throne,
  And all this day an unaccustomed spirit
5  Lifts me above the ground with cheerful thoughts.
  I dreamt my lady came and found me dead—
  Strange dream that gives a dead man leave[3] to think!—
  And breathed such life with kisses in my lips
  That I revived and was an emperor.
10  Ah me, how sweet is love itself possessed,
  When but love's shadows[4] are so rich in joy!

*Enter* BALTHASAR.

  News from Verona!—How now, Balthasar!
  Dost thou not bring me letters from the friar?
  How doth my lady? Is my father well?
15  How fares my Juliet? That I ask again,
  For nothing can be ill if she be well.
BALTHASAR. Then she is well, and nothing can be ill.
  Her body sleeps in Capel's monument,
  And her immortal part with angels lives.
20  I saw her laid low in her kindred's vault,
  And presently took post[5] to tell it you.
  O, pardon me for bringing these ill news,
  Since you did leave it for my office,[6] sir.
ROMEO. Is it even so? Then I defy you, stars![7]
25  Thou know'st my lodging; get me ink and paper,

**1.** *flattering . . . sleep,* pleasant dreams that seem true.
**2.** *bosom's lord,* heart.

**3.** *gives . . . leave,* allows a dead man.

**4.** *shadows,* unreal images of the imagination.

**5.** *presently took post,* soon set out with post horses.
**6.** *office,* duty.
**7.** *Then . . . stars.* Romeo defies the destiny that has fated him to live without Juliet.

And hire post horses; I will hence tonight.
BALTHASAR. I do beseech you, sir, have patience;
    Your looks are pale and wild, and do import
    Some misadventure.
ROMEO.               Tush, thou art deceived.
    Leave me, and do the thing I bid thee do.
    Hast thou no letters to me from the friar?
BALTHASAR. No, my good lord.
ROMEO.           No matter. Get thee gone,
    And hire those horses; I'll be with thee straight.

                      *(Exit* BALTHASAR.*)*

    Well, Juliet, I will be with thee tonight.
    Let's see for means. O mischief, thou art swift
    To enter in the thoughts of desperate men!
    I do remember an apothecary—
    And hereabouts he dwells—which late I noted
    In tattered weeds,[8] with overwhelming[9] brows,
    Culling of simples.[10] Meager were his looks,
    Sharp misery had worn him to the bones;
    And in his needy shop a tortoise hung,
    An alligator stuffed, and other skins
    Of ill-shaped fishes; and about his shelves
    A beggarly account[11] of empty boxes,
    Green earthen pots, bladders, and musty seeds,
    Remnants of packthread[12] and old cakes of roses,[13]
    Were thinly scattered to make up a show.
    Noting this penury, to myself I said,
    "An if a man did need a poison now
    Whose sale is present[14] death in Mantua,
    Here lives a caitiff[15] wretch would sell it him."
    O, this same thought did but forerun my need,
    And this same needy man must sell it me.
    As I remember, this should be the house.
    Being holiday, the beggar's shop is shut.
    What, ho, apothecary!

                    *Enter* APOTHECARY.

APOTHECARY.         Who calls so loud?
ROMEO. Come hither, man. I see that thou art poor.
    Hold, there is forty ducats; let me have
    A dram of poison, such soon-speeding gear[16]
    As will disperse itself through all the veins
    That the life-weary taker may fall dead
    And that the trunk[17] may be discharged of breath
    As violently as hasty powder fired
    Doth hurry from the fatal cannon's maw.
APOTHECARY. Such mortal drugs I have; but Mantua's law
    Is death to any he that utters them.[18]
ROMEO. Art thou so bare and full of wretchedness,
    And fear'st to die? Famine is in thy cheeks,

8. *weeds,* clothes.
9. *overwhelming,* overhanging.
10. *Culling of simples,* selecting medicinal herbs.

11. *beggarly account,* poor array.

12. *packthread,* twine.
13. *cakes of roses,* rose petals caked together for use as a perfume.

14. *present,* immediate.
15. *caitiff,* poor.

16. *soon-speeding gear,* stuff that will begin to act quickly.

17. *trunk,* body.

18. *any . . . utters them,* anyone who distributes them.

70 Need and oppression starveth[19] in thine eyes,
  Contempt and beggary hangs upon thy back;
  The world is not thy friend, nor the world's law;
  The world affords no law to make thee rich;
  Then be not poor, but break it, and take this.
75 APOTHECARY. My poverty, but not my will, consents.
  ROMEO. I pay thy poverty, and not thy will.
  APOTHECARY. Put this in any liquid thing you will
    And drink it off; and, if you had the strength
    Of twenty men, it would dispatch you straight.
80 ROMEO. There is thy gold, worse poison to men's souls.
    Farewell. Buy food, and get thyself in flesh.
    Come, cordial[20] and not poison, go with me
    To Juliet's grave, for there must I use thee.          (*Exeunt.*)

**19.** *starveth,* show hunger.

**20.** *cordial,* a heart stimulant.

*Scene 2: Friar Laurence's cell.*

                              *Enter* FRIAR JOHN.

FRIAR JOHN. Holy Franciscan friar! Brother, ho!

                              *Enter* FRIAR LAURENCE.

FRIAR LAURENCE. This same should be the voice of Friar John.
  Welcome from Mantua. What says Romeo?
  Or, if his mind be writ,[1] give me his letter.
5 FRIAR JOHN. Going to find a barefoot brother out,
  One of our order, to associate[2] me,
  Here in this city visiting the sick,
  And finding him, the searchers[3] of the town,
  Suspecting that we both were in a house
10 Where the infectious pestilence did reign,
  Sealed up the doors, and would not let us forth,
  So that my speed to Mantua there was stayed.
FRIAR LAURENCE. Who bare my letter, then, to Romeo?
FRIAR JOHN. I could not send it—here it is again—
15 Nor get a messenger to bring it thee,
  So fearful were they of infection.
FRIAR LAURENCE. Unhappy fortune! By my brotherhood,
  The letter was not nice[4] but full of charge
  Of dear import,[5] and the neglecting it
20 May do much danger. Friar John, go hence;
  Get me an iron crow,[6] and bring it straight
  Unto my cell.
FRIAR JOHN. Brother, I'll go and bring it thee.          (*Exit.*)
FRIAR LAURENCE. Now must I to the monument alone.
25 Within this three hours will fair Juliet wake.
  She will beshrew me much that Romeo
  Hath had no notice of these accidents;[7]
  But I will write again to Mantua,

**1.** *if . . . writ,* if he has sent a written message.
**2.** *associate,* accompany.

**3.** *searchers,* officials who sought out those suspected of having a highly contagious disease (the "infectious pestilence," in line 10).

**4.** *nice,* trivial.
**5.** *Of dear import,* having dreadful significance.
**6.** *iron crow,* crowbar.

**7.** *accidents,* happenings.

And keep her at my cell till Romeo come;
30  Poor living corse, closed in a dead man's tomb!          (*Exit.*)

## CONSIDERING ACT FIVE, SCENES 1 AND 2

1. (a) What is Romeo's mood at the beginning of Scene 1? (b) What causes Romeo's mood to change quickly?

2. What arguments does Romeo use in persuading the apothecary to sell him a dram of poison? Explain why you do or do not agree with these arguments.

3. (a) Why has Friar John been unable to deliver Friar Laurence's letter to Romeo? (b) Explain the irony of Romeo's indifferent comment, "No matter," when Balthasar tells him he has brought no letters from Friar Laurence.

*Scene 3: The churchyard in Verona where the Capulets' tomb is located. It is nighttime.*

Enter PARIS *and his* PAGE *bearing flowers and a torch.*
PARIS. Give me thy torch, boy; hence, and stand aloof.
    Yet put it out, for I would not be seen.
                    (*The* PAGE *extinguishes the torch.*)
    Under yond yew trees lay thee all along,[1]          1. *all along,* at full length.
    Holding thine ear close to the hollow ground;
5   So shall no foot upon the churchyard tread—
    Being loose, infirm, with digging up of graves—
    But thou shalt hear it; whistle then to me,
    As signal that thou hear'st something approach.
    Give me those flowers. Do as I bid thee, go.
10  PAGE (*speaking aside*). I am almost afraid to stand alone
    Here in the churchyard; yet I will adventure. (*He retires.*)
PARIS. Sweet flower, with flowers thy bridal bed I strew.
    O woe! Thy canopy is dust and stones,
    Which[2] with sweet[3] water nightly I will dew,          2. *Which.* The antecedent is "flowers," line 12.
15  Or, wanting[4] that, with tears distilled by moans.          3. *sweet,* perfumed.
    The obsequies that I for thee will keep          4. *wanting,* lacking.
    Nightly shall be to strew thy grave and weep.
                    (*The* PAGE *whistles off-stage.*)
    The boy gives warning something doth approach.
    What cursèd foot wanders this way tonight
20  To cross[5] my obsequies and true love's rite?          5. *cross,* interfere with.
    What, with a torch! Muffle[6] me, night, awhile. (*He retires.*)          6. *Muffle,* hide.

            Enter ROMEO *and* BALTHASAR *carrying tools*
                *to open the tomb. They cannot see* PARIS.
ROMEO. Give me that mattock[7] and the wrenching iron.          7. *mattock,* pickax.
    Hold, take this letter; early in the morning

See thou deliver it to my lord and father.
25  Give me the light. Upon thy life, I charge thee,
Whate'er thou hear'st or seest, stand all aloof,
And do not interrupt me in my course.
Why I descend into this bed of death
Is partly to behold my lady's face,
30  But chiefly to take thence from her dead finger
A precious ring—a ring that I must use
In dear employment. Therefore hence, be gone.
But if thou, jealous,[8] dost return to pry
In what I further shall intend to do,
35  By heaven I will tear thee joint by joint
And strew this hungry churchyard with thy limbs.
The time and my intents are savage, wild,
More fierce and more inexorable far
Than empty tigers or the roaring sea.
40 BALTHASAR. I will be gone, sir, and not trouble you.
ROMEO. So shalt thou show me friendship. (*Offering money.*)
    Take thou that.
Live and be prosperous, and farewell, good fellow.
BALTHASAR (*speaking aside*). For all this same, I'll hide me
    hereabout.
His looks I fear, and his intents I doubt.[9]       (*He retires.*)
45 ROMEO. Thou detestable maw, thou womb of death,
Gorged with the dearest morsel of the earth,
Thus I enforce thy rotten jaws to open,
And, in despite,[10] I'll cram thee with more food!
        (*He succeeds in opening the tomb.*)
PARIS. This is that banished haughty Montague
50  That murdered my love's cousin, with which grief,
It is supposed, the fair creature died,
And here is come to do some villainous shame
To the dead bodies. I will apprehend him.
        (*He comes forward.*)
Stop thy unhallowed toil, vile Montague!
55  Can vengeance be pursued further than death?
Condemnèd villain, I do apprehend thee;
Obey and go with me, for thou must die.
ROMEO. I must indeed; and therefore came I hither.
Good gentle youth, tempt not a desperate man;
60  Fly hence, and leave me. Think upon these gone;
Let them affright thee. I beseech thee, youth,
Put not another sin upon my head,
By urging me to fury. O, be gone!
By heaven, I love thee better than myself;
65  For I come hither armed against myself.
Stay not, be gone; live, and hereafter say
A madman's mercy bade thee run away.
PARIS. I do defy thy conjurations,[11]
And apprehend thee for a felon here.

8. *jealous,* suspicious.

9. *doubt,* suspect.

10. *in despite,* in defiance.

11. *conjurations,* solemn appeals.

ROMEO. Wilt thou provoke me? Then have at thee, boy!
PAGE. O Lord, they fight! I will go call the watch.          (*Exit.*)
PARIS. O, I am slain! (*He falls.*) If thou be merciful,
    Open the tomb, lay me with Juliet.          (*He dies.*)
ROMEO. In faith, I will. Let me peruse this face.
    Mercutio's kinsman, noble County Paris!
    What said my man when my betossèd soul
    Did not attend[12] him as we rode? I think
    He told me Paris should have married[13] Juliet.
    Said he not so? Or did I dream it so?
    Or am I mad, hearing him talk of Juliet,
    To think it was so? O, give me thy hand,
    One writ with me in sour misfortune's book!
    I'll bury thee in a triumphant[14] grave;
    A grave? O, no; a lantern,[15] slaughtered youth,
    For here lies Juliet, and her beauty makes
    This vault a feasting presence[16] full of light.
    Death,[17] lie thou there, by a dead man interred.
          (*He lays* PARIS *in the tomb, not far from* JULIET.)
    How oft when men are at the point of death
    Have they been merry, which their keepers call
    A lightning[18] before death. O, how may I
    Call this a lightning? O my love! my wife!
    Death, that hath sucked the honey of thy breath,
    Hath had no power yet upon thy beauty:
    Thou art not conquered; beauty's ensign yet
    Is crimson in thy lips and in thy cheeks,
    And death's pale flag is not advancèd there.
    Tybalt, liest thou there in thy bloody sheet?
    O, what more favor can I do to thee
    Than with that hand that cut thy youth in twain
    To sunder his that was thine enemy?
    Forgive me, cousin! Ah, dear Juliet,
    Why art thou yet so fair? Shall I believe
    That unsubstantial death is amorous,
    And that the lean abhorrèd monster keeps
    Thee here in the dark to be his paramour?
    For fear of that, I still will stay with thee
    And never from this palace of dim night
    Depart again. Here, here will I remain
    With worms that are thy chambermaids. O, here
    Will I set up my everlasting rest,
    And shake the yoke of inauspicious stars
    From this world-wearied flesh. Eyes, look your last!
    Arms, take your last embrace! And, lips, O you
    The doors of breath, seal with a righteous kiss
    A dateless[19] bargain to engrossing[20] death!
    Come, bitter conduct, come, unsavory guide!
    Thou desperate pilot, now at once run on
    The dashing rocks thy seasick weary bark!

12. *attend,* pay attention to.
13. *should have married,* was intended to marry.

14. *triumphant,* glorious, honorable.
15. *lantern,* a tower filled with many windows.
16. *feasting presence,* a splendid reception room in a regal mansion.
17. *Death,* the corpse of Paris.

18. *lightning,* a revival of spirit.

19. *dateless,* everlasting.
20. *engrossing,* all-demanding.

Here's to my love! *(He drinks the poison.)* O true apothecary!
120 Thy drugs are quick. Thus with a kiss I die.          *(Falls.)*

*Enter, at the other end of the churchyard,*
FRIAR LAURENCE, *with a lantern,*
*crowbar, mattock, and spade.*

FRIAR LAURENCE. Saint Francis be my speed![21] How oft tonight
Have my old feet stumbled at graves![22] Who's there?
BALTHASAR. Here's one, a friend, and one that knows you well.
FRIAR LAURENCE. Bliss be upon you! Tell me, good my friend,
125 What torch is yond that vainly lends his light
To grubs and eyeless skulls? As I discern,
It burneth in the Capels' monument.
BALTHASAR. It doth so, holy sir; and there's my master,
One that you love.
FRIAR LAURENCE.          Who is it?
BALTHASAR.                    Romeo.
130 FRIAR LAURENCE. How long hath he been there?
BALTHASAR.                              Full half an hour.
FRIAR LAURENCE. Go with me to the vault.
BALTHASAR.                          I dare not, sir.
My master knows not but I am gone hence,
And fearfully did menace me with death
If I did stay to look on his intents.
135 FRIAR LAURENCE. Stay, then; I'll go alone. Fear comes upon me;
O, much I fear some ill unlucky thing.
BALTHASAR. As I did sleep under this yew tree here,
I dreamt my master and another fought,
And that my master slew him.
FRIAR LAURENCE.                    Romeo! *(He goes forward.)*
140 Alack, alack, what blood is this which stains
The stony entrance of this sepulcher?
What mean these masterless and gory swords
To lie discolored by this place of peace?

                          *(He enters the tomb.)*

Romeo! O, pale! Who else? What, Paris too?
145 And steeped in blood? Ah, what an unkind hour
Is guilty of this lamentable chance!
The lady stirs. *(Slowly JULIET comes out of her trance.)*
JULIET. O comfortable[23] friar! Where is my lord?
I do remember well where I should be,
150 And there I am. Where is my Romeo?
                    *(Off-stage noise of the WATCH approaching.)*
FRIAR LAURENCE. I hear some noise. Lady, come from that nest.
Of death, contagion, and unnatural sleep.
A greater power than we can contradict
Hath thwarted out intents. Come, come away.
155 Thy husband in thy bosom there lies dead;
And Paris too. Come, I'll dispose of thee
Among a sisterhood of holy nuns.

21. *speed,* protector.
22. *stumbled at graves.* This was an unlucky omen.

23. *comfortable,* comforting.

Stay not to question, for the watch is coming;
Come, go, good Juliet. I dare no longer stay.
              (*He leaves* JULIET *alone with her dead husband.*)
160 JULIET. Go, get thee hence, for I will not away.
                                  (*Exit* FRIAR LAURENCE.)
What's here? A cup closed in my true love's hand?
Poison, I see, hath been his timeless[24] end.
O churl![25] Drunk all, and left no friendly drop
To help me after? I will kiss thy lips;
165 Haply[26] some poison yet doth hang on them,
To make me die with a restorative.[27] (*Kisses him.*)
Thy lips are warm.
FIRST WATCHMAN (*off-stage*). Lead, boy. Which way?
JULIET. Yea, noise? Then I'll be brief. O happy[28] dagger
                          (*She snatches* ROMEO'S *dagger.*)
170 This is thy sheath (*Stabs herself.*); there rust, and let me die.
                      (*She falls on* ROMEO'S *body and dies.*)

                  *Enter* WATCH, *with the* PAGE *of* PARIS.
PAGE. This is the place; there, where the torch doth burn.
FIRST WATCHMAN. The ground is bloody; search about the church-
    yard.
Go, some of you; whoe'er you find, attach.[29]
Pitiful sight! Here lies the county slain,
175 And Juliet bleeding, warm, and newly dead,
Who here hath lain these two days buried.
Go, tell the prince; run to the Capulets;
Raise up the Montagues; some others search.
We see the ground whereon these woes[30] do lie,
180 But the true ground[31] of all these piteous woes
We cannot without circumstance descry.[32]

          *Enter some members of the* WATCH, *with* BALTHASAR.
SECOND WATCHMAN. Here's Romeo's man; we found him in the
    churchyard.
FIRST WATCHMAN. Hold him in safety till the prince come hither.

          *Re-enter* FRIAR LAURENCE *and a third* WATCHMAN.
THIRD WATCHMAN. Here is a friar that trembles, sighs, and weeps.
185 We took this mattock and this spade from him
As he was coming from this churchyard side.
FIRST WATCHMAN. A great suspicion;[33] stay the friar too.

          *Enter* PRINCE ESCALUS *and* ATTENDANTS.
PRINCE. What misadventure is so early up,
That calls our person from our morning's rest?

              *Enter* LORD *and* LADY CAPULET.
190 CAPULET. What should it be that is so shrieked abroad?
LADY CAPULET. The people in the street cry "Romeo,"

24. *timeless*, untimely.
25. *churl*, miser.

26. *Haply*, perhaps.
27. *To make . . . restorative.*
The very thing (a kiss) that had
been a means of renewing
good cheer when Romeo was
alive, may now bring about
Juliet's death.
28. *happy*, timely.

29. *whoe'er . . . attach.* Arrest
anyone you find.

30. *woes*, the bodies of Romeo
and Juliet.
31. *ground*, cause.
32. *circumstance descry*, note
the details.

33. *A great suspicion*, a most
suspicious thing.

Some "Juliet," and some "Paris"; and all run
With open outcry toward our monument.
PRINCE. What fear is this which startles in our ears?
95 FIRST WATCHMAN. Sovereign, here lies the County Paris slain,
And Romeo dead, and Juliet, dead before,
Warm and new killed.
PRINCE. Search, seek, and know how this foul murder comes.
FIRST WATCHMAN. Here is a friar, and slaughtered Romeo's man,
00 With instruments upon them fit to open
These dead men's tombs.
CAPULET. O heavens! O wife, look how our daughter bleeds!
This dagger hath mista'en[34]—for, lo, his house[35]
Is empty on the back of Montague—
05 And it missheathed in my daughter's bosom!
LADY CAPULET. O me! This sight of death is as a bell
That warns[36] my old age to a sepulcher.

*Enter* MONTAGUE *and* OTHERS.

PRINCE. Come, Montague; for thou art early up
To see thy son and heir more early down.
210 MONTAGUE. Alas, my liege, my wife is dead tonight;
Grief of my son's exile hath stopped her breath.
What further woe conspires against mine age?
PRINCE. Look, and thou shalt see.
MONTAGUE. O thou untaught! What manners is in this,
215 To press before thy father to a grave?
PRINCE. Seal up the mouth of outrage[37] for a while,
Till we can clear these ambiguities
And know their spring,[38] their head, their true descent;
And then will I be general of your woes,
220 And lead you even to death. Meantime, forbear
And let mischance be slave to patience.[39]
Bring forth the parties of suspicion.
FRIAR LAURENCE. I am the greatest, able to do least,
Yet most suspected, as the time and place
225 Doth make against me, of this direful murder;
And here I stand, both to impeach and purge[40]
Myself condemned and myself excused.
PRINCE. Then say at once what thou dost know in this.
FRIAR LAURENCE. I will be brief, for my short date of breath
230 Is not so long as is a tedious tale.
Romeo, there dead, was husband to that Juliet,
And she, there dead, that Romeo's faithful wife.
I married them, and their stol'n marriage day
Was Tybalt's doomsday, whose untimely death
235 Banished the new-made bridegroom from this city,
For whom, and not for Tybalt, Juliet pined.
You, to remove that siege of grief from her,
Betrothed and would have married her perforce
To County Paris. Then comes she to me

34. *mista'en*, mistaken its right target.

35. *his house*, its scabbard.

36. *warns*, orders.

37. *mouth of outrage*, outcry.

38. *spring*, source.

39. *let mischance . . . patience.* Let patience control your hasty reaction to these mishaps.

40. *impeach and purge*, accuse and free from blame.

240 And with wild looks bid me devise some means
    To rid her from this second marriage,
    Or in my cell there would she kill herself.
    Then gave I her, so tutored by my art,
    A sleeping potion; which so took effect
245 As I intended, for it wrought on her
    The form of death. Meantime I writ to Romeo
    That he should hither come as this[41] dire night,
    To help to take her from her borrowed[42] grave,
    Being the time the potion's force should cease.
250 But he which bore my letter, Friar John,
    Was stayed by accident, and yesternight
    Returned my letter back. Then all alone
    At the prefixèd hour of her waking,
    Came I to take her from her kindred's vault,
255 Meaning to keep her closely[43] at my cell
    Till I conveniently could send to Romeo.
    But when I came, some minute ere the time
    Of her awaking, here untimely lay
    The noble Paris and true Romeo dead.
260 She wakes, and I entreated her come forth
    And bear this work of heaven with patience.
    But then a noise did scare me from the tomb,
    And she, too desperate, would not go with me,
    But, as it seems, did violence on herself.
265 All this I know; and to the marriage
    Her nurse is privy;[44] and, if aught in this
    Miscarried by my fault, let my old life
    Be sacrificed, some hour before his time,
    Unto the rigor of severest law.
270 PRINCE. We still have known thee for a holy man.
    Where's Romeo's man? What can he say in this?
    BALTHASAR. I brought my master news of Juliet's death;
    And then in post[45] he came from Mantua
    To this same place, to this same monument.
275 This letter he early bid me give his father,
    And threatened me with death going in the vault,
    If I departed not and left him there.
    PRINCE. Give me the letter; I will look on it.
    Where is the county's page that raised the watch?
280 Sirrah, what made[46] your master in this place?
    PAGE. He came with flowers to strew his lady's grave,
    And bid me stand aloof, and so I did.
    Anon comes one with light to ope the tomb,
    And by and by my master drew on[47] him;
285 And then I ran away to call the watch.
    PRINCE. This letter doth make good the friar's words,
    Their course of love, the tidings of her death;
    And here he writes that he did buy a poison
    Of a poor 'pothecary, and therewithal

41. *as this,* this very.
42. *borrowed,* used temporarily.

43. *closely,* secretly.

44. *privy,* sharing secret knowledge of something.

45. *in post,* with the greatest possible speed.

46. *made,* did.

47. *drew on,* approached.

290　Came to this vault to die and lie with Juliet.
　　Where be these enemies? Capulet! Montague!
　　See, what a scourge is laid upon your hate,
　　That heaven finds means to kill your joys[48] with love!
　　And I, for winking at your discords, too,
295　Have lost a brace of kinsmen.[49] All are punished.
　CAPULET. O brother Montague, give me thy hand.
　　This is my daughter's jointure,[50] for no more
　　Can I demand.
　MONTAGUE. 　　But I can give thee more;
　　For I will raise her statue in pure gold,
300　That while Verona by that name is known,
　　There shall no figure at such rate be set[51]
　　As that of true and faithful Juliet.
　CAPULET. As rich shall Romeo's by his lady's lie,
　　Poor sacrifices of our enmity.
305　PRINCE. A glooming peace this morning with it brings;
　　The sun, for sorrow, will not show his head.
　　Go hence, to have more talk of these sad things;
　　Some shall be pardoned, and some punished,
　　For never was a story of more woe
310　Than this of Juliet and her Romeo. 　　　　　(Exeunt.)

**48.** *your joys,* your children.

**49.** *brace of kinsmen,*
Mercutio and Paris.

**50.** *jointure,* dowry.

**51.** *at such . . . set,* be valued
so greatly.

## CONSIDERING ACT FIVE, SCENE 3

**1. (a)** Why has Paris come to the Capulets' tomb? **(b)** Why has Romeo also come there? **(c)** What mistaken idea do both Paris and Romeo have about Juliet? How has each of them gained that idea?

**2. (a)** Why does Paris feel justified in his determination to slay Romeo? **(b)** How does Romeo try to persuade Paris to leave? **(c)** What happens when Paris refuses to heed Romeo's plea?

**3. (a)** What two tragic discoveries does Friar Laurence make when he enters the tomb? **(b)** What does he urge Juliet to do when she awakens? **(c)** Why does he leave the tomb? Explain why you think he should or should not be blamed for leaving.

**4. (a)** How does Juliet first attempt to end her life and join her husband in death? **(b)** How does she eventually achieve her aim?

**5.** How, at long last, do old Montague and Capulet show that they have learned the price of enmity between their families?

**6.** Complete your outline of the important events in the play.

## A Little Stage History

From its first staging in the 1590's, *Romeo and Juliet* has been one of the most often and most successfully produced of Shakespeare's plays. From the beginning, however, the play was not always produced in its entirety nor the intent of the script followed precisely. Changes were made to suit the abilities of the actors or the tastes of various audiences. The first printed texts of the play (made from actors' copies) indicated, for example, that Elizabethan acting companies didn't hesitate to shorten the play considerably.

London theaters were closed from 1642 to 1660 during the reign of Cromwell, but the first recorded revival of the play occurred in 1662. Samuel Pepys, the famous British diarist, said of this production: ". . . the worst I have ever heard in my life and the worst acted. . . ." Perhaps because of reactions like this, the play was turned into a tragicomedy with Romeo and Juliet miraculously saved at the end and allowed to live happily ever after. To satisfy both those who preferred the original and those who preferred a happy ending, acting companies often presented the tragic version one night and the tragicomic version the next.

During the eighteenth century, *Romeo and Juliet* was performed more times in London and New York than any other Shakespearean play. The most significant change in the text during this period was having Juliet awaken before Romeo died so that they might engage in a tear-evoking farewell.

Modern audiences, however, are too familiar with the original text to permit such tampering. They will tolerate eliminating scenes to shorten playing time, adding stage business, and interpreting a character in an up-to-date way, but even these modifications are not always well received.

The sex of the actors playing the principal roles has a curious history. During Shakespeare's time, women were not allowed to act on the stage; thus a boy always took the role of Juliet. In the nineteenth century, however, it became the practice for a woman to play the role of Romeo. Often an actress, to show her versatility, would play Romeo in one production and Juliet in another. The most famous feminine Romeo was Charlotte Cushman, a leading actress of the London stage in the 1840's and 1850's, who played opposite her sister Susan's Juliet in at least three important productions of the play.

This custom waned markedly after a 1907 production, with a seventeen-year-old girl playing Romeo and a fourteen-year-old girl, Juliet, met with very limited success.

### . . . and Film History

Equally durable as a movie, *Romeo and Juliet* has been produced on film more often than any other Shakespearean play. At least four silent film versions were produced, the first in 1908 when movies were still in the nickelodeon stage. Paul Panzer and Florence Lawrence starred in the title roles. Two competing silent film versions appeared in 1916:

one featuring Theda Bara, the famous vamp of the silent screen, as Juliet; the other starring Francis X. Bushman and Beverly Bayne, the first screen "love team." (They kept their marriage secret for fear it would lessen their popularity.)

The most lavish sound version was a 1936 MGM production with Norma Shearer as Juliet, Leslie Howard as Romeo, and John Barrymore as Mercutio. This film was shot entirely within a studio and emphasized rich costumes, elaborate staging, and ornate sets at the expense of dramatic force. A 1954 British production was chiefly notable for its use of natural settings (it was filmed on location in Italy) and for Laurence Harvey's portrayal of Romeo.

Of more recent interest is director Franco Zeffirelli's 1968 film of the play. A seventeen-year-old actor, Leonard Whiting, played Romeo and a sixteen-year-old actress, Olivia Hussey, Juliet, in this version which used realistic settings and emphasized energetic action in its staging (much brawling, shouting, and rough-housing). Zeffirelli pits the tender awakening of adolescent love, ideal and physical, against the obtuseness and indifference of the older generation. Some critics praised Zeffirelli for making a *Romeo and Juliet* that is understandable to today's audiences. Others criticized him for turning the play into a generation-gap flick. In his defense Zeffirelli said that he made a film about young people for young people. The force of the contrasting views, however, once again testifies to the continuing interest among critics and theatergoers in Shakespeare's star-crossed lovers.

# UNIT 4 REVIEW

**1.** Some critics have maintained that a tragedy should never cover a period longer than a single day. Such a brief time limit was generally ignored by Shakespeare, who sometimes stretched a play (*Julius Caesar*, for example) over several years. He did, however, limit *Romeo and Juliet* to a period of only a few days. Trace the time-scheme of the play. On what day of the week does the action begin? You can find a clue by rereading Act Three, Scene 4, in which Capulet asks, "What day is this?" and Paris replies, "Monday, my lord." How much time has elapsed between the opening of the play and this conversation between Capulet and Paris? What days are taken up by the events that occur during the remainder of the play?

**2.** Any first-rate dramatist is aware of the fact that an occasional change in the mood of a play—a dash of humor, say, in a tragedy, or a temporary threat of disaster in a comedy—tends to sharpen the spectators' enjoyment of the play. Shakespeare was unusually suc-cessful in providing such a change of pace in his plays. Point out some notable examples of Shakespeare's use of humorous characters and situations in *Romeo and Juliet* to relieve the atmosphere of tragedy that pervades the play as a whole.

**3.** The play contains a number of scenes in which a character on stage says or does things the audience knows he or she would not do if the true situation were known. What instances of such dramatic irony can you find in the play? (See the Handbook entry for *irony*.)

**4.** Shakespearean critic Caroline F. E. Spurgeon has suggested that each of Shakespeare's tragedies has a dominant image or set of images that recur throughout the play. The dominant image in *Romeo and Juliet*, according to Spurgeon, is *light* in a variety of forms: torches, sun, moon, stars, the flash of gunpowder, and so on.

a. Which characters and situations in the play are associated with images of light? Which with darkness?

b. Do you agree or disagree with Spurgeon's suggestion that the play presents an "atmosphere of brilliance swiftly quenched"? Explain. (See the Handbook entries for *imagery* and *atmosphere*.)

**5.** At several points in the play Romeo, Juliet, and other characters express feelings of foreboding. Find several examples of premonitions that foreshadow the tragic end of the play. (See the Handbook entry for *foreshadowing*.)

**6.** Throughout the play there are many references to the control of the stars or the heavens over the fate of the two lovers. A modern audience would probably look for other causes of the tragedy. Discuss the influence on the lovers' lives of:

a. fate

b. chance or circumstance

c. family

d. friends

e. the customs of society in that place at that time

f. the character of Juliet

g. the character of Romeo

h. personal choice

Myth
Epic
Philosophy and Poetry
Drama

# Classical Heritage

The earliest stories of Greek literature are tales of the adventures of heroes, both real and imaginary, and of the gods and goddesses of ancient Greek religion. Such stories are called *myths.* Originally myths were enacted in song and dance at religious ceremonies, the earliest of which were believed to increase the fertility of the land. By joining people in common beliefs and rituals, they promoted the unity and stability of a queendom or kingdom.

The earliest known Greek deity was an earth-mother-goddess who personified nature. She preceded the father-god, Zeus, in Greek religion, just as queendoms preceded kingdoms in Greek political life. As cities rose and fell, new gods and goddesses were added from other cultures, and myths were embroidered with history. As the stories were passed on from one generation to another, gods and heroes changed, the gods becoming more human, the heroes becoming godlike.

### Gods and Goddesses

Greek deities experienced human emotions—they became jealous and angry, they fell in and out of love, they quarreled with each other and with humans. But they had godlike powers—they were immortal, they could change form, and they had magical powers over the natural universe. Gods and goddesses often became involved in human affairs, sometimes even assuming human form. Like humans they were unpredictable. They could be generous and kind but were often deceitful and cruel. Although the Greeks believed it wise not to offend the gods, it was hard to know which actions would offend, and "good" conduct was not always rewarded. There were, after all, many gods and goddesses, sometimes with conflicting demands, for each deity had an area of special concern. Poseidon, who ruled the sea, might cause great storms if his wrath were aroused. Aphrodite, the goddess of love and beauty, could help or hinder an affair of the heart. The power of the gods extended even beyond the grave, for Hades ruled the underworld, destination of the spirits of the dead.

Named for Mount Olympus in northern Greece where they were believed to dwell, the Olympian gods were later adopted by the Romans, who called them by Roman rather than Greek names. By the eighth century A.D., when the Roman poet Ovid retold the myths in a long narrative poem called the *Metamorphoses,* the ancient stories were no longer viewed as religiously as they once were.

### Ovid's *Metamorphoses*

Ovid retold the ancient myths and historical legends with wit and irreverence. Nearly every story involves a transformation of some kind—the transformation of a beautiful statue into a living woman, the transformation of a skillful weaver into a spider, the transformation of a god into a golden bull, and so on. It was this theme of changes that gave the poem its title, *Metamorphoses,* which means *transformations.* "The Story of Daedalus and Icarus" and "The Story of Cadmus" are two such stories from Ovid's poem.

# Glossary of Mythology

APHRODITE (af rə dī′tē), *goddess of love and beauty; daughter of* ZEUS. *Roman name:* VENUS (vē′nəs).

APOLLO (ə pol′ō), *god of the sun, healing, poetry, and music; son of* ZEUS.

ARES (ar′ēz *or* er′ēz), *god of war; son of* ZEUS *and* HERA. *Roman name:* MARS (märz).

ARTEMIS (är′tə mis), *goddess of the hunt and the moon; twin sister of* APOLLO. *Roman name:* DIANA (dī an′ə).

ATHENA. *See* Pallas Athena.

DEMETER (di mē′tər), *goddess of agriculture and the fertility of the earth; sister of* ZEUS *and* POSEIDON *and mother of* PERSEPHONE. *Roman name:* CERES (sir′ēz).

DIONYSUS (dī′ə nī′səs), *god of wine and vegetation; son of* ZEUS. *Roman name:* BACCHUS (bak′əs).

FATES (fāts), *three goddesses who controlled human destiny: one spun the thread of life, the second determined its length, and the third cut it off.*

FURIES (fyúr′ēz), *three female spirits with snaky hair who avenged the victims of those who had escaped punishment for their crimes.*

HADES (hā′dēz), *god of the underworld and ruler of the spirits of the dead; husband of* PERSEPHONE *and brother of* ZEUS *and* POSEIDON. *Roman name:* PLUTO (plü′tō).

HERA (hir′ə), *goddess of marriage and the family; queen of the gods and wife of* ZEUS. *Roman name:* JUNO (jü′nō).

HERMES (hėr′mēz), *god of thieves, travel, commerce, and quickness of wit; messenger to the gods and son of* ZEUS. *Roman name:* MERCURY (mėr′kyər ē).

NYMPHS (nimfs), *minor goddesses of nature, represented as beautiful maidens who lived in seas, rivers, mountains, or woods.*

OLYMPUS (ō lim′pəs), *mountain in northeastern Greece where the gods were believed to dwell.*

PALLAS ATHENA (pal′əs ə thē′nə), *also* ATHENA, *goddess of wisdom, the arts, and defensive war; daughter of* ZEUS. *Roman name:* MINERVA (mə ner′və).

PERSEPHONE (pər sef′ə nē), *queen of the dead; wife of* HADES *and daughter of* DEMETER. *Roman name:* PROSERPINA (prō sėr′pə nə).

POSEIDON (pə sīd′n), *god of the sea; brother of* ZEUS *and* HADES. *Roman name:* NEPTUNE (nep′tün).

ZEUS (züs), *chief of the Olympian gods, ruler of the sky and the earth, husband of* HERA *and brother of* HADES *and* POSEIDON. *Roman names:* JUPITER (jü′pə tər) *or* JOVE (jōv).

# THE STORY
## of
# DÆDALUS and ICARUS

*Ovid*

*Translated by Rolfe Humphries*

*A legendary architect, sculptor, and inventor, Daedalus (ded'ə ləs) is said to have fled from Athens when he was accused of murdering a young pupil whose skill rivaled his own. He found sanctuary in Crete, where King Minos commissioned him to build the Labyrinth, a maze which housed the Minotaur, a monster said to be half man and half bull. Eventually Daedalus lost favor with Minos and was imprisoned. As Ovid's story begins, Daedalus hopes to escape with Icarus (ik'ə-rəs), his son.*

Homesick for homeland, Daedalus hated Crete
And his long exile there, but the sea held him.
"Though Minos blocks escape by land or water,"
Daedalus said, "surely the sky is open,
And that's the way we'll go. Minos' dominion
Does not include the air." He turned his thinking
Toward unknown arts, changing the laws of nature.
He laid out feathers in order, first the smallest,
A little larger next it, and so continued,
The way that panpipes rise in gradual sequence.
He fastened them with twine and wax, at middle,
At bottom, so, and bent them, gently curving,
So that they looked like wings of birds, most surely.
And Icarus, his son, stood by and watched him,
Not knowing he was dealing with his downfall,

Stood by and watched, and raised his shiny face
To let a feather, light as down, fall on it,
Or stuck his thumb into the yellow wax,
Fooling around, the way a boy will, always,
20 Whenever a father tries to get some work done.
Still, it was done at last, and the father hovered,
Poised, in the moving air, and taught his son:
"I warn you, Icarus, fly a middle course:
Don't go too low, or water will weigh the wings
down;
25 Don't go too high, or the sun's fire will burn them.
Keep to the middle way. And one more thing,
No fancy steering by star or constellation,
Follow my lead!" That was the flying lesson,
And now to fit the wings to the boy's shoulders.
30 Between the work and warning the father found
His cheeks were wet with tears, and his hands
trembled.
He kissed his son (*Good-by,* if he had known it),

Rose on his wings, flew on ahead, as fearful
As any bird launching the little nestlings
35 Out of high nest into thin air. *Keep on,*
*Keep on,* he signals, *follow me!* He guides him
in flight—O fatal art!—and the wings move
And the father looks back to see the son's wings
    moving.
Far off, far down, some fisherman is watching
40 As the rod dips and trembles over the water,
Some shepherd rests his weight upon his crook,
Some ploughman on the handles of the plough-
    share,
And all look up, in absolute amazement,
At those air-borne above. They must be gods!
45 They were over Samos, Juno's sacred island,
Delos and Paros toward the left, Lebinthus
Visible to the right, and another island,

Calymne, rich in honey. And the boy
Thought *This is wonderful!* and left his father,
50 Soared higher, higher, drawn to the vast heaven,
Nearer the sun, and the wax that held the wings
Melted in that fierce heat, and the bare arms
Beat up and down in air, and lacking oarage
Took hold of nothing. *Father!* he cried, and
    *Father!*
55 Until the blue sea hushed him, the dark water
Men call the Icarian now. And Daedalus,
Father no more, called "Icarus, where are you!
Where are you, Icarus? Tell me where to find
    you!"
And saw the wings on the waves, and cursed his
    talents,
60 Buried the body in a tomb, and the land
Was named for Icarus.

---

## DISCUSSION

1. Why and how does Daedalus change the laws of nature?

2. (a) What fatherly behavior
does Daedalus display? (b) What
boyish behavior does Icarus
display?

3. Why does Daedalus curse
his talents (line 59)?

4. Even in a tale as brief as this
one a writer can direct our sympathies so that we side with or
against his characters. Refer to
specific lines in the poem that reveal the personalities of Daedalus
and of Icarus and tell whether they
enlist your sympathy for or against
the character.

5. Myths were sometimes told
to illustrate right conduct or to
teach a moral lesson. Which of
the following lessons might
"The Story of Daedalus and Icarus" illustrate? Explain. Can you
suggest other lessons that might
apply?

a. Pride goeth before a fall.
b. If the gods had meant us to
fly, they would have given us
wings.
c. Take your father's advice.
d. Don't set your sights too high.

6. (a) How might Daedalus's
advice to "fly a middle course" be
applied to life generally rather
than to flying? (b) Do you think it
is good or bad advice?

## WORD STUDY

Each of the italicized words in
the following sentences is derived
from the name of a character or
a place in Greek or Roman mythology. Use a dictionary to find
(a) the meaning of the italicized
word and (b) the name of the mythological character or place from
which the word is derived. Be prepared to explain the connection
between the meaning of the word
and the mythological character
or place.

1. Schmidt's final, *Icarian* run

in the men's slalom won a silver
medal for the German ski team at
the Winter *Olympics*.

2. If she couldn't find her way
through the *labyrinthine* network
of tunnels before her air supply
gave out, Janet knew she was finished.

3. The *jovial* Dr. Culpepper
was a great favorite with the hospital staff.

4. The *bacchanalian* party ended abruptly when the police arrived.

5. Clifford's *mercurial* temperament confused Annette.

6. The band's *martial* music interrupted Paul's daydreaming,
calling him back to the harsh reality of his arrival at boot camp.

7. Juanita sounded the horn inside the tunnel and listened for
the *echo*.

8. Facing those four *titans* in
the opposing line, Bronkowski
knew the Tigers didn't have a
chance.

# THE STORY of CADMUS

Ovid

*Translated by Rolfe Humphries*

*Attracted by the beauty of Europa, the daughter of King Agenor of Phoenicia, Jove disguised himself as a beautiful golden bull, enticed Europa to climb onto his back, and swam away with her to Crete. When King Agenor discovered that his daughter was missing, he sent his son Cadmus to find her.*

. . . King Agenor,
Unknowing what had happened to his daughter,
Ordered his son, named Cadmus, to go and find her,
Threatening exile as a punishment
5  For failure, in that single action showing
Devotion toward his daughter, toward his son
Harsh wickedness. And Cadmus roamed the world
In vain—for who is good enough detective
To catch Jove cheating?—and became an exile
10  Leaving both fatherland and father's anger.
He sought Apollo's oracle,[1] a suppliant
Asking what land to live in, and Apollo
Replied: "In lonely lands there will come to meet
       you
A heifer, one who has never worn the yoke
15  Nor drawn the curve of the plough. Follow the
       creature
Till she lies down to rest, and there establish
The city walls, and call the land Boeotia."[2]
Scarcely had Cadmus left the sacred cavern
When he saw the heifer, moving slow, unguarded,
20  Wearing no mark of servitude. He followed
Slowly, and silently adored Apollo
For showing him the way. And now the heifer
Had passed Cephisus and Panopean acres,[3]
Halted and raised her handsome head, with horns

---

"The Story of Cadmus" translated by Rolfe Humphries from Ovid's *Metamorphoses.* Copyright 1955, Indiana University Press. Reprinted by permission.

**1.** *Apollo's oracle.* Cadmus visited a shrine to the god Apollo to ask the oracle (a priest or priestess) for advice. The oracle was believed to speak the god's reply.

**2.** *Boeotia* (bē ō′shə).

**3.** *Cephisus and Panopean acres* (sē fis′əs, pa nō′pē ən). In ancient geography, Cephisus was a river flowing through Phocis (fō′sis) and Boeotia, Greece. Panopeus (pan′ō püs) was a city in Phocis, which was bounded on the east by Boeotia.

25 Widespread, and lowed, and looked back at those
      people
    Coming behind, and kneeled, and let her side
    Sink down in the green meadow land, and Cadmus
    Gave thanks, and kissed that foreign ground, and
      greeted
    The unknown fields and mountains.
                        For libation
30 To Jove, he ordered serving-men to go
    Find living water for the sacrifice.
    An ancient forest stood there, undespoiled
    By any axe, and in its midst a cave
    Thick set with bushes. Tightly fitted stones
35 Made a low archway, under which the water
    Poured from abundant springs, and there a serpent,
    Sacred to Mars, was dwelling. His crest was gold,
    His eyes flashed fire, his body swelled with poison;
    Three darting tongues he had, three rows of teeth.
40 The men of Cadmus reached this grove, ill-omened;
    Their lowered vessels broke the water's silence,
    Answered by hissing, for the long head, thrusting,
    Reached out from the long darkness of the cavern.
    The urns sank through the water, and the men
45 Felt blood run cold and limbs turn weak and
      tremble.
    Twisting his scaly coils in writhing loops,
    Curving in undulant arcs and semicircles,
    The serpent lifts himself erect; he towers,
    Half of him anyway, as high, as huge,
50 As the great serpent of the constellations.
    The whole wood lies beneath him, and he strikes,
    Coils, or constricts, and all the men are victims.
    It makes no difference what they try, to fight,
    To run, to stand, too numb for either.

55 High noon arrived, with shadows at their shortest.
    Cadmus began to wonder: what had happened,
    Why had they not come back? He went to find them.
    For shield, he had a lion's skin, for weapon,
    A lance with shining point of steel, a javelin,

60 And, his best armor, a courageous spirit.
    He entered the dark wood, he saw the bodies,
    He saw the great victorious serpent, gloating,
    Licking the wounds with bloody tongue. He cried:
    "I will avenge your death, poor faithful bodies,
65 Or be your comrade in that death!" So saying,
    With all the strength he had, he raised a boulder,
    Lifted it shoulder-high, and hurled it from him
    With force that would have shattered walls and
      towers,
    But the serpent took no wound at all, protected
70 By scales of iron and the skin's dark hardness,
    Not hard enough, however, for the javelin
    Which pierced the middle of the back, the steel
    Biting down into the middle of the belly.
    He is wild with pain, twists back his head, he sees
75 The wounds, he bites the spear shaft, and he loosens
    Wood from the iron, but the iron stays there,
    Stuck in the spine. His rage is more than doubled,
    The throat is swollen, veins stand out, the jaws
    Froth with white poison, and the sound of metal
80 Clangs from the ground as the great scales rasp
      across it.
    The smell of his breath infects the noisome air.
    He coils, he writhes, he straightens, like a beam
    Or battering ram, comes on, like a flooding river
    Sweeping the trees before it. Cadmus yields
85 Only a little, holding up against him
    The lion's skin, and jabbing with the spear point.
    Maddened, the serpent snaps the steel, and catches
    The point between the teeth. The poisonous mouth
    Begins to dribble blood, and the green grass
90 Is sprayed another color, but the wound
    Is slight, the monster yielding, going with it,
    And Cadmus, following hard, keeps pointing,
      pressing,
    Backing the serpent up against an oak tree,
    Pinning him there, and the oak tree bends,
      protesting
95 Under that weight and all that furious lashing.

And as he stood there, gazing at his victim,
A voice was heard, coming from where, he knew not,
But he could hear it saying: "Why, O Cadmus,
Stare at the serpent slain? You also, some day,
100 Will be a serpent for mortal men to stare at."[4]
For a long time he stood there, pale and trembling
And cold with apprehension, but a helper,
Minerva, through the air descending, came
And stood beside him, and she gave him orders
105 To plow the earth, to sow the teeth of the serpent
Which would become the seed of future people.
Cadmus obeyed; he opened the long furrows
And sowed the mortal seed. Could you believe it?
The covered earth broke open, and the clods
110 Began to stir, and first the points of spears
Rose from the ground, then colored plumes, and
        helmets,
Shoulders of men, and chests, arms full of weapons,
A very harvest of the shields of warriors,
The opposite of the way a curtain rises,
115 Showing feet first, then knees, and waists, and
        bodies
And faces last of all.

---

4. *You also . . . stare at.* Because Cadmus killed the serpent
sacred to the god Mars, the angry god later inflicted many sorrows
on Cadmus and his family. In old age, mourning his misfortunes
and the deaths of his children and grandchildren, Cadmus is said
to have cried, "If a serpent's life is so dear to the gods, I would
I were myself a serpent." Having so wished, he began to change
into a serpent. His wife prayed to the gods to let her share her
husband's fate, and she, too, became a serpent.

Cadmus was frightened
By this new menace, got his weapons ready,
And heard a cry, one of the earth-born people
Calling out, "Do not arm! Keep out of this,
120 Our civil warfare." As he spoke, he struck
One of his brothers, and himself was murdered
By a dart, flung far, whose thrower, too, went down
Dying as soon as living. And that madness
Raged through them all; the sudden brothers
        perished
125 By wounds they gave each other, and the earth,
Their mother, felt their short-lived blood upon her,
Warm from their brief existence. Only five
Were left at last, and one of these, Echion,[5]
Let fall his weapons, as Minerva ordered,
130 Asked peace, and won it, from the other brothers,
And Cadmus found them helpers and companions
In the building of the town Apollo promised.

That was the city Thebes, and now the exile
Might seem a happy man. Venus and Mars
135 Were parents of his bride,[6] and there were children
Who turned out well, and children of the children,
Grown to maturity. But always, always,
A man must wait the final day, and no man
Should ever be called happy before burial.

---

5. *Echion* (ē kī′on).
6. *Venus and Mars . . . his bride.* Cadmus married Harmonia,
the daughter of the goddess Venus and the god Mars.

---

## DISCUSSION

1. (a) Why does Cadmus leave his homeland? (b) Why does he follow the heifer?

2. Why does Cadmus kill the serpent?

3. (a) What orders does the goddess Minerva give Cadmus? (b) What transformation takes place as a result?

4. (a) What result of the transformation made Cadmus "seem a happy man"? (b) Considering the information in the footnote for lines 99–100, what do you think is the significance of the last two lines in the selection?

## OVID
### (PUBLIUS OVIDIUS NASO)

Born in 43 B.C., the son of a middle-class landowner, Ovid (ov′id) was educated in Rome and Athens. Resisting his father's efforts to push him into a political career, he became one of Rome's most popular poets.

Among his early verse was a group of short love poems, the *Amores*, recording his attachment to an unidentified older woman. His reputation grew with *The Art of Love*, a long poem giving detailed practical instructions about falling in and out of love and marriage. He treated the subject with more wit and frankness, however, than some members of his society could tolerate. The poem was one of the items used in evidence against Ovid when, in A.D. 8, the emperor Augustus banished him to a town on the Black Sea. Although the *Metamorphoses*, completed in Rome just before his banishment, had assured his fame, Ovid's last years of bitter exile prevented him from enjoying its rewards. He died in A.D. 17.

**Greek and Roman Epics**

Although tales of the Trojan War were probably told in story and song for several generations, the first written accounts are found in the *Iliad* and the *Odyssey,* two epic poems by the Greek poet Homer, who is believed to have lived during the eighth century B.C. An *epic* is a long poem about the adventures of one or more great heroes; it is often an account of the history and ideals of a nation. Since the first epics were recited or sung to the accompaniment of stringed instruments, Homer probably recited the *Iliad* and the *Odyssey* to an audience of nobles, accompanying himself on a harp. There are references in these two epics to some of the same myths later retold by Ovid; however, the poems are based on an actual historical event, a war between two ancient cities.

According to the *Iliad,* the Trojan War started over a woman, the beautiful Helen, wife of the Greek king, Menelaus. With the aid of Aphrodite, the goddess of love, Helen was persuaded to elope with Paris, the son of King Priam of Troy. The Greek armies set out to recapture Helen from the Trojans and return her to her husband and her native land. The *Iliad* narrates the progress of the ten-year war, finally won by the Greeks, who burned Troy and returned Helen to her husband.

The *Odyssey* is an account of the long and adventurous homeward journey of Odysseus, one of the conquering Greeks, after the fall of Troy.

### Schliemann's Excavations

For years scholars thought that the events related in the *Iliad* and the *Odyssey* were pure fiction, that the Greek and Trojan cities described in the poems were mythical. But an archaeologist named Heinrich Schliemann believed Homer's cities were real, and in 1870, using Homer's descriptions as a guide, Schliemann began to dig at a site in Turkey. He uncovered the ruins of an ancient burned city which he declared to be the Troy of Homer's epic. Later digs at the same site revealed that he had actually unearthed a much later city built over the ruins of a city that had been destroyed around 1184 B.C. This is probably the Troy of which Homer wrote. Schliemann later excavated a site on the Greek mainland and uncovered Mycenae, the home of the Greeks who had invaded Troy. The weapons, armor, vases, and gold jewelry Schliemann dug up in Mycenae are strikingly similar to articles described in the *Iliad* and the *Odyssey;* furthermore, the geography of the sites found in modern Turkey and Greece is so similar to that of Homer's cities, that it is now generally accepted that Homer's epics are based at least partly on historical fact, although they were written several centuries after the war they describe.

### Virgil's *Aeneid*

For centuries Homer's epics were popular not only in Greece but also in Rome. The emperor Augustus, hoping to glorify the history of the Roman Empire and his own role in shaping it, urged the Roman poet Virgil (70-19 B.C.) to write an epic in the manner of Homer. Virgil's *Aeneid,* modeled after Homer's poems, is the result of the emperor's request.

According to Virgil's poem, Aeneas was a Trojan prince who fled from his burning city at the end of the war and wandered for years through the Mediterranean. Finally he arrived in Italy, where he and his companions established a civilization which led to the founding of Rome.

The three selections which follow are translations or retellings of episodes from these three epic poems.

# THE SURPRISE

*John Masefield*

Homer's Iliad *has served as a basis for the work of many other writers, including the British poet John Masefield, who, in "The Surprise," retells the last episode of the Trojan War.*

*For nine years the Greeks laid siege to Troy, but the city held fast. In the tenth year, force having failed, the Grecian leaders decided to try craft. At the suggestion of Odysseus (ō dis′ē əs), the cleverest of their leaders, the Greeks secretly constructed a huge wooden horse, hollow inside and furnished with a trap door. Through this door climbed a band of* Grecian soldiers. The remaining Greeks then boarded their ships as though they intended to sail home; actually they sailed to a nearby island.

*The Trojans believed that the Greeks had at last given up. Joyfully, they flung open the city gates and swarmed out over the surrounding plain. There they spied the wooden horse and, proclaiming it a trophy of war, dragged it into the city.*

*Meanwhile, the Greek ships had returned, and the Greek soldiers landed to play their part in the trick designed to surprise the Trojans.*

You have heard the story of the Horse of Troy,
We left him on the sea-beach when we sailed.
We sailed all day, but when the darkness fell
The captains ordered all the fleet ashore.
5 We beached the black ships out of sight of Troy.

Then quietly the captains of the hundreds[1]
Were told that a surprise would be attempted.
Orders were given: then most stringent watch
Was made, lest any traitor should give warning.

10 We supped and slept, till somewhere after midnight,
Then roused, and tied bleached linen on our arms,[2]
And took short spears and swords: no other weapons:
And forth we went by fifties toward Troy.
Absolute silence upon pain of death
15 The order was: we crept along like ghosts.

Soon we were in the Plain among the graves
Of men half-buried, whom we used to know,
And how they died, a dozen known to me.
And Trojan bodies, too; familiar landmarks.
20 It was all cold and windy, with bright stars,
No moon, dry summer going, and the wind
Beating the withered grass and shriveled leaves.

Then we were at the ford and passing through.
I remember water gurgling at a flag-root.

25 Beyond the ford we were in Trojan land.
There was the black mass of the walls of Troy
With towers (and a light in one of them).
No other sign of life, except a glow,
Before Apollo's temple as we judged,
30 Some sacrificial fire not yet quenched.
The city was dead still, but for the wind.

They halted us below the wagon track
Between the Spartans and the Ithacans.[3]
And there we huddled in the bitter cold,
35 Wondering what had happened in the city
And why the city should be still as death:
Whether the Horse were burning in the fire
With all our men inside it sacrifice:
Whether the trap door in the Horse had jammed
40 So that they could not leave it: or perhaps
(We thought) the Horse is guarded in the temple,
Surrounded by men praying all night long.
Or had they ventured out, and all been killed?
And if the men were killed, the stratagem
45 Was surely known, and we half-armed and freezing,
Would be attacked at dawn and ridden down.
A temple bell jangled within the city,
A lesser bell tinkled; then all was silent.

"The Surprise" by John Masefield from *A Tale of Troy*. Copyright 1932 by John Masefield, renewed 1960 by John Masefield. Reprinted with permission of the Macmillan Company and The Society of Authors as the literary representative of the Estate of John Masefield.
1. *captains of the hundreds.* The Greek army was organized in hundreds.
2. *tied . . . our arms,* for purposes of identification.

3. *They halted us . . . Ithacans.* The soldiers were halted near a road, on either side of which were encamped Greek soldiers, the Spartans and the Ithacans.

And all this time the little owls from Ida[4]
50 Came hooting over us: and presently
A mighty, savage owl perched upon Troy[5]
And snapped his iron lips, and flapped, and screamed,
Almost one saw the yellow of his eyes.
Then he launched forth, stealing into the air.
55 It seemed like many ages in the cold
Before the whisper reached the Ithacans
To creep a little nearer to the wall.
When they had passed, unchallenged, others went.
Word passed that there were sentries on the wall.
60 And though the orders were against all speech,
Yet whispers let us know that Diomed[6]
Was at the South Gate underneath the tower,[7]
With the picked fighters.
                Hours seemed to pass
While we froze slowly in our companies.
65 My eyes were so accustomed to the dark
That I could see the great wall with its ramparts,
A tower, and a gate, close-fastened, brazen,
With men of ours heaped near it like to stones.

Then there was whispering in the ranks behind me:
70 A captain whispered, "Who knows Diomed?
Do you?" I whispered, "Yes."

                               "Why, then," he
    whispered,
"Creep forward there, and find him by the gate
Under the tower with the forward party.
Tell him *King Agamemnon*[8] *is convinced*
75 *That this has failed, and that we must withdraw.*
*Be ready to fall back as we retire."*

I crept the seventy yards up to the front.
One whispered, "Diomed is on the right,
Nearest the wall." I found him lying there
80 And whispered him the message of the King.
"What?" he said, "What? Withdraw from where
       we are?
Who says so? What authority have you?"
I told him, "Verbal orders from a captain."
"Lie still," he said, "and not another word.
85 I'll learn of your authority when day dawns."

Then suddenly there came a little noise.

---

4. *Ida,* a mountain overlooking the city of Troy.
5. *a mighty, savage owl . . . Troy.* The owl was the symbol of
Athena who favored the Greeks. Its presence on the gates of Troy
symbolized woe to its defenders.
6. *Diomed* (dī′ə med), leader of an advance party of Grecian
warriors.
7. *South Gate . . . tower.* The city was surrounded by a high wall
surmounted by a rampart. Beside each gate in the wall were square
towers for defense.

---

8. *King Agamemnon* (ag′ə mem′non), older brother of Menelaus
and commander in chief of the Greeks.

105 The dogs had all been killed some weeks before,
There were no watchdogs. When we reached the
Ways,[9]
The Wide Ways running round within the walls,
Some horses, tethered there, whinnied and stamped,
And drowsy horse-boys mumbled in their sleep,
110 But no one challenged; Troy was in a drowse
In the deep morning sleep before the dawn
Now faint upon the distant tops of Ida.

And we were seen by watchmen on the tower
On that side Troy, but none of them suspected
115 That we were Greeks: they thought that we were
Lycians,
Old allies of the Trojans, mustering
Up to the temples for a sacrifice
Before we marched from Troia[10] to our homes.

We were within the second ring of road,[11]
120 Outside King Priam's palace[12] and the temples,
Before a sentry challenged us, and then
It was too late for the alarm to help.
The man paused at the turning of his beat,
Looked round and saw us, gave a cry, then chal-
lenged,

Someone within the gate was lifting down
The heavy bars that barred it, one by one.
Each of us nudged his fellow and drew breath.
90 Diomed stood: we others raised ourselves.
One half the narrow brazen door moved back,
Showing a dark gash that grew wider and lighter;
A lamp wavered and flickered in a lane,
The damp glistened on wallwork; a man peered
95 Round the half-opened door; and "Sst, Sst, Sst,"
He hissed. It was Odysseus, from the Horse.

Diomed signaled to us: he himself
Was first within the gate: I helped him there
To lay the gate wide open to our men.
100 Then we pressed in, up the steep narrow lane
Past the still flickering lamp, over a Trojan
Sentry or watchman, newly murdered there,
Killed by Odysseus: no one challenged us.
We were in Troy: the city was surprised.

9. *the Ways.* The walled city was circular. Just within the wall
ran a wide avenue (Ways) that encircled the city.
10. *Lycians* (lish'i ənz) . . . *Troia* (trō'yə). The Lycians, who lived
south of the Trojans, had been their allies in the war. When the
watchmen heard the noises of men moving, they thought that it was
the Lycians marching in a body to the temples to offer sacrifices
before leaving Troia (Troy).
11. *second ring of road.* A second avenue encircled the principal
buildings, temples, and the king's palace.
12. *King Priam's* (prī'əmz) *palace.* King Priam was the king of
Troy and the father of Paris.

125 Then died, stabbed through the throat by Diomed.
My party rushed into Apollo's temple
And burst into the palace to the guards
Sleeping in quarters, some of them half drunk,
All without arms: we herded them like sheep.

130 And by the time the guards were bound, the city
Was lit with blazing thatches, and awake,
Dawn coming, fire burning, women screaming,
And war-cries, and loud trumpets and clashed
      armor,
There was hard fighting in a dozen spots.

135 We came out of the guard-room by a gate
Into a blaze all red with fire flying:
A palace court it was, the inner court,
Where Menelaus and his Spartan spearmen
Were killing Priam's sons.
140 Just as we reached the court a dozen spearmen
Were all attacking young Deiphobus.[13]

I knew the lad by sight, for he had come
On embassy to Agamemnon once,
And Menelaus meant to have him killed
145 And flung to the camp-dogs, because of Helen.

There he was, fighting for his life with twelve.

A fine young man, like Hektor[14] in the face,
A bright, clean-cut face, tanned with sun and wind,

---

**13.** *Deiphobus* (di if′ō bəs), son of King Priam.
**14.** *Hektor*, the oldest son of Priam and the greatest of the Trojan warriors. He had been killed earlier by Achilles (ə kil′ēz).

Smiling and cool and swift with parry on parry.
150 He had been surprised: he had no body-armor,
Nothing but spear and shield, and there he stood,
Checking each thrust, swift, marvelously.
                                    One minute
He stood, matchless in skill in the red glare,
Then someone crept above and stabbed him down.

155 The city was all ours in the hour.
Many were killed in fighting; many more
Escaped, during the burning and confusion,
Out, to the mountains, by the Eastern gate.
The rest we took: some of the prisoners,
160 The little children and old men and women,
We drove out of the gates into the wild.
The rest we kept: young women skilled in crafts
And men who might make slaves.
                            We made them
      quench
The fires that were burning here and there
165 And then we sacked the city utterly.

When we had sacked her utterly, we forced
Our Trojan slaves to lever down the ramparts
Over the walls, until the city seemed
A mound of fallen stones and roofless houses.
170 We lit the wreck.

Then as we sailed for home with slaves and plunder,
We saw the ruins burning, and the smoke
Streaming across the sunburnt Trojan plain.
With all that world of murder on our backs
175 We bore our load of misery from Asia.

---

## DISCUSSION

1. (a) Is "The Surprise" told from the Greek or the Trojan point of view? (b) Who is the narrator of the poem?

2. (a) What was the Trojan horse? (b) How was it used in cap-turing the city of Troy? (c) Who prevented the Greek troops from withdrawing before the trick had worked?

3. (a) Who were the chief Greek heroes in this story? (b) In what way did each of them contribute to the success of the battle?

4. In what way does the dia-logue add to the effect of the poem?

5. Point out particular passages in which the poet builds suspense.

6. How does the author draw from the reader sympathy for the Trojans?

# THE FLIGHT
# of AENEAS

*Virgil*
*Translated by C. Day Lewis*

*Several centuries after Homer's* Iliad *had been written, a Latin poet named*
*Virgil took up the Trojan theme in his epic poem, the* Aeneid. *While*
*Homer wrote from the Greek point of view, Virgil approached the story*
*from the viewpoint of Aeneas, one of the famous Trojan heroes.*

    Then first the full horror of it all was borne in upon me. I stood
In a daze: the picture of my dear father came to mind,
As I watched King Priam, a man of the same age, cruelly wounded,
Gasping his life away; I pictured my Creusa[1]
5  Deserted, my home pillaged, and the fate of my little Ascanius.[2]
I glanced round, wishing to see what force of men was left me.
All were gone: utter exhaustion and sickness of heart
Had made them drop from the roof to the ground or into the flames.
    Yes, I was now the one man left of my party. But just then,
10  Hugging close to the threshold of Vesta,[3] speechlessly hiding there,
I noticed the daughter of Tyndareus,[4] Helen. The blaze lit up
The whole scene as I wandered, peering this way and that.
Helen, the scourge of Troy and her own land alike,
In dread anticipation of Trojan wrath at Troy's
15  Downfall, of Greek revenge, of her cuckolded husband's anger,—
Helen, that hateful creature, was crouched by the altar, in hiding.
A fire broke out in my heart, a passion of rage to avenge
My country's fall and punish her crime by a crime upon her.
Was she going to get away with it? see Sparta again and her homeland?
20  Return as a queen, in triumph? be once more reunited
With husband, home, parents and children? use our Trojan
Ladies for her attendants and Trojan men for slaves?—
All this, with Priam put to the sword, and Troy in ashes,
And Troy's shore time and again bathed in a sweat of blood?

---

1. *Creusa* (krē ü′sə).
2. *Ascanius* (as kān′ē əs).
3. *Vesta* (ves′tə), goddess of the hearth.
4. *Tyndareus* (tin dar′ē əs).

25 Not so, I said. For although to kill a woman earns one
No fame, and victory over a female wins no decorations,
I shall be praised for stamping out an iniquity, punishing
One who so richly deserves it; and I shall enjoy fulfilling
My soul with a flame of vengeance, appeasing my people's ashes.

30 Such were my thoughts, the insensate fury that drove me onward,
When to my view—and never before had I seen her so clear—
My gentle mother[5] appeared: all glowing with light she came
Through the gloom, a goddess manifest, oh, high and handsome as
The heaven-dwellers know her. She laid a hand on mine,

35 Restraining me, then shaped these words with her rosy lips:—
  My son, what anguish spurs you to this ungoverned rage?
What madness has driven all thought for love out of your heart?
Will you not first find out if your aged father, Anchises,[6]
Is where you left him, and whether your wife, Creusa, be still

40 Alive, and little Ascanius? A whole Greek army is surging
Round them on every side, and but for my guardian care
The flames would have got them by now, the fell sword drained their blood.
It is not the beauty of hated Helen, it is not Paris,
Though you hold him to blame—the gods, the gods, I tell you, are hostile,

45 It's they who have undermined Troy's power and sent it tumbling.     .
Jove supplies fresh courage and a victorious strength
To the Greeks, inciting the gods against the Trojan cause.
Escape then, while you may, my son, and end this ordeal.
I shall be with you, seeing you safe to your father's house.

50   She had spoken; and now she was vanished into the night's thick darkness.
Terrible shapes loom up, set against Troy, the shapes of
Heaven's transcendent will.
    Then indeed I saw that all Ilium[7] was subsiding
Into the flames, and Neptune's Troy[8] quite overthrown.

55 Well, I went down from the roof, and divinely guided pressed on
Through flame and foe: the weapons gave way, the flames drew back for me.
    But when I reached the door of my father's house, the ancestral
Home, my father Anchises, whom first I looked for, wishing
To get him away first to the safety of the hills—Anchises

---

5. *gentle mother,* Venus, the goddess of love.
6. *Anchises* (an kī′sēz).
7. *Ilium* (il′ē əm), Troy.
8. *Neptune's Troy.* As punishment for an attempted revolt against Zeus, Neptune was forced
to help build the walls of Troy.

60 Flatly refused to prolong his life, now Troy was finished,
Or to endure exile. He said:—

O you, whose blood
Is in the prime, who are strong enough to stand on your own feet,
Do you try for escape!
But as for me, if the gods had meant me to go on living,
65 They'd have preserved this place. Enough, more than enough
To have seen Troy ruined once and once have survived her capture.
Bid me farewell and leave, O leave this body of mine
Where it is! I shall find death in action. The foe will slay me
For pity, or spoils. And to bury me—that will not cost them much.
70 For years now I have been lingering, obnoxious to heaven and useless
To mankind, ever since the ruler of gods and men
Blasted me with the searing breath of his levin-flash.[9]
   So he went on saying. We could not shift him, although
We implored him with floods of tears—I, and my wife Creusa,
75 Ascanius and the whole household—not to ruin everything,
Not to add his weight to the doom which was heavy upon us.
He refused: obstinately he clung to his house and his purpose.
Once again I am moved to fight, yearning for death in my misery,
Since neither luck nor forethought offered a way out now.
80 "Father," I said, "did you really think I could run away
And leave you? Did so shameful a notion escape your lips?
If it's the will of heaven that nothing be left of our city,
And if your mind's made up that you and your family
Shall perish, as well as Troy, a door to that death is wide open:
85 Pyrrhus[10] is coming, all bathed in Priam's blood; he loves
Butchering sons in front of their fathers, fathers at the altar.
Was it for this, dear mother, you fetched me through fire and steel,—
That I should witness the enemy right in our house, witness
Ascanius and my father and my Creusa beside them
90 Lying slaughtered here in one another's blood?
To arms, my men! To arms! Their last hour calls the conquered.
Send me back to the Greeks! Let me go back and renew
The fight! It must never be said we died unavenged this day!"
   My sword was at my side again; I was fitting my left arm

---

9. *levin-flash,* lightning-flash.
10. *Pyrrhus* (pir′əs), son of Achilles, one of the Greek warriors.

95  Through the strap of my shield, and on my way out of the house,
When Creusa clung to me at the door, gripping my ankles,
Holding little Ascanius up to his father, and crying:—
    If it's deathwards you go, take us with you! O take us, and come what may!
But if your experience tells you that something is to be gained by
100  Fighting, protect this house first! Think what you're leaving us to—
Ascanius, your father, and me who loved to be called your wife once!
    Loudly she cried these words, and filled the house with her crying.
Just then a miracle happened, a wonderful miracle.
Imagine it!—our hands and our sad eyes were upon
105  Ascanius, when we beheld a feathery tongue of flame
Luminously alight on his head, licking the soft curls
With fire that harmed them not, and playing about his temples.
Anxious, in great alarm, his mother and I hurried to
Beat out, put out with water, that holy blaze on his hair.
110  But father Anchises, greatly heartened, lifted his eyes up,
Stretched up his hands to heaven, with words of prayer, saying:—
    O god omnipotent, if any prayers can sway you,
Give ear to mine. One thing I ask: if by our goodness
We have deserved it, grant your aid, confirm this omen!
115    The old man had hardly spoken when from our left hand came
A sudden crash of thunder, and a shooting star slid down
The sky's dark face, drawing a trail of light behind it.
We watched that star as it glided high over the palace roof,
And blazing a path, buried its brightness deep in the woods of
120  Ida; when it was gone, it left in its wake a long furrow
Of light, and a sulphurous smoke spread widely over the terrain.
That did convince my father. He drew himself upright,
Addressed the gods above, and worshipped the heaven-sent star:—
    No more, no more lingering! I follow, I'm there, where you guide me!
125  Gods of our fathers, guard this family, guard my grandson!
This sign is yours, and Troy is still in your heavenly keeping.
Yea, I consent. I refuse no longer, my son, to go with you.
    He had spoken; and now more clearly over the town the fire's roar
Was heard, and nearer rolled the tide of its conflagration.
130  "Quick, then, dear father," I said, "climb onto my back, and I will
Carry you on my shoulders—that's a burden will not be burdensome.
However things turn out, at least we shall share one danger,

One way of safety, both of us. Let little Ascanius walk
Beside me, and Creusa follow my steps at a distance.
135  And you, servants, pay careful attention to what I shall tell you.
As you go out of the city, you come to a mound with an ancient
Temple of Ceres upon it, secluded; nearby, an old cypress
Stands, which for many years our fathers preserved in reverence.
Let this be our rendezvous: we'll get there by different routes.
140  Do you, my father, carry the sacred relics and home-gods.[11]
Sinful for me to touch them, when I have just withdrawn
From battle, with blood on my hands, until in running water
I am purified."
    With these words, I laid the pelt of a tawny lion
145  For covering over my broad shoulders and bowed neck;
Then stooped to lift my burden: Ascanius twined his fingers
In mine, hurrying to keep up with his father's longer stride.
My wife came on behind. We fared on, hugging the shadows.
I, who just now had faced the enemy volleys, the Greeks'
150  Concentrated attack, without turning a hair—I was scared by
Every breeze, alarmed by every sound, so strung up
Was I with anxiety for my burden and my companion.
    And now I was nearing the gates and thinking that we had made it,
When on a sudden there came to my ears the sound of many
155  Footsteps—or so it seemed. Then, peering into the gloom,
My father exclaimed:—
                —Run! They're upon us! Run, Aeneas!
I can see the shine of their shields and the bronze accoutrements winking.
    Well, I panicked. My wits were fuddled, were snatched away
By some malignant prompting. For even as I darted off
160  Into byways, off my course among streets I knew not—O god,
The anguish of it!—my wife Creusa, fate took her—did she
Stop there? or lose her way? Did she sink down in exhaustion?
We never knew. We never set eyes on her again.
I did not look back for the lost one, I did not give her a thought
165  Until we had reached the mound, the ancient, hallowed place
Of Ceres. Here at last, when all were assembled, one was
Missing, one had denied husband and son her company.
I was out of my mind. What mortal, what god did I not curse?

---

11.  *home-gods,* images of the household gods, believed to embody the spirits of ancestors.

In all the city's ruin what bitterer thing did I see?
170 Commending Ascanius, Anchises and the Teucrian[12] home-gods
To my friends' care, and hiding them deep in the hollow vale,
I put on my shining armour, I made for the city once more.
To reconstruct those events, to retrace our path through Troy
And expose my life to its perils again—that was my purpose.
175     For a start, I returned to the shadowed gate in the city wall
By which I had sallied forth, noting my tracks and following them
Back through the night, straining my eyes to scan them. Everywhere
Dread and the sheer silence reduced my courage to nothing.
Next, I went home, in case—just on the chance that she might have
180 Gone there. The Greeks had broken in, the whole house was occupied.
That instant, gluttonous fire was fanned by the draught right up to
The roof top; flames burst out there, the blast of the heat roared skywards.
I went on, to revisit Priam's house and the citadel.
Here, in the empty colonnades of Juno's sanctuary,
185 Phoenix and fell Ulysses[13] were engaged on the duty allotted them,
Guarding the loot. To this point from all over Troy had plunder,
Salvaged from burning shrines, been brought: tables of gods,
Solid gold bowls and looted vestments were being piled up here
In heaps. Children and frightened mothers were standing about
190 In a long queue.
I dared (you will hardly believe it) to call out loud through the gloom
And fill the streets with shouting: sadly I cried "Creusa!"—
Called to her over and over again, but it was no good.
As I roamed on that endless, frenzied search through the city buildings,
195 There appeared before my eyes a piteous phantom, yes,
The very ghost of Creusa—a figure larger than life.
I was appalled: my hair stood on end, and my voice stuck
In my throat. It was she who spoke then, and thus relieved my pain:—
    Darling husband, it's madness of you to indulge your grief
200 Like this. These happenings are part of the divine
Purpose. It was not written that you should bring Creusa
Away with you; the great ruler of heaven does not allow it.
For you, long exile is destined, broad tracts of sea to be furrowed;

---

**12.** *Teucrian* (tü′krē ən), Trojan: after Teucer, the first king of Troy.
**13.** *Phoenix and . . . Ulysses* (fē′niks *and* yü lis′ēz), Greek warriors. Ulysses is the Latin name for Odysseus.

Then you will reach Hesperia,[14] where Lydian Tiber[15] flows
205 Gently through a land in good heart, and good men live.
There, your affairs will prosper; a kingdom, a royal bride
Await you. No more tears now for your heart's love, Creusa:
I shall not see the proud halls of the Myrmidons or Dolopes,[16]
Nor work as a slave for Greek women—I, who am Dardan[17]
210 And daughter-in-law to the goddess Venus.
No, the great Mother of the gods is going to keep me here.
Goodbye, Aeneas. Cherish our love in the son it gave us.
      With these words, though I wept and had so much to say
To her, she left me, fading out into thin air.
215 Three times I tried to put my arms round her neck, and three times
The phantom slipped my hands, my vain embrace: it was like
Grasping a wisp of wind or the wings of a fleeting dream.
So in the end I went back to my friends, the night being over.
I was astonished to find, when I got there, a great number
220 Of new arrivals come in, both women and men, a sorry
Concourse of refugees assembled for exile. From all sides
They'd rendezvous'd, their minds made up, their belongings ready
For me to lead them wherever I wished across the sea.
And now was the dawn star rising over the ridges of Ida,
225 Bringing another day. The Greeks were holding the gates of
The city in force. Troy was beyond all hope of aid.
I accepted defeat, picked up my father and made for the mountains.

---

**14.** *Hesperia* (hes pir′ē ə), literally, "the Western Land"; in this case, Italy.
**15.** *Tiber* (tī′bər), a river in central Italy.
**16.** *Myrmidons or Dolopes,* Greek peoples or tribes from Thessaly. They fought under Achilles against the Trojans.
**17.** *Dardan,* Trojan.

## DISCUSSION

1. (a) In what way does the point of view in this poem differ from that of the last? (b) Who is the narrator in this one? (c) What did he have to do with the war?

2. (a) Who was responsible for and what means of persuasion was used in restraining Aeneas from killing Helen? (b) What did the goddess promise Aeneas if he would do what she asked?

3. (a) What unusual occurrence convinced Aeneas's father to flee with him? (b) What happened to Creusa during the family's flight from the city? (c) What did Creusa predict for Aeneas's future?

4. (a) Were the tragedies that befell Aeneas during the Trojan War caused only by the results of the war, or did the gods have a hand in them? (b) How did Aeneas finally accept his misfortune?

5. (a) Did you feel greater sympathy for Aeneas or for the narrator in "The Surprise"? Why? (b) In what sense were both men victims of the war?

## WORD STUDY

Ancient Greeks and Romans would, no doubt, be astonished at the array of products and services in our modern world which are named for characters from mythology or their attributes. Explain why the names below are or are not appropriate to the products. Use an unabridged dictionary if necessary.

Argus (camera)
Mercury (automobile)
Aeolian (piano)
Atlas (van lines)
Hermes (adding machine)
Ajax (cleanser)

If you were deciding on a name for a beauty school, an airline, a housing development, and a steamship company, what names or places from mythology might you use? (Consult the Glossary of Mythology on page 367.)

# ODYSSEUS in ITHACA

*Retold from the ancient authors by*
Roger Lancelyn Green

*The second of Homer's epics, the* Odyssey, *relates the adventures of the Greek hero Odysseus as he journeys homeward after the war. (It was Odysseus who had suggested the wooden horse which allowed the Greeks to defeat the Trojans.)*

*Although the distance was not great, Odysseus's homeward journey was filled with dangerous adventures which delayed his return to his kingdom of Ithaca. He and his shipmates encountered stormy seas, a witch goddess, a one-eyed giant, a six-headed man-eating monster, and other perils. Throughout the journey Odysseus was aided by the goddess Athena, who favored him, but he was hindered by the sea god Poseidon, whom he had angered.*

*In the following retelling of the ending of the* Odyssey, *Odysseus has finally reached Ithaca with the help of the Phaeacians (fē ā′shənz). During his twenty-year absence, his son Telemachus (tə lem′ə-kəs) has grown to manhood and his wife Penelope (pə nel′ə pē) has been harassed by suitors who demand that she accept the idea that Odysseus is dead and choose one of them as her new husband. They desire not only the beautiful Penelope but also the wealth of Odysseus's kingdom.*

WHEN Odysseus awoke from sleep a mist lay over all the place and he did not know where he was. At first he lamented, thinking that the Phaeacians had landed him on some desert island and left him to his fate. But presently Athena came to him and drew back the mist. Then Odysseus knew his home, and kneeling down kissed the soil of Ithaca in his joy and thankfulness.

"There is still much trouble before you," Athena warned him. "For a hundred and eight suitors have gathered in your hall to woo your wife Penelope. They dwell in the town, but come each day and feast riotously on your possessions: your flocks and herds grow few, your wine is well-nigh exhausted. But still your faithful Penelope holds them at bay, though she nears the end of her strength."

Then Athena told Odysseus how Penelope had baulked the suitors for three years with a cunning almost equal to his own.

"I cannot choose a husband," Penelope had said, "until I have woven a fine robe to be the winding shroud[1] of the hero Laertes, father of my lord whom you say is dead. It must be a worthy robe, fit for a hero: alas that I could not weave one for my lord Odysseus!"

So Penelope wove at her loom day by day, working hard to make the shroud for Laertes, but every night she stole secretly to her loom and unravelled all that she had woven during the day. But at the end of three years some of her maids, who had fallen in love with several of the Suitors, betrayed her, and the Suitors lay in wait and caught her unpicking the web.

Then they came in a body and told her that she must make her choice without any more delay. Penelope begged for a few weeks in which to decide, and this they allowed.

"But today is her last day of grace," ended Athena, "and tomorrow they will demand her answer. It was when she knew that the end was near that she sent Telemachus to seek news of you. He is at Sparta, but I have been to him there, and he will return today. Go now to the cottage of Eumaeus[2] the faithful swineherd, whose father was a Prince of Phoenicia from whom he was stolen in childhood and sold as a slave to your father Laertes: him you may trust, and Philoetius[3] the herdsman. But you must go in disguise . . ."

Athena spoke more words of advice to Odysseus, and helped him to make himself like an old beggar. After this she departed to guide Telemachus across the sea from Pylos[4] to Ithaca

"Odysseus in Ithaca" from *The Tale of Troy* by Roger Lancelyn Green. Copyright © 1958 by Roger Lancelyn Green. Reprinted by permission of Penguin Books Ltd.
1.  *winding shroud,* a cloth in which a corpse is wrapped for burial.
2.  *Eumaeus* (yü mē′əs).
3.  *Philoetius* (fi lē′shəs).
4.  *Pylos* (pī′lôs), ancient city in southwest Greece on the Ionian Sea.

in such a way as to avoid a band of Suitors who had laid an ambush for him between two islands: Athena came to Telemachus in the guise of his wise tutor Mentor, and brought him safely home that day.

Meanwhile Odysseus hid all the Phaeacian gifts in a cave, and trudged up the beach in his rags and came after a short walk to the cottage of Eumaeus. Out rushed the dogs to drive off the beggar, and Odysseus sat down hastily, to show that he was a friend—a sign which Greek dogs still understand!

Eumaeus came forth, welcomed the beggar kindly into his cottage and fed him well, though he had no idea whom he was really entertaining. Odysseus did not reveal himself until Telemachus came; but then they rejoiced together and made their plans against the Suitors.

That evening Telemachus returned to the palace, and when the Suitors had gone home to bed, he removed all the weapons and armour which usually hung on the walls and pillars in the great hall where the feasts were held. He did not tell Penelope that Odysseus was in Ithaca, nor anything of the plan, but he suggested that, next day when the Suitors came to demand her hand in marriage for one of them, she should consent to marry whoever could bend the bow of Odysseus and shoot an arrow through the rings in the heads of twelve axes set up in a row—a feat which Odysseus himself had often performed in the days before he sailed to Troy.

Next morning Odysseus the beggar came up to the palace, and on the way he met Melanthius[5] the goatherd who jeered at him and kicked him in the side, calling him vile names.

"If ever the great Odysseus returns," said Eumaeus sternly, "you will suffer for treating a stranger like this."

"Oh, he'll never return," cried Melanthius. "Depend upon it, he lies dead in some foreign field—and I only wish Telemachus was as dead as he is!"

Odysseus passed on to the palace, and at the gate he saw his ancient hound Argus, blind and mangey, lying in the dirt where the Suitors had kicked him out to die. But as he drew near the old dog knew him, even after all those years: he struggled to his feet, sniffed at Odysseus, then licked his hand, whining with joy, and wagging his tail feebly—then sank down dead.

There were tears in his eyes as Odysseus stopped to stroke his old friend and lay him out gently by the palace wall.

Inside the courtyard Odysseus begged food from the Suitors, and was not kindly received. And there a real beggar called Irus tried to drive him out; for Irus was ravenously greedy, and spent all his time eating and drinking, and feared that the new beggar might take some of the food which would otherwise come to him.

Odysseus argued with him gently, but Irus would not be reasonable and challenged him to fight with fists. The Suitors gathered round laughing to watch the duel between the two beggars, and promised to see fair play and reward the winner.

When Odysseus bared his strong arms, Irus was afraid and would have slunk away; but the Suitors jeered at him and made him fight, calling him a bully and a cowardly braggart—as indeed he was.

So Irus rushed in with a yell and struck Odysseus on the shoulder; but Odysseus struck back, though not as strongly as he could have done, and stretched Irus bleeding on the ground. Then he dragged him out of the palace, propped him up against the wall, and left him, saying:

"Sit there now, and scare off the swine and dogs; and do not bully beggars again, or a worse thing may befall you!"

Odysseus then returned to the palace, and Penelope sent for him since she had heard that he could give her news of the fall of Troy, and perhaps even of her lost husband.

Odysseus told her as much as seemed good for her to know at that moment, and when his tale was ended, Penelope bade the old nurse Euryclea[6] wash his feet for him and find him some decent clothes to wear—for she knew that he spoke the truth and had really met her husband on his wanderings as he brought her a sure token.

As Euryclea washed his feet with warm water, she came to the scar from the wound which the boar had made on Mount Parnassus when Odysseus was a boy, and she recognized it and knew then who he was.

---

5. *Melanthius* (mə lan′thē əs).

6. *Euryclea* (yür′ə klē′ə).

She would have cried out with joy, but Odysseus put his hand over her mouth quickly:

"Do you want to cause my death?" he whispered. "If the Suitors know, they will murder me at once. Keep my return a secret, even from the Queen: the time will soon come when justice shall be done."

After this he slipped back into the hall and waited quietly. Presently Penelope came in, fair and stately, carrying the great black bow and a quiverful of arrows. At her command twelve axes were set up in a line, and then she said:

"Princes and nobles, I can stand out against you no longer. Therefore whoever among you can string the bow of Odysseus and shoot an arrow through the rings in the axe-heads as he used to do, the same shall be my husband and the lord of rugged Ithaca, and Zacynthos and wooded Same."[7]

So the Suitors began in turn to handle the great bow; but not one of them could so much as string it. Then they grew angry, and declared that it was some trick of Penelope's, and that the bow could not be strung by any mortal man.

"Let me try," said Odysseus, but the Suitors cried out at the impudence of the beggar, and one of them flung a stool at him.

"He shall try if he likes," cried Telemachus, and it seemed as if a quarrel were about to begin. So he turned to Penelope and bade her go to her room with all her maidens; and when she had gone he sent Euryclea to lock them in. While this was happening Philoetius slipped into the courtyard and locked the gates also, that none might come out or in.

Then, at a word from Telemachus, Eumaeus picked up the bow and carried it to Odysseus. He took it in his hands, turning this way and that lovingly, testing it to see that all was well with it; then suddenly he bent it and slipped the string into place as easily as a minstrel strings his lyre. And beneath his fingers the bow-string sang like a swallow, yet with a deeper, fiercer note telling of war and of the death of men.

While the Suitors sat back in anger and amazement Odysseus set an arrow to the string, drew, and loosed so surely that it sped through all twelve of the rings without touching one with its brazen barb.

"Telemachus, your guest does you no shame!" cried Odysseus, and with a bound he was on the high threshold with the arrows ready to his hand and the beggar's rags cast from him. "Lo, now is the terrible trial ended at last," he continued, "and I aim at another mark!"

Even as he spoke an arrow hummed from the bow, and one of the Suitors fell back dead in his seat, pierced through the throat.

"Mind where you're shooting!" shouted some of the Suitors, still not recognizing him and thinking that the last shot had been a mistake.

"That will I indeed," was the answer, "for you have much to answer, you who thought that I would never come back from the land of the Trojans, and therefore wasted my goods and insulted my wife. Now death waits for you, one and all, at the hand of Odysseus the sacker of cities!"

Then, while the great bow sang and the swift shafts hummed the Suitors strove vainly to get at him and pull him down. First they sought for weapons, but these were not in the usual places on the walls. Then such as carried swords attacked him, using tables as shields; but Telemachus brought helmets, spears, and shields for himself and faithful Eumaeus and Philoetius, and armour for Odysseus also, and the battle raged furiously.

Once it was almost lost, for false Melanthius the goatherd slipped into the storeroom and brought out several weapons for the Suitors: but Telemachus caught him in time and tied him up, to be punished afterwards.

On and on shot Odysseus, and Athena spread panic among the Suitors so that they did not rush the four all in a single body as they might have done. When his arrows were exhausted, Odysseus took up the spears which had been flung at him and returned them to the Suitors with deadly aim; and drawing his sword he leapt amongst them, crying his terrible war-cry. At his side fought brave young Telemachus, and Eumaeus the faithful swineherd, and Philoetius the cowherd; and all of them were wounded in that terrible fray.

---

7. *Zacynthos and . . . Same* (zə kin′thôs *and* sā′mē), islands in the Ionian Sea, parts of the kingdom of Odysseus.

At length the Suitors lay dead, every man of them; but Odysseus spared Phemius the minstrel who had done no harm, and a slave who chanced to be in the hall and hid under an ox-hide.

Then Odysseus called for Euryclea, and she brought the handmaidens, and together they carried the bodies out of the palace, and cleansed the hall, and set all in order.

When this was done, Euryclea went to fetch Penelope who all the while had been sleeping peacefully in her inner chamber.

"Awake, dear child!" cried the old nurse. "Awake and see the day for which you have prayed so long! For Odysseus has come—he is here in his own house, and has slain the proud Suitors who troubled you so and devoured all his substance!"

But Penelope would not believe the good news, not even when she came into the hall and found Odysseus waiting for her.

"I have heard it said," she replied when Telemachus reproached her, "that traitor Paris put on the form of Menelaus[8] and so beguiled fair Helen my cousin. And well I know that the Immortals can wear what shape they will!"

Then Odysseus said to Telemachus: "Son, your mother speaks wisely: for we have tokens that we twain know, secret from all others."

Then Odysseus was bathed and clad in fair garments, and Penelope felt almost sure that he

---

8. *Menelaus* (men′ə lā′əs), king of Sparta and husband of Helen. Penelope refers to the incident which started the Trojan War, the elopement of Paris and Helen.

---

was indeed her husband. But still she doubted, and as a test she said:

"Noble sir, let us wait until tomorrow before we test one another further. But now I will command my maidens to bring forth the bed of Odysseus, whom you swear that you are—even his bridal bed and mine, which stands in the innermost chamber."

Then Odysseus turned upon her, saying:

"This is a bitter word that you speak! Who has been interfering with my bed? For there is no man living, however strong, who could lift it and bring it here. And I will tell you why: when I married you, and built on our chamber to the palace, there stood an olive tree as thick as a pillar; round this I built the room, and roofed it over, but the lower branches of the tree I lopped off, and used the tree, still growing, as one of the corner posts of the bed. Lady, here is a token for you! I say that the bed cannot be brought out to me, unless some man has cut away the stem of the olive tree."

When she heard this, Penelope's last doubt was gone. She broke into weeping, and ran up to him, cast her arms about his neck and kissed him, saying:

"Odysseus, my husband! None but you and I knew of the olive tree that is part of the bed in our secret bridal chamber. Now I know you indeed, and now I am truly happy once more!"

Then Odysseus held her in his arms; and in the happiness of that moment it seemed that all his toils and all his wanderings were but little things compared with so great and true a joy.

---

## DISCUSSION

1. How had Penelope delayed choosing one of the suitors?

2. (a) What contest does Telemachus suggest to determine which suitor will marry his mother? (b) Why does he suggest the contest at this time?

3. By whom is Odysseus recognized even when he is disguised?

4. How does Odysseus reveal his identity to the suitors?

5. Why does Odysseus kill the suitors?

6. What second test does Odysseus pass to prove his identity to Penelope?

7. How does the goddess Athena aid Odysseus?

8. Odysseus is characterized throughout the *Odyssey* as a man who survives by using his wits, by thinking his way out of

dangerous situations. What evidence is there in this episode that he relies more on his intellect than on his strength?

9. The plot of this episode depends largely on the device of Odysseus's disguise. (a) What does the disguise contribute to the suspense of the episode? (b) What dramatic irony results from the disguise? (Refer to the Handbook entry on *irony* if necessary.)

# Philosophers and Poets

It would be wrong to assume that the literature of ancient Greece and Rome dealt exclusively with myth and legend. Among the manuscripts preserved from those civilizations are many written by scientists, historians, philosophers, and poets who wrote of the realities of daily life. We owe to these early thinkers many of our modern ideas about ethics, education, politics, and other human affairs.

One of the classical philosophers was an Athenian named Socrates (469?–399 B.C.), who wrote no books and kept no schools. He called himself the Gadfly and wandered about the town, mingling with the crowds in the public squares, talking with people, and asking questions. Through his questioning he tried to arrive at underlying principles of truth.

However, because he introduced ideas and methods that challenged established beliefs, Socrates, at the age of seventy, was put to death. At his trial he was convicted of impiety and of corrupting the youth of Athens—charges that grew out of his refusing to worship the gods publicly and his encouraging young people to question existing ideas.

Since Socrates wrote nothing, it is from others that we must learn of him. Chief among his biographers is his friend and student, Plato, another familiar name in Greek literature. In the following selection, Plato gives his version of what Socrates said to the courtroom audience after he had received his sentence. The second selection is Plato's account of Socrates' final hours in prison.

# the prophecy of socrates

*Plato*
*Translated by Benjamin Jowett*

NOT much time will be gained, O Athenians, in return for the evil name which you will get from the detractors of the city, who will say that you killed Socrates, a wise man; for they will call me wise, even although I am not wise, when they want to reproach you. If you had waited a little while, your desire would have been fulfilled in the course of nature. For I am far advanced in years, as you may perceive, and not far from death. I am speaking now not to all of you, but only to those who have condemned me to death. And I have another thing to say to them: You think that I was convicted because I had no words of the sort which would have procured my acquittal —I mean, if I had thought fit to leave nothing undone or unsaid. Not so; the deficiency which led to my conviction was not of words—certainly not. But I had not the boldness or impudence or inclination to address you as you would have liked me to do, weeping and wailing and lamenting, and saying and doing many things which you have been accustomed to hear from others, and which, as I maintain, are unworthy of me. I thought at the time that I ought not to do anything common or mean when in danger: nor do I now repent of the style of my defence; I would rather die having spoken after my manner, than speak in your manner and live. For neither in war nor yet at law ought I or any man to use every way of escaping death. Often in battle there can be no doubt that if a man will throw away his arms, and fall on his knees before his pursuers, he may escape death; and in other dangers there are other ways of escaping death, if a man is willing to say and do anything. The difficulty, my friends, is not to avoid death, but to avoid unrighteousness; for that runs faster than death. I am old and move slowly, and the slower runner has overtaken me, and my accusers are keen and quick, and the faster runner, who is unrighteousness, has overtaken them. And now I depart hence condemned by you to suffer the penalty of death,—they too go their ways condemned by the truth to suffer the penalty of villainy and wrong; and I must abide by my award—let them abide by theirs. I suppose that these things may be regarded as fated,— and I think that they are well.

And now, O men who have condemned me, I would fain prophesy to you; for I am about to die, and in the hour of death men are gifted with prophetic power. And I prophesy to you who are my murderers, that immediately after my departure punishment far heavier than you have inflicted on me will surely await you. Me you have killed because you wanted to escape the accuser, and not to give an account of your lives. But that will not be as you suppose: far otherwise. For I say that there will be more accusers of you than there are now; accusers whom hitherto I have restrained: and as they are younger they will be more inconsiderate with you, and you will be more offended at them. If you think that by killing men you can prevent someone from censuring your evil lives, you are mistaken; that is not a way of

"The Prophecy of Socrates" from *The Dialogues of Plato*, translated by Benjamin Jowett. Reprinted by permission of Clarendon Press, Oxford. Fourth Edition (1953).

escape which is either possible or honourable; the easiest and noblest way is not to be disabling others, but to be improving yourselves. This is the prophecy which I utter before my departure to the judges who have condemned me.

Friends, who have acquitted me, I would like also to talk with you about the thing which has come to pass, while the magistrates are busy, and before I go to the place at which I must die. Stay then a little, for we may as well talk with one another while there is time. You are my friends, and I should like to show you the meaning of this event which has happened to me. O my judges—for you I may truly call judges—I should like to tell you of a wonderful circumstance. Hitherto the divine faculty of which the internal oracle is the source has constantly been in the habit of opposing me even about trifles, if I was going to make a slip or error in any matter; and now as you see there has come upon me that which may be thought, and is generally believed to be, the last and worst evil. But the oracle made no sign of opposition, either when I was leaving my house in the morning, or when I was on my way to the court, or while I was speaking, at anything which I was going to say; and yet I have often been stopped in the middle of a speech, but now in nothing I either said or did touching the matter in hand has the oracle opposed me. What do I take to be the explanation of this silence? I will tell you. It is an intimation that what has happened to me is a good, and that those of us who think that death is an evil are in error. For the customary sign would surely have opposed me had I been going to evil and not to good.

Let us reflect in another way, and we shall see that there is great reason to hope that death is a good; for one of two things—either death is a state of nothingness and utter unconsciousness, or, as men say, there is a change and migration of the soul from this world to another. Now, if you suppose that there is no consciousness, but a sleep like the sleep of him who is undisturbed even by dreams, death will be an unspeakable gain. For if a person were to select the night in which his sleep was undisturbed even by dreams, and were to compare with this the other days and nights of his life, and then were to tell us how many days and nights he had passed in the course of his life better and more pleasantly than this one, I think that any man, I will not say a private man, but even the great king will not find many such days or nights, when compared with the others. Now, if death be of such a nature, I say that to die is gain; for eternity is then only a single night. But if death is the journey to another place, and there, as men say, all the dead abide, what good, O my friends and judges, can be greater than this? If, indeed, when the pilgrim arrives in the world below, he is delivered from the professors of justice in this world, and finds the true judges who are said to give judgment there, Minos and Rhadamanthus and Aeacus and Triptolemus, and other sons of God who were righteous in their own life, that pilgrimage will be worth making. Above all, I shall then be able to continue my search into true and false knowledge; as in this world, so also in the next; and I shall find out who is wise, and who pretends to be wise, and is not. What would not a man give, O judges, to be able to examine the leader of the great Trojan expedition; or Odysseus or Sisyphus, or numberless others, men and women too! What infinite delight would there be in conversing with them and asking them questions! In another world they do not put a man to death for asking questions: assuredly not. For besides being happier than we are, they will be immortal, if what is said is true.

Wherefore, O judges, be of good cheer about death, and know of a certainty, that no evil can happen to a good man, either in life or after death. He and his are not neglected by the gods; nor has my own approaching end happened by mere chance. But I see clearly that the time had arrived when it was better for me to die and be released from trouble: wherefore the oracle gave no sign. For which reason, also, I am not angry with my condemners, or with my accusers; they have done me no harm, although they did not mean to do me any good; and for this I may gently blame them.

The hour of departure has arrived, and we go our ways—I to die, and you to live. Which is better God only knows.

# the death of socrates

*Plato*

IT seemed to us as if we were going to lose a father, and to be orphans for the rest of our life.

When Socrates had bathed, and his children had been brought to him—he had two sons quite little, and one grown up—and the women of his family were come, he spoke with them in Crito's[1] presence, and gave them his last commands. Then he sent the women and children away, and returned to us.

Presently the servant of the governing council which had condemned him to death came and stood before him and said, "I know that I shall not find you unreasonable like other men, Socrates. They are angry with me and curse me when I bid them drink the poison because the authorities make me do it. But I have found you all along the noblest and gentlest and best man that has ever come here; and now I am sure that you will not be angry with me, but with those who you know are to blame. And so farewell, and try to bear what must be as lightly as you can; you know why I have come." With that he turned away weeping, and went out.

Socrates looked up at him, and replied, "Farewell—I will do as you say." Then he turned to us and said, "How courteous the man is. And the whole time that I have been here, he has constantly come in to see me, and sometimes he has talked to me, and has been the best of men; and now, how generously he weeps for me. Come, Crito, let us obey him—let the poison be brought if it is ready; and if it is not ready, let it be prepared."

1. *Crito,* a follower of Socrates.

Crito replied: "Nay, Socrates, I think that the sun is still upon the hills—it has not set. Besides, I know that other men take the poison quite late, and eat and drink heartily, and even enjoy the company of their chosen friends, after the announcement has been made. So do not hurry, there is still time."

Socrates replied: "And those whom you speak of, Crito, naturally do so; for they think that they will be gainers by so doing. And I naturally shall not do so for I think that I should gain nothing by drinking the poison a little later, by my own contempt for so greedily saving up a life which is already spent. So do not refuse to do as I say."

Then Crito made a sign to his slave who was standing by, and the slave went out, and after some delay returned with the man who was to give the poison, carrying it prepared in a cup. When Socrates saw him, he asked, "You understand these things, my good sir, what have I to do?"

"You have only to drink this," he replied, "and to walk about until your legs feel heavy, and then lie down, and it will act of itself."

With that he handed the cup to Socrates, who took it quite cheerfully, without trembling, and without any change of colour or of feature, and looked up at the man with that fixed glance of his, and asked, "What say you to pouring out a libation to the gods from this draught? May I, or not?"

"We only prepare so much as we think sufficient, Socrates," he answered.

"I understand," said Socrates, "but I suppose

that I may, and must, pray to the gods that my journey hence may be prosperous. That is my prayer—be it so."

With these words he put the cup to his lips and drank the poison quite calmly and cheerfully. Till then most of us had been able to control our grief fairly well. But when we saw him drinking, and then the poison finished, we could do so no longer. My tears came fast in spite of myself, and I covered my face and wept for myself—it was not for him, but at my own misfortune in losing such a friend. Even before that Crito had been unable to restrain his tears, and had gone away. And Apollodorus, who had never once ceased weeping the whole time, burst into a loud cry, and made us one and all break down by his sobbing and grief, except only Socrates himself.

"What are you doing, my friends?" he exclaimed. "I sent away the women chiefly in order that they might not offend in this way for I have heard that a man should die in silence. So calm yourselves and bear up."

When we heard that we were ashamed and we ceased from weeping. But he walked about, until he said that his legs were getting heavy, and then he lay down on his back, as he was told. And the man who gave the poison began to examine his feet and legs from time to time. Then he pressed his foot hard, and asked if there was any feeling in it, and Socrates said, No. And then his legs, and so higher and higher, and showed us that he was cold and stiff.

And Socrates felt himself, and said that when it came to his heart, he should be gone. He was already growing cold about the groin, when he uncovered his face, which had been covered, and spoke for the last time.

"Crito," he said, "I owe a cock to Asclepius; do not forget to pay it."

"It shall be done," replied Crito. "Is there anything else that you wish?"

He made no answer to this question, but after a short interval there was a movement, and the man uncovered him, and his eyes were fixed. Then Crito closed his mouth, and his eyes.

Such was the end of our friend, a man, I think, who was the wisest and justest, and the best man I have ever known.

---

## DISCUSSION

### The Prophecy of Socrates

1. (a) If Socrates had chosen to avoid his penalty, what defense did he say he could have used? (b) In what way would this have differed from the defense he did use? (c) Why did he choose not to save himself?

2. (a) What did Socrates mean by his metaphors, the *slower runner* and the *faster runner?* (b) Which runner overtook him? (c) Which overtook his judges? (d) Which did Socrates say was more to be feared? Why?

3. (a) What prophecy did Socrates make? (b) To whom did he make this prophecy?

4. (a) What were the two concepts of death presented by Socrates? (b) Which of these ideas of death did he prefer? Why?

5. (a) What interpretation did Socrates give to the silence of the oracle? (b) What did he mean when he said that "no evil can happen to a good man, either in life or after death"? (c) In what ways was death a gain, according to his two concepts of death?

6. (a) In what ways did Socrates show that he was opposed to existing beliefs? (b) In what ways did he show that he supported existing beliefs? (c) Was there evidence that Socrates actually considered himself a wiser man than most others? Explain.

### The Death of Socrates

1. (a) In what way are Socrates' ideals reinforced by his refusal to await the setting of the sun before taking the poison? (b) In what spirit does Socrates drink the poison? (c) What is the attitude of his followers toward his death? (d) Do they share Socrates' own attitude and strength of character? Explain.

2. (a) What reference to *gainers* does Socrates make in this selection? (b) In what way does this reference reinforce ideas set forth in his speech after his trial?

3. (a) Which of Socrates' words in this selection seem to indicate that he was not guilty of the charges of impiety that were leveled against him? (b) What further light did these words shed upon Socrates' view of death?

4. In what ways was Socrates shown to be a practical man, as well as a man of strength and lofty ideals?

## Dedication of a Mirror

*Plato*
*Translated by Dudley Fitts*

I Laïs[1] whose laughter was scornful in Hellas,[2]
Whose doorways were thronged daily with young
    lovers,
I dedicate my mirror to Aphroditê:

For I will not see myself as I am now,
And can not see myself as once I was.

## Inscription for the Tomb of Timon[3]

*Ptolemaios the Astronomer*
*Translated by Dudley Fitts*

Ask neither my name nor my country, passers-by:
My sole wish is that all of you may die.

## Hesiod,[4] Fortunate Deliverance From

*Marcus Argentarius*
*Translated by Dudley Fitts*

Lately thumbing the pages of *Works and Days,*
I saw my Pyrrhê[5] coming.
                   Goodbye book!
"Why in the world should I cobweb my days," I
    cried,
"With the works of Old Man Hesiod?"

## Epitaph for Slain Spartans

*Simonides of Ceos*
*Translated by Richmond Lattimore*

Traveler, take this word to the men of Lakedaímon:[6]
We who lie buried here did what they told us to do.

"Epitaph for Slain Spartans" from *Greek Lyrics* translated by Richmond Lattimore. Copyright 1949, 1955, and © 1960 by Richmond Lattimore. All rights reserved. Reprinted by permission of The University of Chicago Press and the author.
1. *Laïs* (lā′is). A celebrated beauty of ancient Greece, Laïs is said to have been killed by jealous wives.
2. *Hellas* (hel′əs), in ancient geography, a town and small district in northeastern Greece. Later Hellas became a name applied to all of ancient Greece.
3. *Timon* (tī′ mən), a famous Athenian misanthrope (one who hates and distrusts everyone), later the subject of a play by Shakespeare, *Timon of Athens.*

"Dedication of a Mirror" by Plato, "Inscription for the Tomb of Timon" by Ptolemaios the Astronomer, "Hesiod, Fortunate Deliverance From" by Marcus Argentarius, from *Poems from the Greek Anthology* by Dudley Fitts. Copyright 1938, 1941 © 1956 by New Directions Publishing Corporation. Reprinted by permission of New Directions Publishing Corporation.
4. *Hesiod* (hē′sē əd *or* hes′ē əd), eighth-century Greek poet, author of a long, morally instructive poem, *Works and Days.*
5. *Pyrrhê* (pir′ē).
6. *Lakedaímon* (lak′ə dī′mon), an early king of Sparta in Greece. Also a name sometimes applied to the kingdom of Sparta.

## On a Fortune-Teller

*Lucilius*
*Translated by Dudley Fitts*

Firmly, as with one voice,
The entire Faculty of the College of Applied Astrology
Foretold a healthy old age for my father's brother.

Hermokleidês[1] alone
Maintained that he would die young:
              but he made this statement
At the funeral service we held for my father's brother.


## On Mauros the Rhetor[4]

*Palladas*
*Translated by Dudley Fitts*

Lo, I beheld Mauros,
Professor of Public Speaking,
Raise high his elephant-snout
And from between his lips
(12 oz. apiece) give vent
To a voice whose very sound is accomplished murder.

I was impressed.


## The Warrior of the Past

*Mimnermus of Colophon*
*Translated by Richmond Lattimore*

None could match the strength of him and the pride of his courage.
    Thus the tale told of my fathers who saw him there
breaking the massed battalions of armored Lydian[2] horsemen,
    swinging the ashwood spear on the range of the Hermos[3] plain.
Pallas Athene, goddess of war, would have found no fault with
    this stark heart in its strength, when at the first-line rush
swift in the blood and staggered collision of armies in battle
    all through the raining shafts he fought out a bitter path.
No man ever in the strong encounters of battle was braver
    than he, when he went still in the gleaming light of the sun.

"The Warrior of the Past" from *Greek Lyrics* translated by Richmond Lattimore. Copyright 1949, 1955, and © 1960 by Richmond Lattimore. All rights reserved. Reprinted by permission of The University of Chicago Press and the author.
1. *Hermokleidês* (hėr'mō klī'dēz).
2. *Lydian* (lid'ē ən), from Lydia, an ancient country on the west coast of Asia Minor.

"On a Fortune-Teller" by Lucilius and "On Mauros the Rhetor" by Palladas, from *Poems from the Greek Anthology* by Dudley Fitts. Copyright 1938, 1941, © 1956 by New Directions Publishing Corporation. Reprinted by permission of New Directions Publishing Corporation.
3. *Hermos* (hėr'mos), in ancient geography, a river of Asia Minor.
4. *Rhetor* (rē'tôr), a public speaker, an orator.

## I Do Despise a Tall General

*Archilochos*
*Translated by Guy Davenport*

I do despise a tall general,
One of those swaggerers,
A curly-haired, cheek-frilled
Whisker dandy.

For me a proper officer's
Short and bow-legged,
Both feet planted well apart,
Tough in the guts.

## Some Saian Mountaineer

*Archilochos*
*Translated by Guy Davenport*

Some Saian mountaineer
Struts today with my shield.
I threw it down by a bush and ran
When the fighting got hot.
Life seemed somehow more precious.
It was a beautiful shield.
I know where I can buy another
Exactly like it, just as round.

## The Fox and the Hedgehog

*Archilochos*
*Translated by Guy Davenport*

Fox knows many,
Hedgehog one
Solid trick.

*Aliter,*[1]
Fox knows
Eleventythree
Tricks and still
Gets caught;
Hedgehog knows
One but it
Always works.

From Carmina Archilochi: *The Fragments of Archilochos*, translated from the Greek by Guy Davenport. Originally published by the University of California Press. Reprinted by permission of The Regents of the University of California.
**1.** *Aliter,* in other words.

## The Good-Natured

*Archilochos*
*Translated by Guy Davenport*

The good-natured need no cutlery
In their vocabulary.


## There's Nothing Now

*Archilochos*
*Translated by Guy Davenport*

There's nothing now
We can't expect to happen!
Anything at all, you can bet,
Is ready to jump out at us.
No need to wonder over it.
Father Zeus has turned
Noon to night, blotting out
The sunshine utterly,
Putting cold terror
At the back of the throat.
Let's believe all we hear.
Even that dolphins and cows
Change place, porpoises and goats,
Rams booming along in the offing,
Mackerel nibbling in the hill pastures.
I wouldn't be surprised,
I wouldn't be surprised.


## When You Upbraid Me

*Archilochos*
*Translated by Guy Davenport*

When you upbraid me
For my poems,
Catch also a cricket
By the wings,
And shout at him
For chirping.

From Carmina Archilochi: *The Fragments of Archilochos*, translated
from the Greek by Guy Davenport. Originally published by the
University of California Press. Reprinted by permission of The
Regents of the University of California.

## Suffenus, Varus, Whom You Know So Well

*Catullus*
*Translated by C. H. Sisson*

Suffenus, Varus, whom you know so well,
Is not only witty, polite, acceptable,
He even writes more verses than other people.
I believe he has at least ten thousand, perhaps more,
All copied out, not just on bits of paper
—Royal parchment, beautiful bindings,
Lines ruled with lead, and all smoothed out with
     pumice.
But when you read him, the elegant Suffenus
Turns out to be a goatherd or a ditcher,
He is so unlike himself, so changed.
What can one make of it? This charming wit,
This expert in civilized conversation
Is about as dull as a row of turnips
Once he touches poetry. However
He is never so happy as when he is writing it;
Then he can love himself and admire his talents.
Still, we all imagine that we have gifts,
And everyone is a bit like Suffenus;
Everyone has his special delusion—
Our view of ourselves is a bit different from other
     people's.

## Living, Dear Lesbia, Is Useless Without Loving

*Catullus*
*Translated by C. H. Sisson*

Living, dear Lesbia, is useless without loving:
The observations of the censorious old
Are worth a penny every piece of advice.
One day follows another, the sun comes back
But when once we have gone away we do not;
Once night comes for us, it is night for ever.
Give me a thousand kisses, and then a hundred,
Then give me a second thousand, a second hundred
And then another thousand, and then a hundred
And when we have made up many, many thousands
Let us forget to count. Better not to know—
It will bring someone's jealous eye upon us
If people know we give so many kisses.

## Lesbia Is Always Talking Scandal About Me

*Catullus*
*Translated by C. H. Sisson*

Lesbia is always talking scandal about me
And never stops: which proves that Lesbia loves me.
How does it prove it? I am in the same case: I abuse her
All the time: and one could not say I do not love her.

## My Woman Says There Is No One She Would Rather Marry

*Catullus*
*Translated by C. H. Sisson*

My woman says there is no one she would rather marry
Than me, not even if Jupiter were to propose to her.
She says: but what a woman says to an eager lover
Ought to be recorded in wind and water.

## DISCUSSION

1. Several of the poems in this section are *lampoons*. A lampoon is a satirical piece of writing, one that attacks or ridicules a person. (a) Which of the poems are lampoons? (b) What human characteristics do the lampoons ridicule?

2. The sentiment expressed in Archilochos's "There's Nothing Now" is a common one. You may have heard someone declare that "This old world is going to the dogs," or "Nothing seems impossible these days!" If the speaker lived in the twentieth century A.D. instead of the seventh century B.C., what details might he offer as proof that "There's nothing now/ We can't expect to happen"?

3. (a) Compare or contrast the attitudes toward war expressed in "The Warrior of the Past," "Epitaph for Slain Spartans," and "Some Saian Mountaineer." (b) Look again at the section of war poems in the Poetry Unit, pages 226–233. Do any of those poems express similar attitudes? Explain.

4. (a) How would you characterize the speaker in Catullus's three poems to Lesbia? Is he, for example, a starry-eyed romantic, a clear-eyed realist, neither? Explain. (b) Knowing what you do about both the speaker and Lesbia, speculate about the kind of husband he would make and the kind of wife she would make. Would theirs be a "good" marriage? Explain.

5. Restate the themes of "The Fox and the Hedgehog," "When You Upbraid Me," and "The Good-Natured" in your own words.

## ARCHILOCHOS

*Archilochos*, which means "First Sergeant," was perhaps a pen name, and an appropriate one, for the poet was also a soldier. Born on the Aegean island of Paros in the seventh century B.C., he traveled widely, earning his living as a soldier-for-hire.

Translators of Archilochos have only fragments of many of his poems, found on tattered scraps of papyrus that had been used to wrap mummies in Alexandria, the ancient Greek capital of Egypt. From these fragments and from quotations of his verses in the works of other early writers, we know that his poems were often angry and satirical. Perhaps it was his stinging verse that gave rise to the legend that wasps hover over his grave.

Although he is credited with inventing several new verse forms, Archilochos's major contribution to the poetry of his time may have been the intensely personal nature of his verse. He is the first poet known to have written so openly and so passionately of his own feelings and experiences.

## CATULLUS
## (GAIUS VALERIUS CATULLUS)

The little that is known of Catullus's life has been inferred from his poems and from references to him by other writers of his time. He was born sometime in the eighties of the first century B.C. and died thirty years later during the reign of Julius Caesar. A member of a prosperous family of Verona, Catullus spent most of his adult life in Rome, where he had a circle of friends who shared with him a liking for wit, sophistication, freedom and spontaneity in art and in living.

From his poems we know that he fell in love with an older woman he calls Lesbia. When this painful relationship ended, Catullus wrote some of his bitterest poems. Early scholars rejected many of his poems as too slangy and direct for serious consideration, but his reputation as a poet has grown over the years. Those qualities for which his verse was once condemned are the very qualities now admired by many critics.

Drama in the Western world was invented by the ancient Greeks. Greek dramas were first performed in connection with the worship of Dionysus, the god of wine. Information about the earliest of these religious festivals is scarce, but most authorities believe that early performances featured a chorus, singing and dancing in a ritual to honor Dionysus. The choral song probably contained a myth about the god. At some later point actors began to perform the actions narrated in the choral song, and eventually spoken dialogue was introduced. At that point drama, as we know it, had come into being.

At the annual festival of Dionysus, held in the spring, competing playwrights presented new tragedies. Comedies were usually presented at another festival, held during the winter. At the spring festival, tragedies were performed before the citizens of Athens in a three-day competition, and prizes were awarded to playwrights whose plays were judged the best. Sophocles, who wrote *Antigone,* the tragedy you are about to read, was a frequent winner at the competitions.

## The Theater

Attending the theater in ancient Greece was not merely an occasion for entertainment. The festival of Dionysus was an annual event of considerable civic and religious significance, attended by nearly all the citizens of Athens. Spectators sat in semicircular rows of seats built into a hillside which formed a natural outdoor amphitheater. At the bottom was a round space called the *orchestra* in which the chorus danced and sang. Later, when the playwrights began to use actors in addition to the chorus, a raised platform and a backdrop of simple scenery were constructed behind the orchestra. The actors in these later plays wore large masks with fixed and exaggerated expressions that could be identified even in the upper rows.

## The Chorus

In the earliest Greek plays the chorus was a large group of men dancing and chanting or singing in unison. Eventually the number was reduced to twelve or fifteen, and one member, the chorus leader, was given individual lines. Some playwrights used the chorus to interpret and recall past events, to comment on the actions of the characters in the play, or to foretell the future. Although its role and importance varied from play to play, the chorus, usually representing the senior citizens of the community, often gave voice to the emotions experienced by the audience.

## Tragedy

To many people a tragedy is merely an unhappy sort of play in which one or more characters have a run of bad luck and eventually meet a sad end. But the ancient Greeks had no such simple idea. To understand what tragedy was to the Greeks, it is necessary to review some basic concepts central to ancient Greek culture.

First of all, the Greeks believed that every person's life was ruled by a predetermined fate—a natural force set in motion by the gods. Furthermore, they believed that every person's fate held in store a personal allotment of unavoidable misery that would come about naturally. Misery in itself was not tragic but expected.

The Greeks also believed, however, that each person possessed a certain freedom of will and action—a concept often touched upon by Socrates in his teachings. By wisely making use of his personal freedom, a person could fulfill his fate with dignity, suffering no more than his allotted share of grief. On the other hand, a person always stood in danger of misusing this freedom. Through some tragic flaw in his own character, he might tempt fate in such a way that he would come to lose all personal dignity; in the process, he would bring upon himself more pain and suffering than his fate had originally held in store for him.

A Greek tragedy, then, is the story of the downfall of a basically good and noble individual who, because of some personal flaw in character, unwittingly tempts fate and brings upon himself extraordinary amounts of sorrow and suffering. Such a play is *Antigone*.

## A Cycle of Tragedy

Although *Antigone* is a complete play in itself, it is closely associated with two other of Sophocles' plays, *Oedipus the King* and *Oedipus at Colonus*. Oedipus, separated as a child from his parents, fulfilled a dreadful prophecy that had been cast at his birth: when he became an adult, he killed his father without recognizing him and later married his mother, whom he did not remember. When he discovered the truth, Oedipus put out his own eyes and banished himself from his kingdom of Thebes. He wandered about for many years, blind and tormented, until he finally died in Colonus, as the oracle had prophesied.

*Antigone* begins after the death of Oedipus, but in a sense the play completes the cycle of tragedy that started with the birth of this great king of Thebes. The fate of Oedipus continues to be fulfilled by his daughter, Antigone.

Antigone is not, however, the only important character in the play. It is equally about Creon, the brother-in-law of Oedipus and the new king of Thebes. Some readers have said that the play should be called *Creon* instead of *Antigone,* arguing that because Creon has more lines than Antigone and because Antigone disappears halfway through the play, it is Creon, not Antigone, who is the tragic hero of the play. Others argue that the play is equally about both characters, each of whom has a tragic flaw and suffers a tragic fate. When you have read the play, decide which view seems right to you.

# Antigone

*Sophocles*

*Translated by E. F. Watling*

## Characters

ISMENE  
ANTIGONE } *daughters of Oedipus*

CREON, *King of Thebes*

HAEMON, *son of Creon*

TEIRESIAS, *a blind prophet*

A SENTRY

A MESSENGER

EURYDICE, *wife of Creon*

CHORUS *of Theban elders*

*King's attendants*

*Queen's attendants*

*A boy leading Teiresias*

*Soldiers*

*Antigone* from *Sophocles: The Theban Plays,* translated by E. F. Watling. Copyright E. F. Watling, 1947. Reprinted by permission of Penguin Books Ltd.

*Scene: Before the Palace at Thebes.*

> *Enter* ISMENE *from the central door of the Palace.*
> ANTIGONE *follows, anxious and urgent; she closes*
> *the door carefully, and comes to join her sister.*

ANTIGONE. O sister! Ismene dear, dear sister Ismene!
  You know how heavy the hand of God is upon us;
  How we who are left must suffer for our father, Oedipus.
  There is no pain, no sorrow, no suffering, no dishonour
5 We have not shared together, you and I.
  And now there is something more. Have you heard this order,
  This latest order that the King has proclaimed to the city?
  Have you heard how our dearest are being treated like
     enemies?
ISMENE. I have heard nothing about any of those we love,
10 Neither good nor evil—not, I mean, since the death
  Of our two brothers, both fallen in a day.
  The Argive army,[1] I hear, was withdrawn last night.
  I know no more to make me sad or glad.
ANTIGONE. I thought you did not. That's why I brought you out
     here,
15 Where we shan't be heard, to tell you something alone.
ISMENE. What is it, Antigone? Black news, I can see already.
ANTIGONE. O Ismene, what do you think? Our two dear
     brothers . . .

1. *Argive army* (är′jīv or är′gīv), the army which attacked Thebes; from Argos (är′gos), a city in southern Greece.

Creon has given funeral honours to one,[2]
And not to the other; nothing but shame and ignominy.
20   Eteocles[3] has been buried, they tell me, in state,
With all honourable observances due to the dead.
But Polynices,[4] just as unhappily fallen—the order
Says he is not to be buried, not to be mourned;
To be left unburied, unwept, a feast of flesh
25   For keen-eyed carrion birds. The noble Creon!
It is against you and me he has made this order.
Yes, against me. And soon he will be here himself
To make it plain to those that have not heard it,
And to enforce it. This is no idle threat;
30   The punishment for disobedience is death by stoning.
So now you know. And now is the time to show
Whether or not you are worthy of your high blood.
ISMENE. My poor Antigone, if this is really true,
What more can *I* do, or undo, to help you?
35  ANTIGONE. *Will* you help me? Will you do something with me?
      Will you?
ISMENE. Help you do what, Antigone? What do you mean?
ANTIGONE. Would you help me lift the body . . . you and me?
ISMENE. You cannot mean . . . to bury him? Against the order?
ANTIGONE. Is he not my brother, and yours, whether you like it
40   Or not? *I* shall never desert him, never.
ISMENE. How could you dare, when Creon has expressly for-
      bidden it?
ANTIGONE. He has no right to keep me from my own.
ISMENE. O sister, sister, do you forget how our father
Perished in shame and misery, his awful sin
45   Self-proved, blinded by his own self-mutilation?
And then his mother, his wife—for she was both—
Destroyed herself in a noose of her own making.[5]
And now our brothers, both in a single day
Fallen in an awful exaction of death for death,
50   Blood for blood, each slain by the other's hand.
Now we two left; and what will be the end of us,
If we transgress the law and defy our king?
O think, Antigone; we are women; it is not for us
To fight against men; our rulers are stronger than we,
55   And we must obey in this, or in worse than this.
May the dead forgive me, I can do no other
But as I am commanded; to do more is madness.
ANTIGONE. No; then I will not ask you for your help.
Nor would I thank you for it, if you gave it.
60   Go your own way; I will bury my brother;
And if I die for it, what happiness!
Convicted of reverence—I shall be content
To lie beside a brother whom I love.
We have only a little time to please the living,
65   But all eternity to love the dead.

2. *funeral honours to one.* In Greek mythology, the souls of unburied human beings could not cross the River Styx to the realm of the dead but were compelled to wander forever with no permanent resting place. Consequently, burial of the dead was an important sacred duty of surviving friends and relatives.
3. *Eteocles* (i tē′ə klēz).
4. *Polynices* (pol i nī′sēz).

5. *his mother . . . own making,* Jocasta (jō kas′tə), realizing that she was both wife and mother to Oedipus, hanged herself.

There I shall lie for ever. Live, if you will;
  Live, and defy the holiest laws of heaven.
ISMENE. I do not defy them; but I cannot act
  Against the State. I am not strong enough.
70 ANTIGONE. Let that be your excuse, then. I will go
  And heap a mound of earth over my brother.
ISMENE. I fear for you, Antigone; I fear——
ANTIGONE. You need not fear for me. Fear for yourself.
ISMENE. At least be secret. Do not breathe a word.
75  I'll not betray your secret.
ANTIGONE.                    Publish it
  To all the world! Else I shall hate you more.
ISMENE. Your heart burns! Mine is frozen at the thought.
ANTIGONE. I know my duty, where true duty lies.
ISMENE. If you can do it; but you're bound to fail.
80 ANTIGONE. When I have *tried* and failed, I shall have failed.
ISMENE. No sense in starting on a hopeless task.
ANTIGONE. Oh, I shall hate you if you talk like that!
  And *he*[6] will hate you, rightly. Leave me alone
  With my own madness. There is no punishment
85  Can rob me of my honourable death.
ISMENE. Go then, if you are determined, to your folly.
  But remember that those who love you . . . love you still.
                    (ISMENE *goes into the Palace.* ANTIGONE
                      *leaves the stage by a side exit.*)


                    *Enter the* CHORUS *of Theban elders.*
CHORUS. Hail the sun! the brightest of all that ever
  Dawned on the City of Seven Gates, City of Thebes!
90  Hail the golden dawn over Dirce's river[7]
  Rising to speed the flight of the white invaders
      Homeward in full retreat!

  The army of Polynices was gathered against us,
  In angry dispute his voice was lifted against us,
95  Like a ravening bird of prey he swooped around us
  With white wings flashing, with flying plumes,
      With armed hosts ranked in thousands.

  At the threshold of seven gates in a circle of blood
  His swords stood round us, his jaws were opened against us;
100  But before he could taste our blood, or consume us with fire,
  He fled, fled with the roar of the dragon behind him
      And thunder of war in his ears.

  The Father of Heaven abhors the proud tongue's boasting;
  He marked the oncoming torrent, the flashing stream
105  Of their golden harness, the clash of their battle gear;
  He heard the invader cry Victory over our ramparts,
      And smote him with fire to the ground.[8]

6. *he,* Polynices.

7. *Dirce's river.* Dirce (dėr′sē), the
wife of a previous ruler of Thebes,
was brutally murdered and her
corpse thrown into a stream thereafter called by her name.

8. *The Father of Heaven . . . smote
him with fire to the ground.* Zeus,
who favored the Thebans in the
battle, struck down the invading
Argive army with thunderbolts.

Down to the ground from the crest of his hurricane on-
    slaught
He swung, with the fiery brands of his hate brought low:
Each and all to their doom of destruction appointed
    By the god that fighteth for us.

Seven invaders at seven gates seven defenders
Spoiled of their bronze for a tribute to Zeus;[9] save two
Luckless brothers in one fight matched together
    And in one death laid low.[10]

Great is the victory, great be the joy
In the city of Thebes, the city of chariots.
Now is the time to fill the temples
With glad thanksgiving for warfare ended;
Shake the ground with the night-long dances,
Bacchus afoot and delight abounding.

But see, the King comes here,
Creon, the son of Menoeceus,[11]
Whom the gods have appointed for us
In our recent change of fortune.
What matter is it, I wonder,
That has led him to call us together
By his special proclamation?

    *The central door is opened, and* CREON *enters.*
CREON. My councillors: now that the gods have brought our city
Safe through a storm of trouble to tranquillity,
I have called you especially out of all my people
To conference together, knowing that you
Were loyal subjects when King Laius[12] reigned,
And when King Oedipus so wisely ruled us,
And again, upon his death, faithfully served
His sons, till they in turn fell—both slayers, both slain,
Both stained with brother-blood, dead in a day—
And I, their next of kin, inherited
The throne and kingdom which I now possess.
No other touchstone can test the heart of a man,
The temper of his mind and spirit, till he be tried
In the practice of authority and rule.
For my part, I have always held the view,
And hold it still, that a king whose lips are sealed
By fear, unwilling to seek advice, is damned.
And no less damned is he who puts a friend
Above his country; I have no good word for him.
As God above is my witness, who sees all,
When I see any danger threatening my people,
Whatever it may be, I shall declare it.
No man who is his country's enemy

9. *Seven invaders . . . tribute to
Zeus.* Polynices and six Argive chiefs
each attacked one of Thebes' seven
gates, which were successfully defended by seven Theban heroes. The
Theban defenders offered the armor
of the slain Argive chiefs as a tribute
to Zeus.
10. *Luckless brothers . . . laid low.*
Antigone's brothers, Polynices and
Eteocles, killed each other in single
combat, ending the war.

11. *Menoeceus,* (mə nē′sē əs).

12. *King Laius* (lā′əs), a former king
of Thebes and father of Oedipus.

Shall call himself my friend. Of this I am sure—
Our country is our life; only when she[13]
Rides safely, have we any friends at all.

13. *she*, Thebes.

155 Such is my policy for our common weal.
In pursuance of this, I have made a proclamation
Concerning the sons of Oedipus, as follows:
Eteocles, who fell fighting in defence of the city,
Fighting gallantly, is to be honoured with burial
160 And with all the rites due to the noble dead.
The other—you know whom I mean—his brother Polynices,
Who came back from exile intending to burn and destroy
His fatherland and the gods of his fatherland,
To drink the blood of his kin, to make them slaves—
165 He is to have no grave, no burial,
No mourning from anyone; it is forbidden.
He is to be left unburied, left to be eaten
By dogs and vultures, a horror for all to see.
I am determined that never, if I can help it,
170 Shall evil triumph over good. Alive
Or dead, the faithful servant of his country
Shall be rewarded.

CHORUS.                Creon, son of Menoeceus,
You have given your judgment for the friend and for the
     enemy.
As for those that are dead, so for us who remain,
175 Your will is law.

CREON.           See then that it be kept.

CHORUS. My lord, some younger would be fitter for that task.

CREON. Watchers are already set over the corpse.

CHORUS. What other duty then remains for us?

CREON. Not to connive at any disobedience.

180 CHORUS. If there were any so mad as to ask for death——

CREON. Ay, that is the penalty. There is always someone
Ready to be lured to ruin by hope of gain.

        (*He turns to go. A* SENTRY *enters from the side of
            the stage.* CREON *pauses at the Palace door.*)

SENTRY. My lord: if I am out of breath, it is not from haste.
I have not been running. On the contrary, many a time
185 I stopped to think and loitered on the way,
Saying to myself "Why hurry to your doom,
Poor fool?" and then I said "Hurry, you fool.
If Creon hears this from another man,
Your head's as good as off." So here I am,
190 As quick as my unwilling haste could bring me;
In no great hurry, in fact. So now I am here . . .
But I'll tell my story . . . though it may be nothing after all.
And whatever I have to suffer, it can't be more
Than what God wills, so I cling to that for my comfort.

195 CREON. Good heavens, man, whatever is the matter?

SENTRY. To speak of myself first—I never did it, sir;
  Nor saw who did; no one can punish me for that.
CREON. You tell your story with a deal of artful precaution.
  It's evidently something strange.
SENTRY.                                    It is.
200   So strange, it's very difficult to tell.
CREON. Well, out with it, and let's be done with you.
SENTRY. It's this, sir. The corpse . . . someone has just
  Buried it and gone. Dry dust over the body
  They scattered, in the manner of holy burial.
205 CREON. What! Who dared to do it?
SENTRY.                                    I don't know, sir.
  There was no sign of a pick, no scratch of a shovel;
  The ground was hard and dry—no trace of a wheel;
  Whoever it was has left no clues behind him.
  When the sentry on the first watch showed it us,
210   We were amazed. The corpse was covered from sight—
  Not with a proper grave—just a layer of earth—
  As it might be, the act of some pious passer-by.
  There were no tracks of an animal either, a dog
  Or anything that might have come and mauled the body.
215   Of course we all started pitching in to each other,
  Accusing each other, and might have come to blows,
  With no one to stop us; for anyone might have done it,
  But it couldn't be proved against him, and all denied it.
  We were all ready to take hot iron in hand
220   And go through fire and swear by God and heaven
  We hadn't done it, nor knew of anyone
  That could have thought of doing it, much less done it.
    Well, we could make nothing of it. Then one of our men
  Said something that made all our blood run cold—
225   Something we could neither refuse to do, nor do,
  But at our own risk. What he said was "This
  Must be reported to the King; we can't conceal it."
  So it was agreed. We drew lots for it, and I,
  Such is my luck, was chosen. So here I am,
230   As much against my will as yours, I'm sure;
  A bringer of bad news expects no welcome.
CHORUS. My lord, I fear—I feared it from the first—
  That this may prove to be an act of the gods.
CREON. Enough of that! Or I shall lose my patience.
235   Don't talk like an old fool, old though you be.
  Blasphemy, to say the gods could give a thought
  To carrion flesh! Held him in high esteem,
  I suppose, and buried him like a benefactor—
  A man who came to burn their temples down,
240   Ransack their holy shrines, their land, their laws?
  Is that the sort of man you think gods love?
  Not they. No. There's a party of malcontents
  In the city, rebels against my word and law,

Shakers of heads in secret, impatient of rule;
245 *They* are the people, I see it well enough,
Who have bribed their instruments to do this thing.
Money! Money's the curse of man, none greater.
That's what wrecks cities, banishes men from home,
Tempts and deludes the most well-meaning soul,
250 Pointing out the way to infamy and shame.
Well, they shall pay for their success. *(To the* SENTRY.*)* See
    to it!
See to it, you! Upon my oath, I swear,
As Zeus is my god above: either you find
The perpetrator of this burial
255 And bring him here into my sight, or death—
No, not your mere death shall pay the reckoning,
But, for a living lesson against such infamy,
You shall be racked and tortured till you tell
The whole truth of this outrage; so you may learn
260 To seek your gain where gain is yours to get,
Not try to grasp it everywhere. In wickedness
You'll find more loss than profit.

SENTRY.                   May I say more?
CREON. No more; each word you say but stings me more.
SENTRY. Stings in your ears, sir, or in your deeper feelings?
265 CREON. Don't bandy words, fellow, about my feelings.
SENTRY. Though I offend your ears, sir, it is not I
    But he that's guilty that offends your soul.
CREON. Oh, born to argue, were you?
SENTRY.                  Maybe so;
    But still not guilty in this business.
270 CREON. Doubly so, if you have sold your soul for money.
SENTRY. To think that thinking men should think so wrongly!
CREON. Think what you will. But if you fail to find
    The doer of this deed, you'll learn one thing:
    Ill-gotten gain brings no one any good.
                     *(He goes into the Palace.)*
275 SENTRY. Well, heaven send they find him. But whether or no,
    They'll not find me again, that's sure. Once free,
    Who never thought to see another day,
    I'll thank my lucky stars, and keep away.
                            *(Exit.)*

CHORUS. Wonders are many on earth, and the greatest of these
280 Is man, who rides the ocean and takes his way
Through the deeps, through wind-swept valleys of perilous
    seas
    That surge and sway.

    He is master of ageless Earth, to his own will bending
The immortal mother of gods by the sweat of his brow,
285 As year succeeds to year, with toil unending
    Of mule and plough.

He is lord of all things living; birds of the air,
Beasts of the field, all creatures of sea and land
He taketh, cunning to capture and ensnare
    With sleight of hand;

    Hunting the savage beast from the upland rocks,
Taming the mountain monarch in his lair,
Teaching the wild horse and the roaming ox
    His yoke to bear.

    The use of language, the wind-swift motion of brain
He learnt; found out the laws of living together
In cities, building him shelter against the rain
    And wintry weather.

    There is nothing beyond his power. His subtlety
Meeteth all chance, all danger conquereth.
For every ill he hath found its remedy,
    Save only death.

    O wondrous subtlety of man, that draws
To good or evil ways! Great honour is given
And power to him who upholdeth his country's laws
    And the justice of heaven.

    But he that, too rashly daring, walks in sin
In solitary pride to his life's end.
At door of mine shall never enter in
    To call me friend.

(*Severally*,[14] *seeing some persons approach from a distance.*)
O gods! A wonder to see!
Surely it cannot be———
It is no other———
Antigone!
Unhappy maid———
Unhappy Oedipus' daughter; it is she they bring.
Can she have rashly disobeyed
The order of our King?

14. *Severally.* Each of the following lines is spoken by a different member of the Chorus.

                    Enter the SENTRY, *bringing* ANTIGONE
                        *guarded by two more soldiers.*
SENTRY. We've got her. Here's the woman that did the deed.
    We found her in the act of burying him. Where's the King?
CHORUS. He is just coming out of the palace now.

                    *Enter* CREON.
CREON. What's this? What am I just in time to see?
SENTRY. My lord, an oath's a very dangerous thing.
    Second thoughts may prove us liars. Not long since

325 I swore I wouldn't trust myself again
To face your threats; you gave me a drubbing the first time.
But there's no pleasure like an unexpected pleasure,
Not by a long way. And so I've come again,
Though against my solemn oath. And I've brought this lady,
330 Who's been caught in the act of setting that grave in order.
And no casting lots for it this time—the prize is mine
And no one else's. So take her; judge and convict her.
I'm free, I hope, and quit of the horrible business.
CREON. How did you find her? Where have you brought her from?
335 SENTRY. She was burying the man with her own hands, and that's
the truth.
CREON. Are you in your senses? Do you know what you are
saying?
SENTRY. I saw her myself, burying the body of the man
Whom you said not to bury. Don't I speak plain?
CREON. How did she come to be seen and taken in the act?
340 SENTRY. It was this way. After I got back to the place,
With all your threats and curses ringing in my ears,
We swept off all the earth that covered the body,
And left it a sodden naked corpse again;
Then sat up on the hill, on the windward side,
345 Keeping clear of the stench of him, as far as we could;
All of us keeping each other up to the mark,
With pretty sharp speaking, not to be caught napping this time.
So this went on some hours, till the flaming sun
Was high in the top of the sky, and the heat was blazing.
350 Suddenly a storm of dust, like a plague from heaven,
Swept over the ground, stripping the trees stark bare,
Filling the sky; you had to shut your eyes
To stand against it. When at last it stopped,
There was the girl, screaming like an angry bird,
355 When it finds its nest left empty and little ones gone.
Just like that she screamed, seeing the body
Naked, crying and cursing the ones that had done it.
Then she picks up the dry earth in her hands,
And pouring out of a fine bronze urn she's brought
360 She makes her offering three times to the dead.[15]
Soon as we saw it, down we came and caught her.
She wasn't at all frightened. And so we charged her
With what she'd done before, and this. She admitted it,
I'm glad to say—though sorry too, in a way.
365 It's good to save your own skin, but a pity
To have to see another get into trouble,
Whom you've no grudge against. However, I can't say
I've ever valued anyone else's life
More than my own, and that's the honest truth.
370 CREON (to ANTIGONE). Well, what do you say—you, hiding your
head there:
Do you admit, or do you deny the deed?

15. *And pouring . . . to the dead,*
pouring wine or water as an offering
to the gods.

ANTIGONE. I do admit it. I do not deny it.

CREON (*to the* SENTRY). You—you may go. You are discharged
    from blame.

                               (*Exit* SENTRY.)

    Now tell me, in as few words as you can,

375    Did you know the order forbidding such an act?

ANTIGONE. I knew it, naturally. It was plain enough.

CREON. And yet you dared to contravene it?

ANTIGONE.                       Yes.

    That order did not come from God. Justice,

    That dwells with the gods below, knows no such law.

380    I did not think your edicts strong enough

    To overrule the unwritten unalterable laws

    Of God and heaven, you being only a man.

    They are not of yesterday or today, but everlasting,

    Though where they came from, none of us can tell.

385    Guilty of their transgression before God

    I cannot be, for any man on earth.

    I knew that I should have to die, of course,

    With or without your order. If it be soon,

    So much the better. Living in daily torment

390    As I do, who would not be glad to die?

    This punishment will not be any pain.

    Only if I had let my mother's son

    Lie there unburied, then I could not have borne it.

    This I can bear. Does that seem foolish to you?

395    Or is it you that are foolish to judge me so?

CHORUS. She shows her father's stubborn spirit: foolish

    Not to give way when everything's against her.

CREON. Ah, but you'll see. The over-obstinate spirit

    Is soonest broken; as the strongest iron will snap

400    If over-tempered in the fire to brittleness.

    A little halter is enough to break

    The wildest horse. Proud thoughts do not sit well

    Upon subordinates. This girl's proud spirit

    Was first in evidence when she broke the law;

405    And now, to add insult to her injury,

    She gloats over her deed. But, as I live,

    She shall not flout my orders with impunity.

    My sister's child—ay, were she even nearer,

    Nearest and dearest, she should not escape

410    Full punishment—she, and her sister too,

    Her partner, doubtless, in this burying.

      Let her be fetched! She was in the house just now;

    I saw her, hardly in her right mind either.

    Often the thoughts of those who plan dark deeds

415    Betray themselves before the deed is done.

    The criminal who being caught still tries

    To make a fair excuse, is damned indeed.

ANTIGONE. Now you have caught, will you do more than kill me?

CREON. No, nothing more; that is all I could wish.

420 ANTIGONE. Why then delay? There is nothing that you can say
That I should wish to hear, as nothing I say
Can weigh with you. I have given my brother burial.
What greater honour could I wish? All these
Would say that what I did was honourable,

425 But fear locks up their lips. To speak and act
Just as he likes is a king's prerogative.

CREON. You are wrong. None of my subjects thinks as you do.

ANTIGONE. Yes, sir, they do; but dare not tell you so.

CREON. And you are not only alone, but unashamed.

430 ANTIGONE. There is no shame in honouring my brother.

CREON. Was not his enemy, who died with him, your brother?

ANTIGONE. Yes, both were brothers, both of the same parents.

CREON. You honour one, and so insult the other.

ANTIGONE. He that is dead will not accuse me of that.

435 CREON. He will, if you honour him no more than the traitor.

ANTIGONE. It was not a slave, but his brother, that died with him.

CREON. Attacking his country, while the other defended it.

ANTIGONE. Even so, we have a duty to the dead.

CREON. Not to give equal honour to good and bad.

440 ANTIGONE. Who knows? In the country of the dead that may be
the law.

CREON. An enemy can't be a friend, even when dead.

ANTIGONE. My way is to share my love, not share my hate.

CREON. Go then, and share your love among the dead.
We'll have no woman's law here, while I live.

*Enter* ISMENE *from the Palace.*

445 CHORUS. Here comes Ismene, weeping
In sisterly sorrow; a darkened brow,
Flushed face, and the fair cheek marred
With flooding rain.

CREON. You crawling viper! Lurking in my house

450 To suck my blood! Two traitors unbeknown
Plotting against my throne. Do you admit
To a share in this burying, or deny all knowledge?

ISMENE. I did it—yes—if she will let me say so.
I am as much to blame as she is.

ANTIGONE.                    No.

455 That is not just. You would not lend a hand
And I refused your help in what I did.

ISMENE. But I am not ashamed to stand beside you
Now in your hour of trial, Antigone.

ANTIGONE. Whose was the deed, Death and the dead are witness.

460 I love no friend whose love is only words.

ISMENE. O sister, sister, let me share your death,
Share in the tribute of honour to him that is dead.

ANTIGONE. You shall not die with me. You shall not claim
That which you would not touch. One death is enough.

165 ISMENE. How can I bear to live, if you must die?
ANTIGONE. Ask Creon. Is not he the one you care for?
ISMENE. You do yourself no good to taunt me so.
ANTIGONE. Indeed no: even my jests are bitter pains.
ISMENE. But how, O tell me, how can I still help you?
170 ANTIGONE. Help yourself. I shall not stand in your way.
ISMENE. For pity, Antigone—can I not die with you?
ANTIGONE. You chose; life was your choice, when mine was
        death.
ISMENE. Although I warned you that it would be so.
ANTIGONE. Your way seemed right to some, to others mine.
175 ISMENE. But now both in the wrong, and both condemned.
ANTIGONE. No, no. You live. My heart was long since dead,
    So it was right for me to help the dead.
CREON. I do believe the creatures both are mad;
    One lately crazed, the other from her birth.
180 ISMENE. Is it not likely, sir? The strongest mind
    Cannot but break under misfortune's blows.
CREON. Yours did, when you threw in your lot with hers.
ISMENE. How could I wish to live without my sister?
CREON. You have no sister. Count her dead already.
185 ISMENE. You could not take her—kill your own son's bride?
CREON. Oh, there are other fields for him to plough.
ISMENE. No truer troth was ever made than theirs.
CREON. No son of mine shall wed so vile a creature.
ANTIGONE. O Haemon, can your father spite you so?
490 CREON. You and your paramour, I hate you both.
CHORUS. Sir, would you take her from your own son's arms?
CREON. Not I, but death shall take her.
CHORUS.                                    Be it so.
    Her death, it seems, is certain.
CREON.                                    Certain it is.
    No more delay. Take them, and keep them within—
495 The proper place for women. None so brave
    As not to look for some way of escape
    When they see life stand face to face with death.
                        (The women are taken away.)
CHORUS. Happy are they who know not the taste of evil.
    From a house that heaven hath shaken
500 The curse departs not
    But falls upon all of the blood,[16]
    Like the restless surge of the sea when the dark storm drives
    The black sand hurled from the deeps
    And the Thracian gales boom down
505 On the echoing shore.

    In life and in death is the house of Labdacus[17] stricken.
    Generation to generation,
    With no atonement,
    It is scourged by the wrath of a god.

16. *The curse . . . upon all of the
blood.* The curse on Oedipus has
passed on to his descendants.

17. *the house of Labdacus* (lab'-
də kəs), the ruling family of Thebes.
Labdacus, a former king, was the
grandfather of Oedipus.

510 And now for the dead dust's sake is the light of promise,
The tree's last root, crushed out
By pride of heart and the sin
Of presumptuous tongue.

For what presumption of man can match thy power,
515 O Zeus, that art not subject to sleep or time
Or age, living for ever in bright Olympus?
Tomorrow and for all time to come,
As in the past,
This law is immutable:
520 For mortals greatly to live is greatly to suffer.

Roving ambition helps many a man to good,
And many it falsely lures to light desires,
Till failure trips them unawares, and they fall
On the fire that consumes them. Well was it said,
525 Evil seems good
To him who is doomed to suffer;
And short is the time before that suffering comes.[18]

But here comes Haemon,
Your youngest son.
530 Does he come to speak his sorrow
For the doom of his promised bride,
The loss of his marriage hopes?
CREON. We shall know it soon, and need no prophet to tell us.

*Enter* HAEMON.

Son, you have heard, I think, our final judgment
535 On your late betrothed. No angry words, I hope?
Still friends, in spite of everything, my son?
HAEMON. I am your son, sir; by your wise decisions
My life is ruled, and them I shall always obey.
I cannot value any marriage tie
540 Above your own good guidance.
CREON.                            Rightly said.
Your father's will should have your heart's first place.
Only for this do fathers pray for sons
Obedient, loyal, ready to strike down
Their fathers' foes, and love their fathers' friends.
545 To be the father of unprofitable sons
Is to be the father of sorrows, a laughingstock
To all one's enemies. Do not be fooled, my son,
By lust and the wiles of a woman. You'll have bought
Cold comfort if your wife's a worthless one.
550 No wound strikes deeper than love that is turned to hate.
This girl's an enemy; away with her,
And let her go and find a mate in Hades.
Once having caught her in a flagrant act—

**18.** *Evil seems good . . . suffering comes.* Although a man may convince himself that the evil he does is good, he must eventually suffer punishment for his wrongdoing.

The one and only traitor in our State—
555  I cannot make myself a traitor too;
So she must die. Well may she pray to Zeus,
The god of family love. How, if I tolerate
A traitor at home, shall I rule those abroad?
   He that is a righteous master of his house
560  Will be a righteous statesman. To transgress
Or twist the law to one's own pleasure, presume
To order where one should obey, is sinful,
And I will have none of it.
He whom the State appoints must be obeyed
565  To the smallest matter, be it right—or wrong.
And he that rules his household, without a doubt,
Will make the wisest king, or, for that matter,
The staunchest subject. He will be the man
You can depend on in the storm of war,
570  The faithfullest comrade in the day of battle.
There is no more deadly peril than disobedience;
States are devoured by it, homes laid in ruins,
Armies defeated, victory turned to rout.
While simple obedience saves the lives of hundreds
575  Of honest folk. Therefore, I hold to the law,
And will never betray it—least of all for a woman.
Better be beaten, if need be, by a man,
Than let a woman get the better of us.
CHORUS. To me, as far as an old man can tell,
580  It seems your Majesty has spoken well.
HAEMON. Father, man's wisdom is the gift of heaven,
The greatest gift of all. I neither am
Nor wish to be clever enough to prove you wrong,
Though all men might not think the same as you do.
585  Nevertheless, I have to be your watchdog,
To know what others say and what they do,
And what they find to praise and what to blame.
Your frown is a sufficient silencer
Of any word that is not for your ears.
590  But *I* hear whispers spoken in the dark;
On every side I hear voices of pity
For this poor girl, doomed to the cruellest death,
And most unjust, that ever woman suffered
For an honourable action—burying a brother
595  Who was killed in battle, rather than leave him naked
For dogs to maul and carrion birds to peck at.
Has she not rather earned a crown of gold?—
Such is the secret talk about the town.
   Father, there is nothing I can prize above
600  Your happiness and well-being. What greater good
Can any son desire? Can any father
Desire more from his son? Therefore I say,
Let not your first thought be your only thought.

Think if there cannot be some other way.
Surely, to think your own the only wisdom,
And yours the only word, the only will,
Betrays a shallow spirit, an empty heart.
It is no weakness for the wisest man
To learn when he is wrong, know when to yield.
So, on the margin of a flooded river
Trees bending to the torrent live unbroken,
While those that strain against it are snapped off.
A sailor has to tack and slacken sheets
Before the gale, or find himself capsized.
 So, father, pause, and put aside your anger.
I think, for what my young opinion's worth,
That, good as it is to have infallible wisdom,
Since this is rarely found, the next best thing
Is to be willing to listen to wise advice.

CHORUS. There is something to be said, my lord, for his point
  of view,
 And for yours as well; there is much to be said on both
  sides.
CREON. Indeed! Am I to take lessons at my time of life
 From a fellow of his age?
HAEMON. No lesson you need be ashamed of.
 It isn't a question of age, but of right and wrong.
CREON. Would you call it right to admire an act of disobedience?
HAEMON. Not if the act were also dishonourable.
CREON. And was not this woman's action dishonourable?
HAEMON. The people of Thebes think not.
CREON.          The people of Thebes!
 Since when do I take my orders from the people of Thebes?
HAEMON. Isn't that rather a childish thing to say?
CREON. No. I am king, and responsible only to myself.
HAEMON. A one-man state? What sort of a state is that?
CREON. Why, does not every state belong to its ruler?
HAEMON. You'd be an excellent king—on a desert island.
CREON. Of course, if you're on the woman's side——
HAEMON.           No, no——
 Unless you're the woman. It's you I'm fighting for.
CREON. What, villain, when every word you speak is against me?
HAEMON. Only because I know you are wrong, wrong.
CREON. Wrong? To respect my own authority?
HAEMON. What sort of respect tramples on all that is holy?
CREON. Despicable coward! No more will than a woman!
HAEMON. I have nothing to be ashamed of.
CREON.         Yet you plead her
  cause.
HAEMON. No, *yours*, and mine, and that of the gods of the dead.
CREON. You'll never marry her this side of death.
HAEMON. Then, if she dies, she does not die alone.
CREON. Is that a threat, you impudent——

HAEMON.                             Is it a threat
   To try to argue against wrong-headedness?
CREON. You'll learn what wrong-headedness is, my friend, to
   your cost.
650  HAEMON. O father, I could call you mad, were you not my father.
CREON. Don't toady me, boy; keep that for your lady-love.
HAEMON. You mean to have the last word, then?
CREON.                              I do.
   And what is more, by all the gods in heaven,
   I'll make you sorry for your impudence.
                            *(Calling to those within.)*
655  Bring out that she-devil, and let her die
   Now, with her bridegroom by to see it done!
HAEMON. That sight I'll never see. Nor from this hour
   Shall you see me again. Let those that will
   Be witness of your wickedness and folly.          *(Exit.)*
660  CHORUS. He is gone, my lord, in very passionate haste.
   And who shall say what a young man's wrath may do?
CREON. Let him go! Let him do! Let him rage as never man raged,
   He shall not save those women from their doom.
CHORUS. You mean, then, sire, to put them both to death?
665  CREON. No, not the one whose hand was innocent.
CHORUS. And to what death do you condemn the other?
CREON. I'll have her taken to a desert place
   Where no man ever walked, and there walled up
   Inside a cave, alive, with food enough
670  To acquit ourselves of the blood-guiltiness
   That else would lie upon our commonwealth.
   There she may pray to Death, the god she loves,
   And ask release from death; or learn at last
   What hope there is for those who worship death.[19]
                                 *(Exit.)*
675  CHORUS. Where is the equal of Love?
   Where is the battle he cannot win,
   The power he cannot outmatch?
   In the farthest corners of earth, in the midst of the sea,
   He is there; he is here
680  In the bloom of a fair face
   Lying in wait;
   And the grip of his madness
   Spares not god or man,

    Marring the righteous man,
685  Driving his soul into mazes of sin
   And strife, dividing a house.
   For the light that burns in the eyes of a bride of desire
   Is a fire that consumes.
   At the side of the great gods
690  Aphrodite immortal
   Works her will upon all.

**19.** *I'll have her taken . . . worship death.* If Antigone is provided with enough food to enable her to pray for her life, then whether or not she dies is up to the gods, and Creon and the state are blameless.

*The doors are opened and* ANTIGONE *enters, guarded.*

But here is a sight beyond all bearing,
At which my eyes cannot but weep;
Antigone forth faring

5    To her bridal bower of endless sleep.

ANTIGONE. You see me, countrymen, on my last journey,
Taking my last leave of the light of day;
Going to my rest, where death shall take me
Alive across the silent river.[20]

10   No wedding day; no marriage music;
Death will be all my bridal dower.

CHORUS. But glory and praise go with you, lady,
To your resting place. You go with your beauty
Unmarred by the hand of consuming sickness,

15   Untouched by the sword, living and free,
As none other that ever died before you.

ANTIGONE. The daughter of Tantalus,[21] a Phrygian maid,
Was doomed to a piteous death on the rock
Of Sipylus, which embraced and imprisoned her,

20   Merciless as the ivy; rain and snow
Beat down upon her, mingled with her tears,
As she wasted and died. Such was her story,
And such is the sleep that I shall go to.

CHORUS. She was a goddess of immortal birth,

25   And we are mortals; the greater the glory,
To share the fate of a god-born maiden,
A living death, but a name undying.

ANTIGONE. Mockery, mockery![22] By the gods of our fathers,
Must you make me a laughingstock while I yet live?

20   O lordly sons of my city! O Thebes!
Your valleys of rivers, your chariots and horses!
No friend to weep at my banishment
To a rock-hewn chamber of endless durance,
In a strange cold tomb alone to linger

25   Lost between life and death for ever.

CHORUS. My child, you have gone your way
To the outermost limit of daring
And have stumbled against Law enthroned.
This is the expiation

30   You must make for the sin of your father.

ANTIGONE. My father—the thought that sears my soul—
The unending burden of the house of Labdacus.
Monstrous marriage of mother and son . . .
My father . . . my parents . . . O hideous shame!

35   Whom now I follow, unwed, curse-ridden,
Doomed to this death by the ill-starred marriage
That marred my brother's life.

CHORUS. An act of homage is good in itself, my daughter;
But authority cannot afford to connive at disobedience.

40   You are the victim of your own self-will.

20. *silent river,* in Greek mythology, one of the rivers which separated the land of the dead from the land of the living.

21. *the daughter of Tantalus,* Niobe (nī′ō bē), whose children were slain by the gods to punish her for her excessive pride. Overcome with grief, she turned into a stone from which tears continued to flow. The stone was carried by a whirlwind to Mount Sipylus (si′pi ləs) in Phrygia (frij′i ə), the kingdom of Niobe's father.

22. *mockery.* Antigone mistakenly thinks that the Chorus, in comparing her to the gods, is making fun of her.

ANTIGONE. And must go the way that lies before me.
No funeral hymn; no marriage music;
No sun from this day forth, no light,
No friend to weep at my departing.

*Enter* CREON.

745 CREON. Weeping and wailing at the door of death!
There'd be no end of it, if it had force
To buy death off. Away with her at once,
And close her up in her rock-vaulted tomb.
Leave her and let her die, if die she must,
750 Or live within her dungeon. Though on earth
Her life is ended from this day, her blood
Will not be on our hands.
ANTIGONE.                    So to my grave,
My bridal bower, my everlasting prison,
I go, to join those many of my kinsmen
755 Who dwell in the mansions of Persephone,
Last and unhappiest, before my time.
Yet I believe my father will be there
To welcome me, my mother greet me gladly,
And you, my brother, gladly see me come.
760 Each one of you my hands have laid to rest,
Pouring the due libations on your graves.
It was by this service to your dear body, Polynices,
I earned the punishment which now I suffer,
Though all good people know it was for your honour.
765     O but I would not have done the forbidden thing
For any husband or for any son.
For why? I could have had another husband
And by him other sons, if one were lost;
But, father and mother lost, where would I get
770 Another brother? For thus preferring you,
My brother, Creon condemns me and hales me away,
Never a bride, never a mother, unfriended,
Condemned alive to solitary death.
What law of heaven have I transgressed? What god
775 Can save me now? What help or hope have I,
In whom devotion is deemed sacrilege?
If this is God's will, I shall learn my lesson
In death; but if my enemies are wrong,
I wish them no worse punishment than mine.
780 CHORUS. Still the same tempest in the heart
Torments her soul with angry gusts.
CREON. The more cause then have they that guard her
To hasten their work; or they too suffer.
CHORUS. Alas, that word had the sound of death.
785 CREON. Indeed there is no more to hope for.
ANTIGONE. Gods of our fathers, my city, my home,
Rulers of Thebes! Time stays no longer.

Last daughter of your royal house
Go I, *his* prisoner, because I honoured
90    Those things to which honour truly belongs.

                    (ANTIGONE *is led away.*)

CHORUS. So, long ago, lay Danae[23]
    Entombed within her brazen bower;
Noble and beautiful was she,
    On whom there fell the golden shower
95    Of life from Zeus. There is no tower
So high, no armoury so great,
    No ship so swift, as is the power
Of man's inexorable fate.

There was the proud Edonian king,
00    Lycurgus,[24] in rock-prison pent
For arrogantly challenging
    God's laws: it was his punishment
    Of that swift passion to repent
In slow perception, for that he
05    Had braved the rule omnipotent
Of Dionysus' sovereignty.

On Phineus' wife[25] the hand of fate
    Was heavy, when her children fell
Victims to a stepmother's hate,
10    And she endured a prison-cell
    Where the North Wind stood sentinel
In caverns amid mountains wild.
    Thus the grey spinners wove their spell
On her, as upon thee, my child.[26]

        *Enter* TEIRESIAS, *the blind prophet, led by a boy.*
315 TEIRESIAS. Gentlemen of Thebes, we greet you, my companion
    and I,
Who share one pair of eyes on our journeys together—
For the blind man goes where his leader tells him to.
CREON. You are welcome, father Teiresias. What's your news?
TEIRESIAS. Ay, news you shall have; and advice, if you can heed it.
320 CREON. There was never a time when I failed to heed it, father.
TEIRESIAS. And thereby have so far steered a steady course.
CREON. And gladly acknowledge the debt we owe to you.
TEIRESIAS. Then mark me now; for you stand on a razor's edge.
CREON. Indeed? Grave words from your lips, good priest. Say on.
325 TEIRESIAS. I will; and show you all that my skill reveals.
    At my seat of divination,[27] where I sit
    These many years to read the signs of heaven,
    An unfamiliar sound came to my ears
    Of birds in vicious combat, savage cries
330    In strange outlandish language, and the whirr
    Of flapping wings; from which I well could picture

**23.** *Danae* (dan′ə ē), a maiden imprisoned in a bronze chamber by her father, who feared a prophecy that a child born to Danae would someday kill him. Zeus entered her bronze chamber as a golden rain, and from their union Perseus, who eventually did kill his grandfather, was born.

**24.** *Lycurgus* (lī kèr′gəs), a Greek king who opposed the worship of Dionysus and was punished by being imprisoned in a cave and driven insane.

**25.** *Phineus' wife* (fin′ē əs). King Phineus imprisoned his former wife and their two sons when he believed false accusations about them made by their stepmother, Idaea (ī dē′ə).

**26.** *So, long ago, lay Danae . . . as upon thee, my child.* In this speech the Chorus compares Antigone's fate to that of three other mortals who had been imprisoned.

**27.** *seat of divination,* the place where Teiresias sat to listen to the birds, which were believed to tell him the future.

The gruesome warfare of their deadly talons.
Full of foreboding then I made the test
Of sacrifice upon the altar fire.
835 There was no answering flame; only rank juice
Oozed from the flesh and dripped among the ashes,
Smouldering and sputtering; the gall vanished in a puff,
And the fat ran down and left the haunches bare.
Thus (through the eyes of my young acolyte,
840 Who sees for me, that I may see for others)
I read the signs of failure in my quest.
    And why? The blight upon us is *your* doing.
The blood that stains our altars and our shrines,
The blood that dogs and vultures have licked up,
845 It is none other than the blood of Oedipus
Spilled from the veins of his ill-fated son.
Our fires, our sacrifices, and our prayers
The gods abominate. How should the birds
Give any other than ill-omened voices,
850 Gorged with the dregs of blood that man has shed?
Mark this, my son: all men fall into sin.
But sinning, he is not forever lost
Hapless and helpless, who can make amends
And has not set his face against repentance.
855 Only a fool is governed by self-will.
    Pay to the dead his due. Wound not the fallen.
It is no glory to kill and kill again.
My words are for your good, as is my will,
And should be acceptable, being for your good.
860 CREON. You take me for your target, reverend sir,
Like all the rest. I know your art of old,
And how you make me your commodity
To trade and traffic in for your advancement.
Trade as you will; but all the silver of Sardis
865 And all the gold of India will not buy
A tomb for yonder traitor. No. Let the eagles
Carry his carcass up to the throne of Zeus;
Even that would not be sacrilege enough
To frighten me from my determination
870 Not to allow this burial. No man's act
Has power enough to pollute the goodness of God.
But great and terrible is the fall, Teiresias,
Of mortal men who seek their own advantage
By uttering evil in the guise of good.
875 TEIRESIAS. Ah, is there any wisdom in the world?
CREON. Why, what is the meaning of that wide-flung taunt?
TEIRESIAS. What prize outweighs the priceless worth of prudence?
CREON. Ay, what indeed? What mischief matches the lack of it?
TEIRESIAS. And there you speak of your own symptom, sir.
880 CREON. I am loth to pick a quarrel with you, priest.
TEIRESIAS. You do so, calling my divination false.

CREON. I say all prophets seek their own advantage.

TEIRESIAS. All kings, say I, seek gain unrighteously.

CREON. Do you forget to whom you say it?

TEIRESIAS.                                          No.
885  Our king and benefactor, by my guidance.

CREON. Clever you may be, but not therefore honest.

TEIRESIAS. Must I reveal my yet unspoken mind?

CREON. Reveal all; but expect no gain from it.

TEIRESIAS. Does that still seem to you my motive, then?

890  CREON. Nor is my will for sale, sir, in your market.

TEIRESIAS. Then hear this. Ere the chariot of the sun
     Has rounded once or twice his wheeling way,
     You shall have given a son of your own loins
     To death, in payment for death—two debts to pay:
895  One for the life that you have sent to death,
     The life you have abominably entombed;
     One for the dead still lying above ground
     Unburied, unhonoured, unblest by the gods below.
     You cannot alter this. The gods themselves
900  Cannot undo it. It follows of necessity
     From what you have done. Even now the avenging Furies,
     The hunters of Hell that follow and destroy,
     Are lying in wait for you, and will have their prey,
     When the evil you have worked for others falls on you.
905  Do I speak this for my gain? The time shall come,
     And soon, when your house will be filled with the
            lamentation
     Of men and of women; and every neighbouring city
     Will be goaded to fury against you, for upon them
     Too the pollution falls when the dogs and vultures
910  Bring the defilement of blood to their hearths and altars.[28]
        I have done. You pricked me, and these shafts of wrath
     Will find their mark in your heart. You cannot escape
     The sting of their sharpness. Lead me home, my boy.
     Let us leave him to vent his anger on younger ears,
915  Or school his mind and tongue to a milder mood
        Than that which now possesses him. Lead on.        (Exit.)

CHORUS. He has gone, my lord. He has prophesied terrible things.
     And for my part, I that was young and now am old
     Have never known his prophecies proved false.

920  CREON. It is true enough; and my heart is torn in two.
     It is hard to give way, and hard to stand and abide
     The coming of the curse. Both ways are hard.

CHORUS. If you would be advised, my good lord Creon——

CREON. What must I do? Tell me, and I will do it.

925  CHORUS. Release the woman from her rocky prison.
     Set up a tomb for him that lies unburied.

CREON. Is it your wish that I consent to this?

CHORUS. It is, and quickly. The gods do not delay
     The stroke of their swift vengeance on the sinner.

**28.** *The time shall come . . . and altars.* This prophecy by Teiresias later came true when the families of the slain Argive chiefs enlisted the aid of the Athenian king, Theseus (thē′sē əs), to obtain burial rites for their dead. The Athenian army marched against Thebes and conquered it.

CREON. It is hard, but I must do it. Well I know
930    There is no armour against necessity.
CHORUS. Go. Let your own hand do it, and no other.
CREON. I will go this instant. Slaves there! One and all.
    Bring spades and mattocks out on the hill!
935    My mind is made; 'twas I imprisoned her,
    And I will set her free. Now I believe
    It is by the laws of heaven that man must live.

                                                            (Exit.)

CHORUS. O Thou whose name is many,[29]
    Son of the Thunderer, dear child of his Cadmean bride,
940    Whose hand is mighty
    In Italia,
    In the hospitable valley
    Of Eleusis,
    And in Thebes,
945    The mother-city of thy worshippers,
    Where sweet Ismenus gently watereth
    The soil whence sprang the harvest of the dragon's teeth;[30]

    Where torches on the crested mountains gleam,
    And by Castalia's stream
950    The nymph-train in thy dance rejoices,
    When from the ivy-tangled glens
    Of Nysa[31] and from vine-clad plains
    Thou comest to Thebes where the immortal voices
    Sing thy glad strains.

955    Thebes, where thou lovest most to be,
    With her, thy mother, the fire-stricken one,[32]
    Sickens for need of thee.
    Healer of all her ills;
    Come swiftly o'er the high Parnassian hills,[33]
960    Come o'er the sighing sea.

    The stars, whose breath is fire, delight
    To dance for thee; the echoing night
    Shall with thy praises ring.
    Zeus-born, appear! With Thyiads[34] revelling
965    Come, bountiful
    Iacchus, King!

    Enter a MESSENGER, *from the side of the stage.*
MESSENGER. Hear, men of Cadmus' city, hear and attend,
    Men of the house of Amphion,[35] people of Thebes!
    What is the life of man? A thing not fixed
970    For good or evil, fashioned for praise or blame.
    Chance raises a man to the heights, chance casts him down,
    And none can foretell what will be from what is.
    Creon was once an enviable man;

29. *Thou whose name is many*. The Chorus invokes the god Dionysus, whose native city of Thebes was under his special protection. Bacchus, Iacchus, and God of Wine are three of his many names.

30. *Ismenus . . . dragon's teeth*. Cadmus, the founder of Thebes, sowed dragon's teeth in the soil from which sprang armed men who helped him build the city near the river Ismenus (is mē′nəs).

31. *nymph-train . . . Nysa*. When Semele (sem′ə lē), the mother of Dionysus, died, Zeus took his infant son to the nymphs of Nysa (nī′sə), who cared for him during his childhood.

32. *thy mother, the fire-stricken one*. Zeus had promised Semele that he would grant her one wish. Her wish was to see him in his full splendor as the king of gods and men. Being mortal, she could not endure the sight and was consumed to ashes.

33. *Parnassian hills*. Parnassus (pär-nas′əs), a mountain in southern Greece, was sacred to Apollo and the Muses.

34. *Thyiads* (thī′yadz), women driven mad by wine and the power of Dionysus. Also called Maenads (mē′nadz).

35. *Amphion* (am fī′ən), a former king of Thebes.

He saved his country from her enemies,
975 Assumed the sovereign power, and bore it well,
The honoured father of a royal house.
Now all is lost; for life without life's joys
Is living death; and such a life is his.
Riches and rank and show of majesty
980 And state, where no joy is, are empty, vain
And unsubstantial shadows, of no weight
To be compared with happiness of heart.
CHORUS. What is your news? Disaster in the royal house?
MESSENGER. Death; and the guilt of it on living heads.
985 CHORUS. Who dead? And by what hand?
MESSENGER.                                           Haemon is dead,
    Slain by his own——
CHORUS.                         His father?
MESSENGER.                                      His own hand.
    His father's act it was that drove him to it.
CHORUS. Then all has happened as the prophet said.
MESSENGER. What's next to do, your worships will decide.
                                   (*The Palace door opens.*)
990 CHORUS. Here comes the Queen, Eurydice. Poor soul,
    It may be she has heard about her son.

                    Enter EURYDICE, *attended by women.*
EURYDICE. My friends, I heard something of what you were
        saying
    As I came to the door. I was on my way to prayer
    At the temple of Pallas, and had barely turned the latch
995 When I caught your talk of some near calamity.
    I was sick with fear and reeled in the arms of my women.
    But tell me what is the matter; what have you heard?
    I am not unacquainted with grief,[36] and I can bear it.
MESSENGER. Madam, it was I that saw it, and will tell you all.
1000 To try to make it any lighter now
    Would be to prove myself a liar. Truth
    Is always best.
                    It was thus. I attended your husband,
    The King, to the edge of the field where lay the body
    Of Polynices, in pitiable state, mauled by the dogs.
1005 We prayed for him to the Goddess of the Roads,[37] and to Pluto,
    That they might have mercy upon him. We washed the re-
        mains
    In holy water, and on a fire of fresh-cut branches
    We burned all that was left of him, and raised
    Over his ashes a mound of his native earth.
1010 That done, we turned toward the deep rock-chamber
    Of the maid that was married with death.
                                   Before we reached it,
    One that stood near the accursed place had heard
    Loud cries of anguish, and came to tell King Creon.

**36.** *I am not unacquainted with grief.* Menoeceus, a son of Creon and Eurydice, had sacrificed himself at the beginning of the war because of a prophecy that Thebes would be saved only if he were killed.

**37.** *Goddess of the Roads,* Hecate (hek′ə tē), a goddess of the underworld who sent apparitions to frighten travelers at night.

As he approached, came strange uncertain sounds
Of lamentation, and he cried aloud:
"Unhappy wretch! Is my foreboding true?
Is this the most sorrowful journey that ever I went?
My son's voice greets me. Go, some of you, quickly
Through the passage where the stones are thrown apart,
Into the mouth of the cave, and see if it be
My son, my own son Haemon that I hear.
If not, I am the sport of gods."
                              We went
And looked, as bidden by our anxious master.
There in the furthest corner of the cave
We saw her hanging by the neck. The rope
Was of the woven linen of her dress.
And, with his arms about her, there stood he
Lamenting his lost bride, his luckless love,
His father's cruelty.
                    When Creon saw them,
Into the cave he went, moaning piteously.
"O my unhappy boy," he cried again,
"What have you done? What madness brings you here
To your destruction? Come away, my son,
My son, I do beseech you, come away!"
His son looked at him with one angry stare,
Spat in his face, and then without a word
Drew sword and struck out. But his father fled
Unscathed. Whereon the poor demented boy
Leaned on his sword and thrust it deeply home
In his own side, and while his life ebbed out
Embraced the maid in loose-enfolding arms,
His spurting blood staining her pale cheeks red.
              (EURYDICE *goes quickly back into the Palace.*)
Two bodies lie together, wedded in death,
Their bridal sleep a witness to the world
How great calamity can come to man
Through man's perversity.
CHORUS.                      But what is this?
The Queen has turned and gone without a word.
MESSENGER. Yes. It is strange. The best that I can hope
Is that she would not sorrow for her son
Before us all, but vents her grief in private
Among her women. She is too wise, I think,
To take a false step rashly.
CHORUS.                      It may be.
Yet there is danger in unnatural silence
No less than in excess of lamentation.
MESSENGER. I will go in and see, whether in truth
There is some fatal purpose in her grief.
Such silence, as you say, may well be dangerous.
                              (*He goes in.*)

*Enter Attendants preceding the King.*

CHORUS. The King comes here.
What the tongue scarce dares to tell
1060  Must now be known
By the burden that proves too well
The guilt, no other man's
But his alone.

*Enter* CREON *with the body of* HAEMON.

CREON. The sin, the sin of the erring soul
1065  Drives hard unto death.
Behold the slayer, the slain,
The father, the son.
O the curse of my stubborn will!
Son, newly cut off in the newness of youth,
1070  Dead for my fault, not yours.
CHORUS. Alas, too late you have seen the truth.
CREON. I learn in sorrow. Upon my head
God has delivered this heavy punishment,
Has struck me down in the ways of wickedness,
1075  And trod my gladness under foot.
Such is the bitter affliction of mortal man.

*Enter the* MESSENGER *from the Palace.*

MESSENGER. Sir, you have this and more than this to bear.
Within there's more to know, more to your pain.
CREON. What more? What pain can overtop this pain?
1080  MESSENGER. She is dead—your wife, the mother of him that is
dead—
The death wound fresh in her heart. Alas, poor lady!
CREON. Insatiable Death, wilt thou destroy me yet?
What say you, teller of evil?
I am already dead,
1085  And is there more?
Blood upon blood?
More death? My wife?
   (*The central doors open, revealing the body of* EURYDICE.)
CHORUS. Look then, and see; nothing is hidden now.
CREON. O second horror!
1090  What fate awaits me now?
My child here in my arms . . . and there, the other . . .
The son . . . the mother . . .
MESSENGER. There at the altar with the whetted knife
She stood, and as the darkness dimmed her eyes
1095  Called on the dead, her elder son and this,
And with her dying breath cursed you, their slayer.
CREON. O horrible . . .
Is there no sword for me,
To end this misery?

1100 MESSENGER. Indeed you bear the burden of two deaths.
　　　It was her dying word.
　　CREON. And her last act?
　　MESSENGER. Hearing her son was dead, with her own hand
　　　She drove the sharp sword home into her heart.
1105 CREON. There is no man can bear this guilt but I.
　　　It is true, I killed him.
　　　Lead me away, away. I live no longer.
　　CHORUS. 'Twere best, if anything is best in evil times.
　　　What's soonest done, is best, when all is ill.
1110 CREON. Come, my last hour and fairest,
　　　My only happiness . . . come soon.
　　　Let me not see another day.
　　　Away . . . away . . .
　　CHORUS. The future is not to be known; our present care
1115 Is with the present; the rest is in other hands.
　　CREON. I ask no more than I have asked.
　　CHORUS. Ask nothing.
　　　What is to be, no mortal can escape.
　　CREON. I am nothing. I have no life.
1120 Lead me away . . .
　　　That have killed unwittingly
　　　My son, my wife.
　　　I know not where I should turn,
　　　Where look for help.
1125 My hands have done amiss, my head is bowed
　　　With fate too heavy for me.

*(Exit.)*

　　CHORUS. Of happiness the crown
　　　And chiefest part
　　　Is wisdom, and to hold
1130 The gods in awe.
　　　This is the law
　　　That, seeing the stricken heart
　　　Of pride brought down,
　　　We learn when we are old.

*(Exeunt)*

# DISCUSSION

1. (a) Why does Creon order burial honors for Eteocles but forbid burial for Polynices? (b) Why does Antigone refuse to obey?

2. What is the attitude of Ismene toward Antigone? Of Antigone toward Ismene?

3. In what ways are Creon and Antigone alike?

4. (a) What does the scene between Haemon and his father reveal about the character of Haemon? Of Creon? (b) With what arguments does Haemon try to persuade Creon to change his order?

5. (a) What similarities exist between the character and function of the Sentry in *Antigone* and the Nurse in *Romeo and Juliet*? Explain. (b) What other similarities are there between the two plays?

6. (a) What purpose does Teiresias serve in the play? (b) Teiresias says, "Only a fool is governed by self-will." Do his words apply to Creon, to Antigone, or to both?

7. On one level this play is a personal contest between a willful king and an equally willful subject over the burial of a slain soldier, but the opposition of king and subject represents several larger conflicts as well. Referring to specific lines from the play to support your opinions, discuss how Creon and Antigone are in basic disagreement about the following issues: (a) the law of the state vs. individual conscience, (b) youth vs. age, (c) man vs. woman. Which side do you favor on each issue? Why?

8. (a) At what points in the play does the Chorus sympathize with Creon? With Antigone? (b) In each case, what causes the Chorus to change its attitude?

9. (a) How long is the time span of this play? (b) Is the action continuous, or is it interrupted by lapses of time? (c) Does the action take place in more than one setting? (d) How does the audience find out what happens "off stage," that is, in another location? What particular actions in *Antigone* are revealed in this way?

10. The following statements offer three views of *Antigone*. Select the one that seems to you to best account for the meaning of the play. If none of the following statements satisfies you, offer your own view. In any case, support your opinion with evidence from the play.

a. The tragedy in *Antigone* results from Creon's stubbornly insisting that the law of the state be obeyed even when it conflicts with the higher moral law of the gods. Although Creon has forbidden the burial of the enemies of Thebes, Antigone is willing to sacrifice her life in order to obey the higher law, which requires that she give her brother a proper burial. When Creon cannot make Antigone bend to his will, he not only causes her death, but he also brings tragedy on himself by causing the deaths of his wife and his son.

b. The tragedy in *Antigone* results from Antigone's desire to play the role of lonely martyr. Like most people who are fanatically devoted to a cause, she has no understanding of or regard for the well-being of others. She treats even her sister cruelly when Ismene offers to share her punishment. Her blind insistence on the rightness of her action brings about not only her death but also the deaths of Haemon and Eurydice. While Creon's pride and stubbornness unquestionably contribute to the final disaster, ultimately he does try to reverse his order and release Antigone. It is not Creon, then, but Antigone, who must bear primary responsibility for the tragedy.

c. The tragedy in *Antigone* results from a conflict between the highest moral laws and the laws that govern the day-to-day affairs of a society. Neither Creon nor Antigone is "right" or "wrong," or, to put it another way, *both* Creon and Antigone are "right" *and* "wrong." We must have moral laws that provide a foundation for religion or ethics or what we call conscience, but we must also have the laws of the state that prevent the chaos which might result if everyone did what he or she thought was right. The two kinds of law are not usually in opposition, but Antigone and Creon are trapped in a situation in which the laws conflict, a situation in which neither can back down, a situation which leads not only to the death of one and the ruin of the other, but also to the deaths of innocent people. The cause of the tragedy is neither Creon nor Antigone but the situation which traps them between two irreconcilable principles.

## WORD STUDY

The words listed below have become a part of the English language, but each has its origin in the language of Greek drama and theater. Give the modern meaning of each word before using it in one of the following sentences. Use a dictionary if necessary.

| | |
|---|---|
| scene | Thespian |
| tragedy | theater |
| comedy | drama |
| orchestra | chorus |

1. Margarita didn't sing one of the solo parts, but at least she was a member of the _____ .

2. He had never tried acting, but his love of the theater made him a _____ at heart.

3. Although the play was funny in part, it could not truly be called a _____ .

4. Before the opening _____ , an actor stepped on stage to deliver a prologue.

5. Strictly speaking, an auditorium is not exactly the same thing as a _____ .

6. The most expensive seats are usually on the main floor in the _____ .

7. Although *Romeo and Juliet* has some humorous scenes, it is nevertheless a _____ .

8. The screenplay is an adaptation of British playwright Reginald Marlowe's _____ , *The Butler Takes a Bride,* first performed on Broadway in 1948.

## SOPHOCLES

Born near Athens about 495 B.C., Sophocles lived at a time when Greece was at its height of political power and of creation in the arts and philosophy. He was one of Athens' most distinguished citizens—an accomplished musician and athlete as well as a successful and respected playwright. Elected one of the ten generals of Athens, the highest elective office of the state, he also held priesthoods in several religious cults. In the dramatic festivals of his age he won the first prize twenty-four times, more than any other dramatist, but of the more than one hundred plays he wrote before his death in 406 B.C., only seven remain.

## From Greek and Latin into English

For the great majority of readers, language is an obvious barrier to the study of classical literature. Although classical scholars are able to study early Greek and Latin literature in the original languages, most people must depend on translators.

The problems of translating poetry are especially difficult, for a translator must contend not only with words and thoughts but also with poetic elements such as rhythm, rhyme, alliteration, and meter. Because of these problems, some translators settle for conveying the essence of a poem through a prose rather than a poetic version.

Compare the following translations of the same passage from Ovid's "Story of Daedalus and Icarus."

### I.

Now in this while gan Dædalus
   a wearinesse to take
Of living like a banist man and
   prisoner such a time
In Crete, and longed in his heart
   to see his native Clime.
But Seas enclosed him as if he had
   in prison be.
Then thought he: though both Sea
   and land King Minos stop
   fro me,
I am assurde he cannot stop the
   Aire and open Skie:
To make my passage that way then
   my cunning will I trie.
Although that Minos like a Lord
   held all the world beside:
Yet doth the Aire from Minos yoke
   for all men free abide.
This sed: to uncoth Arts he bent
   the force of all his wits
To alter natures course by craft.
      Arthur Golding (1567)

### II.

In tedious exile now too long
   detain'd,
Dædalus languish'd for his native
   land:
The sea foreclos'd his flight; yet
   thus he said;
"Though earth and water in
   subjection laid,
O cruel Minos, thy dominion be,
We'll go through air; for sure the
   air is free."
Then to new arts his cunning
   thought applies,
And to improve the work of nature
   tries.
      Samuel Croxall (1717)

### III.

Homesick for homeland, Daedalus
   hated Crete
And his long exile there, but the
   sea held him.
"Though Minos blocks escape by
   land or water,"

Daedalus said, "surely the sky is open,
And that's the way we'll go. Minos' dominion
Does not include the air." He turned his thinking
Toward unknown arts, changing the laws of nature.
                    Rolfe Humphries (1955)

The first translation, from the age of Shakespeare, uses a rhymed fourteen-beat iambic line. (An iambic consists of two syllables, an unaccented followed by an accented.) The second translation uses a rhymed ten-beat iambic line. The third uses a loose ten-beat unrhymed line. Since Ovid used none of these verse forms, only someone who knows the Latin original could decide which translation is more faithful to the meaning, tone, and effect of Ovid's poem. Translations vary according to the purposes and abilities of the translator and the literary fashions of the time in which the translator is writing.

Some translators depart almost entirely from the language of the original, as in the following passage:

Dædalus built the labyrinth for King Minos, but afterwards lost the favour of the king, and was shut up in a tower. He contrived to make his escape from his prison, but could not leave the island by sea, as the king kept strict watch on all the vessels, and permitted none to sail without being carefully searched. "Minos may control the land and sea," said Dædalus, "but not the regions of the air. I will try that way." So he set to work to fabricate wings for himself and his young son Icarus.
                    Thomas Bulfinch (1913)

This is not truly a translation but a retelling of the story in prose. A storyteller like Bulfinch is freer than a translator in matters of language, style, and even content; but a good prose retelling retains the essential meaning and effect of the original.

Computers have been programed to translate from one language into another, but, like other translators, they find it difficult to convey the essence of the original. A computer once translated the proverb "Out of sight, out of mind" into Japanese. When the Japanese was translated back into English, it had become "Invisible, insane."

## UNIT 5 REVIEW

**1.** Briefly identify each of the following:

a. Zeus          h. Odysseus
b. Icarus         i. *Iliad*
c. Cadmus      j. *Odyssey*
d. Ovid           k. *Aeneid*
e. Socrates     l. Homer
f. Sophocles   m. Virgil
g. Dionysus    n. Trojan horse

**2.** Throughout the *Iliad* and the *Odyssey*, Homer attaches to the names of characters a descriptive word or phrase expressing some characteristic of that person. Odysseus, for example, is repeatedly referred to as "wily Odysseus" and "Odysseus the great tactician." Imagine that you are a writer faced with the task of choosing an epithet for each of the following characters. In each case choose the word or phrase that you think most accurately characterizes the person.

a. Creon        e. Icarus
b. Antigone    f. Aeneas
c. Ismene       g. Socrates
d. Haemon     h. Penelope

**3.** If you could spend an evening talking with one character or author from this unit, with whom would you choose to spend it?

a. Why would you choose that person?

b. What would be your first few questions or comments to that person?

**4.** On the basis of what you have read in this unit, what do you think are some of the human values that were important to ancient Greeks and Romans? There follow some categories that may help you organize your thoughts.

a. parents and children ("The Story of Daedalus and Icarus," "The Flight of Aeneas," "Odysseus in Ithaca," *Antigone*)

b. war ("The Surprise," "The Flight of Aeneas," "The Warrior of the Past," "Epitaph for Slain Spartans," "Some Saian Mountaineer")

c. love ("The Flight of Aeneas"; "Odysseus in Ithaca"; "Living, Dear Lesbia, Is Useless Without Loving"; *Antigone*)

d. death ("The Prophecy of Socrates," *Antigone*, "Some Saian Mountaineer")

e. the nature of heroism ("The Story of Cadmus," "The Warrior of the Past," "Some Saian Mountaineer," "Odysseus in Ithaca," *Antigone*, "The Death of Socrates")

From "Daedalus and Icarus" from *Bulfinch's Mythology*. Permission granted by the publisher, Thomas Y. Crowell Company, Inc., New York.

At Random is different from any other unit in this book. It is an anthology within an anthology. Its keynote is variety. Here are short stories, poetry, nonfiction, and two plays written for television. These various types of literature include selections which vary in tone, mood, style, time, and place. Studying these selections will enable you to review, reapply, and extend what you have learned.

**Short Story**
**Poetry**
**Autobiography**
**Article and Essay**
**Drama**

# At Random

# THE HIGHLAND BOY

*Leslie Norris*

*He was clever, deceitful, and shameless. He could reduce a race to chaos.*

THE first greyhound I ever owned was a black-brindled dog called Highland Boy. He was a small dog, weighing perhaps fifty-three pounds, and his coat was a dull black with sparse streaks of rust-colored hair running through it. He was not attractive at first glance, and his expression was at once conciliatory and untrustworthy. I had known him for a year before I became his owner, because he belonged to my Uncle Cedric.

My Uncle Cedric owned a tobacconist's and confectionery shop in Victoria Road, very near to our house, and it was my habit to visit this shop on Saturday evenings to buy a quarter of a pound of chocolate caramels. Cedric would take a paper bag as big as a pillowcase, and thrusting his hand into all the glass jars around him, would fill it with a sweet assortment of flavors enough to last a week. This situation was not as perfect as it seems, for Bertie Christopher soon discovered my Saturday evening fortune, and he and his gang would perch like a row of twelve-year-old vultures on the railings

opposite my uncle's shop, waiting for me to emerge. Fighting was out of the question since the very weight of the sweets was an embarrassment. I used to hover patiently behind the door of the shop until something broke momentarily their brooding concentration, and then I'd run for it. Sprinting and jinking like a startled buck, I'd break past three or four fairly easily. After that it was head down and knock my way through. Most Saturdays at that time I could be found fingering a swollen eye or some other temporary and violent blemish, gloomily eating a chocolate-covered almond or a marzipan whirl, wondering if it was worth it.

Highland Boy was often in the shop with my Uncle Cedric on Saturday evenings. They would both have been to the unlicensed track at the top of the town, and my uncle would usually be staring in a bewildered fashion at Highland Boy. All the dog ever did was to whisk his thin tail once or twice and then look shyly and resignedly at the floor. I often thought my uncle took a kind of defiant pride in the dog.

Uncle Cedric was a tall, thin man, almost completely bald although he was only twenty-eight. He had the most ferocious eyebrows I have ever seen, and my grandmother said that if he were to comb them back over his bare skull they would offer more than adequate compensation. She never said this in Cedric's hearing because he was sensitive. Cedric wore checked suits, and he would stand with his hands, his fingertips anyway, in the little pockets of his waistcoat, which made his elbows stick out like the stubby wings of a sparrow and his shoulders lift almost up to his ears. He was mild and slow-moving enough normally, but phenomenally strong and brisk when angry. Nobody cared to argue with Cedric. I once saw him argue with three Irishmen who had decided to contest, as a matter of entertainment, a debt of honor. Cedric stood against a shop window in case they should attempt to attack him from behind and set about dealing with them.

"B'Jasus, he's a daisy," cried the admiring Irishmen as they reeled and staggered away. "Didja ever see the dint he gave Paddy, now?"

They all four went into a public house, and I was left to mind Cedric's van.

On a golden Saturday in late August, at eight-thirty in the evening, I went as usual for my trove of sugar. Bertie Christopher and his gang watched my every step with cold, unblinking eyes. The shop door was open, and Cedric and Highland Boy stood inside. I knew at once that there was some serious trouble. The dog was absolutely still, head and tail hanging low, and he did not give me even a hint of a greeting. I looked up at Cedric. Great, silent tears were rolling down his face.

"What's wrong?" I asked. "Uncle Cedric, what's the matter?"

He was shaking with anger, but his voice was remote and controlled.

"This bloody dog," he said, "has kept the bookmakers in affluence, with my money, since the day I bought him. I have been involved in many a disgraceful and undignified scene because of the deceitful manner in which he races, people believing that I, in some devilish way, have control over his actions. All this I have put up with because of my love of animals. But he has killed my cat, and that is the end."

Cedric loved his cat, a large, somnolent ginger creature. This was gasping tragedy. I looked at Highland Boy. His eye was mild and distant, and there were flecks of ginger fur about his mouth.

A small, nervous man came in for cigarettes, and Cedric wept unashamed as he served him with a packet of the wrong brand.

"What are you going to do?" I asked.

"Take him out of my sight, boy," said Cedric. "I make him over to you as a present. Tomorrow I'll give you his pedigree and registration papers, but take him out of my sight."

I hooked my fingers behind Highland Boy's collar and went. Bertie Christopher was surprised enough to let me pass without a struggle, and then Highland Boy and I trotted down the garden and into the house.

My father was sitting in his armchair reading Dickens, which is what he always did when he wasn't busy.

"What's this?" he said.

"A dog," I said, "Highland Boy."

"He needs feeding. You can keep him in the washhouse," said my father. The dog looked at him, and he looked at the dog. They liked each other.

So began my career as a greyhound owner.

I used to get up very early each morning and exercise that dog over the moors. I became hard and stringy, able to run for prodigious distances without distress, but Highland Boy seemed completely unaffected. When I had enough money—the fee was five shillings—I would enter him for a race on one of the unlicensed tracks either in our town or in one of the neighboring towns. Neither he nor I was popular on these tracks.

I have thought since that the dog was an imaginative genius. There may be ways of reducing a race to chaos that he didn't invent, but I doubt it. Sometimes he would shoot away with every appearance of running an orthodox and blameless five hundred and twenty-five yards, which was the usual length of a race, only to feel lonely up there in front. He would wait for the second dog and gambol along beside him, smiling and twisting in an ecstasy of friendship. This commonly so upset the other dog that he ran wide, turned round, or lost ground so rapidly that he was effectively out of the running; I'd have to avoid the owner of such a dog for months. He won a solitary race, in Aberdare, in so strange a fashion that I was almost ashamed to collect the prize money. Running with a controlled abandon which left the honest journeymen who were his competitors far behind, he got to within a foot of the winning post and stopped dead. The second dog, laboring along twenty lengths behind, ran heavily into him and knocked Highland Boy over the line. Four Chinamen, heavy and regular gamblers, leaped and capered as they ran for the bookmakers. They were the most scrutable men I ever saw, and the only men who ever made a killing on my dog. After this race, Benny Evans, who was the handicapper at the track, suggested that it might be sensible if I kept my dog away until people's memories grew dim. I could see his point.

Every September, as if to give an added splendor to the death of summer, a great open competition was held at the Tredegar track, twelve miles away over the hills. The prize was twenty-five pounds and a silver cup. My Uncle Cedric now possessed a marvelous dog, the beautiful Special Request, and he would certainly enter him. He spoke to my father and me of his well-founded hopes.

"When I went over to Ireland," he said, "to buy this dog from Father Seamus Riordan, I was assured there wasn't a dog to touch him. And they were right. That silver cup is as good as in my hands, barring accidents, and the twenty-five pounds too."

He beamed at the glorious tan-and-white greyhound, silken-coated and sided like a bream.[1]

"He's a beauty," I said.

"You ought to take your dog. I'll pay for his entry," my father said.

"Why not?" said Cedric, with the large generosity of a man who knows he is not to be affected by the decisions of lesser men.

I went over to Tredegar on the bus, on the Thursday night of the qualifying races. Highland Boy behaved admirably, running second to a very good dog which had been specially imported from Bristol.[2] This meant that he went into the semifinals the next evening. Cedric's dog won his heat very easily and broke the track record. Almost everybody from our town was on him to win the final, and our hopes were high.

When we got to the track on the Friday evening, we found that the two semifinals were to be held last on the program. Cedric was amused to find that our dogs were in the same race, Special Request in Box 6, which was lucky since he was a superbly fast starter, and Highland Boy in Box 3. The first three dogs in each race would go on to the final, to be held a week later. I knew I had no chance. Highland Boy was too small to stand the buffeting that would certainly go on in the middle of the track.

"Never mind," said Cedric, "he's done very well to get as far as this."

The lights were shining on the track by the time our race was announced. I went down to the paddock and put the racing coat with the large number three on it around Highland Boy, taking care not to fasten it too tightly under his stomach. He seemed only half the size of the other dogs. I felt like crying. I put his racing

muzzle on. He was unperturbed, perfectly at ease among the eager whining of the other dogs. The stewards made me wear a long white coat to walk him down to the boxes. It was too long and I had to hold it up with one hand and everybody laughed.

"It's ridiculous to allow a boy to put his dog in an important race like this," said Paul Davies, a thin lame man, as we walked down the track. "Particularly a dog like that thing; he can ruin any race."

My uncle gave him a red look.

"The cure for your lameness, Paul, is to break the good leg," he said.

Paul, whose disability had given him guile and cunning, thought of the three Irishmen and gulped.

"I hope you don't think I was talking of your nephew here," he said. "Why, this boy is a credit. He has a real sense of vocation and will be just like you, Ced, in a couple of years."

We walked silently down to the line of six boxes, put our dogs in one by one, and ran across the field over to the finish, so that we would be ready to collect them after the race.

They flew out of the traps, and Special Request was well in front by the second bend. I couldn't even see my dog. On the back straight he was last and not moving very freely, but as they hit the last bend he began to run, weaving through the field with breathtaking speed. I was proud of him. He finished third, well behind the first two, but he was in the final.

Now I had a week before the great day. I gave Highland Boy two raw eggs a day, fed him on minced beef before putting him in his straw, walked him until my feet were raw. He didn't seem an ounce different.

On the night of the final we went in a hired bus. We carried with us all the loose money in the town, and we were thick with strategies for getting good odds from the bookmakers. I sat in a front seat, behind the driver where I could get a good view of the road, and Highland Boy sat between my feet. I wore my best suit, the one with a gray stripe, and I wasn't going to wear a long white coat whatever happened.

We got to the track, and I waited about through the dragging tedium of the earlier

---

1. *bream,* a freshwater fish with a laterally flattened, deep body.
2. *Bristol,* a seaport in southwestern England.

races. I could see my uncle's friends, jovial with expectation, their eyes full of money. Highland Boy was drawn in Box 1, a good position if he got away quickly enough, right on the rail. Cedric's dog was in Box 5, which was perfectly all right for him. He was a big dog and could barge his way through.

I went down to the paddock in a dream, my fingers shaking so that I couldn't fasten the racing coat, and Cedric did it for me.

"Good luck, Uncle," I said.

"He'll dawdle it,"[3] said Cedric. "My Special Request will dawdle it. The only interesting question is, Who's going to be second?"

I put Highland Boy into the first box and he went in like a gentleman. When I popped around the front to have a look at him, he gave me a serious and apologetic glance, and I knew how he felt.

"It doesn't matter, you've done well," I said.

The bell went, and the hare began its run from behind the starting line. I could have sworn that Highland Boy's box opened seconds before the others, but I know that's impossible. He was fifteen yards clear at the end of the first straight and fled around the bend, tracking so closely to the inner fence that I thought he would leave the color of his skin on every inch of it. He coiled and stretched with brilliant suppleness and vigor, throwing his length into a stride like a flying dive, balling himself tight, his back arched high, then unleashing again. I knew, everybody in the stadium knew, that the race was over before it was halfway run. My dog won by fifteen easy lengths, and I had collected him, put on his lead, and begun to walk away when the second dog reached us, panting and exhausted. I was spring-heeled with elation, but I held my face stiff because I knew it was wrong of me to feel even remotely happy. I thought of Uncle Cedric, his pockets full of red and white ribbon he'd bought especially to decorate the cup. I wondered how we could go home to our friends to tell them that all their money was lost, that the wrong dog had won the cup. I looked down at Highland Boy. The muscles on his quarters were shivering, but he seemed all right otherwise. He was a heartless dog.

They made me walk him around the track, and he danced on his toes every inch of it. He knew he'd won. They gave me a check for twenty-five pounds and a dented cup, said to be silver. Everybody cheered derisively, except the relieved bookmakers and the silent, ominous party of my uncle's friends. People jeered Uncle Cedric, and he had no reply. We filed into our cheerless coach. Nobody congratulated me. I held the unwanted cup on my knee until it began to get heavy, and then I put it under the seat.

We sat together, Uncle Cedric and I, on the seat nearest the door, and Highland Boy coiled himself into a tactful ball at our feet. My uncle put Special Request on the seat between us and then hunched into his overcoat, dark with gloom, unmoving except for the fingers of his left hand, which absentmindedly fondled the folded ear of his defeated champion. Behind us, from the back seat where he sat with four of his friends, I could hear the bitter voice of big Carl Jenkins. He spoke quietly at first, but now his voice grew heavy and bold.

He was very nasty. He said that although he had known my uncle to be the biggest crook in four valleys, he had not thought Cedric would swindle his own friends of their hard-earned money. This, said Carl Jenkins, was the lowest of my uncle's many abominable tricks. He reasoned that my uncle was bald only because nothing as honest and natural as hair would live on him. "And," added Carl Jenkins, "like master, like dog. We all know that Highland Boy could never be trusted."

There was a lot of muttered support for this opinion, and one or two bolder spirits began to threaten my uncle with violence. He sat unmoved, as if deaf.

"Oh, he's a fly[4] one," said Carl Jenkins. "You won't find many as fly as Cedric. Have you ever known him to do an honest day's work? Never. All he does is sit in his shop, growing rich and planning the schemes and tricks by which he robs his friends of their money. He pretends," continued Carl Jenkins with a sour irony, "that the dog belongs to the boy there, but we all know the boy will do whatever Cedric tells him."

---

3. *He'll dawdle it.* He'll win without having to use all his speed.

4. *fly,* clever.

The bus swung slowly round the corner at the end of Bennett Street and hung above the hill into High Street. My uncle tapped the driver on the shoulder as a signal that he should stop. The bus sidled in to the curb.

"How much money did he take over to Tredegar?" trumpeted Carl Jenkins, swollen with eloquence and sorrow, "money which his trusting friends had asked him to put on that fine dog Special Request, which would have won if he hadn't been up to his criminal tricks? How much money did you steal from us, Cedric?"

The bus stopped, and my uncle stood up. His smile was genial and terrible. He looked slowly about him, nodding his head here and there, as if thoughtfully recognizing certain people in front of him. His hands were deep in the pockets of his overcoat.

"Jump off, boy," he said, "and trot home all the way. The dog could do with a loosener."

He didn't look at me at all. I scuffled under the seat for the rolling trophy, grabbed Highland Boy's lead, and prepared to jump.

"Two hundred and forty-one pounds," my uncle said, very mildly. "I took two hundred and forty-one pounds to Tredegar with me tonight, and a hundred of them were my own."

He sighed deeply.

"Has anybody on this bus lost as much as I have?" he asked. "A hundred pounds? Because I left the whole of that money, the whole two hundred and forty-one pounds, in the hands of the bookmakers. I've cheated nobody, and I've lost more money than anybody else. If there is a villain, then it's Highland Boy. But he ran a good race, he ran a fine race, and he beat us all. Hurry up, boy. And now, Carl Jenkins, I'll push your nose through the back of your neck and tie your lying mouth in a knot."

As I jumped from the bus, already moving slowly, I saw my uncle advancing majestically upon his enemy, but although I pounded downhill after the bus, I saw no more.

I went home and told my father. He was sitting by the fire reading P. G. Wodehouse,[5] which is what he did when he was very happy, usually on Saturday evenings and at Christmas,

but when I told him that Uncle Cedric was fighting Carl Jenkins in the bus, he got up, put on his hat and coat, and left. I could not remember my father ever having left the house at night before.

Later, after perhaps an hour, he returned.

"Did you see Uncle Cedric?" I asked.

My father nodded.

"Was the fight over?"

My father thought about that one; he was a very precise man.

"It was all over as far as Carl Jenkins was concerned," he answered, "but there were one or two others your uncle felt aggrieved with. However, the police were about to arrive, and I persuaded Cedric that he ought to catch the late train to Cardiff, to stay with his cousins, just for a while. Now you'd better go to bed."

For some weeks my grandmother kept behind the counter in my uncle's shop. When I went on Saturdays for my quarter of a pound of chocolate caramels, she would weigh them out with hairbreadth accuracy, five to the ounce, as if I were any casual customer. Life seemed to have lost much of its savor, and I was too dispirited to avoid Bertie Christopher wholeheartedly. I took to fighting him so often that I soon knew every move he was likely to make, although his right swing was always risky. In the end we knocked each other into a grudging friendship, and when Uncle Cedric came back from Cardiff after a month, I rather liked sharing my Saturday candy with Bertie and the other boys.

By that time my father had taken Highland Boy to live in the house. Without anybody saying anything, it was somehow agreed that his racing career was over. He had a basket down by the fire, but most of the time he'd be leaning against my father's knees, fawning on my old man in the most shameless manner. It used to be sickening to see them together, watching them walk down the garden with leisurely dignity, or stand silently together while they contemplated some gentle problem. It was annoying to see Highland Boy a reformed scoundrel, wearing his drab color with the proud humility and decency of a deacon.

He lived with us for another twelve years, dying the month after Bertie Christopher went to work in London, but it was longer than that before I owned another greyhound.

---

5. *P. G. Wodehouse,* British humorist and novelist.

## DISCUSSION

1. Seen through the eyes of the narrator, Uncle Cedric is an admirable person. Find incidents in the story that show him to be (a) generous, (b) proud, and (c) fearless.

2. The narrator describes Highland Boy as an imaginative genius. What illustrations does he give of the dog's imaginativeness?

3. Were you completely surprised by Highland Boy's winning the final race of the open competition at Tredegar track? If you were, explain why. If you were not, explain what in the story prepared you for anticipating his winning.

4. Why can't the narrator show his elation when Highland Boy wins the big race?

5. Why, at the end of the story, does the narrator find Highland Boy "shameless," "sickening," and "annoying"?

6. How does this story differ from the usual "racing-underdog-wins" story?

## LESLIE NORRIS

Leslie Norris grew up in the industrial town of Merthyr in South Wales, where he was born in 1921, and though he now lives in England, much of his poetry and fiction draws upon incidents from Merthyr schooldays and time spent roaming nearby moorlands.

His works include volumes of poetry—his best-known poem being "The Ballad of Billy Rose," a tribute to a blind boxer—short radio plays, short stories, and verse translations from medieval Welsh. He currently teaches at the College of Education, Bognor Regis, Sussex, and lives with his wife in nearby Chichester.

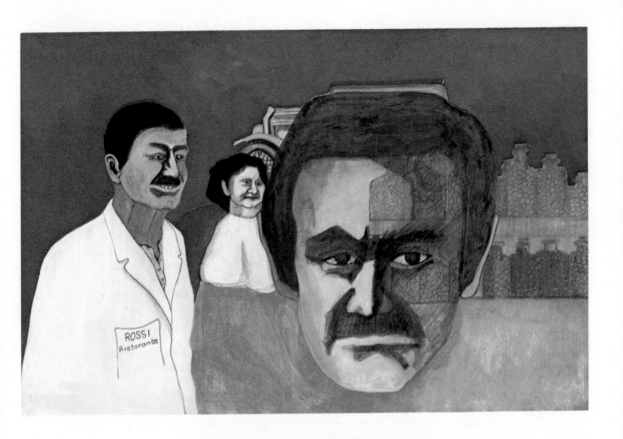

# FORBIDDEN FRIES

*Giovanni Guareschi*
*Translated from the Italian by Gordon Sager*

I was as dilapidated as an old Ford: defective carburetor, stomach cylinder out of order, irregular flow of oil, heart beating in the head, wiring that kept fusing. Now a foot, now a hand, now an elbow or knee, now a headlight burned out, now the nose, now the teeth, now the spine. Nothing was right.

I tried bicarbonate of soda, pills, pomades, gargles, powders, DDT, alcohol, iodine, tablets, purges, tonics, sulfa drugs, mustard plasters, compresses, inhalations, fumes, oil, naphtha, milk, mineral water, fruit salts, infusions, phosphates, and yogurt.

One day I called my family together, and I said: "The situation is serious. The machine keeps going by dint of wire and string, and I can't send it to the garage because I can't take it out of use. So everybody's got to do his bit to help. From today on, the house is going to be reorganized. For six days of the week everybody behaves as his own sense and discretion dictate, but on Monday Papa has to be allowed to run like clockwork. Papa works Sunday night, and he works Monday night, and inasmuch as he also works all day Monday, nothing, all day Monday, must be allowed to interfere with him. Now, to go like clockwork, he needs two things: absolute tranquillity and adequate food. Six days of the week Papa can have a stomachache, Monday he can't."

Albertino and the Pasionaria[1] accepted this without thinking that it was an attempt to inaugurate a dictatorship on my part. And they agreed to cooperate.

To avoid all misunderstanding, the Pasionaria asked for elucidation of certain details.

"Monday," she said "is it all right for you to get mad if you don't find the paste on your desk? Or if I'm using the drawing paper and the India ink?"

"No," I replied. "I can get mad only on account of the paste, which is something I don't need very often. But since I've got to do some drawings every Monday, the absence of the essential materials, such as paper and ink, will not be tolerated."

"That's all right," agreed the Pasionaria. "That only means I'll have to change days."

Albertino had only one question. "Is it all right for you to get mad on Monday if you don't find any more oranges to make an orangeade with?"

"No," I replied, "it is not. The absence of orangeade could endanger the entire working operation."

"Very well," Albertino said in an easy voice. "Mondays I'll make do with apples or pears."

Margherita appeared to have no objections. But when I thought I had everything arranged, she cried: "So I'm a Lucrezia Borgia,[2] am I? Seven days of the week I poison my husband, and now he asks, as a special favor, that I don't poison him on Mondays."

This was not what I meant.

"It's merely a question," I said clearly, "at Monday's meals, of avoiding foods that are not suitable to my particular gastric disturbances. For instance, absolutely no fried foods on Mondays."

We were in the kitchen, and my India ink and brushes were, naturally enough, on the kitchen table, where the Pasionaria was making use of them for her own purposes.

"Today's not Monday," the Pasionaria told me when I asked her for the ink and a brush.

"I know that," I replied. "I only want my ink as a temporary loan, so I can write on the wall above the gas stove: 'Mondays in this house, nothing gets fried.'"

After I had posted this announcement, Margherita shook her head in a melancholy manner. "So we're going to start all over again with writing on the wall, are we? Why don't you also write that Italy's destiny lies on the sea and that she'll never turn back?"

With a sad heart I felt constrained to rebuke her for her inopportune sarcasm. "By safeguarding my stomach on Mondays, I'm safeguarding my work, and the future of our children!"

It was the first Monday after the reform.

I had worked all night Sunday, and when I got up from my chair, I found enough oranges to quench my thirst.

I went back upstairs and sat down at my drawing table. All the brushes were in the yellow jar, and beside them stood the bottle of India ink. Instead of the pot of paste, I found a note from the Pasionaria: "The paste is on my desk. Don't worry, go and get it."

---

1. *Albertino and Pasionaria,* the narrator's children. "The Pasionaria" is a nickname for the daughter.

2. *Lucrezia Borgia* (lü krē′tsyä bôr′jä), an Italian noblewoman (1480–1519) whose reputation as a poisoner, although never proved, has been preserved in several plays and operas based on her life.

I had no need for it, so I didn't worry and I didn't go and get it.

Everything went wonderfully well. At one o'clock the inside telephone rang, and when I picked up the receiver, Margherita said that if I wanted to come down, luncheon was served. But before I heard Margherita's voice, I smelled the hideous odor of frying food. Some people would doubtless say the smell did not come into the studio along the telephone wire but through the crack under the door, but I am convinced the stench was so strong I smelled it through the telephone.

I went down, and coughing my way through the smoke in the kitchen, sat down at my place. I said nothing, but the Pasionaria, who had just come home from school, threw her satchel on a chair and shouted: "I could smell it as soon as I turned off Viale Romagna. 'Mondays in this house, nothing gets fried!'"

Margherita, who had just finished burning God knows what in the frying pan, turned.

"Monday?" she cried. "I thought today was Saturday. It's extraordinary how much Saturday is like Monday here in Milan!"

I was not going to get excited.

"The days pass, one after the other," I said, "and so much alike, it's easy to lose all idea of time. Anyway, it won't happen again. Every Monday morning I'm going to put up a sign saying, 'Notice: Today is Monday.'"

I ate the fried food and soon had a stomachache, but I didn't feel too bad, for I was convinced it was my last Monday stomachache.

It was the following Monday. Early in the morning I went down to the kitchen to squeeze some oranges, and on the rack above the stove I affixed the sign: "Notice: Today is Monday."

I came down again at one, and Margherita was at the stove, frying something.

I got angry.

"Margherita," I asked, "did you happen to see a sign reading, 'Notice: Today is Monday'?"

"Yes," she replied cheerfully. "It was a kind thought. Of course you might also have written, 'Tomorrow is Tuesday.' But I couldn't understand why you wanted to tell me that today is Monday."

"Mondays in this lousy house, nothing gets fried!" cried the Pasionaria, throwing her satchel into a corner of the room.

Then Margherita remembered, and so great was her consternation that I said nothing more. Once again I ate fried food and had a stomachache and a hard time working that afternoon and night.

It was the third Monday after the reform, and I went downstairs at lunchtime to find that Margherita was not frying anything—because she'd already finished.

In silence I awaited the return of the Pasionaria. She tossed her satchel on the radiator.

"Mondays in this house, nothing gets fried!" cried the Pasionaria in a disgusted tone. "Only on the day after Sunday and the day before Tuesday."

I turned to Margherita.

"Didn't you see the sign," I asked, "telling you what day it is?"

Margherita spread out her arms and raised her eyes to the ceiling.

"Yes," she answered, "yes, I saw the Monday notice, I read the notice that Monday nothing gets fried, but I decided for once I'd allow myself to disobey the order. How's a poor woman to prepare lunch and dinner if she's not allowed to fry anything? A poor woman who's never taken courses in cooking, who racks her brain trying to think of dishes that aren't fried, isn't she allowed once in her life to make some fried food? It's inhuman!"

The fourth Monday after the reform, I sat down at the table at one o'clock in the best of humor. Margherita had cooked up a panful of fried stuff that could be smelled as far away as San Babila, but I was in the best of humor. When the Pasionaria came home and cried, "Mondays in this house, nothing gets fried," I didn't get angry, I felt more cheerful than ever. Margherita brought to the table the customary vat of minestrone, the kind I love, which bloats me so and which I must never eat.

"No, thank you," I said when the soup was passed to me.

"Aren't you eating?" Margherita asked. "Aren't you feeling well?"

"I'll eat. I'm waiting."

I didn't have long to wait. After about five minutes there was a ring at the door and a waiter in a white jacket appeared, carrying a tray in his hands. He took from the tray a plate of baked pasta, a plate of plain meat with vegetables, and a saucer of stewed fruit. With something of a flourish, he arranged it all in front of me, and left. I began to eat quietly, pretending not to see the look on Margherita's face.

"This," she said, vibrating with indignation, "is the most frightful insult a man can pay the mother of his children! He may go out to eat in a restaurant—all right—but having a restaurant bring food into his own house, that, I honestly believe, has never happened before!"

The baked pasta was just as I like it: a small portion, not at all rich, and very tasty. I went on to the rest of the meal, paying not the slightest heed to Margherita. When I finished, I said: "Margherita, on Mondays I have to run like clockwork—not for myself but for the future of my children, and also for yours. If by some evil chance we always have to have fried food on Monday, then that's an obstacle I must overcome—at any cost!"

"Don't try to cover up what you've done," she said bitterly. "I consider it a gross offense."

And that's the way things stood when I went back upstairs to work. It was rather unpleasant, but my stomach was fine.

The fifth Monday I went downstairs prepared for combat. Entering the kitchen, I smelled nothing frying. I smelled nothing, in fact. Somebody had laid the table, but the general impression was that no meal had been cooked. Margherita was listening to the radio. Albertino was outside in the garden. When the Pasionaria arrived, even she was dumfounded.

"Well!" she cried crossly. "Isn't there ever going to be anything more to eat in this horrible house?"

Margherita paid no attention to her. Obviously the storm was going to break with the arrival of the waiter bringing my lunch.

But nothing broke. The waiter arrived with a large hamper, brought out four plates of baked pasta, four plates of boiled meat with vege-tables, and four bowls of stewed fruit. He arranged them on the table and left.

We sat down to eat in silence.

At last, with the fruit, Margherita explained: "What a relief, once a week, not to have to mess around with pots and pans! I needed a holiday. Besides, I think it's a good idea to have a change once a week."

Nothing more was said.

The days passed, and it was the sixth Monday after the reform.

At one o'clock I came downstairs and sat down to wait at the table, which had already been set. The boy from the restaurant arrived and arranged the plates: baked pasta, fried brains . . .

"What's this?" I cried. "Fried stuff?"

"I brought what the lady ordered on the telephone," the boy said.

When we were alone, Margherita turned to me.

"Boiled meat! Boiled meat! Always boiled meat!" she cried. "A person gets tired of it. You need a change once in a while!"

The seventh Monday the boy from the restaurant didn't come, because nobody called him. I went downstairs at one o'clock and the house was impregnated with the smell of frying.

When the Pasionaria arrived, she wrinkled up her nose.

"If this frying doesn't stop," she cried, "it's going to end up with me going to a restaurant on Mondays!"

After lunch I took bicarbonate and went upstairs to finish my drawing. I found neither brushes nor pencils nor India ink. Instead there was a note from the Pasionaria: "If the others are going to do what they want, so will I!"

So I came to the conclusion that if that's the way things had to go, maybe it was just as well that that's the way they went and I cheered up. Today is the thirteenth Monday, and out of the kitchen billow gusts of black smoke bearing such an odor of frying as the human nose has never smelled before.

And I thank God that today I have a cold that makes that infernal stench seem altogether innocuous.

## DISCUSSION

1. What is your reaction to the father's run-down condition (as described in the opening paragraph)? Do you take it seriously, lightly, or how? What accounts for your reaction?

2. What effect is created by including such things as DDT, pomades, and naphtha in the list of remedies the father tried?

3. The father says he needs two things on Monday: absolute tranquillity and adequate food. How do the Pasionaria's and Margherita's responses to his request suggest that he is not likely to get what he wants?

4. How is the father's attempt to get the kind of food he wants from a restaurant thwarted?

5. (a) Would you describe the Pasionaria as being sympathetic with or indifferent to what her father wants? Or is her reaction a mixed one? Point out instances in the story that illustrate her attitude. (b) To whom does the Pasionaria's oft-repeated remark that nothing ever gets fried in the house on Mondays seem to be directed—her mother, her father, or both of them? What seems to be the purpose of the remark?

6. The conflict described in the story is one that could have led to bitter family strife. Why didn't it?

7. Would you describe the tone of the story as (a) sarcastic, (b) bitter, (c) vindictive, (d) ironic, or (e) indignant? Explain.

## GIOVANNI GUARESCHI

Giovanni Guareschi is best known for his stories about Don Camillo, the contentious village priest who carries on a running battle with the local Communist mayor for the minds and hearts of the villagers. Don Camillo, a rather physical priest who believes in direct action, finds a worthy adversary in the mayor, who is every bit as agressive and physical; and the two engage in a series of humorous skirmishes. The first book of Don Camillo stories appeared under the title *The Little World of Don Camillo*. The most recent collection is *Don Camillo Meets the Flower Children*.

Guareschi was born in Italy in 1908 and died in 1968. Though his parents wanted him to be a naval engineer, he elected to study law but got sidetracked by an interest in drawing caricatures. This interest led him into newspaper and magazine work (some of the hazards of which are described in "Forbidden Fries.").

World War II interrupted his literary career. Not being sympathetic to the Axis cause, he spent most of the war in German concentration camps. He described this period as the busiest in his life, wryly remarking that he had to work very hard to stay alive. After the war he returned to Milan and founded the weekly satirical review *Candido* ("candid" or "frank"). He noted that the work he did for *Candido* was highly regarded by the staff members, possibly because he was editor-in-chief. It was in this journal that the stories of Don Camillo and of the Pasionaria and Margherita first appeared.

# between the dark and the daylight

*Nancy Hale*

THIS was the bed where Sara had always been put when she was sick. Not her own bed, narrow and tidy against the wall of her room, among her own books, her own furniture, so well known to her that she did not see them any more. This bed was different. This was the guest-room bed, a double bed with white-painted iron from head to foot. All her fifteen years she had been put here when she had a cold, or tonsillitis, or measles. It was higher, and broader, and softer than her own bed, and being here pulled her back to the books she had read when she had been sick, or that had been read to her; to the long, unlabored trains of fantasy that had swung in her mind like slow, engrossing ocean swells.

Within the enchantment of the bed in the guest room her mind was released over centuries and into palaces and into the future, and she could alter her person from small to tall, from quiet to commanding. In this bed she had been by turns a queen, a Roman, a man during the Massacre of St. Bartholomew.[1] Here she had imagined herself grown-up and having five children, had given them names and learned their separate faces and spoken to them and punished them. She had always dreamed in this bed of new things and new feelings. She had never reached backward for anything within her own experience.

She had not been sick in several months, but she had bronchitis now, and since she had been sick last something had dropped away from her. She had changed. Without questioning what was happening to her, or even being con-

scious of it, she had stopped playing in brooks and running fast in sneakers and wearing her hair in two pigtails. In these autumn months the girls she played with had changed too. They bought sodas in the drugstore. They walked slowly, eternally, along the tarred New England sidewalks, with their arms around each other's waists. Suddenly they would laugh together helplessly for a moment; at what, they did not know. They cut their hair and curled it, or brushed it out smooth and tied a hair ribbon around it. They watched themselves pass in the shop windows of the town. And all of it had come like a natural change and occupied her fully.

It was not that she turned her head away from one side and looked toward the other. The old things she had known so many years now stood still without a sound to call her as they used, and until she took sick she did not think of them. But as she lay in the guest-room bed she resented more and more what was happening to her. She had no pleasure in remembering the shop windows, the drugstore, the boys— only a sort of weariness and distaste. She did not want to go that way. It all began when she read the Indian book.

After three days her fever went down and she stopped coughing so much and was allowed to go from the guest room into her own room, in her nightgown and wrapper, and take books out of the shelves and bring them back to bed. The first day she brought a book of Poe's short

---

1.  *Massacre of St. Bartholomew,* a massacre of over 3,000 Huguenots in Paris on St. Bartholomew's Day, August 24, 1572.

stories that she loved, and two of the Little Colonel books, and a book about English history, and an old book that she had not read for years, about Indians and wood lore. Her Uncle Lyman had sent it to her one autumn after he had been at their house for a visit. That was when she was eleven.

He belonged to a mountain-climbing club and took long walks in the woods behind their house and she used to go with him. She felt something wonderful in the way he walked without noise along the smooth brown paths, and liked to walk behind, watching him. When it grew dark early in those fall afternoons he would still follow the path without hesitation.

One afternoon when it was cold and frosty and the sun was setting, they came out on a hillside that ran down to the road. There was a clump of birches at the top and he took a knife out of his pocket and showed her how to cut away a strip of birch bark and then to pare its delicate, pale-pink paper from within. That was Indian paper, he said. He took up a rock with big spots of mica and held it up into the shining of the late sun. "If there was someone over on that far hill, I could signal to him with this," he said, "if we were Indians."

What he had said about the Indians filled her mind after he was gone. Through the winter and through the spring she went to the woods. In the winter it was only in the afternoons that she could go, late, after she got home from school. But when the spring came there was more time; it didn't get dark so early. She found a pool beside a rock, covered with green slime, and at the edges the ice-cold water was full of the blobs of transparent jelly that held a million black spots: frogs' eggs. She took them home with her in a tin lard pail and put them in a glass bowl, to watch the polliwogs hatch out. They turned from eggs to tadpoles, to strange creatures with a tail and two legs. And one morning they jumped out of the bowl and hopped about the dining-room floor and had to be thrown out in the garden.

When it was summer she could go all day. She asked for Indian clothes and was given them for her birthday: a fringed coat and skirt, and a leather band for her head, with a feather in it. The skirt had a pocket in the side, where she carried her lunch, done up in waxed paper. When she was alone, on the long paths that had been there for a hundred years and led, if you could follow them, to other states, to other woods and meadows miles away, she was satisfied and at home. She lived within her own private world—this world with a pine-needle floor, peopled by the shadow shapes of men who moved without noise, surmounted by tall plumes. This world was beautiful and intricate and still. The ground pine ran along under the dead leaves in secret; the shallows of the little ponds were filled with a minute and busy life, tiny fish and frogs and "rowboats" that skittered across the slimy surface into the shade. The grouse hid in the underbrush, and the small animals, the rabbits and the sudden moles, ran at intervals across the path, into the sunlight and out of it.

When she went home late in the afternoons it was walking out of one world into another. It required a readjustment of the hearing. From the minute sounds of the woods to which she was acute all day, she walked down along the road past the cultivated meadows, where the sounds were bolder—loud crickets and the long squeal of the cicada—past the hunting dogs that were penned up behind their neighbor's house and barked at all passers, past the hired man putting his tools away in the barn.

Finally there was the house, and she would have supper with her mother and father. In a cotton dress and socks and sneakers, she would sit at the round table and talk and eat and watch the sun going down at last through the west window. The door stood open on the garden and the smell of early-evening grass, the sound of birds, came in as they finished supper. Much later, when she was going to bed, she would kneel down on the floor in her room and crane her head far out of the window to smell the smell that came across the fields, to see through the light summer night the dark, irregular silhouette against the sky; that was the smell and the shape of the woods.

But somehow it had sifted away, melted into the next year of her life, and become like a streak of old color in the long stream of being alive. Now, as she read that book, which had been a Bible to her, everything she had been doing for months seemed dingy and dull and unbeautiful. The Indian book awoke in her the recollection of the woods and being in the woods. For the first time in her life, now in this bed, she thought longingly of something that she had already experienced. She felt her mind entering the woods and inhabiting them again. She had never finished with the woods, she decided. She had left them for no reason, and when she was well again she would go back to them. That was what she wanted. She did not know why she had penetrated that other world, the new, sharp, bright-lit life that she had begun lately, but it was not what she wanted. She did not want to grow up and be with people. It was not suited to her, and she rejected it now, lying free to choose in bed.

She lay with her legs spread comfortably beneath the smooth, cool sheet and stared sightless at the bare yellow-and-white buttonwood branches outside her window. Trays were brought to her and she ate thin soup with lemon in it, and hot buns, and scrambled eggs, and ice cream. The sunshine moved regularly across the floor of the guest room, from beside her bed in the morning to the farthest corner by the window at sunset. Then it disappeared and twilight filled the room. In the house across the road the lights went on for supper and the lights went out for sleep. And there were stars in the black square of her window.

She was in bed six days and at the end of that time she got up. She saw things again vertically and shook herself like a dog and went outside on the side porch, where the November sunshine lay in pale, lemon-colored stripes. The outdoors smelled sharp and sunny, and her muscles came to life and itched to move. She ran down through the garden to the apple tree and climbed it as she had always done for years, up through its round, rough, pinky-gray branches to a crotch high up, where she sat and surveyed the land. The swamp lay beyond, all still and golden. The apple trees round her were not as high as this one, and she could look down into them. Across the fields the white farmhouse let a thin stream of smoke up through its chimney, where it wavered and turned blue

and vanished into the chilly blue sky. The air smelled of late autumn; the air smelled of dead leaves; the air was sharp and lively and wishful. Sara sat in the tree and swung her legs and thought about nothing until somebody called her and she looked down. It was her friend Catherine, who lived in the farmhouse. She stood under the tree and squinted her eyes up at Sara.

"Hi!" Sara said.
"You all well?"
"Sure!"
"Let's go for a walk."
"O.K."

She clambered down the tree and they left the orchard and started to walk down the road to the town, along the lumpy sidewalk made of tar and pebbles. The trees beside the road were bare and clean, and the sky was blue, and the cars drove by gaily. In this November day there was a feeling of activity and of happiness, the brisk, anticipatory feeling of winter coming. Sara and Catherine put their arms around each other's waist and strolled, smiling and talking about what had been happening in school, and about boys.

It was exciting to talk about school. Talking about it, Sara smelled the smell of the classroom, of new, freshly sharpened lead pencils. The impetus of living took hold of her and she was eager and ready for it. She looked at Catherine's plaid wool skirt switching beside her own blue one, casting a thin, swaying shadow on the sidewalk. They strolled on into the town. All the plate-glass windows of the stores glittered in the sun and there was a busy air about the town, of things to be done, of putting on storm doors, of settling down to wait for winter. They passed Tracey's newsstand, where the boys stood in a group looking around. Catherine waved and Sara looked over her shoulder.

"Ha ya?" the Tracey boy said.
"Ha ya doing?" Sara said. She and Catherine laughed lightly, meaningfully, and walked on down the street to the drugstore. They went inside and sat at one of the black glass-topped tables with triangular seats. The store smelled of soda and drugs and candy. The soda clerk walked over to their table.

"What are you having?" he asked.

"Chocolate float," Catherine said.

"Chocolate float, too," Sara said.

It was somehow delightful in the drugstore, full of promise and undisclosed things. To sit, elbows on the damp black glass, and watch the solid glass door and the people who went in and out was somehow exciting. Sara looked at the other customers out of the corner of her eyes, wisely, with poise, and drank her drink through a straw without looking down at it.

"Gee, I'm glad you're over that old bronchitis," Catherine said.

"Gee, so am I."

"I thought you'd never be out. You must have been in the house a whole week."

"Pretty near."

"Don't you just *hate* being sick?"

"I certainly do. Just lying there in bed."

"My mother's going to buy me four new dresses for school. She said I could pick them out myself."

"That's keen. My mother says . . ."

Sara went on talking, eagerly, with satisfaction. She was glad to be well and out and doing things. She felt new vistas opening up before her: school, the girls at school, boys, and beyond that unimaginable things, growing up. For an instant her thought trembled alone, apart from what she was saying.

She thought it was nice to be well and going on with living. It was horrid to be sick and just lie and think. Then her mind switched away from that, the inaction of it, and back into the occupying present, and was happy.

## DISCUSSION

1. The narrator tells us that Sara had changed since her last illness. In what ways had she changed?

2. (a) What is Sara's attitude toward these changes after she has spent a few days in the guest-room bed? (b) What led her to develop this attitude?

3. (a) During her six days' convalescence in the guest room what does Sara experience for the first time? (b) What are the causes of this new experience?

4. When Sara was younger she spent a great deal of time alone in the woods, living "within her own private world." What did she find attractive about that world?

5. (a) After recovering from her illness, Sara is described as seeing things again vertically and shaking herself like a dog. What do these descriptions suggest about both Sara's physical condition and her state of mind? (b) In view of what hap-

pens in the remainder of the story, are these descriptions appropriate? Explain.

6. (a) How do Sara's ideas and attitudes change once she becomes well? (b) In spite of these changes, in what ways is Sara consistent in her responses to the world around her?

7. (a) Is the conflict in the story just Sara's, or is her personal conflict representative of something larger, of, say, conflicting ways of life, conflicting values, conflicting cultures? Explain. (b) Tell why you agree or disagree with the way Sara resolved her conflict.

8. What possible meanings might the title "Between the Dark and the Daylight" have in relation to the story?

## NANCY HALE

Born in Boston in 1908, Nancy Hale grew up in Dedham, Massachusetts, studied at the Boston Museum of Fine Arts, and at the age of twenty went to New York

to work as an assistant editor for *Vogue*.

In 1934 she joined *The New York Times* as a reporter, the first woman to do so. She has since produced short stories and novels, in addition to critical and autobiographical writings. One novel, *The Prodigal Women*, has sold over a million copies.

# Poetry

**Running**

*Richard Wilbur*

What were we playing? Was it prisoner's base?
I ran with whacking keds
Down the cart-road past Rickard's place,
And where it dropped beside the tractor-sheds

5 Leapt out into the air above a blurred
Terrain, through jolted light,
Took two hard lopes, and at the third
Spanked off a hummock-side exactly right,

And made the turn, and with delighted strain
10 Sprinted across the flat
By the bull-pen, and up the lane.
Thinking of happiness, I think of that.

## DISCUSSION

1. What is implied by the uncertainty of the information given the reader in the first line of the poem?

2. The "running" is described in one long sentence. Would the description be more effective if this sentence were broken up into two or three short sentences? Why or why not?

3. Point out words and phrases that help the reader re-create the sensations the speaker experienced when he was running.

4. May Swenson has said that poetry doesn't tell; it shows. What is "shown" in the poem? What is "told"? Would the poem be more effective if the parts that "tell" were omitted? Explain.

## RICHARD WILBUR

Richard Wilbur was born in 1921 in New York City and grew up in rural New Jersey. His literary interests developed at Amherst College, where he served as an editor for the campus newspaper.

Wilbur has published steadily since 1947. His *Things of This World* won both the 1957 Pulitzer Prize for poetry and the National Book Award. He wrote the lyrics for Leonard Bernstein's comic opera version of Voltaire's *Candide,* and his translations of two of Moliere's plays, *The Misanthrope* and *Tartuffe,* have been widely performed throughout the U.S.

*Walking to Sleep* is one of his most recent volumes of poetry.

## Daybreak in Alabama

*Langston Hughes*

When I get to be a composer
I'm gonna write me some music about
Daybreak in Alabama
And I'm gonna put the purtiest songs in it
5  Rising out of the ground like a swamp mist
And falling out of heaven like soft dew.
I'm gonna put some tall tall trees in it
And the scent of pine needles
And the smell of red clay after rain
10  And long red necks
And poppy colored faces
And big brown arms
And the field daisy eyes
Of black and white black white black people
15  And I'm gonna put white hands
And black hands and brown and yellow hands
And red clay earth hands in it
Touching everybody with kind fingers
And touching each other natural as dew
20  In that dawn of music when I
Get to be a composer
And write about daybreak
In Alabama.

## DISCUSSION

1. Of the things the speaker intends to put into his music, which appeal to (a) the sense of sight, (b) the sense of smell, (c) the sense of touch?

2. Music is said to be the universal language. How might this idea influence the speaker's desire to compose music about daybreak in Alabama?

3. One thinks of music as combining different sounds into a harmonious whole. How is the poem an attempt to combine different elements into a harmonious whole?

4. (a) What feelings, thoughts, and images are suggested by daybreak and dawn? (b) What figurative daybreak is suggested by the poem?

## LANGSTON HUGHES

Langston Hughes was a versatile writer who, in spite of much early hardship, enjoyed a long and productive career. He is perhaps best known as a poet and as the creator of the short-story character Jesse B. Semple, a not-so-simple character who invariably met adversity with dignity, wisdom, and humor.

Born in Joplin, Missouri, in 1902, Hughes attended high school in Cleveland, Ohio, where he began writing poetry. After he published a play and some poems in 1921, he soon became part of the Harlem Renaissance, a movement dedicated to finding and publishing black authors.

Toward the end of his career (he died in 1967) he devoted his energies to encouraging and introducing new black writers and to recording the history and culture of black Americans.

### freddy the rat perishes

*Don Marquis*

*At night, archy, who is a cockroach, climbs up on the
typewriter in the newspaper office and writes reports to the boss, a newspaper columnist.*

listen to me there have
been some doings here since last
i wrote there has been a battle
behind that rusty typewriter cover
5 in the corner
you remember freddy the rat well
freddy is no more but
he died game the other
day a stranger with a lot of
10 legs came into our little circle a
    tough looking kid
he was with a bad eye

who are you said a thousand legs
if i bite you once
said the stranger you won t ask
15 again he he little poison tongue said
the thousand legs who gave you
    hydrophobia
i got it by biting myself said
the stranger i m bad keep away
from me where i step a weed dies
20 if i was to walk on your forehead it
    would
raise measles and if
you give me any lip i ll do it

they mixed it then
and the thousand legs succumbed
25 well we found out this fellow
was a tarantula he had come up from
south america in a bunch of bananas
for days he bossed us life

was not worth living he would stand in
30 the middle of the floor and taunt
us ha ha he would say where i
step a weed dies do
you want any of my game i was
raised on red pepper and blood i am
35 so hot if you scratch me i will light
like a match you better
dodge me when i m feeling mean and
i don t feel any other way i was nursed
on a tabasco bottle if i was to slap
40 your wrist in kindness you
would boil over like job[1] and heaven
help you if i get angry give me
room i feel a wicked spell coming on

last night he made a break at freddy
45 the rat keep your distance
little one said freddy i m not
feeling well myself somebody poisoned
    some
cheese for me i m as full of
death as a drug store i
50 feel that i am going to die anyhow
come on little torpedo come on don t stop
to visit and search then they
went at it and both are no more please
throw a late edition on the floor i
    want to
55 keep up with china we dropped freddy
off the fire escape into the alley with
military honors

            archy

---

From *archy and mehitabel* by Don Marquis. Copyright 1927 by
Doubleday and Company, Inc. Reprinted by permission of the
publisher.

**1.** *job* (jōb), a Biblical figure who was afflicted with boils.

## dying is fine)but Death

*E. E. Cummings*

dying is fine)but Death

?o
baby
i

wouldn't like

Death if Death
were
good:for

when(instead of stopping to think)you

begin to feel of it,dying
's miraculous
why?be

cause dying is

perfectly natural;perfectly
putting
it mildly lively(but

Death

is strictly
scientific
& artificial &

evil & legal)

we thank thee
god
almighty for dying

(forgive us,o life!the sin of Death

## DISCUSSION

*freddy the rat perishes*

1. Why do you suppose there are no capitals and punctuation marks in archy's typewriting?

2. What might be a reason for the irregularity of the lines?

3. Where did the battle archy describes take place?

4. (a) Who were the first two contestants? (b) What happened?

5. (a) Why did freddy decide to take on the tarantula? (b) What was the outcome? (c) Why was freddy given "military honors"?

6. Why did archy want a late edition?

7. The creatures that inhabit archy's world often behave more like people than like insects and animals. What characteristics of the tarantula make him a recognizable human "type"? What human characteristics does archy display? freddy?

*dying is fine)but Death*

1. In what sense is the opening statement of the poem ("dying is fine") unusual?

2. (a) With what does the poet contrast dying? (b) What are the attributes of dying that make it "fine"? (c) How does the poet characterize Death? What are the unfavorable connotations of the characteristics attributed to Death? (d) In his poetry E. E. Cummings does not use capitals where they would customarily be used. What is the effect, then, of capitalizing *Death*?

3. In each of the following pairs, which item would the speaker in the poem probably prefer? Why? (a) process – product (b) thinking – feeling (c) love – loving (d) body – mind.

4. Why is it paradoxical to say that "dying is . . . lively"?

5. Reread aloud from the colon in line 8 to the parenthesis in line 21, following carefully the poet's signals for "sounding" the poem. How do the arrangement of the lines and the manner of expression contribute to the contrasting ideas about dying and Death?

6. How do the last four lines differ in tone from the rest of the poem? Why might the narrator thank God for dying?

## DON MARQUIS

Don Marquis (mär′kwis) is remembered primarily as a humorous newspaper columnist, but he was also the author of novels, short stories, poems, and several successful plays. He once remarked, "It would be one up on me if I should be remembered longest for creating a cockroach character." Ironically, his remark seems to have come true, for of all his works the archy-mehitabel poems are the ones still read widely today.

Marquis held many jobs before he was able to devote himself exclusively to journalism and creative writing. He taught at a country school, clerked, bailed hay, was a member of a traveling theatrical group, and worked for the Census Bureau in Washington D.C. While with the Census Bureau he began working as a part-time reporter. This led to jobs with a number of newspapers throughout the country and finally to the *New York Sun*, where, after working as a reporter and an editorial writer, he became a columnist and introduced his cockroach character to the reading public. Beneath Marquis's light humor is a vein of cynicism, a sense that life never works out as one expects (an attitude reflected in his remark about being remembered for the archy poems rather than for his more serious work). He died in 1937 at the age of fifty-nine, after spending the last six years of his life penniless and hopelessly crippled.

## E. E. CUMMINGS

E(dward) E(stlin) Cummings resisted standardization and conformity and celebrated the spontaneous response. He experimented with poetic form—coining words, scrambling word order, using irregular line length, running words together to increase tempo, spacing them to slow it.

Cummings was born in Cambridge, Massachusetts, in 1894 and was educated at Harvard University. Before the United States entered World War I, he joined a volunteer ambulance corps and served in France, where he was erroneously convicted of treasonable correspondence and imprisoned for several months. His first book, *The Enormous Room* (1922), records these experiences. After the war he studied art for a time in Paris, but eventually took up more or less permanent residence in New York's Greenwich Village. Until his death in 1962, Cummings devoted his energies to both painting and poetry.

His first book of poetry, *Tulips and Chimneys*, established the individual tone that characterizes Cummings's works. He received the National Book Award for *Poems: 1923 – 54*.

## *Vale* from Carthage (Spring, 1944)

*Peter Viereck*

I, now at Carthage. He, shot dead at Rome.
Shipmates last May. "And what if one of us,"
I asked last May, in fun, in gentleness,
"Wears doom, like dungarees, and doesn't know?"
5  He laughed, *"Not see Times Square again?"* The foam,
Feathering across that deck a year ago,
Swept those five words—like seeds—beyond the seas
　　　Into his future. There they grew like trees;
　　　And as he passed them there next spring, they laid
10 　　Upon his road of fire their sudden shade.
Though he had always scraped his mess-kit pure
And scrubbed redeemingly his barracks floor,
Though all his buttons glowed their ritual-hymn
Like cloudless moons to intercede for him,
15 No furlough fluttered from the sky. He will
Not see Times Square—he will not see—he will
Not see Times
　　　change; at Carthage (while my friend,
Living those words at Rome, screamed in the end)
I saw an ancient Roman's tomb and read
20 *"Vale"* in stone. Here two wars mix their dead:
　　　Roman, my shipmate's dream walks hand in hand
　　　With yours tonight ("New York again" and "Rome"),
　　　Like widowed sisters bearing water home
　　　On tired heads through hot Tunisian sand
25 　　In good cool urns, and says, "I understand."
Roman, you'll see your Forum Square no more;
What's left but this to say of any war?

---

## DISCUSSION

1. (a) What information about time, place, and circumstance does the reader learn from the first three sentences in the poem?

First published in Peter Viereck's book *Terror and Decorum*, N.Y., Scribners, 1948; Pulitzer prize for verse, 1949; out of print. Included in reprint of *Terror and Decorum*, 1973, by Greenwood Press, Westport, Conn. and in Peter Viereck's *New and Selected Poems*, Bobbs-Merrill Co., N.Y. 1967, as well as other collections.

(b) What contrasts are presented in these sentences?

2. (a) What is the shipmate's response to the speaker's question about wearing doom? (b) What attitude is implied in this response? (c) How did the friend "live the words" of the response?

3. What point is the speaker making in lines 11–17?

4. (a) How are the three place names—Carthage, Rome, Times Square—used to mix two wars, to draw parallels between the past and the present? (b) How do the connotations of Times Square contrast with those of Carthage and Rome?

5. To what does "this" refer in the final line of the poem?

6. *Vale* is the Latin word for farewell. In what sense(s) is the poem a farewell?

*Who knows what fruit the tree of knowledge may bear? Is*
*there only one way of "knowing," one source of knowledge?*
*In the opening lines of this poem, the speaker suggests that*
*knowledge (the "fig" and the "grape") may come from many*
*unlikely sources. Her story, which she begins to relate in line*
*7, recounts the frightening experience that served as her*
*"first step in knowledge."*

### Wild Grapes

*Robert Frost*

What tree may not the fig be gathered from?
The grape may not be gathered from the birch?
It's all you know the grape, or know the birch.
As a girl gathered from the birch myself
5 Equally with my weight in grapes, one autumn,
I ought to know what tree the grape is fruit of.

I was born, I suppose, like anyone,
And grew to be a little boyish girl
My brother could not always leave at home.
10 But that beginning was wiped out in fear
The day I swung suspended with the grapes,
And was come after like Eurydice[1]
And brought down safely from the upper regions;
And the life I live now's an extra life
15 I can waste as I please on whom I please.
So if you see me celebrate two birthdays,
And give myself out as two different ages,
One of them five years younger than I look—

One day my brother led me to a glade
20 Where a white birch he knew of stood alone,
Wearing a thin headdress of pointed leaves,
And heavy on her heavy hair behind,
Against her neck, an ornament of grapes.
Grapes, I knew grapes from having seen them last year.
25 One bunch of them, and there began to be
Bunches all round me growing in white birches,
The way they grew round Leif the Lucky's German;[2]
Mostly as much beyond my lifted hands, though,
As the moon used to seem when I was younger,
30 And only freely to be had for climbing.
My brother did the climbing; and at first
Threw me down grapes to miss and scatter
And have to hunt for in sweet fern and hardhack;
Which gave him some time to himself to eat,
35 But not so much, perhaps, as a boy needed.
So then, to make me wholly self-supporting,
He climbed still higher and bent the tree to earth
And put it in my hands to pick my own grapes.
"Here, take a treetop, I'll get down another.
40 Hold on with all your might when I let go."
I said I had the tree. It wasn't true.
The opposite was true. The tree had me.
The minute it was left with me alone,
It caught me up as if I were the fish
45 And it the fishpole. So I was translated,
To loud cries from my brother of "Let go!
Don't you know anything, you girl? Let go!"
But I, with something of the baby grip

---

**1.** *Eurydice* (yū rid′ə sē). According to Greek mythology, when Eurydice died, her husband Orpheus went to Hades seeking her. He freed her by the charm of his music, but lost her again because he disobeyed Pluto's order not to look at Eurydice until they reached the upper world.

**2.** *Leif the Lucky's German.* With Leif Ericson's Viking crew was a German who lived with Leif's family in Greenland. When they reached what may have been North America, he was overjoyed to find grapes, a fruit unknown in Greenland.

Acquired ancestrally in just such trees
50 When wilder mothers than our wildest now
Hung babies out on branches by the hands
To dry or wash or tan, I don't know which
(You'll have to ask an evolutionist)—
I held on uncomplainingly for life.
55 My brother tried to make me laugh to help me.
"What are you doing up there in those grapes?
Don't be afraid. A few of them won't hurt you.
I mean, they won't pick you if you don't them."
Much danger of my picking anything!
60 By that time I was pretty well reduced
To a philosophy of hang-and-let-hang.
"Now you know how it feels," my brother said,
"To be a bunch of fox grapes, as they call them,
That when it thinks it has escaped the fox
65 By growing where it shouldn't—on a birch,
Where a fox wouldn't think to look for it—
And if he looked and found it, couldn't reach it—
Just then come you and I to gather it.
Only you have the advantage of the grapes
70 In one way: you have one more stem to cling by,
And promise more resistance to the picker."

One by one I lost off my hat and shoes,
And still I clung. I let my head fall back,
And shut my eyes against the sun, my ears
75 Against my brother's nonsense. "Drop," he said,
"I'll catch you in my arms. It isn't far."
(Stated in lengths of him it might not be.)
"Drop or I'll shake the tree and shake you down."
Grim silence on my part as I sank lower,
80 My small wrists stretching till they showed the banjo strings.
"Why, if she isn't serious about it!
Hold tight awhile till I think what to do.
I'll bend the tree down and let you down by it."
I don't know much about the letting down;
85 But once I felt ground with my stocking feet
And the world came revolving back to me,
I know I looked long at my curled-up fingers,
Before I straightened them and brushed the bark off.
My brother said: "Don't you weigh anything?
90 Try to weigh something next time, so you won't
Be run off with by birch trees into space."

It wasn't my not weighing anything
So much as my not knowing anything—
My brother had been nearer right before.
95 I had not taken the first step in knowledge;
I had not learned to let go with the hands,

As still I have not learned to with the heart,
And have no wish to with the heart—nor need,
That I can see. The mind—is not the heart.
100  I may yet live, as I know others live,
To wish in vain to let go with the mind—
Of cares, at night, to sleep; but nothing tells me
That I need learn to let go with the heart.

## DISCUSSION

*Lines 7–18*

1. (a) What was it that was "wiped out in fear"? (b) What caused this beginning, this way of behaving, to change? (c) How old was the girl when this change occurred? (line 18)

2. (a) In what sense was the girl like Eurydice? (See footnote 1.) Is there a pun in this allusion? Explain. (b) In what sense did the girl gain an extra life? (If you have difficulty answering questions 1 and 2 initially, return to them after you have discussed the entire poem.)

*Lines 19–30 (Now begins the specific experience the speaker referred to in the previous lines.)*

3. (a) Why did the girl and her brother go to the glade? (b) How does the scene described in lines 19–30 provide one kind of answer to the question posed in line 2 of the poem?

4. (a) To what are the pointed leaves and the grapes compared? How effective do you find this image? Explain. Try to describe in your own words the appearance of the tree. (b) To what is the tree itself implicitly compared?

*Lines 31–54*

5. (a) Why does the brother decide to bend branches of the tree down to the girl? (b) What does the speaker mean when she says, "The tree had me"? (c) To what does the speaker compare herself when she is hanging on to the branches?

*Lines 55–91*

6. (a) What does the brother do to try to relieve his sister's fear? (b) Is he successful? (c) What is your reaction to his remarks? Explain.

7. (a) Why doesn't the girl release her hold and drop into her brother's arms? (b) What are the "banjo strings" referred to in line 80? What is the point of referring to them? (c) About how old would you take the brother to be? On what do you base your estimate? What is your opinion of the brother? Why?

*Lines 92–103*

8. (a) What are possible meanings of "letting go with the hands"? (b) Why might this be construed as the first step in knowledge? (c) How does letting go with the hands differ from letting go with the mind?

9. (a) What is the speaker's attitude toward letting go with the mind? Toward letting go with the heart? (b) What is the difference between the two?

10. Of the following statements, which do you prefer as an expression of the central idea of the poem? If you prefer none of them, prepare your own statement of the central idea of the poem. Reread the entire poem before you attempt an answer. Be prepared to defend your choice.

(a) We learn through the body, the mind, the affections. A different wisdom applies to each kind of knowing. The certainty or the pleasure of the senses may endanger us. The concerns of the mind may become obsessions. But the affections (love) are not lightly relinquished, indeed, should not be relinquished.

(b) Wisdom consists of learning when to let go—of possessions, of cares, of people. The heart, however, has reasons the mind knows nothing of. The wisdom of letting go does not apply to the experience of the affections.

(c) Knowledge comes in stages. The first stage is to learn, perhaps through fear or disappointment, not to trust instinctive physical reaction. The next stage is to learn that the objects of thought (ideas) may not be constant, may have to be modified. The final wisdom is to trust the affections, the heart.

(d) Love stands on a different plane from common sense and from knowledge; while it may be necessary to relinquish possessions or to modify ideas, one must never turn from love.

# Autobiography

FROM

# Barrio Boy

*Ernesto Galarza*

*Ernesto Galarza's life began in Jalcocotán (häl′ cō-cō tän′), a mountain village in western Mexico. His parents had been divorced just before his birth, and his mother, Doña Henriqueta (dō′nyä en rē kā′tä), had gone to Jalcocotán to live with her sister Esther and her two brothers, Gustavo and José. The turmoil of the revolution in Mexico, which began in 1910, forced the family to make several moves, finally bringing them to the barrio in Sacramento, California, where Ernesto's uncles tried to find work and keep the family together. Ernesto Galarza eventually left the barrio, received his Ph.D. from Columbia University, and at the time of this printing lives in San Jose, California, where he is a teacher, writer, and lecturer. In Barrio Boy, he tells what life was like for a child of two cultures, growing toward manhood in his adopted country. (A Spanish-English glossary appears on page 482.)*

WE found the Americans as strange in their customs as they probably found us. Immediately we discovered that there were no *mercados* and that when shopping you did not put the groceries in a *chiquihuite*. Instead everything was in cans or in cardboard boxes or each item was put in a brown paper bag. There were neighborhood grocery stores at the corners and some big ones uptown, but no *mercado*. The grocers did not give children a *pilón*, they did not stand at the door and coax you to come in and buy, as they did in Mazatlán. The fruits and vegetables were displayed on counters instead of being piled up on the floor. The stores smelled of fly spray and oiled floors, not of fresh pineapple and limes.

Neither was there a plaza, only parks which had no bandstands, no concerts every Thursday, no Judases exploding on Holy Week,[1] and no promenades of boys going one way and girls the other. There were no parks in the *barrio*; and the ones uptown were cold and rainy in winter, and in summer there was no place to sit except on the grass. When there were celebrations nobody set off rockets in the parks, much less on the street in front of your house to announce to the neighborhood that a wedding or a baptism was taking place. Sacramento did not have a *mercado* and a plaza with the cathedral to one side and the Palacio de Gobierno on another to make it obvious that there and nowhere else was the center of the town.

It was just as puzzling that the Americans did not live in *vecindades*, like our block on Leandro Valle. Even in the alleys, where people knew one another better, the houses were fenced apart, without central courts to wash clothes, talk, and play with the other children. Like the city, the Sacramento *barrio* did not have a place which was the middle of things for everyone.

In more personal ways we had to get used to the Americans. They did not listen if you did not speak loudly, as they always did. In the Mexican style, people would know that you were enjoying their jokes tremendously if you merely smiled and shook a little, as if you were trying to swallow your mirth. In the American style there was little difference between a laugh and a roar, and until you got used to them you could hardly tell whether the boisterous Americans were roaring mad or roaring happy.

It was Doña Henriqueta more than Gustavo or José who talked of these oddities and classified them as agreeable or deplorable. It was she also who pointed out the pleasant surprises of the American way. When a box of rolled oats with a picture of red carnations on the side was emptied, there was a plate or a bowl or a cup with blue designs. We ate the strange stuff regularly for breakfast and we soon had a set of the beautiful dishes. Rice and beans we bought in cotton bags of colored prints. The bags were unsewed, washed, ironed, and made into gaily designed towels, napkins, and handkerchiefs. The American stores also gave small green stamps which were pasted in a book to exchange for prizes. We didn't have to run to the corner with the garbage; a collector came for it.

With remarkable fairness and never-ending wonder we kept adding to our list the pleasant and the repulsive in the ways of the Americans. It was my second acculturation.

The older people of the *barrio*, except in those things which they had to do like the Americans because they had no choice, remained Mexican. Their language at home was Spanish. They were continuously taking up collections to pay somebody's funeral expenses or to help someone who had had a serious accident. Cards were sent to you to attend a burial where you would throw a handful of dirt on top of the coffin and listen to tearful speeches at the graveside. At every baptism a new *compadre* and a new *comadre* joined the family circle. New Year greeting cards were exchanged, showing angels and cherubs in bright colors sprinkled with grains of mica so that they glistened like gold dust. At the family parties the huge pot of steaming tamales was still the center of attention, the *atole* served on the side with chunks of brown sugar for sucking and crunching. If the party lasted long enough, someone produced a guitar, the men took over, and the singing of *corridos* began.

In the *barrio* there were no individuals who had official titles or who were otherwise recognized by everybody as important people. The reason must have been that there was no place in the public business of the city of Sacramento for the Mexican immigrants. We only rented a corner of the city, and as long as we paid the rent on time everything else was decided at City Hall or the County Court House, where Mexicans went only when they were in trouble. Nobody from the *barrio* ever ran for mayor or city councilman. For us the most im-

---

1. *Judases exploding on Holy Week.* In Mexico on the day before Easter, papier-mâché effigies of Judas are hung with firecrackers and exploded.

portant public officials were the policemen who walked their beats, stopped fights, and hauled drunks to jail in a paddy wagon we called *La Julia.*

The one institution we had that gave the *colonia* some kind of image was the *Comisión Honorífica,* a committee picked by the Mexican Consul in San Francisco to organize the celebration of the *Cinco de Mayo*[2] and the Sixteenth of September, the anniversaries of the battle of Puebla and the beginning of our War of Independence. These were the two events which stirred everyone in the *barrio,* for what we were celebrating was not only the heroes of Mexico but also the feeling that we were still Mexicans ourselves. On these occasions there was a dance preceded by speeches and a concert. For both the *cinco* and the sixteenth, queens were elected to preside over the ceremonies.

Between celebrations neither the politicians uptown nor the *Cosmisión Honorífica* attended to the daily needs of the *barrio.* This was done by volunteers—the ones who knew enough English to interpret in court, on a visit to the doctor, a call at the county hospital, and who could help make out a postal money order. By the time I had finished the third grade at the Lincoln School I was one of these volunteers. My services were not professional but they were free, except for the IOU's I accumulated from families who always thanked me with "God will pay you for it."

My clients were not *pochos,* Mexicans who had grown up in California, probably had even been born in the United States. They had learned to speak English of sorts and could still speak Spanish, also of sorts. They knew much more about the Americans than we did, and much less about us. The *chicanos* and the *pochos* had certain feelings about one another. Concerning the *pochos,* the *chicanos* suspected that they considered themselves too good for the *barrio* but were not, for some reason, good enough for the Americans. Toward the *chicanos,* the *pochos* acted superior, amused at our confusions but not especially interested in explaining them to us. In our family when I

2. *Cinco de Mayo* (sēng′kō ᴛHā mä′yō), the fifth of May, a major national holiday in Mexico. The date commemorates the Battle of Puebla, May 5, 1862, when invading French forces were defeated by a much smaller Mexican army.

forgot my manners, my mother would ask me if I was turning *pochito.*

Turning *pocho* was a half-step toward turning American. And America was all around us, in and out of the *barrio.* Abruptly we had to forget the ways of shopping in a *mercado* and learn those of shopping in a corner grocery or in a department store. The Americans paid no attention to the Sixteenth of September, but they made a great commotion about the Fourth of July. In Mazatlán Don Salvador had told us, saluting and marching as he talked to our class, that the *Cinco de Mayo* was the most glorious date in human history. The Americans had not even heard about it.

In Tucson, when I had asked my mother again if the Americans were having a revolution, the answer was: "No, but they have good schools, and you are going to one of them." We were by now settled at 418 L Street [Sacramento] and the time had come for me to exchange a revolution for an American education.

The two of us walked south on Fifth Street one morning to the corner of Q Street and turned right. Half of the block was occupied by the Lincoln School. It was a three-story wooden building, with two wings that gave it the shape of a double-T connected by a central hall. It was a new building, painted yellow, with a shingled roof that was not like the red tile of the school in Mazatlán. I noticed other differences, none of them very reassuring.

We walked up the wide staircase hand in hand and through the door, which closed by itself. A mechanical contraption screwed to the top shut it behind us quietly.

Up to this point the adventure of enrolling me in the school had been carefully rehearsed. Mrs. Dodson[3] had told us how to find it, and we had circled it several times on our walks. Friends in the *barrio* explained that the director was called a principal, and that it was a lady and not a man. They assured us that there was always a person at the school who could speak Spanish.

Exactly as we had been told, there was a sign on the door in both Spanish and English: "Principal." We crossed the hall and entered the office of Miss Nettie Hopley.

3. *Mrs. Dodson,* the landlady at 418 L Street, where Ernesto lived.

Miss Hopley was at a roll-top desk to one side, sitting in a swivel chair that moved on wheels. There was a sofa against the opposite wall, flanked by two windows and a door that opened on a small balcony. Chairs were set around a table, and framed pictures hung on the walls of a man with long white hair and another with a sad face and a black beard.

The principal half turned in the swivel chair to look at us over the pinch glasses crossed on the ridge of her nose. To do this she had to duck her head slightly as if she were about to step through a low doorway.

What Miss Hopley said to us we did not know, but we saw in her eyes a warm welcome, and when she took off her glasses and straightened up, she smiled wholeheartedly, like Mrs. Dodson. We were, of course, saying nothing, only catching the friendliness of her voice and the sparkle in her eyes while she said words we did not understand. She signaled us to the table. Almost tiptoeing across the office, I maneuvered myself to keep my mother between me and the gringo lady. In a matter of seconds I had to decide whether she was a possible friend or a menace. We sat down.

Then Miss Hopley did a formidable thing. She stood up. Had she been standing when we entered she would have seemed tall. But rising from her chair she soared. And what she carried up and up with her was a buxom superstructure, firm shoulders, a straight sharp nose, full cheeks slightly molded by a curved line along the nostrils, thin lips that moved like steel springs, and a high forehead topped by hair gathered in a bun. Miss Hopley was not a giant in body, but when she mobilized it to a standing position she seemed a match for giants. I decided I liked her.

She strode to a door in the far corner of the office, opened it and called a name. A boy of about ten years appeared in the doorway. He sat down at one end of the table. He was brown like us, a plump kid with shiny black hair combed straight back, neat, cool, and faintly obnoxious.

Miss Hopley joined us with a large book and some papers in her hand. She, too, sat down, and the questions and answers began by way of our interpreter. My name was Ernesto.

My mother's name was Henriqueta. My birth certificate was in San Blas. Here was my last report card from the Escuela Municipal Numero 3 para Varones of Mazatlán, and so forth. Miss Hopley put things down in the book and my mother signed a card.

As long as the questions continued, Doña Henriqueta could stay and I was secure. Now that they were over, Miss Hopley saw her to the door, dismissed our interpreter, and without further ado took me by the hand and strode down the hall to Miss Ryan's first grade.

Miss Ryan took me to a seat at the front of the room, into which I shrank—the better to survey her. She was, to skinny, somewhat runty me, of a withering height when she patrolled the class. And when I least expected it, there she was, crouching by my desk, her blond radiant face level with mine, her voice patiently maneuvering me over the awful idiocies of the English language.

During the next few weeks Miss Ryan overcame my fears of tall, energetic teachers as she bent over my desk to help me with a word in the pre-primer. Step by step, she loosened me and my classmates from the safe anchorage of the desks for recitations at the blackboard and consultations at her desk. Frequently she burst into happy announcements to the whole class. "Ito can read a sentence," and small Japanese Ito, squint-eyed and shy, slowly read aloud while the class listened in wonder: "Come, Skipper, come. Come and run." The Korean, Portuguese, Italian, and Polish first graders had similar moments of glory, no less shining than mine the day I conquered *butterfly*, which I had been persistently pronouncing in standard Spanish as *boo-ter-flee*. "Children," Miss Ryan called for attention. "Ernesto has learned how to pronounce *butterfly!*" And I proved it with a perfect imitation of Miss Ryan. From that celebrated success, I was soon able to match Ito's progress as a sentence reader with "Come, butterfly, come fly with me."

Like Ito and several other first graders who did not know English, I received private lessons from Miss Ryan in the closet, a narrow hall off the classroom with a door at each end. Next to one of these doors Miss Ryan placed a large chair for herself and a small one for me. Keeping an eye on the class through the open door, she read with me about sheep in the meadow and a frightened chicken going to see the king, coaching me out of my phonetic ruts in words like *pasture, bow-wow-wow, hay*, and *pretty*, which to my Mexican ear and eye had so many unnecessary sounds and letters. She made me watch her lips and then close my eyes as she repeated words I found hard to read. When we came to know each other better, I tried interrupting to tell Miss Ryan how we said it in Spanish. It didn't work. She only said "oh" and went on with *pasture, bow-wow-wow*, and *pretty*. It was as if in that closet we were both discovering together the secrets of the English language and grieving together over the tragedies of Bo-Peep. The main reason I was graduated with honors from the first grade was that I had fallen in love with Miss Ryan. Her radiant, no-nonsense character made us either afraid not to love her or love her so we would not be afraid, I am not sure which. It was not only that we sensed she was with it, but also that she was with us.

Like the first grade, the rest of the Lincoln School was a sampling of the lower part of town where many races made their home. My pals in the second grade were Kazushi, whose parents spoke only Japanese; Matti, a skinny Italian boy; and Manuel, a fat Portuguese who would never get into a fight but wrestled you to the ground and just sat on you. Our assortment of nationalities included Koreans, Yugoslavs, Poles, Irish, and home-grown Americans.

Miss Hopley and her teachers never let us forget why we were at Lincoln: for those who were alien, to become good Americans; for those who were so born, to accept the rest of us. Off the school grounds we traded the same insults we heard from our elders. On the playground we were sure to be marched up to the principal's office for calling someone a wop, a chink, a dago, or a greaser. The school was not so much a melting pot as a griddle where Miss Hopley and her helpers warmed knowledge into us and roasted racial hatreds out of us.

At Lincoln, making us into Americans did not mean scrubbing away what made us originally foreign. The teachers called us as our parents did, or as close as they could pronounce our names in Spanish or Japanese. No one was ever scolded or punished for speaking in his native tongue on the playground. Matti told the class about his mother's down quilt, which she had made in Italy with the fine feathers of a thousand geese. Encarnación acted out how boys learned to fish in the Philippines. I astounded the third grade with the story of my travels on a stagecoach, which nobody else in the class had seen except in the museum at Sutter's Fort. After a visit to the Crocker Art Gallery and its collection of heroic paintings of the golden age of California, someone showed a silk scroll with a Chinese painting. Miss Hopley herself had a way of expressing wonder over these matters before a class, her eyes wide open until they popped slightly. It was easy for me to feel that becoming a proud American, as she said we should, did not mean feeling ashamed of being a Mexican.

The Americanization of Mexican me was no smooth matter. I had to fight one lout who made fun of my travels on the *diligencia*, and my barbaric translation of the word into "diligence." He doubled up with laughter over the word until I straightened him out with a kick. In class I made points explaining that in Mexico roosters said "qui-qui-ri-qui" and not "cock-a-doodle-doo," but after school I had to put up with the taunts of a big Yugoslav who said Mexican roosters were crazy.

But it was Homer who gave me the most lasting lesson for a future American.

Homer was a chunky Irishman who dressed as if every day was Sunday. He slicked his hair between a crew cut and a pompadour. And Homer was smart, as he clearly showed when he and I ran for president of the third grade.

Everyone understood that this was to be a demonstration of how the American people vote for president. In an election, the teacher explained, the candidates could be generous and vote for each other. We cast our ballots in a shoe box and Homer won by two votes. I polled my supporters and came to the conclusion that I had voted for Homer and so had he. After class he didn't deny it, reminding me of what the teacher had said—we could vote for each other but didn't have to. . . .

One thing that wasn't taught at the Lincoln School, but which I learned from experience, was that a place has to have somebody in charge to decide things and organize them. At 418 L that somebody was Mrs. Dodson, and she organized matters from her apartment on the second floor rear. Running errands for her, I went in and out of the apartment often. I stepped softly on the rug, afraid to scuff it. There was a mahogany console with a record player and on the inside of the cover a picture of a white dog listening to the music coming from a tin horn. Above the victrola there was a picture of a naked lady standing ankle deep in a pool, which looked cold because the lady was holding her arms in front of her, her hands on her knees. In one corner of the parlor sat a huge brown teddy bear watching the glass bead curtain between the parlor and the kitchen that tinkled every time you went through it. The apartment was a decorated, cozy place I liked to visit except for Pinkey, Mrs. Dodson's pint-sized lap dog with toothpick legs and a nasty temper. He annoyed me with his squeaky bark which said plainly he didn't want me there.

Except for ourselves, the tenants of 418 L were far from being a family; they were more like a collection. There was something peculiar about each one; they were people who stayed out of each other's way but who didn't mind being noticed and who noticed you. I went for Mr. Howard's laundry and he loaned me a book called *Enoch Arden*. The Old Gentleman knocked on our wall when he was ready to put on his necktie and coat, a signal for me to go and help him. Every now and then he pressed a dime into my hand or bought me a chocolate bar when I walked with him to the corner and back. My mother helped the Indian lady with her wash, and she took me to the State Fair one summer where she bought me a whip and a cowboy belt. Tenants came and went, but the familiar characters like us stayed on. From them my circle of acquaintances and friends began to spread around the block.

One of the first of these was Big Singh, the brawny Hindu who ran a boarding house next door for his fellow countrymen. Big Singh with his thick black beard always wore a dark turban wound around his head and a white apron from his neck to his ankles. His side porch looked over our yard and Big Singh would lean on the railing chatting with us in the few English words he knew. I became Big Singh's tutor, for he often asked me how to say certain words in English, which I supplied with complete confidence. As a show of appreciation he hired me to work in his kitchen on Saturday afternoons to turn over the thick flour cakes he prepared for his boarders and which he called *ruti*. On weekends many of the Sikh[4] laborers came there to eat and sleep. They were all enormous, like Big Singh, and all wore beards and turbans of different colors.

Up the street from us, toward Fourth, there was Miss Florence, who lived in a second-story flat and accompanied herself on the piano. She sang, very loudly, a song called "I Want Sympathy," swooping up and down the bars melodiously like someone on a long, high swing. She beat rugs on her front porch and called out to me when she saw me pass by. Her rugged, unlovely face broke into smiles when I called back, as I always did, "Miss Florence, sing 'Sympathy'." . . .

Halfway down the alley lived a Yugoslav who worked in the railroad shops and ran a bowling alley. It was a dirt strip, tamped down, with a border of planks. On Sundays the Slavs gathered to play bocce,[5] and once a year the alley was covered with boards and turned into a winery. A large press was brought out of the cellar, and the men, chattering and drinking, pressed the grapes with their bare feet, their pants rolled up above the knees. They offered me nips of wine and lowered me into the press to tramp grapes myself.

At the Fourth Street end of the alley there was a fish shop run by a Japanese who sometimes bought from me the catfish I caught in the river. We never argued about the price. As with the laundryman, ours was a speechless acquaintance, my fish and his nickels crossing

---

**4.** *Sikh* (sēk), member of a Hindu religious sect of Northern India.
**5.** *bocce* (boch′ē), lawn bowling on a narrow court.

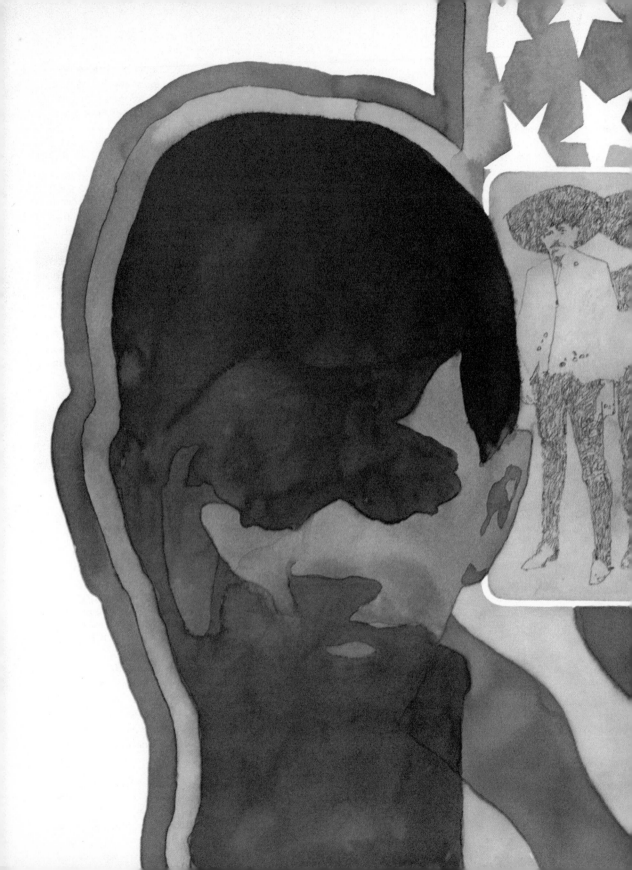

the counter in opposite directions, without a word being said.

This was our alley, along with the shanties, the barns, and the sagging cottages behind picket or plank fences. It was a refuge for sleeping drunks, and I often passed by them looking for gunny sacks, beer bottles, and scraps of tinfoil.

A different type altogether was Lettie, who lived next door in a rooming house very much like 418 L. She was petite, dark skinned, sculptured, and vivacious. She performed every night at a dance hall near Second Street. If I wasn't off on an errand I made it a point to sit on the flat-topped newel post of the front staircase of our house. When she passed on her way to work—with a red rose in her hair, lips rouged like her flower, eyelashes painted like coal, a tight velvet jacket with silver buttons, a flouncy miniskirt, lace stockings and black slippers—she always mesmerized me. People on the second-story porch followed Miss Lettie with their eyes as long as they could. I could see her until she turned into the dance hall. I ran errands for her and taught Albert, her son who was several years younger than I, to play marbles and whittle. When I was baby-sitting with Albert we played the victrola and looked at pictures of his mother in dancing poses tacked on the walls.

Less familiar to me were other characters of the lower part of town, people like Frisco, Speedy, and Shorty Lopez. Frisco played the piano in the saloon at the corner, always wearing a black vest and a straw hat. I couldn't watch him through the swinging doors of the saloon, but I often saw him walk in and out, and I could hear him banging out his tunes. Mr. Hans, who knew music, said that nobody could play "1912" and "Alexander's Ragtime Band" like Frisco. Speedy was a messenger boy who carried trays with dinners to hotels and rooming houses, balancing them on a flat cap with an upraised visor as he pedaled full speed on a bicycle.

But by far most of my admiration was for Lopez, a Mexican known to the gringos as Shorty and to us as Cho-ree. The nickname was unavoidable for he was several inches short of legs to match his barrel chest and the head and arms of a tall, powerful man. For that kind of a body Cho-ree had the perfect job. He drove a team of regal percherons harnessed to a beer truck with a platform that hung low over the street. Shorty delivered beer to the saloons, driving his team perched high on the truck, slapping them with the reins and himself jouncing from side to side like a prize rider at a horse show. He wrestled beer kegs on and off his truck all day long, but when he passed by 418 L, he was a charioteer master of two magnificent chargers.

Just as Cho-ree excited me to become a beer truck driver and Mr. Hans a horn player, Mr. Howard was affectionately trying to make me a scholar. He loved books and was always buying used ones on his travels. After *Enoch Arden* he gave me a Horatio Alger, reading paragraphs here and there to get me started. On the shelf of the wooden box that stood by my bunk I lined up Mr. Howard's gifts, which I read after I was sent to bed. Next to them stood the cloak-and-dagger novels in Spanish my mother handed on to me in which I read of noble ladies whose husbands were murdered and avenged, good guys and bad ones killing one another in moonlight duels; and the adventures of Cacaseno, who saved himself from being hanged by getting a promise from the King of Spain that he could choose the tree from which to be strung up, and never finding one that was quite suitable.

To this select, bilingual library Mr. Howard one day added a frayed copy of Blackstone's *Commentaries on the Common Law of England,* a thick book with black covers, small print, broken corners, and no pictures except one of the formidable, bewigged Lord Justice himself. Mr. Howard explained that he had bought it for me to read, if I should decide to become a lawyer. As I did with everything he gave me, I tried making sense of the *Commentaries,* finally leaving it on the bookshelf to read later, much later. I asked Mr. Howard to be on the lookout for a copy of Tio Tonche[6] which we had lost somewhere between Mazatlán and Sacramento. He had never heard of the work and never turned one up.

---

6. *Tio Tonche* (tē′ō tōn′chä), the main character in the first book Ernesto owned, *The Tales of Tio Tonche.*

Our block provided me with adventurers as well as scholars. Mr. Charley, who lived in a basement room with a dirt floor under Big Singh's boarding house, introduced me to history with a bang.

Mr. Charley was an elderly, slouching man who wore loose clothes and a cavalry hat slanted over his right ear. His moustache was enormous, twice as long as Mr. Brien's and a match for his thick eyebrows. On the Fourth of July we celebrated privately and secretly in his dark and stuffy little room. He invited me, Catfish, and Russell, two neighborhood boys of about my age, to what he called his own fireworks.

Mr. Charley sat us on the floor and told the story of his charge up San Juan Hill with Colonel Teddy Roosevelt. He dispatched, so he said, dozens of Spaniards with his two horse pistols. Pointing to the wall he exclaimed: "With them," and he took the two enormous irons carefully out of the holsters. Holding one in each hand he fired them by turns into the ground. The little room shook and filled with the smell of burnt powder. The explosions sounded like the torpedoes that people were setting off in the street above us so that no one could suspect that some real shooting was going on.

Choking delightfully from the gunsmoke and shaken wonderfully by the blasts, we sat and listened to Mr. Charley's glorious account of how he and Colonel Roosevelt won the war. When the pistols were back in the holsters he let us out with a caution not to tell anybody. "The pistols," he said, "make a hell of a bang. I can't shoot them except on the Fourth of July, when everybody thinks they are torpedoes." On the promise that he would show us more fireworks the next Fourth, we kept his secret.

Girolamo, who worked at the pasta factory three blocks from our place, had not read Blackstone or fought at San Juan, but he made macaroni. A barrel stood in the alley behind the factory into which "seconds" of macaroni, spaghetti, tagliarini, and vermicelli, were dropped. By sorting through these discards I could gather a bag of clean, fresh pasta, which my mother made into soup.

Whenever Girolamo saw me at my gleaning he came over with a fistful of whatever he was making at the moment and put it in my paper bag. We talked, he in Italian, I in Spanish. When he went back to his machines I could see him pouring flour dough into a metal tub high on an iron frame, squeezing it through a mold and cutting with a large knife the white threads of macaroni that came out below. Girolamo, who talked to me with waving arms and gentle pinches to make a point, shouting and making musical grunts all the while, made me think that perhaps the life of a macaroni maker was just as interesting as that of a lawyer or a Rough Rider.[7]

The *barrio*, without particularly planning it that way, was providing me with an education out of school as well as in. I did not think of 418 L Street and the Lincoln School as in any way alike, but both had a principal, Miss Hopley and Mrs. Dodson. From Miss Hopley I learned that the man with the black beard and the sad eyes pictured on her wall was Abraham Lincoln, for whom our school was named. From Mrs. Dodson I found out that the picture of the nude lady was *September Morn* and that it was a famous painting. Miss Hopley conducted me firmly and methodically through the grades into the new world of books and manners she called America. Mrs. Dodson adopted us into the odd company of the rooming house, from which I found my way through the *barrio*.

When the Sumo wrestlers from Japan put on a match in a tent raised on a vacant lot, somebody in the house got me a job giving out handbills and a pass for my work. Wedged in a Japanese audience I saw two mountains of fat dressed in loincloths trying to kill each other. At 418 L with the help of my neighbors, I lined up business for a traveling photographer who took pictures of children sitting on a donkey that reminded me, joyfully, of our Relámpago in Jalcocotán. Mr. Hans gave us front porch lectures on the electric automobiles that passed by—stiff black boxes gliding by without a sound and without a smell with stiff ladies at the steering bar, also in black. There was an arrangement with the bartender on Fourth

---

7. *Rough Rider*, member of a volunteer regiment of cavalry, organized by Theodore Roosevelt for service in the Spanish-American War.

Street by which I could buy a pail of draught beer by signaling him from the alley door marked "Family Entrance." The cop on the beat objected mildly to this, as he did to Choree's allowing me to nip rides on his truck. To please him we did it only when he was somewhere else in the *barrio*.

Once in a while, I also managed to get around the rule that I was not to run to skid row whenever a street fight was on. These fights were regular, especially on Saturday nights, and the news of a brawl spread fast. If they happened when I was on the waterfront my attendance at these bloody events was no problem. I simply joined the crowd. In one of these fights I saw Speedy and another American battle with their fists, both men streaming blood from their faces. The fight between two Mexicans was something memorable. I arrived in time to see the police loading the winner into the paddy wagon, and the loser lying in the alley in a bloody shirt. And there was the fire in our alley that burned down a shack and cremated an old man who lived there. A house was blown up on T Street, by the Black Hand,[8] it was said. I walked by the place with Catfish stealthily. We thought we could see the smudged imprint of the Hand on the blasted chimney.

When there was a fight, a fire, or a murder the government paid a great deal of attention to the *barrio*. Police and firemen swarmed around for a while. We never called the police, they just came. José explained the wisdom of this to me. "When *los chotas* start asking questions," he said, "you never know what they will ask next." About one thing the entire *barrio* seemed to be in agreement: the dirtiest, most low-down human being was the stool pigeon, the sneak who turned you in to the Authorities. . . .

Going to school did not prevent me from continuing my career as a working member of the family, which I had started as apprentice to La Pozolera.[9] Whatever the surprising differences between Mazatlán and the *barrio* in Sacramento, in one thing they were powerfully the same—*trabajo*. If you didn't have it you spent the days looking for it. If you had it, you worried about how long it would last. You didn't spoil your chances of being hired by asking questions about wages or food or paydays. The thing to avoid was to pass the winter in the *barrio* without money, *de oquis*—without a job. New *chicanos* kept coming. They tramped the muddy alleys and the streets, gathering in small groups on the sidewalks of skid row when it was sunny, inside the poolhalls when it was hot. All this they found out, and other important things: that if you got to know a labor contractor well he would lend you money to carry you over the winter; that once you became a regular customer of the pawnbroker you could hock tools, musical instruments, and even clothes; that there were Mexican families who would feed you on credit until spring; that in cold weather several men could sleep in a small room without heat.

Taking stock of the situation, the family was already minus my mother's wages as a seamstress. The letters to the neighbor who had kept the Ajax[10] for us in Mazatlán were never answered, and we at last realized we had lost it. Besides, nobody in the *barrio* had money to pay for sewing. Our apartment at 418 L became more of a base than a home for Gustavo and José. When they could they worked on the riverfront, in the railroad shops, the canneries, lumber yards, pipe plants, stables, and nearby rice mills. When they couldn't, they rolled their clothes and blankets into bindles, hobo style, and walked the railway tracks to Woodland, Roseville, Stockton, Marysville, or Folsom for fruit picking, building construction, wood chopping, or sand hogging. When river traffic was at the peak in the summer and fall, they loaded grain on the barges or shipped as deckhands on the stern-wheelers that paddled between Colusa and San Francisco Bay. And one winter they walked to Truckee for a week's wages at a lumber mill.

We still called it *hacerle la lucha*, the daily match with the job givers, layoffs, the rent, groceries, and the seasons. I was never told, and I never asked, about getting into the *lucha*.

---

**8.** *the Black Hand,* the name and symbol of a secret criminal society organized for blackmail and acts of violence.
**9.** *La Pozolera* (lä pō'sō lā'ra), the owner of a sidewalk restaurant in Mazatlán (mä'sät län'), Mexico, where Ernesto had his first job.

**10.** *the Ajax,* Ernesto's mother's sewing machine.

I simply asked permission to do the *trabajos* that I found, one by one, in the *barrio*.

Matti, my Italian buddy, coached me into selling the *Sacramento Union* on Sixth and K, where he made room on one corner for me. He showed me how to manage the small change. The rest I learned watching and listening to him yell the headlines and rush his customers. By school time I was through, had reported home, counted out my cash on the kitchen table, turned it over to my mother, and had breakfast. It was Matti also who pointed out that I could keep a copy of the *Union* to take home, the first regular newspaper we had in the house. At night I picked out words from the headlines and read them to whoever would listen. It was I who brought the headlines home that said an Austrian duke had been assassinated and that there was a war.[11]

Lincoln School and the *barrio* cooperated to help me get further into *la lucha*. I never had any homework. I took my books home to show off but never to prepare lessons. This meant that Miss Campbell or Miss Delahunty or Mrs. Wood did not interfere with my free working time after school or on Saturdays.

I worked up a small income as a part-time bellhop and house boy in the rooming house. Nobody at 418 L could scamper up and down the three stories or relay a laundry package to the alley and back as fast as I, or beat rugs with a stick on the laundry wire and hang blankets out to air. I wasn't paid in tips, but on Saturdays people flipped a nickel or a dime at me, and on holidays as much as a quarter. For me there was a smooth flow between these money-making employments and my tasks in our apartment—making my bed, sweeping the backyard, and checking the rat traps under the floor.

My services as a valet to the Old Gentleman next door brought ten cents a week, for nothing more than a fast hand when he dressed and undressed. After I noticed Big Singh cooking some round cakes on a grill in his kitchen, he offered me one through the window, saying "*Ruti, ruti.*" I climbed the fence to the window, took the cake, examined it and said, "No, tortilla." Big Singh roared, asked me to come in, and offered me a part-time job helping him with the baking. I checked with my mother, she checked with Mrs. Dodson, and permission was granted. I flipped the *ruti* on the griddle with my fingernails in a way that astounded the Sikh giant. On Saturdays I cooked *ruti* for him which the boarders ate by the basket, not unlike Mexicans ate tortillas.

After the Saturday morning chores and errands at the house I had almost the whole of Saturday to myself. With Matti, Catfish, and Russell as my instructors and guides, the entire *barrio* became my bonanza. With a gunny sack over my shoulder I collected empty beer bottles, tinfoil, discarded rags, bits of copper wire the linemen dropped around telephone poles, and pieces of scrap iron.

This was how I met the Negro lady who lived in the shanty on the alley behind our house. She was jet black, bigger sidewise than up and down, with eyes as bright as agates. Her backyard was noisy with laughter and loud talk, especially on Saturday nights, and the police sometimes came and took her away for a few days. One morning I asked for some empty beer bottles I spotted in the corner of her yard just inside the picket fence. I had to explain to her where I lived, why I wanted the bottles, and who my folks were. We turned out to be such close neighbors that she offered to pile all her empties in a box by the gate. The only condition was that I was not to come into the yard, but to call her. As long as she was allowed to live in the alley, I collected enough empties from her to give me a good start on my Saturday rounds. Next to her bottles I liked her musical, hooting laugh that seemed to explode merrily out of her whole body.

The alleys, I discovered, were the poorer part of my claim. The best payoff was along the riverfront, the railway tracks, the wharves, the produce markets, and the warehouses. Sacks and crates were moved about on handtrucks over iron sheets placed between the freight cars and the loading platforms. When a sack ripped or a crate broke, potatoes, onions, beets, and apples rolled about. The stevedores kicked

---

11. *Austrian duke . . . war.* The assassination of Archduke Francis Ferdinand of Austria-Hungary by a Serbian nationalist in 1914 precipitated World War I (1914–1918).

them aside so they would spill to the ground, where I salvaged them. On the wharves where the company guards were friendly, we were allowed to scrounge in the unloaded box cars for specialties like cracked watermelons or bouquets of carrots. On a good Saturday, combing the waterfront all day, I could supply the family with all our needs of potatoes or onions for the week.

José taught me to fish, and I carried a line in my pants pocket on my rounds. If the pickings were light on the wharves I climbed down the bank of the river between the warehouses and threw my line close to where the cooks on the stern wheelers threw the garbage into the water. Waiting for a bite, I sat on the rocks, listening to the lap of the river against the barges and the piles, and to the rumble of the handtrucks the stevedores pushed back and forth on the plank floors high above me. It was cool under the wharves. Through the tall black piles I could see framed pictures of tugboats straining their hawsers towing barges piled high with sacks of grain; the *Fort Sutter* or the *Capital City*, the floating palaces that sailed every night for San Francisco from their moorings at the M Street bridge; the struts and girders of the bridge above the muddy brown sweep of the Sacramento; and the wooded shore of Yolo beyond. There was a mile or so of riverfront like this, and I possessed it all.

*Haciendole la lucha* in my own way I found out how jobs are lost, and sometimes friends along with the jobs. One day the black lady was taken off by the police and never came back. Big Singh, during a Saturday carousal, threw one of his drunken guests over the railing of his porch to the sidewalk. My mother and Mrs. Dodson decided to end my employment as kitchen assistant because of the danger of my being trapped under a falling Sikh. . . .

Rules were laid down to keep me, as far as possible, *un muchacho bien educado*. If I had to spit I was to do it privately, or if in public, by the curb, with my head down and my back to people. I was never to wear my cap in the house and I was to take it off even on the porch if ladies or elderly gentlemen were sitting. If I wanted to scratch, under no circumstances was I to do it right then and there, in company, like the Americans, but I was to excuse myself. If Catfish or Russell yelled to me from across the street, I was not to shout back. I was never to ask for tips for my errands or other services to the tenants of 418 L, for these were *atenciones* expected of me.

Above all I was never to fail in *respeto* to grown-ups, no matter who they were. It was an inflexible rule; I addressed myself to *Señor* Big Singh, *Señor* Big Ernie, *Señora* Dodson, *Señor* Cho-ree Lopez.

My standing in the family, but especially with my mother depended on my keeping these rules. I was not punished for breaking them. She simply reminded me that it gave her acute *vergüenza* to see me act thus, and that I would never grow up to be a correct *jefe de familia* if I did not know how to be a correct boy. I knew what *vergüenza* was from feeling it time and again; and the notion of growing up to keep a tight rein over a family of my own was somehow satisfying.

In our musty apartment in the basement of 418 L, ours remained a Mexican family. I never lost the sense that we were the same, from Jalco[12] to Sacramento. There was the polished cedar box, taken out now and then from the closet to display our heirlooms. I had lost the rifle shells of the revolution, and Tio Tonche, too, was gone. But there was the butterfly serape, the one I had worn through the Battle of Puebla; a black lace mantilla Doña Henriqueta modeled for us; bits of embroidery and lace she had made; the tin pictures of my grandparents; my report card signed by Señorita Bustamante and Don Salvador; letters from Aunt Esther; and the card with the address of the lady who had kept the Ajax for us. When our mementos were laid out on the bed I plunged my head into the empty box and took deep breaths of the aroma of *puro cedro*, pure Jalcocotán mixed with camphor.

12. *Jalco*, Jalcocotán, the village where Ernesto was born.

## DISCUSSION

1. What were some of the strange American customs that Doña Henriqueta and her family found agreeable? Why were they pleased with these customs?

2. What American customs did they classify as deplorable? How did these customs contrast with Mexican customs that they missed?

3. What was the difference between the *chicanos* and the *pochos*? What "certain feelings" did the *chicanos* and the *pochos* have about one another?

4. (a) What does the author mean when he says that Lincoln School was ". . . not so much a melting pot as a griddle . . ."? (b) What methods did the school practice to Americanize the students? (c) How did the teachers make it possible for the students to maintain pride in their original cultures? (d) Why did Ernesto regard the lesson he learned from Homer as his most lasting lesson in Americanization?

5. What did Ernesto learn from each of the following people? (a) Mrs. Dodson, (b) Mr. Howard, (c) Cho-ree Lopez, (d) Mr. Charley.

6. (a) In what ways did Ernesto contribute to the family fortunes? (b) Would a young boy living in a *barrio* today be likely to do some of the same jobs? Why or why not?

7. What advantages were there to the *barrio* Ernesto lived in that would probably not be present in a *barrio* today?

# spanish-english glossary

(See page 594 for pronunciation key.)

**atenciones** (ä′ten syō′näs), attentions, acts of courtesy, duties, responsibilities.

**atole** (ä tō′lä), corn gruel, about the consistency of thin mush.

**barrio** (bär′yō), a chiefly Spanish-speaking community or neighborhood in a U.S. city.

**chiquihuite** (chē′kē wē′tä), a wicker basket with a looped handle, used for shopping in the *mercado*.

**chota** (chō′tä), the police, a policeman.

**colonia** (kō lō′nyä), that part of a city where foreigners live, more or less apart and according to nationality; the members of such a nationality; for instance, the *colonia americana de Mazatlán*.

**comadre** (kō mä′ℱHrä), in this context, a lady's relationship to parents whose baby she has presented for baptism, of whom she is the *madrina*.

**Comision Honorifica** (kō′mē syō′nō nō rē′-fē kä), honorable committee.

**compadre** (kôm pä′ℱHrä), a gentleman's relationship to the parents of a baby he has presented for baptism, of whom he is the *padrino*; two adult males may bestow the honorary title of *compadre* on each other to indicate fondness.

**corrido** (kô rē′ℱHō), a dramatic or heroic story sung to the accompaniment of guitars; a sort of Mexican folk opera on subjects such as The Disobedient Son, The Great Flood of Papasquiaro, Juan Charrasqueado the Valiant One.

**diligencia** (dē′lē hen′syä), stagecoach.

**gringo** (grēng′gō), a white-skinned foreigner, but especially an American.

**hacerle la lucha** (ä ser′lä lä lü′chä), to make one's living, to try hard.

**jefe de familia** (hä′fä ℱHä fä mē′lyä), the head of the family, called *el jefe* for short.

**mercado** (mer kä′ℱHō), marketplace.

**muchacho bien educado** (mü chä′chō bye′nä dü kä′ℱHō), well-educated or well-brought-up boy.

**Palacio de Gobierno** (pä lä′syō ℱHä gō byer′-nō), in Mexico, a capitol building, a seat of government.

**pilón** (pē lōn′), a bonus given to children by grocerymen, such as a chip of *panocha* or a jelly bean.

**puro cedro** (pü′rō sä′ℱHrō), pure cedar.

**respeto** (räs pä′tō), consideration and esteem for one's elders, and all the ways in which such esteem is shown.

**trabajo** (trä bä′hō), work.

**vecindades** (bä′sēn dä′ℱHäs), neighborhoods.

**verguenza** (ber gwen′sä), a sense of shame, of personal dignity; conscience; doing right; modesty; responsible behavior; trustworthiness not based on the fear of being caught.

# VULTURE COUNTRY

*John D. Stewart*

SPAIN is the stronghold of the vultures. There are four listed species in Europe, two common and two rare; if they are anywhere, they are in Spain. The bearded vulture and the black survive there, the Egyptian flourishes, and the great griffon swarms. The further south you go the more numerous they become, until you reach the hot grazing plains of Andalusia.[1] There, summer and winter through, they hang in hordes in the roofless sky, for Andalusia is the vulture country.

1.  *Andalusia,* a plainlike region in the southern Spanish province of Seville.

There are three essential qualities for vulture country: a rich supply of unburied corpses, high mountains, a strong sun. Spain has the first of these, for in this sparsely populated and stony land it is not customary, or necessary, to bury dead animals. Where there are vultures in action such burial would be a self-evident waste of labor, with inferior sanitary results. Spain has mountains, too, in no part far to seek; and the summer sun is hot throughout the country. But it is hottest in Andalusia, and that is the decisive factor.

The sun, to the vulture, is not just something which makes life easier and pleasanter, a mere matter of preference. His mode of life is impossible without it. Here in Andalusia the summer sun dries up every pond and lake and almost every river. It drives the desperate frogs deep into the mud cracks and forces the storks to feed on locusts. It kills the food plants and wilts the fig trees over the heads of the panting flocks. Andalusia becomes like that part of ancient Greece, "a land where men fight for the shade of an ass."

All animals, both tame and wild, weaken in these circumstances, and the weakest go to the wall and die. The unpitying sun glares down on the corpses and speeds their putrefaction, rotting the hide and softening the sinews and the meat, to the vulture's advantage. But the sun plays a still greater part in his life. Its main and vital function, for him, is the creation of thermal currents in the atmosphere, for without these he would be helpless.

The vulture must fly high—high enough to command a wide territory, for, except at times of catastrophe, dead animals are never thick on the ground. His task is to soar to ten thousand feet, more or less, two or three times in a day, and to hang there and keep constant survey. A male griffon weighs up to sixteen pounds, so that to hoist himself up to that necessary viewpoint would call for fifty-three thousand calories, the equivalent of fifty pounds of meat. To find and eat three times his own weight in a day is clearly impossible; a short cut must be made. In the dawn of any day, in Andalusia, you may see the vulture discovering that short cut.

The eagles, buzzards, kites, and falcons are already on the wing, quartering the plain fast and low, seeking reptiles and small game. But the vulture sits on a crag and waits. He sees the sun bound up out of the sierra, and still he waits. He waits until the sun-struck rocks and the hard earth heat up and the thermal currents begin to rise. When the upstream is strong enough, he leaps out from the cliff, twists into it, and without one laborious wingbeat, spirals and soars.

By the time the vulture reaches his station, a half hour later and maybe more, the sun is blazing down on the plain and betraying every detail to his telescopic eye, and the updraft is strengthening as the day approaches its zenith. His ceiling for this day is fixed by two factors. One is the strength and buoyancy of his chosen thermal, which will vary with the strength of the sun and the behavior of the upper winds. But the more important factor, for it fixes his horizontal bearings as well, is the distribution of neighboring vultures in the sky, his colleagues and competitors.

He cocks his head from side to side and checks their various positions. There they hang, dotted across the clear sky at intervals of a mile or so—at the corners of one-mile squares. Height and lateral distances all adjusted, the vulture settles, circling slowly on his invisible support, and begins his long and lonely vigil.

This griffon vulture, which I select from the four species as being by far the most prevalent and typical, is almost sure to be a male. The female rarely leaves her nest from early March, when she lays her rough white egg, until August, when her huge poult is fledged and flying. The father has to feed and carry for all three.

At first glance, from below, he appears as one great wing, ten feet from tip to tip and two feet broad. His tail is square and very short, which is all it needs to be, for there are no sharp or sudden quirks in his flight that would call for a strong rudder. His movements are premeditated, stressless, and leisurely, for his energy must be conserved at all costs and never wasted on aerobatics.

The vulture's head and neck, too, protrude very little in front of his wing plane, and this distinguishes his flight silhouette from the eagle's. His neck is, in fact, some two feet long, but since it is bare—and must be bare—he folds it back into his collar to keep it warm. His head, apart from its nakedness, is like an eagle's; his yellow claws, which never kill and rarely carry, are shorter and not so strong. His plumage is a uniform sandy color, faded and tattered by work and waiting and, perhaps, by old age. It is relieved only by his coffee-colored ruff and the broad black primary wing feathers fingering the air.

The vulture sails in silence, for no vocal signals could serve him at such a distance from his fellows. He croaks, growls, and whistles only in his family circle, and at his feasts. He circles by almost imperceptible adjustments of his wing planes, aided by slight twists of his tail. But his head is in constant and active movement. He swivels it from one side to the other, bringing each eye in turn to bear on the earth. Then he bends his neck to right or left to check on one of his neighbors to north, south, east, or west.

The whole vulture network is interdependent. Each vulture can give and receive two signals or, as the scientists call them, "visual stimuli." Circling means "Nothing doing"; dropping, or its resultant hole in the sky, calls "Come here!" Like all other vultures, he rests reassured by the first and is rapidly and relentlessly drawn by the second.

It is demonstrable how, with a special density of nerve endings on his retina, the vulture can see a small animal from a great height. Many other birds—gannets, for example—have the same propensity. Their eyesight is surprising only when we compare it with the poor standards of our own. But a mystery remains: how does the bird know that the animal is dead? The sense of smell is to be ruled out straightway. It is impossible that it would operate at such a distance, even allowing for the upward current of air. Birds are not, generally, well endowed in this respect, and in the vulture's case this may be especially fortunate.

No book, no expert, could answer this question for me, and I carried it through the vulture country for years, the one tantalizing imponderable, the broken link. Then, one hot afternoon, I lay down beside an old swineherd in the shade

of a cork oak on the foothills overlooking the great plain of La Janda. For fifty years, he told me, he had watched pigs on that plain—the pigs, yes, and the vultures. I put my problem to him.

The swineherd's theory is not to be proved, but it is a wise one and I shall hold it until I find a better. No, he said, it is not the white belly skin that distinguishes the dead animals. White fur may fix the vulture's eye, but it does not offer him evidence of death. All herds and flocks, said the old man, lie down together and at one time. They have their place and their hour of rest. When a vulture sees an animal lying alone and apart, he is bound to notice it. The next time he crosses, the same image strikes his eye and startles him again. Over and over again he marks it and waits and watches; but now, alerted, he watches it more closely.

The next day the animal is still there; his attention is fixed upon it now; so he circles a little lower, his eye riveted, seeking the slightest movement of limb or lung. He sees none, but he continues to wait, said the old man. It takes him two days, at least, to confirm death. He goes on circling, but lower. He becomes more engrossed, and more sure. The other vultures note his behavior and move over a little in the sky. Every time he falls, they move closer. Now he is very low. He seeks the heaving of the flanks or eye movements; he sees neither. At some point, perhaps, he receives a visual stimulus in some death sign—the protruding tongue or the wide and whitened eye. Then he falls quickly, landing heavily at a little distance from the corpse.

The swineherd and I watched the first vulture land. We watched him sidling and circling the dead goat, standing erect to see better, wing tips trailing, naked neck stretched to the full, head swiveling rapidly to bring alternate eyes to bear. He hopped closer and paused, peering intently. If he could smell, even as well as we, his doubts would have been over. But he stood there, irresolute, famished yet fearful, with his bill open and his wings ready for use.

Then a big shadow swept across the brown grass, and the vulture glanced upwards. His involuntary signal had been answered, and a tall column of vultures wheeled overhead. He hopped to close quarters, stretched forward, pecked the corpse, and leapt back. He watched it for a second more; no movement. Then he croaked once, as though to bless himself, and threw himself on the body. He struck his heavy beak into the flank, flapped for balance, and thrust backwards with feet and wings to strip the hide from the ribs and belly.

Almost immediately there were eight more vultures at the corpse, and we saw that all of them sought and fought for the same place. Their aim was to penetrate, their object the viscera. Watching them thrusting their long necks deep into the belly cavity and withdrawing them befouled and bloodstained, I saw why those necks must be bare. Yes, said the swineherd, and that is the one part the vulture cannot reach to clean. His mate may clean it for him later, for pure greed, but if he had feathers there he would have maggots in them.

Now sixteen more vultures swept down, landing heavily in their haste and flaphopping to the feast—the second square from the sky pattern. The corpse was covered, submerged in a heaving, struggling mass of broad brown wings. A new column wheeled above us, circling lower. There should be twenty-four up there, I reckoned. There were twenty-three.

The latecomers landed on nearby trees, including ours, and their weight bent thick limbs to the ground. From points four miles distant, we could expect thirty-four more, and at the height of the carnival I counted just short of one hundred birds.

A mule lasts two hours, said the old man, and an ox, three. This goat became bones in the sun in half an hour.

As the hundred fed, or hoped and waited, many more vultures circled high above, assessing the situation and the prospects and treasuring their altitude. Toward the end, when the feasters scattered and exposed the small skeleton, the watchers flapped and drifted wearily away to resume their distant stations. But they had fulfilled their function. They had marked the spot and drawn the Egyptian vultures and the kites.

Now the little Egyptian vultures landed daintily and dodged nimbly through the throng of giants. They are bare on the face and throat only, with well-feathered head and neck, and so, perforce, they are cleaner feeders. The dirty work has been done; now the long and delicate beak comes into play. The Egyptian vultures attack the skull, the large joints, and the crevices of the pelvic girdle—all parts inaccessible to the griffon's heavy beak. They extract brains, membranes, and the spinal cord, and clip out tendons and ligaments. They dodge out through the encircling griffons with their spoils, gobble them swiftly, and dance back for more. The griffons, gorged with meat and panting in the sun, pay them scant attention.

Finally, when all but the whistling kites have left the scene, comes the great solitary bearded vulture, the fierce lammergeier.[2] His whole head is feathered, so he despises carrion. He lives aloof from all the rest of the vulture tribe, but they serve his interests, so he keeps them within sight. The old swineherd calls him Quebrantahuesos[3]—the bone smasher—and Aeschylus[4] noted him, long ago, for the same behavior. The lammergeier seizes the largest bones, carries them high, in his claws, and drops them on the rocks. Then he swoops down and rakes out the marrow.

Like an eagle, he can kill as well as carry with his claws, and he has not the true vulture's patient, soaring habit. He attacks flocks and herds and carries off the lambs and kids and piglets. After his work has been done nothing will remain except an empty skull and some small bones, which the ants and carrion beetles pick and polish.

Our griffon, first on the scene, will not be the first to leave it. He is sure to have gorged himself with his advantage. Crop, throat, and neck distended, he squats back on his tail, with his wings spread to steady him and his beak hanging open. From time to time he chokes and belches and gags, and it is an hour, maybe, before the meat subsides in him.

When he is ready, the griffon runs and leaps across the plain, thrashing heavily with his big wings, and labors into the air. He finds a thermal, circles in it to his altitude, then slips

2. *lammergeier* (lam′ər gī′ər).
3. *Quebrantahuesos* (kā brän′tä hwā′sōs).
4. *Aeschylus* (es′kə ləs), a Greek dramatist who lived from 525–456 B.C.

sideways and sweeps gently across the sierra to his distant nest.

The griffon vultures are gregarious in nesting, with colonies throughout the mountains at fairly regular intervals of thirty miles. They are said to pair for life. Certainly they return every year to the same nest. In January they begin to repair the nest, a broad and battered saucer of strong branches, topped with twigs and grass. They are careless builders, and many nests have bare rock protruding in them. No attempt is made to cover it. The egg is laid in late February and incubated for forty days. The new chick is bare and blue-skinned and looks as though he might become a dragon, but soon he sprouts white down and begins to assert the characteristics of his race. In a month he is voracious, and by the end of April he will demand four pounds of meat every day. Before he is fledged he will need eight pounds. Providentially, his demands coincide with the heyday of death.

When the male vulture arrives at the nest he settles on a nearby ledge, vomits, and sorts out the result with his beak. The female helps with this assessment, feeding herself hungrily on the larger relics. Then she offers her gape and crop to her cowering, whistling infant. The chick gobbles madly. With vultures it can never be "little and often," for animals dine irregularly, as they must, so the birds, young and old, must gorge to the neck when opportunity offers. That is their instinct and their nature.

A male vulture with family responsibilities cannot rest for long. Now that his load is delivered and eaten, he is likely to be the hungriest of the family. This, too, is as it should be, for the hunger sends him out and up again, however little daylight may remain, to circle in the sky until the sunset reddens the sierra.

Time was when the summer drought killed thousands of beasts every year and the floods of winter hundreds more. Nowadays there are fewer casualties, but the vultures still have a fairly constant food supply in the charnel gorges, which lie below most mountain villages. Grazalema, Arcos, Casares,[5] and a hundred

more were built, for protection from the raiding Moors,[6] on the edge of the precipice. All dead and dying animals, as well as all the garbage of the town, are simply pushed over the cliff and left to the birds. There is a bird in Andalusia for every class and size of refuse. From the escarpment you can watch all the scavengers of the air, soaring below you or fighting on the feast. The great black vulture may be here, the griffon and Egyptian for sure, and two kinds of kites. The cunning ravens and carrion crows wait on the outskirts, dashing in to snatch their choice. Clouds of choughs and jackdaws[7] wheel and cry above them.

There is a new feeding ground in the unfenced highways of Andalusia. As motor traffic increases, these offer more and more dead dogs, cats, kids, pigs, and rabbits. If you are abroad at dawn, it is a common thing to run down a vulture intent on scraping a dead dog off the asphalt. Even so, with an apparently limitless population of these great birds, each looking for some thirty pounds of meat every day, one wonders how they flourish.

Their wonderful feeding system has, it seems to me, one fatal flaw. They can signal "Food here," but not how much. At the feast which I have described only some succeeded in feeding at all, and only two or three ate their fill. A majority came the distance and lost their height for little or for nothing.

In Africa, also vulture country, there is no such difficulty, for there all the game is big game, and every funeral is worth attending. It may be that some of our Andalusian vultures go there in the winter. Certainly our vulture population increases here, but that is because the vultures from further north crowd in as the heat decreases and the air currents weaken in their homelands. Fortunately, there is a seasonal food supply ready for them all, for it is the time of birth, with all its failures and fatalities. After the winter storms, too, the torrents offer up their toll of corpses. And in winter, each bird has only himself to feed. But you would not doubt, if you knew the constant panic for food which dominates him summer and winter alike, that

---

5. *Grazalema, Arcos, Casares.* Grazalema and Arcos are cities of Cadiz, the southernmost province of Spain; Casares is a province in the central part of Spain.

6. *Moors,* a dark-skinned North African people who conquered Spain in the eighth century A.D.

7. *choughs* (chufs) *and jackdaws,* small birds which are similar to crows in appearance.

the vulture leads a competitive and anxious life. He has strong forces for survival. It is held—and we know it to be true of eagles—that the vulture has a very long life. If this longevity is a fact, then the solitary chick each year may add up to a good replacement rate.

The nest is inaccessible, and the hen guards it constantly against the only possible natural enemy—other vultures or raptors. So the survival rate must be high, as is proved by the evident increase toward saturation point.

At times, lying on my back on the plain with binoculars trained on the sky, I have seen vultures circling in two or three layers, each one high above the other. What can this mean? A hungry duplication, or triplication, hopelessly covering the same feeding ground and using the only available thermals? Or the opposite—idle and well-fed reserves standing by for surplus?

No one can tell me. But here in the vulture country there are no birds more spectacular, more fascinating to watch and to study. In time we may find out the last of their secrets. I lie on the plains and keep on watching them. And they, I know, keep on watching me.

## DISCUSSION

1. (a) What three essential qualities does the Andalusian countryside offer that vultures need? (b) In what ways does the sun help the vulture survive?

2. How do the various parts of the anatomy of the vulture fit him for the life he must lead?

3. (a) What was the swineherd's theory of how a vulture can detect a dead animal from a great height? (b) According to this theory what steps does a vulture take to make certain an animal is dead? (c) Why should a vulture not risk a trip to the ground for nothing?

4. (a) How do vultures help one another in "cooperative" living?

5. (a) In this essay, the author has chosen a subject interesting to him, has described his experiences, and at the same time has given us insight into his own personality. What have you learned about the author from his essay? (b) How does the author feel about vultures in general? What purpose do they serve?

6. How would you describe the style and tone of this selection? Is it simple and direct, flowery, emotional? Quote lines to support your answer.

7. What is the author suggesting in the last sentence of his essay?

# outwitting the lightning

*Wolcott Gibbs*

THERE was an article somewhere a while ago about how to keep from getting hit by lightning. I don't remember much that it said, because our cook was reading a serial in the same issue about a girl who fell in love with a jai-alai[1]

1. *jai-alai* (hī´ə lī´), a game like handball, played with a basket-like racquet fastened to the arm.

player, and took the magazine up to bed with her every night, so that I didn't get very far with the lightning article except to learn that you mustn't stand around under trees, and I knew that already.

It reminded me, though, of the times my aunt and I used to have with thunderstorms when I was a child. My aunt's major obsession is cats, which she thinks climb up on people's beds at night and smother them, but lightning comes next. I have heard that the fear of lightning is congenital, but I doubt it, because I can't remember that it ever bothered me until I went to stay with her on Long Island.

On the South Shore, storms come up very quickly. The clouds mount, purple on black, in the west. There is a stiff, hot wind that turns up the undersides of the leaves, giving everything a strange, end-of-the-world effect, and the next thing you know you're in the middle of it. Sometimes, of course, the storms go rumbling and flashing out to sea, but not often, and when they do, they're as likely as not to come back treacherously from the east, where you least expect them. These storms are hardest of all for my aunt to bear. They put her in a sort of double jeopardy and her nerves go all to pieces, so that she usually ends up sitting on a raincoat in the cellar.

I was about eight when I had my first experience with Long Island lightning. I was sitting on the floor cutting out the wings for a cardboard airplane with a pair of scissors when my aunt came into the room. She was wearing a pair of my uncle's rubbers and her head was wrapped in a towel, because thunderstorms always made it ache. She looked unusual and mildly deranged, like the White Queen.[2] When she saw me, she gave a negligible squeal.

"Put down those scissors!" she said.

"They haven't any points," I said hastily. My mother was almost as theatrical about scissors as my aunt was about cats, her theory being that an enormous number of people committed involuntary hara-kiri every year by falling on the points.

"It isn't the points," said my aunt. "They're *steel*. Put them down before—oh, *dear!*"

There had been a violent crash just then, apparently directly outside the window. My aunt leaned against the door, shuddering.

"My, but that was close!" she gasped. "It must have hit one of the maples."

I got up and ran to the window, but there wasn't much to see. The rain was coming down straight and blinding, and everything looked very queer in the yellow glare. The trees seemed all right, though.

2. *White Queen,* a character in Lewis Carroll's *Through the Looking-Glass.*

"I don't see———" I began, but she caught me by the shoulder.

"Come away from that window," she whispered fiercely. "Do you want to get killed? Never, *never* stand near a window when there's a thunderstorm."

It was a bad storm and it lasted all afternoon. By the time it had gone muttering off to sea, I knew everything that you mustn't do during a thunderstorm.

In the first place, you mustn't use the telephone. If it rings, don't answer it. In spite of uninformed persons who imagine telephone receivers are rubber, they are made of steel. Touch one, and up you go. My aunt's explanation of that is quite simple: anything steel (and all the metal in the house automatically becomes steel with the first gathering thunderheads) attracts electricity. When it attracts enough, it blows up, along with anyone imprudent enough to be attached to it. My aunt's horror of the telephone extends to everything else that works by electricity. No matter how dark it gets, she never turns on the lights; she uses candles. If she happens to be in her car when a storm breaks, she turns off the switch and sits there, to the confusion of traffic, until it is over. This is purest agony, because the car is steel too, and liable to go wham with her at any moment.

Next to steel, water is the most dangerous thing in a thunderstorm. It conducts electricity. This is a somewhat vague term in her mind. She doesn't mean that water conveys electricity from one place to another. She means, in a large way, that any body of water becomes impregnated with electricity at the outset of a storm and stays that way until it is over. Anyone foolish enough to get in it is briskly and competently electrocuted. This theory applies equally to our bathtub and to the Great South Bay, except that the bay, being larger, holds its electricity longer. She considers it very unwise to go swimming for at least an hour after a storm is over.

Drafts are another thing. In spite of the shattering violence of which it is capable, lightning strays like smoke along the faintest current of air. When a storm begins, she shuts and locks every door and window in the house. That makes everyone pretty hot and uncomfortable, but it doesn't do much good. There are always strange breezes around her ankles, any of which may easily carry a bolt which will demolish the house. The fireplace is the most perilous source of drafts. It is an open, almost suicidal invitation to destruction, and she avoids it carefully. As a matter of fact, a fireplace had very nearly been the end of my grandfather, who had been sitting in front of one when a ball of fire rolled down the chimney and out on the hearth, where it oscillated for some time, looking at him, before it rolled thoughtfully away and disappeared in the cellar.

That is another of the perils of lightning: its ability to assume practically any form you can think of. It can be a bolt, or a ball, or even a thin mist, luminous but deadly. You can take all the negative precautions you want—avoiding metal and drafts and water—but it will get you anyway if it's in the mood. There is only one positive cure for lightning, and that is rubber. My aunt has the utmost faith in rubber, which she thinks confers a sort of magic immunity. If you wear rubber, lightning can't get at you, not even if it strikes in the same room. Like all her precautions, however, even that has one miserable flaw. You have to be all rubber. If there is a single chink, however small, the lightning gets in, and you're done for. When a storm gets really bad, my aunt always spreads one raincoat on the floor and sits on it. Then she puts another one over her head, like a tent. She sits that way until the storm is over, when she reappears tentatively, a little at a time. It always seems to astonish her mildly to find the rest of us alive and unsinged, but I think she puts it down mostly to luck, and is convinced that in the end we'll pay for our mad and unprecedented recklessness. It is a tribute to her training that even now, with the first far away roll of thunder, I think so, too.

---

## DISCUSSION

1. How does the author make it clear at the outset of the article that his aunt is something of a "character"?

2. With what amusing visual impressions of his aunt does the author supply the reader?

3. How are the aunt's fears of steel, water, and drafts ridiculed?

4. Is the author harsh or gentle in his criticism of his aunt? Explain.

5. What is implied by the last sentence in the article?

## WOLCOTT GIBBS

"Year in and year out, regardless of the world's condition or my own, I thumped away," commented Wolcott Gibbs about his more than thirty years on the staff of the New Yorker.

A native New Yorker, born in 1902, Gibbs spent three years working for the Long Island Railroad and a short time as a writer on a small Long Island publication before joining the New Yorker as a copy reader. He worked in many capacities on the magazine, being "professionally ambidextrous"—a good editor and a versatile writer; and his obituary in the New Yorker noted with gratitude, "he filled our gaping pages with satirical sketches, profiles, parodies, reminiscences, and comment."

From 1940 to 1958, the year of his death, he was the New Yorker's drama critic. "I've always felt," he is quoted as having said, "that play criticism was a silly occupation for a grown man."

Wolcott Gibbs spent his winters in Manhattan and his summers on Fire Island, a sandbar off Long Island which became a gathering place for the literary and artistic, and about which Gibbs wrote Season in the Sun, the 1950 Broadway hit comedy. Other works include Bed of Neuroses (1937) and More in Sorrow.

# FIRE WALKING IN CEYLON

*Leonard Feinberg*

ALTHOUGH we had seen men walking barefoot on burning embers twice before, we were not prepared for the mass fire walk at Kataragama.[1] The first time, on a pleasant summer afternoon, surrounded by playing children and laughing family groups, we watched four men walk quickly through a twelve-foot fire pit. The occasion was a Hindu festival, and the atmosphere was similar to that of a state fair in the United States. The second time we had been among the guests of a Ceylonese planter who included in the evening's entertainment a fire-walking exhibition by six men.

But at the temple of Kataragama everything was different. There, on the night of the full moon in August, fire walking climaxes a week's ceremonies in honor of the Hindu god Kataragama. From all over the island, worshipers and spectators (Buddhist as well as Hindu, although theoretically Buddhists do not believe in gods) had been converging on the little settlement in the jungle of southeastern Ceylon. During the early part of the week, devotees had paid tribute to Kataragama by hanging colored papers on trees near the temple or by breaking sacrificial coconuts on a rock provided for that purpose. Toward the week's end, the nature of the sacrifices was intensified, and zealous worshipers perforated their cheeks with pins, or walked on nails, or imbedded into their naked shoulders meat hooks with which they pulled heavy carts along a pitted dirt road.

By midnight the crowd was feverishly tense. Since the logs in the twenty-by-six-foot pit had been burning for four hours, the fire walking would presumably take place about 4 A.M. But the tradition against making any sort of

prediction about the immediate future is so strong at Kataragama that the local priest, asked by an American tourist when the fire walking would begin, replied that there probably would not be any walking at all. The crowd surged away from the pit slowly and steadily— slowly because every inch of the temple grounds had been packed for hours, and steadily because the heat from the pit was becoming unbearable. The men and women nearest the pit had held their places for days, eating and sleeping in one spot. The Ceylonese are ordinarily very clean, but the activity at Kataragama is more important than sanitation, and as the hours passed everything intensified: the heat, the tension, the odors of sweat and urine and incense. A wave of malevolent expectation permeated the air, a powerful undercurrent of suppressed sadism that made intruders like ourselves feel dilettantish, uncomfortable, and slightly ashamed. Fire walking is far more than just a spectacle to most of these people; it is a concrete symbol of intimate identification with a supernatural power. From time to time men would shout "Hora Hora," an Oriental form of "Amen" in honor of the god whose power transcends the science of the West.

About 2 A.M. people near us suddenly scurried to make room for a young woman carrying in her bare hands a clay pot full of burning coconut husks. She did not seem to be feeling any pain, but she was abnormally excited as she staggered to the outer sanctum of the temple. There she threw the pot down, exultantly showed the crowd her hands—they were gray, but not burned—and began knocking on the temple door. She apparently wanted to demonstrate to the priest, or the god, what she had accomplished, but no one was being admitted that night, and she was still pounding frantically

"Fire Walking in Ceylon" by Leonard Feinberg. Originally appeared in *The Atlantic Monthly*. Copyright 1966 Leonard Feinberg. Reprinted by permission of the Evelyn Singer Agency.

1. *Kataragama* (kut′ə rə gum′ə), Hindu pilgrimage center in southeast Ceylon.

at the massive door when the attention of the crowd shifted to another woman. This one too had a red-hot pot full of burning husks, but she carried it in the conventional Ceylonese fashion —on top of her head. And when she removed the pot, neither her hair nor her hands showed any sign of scorching.

Shortly before four o'clock an ominous grumbling swept through the crowd. Then angry shouts, threatening arms, protests. By climbing a stone wall I was able to see what the trouble was. A row of chairs had been reserved for several wealthy Ceylonese from Colombo and their European guests. But when they arrived they found that a group of Buddhist monks had occupied the seats and refused to move. (For more than a year, as a calculated technique of growing nationalism, monks had been usurping reserved seats at public gatherings.) The police officer tried to persuade the monks to give up the seats, but the yellow-robed figures leaned placidly on their umbrellas and pretended that he did not exist. There was no question where the sympathy of the mob lay, and when their protests became loud the police officer shrugged his shoulders and motioned to the legal holders of the seats. They dispersed to the edges of the standing mob, far away from the pit.

At four in the morning wailing flutes and pounding drums announced the arrival of the walkers. The long procession was led by white-robed priests, their faces streaked with red and yellow and white ash. By this time the flames had stopped spurting and the pit consisted of a red-hot mass of burning wood, which attendants were leveling with long branches. The heat of the fire was still intense; within ten feet of the pit it was difficult to breathe. Then the priests muttered incantations, the drums built up to a crescendo, and the fire walking began.

Among the eighty persons who walked the fire that night there were ten women. But in the mad excitement of the crowd's cheers, the drumbeats, the odors, the tension, it was difficult to identify individuals. Some men skipped lightly through the fire, as if doing a restrained version of the hop, skip, and jump in three or four steps. Some raced through, determined,

somber. Some ran through exultantly, waving spears. One man danced gaily into the center of the pit, turned, did a kind of wild jig for a few moments, then turned again and danced on through. Another man stumbled suddenly and the crowd gasped; he fell forward, hung for a ghastly moment on the coals, then straightened and stumbled on. The crowd sighed. Two women ran through, close together, holding hands, taking five or six steps. In the phantasmagoric blur of roars, screams, and incantations, the fire walkers looked less like human beings than grotesque puppets in a macabre shadow play. For a long moment one person stood out in the hectic cavalcade of charging, gyrating figures: a short, slim man in a white sarong strolled slowly and serenely through the fire, stepping on the solid earth at the end of the pit as gently as he had stepped on the embers.

After going through the fire, the walkers, some shuffling, some running, a few helped or led by attendants, proceeded to a spot beside the temple where the head priest placed a smear of saffron ash on the forehead of each participant. The ash had been taken from the pit and blessed, and the fire walkers strode off proudly.

There are two types of fire walking, on stones (usually of volcanic origin) in Polynesia, and on embers in Asia and Africa. Theories which try to explain the secret of fire walking fall into three categories: physical, psychological, and religious. The most publicized attempts of scientists to find the solution took place in 1935 and 1936, when the London Council for Psychical Investigation arranged two series of fire walks at Surrey, England. The council took charge of building the pit and burning the logs, it provided a number of physicians, chemists, physicists, and Oxford professors to examine every stage of the proceedings, and it published an official report of its conclusions. Some of the scientists published individual reports, in general agreeing that fire walking can be explained in terms of certain physical facts, but they did not agree on precisely what those physical facts were.

At the first series of Surrey tests, an Indian

named Kuda Bux walked uninjured through a fire pit the surface temperature of which was 430° C., the interior temperature, 1400° C. In the 1936 test, for Ahmed Hussain, the surface temperature was over 500° C. Both Bux and Hussain insisted that the secret was "faith," and Hussain claimed that he could convey immunity to anyone who would walk the fire with him. A half-dozen English amateurs, who had answered the council's advertisement for volunteers, did walk the fire behind Hussain and were "slightly burned." One of these amateurs managed, a few days later, to walk through the fire pit alone, in three steps, without suffering the slightest injury.

In brief, the official report of the council stated that fire walking is a gymnastic feat operating on this principle: a limited number of quick and even steps on a poor conductor of heat does not result in burning of the flesh. "The secret of fire walking," the report said, "lies in the low thermal conductivity of the burning wood. . . . The quantity of heat transferred may remain small if . . . the time of contact is very short. . . . The time of contact is not above half a second in normal quick walking." To put it another way, it is safe to take three even steps, limiting each contact to half a second, on wood embers ("The thermal conductivity of copper . . . is about 1,000 times greater than that of wood"). The report conceded that "successive contacts . . . cause an accumulation of heat sufficient to cause injury, and . . . with fires whose temperature is 500° Centigrade or more, only two contacts can be made with each foot without erythema or blistering."

The weight of the walker makes a difference, the report suggested, each of the Indians weighing less than 126 pounds and sinking into the embers to a lesser degree, and for a shorter time, than the heavier English amateurs. An expert also has the advantage of walking steadily and distributing his weight evenly, whereas the inexperience and undue haste of the beginner make it difficult for him to avoid resting a part of his foot more heavily than he should. When the amateur walker took an uneven number of steps, the foot which had taken more steps suffered more burns.

Other observers of fire walking have offered various explanations, the most popular being that Orientals have very tough soles. They walk barefoot all their lives, often on hot surfaces. Sometimes they put out cigarette butts with their toes and, when marching in parades, step on burning husks which have fallen out of torch-bearers' fires. This is true. But the English physicians who examined Bux and Hussain described their feet as very soft, not at all calloused.

Another familiar conjecture is that fire walkers use chemical preparations to protect their feet. An American magician believes that a paste of alum and salt is applied, and other experts have speculated that soda, or soap, or juice of mysterious plants, or an anesthetic of some sort is used. But the physician and the chemist who examined Bux and Hussain at Surrey were positive that nothing had been applied to the feet; for control purposes, they washed one of Bux's feet and dried it carefully before he walked.

The "water-vapor protection" theory has a number of supporters. An American chemist recently wrote, in a popular magazine, that he could walk comfortably on burning coals and apply his tongue painlessly to a red-hot iron bar by utilizing this principle: at a certain range of high temperature, a thin film of water acts as absolute protection against heat. The trouble with this theory, as the Surrey tests showed, is (1) the fire walkers' feet were dry, (2) it would be difficult, under any conditions, to supply a uniform amount of water to the soles during a fire walk, and (3) moisture is not advisable, because embers are likely to stick to wet soles and cause blisters.

Still another explanation was offered by Joseph Dunninger. He asserts that the trick used by fire-walking Shinto priests in Japan consisted of making the fuel in the trench shallow in the center and deep on the sides, and starting the fire in the center. By the time the walking begins, the fire has burned out in the center, is still blazing at the edges, and the priests step on the cool ashes of the center. That may be the secret of the Shinto priests, but the pit at Surrey was filled evenly under the supervision of scientists. And an English planter in the Marquesas Islands, who was once teased by a local chief into fire walking, reported that the fire was hottest in the center.

These are the physical explanations. The psychological theories are more difficult to test. Having watched fire walking in Japan some years ago, Percival Lowell of Harvard concluded that the feat was made possible by the less sensitive nervous organism of the Oriental and the ecstasy of the walker (as well as the extremely tough calluses on his soles). A variation on the "ecstasy" theory is the suggestion of one psychologist that hypnosis is the secret. The fire walker, he says, has been hypnotized and provided with the same immunity to pain that can be observed even in a classroom demonstration of hypnosis. The fire walker may not know that he is hypnotized, but hypnosis is what the priest is actually practicing when he gives the walker his last-minute instructions. After the performance, while ostensibly putting a mark of holy ash on the fire walker's forehead, the priest breaks the hypnosis. Most psychologists, however, reject this explanation on the grounds that hypnosis may lessen the subjective feeling of pain but cannot prevent skin from burning.

It is well known in the East that yogis and fakirs[2] can attain so profound a state of concentration on a single object that nothing else distracts them. In this state, the practitioner may lie on a bed of nails, keep a hand outstretched for days, remain motionless for a week, or perform other feats whose practical value is limited but which do demonstrate a control over the body that most human beings are unable to achieve. According to some yogis, he who masters concentration can separate the soul from the body, so that the vacant shell does not feel pain. But since even a dead body will burn, this explanation is not satisfactory.

As far as the devout Ceylonese believer is concerned, the secret is simple: complete faith in Kataragama. Kataragama is a very powerful god. If, in desperation—at a time of serious illness, near-bankruptcy, dangerous competition from a hated rival—a man or woman vows to walk the fire in exchange for Kataragama's help, Kataragama may give that help. The

---

2. *yogis* (yō'gēz) and *fakirs* (fə kirz'), Hindu holy men who lead lives of contemplation and self-denial.

amateur walker, then, is either a petitioner for supernatural assistance or a grateful recipient of it. His preparation may begin as early as May, when he arrives at Kataragama and puts himself under the direction of the chief priest. For three months he lives ascetically, abstaining from all sensual pleasures, eating only vegetables, drinking only water, bathing in the holy river near the temple, and going through religious rituals conducted by the priest. If he does all this, and if he has *absolute, unquestioning, complete* faith in Kataragama's power, he walks the fire unafraid and unharmed.

On the night we watched the fire walking at Kataragama, twelve people were burned badly enough to go to the hospital, and one of them died. These people, the devout believer will tell you, lacked either faith or preparation. Another man who lacked at least one of these ingredients was a young English clergyman who visited Ceylon a few years ago. This Protestant minister reasoned that the faith of a Christian was at least as strong as that of a Hindu, and he volunteered to walk the fire with the others. He did, and spent the next six months in a hospital, where doctors barely managed to save his life.

It is believed by the Ceylonese that Kataragama exercises absolute and somewhat whimsical control of the area within a fourteen-mile radius of his temple. His portrait, presumably life-size, shows a handsome, seven-foot-tall, six-headed and twelve-armed god, with two women and a blue peacock for companionship and transportation. Although he is technically a Hindu god, many Buddhists also worship him, or at least ask for his help when they are in trouble. Officially the god of war and revenge, he is probably more fervently worshiped and more genuinely feared than any other god in Ceylon. He has an A-1 reputation for protecting his congregation and, according to numerous legends, exhibits a genial playfulness in devising disconcerting mishaps for those who violate his minor taboos.

Most Ceylonese try to make at least one visit a year to his temple, not necessarily during the August ceremonies, but at some other time of the year when the settlement in the jungle is sparse, quiet, and suitable for meditation. Everyone manages to get to Kataragama sooner or later, it seems. My Hindu friend in the police department went one week, my wife's Muslim jeweler another, my Buddhist tailor a third. It is considered especially commendable to walk all the way to Kataragama, and many Ceylonese do walk there, sometimes carrying a large, colorful, paper-and-wood contraption in the form of an arch, which indicates that they are fulfilling a vow.

Our driver on the trip to Kataragama was a young Singhalese[3] who told us that his name was Elvis. (He told Englishmen that his name was Winston.) His driving got a little erratic as the day wore on, and he finally admitted that, though a Buddhist, he was taking no chances with Kataragama and had been fasting all day. While we were eating, he warned our friends and us about certain taboos that visitors to the Kataragama territory were supposed to observe. One local rule forbade announcing an expected arrival time; that, said Elvis, was an infallible way of being delayed. Another dangerous thing to do was to speak disrespectfully of Kataragama. A Buddhist in a Renault immediately remarked that, the weather being ideal, we ought to arrive at Kataragama by six o'clock.

3. *Singhalese* (sing′gə lēz′), member of the principal native race of Ceylon.

And a Christian woman in a Vauxhall said that all this fear of Kataragama was nonsense; she had been there the previous year and had ridiculed the entire procedure, but nothing had happened.

When we finished eating we got into our Volkswagen and followed the other two cars. Suddenly it began to rain. It rained only for five minutes and, we learned later, only within a few hundred yards. As we carefully rounded a curve on the slick road we saw that the two other cars were now facing us. The Renault's hood was stuck halfway into a rock fence, and the Vauxhall was resting its side on the same fence. It turned out that the Renault had skidded and started turning in the road, and to avoid hitting it the driver of the Vauxhall put on her brakes. By the time the cars stopped skidding they had smashed into the fence. No one was injured except the scoffing woman, who had a painful but not serious bruise on the spot where an irritated parent might have been expected to spank his child. It took a long time to improvise pulling cables, disengage the cars, and tow them to a garage. We eventually reached the temple just before midnight, and although all of these coincidences and superstitions can be logically accounted for, no one in our party made any more jeering remarks about Kataragama.

## DISCUSSION

1. Of the five physical theories advanced to explain fire walking, which appears soundest? Why?

2. (a) What are the psychological explanations of fire walking? (b) What evidence does the author cite in accepting or rejecting these explanations?

3. (a) How do the Ceylonese explain fire walking? (b) What preparations does a believer make before a fire walk? (c) How do the Ceylonese account for believers who are seriously burned in a fire walk?

4. (a) The author says that to most of the people at Kataragama fire walking ". . . is a concrete symbol of the intimate identification with a supernatural power." Explain in your own words what this means. (b) Point out practices in other religions intended to serve a similar purpose.

5. How do the opening and closing sections of the article differ from the section in which the theories explaining fire walking are discussed? What do the episodes described in the opening and closing sections add to the article?

6. Which of the theories that attempt to explain fire walking do you prefer? Why?

# Drama

# Visit to a Small Planet

*Gore Vidal*

## Characters

KRETON
ROGER SPELDING
ELLEN SPELDING
MRS. SPELDING
JOHN RANDOLPH
GENERAL POWERS

# Act One

AIDE

PAUL LAURENT

SECOND VISITOR

PRESIDENT OF PARAGUAY

TECHNICIANS

(*Stock Shot:*[1] *The night sky, stars. Then slowly a luminous object arcs into view. As it is almost upon us, dissolve to*[2] *the living room of the Spelding house in Maryland.*

*Superimpose card:* The Time: The Day After Tomorrow.[3]

*The room is comfortably balanced between the expensively decorated and the homely.* ROGER SPELDING *is concluding his TV broadcast. He is middle-aged, unctuous, resonant. His wife, bored and vague, knits passively while he talks at his desk. Two* TECHNICIANS *are on hand, operating the equipment. His daughter,* ELLEN, *a lively girl of twenty, fidgets as she listens.*)

SPELDING (*into microphone*). . . . and so, according to General Powers . . . who should know if anyone does . . . the flying object which has given rise to so much irresponsible conjecture is nothing more than a meteor passing through the earth's orbit. It is not, as many believe, a secret weapon of this country. Nor is it a spaceship as certain lunatic elements have suggested. General Powers has assured me that it is highly doubtful there is any form of life on other planets capable of building a spaceship. "If any traveling is to be done in space, we will do it first." And those are his exact words. . . . Which winds up another week of news.

*Visit to a Small Planet* by Gore Vidal. Copyright © 1956, 1957, by Gore Vidal. Reprinted by permission of Little, Brown and Co. and William Morris Agency, Inc.
1.  *Stock Shot*, a piece of film, often from a newsreel or travelogue, kept and used as an insert or background shot for other films or television productions.
2.  *dissolve to*. One picture fades out as another fades in.
3.  *The Time: . . . Tomorrow*. These words appear over the scene.

*(Crosses to pose with wife and daughter)* This is Roger Spelding, saying good night to Mother and Father America, from my old homestead in Silver Glen, Maryland, close to the warm pulsebeat of the nation.

TECHNICIAN. Good show tonight, Mr. Spelding.

SPELDING. Thank you.

TECHNICIAN. Yes sir, you were right on time. *(SPELDING nods wearily, his mechanical smile and heartiness suddenly gone.)*

MRS. SPELDING. Very nice, dear. Very nice.

TECHNICIAN. See you next week, Mr. Spelding.

SPELDING. Thank you, boys.

*(TECHNICIANS go.)*

SPELDING. Did you like the broadcast, Ellen?

ELLEN. Of course I did, Daddy.

SPELDING. Then what did I say?

ELLEN. Oh, that's not fair.

SPELDING. It's not very flattering when one's own daughter won't listen to what one says while millions of people . . .

ELLEN. I always listen, Daddy, you know that.

MRS. SPELDING. We love your broadcasts, dear. I don't know what we'd do without them.

SPELDING. Starve.

ELLEN. I wonder what's keeping John?

SPELDING. Certainly not work.

ELLEN. Oh, Daddy, stop it! John works very hard and you know it.

MRS. SPELDING. Yes, he's a perfectly nice boy, Roger. I like him.

SPELDING. I know. I know: He has every virtue except the most important one: he has no get-up-and-go.

ELLEN *(precisely)*. He doesn't want to get up and he doesn't want to go because he's already where he wants to be on his own farm which is exactly where *I'm* going to be when we're married.

SPELDING. More thankless than a serpent's tooth is an ungrateful child.[4]

ELLEN. I don't think that's right. Isn't it "more deadly . . ."

SPELDING. Whatever the exact quotation is, I stand by the sentiment.

MRS. SPELDING. Please don't quarrel. It always gives me a headache.

---

4. *More thankless . . . an ungrateful child.* Spelding is misquoting a line from Shakespeare's *King Lear*, Act I, Scene 4: "How sharper than a serpent's tooth it is to have a thankless child!"

SPELDING. I never quarrel. I merely reason, in my simple way, with Miss Know-it-all here.

ELLEN. Oh, Daddy! Next you'll tell me I should marry for money.

SPELDING. There is nothing wrong with marrying a wealthy man. The horror of it has always eluded me. However, my only wish is that you marry someone hard-working, ambitious, a man who'll make his mark in the world. Not a boy who plans to sit on a farm all his life, growing peanuts.

ELLEN. English walnuts.

SPELDING. Will you stop correcting me?

ELLEN. But, Daddy, John grows walnuts . . . *(JOHN enters, breathlessly.)*

JOHN. Come out! Quick! It's coming this way. It's going to land right here!

SPELDING. *What's* going to land?

JOHN. The spaceship. Look!

SPELDING. Apparently you didn't hear my broadcast. The flying object in question is a meteor not a spaceship.

*(JOHN has gone out with ELLEN. SPELDING and MRS. SPELDING follow.)*

MRS. SPELDING. Oh, my! Look! Something *is* falling! Roger, you don't think it's going to hit the house, do you?

SPELDING. The odds against being hit by a falling object that size are, I should say, roughly, ten million to one.

JOHN. Ten million to one or not it's going to land right here and it's *not* falling.

SPELDING. I'm sure it's a meteor.

MRS. SPELDING. Shouldn't we go down to the cellar?

SPELDING. If it's not a meteor, it's an optical illusion . . . mass hysteria.

ELLEN. Daddy, it's a real spaceship. I'm sure it is.

SPELDING. Or maybe a weather balloon. Yes, that's what it is. General Powers said only yesterday . . .

JOHN. It's landing!

SPELDING. I'm going to call the police . . . the army! *(Bolts inside)*

ELLEN. Oh look how it shines!

JOHN. Here it comes!

MRS. SPELDING. Right in my rose garden!

ELLEN. Maybe it's a balloon.

JOHN. No, it's a spaceship and right in your own backyard.

ELLEN. What makes it shine so?

JOHN. I don't know but I'm going to find out. (Runs off toward the light)

ELLEN. Oh, darling, don't! John, please! John, John come back!

(SPELDING, wide-eyed, returns.)

MRS. SPELDING. Roger, it's landed right in my rose garden.

SPELDING. I got General Powers. He's coming over. He said they've been watching this thing. They . . . they don't know what it is.

ELLEN. You mean it's nothing of ours?

SPELDING. They believe it . . . (swallows hard) . . . it's from outer space.

ELLEN. And John's down there! Daddy, get a gun or something.

SPELDING. Perhaps we'd better leave the house until the army gets here.

ELLEN. We can't leave John.

SPELDING. I can. (Peers nearsightedly) Why, it's not much larger than a car. I'm sure it's some kind of meteor.

ELLEN. Meteors are blazing hot.

SPELDING. This is a cold one . . .

ELLEN. It's opening . . . the whole side's opening! (Shouts) John! Come back! Quick. . . .

MRS. SPELDING. Why, there's a man getting out of it! (Sighs) I feel much better already. I'm sure if we ask him, he'll move that thing for us. Roger, you ask him.

SPELDING (ominously). If it's really a man?

ELLEN. John's shaking hands with him. (Calls) John darling, come on up here . . .

MRS. SPELDING. And bring your friend . . .

SPELDING. There's something wrong with the way that creature looks . . . if it is a man and not a . . . not a monster.

MRS. SPELDING. He looks perfectly nice to me. (JOHN and the visitor appear. The visitor is in his forties, a mild, pleasant-looking man with side whiskers and dressed in the fashion of 1860. He pauses when he sees the three people, in silence for a moment. They stare back at him, equally interested.)

VISITOR. I seem to've made a mistake. I am sorry. I'd better go back and start over again.

SPELDING. My dear sir, you've only just arrived. Come in, come in. I don't need to tell you what a pleasure this is . . . Mister . . . Mister . . .

VISITOR. Kreton . . . This is the wrong costume, isn't it?

SPELDING. Wrong for what?

KRETON. For the country, and the time.

SPELDING. Well, it's a trifle old-fashioned.

MRS. SPELDING. But really awfully handsome.

KRETON. Thank you.

MRS. SPELDING (to husband). Ask him about moving that thing off my rose bed.

(SPELDING leads them all into living room.)

SPELDING. Come on in and sit down. You must be tired after your trip.

KRETON. Yes, I am a little. (Looks around delightedly) Oh, it's better than I'd hoped!

SPELDING. Better? What's better?

KRETON. The house . . . that's what you call it? Or is this an apartment?

SPELDING. This is a house in the State of Maryland, U.S.A.

KRETON. In the late twentieth century! To think this is really the twentieth century! I must sit down a moment and collect myself. The real thing! (He sits down.)

ELLEN. You . . . you're not an American, are you?

KRETON. What a nice thought! No, I'm not.

JOHN. You sound more English.

KRETON. Do I? Is my accent very bad?

JOHN. No, it's quite good.

SPELDING. Where are you from, Mr. Kreton?

KRETON (evasively). Another place.

SPELDING. On this earth of course.

KRETON. No, not on this planet.

ELLEN. Are you from Mars?

KRETON. Oh dear no, not Mars. There's nobody on Mars . . . at least no one I know.

ELLEN. I'm sure you're teasing us and this is all some kind of publicity stunt.

KRETON. No, I really am from another place.

SPELDING. I don't suppose you'd consent to my interviewing you on television?

KRETON. I don't think your authorities will like that. They are terribly upset as it is.

SPELDING. How do you know?

KRETON. Well, I . . . pick up things. For instance, I know that in a few minutes a number of people from your Army will be here to question me and they . . . like you . . . are torn by doubt.

SPELDING. How extraordinary!

ELLEN. Why did you come here?

KRETON. Simply a visit to your small planet. I've been studying it for years. In fact, one might say, you people are my hobby. Especially, this period of your development.

JOHN. Are you the first person from your . . . your planet to travel in space like this?

KRETON. Oh my no! Everyone travels who wants to. It's just that no one wants to visit you. I can't think why. *I* always have. You'd be surprised what a thorough study I've made. (*Recites*) The planet, Earth, is divided into five continents with a number of large islands. It is mostly water. There is one moon. Civilization is only just beginning. . . .

SPELDING. Just beginning! My dear sir, we have had. . . .

KRETON (*blandly*). You are only in the initial stages, the most fascinating stages as far as I'm concerned . . . I do hope I don't sound patronizing.

ELLEN. Well, we are very proud.

KRETON. I know and that's one of your most endearing, primitive traits. Oh, I can't believe I'm here at last!

(GENERAL POWERS, *a vigorous product of the National Guard, and his* AIDE *enter.*)

POWERS. All right folks. The place is surrounded by troops. Where is the monster?

KRETON. I, my dear General, am the monster.

POWERS. What are you dressed up for, a fancy-dress party?

KRETON. I'd hoped to be in the costume of the period. As you see I am about a hundred years too late.

POWERS. Roger, who is this joker?

SPELDING. This is Mr. Kreton . . . General Powers. Mr. Kreton arrived in that thing outside. He is from another planet.

POWERS. I don't believe it.

ELLEN. It's true. We saw him get out of the flying saucer.

POWERS (*to* AIDE). Captain, go down and look at that ship. But be careful. Don't touch anything. And don't let anybody else near it. (AIDE *goes.*) So you're from another planet.

KRETON. Yes. My, that's a very smart uniform but I prefer the ones made of metal, the ones you used to wear, you know: with the feathers on top.

POWERS. That was five hundred years ago . . . Are you *sure* you're not from the Earth?

KRETON. Yes.

POWERS. Well, I'm not. You've got some pretty tall explaining to do.

KRETON. Anything to oblige.

POWERS. All right, which planet?

KRETON. None that you have ever heard of.

POWERS. Where is it?

KRETON. You wouldn't know.

POWERS. This solar system?

KRETON. No.

POWERS. Another system?

KRETON. Yes.

POWERS. Look, Buster, I don't want to play games: I just want to know where you're from. The law requires it.

KRETON. It's possible that I could explain it to a mathematician but I'm afraid I couldn't explain it to you, not for another five hundred years and by then of course *you'd* be dead because you people do die, don't you?

POWERS. What?

KRETON. Poor fragile butterflies, such brief little moments in the sun. . . . You see *we* don't die.

POWERS. You'll die all right if it turns out you're a spy or a hostile alien.

KRETON. I'm sure you wouldn't be so cruel.

(AIDE *returns; he looks disturbed.*)

POWERS. What did you find?

AIDE. I'm not sure, General.

POWERS (*heavily*). Then do your best to describe what the object is like.

AIDE. Well, it's elliptical, with a fourteen-foot diameter. And it's made of an unknown metal which shines and inside there isn't anything.

POWERS. Isn't anything?

AIDE. There's nothing inside the ship: No instruments, no food, nothing.

POWERS (*to* KRETON). What did you do with your instrument board?

KRETON. With my what? Oh, I don't have one.

POWERS. How does the thing travel?

KRETON. I don't know.

POWERS. You don't know. Now look, Mister, you're in pretty serious trouble. I suggest you do a bit of cooperating. You claim you traveled here from outer space in a machine with no instruments . . .

KRETON. Well, these cars are rather common in my world and I suppose, once upon a time, I must've known the theory on which they operate but I've long since forgotten. After all, General, we're not mechanics, you and I.

POWERS. Roger, do you mind if we use your study?

SPELDING. Not at all. Not at all, General.

POWERS. Mr. Kreton and I are going to have a chat. (*To* AIDE) Put in a call to the Chief of Staff.

AIDE. Yes, General.

(SPELDING *rises, leads* KRETON *and* POWERS *into the next room, a handsomely furnished study, many books and a globe of the world.*)

SPELDING. This way, gentlemen. (KRETON *sits down comfortably beside the globe which he twirls thoughtfully. At the door,* SPELDING *speaks in a low voice to* POWERS.) I hope I'll be the one to get the story first, Tom.

POWERS. There isn't any story. Complete censorship. I'm sorry but this house is under martial law. I've a hunch we're in trouble.

(*He shuts the door.* SPELDING *turns and rejoins his family.*)

ELLEN. I think he's wonderful, whoever he is.

MRS. SPELDING. I wonder how much damage he did to my rose garden . . .

JOHN. It's sure hard to believe he's really from outer space. No instruments, no nothing . . . boy, they must be advanced scientifically.

MRS. SPELDING. Is he spending the night, dear?

SPELDING. What?

MRS. SPELDING. Is he spending the night?

SPELDING. Oh yes, yes, I suppose he will be.

MRS. SPELDING. Then I'd better go make up the bedroom. He seems perfectly nice to me. I like his whiskers. They're so very . . . comforting. Like Grandfather Spelding's. (*She goes.*)

SPELDING (*bitterly*). I *know* this story will leak out before I can interview him. I just know it.

ELLEN. What does it mean, we're under martial law?

SPELDING. It means we have to do what General Powers tells us to do. (*He goes to the window as a soldier passes by.*) See?

JOHN. I wish I'd taken a closer look at that ship when I had the chance.

ELLEN. Perhaps he'll give us a ride in it.

JOHN. Traveling in space! Just like those stories. You know: intergalactic drive stuff.

SPELDING. *If* he's not an impostor.

ELLEN. I have a feeling he isn't.

JOHN. Well, I better call the family and tell them I'm all right. (*He crosses to telephone by the door which leads into hall.*)

AIDE. I'm sorry, sir, but you can't use the phone.

SPELDING. He certainly can. This is my house . . .

AIDE (*mechanically*). This house is a military reservation until the crisis is over: Order General Powers. I'm sorry.

JOHN. How am I to call home to say where I am?

AIDE. Only General Powers can help you. You're also forbidden to leave this house without permission.

SPELDING. You can't do this!

AIDE. I'm afraid, sir, we've done it.

ELLEN. Isn't it exciting!

(*Cut to study.*)

POWERS. Are you deliberately trying to confuse me?

KRETON. Not deliberately, no.

POWERS. We have gone over and over this for two hours now and all that you've told me is that you're from another planet in another solar system . . .

KRETON. In another dimension. I think that's the word you use.

POWERS. In another dimension and you have come here as a tourist.

KRETON. Up to a point, yes. What did you expect?

POWERS. It is my job to guard the security of this country.

KRETON. I'm sure that must be very interesting work.

POWERS. For all I know, you are a spy, sent here by an alien race to study us, preparatory to invasion.

KRETON. Oh, none of my people would *dream* of invading you.

POWERS. How do I know that's true?

KRETON. You don't, so I suggest you believe me. I should also warn you: I can tell what's inside.

POWERS. What's inside?

KRETON. What's inside your mind.

POWERS. You're a mind reader?

KRETON. I don't really read it. I hear it.

POWERS. What am I thinking?

KRETON. That I am either a lunatic from the earth or a spy from another world.

POWERS. Correct. But then you could've guessed that. *(Frowns)* What am I thinking now?

KRETON. You're making a picture. Three silver stars. You're pinning them on your shoulder, instead of the two stars you now wear.

POWERS *(startled)*. That's right. I was thinking of my promotion.

KRETON. If there's anything I can do to hurry it along, just let me know.

POWERS. You can. Tell me why you're here.

KRETON. Well, we don't travel much, my people. We used to but since we see everything through special monitors and recreators, there is no particular need to travel. However, *I* am a hobbyist. I love to gad about.

POWERS *(taking notes)*. Are you the first to visit us?

KRETON. Oh, no! We started visiting you long before there were people on the planet. However, we are seldom noticed on our trips. I'm sorry to say I slipped up, coming in the way I did . . . but then this visit was all rather impromptu. *(Laughs)* I am a creature of impulse, I fear.

*(AIDE looks in.)*

AIDE. Chief of Staff on the telephone, General.

POWERS *(picks up phone)*. Hello, yes, sir. Powers speaking. I'm talking to him now. No, sir. No, sir. No, we can't determine what method of power was used. He won't talk. Yes, sir. I'll hold him here. I've put the house under martial law . . . belongs to a friend of mine, Roger Spelding, the TV commentator. Roger Spelding, the TV . . . What? Oh, no, I'm sure he won't say anything. Who . . . oh, yes, sir. Yes, I realize the importance of it. Yes, I will. Good-by. *(Hangs up)* The President of the United States wants to know all about you.

KRETON. How nice of him! And I want to know all about him. But I do wish you'd let me rest a bit first. Your language is still not familiar to me. I had to learn them all, quite exhausting.

POWERS. You speak *all* our languages?

KRETON. Yes, all of them. But then it's easier than you might think since I can see what's inside.

POWERS. Speaking of what's inside, we're going to take your ship apart.

KRETON. Oh, I wish you wouldn't.

POWERS. Security demands it.

KRETON. In that case *my* security demands you leave it alone.

POWERS. You plan to stop us?

KRETON. I already have . . . Listen.

*(Far-off shouting. AIDE rushes into the study.)*

AIDE. Something's happened to the ship, General. The door's shut and there's some kind of wall all around it, an invisible wall. We can't get near it.

KRETON *(to camera)*. I hope there was no one inside.

POWERS *(to KRETON)*. How did you do that?

KRETON. I couldn't begin to explain. Now if you don't mind, I think we should go in and see our hosts.

*(He rises, goes into living room. POWERS and AIDE look at each other.)*

POWERS. Don't let him out of your sight.

*(Cut to living room as POWERS picks up phone. KRETON is with JOHN and ELLEN.)*

KRETON. I don't mind curiosity but I really can't permit them to wreck my poor ship.

ELLEN. What do you plan to do, now you're here?

KRETON. Oh, keep busy. I have a project or two . . . *(Sighs)* I can't believe you're real!

JOHN. Then we're all in the same boat.

KRETON. Boat? Oh, yes! Well, I should have come ages ago but I . . . I couldn't get away until yesterday.

JOHN. Yesterday? It only took you a *day* to get here?

KRETON. One of *my* days, not yours. But then you don't know about time yet.

JOHN. Oh, you mean relativity.

KRETON. No, it's much more involved than that. You won't know about time until . . . now let me see if I remember . . . no, I don't, but it's about two thousand years.

JOHN. What do we do between now and then?

KRETON. You simply go on the way you are, living your exciting primitive lives . . . you have no idea how much fun you're having now.

ELLEN. I hope you'll stay with us while you're here.

KRETON. That's very nice of you. Perhaps I will. Though I'm sure you'll get tired of having a visitor under foot all the time.

ELLEN. Certainly not. And Daddy will be deliriously happy. He can interview you by the hour.

JOHN. What's it like in outer space?

KRETON. Dull.

ELLEN. I should think it would be divine! (POWERS *enters.*)

KRETON. No, General, it won't work.

POWERS. What won't work?

KRETON. Trying to blow up my little force field. You'll just plough up Mrs. Spelding's garden. (POWERS *snarls and goes into study.*)

ELLEN. Can you tell what we're *all* thinking?

KRETON. Yes. As a matter of fact, it makes me a bit giddy. Your minds are not at all like ours. You see we control our thoughts while you . . . well, it's extraordinary the things you think about!

ELLEN. Oh, how awful! You can tell *everything* we think?

KRETON. Everything! It's one of the reasons I'm here, to intoxicate myself with your primitive minds . . . with the wonderful rawness of your emotions! You have no idea how it excites me! You simply seethe with unlikely emotions.

ELLEN. I've never felt so sordid.

JOHN. From now on I'm going to think about agriculture.

SPELDING (*entering*). You would.

ELLEN. Daddy!

KRETON. No, no. You must go right on thinking about Ellen. Such wonderfully *purple* thoughts.

SPELDING. Now see here, Powers, you're carrying this martial law thing too far . . .

POWERS. Unfortunately, until I have received word from Washington as to the final disposition of this problem, you must obey my orders: no telephone calls, no communication with the outside.

SPELDING. This is unsupportable.

KRETON. Poor Mr. Spelding! If you like, I shall go. That would solve everything, wouldn't it?

POWERS. You're not going anywhere, Mr. Kreton, until I've had my instructions.

KRETON. I sincerely doubt if you could stop me. However, I put it up to Mr. Spelding. Shall I go?

SPELDING. Yes! (POWERS *gestures a warning.*) Do stay, I mean, we want you to get a good impression of us . . .

KRETON. And of course you still want to be the first journalist to interview me. Fair enough. All right, I'll stay on for a while.

POWERS. Thank you.

KRETON. Don't mention it.

SPELDING. General, may I ask our guest a few questions?

POWERS. Go right ahead, Roger. I hope you'll do better than I did.

SPELDING. Since you read our minds, you probably already know what our fears are.

KRETON. I do, yes.

SPELDING. We are afraid that you represent a hostile race.

KRETON. And I have assured General Powers that my people are not remotely hostile. Except for me, no one is interested in this planet's present stage.

SPELDING. Does this mean you might be interested in a *later* stage?

KRETON. I'm not permitted to discuss your future. Of course my friends think me perverse to be interested in a primitive society but there's no accounting for tastes, is there? You are my hobby. I love you. And that's all there is to it.

POWERS. So you're just here to look around . . . sort of going native.

KRETON. What a nice expression! That's it exactly. I am going native.

POWERS (*grimly*). Well, it is my view that you have been sent here by another civilization for the express purpose of reconnoitering prior to invasion.

KRETON. That *would* be your view! The wonderfully primitive assumption that all strangers are hostile. You're almost too good to be true, General.

POWERS. You deny your people intend to make trouble for us?

KRETON. I deny it.

POWERS. Then are they interested in establish-

ing communication with us? Trade? That kind of thing?

KRETON. We have always had communication with you. As for trade, well, we do not trade . . . that is something peculiar only to your social level. (*Quickly*) Which I'm not criticizing! As you know, I approve of everything you do.

POWERS. I give up.

SPELDING. You have no interest then in . . . well, trying to dominate the earth.

KRETON. Oh, yes!

POWERS. I thought you just said your people weren't interested in us.

KRETON. *They're* not, but *I* am.

POWERS. You!

KRETON. Me . . . I mean I. You see I've come here to take charge.

POWERS. Of the United States?

KRETON. No, of the whole world. I'm sure you'll be much happier and it will be great fun for me. You'll get used to it in no time.

POWERS. This is ridiculous. How can one man take over the world?

KRETON (*gaily*). Wait and see!

POWERS (*to* AIDE). Grab him!

(POWERS *and* AIDE *rush* KRETON *but within a foot of him, they stop, stunned.*)

KRETON. You can't touch me. That's part of the game. (*He yawns.*) Now, if you don't mind, I shall go up to my room for a little lie-down.

SPELDING. I'll show you the way.

KRETON. That's all right. I know the way. (*Touches his brow*) Such savage thoughts! My head is vibrating like a drum. I feel quite giddy, all of you thinking away. (*He starts to the door; he pauses beside Mrs. Spelding.*) No, it's not a dream, dear lady. I shall be here in the morning when you wake up. And now, good night, dear, wicked children . . .

(*He goes as we fade out.*)

# Act Two

(*Fade in on* KRETON'S *bedroom next morning. He lies fully clothed on bed with cat on his lap.*)

KRETON. Poor cat! Of course I sympathize with you. Dogs *are* distasteful. What? Oh, I can well believe they do: yes, yes, how disgusting. They don't ever groom their fur! But you do *constantly*, such a fine coat. No, no, I'm not just saying that. I really mean it: exquisite texture. Of course, I wouldn't say it was *nicer* than skin but even so. . . . What? Oh, no! They *chase* you! Dogs chase you for no reason at all except pure malice? You poor creature. Ah, but you *do* fight back! That's right! give it to them: slash, bite, scratch! Don't let them get away with a trick. . . . No! Do dogs really do that? Well, I'm sure *you* don't. What . . . oh, well, yes I completely agree about mice. They *are* delicious! (Ugh!) Pounce, snap and there is a heavenly dinner. No, I don't know any mice yet . . . they're not very amusing? But after all think how you must terrify them because you are so bold, so cunning, so beautifully predatory! (*Knock at door*) Come in.

ELLEN (*enters*). Good morning. I brought you your breakfast.

KRETON. How thoughtful! (*Examines bacon*) Delicious, but I'm afraid my stomach is not like yours, if you'll pardon me. I don't eat. (*Removes pill from his pocket and swallows it*) This is all I need for the day. (*Indicates cat*) Unlike this creature, who would eat her own weight every hour, given a chance.

ELLEN. How do you know?

KRETON. We've had a talk.

ELLEN. You can *speak* to the cat?

KRETON. Not speak exactly but we communicate. I look inside and the cat cooperates. Bright red thoughts, very exciting, though rather on one level.

ELLEN. Does kitty like us?

KRETON. No, I wouldn't say she did. But then she has very few thoughts not connected with food. Have you, my quadruped criminal? (*He strokes the cat, which jumps to the floor.*)

ELLEN. You know you've really upset everyone.

KRETON. I supposed that I would.

ELLEN. Can you really take over the world, just like that?

KRETON. Oh, yes.

ELLEN. What do you plan to do when you *have* taken over?

KRETON. Ah, that is my secret.

ELLEN. Well, I think you'll be a very nice President, *if* they let you of course.

KRETON. What a sweet girl you are! Marry him right away.

ELLEN. Marry John?

KRETON. Yes. I see it in your head *and* in his. He wants you very much.

ELLEN. Well, we plan to get married this summer, if father doesn't fuss too much.

KRETON. Do it before then. I shall arrange it all if you like.

ELLEN. How?

KRETON. I can convince your father.

ELLEN. That sounds awfully ominous. I think you'd better leave poor Daddy alone.

KRETON. Whatever you say. *(Sighs)* Oh, I love it so! When I woke up this morning I had to pinch myself to prove I was really here.

ELLEN. We were all doing a bit of pinching too. Ever since dawn we've had nothing but visitors and phone calls and troops outside in the garden. No one has the faintest idea what to do about you.

KRETON. Well, I don't think they'll be confused much longer.

ELLEN. How do you plan to conquer the world?

KRETON. I confess I'm not sure. I suppose I must make some demonstration of strength, some colorful trick that will frighten everyone . . . though I much prefer taking charge quietly. That's why I've sent for the President.

ELLEN. The President? *Our* President?

KRETON. Yes, he'll be along any minute now.

ELLEN. But the President just doesn't go around visiting people.

KRETON. He'll visit me. *(Chuckles)* It may come as a surprise to him, but he'll be in this house in a very few minutes. I think we'd better go downstairs now. *(To cat)* No, I will not give you a mouse. You must get your own. Be self-reliant. Beast!

*(Dissolve to the study.* POWERS *is reading book entitled* The Atom and You. *Muffled explosions off-stage.)*

AIDE *(entering).* Sir, nothing seems to be working. Do we have the General's permission to try a fission bomb on the force field?

POWERS. No . . . no. We'd better give it up.

AIDE. The men are beginning to talk.

POWERS *(thundering).* Well, keep them quiet! *(Contritely)* I'm sorry, Captain. I'm on edge. Fortunately, the whole business will soon be in the hands of the World Council.

AIDE. What will the World Council do?

POWERS. It will be interesting to observe them.

AIDE. You don't think this Kreton can really take over the world, do you?

POWERS. Of course not. Nobody can.

*(Dissolve to living room.* MRS. SPELDING *and* SPELDING *are talking.)*

MRS. SPELDING. You still haven't asked Mr. Kreton about moving that thing, have you?

SPELDING. There are too many *important* things to ask him.

MRS. SPELDING. I hate to be a nag but you know the trouble I have had getting anything to grow in that part of the garden . . .

JOHN *(enters).* Good morning.

MRS. SPELDING. Good morning, John.

JOHN. Any sign of your guest?

MRS. SPELDING. Ellen took his breakfast up to him a few minutes ago.

JOHN. They don't seem to be having much luck, do they? I sure hope you don't mind my staying here like this.

*(*SPELDING *glowers.)*

MRS. SPELDING. Why, we love having you! I just hope your family aren't too anxious.

JOHN. One of the G.I.'s finally called them, said I was staying here for the weekend.

SPELDING. The rest of our *lives*, if something isn't done soon.

JOHN. Just how long do you think that'll be, Dad?

SPELDING. Who knows?

*(*KRETON *and* ELLEN *enter.)*

KRETON. Ah, how wonderful to see you again! Let me catch my breath. . . . Oh, your minds! It's not easy for me, you know. So many crude thoughts blazing away! Yes, Mrs. Spelding, I will move the ship off your roses.

MRS. SPELDING. That's awfully sweet of you.

KRETON. Mr. Spelding, if any interviews are to be granted you will be the first. I promise you.

SPELDING. That's very considerate, I'm sure.

KRETON. So you can stop thinking *those* particular thoughts. And now where is the President?

SPELDING. The President?

KRETON. Yes, I sent for him. He should be here. (*He goes to the terrace window.*) Ah, that must be he. (*A swarthy man in uniform with a sash across his chest is standing bewildered, on the terrace.* KRETON *opens the glass door.*) Come in, sir, come in, Your Excellency. Good of you to come on such short notice. (*Man enters.*)

MAN (*in Spanish accent*). Where am I?

KRETON. You *are* the President, aren't you?

MAN. Of course I am the President. What am I doing here? I was dedicating a bridge and I find myself . . .

KRETON (*aware of his mistake*). Oh, dear! *Where* was the bridge?

MAN. Where do you think, you idiot, in Paraguay!

KRETON (*to others*). I seem to've made a mistake. Wrong President. (*Gestures and the man disappears*) Seemed rather upset, didn't he?

JOHN. You can make people come and go just like that?

KRETON. Just like that.
(POWERS *looks into room from the study.*)

POWERS. Good morning, Mr. Kreton. Could I see you for a moment?

KRETON. By all means. (*He crosses to the study.*)

SPELDING. I believe I am going mad.
(*Cut to study. The* AIDE *stands at attention while* POWERS *addresses* KRETON.)

POWERS. . . . and so we feel, the government of the United States feels, that this problem is too big for any one country, therefore we are turning the whole affair over to Paul Laurent, the Secretary-General of the World Council.

KRETON. Very sensible. I should've thought of that myself.

POWERS. Mr. Laurent is on his way here now. And I may add, Mr. Kreton, you've made me look singularly ridiculous.

KRETON. I'm awfully sorry. (*Pause*) No, you can't kill me.

POWERS. You were reading my mind again.

KRETON. I can't really help it, you know. And such *black* thoughts today, but intense, very intense.

POWERS. I regard you as a menace.

KRETON. I know you do and I think it's awfully unkind. I do mean well.

POWERS. Then go back where you came from and leave us alone.

KRETON. I'm afraid I can't do that just yet . . . (*Phone rings, the* AIDE *answers it.*)

AIDE. He's outside? Sure, let him through. (*To* POWERS) The Secretary-General of the World Council is here, sir.

POWERS (*to* KRETON). I hope you'll listen to *him*.

KRETON. Oh, I shall, of course. I love listening. (*The door opens and* PAUL LAURENT, *middle-aged and serene, enters.* POWERS *and his* AIDE *stand to attention.* KRETON *goes forward to shake hands.*)

LAURENT. Mr. Kreton?

KRETON. At your service, Mr. Laurent.

LAURENT. I welcome you to this planet in the name of the World Council.

KRETON. Thank you sir, thank you.

LAURENT. Could you leave us alone for a moment, General?

POWERS. Yes, sir.
(POWERS *and* AIDE *go.* LAURENT *smiles at* KRETON.)

LAURENT. Shall we sit down?

KRETON. Yes, yes I love sitting down. I'm afraid my manners are not quite suitable, yet. (*They sit down.*)

LAURENT. Now, Mr. Kreton, in violation of all the rules of diplomacy, may I come to the point?

KRETON. You may.

LAURENT. Why are you here?

KRETON. Curiosity. Pleasure.

LAURENT. You are a tourist then in this time and place?

KRETON (*nods*). Yes. Very well put.

LAURENT. We have been informed that you have extraordinary powers.

KRETON. By your standards, yes, they must seem extraordinary.

LAURENT. We have also been informed that it is your intention to . . . to take charge of this world.

KRETON. That is correct. . . . What a remarkable mind you have! I have difficulty looking inside it.

LAURENT (*laughs*). Practice. I've attended so

many conferences. . . . May I say that your conquest of our world puts your status of tourist in a rather curious light?

KRETON. Oh, I said nothing about *conquest*.

LAURENT. Then how else do you intend to govern? The people won't allow you to direct their lives without a struggle.

KRETON. But I'm sure they will if I ask them to.

LAURENT. You believe you can do all this without, well, without violence?

KRETON. Of course I can. One or two demonstrations and I'm sure they'll do as I ask. *(Smiles)* Watch this.

*(Pause. Then shouting.* POWERS *bursts into room.)*

POWERS. Now what've you done?

KRETON. Look out the window, your Excellency. (LAURENT *goes to window. A rifle floats by, followed by an alarmed soldier.)* Nice, isn't it? I confess I worked out a number of rather melodramatic tricks last night. Incidentally, all the rifles of all the soldiers in all the world are now floating in the air. *(Gestures)* Now they have them back.

POWERS *(to* LAURENT). You see, sir, I didn't exaggerate in my report.

LAURENT *(awed)*. No, no, you certainly didn't.

KRETON. You were skeptical, weren't you?

LAURENT. Naturally. But now I . . . now I think it's possible.

POWERS. That this . . . this gentleman is going to run everything?

LAURENT. Yes, yes I do. And it might be wonderful.

KRETON. You *are* more clever than the others. You begin to see that I mean only good.

LAURENT. Yes, only good. General, do you realize what this means? We can have one government . .

KRETON. With innumerable bureaus, and intrigue. . . .

LAURENT *(excited)*. And the world could be incredibly prosperous, especially if he'd help us with his superior knowledge.

KRETON *(delighted)*. I will, I will. I'll teach you to look into one another's minds. You'll find it devastating but enlightening: all that self-interest, those *lurid* emotions . . .

LAURENT. No more countries. No more wars . . .

KRETON *(startled)*. What? Oh, but I like a lot of countries. Besides, at this stage of your development you're supposed to have lots of countries and lots of wars . . . innumerable wars . . .

LAURENT. But you can help us change all that.

KRETON. *Change* all that! My dear sir, I am your friend.

LAURENT. What do you mean?

KRETON. Why, your deepest pleasure is violence. How can you deny that? It is the whole point to you, the whole point to my hobby . . . and you are my hobby, all mine.

LAURENT. But our lives are devoted to *controlling* violence, and not creating it.

KRETON. Now, don't take me for an utter fool. After all, I can see into your minds. My dear fellow, don't you *know* what you are?

LAURENT. What are we?

KRETON. You are savages. I have returned to the dark ages of an insignificant planet simply because I want the glorious excitement of being among you and reveling in your savagery! There is murder in all your hearts and I love it! It intoxicates me!

LAURENT *(slowly)*. You hardly flatter us.

KRETON. I didn't mean to be rude but you did ask me why I am here and I've told you.

LAURENT. You have no wish then to . . . to help us poor savages.

KRETON. I couldn't even if I wanted to. You won't be civilized for at least two thousand years and you won't reach the level of my people for about a million years.

LAURENT *(sadly)*. Then you have come here only to . . . to observe?

KRETON. No, more than that. I mean to regulate your past times. But don't worry: I won't upset things too much. I've decided I don't want to be known to the people. You will go right on with your countries, your squabbles, the way you always have, while I will *secretly* regulate things through you.

LAURENT. The World Council does not govern. We only advise.

KRETON. Well, I shall advise you and you will advise the governments and we shall have a lovely time.

LAURENT. I don't know what to say. You obviously have the power to do as you please.

KRETON. I'm glad you realize that. Poor General Powers is now wondering if a hydrogen bomb might destroy me. It won't, General.

POWERS. Too bad.

KRETON. Now, your Excellency, I shall stay in this house until you have laid the groundwork for my first project.

LAURENT. And what is that to be?

KRETON. A war! I want one of your really splendid wars, with all the trimmings, all the noise and the fire . . .

LAURENT. A war! You're joking. Why at this moment we are working as hard as we know how *not* to have a war.

KRETON. But secretly you want one. After all, it's the one thing your little race does well. You'd hardly want me to deprive you of your simple pleasures, now would you?

LAURENT. I think you must be mad.

KRETON. Not mad, simply a philanthropist. Of course I myself shall get a great deal of pleasure out of a war (the vibrations must be incredible!) but I'm doing it mostly for you. So, if you don't mind, I want you to arrange a few incidents, so we can get one started spontaneously.

LAURENT. I refuse.

KRETON. In that event, I shall select someone else to head the World Council. Someone who *will* start a war. I suppose there exist a few people here who might like the idea.

LAURENT. How can you do such a horrible thing to us? Can't you see that we don't want to be savages?

KRETON. But you have no choice. Anyway, you're just pulling my leg! I'm sure you want a war as much as the rest of them do and that's what you're going to get: the biggest war you've ever had!

LAURENT (stunned). Heaven help us!

KRETON (exuberant). Heaven won't! Oh, what fun it will be! I can hardly wait! (He strikes the globe of the world a happy blow as we fade out.)

# Act Three

(Fade in on the study, two weeks later. KRE-TON is sitting at desk on which a map is spread out. He has a pair of dividers, some models of jet aircraft. Occasionally he pretends to dive bomb, imitating the sound of a bomb going off. POWERS enters.)

POWERS. You wanted me, sir?

KRETON. Yes, I wanted those figures on radio-active fallout.

POWERS. They're being made up now, sir. Anything else?

KRETON. Oh, my dear fellow, why do you dislike me so?

POWERS. I am your military aide, sir: I don't have to answer that question. It is outside the sphere of my duties.

KRETON. Aren't you at least happy about your promotion?

POWERS. Under the circumstances, no, sir.

KRETON. I find your attitude baffling.

POWERS. Is that all, sir?

KRETON. You have never once said what you thought of my war plans. Not once have I got a single word of encouragement from you, a single compliment . . . only black thoughts.

POWERS. Since you read my mind, sir, you know what I think.

KRETON. True, but I can't help but feel that deep down inside of you there is just a twinge of professional jealousy. You don't like the idea of an outsider playing your game better than you do. Now confess!

POWERS. I am acting as your aide only under duress.

KRETON (sadly). Bitter, bitter . . . and to think I chose you especially as my aide. Think of all the other generals who would give anything to have your job.

POWERS. Fortunately, they know nothing about my job.

KRETON. Yes, I do think it wise not to advertise my presence, don't you?

POWERS. I can't see that it makes much difference, since you seem bent on destroying our world.

KRETON. I'm not going to destroy it. A few dozen cities, that's all, and not very nice cities either. Think of the fun you'll have building new ones when it's over.

POWERS. How many millions of people do you plan to kill?

KRETON. Well, quite a few, but they love this sort of thing. You can't convince me they don't. Oh, I know what Laurent says. But he's a misfit, out of step with his time. Fortunately, my new World Council is more reasonable.

POWERS. Paralyzed is the word, sir.

KRETON. You don't think they like me either?

POWERS. You *know* they hate you, sir.

KRETON. But love and hate are so confused in your savage minds and the vibrations of the one are so very like those of the other that I can't always distinguish. You see, we neither love nor hate in my world. We simply have hobbies. (*He strokes the globe of the world tenderly.*) But now to work. Tonight's the big night: first, the sneak attack, then: boom! (*He claps his hands gleefully.*)

(*Dissolve to the living room, to* JOHN *and* ELLEN.)

ELLEN. I've never felt so helpless in my life.

JOHN. Here we all stand around doing nothing while he plans to blow up the world.

ELLEN. Suppose we went to the newspapers.

JOHN. He controls the press. When Laurent resigned they didn't even print his speech. (*A gloomy pause*)

ELLEN. What are you thinking about, John?

JOHN. Walnuts. (*They embrace.*)

ELLEN. Can't we do anything?

JOHN. No, I guess there's nothing.

ELLEN (*vehemently*). Oh! I could kill him! (KRETON *and* POWERS *enter.*)

KRETON. Very good, Ellen, *very* good! I've never felt you so violent.

ELLEN. You heard what I said to John?

KRETON. Not in words, but you were absolutely bathed in malevolence.

POWERS. I'll get the papers you wanted, sir. (POWERS *exits.*)

KRETON. I don't think he likes me very much but your father does. Only this morning he offered to handle my public relations and I said I'd let him. Wasn't that nice of him?

JOHN. I think I'll go get some fresh air. (*He goes out through the terrace door.*)

KRETON. Oh, dear! (*Sighs*) Only your father is really entering the spirit of the game. He's a much better sport than you, my dear.

ELLEN (*exploding*). Sport! That's it! You think we're sport. You think we're animals to be played with: well, we're not. We're people and we don't want to be destroyed.

KRETON (*patiently*). But I am not destroying you. You will be destroying one another of your own free will, as you have always done. I am simply a . . . a kibitzer.

ELLEN. No, you are a vampire!

KRETON. A vampire? You mean I drink blood? Ugh!

ELLEN. No, you drink emotions, our emotions. You'll sacrifice us all for the sake of your . . . your vibrations!

KRETON. Touché. Yet what harm am I really doing? It's true I'll enjoy the war more than anybody; but it will be *your* destructiveness after all, not mine.

ELLEN. You could stop it.

KRETON. So could you.

ELLEN. I?

KRETON. Your race. They could stop altogether but they won't. And I can hardly intervene in their natural development. The most I can do is help out in small, practical ways.

ELLEN. We are not what you think. We're not so . . . so primitive.

KRETON. My dear girl, just take this one household: your mother dislikes your father but she is too tired to do anything about it so she knits and she gardens and she tries not to think about him. Your father, on the other hand, is bored with all of you. Don't look shocked: he doesn't like you any more than you like him . . .

ELLEN. Don't say that!

KRETON. I am only telling you the truth. Your father wants you to marry someone important; therefore he objects to John while you, my girl . . .

(*With a fierce cry,* ELLEN *grabs vase to throw.*)

ELLEN. You devil! (*Vase breaks in her hand.*)

KRETON. You see? That proves my point perfectly. (*Gently*) Poor savage, I cannot help what you are. (*Briskly*) Anyway, you will soon be distracted from your personal problems. Tonight is the night. If you're a good girl, I'll let you watch the bombing.

(*Dissolve to study. Eleven forty-five.* POWERS *and the* AIDE *gloomily await the war.*)

AIDE. General, isn't there anything we can do?

POWERS. It's out of our hands.

(KRETON, *dressed as a Hussar with shako, enters.*)

KRETON. Everything on schedule?

POWERS. Yes, sir. Planes left for their targets at twenty-two hundred.

KRETON. Good . . . good. I myself shall take off shortly after midnight to observe the attack first-hand.

POWERS. Yes, sir.

(KRETON *goes into the living room where the family is gloomily assembled.*)

KRETON (*enters from study*). And now the magic hour approaches! I hope you're all as thrilled as I am.

SPELDING. You still won't tell us who's attacking whom?

KRETON. You'll know in exactly . . . fourteen minutes.

ELLEN (*bitterly*). Are we going to be killed too?

KRETON. Certainly not! You're quite safe, at least in the early stages of the war.

ELLEN. Thank you.

MRS. SPELDING. I suppose this will mean rationing again.

SPELDING. Will . . . will we see anything from here?

KRETON. No, but there should be a good picture on the monitor in the study. Powers is tuning in right now.

JOHN (*at window*). Hey look, up there! Coming this way!

(ELLEN *joins him.*)

ELLEN. What is it?

JOHN. Why . . . it's *another* one! And it's going to land.

KRETON (*surprised*). I'm sure you're mistaken. No one would dream of coming here. (*He has gone to the window, too.*)

ELLEN. It's landing!

SPELDING. Is it a friend of yours, Mr. Kreton?

KRETON (*slowly*). No, no, not a friend . . .

(KRETON *retreats to the study; he inadvertently drops a lace handkerchief beside the sofa.*)

JOHN. Here he comes.

ELLEN (*suddenly bitter*). Now we have two of them.

MRS. SPELDING. My poor roses.

(*The new* VISITOR *enters in a gleam of light from his ship. He is wearing a most futuristic costume. Without a word, he walks past the awed family into the study.* KRETON *is cowering behind the globe.* POWERS *and the* AIDE *stare, bewildered, as the* VISITOR *gestures sternly and* KRETON *reluctantly removes shako and sword. They communicate by odd sounds.*)

VISITOR (*to* POWERS). Please leave us alone.

(*Cut to living room as* POWERS *and the* AIDE *enter from the study.*)

POWERS (*to* ELLEN). Who on earth was that?

ELLEN. It's another one, another visitor.

POWERS. Now we're done for.

ELLEN. I'm going in there.

MRS. SPELDING. Ellen, don't you dare!

ELLEN. I'm going to talk to them. (*Starts to door*)

JOHN. I'm coming, too.

ELLEN (*grimly*). No, alone. I know what I want to say.

(*Cut to interior of the study, to* KRETON *and the other* VISITOR *as* ELLEN *enters.*)

ELLEN. I want you both to listen to me . . .

VISITOR. You don't need to speak. I know what you will say.

ELLEN. That you have no right here? That you mustn't . . .

VISITOR. I agree. Kreton has no right here. He is well aware that it is forbidden to interfere with the past.

ELLEN. The past?

VISITOR (*nods*). You are the past, the dark ages: we are from the future. In fact, we are *your* descendants on another planet. We visit you from time to time but we never interfere because it would change *us* if we did. Fortunately, I have arrived in time.

ELLEN. There won't be a war?

VISITOR. There will be no war. And there will be no memory of any of this. When we leave here you will forget Kreton and me. Time will turn back to the moment before his arrival.

ELLEN. Why did you want to hurt us?

KRETON (*heartbroken*). Oh, but I didn't! I only wanted to have . . . well, to have a little fun, to indulge my hobby . . . against the rules of course.

VISITOR (*to* ELLEN). Kreton is a rarity among us. Mentally and morally he is retarded. He is a child and he regards your period as his toy.

KRETON. A child, now really!

VISITOR. He escaped from his nursery and came back in time to you . . .

KRETON. And *every*thing went wrong, everything! I wanted to visit 1860 . . . that's my *real* period but then something happened to the car and I ended up here, not that I don't find you nearly as interesting but . . .

VISITOR. We must go, Kreton.

KRETON (*to* ELLEN). You did like me just a bit, didn't you?

ELLEN. Yes, yes I did, until you let your hobby get out of hand. (*To* VISITOR) What is the future like?

VISITOR. Very serene, very different . . .

KRETON. Don't believe him: it is dull, dull, dull beyond belief! One simply floats through eternity: no wars, no excitement . . .

VISITOR. It is forbidden to discuss these matters.

KRETON. I can't see what difference it makes since she's going to forget all about us anyway.

ELLEN. Oh, how I'd love to see the future . . .

VISITOR. It is against . . .

KRETON. Against the rules: how tiresome you are. (*To* ELLEN) But, alas, you can never pay us a call because you aren't born yet! I mean where we are you are not. Oh, Ellen, dear, think kindly of me, until you forget.

ELLEN. I will.

VISITOR. Come. Time has begun to turn back. Time is bending.

(*He starts to door.* KRETON *turns conspiratorially to* ELLEN.)

KRETON. Don't be sad, my girl. I shall be back one bright day, but a bright day in 1860. I dote on the Civil War, so exciting . . .

VISITOR. Kreton!

KRETON. Only next time I think it'll be more fun if the *South* wins! (*He hurries after the* VISITOR.)

(*Cut to clock as the hands spin backwards. Dissolve to the living room, exactly the same as the first scene:* SPELDING, MRS. SPELDING, ELLEN.)

SPELDING. There is nothing wrong with marrying a wealthy man. The horror of it has always eluded me. However, my only wish is that you marry someone hard-working, ambitious, a man who'll make his mark in the world. Not a boy who is content to sit on a farm all his life, growing peanuts. . .

ELLEN. English walnuts! And he won't just sit there.

SPELDING. Will you stop contradicting me?

ELLEN. But, Daddy, John grows walnuts . . .

(JOHN *enters.*)

JOHN. Hello, everybody.

MRS. SPELDING. Good evening, John.

ELLEN. What kept you, darling? You missed Daddy's broadcast.

JOHN. I saw it before I left home. Wonderful broadcast, sir.

SPELDING. Thank you, John.

(JOHN *crosses to window.*)

JOHN. That meteor you were talking about, well, for a while it looked almost like a spaceship or something. You can just barely see it now.

(ELLEN *joins him at window. They watch, arms about one another.*)

SPELDING. Spaceship! Nonsense! Remarkable what some people will believe, *want* to believe. Besides, as I said in the broadcast: if there's any traveling to be done in space we'll do it first.

(*He notices* KRETON'S *handkerchief on sofa and picks it up. They all look at it, puzzled, as we cut to stock shot of the starry night against which two spaceships vanish in the distance, one serene in its course, the other erratic, as we fade out.*)

## DISCUSSION

*Act One*

1. What is the time and setting?
2. How would you describe the spaceship?
3. What characters are introduced, and what are their relationships to one another?
4. What are the clues to Mrs. Spelding's character?
5. (a) What are the main interests of Roger Spelding? (b) What do these interests tell you about his character?
6. How is Kreton dressed?
7. What is going on in the Spelding house at the time John announces that the spaceship is going to land?
8. (a) Why has Kreton come to visit earth? (b) What is his attitude toward earth people? (c) What does Powers suspect of Kreton? (d) In what ways are the earth people at a disadvantage with Kreton? (e) What clues show that Kreton was an odd person on his own planet?

*Act Two*

1. What various reactions do the other characters show toward Kreton?
2. (a) In Kreton's mind what is the status of earth's "civilization"? (b) How far have earth people progressed compared with his own people?
3. (a) By what powers can Kreton conquer the world? Bring peace if he wishes? (b) What are his plans?

*Act Three*

1. (a) As Act Three opens, what is the relationship of Powers to Kreton? (b) What is Powers's feeling about his "promotion"?
2. What leads up to Ellen's throwing a vase at Kreton?
3. (a) When does the play's crisis come, the point at which the action can go either way? (b) During the crisis, how are the reactions of the Spelding family members consistent with their characters as earlier established?
4. What does the second Visitor reveal about Kreton that makes his visit to the earth even more ironic?
5. (a) How is the plot resolved? (b) What do you make of the fact that the earth people and the visitors part in the end without apparently having changed each other?
6. What are some of the targets for satire in this play? (See the Handbook entry for *satire*.)

## GORE VIDAL

Gore Vidal has a first-hand knowledge of practical politics, a knowledge gained from his family and

from his own political activities. His father served under Franklin D. Roosevelt as Director of Air Commerce; his maternal grandfather, Thomas Gore, was a senator from Oklahoma for twenty years; and his stepsister is the widow of President Kennedy. Vidal, himself, in an unexpectedly close race, ran for Congress in 1960 from his district in New York. This knowledge he has put to effective use in *Visit to a Small Planet, The Best Man, An Evening with Richard Nixon,* and his novel, *Washington D.C.*

Vidal was born in 1925 and wrote his first novel in 1944 when he was nineteen. He has since enjoyed success as a novelist, essayist, playwright, and television personality.

# THE MOTHER

*Paddy Chayefsky*

## Characters

OLD LADY

DAUGHTER

BOSS

SON-IN-LAW

NEGRO WOMAN

SISTER

MRS. GEEGAN

MRS. KLINE

BOOKKEEPER

PUERTO RICAN GIRL

# Act One

(Fade in: Film—a quick group of shots showing New York in a real thunderstorm—rain
whipping through the streets—real miserable
weather.

Dissolve to: Close-up of an old woman, aged
sixty-six, with a shock of gray-white hair,
standing by a window in her apartment, looking out, apparently deeply disturbed by the
rain slashing against the pane.

We pull back to see that the old woman is
wearing an old kimono, under which there
is evidence of an old white batiste nightgown. Her gray-white hair hangs loosely
down over her shoulders. It is early morning, and she has apparently just gotten out
of bed. This is the bedroom of her two-and-a-
half-room apartment in a lower-middle-
class neighborhood in the Bronx. The bed
is still unmade and looks just slept in. The
furniture is old and worn. On the chest of
drawers there is a galaxy of photographs

and portrait pictures, evidently of her various
children and grandchildren. She stands looking out the window, troubled, disturbed. Suddenly the alarm, perched on the little bed
table, rings. Camera moves in for closeup of
the alarm clock. It reads half-past six. The
OLD LADY's hand comes down and shuts the
alarm off.

Cut to: Close-up of another alarm clock, ringing in another apartment. It also reads half-
past six; but it is obviously a different clock,
on a much more modern bed table. This one
buzzes instead of clangs. A young woman's
hand reaches over and turns it off.

Camera pulls back to show that we are in
the bedroom of a young couple. The young
woman who has turned the clock off is a
rather plain girl of thirty. She slowly sits
up in bed, assembling herself for the day.
On the other half of the bed, her husband
turns and tries to go back to sleep.)

SON-IN-LAW (*from under the blankets*). What time is it?

DAUGHTER (*still seated heavily on the edge of the bed*). It's half-past six.

SON-IN-LAW (*from under the blankets*). What did you set it so early for?

DAUGHTER. I wanna call my mother. (*She looks out at the window, the rain driving fiercely against it.*) For heaven's sake, listen to that rain! She's not going down today, I'll tell you that, if I have to go over there and chain her in her bed. . . . (*She stands, crosses to the window, studies the rain.*) Boy, look at it rain.

SON-IN-LAW (*still under the covers*). What?

DAUGHTER. I said, it's raining. (*She makes her way, still heavy with sleep, out of the bedroom into the foyer of the apartment. She pads in her bare feet and pajamas down the foyer to the telephone table, sits on the little chair, trying to clear her head of sleep. A baby's cry is suddenly heard in an off room. The young woman absently goes "Sshh." The baby's cry stops. The young woman picks up the receiver of the phone and dials. She waits. Then . . .*)

DAUGHTER. Ma? This is Annie. Did I wake you up? . . . I figured you'd be up by now. . . . Ma, you're not going downtown today, and I don't wanna hear no arguments . . . Ma, have you looked out the window? It's raining like . . . Ma, I'm not gonna let you go downtown today, do you hear me? . . . I don't care, Ma . . . Ma, I don't care . . . Ma, I'm coming over. You stay there till . . . Ma, stay there till I come over. I'm getting dressed right now. I'll drive over in the car. It won't take me ten minutes . . . Ma, you're not going out in this rain. It's not enough that you almost fainted in the subway yesterday . . . Ma, I'm hanging up, and I'm coming over right now. Stay there . . . all right, I'm hanging up . . . (*She hangs up, sits for a minute, then rises and shuffles quickly back up the foyer and back into her bedroom. She disappears into the bathroom, unbuttoning the blouse of her pajamas. She leaves the bathroom door open, and a shaft of light suddenly shoots out into the dark bedroom.*)

SON-IN-LAW (*awake now, his head visible over the covers*). Did you talk to her?

DAUGHTER (*off in bathroom*). Yeah, she was all practically ready to leave.

SON-IN-LAW. Look, Annie, I don't wanna tell you how to treat your own mother, but why don't you leave her alone? It's obviously very important to her to get a job for herself. She wants to support herself. She doesn't want to be a burden on her children. I respect her for that. An old lady, sixty-six years old, going out and looking for work. I think that shows a lot of guts.

(*The* DAUGHTER *comes out of the bathroom. She has a blouse on now and a half-slip.*)

DAUGHTER (*crossing to the closet*). George, please, you don't know what you're talking about, so do me a favor, and don't argue with me. I'm not in a good mood. (*She opens the closet, studies the crowded rack of clothes.*) I'm turning on the light, so get your eyes ready. (*She turns on the light. The room is suddenly bright. She blinks and pokes in the closet for a skirt, which she finally extracts.*) My mother worked like a dog all her life, and she's not gonna spend the rest of her life bent over a sewing machine. (*She slips into the skirt.*) She had one of her attacks in the subway yesterday. I was never so scared in my life when that cop called yesterday. (*She's standing in front of her mirror now, hastily arranging her hair.*) My mother worked like a dog to raise me and my brother and my sister. She worked in my old man's grocery store till twelve o'clock at night. We owe her a little peace of mind, my brother and my sister and me. She sacrificed plenty for us in her time. (*She's back at the closet, fishing for her topcoat.*) And I want her to move out of that apartment. I don't want her living alone. I want her to come live here with us, George, and I don't want any more arguments about that either. We can move Tommy in with the baby, and she can have Tommy's room. And that reminds me—the baby cried for a minute there. If she cries again, give her her milk because she went to sleep without her milk last night. (*She has her topcoat on now and is already at the door to the foyer.*) All right, I'll probably be back in time to make your breakfast. Have you got the keys to the car? . . . (*She nervously pats the pocket of her coat.*) No, I got them. All right, I'll see you. Good-by, George . . . (*She goes out into the foyer.*)

SON-IN-LAW. Good-by, Annie . . . (*Off in some other room, the baby begins to cry again, a little more insistently. The husband raises his eyebrows and listens for a moment. When it becomes apparent that the baby isn't going to stop, he sighs and begins to get out of bed.*

*Dissolve to: The* OLD LADY *standing by the window again. She is fully dressed now, however, even to the black coat and hat. The coat is unbuttoned. For the first time, we may be aware of a black silk mourning band that the* OLD LADY *has about the sleeve of her coat. Outside, the rain has abated considerably. It is drizzling lightly now. The* OLD LADY *turns to her* DAUGHTER, *standing at the other end of the bedroom, brushing the rain from her coat. When the* OLD LADY *speaks, it is with a mild, but distinct, Irish flavor.*)

OLD LADY. It's letting up a bit.

DAUGHTER (*brushing off her coat*). It isn't letting up at all. It's gonna stop and start all day long.

(*The* OLD LADY *starts out of her bedroom, past her* DAUGHTER, *into her living room.*)

OLD LADY. I'm going to make a bit of coffee for myself and some Rice Krispies. Would you like a cup?

(*The* DAUGHTER *turns and starts into the living room ahead of her mother.*)

DAUGHTER. I'll make it for you.

OLD LADY. You won't make it for me. I'll make it myself. (*She crowds past the* DAUGHTER *and goes to the kitchen. At the kitchen doorway, she turns and surveys her* DAUGHTER.*)

OLD LADY. Annie, you know, you can drive somebody crazy, do you know that?

DAUGHTER. I can drive somebody crazy! *You're* the one who can drive somebody crazy.

OLD LADY. Will you stop hovering over me like I was a cripple in a wheel chair? I can make my own coffee, believe me. Why did you come over here? You've got a husband and two kids to take care of. Go make coffee for them, for heaven's sakes. (*She turns and goes*

*into the kitchen, muttering away. She opens a cupboard and extracts a jar of instant coffee.*)

OLD LADY. I've taken to making instant coffee, would you like a cup?

(*The* DAUGHTER *is standing on the threshold of the kitchen now, leaning against the door-jamb.*)

DAUGHTER. All right, make me a cup, Ma.

(*The* OLD LADY *takes two cups and saucers out and begins carefully to level out a tea-spoonful of the instant coffee into each. The* DAUGHTER *moves into the kitchen, reaches up for something in the cupboard.*)

DAUGHTER. Where do you keep your saccharin, Ma?

(*The* OLD LADY *wheels and slaps the* DAUGHTER'S *outstretched arms down.*)

OLD LADY. Annie, I'll get it myself! (*She points a finger into the living room.*) Go in there and sit down, will you? I'll bring the cup in to you!

(*The* DAUGHTER *leans back against the door-jamb, a little exasperated with the* OLD LADY'S *petulent independence. The* OLD LADY *now takes an old teapot and sets it on the stove and lights a flame under it.*)

OLD LADY. You can drive me to the subway if you want to do something for me.

DAUGHTER. Ma, you're not going downtown today.

OLD LADY. I want to get down there extra early today on the off-chance that they haven't given the job to someone else. What did I do with that card from the New York State Employment Service? . . . (*She shuffles out of the kitchen, the* DAUGHTER *moving out of the doorway to give her passage. The* OLD LADY *goes to the table in the living room on which sits her battered black purse. She opens it and takes out a card.*)

OLD LADY. I don't want to lose that. (*She puts the white card back into her purse.*) I'm pretty sure I could have held onto this job, because the chap at the Employment Service called up the boss, you see, over the phone, and he explained to the man that I hadn't worked in quite a number of years . . .

DAUGHTER (*muttering*). Quite a number of years . . .

OLD LADY. . . . and that I'd need a day or so to get used to the machines again.

DAUGHTER. Did the chap at the Employment Service explain to the boss that it's forty years that you haven't worked?

OLD LADY (crossing back to the kitchen). . . . and the boss understood this, you see, so he would have been a little lenient with me. But then, of course, I had to go and faint in the subway, because I was in such a hurry to get down there, you know, I didn't even stop to eat my lunch. I had brought along some sandwiches, you see, cheese and tomatoes. Oh, I hope he hasn't given the job to anyone else . . .

(The OLD LADY reaches into the cupboard again for a bowl of sugar, an opened box of Rice Krispies, and a bowl. The DAUGHTER watches her as she turns to the refrigerator to get out a container of milk.)

DAUGHTER. Ma, when are you gonna give up? (The OLD LADY frowns.)

OLD LADY. Annie, please . . . (She pours some Rice Krispies into the bowl.)

DAUGHTER. Ma, you been trying for three weeks now. If you get a job, you get fired before the day is over. You're too old, Ma, and they don't want to hire old people . . .

OLD LADY. It's not the age . . .

DAUGHTER. They don't want to hire white-haired old ladies.

OLD LADY. It's not the age at all! I've seen plenty old people with white hair and all, sitting at those machines. The shop where I almost had that job and he fired me the other day, there was a woman there, eighty years old if she was a day, an old crone of a woman, sitting there all bent over, her machine humming away. The chap at the Employment Service said there's a lot of elderly people working in the needle trades. The young people nowadays don't want to work for thirty-five, forty dollars a week, and there's a lot of old people working in the needle trades.

DAUGHTER. Well, whatever it is, Ma . . .

OLD LADY (leaning to her DAUGHTER). It's my fingers. I'm not sure of them any more. When you get old, y'know, you lose the sureness in your fingers. My eyes are all right, but my fingers tremble a lot. I get excited, y'know,

when I go in for a tryout, y'know. And I'll go in, y'know, and the boss'll say: "Sit down, let's see what you can do." And I get so excited. And my heart begins thumping so that I can hardly see to thread the needle. And they stand right over you, y'know, while you're working. They give you a packet of sleeves or a shirt or something to put a hem on. Or a seam or something, y'know. It's simple work, really. Single-needle machine. Nothing fancy. And it seems to me I do it all right, but they fire me all the time. They say: "You're too slow." And I'm working as fast as I can. I think, perhaps, I've lost the ability in my fingers. And that's what scares me the most. It's not the age. I've seen plenty of old women working in the shops. (She has begun to pour some milk into her bowl of cereal; but she stops now and just stands, staring bleakly down at the worn oilcloth on her cupboard.)

DAUGHTER (gently). Ma, you worked all your life. Why don't you take it easy?

OLD LADY. I don't want to take it easy. Now that your father's dead and in the grave I don't know what to do with myself.

DAUGHTER. Why don't you go out, sit in the park, get a little sun like the other old women?

OLD LADY. I sit around here sometimes, going crazy. We had a lot of fights in our time, your father and I, but I must admit I miss him badly. You can't live with someone forty-one years and not miss him when he's dead. I'm glad that he died for his own sake—it may sound hard of me to say that—but I am glad. He was in nothing but pain the last few months, and he was a man who could never stand pain. But I do miss him.

DAUGHTER (gently). Ma, why don't you come live with George and me?

OLD LADY. No, no, Annie, you're a good daughter. . . .

DAUGHTER. We'll move Tommy into the baby's room, and you can have Tommy's room. It's the nicest room in the apartment. It gets all the sun . . .

OLD LADY. I have wonderful children. I thank God every night for that. I . . .

DAUGHTER. Ma, I don't like you living here alone . . .

OLD LADY. Annie, I been living in this house for eight years, and I know all the neighbors and the store people, and if I lived with you, I'd be a stranger.

DAUGHTER. There's plenty of old people in my neighborhood. You'll make friends.

OLD LADY. Annie, you're a good daughter, but I want to keep my own home. I want to pay my own rent. I don't want to be some old lady living with her children. If I can't take care of myself, I just as soon be in the grave with your father. I don't want to be a burden on my children . . .

DAUGHTER. Ma, for heaven's sakes . . .

OLD LADY. More than anything else, I don't want to be a burden on my children. I pray to God every night to let me keep my health and my strength so that I won't have to be a burden on my children . . . (*The teapot suddenly hisses. The* OLD LADY *looks up.*) Annie, the pot is boiling. Would you pour the water in the cups?

(*The* DAUGHTER *moves to the stove. The* OLD LADY, *much of her ginger seemingly sapped out of her, shuffles into the living room. She perches on the edge of one of the wooden chairs.*)

OLD LADY. I been getting some pains in my shoulder the last week or so. I had the electric heating pad on practically the whole night. . . . (*She looks up toward the windows again.*) It's starting to rain a little harder again. Maybe, I won't go downtown today after all. Maybe, if it clears up a bit, I'll go out and sit in the park and get some sun.

(*In the kitchen, the* DAUGHTER *pours the boiling water into each cup, stirs.*)

DAUGHTER (*to her mother, off in the living room*). Is this all you're eating for breakfast, Ma? Let me make you something else . . .

(*Dissolve to: A park bench. The* OLD LADY *and two other old ladies are seated, all bundled up in their cheap cloth coats with the worn fur collars. The second old lady is also Irish. Her name is* MRS. GEEGAN. *The third old lady is possibly Jewish, certainly a New Yorker by intonation. Her name is* MRS. KLINE. *The rain has stopped; it is a clear, bright, sunny March morning.*)

OLD LADY. . . . Well, it's nice and clear now, isn't it? It was raining something fierce around seven o'clock this morning.

MRS. GEEGAN (*grimacing*). It's too ruddy cold for me. I'd go home except my daughter-in-law's cleaning the house, and I don't want to get in her way.

MRS. KLINE. My daughter-in-law should drop dead tomorrow.

MRS. GEEGAN. My daughter-in-law gets into an awful black temper when she's cleaning.

MRS. KLINE. My daughter-in-law should grow rich and own a hotel with a thousand rooms and be found dead in every one of them.

MRS. GEEGAN (*to the* OLD LADY). I think I'll go over and visit Missus Halley in a little while, would you like to go? She fell down the stairs and broke her hip, and they're suing the owners of the building. I saw her son yesterday, and he says she's awful weak. When you break a hip at that age, you're as good as in the coffin. I don't like to visit Missus Halley. She's always so gloomy about things. But it's a way of killing off an hour or so to lunch. A little later this afternoon, I thought I'd go to confession. It's so warm and solemn in the church. Do you go to Saint John's? I think it's ever so much prettier than Our Lady of Visitation. Why don't you come to Missus Halley's with me, Missus Fanning? Her son's a sweet man, and there's always a bit of fruit they offer you.

OLD LADY. I don't believe I know a Missus Halley.

MRS. GEEGAN. Missus Halley, the one that fell down the stairs last week and dislocated her hip. They're suing the owners of the building for forty thousand dollars.

MRS. KLINE. They'll settle for a hundred, believe me.

MRS. GEEGAN. Oh, it's chilly this morning. I'd go home, but my daughter-in-law is cleaning the house, and she doesn't like me to be about when she's cleaning. I'd like a bottle of beer, that's what I'd like. Oh, my mouth is fairly watering for it. I'm not allowed to have beer, you know. I'm a diabetic. You don't happen to have a quarter on you, Missus Fanning? We could buy a bottle and split it between us. I'd ask my son for it, but they always want to know what I want the money for.

OLD LADY (*looking sharply at* MRS. GEEGAN). Do you have to ask your children for money?

MRS. GEEGAN. Oh, they're generous. They always give me whenever I ask. But I'm not allowed to have beer, you see, and they wouldn't give me the twenty-five cents for that. What do I need money for anyway? Go to the movies? I haven't been to the movies in more than a year, I think. I just like a dollar every now and then for an offering at mass. Do you go to seven o'clock novena, Missus Fanning? It's a good way to spend an hour, I think.

OLD LADY. Is that what you do with your day, Missus Geegan? Visit dying old ladies and go to confession?

MRS. GEEGAN. Well, I like to stay in the house a lot, watching television in the afternoons, with the kiddie shows and a lot of dancing and Kate Smith and shows like that. But my daughter-in-law's cleaning up today, and she doesn't like me around the house when she's cleaning, so I came out a bit early to sit in the park.

(*The* OLD LADY *regards* MRS. GEEGAN *for a long moment.*)

MRS. KLINE. My daughter-in-law, she should invest all her money in General Motors stock, and they should go bankrupt.

(*A pause settles over the three old ladies. They just sit, huddled, their cheeks pressed into the fur of their collars. After a moment, the* OLD LADY *shivers noticeably.*)

OLD LADY. It's a bit chilly. I think I'll go home. (*She rises.*) Good-by, Missus Geegan . . . Good-by, Missus . . .

(*The other two old ladies nod their good-bys. The* OLD LADY *moves off screen. We hold for a moment on the remaining two old ladies, sitting, shoulders hunched against the morning chill, faces pressed under their collars, staring bleakly ahead.*

*Dissolve to: Door of the* OLD LADY's *apartment. It opens, and the* OLD LADY *comes in. She closes the door behind her, goes up the small foyer to the living room. She unbuttons her coat and walks aimlessly around the room, into the bedroom and out again, across the living room and into the kitchen, and then out of the kitchen. She is frowning as she walks and rubs her hands continually as if she is quite cold. Suddenly she goes to the telephone, picks it up, dials a number, waits.*)

OLD LADY (*snappishly*). Is this Mister McCleod? This is Missus Fanning in Apartment 3F! The place is a refrigerator up here! It's freezing! I want some steam! I want it right now! That's all there is to it! I want some steam right now! (*She hangs up sharply, turns—scowling—and sits heavily down on the edge of a soft chair, scowling, nervous, rocking a little back and forth. Then abruptly she rises, crosses the living room to the television set, clicks it on. She stands in front of it, waiting for a picture to show. At last the picture comes on. It is the WPIX station signal, accompanied by the steady high-pitched drone that indicates there are no programs on yet. She turns the set off almost angrily.*

She is beginning to breathe heavily now. She turns nervously and looks at the large ornamental clock on the sideboard. It reads ten minutes after eleven. She goes to the small dining table and sits down on one of the hardback chairs. Her black purse is still on the table, as it was during the scene with her DAUGHTER. Her eyes rest on it for a moment; then she reaches over, opens the purse, and takes out the white employment card. She looks at it briefly, expressionlessly. Then she returns it to the purse and reclasps the purse. Again she sits for a moment, rigid, expressionless. Then suddenly she stands, grabs the purse, and starts out the living room, down the foyer, to the front door of her apartment—buttoning her coat as she goes. She opens the door, goes out.

Camera stays on door as it is closed. There is the noise of a key being inserted into the lock. A moment later the bolts on the lock shift into locked position. Hold.

Fade out.)

# Act Two

(Fade in: Film. Lunchtime in the needle-trade district of New York—a quick montage of shots of the streets, jammed with traffic, trucks, and working people hurrying to the dense little luncheonettes for their lunch.

Dissolve to: Interior of the Tiny Tots Sportswear Co., Inc., 137 West Twenty-seventh Street, on the eighth floor. It is lunchtime. We dissolve in on some of the women operators at their lunch. They are seated at their machines, of which there are twenty—in two rows of ten, facing each other. Not all of the operators eat their lunch in: about half go downstairs to join the teeming noontime crowds in the oily little restaurants of the vicinity. The ten-or-so women whom we see —munching their sandwiches and sipping their containers of coffee and chattering shrilly to one another—all wear worn housedresses. A good proportion of the operators are Negro and Puerto Rican. Not a few of them are gray-haired, or at least unmistakably middle-aged.

The rest of the shop seems to consist of endless rows of pipe racks on which hang finished children's dresses, waiting to be shipped. In the middle of these racks is a pressing machine and sorting table at which two of the three men who work in the shop eat their lunch. At the far end of the loft—in a corner so dark that a light must always be on over it—is an old, battered roll-top desk at which sits the BOOKKEEPER, an angular woman of thirty-five, differentiated from the hand workers in that she wears a clean dress.

Nearby is the BOSS, a man in his thirties. He is bent over a machine, working on it with a screw driver. The BOSS is really a pleasant man; he works under the illusion, however, that gruffness is a requisite quality of an executive.

Somehow, a tortured passageway has been worked out between the racks leading to the elevator doors; it is the only visible exit and entrance to the loft.

As we look at these doors, there is a growing whirring and clanging announcing the arrival of the elevator. The doors slide reluctantly open, and the OLD LADY enters the shop. The elevator doors slide closed behind her. She stands surrounded by pipe racks, a little apprehensive. The arrival of the elevator has caused some of the people to look up briefly. The OLD LADY goes to the presser, a Puerto Rican.)

OLD LADY. Excuse me, I'm looking for the boss. (The presser indicates with his hand the spot where the BOSS is standing, working on the machine. The OLD LADY picks her way through the cluttered pipe racks to the BOOKKEEPER, who looks up at her approach. The BOSS also looks up briefly at her approach, but goes back to his work. The OLD LADY opens her purse, takes out the white card, and proffers it to the BOOKKEEPER. She mutters something.)

BOOKKEEPER. Excuse me, I can't hear what you said.

OLD LADY. I said, I was supposed to be here yesterday, but I was sick in the subway I—fainted, you see and . . .

(*The* BOSS *now turns to the* OLD LADY.)

BOSS. What? . . . What? . . .

OLD LADY. I was sent down from the . . .

BOSS. What?

OLD LADY (*louder*). I was sent down from the New York State Employment Service. I was supposed to be here yesterday.

BOSS. Yes, so what happened?

OLD LADY. I was sick, I fainted in the subway.

BOSS. What?

OLD LADY (*louder*). I was sick. The subway was so hot there, you see—there was a big crush at a Hundred and Forty-ninth Street . . .

BOSS. You was supposed to be here yesterday.

OLD LADY. I had a little trouble. They had my daughter down there and everything. By the time I got down here, it was half-past five, and the fellow on the elevator—not the one that was here this morning—another fellow entirely. An old man it was. He said there was nobody up here. So I was going to come down early this morning, but I figured you probably had the job filled anyway. That's why I didn't come down till now.

BOSS. What kind of work do you do?

OLD LADY. Well, I used to do all sections except joining and zippers, but I think the fellow at the Employment Service explained to you that it's been a number of years since I actually worked in a shop.

BOSS. What do you mean, a number of years?

OLD LADY (*mumbling*). Well, I did a lot of sewing for the Red Cross during the war, y'know, but I haven't actually worked in a shop since 1916.

BOSS (*who didn't quite hear her mumbled words*). What?

OLD LADY (*louder*). Nineteen sixteen. October.

BOSS. Nineteen sixteen.

OLD LADY. I'm sure if I could work a little bit, I would be fine. I used to be a very fast worker

BOSS. Can you thread a machine?

(*The* OLD LADY *nods.*)

*He starts off through the maze of pipe racks*

*to the two rows of machines. The* OLD LADY *follows after him, clutching her purse and the white card, her hat still sitting on her head, her coat still buttoned. As they go up the rows of sewing machines, the other operators look up to catch covert glimpses of the new applicant. The* BOSS *indicates one of the open machines.)*

BOSS. All right. Siddown. Show me how you thread a machine.

*(The* OLD LADY *sets her purse down nervously and takes the seat behind the machine. The other operators have all paused in their eating to watch the test. The* OLD LADY *reaches to her side, where there are several spools of thread.)*

OLD LADY. What kind of thread, white or black? . . .

BOSS. White! White!

*(She fumblingly fetches a spool of white thread and, despite the fact she is obviously trembling, she contrives to thread the machine—a process which takes about half a minute. The* BOSS *stands towering over her.)*

BOSS. Can you sleeve?

*(The* OLD LADY *nods, desperately trying to get the thread through the eye of the needle and over the proper holes.)*

BOSS. It's a simple business. One seam. (He reaches into the bin belonging to the machine next to the one the* OLD LADY *is working on and extracts a neatly tied bundle of sleeve material. He drops it on the table beside the* OLD LADY.)

BOSS. All right, make a sleeve. Let's see how you make a sleeve.

*(He breaks the string and gives her a piece of sleeve material. She takes it, but is so nervous it falls to the floor. She hurriedly bends to pick it up, inserts the sleeve into the machine, and hunches into her work—her face screwed tight with intense concentration. She has still not unbuttoned her coat, and beads of sweat begin to appear on her brow. With painstaking laboriousness, she slowly moves the sleeve material into the machine. The* BOSS *stands, impatient and scowling.)*

BOSS. Mama, what are you weaving there, a carpet? It's a lousy sleeve, for Pete's sake.

OLD LADY. I'm a little unsure. My fingers are a little unsure . . .

BOSS. You gotta be fast, Mama. This is week work. It's not piecework. I'm paying you by the hour. I got twenny dozen cottons here, gotta be out by six o'clock. The truckman isn't gonna wait, you know . . . Mama, Mama, Mama, watch what you're doing there . . . (He leans quickly forward and reguides the material.) A straight seam, for heaven's sake! You're making it crooked . . . Watch it! Watch it! Watch what you're doing there, Mama . . . All right, sew. Don't let me make you nervous. Sew . . . Mama, wadda you sewing there, an appendicitis operation? It's a lousy sleeve. How long you gonna take? I want operators here, not surgeons . . . (Through all this, the terrified* OLD LADY *tremblingly pushes the material through the machine. Finally she's finished. She looks up at the* BOSS, *her eyes wide with apprehension, ready to pick up her purse and dash out to the street. The* BOSS *picks up the sleeve, studies it, then drops it on the table, mutters.)*

BOSS. All right, we'll try you out for a while . . .

*(He turns abruptly and goes back through the pipe racks to the desk. The* OLD LADY *sits, trembling, a little slumped, her coat still buttoned to the collar. A middle-aged* NEGRO WOMAN, *sitting at the next machine over her lunch, leans over to the* OLD LADY.)*

NEGRO WOMAN (gently). Mama, what are you sitting there in your hat and coat for? Hang them up, honey. You go through that door over there.

*(She points to a door leading into a built-in room. The* OLD LADY *looks up slowly at this genuine sympathy.)*

NEGRO WOMAN. Don't let him get you nervous, Mama. He likes to yell a lot, but he's okay.

*(The tension within the* OLD LADY *suddenly bursts out in the form of a soft, staccato series of sighs. She quickly masters herself.)*

OLD LADY (smiling at the NEGRO WOMAN). I'm a little unsure of myself. My fingers are a little unsure.

*(Cut to: The* BOSS, *standing by the desk. He leans down to mutter to the* BOOKKEEPER.)*

BOSS (muttering). How could I say no, will you tell me? How could I say no? . . .

BOOKKEEPER. Nobody says you should say no.

BOSS. She was so nervous, did you see how nervous she was? I bet you she's seventy years old. How could I say no? *(The telephone suddenly rings.)* Answer . . . *(The BOOKKEEPER picks up the receiver.)*

BOOKKEEPER *(on the phone)*. Tiny Tots Sportswear . . .

BOSS *(in a low voice)*. Who is it?

BOOKKEEPER *(on phone)*. He's somewhere on the floor, Mister Raymond. I'll see if I can find him . . .

BOSS *(frowning)*. Which Raymond is it, the younger one or the older one?

BOOKKEEPER. The younger one.

BOSS. You can't find me.

*(The BOOKKEEPER starts to relay this message, but the BOSS changes his mind. He takes the receiver.)*

BOSS. Hello, Jerry? This is Sam . . . Jerry, for heaven's sake, the twenty dozen just came at half-past nine this morning . . . Jerry, I told you six o'clock; it'll be ready six o'clock . . . *(Suddenly lowers his voice, turns away from the BOOKKEEPER, embarrassed at the pleading he's going to have to go through now)* Jerry, how about that fifty dozen faille sports suits . . . Have a heart, Jerry, I need the work. I haven't got enough work to keep my girls. Two of them left yesterday . . . Jerry, please, what kind of living can I make on these cheap cottons? Give me a fancier garment . . . It's such small lots, Jerry. At least give me big lots . . . *(Lowering his voice even more)* Jerry, I hate to appeal to you on this level, but I'm your brother-in-law, you know. . . . Things are pretty rough with me right now, Jerry. Have a heart. Send me over the fifty dozen failles you got in yesterday. I'll make a rush job for you . . . please, Jerry, why do you have to make me crawl? All right, I'll have this one for you five o'clock . . . I'll call up the freight man now. How about the failles? . . . Okay, Jerry, thank you, you're a good fellow . . . All right, five o'clock. I'll call the freight man right now . . . Okay . . . *(He hangs up, stands a moment, sick at his own loss of dignity. He turns to the BOOKKEEPER, head bowed.)*

BOSS. My own brother-in-law . . .

*(He shuffles away, looks up. The OLD LADY, who had gone into the dressing room to hang up her coat and hat, comes out of the dressing room now. The BOSS wheels on her.)*

BOSS. Watsa matter with you? I left you a bundle of sleeves there! You're not even in the shop five minutes, and you walk around like you own the place! *(He wheels to the other operators.)* All right! Come on! Come on! What are you sitting there? Rush job! Rush job! Let's go! Five o'clock the freight man's coming! Let's go! Let's go!

*(Cut to: The bedroom of the DAUGHTER's and SON-IN-LAW's apartment. The bed has been made, the room cleaned up. The blinds have been drawn open, and the room is nice and bright. The SON-IN-LAW sits on one of the straight-back chairs, slumped a little, surly, scowling. The DAUGHTER sits erectly on the bed, her back to her husband, likewise scowling. Apparently, angry words have passed between them. The doorbell buzzes off. Neither of them moves for a moment. Then the DAUGHTER rises. At her move, the SON-IN-LAW begins to gather himself together.)*

SON-IN-LAW. I'll get it.

*(The DAUGHTER moves—in sullen, quick silence—past him and out into the foyer. The SON-IN-LAW, who has started to rise, sits down again.*

*In the hallway, the DAUGHTER pads down to the front door of the apartment. She is wearing a housedress now and house slippers. She opens the door. Waiting at the door is an attractive young woman in her early thirties, in coat and hat.)*

DAUGHTER. Hello, Marie, what are you doing here?

SISTER. Nothing. I just came by for a couple of minutes, that's all. I just brought the kids back to school. I thought I'd drop in for a minute, that's all. How's George? *(She comes into the apartment. The DAUGHTER closes the door after her. The SISTER starts down the hallway.)*

DAUGHTER. You came in right in the middle of an argument.

*(The SON-IN-LAW is now standing in the bedroom doorway.)*

SON-IN-LAW (*to the* SISTER). Your sister drives me crazy.

SISTER. Watsa matter now?

DAUGHTER (*following her* SISTER *up the foyer*). Nothing's the matter. How's Jack? The kids? (*The two women go into the bedroom, the* SON-IN-LAW *stepping back to let them in.*)

SISTER. They're fine. Jack's got a little cold, nothing important. I just took the kids back to school, and I thought I'd drop in, see if you feel like going up to Fordham Road, do a little shopping for a couple of hours. (*To the* SON-IN-LAW) What are you doing home?

SON-IN-LAW. It's my vacation. We were gonna leave the kids with my sister, drive downna Virginia, North Carolina, get some warm climate. But your crazy sister don't wanna go. She don't wanna leave your mother . . . (*Turning to his wife*) Your mother can take care of herself better than we can. She's a tough old woman. . . . How many vacations you think I get a year? I don't wanna sit in New York for two weeks, watching it rain.

SISTER. Go ahead, Annie. Me and Frank will see that Mom's all right.

DAUGHTER. Sure, you and Frank. Look, Marie, I was over to see Mom this morning . . .

SON-IN-LAW. Half-past six she got up this morning, go over to see your mother.

DAUGHTER. After what happened yesterday, I decided to put my foot down. Because Mom got no business at her age riding up and down in the subways. You know how packed they are. Anyway, I called Mom on the phone, and she gave me the usual arguments. You know Mom. So anyway, I went over to see her, and she was very depressed. We talked for about an hour, and she told me she's been feeling very depressed lately. It's no good Mom living there alone, and you know it, Marie. Anyway, I think I finally convinced her to move out of there and come and live over here.

SON-IN-LAW. You didn't convince me.

DAUGHTER. George, please . . .

SON-IN-LAW. Look, Annie, I like your mother. We get along fine. We go over visit her once, twice a week, fine. What I like about her is that she doesn't hang all over you like my mother does.

DAUGHTER. This is the only thing I ever asked you in our whole marriage . . .

SON-IN-LAW. This is just begging for trouble. You know that in the bottom of your heart. . .

DAUGHTER. I don't wanna argue any more about it . . .

SISTER. Look, Annie, I think George is right, I think . . .

(*The* DAUGHTER *suddenly wheels on her* SISTER, *a long-repressed fury trembling out of her.*)

DAUGHTER (*literally screaming*). You keep outta this! You hear me? You never cared about Mom in your whole life! How many times you been over there this week? How many times? I go over every day! Every day! And I go over in the evenings too sometimes!

(*The* SISTER *turns away, not a little shaken by this fierce onslaught. The* DAUGHTER *sits down on the bed again, her back to both her husband and* SISTER, *herself confused by the ferocity of her outburst. The* SON-IN-LAW *looks down, embarrassed, at the floor. A moment of sick silence fills the room. Then without turning, but in a much lower voice, the* DAUGHTER *goes on.*)

DAUGHTER. George, I been a good wife to you. Did I ever ask you for mink coats or anything? Anything you want has always been good with me. This is the only thing I ever ask of you. I want my mother to live here with me where I can take care of her.

(*The* SON-IN-LAW *looks up briefly at his wife's unrelenting back and then back to the floor again.*)

SON-IN-LAW. All right, Annie. I won't argue any more with you about it.

SISTER. I guess I better go because I want to get back in the house before three o'clock when the kids come home from school.

(*Nobody says anything, so she starts for the door. The* SON-IN-LAW, *from his sitting position, looks up briefly at her as she passes, but she avoids his eyes. He stands, follows her out into the foyer. They proceed silently down the foyer to the doorway. Here they pause a minute. The scene is conducted in low, intense whispers.*)

SON-IN-LAW. She don't mean nothing, Marie. You know that.

SISTER. I know, I know . . .

SON-IN-LAW. She's a wonderful person. She'd get up at three o'clock in the morning for you. There's nothing she wouldn't do for her family.

SISTER. I know, George. I know Annie better than you know her. When she's sweet, she can be the sweetest person in the world. She's my kid sister but many's the time I came to her to do a little crying. But she's gonna kill my mother with all her sacrifices. She's trying to take away my mother's independence. My mother's been on her own all her life. That's the only way she knows how to live. I went over to see my mother yesterday. She was depressed. It broke my heart because I told Jack; I said: "I think my mother's beginning to give up." My mother used to be so sure of herself all the time, and yesterday she was talking there about how maybe she thinks she is getting a little old to work. It depressed me for the rest of the day . . .

SON-IN-LAW. Marie, you know that I really like your mother. If I thought it would work out at all, I would have no objection to her coming to live here. But the walls in this place are made out of paper. You can hear everything that goes on in the next room, and . . .

SISTER. It's a big mistake if she comes here. She'll just dry up into bones inside a year.

SON-IN-LAW. Tell that to Annie. Would you do that for me, please?

SISTER. You can't tell Annie nothing. Annie was born at a wrong time. The doctor told my mother she was gonna die if she had Annie, and my mother has been scared of Annie ever since. And if Annie thinks she's gonna get my mother to love her with all these sacrifices, she's crazy. My mother's favorite was always our big brother Frank, and Annie's been jealous of him as long as I know. I remember one time when we were in Saint John's school on Daly Avenue—I think Annie was about ten years old, and . . . oh, well, look, I better go. I'm not mad at Annie. She's been like this as long as I know her. (*She opens the door.*) She's doing the worst thing for my mother, absolutely the worst thing. I'll see you, George.

SON-IN-LAW. I'll see you.

(*The* SISTER *goes out, closing the door after her. The* SON-IN-LAW *stands a moment. Then, frowning, he moves back up the foyer to the bedroom. His wife is still seated as we last saw her, her back to the door, her hands in her lap—slumped a little, but with an air of rigid stubbornness about her. The* SON-IN-LAW *regards her for a moment. Then he moves around the bed and sits down beside his wife. He puts his arm around her and pulls her to him. She rests her head on his chest. They sit silently for a moment.*

*Dissolve to: Interior, the shop. The full complement of working operators are there, all hunched over their machines, and the place is a picture of industry. The women chatter shrilly with each other as they work. A radio plays in the background. Occasionally, one of the operators lifts her head and bellows out: "Work! Work! Jessica! Gimme some work!" . . . The* BOOKKEEPER, *Jessica, scurries back and forth from her desk to the sorting table—where she picks up small cartons of materials, bringing them to the operators—and back to her desk.*

*Dissolve to: The* OLD LADY *and her immediate neighbor, the* NEGRO WOMAN, *both bent over their machines, sewing away. The motors hum. The two women move their materials under the plunging needles. The* OLD LADY *hunches, intense and painfully concentrated, over her work. They sew in silent industry for a moment. Then . . .*)

OLD LADY (*without daring to look up from her work*). I'm getting the feel back, you know?

NEGRO WOMAN (*likewise without looking up*). Sure, you're gonna be all right, Mama.

OLD LADY. I used to be considered a very fast operator. I used to work on the lower East Side in those sweatshops, y'know. Six dollars a week. But I quit in October, 1916, because I got married and, in those days, y'know, it was a terrible disgrace for a married woman to work. So I quit. Not that we had the money. My husband was a house painter when we got married, which is seasonal work at best, and he had to borrow money to go to Atlantic City for three days. That was our honeymoon.

*(They lapse into silence. A woman's shrill voice from farther down the row of machines calls out: "Work! Hey, Jessica! Bring me some work!" The two women sew silently. Then . . .)*

OLD LADY. I got a feeling he's going to keep me on here. The boss, I mean. He seems like a nice enough man.

NEGRO WOMAN. He's nervous, but he's all right.

OLD LADY. I've been looking for almost four weeks now, y'know. My husband died a little more than a month ago.

NEGRO WOMAN. My husband died eighteen years ago.

OLD LADY. He was a very sick man all his life—lead poisoning, you know, from the paints. He had to quit the trade after a while, went into the retail grocery business. He was sixty-seven when he died, and I wonder he lived this long. In his last years, the circulation of the blood in his legs was so bad he could hardly walk to the corner.

NEGRO WOMAN. My big trouble is arthritis. I get terrible pains in my arms and in my shoulders sometimes.

OLD LADY. Oh, I been getting a lot of pains in my back, in between my shoulder blades.

NEGRO WOMAN. That's gall bladder.

OLD LADY. Is that what it is?

NEGRO WOMAN. I had that. When you get to our age, Missus Fanning, you gotta expect the bones to rebel.

OLD LADY. Well, now, you're not such an old woman.

NEGRO WOMAN. How old do you think I am?

OLD LADY. I don't know. Maybe forty, fifty.

NEGRO WOMAN. I'm sixty-eight years old.

*(For the first time, the OLD LADY looks up. She pauses in her work.)*

OLD LADY. I wouldn't believe you were sixty-eight.

NEGRO WOMAN. I'm sixty-eight. I got more white hair than you have. But I dye it. You oughtta dye your hair too. Just go in the five-and-ten, pick up some kind of hair dye. Because most people don't like to hire old people with white hair. My children don't want me to work no more, but I'm gonna work until I die. How old do you think that old Greek woman over there is?

OLD LADY. How old?

NEGRO WOMAN. She's sixty-nine. She got a son who's a big doctor. She won't quit working either. I like working here. I come in here in the morning, punch the clock. I'm friends with all these women. You see that little Jewish lady down there? That's the funniest little woman I ever met. You get her to tell you some of her jokes during lunch sometime. She gets me laughing sometimes I can hardly stop. What do I wanna sit around my dirty old room for when I got that little Jewish woman there to tell me jokes all day? That's what I tell my children.

*(The OLD LADY turns back to her sewing.)*

OLD LADY. Oh, I'd like to hear a couple of jokes.

*(At this moment there is a small burst of high-pitched laughter from farther down the rows of machines. Camera cuts to long shot of the rows of operators, singling out a group of three Puerto Rican girls in their twenties. One of them has apparently just said something that made the other two laugh. A fourth Puerto Rican girl, across the table and up from them, calls to them in Spanish: "What happened? What was so funny?" The Puerto Rican girl who made the others laugh answers in a quick patter of high-pitched Spanish. A sudden gust of laughter sweeps all the Puerto Rican girls at the machines. Another woman calls out: "What she say?" One of the Puerto Rican girls answers in broken English.)*

PUERTO RICAN GIRL. She say, t'ree week ago, she make a mistake, sewed the belts onna dress backward. Nobody found out. Yesterday, she went in to buy her little girl a dress inna store. They tried to sell her one-a these dresses . . . *(A wave of laughter rolls up and down the two rows of operators.)* She say, the label onna dress say: "Made in California." *(They absolutely roar at this.)*

*(Close-up: The OLD LADY joining in the general laughter. She finishes the sleeve she has been working on. It is apparently the last of the bunch. She gathers together in front of her the two dozen other sleeves she has just finished and begins to tie them up with a black ribbon. She lifts her head up and—with magnificent professionalism—calls out.)*

OLD LADY. Work! Work! . . .
(Camera closes down on the bundle of sleeves she has tied together with the black ribbon.

Dissolve to: The same bundle of sleeves. We pull back and see it is now being held by the BOSS. He is frowning down at them. At his elbow is standing one of the Puerto Rican girls. She is muttering in broken English.)
PUERTO RICAN GIRL. So what I do? The whole bunch, same way . . .
BOSS (scowling). All right, all right. Cut them open, resew the whole bunch . . .
PUERTO RICAN GIRL. Cut! I didn't do! I can't cut, sew, five o'clock the truckman . . . I gotta sew them on the blouse. Take two hours . . .
BOSS. All right, all right, cut them open, sew them up again . . .
(The girl takes the bundle of sleeves and shuffles away. The BOSS turns, suddenly deeply weary. He goes to the desk.)
BOSS (to the BOOKKEEPER). The old lady come in today, she sewed all the sleeves for the left hand. She didn't make any rights. All lefts . . .
BOOKKEEPER. So what are you gonna do? It's half-past four.
BOSS. Call up Raymond for me.
(The BOOKKEEPER picks up the phone receiver, dials. The BOSS looks up and through the pipe racks at the OLD LADY, sitting hunched and intense over her machine, working with concentrated meticulousness. The BOSS's attention is called back to the phone by the BOOKKEEPER. He takes the phone from her.)
BOSS (in a low voice). Jerry? This is Sam. Listen. I can't give you the whole twenty dozen at five o'clock. . . . All right, wait a minute, lemme . . . All right, wait a minute. I got fifteen dozen on the racks now . . . Jerry, please. I just got a new operator in today. She sewed five dozen sleeves all left-handed. We're gonna have to cut the seams open, and resew them . . . Look, Jerry, I'm sorry, what do you want from me? I can get it for you by six . . . Jerry, I'll pay the extra freight fee myself . . . Jerry . . . Listen, Jerry, how about those fifty dozen faille sport suits? This doesn't change your mind, does it . . . Jerry, it's an accident. It could happen to anyone . . . (A fury begins to take hold of the BOSS.) Look, Jerry, you promised me the fifty dozen fai . . . Look, Jerry, you know what you can do with those fifty dozen failles? You think I'm gonna crawl on my knees to you? (He's shouting now. Every head in the shop begins to look up.) You're a miserable human being, you hear that? I'd rather go bankrupt

than ask you for another order! And don't come over to my house no more! You hear? I ain't gonna crawl to you! You hear me? I ain't gonna crawl to you! . . . (He slams the receiver down, stands, his chest heaving, his face flushed. He looks down at the BOOKKEEPER, his fury still high.)
BOSS. Fire her! Fire her! Fire her! (He stands, the years of accumulated humiliation and resentment flooding out of him.

Fade out.)

# Act Three

(Fade in: Interior of a subway car heading north to the Bronx during the rush hour—absolutely jam-packed. The camera manages to work its way through the dense crowd to settle on the OLD LADY, seated in her black coat and hat, her hands folded in her lap, her old purse dangling from her wrist. She is staring bleakly straight ahead of herself, as if in another world. The train hurtles on.

Dissolve to: Interior of the OLD LADY's apartment—dark—empty. Night has fallen outside. The sound of a key being inserted into the lock. The bolts unlatch, and the door is pushed open. The OLD LADY enters. She closes the door after herself, bolts it. She stands a moment in the dark foyer, then shuffles up the foyer to the living room. She unbuttons her coat, sits down by the table, places her purse on the table. For a moment she sits. Then she rises, goes into the kitchen, turns on the light.

It takes her a moment to remember what she came into the kitchen for. Then, collecting herself, she opens the refrigerator door, extracts a carton of milk, sets it on the cupboard shelf. She opens the cupboard door, reaches in, extracts the box of Rice Krispies and a bowl. She sets the bowl down, begins to open the box of cereal. It falls out of her hands to the floor, a number of the pebbles of cereal rolling out to the floor. She starts to bend to pick the box up, then suddenly straightens and stands breathing heavily, nervously wetting her lips. She moves out of the kitchen quickly now, goes to the table, sits down again, picks up the phone, and dials. There is an edge of desperation in her movements. She waits. Then . . .)

OLD LADY. Frank? Who's this, Lillian? Lillian, dear, this is your mother-in-law, and I . . . oh, I'm sorry, what? . . . Oh, I'm sorry . . . Who's this, the baby sitter? . . . This is Missus Fanning, dear—Mister Fanning's mother, is he in? . . . Is Missus Fanning in? . . . Well, do you expect them in? I mean, it's half-past six. Did they eat their dinner already? . . . Oh, I see. Well, when do you . . . Oh, I see . . . No, dear, this is Mister Fanning's mother. Just tell him I called. It's not important. (She hangs up, leaving her hand still on the phone. Then she lifts the receiver again and dials

another number. She places a smile on her face and waits. Then . . .)

OLD LADY. Oh, Marie, dear, how are you . . . this is Mother . . . Oh, I'm glad to hear your voice . . . Oh, I'm fine . . . fine. How's Jack and the kids? . . . Well, I hope it's nothing serious . . . Oh, that's good . . . (She is mustering up all the good humor she has in her.) Oh my, what a day I had. Oh, wait'll I tell you. Listen, I haven't taken you away from your dinner or anything . . . Oh, I went down to look for a job again . . . Yes, that's right, Annie was here this morning . . . how did you know? . . . Oh, is that right? Well, it cleared up, you know, and I didn't want to just sit around, so I went down to this job, and I got fired again . . . The stupidest thing, I sewed all left sleeves . . . Well, you know you have to sew sleeves for the right as well as the left unless your customers are one-armed people . . . (She is beginning to laugh nervously.) Yes, it's comical, isn't it? . . . Yes, all left-handed . . . (She bursts into a short, almost hysterical laugh. Her lip begins to twitch, and she catches her laughter in its middle and breathes deeply to regain control of herself.) Well, how's Jack and the kids? . . . Well, that's fine . . . What are you doing with yourself tonight? . . . (A deep weariness seems to have taken hold of her. She rests her head in the palm of her free hand. Her eyes are closed.) Oh, do you have a baby sitter? . . . Well, have a nice time, give my regards to your mother-in-law . . . No, no, I'm fine . . . No, I was just asking . . . No, no, listen, dear, I'm absolutely fine. I just come in the house, and I'm going to make myself some Rice Krispies, and I've got some rolls somewhere, and I think I've got a piece of fish in the refrigerator, and I'm going to make myself dinner and take a hot tub, and then I think I'll watch some television. What's tonight, Thursday? . . . Well, Groucho Marx is on tonight . . . No, no, I just called to ask how everything was. How's Jack and the kids? . . . That's fine, have a nice time . . . Good-by, dear . . . (She hangs up, sits erectly in the chair now. Her face wears an expression of the most profound weariness. She rises now and shuffles with no purpose into *the center of the dark room, her coat flapping loosely around her. Then she goes to the television set, turns it on. In a moment a jumble of lines appear, and the sound comes up. The lines clear up into Faye and Skitch Henderson engaging each other in very clever chitchat. The* OLD LADY *goes back to a television-viewing chair, sits down stiffly—her hands resting on the armrests—and expressionlessly watches the show. Camera comes in for a close-up of the* OLD LADY, *staring wide-eyed right through the television set, not hearing a word of the chitchat. She is breathing with some difficulty. Suddenly she rises and almost lurches back to the table. She takes the phone, dials with obvious trembling, waits . . .)*

OLD LADY. Annie? Annie, I wonder if I could spend the night at your house? I don't want to be alone . . . I'd appreciate that very much . . . All right, I'll wait here . . .

*(Dissolve to: Interior of the* OLD LADY's *bedroom. The* SON-IN-LAW, *in his hat and jacket, is snapping the clasps of an old valise together. Having closed the valise, he picks it off the bed and goes into the living room. The* OLD LADY *is there. She is seated in one of the straight-back chairs by the table, still in her coat and hat, and she is talking to the* DAUGHTER—*who can be seen through the kitchen doorway, reaching up into the pantry for some of her mother's personal groceries.)*

OLD LADY. . . . Well, the truth is, I'm getting old, and there's no point in saying it isn't true. *(To her* SON-IN-LAW *as he sets the valise down beside her)* Thank you, dear. I always have so much trouble with the clasp. . . . Did you hear the stupid thing I did today? I sewed all left-handed sleeves. That's the mark of a wandering mind, a sure sign of age. I'm sorry, George, to put you to all this inconvenience . . .

SON-IN-LAW. Don't be silly, Ma. Always glad to have you.

OLD LADY. Annie dear, what are you looking for?

DAUGHTER *(in the kitchen)*. Your saccharin.

OLD LADY. It's on the lower shelf, dear. . . . This isn't going to be permanent, George. I'll just stay with you a little while till I get a room somewheres with some other old woman . . .

DAUGHTER *(in the kitchen doorway)*. Ma, you're gonna stay with us, so, for heaven's sakes, let's not have no more arguments.

OLD LADY. What'll we do with all my furniture? Annie, don't you want the china closet?

DAUGHTER. No, Ma, we haven't got any room for it . . .

OLD LADY. It's such a good-looking piece. What we have to do is to get Jack and Marie and Frank and Lillian and all of us together, and we'll divide among the three of you whatever you want. I've got that fine set of silver—well, it's not the best, of course, silver plate, y'know—it's older than you are, Annie. *(To her* SON-IN-LAW*)* It was a gift of the girls in my shop when I got married. It's an inexpensive set, but I've shined it every year, and it sparkles. *(To her* DAUGHTER *in the kitchen)* Yes, that's what we'll have to do. We'll have to get all of us together one night and I'll apportion out whatever I've got. And whatever you don't want, well, we'll call a furniture dealer . . . *(to her* SON-IN-LAW*)* . . . although what would he pay me for these old things here? . . . *(To her* DAUGHTER*)* Annie, take the china closet . . . It's such a fine piece . . .

DAUGHTER. Ma, where would we put it?

OLD LADY. Well, take that soft chair there. You always liked that chair . . .

DAUGHTER. Ma . . .

OLD LADY. There's nothing wrong with it. It's not torn or anything. The upholstery's fine. Your father swore by that chair. He said it was the only chair he could sit in.

DAUGHTER. Ma, let's not worry about it now. We'll get together sometime next week with Marie and Lillian.

OLD LADY. I want you to have the chair . . .

DAUGHTER. Ma, we got all modern furniture in our house . . .

OLD LADY. It's not an old chair. We just bought it about six years ago. No, seven . . .

DAUGHTER. Ma, what do we need the . . .

OLD LADY. Annie, I don't want to sell it to a dealer! It's my home. I don't want it to go piece by piece into a second-hand shop.

DAUGHTER. Ma . . .

SON-IN-LAW. Annie! we'll take the chair!

DAUGHTER. All right, Ma, the chair is ours.

OLD LADY. I know that Lillian likes those lace linens I've got in the cedar chest. And the carpets. Now these are good carpets, Annie. There's no sense just throwing them out. They're good broadloom. The first good money your father was making we bought them. When we almost bought that house in Passaic, New Jersey. You ought to remember that, Annie, you were about seven then. But we bought the grocery store instead. Oh, how we scraped in that store. In the heart of the depression. We used to sell bread for six cents a loaf. I remember my husband said: "Let's buy a grocery store. At least we'll always have food in the house." It seems to me my whole life has been hand-to-mouth. Did we ever not worry about the rent? I remember as a girl in Cork, eating boiled potatoes every day. I don't know what it all means, I really don't . . . (*She stares rather abstractedly at her* SON-IN-LAW.) I'm sixty-six years old, and I don't know what the purpose of it all was.

SON-IN-LAW. Missus Fanning . . .

OLD LADY. An endless, endless struggle. And for what? For what? (*She is beginning to cry now.*) Is this what it all comes to? An old woman parceling out the old furniture in her house . . .? (*She bows her head and stands, thirty years of repressed tears torturously working their way through her body in racking shudders.*)

DAUGHTER. Ma . . .

(*The* OLD LADY *stands, her shoulders slumped, her head bowed, crying with a violent agony.*)

OLD LADY (*the words tumbling out between her sobs*). Oh, I don't care . . . I don't care . . .

(*Hold on the* OLD LADY, *standing, crying.*

*Dissolve to: Film. Rain whipping through the streets of New York at night—same film we opened the show with—a frightening thunderstorm.*

*Dissolve to: The* OLD LADY'S *valise, now open, lying on a narrow single bed. We pull back to see the* OLD LADY—*in a dress, but with her coat off—rummaging in the valise for something. The room she is in is obviously a little boy's room. There are a child's paintings and drawings and cutouts Scotch-taped to the wall, and toys and things on the floor. It is dark outside, and the rain whacks against the window panes. The* OLD LADY *finally extracts from out of the valise a long woolen nightgown and, holding it in both arms, she shuffles to the one chair in the room and sits down. She sets the nightgown in her lap and bends to remove her shoes. This is something of an effort and costs her a few moments of quick breathing. She sits, expressionless, catching her breath, the white nightgown on her lap, her hands folded on it. Even after she regains her breath, she sits this way, now staring fixedly at the floor at her feet.*
Hold.*

*Dissolve to: The window of the child's bedroom. It is daylight now, and the rain has stopped. The cold morning sun shines thinly through the white chintz curtains. The camera pulls slowly back and finally comes to rest on the* OLD LADY *sitting just as we saw her last, unmoving, wrapped in thought, the white nightgown on her lap, her hands folded. From some room off, the thin voice of a baby suddenly rises and abruptly falls. The* OLD LADY *looks slowly up.*

*Then she bends and puts her shoes on. She rises, sets the nightgown on the chair from which she has just risen, moves with a slight edge of purpose down the room to the closet, opens the door, reaches in, and takes out her coat. She puts it on, stands a moment, looking about the room for something. She finds her hat and purse sitting on the chest of drawers. She picks them up. Then she turns to the door of the room and carefully opens it. She looks out onto the hallway. Across from her, the door to her* DAUGHTER'S *and* SON-IN-LAW'S *bedroom stands slightly ajar. She crosses to the door, looks in. Her* DAUGHTER *and* SON-IN-LAW *make two large bundles under their blankets. For a moment she stands and surveys them. Then the* DAUGHTER *turns in her bed so that she faces her mother. Her eyes are open; she has not been asleep. At the sight of her mother in the doorway, she leans upon one elbow.*)

OLD LADY (*in an intense whisper*). Annie, it just wasn't comfortable, you know? I just can't sleep anywheres but in my own bed, and that's the truth. I'm sorry, Annie, honest. You're a fine daughter, and it warms me to know that I'm welcome here. But what'll I do with myself, Annie, what'll I do? . . .

(*The DAUGHTER regards her mother for a moment.*)

DAUGHTER. Where are you going, Ma, with your coat on?

OLD LADY. I'm going out and look for a job. And, Annie, please don't tell me that everything's against me. I know it. Well, I'll see you, dear. I didn't mean to wake you up . . . (*She turns and disappears from the doorway. The DAUGHTER starts quickly from the bed.*)

DAUGHTER. Ma . . . (*She moves quickly across the room to the door of the hallway. She is in her pajamas. She looks down the hallway, which is fairly dark. Her mother is already at the front door, at the other end.*)

DAUGHTER. Ma . . .

OLD LADY. I'm leaving the valise with all my things. I'll pick them up tonight. And please don't start an argument with me, Annie, because I won't listen to you. I'm a woman of respect. I can take care of myself. I always

have. And don't tell me it's raining because it stopped about an hour ago. And don't say you'll drive me home because I can get the bus two blocks away. Work is the meaning of my life. It's all I know what to do. I can't change my ways at this late time.

(*For a long moment the mother and DAUGHTER regard each other. Then the DAUGHTER pads quietly down to the OLD LADY.*)

DAUGHTER (*quietly*). When I'm your age, Ma, I hope I'm like you.

(*For a moment the two women stand in the dark hallway. Then they quickly embrace and release each other. The OLD LADY unbolts the door and disappears outside, closing the door after her. The DAUGHTER bolts it shut with a click. She turns and goes back up the dark foyer to her own bedroom. She goes in, shuffles to the bed, gets back under the covers. For a moment she just lies there. Then she nudges her sleeping husband, who grunts.*)

DAUGHTER. George, let's drop the kids at your sister's for a week or ten days and drive down to Virginia. You don't want to spend your one vacation a year sitting in New York, watching it rain.

(*The SON-IN-LAW, who hasn't heard a word, grunts once or twice more. The DAUGHTER pulls the blankets up over her shoulders, turns on her side, and closes her eyes. Fade out.*)

---

## DISCUSSION

*Act One*

1. (a) What conflicts are introduced in Act One? (b) Between what two characters is the main conflict? (c) How is it dramatically suggested by camera action at the opening of the act?

2. Whom is the Old Lady mourning?

3. What clues reveal the social-economic class to which the characters belong?

4. (a) What does the Son-in-law

say would happen to the Old Lady if she were to move in with his family? (b) Do you think he is right? (c) What does the Daughter say would happen to the Old Lady if she got a job?

5. How does the Old Lady want to live?

6. What makes the Old Lady decide to go for the job after all?

*Act Two*

1. (a) While the Sister is in the apartment, what do you learn

about the character of both the Daughter and the Old Lady? (b) What additional information do you get about the cause of the conflict between them?

2. (a) What kind of man is the Boss? (b) How does the Old Lady's work affect his production problem? (c) How is the Daughter's prophecy in Act One fulfilled?

*Act Three*

1. (a) At the beginning of Act Three, what state of mind prompts

the Old Lady to make the telephone calls? (b) What is the significance of the sequence of her calls? (c) Of what prophecy by the Son-in-law in Act One are you reminded?

2. (a) The last scene parallels the first part of Act One. What are the similarities? The differences? (b) What discoveries have the Old Lady and the Daughter made about themselves and about each other? (c) Has the Daughter won any kind of "victory"? Explain.

3. (a) What do you think of the Old Lady's final decision? (b) Had she surrendered and retired to live with the Daughter, what might have resulted?

4. What TV techniques contribute dramatic effects that would not be possible in a stage production of *The Mother?*

## PADDY CHAYEFSKY

Paddy Chayefsky has said of *The Mother* that it deals ". . . with the world of the mundane, the ordinary, and the untheatrical. The main relationships are as common as people." Known for his natural dialogue, Chayefsky strives to have his characters' language sound tape-recorded.

Chayefsky was born in the Bronx in 1923 and grew up there. After high school he briefly played semi-professional football, then attended City College of New York. During World War II he served with the army in Germany.

Chayefsky has written radio scripts, television mysteries, and serious television drama. *Marty* was both an award-winning television drama and an Academy Award-winning film. His *Middle*

*of the Night* ran for almost two years on Broadway, and in 1971 he won an Academy Award for his screenplay for the film *Hospital.*

# Composition Guide

**James Pierce**

Writing, composing with words, not only enables one to communicate, to connect with other human beings, but also helps one understand himself. The noted short story writer and critic V. S. Pritchett once said that he writes to find out what he thinks and feels. Our feelings are indeed often vague and ill-defined, our thoughts disconnected and rambling until we try to put them into some written form, say, a re-creation of a past experience or an exploration of an idea. When we write we find out more about ourselves. Yet writing is also a social instrument, a means of communicating with others. Our written words are intended to evoke a favorable response from our readers. Thus, we take care to observe the conventions of writing, to be clear and forceful, and not to offend our readers unintentionally.

The assignments in this composition guide reflect the twofold nature of writing: some emphasize the personal, others the social function of writing. Some of the assignments ask you to re-create your own experience or to refine your ideas; others ask you to create fictional experiences or to provide information for your readers or to take a public stance on a question. Most of the assignments offer you a choice of topic or technique. The overall aim of the composition guide is to enable you to compose in a wide variety of writing situations. Below are listed the unit titles and the assignments designed to accompany each unit.

**UNIT 1: The Short Story**
One: *Explanation*
Two: *Opinions*
Three: *Character Sketch*
Four: *Explanation*
Five: *Description*
Six: *Opinions*
Seven: *Criticism*
Eight: *Evaluation*

**UNIT 2: Nonfiction**
Nine: *Persuasion*
Ten: *Personal Experience*
Eleven: *Opinions*

**UNIT 3: Poetry**
Twelve: *Description*
Thirteen: *Opinions*
Fourteen: *Comparison and Contrast*
Fifteen: *Character Sketch*
Sixteen: *Interpretation*
Seventeen: *Interpretation*
Eighteen: *Personal Experience*
Nineteen: *Interpretation*

**UNIT 4: Romeo and Juliet**
Twenty: *Analysis of Character*
Twenty-one: *Dialogue*
Twenty-two: *Interpretation*

**UNIT 5: Classical Heritage**
Twenty-three: *Myths*
Twenty-four: *Explanation*
Twenty-five: *Persuasion*
Twenty-six: *Persuasion*

**UNIT 6: At Random**
Twenty-seven: *Script Writing*
Twenty-eight: *Description*
Twenty-nine: *Character Sketch*
Thirty: *Explanation*

# LESSON ONE: *Explanation*

*Based on "Peter Two" and "The Most Dangerous Game," pages 2–21.*
Peter Two undergoes a definite change, a change reflected in his attitude toward television adventure programs. In the beginning of the story he is enthralled by such programs; at the end of the story he turns the television set off in the midst of a program and says to himself, "... ah, they can have that, that's for kids." About Sanger Rainsford the reader cannot be so certain. It's possible he changed his attitude toward the hunted, but the story doesn't explicitly tell the reader that he has changed.

Choose as the subject of your composition either the change that occurred in Peter or the change you believe occurred in Sanger Rainsford, and in a paragraph explain how the change came about. Make the first sentence of your paragraph a brief statement of this change: for example, "Peter saw himself as ..., but came to realize that ..."; "Sanger Rainsford undoubtedly changed his mind about. ..." If necessary, use the next sentence to make clear the character's point of view before he changed. Then, referring to specific details and events in the story, explain what caused the change. (No need to retell the story; just select those events that significantly influenced the main character and show him modifying the way he thinks or behaves.) Conclude your paragraph with a statement of the character's point of view after he changed.

(If you strongly disagree with the view that Sanger Rainsford changed, write a paragraph explaining why there is no evidence in the story to indicate that he did change his attitude in any significant way.)

After you have finished your paragraph, exchange papers with a classmate and read and discuss each other's paper with the following points in mind: (*a*) Is the change attributed to the character clearly stated? (*b*) Can the reader understand the character's before and after states? (*c*) Do the events cited from the story show why the character changed? Is there enough supporting evidence? (*d*) Need any changes in sentence structure, spelling, punctuation, etc., be made to prepare the paper for

other readers? After the discussion revise your paper, if necessary.

## ALTERNATE ASSIGNMENTS

1. Our ideas, our attitudes, our likes and dislikes change. Think back to a change you have undergone. It can be a change in taste or behavior, a change in thinking or feeling—whatever seems of significance to you and of likely interest to others. Write a paragraph in which you describe the change and explain how it came about. Assume you are writing to a friend who thinks of you in the old way and you are trying to make clear to him your present point of view and why you have changed. If you wish, you can cast your first sentence in the form of "I used to ..., but now. ..."

2. Assume you are Sanger Rainsford. You have left Ship-Trap Island and are now in Rio. Your partner Whitney has gone ahead with the jaguar hunt and is now at a camp up the Amazon. You want to send him a message assuring him that you are all right, but also explaining to him what you now feel about hunting and what your present attitude toward the hunted is. Write the message.

# LESSON TWO: *Opinions*

*Based on "Claudine's Book," pages 23–34.*
Claudine is a rather severe critic of both grown-ups and young people. Turn back to pages 26 and 27 and reread what she writes in her diary. Is Claudine just being superior, just being "stuck-up," as her classmates might say, or is there some truth in her observations? Is she even being clear? What does she mean by saying that grownups *worry about* children but they don't *think of* them? And how can kids act wise and think stupid? Select either her observation about grownups or her observation about kids, and write a paragraph or two expressing your opinion about what she says. First indicate what you think she means. Then explain to what extent you agree or disagree with what she says. On what do you base your opinion: what you have read, what you have seen (TV programs, movies), what you have

actually experienced or witnessed? Can you cite examples from your own experience that support your opinion? Are they typical examples or unique ones?

Assume that you have read *Claudine's Book* and that you are addressing your words of agreement ("I know what you mean") or disagreement ("You couldn't have meant what you said about . . .") to her, the author.

## LESSON THREE: *Character Sketch*

*Based on "Luther," "Bargain," and "The Endless Streetcar Ride into the Night and the Tinfoil Noose," pages 37–59.*
One of the techniques an author uses to help the reader understand a character is to describe his appearance. A description of a character's appearance—his prominent facial features, his build, the way he walks, the way he stands or sits, the clothes he wears—can tell the reader a great deal. It can provide insight into the kind of person the character is meant to be (see, for example, the descriptions of Freighter Slade and Mr. Baumer); it can signal a change in behavior (as is the case with Luther); or it can humorously ridicule the character (recall the description of the narrator's clothes in "The Endless Streetcar Ride . . .").

Select someone you know and can observe firsthand. Study this person for ten minutes or so, taking notes on his or her facial features, hair style, body proportions, walk, posture, gestures, and dress. These notes will serve as the raw material for a written description of this person. Now decide what you intend to accomplish with the description: To suggest the kind of person he or she is by external details? (What traits will the description reveal?) To show a change in the person? (Will the notes suffice for this?) To criticize or praise the person?

After you have determined your purpose, select the details from your notes that will help you achieve the emphasis you intend. (For example, if you hope to emphasize the person's vitality, you will probably want to describe his movements, his gestures, his stance, his eyes, etc.; details of dress may be of minor importance.) Now decide on an order for your description (e.g., face, then body; body, then clothes; specific to general; top to bottom; then and now—whatever is appropriate to your purpose), and prepare a first draft. Keep the person you are describing anonymous, if you wish.

Have a classmate or, if possible, the subject of your description read your draft to help you determine if the emphasis you intended is clear. Ask the reader what impression he gets of the person you have described. What in the description accounts for the impression? Revise if necessary.

ALTERNATE ASSIGNMENT

If you are unable to observe someone firsthand, select a character from one of the three stories whose appearance is not described. Possibilities would be Mr. Carter, Al, Schwartz, or Helen. Then create a description of the character that you would imagine to be appropriate to the situation and to what you know of the character from having read the story.

## LESSON FOUR: *Explanation*

*Based on "The Sky Is Gray," "The Lottery Ticket," and "The Idealist," pages 61–87.*
Through their actions and thoughts the characters in these stories reveal the values they regard as important. Delaney takes a beating from Murderer Moloney rather than tell a lie. He makes quite clear the values, the code of conduct he is trying to live up to. The possibility of sudden wealth leads Ivan Dmitritch to envision the kind of life he admires. Mama wants James to "be a man" and trains him accordingly. Given what they value, how might these characters act in other situations?

Imagine a situation not depicted in the story for *one* of these characters: (a) Mama finds that the fee for extracting a tooth is now $2.00 rather than $1.50. (b) Upon returning home late at night, Mama and James find that the hog has gotten out and that Ty and Val have been unable to retrieve it. (c) Ivan comes home from the office after having learned that he is to be promoted to a better-paying position. (d) Ivan and Masha spend a week at a resort in the south of France. *(e)* In the schoolyard Delaney sees Gorman picking on Flanagan—tripping him, pushing him, making fun of his back.

Describe in a paragraph what you think the character would do in the situation you have selected. The character should act consistently, that is, in accord with the way he acts in the story. In a second paragraph explain why you think the character would act in the manner you describe.

ALTERNATE ASSIGNMENTS

1. You may prefer to *show* the character acting in the situation you have imagined rather than tell about how and why he might act. In that case, narrate the scene as if it were a part of the story from which it is derived. If your scene is based on "The Sky Is Gray," you will need to assume the character of James to narrate it. If it is based on "The Idealist," you will narrate the scene through the character of Delaney. If it derives from "The Lottery Ticket," you will be an anonymous narrator focusing on the actions and thoughts of Ivan. (Review the Handbook entry on *point of view* before you attempt this assignment.)

2. "The Lottery Ticket" is essentially one brief scene: a conversation between a husband and wife after dinner. "The Sky Is Gray" is a series of scenes: waiting for the bus, flashbacks to Monsieur Bayonne's attempts to cure the toothache and to getting up in the morning, the bus ride, waiting in the dentist's office, and so on. "The Idealist" alternates between the narrator's reflections and scenes in the classroom and elsewhere. Notice that the scenes in these stories are not strange or unusual; they are built from familiar materials. One of them may suggest an episode you would like to narrate: a conversation in the dentist's waiting room, a ride on the school bus (or any public conveyance), a classroom or schoolyard episode, an argument at the dinner table, an after-dinner discussion.

Create an episode based on material familiar to you and present it as if it were a scene in a short story. Decide whether you are a character (an "I") in the scene or whether you are reporting it from the outside (as in "The Lottery Ticket"). Then present what the characters say, their necessary actions, and the thoughts that are pertinent and possible given your point of view.

## LESSON FIVE: *Description*

*Based on "Rain on Tanyard Hollow" and "A Reading Problem," pages 89–109.*

The weather is a commonplace of conversation, but because it does influence our lives in general and specific ways, it is often an important element in stories. Emily Vanderpool's search for a place to read, for example, is influenced by the season: only in the fall can she read up in the mountains. Mammie and Pappie and Tracey need a break in the hot spell, need the rain to save at least a part of their crops.

The effects of the weather are also rendered in these stories. On the day that Emily meets the Gerlashes, a heat haze hangs over the summits of the mountains, the pavement is soft, the sidewalk shimmering, and the red dirt road so dusty that after a few steps Emily's legs look burned. When Tracey and Pappie walk down the hill, the sweat runs off Pappie's beard and Tracey's nose, gets in their eyes, completely envelops them; and they notice that the trees are dying, the leaves turning brown. Such descriptive details help the reader feel the intense heat.

This assignment will give you an opportunity to recreate an experience you have had with a particular kind of weather—intense dry heat, muggy heat, the refreshing warmth of a spring day, a gentle spring rain, a driving wintry rain, snow, fog. Describe this experience so that the reader *(a)* can visualize the setting and your relationship to it (e.g., a city street, a park, a suburban street, a country road, a field, a crowded beach, a deserted beach; what are you doing? walking, running, standing, lying down?) *(b)* can feel the effect of the weather on you and the things around you. Include images of touch or feel, of smell, of sight, of sound. (Can you "taste" the weather?) *(c)* can perceive the mood the weather induced in you (e.g., dreariness, lightness of heart, exhaustion, invigoration). You may want to review the Handbook entry on *imagery*.

Have a classmate read your description of the experience and suggest a title for it that reflects the mood it expresses.

## LESSON SIX: *Opinions*

*Based on "The Scarlet Ibis" and "To Da-duh, in Memoriam," pages 111–127.*
According to the author of "The Scarlet Ibis," the narrator's observation ". . . that pride is a wonderful, terrible thing, a seed that bears two vines, life and death" is central to the meaning of the story. The observation is stated as a general truth that the narrator learned later in life.

What is your reaction to this "truth"? How does it apply to the narrator's treatment of Doodle? Can it be applied without distortion to the actions of Da-duh and her granddaughter? Or need it be qualified? Is it borne out by your own experience?

Prepare a response to the author, Mr. Hurst, in which you express your thoughts on the narrator's observation about pride. You might consider the following questions before beginning to write: Is this idea central to the meaning of the story? How? How does it hold up as a general truth? Can it be applied to the actions of others, either fictitious (e.g., Da-duh and her granddaughter) or real? In your own experience, does pride sustain *and* destroy?

## LESSON SEVEN: *Criticism*

*Based on "The Fifty-first Dragon" and "By the Waters of Babylon," pages 128–141.*
From reading and discussing these two stories and from studying the Handbook entry on *fantasy*, you are aware that writers sometimes create improbable situations and characters to criticize the present. As the two stories illustrate, a writer may (among a number of possibilities) project present tendencies into a prophetic future, or he may create a mythical past in which present customs, patterns of behavior, values, or habits of thought are ridiculed.

If the improbable, the fantastic, interest you as a way of commenting on the present, select one of these approaches—a setting in the future or one in the legendary past—and create a narrative that will serve to criticize a present custom, way of behaving, value, or popular idea that you regard as stupid or possibly dangerous.

## LESSON EIGHT: *Evaluation*

*Based on Unit 1, "The Short Story."*
One of the author/consultants of this book (me) wrote the following when recommending selections for the short story unit:

I've had to remind myself that we're selecting stories for thirteen-and fourteen-year-olds to read and study and that our touchstones are interest and instruction for them: what will appeal to them and will enlighten them. To me, this implies that we should have some stories that are strong in the storytelling element, the what-happens-next; some stories that give the students insight into themselves (either at their present age or at an earlier age); some that enlarge their social vision, that extend their sympathies (help them understand the complexities of character or understand people that are different); some that extend their imaginations; and some that cause them to reflect on the meaning and purpose of life.

Assume that you are writing to me (send the letter if you wish; would be pleased to receive it) to tell me *(a)* whether or not you agree with my assumptions about the kind of stories that should be in a unit of this sort (why do you agree or disagree?) and *(b)* whether or not the unit achieves what I've recommended. Are there stories for each category I've suggested? If so, which ones? Are there some stories that don't seem to fit any of the purposes listed above? Which ones? Why don't they fit? This book will be revised in time; some of the stories will be retained, others will be replaced. Which stories would you recommend keeping in the book? Which would you recommend removing? Of the latter, why would you recommend their removal? After having read and discussed the stories, what's your over-all impression of the unit ("Great," "Good," "O.K.," "Well . . .")?

Thanks in advance for your criticisms.

## LESSON NINE: *Persuasion*

*Based on "From Portrait of Myself," "From Black Elk Speaks," and "From Narrative of the Life of Frederick Douglass," pages 146–166.*
The people presented to you in these selections exhibited determination, strength of character, force of will. They held convictions, strong convictions, about freedom, unrecognized beauty, injustice, right conduct; and they didn't hesitate to express their convictions and to act on them. These people accomplished something, had an overpowering drive or a unique vision or participated and played a role in momentous events. To people with such strength of character we seldom react neutrally. Most often we react in any of a number of ways: We are favorably impressed or unfavorably impressed; we admire what they did but perhaps dislike them; we don't necessarily admire what they did, but we respect, say, their singleness of purpose, their straightforwardness, their endurance.

How we react depends partly on ourselves, of course, on our individual personalities and values. But what primarily influences our reaction is how the people present themselves to us: how they describe their actions and accomplishments (with arrogance, with humility, with pride, with wonder, etc.), what their attitude toward themselves is, and what it is they actually did or tried to do.

Select one of the three figures—Margaret Bourke-White, Black Elk, or Frederick Douglass —and in a sentence state your reaction to that person as presented in the selection. Give a full reaction; don't limit yourself to an either/or response (e.g., admire/detest). Seldom, if ever, do we react to any person with a single, unified response: admiration, respect, irritation, pity, envy—they're all mixed together.

Use your statement as a thesis sentence for a composition in which you will persuade the rest of the class that your reaction is an appropriate one. Indicate what your reaction is based on. What specific actions, thoughts, expressions of the person account for your attitudes? What is your response to what the person accomplished or tried to achieve, to the person as a person, to the way the person describes his actions? Indicate as well how your values and tastes temper your reaction.

Your aim is to convince the rest of the class that your reaction to this person is appropriate and fair.

## LESSON TEN: *Personal Experience*

*Based on "The Rose-Beetle Man" (page 179) and "The Dog That Bit People" (page 194).*
Gerald Durrell tells us that Achilles the tortoise was sprightly, intelligent, and lovable and that he had a peculiar sense of humor. The incidents he describes illustrate these characteristics of the tortoise. Similarly, James Thurber recounts examples of Muggs's behavior that illustrate his bad humor, his irascibility, his "seeing things." Through telling and showing, the authors entertainingly portray the unique personalities of their pets.

This assignment gives you an opportunity to portray an animal whose "personality" has made an impression on you. (It can be one of your pets or one belonging to someone else, a farm animal, a zoo animal, a squirrel in the park—whatever.) In planning your portrait determine first the animal's dominant traits, those that make up his personality; then make a list of incidents that will illustrate those traits. In the actual writing of the portrait, you can start with a general characterization, with background information (e.g., how you came to know the animal), or with the narrating of an incident that illustrates one of the animal's traits.

In this assignment you are drawing on personal experience, telling about what you know from firsthand observation. Assume that your audience is the class: you are writing to entertain and enlighten your classmates.

## LESSON ELEVEN: *Opinions*

*Based on "My Planet, 'Tis of Thee" (page 186) and "The Risk Takers" (page 198).*
Articles like the two listed above challenge our accepted ways of thinking, provoke us into thinking about topics we aren't normally aware of or about problems we'd just as soon forget. Robert Daley, for example, says we can't just dismiss risk takers as some special kind of nuts; in their own ways they contribute to the advancement of society. "Cut off the right to risk one's life, and progress would end and society would atrophy and die." Yet Isaac Asimov argues that "progress," as we commonly understand it, must be resisted. We can't have it better and survive. While these two viewpoints do not necessarily contradict one another, they do illustrate the argumentative nature of such articles. Each author asks the reader to agree with him, to accept his explanations and arguments.

Below are some statements from the two articles that you may or may not agree with. Select the one that interests you most (or you may choose from one of the articles another statement that provokes your assent or disagreement), and write a response to the author; he is your assumed audience.

If you agree with the statement, on what is your agreement based? Evidence and arguments that the author himself supplies (cite them)? Your own experience? Material from other writings? Happenings in the environment? If you disagree with the statement, supply counter arguments and evidence supporting those arguments.

1. ". . . in viewing the future, I am forced to be guided by a certain cynicism because so many people, however lovable, seem to be immune to reason."

2. "It is really irrelevant that we think the Russians are a bunch of Commies or that they think we are a bunch of Imperialists."

3. "Let us have the space effort become multi-national in the future, let there be a planetary flag thrust into the soil of Mars. . . ."

4. ". . . nobody has a right to risk his life very much. We have a lot of laws against suicide."

5. "Most men who search out danger do it for money and for the pure pleasure of it."

6. ". . . you can't have a safe world and a progressive one."

## LESSON TWELVE: *Description*

*Based on "Responses," pages 214–221.*
The poems in this section rivet the reader's attention on commonplace things: snow, clods, a barn, a shed, an axehandle, morning and evening light, rain, birds, grass, a parking lot, a billboard, popcorn wrappers, crushed cigars, fog.

These are familiar objects and events, but the poets help us see them in fresh, unique ways through precise observation (the perfect symmetry of two starlings turning in the air to land backwards on a wire, the way the snow falls), through apt comparisons (fog is like a cat), and through describing their effects (the snow can soften the harsh contours of the city, or a bit of it shaken down by a crow can change a man's mood). The commonplace can be of interest if observed closely and imaginatively.

Select some place to observe, either a static or an active scene (e.g., a subway stop, a bus stop, a store front, a counter in a department store, a field, a parking lot, a boat dock, a schoolyard, a classroom), and for ten minutes write down, pell-mell, everything you see, hear, smell, feel. Use the first words that come to you; at this stage don't worry about spelling, grammar, style, form. You may do any one of the following with your raw notes:

(*a*) Select two or three of the most vivid sense impressions you have recorded (the way a place or an object looked or sounded or smelled or felt), and make each one into a one sentence poem, possibly after the manner of a Haiku, (three short lines) or after the manner of "Dust of Snow." Your poems may be rhymed or unrhymed.

(*b*) Select a cluster of impressions you have recorded that seem to form a pattern or lead to a single impression or suggest a comparison, and transform the impressions into a poem of from four to eight lines. Lines may be any length; the poem may be rhymed or unrhymed.

If you wish, pattern your poem after one of the poems in the "Responses" section.

*(c)* Take the sense impressions you have recorded and rewrite them to make them understandable and interesting to other people. If the scene you recorded was static, describe it from a specific point of observation; through selection of detail and choice of words, suggest the mood induced by the scene. If the scene was active, decide on a point of view and an appropriate time order; include dialogue if you have it recorded, and try to make a point with your narrative.

Whichever assignment you select, assume you are writing to your classmates. Your paper will be read and discussed by them.

## LESSON THIRTEEN: *Opinions*

*Based on "Curses," pages 222–225.*
The "curses" in this section express various shades of displeasure: exasperation at having been misdirected, hatred of one who has broken his word, indignation at the senseless killing of animals, and irritation with a talkative member of an audience. When we are angered by what we consider senseless or cruel, or when we feel we have been wronged or mistreated, expressing our displeasure can be healthy and, indeed, enjoyable. Think of something that irritates or exasperates you or arouses your indignation (e.g., a parent's constant reminders, a little brother's or sister's questions, a particular mannerism or practice of a teacher, a friend's always being late, a specific type of TV commercial, football fans, hot-car addicts), and write a curse of your own.

Notice that the curses you have read are written in different poetic forms. Feel free to use any form you find suitable. The traditional opening of such a poem, however, is a "may" construction ("May he . . . ," "May she . . . ," "May they . . . ," "May the mangy cur . . . ," "May the stiff-necked fool . . ."). Use this construction if it helps you get started and if it is appropriate to the shade of displeasure you are trying to express.

Try to compose a curse that others would sympathize with, one that could be part of an anthology of curses to be compiled by your class.

## LESSON FOURTEEN: *Comparison and Contrast*

*Based on "Battlegrounds," pages 226–233.*
The poems in this section express various attitudes toward war, man's destructiveness, and the meaning of death—subjects common to poetry from its beginnings. Though contemporary attitudes toward these subjects may fluctuate, the dilemmas they present confront every age. How should a fighting man conduct himself? How should we honor the dead? What can we say of them? (Compare Housman's "Here Dead Lie We . . . ," (page 226) with Simonides of Ceos's "Epitaph for Slain Spartans," page 398.) How will the living accept the death of those killed in war? Do wars ever accomplish anything? Should we or should we not support a given conflict?

Writing about the poems in this section will give you an opportunity to sharpen your understanding of some of the possible attitudes toward these subjects through expressing your own thoughts about them. You may choose either of the following assignments:

*(a)* The speaker in "The Mother" is accepting —resigned, yes, but accepting. The speaker in "The Conscientious Objector" is resistant, even defiant. Yet, are they really so very different? Compare and contrast the mother and the conscientious objector. What character traits do they have in common? How do they differ? Are their ideas similar or different? In what ways? How do their circumstances differ (concrete-abstract, specific-general)? Which do you prefer? Why?

*(b)* Reread the poems in the "Battlegrounds" section and select the two that contain the most meaning for you. Then write a brief composition (two or three paragraphs) in which you compare or contrast the two and explain why the poems are meaningful to you. Do the poems express the same or different ideas? Is it the human content of the poems that engages you? The ideas? The *way* the ideas are expressed (use of figurative language, imagery, descriptive

details, etc.)? What are the attitudes toward the subjects of the poems? The character of the speakers? Explain specifically what it is about each poem that interests you and why it interests you.

## LESSON FIFTEEN: *Character Sketch*

*Based on "Portraits," pages 234–239.*
How would you describe one of the people presented in this group of poems? What picture do you have of Melora Vilas, the mother with granite-like courage, the bean eaters, Miss Rosie, the certain gentleman?

You know something of their qualities, of their traits: courage, "Mostly Good," uncertainty; of their longings: for self-knowledge, for security; of the articles that surround them: tools and quilts, mahogany dressers, beads and receipts, tobacco crumbs, old man's shoes; of what they resemble: "small face cut like a heart," "wet brown bag of a woman." From what you know, how would you imagine their physical features? How, for example, would you visualize the facial features of the certain gentleman? Would you pay special attention to his eyes? How might he carry himself? How old might he be? What clothes would he wear?

Create a visual description of one of the people presented in this group of poems (do both the bean eaters, if you wish). Describe the facial features, the stature, the clothes that you imagine would be fitting for this person; tell, or better yet, suggest his age.

### ALTERNATE ASSIGNMENT

If you wish, create a poem describing a specific person (real or imaginary) or a type. Think of the character in a particular setting doing something. Then decide what your portrait will contain—qualities, longings, articles that characterize, comparisons? What will be the relationship of the speaker of your poem to the person being portrayed (close, as in "Miss Rosie," or relatively distant, as in "The Bean Eaters")?

## LESSON SIXTEEN: *Interpretation*

*Based on "Blues" pages 240–247.*
Sometimes a line or an observation in a poem strikes us as especially apt. Its meaning for us may differ somewhat from its meaning within the context of the poem, but it catches our interest, we find ourselves responding to it. We think, "Yes, that's just the way I feel," or "That's the way it is, all right," or "I never thought about it that way before," or "I never heard it put that way before." Choose a line from one of the poems in this group that caught your interest in this way.

Now write a paragraph in which you explain why the observation you have selected interests you. How would you interpret its meaning? What special reference does it have for you? What, if anything, about the way it is stated pleases you? You may limit the audience for this paper to your teacher, if you wish.

### ALTERNATE ASSIGNMENT

One of the questions after "The Housewife's Lament" asks you to think of the details that might be included in "The Student's Lament." If composing a lament appeals to you, go ahead and write "The Student's Lament." Or compose some other lament that fits your situation: "The Daughter's Lament," "The Son's Lament," "The Big Sister's (Brother's) Lament," "The Little Sister's (Brother's) Lament," "The Only Child's Lament," "The Paperboy's Lament," "The Baby-sitter's Lament." Or put yourself in someone else's place: "The Parent's Lament," "The Teacher's Lament," "The Supermarket-Checker's Lament," "The Barber's Lament," "The Milkman's Lament," "The Mail Carrier's Lament."

## LESSON SEVENTEEN: *Interpretation*

*Based on "Destinations," pages 248–255.*
Selecting a title for the poems in this section is an exercise in generalization. What concept, summed up in a word or a phrase, will suitably apply to the five poems in the section? The editors selected "Destinations." You may agree

that that's what the poems, in their various ways, are about. Or you may feel that some other title would be more appropriate, something like "Ends and Means" or "Lessons" or "Stacking Up/Pulling Back" or "Anticipations."

Create a title of your own for the poems in this section or select the present title or one of the possibilities suggested in the previous paragraph, and then write a paragraph defending your choice of title. Assume that you are writing to one of the editors of *Outlooks through Literature* attempting to persuade him or her either to keep "Destinations" as the title or to use a different title. In either case, you will want to show how well the title you are defending applies to each of the five poems in the section.

ALTERNATE ASSIGNMENT

One of the questions following "The Most Perilous Moment in Life" asks you to describe your most perilous moment. Perhaps it is not your most perilous moment that interests you but some other "moment" : your most *absurd,* your most *ludicrous,* your most *visionary,* your most *liberating,* your most *mind-bending,* your most *gourd-zonking.* If the notion appeals to you, select some "moment" of particular interest to you and write a paragraph or two or, if you prefer, a poem, describing it.

## LESSON EIGHTEEN: *Personal Experience*

*Based on "Phantoms" pages 256–261.*
The poems in this section present some uncanny happenings: ghosts of the dead complaining about the actions of the living, a witch insinuating that the imp of the perverse is in us all, a weird presence haunting someone, skaters on a spectral lake, photographs that reflect life or death.

Perhaps the poems remind you of an uncanny experience you have had: the feeling that someone was following you or watching you, the certainty that someone or something was outside your bedroom window at night, an eerie, inexplicable sound occurring in your house in the middle of the night, a prophetic dream?

If you have not had such an incident happen to you, imagine some uncanny experience that could happen to you. Now narrate this incident so that it will be clear and vivid to your classmates, so that its weirdness comes through. Establish a setting (where and when and under what circumstances the incident occurred); describe the uncanny happening(s); record your thoughts, speech, actions; and tell how the incident concluded.

## LESSON NINETEEN: *Interpretation*

*Based on* The Rime of the Ancient Mariner, *pages 262–281.*
After having read and discussed *The Rime of the Ancient Mariner,* you know that it can be approached in a number of ways: as a series of vivid scenes rich in imagery and sensory detail; as a miraculous tale, a fantastic adventure with supernatural beings and unnatural happenings; as a "night journey" of the spirit; as a moral fable.

Of course, it is not necessary to respond to the poem in any one way or in all of the ways suggested above. Your reading of the poem depends on your own preferences, on the way you react to the literal and the figurative. Therefore, among the assignments below, choose the one that gives you the most opportunity to write about the way the poem affects you.

(a) The emotional impact of the various scenes in the poem depends not only on the mariner's telling how he feels but also on the use of vivid descriptive words (which create images of sight, sound, touch, etc.) and the device of repetition. Select one of the scenes listed below and write an analysis in which you show how the predominant emotions in the scene (e.g., desolation, despair, relief) are reinforced through apt word choice, imagery, and repetition:

(1) Storm Blast/Land of Ice, lines 41–62
(2) The Becalming, lines 107–138
(3) The Skeleton Ship, lines 171–198
(4) The Mariner Alone, lines 232–256
(5) Breaking of the Spell, lines 263–291
(6) The Refreshing Storm, lines 297–326

(7) Sighting Home Port, lines 452–479

(b) Write a brief paper in which you show how the poem may be regarded as a tale of the supernatural. How does the *way* it is told contribute to its eerieness? What purpose does the story "frame" serve? The flashback technique? What are its miraculous elements? What characteristics does it have in common with other supernatural tales you have read or seen?

(c) Put yourself in the role of a script writer trying to sell this story to a television producer. What would you say in a memo to convince him that the tale would make a good television play for one of the programs that specializes in the weird and the unusual?

(d) A symbol, you will recall, means what it is as well as something more. For example, the peach tree in "Birthday in the House of the Poor" is a peach tree, but it also stands for the barrenness of the speaker in the poem. The albatross in *The Rime of the Ancient Mariner* is an albatross, but it also has additional force. Write a paper in which you show how the albatross acquires symbolic meanings in the poem. Before beginning to write, consider these questions: What is the literal use of the albatross in the poem? When does it begin to take on meanings other than its literal one? By the end of the narrative, what meanings have been suggested by the albatross? How might it be said that we all carry an albatross around our necks? (Or can this be said of all generations?)

# LESSON TWENTY: *Analysis of Character*

*Based on* Romeo and Juliet, *pages 286–361.*
The philosopher Karl Jaspers has said that a crisis enables a person to become aware of his inner resources. The death of someone close, forced separation from a loved one, a friend's betrayal, hopes for a career dashed, a brush with death—these are critical situations that force one to call upon his inner reserves, to assess what is worthwhile. They therefore enable one to grow. While no certainty exists that growth will occur, such crises provide the conditions for growth.

Using as your touchstone the idea that a crisis enables a person to grow in strength of character, write a paper in which you evaluate the reactions of both Juliet and Romeo to the news of Romeo's banishment (Act III, Scenes 2 and 3). How would you assess the character of each prior to the news of the banishment? How does each react to the news? How would you characterize their reactions? Is there any development in these reactions, any progression from shock and despair to strength and firm resolve? Explain. Does one show more strength of character than the other? How?

OR

A character in a play is defined not so much by the playwright's description (if he provides one) as by what the character does, his actions; by what he says; by what other characters say about him; and by the setting in which he moves. If we want to understand a character, we have to pay attention to the various ways in which his personality is defined.

Assume that your class is going to produce some scenes from *Romeo and Juliet* and that you have been asked to help prepare analyses of the characters, the aim being to give the student-actors sound understandings of the characters so that they may interpret their parts perceptively. Select one of the minor characters listed below:

| | | |
|---|---|---|
| Capulet | | Mercutio |
| | Nurse | |
| Tybalt | | Friar Laurence |

Now prepare a written analysis of the character you have selected that will make clear the position he occupies in the play and the sort of person he is. Is the character generous of spirit or mean-spirited, wise or foolish, rash or prudent, honorable or knavish, witty or laughable, etc.? Why does he act as he does?

Review the scenes in which the character appears or is referred to, and base your analysis on what he does and says, what others say about him (or how others treat him), and the position he occupies in the social setting of the play. Be prepared to discuss your analysis with other students who have analyzed the same character.

## LESSON TWENTY-ONE: *Dialogue*

*Based on* Romeo and Juliet, *pages 286–361.*
Imagine the following discussion:

ALLEN: *(hard-headed, realistic):* Well, really, the play is absurd: love at first sight (straight out of fairyland); married within a day of meeting; secret potions; missed messages. It's all contrived. The work of a hack. Besides, there's no real motivation for anything. It's all chance; everything happens by accident.

BERTRAND *(philosophical; used to baiting Allen):* Now, Allen, let's not always reduce everything to the law of probability, eh? The play isn't *meant* to be realistic. It isn't about the death of a salesman but about the death of two very idealistic adolescents. The point is: what brings about their tragedy? It isn't chance, as you say (nothing happens by chance); it's fate. Remember the opening note of the play: the lovers are "star-crossed." Their destiny is written in the stars; it's in the nature of things.

ALLEN: Well, what's that supposed to mean?

BERTRAND: Well, ah, let's see: it means that given the circumstances in which they lived, the tragic outcome of their love was inevitable.

CATHERINE *(sensitive, sympathetic; not romantic, but willing to grant the play its assumptions):* For once I'm not going to let you two argue on and on without hearing someone else's point of view. You never *listen* to each other, anyway. You're both so willing to dismiss the characters in the play. Allen, to you they're just cardboard "literary" figures. Would you feel that way if you saw the play acted on the stage or saw a film of it? Saw the characters embracing, fighting, dying? I don't think so. And Bertrand, you just see the characters as pawns in some sort of cosmic game. What happens to Romeo and Juliet happens because of them, because of the kind of people they are. Remember what Cassius says to Bru-

tus in *Julius Caesar:* "The fault, dear Brutus, is not in our stars / But in ourselves. . . ."

Allen, Bertrand, and Catherine express three different views of *Romeo and Juliet:* that the tragic events are caused *(a)* by chance, *(b)* by fate, *(c)* by character. Complete either of the two assignments below.

1. Continue in dialogue form the Allen-Bertrand-Catherine discussion, forcing each one to supply evidence for his point of view. How would Allen go about proving that everything happens by chance? What are the accidental happenings in the play? Do they lead to the tragedy? How would Bertrand prove his case? What in the play supports his view that Romeo and Juliet never had a chance? What about Catherine? How could she show that Romeo and Juliet cause their own downfall? What would she have to illustrate about their characters? What conclusion the discussion comes to is up to you.

2. Create your own dialogue (this form of writing is called a Socratic dialogue) in which characters other than Allen, Bertrand, and Catherine discuss and argue their interpretations of the play. There may be other views of the play that you want to argue, and you may be more comfortable with characters of your own creation. If you find three characters too difficult to sustain, you may limit the dialogue to two characters.

## LESSON TWENTY-TWO: *Interpretation*

*Based on* Romeo and Juliet, *pages 286–361.*
Seldom do we see a full-length version of a Shakespearean play in a modern production. Because the nature of the modern stage does not allow, as did the Elizabethan stage, for the quick playing of many scenes, a full-length version of a Shakespearean play is usually considered too long for modern audiences. Thus the director faces the problem of what to cut from the original script—parts of scenes, whole scenes, some combination of both?

Assume that the drama class in your school is going to produce *Romeo and Juliet* and that the director has proposed cutting the following scenes from the play in order not to make the playing time of the production too long:

Act I, Scene 4 (Benvolio and Mercutio attempt to lighten Romeo's gloom.)

Act II, Scene 1 (Immediately after the party.)

Act II, Scene 5 (Nurse returns with Romeo's message for Juliet.)

Act IV, Scene 2 (Juliet appears to agree to marry Paris.)

Act IV, Scene 4 (Preparations for the wedding.)

Select the one scene from the list which, in your judgment, would do the most damage to the play if it were eliminated. Then write a note to the director attempting to convince him to retain the scene. In composing your note, consider the functions the scene performs. (Does it advance the plot? What necessary information, if any, does it give the audience? Does it provide insight into character? Does it establish a mood or help develop an idea or theme? Which functions make it necessary to retain the scene?)

# LESSON TWENTY-THREE: *Myths*

*Based on "The Story of Daedalus and Icarus" and "The Story of Cadmus," pages 369–374.* Sometimes a myth—a story invoking events supernatural and beings superhuman—helps us understand the meaning of the works of humans and the events of the natural world more readily than does a factual, objective explanation.

There is, for example, more to the story of Cadmus than an explanation of how the city of Thebes was founded. The modern writer Marshall McLuhan has pointed out that the story of Cadmus and the sowing of the serpent's teeth may be viewed as a myth about the meaning of the alphabet, for Cadmus was the king who reputedly introduced the phonetic letters into Greece.

On the one hand, teeth and the letters of the alphabet are alike in that they are both visual in impact; they follow one another in a precise linear order. And just as teeth are agents of power in humans and in many animals, so are the letters of the alphabet agents of power and aggression as used by literate people.

On the other hand, the letters of the alphabet are like armed men (what the serpent's teeth became) in that at the time they ". . . meant power and authority and control of military structures at a distance." Prealphabetic writing was difficult to master; the alphabet, however, could be learned rather easily, thus making it possible for many people to read and write and to share in the giving and receiving of orders at a distance. With the coming of the alphabet, knowledge ceased to be a monopoly for one small, highly-trained class.

In a similar manner the story of Daedalus and Icarus could be viewed as a myth about the grandeur and folly of the human desire for flight or about the gain and loss created by any invention.

Thus, while a myth may tell an imaginative story with a simple moral (e.g., obey the will of the gods; follow the advice of your father), it may also imply other meanings.

This assignment gives you an opportunity to create a myth of your own to explain the origin or meaning of something we now more or less take for granted. You may write a story explaining one of the items on the list of possibilities below, or you may choose not to be limited by the list. If you would rather compose a myth explaining, say, some element of human nature, something historical, a feature of the landscape, a common household article, feel free to do so.)

| | |
|---|---|
| roads | camera |
| clock | telegraph |
| motorcycle | phonograph |
| airplane | radio |
| games | money |
| telephone | automobile |
| movies | ship |
| numbers | typewriter |
| bicycle | tape recorder |
| train | television |

Your hero may be on a quest, a journey in search of something. She or he may be in a difficult situation, trapped in some way. The intervention of gods and goddesses and the creation of the "thing" being explained may be used to help the hero either in the search or out of the predicament.

Be prepared to have your myth read by other members of your class. You may wish to work in committees or small groups to prepare all the myths for duplication so that they may be compiled into a Book of Myths, each member of the class to receive a copy.

## LESSON TWENTY-FOUR: *Explanation*

*Based on Greek and Latin Poems, pages 398–403.*

Were the concerns of the Greeks and Romans so different from our own? Some of the poems in this section seem timeless or, at least, contemporary. "On a Fortune-Teller," with its reference to astrology, its note of really-don't-believe-in-it-but, could just as readily have been written today as two thousand years ago.

Review the poems in this section. Select the one that appeals to you the most. Then write a paragraph in which you quote the observation made, explain what it means, and illustrate (with reference to specific events and happenings) how it might apply to life today. If you know of other similar observations from literature of the past and present, refer to those as well in your paragraph.

ALTERNATE ASSIGNMENT

Instead of writing about the modernity of a single observation, you may wish to show how one of the Greek or Latin poems is similar to one of the more modern poems found in the Poetry Unit. Some possible comparisons are:

1. "Dedication of a Mirror" and "Melora Vilas"

2. "Epitaph for Slain Spartans" and "Here Dead Lie We . . ."

3. "Suffenus, Varus, Whom You Know So Well" and "Lots of Lakes"

If you elect this assignment, you will want to show how the two poems are alike: for example, in theme, in content, in tone, in the use of imagery, in the way statements are made (by contrast, by illustration, by paradox, etc.). To complete the comparison of the two poems,

you would also need to show how they differ: Do they say the same thing, or are they variations of a common theme? How do they differ in circumstance or occasion? Other differences?

## LESSON TWENTY-FIVE: *Persuasion*

*Based on* Antigone, *pages 406–436.*

Assume that a representative of the National Organization of Women has filed a complaint against *Antigone*, demanding that students not be required to study the play. She maintains that Sophocles was a male chauvinist pig and that the play is obviously anti-feminist, placing women in the position of second-class citizens and perpetuating the myth that women are inferior, either submissively weak or hysterically irrational. Studying such a play merely ingrains such unconscious attitudes in the minds of the students, she concludes; therefore, the play should be removed from the course of study.

The principal of your school has refused to remove the play from the course of study. He argues that we don't know what Sophocles' personal views on women were. Even if we did have evidence that in his personal life he was anti-feminist, it would be of no consequence. We should give our attention to the play itself. And far from portraying women unfavorably, it shows them to be above the narrow concerns of men. Antigone is the most admirable character in the play, the strongest and at the same time the least self-serving. Her actions serve to show how limited are the views of Creon. While the play is not consciously studied as a document of pro-feminist literature, it does portray women in a favorable light. Therefore, complaint denied.

Do you agree or disagree with the principal's action? If you agree, write a letter to him supporting his position. Urge him to stand fast, and help him by supplying evidence from the play that will enable him to defend his position. If you disagree, write a letter to the principal attacking his position. Supply counter-arguments, supported by evidence from the play, and urge him to give way.

## LESSON TWENTY-SIX: *Persuasion*

*Based on* Antigone, *pages 406–436.*
If you were trying to urge people unfamiliar with *Antigone* to see a production of the play, what points would you stress?

Assume that you are the publicity agent for a dramatic company that is going to put on a production of *Antigone* at your school. Your job is to advertise the production and interest students in seeing it. Prepare a one-page promotional flyer about the production that can be posted around the school. The flyer will, of course, include information about the details of the production (title, author, performance dates and times, etc.), but it should prominently feature information that will make young people want to see the play.

Some possible leads: Civil Disobedience in Ancient Thebes, Defying the Establishment, Authoritarian Administrator Learns the Hard Way, Conflict Between the Generations.

## LESSON TWENTY-SEVEN: *Script Writing*

*Based on "The Highland Boy" and "Forbidden Fries," pages 442–452.*
Dramatizing a scene from a short story can be instructive as well as entertaining. It gives you a chance to crystallize your understanding of character, theme, and situation. Assume that your class is going to act out the following scenes from the two short stories listed above:

"Forbidden Fries"

1. The opening scene, in which the father explains to the family why he must have tranquillity and the right kind of food on Mondays.

2. The fourth Monday after the reform—the scene in which the waiter brings special food for the father's lunch.

3. The fifth Monday—the scene in which the waiter brings food for the entire family.

"The Highland Boy"

1. The scene in the shop when Uncle Cedric gives Highland Boy to his nephew.

2. The scene on the bus when Uncle Cedric is taunted by Carl Jenkins.

Prepare a script for one of these scenes. You may have to invent some dialogue to make the scene clear and to realize its dramatic potential. For example, you will probably want to translate into dialogue such narrator comments as "One day I called my family together. . . ." and ". . . one or two of the bolder spirits began to threaten my uncle with violence." In your stage directions describe what can be seen (the setting), any sounds the audience will hear (knock on the door, etc.), the movements of the actors, and any directions to the actors (e.g., how a line should be spoken; an emotion that should be shown) you think necessary. Give your scene a title.

(Your teacher may want to modify this assignment by dividing the class into five groups and having each group not only prepare the script for a scene but also present the scene to the class.)

## LESSON TWENTY-EIGHT: *Description*

*Based on At Random: Poetry, pages 458–467.*
Why is dying fine? Because it is a process, a happening, "perfectly natural." What is happiness? Feeling the thwack of your Keds as you are running to the baseball diamond. How do you take the first step in knowledge? Through a specific frightening experience. The poems in this section emphasize the concreteness of experience: tasting, touching, smelling, hearing, and seeing the world. We can use our senses, as May Swenson said, " . . . to get through the curtains of things as they *appear*, to things as they *are* . . . . "

We can use the poet's technique of emphasizing the concrete to recapture experiences of our own. Think of a time when you were doing one of the activities listed below. Then describe in a paragraph (or a poem, if you wish) the sensations you had while engaged in this activity. What did you taste, touch, smell, hear, see? What did the activity really "feel" like?

| | |
|---|---|
| walking | skiing |
| skating | cooking |
| sewing | digging |
| swimming | knitting |

| | |
|---|---|
| fighting | horseback riding |
| climbing | skin diving |
| sailing | sledding |
| cycling | eating |
| plowing | surfing |
| hunting | fishing |

## LESSON TWENTY-NINE: *Character Sketch*

*Based on "Outwitting the Lightning," pages 489–491.*
Wolcott Gibbs's portrait of his aunt suggests how closeness to a subject may affect not only the content of what one writes but also one's style of writing. Writing from personal experience, Gibbs is himself a character in the article, both in the present and the past. He focuses on just one of his aunt's traits, her obsession about lightning, and he illustrates this not with something he heard about but with a specific happening he experienced. He writes about his aunt in a casual, familiar style, as if he were talking to the reader. In portraying her oddness, he adopts a light, gently humorous tone. What he tells us and how he tells us about his aunt may serve as a model for the short portrait based on personal experience.

Select someone you know—a friend, a relative, an acquaintance—who has a striking characteristic or a peculiar obsession or an unusual way of confronting life, someone who is not famous but is admirable or amusing or eccentric in his own way. Write a brief sketch of this person in which you define his or her distinctive trait and illustrate it with a specific incident. Use the casual, familiar style ("talking" writing rather than "writing" writing). Show how you are personally involved; put yourself in the sketch. After you have finished the sketch, ask yourself: Would my classmates enjoy reading about this "character"?

### ALTERNATE ASSIGNMENT

Instead of writing about someone you know firsthand, you may prefer to write about a public figure who interests you and about whom you would like to know more. Often the people we know *about* (have heard about, read about, perhaps observed) who capture our imagination and admiration are those who have brought about or are trying to bring about change.

Whoever the public figure is who interests you, you will want to find out what you can about the person. Consult the information available: articles and books about or by the figure, printed interviews. As you read through this material, take notes on the following: (1) What are the important biographical facts about this person? Early life? Significant influences? What makes him tick? (2) How did he or she happen to become the leader of a cause? (3) What is he or was he trying to accomplish? What is his "program"? What specific changes is he working for? (4) To what degree has the "cause" this person fought for, or is fighting for, been achieved? From your notes compose a biographical sketch of this person. Try to keep your sketch within eight-hundred words; list at the end the books and articles you consulted. Your purpose here is to convey information. After reading your sketch, your classmates should have a clear understanding of just who this person is and what he is fighting for.

(Since this is a more ambitious assignment than the brief personal portrait, it may be done as a group project, with students working together on the same public figure, each member of the group being responsible for a section of the biographical sketch. This is the way many "profiles" are put together for magazines. Each group could consider itself a writing team for a news magazine.)

## LESSON THIRTY: *Explanation*

*Based on* Visit to a Small Planet *and* The Mother, *pages 498–539.*
While a television play is very similar to a play written for the stage, it has the use of one additional dramatic element: the camera. Without the use of any dialogue, the camera may provide information (where are we, what is happening, the nature of the scene—busy, sleepy, etc.), may help to characterize (through the

use of close-ups, for example), may comment on or interpret the action. Like the narrator in a short story, the camera supplies a point of view.

The camera as a special dramatic device is used sparingly in *Visit to a Small Planet*. The fantasy is quickly established at the opening of the play with a shot of a strange space ship and the legend: "THE TIME: THE DAY AFTER TOMORROW." The characterization of Kreton is given an added fillip with the closing shot of the two space ships, one straight on course, the other erratic. Because the camera allows for quick transition, there are many short scenes in the play. The camera is used to much greater dramatic effect in *The Mother*. Just one example: The Mother's defeat is forcefully rendered with the shot of her riding home on the subway.

Reread the garment-shop scenes in Act II of *The Mother*, and note the descriptions of camera shots in those scenes ("Fade in," "Dissolve to," "Close-up," etc.). Write a brief paper in which you explain how these shots provide information to the viewer, interpret or comment on the action, and help to characterize the Mother and the Boss.

## ALTERNATE ASSIGNMENT

Assume that your class is going to videotape "The Lottery Ticket" *(page 78)*. You are the director. While the dialogue is virtually all there for you, you will have to use the camera to depict what the narrator of the story supplies beyond the dialogue. Write a description of the camera shots you will use to establish scene, to reflect unspoken emotion or change in attitude, to convey the meaning of the episode. How, for example, will you use the camera to comment on the shabbiness of the surroundings, the frustration and irritation of Ivan, the unspoken thoughts of his wife? How might the camera be used to render the imaginings of Ivan?

# Handbook of Literary Terms

James Pierce

## ATMOSPHERE

It is twilight. A thick wet snow is twirling around the newly lighted street lamps, and lying in soft thin layers on the roofs, the horses' backs, people's shoulders and hats. The cabdriver, Iona Potapov, is quite white, and looks like a phantom; he is bent double as far as a human body can bend double; he is seated on his box; he never makes a move. If a whole snowdrift fell on him, it seems as if he would not find it necessary to shake it off. His little horse is also quite white, and remains motionless; its immobility, its angularity, and its straight wooden-looking legs, even close by, give it the appearance of a gingerbread horse worth a kopek. It is, no doubt, plunged in deep thought. If you were snatched from the plow, from your usual gray surroundings, and were thrown into this slough full of monstrous lights, unceasing noise, and hurrying people, you too would find it difficult not to think.

Anton Chekhov's short story "Lament" opens with the preceding paragraph. One purpose the paragraph serves is to prepare the reader emotionally for the events of the story, to set up expectations of feeling that will be in harmony with what happens in the story. The author does this by establishing an emotional atmosphere, a mood. The atmosphere suggested by the paragraph is—what? One of happiness? One of terror? Of outraged anger? Of quietude and isolation, and, perhaps, loneliness? What feeling does the reader get from the paragraph? How does the author communicate it to him?

1. What objects—human and non-human— are described most fully in the paragraph?

The reader's attention is focused on the cabdriver and his horse and the snow that is blanketing them, not on the street lamps, not on the shops or houses lining the street, not on the people who are probably passing by.

2. How are the objects described?

The snow is "twirling," "lying in soft thin layers." The effect is that of a soft blanket deadening sound and motion. The cabdriver looks like "a phantom"; he is "bent double" and "never makes a move." The bent-double image suggests age, care, perhaps a burden of some sort. The horse, too, is white with snow and motionless.

3. In what setting are the objects placed?

It is winter, of course. The time of day is twilight, traditionally the low point of the day, the time of exhaustion and loneliness. And the place is a well-lighted city street, full of sound and motion. The stillness and isolation of the cabdriver and his horse are emphasized by being placed in this bustling setting.

The scene, the prominent objects within it, and their characteristics combine to establish an atmosphere of lonely isolation.

> **ATMOSPHERE:** the climate of feeling, or mood, of a literary work. The author establishes the atmosphere by the objects he selects to describe, by how he describes them, and by the setting in which he places them.

# AUTOBIOGRAPHY AND BIOGRAPHY

Autobiography and biography are similar; both recount the events in the life of an actual person. In an autobiography, someone writes about his own life; in a biography, about the life of another person. Yet, as illustrated in the following two accounts of an episode in Mark Twain's courtship of Olivia Langdon, the forms can have different emphases as well as different sources of information.

## from The Autobiography of Mark Twain

It sounds easy and swift and unobstructed but that was not the way of it. It did not happen in that smooth and comfortable way. There was a deal of courtship. There were three or four proposals of marriage and just as many declinations. I was roving far and wide on the lecture beat but I managed to arrive in Elmira every now and then and renew the siege. Once I dug an invitation out of Charley Langdon to come and stay a week. It was a pleasant week but it had to come to an end. I was not able to invent any way to get the invitation enlarged. No schemes that I could contrive seemed likely to deceive. They did not even deceive *me*, and when a person cannot deceive himself the chances are against his being able to deceive other people. But at last help and good fortune came and from a most unexpected quarter. It was one of those cases so frequent in the past centuries, so infrequent in our day—a case where the hand of Providence is in it.

I was ready to leave for New York. A democrat wagon stood outside the main gate with my trunk in it, and Barney, the coachman, in the front seat with the reins in his hand. It was eight or nine in the evening and dark. I bade good-by to the grouped family on the front porch, and Charley and I went out and climbed into the wagon. We took our places back of the coachman on the remaining seat, which was aft toward the end of the wagon and was only a temporary arrangement for our accommodation and was not fastened in its place; a fact which—most fortunately for me—we were not aware of. Charley was smoking. Barney touched up the horse with the whip. He made a sudden spring forward. Charley and I went over the stern of the wagon backward. In the darkness the red bud of fire on the end of his cigar described a curve through the air which I can see yet. This was the only visible thing in all that gloomy scenery. I struck exactly on the top of my head and stood up that way for a moment, then crumbled down to the earth uncon-

scious. It was a very good unconsciousness for a person who had not rehearsed the part. It was a cobblestone gutter and they had been repairing it. My head struck in a dish formed by the conjunction of four cobblestones. That depression was half full of fresh new sand and this made a competent cushion. My head did not touch any of those cobblestones. I got not a bruise. I was not even jolted. Nothing was the matter with me at all.

Charley was considerably battered, but in his solicitude for me he was substantially unaware of it. The whole family swarmed out, Theodore Crane in the van with a flask of brandy. He poured enough of it between my lips to strangle me and make me bark but it did not abate my unconsciousness. I was taking care of that myself. It was very pleasant to hear the pitying remarks trickling around over me. That was one of the happiest half dozen moments of my life. There was nothing to mar it—except that I had escaped damage. I was afraid that this would be discovered sooner or later and would shorten my visit. I was such a dead weight that it required the combined strength of Barney and Mr. Langdon, Theodore and Charley to lug me into the house, but it was accomplished. I was there. I recognized that this was victory. I was there. I was safe to be an incumbrance for an indefinite length of time—but for a length of time, at any rate, and a Providence was in it.

They set me up in an armchair in the parlor and sent for the family physician. Poor old creature, it was wrong to rout him out but it was business, and I was too unconscious to protest. Mrs. Crane—dear soul, she was in this house three days ago, gray and beautiful and as sympathetic as ever—Mrs. Crane brought a bottle of some kind of liquid fire whose function was to reduce contusions. But I knew that mine would deride it and scoff at it. She poured this on my head and pawed it around with her hand, stroking and massaging, the fierce stuff dribbling down my backbone and marking its way, inch by inch, with the sensation of a forest fire. But *I* was satisfied. When she was getting worn out, her husband, Theodore, suggested that she take a rest and let Livy carry on the assuaging for a while. That was very pleasant. I should have been obliged to recover presently if it hadn't been for that. But under Livy's manipulations—if they had continued—I should probably be unconscious to this day. It was very delightful, those manipulations. So delightful, so comforting, so enchanting, that they even soothed the fire out of that fiendish successor to Perry Davis's "Pain-Killer."

Then that old family doctor arrived and went at the matter in an educated and practical way—that is to say, he started a search expedition for contusions and humps and bumps and announced that there were none. He said that if I would go to bed and forget my adventure I would be all right in the morning—which was not so. I was *not* all right in the morning. I didn't intend to be all right and I was far from being all right. But I said I only needed rest and I didn't need that doctor any more.

I got a good three days' extension out of that adventure and it helped a good deal. It pushed my suit forward several

From pp. 106–109 in *Mark Twain's Autobiography*, Volume II. Copyright, 1924, by Clara Gabrilowitsch. Copyright, 1952, by Clara Clemens Samossoud. By permission of Harper & Row Publishers, Inc.

steps. A subsequent visit completed the matter and we became engaged conditionally; the condition being that the parents should consent.

## from Mr. Clemens and Mark Twain

*Justin Kaplan*

Visiting his family in St. Louis after Livy first refused him, he felt "savage and crazy," was angry and low-spirited, defied Pamela's temperance pledges, drank, and became even gloomier. The whole visit was a "ghastly infliction," he wrote to Mary Fairbanks on September 24; "I am afraid I do not always disguise it, either." The only good news came in a letter from Livy along with her picture: she assured him that he was in her prayers, and she said he could come for a second visit at the end of the month. He spent a night and a day in Elmira, and she seemed to give him some grounds for hope; at least she did not object to his increasing persistence within the relationship of brother and sister. Then he had a lucky accident. Early in the evening, as he was climbing into the democrat wagon which was to take him to the depot, the horse suddenly started and he fell over backward into the gutter. He was carried into the house, and there he stayed another day or two, nursed by Livy. It was one of those episodes in his life which, like his first sight of Livy's miniature on board the *Quaker City,* had the shape of daydream to begin with and which he made part of his own mythology. By the time he came to this episode in his *Autobiography,* he had turned it into an even better story, in which he played the role of wily suitor: "I got not a bruise. I was not even jolted. Nothing was the matter with me at all. . . . That was one of the happiest half dozen moments of my life." This was his version of it in 1906, but only a week after it happened he told Mary Fairbanks that he had actually been knocked unconscious, and he even wrote it up for the *Alta California:* "I fell out of a wagon backwards, and broke my neck in two places." The episode liberated the heroically masochistic Tom Sawyer within him. In a fragment which he wrote shortly after his marriage, his first explicit attempt to write fiction about the experience of boyhood filtered through the nostalgia of manhood, his boy hero stands outside the house of the girl he loves and is very nearly run over by a wagon; he is sorry that he was not hit, "because then I would have been crippled and they would have carried me into her house all bloody and busted up, and she would have cried, and I would have been per-fectly happy, because I would have had to stay there till I got well, which I wish I never would get well."

1. In Twain's account of the accident, how seriously was he hurt? How does his version of the accident differ from the biographer's? What additional sources of information does the biographer use to support his claim that Twain was indeed hurt in the accident?

2. Can you point out other factual differences in the two accounts? (For example, how does the occasion for the visit differ in the two accounts?)

3. In Twain's account, what purpose did the accident and the consequent period of convalescence serve? According to the biographer, however, what additional purpose did the accident serve?

A person writing about his own life can rely on his memory; he knows what was important to him, and he can select and arrange the events to reflect that importance. To Twain, the accident was important in forwarding his courtship of Livy, and he gives a rather full account of the accident and how he used it. Some of the details, being recalled by Twain thirty-eight years after the event, may not be quite accurate, but the importance of the event is reflected in the way it is rendered.

A biographer, if he is writing about someone who is not alive, has the disadvantage of not being able to call directly on the memory of his subject. He can't talk to him. (Mr. Kaplan, for example, was not able to ask Twain if the accident served a literary as well as a romantic purpose.) On the other hand, the biographer has the advantage, usually, of drawing information about his subject from many sources: accounts by people who knew the subject, letters, newspaper articles, etc. The factual differences in the two accounts of the accident are obviously owing to the many sources of information consulted by Mr. Kaplan but forgotten or overlooked by Twain. One other point: a biographer usually tries to show how the happenings he chooses to describe influenced the life or work of his subject. Thus, Kaplan maintains that the accident not only influenced Twain's courting of Livy but also his literary imagination.

# CHARACTERIZATION

Our interest in reading stories is primarily an interest in finding out about people, about what happens to them and why they act as they do. Sometimes a character in a story helps us understand ourselves, why we did or did not act the same way in a similar situation. More often, the characters created by writers reveal to us the variety of human responses to the desires and hopes, the concerns and cares, the frustrations and confusions common to us all.

To characterize the people in a story, to reveal how and why they act as they do, an author may use a number of methods. The following scene from Guy de Maupassant's story "The Necklace" illustrates the principal methods of characterization.

She had no dresses, no jewels, nothing; and she loved only that, she felt made for that. She was filled with a desire to please, to be envied, to be bewitching and sought after. She had a rich friend, a former schoolmate at the convent, whom she no longer wished to visit because she suffered so much when she came home. For whole days at a time she wept without ceasing in bitterness and hopeless misery.

Now, one evening her husband came home with a triumphant air, holding in his hand a large envelope.

"There," said he, "there is something for you."

She quickly tore open the paper and drew out a printed card, bearing these words:

"The Minister of Public Instruction and Mme. Georges Rampouneau request the honor of M. and Mme. Loisel's company at the palace of the Ministry, Monday evening, January 18th."

Instead of being overcome with delight, as her husband expected, she threw the invitation on the table with disdain, murmuring:

"What do you wish me to do with that?"

"Why, my dear, I thought you would be pleased. You never go out, and it is such a fine opportunity, this! I had awful trouble getting it. Everyone wants to go; it is very select, and they are not giving many invitations to clerks. You will see the whole official world."

She looked at him with irritation, and said, impatiently:

"What do you wish me to put on my back if I go?"

He had not thought of that. He stammered:

"Why, the dress you go to the theatre in. It seems all right to me."

He stopped, stupefied, distracted, on seeing that his wife was crying. Two great tears descended slowly from the corners of her eyes toward the corners of her mouth. He stuttered:

"What's the matter? What's the matter?"

By a violent effort she subdued her feelings and replied in a calm voice, as she wiped her wet cheeks:

"Nothing. Only I have no dress and consequently I cannot go to this ball. Give your invitation to some friend whose wife is better equipped than I."

He was in despair. He replied:

"Let us see, Mathilde. How much would it cost, a suitable dress, which you could wear again on future occasions, something very simple?"

She reflected for some seconds, computing the cost, and also wondering what sum she could ask without bringing down upon herself an immediate refusal and an astonished exclamation from the economical clerk.

At last she answered hesitatingly:

"I don't know exactly, but it seems to me that with four hundred francs I could manage."

He turned a trifle pale, for he had been saving just that sum to buy a gun and treat himself to a little hunting the following summer, in the country near Nanterre, with a few friends who went there to shoot larks of a Sunday.

However, he said:

"Well, I think I can give you four hundred francs. But see that you have a pretty dress."

The day of the ball drew near, and Madame Loisel seemed sad, unhappy, anxious. Her dress was ready, however. Her husband said to her one evening:

"What is the matter? Come, you've been looking queer these last three days."

And she replied:

"It worries me that I have no jewels, not a single stone, nothing to put on. I shall look wretched enough. I would almost rather not go to the party."

He answered:

"You might wear natural flowers. They are very fashionable this season. For ten francs you can get two or three magnificent roses."

She was not convinced.

"No; there is nothing more humiliating than to look poor among women who are rich."

But her husband cried:

"How stupid of you! Go and find your friend Madame Forestier and ask her to lend you some jewels. You are intimate enough with her for that."

She uttered a cry of joy.

"Of course. I had not thought of that."

The next day she went to her friend's house and told her distress. Madame Forestier went to her handsome wardrobe, took out a large casket, brought it back, opened it, and said to Madame Loisel:

"Choose, my dear."

She saw first of all some bracelets, then a pearl necklace, then a Venetian cross, gold and precious stones of wonderful workmanship. She tried on the ornaments before the glass, hesitated, could not make up her mind to part with them, to give them back. She kept asking:

"Have you nothing else?"

"Why, yes. See, I do not know what will please you."

All at once she discovered, in a black satin box, a splendid diamond necklace, and her heart began to beat with immoderate desire. Her hands trembled as she took it. She fastened it around her throat, over her high-necked dress, and stood lost in ecstasy as she looked at herself.

"Would you lend me that,—only that?"

"Why, yes, certainly."

She sprang upon the neck of her friend, embraced her rapturously, then fled with her treasure.

1. What was it that Madame Loisel "loved only"? What did she feel made for?

2. Why did she no longer wish to visit her rich friend?

3. As the day of the ball drew near, was Madame Loisel happy? Frightened? Sad and anxious?

The reader learns of Madame Loisel's longings, her vanity, her acute discontent, her lack of pleasure in her possessions, directly from the author. *An author may directly describe or explain a character.*

4. What did Madame Loisel do with the invitation after she had read it?

5. How did she react to her husband's suggestion that she wear her theater dress to the ball?

6. What does her hesitation while trying on the jewelry tell us about her?

Madame Loisel's actions complement the picture of her personality drawn directly by the author. She is disdainful of what she has, has no thought for her husband, wants, wants, wants. *An author may reveal a character through his or her actions.*

7. Why was Madame Loisel not delighted with the invitation to the ball?

8. What reasons did she give for rejecting her husband's suggestion that she wear flowers on her dress?

What Madame Loisel says makes evident her vanity, her concern for her appearance, her acute sense of what is appropriate. *An author may reveal a character through his or her speech.*

9. How did Madame Loisel arrive at the figure of four hundred francs for the dress?

Through her reflecting, the reader sees that Madame Loisel is thinking not only of the cost

of the dress but also of how much she can get out of her husband. *An author may reveal a character through his or her thoughts.*

10. What effect did Monsieur Loisel hope the invitation would have on his wife?

11. What made him despair?

12. What had he intended to do with the four hundred francs?

The reactions of Monsieur Loisel to his wife's behavior reinforce the reader's impression that she is difficult to please and thinks only of herself. Although his reasons for wanting the four hundred francs may be as selfish as hers, it is clear that Madame Loisel expects her husband to make the sacrifices necessary for domestic harmony. *An author may reveal a character through the reactions of other characters.*

---

**CHARACTERIZATION:** the methods an author uses to reveal the character and personality of a person in a story. An author may explain the character directly or reveal a character through describing his or her actions, speech, thoughts, or the reaction of others.

---

# DIALOGUE

*Cottage kitchen, with nets, oilskins, spinning wheel, some new boards standing by the wall, etc.* CATHLEEN, *a girl of about twenty, finishes kneading cake, and puts it down in the pot-oven by the fire; then wipes her hands, and begins to spin at the wheel.* NORA, *a young girl, puts her head in at the door.*

NORA (*in a low voice*). Where is she?

CATHLEEN. She's lying down, God help her, and may be sleeping, if she's able.

(NORA *comes in softly, and takes a bundle from under her shawl.*)

CATHLEEN (*spinning the wheel rapidly*). What is it you have?

NORA. The young priest is after bringing them. It's a shirt and a plain stocking were got off a drowned man in Donegal.

(CATHLEEN *stops her wheel with a sudden movement, and leans out to listen.*)

NORA. We're to find out if it's Michael's they are, some time herself will be down looking by the sea.

CATHLEEN. How would they be Michael's, Nora? How would he go the length of that way to the far north?

NORA. The young priest says he's known the like of it. "If it's Michael's they are," says he, "you can tell herself he's got a clean burial by the grace of God, and if they're not his, let no one say a word about them, for she'll be getting her death," says he, "with crying and lamenting."

(*The door which* NORA *half closed is blown open by a gust of wind.*)

CATHLEEN (*looking out anxiously*). Did you ask him would he stop Bartley going this day with the horses to the Galway fair?

NORA. "I won't stop him," says he, "but let you not be afraid. Herself does be saying prayers half through the night, and the Almighty God won't leave her destitute," says he, "with no son living."

CATHLEEN. Is the sea bad by the white rocks, Nora?

NORA. Middling bad, God help us. There's a great roaring in the west, and it's worse it'll be getting when the tide's turned to the wind. (*She goes over to the table with the bundle.*) Shall I open it now?

CATHLEEN. Maybe she'd wake up on us, and come in before we'd done. (*Coming to the table.*) It's a long time we'll be, and the two of us crying.

NORA (*goes to the inner door and listens*). She's moving about on the bed. She'll be coming in a minute.

CATHLEEN. Give me the ladder, and I'll put them up in the turf-loft,[1] the way she won't know of them at all, and maybe when the tide turns she'll be going down to see would he be floating from the east.

(*They put the ladder against the gable of the chimney;* CATHLEEN *goes up a few steps and hides the bundle in the turf-loft.* MAURYA *comes from the inner room.*)

MAURYA (*looking up at* CATHLEEN *and speaking querulously*). Isn't it turf enough you have for this day and evening?

CATHLEEN. There's a cake baking at the fire for a short space

(*throwing down the turf*) and Bartley will want it when the tide turns if he goes to Connemara.

(NORA *picks up the turf and puts it round the pot-oven.*)

MAURYA (*sitting down on a stool at the fire*). He won't go this day with the wind rising from the south and west. He won't go this day, for the young priest will stop him surely.

NORA. He'll not stop him, mother, and I heard Eamon Simon and Stephen Pheety and Colum Shawn saying he would go.

MAURYA. Where is he itself?

NORA. He went down to see would there be another boat sailing in the week, and I'm thinking it won't be long till he's here now, for the tide's turning at the green head, and the hooker's tacking[2] from the east.

CATHLEEN. I hear someone passing the big stones.

NORA (*looking out*). He's coming now, and he in a hurry.

1. Who are Nora and Cathleen?
2. What has happened to Michael before the opening of the scene?
3. What does Nora bring? Where did she get them?
4. What do Nora and Cathleen plan to do? When will they do it?
5. Who is Maurya?
6. Who is Bartley? Where is he planning to go? What is Maurya's reaction to this?

*Dialogue* is the conversation of two or more people as it occurs in a play, a novel, a short story, a poem, or a work of nonfiction. As the brief exchange from the opening scene of "Riders to the Sea" illustrates, dialogue serves a number of dramatic purposes.

1. It can establish setting, (Ireland, near the sea) supply necessary background information (Michael has been lost at sea) and establish the dramatic situation (there is but one son left to Maurya).

2. It can identify characters and reveal the relationships among them. (Nora and Cathleen are sisters; Michael and Bartley are their brothers; Maurya is the mother.)

3. It can be used to reveal personality and motivation and to characterize. (Nora and Cathleen hope to spare their mother from the anguish of identifying the clothes found.)

---

1. *turf-loft,* place where slabs of peat used for fuel are stored.

2. *hooker's tacking.* A one-masted fishing boat is running against the wind.

4. It can advance the action (Bartley plans to go to Connemara despite the rising seas) as well as establish mood and express ideas.

While we would expect to find a concentrated use of dialogue in plays and television scripts, sometimes a novelist, a short-story writer, or a poet will use dialogue in much the same way as a playwright. The short story "The Most Dangerous Game" (page 9) for example, opens with a dialogue that quickly establishes setting, identifies the profession of the major character, provides an expression of his view of life, and imparts an air of mystery and danger.

> **DIALOGUE:** the conversation of two or more characters in a short story, novel, play, poem, or work of nonfiction. Dialogue may be used to establish setting, provide background information, identify characters and their relationships with one another, reveal personality and motivation, establish tone, express ideas, or advance the action.

# FANTASY

Consider the following:

1. A knight makes his living slaying dragons. One of his victims not only breathes fire but tries to disarm his attackers by making puns.

2. A priest's son has a vision of a great river and, beyond it, the Place of the Gods. To fulfill his priesthood, he sets out alone in quest of his vision. After a long journey he crosses a great river and inspects the Place of the Gods. It is the ancient city of New York, now in ruins and without human life.

3. The dead complain that the people who walk past their graveyard at night make horrible whistling sounds.

4. A witch explains how she enjoys upsetting man's expectations, thwarting his wishes and desires.

5. A skeleton ship with a crew of two, Life-in-Death and Death, comes alongside a becalmed ship. Life-in-Death and Death cast dice for the souls of the men on the becalmed ship.

6. A cockroach types a note to a newspaper

reporter describing the fatal fight between freddy the rat and a tarantula.

7. A stranger from another planet, one outside the solar system, unexpectedly arrives in a spaceship at the home of a television commentator and announces that he intends to take charge of the world.

Are the foregoing examples of (a) comedy, (b) realistic fiction, (c) fantasy, (d) tragedy? If you selected (c), you already have a good understanding of the meaning of *fantasy:* the conscious breaking free from experienced reality.

The desire not to limit the imagination to what can be experienced—to depict instead what might be, what could be, what should be—is a strong impulse in many authors.

An author creates fantasy when he depicts a nonexistent or unreal world, such as a fairyland or a world set in the future; when he creates incredible or unreal characters, such as animals that do not exist, talking animals, or supernatural beings; or when he describes technological, biological, or social advancements contrary to present experience, such as spaceships from other planets, people who do not deteriorate with age, or completely harmonious societies.

An author may employ fantasy simply to delight the reader, to impress with his ingenuity; he may wish to appeal to the reader's imagination, to provide a vision of the possibilities of human existence; or he may use fantasy as a means of criticizing present reality.

The examples given at the beginning of this entry are all derived from selections in this book. As you read the selections, try to identify the kind of fantasy employed in each as well as the purposes served by each fantasy.

> **FANTASY:** fiction that departs from experienced reality by depicting nonexistent or unreal settings, situations, happenings, or characters. Fantasy includes fables, fairy tales, ghost stories, and science fiction. Fantasy may or may not be employed as a means of criticizing present reality.

W Miller

*"It never fails, dearie. When you really need a knight, there's never one around."*

# FIGURATIVE LANGUAGE

### The Skaters

*John Gould Fletcher*

Black swallows swooping or gliding
In a flurry of entangled loops and curves;
The skaters skim over the frozen river.
And the grinding click of their skates as they
      impinge upon the surface,
Is like the brushing together of thin wing-tips
      of silver.

1. Who are the "black swallows"?
2. What different movements of the skaters are described by "swooping and gliding"?
3. Is the skating scene tranquil and dreamlike or active? Which line tells you?

"The Skaters" is not about black swallows but about a group of skaters on a frozen river. The poet has therefore not used the image of the black swallows literally. He has used the image of the swallows *figuratively* to describe the movements of the skaters. He presents the skaters *as if* they were a flock of black swallows. What does this accomplish?

The implied comparison makes it easy for us to visualize the skaters, standing out against the white of the ice, graceful in their movements, seeming to intersect and entwine. Because two things essentially unlike—a flock of birds and a group of skaters—are shown to have similarities, the comparison appeals to our imagination. The use of the image in a figurative way enables the poet to present a complicated scene vividly yet economically through an apt comparison.

Figurative language, then, is language used in non-literal ways to achieve vividness and intensity. Whenever we use words to represent something other than their literal meaning we are employing a figure of speech. There are several types of figures of speech, some of the more common of which are *simile, metaphor, personification,* and *hyperbole.*

### Simile

A *simile* (sim′ə lē′) is a stated comparison between two dissimilar things that are shown to have some element in common. Similes are stated rather than implied comparisons because they are introduced by "like" or "as." ("The grinding click of their skates . . ./Is *like* the brushing together of thin wing-tips of silver.")

What element in common do the click of the skates and the brushing together of silver wing-tips have? How does the comparison modify our impression of the sound of the click of the skates?

### Metaphor

A *metaphor* (met′ə fôr) is an implied comparison between things essentially unlike. For example, the first comparison in "The Skaters" is a metaphor: the black swallows stand for the skaters. A comparison need not, however, be expressed so directly. If, for example, a writer says, "The villagers flocked to the meeting," he has compressed the implied comparison of

"The Skaters" from *Preludes and Symphonies* by John Gould Fletcher. Reprinted by permission of Mrs. John Gould Fletcher.

the villagers to a flock of birds into the verb "flocked."

Notice how in the following poem the author uses both simile and metaphor to give a fresh perspective to a commonplace scene.

### Central Park Tourney

*Mildred Weston*

Cars
In the Park
With long spear lights
Ride at each other
5 Like armored knights;
Rush,
Miss the mark,
Pierce the dark,
Dash by!
10 Another two
Try.

Staged
In the Park
From dusk
15 To dawn,
The tourney goes on:
Rush,
Miss the mark,
Pierce the dark,
20 Dash by!
Another two
Try.

1. What comparison is made in lines 4 and 5? Is it a simile or a metaphor?

2. The central comparison or metaphor of the poem is expressed in the title and repeated in line 16. The cars approaching one another with their lights on are equated with what?

### Personification

*Personification* (per son′ə fə kā′shən), occurs when human characteristics are given to something non-human. If one's car, for example, is

"Central Park Tourney" by Mildred Weston from *The New Yorker*, May 9, 1953. Reprinted by permission; Copyright © 1953 The New Yorker Magazine, Inc.

given a personal name and described as an erratic old bag, then the car has been personified.

The purpose of personification is to give vividness and intensity to the impersonal or the abstract. An example of personification occurs in the poem "Conscientious Objector" (page 227). There an abstraction (Death) is turned into a human being. The narrator of the poem could have said, "I'm against killing," and let it go at that. What would have been lost if this approach had been taken?

### Hyperbole

*Hyperbole* (hī pėr′bə lē′) is an exaggerated statement used to achieve emphasis. "He couldn't punch his way out of a paper bag" and "It's raining golf balls" are hyperboles, deliberate exaggerations designed to emphasize lack of physical strength on the one hand, and severity of a storm on the other.

What is the purpose of the hyperbole in the following lines from Robert Burns's "A Red, Red Rose"?

> As fair art thou, my bonnie lass,
>   So deep in luve am I,
> And I will luve thee still, my dear,
>   Till a' the seas gang dry.
>
> Till a' the seas gang dry, my dear,
>   And the rock melt wi' the sun!
> And I will luve thee still, my dear,
>   While the sands o' life shall run.

---

**FIGURATIVE LANGUAGE:** language expanded beyond its usual literal meaning to achieve emphasis or to express a fitting relationship between things essentially unlike. A figurative expression usually contains a stated or implied comparison. Among the more common figures of speech are *simile, metaphor, personification,* and *hyperbole.* An effective figure of speech is brief and forceful, surprising but appropriate.

---

# FORESHADOWING

Alice was beginning to get very tired of sitting by her sister on the bank, and of having nothing to do: once or twice she had peeped into the book her sister was reading, but it had no pictures or conversations in it, "and what is the use of a book," thought Alice, "without pictures or conversations?"

So she was considering, in her own mind (as well as she could, for the hot day made her feel very sleepy and stupid), whether the pleasure of making a daisy-chain would be worth the trouble of getting up and picking daisies, when suddenly a white rabbit with pink eyes ran close by her.

There was nothing so *very* remarkable in that; nor did Alice think it so *very* much out of the way to hear the Rabbit say to itself, "Oh dear! Oh dear! I shall be too late!" (when she thought it over afterwards, it occurred to her that she ought to have wondered at this, but at the time it all seemed quite natural); but when the Rabbit actually *took a watch out of its waistcoat-pocket,* and looked at it, and then hurried on, Alice started to her feet, for it flashed across her mind that she had never before seen a rabbit with either a waistcoat-pocket, or a watch to take out of it, and, burning with curiosity, she ran across the field after it, and was just in time to see it pop down a large rabbit-hole under the hedge.

One purpose of this strange encounter is to prepare the reader for the events that will follow.

1. When do you *first* suspect that Alice is about to have some unusual adventures?

2. At this point do you have any definite idea of what direction the story will take?

The practice of preparing the reader for what is to come in a story is called *foreshadowing*. The purpose of foreshadowing is usually two-fold: *(1)* to stimulate in the reader an interest in what happens next and *(2)* to give an air of plausibility to the twists and turns of the plot by avoiding complete surprise.

Sometimes foreshadowing takes the form of a hint or a clue, the meaning of which does not become clear until much later in the story. In the opening scene of "Bargain" (page 47), for example, Mr. Baumer offers the young narrator the following advice: "Better study, Al. Is good to know to read and write and figure." The significance of these lines does not become apparent until the end of the story, when the reader learns that the resolution of the conflict turns on the ability to read. Moreover, the author deliberately does not emphasize the re-

lationship of the lines to the plot, for he has Al, the narrator, interpret them in the following way: "I guess he felt he had to push me a little, my father being dead."

The type of foreshadowing used in "Bargain" subtly prepares the reader for what is to come by planting in his consciousness an idea that will be central to the working out of the plot.

> **FORESHADOWING:** the author's use of hints, clues, or information suggesting impending events. While foreshadowing helps to create suspense, it also enables the reader to anticipate the behavior of characters and the turn of events in a story.

# IMAGERY

At any waking moment you are filtering experience through all your senses. If you are in a classroom, for example, you *see* your classmates, the teacher, the forms of the room, the furniture, the view from the windows; you *hear* whoever is speaking, perhaps the teacher or other students, but also the undercurrent of sound within the room—chair scraping, book opening, paper rustling, whispering—as well as the faint sounds outside the room; you *feel* the desk against your leg, the book or pencil in your hand as well as subtle, almost unconscious pressure, such as the fit of the shoes on your feet or the weight of the clothes on your shoulders; you *smell* the odors rising from the bodies and objects in the room and, if it is a mild day and the windows are open, the city or country odors gently infiltrating the room; and you *taste*, say, the residue of food you have last eaten or the pencil you are nibbling or the gum you are chewing. The world in all its variety comes to you through your senses.

When a writer presents what can be seen, heard, touched, tasted, smelled, as well as what can be felt inside (e.g., hunger, pain), he creates *images*—collectively, *imagery*. The writer of imaginative literature attempts to communicate experience, not give information; he aims to make us hear, feel, see. To achieve that aim, to make it possible for the reader to participate in the experience, a writer appeals to the senses, directly through the sounds and rhythms of the words used and indirectly through the *images* presented to the reader. The images, in a sense, re-create the experience so that the reader is not told what to think or feel but can arrive at his own response. Notice how this happens in the following poem.

## Little Exercise
(*for Thomas Edwards Wanning*)

*Elizabeth Bishop*

Think of the storm roaming the sky uneasily
like a dog looking for a place to sleep in,
listen to it growling.

Think how they must look now, the mangrove keys
lying out there unresponsive to the lightning
in dark, coarse-fibred families,

where occasionally a heron may undo his head,
shake up his feathers, make an uncertain comment
when the surrounding water shines.

Think of the boulevard and the little palm trees
all stuck in rows, suddenly revealed
as fistfuls of limp fish-skeletons.

It is raining there. The boulevard
and its broken sidewalks with weeds in every crack,
and relieved to be wet, the sea to be freshened

Now the storm goes away again in a series
of small, badly lit battle-scenes,
each in 'Another part of the field.'

Think of someone sleeping in the bottom of a
        row-boat
tied to a mangrove root or the pile of a bridge;
think of him as uninjured, barely disturbed.

1. What images of sight and sound are presented in the first three stanzas? Is the figurative language used effective in your opinion? Why or why not?

2. Why might the heron's comment be "uncertain"?

3. What images are presented in stanzas four and five?

4. In a battle scene in a Shakespearean play, a change of setting is indicated by the words "Another part of the field." How does this help to explain the image developed in the sixth stanza?

5. What is the setting for this poem?

6. What new element in the "exercise" is introduced in the last stanza? What does it add to the poem as a whole?

Notice that the poet does not tell us *about* the progress of a storm but instead presents the sights and sounds that enable a reader to experience the storm.

Reprinted with the permission of Farrar, Straus & Giroux, Inc. from *The Complete Poems* by Elizabeth Bishop, copyright © 1946, 1969 by Elizabeth Bishop.

# INFERENCE

. . . With a resigned air and a somewhat weary smile, Holmes begged the beautiful intruder to take a seat, and to inform us what it was that was troubling her.

"At least it cannot be your health," said he, as his keen eyes darted over her; "so ardent a bicyclist must be full of energy."

She glanced down in surprise at her own feet, and I observed the slight roughening of the side of the sole caused by the friction of the edge of the pedal.

"Yes, I bicycle a good deal, Mr. Holmes. . . ."

My friend took the lady's ungloved hand, and examined it with as close an attention and as little sentiment as a scientist would show to a specimen.

"You will excuse me, I am sure. It is my business," said he, as he dropped it. "I nearly fell into the error of supposing you were typewriting. Of course, it is obvious that it is music. You observe the spatulate finger-ends, Watson, which is common to both professions? There is a spirituality about the face, however"—she gently turned it towards the light—"which the typewriter does not generate. This lady is a musician."

"Yes, Mr. Holmes, I teach music."

"In the country, I presume, from your complexion."

"Yes, sir, near Farnham, on the borders of Surrey."

From "The Adventure of the Solitary Cyclist" from *The Complete Sherlock Holmes* by Sir Arthur Conan Doyle. Reprinted by permission of the Trustees of the Estate of Sir Arthur Conan Doyle and John Murray (Publishers) Ltd.

1. How does Sherlock Holmes come to the conclusion that the woman is an ardent bicyclist?

2. What do the woman's finger-ends tell Holmes? Why does he decide she is not a typist?

3. How does he know that she lives in the country rather than the city?

From a few hints and bits of evidence—a slight roughening in a telltale place on the woman's shoes, wide fingertips, a "spiritual" face, and a healthy complexion—Sherlock Holmes determines a good deal about the woman before him. He illustrates the process of *making inferences,* drawing conclusions from limited information.

Like Holmes, the reader of fiction must make inferences about the personalities of characters and the meaning of happenings, for often the author presents characters and events directly without telling the reader about them, without explaining what kind of people the characters are or what the events illustrate. Instead, he relies on the reader's ability to make reasonable inferences from what he has presented. In the following excerpt from Ring Lardner's story "I Can't Breathe," for example, Lardner does not tell the reader *about* the girl; he presents her in her own words. (The excerpt is a diary entry.)

July 18

I have skipped a day. I was busy every minute of yesterday and so exhausted when I came upstairs that I was tempted to fall into bed with all my clothes on. First Gordon called me up from Chicago to remind me that he would be in New York the day I got there and that when he comes he wants me all to himself all the time and we can make plans for our wedding. The connection was bad again and I just couldn't explain to him about Walter.

I had an engagement with Frank for lunch and just as we were going in another long distance call came, from Walter this time. He wanted to know why I haven't written more letters and sent him more telegrams and asked me if I still loved him and of course I told him yes because I really do. Then he asked if I had met any men here and I told him I had met one, a friend of Uncle Nat's. After all it was Uncle Nat who introduced me to Frank. He reminded me that he

Reprinted by permission of Charles Scribner's Sons and Chatto and Windus Ltd. from "I Can't Breathe" (Copyright 1926 International Magazines, Co., Inc., renewal copyright 1954 Ellis A. Lardner) from *The Best Stories of Ring Lardner* (pp. 18–19).

would be in New York on the 25th which is the day I expect to get home, and said he would have theater tickets for that night and we would go somewhere afterwards and dance.

Frank insisted on knowing who had kept me talking so long and I told him it was a boy I had known a long while, a very dear friend of mine and a friend of my family's. Frank was jealous and kept asking questions till I thought I would go mad. He was so serious and kind of cross and gruff that I gave up the plan of telling him the truth till some time when he is in better spirits.

I played golf with Frank in the afternoon and we took a ride last night and I wanted to get in early because I had promised both Walter and Gordon that I would write them long letters, but Frank wouldn't bring me back to the Inn till I had named a definite date in December. I finally told him the 10th and he said all right if I was sure that wasn't a Sunday. I said I would have to look it up, but as a matter of fact I know the 10th falls on a Friday because the date Walter and I have agreed on for our wedding is Saturday the 11th.

Today has just been the same thing over again, two more night letters, a long distance call from Chicago, golf and a ride with Frank, and the room full of flowers. But tomorrow I am going to tell Frank and I am going to write Gordon a long letter and tell him, too, because this simply can't go on any longer. I can't breathe. I can't live.

1. What is it that the girl would tell Gordon about Walter? Has she had other opportunities to tell him?

2. What impression does she give Walter when she tells him that the one man she has met is a friend of her uncle?

3. What is the "truth" she plans to tell Frank? In the two days described in the entry, how many opportunities does she have to tell him?

4. Why is she likely or not likely to carry through her plans for the next day?

5. The girl (a) is very concerned about disappointing Gordon and Frank, (b) is *really* in love with Walter, (c) enjoys being engaged to three men, (d) seriously wants to be honest and straightforward with all three.

> **INFERENCE:** a reasonable conclusion about the behavior of a character or the meaning of an event drawn from the limited information presented by the author.

# IRONY

## Verbal Irony

In the following excerpt from *Oliver Twist* by Charles Dickens, Oliver, who is a young orphan, has just been brought to a workhouse by the beadle of the parish, Mr. Bumble.

Oliver had not been within the walls of the workhouse a quarter of an hour, and had scarcely completed the demolition of a second slice of bread, when Mr. Bumble, who had handed him over to the care of an old woman, returned; and, telling him it was a board night, informed him that the board had said he was to appear before it forthwith.

Not having a very clearly defined notion of what a live board was, Oliver was rather astounded by this intelligence, and was not quite certain whether he ought to laugh or cry. He had no time to think about the matter, however; for Mr. Bumble gave him a tap on the head, with his cane, to wake him up: and another on the back to make him lively: and bidding him follow, conducted him into a large white-washed room, where eight or ten fat gentlemen were sitting round a table. At the top of the table, seated in an armchair rather higher than the rest, was a particularly fat gentleman with a very round, red face.

'Bow to the board,' said Bumble. Oliver brushed away two or three tears that were lingering in his eyes; and seeing no board but the table, fortunately bowed to that.

'What's your name, boy?' said the gentleman in the high chair.

Oliver was frightened at the sight of so many gentlemen, which made him tremble: and the beadle gave him another tap behind, which made him cry. These two causes made him answer in a very low and hesitating voice; whereupon a gentleman in a white waistcoat said he was a fool. Which was a capital way of raising his spirits, and putting him quite at his ease.

'Boy,' said the gentleman in the high chair, 'listen to me. You know you're an orphan, I suppose?'

'What's that, sir?' inquired poor Oliver.

'The boy *is* a fool—I thought he was,' said the gentleman in the white waistcoat.

'Hush!' said the gentleman who had spoken first. 'You know you've got no father or mother, and that you were brought up by the parish, don't you?'

'Yes, sir,' replied Oliver, weeping bitterly.

'What are you crying for?' inquired the gentleman in the white waistcoat. And to be sure it was very extraordinary. What *could* the boy be crying for?

'I hope you say your prayers every night,' said another gentleman in a gruff voice; 'and pray for the people who feed you, and take care of you—like a Christian.'

'Yes, sir,' stammered the boy. The gentleman who spoke last was unconsciously right. It would have been *very* like a Christian, and a marvellously good Christian, too, if Oliver had prayed for the people who fed and took care of *him*. But he hadn't, because nobody had taught him.

'Well! You have come here to be educated, and taught a useful trade,' said the red-faced gentleman in the high chair.

'So you'll begin to pick oakum[1] to-morrow morning at six o'clock,' added the surly one in the white waistcoat.

For the combination of both these blessings in the one simple process of picking oakum, Oliver bowed low by the direction of the beadle, and was then hurried away to a large ward: where, on a rough, hard bed, he sobbed himself to sleep. What a noble illustration of the tender laws of England! They let the paupers go to sleep!

Poor Oliver! He little thought, as he lay sleeping in happy unconsciousness of all around him, that the board had that very day arrived at a decision which would exercise the most material influence over all his future fortunes. But they had. And this was it:

The members of this board were very sage, deep, philosophical men; and when they came to turn their attention to the workhouse, they found out at once, what ordinary folks would never have discovered—the poor people liked it! It was a regular place of public entertainment for the poorer classes; a tavern where there was nothing to pay; a public breakfast, dinner, tea, and supper all the year round; a brick and mortar elysium, where it was all play and no work. 'Oho!' said the board, looking very knowing; 'we are the fellows to set this to rights; we'll stop it all, in no time.' So, they established the rule, that all poor people should have the alternative (for they would compel nobody, not they), of being starved by a gradual process in the house, or by a quick one out of it. With this view, they contracted with the water-works to lay on an unlimited supply of water; and with a corn-factor to supply periodically small quantities of oatmeal; and issued three meals of thin gruel a day, with an onion twice a week, and half a roll on Sundays. They made a great many other wise and humane regulations, having reference to the ladies, which it is not necessary to repeat; kindly undertook to divorce poor married people, in consequence of the great expense of a suit in Doctors' Commons; and, instead of compelling a man to support his family, as they had theretofore done, took his family away from him, and made him a bachelor! There is no saying how many applicants for relief, under these last two heads, might have started up in all classes of society, if it had not been coupled with the workhouse; but the board were long-headed men, and had provided for this difficulty. The relief was inseparable from the workhouse and the gruel; and that frightened people.

For the first six months after Oliver Twist was removed, the system was in full operation. It was rather expensive at first, in consequence of the increase in the undertaker's bill, and the necessity of taking in the clothes of all the paupers, which fluttered loosely on their wasted, shrunken forms, after a week or two's gruel. But the number of workhouse inmates got thin as well as the paupers; and the board were in ecstasies.

---

**1.** *oakum*, a loose fiber obtained by picking apart old ropes; once used for calking the seams of ships.

1. Does Dickens really think that the laws of England are noble, that Oliver is taken care of in a Christian fashion, and that the members of the board are philosophical, wise, and humane?

2. Does he expect the reader to believe that poor people liked the workhouse?

3. How would you describe Dickens's attitude toward treatment of the poor?

You have probably heard the expression "Thanks a lot" used sarcastically, spoken in a way to mean, "Thanks—for nothing." Dickens does something similar; he says one thing but means another. His seeming to praise the wisdom and charity of the board while actually criticizing them illustrates *verbal irony,* a form of expression in which one says the opposite of what he means. Irony is an indirect, sometimes bitter, sometimes humorous form of criticism.

The poem "The Conquerors" (page 228) praises man's ability through the ages to kill great masses of people and criticizes modern man's pride in atomic weapons. In what ways is the poem ironic?

**Irony of Situation**

The content of this excerpt illustrates another form of irony, *irony of situation,* wherein the opposite of what is expected or intended occurs. The board, we are told, has decided to educate Oliver and teach him a useful trade but instead of sending Oliver to school, as might be expected, he is to begin work at six the next morning picking oakum.

As you may recall, the author of "The Endless Streetcar Ride . . ." (page 55) uses irony of situation in a humorous, yet somewhat sobering way. What was the narrator's attitude toward blind dates? Why did he agree to go on a blind date? Why is he pleased when he meets his blind date? What reversal, what irony of situation occurs during the evening?

**Dramatic Irony**

Dramatic irony occurs in fiction or drama when the reader or spectator knows more about the true state of affairs than the characters do. In "By the Waters of Babylon" (page 134), for example, the narrator is not aware that he has found what remains of New York after a war. The reader soon realizes the situation, however, and the narrator's discoveries, actions, and thoughts therefore have an additional meaning he is not aware of. Is there dramatic irony in this short excerpt from *Oliver Twist*? What is the reader aware of that Oliver is not?

> **IRONY:** In general, a contrast between what appears to be and what really is. *Verbal irony* occurs when the surface meaning of what one says or writes is the opposite of the intended meaning. *Irony of situation* exists when the opposite of what is expected or intended occurs. *Dramatic irony* occurs in fiction or drama when the reader or spectator knows more about the true state of affairs than the characters do.

# PLOT

## The Sniper

*LIAM O'FLAHERTY*

The long June twilight faded into night. Dublin lay enveloped in darkness but for the dim light of the moon that shone through fleecy clouds, casting a pale light as of approaching dawn over the streets and the dark waters of the Liffey. Around the beleaguered Four Courts the heavy guns roared. Here and there through the city, machine guns and rifles broke the silence of the night, spasmodically, like dogs barking on lone farms. Republicans and Free Staters were waging civil war.

On a roof top near O'Connell Bridge, a Republican sniper lay watching. Beside him lay his rifle and over his shoulders were slung a pair of field glasses. His face was the face of a student, thin and ascetic, but his eyes had the cold gleam of the fanatic. They were deep and thoughtful, the eyes of a man who is used to looking at death.

He was eating a sandwich hungrily. He had eaten nothing since morning. He had been too excited to eat. He finished the sandwich, and, taking a flask of whisky from his pocket, he took a short draught. Then he returned the flask to his pocket. He paused for a moment, considering whether he should risk a smoke. It was dangerous. The flash might be seen in the darkness, and there were enemies watching. He decided to take the risk.

Placing a cigarette between his lips, he struck a match, inhaled the smoke hurriedly and put out the light. Almost immediately, a bullet flattened itself against the parapet of the roof. The sniper took another whiff and put out the cigarette. Then he swore softly and crawled away to the left.

Cautiously he raised himself and peered over the parapet. There was a flash and a bullet whizzed over his head. He dropped immedi- ately. He had seen the flash. It came from the opposite side of the street.

He rolled over the roof to a chimney stack in the rear, and slowly drew himself up behind it, until his eyes were level with the top of the parapet. There was nothing to be seen—just the dim outline of the opposite housetop against the blue sky. His enemy was under cover.

Just then an armored car came across the bridge and advanced slowly up the street. It stopped on the opposite side of the street, fifty yards ahead. The sniper could hear the dull panting of the motor. His heart beat faster. It was an enemy car. He wanted to fire, but he knew it was useless. His bullets would never pierce the steel that covered the gray monster.

Then round the corner of a side street came an old woman, her head covered by a tattered shawl. She began to talk to the man in the turret of the car. She was pointing to the roof where the sniper lay. An informer.

The turret opened. A man's head and shoulders appeared, looking toward the sniper. The sniper raised his rifle and fired. The head fell heavily on the turret wall. The woman darted toward the side street. The sniper fired again. The woman whirled round and fell with a shriek into the gutter.

Suddenly from the opposite roof a shot rang out and the sniper dropped his rifle with a curse. The rifle clattered to the roof. The sniper thought the noise would wake the dead. He stopped to pick the rifle up. He couldn't lift it. His forearm was dead. "I'm hit," he muttered.

Dropping flat onto the roof, he crawled back to the parapet. With his left hand he felt the injured right forearm. The blood was oozing through the sleeve of his coat. There was no pain—just a deadened sensation, as if the arm had been cut off.

Quickly he drew his knife from his pocket, opened it on the breastwork of the parapet, and ripped open the sleeve. There was a small hole where the bullet had entered. On the other side there was no hole. The bullet had lodged in the bone. It must have fractured it. He bent the arm below the wound. The arm bent back

---

"The Sniper" from *Spring Sowing* by Liam O'Flaherty. Reprinted by permission of Harcourt Brace Jovanovich, Inc. and Jonathan Cape Ltd.

easily. He ground his teeth to overcome the pain.

Then taking out his field dressing, he ripped open the packet with his knife. He broke the neck of the iodine bottle and let the bitter fluid drip into the wound. A paroxysm of pain swept through him. He placed the cotton wadding over the wound and wrapped the dressing over it. He tied the ends with his teeth.

Then he lay still against the parapet, and, closing his eyes, he made an effort of will to overcome the pain.

In the street beneath all was still. The armored car had retired speedily over the bridge, with the machine gunner's head hanging lifeless over the turret. The woman's corpse lay still in the gutter.

The sniper lay still for a long time nursing his wounded arm and planning escape. Morning must not find him wounded on the roof. The enemy on the opposite roof covered his escape. He must kill that enemy and he could not use his rifle. He had only a revolver to do it. Then he thought of a plan.

Taking off his cap, he placed it over the muzzle of his rifle. Then he pushed the rifle slowly upward over the parapet, until the cap was visible from the opposite side of the street. Almost immediately there was a report, and a bullet pierced the center of the cap. The sniper slanted the rifle forward. The cap slipped down into the street. Then catching the rifle in the middle, the sniper dropped his left hand over the roof and let it hang, lifelessly. After a few moments he let the rifle drop to the street. Then he sank to the roof, dragging his hand with him.

Crawling quickly to the left, he peered up at the corner of the roof. His ruse had succeeded. The other sniper, seeing the cap and rifle fall, thought that he had killed his man. He was now standing before a row of chimney pots, looking across, with his head clearly silhouetted against the western sky.

The Republican sniper smiled and lifted his revolver above the edge of the parapet. The distance was about fifty yards—a hard shot in the dim light, and his right arm was paining him like a thousand devils. He took a steady aim. His hand trembled with eagerness. Pressing his lips together, he took a deep breath through his nostrils and fired. He was almost deafened with the report and his arm shook with the recoil.

Then when the smoke cleared he peered across and uttered a cry of joy. His enemy had been hit. He was reeling over the parapet in his death agony. He struggled to keep his feet, but he was slowly falling forward, as if in a dream. The rifle fell from his grasp, hit the parapet, fell over, bounded off the pole of a barber's shop beneath and then clattered on the pavement.

Then the dying man on the roof crumpled up and fell forward. The body turned over and over in space and hit the ground with a dull thud. Then it lay still.

The sniper looked at his enemy falling and he shuddered. The lust of battle died in him. He became bitten by remorse. The sweat stood out in beads on his forehead. Weakened by his wound and the long summer day of fasting and watching on the roof, he revolted from the sight of the shattered mass of his dead enemy. His teeth chattered, he began to gibber to himself, cursing the war, cursing himself, cursing everybody.

He looked at the smoking revolver in his hand, and with an oath he hurled it to the roof at his feet. The revolver went off with the concussion and the bullet whizzed past the sniper's head. He was frightened back to his senses by the shock. His nerves steadied. The cloud of fear scattered from his mind and he laughed.

Taking the whisky flask from his pocket, he emptied it at a draught. He felt reckless under the influence of the spirit. He decided to leave the roof now and look for his company commander, to report. Everywhere around was quiet. There was not much danger in going through the streets. He picked up his revolver and put it in his pocket. Then he crawled down through the skylight to the house underneath.

When the sniper reached the laneway on the street level, he felt a sudden curiosity as to the identity of the enemy sniper whom he had killed. He decided that he was a good shot, whoever he was. He wondered did he know him. Perhaps he had been in his own company before the split in the army. He decided to risk going over to have a look at him. He peered around the corner into O'Connell Street. In the upper part of the street there was heavy firing, but around here all was quiet.

The sniper darted across the street. A machine gun tore up the ground around him with a hail of bullets, but he escaped. He threw himself face downward beside the corpse. The machine gun stopped.

Then the sniper turned over the dead body and looked into his brother's face.

## Conflict

1. What risk does the Republican sniper take in the beginning of the story? How does this action endanger his life?

2. What problem is he therefore confronted with? What ways are open to him to eliminate or escape the danger?

3. On what level(s) of action—physical, mental, emotional, moral—does this problem occur?

In every story there is a conflict of opposing forces, a struggle, a problem to be resolved. In "The Sniper" there is an obvious conflict on the physical plane of action: two snipers confront one another; one must shoot the other to resolve the conflict. In many stories, however, the conflict is not so obviously physical: a main character may struggle with conflicting emotions of, say, love and hate, attraction and repulsion, or with conflicting duties or values.

Conflicts that pit the main character against something outside himself—another character, the forces of nature, the power of society—are called *external* conflicts. Conflicts that occur within the main character—struggles of conscience or emotion—are called *internal* conflicts. Seldom is the conflict in a story entirely external or internal. What feelings, for example, overwhelm the sniper after he has killed his enemy?

The *plot* of a story refers to the related events that present and eventually resolve some problem or conflict. (Some stories are said to have little plot. This means that the focus in such stories is not on the resolving of some problem or conflict but perhaps on a mood or a theme or a particular social setting.)

## Pattern of Events/Complications

The conflict having been established, the author presents events that are related to it—that clarify the significance of the conflict, for example, or intensify it or work toward its resolution. In "The Sniper" the author concentrates on presenting the action of the sniper as he attempts to outwit his enemy.

1. Why does the sniper peer over the parapet after he has put out his cigarette?

2. How does the arrival of the armored car increase the danger facing the sniper?

3. What purpose is served by introducing the old lady, the informer?

4. After the episode of the armored car how have the odds against the sniper been increased?

5. Why can't the sniper remain on the roof until morning?

The events selected by the author intensify the conflict and work toward its resolution. The sniper must locate his enemy. He peers over the parapet and is shot at again. The second shot reinforces in the reader's mind the danger facing the sniper. The introducing of complications is a typical plot development. The arrival of the armored car and the appearance of the informer complicate the sniper's problem. He overcomes this danger but in the process is wounded by the opposing sniper—a further complication. Now he must either kill the opposing sniper or perish himself. Thus the events form a pattern leading to a conclusion.

## Climax and Conclusion

The *climax* of a story occurs when the main character takes decisive action to end the conflict or when the situation is such that the problem must be resolved one way or another. The climax in "The Sniper" occurs when the main character sets his plan of deception into action. He doesn't know how it will work out, but it should decide the issue one way or another. (Not every story contains a climax in this sense; sometimes no decisive action is taken or the problem is left unresolved.)

The *conclusion* of a story includes the resolving of the conflict and any events following it. Sometimes the conclusion contains a direct or oblique comment on the significance of the conflict.

1. What does the sniper decide to do after he has killed his opponent?

2. What meaning is given to his triumph when he turns over the dead body of his opponent and discovers his brother?

---

**PLOT:** a series of related events selected by the author to present and bring about the resolution of some conflict or problem. In a strongly plotted story, the events usually follow a pattern: the conflict or problem is established; complications arise from the conflict; the main character takes decisive action, or the situation itself brings about a climax; the conflict is resolved.

---

# POINT OF VIEW

## First Person

The following paragraphs are from the short story "Bargain" (page 47).

Mr. Baumer stooped and picked up the bill and put it on top of the rest and smoothed it out for mailing. When he straightened up I could see tears in his eyes from having his nose screwed around.

He didn't say anything to me, and I didn't say anything to him, being so much younger and feeling embarrassed for him. He went into the post office and slipped the bills in the slot, and we walked on home together. At the last, at the crossing where I had to leave him, he remembered to say, "Better study, Al. Is good to know to read and write and figure." I guess he felt he had to push me a little, my father being dead.

1. Who is the "he"?
2. Who is the "I"?

3. Who, therefore, is telling the story?

The writer of a short story selects a narrator to tell his story. In this instance the narrator is a character in the story—Al, the boy who works at Mr. Baumer's store. The story is told from his *point of view.*

Because the story is told through an "I," it is an instance of *first person* point of view. The choice of narrator, of point of view, is important, for it determines the amount and kind of information that will be given to the reader. What would happen, for example, if "Bargain" were told from the point of view of Mr. Baumer? Could the story be told by Freighter Slade? What does the author gain by telling the story through Al?

"The Endless Streetcar Ride into the Night,

and the Tinfoil Noose" (page 55) is another example of a story told through the first person point of view. But the point of view in the two stories differs in a significant way. In leading up to the action, the narrator makes the following observation:

The fourteenth summer is a magic one for all kids. You have just slid out of the pupa stage, leaving your old baby skin behind, and have not yet become a grizzled, hardened, tax-paying beetle. At fourteen you are made of cellophane. You curl easily and everyone can see through you.

You will not find this type of observation in "Bargain." The point in time from which the narrators tell the stories differs. In "The Endless Streetcar Ride . . ." the narrator is recalling the events; they happened a long time ago. He knows what they mean. In "Bargain," on the other hand, the narrator is telling the story *as if* the events had just occurred. He doesn't know their full meaning. The reader, therefore, does not know *more* than the narrator.

Still another type of first person narration can be seen in "Luther" (page 37):

Luther arrived at Booker T. Washington Junior High School (Columbus Avenue and 107th Street, Manhattan) in September of 1955, six months before I did. I met him at the end of February, the third week I taught there, when one of the assistant principals asked me to cover the cafeteria during fifth period for a teacher who had to be at a conference. "Good luck with the animals," I remember him saying.

1. In what way is the "I" of this story (Mr. Carter) similar to the "I" of "Bargain"?
2. In what way is he similar to the "I" of "The Endless Streetcar Ride . . ."?
3. How does he differ from these two other first person narrators?

Like Al in "Bargain" Mr. Carter is not the main character and is in the position of an observer. His sources of information are what he hears and sees and what the main character tells him. Like the "I" in "The Endless Streetcar Ride . . ." however, Mr. Carter has the advantage of looking back on the events of the story from a point in time.

Thus, the first person narrator may be a major

or minor character who reports the events of the story *as if* they had just occurred or from a *subjective* point of view. He may be the main character who tells the story from the vantage point of maturity, that is, from a *detached* point of view. And finally, he may be a minor character who tells the story from the point of view of an *observer*, reporting events that have occurred in the past.

### Third Person

Sometimes a writer chooses not to tell a story through one of the characters, as did Margaret Deland, the author of "At the Stuffed-Animal House":

Willy King's buggy, splashed to the top of the hood with mud and sagging sidewise on its worn old springs, came pulling up the hill past the burial-ground. The doctor, himself, curled in one corner, rested a leg on the dashboard and hung his reins on the hook over his head. He was very sleepy, for he had been up until three with an old woman who thought she was sick, and he had been routed out of bed again at five because she told her family that she was going to die. William King was not given to sarcasm, but he longed to say to the waiting relatives, "There is no hope!— she'll live." Instead, he looked seriously sympathetic and kept his thoughts to himself. . . .

We find no "I" in this excerpt. Who, then, is telling the story? Somebody outside the story, a *third person*. Unlike a first person narrator, an anonymous narrator may reveal the thoughts of any of the characters. He is also free to comment on the actions of the characters. (He can tell the reader whether the characters are acting in, say, a sensible or a foolish manner.)

On the other hand, the third person narrator may simply report what the characters say and do, as does the narrator in "The Fifty-first Dragon" on page 128. Although the narrator is "out there," he does not enter the minds of any of the characters; nor does he necessarily comment on their actions. He leaves it to the reader to interpret the events.

Thus, the third person narrator may tell the story from an *omniscient (all-knowing) point of view*, entering the minds of the characters and commenting on their actions; or from an *ob-*

*jective point of view*, reporting only what the characters do and say.

**POINT OF VIEW:** This term refers to the way a story is told, the way it is narrated. A story is usually told by a character in the story, an "I", or by an anonymous person outside the story. The author's choice of narrator determines the amount of information a reader will be given. The principal points of view are first person and third person. Within these two broad categories, the following types of narration may be found:

*First Person Subjective:* The narrator is a major or minor character in the story who reports the events as if they had just happened and who appears to be unaware of the full meaning of the events. The reader knows more than the narrator.

*First Person Detached:* The narrator is a major character in the story who recalls the events from the vantage point of maturity. He has had time to reflect on the meaning of the events.

*First Person Observer:* The narrator is a minor character in the story who plays the roles of eyewitness and confidant. His sources of information are what he hears and sees and what the main character tells him.

*Third Person Omniscient:* The narrator is an anonymous person outside the story who plays an all-knowing role. He not only reports what the characters do and say but also enters the minds of the characters and comments on their actions.

*Third Person Objective:* The narrator is an anonymous person outside the story who reports only what the characters do and say.

# RHYME AND SOUND DEVICES

One of the pleasures to be derived from poetry is auditory, a pleasure in the *sound* of the words in a poem. One of the poems in the poetry unit that strikingly emphasizes sound qualities is "The Skater of Ghost Lake" (page 258). Notice, for example, the many sound repetitions in the first stanza.

Ghost Lake's a dark lake, a deep lake and cold:
Ice black as ebony, frostily scrolled;
Far in its shadows a faint sound whirrs;
Steep stand the sentineled deep, dark firs.

1. Which words are repeated in the four lines?
2. Which sounds are repeated at the ends of lines?
3. In the first line, aside from the *l* in *lake* what beginning sound of a word is repeated?
4. In the fourth line, which beginning sounds of words are repeated? What accented vowel sound is repeated?
5. Pronounce the last word in the third line aloud slowly. What sense do you get from the sound itself?

One obvious way to emphasize certain sounds is to repeat whole words, as occurs with the repeating of *lake, dark,* and *deep* in the first stanza. (The words are not repeated for their sound values alone, of course; they are obviously repeated to emphasize their sense, what they stand for, as well.) But sound repetition would become monotonous if it were limited to this method.

A second method is rhyming, repeating sounds (the accented vowel plus succeeding sounds) at the end of lines. The *-old* sound of *cold* is repeated at the end of the second line, and the *-irrs* sound of *whirrs* is repeated at the end of the fourth line. (Notice that rhyming has nothing to do with spelling.) If one were to

chart the pattern of this rhyming, one would represent the first rhyming sound as *a* and the second rhyming sound as *b*. Thus, the pattern of rhyme, or the *rhyme scheme,* of the first stanza of the poem would be expressed as *a a b b*.

What would be the rhyme scheme of the following stanza from "At Magnolia Cemetery"?

Sleep sweetly in your humble graves,
Sleep, martyrs of a fallen cause;
Though yet no marble column craves
The pilgrim here to pause.

More intricate rhyme schemes are possible in longer stanzas or in such poetic forms as the sonnet. Try to chart the rhyme scheme of "The Conquerors" (page 228).

It is possible to have rhyming sounds *within* a line of poetry, as in the fourth line from "The Skater of Ghost Lake" stanza:

St*eep* stand the sentineled d*eep*, dark firs.

This form of rhyme is referred to as *internal rhyme.* It is used sparingly, especially when end rhyme is employed, because it tends to create a sing-song effect.

Another technique a poet can use is to repeat the beginning consonant sounds of words, as Benét does with "*d*ark-*d*eep" in the first line, with "*f*ar-*f*aint" in the third line, and with "*s*teep-*s*tand" and "*d*eep-*d*ark" in the fourth line. This form of sound repetition is called *alliteration,* and is popular in our language (do or die, bed and breakfast, safe and sound, time and tide) because it gives pleasure in itself. But it is also used where possible to echo the sense and to provide emphasis. For example "deep, dark firs" and "dark lake-deep lake" emphasize the mystery, the treacherousness of the scene and therefore help prepare the reader for the story that is about to unfold.

What is the effect of the alliteration in the first two lines from "At Magnolia Cemetery"?

When the sound of a word provides an illustration of its sense, we have an instance of

From "The Skater of Ghost Lake". Reprinted by permission of Dodd, Mead & Company, Inc. from *Golden Fleece* by William Rose Benét. Copyright 1933, 1935 by Dodd, Mead & Company, Inc. Copyright renewed.

# RHYTHM

*onomatopoeia* (on′ə mat′ə pē′ə). Common examples are *ouch, murmur, buzz, gurgle,* and *purr.* This is yet another device used by a poet to help achieve harmony between sound and sense. The word at the end of the third line, *whirrs,* is onomatopoetic; the sound of the word itself suggests the sound that the word stands for.

Point out instances of *(a)* internal rhyme, *(b)* alliteration, and *(c)* onomatopoeia in the following stanzas from "The Rime of the Ancient Mariner." What is the rhyme scheme for each stanza? How does it differ from the rhyme schemes for the stanzas from "The Skater of Ghost Lake" and "At Magnolia Cemetery"? What might be the reason for the difference?

The ice was here, the ice was there,
 The ice was all around;
It cracked and growled, and roared and howled;
 Like noises in a swound!

The fair breeze blew, the white foam flew,
 The furrow followed free;
We were the first that ever burst
 Into that silent sea.

---

**RHYME:** the repetition of word-ending sounds; specifically, the repetition of accented vowel sounds plus any succeeding sounds (*first-burst,* de*lightful*-sp*iteful*). When sounds are repeated at the ends of lines (end rhymes), they are arranged in a pattern within the poem called a *rhyme scheme.* One may describe a rhyme scheme by representing sounds with letters of the alphabet. A rhyme occurring within a line is called an *internal rhyme.*

**ALLITERATION:** the repetition of initial consonant sounds. (*s*torm and *s*tress; *l*ong, *l*ean, and *l*anky)

**ONOMATOPOEIA:** the correspondence of sound and sense in a word; the sound of the word suggests what the word stands for.

---

*Rhythm* is the arrangement of stressed and unstressed sounds in speech or writing. The rhythm in some pieces of writing has a definite pattern or cadence; in others it is irregular. Read the following limerick aloud:

> There was a young lady from Austin,
> Who started to cycle to Boston.
>  By Platte she was cross-eyed
>  From too much monoxide,
> Said she, "This is very exhaustin'."

Did you find yourself naturally stressing certain words or syllables after the first few readings? The limerick is a poetic form with a fairly definite structure. For example, the first line usually starts with "There was a . . ."; the first, second, and last lines rhyme; the third and fourth lines rhyme. The reading of any limerick tends to fall into a cadence, as in this instance (capital letters indicate stressed words or syllables):

> There WAS a young LAdy from AUStin,
> Who STARted to CYcle to BOSton.
>  By PLATTE she was CROSS-eyed
>  From TOO much moNOXide,
> Said SHE, "This is VERy exHAUStin'."

While there is some slight variation in the number of unstressed syllables preceding stressed syllables, this limerick exhibits a patterned rhythm: three stresses in the first, second, and last lines; two stresses in the third and fourth lines. This sort of regular rhythm is suitable for a short, humorous verse; but in more serious poetry, writers often vary the beat to achieve emphasis and to avoid monotony. (Notice, for instance, how A. E. Housman departs from the basic rhythm in his poem on page 226.)

A regular rhythm is a technique—like imagery, figurative language, alliteration, or rhyme—that a poet may or may not use. Many modern poems do not have the marked pattern of sound that limericks and the poem by Housman exhibit. The poet may choose not to employ a regular beat but instead to use an irregular rhythm, similar to that of speech, or to vary the rhythm widely to suit the different situations in the poem. How would you describe the rhythm in the following lines by Walt Whitman?

Afoot and light-hearted I take to the open road,
Healthy, free, the world before me,
The long brown path before me leading wherever
    I choose.

Henceforth I ask not good-fortune, I myself am
    good-fortune,
Henceforth I whimper no more, postpone no more,
    need nothing,
Done with indoor complaints, libraries, querulous
    criticisms,
Strong and content I travel the open road.

1. What words or syllables would you stress in the first three lines? Does the arrangement of stressed and unstressed syllables fall into a regular pattern?

2. Is the last syllable in each line stressed?

3. Is there a natural pause at the end of each line?

While there is rhythm in the poem, of course, it is the casual, irregular rhythm of speech rather than the measured rhythm of a regular beat. The poem's irregular pattern of sound helps the reader focus on the poet's thoughts more than on the rhythm of the words.

Rhythm in poetry and in prose can be used simply for enjoyment in the sound. We take pleasure in nursery rhymes and nonsensical schoolyard chants because we enjoy the cadences of such expressions. We can experience this kind of pleasure in the following lines from an old folk song:

Eyes like the morning star,
Cheeks like a rose,
Annie was a pretty girl,
God Almighty knows,
Weep all you little rains,
Wail, winds, wail——
All along, along, along,
The Colorado Trail.

Secondly, rhythm can be used to echo the sense, as in the poem "Lessons" (page 248) in which the rushing rhythm complements the rushing of people trying to get ready, or in these drowsy lines about a flowing river by Robert Burns:

Flow gently, sweet Afton! among thy green braes,
Flow gently, I'll sing thee a song in thy praise;
My Mary's asleep by thy murmuring stream,
Flow gently, sweet Afton, disturb not her dream.

Finally, rhythm can be used to emphasize important words, as in the following lines from "The Rime of the Ancient Mariner," where the word "ice" is emphasized by being in the stressed position each time it is used:

The ICE was HERE, the ICE was THERE,
    The ICE was ALL aROUND

---

**RHYTHM:** the arrangement of stressed and unstressed sounds in speech and writing. The rhythm in a poem may have a single, dominant beat; it may be varied within the poem to fit different situations and moods; or it may be casual and irregular like speech.

---

## SATIRE

Satire is the art of ridiculing a subject, of making fun of it, of bringing it down in order to evoke toward it attitudes of amusement, contempt, or scorn. For instance, George S. Kaufman once wrote in a review of a short-lived comedy: "There was laughter in back of the theater, leading to the belief that someone was telling jokes back there."

A satirist usually desires to effect a change in society—to get people to stop taking seriously what he has ridiculed or to stop committing the stupidities he has exposed. Mark Twain's statement that "A classic is something that everybody wants to have read and nobody wants to read" is an example of this.

A satirist attacks what he considers to be foolish (e.g., clothing fads taken seriously, the superficialities and stupidities of the television industry) or evil (e.g., man's inhumanity to man, his greed, his lust for power) or in bad taste. His tone may range from the gently humorous to the savagely indignant. What is the tone of George Bernard Shaw's statement: "We don't bother much about dress and manners in England, because, as a nation we don't dress well and we've no manners"?

The poem "Item" by Howard Nemerov on page 253 is satirical. How would you characterize the author's tone, his attitude toward the subject? (Is he amused? indignant? mocking? See the entry for *tone* in this Handbook.)

> **SATIRE:** the art of bringing a subject down by ridiculing it and evoking toward it attitudes of amusement, contempt, or scorn.

The short story "The Purloined Letter" by Edgar Allan Poe opens with the following paragraph:

At Paris, just after dark one gusty evening in the autumn of 18____, I was enjoying the twofold luxury of meditation and a meerschaum, in company with my friend, C. Auguste Dupin, in his little back library, or book-closet, *au troisième*, No. *33 Rue Dunôt, Faubourg St. Germain.* For one hour at least we had maintained a profound silence; while each, to any casual observer, might have seemed intently and exclusively occupied with the curling eddies of smoke that oppressed the atmosphere of the chamber. For myself, however, I was mentally discussing certain topics which had formed matter for conversation between us at an earlier period of the evening; I mean the affair of the Rue Morgue, and the mystery attending the murder of Marie Rogêt. I looked upon it, therefore, as something of a coincidence, when the door of our apartment was thrown open and admitted our old acquaintance, Monsieur G____, the Prefect of the Parisian police.

1. What time of day is it?
2. In what city does the story take place?
3. What time of year is it?
4. Does the story take place in this century?
5. In what kind of room are the characters meditating?

The opening paragraph helps the reader locate the story in space and time—a windy evening in autumn in the library of C. Auguste Dupin in Paris of the 1800's. Locating a story in a given time and place establishes its *setting*.

What are some of the purposes a setting may serve? Locating the characters of a story in a specific time and place helps to make their actions believable. While the narrator and Dupin might not be believable in Los Angeles, California, in the 1970's, they are, as you would discover if you continued the story, believable in Paris in the last century.

Read the opening paragraph of "Bargain" on page 47. Does Freighter Slade seem believable in this setting?

A setting may also help create the atmosphere of a story. In the opening paragraphs of "The Scarlet Ibis" (page 111), for example, the setting contributes an atmosphere of loneliness, gentle nostalgia, and reminiscence. Another purpose the setting may serve is to focus the expectations of the reader. Because "Bargain" has the setting of a "western," the reader may expect to encounter a rough code of behavior, a reliance on force to settle disputes. We would expect just the opposite after reading the opening of "The Purloined Letter" above.

Finally, the setting may be vital to the unraveling of the plot or the revealing of character: only in that particular time or place could the problem have occurred or the character have behaved in a certain way. This is often true in science fiction or detective stories.

Notice in the following excerpts from "The Purloined Letter" how the setting forms a vital part of the problem posed for Dupin and the Prefect, who is looking for a stolen letter. (The narrator is conversing with the Prefect.)

"Suppose you detail," said I, "the particulars of your search."

"Why, the fact is, we took our time, and we searched *everywhere*. I have had long experience in these affairs. I took the entire building, room by room; devoting the nights of a whole week to each. We examined, first, the furniture of each apartment. We opened every possible drawer; and I presume you know that, to a properly trained police-agent, such a thing as a 'secret' drawer is impossible. Any man is a dolt who permits a 'secret' drawer to escape him in a search of this kind. The thing is *so* plain. There is a certain amount of bulk—of space—to be accounted for in every cabinet. Then we have accurate rules. The fiftieth part of a line could not escape us. After the cabinets we took the chairs. The cushions we probed with the fine long needles you have seen me employ. From the tables we removed the tops. . . ."

The Prefect continues to describe how every inch of the hotel was searched. Some weeks later he returns to tell Dupin that the letter still has not been found. Dupin, however, thinks the policeman has overlooked an obvious hiding place, and he, himself, goes to visit the apartments of the man who is accused of stealing the letter. Dupin, in telling of his visit, says:

"At length my eyes, in going the circuit of the room, fell upon a trumpery filigree card-rack of pasteboard, that hung dangling by a dirty blue ribbon, from a little brass knob just beneath the middle of the mantelpiece. In this rack, which had three or four compartments, were five or six visiting cards and a solitary letter. This last was much soiled and crumpled. . . . It was thrust carelessly, and even, as it

seemed, contemptuously, into one of the uppermost divisions of the rack.

"No sooner had I glanced at this letter than I concluded it to be that of which I was in search. . . ."

In this instance, a particular setting is vital to the development of the plot. How could a letter, which is known to be on certain premises, have escaped a detailed search by the police?

---

**SETTING:** the time and place in which the events of a narrative occur. The setting may be described specifically by the narrator or one of the characters, or it may be suggested through dialogue and action. A realistic setting—whether in the past, present, or future—lends an air of credibility to the characters and actions depicted in a story. The setting helps to limit the expectations of a reader (only certain actions are possible in a given time and place), may serve to create an appropriate atmosphere for the events of a story, and may be vital to the development of the plot or the revealing of character.

---

## SOLILOQUY

*Why, thank you so much. I'd adore to.*

I don't want to dance with him. I don't want to dance with anybody. And even if I did, it wouldn't be with him. He'd be well down among the last ten. I've seen the way he dances; it looks like something you do on St. Walpurgis Night. Just think, not a quarter of an hour ago, here I was sitting, feeling so sorry for the poor girl he was dancing with. And now *I'm* going to be the poor girl. Well, well. Isn't it a small world?

This is an excerpt from the short story "The Waltz" by Dorothy Parker. The first line tells us what the girl says; the remaining lines tell us what she is thinking.

1. How does the girl really feel about dancing with the boy who has asked her?

2. What do we find out about the girl from her thoughts? Does she view the situation tragically, comically, ironically? How do you think she will act toward her partner during the dance?

We are able to appreciate the contrast between what the girl says and how she really feels because the author presents the girl's thoughts directly to us.

It is a bit more difficult for the dramatist, however, to present the thoughts of characters in a play. There have been some attempts in modern drama, and especially in films, to record the thoughts of a character on tape or a sound track and play the sound to the audience. But dramatists of earlier times adopted the "dramatic convention" of simply having a character, alone on the stage, speak his thoughts aloud. This way of presenting a character's thoughts is called a *soliloquy*, and it was used with special effectiveness by Shakespeare.

The purpose of a soliloquy is to give the audience greater insight into a character. As used by Shakespeare, the soliloquy helps the audience understand the doubts and confusions in a character's mind, the alternative courses of action he is considering, and his reasons for acting as he does. The function of this dramatic technique is well illustrated, for example, by Juliet's "potion" soliloquy from Act IV, Scene Three of *Romeo and Juliet*:

(Friar Laurence has given Juliet the potion which will make her appear to be dead for forty-two hours so that she can avoid having to marry Paris and can be reunited with Romeo. She is alone in her chamber, contemplating taking the potion.)

Come, vial.
What if this mixture do not work at all?
Shall I be married then tomorrow morning?
No, no; this shall forbid it. Lie thou there.
*(She lays down her dagger.)*
What if it be a poison which the friar
Subtly hath ministered to have me dead,
Lest in this marriage he should be dishonored

Because he married me before to Romeo?
I fear it is, and yet methinks it should not,
For he hath still been tried a holy man.
How if, when I am laid into the tomb,
I wake before the time that Romeo
Come to redeem me?—There's a fearful point!
Shall I not then be stifled in the vault,
To whose foul mouth no healthsome air breathes in,
And there die strangled ere my Romeo comes?
Or, if I live, is it not very like
The horrible conceit of death and night,
Together with the terror of the place—
As in a vault, an ancient receptacle
Where, for these many hundred years, the bones
Of all my buried ancestors are packed;
Where bloody Tybalt, yet but green in earth,
Lies festering in his shroud; where, as they say,
At some hours in the night spirits resort;—
Alack, alack, is it not like that I,
So early waking, what with loathsome smells,
And shrieks like mandrakes' torn out of the earth,
That living mortals, hearing them, run mad:—
O, if I wake shall I not be distraught,
Environed with all these hideous fears,
And madly play with my forefathers' joints,
And pluck the mangled Tybalt from his shroud,
And, in this rage, with some great kinsman's bone,
As with a club, dash out my desperate brains?
O, look! Methinks I see my cousin's ghost
Seeking out Romeo, that did spit his body
Upon a rapier's point.—Stay, Tybalt, stay!
Romeo, I come! This do I drink to thee.
*(She drinks and falls upon her curtained bed.)*

1. With what "insurance" does Juliet provide herself in case the potion does not work?

2. Why does she think the potion might actually be a poison that will kill her?

3. What convinces her that Friar Laurence would not give her a poison?

4. Juliet fears that she will awake in the burial vault before Romeo comes. What does she first imagine might happen to her if this were the case? What does she fear that the idea of death and the terror of the burial vault might do to her? What does she fear she might do to herself? What is the progression of Juliet's imagined fears? What is their purpose? How do they prepare us for what she next imagines?

5. How does she finally convince herself to take the potion?

The potion that Friar Laurence gives Juliet offers her a way out of her difficulties (her father has insisted that she marry Paris the next day; yet she is secretly married to Romeo, who is in exile). If she had taken it directly, without thinking about it, the potion would be no more than a plot device, a contrivance; and the incident would lack dramatic force. Juliet's soliloquy helps the audience understand the magnitude of the event: Here is a confused and frightened young girl—caught between powerful loyalties, poised between salvation and damnation—whose vivid imagination works on her fears until she is in a state of near hysteria before she can take the potion.

---

**SOLILOQUY:** The dramatic convention of a character's speaking his or her thoughts aloud while alone on the stage. The purpose of a soliloquy is to help the audience understand a character's motives and the significance of his actions. Although the soliloquy is not often used in modern plays, Shakespeare and other Elizabethan dramatists readily employed it as a dramatic technique.

---

1. What effect are the references to the French, the Chinese, and the English intended to have?

2. What is the purpose of claiming that gourmets the world over enjoy this soup?

3. What is the purpose of stating that "it may cost a little more"?

4. What effect is the word "imported" intended to have?

5. Is Johnson's & Brown's soup just a soup? What else is it supposed to stand for?

This advertisement illustrates the modern copywriter's practice of investing a product with *symbolic* value, of making it stand for something else. In the advertisement, Johnson's & Brown's soup stands for aristocratic taste, knowledge of the world, and affluence. The copywriter has made a can of soup a *symbol* of these things. A *symbol* is any object, happening, place, or person that not only represents itself but also stands for something else.

Literary symbols serve a similar purpose: to invest a poem, play, short story, or novel with more than surface meaning; to give a literary work or some part of it a variety of meanings and applications. Some symbols have been used so often that we almost immediately recognize

their significance when they appear in literary works: a white dove stands for peace, for example; a crown for majesty, a forked road for a choice, usually a difficult one. Other literary symbols, however, are not so obvious and gain their significance from the context in which they appear. The symbol of the bird in the story "The Scarlet Ibis" (page 111) is an example. The scarlet ibis is a rare, exotic bird, but it is not always regarded as a symbol for a courageous spirit. Yet as it is used in that story, it stands for the spirit of Doodle, the narrator's frail brother.

Once we recognize the power of symbolism, the ability of the symbol to radiate meaning, to invest the poem or the short story with a rich suggestiveness, we must be on guard against symbol hunting, against seeing more in the image or the situation than the context allows. As Robert Frost reminds us in one of his poems, "The rose is a rose . . ."; and that's all it may be. A fire, for example, may stand for the raging spirit, for a social upheaval, for the surging and ebbing of enthusiasm, for the consumption of energy; or it may be just a fire. It all depends.

In the poem that follows, is "the seed of the fire" a symbol, or isn't it? How do you know?

### The Song of the Old Mother

*William Butler Yeats*

I rise in the dawn, and I kneel and blow
Till the seed of the fire flicker and glow.
And then I must scrub, and bake, and sweep,
Till the stars are beginning to blink and peep;
But the young lie long and dream in their bed
Of the matching of ribbons, for bosom and head,
And their day goes over in idleness,
And they sigh if the wind but lift a tress.
While I must work, because I am old
And the seed of the fire gets feeble and cold.

Reprinted with permission of The Macmillan Company and M. B. Yeats from "The Song of the Old Mother" by William Butler Yeats. Copyright 1906 by The Macmillan Company, renewed 1934 by William Butler Yeats.

# THEME

1. When the Old Mother says, ". . . I kneel and blow / Till the seed of the fire flicker and glow" what, literally, is she doing? At this point, is there any reason to regard "the seed of the fire" as anything more than the embers that have been banked for the night?

2. How does the use of "the seed of the fire" in the last line differ from its use in the second line? What added meaning does the image take on at this point?

If the poet had not repeated "the seed of the fire" in the last line and connected its feebleness and coldness with the age of the mother, there would be little reason to regard it as a symbol. His having done this, however, makes it reasonable to interpret the image as a symbol for the waning life force of the Old Mother.

---

**SYMBOL:** any object, happening, person, or place which signifies not only itself but also something more abstract or general. For example, in the expression, "You can lead a horse to water, but you can't make him drink," "horse" literally signifies a horse but also stands for anybody who is given opportunity but refuses to take advantage of it.

---

The central idea or *theme* of a literary work is usually some observation about life, about the world we live in. It is simply a comment on life, not a direction on how to live. Sometimes the theme is explicitly stated in the literary work. More often than not, however, the theme is implied from what has occurred in the poem, the short story, the novel, the play. As readers, we want to understand a literary work as best we can. We want not only to understand the *how* of a literary work (how it's put together, its techniques, its use of literary conventions, etc.), but also to understand the *why*, the what's-it-all-about. When we try to answer this question for ourselves, we are trying to express the theme of the work.

Here is a modern version of Little Red Riding Hood. What comment on life does it make?

### The Little Girl and the Wolf

*James Thurber*

One afternoon a big wolf waited in a dark forest for a little girl to come along carrying a basket of food to her grandmother. Finally a little girl did come along and she was carrying a basket of food. "Are you carrying that basket to your grandmother?" asked the wolf. The little girl said yes, she was. So the wolf asked her where her grandmother lived and the little girl told him and he disappeared into the wood.

When the little girl opened the door of her grandmother's house she saw that there was somebody in bed with a nightcap and nightgown on. She approached no nearer than twenty-five feet from the bed when she saw that it was not her grandmother but the wolf, for even in a nightcap a wolf does not look any more like your grandmother than the Metro-Goldwyn lion looks like Calvin Coolidge. So the little girl took an automatic out of her basket and shot the wolf dead.

Which of the following statements would you select as the theme of this modern fable? *(a)* Success requires careful planning and attention to detail; *(b)* Watch out for sharp-eyed little girls; *(c)* It is not so easy to fool little girls nowadays as it used to be.

Item *(c)* is the author's statement of the theme. Do you agree?

> **THEME:** The central idea of a literary work, usually expressed as a general observation about people or the world we live in. The theme is a statement of the way things are (a statement derived from what occurs in a literary work), not a statement telling the reader how to live. A theme may be stated or implied.

# TONE

When someone speaks to you, you hear not only what he says but also how he says it. The *tone* of the speaker's voice can be just as important as what he says. The "good morning" of your father, your teacher, or your employer can be said in such a way to make you glad you are alive or to make you wish you hadn't gotten out of bed. In other words, the speaker not only says something, but usually expresses a definite attitude toward what he says. He makes clear, for instance, whether the "good morning" is meant as praise or blame or is merely a perfunctory greeting.

Tone of voice is largely a matter of emphasis and inflection (rising and falling of the voice). Consider the different meanings that can be given to the same sentence merely by shifting the emphasis and inflection:

*George* completed two jobs yesterday. [The rest of you didn't.]
George *completed* two jobs yesterday. [He left several jobs uncompleted.]
George completed *two* jobs yesterday. [He did more than usual.]
George completed two *jobs* yesterday. [George is wonderful.]
George completed two jobs *yesterday*. [He didn't do as well today.]

A writer, too, has a *tone,* an attitude toward what he writes; and just as tone of voice contributes to the meaning of what is spoken, so the writer's tone contributes to his meaning. His attitude, among many possibilities, can be serious, bitter, satirical, whimsical, lighthearted, mocking, indignant, or reminiscent. The writer, however, cannot rely on voice emphasis and inflection to express his attitude; he has to use other means. Notice the different attitudes expressed toward the same woman and coat in the following descriptions:

The coat was exquisitely tailored and flowed from her shoulders with casual grace, as if it were a natural complement to her reed-like figure.

The coat was well-tailored but hung loosely about her stick-like frame, as if somehow a tent had imploded but was still held aloft by its centerpole.

The coat must have cost more than the average workman makes in a month. And what was its use? To enhance this useless stick of a woman, who starved herself in the interest of fashion.

1. What does "exquisitely tailored" suggest that "well-tailored" does not?
2. What is the difference in suggestion between "reed-like" and "stick-like"?
3. In the third description, what is emphasized about the coat? About the woman?
4. Match the following attitudes to the appropriate descriptions: *(a)* admiring, *(b)* indignant, *(c)* disapproving.

Thus a writer expresses his *tone,* his attitude toward what he writes, through his choice of words (e.g., "flowed from her shoulders" instead of "hung loosely") and his selection of details (e.g., relative cost of the coat rather than how it looked).

How would you characterize the tone of the following description from Charles Dickens's *Hard Times:*

## Coketown

It was a town of red brick, or of brick that would have been red if the smoke and ashes had allowed it; but as matters stood it was a town of unnatural red and black like the painted face of a savage.

It was a town of machinery and tall chimneys, out of which interminable serpents of smoke trailed themselves for ever and ever, and never got uncoiled.

It had a black canal in it, and a river that ran purple with ill-smelling dye, and vast piles of building full of windows where there was a rattling and a trembling all day long, and where the piston of the steam-engine worked monotonously up and down, like the head of an elephant in a state of melancholy madness. It contained several large streets all very like one another, and many small streets still more like one another, inhabited by people equally like one another, who all went in and out at the same hours, with the same sound upon the same pavements, to do the same work, and to whom every day was the same as yesterday and tomorrow, and every year the counterpart of the last and the next.

1. What kind of a town is Coketown (a farm town? a factory town? a business and commercial center?)

2. Is the town described as a pleasant or unpleasant place? Select words and phrases that serve to characterize the town.

3. What is the effect of the repetitions ("... large streets ... like one another, ... small streets ... like one another, ... people ... like one another, ... the same hours, ... the same sound ... the same pavements, ... the same work ....") in the last sentence?

4. Does the author approve or disapprove of the town? How can you tell?

In one sense, Dickens's attitude toward the manufacturing town he has described is clear enough: he disapproves, and he wants his readers to disapprove. He ridicules its ugliness, its assault upon the senses, its monotonous sameness. Yet he does not seem to be solemnly earnest or bitter or highly indignant. There is an element of humorous exaggeration in the description (the effect of the repetitions); this is not quite the way it is, but the way it appears to an imaginative observer. And as long as the element of humor is there, the reader is not likely to expect a strictly realistic story. We may, therefore, characterize the tone of the description as grimly humorous.

---

**TONE:** The author's attitude, stated or implied, toward what he has written. Some possible attitudes are earnestness, seriousness, bitterness, indignation, joy, lightheartedness, whimsicality, mockery, cynicism, irony. The author reveals his attitude through his choice of words and details. The tone of a literary work may differ, however, from the *narrator's* attitude toward the events described.

---

# Glossary
## COMPLETE PRONUNCIATION KEY

The pronunciation of each word is shown just after the word, in this way: **ab bre vi ate** (ə brē′vē āt). The letters and signs used are pronounced as in the words below. The mark ′ is placed after a syllable with primary or strong accent, as in the example above. The mark ′ after a syllable shows a secondary or lighter accent, as in **ab bre vi a tion** (ə brē′vē ā′shən).

Some words, taken from foreign languages, are spoken with sounds that otherwise do not occur in English. Symbols for these sounds are given at the end of the table as "Foreign Sounds."

| | | | | | | | |
|---|---|---|---|---|---|---|---|
| a | hat, cap | j | jam, enjoy | th | thin, both | | |
| ā | age, face | k | kind, seek | ᴛʜ | then, smooth | | |
| ä | father, far | l | land, coal | | | | |
| | | m | me, am | | | | |
| | | n | no, in | u | cup, butter | | |
| b | bad, rob | ng | long, bring | u̇ | full, put | | |
| ch | child, much | | | ü | rule, move | | |
| d | did, red | | | | | | |
| | | | | v | very, save | | |
| e | let, best | o | hot, rock | w | will, woman | | |
| ē | equal, see | ō | open, go | y | young, yet | | |
| ėr | term, learn | ô | order, all | z | zero, breeze | | |
| | | oi | oil, voice | zh | measure, seizure | | |
| | | ou | house, out | | | | |
| f | fat, if | | | | | | |
| g | go, bag | | | ə represents: | | | |
| h | he, how | p | paper, cup | a in about | | | |
| | | r | run, try | e in taken | | | |
| | | s | say, yes | i in April | | | |
| | | sh | she, rush | o in lemon | | | |
| i | it, pin | t | tell, it | u in circus | | | |
| ī | ice, five | | | | | | |

**foreign sounds**

Y as in French *du*. Pronounce ē with the lips rounded as for English ü in **rule**.

œ as in French *peu*. Pronounce ā with the lips rounded as for ō.

N as in French *bon*. The N is not pronounced, but shows that the vowel before it is nasal.

H as in German *ach*. Pronounce k without closing the breath passage.

From *Thorndike-Barnhart High School Dictionary* by E. L. Thorndike and Clarence L. Barnhart. Copyright © 1968 by Scott, Foresman and Company. Reprinted by permission.

# PARTS OF SPEECH

| | | | | | |
|---|---|---|---|---|---|
| *n.* | noun | *adj.* | adjective | *prep.* | preposition |
| *v.* | verb | *adv.* | adverb | *conj.* | conjunction |
| *pron.* | pronoun | | | *interj.* | interjection |

# ETYMOLOGY KEY

| | | | |
|---|---|---|---|
| < | from, derived from, taken from | **gen.** | genitive |
| **?** | possibly | **lang.** | language |
| **abl.** | ablative | **masc.** | masculine |
| **accus.** | accusative | **neut.** | neuter |
| **cf.** | compare | **pp.** | past participle |
| **dial.** | dialect | **ppr.** | present participle |
| **dim.** | diminutive | **pt.** | past tense |
| **fem.** | feminine | **ult.** | ultimately |
| | | **var.** | variant |

# LANGUAGE ABBREVIATIONS

| | |
|---|---|
| AF | Anglo-French (=Anglo-Norman, the dialect of French spoken by the Normans in England, esp. 1066-c.1164) |
| Am.E | American English (originating in U.S.) |
| Am.Ind. | American Indian |
| Am.Sp. | American Spanish |
| E | English |
| F | French |
| G | German |
| Gk. | Greek (from Homer to 300 A.D.) |
| Gmc. | Germanic (parent language of Gothic, Scandinavian, English, Dutch, German) |
| HG | High German (speech of Central and Southern Germany) |
| Hindu. | Hindustani (the commonest language of India) |
| Ital. | Italian |
| L | Latin (Classical Latin 200 B.C.–300 A.D.) |
| LG | Low German (speech of Northern Germany) |
| LGk. | Late Greek (300–700) |
| LL | Late Latin (300–700) |
| M | Middle |
| ME | Middle English (1100–1500) |
| Med. | Medieval |
| Med.Gk. | Medieval Greek (700–1500) |
| Med.L | Medieval Latin (700–1500) |
| MF | Middle French (1400–1600) |
| MHG | Middle High German (1100–1450) |
| MLG | Middle Low German (1100–1450) |
| NL | New Latin (after 1500) |
| O | Old |
| OE | Old English (before 1100) |
| OF | Old French (before 1400) |
| OHG | Old High German (before 1100) |
| Pg. | Portuguese |
| Scand. | Scandinavian (one of the Germanic languages of Northern Europe before Middle English times; Old Norse unless otherwise specified) |
| Skt. | Sanskrit (the ancient literary language of India, from the same parent language as Persian, Greek, Latin, Germanic, Slavonic, and Celtic) |
| Sp. | Spanish |
| VL | Vulgar Latin (a popular form of Latin, the main source of French, Spanish, Italian, Portuguese, and Romanian) |

**a bash** (ə bash′), v. embarrass and confuse; make uneasy and somewhat ashamed: *The shy girl was abashed when she saw the room filled with strangers.* [< OF *esbaïss-*, stem of *esbaïr* be astonished < VL *batare* gape]

**a bate** (ə bāt′), v., **a bat ed, a bat ing.** 1. make less in amount, intensity, etc.: *The medicine abated his pain.* 2. become less violent, intense, etc.: *The storm has abated.* 3. put an end to.

**ab bey** (ab′ē), n., pl. **-beys.** 1. the building or buildings where monks or nuns live a religious life ruled by an abbot or abbess; a monastery or convent. 2. the monks or nuns living there. [< OF < LL *abbatia* < *abbas* abbot]

**ab hor** (ab hôr′), v., **-horred, -hor ring.** shrink away from with horror; feel disgust or hate for; detest: *Some people abhor snakes.* [< L *abhorrere* < *ab-* from + *horrere* shrink, bristle with fear] **—ab hor′red,** adj.

**a bide** (ə bīd′), v., **a bode** or **a bid ed, a bid ing.** 1. stay; remain. 2. dwell; continue to live (in a place). 3. put up with; endure; tolerate. 4. stand firm. [OE *ābīdan* stay on, and *onbīdan* wait for]

**a bom i na ble** (ə bom′ə nə bl or ə-bom′nə bl), adj. 1. disgusting; hateful; loathsome. 2. very unpleasant; distasteful. [< F < L *abominabilis* < *abominari*. See ABOMINATE.] **—a bom′i na bly,** adv.

**a bom i nate** (ə bom′ə nāt), v., **-nat ed, -nat ing.** 1. feel disgust for; hate very much; abhor; detest. 2. dislike. [< L *abominari* deplore as an ill omen < *ab-* off + *ominari* prophesy < *omen* omen]

**ab stract** (ab′strakt or ab strakt′), adj. 1. thought of apart from any particular object or real thing; not concrete: *Sweetness is abstract; sugar is concrete.* 2. expressing a quality that is thought of apart from any particular object or real thing. In "Honesty is the best policy," *honesty* is an abstract noun. 3. not practical; ideal; theoretical. 4. hard to understand; difficult: *abstract theories about the nature of the soul.* **—ab′stract ly,** adv.

**ac cen tu ate** (ak sen′chù āt), v., **-at ed, -at ing.** emphasize: *Her black hair accentuated the whiteness of her skin.*

**ac o lyte** (ak′ə līt), n. 1. person who helps a priest during certain religious services; altar boy. The acolyte lights the candles on the altar. 2. attendant; assistant. [< Med. L *acolitus* < Gk. *akolouthos* follower]

**a dieu** (ə dü′ or ə dyü′), interj., n., pl. **a dieus** or **a dieux** (ə düz′ or ə dyüz′). good-by; farewell. [< F *à dieu* to God]

**Ad i ron dacks** (ad′ə ron′daks), n.pl. mountain range in NE New York. The highest peak is 5344 feet. The Adirondacks are a part of the Appalachian mountain chain. [Am.E; < Mohawk Indian term meaning "they eat trees," applied to a tribe of Canadian Indians]

**ad mon ish** (ad mon′ish), v. 1. advise against something; warn: *The policeman admonished him not to drive too fast.* 2. reprove gently: *The teacher admonished the student for his careless work.* 3. urge strongly; advise.

**ad ver sar y** (ad′vər ser′ē), n., pl. **-sar ies.** 1. person opposing or resisting another person; enemy. 2. person or group on the other side in a contest. [< L *adversarius*] **—Syn.** 1. foe.

**ad ver si ty** (ad vėr′sə tē), n., pl. **-ties.** 1. condition of unhappiness, misfortune, or distress. 2. stroke of misfortune; unfavorable or harmful thing or event.

**adz** or **adze** (adz), n. tool somewhat like an ax but with a blade set across the end of the handle and curving inward. [OE *adesa*]

**aer i al ist** (ar′ē ə list, er′ē ə list, or ā ėr′ē-ə list), n. a trapeze artist.

**af fa ble** (af′ə bl), adj. easy to talk to; courteous and pleasant. [< F < L *affabilis* easy to speak to < *affari* < *ad-* to + *fari* speak]

**af flic tion** (ə flik′shən), n. 1. state of pain or distress. 2. cause of pain, trouble, or distress. **—Syn.** 1. misery, wretchedness. 2. misfortune.

**af flu ent** (af′lù ənt), adj. 1. very wealthy. 2. abundant; plentiful. **—af′flu ent ly,** adv.

**af front** (ə frunt′), n. 1. a word or act that openly expresses intentional disrespect. 2. a slight or injury to one's dignity. [< v.] **—v.** 1. insult openly; offend purposely: *The boy affronted the teacher by making a face at her.* 2. meet face to face; confront.

**af ter deck** (af′tər dek′ or äf′tər dek′), n. deck toward or at the stern of a ship.

**a gape** (ə gāp′ or ə gap′), adv., adj. 1. gaping; with the mouth wide open in wonder or surprise. 2. wide open.

**ag ile** (aj′əl), adj. moving quickly and easily; active; lively; nimble: *An acrobat has to be agile.* [< L *agilis* < *agere* move] **—ag′ile ly,** adv.

**a gil i ty** (ə jil′ə tē), n. ability to move quickly and easily; activeness; liveliness; nimbleness.

**ag i tate** (aj′ə tāt), v., **-tat ed, -tat ing.** 1. move or shake violently. 2. disturb; excite (the feelings or the thoughts of): *She was much agitated by the news of her brother's illness.* 3. keep arguing about and discussing a matter to arouse public interest: *agitate for a shorter working day.* [< L *agitare* move to and fro < *agere* drive, move] **—ag′i tat′ed ly,** adv.

**ag nos tic** (ag nos′tik), n. person who believes that nothing is known or can be known about the existence of God or about things outside of human experience. **—adj.** of agnostics or their beliefs. [< Gk. *agnostos* < *a-* not + *gnostos* (to be) known]

**a gue** (ā′gyü), n. 1. a malarial fever with chills and sweating that occur at regular intervals. 2. a fit of shivering; chill. [< OF < L *acuta* (*febris*) severe (fever)]

**al ba tross** (al′bə trôs or al′bə tros), n. any of various large web-footed sea birds related to the petrel, that can fly long distances.

**al der man** (ôl′dər mən), n., pl. **-men.** 1. in the U.S., a member of a council that governs a city. 2. *Early Eng. Hist.* a chief; the chief magistrate of a county or group of counties.

**al ien** (āl′yən or ā′lē ən), n. 1. person who is not a citizen of the country in which he lives. 2. foreigner; stranger. **—adj.** 1. of another country; foreign. 2. entirely different; not in agreement; strange: *Unkindness is alien to her nature.* [< L *alienus* < *alius* other]

**al ien ate** (āl′yən āt or ā′lē ən āt), v., **-at ed, -at ing.** turn away in feeling or affection; make unfriendly: *He was alienated from his sister by her foolish acts.*

**al ka li** (al′kə li), n., pl. **-lis** or **-lies.** 1. any base or hydroxide that is soluble in water, neutralizes acids and forms salts with them, and turns red litmus blue. Lye and ammonia are alkalis. 2. any salt or mixture of salts that neutralizes acids. Some desert soils contain much alkali. [< MF *alcali* < Arabic *al-qalī* the ashes of saltwort (a genus of plants)]

**al ly** (al′i or ə li′), n., pl. **-lies.** 1. person or nation united with another for some special purpose. 2. helper; supporter.

**al ma ma ter** or **Al ma Ma ter** (al′mə mä′tər, äl′mə mä′tər, or al′mə mä′tər), person's school, college, or university. [< L *alma mater* bounteous mother]

**a loof** (ə lüf′), adv. at a distance; withdrawn; apart: *One boy stood aloof from all the others.* **—adj.** unsympathetic; not interested; reserved.

**al ter nate** (ôl′tər nāt or al′tər nāt), v., **-nat ed, -nat ing.** 1. occur by turns, first one and then the other; happen or be arranged by turns. 2. arrange by turns; do by turns: *alternate work and pleasure.* 3. take turns. 4. interchange regularly. [< L *alternare* < *alternus* every second < *alter* other]

**al um** (al′əm), n. a white mineral salt used in medicine and in dyeing. Alum is sometimes used to stop the bleeding of a small cut. *Formula:* KA1 (SO$_4$)$_2$·12H$_2$O

**Am a zon** (am′ə zon or am′ə zən), n. the largest river in the world, flowing from the Andes Mountains in NW South America across Brazil into the Atlantic. 3900 mi.

**am ber** (am′bər), n. 1. a hard, translucent yellow or yellowish brown fossil resin, used for jewelry and in making stems of pipes. 2. color of amber; yellow; yellowish brown.

**am big u ous** (am big′yü əs), adj. 1. having more than one possible meaning. 2. doubtful; not clear; uncertain. **—am big′u ous ly,** adv.

**am bro sia** (am brō′zhə), n. 1. food of the ancient Greek and Roman gods. 2. something especially pleasing to taste or smell. [< L < Gk. *ambrosia* < *ambrotos* < *a-* not + *brotos* mortal]

**a mend** (ə mend′), v. 1. change the form of (a law, bill, motion, etc.) by addition, omission, etc.: *Our Constitution was amended so that women could vote.* 2. change for the better; improve. 3. free from faults; make right; correct. [< OF *amender* < L *emendare* < *ex-* out of + *mendum, menda* fault]

**a men i ty** (ə men′ə tē or ə mē′nə tē), n., pl. **-ties.** 1. pleasant way; polite act: *Saying "Thank you" and holding the door open*

for a person to pass through are amenities.
2. pleasantness; agreeableness: *the amenity of a warm climate.* [< L *amoenitas* < *amoenus* pleasant]

**a mi a ble** (ā′mē ə bl), *adj.* good-natured and friendly; pleasant and agreeable. [< OF *amiable* < LL *amicabilis* < L *amicus* friend] **—a′mi a bly,** *adv.*

**a miss** (ə mis′), *adv.* wrongly; out of order; at fault. —*adj.* improper; wrong. [ME *a mis* by (way of) fault]

**am or ous** (am′ər əs), *adj.* 1. inclined to love. 2. showing love; loving. 3. having to do with love or courtship. [< OF *amorous* < *amour* love < L *amor*] **—am′o rous ly,** *adv.*

**am phi the a ter** or **am phi the a tre** (am′fə thē′ə tər), *n.* 1. a circular or oval building with tiers of seats around a central open space. 2. something resembling an amphitheater in shape. [< L < Gk. *amphitheatron* < *amphi-* on all sides + *theatron* theater]

**a nal o gy** (ə nal′ə jē), *n., pl.* **-gies.** 1. likeness in some ways between things that are otherwise unlike; similarity: *the analogy between words like man and pan.* 2. comparison of such things. [< L < Gk. *analogia* equality of ratios, proportion]

**a nal y sis** (ə nal′ə sis), *n., pl.* **-ses** (-sēz). separation of a thing into its parts; examination of a thing's parts to find out their essential features. An analysis can be made of a book, a person's character, a medicine, soil, etc. [< Med.L < Gk. *analysis* a breaking up < *analyein* unloose < *ana-* up + *lyein* loose]

**an a lyt i cal** (an′ə lit′ə kl), *adj.* of analysis; using analysis. **—an′a lyt′i cal ly,** *adv.*

**a nat o my** (ə nat′ə mē), *n., pl.* **-mies.** 1. structure of an animal or plant: *The anatomy of an earthworm is much simpler than that of a man.* 2. science of the structure of animals and plants.

**an gu lar** (ang′gyə lər), *adj.* 1. having angles; sharp-cornered. 2. not plump; bony. 3. stiff and awkward. [< L *angularis* < *angulus* angle]

**an i mate** (an′ə māt), *v.,* **-mat ed, -mat ing.** 1. give life to; make alive. 2. make lively, gay, or vigorous. 3. inspire; encourage: *The soldiers were animated by their captain's brave speech.* 4. put into action; cause to act or work. [< L *animare* < *anima* life, breath]

**a non** (ə non′), *adv.* 1. in a little while; soon. 2. at another time; again. 3. **ever and anon,** now and then. [OE *on ān* into one, *on āne* in one, at once]

**a non y mous** (ə non′ə məs), *adj.* 1. by or from a person whose name is not known or given: *An anonymous book is one published without the name of the author.* 2. having no name; nameless. [< Gk. *anonymos* < *an-* without + (dialectal) *onyma* name] **—a non′y mous ly,** *adv.*

**an te room** (an′ti rüm′ or an′ti rùm′), *n.* a small room leading to a larger one; a waiting room.

**an tic** (an′tik), *n.* 1. Often, **antics,** *pl.* a grotesque gesture or action; a silly trick: *The clown amused us by his antics.* 2.

Archaic. clown. [< Ital. *antico* old (with sense of *grottesco* grotesque) < L *antiquus* ancient]

**a pos tro phe** (ə pos′trə fē), *n.* words addressed to an absent person as if he were present or to a thing or idea as if it could appreciate them.

**a poth e car y** (ə poth′ə ker′ē), *n., pl.* **-car ies.** 1. person who prepares and sells drugs and medicines; druggist. 2. *Brit.* formerly, a person who prescribed medicines and sold them.

**ap pa ri tion** (ap′ə rish′ən), *n.* 1. ghost; phantom. 2. something strange, remarkable, or unexpected which comes into view. 3. act of appearing; appearance.

**ap point ments** (ə point′mənts), *n. pl.* furniture; equipment.

**ap pre hen sion** (ap′ri hen′shən), *n.* 1. expectation of evil; fear; dread. 2. a seizing; being seized; arrest. 3. understanding; grasp by the mind.

**ap pre hen sive** (ap′ri hen′siv), *adj.* 1. afraid; anxious; worried. 2. quick to understand; able to learn. **—ap′pre hen′sive ly,** *adv.*

**ap pren tice** (ə pren′tis), *n.* 1. person learning a trade or art. In return for instruction the apprentice agrees to work for his employer a certain length of time with little or no pay. 2. beginner; learner. [< OF *aprentis* < *aprendre* learn < L *apprehendere*]

**aq ua vi tae** (ak′wə vī′tē), *n.* 1. alcohol. 2. brandy; whiskey, etc. [< NL *aqua vitae* water of life]

**ar bi trate** (är′bə trāt), *v.,* **-trat ed, -trat ing.** 1. give a decision in a dispute: *arbitrate between two persons in a quarrel.* 2. settle by arbitration; submit to arbitration.

**ar chi tect** (är′kə tekt), *n.* 1. person skilled in architecture. 2. person who makes plans for buildings and sees that these plans are followed by the contractors and workers who actually put up the buildings. [< L *architectus* < Gk. *architekton* < *archi-* chief + *tekton* builder]

**ar dent** (ärd′nt), *adj.* 1. full of zeal; very enthusiastic; eager. 2. burning; fiery; hot. 3. glowing.

**a ris to crat** (ə ris′tə krat or ar′is tə krat), *n.* 1. person who belongs to the aristocracy; noble. 2. person who has the tastes, opinions, manners, etc., of the upper classes.

**ar ma da** (är mä′də or är mā′də), *n.* 1. fleet of warships. 2. fleet of airplanes. [< Sp. < L *armata* armed force, originally pp. neut. pl. of *armare* to arm]

**ar ni ca** (är′nə kə), *n.* 1. a healing liquid used on bruises, sprains, etc., prepared from the dried flowers, leaves, or roots of a plant of the aster family. 2. the plant itself. It has showy yellow flowers. [< NL]

**ar ti choke** (är′tə chōk), *n.* 1. a thistlelike plant whose flowering head is cooked and eaten. 2. the flowering head.

**ar tic u late** (*adj.* är tik′yə lit; *v.* är tik′yə lāt), *v.,* **-lat ed, -lat ing.** —*adj.* 1. uttered in distinct syllables of words: *A baby cries and gurgles, but does not use articulate speech.* 2. able to put one's

**attribute**

hat, āge, fär; let, ēqual, tėrm;
it, īce; hot, ōpen, ôrder;
oil, out; cup, pùt, rüle;
ch, child; ng, long; sh, she;
th, thin; ᴛʜ, then; zh, measure;

ə represents *a* in about, *e* in taken,
*i* in pencil, *o* in lemon, *u* in circus.

< = from, derived from, taken from.

thoughts into words: *Julia is the most articulate of the sisters.* —*v.* 1. speak distinctly: *Be careful to articulate your words so that everyone in the room can understand you.* 2. give clarity or distinction to.

**as cet ic** (ə set′ik), *n.* 1. person who practices unusual self-denial and devotion, or severe discipline of self for religious reasons. 2. person who refrains from pleasures and comforts. —*adj.* refraining from pleasures and comforts; self-denying. [< Gk. *asketikos* < *askeein* exercise; hence, discipline] **—as cet′i cal ly,** *adv.*

**as per i ty** (as per′ə tē), *n., pl.* **-ties.** roughness; harshness; severity. [< OF *asprete* < L *asperitas* < *asper* rough]

**as sail** (ə sāl′), *v.* 1. set upon with violence; attack: *assail a fortress.* 2. set upon vigorously with arguments, abuse, etc. 3. undertake with the purpose of mastering. **—as sail′ing,** *adj.*

**as sent** (ə sent′), *v.* express agreement; agree. —*n.* acceptance of a proposal, statement, etc.; agreement. [< OF < L *assentare* < *ad-* along with + *sentire* feel, think]

**as sess** (ə ses′), *v.* 1. estimate the value of (property or income) for taxation. 2. estimate or judge the value, character, etc., of; evaluate: *assess the situation.*

**asth ma** (az′mə or as′mə), *n.* a chronic disease that causes difficulty in breathing, a feeling of suffocation, and coughing. [< Gk. *asthma* panting < *azein* breathe hard]

**asth mat ic** (az mat′ik or as mat′ik), *adj.* 1. of or having to do with asthma. 2. suffering from asthma.

**as tra khan** or **as tra chan** (as′trə kən), *n.* 1. the curly furlike wool on the skin of young lambs from Astrakhan. 2. a woolen cloth that looks like this.

**As tra khan** (as′trə kən), *n.* 1. district in SW Soviet Union. 2. capital of this district. 294,000.

**as tute** (əs tüt′ or əs tyüt′), *adj.* shrewd; crafty; sagacious: *Many lawyers are astute.* [< L *astutus* < *astus* sagacity]

**a sun der** (ə sun′dər), *adv.* apart; widely separated. —*adj.* apart; separate.

**at ro phy** (at′rə fē), *n., v.,* **-phied, -phy ing.** —*n.* wasting away; wasting away of a part or parts of the body. —*v.* waste away. [< LL < Gk. *atrophia* < *a-* without + *trophe* nourishment]

**at tain** (ə tān′), *v.* 1. arrive at; reach: *attain years of discretion.* 2. gain; accomplish. [< OF *ataindre* < VL *attangere* < L *ad-* to + *tangere* touch] **—Syn.** 2. achieve.

**at trib ute** (at′rə byüt), *n.* a quality considered as belonging to a person or thing; a characteristic: *Kindness is an attribute of a good teacher.*

**aught** (ôt), *n.* anything: *You may go for aught I care.* —*adv.* in any way; to any degree; at all: *Help came too late to avail aught.* [OE *āwiht* < *ā-* ever + *wiht* a thing]

**aug ment** (ôg ment′), *v.* increase; enlarge: *The king augmented his power by taking over rights that had belonged to the nobles.* [< L *augmentare* < *augmentum* < *augere* increase]

**au ra** (ô′rə), *n., pl.* **au ras, au rae** (ô′rē). something supposed to come from a person or thing and surround him or it as an atmosphere: *An aura of holiness surrounded the saint.* [< L < Gk.]

**aus tere** (ôs tir′), *adj.* **1.** harsh; stern. **2.** strict in morals: *The Puritans were austere.* **3.** severely simple: *The tall, plain columns stood against the sky in austere beauty.* [< L < Gk. *austeros* < *auein* dry]

**a venge** (ə venj′), *v.*, **a venged, a veng ing. 1.** get retribution for: *The Indian will avenge the murder of his brother by killing the murderer.* **2.** take vengeance on behalf of: *The clan avenged their slain chief.* **3.** get revenge. [< OF *avengier* < *a-* to (< L *ad-*) + *vengier* < L *vindicare* punish < *vindex* champion] —**a veng′er,** *n.*

**a ver** (ə vėr′), *v.*, **a verred, a ver ring.** state to be true; assert. [< OF *averer*, ult. < L *ad-* + *verus* true]

**a ver sion** (ə vėr′zhən or ə vėr′shən), *n.* **1.** a strong or fixed dislike; antipathy. **2.** thing or person disliked.

**a vert** (ə vėrt′), *v.* **1.** prevent; avoid: *He averted the accident by a quick turn of his car.* **2.** turn away; turn aside: *She averted her eyes from the wreck.* [< OF < L *avertere* < *ab-* from + *vertere* turn]

**av id** (av′id), *adj.* eager; greedy: *The miser was avid for gold.* [< L *avidus* < *avere* desire eagerly] —**av′id ly,** *adv.*

**a vow al** (ə vou′əl), *n.* frank or open declaration; confession; admission; acknowledgment.

**awe** (ô), *n., v.*, **awed, aw ing.** —*n.* great fear and wonder; fear and reverence. —*v.* **1.** cause to feel awe; fill with awe: *The majesty of the mountains awed us.* **2.** influence or restrain by awe. [< Scand. *agi*]

**awe-strick en** (ô′strik′ən), *adj.* filled with awe.

**bail i wick** (bāl′ə wik), *n.* **1.** a person's field of knowledge, work, or authority. **2.** the special domain or territory in which one has superior aptitude or experience or in which one has a particular right to exercise authority and respect.

**bale ful** (bāl′fəl), *adj.* evil; harmful.

**Bal kans** (bôl′kənz), *n.* the Balkan States; countries on the Balkan Peninsula; Yugoslavia, Romania, Bulgaria, Albania, Greece, and European Turkey.

**ban ish** (ban′ish), *v.* **1.** condemn to leave a country; exile. **2.** force to go away; send away; drive away. [< OF *baniss-*, stem of *banir* < LL *bannire* ban < Gmc.]

**bar bar ous** (bär′bər əs), *adj.* **1.** not civilized; savage. **2.** rough and rude; coarse; unrefined. **3.** cruelly harsh; brutal.

**bark** (bärk), *n.* **1.** ship with three masts, square-rigged on the first two masts and fore-and-aft-rigged on the other. **2.** *Poetic.* boat; ship. Also, **barque.**

**bar on** (bar′ən), *n.* nobleman; man of noble rank, title, or birth. [<OF<OHG *baro* man, fighter]

**ba ro ni al** (bə rō′nē əl), *adj.* **1.** of a baron; of barons. **2.** suitable for a baron; splendid; stately; magnificent.

**bar racks** (bar′əks), *n. pl.* **1.** a building or group of buildings for soldiers to live in. **2.** a large, plain building in which many people live. Also, **barrack.**

➔**Barracks** appears with either a singular or plural verb: *John wrote that his barracks was a lively place. The barracks were inspected daily.*

**bar re ra** (bə re′rə or bä re′rə), *n.* **1.** the red wooden fence surrounding a bull ring. **2.** the first row of seats in the amphitheater of a bull ring.

**bash** (bash), *Dialect and Slang.* —*v.* strike with a smashing blow. —*n.* a smashing blow. [? imitative]

**Bat on Rouge** (bat′n rüzh′), *n.* capital of Louisiana, in the SE part, on the Mississippi. 152,000.

**be deck** (bi dek′), *v.* adorn; decorate.

**be guile** (bi gīl′), *v.*, **-guiled, -guil ing. 1.** deceive; cheat: *His pleasant ways beguiled me into thinking that he was my friend.* **2.** take away from deceitfully or cunningly. **3.** entertain; amuse. —**Syn. 1.** delude.

**bel lig er ence** (bə lij′ər əns), *n.* **1.** being warlike; fondness for fighting. **2.** fighting; war.

**be muse** (bi myüz′), *v.*, **-mused, -mus ing.** confuse; bewilder; stupefy.

**berth** (bėrth), *n.* **1.** place to sleep on a ship, train, or airplane. **2.** place for a ship to anchor. **3. give a wide berth to,** keep well away from.

**be seech** (bi sēch′), *v.*, **-sought** or **-seeched, -seech ing.** ask earnestly; beg. [ME *biseche* (*n*) < *be-* thoroughly + *seche* (*n*) seek] —**Syn.** entreat; implore.

**be seech ing** (bi sēch′ing), *adj.* that beseeches. —**be seech′ing ly,** *adv.*

**be trothed** (bi trōᴛʜd′ or bi trôtht′), *n.* person engaged to be married.

**bev y** (bev′ē), *n., pl.* **bev ies.** a small group: *a bevy of quail, a bevy of girls.*

**bier** (bir), *n.* a movable stand on which a coffin or dead body is placed.

**biv ouac** (biv′wak or biv′ü ak), *n., v.*, **-acked, -ack ing.** camp outdoors without tents or with very small tents: *The soldiers made a bivouac for the night in a field. They bivouacked there until morning.* [< F, probably < Swiss G *biwache* < *bi* by + *wache* watch]

**bi zarre** (bə zär′), *adj.* odd; queer; fantastic; grotesque. [< F < Sp. *bizarro* brave < Basque *bezar* beard]

**bland** (bland), *adj.* **1.** smooth; mild; gentle; soothing: *A warm spring breeze is bland.* **2.** agreeable; polite. [< L *blandus* soft] —**bland′ly,** *adv.*

**blas phe my** (blas′fə mē), *n., pl.* **-mies.** abuse or contempt for God or sacred things. —**Syn.** profanity.

**blight** (blīt), *n.* **1.** any disease that causes plants to wither or decay. **2.** anything that causes destruction or ruin. —*v.* **1.** cause to wither or decay. **2.** destroy; ruin.

**blu cher** (blü′chər or blü′kər), *n.* shoe whose tongue and front part are one piece of leather. [named after Field Marshal von *Blücher*]

**bod ice** (bod′is), *n.* **1.** the close-fitting waist of a dress. **2.** a wide girdle worn over a dress and laced up the front. Some European peasant women wear bodices. [var. of pl. of *body*, part of a dress]

**boon dog gle** (bün′dog′l), *v.*, **-gled, -gling,** *n. U.S. Informal.* —*v.* do useless work. —*n.* a worthless work or product. [Am.E]

**boot leg** (büt′leg′), *v.*, **-legged, -leg ging,** *adj.*, *n. U.S.* —*v.* sell, transport, or make unlawfully. —*adj.* made, transported, or sold unlawfully. —*n. Slang.* alcoholic liquor made, sold, or transported unlawfully. [modern use from practice of smuggling liquor in boot legs]

**boot leg ger** (büt′leg′ər), *n. Slang.* person who bootlegs.

**bow** (bou), *n.* **1.** the forward part of a ship or boat. **2.** person who rows with the oar nearest the bow of a boat.

**bow er** (bou′ər), *n.* **1.** shelter of leafy branches. **2.** summerhouse or arbor. **3.** *Archaic.* bedroom. [OE *būr* dwelling]

**brace** (brās), *n.* pair; couple: *a brace of ducks.*

**bran dish** (bran′dish), *v.* wave or shake threateningly; flourish: *The knight drew his sword and brandished it at his enemy.* —*n.* a threatening shake; flourish. [< OF *brandiss-*, stem of *brandir* < *brand* sword < Gmc.]

**brash** (brash), *adj.* **1.** hasty; rash. **2.** impudent; saucy.

**breach** (brēch), *n.* **1.** an opening made by breaking down something solid; gap. **2.** a breaking (of a law, promise, duty, etc.); neglect: *For me to go away today would be a breach of duty.* —*v.* break through; make an opening in. —**Syn.** *n.* **1.** fracture, crack.

**bread fruit** (bred′früt′), *n.* **1.** a large, round, starchy, tropical fruit of the Pacific Islands, much used for food. When baked, it tastes somewhat like bread. **2.** tree that it grows on.

**Bridge town** (brij′toun), *n.* capital of Barbados in the West Indies. 11,000.

**bri er**[1] (brī′ər), *n.* thorny or prickly bush with a woody stem, especially the wild rose. Also, **briar.** [OE *brēr*]

**bri er**[2] (brī′ər), *n.* **1.** a white heath tree found in S Europe. Its root is used in making tobacco pipes. **2.** a tobacco pipe made of this. Also, **briar.** [< F *bruyère* heath < Celtic]

**bril lig** (bril′ig), *adj.* a nonsense word from Lewis Carroll's poem "Jabberwocky."

**brim stone** (brim′stōn′), *n.* **1.** sulfur.

2. fuel of hellfire. [ME *brinston* < *brinn-burn* + *ston* stone]

**brine** (brīn), *n.* 1. very salty water: *Pickles are often kept in brine.* 2. a salt lake or sea; ocean.

**bro gan** (brō′gən), *n.* a coarse, strong shoe. [< Irish, Scotch Gaelic *brōgan,* dim. of *brōg* shoe]

**brooch** (brōch or brüch), *n.* an ornamental pin having the point secured by a catch.

**Bru lé** (brü lā′), *n.* a subtribe of the Sioux.

**bulb ous** (bul′bəs), *adj.* 1. having bulbs; growing from bulbs: *Daffodils are bulbous plants.* 2. shaped like a bulb; rounded and swelling: *a bulbous nose.*

**bumblebee corn,** corn stunted from lack of water.

**buoy ant** (boi′ənt or bü′yənt), *adj.* 1. able to float. 2. able to keep things afloat: *Air is buoyant; balloons float in it.* 3. light-hearted; cheerful; hopeful: *Children are usually more buoyant than old people.* —**buoy′ant ly,** *adv.*

**bur ly** (ber′lē), *adj.,* **-li er, -li est.** 1. strong; sturdy; big. 2. bluff; rough. [OE *borlīce* excellently]

**butte** (byüt), *n.* in western U.S., a steep hill standing alone. [Am.E; < F]

**ca jole** (kə jōl′), *v.,* **-joled, -jol ing.** persuade by pleasant words, flattery, or false promises; coax. [< F *cajoler*]

**Ca lym ne** (ka lim′na), *n.* an island in the Aegean Sea. 49 sq. mi. Also, **Kalimnos** (modern), **Calymna,** or **Kalymna.**

**can o py** (kan′ə pē), *n., pl.* **-pies,** *v.,* **-pied, -py ing.** —*n.* 1. a covering fixed over a bed, throne, entrance, etc.; covering carried on poles over a person. 2. a rooflike covering; shelter; shade. 3. sky. —*v.* cover with a canopy. [< F *canapé* < Med.L < L *conopeum* < Gk. *konopeion* a couch with curtains of mosquito netting < *konops* gnat]

**can tan ker ous** (kan tang′kər əs), *adj.* hard to get along with because ready to make trouble and oppose anything suggested; ill-natured. [alteration, influenced by *rancorous,* of earlier unrecorded *con-teckerous* < ME *contecker* contentious person < *conteck* strife, quarreling]

**cap i tal** (kap′ə tl), *n.* 1. amount of money or property that a company or a person uses in carrying on a business: *The Smith Company has a capital of $30,000.* 2. source of power or advantage; resources.

**ca reen** (kə rēn′), *v.* 1. lean to one side; tilt; tip: *The ship careened in the strong wind.* 2. cause to lean to one side: *The strong wind careened the ship.* [< F < L *carina* keel]

**Car ib be an** (kar′ə bē′ən or kə rib′ē ən), *n.* sea between Central America, the West Indies, and South America. 750,000 sq. mi. —*adj.* of or having to do with this sea or the islands in it.

**car ri on** (kar′ē ən), *n.* 1. dead and decaying flesh. 2. rottenness; filth. —*adj.* 1. dead and decaying. 2. feeding on dead and decaying flesh. 3. rotten; filthy. [< OF

*carogne* < VL *caronia,* ult. < L *caries* decay]

**Cas ta li a** (kas tā′li ə), *n.* a spring on Mount Parnassus, sacred to Apollo and the Muses; its waters were considered to be a source of poetic inspiration.

**cat a pult** (kat′ə pult), *n.* an ancient weapon for shooting stones, arrows, etc. —*v.* shoot from a catapult; throw; hurl. [< L *catapulta* < Gk. *katapeltes,* probably < *kata-* down + *pallein* hurl]

**cat a ract** (kat′ə rakt), *n.* an opaque condition in the lens of the eye, or its capsule, that causes partial or total blindness. [< L *cataracta* < Gk. *kataraktes* < *kata-* down + *arassein* dash]

**cat walk** (kat′wôk′), *n.* a narrow place to walk, as on a bridge or over an engine room.

**caul** (kôl), *n.* membrane sometimes covering the head of a child at birth. It was supposed to bring good luck and to safeguard against drowning. [< OF *cale* a kind of little cap]

**cen so ri ous** (sen sô′rē əs or sen sō′rē-əs), *adj.* too ready to find fault; severely critical. —**cen so′ri ous ly,** *adv.* —**Syn.** hypercritical, carping.

**chafe** (chāf), *v.,* **chafed, chaf ing,** *n.* —*v.* 1. rub to make warm: *She chafed her cold hands.* 2. wear or be worn away by rubbing. 3. make or become sore by rubbing: *The stiff collar chafed the man's neck.* 4. make angry: *His big brother's teasing chafed him.* 5. become angry: *He chafed under his big brother's teasing.* —*n.* a chafing; irritation. [< OF *chaufer* < L *calefacere* < *calere* be warm + *facere* make] —**Syn.** *v.* 4. irritate, gall, annoy, vex, exasperate.

**cha grin** (shə grin′), *n.* a feeling of disappointment, failure, or humiliation. —*v.* cause to feel chagrin. [< F *chagrin* grained leather, vexation < Turkish *çāghrī* rump of a horse; shift of meaning comes from idea of being ruffled] —**Syn.** *n.* mortification, vexation.

**cham ois** (sham′ē), *n., pl.* **-ois.** 1. a small, goatlike antelope that lives in the high mountains of Europe and SW Asia. 2. a soft leather made from the skin of sheep, goats, deer, etc. [< F < LL *camox*]

**char nel** (chär′nl), *adj.* 1. of or used for a place where dead bodies or bones are laid. 2. deathlike; ghastly. [< OF < LL *carnale,* originally neut. of L *carnalis*]

**chaste** (chāst), *adj.* 1. pure; virtuous. 2. decent; modest. 3. simple in taste or style; not too much ornamented. [< OF < L *castus* pure] —**chaste′ly,** *adv.*

**châ teau** (sha tō′), *n., pl.* **-teaux** (-tōz′). 1. a French castle. 2. a large country house, usually in France. [< F *château* < L *castellum* castle]

**chide** (chīd), *v.,* **chid ed** or **chid, chid ed, chid,** or **chid den, chid ing.** reproach; blame; scold: *She chided the little girl for soiling her dress.* [OE *cīdan*]

**chol er ic** (kol′ər ik), *adj.* easily made angry; irritable.

**chris ten ing** (kris′n ing or kris′ning), *n.* act or ceremony of baptizing and naming; baptism.

hat, āge, fär; let, ēqual, tėrm;
it, īce; hot, ōpen, ôrder;
oil, out; cup, put, rüle;
ch, child; ng, long; sh, she;
th, thin; ᴛʜ, then; zh, measure;

ə represents *a* in about, *e* in taken,
*i* in pencil, *o* in lemon, *u* in circus.

< = from, derived from, taken from.

**cinch** (sinch), *U.S.* —*n.* 1. a strong girth for fastening a saddle or pack on a horse. 2. *Informal.* a firm hold or grip. —*v.* fasten on with a cinch; bind firmly. [Am.E; < Sp. *cincha* < L *cincta* girdle < *cingere* bind]

**ci pher** (sī′fər), *n.* 1. zero; 0. 2. person or thing of no importance. 3. something in secret writing or code. 4. key to a method of secret writing or code. Also, **cypher.** [< Med.L *ciphra* < Arabic *sifr* empty]

**clair voy ant** (klar voi′ənt or kler voi′-ənt), *adj.* 1. having the power of seeing things that are out of sight. 2. exceptionally keen. —*n.* person who has, or claims to have, the power of seeing things that are out of sight: *The clairvoyant claimed to be able to locate lost articles, and to give news of faraway people.* [< F *clairvoyant* < *clair* clear + *voyant,* ppr. of *voir* see (< L *videre*)]

**cleft** (kleft), *v.* a pt. and a pp. of **cleave.** —*adj.* split; divided. —*n.* space or opening made by splitting; crack. [OE *(ge)clyft*]

**clod** (klod), *n.* 1. lump of earth; lump. 2. earth; soil. [OE *clod*]

**cob ble** (kob′l), *n., v.,* **-bled, -bling.** —*n.* cobblestone. —*v.* pave with cobblestones.

**cod dle** (kod′l), *v.,* **-dled, -dling.** 1. treat tenderly; pamper: *coddle sick children.* 2. cook in hot water without boiling: *coddle an egg.* [var. of *caudle,* n., gruel < OF < L *calidus* hot] —**Syn.** 1. humor, indulge.

**co in cide** (kō′in sīd′), *v.,* **-cid ed, -cid ing.** 1. occupy the same place in space: *If these triangles △ △ were placed one on top of the other, they would coincide.* 2. occupy the same time: *The working hours of the two friends coincide.* 3. correspond exactly; agree: *Her opinion coincides with mine.* [< Med.L *coincidere* < L *co-* together + *in* upon + *cadere* fall] —**Syn.** 3. concur, harmonize, tally.

**col lat er al** (kə lat′ər əl), *adj.* 1. parallel; side by side. 2. related but less important; secondary; indirect. 3. additional. —**col-lat′er al ly,** *adv.*

**com merce** (kom′ərs or kom′ėrs), *n.* buying and selling in large amounts between different places; business. [< F < L *commercium,* ult. < *com-* with + *merx* wares]

**com mod i ty** (kə mod′ə tē), *n., pl.* **-ties.** 1. anything that is bought and sold. 2. a useful thing.

**com pla cent** (kəm plā′snt), *adj.* pleased with oneself; self-satisfied: *The winner's complacent smile annoyed some people.* [< L *complacens, -entis,* ppr. of *complacere* < *com-* + *placere* please]

**com pul sive** (kəm pul′siv), *adj.* 1. using force. 2. having an irresistible impulse to perform some irrational act. —**compul′sive ly,** *adv.*

**con cede** (kən sēd′), *v.,* **-ced ed, -ced ing.** 1. admit as true; admit: *Everyone concedes that 2 and 2 make 4.* 2. give (what is asked or claimed); grant; yield: *He conceded us the right to walk through his land.* [< L *concedere* < *com-* altogether + *cedere* yield]

**con ceive** (kən sēv′), *v.,* **-ceived, -ceiv ing.** 1. form in the mind; think up; imagine. 2. have an idea or feeling; think. 3. put in words; express: *The warning was conceived in the plainest language.* 4. become pregnant.

**con crete** (kon′krēt or kon krēt′), *adj.* 1. existing of itself in the material world, not merely in idea or as a quality; real. All actual objects are concrete. 2. not abstract or general; specific; particular: *The lawyer gave concrete examples of the prisoner's cruelty.* 3. naming a thing, especially something perceived by the senses: *"Sugar" and "people" are concrete nouns; "sweetness" and "humanity" are abstract nouns.* 4. formed into a mass; solid; hardened. [< L *concretus,* pp. of *concrescere* < *com-* together + *crescere* grow] —**con crete′ly,** *adv.*

**con dens er** (kən den′sər), *n.* 1. person or thing that condenses something. 2. a strong lens or lenses for concentrating light upon a small area.

**con done** (kən dōn′), *v.,* **-doned, -don ing.** forgive; overlook. [< L *condonare* < *com-* up + *donare* give]

**con du cive** (kən dü′siv or kən dyü′siv), *adj.* helpful; favorable: *Exercise is conducive to health.*

**con duc tiv i ty** (kon′duk tiv′ə tē), *n.* power of conducting heat, electricity, etc.

**con gen i tal** (kən jen′ə tl), *adj.* inborn; present at birth. [< L *congenitus* born with < *com-* with + *genitus* born]

**con jec ture** (kən jek′chər), *n., v.,* **-tured, -tur ing.** —*n.* 1. formation of an opinion admittedly without sufficient evidence for proof; guessing. 2. a guess. —*v.* guess.

**con jure** (kun′jər or kon′jər), *v.,* **-jured, -jur ing.** 1. **conjure up, a.** cause to appear in a magic way. **b.** cause to appear in the mind. 2. compel (a spirit, devil, etc.) to appear or disappear by magic words. 3. cause to be or happen by magic or as if by magic. [< OF < L *conjurare* make a compact < *com-* together + *jurare* swear]

**con nive** (kə nīv′), *v.,* **-nived, -niv ing.** 1. shut one's eyes to something wrong; give aid to wrongdoing by not telling of it, or by helping it secretly. 2. cooperate secretly. [< L *connivere* shut the eyes, wink < *com-* together + *niv-* press (related to *nictere* wink)]

**con sci en tious** (kon′shē en′shəs), *adj.* 1. careful to do what one knows is right; controlled by conscience. 2. done with care to make it right: *Conscientious work is careful and exact.* —**con′sci en′tious ly,** *adv.*

**con sign** (kən sīn′), *v.* 1. hand over; deliver: *The man was consigned to prison. The father consigned the child to his sister's care.* 2. transmit; send: *We will consign the goods to him by express.* 3. set apart; assign.

**con stel la tion** (kon′stə lā′shən), *n.* 1. a group of stars: *The Big Dipper is the easiest constellation to locate.* 2. division of the heavens occupied by such a group. [< LL *constellatio, -onis* < L *com-* together + *stella* star]

**con ster na tion** (kon′stər nā′shən), *n.* great dismay; paralyzing terror: *To our consternation the train rushed on toward the burning bridge.*

**con strain** (kən strān′), *v.* 1. force; compel. 2. confine; imprison. 3. repress; restrain. [< OF *constreindre* < L *constringere* < *com-* together + *stringere* pull tightly]

**con ta gion** (kən tā′jən), *n.* 1. the spreading of disease by contact. 2. disease spread in this way; contagious disease. 3. means by which disease is spread. 4. the spreading of any influence from one person to another: *A contagion of fear swept through the audience and caused a panic.* 5. evil influence; moral corruption. [< L *contagio, -onis* a touching < *contingere*]

**con temp tu ous** (kən temp′chü əs), *adj.* showing contempt; scornful: *a contemptuous look.*

**con tral to** (kən tral′tō), *n., pl.* **-tos,** *adj.* —*n.* 1. the lowest woman's voice. 2. in music, a part to be sung by the lowest woman's voice. 3. person who sings this part. —*adj.* of or for a contralto.

**con tra vene** (kon′trə vēn′), *v.,* **-vened, -ven ing.** 1. conflict with; oppose: *A dictatorship contravenes the liberty of individuals.* 2. contradict. 3. violate; infringe. [< LL *contravenire* < L *contra-* against + *venire* come]

**con trite** (kən trīt′ or kon′trīt), *adj.* 1. broken in spirit by a sense of guilt; penitent. 2. showing deep regret and sorrow: *He wrote an apology in contrite words.* —**con trite′ly,** *adv.*

**co ro na** (kə rō′nə), *n., pl.* **-nas, -nae** (-nē). 1. ring of light seen around the sun or moon. 2. halo of light around the sun, seen only during an eclipse. 3. a crownlike part; crown. [< L *corona* crown]

**cos mic** (koz′mik), *adj.* 1. of or belonging to the universe; having to do with the whole universe: *Cosmic forces produce stars and meteors.* 2. vast. [< Gk. *kosmikos* < *kosmos* order, world]

**cos mop o lite** (koz mop′ə līt), *n.* a cosmopolitan person; a worldly person; person who feels at home in any part of the world. [< Gk. *kosmopolites* < *kosmos* world + *polites* citizen < *polis* city]

**coun te nance** (koun′tə nəns), *n.* 1. expression of the face: *His angry countenance frightened us all.* 2. face; features: *The king had a noble countenance.* 3. approval; encouragement: *He gave countenance to our plan, but no active help.* 4. calmness; composure. [< OF *conte-*

*nance* < Med.L *continentia* demeanor < L *continentia* self-control < *continere*]

**coun ter** (koun′tər), *v.* 1. go or act counter to; oppose: *She did not like our plan; so she countered it with one of her own.* 2. act in retaliation. 3. speak in defense of oneself or one's ideas. [< F < L *contra* against]

**cour ti er** (kôr′tē ər or kōr′tē ər), *n.* 1. person often present at the court of a king, prince, etc.; court attendant. 2. person who tries to win the favor of another by flattering and pleasing him.

**Cov en try** (kuv′ən trē or kov′ən trē), *n.* city in central England. 277,000.

**cov ert** (kuv′ərt), *adj.* secret; hidden; disguised: *covert glances.* —*n.* 1. shelter; hiding place. 2. thicket in which animals hide.

**cow er** (kou′ər), *v.* 1. crouch in fear or shame. 2. draw back tremblingly from another's threats, blows, etc.

**cra vat** (krə vat′), *n.* 1. necktie. 2. neckcloth; scarf.

**Cre ole** or **cre ole** (krē′ōl), *n.* 1. a white person who is a descendant of the French who settled in Louisiana. 2. the French language as spoken in Louisiana. 3. a French or Spanish person born in Spanish America or the West Indies. 4. *creole,* person who is part Negro and part Creole. —*adj.* of or having to do with the Creoles.

**cre scen do** (krə shen′dō), *adj., adv., n., pl.* **-dos.** —*adj., adv.* gradually increasing in force or loudness. —*n.* a gradual increase in force or loudness. [< Ital. *crescendo,* ppr. of *crescere* increase < L]

**crick et** (krik′it), *n.* 1. an outdoor game played by two teams of eleven players each, with ball, bats, and wickets. Cricket is very popular in England. 2. *Informal.* fair play; good sportsmanship. [< OF *criquet* goal post, stick, probably < MDutch *cricke* stick to lean on]

**crook** (krůk), *n.* 1. hook; bend; curve: *a crook in a stream.* 2. a shepherd's staff. Its upper end is curved or bent into a hook. [apparently < Scand. *krókr*]

**crop** (krop), *n.* a baglike swelling of a bird's food passage where food is prepared for digestion. [OE *cropp* sprout, craw]

**cu beb** (kyü′beb), *n.* 1. a dried, unripe berry of a tropical shrub, used in medicine. 2. cigarette containing the crushed berries.

**cud** (kud), *n.* 1. mouthful of food that cattle and similar animals bring back into the mouth from the first stomach for a slow, second chewing. 2. a quid of chewing tobacco; bite to be chewed. [OE *cudu,* var. of *cwidu*]

**cull** (kul), *v.* 1. pick out; select: *The lawyer culled important facts from the mass of evidence.* 2. pick over; make selections from.

**cu po la** (kyü′pl ə), *n.* 1. a rounded roof; dome. 2. a small dome or tower on a roof. [< Ital. < LL *cupula,* dim. of L *cupa* tub]

**cur ate** (kyür′it), *n. Esp. Brit.* clergyman who is an assistant to a pastor, rector, or vicar.

**curd** (kèrd), *n.* Often, **curds,** *pl.* the thick part of milk which separates from the watery part when milk sours. —*v.* form into curds; curdle. [ME *curd, crud*]

**cur few** (kėr′fyü), *n.* 1. a ringing of a bell at a fixed time every evening as a signal. In the Middle Ages, it was a signal to put out lights and cover fires. More recently it has been used as a signal for children to come in off the streets. 2. bell ringing such a signal. 3. time when it is rung. [< AF *coeverfu* < *covrir* cover (< L *cooperire*) + *feu* fire < L *focus* hearth]

**curt** (kėrt), *adj.* short; rudely brief; abrupt: *a curt way of talking.* [< L *curtus* cut short] —**curt′ly,** *adv.*

**cus pi dor** (kus′pə dôr′), *n.* container to spit into; spittoon. [Am.E; < Pg. *cuspidor* spitter < *cuspir* spit < L *conspuere* spit on < *com-* + *spuere* spit]

**cut ler y** (kut′lər ē), *n.* 1. knives, scissors, and other cutting instruments. 2. knives, forks, spoons, etc., for table use.

**cyn i cal** (sin′ə kl), *adj.* 1. doubting the sincerity and goodness of others. 2. sneering; sarcastic.

**cyn i cism** (sin′ə siz əm), *n.* 1. cynical quality or disposition. 2. a cynical remark.

**czar** (zär), *n.* 1. emperor. It was the title of the former emperors of Russia. 2. autocrat; person with absolute power. Also, **tsar, tzar.** [< Russian *tsar* < Old Church Slavic < Gothic < L *Caesar* Caesar]

**dan dy** (dan′dē), *n., pl.* **-dies.** man who is too careful of his dress and appearance. [originally Scottish, ? < *Dandy*, a Scottish var. of *Andrew*]

**dank** (dangk), *adj.* unpleasantly damp; moist; wet: *The cave was dark, dank, and chilly.* [ME. Cf. Swedish *dank* marshy spot.]

**da ta** (dā′tə, dat′ə, or dä′tə), *n. pl.* of **datum.** things known or granted; information from which conclusions can be drawn; facts.

**dear** (dir), *adj.* 1. much loved; precious. 2. much valued; highly esteemed. 3. high-priced; costly. —*adv.* 1. with affection; fondly. 2. at a high price; at a great cost. [OE *dēore*] —**dear′ly,** *adv.*

**de bauch** (di bôch′), *n.* 1. excessive indulgence in sensual pleasures; excess in eating or drinking. 2. bout or period of seduction from duty, virtue, or morality. [< F *débaucher* entice from duty]

**de crep it** (di krep′it), *adj.* broken down or weakened by old age; old and feeble. [< L *decrepitus* broken down < *de-* + *crepare* creak] —**de crep′it ly,** *adv.*

**deem** (dēm), *v.* think; believe; consider. [OE *dēman* < *dōm* judgment]

**de file** (di fīl′), *v.,* **-filed, -fil ing.** 1. make filthy or dirty; make disgusting in any way. 2. destroy the purity or cleanness of; corrupt. [alteration of *defoul* (< OF *defouler* trample down, violate) after obsolete *file* befoul < OE *fylan* < *fūl* foul] —**de fil′er,** *n.*

**de file ment** (di fīl′mənt), *n.* 1. act of defiling. 2. state of being defiled. 3. thing that defiles. [< *defile*]

**de lir i um** (di lir′ē əm), *n., pl.* **-lir i ums, -lir i a** (-lir′ē ə). 1. a temporary disorder of the mind that occurs during fevers, insanity, drunkenness, etc. Delirium is characterized by excitement, irrational talk, and hallucinations. 2. any wild excitement that cannot be controlled. [< L *delirium* < *delirare* rave, be crazy < *de lira* (*ire*) (go) out of the furrow (in plowing)]

**De los** (dē′los), *n.* small island in the S Aegean Sea, the legendary birthplace of Apollo and Artemis.

**de lude** (di lüd′), *v.,* **-lud ed, -lud ing.** mislead; deceive. [< L *deludere* < *de-* (to the detriment of) + *ludere* play] —**de lud′er,** *n.*

**de lu sion** (di lü′zhən), *n.* 1. act of deluding. 2. state of being deluded. 3. a false notion or belief: *The insane man had a delusion that he was the king.* 4. a fixed belief maintained in spite of unquestionable evidence to the contrary. [< L *delusio, -onis* < *deludere*]

**de ment ed** (di men′tid), *adj.* insane; crazy. [< L *dementare* < *demens* mad < *de-* out of + *mens* mind]

**de mesne** (di mān′ or di mēn′), *n.* 1. land or land and buildings possessed as one's own; real estate. 2. house and land belonging to a lord and used by him. 3. domain; realm. [< AF *demesne*, a respelling of OF *demeine* domain]

**de mon stra ble** (di mon′strə bl or dem′ən strə bl), *adj.* capable of being proved.

**de note** (di nōt′), *v.,* **-not ed, -not ing.** be the sign of; indicate: *A fever usually denotes sickness.* [< F *dénoter* < L *denotare* < *de-* + *nota* mark]

**de plor a ble** (di plôr′ə bl or di plōr′ə bl), *adj.* 1. regrettable; lamentable: *a deplorable accident.* 2. wretched; miserable. —**de plor′a bly,** *adv.*

**de pot** (dē′pō), *n. U.S.* a railroad station.

**de range** (di rānj′), *v.,* **-ranged, -rang ing.** 1. disturb the order or arrangement of; throw into confusion. 2. make insane. [< F *déranger* < *dé-* (< L *dis-*) + *ranger* range]

**de rive** (di rīv′), *v.,* **-rived, -riv ing.** get; receive; obtain: *A scholar derives knowledge from reading books.* [< F < L *derivare* lead off, draw off < *de-* + *rivus* stream] —**de riv′a ble,** *adj.*

**der rick** (der′ik), *n.* 1. machine for lifting and moving heavy objects. A derrick has a long arm that swings at an angle from the base of an upright post or frame. 2. a towerlike framework over an oil well, gas well, etc., that holds the drilling and hoisting machinery. [named after *Derrick*, a hangman at Tyburn, London]

**des o late** (des′ə lit), *adj.* 1. laid waste; devastated; barren: *desolate land.* 2. not lived in; deserted: *a desolate house.* 3. unhappy; wretched; forlorn: *The ragged, hungry child looked desolate.* [< L *desolatus*, pp. of *desolare* < *de-* + *solus* alone]

**des o la tion** (des′ə lā′shən), *n.* 1. act of making desolate. 2. a ruined, lonely, or deserted condition. 3. a desolate place. 4. sadness; lonely sorrow.

**des pe ra do** (des′pə rä′dō), *n., pl.* **-does** or **-dos.** a bold, reckless criminal; dangerous outlaw.

hat, āge, fär; let, ēqual, tėrm;
it, īce; hot, ōpen, ôrder;
oil, out; cup, pút, rüle;
ch, child; ng, long; sh, she;
th, thin; ᴛʜ, then; zh, measure;

ə represents *a* in about, *e* in taken, *i* in pencil, *o* in lemon, *u* in circus.

< = from, derived from, taken from.

**de spond ent** (di spon′dənt), *adj.* without courage or hope; discouraged; dejected. —**de spond′ent ly,** *adv.*

**des ul to ry** (des′əl tô′rē or des′əl tō′-rē), *adj.* jumping from one thing to another; unconnected; without aim or method: *The careful study of a few books is better than the desultory reading of many.* [< L *desultorius* of a leaper, ult. < *de-* down + *salire* leap] —**des′ul to′ri ly,** *adv.*

**det o na tion** (det′ə nā′shən or dē′tə nā′shən), *n.* 1. explosion with a loud noise. 2. a loud noise.

**de vi ous** (dē′vē əs), *adj.* 1. winding; twisting; roundabout: *We took a devious route through side streets and alleys.* 2. straying from the right course; not straightforward; going astray: *His devious nature was shown in half-lies and small dishonesties.* [< L *devius* < *de-* out of + *via* the way] —**de′vi ous ness,** *n.*

**dev o tee** (dev′ə tē′), *n.* 1. person deeply devoted to something. 2. person earnestly devoted to religion.

**dex ter i ty** (deks ter′ə tē), *n.* 1. skill in using the hands. 2. skill in using the mind; cleverness.

**dic ta** (dik′tə), *n.* pl. of **dictum.**

**dic tum** (dik′təm), *n., pl.* **-tums, -ta.** 1. a formal comment; authoritative opinion: *The dictum of the critics was that the play was excellent.* 2. maxim; saying. [< L *dictum* (thing) said, pp. neut. of *dicere* say]

**di gress** (də gres′ or dī gres′), *v.* turn aside; get off the main subject in talking or writing. [< L *digressus*, pp. of *digredi* deviate < *dis-* aside < *gradi* to step]

**di lap i dat ed** (də lap′ə dāt′id), *adj.* falling to pieces; partly ruined or decayed through neglect: *a dilapidated house.* [< L *dilapidatus*, pp. of *dilapidare* lay low (with stones) < *dis-* (intensive) + *lapis* stone]

**dil et tante** (dil′ə tänt or dil′ə tan′tē), *n., pl.* **-tes, -ti.** 1. lover of the fine arts. 2. person who follows some art or science as an amusement or in a trifling way. 3. trifler.

**dil i gent** (dil′ə jənt), *adj.* 1. hardworking; industrious. 2. careful and steady —**dil′i gent ly,** *adv.*

**din gle** (ding′gl), *n.* a small, deep, shady valley.

**dint** (dint), *n.* 1. force: *By dint of hard work the man became successful.* 2. dent.

**dire** (dīr), *adj.,* **dir er, dir est.** causing great fear or suffering; dreadful.

**dire ful** (dīr′fəl), *adj.* dire; dreadful; terrible. —**dire′ful ly,** *adv.*

**dirge** (dėrj), *n.* a funeral song or tune.

[contraction of L *dirige* direct (imperative of *dirigere*), first word in office for the dead]

**dis cern** (də zėrn′ or də sėrn′), *v.* perceive; see clearly; distinguish; recognize. [< F < L *discernere* < *dis*- off + *cernere* separate]

**dis cord** (dis′kôrd), *n.* 1. difference of opinion; disputing; disagreement. 2. in music, a lack of harmony in notes sounded at the same time. 3. harsh, clashing sounds.

**dis course** (*n.* dis′kôrs or dis′kōrs; *v.* dis kôrs′ or dis kōrs′), *n., v.,* **-coursed, -cours ing.** —*n.* 1. a formal speech or writing: *Lectures and sermons are discourses.* 2. conversation; a talk. —*v.* 1. speak or write formally. 2. converse; talk. [< F *discours* < Med.L < L *discursus* < *dis*- in different directions + *currere* run]

**dis cre tion** (dis kresh′ən), *n.* 1. freedom to judge or choose: *Making final plans was left to the president's discretion.* 2. quality of being discreet; good judgment; carefulness in speech or action; wise caution. —**Syn.** 1. choice.

**dis dain** (dis dān′), *v.* look down on; consider beneath oneself; scorn: *The honest official disdained the offer of a bribe.* —*n.* act of disdaining; feeling of scorn.

**dis dain ful** (dis dān′fəl), *adj.* feeling or showing disdain. —**dis dain′ful ly,** *adv.*

**dis par age ment** (dis par′ij mənt), *n.* something that lowers a thing or person in worth or importance.

**dis po si tion** (dis′pə zish′ən), *n.* 1. habitual ways of acting toward others or of thinking about things; nature: *a cheerful disposition, a selfish disposition.* 2. tendency; inclination: *a disposition to argue.*

**dis pu tant** (dis′pyə tənt or dis pyüt′nt), *n.* person who takes part in a dispute or debate.

**dis sem ble** (di sem′bl), *v.,* **-bled, -bling.** 1. disguise or hide (one's real feelings, thoughts, plans, etc.): *She dissembled her anger with a smile.* 2. conceal one's motives, etc.; be a hypocrite. 3. pretend not to see or notice; disregard; ignore. [alteration, after *resemble,* of obsolete *dissimule* dissimulate] —**dis sem′bler,** *n.*

**dis so nant** (dis′ə nənt), *adj.* 1. harsh in sound; clashing; not harmonious. 2. out of harmony with other views or persons; disagreeing. [< L *dissonans, -antis,* ppr. of *dissonare* < *dis*- differently + *sonare* sound]

**dis tem per** (dis tem′pər), *n.* 1. an infectious disease of dogs and other animals, accompanied by a short, dry cough and a loss of strength. 2. sickness of the mind or body; disorder; disease. 3. disturbance. [< v.] —*v.* make unbalanced; disturb; disorder. [< LL *distemperare* mix improperly < L *dis*- not + *temperare* mix in proper proportion]

**dis traught** (dis trôt′), *adj.* 1. in a state of mental conflict and confusion. 2. crazed.

**di vers** (dī′vərz), *adj.* several different; various.

**doc trine** (dok′trən), *n.* 1. what is taught as the belief of a church, nation, or group of persons; belief; principle. 2. what is taught; teachings.

**doff** (dof or dôf), *v.* 1. take off; remove: *He doffed his hat as the flag passed by.* 2. get rid of; throw aside. [contraction of *do off*]

**dog ged** (dôg′id or dog′id), *adj.* stubborn; persistent; not giving up: *In spite of failures he kept on with dogged determination to succeed.* [< *dog*] —**dog′ged ly,** *adv.*

**do min ion** (də min′yən), *n.* 1. supreme authority; rule; control. 2. territory under the control of one ruler or government. [< obsolete F < Med.L *dominion, -onis,* alteration of L *dominium* ownership]

**dos si er** (dos′ē ā or dos′ē ər), *n.* collection of documents or papers about some subject. [< F]

**dou blet** (dub′lit), *n.* a man's close-fitting jacket. Men in Europe wore doublets in the 15th, 16th, and 17th centuries.

**douche** (düsh), *n.* 1. jet of water applied on or into any part of the body: *A douche of salt water up my nose helped relieve my cold in the head.* 2. application of a douche. [< F < Ital. *doccia,* ult. < L *ducere* lead]

**dow er** (dou′ər), *n.* 1. a widow's share for life of her dead husband's property. 2. dowry. 3. a natural gift, talent, or quality; endowment. [< OF *douaire* < Med.L *dotarium* < L *dotare* endow < *dos* dowry]

**dram** (dram), *n.* 1. a small weight. In apothecaries' weight, 8 drams make one ounce; in avoirdupois weight, 16 drams make one ounce. 2. fluid dram. 3. *Esp. Brit.* a small drink of intoxicating liquor. 4. *Esp. Brit.* a small amount of anything. Also, *Brit.* **drachm.**

**dregs** (dregz), *n. pl.* 1. solid bits of matter that settle to the bottom of a liquid: *After pouring the tea she rinsed the dregs out of the teapot.* 2. the most worthless part: *Thieves and murderers are the dregs of humanity.* [< Scand. *dreggjar*]

**droll** (drōl), *adj.* amusingly odd; humorously quaint; laughable: *We smiled at the monkey's droll tricks.* [< F *drôle* (originally n.) good fellow < Dutch *drol* little fat fellow]

**drought** (drout), *n.* 1. a long period of dry weather; continued lack of rain. 2. lack of moisture; dryness. 3. *Archaic or Dialect.* thirst. [OE *drūgath.* Related to *dry.*]

➔ **drought, drouth.** Both forms are in good use, *drought* probably more common in formal English, and *drouth* in informal.

**drouth** (drouth), *n.* drought.

**drudge** (druj), *n., v.,* **drudged, drudging.** —*n.* person who does hard, tiresome, or disagreeable work. —*v.* do hard, tiresome, or disagreeable work. [ME *drugge* (n); cf. OE *drēogan* work, suffer]

**du bi ous** (dü′bē əs or dyü′bē əs), *adj.* 1. doubtful; uncertain: *a dubious compliment, dubious authorship, a dubious friend.* 2. of questionable character; probably bad: *a dubious scheme for making money.* [< L *dubiosus* < *dubius* doubtful < *du-* two] —**du′bi ous ly,** *adv.*

**duc at** (duk′ət), *n.* a gold or silver coin formerly used in some European countries.

Its value varied, being at most about $2.30. [< F < Ital. *ducato* < Med.L < L′ *dux* leader]

**dumb** (dum), *adj.* 1. not able to speak: *dumb animals.* 2. silenced for the moment by fear, surprise, shyness, etc. 3. that does not speak; silent. 4. *U.S. Informal.* stupid; dull. [(defs. 1-3) OE; (def. 4) < G *dumm* stupid] —**dumb′ly,** *adv.*

**dumb wait er** (dum′wāt′ər), *n. U.S.* a small box with shelves, pulled up and down a shaft to send dishes, food, rubbish, etc., from one floor to another.

**dupe** (düp or dyüp), *n., v.,* **duped, duping.** —*n.* 1. person easily deceived or tricked. 2. one who is being deluded or tricked: *The young politician's inexperience is making him the dupe of some unscrupulous schemers.* —*v.* deceive; trick. [< F < L *upupa* hoopoe (a bird)]

**dur ance** (dùr′əns or dyür′əns), *n.* imprisonment. [< OF *durance* duration]

**du ress** (dù res′, dyü res′, dùr′es, or dyür′es), *n.* 1. force; force used to make one do something against his will. 2. imprisonment. [< OF *duresse* < L *duritia* hardness < *durus* hard]

**ea sel** (ē′zl), *n.* a support or upright frame for holding a picture, blackboard, etc.

**eaves** (ēvz), *n. pl.* the lower edges of a roof projecting beyond the wall of a building. [OE *efes*]

➔ **Eaves,** originally singular, is now understood as plural, and a new singular, *eave,* is sometimes found.

**eb on y** (eb′ən ē), *n., pl.* **-on ies,** *adj.* —*n.* 1. a hard, heavy, durable wood, used for the black keys of a piano, the backs and handles of brushes, ornamental woodwork, etc. 2. a tropical tree that yields this wood. —*adj.* 1. made of ebony. 2. like ebony; black; dark.

**e dict** (ē′dikt), *n.* a public order or command by some authority; decree. [< L *edictum* < *edicere* < *ex*- out + *dicere* say]

**ef fem i nate** (ə fem′ə nit), *adj.* lacking in manly qualities; showing weakness or delicacy that is not manly. [< L *effeminatus,* pp. of *effeminare* make a woman of < *ex-* + *femina* woman] —**Syn.** womanish.

**el lip ti cal** (i lip′tə kl), *adj.* shaped like an ellipse, an oval having both ends alike; of an ellipse.

**el o quent** (el′ə kwənt), *adj.* 1. having gracefulness and force of expression. 2. very expressive. [< L *eloquens, -entis,* ppr. of *eloqui* < *ex*- out + *loqui* speak] —**el′o quent ly,** *adv.*

**e lu ci da tion** (i lü′sə dā′shən), *n.* a making clear; explanation.

**e lude** (i lüd′), *v.,* **e lud ed, e lud ing.** 1. slip away from; avoid or escape by cleverness, quickness, etc.: *The sly fox eluded the dogs.* 2. escape discovery by; baffle: *The cause of cancer has eluded all research.* [< L *eludere* < *ex*- out + *ludere* play]

**em boss** (em bôs′ or em bos′), *v.* 1. decorate with a design, pattern, etc., that stands out from the surface: *Our coins are* embossed with letters and figures. 2. cause to stand out from the surface: *He ran his finger over the letters to see if they had been embossed.* [< OF *embocer* < *en-* + *boce* swelling, boss]

**em is sar y** (em′ə ser′ē), *n., pl.* **-sar ies.** 1. person sent on a mission or errand. 2. a secret agent; spy.

**em u late** (em′yə lāt), *v.,* **-lat ed, -lat ing.** try to equal or excell: *The proverb tells us to emulate the industry of the ant.* [< L *aemulari* < *aemulus* striving to equal]

**en croach** (en krōch′), *v.* 1. go beyond proper or usual limits: *The sea encroached upon the shore and submerged the beach.* 2. trespass upon the property or rights of another; intrude: *He is a good salesman and will not encroach upon his customer's time.*

**en gross** (en grōs′), *v.* occupy wholly; take up all the attention of: *She was engrossed in a story.*

**en hance** (en hans′ or en häns′), *v.,* **-hanced, -hancing.** make greater; add to; heighten: *The gardens enhanced the beauty of the house.* [< AF var. of OF *enhaucier* < *en-* on, up (< L *in-*) + *haucier* raise, ult. < L *altus* high] —**en hance′ment,** *n.*

**en mi ty** (en′mə tē), *n., pl.* **-ties.** the feeling that enemies have for each other; hate. —**Syn.** hostility, hatred.

**en nui** (än′wē), *n.* a feeling of weariness and discontent from lack of occupation or interest; boredom. [< F. Related to *annoy.*]

**en sem ble** (än säm′bl), *n.* 1. all the parts of a thing considered together; general effect. 2. a complete, harmonious costume. [< F < VL < L *in-* + *simul* at the same time]

**en sign** (en′sīn or en′sən), *n.* 1. flag; banner: *The ensign of the United States is the Stars and Stripes.* 2. sign of one's rank, position, or power; symbol of authority. [< OF *enseigne* < L *insignia* insignia]

**en ti ty** (en′tə tē), *n., pl.* **-ties.** 1. something that has a real and separate existence either actually or in the mind; anything real in itself: *Persons, mountains, languages, and beliefs are distinct entities.* 2. being; existence. [< LL *entitas* < L *ens*, ppr. of *esse* be]

**en trails** (en′trālz or en′trəlz), *n. pl.* the inner parts of a man or animal. [< OF *entrailles* < LL *intralia* < L *interanea* < *inter* within]

**en treat** (en trēt′), *v.* ask earnestly; beg and pray; implore: *The captives entreated the savages not to kill them.* Also, **intreat.**

**e nu me rate** (i nü′mə rāt′ or i nyü′mə-rāt′), *v.,* **-at ed, -at ing.** 1. name one by one; give a list of: *He enumerated the capitals of the 50 states.* 2. count. [< L *enumerare* < *ex-* out + *numerus* number]

**ep i lep sy** (ep′ə lep′sē), *n.* a chronic nervous disease whose attacks cause convulsions and unconsciousness.

**ep i taph** (ep′ə taf or ep′ə täf), *n.* a short statement in memory of a dead person, usually put on his tombstone. [< L < Gk. *epitaphion* funeral oration < *epi-* at + *taphos* tomb]

**ep i thet** (ep′ə thet), *n.* a descriptive expression; adjective or noun, or even a clause, expressing some quality or attribute: *In "crafty Ulysses" and "Richard the Lion-Hearted" the epithets are "crafty" and "the Lion-Hearted."* [< L < Gk. *epitheton* added < *epi-* on + *tithenai* place]

**ep och** (ep′ək; *esp. Brit.* ē′pok), *n.* 1. period of time; era. 2. period of time in which striking things happened. 3. the starting point of such a period: *The invention of the steam engine marked an epoch in the evolution of industry.* [< Med.L < Gk. *epoche* a stopping, fixed point in time < *epechein* < *epi-* up + *echein* hold] —**Syn.** 1. age.

**ere** (ar or er), *prep.* before. —*conj.* 1. before. 2. sooner than; rather than. [OE *ǣr*]

**err** (ėr or er), *v.* 1. go wrong; make mistakes. 2. be wrong; be mistaken or incorrect. 3. do wrong; sin. [< OF < L *errare* wander] —**Syn.** 1. stray, deviate, blunder.

**er rat ic** (ə rat′ik), *adj.* 1. not steady; uncertain; irregular: *An erratic mind jumps from one idea to another.* 2. queer; odd: *erratic behavior.* [< L *erraticus* < *errare* err]

**er y the ma** (er′ə thē′mə), *n.* an abnormal redness of the skin resulting from the congestion of blood vessels.

**es carp ment** (es kärp′mənt), *n.* 1. a steep slope; cliff. 2. ground made into a steep slope as part of a fortification. [< F *escarpement* < *escarper* form into a steep slope < *escarpe* a steep slope < Ital. *scarpa* < Gmc.]

**ev a nesce** (ev′ə nes′), *v.,* **-nesced, -nes cing.** disappear gradually; fade away; vanish. [< L *evanescere* < *ex-* out + *vanescere* vanish < *vanus* insubstantial]

**e van gel ist** (i van′jə list), *n.* 1. preacher of the Gospel. 2. a traveling preacher who stirs up religious feeling in revival services or camp meetings.

**e va sion** (i vā′zhən), *n.* 1. a getting away from something by trickery; an avoiding by cleverness: *Evasion of one's duty is contemptible.* 2. an attempt to escape an argument, a charge, a question, etc.

**e va sive** (i vā′siv or i vā′ziv), *adj.* tending or trying to get away from or avoid by trickery, cleverness, misleading statement, etc.: *"Perhaps" is an evasive answer.* —**e va′sive ly,** *adv.* —**Syn.** shifty, misleading.

**e vict** (i vikt′), *v.* expel by a legal process from land, a building, etc.; eject (a tenant): *The tenant was evicted by the sheriff for not paying his rent.*

**ev o lu tion** (ev′ə lü′shən), *n.* 1. any process of formation or growth; gradual development: *the evolution of the modern steamship from the first crude boat.* 2. something evolved; product of development; not a sudden discovery or creation. 3. theory that all living things developed from a few simple forms of life or from a single form.

**ev o lu tion ist** (ev′ə lü′shən ist), *n.* student of, or believer in, the theory of evolution.

**ex ac er bate** (eg zas′ər bāt or eks as′-ər bāt), *v.,* **-bat ed, -bat ing.** 1. make worse; aggravate (pain, disease, anger). 2. irritate (a person's feelings). [< L *exac-*

hat, āge, fär; let, ēqual, tėrm;
it, īce; hot, ōpen, ôrder;
oil, out; cup, pùt, rüle;
ch, child; ng, long; sh, she;
th, thin; ͯH, then; zh, measure;

ə represents *a* in about, *e* in taken,
*i* in pencil, *o* in lemon, *u* in circus.

< = from, derived from, taken from.

*erbare* < *ex-* completely + *acerbus* harsh, bitter]

**ex hort** (eg zôrt′), *v.* urge strongly; advise or warn earnestly: *The preacher exhorted his congregation to live better lives.* [< L *exhortari* < *ex-* + *hortari* urge strongly] —**ex hort′er,** *n.*

**ex ile** (eg′zīl or ek′sīl), *v.,* **-iled, -il ing,** *n.* —*v.* force (a person) to leave his country or home; banish: *Many people were exiled from the country.* —*n.* 1. a being exiled; banishment: *Napoleon's exile to Elba was brief.* 2. an exiled person. 3. any prolonged absence from one's own country.

**ex pe di en cy** (eks pē′dē ən sē), *n., pl.* **-cies.** 1. usefulness; suitability for bringing about a desired result; desirability or fitness under the circumstances. 2. personal advantage; self-interest: *The crafty lawyer was influenced more by expediency than by the love of justice.*

**ex pi ate** (eks′pē āt), *v.,* **-at ed, -at ing.** make amends for (a wrong, sin, etc.); atone for: *The thief expiated his theft by giving back the amount stolen and by reforming.* [< L *expiare* < *ex-* completely + *piare* appease < *pius* devout]

**ex pi a tion** (eks′pē ā′shən), *n.* 1. a making amends for a wrong, sin, etc.; atonement: *He made a public apology in expiation of his error.* 2. amends; means of atonement.

**ex pire** (ek spīr′), *v.,* **-pired, -pir ing.** 1. come to an end: *You must obtain a new automobile license when your old one expires.* 2. die. [< L *ex(s)pirare* < *ex-* out + *spirare* breathe] —**Syn.** 2. perish.

**ex tant** (eks′tənt or eks tant′), *adj.* still in existence: *Some of Washington's letters are extant.* [< L *ex(s)tans, -antis,* ppr. of *ex(s)tare* < *ex-* out, forth + *stare* stand]

**ex trem i ty** (eks trem′ə tē), *n., pl.* **-ties.** 1. the very end; farthest possible place; last part or point. 2. extreme need, danger, suffering, etc.: *In their extremity the people on the sinking ship bore themselves bravely.* 3. an extreme degree.

**ex u ber ant** (eg zü′bər ənt), *adj.* 1. very abundant; overflowing; lavish: *exuberant health, good nature, or joy; an exuberant welcome.* 2. profuse in growth; luxuriant. [< L *exuberans, -antis,* ppr. of *exuberare* grow luxuriantly < *ex-* thoroughly + *uber* fertile] —**ex u′ber ant ly,** *adv.*

**ex ult** (eg zult′), *v.* be very glad; rejoice greatly: *The winners exulted in their victory.* [< L *ex(s)ultare,* frequentative of *exsilire* leap out or up < *ex-* forth + *salire* leap]

**face** (fās), *n.* 1. the front part of the head. 2. outward appearance. 3. the front part; right side; surface: *the face of a clock.*
**face to face, a.** with faces toward each other. **b.** in the actual presence.
**save face,** avoid disgrace or humiliation.
**in the face of, a.** in the presence of. **b.** in spite of.
**lose face,** lose dignity or self-respect; be humiliated.
**show one's face,** appear; be seen.

**faille** (fīl or fāl), *n., adj.* a soft, ribbed silk or rayon cloth. [< F < MDutch *falie* scarf]

**fain** (fān), *Archaic* and *Poetic.* —*adv.* by choice; gladly. —*adj.* 1. willing, but not eager; forced by circumstances. 2. glad; willing. 3. eager; desirous. [OE *fægen*]

**fal la cy** (fal′ə sē), *n., pl.* **-cies.** 1. a false idea; mistaken belief; error: *It is a fallacy to suppose that riches always bring happiness.* 2. mistake in reasoning; misleading or unsound argument. [< L *fallacia* < *fallax* deceptive < *fallere* deceive]

**far thing** (fär′ฑHing), *n.* 1. a former British coin worth a fourth of a British penny. 2. **not worth a farthing,** having very little value. [OE *fēorthung* < *fēortha* fourth]

**fath om** (faฑH′əm), *n., pl.* **fath oms** or (*esp. collectively*) **fath om.** a unit of measure equal to 6 feet, used mostly in measuring the depth of water and the length of ships' ropes, cables, etc. [OE *fæthm* width of the outstretched arms]

**fawn** (fôn), *v.* cringe and bow; act slavishly: *Many flattering relatives fawned on the rich old man.*

**feign** (fān), *v.* 1. put on a false appearance of; make believe; pretend: *Some animals feign death when in danger.* 2. make up to deceive; invent falsely: *feign an excuse.* 3. imagine: *The phoenix is a feigned bird.*

**feint** (fānt), *n.* 1. a false appearance; pretense: *The boy made a feint of studying hard, though actually he was listening to the radio.* 2. movement intended to deceive; pretended blow; sham attack. —*v.* make a pretended action or movement intended to take an opponent off his guard; make a pretended blow or sham attack: *The fighter feinted with his right hand and struck with his left.* [< F *feinte* < *feindre* feign]

**fel on** (fel′ən), *n.* person who has committed a serious crime; criminal: *Murderers and thieves are felons.*

**fer ro type** (fer′ō tīp′), *n.* a positive photograph taken directly on a thin plate of iron coated with a sensitized film. Also called **tintype.**

**fer vent** (fer′vənt), *adj.* 1. showing warmth of feeling; very earnest: *a fervent plea.* 2. hot; glowing. [< F < L *fervens, -entis,* ppr. of *fervere* boil] —**fer′vent ly,** *adv.* —**Syn.** 1. ardent, zealous, passionate.

**fes toon** (fes tün′), *n.* a hanging curve of flowers, leaves, ribbons, etc.: *The flags were hung on the wall in colorful festoons.* —*v.* 1. decorate with festoons: *The Christmas tree was festooned with tinsel.* 2. form into festoons; hang in curves: *Draperies were festooned over the window.*

**fe tal** (fē′tl), *adj.* 1. of a fetus. 2. like that of a fetus. Also, **foetal.**

**fe tish** (fē′tish or fet′ish), *n.* 1. any material object supposed to have magic power. 2. anything regarded with unreasoning reverence or devotion: *Some people make a fetish of style.* [< F *fétiche* < Pg. *feitiço* charm, originally adj., artificial < L *facticius*]

**fe tus** (fē′təs), *n.* an animal embryo during the later stages of its development. Also, **foetus.** [< L]

**feu dal** (fyü′dl), *adj.* of or having to do with feudalism.

**feu dal ism** (fyü′dl iz əm), *n.* the social, economic, and political system of Europe in the Middle Ages. Under this system vassals (servants) held land on condition of giving military and other services to the lord owning it in return for the protection and the use of the land.

**fi let mi gnon** (fi lā′ min′yon), *n.* broiled steak of the finest cut.

**fi nite** (fī′nīt), *adj.* having limits or bounds; not infinite: *Death ends man's finite existence.*

**fis sion** (fish′ən), *n.* 1. a splitting apart; division into parts. 2. the splitting that occurs when the nucleus of an atom under bombardment absorbs a neutron. Nuclear fission releases tremendous amounts of energy when heavy elements, especially plutonium and uranium, are involved. [< L *fissio, -onis* < *findere* cleave]

**fission bomb,** an atomic bomb that derives its force solely from the splitting of atoms. The original atomic bombs were fission bombs; the newer hydrogen bombs are fusion bombs.

**fit ful** (fit′fəl), *adj.* going on and then stopping awhile; irregular: *a fitful sleep, a fitful conversation.* —**Syn.** spasmodic.

**fiv er** (fiv′ər), *n. Slang.* 1. a five-dollar bill. 2. *esp. Brit.* a five-pound note.

**fla grant** (flā′grənt), *adj.* notorious; outrageous; scandalous. [< L *flagrans, -antis,* ppr. of *flagrare* burn] —**fla′ grant ly,** *adv.*

**flat ware** (flat′wâr′ or flat′wer′), *n.* 1. knives, forks, and spoons. 2. plates, platters, saucers, etc.

**flaunt** (flônt or flänt), *v.* 1. show off. 2. wave proudly: *banners flaunting in the breeze.* [? < Scand. (Norwegian) *flanta* gad about]

**flaw** (flô), *v.* make or become defective; crack.

**fledge** (flej), *v.,* **fledged, fledg ing.** 1. grow the feathers needed for flying. 2. bring up (a young bird) until it is able to fly. 3. provide or cover with feathers. [cf. OE *unflicge* unfledged, unfit to fly]

**fleece** (flēs), *n.* 1. wool that covers a sheep or similar animal. 2. quantity of wool cut from a sheep at one time. 3. something like a fleece: *a fleece of hair, the fleece of new-fallen snow.*

**Flod den** (flod′n), *n.* hill in NE England where the English defeated the Scots in 1513.

**flog** (flog or flôg), *v.,* **flogged, flog ging.** whip very hard; beat with a whip, stick, etc.

[? English school slang for L *flagellare* whip] —**flog′ger,** *n.*

**flour ish** (flėr′ish), *v.* 1. grow or develop with vigor; thrive; do well. 2. wave (a sword, stick, arm, etc.) in the air. 3. make a showy display.

**flout** (flout), *v.* 1. treat with contempt or scorn; mock; scoff at: *The foolish boy flouted his mother's advice.* 2. show contempt or scorn; scoff. —**Syn.** 1. jeer, taunt.

**fod der** (fod′ər), *n.* coarse food for horses, cattle, etc. Hay and cornstalks with their leaves are fodder. [OE *fōdor* < *fōda* food]

**form a tive** (fôr′mə tiv), *adj.* having to do with formation or development; forming; molding: *Home and school are the chief formative influences in a child's life.*

**for mi da ble** (fôr′mə də bl), *adj.* hard to overcome; hard to deal with; to be dreaded. [< L *formidabilis* < *formidare* dread] —**for′mi da bly,** *adv.* —**Syn.** appalling, fearful.

**fort night** (fôrt′nīt or fôrt′nit), *n.* two weeks. [ME *fourtenight,* contraction of OE *fēowertiene niht* fourteen nights]

**fos sil** (fos′l), *n.* 1. the hardened remains or traces of animals or plants of a former age. 2. a very old-fashioned person, set in his ways. [< F < L *fossilis* dug up < *fodere* dig]

**foy er** (foi′ər or foi′ā), *n.* 1. an entrance hall used as a lounging room in a theater or hotel; lobby. 2. an entrance hall. [< F, ult. < L *focus* hearth]

**fray** (frā), *n.* a noisy quarrel; fight.

**fret** (fret), *v.,* **fret ted, fret ting.** 1. be peevish, unhappy, discontented, or worried: *A baby frets in hot weather.* 2. make peevish, unhappy, discontented, or worried. 3. eat away; wear; rub. 4. roughen; disturb. —**Syn.** 2. harass, vex, provoke.

**frond** (frond), *n.* a divided leaf of a fern, palm, etc. [< L *frons, frondis* leaf]

**ful crum** (ful′krəm), *n., pl.* **-crums, -cra** (-krə). support on which a lever turns or is supported in moving or lifting something. [< L *fulcrum* bedpost < *fulcire* to support]

**fu ner e al** (fyü nir′ē əl), *adj.* 1. of or suitable for a funeral. 2. sad; gloomy; dismal. [< L *funereus* < *funus* funeral] —**Syn.** 2. solemn, mournful.

**fur row** (fėr′ō), *n.* 1. a long, narrow groove or track cut in the ground by a plow. 2. any long, narrow groove or track.

**fur tive** (fėr′tiv), *adj.* 1. done stealthily; secret: *a furtive glance into the forbidden room.* 2. sly; stealthy: *The thief had a furtive manner.* [< L *furtivus* < *fur* thief]

**fu tile** (fyü′tl), *adj.* 1. not successful; useless. 2. not important; trifling. [< L *futilis* pouring easily, worthless < *fundere* pour] —**fu′tile ly,** *adv.*

**gad** (gad), *v.,* **gad ded, gad ding.** move about restlessly; go about looking for pleasure or excitement.

**gain say** (gān′sā′), *v.,* **-said** or **-sayed, -say ing.** deny; contradict; dispute. [< *gain-* against + *say*]

**gall** (gôl), *n.* **1.** a bitter yellow, brown, or greenish liquid secreted by the liver and stored in the gall bladder; bile of animals. **2.** gall bladder. **3.** bitterness; hate. [OE *galla*]

**gal lant** (gal′ənt or gə lant′), *n.* **1.** a spirited or courageous man. **2.** man who is gay or wears showy clothes; man of fashion. **3.** man who is very polite and attentive to women. **4.** lover. [< OF *galant*, ppr. of *galer* make a show < *gale*]

**gal ler y** (gal′ər ē or gal′rē), *n., pl.* **-ler ies.** **1.** a long, narrow platform or passage projecting from the wall of a building. **2.** a projecting upper floor in a church, theater, or hall with seats or room for part of the audience; balcony. **3.** a covered walk or porch.

**gan net** (gan′it), *n.* a large, fish-eating sea bird somewhat like a pelican, but with long, pointed wings and a shorter tail. [OE *ganot*]

**gape** (gāp or gap), *v.,* **gaped, gap ing,** *n.* —*v.* **1.** open wide: *A deep hole in the earth gaped before us.* **2.** open the mouth wide; yawn. **3.** stare with the mouth open. —*n.* **1.** a wide opening. **2.** act of opening the mouth wide; yawning. **3.** an open-mouthed stare. [< Scand. *gapa*]

**gar goyle** (gär′goil), *n.* **1.** spout for carrying off rain water, ending in a grotesque head that projects from the gutter of a building. **2.** projection or ornament on a building resembling a gargoyle. [< OF *gargouille;* imitative. Cf. L *gurgulio* gullet.]

**gar ner** (gär′nər), *v.* gather and store away: *Wheat is cut and garnered at harvest time.* [< n.] —*n.* **1.** storehouse for grain. **2.** a store of anything. [< OF *gernier, grenier* < L *granarium* < *granum* grain]

**gas tric** (gas′trik), *adj.* of or near the stomach. [< Gk. *gaster, gastros* stomach]

**gen ial** (jēn′yəl), *adj.* **1.** smiling and pleasant; cheerful and friendly; kindly: *a genial welcome.* **2.** helping growth; pleasantly warming; comforting: *genial sunshine.* [< L *genialis,* literally, belonging to the genius < *genius*]

**gen tile** or **Gen tile** (jen′tīl), *n.* **1.** person who is not a Jew. **2.** heathen; pagan. **3.** among Mormons, a person who is not a Mormon. [< LL *gentilis* foreign < L *gentilis* of a people, national]

**Get tys burg** (get′ēz bėrg), *n.* town in S Pennsylvania. One of the important battles of the Civil War was fought there July 1, 2, and 3, 1863.

**gin ger ly** (jin′jər lē), *adv., adj.* with extreme care or caution.

**girth** (gėrth), *n.* **1.** the measure around anything: *a man of large girth, the girth of a tree.* **2.** strap or band that keeps a saddle, pack, etc., in place on a horse's back. **3.** girdle. [< Scand. *gjörth* girdle]

**glade** (glād), *n.* **1.** an open space in a wood or forest. **2.** a marshy tract of low ground covered with grass.

**glen** (glen), *n.* a small, narrow valley.

**glow er** (glou′ər), *v.* stare angrily; scowl: *The fighters glowered at each other.* —*n.* an angry or sullen look. [? < obsolete *glow,* v., stare] —**glow′er ing ly,** *adv.*

**G-man** (jē′man′), *n., pl.* **-men.** *Informal.* a special agent of the United States Department of Justice; agent of the FBI. [Am.E; for *Government man*]

**gnarled** (närld), *adj.* covered with knots or hard, rough lumps; knotted; twisted; rugged: *The farmer's gnarled hands grasped the plow firmly.*

**goad** (gōd), *n.* **1.** a sharp-pointed stick for driving cattle, etc.; gad. **2.** anything that drives or urges one on. —*v.* drive or urge on; act as a goad to: *Hunger goaded him to steal a loaf of bread.* [OE *gād*] —*Syn. v.* stimulate, spur, impel.

**gon do la** (gon′dl ə), *n.* a long, narrow boat with a high peak at each end, used on the canals of Venice. [< dialectal Ital. *gondola* < *gondolar* rock]

**gorge** (gôrj), *n., v.,* **gorged, gorg ing.** —*n.* a deep, narrow valley, usually steep and rocky. —*v.* **1.** eat greedily until full; stuff with food. **2.** fill full; stuff. [< OF *gorge* throat, ult. < LL *gurges* throat, jaws < L *gurges* abyss, whirlpool]

**gos sa mer** (gos′ə mər), *n.* **1.** film or thread of cobweb. **2.** a very thin, light cloth. **3.** a thin, light, waterproof cloth or coat. [ME *gossomer* goose summer, name for "Indian summer," the season for goose and cobwebs]

**gram o phone** (gram′ə fōn), *n.* a phonograph.

**gran ite** (gran′it), *n.* **1.** a hard igneous rock made of grains of other rocks, chiefly quartz and feldspar. Granite is much used for buildings and monuments. **2.** unyielding firmness or endurance.

**grat is** (grat′is or grā′tis), *adv., adj.* for nothing; free of charge. [< L *gratis,* ult. < *gratia* favor]

**gra tu i tous** (grə tü′ə təs or grə tyü′ə təs), *adj.* **1.** freely given or obtained; free. **2.** without reason or cause; unnecessary; uncalled-for. . —**gra tu′i tous ly,** *adv.* —*Syn.* **2.** unwarranted.

**grease wood** (grēs′wùd′), *n.* a stiff, prickly shrub with narrow leaves, growing in alkaline regions in the western U.S. [Am.E]

**gre gar i ous** (grə gar′ē əs or grə ger′ē əs), *adj.* **1.** living in flocks, herds, or other groups: *Sheep and cattle are gregarious.* **2.** fond of being with others. **3.** of or having to do with a flock or crowd. [< L *gregarius* < *grex* flock]

**gri mace** (grə mās′ or grim′is), *n., v.,* **-maced, -mac ing.** —*n.* a twisting of the face; ugly or funny smile. —*v.* make grimaces.

**grind stone** (grīnd′stōn′), *n.* a flat, round stone set in a frame and turned by a crank, treadle, etc. It is used to sharpen tools, such as axes and knives, or to smooth and polish things.

**gris ly** (griz′lē), *adj.,* **-li er, -li est.** frightful; horrible; ghastly. [OE *grislic*]

**grudge** (gruj), *v.,* **grudged, grudg ing.** **1.** feel anger or dislike toward (a person) because of (something); envy the possession of: *He grudged me my little prize even though he had won a bigger one.* **2.** give or let have unwillingly: *The mean man grudged his horse the food that it ate.* [earlier meaning, grumble, complain; var.

hat, āge, fär; let, ēqual, tėrm;
it, īce; hot, ōpen, ôrder;
oil, out; cup, pùt, rüle;
ch, child; ng, long; sh, she;
th, thin; ᴛʜ, then; zh, measure;

ə represents *a* in about, *e* in taken,
*i* in pencil, *o* in lemon, *u* in circus.

< = from, derived from, taken from.

of obsolete *grutch* < OF *groucher* murmur, grumble] —*Syn.* **1.** envy, begrudge.

**gua va** (gwä′və), *n.* **1.** a tropical American tree or shrub with a yellow or red, round or pear-shaped fruit. **2.** the fruit, used for jelly, jam, etc. [< Sp. *guayaba* < native name]

**guile** (gīl), *n.* crafty deceit; craftiness; sly tricks: *A swindler uses guile; a robber uses force.* [< OF < Gmc.] —*Syn.* cunning, wiliness, trickery.

**gy rate** (jī′rāt or jī rāt′), *v.,* **-rat ed, -rat ing.** move in a circle or spiral; whirl; rotate: *A top gyrates.* [< L *gyrare* < *gyrus* circle < Gk. *gyros*]

**hab it a ble** (hab′ə tə bl), *adj.* fit to live in.

**hap less** (hap′lis), *adj.* unlucky; unfortunate.

**har bor** (här′bər), *v.* **1.** give shelter to; give a place to hide: *The dog's shaggy hair harbors fleas.* **2.** take shelter or refuge. **3.** keep or nourish in the mind: *Don't harbor unkind thoughts.* [OE *hereborg* lodgings < *here* army + *beorg* shelter]

**har mo ni ous** (här mō′nē əs), *adj.* **1.** agreeing in feelings, ideas, or actions; getting along well together: *The children played together in a harmonious group.* **2.** arranged so that the parts are orderly or pleasing; going well together: *A beautiful picture has harmonious colors.* **3.** sweet-sounding; musical.

**har ry** (har′ē), *v.,* **-ried, -ry ing.** **1.** raid and rob with violence: *The pirates harried the towns along the coast.* **2.** keep troubling; worry; torment: *Fear of losing his job harried the clerk.* [OE *hergian* < *here* army]

**Has tings** (hās′tingz), *n.* seaport in SE England. William the Conqueror defeated the Saxons here in 1066. 65,000.

**haunch** (hônch or hänch), *n.* **1.** part of the body around the hip; the hip. **2.** a hind quarter of an animal: *A dog sits on his haunches.* **3.** leg and loin of a deer, sheep, etc., used for food. [< OF *hanche* < Gmc.]

**hav er sack** (hav′ər sak), *n.* bag used by soldiers and hikers to carry food. [< F *havresac* < LG *habersack* oat sack]

**haw ser** (hô′zər or hô′sər), *n.* a large rope or small cable. Hawsers are used for mooring or towing ships.

**hearth** (härth), *n.* **1.** floor of a fireplace. **2.** home; fireside: *The soldiers longed for their own hearths.* [OE *heorth*]

**hea then** (hē′ᴛʜən), *n., pl.* **-thens** or

**-then,** *adj.* —*n.* **1.** person who does not believe in the God of the Bible; person who is not a Christian, Jew, or Moslem. **2.** people who are heathen. **3.** an irreligious or unenlightened person. —*adj.* **1.** of or having to do with heathens. **2.** irreligious; unenlightened. [OE *hǣthen*]

**heed** (hēd), *v.* give careful attention to; take notice of: *Now heed what I say.* [OE *hēdan*]

**heif er** (hef′ər), *n.* a young cow that has not had a calf. [OE *hēahfore*]

**hence** (hens), *adv.* **1.** from now; from this time onward: *years hence.* **2.** from here. —*interj.* **1. hence!** go away! **2. hence with!** take away.

**her ald** (her′əld), *n.* **1.** person who carries messages and makes announcements; messenger. **2.** forerunner; harbinger: *Dawn is the herald of day.*

**her e sy** (her′ə sē), *n., pl.* **-sies. 1.** belief different from the accepted belief of a church, school, profession, etc. **2.** the holding of such a belief. [< OF < L < Gk. *hairesis* a taking, choosing < *haireein* take]

**her on** (her′ən), *n.* a wading bird with a long neck, long bill, and long legs.

**het er o ge ne i ty** (het′ər ə jə nē′ə tē), *n., pl.* **-ties. 1.** a being heterogeneous; wide dissimilarity. **2.** a heterogeneous element or part.

**het er o ge ne ous** (het′ər ə jē′nē əs or het′ər ə jēn′yəs), *adj.* **1.** different in kind; unlike; not at all similar; varied. **2.** made up of unlike elements or parts; miscellaneous. [< Med.L *heterogeneus,* ult. < Gk. *heteros* other + *genos* kind]

**hew** (hyü), *v.,* **hewed, hewed** or **hewn, hew ing. 1.** cut with an ax, sword, etc.: *He hewed down the tree.* **2.** cut into shape; form by cutting with an ax, etc.: *hew stone for building, hew logs into beams.*

**hey day** (hā′dā′), *n.* period of greatest strength, vigor, spirits, prosperity, etc.

**hith er** (hiᴛʜ′ər), *adv.* to this place; toward this place; here. —*adj.* on this side; nearer. [OE *hider.* Related to *here.*]

**hoar frost** (hôr′frôst′, hōr′frôst′, hôr′- frost′, or hōr′frost′), *n.* white frost.

**hoar y** (hôr′ē or hōr′ē), *adj.,* **hoar i er, hoar i est. 1.** white or gray. **2.** white or gray with age. **3.** old; ancient.

**hom age** (hom′ij or om′ij), *n.* respect; reverence; honor: *Everyone paid homage to the great leader.* [< OF *homage* < *hom* man, vassal < L *homo*]

**Ho mo sa pi ens** (hō′mō sā′pē enz), *n.* man; human being; the species including all existing races of mankind. [< L *homo sapiens,* literally, man having sense]

**hoo poe** (hü′pü), *n.* a bright-colored bird with a long, sharp bill and a fanlike crest on its head. Its call sounds like its name. [earlier *hoop* < F *huppe* < L *upupa* (imitative)]

**hoose gow** or **hoos gow** (hüs′gau), *n. Slang.* jail, prison, guardhouse. [< Sp. *juzgado* panel of judges, tribunal, courtroom, < ppr. of *juzgar* to judge < L *judicare*]

**hum mock** (hum′ək), *n.* a very small, rounded hill; knoll; hillock.

**hurl ey** (her′lē), *n., pl.* **hurl eys, hurl ies.** *Brit.* **1.** the game of hurling. **2.** the stick used in hurling, similar to a field hockey stick, but with a wide, flat blade. Also, **hurly.**

**hus sar** (hù zär′), *n.* a European light-armed cavalry soldier. [< Hungarian *huszár,* originally, freebooter < OSerbian *husar,* var of *kursar* < Ital. *corsaro* runner < VL *cursarius* < L *cursus* a run]

**hy dro pho bi a** (hī′drə fō′bē ə), *n.* **1.** an infectious disease of dogs and other flesh-eating mammals that causes convulsions, frothing at the mouth, and madness; rabies. The disease can be transmitted to man and other animals by the bite of an infected animal. **2.** a morbid dread of water.

**hy per bo le** (hī pėr′bl ē), *n.* exaggeration for effect. *Example:* Waves high as mountains broke over the reef. [< L < Gk. *hyperbole*]

**hy per bol ic** (hī′pər bol′ik), *adj.* **1.** of, like, or using hyperbole; exaggerated; exaggerating. **2.** of or having to do with hyperbolas.

**hyp o crite** (hip′ə krit), *n.* **1.** person who puts on a false appearance of goodness or religion. **2.** person who pretends to be what he is not; pretender. [< OF *ypocrite* < L < Gk. *hypokrites* actor]

**hyp o crit i cal** (hip′ə krit′ə kl), *adj.* of or like a hypocrite; insincere. —**hyp′o - crit′i cal ly,** *adv.*

**hy poth e sis** (hī poth′ə sis), *n., pl.* **-ses. 1.** something assumed because it seems likely to be a true explanation; theory. **2.** proposition assumed as a basis for reasoning.

**hy poth e size** (hī poth′ə sīz), *v.,* **-sized, -siz ing. 1.** make a hypothesis. **2.** assume; suppose.

**hys ter i a** (hi stir′ē ə or hi ster′ē ə), *n.* **1.** a nervous disorder that causes violent fits of laughing and crying, imaginary illnesses, or general lack of self-control. **2.** senseless excitement.

**i bis** (ī′bis), *n., pl.* **i bis es** or (*esp. collectively*) **i bis.** a long-legged wading bird like a heron. The ancient Egyptians regarded the ibis as sacred. [<L <Gk. <Egyptian]

**i dol a try** (ī dol′ə trē), *n., pl.* **-tries. 1.** worship of idols. **2.** worship of a person or thing; great love or admiration; extreme devotion. [< OF < L < Gk. *eidololatreia* < *eidolon* image + *latreia* service]

**ig no min y** (ig′nə min′ē), *n., pl.* **-min ies. 1.** loss of one's good name; public shame and disgrace; dishonor. **2.** shameful action or conduct. [< L *ignominia* < *in-* not + *nomen* name; form influenced by OL *gnoscere* come to know]

**im mi nent** (im′ə nənt), *adj.* likely to happen soon; about to occur: *The black clouds show that a storm is imminent.* [< L *imminens, -entis,* ppr. of *imminere* overhang] —**im/mi nent ly,** *adv.*

**im mo late** (im′ə lāt), *v.,* **-lat ed, -lat ing. 1.** kill as a sacrifice. **2.** sacrifice. [< L *immolare* sacrifice, originally, sprinkle with sacrificial meal < *in-* on + *mola* sacrificial meal]

**im mo la tion** (im′ə lā′shən), *n.* sacrifice.

**im mune** (i myün′), *adj.* **1.** protected from disease; not susceptible; inoculated. **2.** exempt: *immune from taxes.* [< L *immunis,* originally, free from obligation]

**im mu ni ty** (i myü′nə tē), *n., pl.* **-ties. 1.** resistance to disease, poison, etc. **2.** freedom; protection.

**im mu ta ble** (i myü′tə bl), *adj.* never changing; unchangeable. —**im mu/ta bly,** *adv.* —**Syn.** unalterable, permanent.

**im pale** (im pāl′), *v.,* **-paled, -pal ing. 1.** pierce through with anything pointed; fasten upon anything pointed: *The butterflies were impaled on small pins stuck in a sheet of cork.* **2.** torture or punish by thrusting upon a pointed stake. [< F *empaler,* ult. < L *in-* on + *palus* stake]

**im pas sive** (im pas′iv), *adj.* **1.** without feeling or emotion; unmoved: *He listened with an impassive face.* **2.** not feeling pain or injury; insensible. —**im pas′sive ly,** *adv.* —**Syn. 1.** indifferent, apathetic, passive.

**im pel** (im pel′), *v.,* **-pelled, -pel ling. 1.** drive; force; cause: *Hunger impelled the lazy man to work.* **2.** cause to move; drive forward; push along: *The wind impelled the boat to shore.* [< L *impellere* < *in-* on + *pellere* push]

**im per cep ti ble** (im′pər sep′tə bl), *adj.* **1.** very slight; gradual. **2.** that cannot be perceived or felt.

**im per i ous** (im pir′ē əs), *adj.* **1.** haughty; arrogant; domineering; overbearing. **2.** imperative; necessary; urgent. [< L *imperiosus* commanding] —**im pe′ri ous ly,** *adv.* —**Syn. 1.** dictatorial.

**im pet u ous** (im pech′ü əs), *adj.* **1.** moving with great force or speed: *the impetuous rush of water over Niagara Falls.* **2.** acting hastily, rashly, or with sudden feeling. [< LL *impetuosus* < L *impetus* attack] —**im pet′u ous ly,** *adv.*

**im pla ca ble** (im plā′kə bl or im plak′- ə bl), *adj.* that cannot be satisfied, pacified, or appeased; relentless. —**im pla′ca bly,** *adv.* —**Syn.** unforgiving, inexorable.

**im ple ment** (im′plə ment), *v.* **1.** provide with tools or other means. **2.** provide the power and authority necessary to accomplish or put (something) into effect: *implement an order.* **3.** carry out; get done. [< LL *implementum* literally, that which fills a need < L *implere* < *in-* in + *-plere* fill]

**im plode** (im plōd′), *v.* burst inward.

**im pon der a ble** (im pon′dər ə bl), *adj.* without weight that can be felt or measured: *Faith and love are imponderable forces.* —*n.* something imponderable.

**im por tune** (im′pôr tün′, im′pôr tyün′, or im pôr′chən), *v.,* **-tuned, -tun ing.** ask urgently or repeatedly; trouble with demands. [< MF < L *importunus* inconvenient]

**im pose** (im pōz′), *v.,* **-posed, -pos ing. 1.** force or thrust oneself or one's authority or influence on another or others. **2. impose on** or **upon, a.** take advantage of; use for selfish purposes. **b.** deceive; cheat;

trick. [< F *imposer* < *in-* on + *poser* put, place]

**im pound** (im pound′), v. 1. shut up; enclose; confine: *A dam impounds water.* 2. put in the custody of a law court: *The court impounded the documents to use as evidence.*

**im preg nate** (im preg′nāt), v., **-nat ed, -nat ing,** *adj.* —v. 1. make pregnant; fertilize. 2. fill (with); saturate: *Sea water is impregnated with salt.* 3. instill into (the mind); inspire; imbue. —*adj.* impregnated. [< LL *impraegnare* make pregnant < *in-* + *praegnas* pregnant]

**im promp tu** (im promp′tü or im-promp′tyü), *adv., adj.* without previous thought or preparation; offhand: *a speech made impromptu.* [< L *in promptu* in readiness] —**Syn.** *adj.* improvised.

**im pru dent** (im prüd′nt), *adj.* not prudent; rash; not discreet. —**im pru′dent ly,** *adv.* —**Syn.** indiscreet.

**im pu dence** (im′pyə dəns), *n.* lack of shame or modesty; rude boldness.

**im pu dent** (im′pyə dənt), *adj.* without shame or modesty; forward; rudely bold. [< L *impudens, -entis,* ult. < *in-* not + *pudere* be modest] —**im′pu dent ly,** *adv.*

**im pu ni ty** (im pyü′nə tē), *n.* freedom from punishment, injury, or other bad consequences: *If laws are not enforced, crimes are committed with impunity.* [< L *impunitas,* ult. < *in-* without + *poena* punishment]

**im pute** (im pyüt′), v., **-put ed, -put ing.** consider as belonging; attribute; charge (a fault, etc.) to a person; blame: *I impute his failure to laziness.*

**in ac ces si ble** (in′ak ses′ə bl), *adj.* 1. not accessible; that cannot be reached or entered. 2. hard to get at; hard to reach or enter: *The fort on top of the steep hill is inaccessible.* 3. that cannot be obtained; hard to obtain.

**in au gu rate** (in ô′gyə rāt), v., **-rat ed, -rat ing.** 1. install in office with a ceremony: *A President of the United States is inaugurated every four years.* 2. make a formal beginning of; begin: *The invention of the airplane inaugurated a new era in transportation.* [< L *inaugurare* < *in-* for + *augur* taker of omens]

**in aus pi cious** (in′ôs pish′əs), *adj.* with signs of failure; unfavorable; unlucky. —**in′aus pi′cious ly,** *adv.* —**Syn.** unpromising.

**in can des cent** (in′kən des′nt), *adj.* 1. glowing with heat; red-hot or white-hot. 2. intensely bright; brilliant. [< L *incandescens,* ppr. of *incandescere* begin to glow < *in-* + *candere* be gleaming white]

**in can ta tion** (in′kan tā′shən), *n.* 1. set of words spoken as a magic charm or to cast a magic spell. 2. use of such words. [< L *incantatio, -onis* < *incantare* chant a magic formula against < *in-* against + *cantare* chant]

**in ces sant** (in ses′nt), *adj.* never stopping; continued or repeated without interruption. [< LL *incessans, -antis* < L *in-* not + *cessare* cease] —**in ces′sant ly,** *adv.* —**Syn.** ceaseless, constant.

**in ci den tal** (in′sə den′tl), *adj.* 1. hap-

pening or likely to happen along with something else more important: *Certain discomforts are incidental to camping out.* 2. occurring by chance.

**in com pre hen si ble** (in′kom pri hen′-sə bl), *adj.* impossible to understand. —**in′com pre hen′si bly,** *adv.*

**in cre du li ty** (in′krə dü′lə tē or in′krə-dyü′lə tē), *n.* lack of belief; doubt.

**in cred u lous** (in krej′ə ləs), *adj.* 1. not ready to believe; not credulous; doubting: *People nowadays are incredulous about ghosts and witches.* 2. showing a lack of belief. —**in cred′u lous ly,** *adv.*

**in del i ble** (in del′ə bl), *adj.* 1. that cannot be erased or removed; permanent: *indelible ink, an indelible disgrace.* 2. making an indelible mark: *an indelible pencil.* [< L *indelebilis* < *in-* not + *delebilis* able to be destroyed < *delere* destroy] —**in del′i bly,** *adv.*

**in dig nant** (in dig′nənt), *adj.* angry at something unworthy, unjust, or mean. [< L *indignans, -antis,* ppr. of *indignari* be indignant (at), regard as unworthy < *indignus* unworthy < *in-* not + *dignus* worthy] —**in dig′nant ly,** *adv.* —**Syn.** incensed, provoked, displeased.

**in dis crim i nate** (in′dis krim′ə nit), *adj.* 1. confused: *He tipped everything out of his suitcase in an indiscriminate mass.* 2. not discriminating; with no feeling for differences: *He is an indiscriminate reader and likes both good books and bad ones.* —**in′dis crim′i nate ly,** *adv.*

**in do lent** (in′dl ənt), *adj.* lazy; disliking work. [< LL *indolens, -entis* < L *in-* not + *dolens,* ppr. of *dolere* be in pain] —**in′do lent ly,** *adv.*

**in duce** (in düs′ or in dyüs′), v., **-duced, -duc ing.** 1. lead on; influence; persuade: *Advertising induces people to buy.* 2. cause; bring about: *Some drugs induce sleep.* [< L *inducere* < *in-* in + *ducere* lead] —**Syn.** 1. incite, impel.

**in ev i ta ble** (in ev′ə tə bl), *adj.* not avoidable; sure to happen; certain to come: *Death is inevitable.* [< L *inevitabilis* < *in-* not + *evitabilis* avoidable < *evitare* avoid < *ex-* + *vitare* avoid] —**in ev′i ta bly,** *adv.*

**in ex o ra ble** (in ek′sər ə bəl), *adj.* relentless; unyielding; not influenced by prayers or entreaties: *The forces of nature are inexorable.* [< L *inexorabilis* < *in-* not + *ex-* successfully + *orare* entreat] —**in ex′o ra bly,** *adv.* —**Syn.** unrelenting, implacable.

**in ex pli ca ble** (in′ik splik′ə bəl or in ek′splə kə bəl), *adj.* impossible to explain or understand; mysterious. [< L *inexplicabilis* ] —**in ex′pli ca bly,** *adv.*

**in ex tri ca ble** (in eks′trə kə bl), *adj.* 1. that one cannot get out of. 2. that cannot be disentangled or solved. [< L *inextricabilis* ] —**in ex′tri ca bly,** *adv.*

**in fal li bil i ty** (in fal′ə bil′ə tē), *n.* absolute freedom from error.

**in fal li ble** (in fal′ə bl), *adj.* 1. free from error; that cannot be mistaken: *an infallible rule.* 2. absolutely reliable; sure: *infallible obedience.* [< Med.L *infallibilis* ] —**in fal′li bly,** *adv.*

**in fi del** (in′fə dl), *n.* 1. person who does

hat, āge, fär; let, ēqual, tėrm;
it, īce; hot, ōpen, ôrder;
oil, out; cup, pùt, rüle;
ch, child; ng, long; sh, she;
th, thin; ŦH, then; zh, measure;

ə represents *a* in about, *e* in taken,
*i* in pencil, *o* in lemon, *u* in circus.

< = from, derived from, taken from.

---

not believe in religion. 2. person who does not accept a particular faith. 3. person who does not accept Christianity. —*adj.* not believing in religion. [< L *infidelis* < *in-* not + *fidelis* faithful < *fides* faith]

**in fi nite** (in′fə nit), *adj.* 1. without limits or bounds, endless. 2. extremely great: *Teaching little children takes infinite patience.* —*n.* that which is infinite. [< L *infinitus* < *in-* not + *finis* boundary]

**in firm** (in fėrm′), *adj.* 1. weak; feeble. 2. weak in will or character; not steadfast. 3. not firm; not stable. —**Syn.** 1. shaky, decrepit, debilitated.

**in fir mar y** (in fėr′mər ē), *n., pl.* **-ries.** 1. place for the care of the infirm, sick, or injured; hospital in a school or institution. 2. hospital.

**in fra red** (in′frə red′), *adj.* of the invisible part of the spectrum whose rays have wave lengths longer than those of the red part of the visible spectrum. Most of the heat from sunlight, incandescent lamps, carbon arcs, resistance wires, etc., is from infrared rays.

**in gen ious** (in jēn′yəs), *adj.* 1. clever; skillful in making; good at inventing: *The ingenious boy made a radio set for himself.* 2. cleverly planned and made: *This mousetrap is an ingenious device.* [< L *ingeniosus* < *ingenium* natural talent] —**in gen′ious ly,** *adv.*

**in gé nue** (aɴ′zhə nü; *French* aɴ zhā nY′), *n., pl.* **-nues.** 1. a simple, innocent girl or young woman, especially as represented on the stage. 2. actress who plays such a part. [< F *ingénue,* originally fem. adj., ingenuous]

**in ge nu i ty** (in′jə nü′ə tē or in′jə-nyü′ə tē), *n., pl.* **-ties.** skill in planning, inventing, etc.; cleverness. [< L *ingenuitas* frankness < *ingenuus* ingenuous; influenced by association with *ingenious*]

**Ingersoll,** a brand of inexpensive watch.

**in got** (ing′gət), *n.* mass of metal, such as gold, silver, or steel, cast into a convenient shape in a mold. [< OE *in-* in + *goten,* pp. of *gēotan* pour]

**in iq ui ty** (in ik′wə tē), *n., pl.* **-ties.** 1. very great injustice; wickedness. 2. a wicked or unjust act. [< L *iniquitas* < *iniquus* < *in-* not + *aequus* just]

**in junc tion** (in jungk′shən), *n.* 1. command; order. 2. a formal order issued by a law court ordering a person or group to do, or refrain from doing, something. [< LL *injunctio, -onis* < L *injungere* enjoin < *in-* in + *jungere* join]

**in noc u ous** (i nok′yü əs), *adj.* harmless.

[< L *innocuus* < *in-* not + *nocuus* hurtful < *nocere* to harm]

**in nu mer a ble** (i nü′mər ə bl or i nyü′-mər ə bl), *adj.* too many to count; very many. —**Syn.** countless, myriad.

**in op por tune** (in op′ər tün′ or in-op′ər tyün′), *adj.* coming at a bad time; unsuitable: *An inopportune call delayed us.* —**in op′por tune′ly,** *adv.* —**Syn.** untimely, unseasonable.

**in sa tia ble** (in sā′shə bl), *adj.* that cannot be satisfied; extremely greedy. —**in sa′tia bly,** *adv.* —**Syn.** unquenchable.

**in som ni a** (in som′nē ə), *n.* inability to sleep; sleeplessness. [< L *insomnia* < *in-* not + *somnus* sleep]

**in ter** (in tėr′), *v.,* **-terred, -ter ring.** put (a dead body) into a grave or tomb; bury. [< OF *enterrer* < L *interrare* < *in-* in + *terra* earth]

**in ter cede** (in′tər sēd′), *v.,* **-ced ed, -ced ing.** 1. plead or beg in another's behalf: *Friends of the condemned man interceded with the governor for a pardon.* 2. interfere in order to bring about an agreement. [< L *intercedere* < *inter-* between + *cedere* go]

**in ter ces sion** (in′tər sesh′ən), *n.* act or fact of interceding. [< L *intercessio, -onis* < *intercedere.* See INTERCEDE.]

**in ter ur ban** (in′tər ėr′bən), *adj.* between cities or towns. [Am.E]

**in ti mate** (in′tə māt), *v.,* **-mat ed, -mat ing.** 1. suggest indirectly; hint. 2. announce; notify.

**in trep id** (in trep′id), *adj.* fearless; dauntless; courageous; very brave. [< L *intrepidus* < *in-* not + *trepidus* alarmed] —**in trep′id ly,** *adv.* —**Syn.** bold, daring.

**in un da tion** (in′un dā′shən), *n.* an overflowing; flood.

**in var i a bly** (in var′ē ə blē or in ver′-ē ə blē), *adv.* always; without change; without exception.

**in vo ca tion** (in′və kā′shən), *n.* 1. act of calling upon in prayer; appeal for help or protection. 2. a calling forth of spirits by magic. 3. set of magic words used to call forth spirits.

**i ras ci ble** (i ras′ə bl), *adj.* 1. easily made angry; irritable. 2. showing anger. [< LL *irascibilis* < L *irasci* grow angry < *ira* anger] —**i ras′ci bly,** *adv.*

**ir i des cent** (ir′ə des′nt), *adj.* 1. displaying colors like those of the rainbow. 2. changing colors according to position. [< L *iris, iridis* rainbow < Gk.] —**ir′i des′cent ly,** *adv.*

**ir res o lute** (i rez′ə lüt), *adj.* unable to make up one's mind; not sure of what one wants; hesitating: *Irresolute persons make poor leaders.* —**ir res′o lute ly,** *adv.*

**i sin glass** (ī′zing glas′ or ī′zing gläs′), *n.* 1. kind of gelatin obtained from air bladders of sturgeon, cod, and similar fishes, used for making glue, clearing liquors, etc. 2. mica, a mineral that divides into thin semitransparent layers. [alteration of MDutch *huysenblas* sturgeon bladder; influenced by *glass*]

**Ith a ca** (ith′ə kə), *n.* 1. a small island W of Greece, the home of Odysseus. 2. city in S New York. 29,000.

**jamb** or **jambe** (jam), *n.* the upright piece forming the side of a doorway, window, fireplace, etc.

**jar gon** (jär′gən or jär′gon), *n.* 1. confused, meaningless talk or writing. 2. language that is not understood. 3. language of a special group, profession, etc. Doctors, actors, and sailors have jargons. 4. chatter. [< OF; probably ult. imitative]

**jave lin** (jav′lən or jav′ə lin), *n.* a light spear thrown by hand. [< F *javeline*]

**jeop ar dy** (jep′ər dē), *n.* risk; danger; peril: *His life was in jeopardy when the tree fell.* [< OF *jeu parti* an even or divided game, ult. < L *jocus* play + *pars* part]

**jer ry-built** (jer′ē bilt′), *adj.* built carelessly of poor materials; flimsy. [? alteration of an earlier *jury-built;* cf. *jury-rigged* rigged for temporary service]

**jest** (jest), *n.* 1. joke. 2. act of poking fun; mockery. 3. thing to be mocked or laughed at.

**joc und** (jok′ənd or jō′kənd), *adj.* cheerful; merry; gay. [< L *jocundus,* var. (influenced by *jocus* a jest) of *jucundus* pleasant < *juvare* please] —**joc′und ly,** *adv.*

**keel** (kēl), *n.* 1. the main timber or steel piece that extends the whole length of the bottom of a ship or boat. 2. *Poetic.* ship. [< Scand. *kjölr*]

**khak i** (kak′ē or kä′kē), *adj., n., pl.* **khak-is.** —*adj.* 1. dull yellowish brown. 2. made of khaki. —*n.* 1. a dull, yellowish brown. 2. a stout twilled cloth of this color, used for soldiers' uniforms. 3. uniform or uniforms made of this cloth. [< Hindi *khākī,* originally, dusty < Persian *khāk* dust]

**kib itz er** (kib′it sər), *n. Informal.* 1. person watching a card game. 2. person who gives unwanted advice; meddler. [Am.E; < Yiddish]

**kil o me ter** (kil′ə mē′tər or kə lom′ə tər), *n.* distance equal to 1000 meters, or 3280.8 feet. [< F *kilomètre*]

**ki mo no** (kə mō′nə), *n., pl.* **-nos.** 1. a loose outer garment held in place by a sash, worn by Japanese men and women. 2. a woman's loose dressing gown. [< Japanese]

**kite** (kīt), *n.* hawk with long pointed wings.

**knave** (nāv), *n.* 1. a tricky, dishonest person; rogue; rascal. 2. *Archaic.* a male servant; man of humble birth or position. [OE *cnafa* boy] —**Syn.** 1. scoundrel.

**knick ers** (nik′ərz), *n.pl.* short loose-fitting trousers gathered in at or just below the knee. [short for *knickerbockers,* < *Knickerbocker*]

**L** (el), *n.* elevated railroad; railroad raised above the ground on a supporting frame

high enough for streetcars, automobiles, etc., to pass underneath.

**la bo ri ous** (lə bô′rē əs or lə bō′rē əs), *adj.* 1. requiring much work; requiring hard work: *Climbing a mountain is laborious.* 2. hard-working; industrious: *Bees and ants are laborious insects.* 3. showing signs of effort; not easy. [< L *laboriosus* < *labor* labor] —**la bo′ri ous ly,** *adv.*

**lac e rate** (las′ə rāt′), *v.,* **-at ed, -at ing.** 1. tear roughly; mangle: *The bear's claws lacerated his flesh.* 2. wound; hurt (the feelings, etc.). [< L *lacerare* < *lacer* mangled]

**lac quer** (lak′ər), *n.* 1. varnish consisting of shellac dissolved in alcohol, used for coating brass. 2. varnish made from the resin of a sumac tree of SE Asia. It gives a very high polish on wood. —*v.* coat with lacquer. [< F < Pg. *laca* lac]

**la dle** (lā′dl), *n.* a large cup-shaped spoon with a long handle, for dipping out liquids. [OE *hlædel* < *hladan* lade]

**la ment** (lə ment′), *v.* 1. express grief for; mourn for: *lament the dead.* 2. express grief; mourn; weep: *Why does she lament?* 3. regret: *We lamented his absence.* —*n.* 1. expression of grief; wail. 2. poem, song, or tune that expresses grief. 3. a regret. [< L *lamentari* < *lamentum* a wailing]

**lam en ta ble** (lam′ən tə bl), *adj.* 1. to be regretted or pitied: *a lamentable accident, a lamentable failure.* 2. sorrowful; mournful. —**lam′en ta bly,** *adv.*

**lam en ta tion** (lam′ən tā′shən), *n.* loud grief; mourning; wailing; cries of sorrow.

**lance** (lans or läns), *n.* 1. a long wooden spear with a sharp iron or steel head. Knights carried lances. 2. any instrument like a soldier's lance. [< F < L *lancea* light Spanish spear]

**lan guish** (lang′gwish), *v.* 1. become weak or weary; lose energy; droop: *The flowers languished from lack of water.* 2. suffer under any unfavorable conditions: *He languished in prison for twenty years.* 3. grow dull, slack, or less intense: *His vigilance never languished.* —**Syn.** 1. wither, fade.

**las si tude** (las′ə tüd or las′ə tyüd), *n.* lack of energy; weakness; weariness. [< L *lassitudo* < *lassus* tired]

**lat er al** (lat′ər əl), *adj.* of the side; at the side; from the side; toward the side. [< L *lateralis* < *latus* side]

**lat i tude** (lat′ə tüd or lat′ə tyüd), *n.* 1. distance north or south of the equator, measured in degrees. 2. place or region having a certain latitude: *Polar bears live in the cold latitudes.* [< L *latitudo* < *latus* wide]

**lau rel** (lô′rəl or lor′əl), *n.* 1. a small evergreen tree with smooth, shiny leaves; bay tree. 2. the leaves. The ancient Greeks and Romans crowned victors with wreaths of laurel.

**lay out** (lā′out′), *n.* 1. act of laying out. 2. arrangement; plan: *This map shows the layout of the camp.* 3. plan or design for an advertisement, book, etc. 4. thing laid or spread out; display.

**Le bin thus** (lə bin′thəs), *n.* an island in the Aegean Sea.

**leek** (lēk), *n.* vegetable somewhat like an onion, but with larger leaves, a smaller bulb shaped like a cylinder, and a milder flavor. [OE *lēac*]

**leer** (lir), *v.* give a sly, sidelong look; glance evilly. [? OE *hlēor* cheek] **—leer′ing ly,** *adv.*

**lest** (lest), *conj.* 1. for fear that: *Be careful lest you fall from that tree.* 2. that: *I was afraid lest he should come too late to save us.* [OE *thȳ læs the* whereby less that]

**li ba tion** (lī bā′shən), *n.* 1. a pouring out of wine, water, etc., as an offering to a god. 2. wine, water, etc., offered in this way. [< L *libatio, -onis* < *libare* pour out]

**li cense** (lī′sns), *n.* 1. permission given to do something. 2. too much liberty; disregard of what is right and proper; abuse of liberty. [< OF *licence* < L *licentia* < *licere* be allowed]

**liege** (lēj), *n.* 1. lord having a right to the homage and loyal service of his vassals. 2. vassal obliged to give homage and loyal service to his lord. [< OF < LL *leticus* < *letus* freedman, ult. < Gmc.]

**lights** (lits), *n.pl.* lungs of sheep, pigs, etc. [so called because of their light weight]

**lilt** (lilt), *v.* sing or play (a tune) in a light, tripping manner. —*n.* 1. a lively song or tune with a swing. 2. a lively, springing movement.

**list less** (list′lis), *adj.* seeming too tired to care about anything; not interested in things; not caring to be active. **—list′less ly,** *adv.* **—Syn.** indifferent, languid.

**loam** (lōm), *n.* rich, fertile earth; earth in which much humus is mixed with clay and sand. [OE *lām*]

**lo cust** (lō′kəst), *n.* any of the grasshoppers with short antennae, certain kinds of which migrate in great swarms, destroying crops. [< L *locusta*]

**loft** (lôft or loft), *n.* 1. attic. 2. room under the roof of a barn. 3. gallery in a church or hall. 4. *U.S.* an upper floor of a business building or warehouse. [< Scand. *lopt* air, sky, loft]

**log ic** (loj′ik), *n.* 1. science of proof. 2. reasoning; use of argument. 3. reason; sound sense. [< LL < Gk. *logike (techne)* reasoning (art) < *logos* word]

**lon gev i ty** (lon jev′ə tē), *n.* long life. [< L *longaevitas* < *longaevus* long-lived < *longus* long + *aevum* age]

**lope** (lōp), *v.,* **loped, lop ing,** *n.* —*v.* run with a long, easy stride. —*n.* a long, easy stride. [< Scand. *hlaupa* leap]

**lore** (lôr or lōr), *n.* 1. facts and stories about a certain subject. 2. learning; knowledge. [OE *lār.* Related to *learn.*]

**lot ter y** (lot′ər ē), *n., pl.* **-ter ies.** scheme for distributing prizes by lot or chance. In a lottery a large number of tickets are sold, some of which draw prizes.

**lout** (lout), *n.* an awkward, stupid fellow; boor. [< Scand. *lūtr* bent down, stooping]

**lu cid** (lü′sid), *adj.* 1. easy to understand: *a lucid explanation.* 2. shining; bright. 3. sane: *An insane person sometimes has lucid intervals.* [< L *lucidus* < *lux* light] **—lu′cid ly,** *adv.*

**lu mi nar y** (lü′mə ner′ē), *n., pl.* **-nar ies.** 1. the sun, moon, or other light-giving body. 2. a famous person. [< Med.L *luminarium* < L *lumen* light]

**lu mi nous** (lü′mə nəs), *adj.* 1. shining by its own light: *The sun and stars are luminous bodies.* 2. full of light; bright. 3. easily understood; clear; enlightening. [< L *luminosus* < *lumen* light] **—lu′mi nous ly,** *adv.*

**lunge** (lunj), *n., v.,* **lunged, lung ing.** —*n.* any sudden forward movement; thrust. —*v.* move suddenly forward; thrust. [ult. < F *allonger,* ult. < L *ad-* toward + *longus* long]

**lu rid** (lùr′id), *adj.* 1. lighted up with a red or fiery glare: *The sky was lurid with the flames of the burning city.* 2. terrible; sensational; startling: *lurid crimes.* [< L *luridus*]

**ma ca bre** (mə kä′brə or mə kä′bər), *adj.* gruesome; horrible; ghastly. [< F]

**mack er el** (mak′ər əl or mak′rəl), *n., pl.* **-el** or (*in reference to different species*) **-els.** a salt-water fish of the N Atlantic much used for food. [< OF *maquerel*]

**mag got** (mag′ət), *n.* legless larva of any of various kinds of flies, often living in decaying matter.

**mag nate** (mag′nāt), *n.* a great man; important person. [< LL *magnas, -atis* < L *magnus* great]

**main tain** (mān tān′), *v.* 1. keep; keep up; carry on: *maintain a business, maintain a family.* 2. support; uphold: *maintain an opinion.* 3. declare to be true: *He maintained that he was innocent.* 4. affirm; assert against opposition: *He maintains his innocence.* [< F *maintenir* < L *manu tenere* hold by the hand]

**mal con tent** (mal′kən tent′), *adj.* discontented; rebellious. —*n.* a discontented person; rebellious person.

**ma lev o lence** (mə lev′l əns), *n.* the wish that evil may happen to others; ill will; spite.

**ma lev o lent** (mə lev′l ənt), *adj.* wishing evil to happen to others; showing ill will; spiteful. [< L *malevolens, -entis,* ult. < *male* ill + *velle* wish]

**mal ice** (mal′is), *n.* active ill will; wish to hurt others; spite. [< OF < L *malitia* < *malus* evil]

**ma li cious** (mə lish′əs), *adj.* showing active ill will; wishing to hurt others; spiteful. **—ma li′cious ly,** *adv.*

**ma lig nant** (mə lig′nənt), *adj.* 1. very evil; very hateful; very malicious. 2. very harmful. 3. very infectious; very dangerous; causing death: *Cancer is a malignant growth.* [< LL *malignans, -antis* acting from malice < *malignus*] **—ma lig′nant ly,** *adv.*

**ma neu ver** (mə nü′vər), *n., v.,* **-vered, -ver ing.** —*n.* 1. a planned movement of troops or warships: *Every year the army and navy hold maneuvers for practice.* 2. a skillful plan; clever trick. —*v.* 1. perform maneuvers. 2. cause to perform maneuvers. 3. plan skillfully; use clever tricks: *A scheming person is always maneuvering for some advantage.* Also, **manoeuvre.** [< F

*manoeuvre,* ult. < L *manu operare* work by hand]

**man go** (mang′gō), *n., pl.* **-goes** or **-gos.** 1. a slightly sour, juicy fruit with a thick, yellowish red rind. Mangoes are eaten ripe or pickled when green. 2. the tropical tree that it grows on. [< Pg. < Malay < Tamil *mānkāy*]

**marl** (märl), *n.* 1. soil containing clay and calcium carbonate, used in making cement and as a fertilizer. 2. *Poetic.* earth. [<OF *marle* < Med.L *margila* < L *marga,* probably < Celtic]

**Marne** (märn), *n.* river flowing from NE France into the Seine River. 325 mi. In two battles of the Marne (September 1914 and July 1918) the Allies checked German offensives.

**ma son ry** (mā′sn rē), *n.* stonework; brickwork.

**mas sa cre** (mas′ə kər), *n., v.,* **-cred, -cring.** —*n.* wholesale, pitiless slaughter of people or animals. —*v.* kill (many people or animals) needlessly or cruelly; slaughter in large numbers. [<F *massacre,* in OF *macecle* shambles, ult. < VL *maccare* beat (<Gmc.) + L *collum* neck]

**mat tock** (mat′ək), *n.* tool like a pickax, but having a flat blade on one side or flat blades on both sides, used for loosening soil and cutting roots. [OE *mattuc*]

**maw** (mô), *n.* 1. mouth. 2. throat. 3. stomach.

**mead** (mēd), *n. Poetic.* meadow. [OE *mæd*]

**mea ger** or **mea gre** (mē′gər), *adj.* 1. poor; scanty: *a meager meal.* 2. thin; lean: *a meager face.* [<OF *maigre* < L *macer* thin]

**Mede** (mēd), *n.* native or inhabitant of Media.

**Me di a** (mē′dē ə), *n.* an ancient country in SW Asia, south of the Caspian Sea.

**me di e val** (mē′dē ē′vl or med′ē ē′vl), *adj.* 1. belonging to or having to do with the Middle Ages (the years from about 500 A.D. to about 1450 A.D.). 2. like that of the Middle Ages. Also, **mediaeval.** [< L *medium* middle + *aevum* age]

**me di o cre** (mē′dē ō′kər or mē′dē ō′kər), *adj.* neither good nor bad; average; ordinary. [< F < L *mediocris,* originally, halfway up < *medius* middle + *ocris* jagged mountain]

**me nag er ie** (mə naj′ər ē or mə nazh′ər ē), *n.* 1. collection of wild animals kept in cages for exhibition. 2. place where such animals are kept. [< F *ménagerie,* literally, management of a household]

---

hat, āge, fär; let, ēqual, tèrm; it, īce; hot, ōpen, ôrder; oil, out; cup, pùt, rüle; ch, child; ng, long; sh, she; th, thin; ŦH, then; zh, measure;

ə represents *a* in about, *e* in taken, *i* in pencil, *o* in lemon, *u* in circus.

< = from, derived from, taken from.

**609**

**mer can tile** (mėr′kən til or mėr′kən tīl), *adj.* of merchants or trade; commercial: *a mercantile firm, mercantile law.* [< F < Ital. *mercantile* < *mercante* merchant]

**me ter** (mē′tər), *n.* unit of length in the metric system; 39.37 inches. Also, *esp. Brit.* **metre.** [< F *mètre* < L < Gk. *metron* measure]

**me tic u lous** (mə tik′yə ləs), *adj.* extremely or excessively careful about small details. [< L *meticulosus* < *metus* fear] **—me tic′u lous ly,** *adv.* **—me tic′u lous ness,** *n.*

**met tle** (met′l), *n.* 1. disposition; spirit; courage. 2. **on one's mettle,** ready to do one's best. [var. of *metal*]

**mewl** (myül), *v.* cry like a baby; whimper. [imitative]

**mid dy** (mid′ē), *n., pl.* **-dies.** middy blouse.

**middy blouse,** a loose blouse like a sailor's.

**min e stro ne** (min′ə strō′nē), *n.* a thick soup containing vegetables, vermicelli, etc. [< Ital.]

**mi nute** (mī nüt′ or mī nyüt′), *adj.* 1. very small. 2. going into or concerned with very small details: *a minute observer, minute instructions.* [< L *minutus* made small < *minus* less] **—Syn.** 1. tiny, diminutive, little. 2. detailed, particular.

**mi nute ly** (mī nüt′lē or mī nyüt′lē), *adv.* in minute manner, form, degree, or detail.

**mi rage** (mə räzh′), *n.* 1. a misleading appearance, usually in the desert or at sea, resulting from a reflection of some distant scene in such a way as to give the impression that it is near. 2. illusion; thing that does not exist. [< F *mirage* < *mirer* look at carefully, se′ *mirer* look at oneself in a mirror, see reflected < L *mirare,* var. of *mirari* wonder (at), admire]

**mode** (mōd), *n.* 1. manner or way in which a thing is done. 2. style, fashion, or custom that prevails; the way most people are doing.

**mod i cum** (mod′ə kəm), *n.* a small or moderate quantity. [< L *modicum,* neut., moderate < *modus* measure]

**mo men tous** (mō men′təs), *adj.* very important. **—Syn.** weighty, serious, critical.

**mon o lith** (mon′ə lith), *n.* 1. a single large block of stone. 2. monument, column, statue, etc., formed of a single large block of stone. [< L < Gk. *monolithos* < *monos* single + *lithos* stone]

**mon o lith ic** (mon′ə lith′ik), *adj.* of a monolith; being a monolith.

**mon o nu cle o sis** (mon′ə nü′klē ō′sis or mon′ə nyü′klē ō′sis), *n.* a disease characterized by fever and enlargement of the lymph nodes.

**moon shin er** (mün′shīn′ər), *n. U.S. Informal.* 1. person who makes intoxicating liquor contrary to law. 2. person who follows an unlawful trade at night.

**moor ing** (mür′ing), *n. usu. pl.* 1. ropes, cables, anchors, etc., by which a ship is fastened. 2. place where a ship is moored.

**mo rale** (mə ral′ or mə räl′), *n.* moral or mental condition as regards courage, confidence, enthusiasm, etc.: *the morale of troops.* [< F *morale,* fem. of *moral* moral]

**mo rose** (mə rōs′), *adj.* gloomy; sullen; ill-humored. [< L *morosus,* originally, set in one's ways < *mos* habit]

**Mount ie** or **Mount y** (moun′tē or moun′ti), *n., pl.* **-ies.** a member of the Royal Canadian Mounted Police.

**mul ti cel lu lar** (mul′ti sel′yə lər), *adj.* having more than one cell.

**mus ter** (mus′tər), *n.* 1. assembly; collection. 2. bringing together of men or troops for review or service.

**mut ton** (mut′n), *n.* meat from a sheep. [< OF *mouton* < Med.L *multo* ram < Celtic]

**na stur tium** (nə stėr′shəm), *n.* 1. plant with yellow, orange, and red flowers, and sharp-tasting seeds and leaves. 2. the flower. [< L *nasturtium* < *nasus* nose + *torquere* twist; from pungent odor]

**naught** (nôt), *n.* 1. nothing. 2. zero; 0. Also, **nought.** [OE *nāwiht* < *nā* no + *wiht* wight]

**neb u lous** (neb′yə ləs), *adj.* 1. hazy; vague; confused. 2. cloudlike. [< L *nebulosus* < *nebula* mist]

**ne gate** (ni gāt′ or nē′gāt), *v.,* **-gat ed, -gat ing.** deny; nullify. [< L *negare* say no]

**neg li gi ble** (neg′lə jə bl), *adj.* that can be disregarded: *In buying a suit, a difference of ten cents in prices is negligible.*

**neth er** (neᴛʜ′ər), *adj.* lower.

**nim ble** (nim′bl), *adj.,* **-bler, -blest.** 1. active and sure-footed; light and quick; quick-moving: *Goats are nimble in climbing among the rocks.* 2. quick to understand and to reply; clever: *a nimble mind.* **—nim′bly,** *adv.*

**nin ny** (nin′ē), *n., pl.* **-nies.** fool.

**noi some** (noi′səm), *adj.* 1. offensive; disgusting; smelling bad: *a noisome slum.* 2. harmful; injurious: *a noisome pestilence.* **—noi′some ly,** *adv.*

**nom i nal** (nom′ə nl), *adj.* 1. being so in name only; not real: *The president is the nominal head of the club, but the secretary really runs its affairs.* 2. so small that it is not worth considering; unimportant compared with the real value: *We paid a nominal rent for the cottage—$5 a month.* [< L *nominalis* < *nomen* name]

**non cha lant** (non′shə lənt or non′shə länt′), *adj.* without enthusiasm; coolly unconcerned; indifferent. [< F *nonchalant* < *non-* not < L) + *chaloir* be warm < L *calere*] **—non′cha lant ly,** *adv.*

**non com pli ance** (non′kəm plī′əns), *n.* fact of not complying; failure to comply.

**no ve na** (nō vē′nə), *n., pl.* **-nas, -nae** (-nē). in the Roman Catholic Church, a religious exercise consisting of prayers or services on nine days, or sometimes nine corresponding days in consecutive months: *a novena of nine first Fridays.* [< Med.L *novena,* ult. < L *novem* nine]

**nub bin** (nub′ən), *n.* 1. a small lump or piece. 2. *U.S.* a small or imperfect ear of corn. 3. an undeveloped fruit.

**nup tial** (nup′shəl), *adj.* of marriage or weddings. **—n. nuptials,** *pl.* a wedding; the wedding ceremony. [< L *nuptialis,* ult. < *nubere* take a husband]

**o bese** (ō bēs′), *adj.* extremely fat. [< L *obesus* < *ob-* in addition + *edere* eat]

**o bliv i ous** (ə bliv′ē əs), *adj.* 1. not mindful: *The book was so interesting that I was oblivious of my surroundings.* 2. bringing or causing forgetfulness. [< L *obliviosus*] **—ob liv′i ous ly,** *adv.* **—Syn.** 1. unmindful, heedless.

**ob scure** (əb skyür′), *adj.,* **-scur er, -scur est.** 1. not expressing meaning clearly. 2. not easily discovered; hidden: *an obscure path, an obscure meaning.* 3. not distinct; not clear: *an obscure form, obscure sounds, an obscure view.* [< OF < L *obscurus* < *ob-*over + *scur-*cover] **—ob scure′ly,** *adv.*

**ob se quies** (ob′sə kwēz), *n.pl.* funeral rites or ceremonies; stately funeral. [< Med.L *obsequiae,* pl., for L *exsequiae* < *ex-*out + *sequi* follow]

**ob trude** (əb trüd′), *v.,* **-trud ed, -trud ing.** 1. put forward unasked and unwanted; force: *Don't obtrude your opinions on others.* 2. come unasked and unwanted; force oneself; intrude. 3. push out; thrust forward: *A turtle obtrudes its head from its shell.* [< L *obtrudere* < *ob-* toward + *trudere* to thrust]

**O'Connor** (ō kon′ər), *n.* **Frank** (*Michael Donovan*), 1903-1966, Irish writer.

**off ing** (ôf′ing or of′ing), *n.* 1. the more distant part of the sea as seen from the shore. 2. position at a distance from the shore. 3. **in the offing, a.** just visible from the shore. **b.** within sight. **c.** not far off.

**o gre** (ō′gər), *n.* giant or monster that supposedly eats people. [< F]

**o men** (ō′mən), *n.* 1. sign of what is to happen; object or event that is believed to mean good or bad fortune: *Spilling salt is said to be an omen of misfortune.* 2. prophetic meaning: *Some people consider a black cat a creature of ill omen.* [< L]

**om i nous** (om′ə nəs), *adj.* of bad omen; unfavorable; threatening: *Those clouds look ominous for our picnic.* [< L *ominosus* < *omen* omen] **—om′i nous ly,** *adv.*

**om nip o tent** (om nip′ə tənt), *adj.* having all power; almighty. [< L *omnipotens, -entis* < *omnis* all + *potens* being able] **—om nip′o tent ly,** *adv.*

**o paque** (ō pāk′), *adj.* 1. not letting light through; not transparent. 2. not shining; dark; dull. 3. obscure; hard to understand. **—n.** something opaque. [< L *opacus* dark, shady] **—o paque′ness,** *n.*

**o pi ate** (ō′pē it or ō′pē āt), *n.* 1. drug that contains opium and so dulls pain or brings sleep. 2. anything that quiets. [< Med.L *opiatus* < L *opium* opium]

**op pres sion** (ə presh′ən), *n.* 1. an oppressing; a burdening: *The oppression of the people by the nobles caused the war.* 2. cruel or unjust treatment. 3. a heavy, weary feeling.

**orb** (ôrb), *n.* 1. sphere; globe. 2. sun,

moon, planet, or star. 3. *Esp. Poetic.* eyeball or eye. [< L *orbis* circle]

**ore** (ôr or ōr), *n.* rock, sand, or dirt containing some metal. [OE *ār* brass]

**or gi as tic** (ôr′jē as′tik), *adj.* of, having to do with, or of the nature of orgies; wild; frenzied.

**or gy** (ôr′jē), *n., pl.* **-gies.** 1. a wild, drunken revel. 2. period of uncontrolled indulgence. [< L < Gk. *orgia* secret rites]

**o ri en ta tion** (ô′rē en tā′shən or ō′rē en tā′shən), *n.* a finding out of the actual facts or conditions and putting oneself in the right relation to them.

**o ri son** (ôr′ə zən), *n. Archaic or Poetic.* prayer. [< OF < LL *oratio, -onis* prayer < L *oratio* speech < *orare* pray]

**or tho dox** (ôr′thə doks), *adj.* 1. having generally accepted views or opinions, especially in religion. 2. approved by convention; usual; customary: *the orthodox Christmas dinner of turkey and plum pudding.* [< LL < Gk. *orthodoxos* < *orthos* correct + *doxa* opinion < *dokein* think]

**os cil late** (os′l āt), *v.,* **-lat ed, -lat ing.** 1. swing to and fro like a pendulum; move to and fro between two points. 2. cause to swing to and fro. 3. vary between opinions, purposes, etc. [< L *oscillare*]

**os ten si bly** (os ten′sə blē), *adv.* apparently; on the face of it; as openly stated or shown.

**pag eant ry** (paj′ənt rē), *n., pl.* **-ries.** 1. a splendid show; gorgeous display; pomp. 2. mere show; empty display.

**pa la tial** (pə lā′shəl), *adj.* like a palace; fit for a palace; magnificent. [< L *palatium* palace]

**pa lav er** (pə lav′ər or pə lä′vər), *n.* 1. parley or conference, especially between travelers and uncivilized natives. 2. talk. 3. smooth, persuading talk; fluent talk; flattery. —*v.* 1. talk. 2. talk fluently or flatteringly. [< Pg. *palavra* < L *parabola* story, parable]

**pal lor** (pal′ər), *n.* lack of color from fear, illness, death, etc.; paleness. [< L]

**pal met to** (pal met′ō), *n., pl.* **-tos** or **-toes.** any of several kinds of palm trees with fan-shaped leaves, abundant on the SE coast of the U.S. [Am.E; < Sp. *palmito,* dim. of *palma* palm]

**pal pa ble** (pal′pə bl), *adj.* 1. readily seen or heard and recognized; obvious: *a palpable error.* 2. that can be touched or felt. [< LL *palpabilis* < L *palpare* feel] —**Syn.** tangible.

**pan pipe** (pan′pīp′), *n.* an early musical instrument made of reeds or tubes of different lengths, fastened together in order of their length. The reeds or tubes were closed at one end; the player blew across their tops.

**pan to mime** (pan′tə mīm), *n.* 1. a play without words, in which the actors express themselves by gestures. 2. gestures without words. [< L < Gk. *pantomimos* < *pas, pantos* all + *mimos* mimic]

**pa paw** (pô′pô), *n.* 1. a small North American tree bearing oblong, yellowish, edible fruit with many beanlike seeds. 2. this fruit. 3. papaya. Also, **pawpaw.** [Am.E; < Sp. *papaya*]

**par a dox i cal** (par′ə dok′sə kl), *adj.* of paradoxes; involving a statement that may be true but seems to say two opposite things; involving a contradiction. —**par′a dox′i cal ly,** *adv.*

**par a mour** (par′ə mùr), *n.* 1. person who takes the place of a husband or wife illegally. 2. *Archaic.* lover. [< OF *paramour* < *par amour* by love < L *per amorem*]

**par a sol** (par′ə sôl or par′ə sol), *n.* umbrella used as a protection from the sun. [< F < Ital. *parasole* < *para* ward off! + *sole* sun]

**parch ment** (pärch′mənt), *n.* 1. the skin of sheep, goats, etc., prepared for use as a writing material. 2. manuscript or document written on parchment. 3. paper that looks like parchment. [< OF *parchemin* < VL *particaminum* (influenced by *parthica pellis* Parthian leather) < LL < Gk. *pergamene* < *Pergamon* Pergamum, whence it came]

**Par os** (par′os or per′os), *n.* a Greek island in the Aegean Sea, noted for its beautiful, white marble. 9000 pop.; 13 mi. long; 10 mi. wide.

**pas ta** (pä′stə), *n.* any of various flour-and-egg food preparations of Italian origin, usually served with a sauce.

**pa tron ize** (pā′trən īz or pat′rən īz), *v.,* **-ized, -iz ing.** 1. be a regular customer of; give regular business to. 2. act as a patron toward; support or protect. 3. treat in a condescending way. —**pa′tron iz′ing ly,** *adv.*

**paunch** (pônch or pänch), *n.* 1. belly; stomach. 2. a large, protruding belly.

**pawn** (pôn), *v.* leave (something) with another person as security that borrowed money will be repaid: *He pawned his watch to buy food until he could get work.* [< n.] —*n.* 1. something left as security. 2. place where something is pawned. 3. a pledge. [< OF *pan*]

**peal** (pēl), *n.* 1. a loud, long sound: *a peal of thunder, peals of laughter.* 2. the loud ringing of bells. —*v.* sound out in a peal; ring: *The bells pealed forth their message of Christmas joy.* [ME *pele*]

**pec tor al** (pek′tər əl), *adj.* of, in, or on the breast or chest. [< L *pectoralis* < *pectus* chest]

**peer** (pir), *n.* 1. person of the same rank, ability, etc., as another; equal. 2. man who has a title; man who is high and great by birth or rank. [< OF *per* < L *par* equal]

**pee vish** (pē′vish), *adj.* cross; fretful; complaining.

**pelvic girdle,** a bony arch that supports the hind limbs of an animal having a backbone.

**pen ance** (pen′əns), *n.* punishment borne to show sorrow for sin, to make up for a wrong done, and to obtain pardon. [< OF *pen(e)ance* < L *paenitentia* penitence]

**pen sive** (pen′siv), *adj.* 1. thoughtful in a serious or sad way. 2. melancholy. [< OF *pensif* < *penser* think < L *pensare* weigh, ponder < *pendere* weigh] —**pen′sive ly,** *adv.*

hat, āge, fär; let, ēqual, tėrm; it, īce; hot, ōpen, ôrder; oil, out; cup, pùt, rüle; ch, child; ng, long; sh, she; th, thin; ᴛн, then; zh, measure;

ə represents *a* in about, *e* in taken, *i* in pencil, *o* in lemon, *u* in circus.

< = from, derived from, taken from.

**Pen te cost** (pen′tə kôst or pen′tə kost), *n.* 1. the seventh Sunday after Easter. Pentecost is a Christian festival in memory of the descent of the Holy Ghost upon the Apostles. Also called **Whitsunday.** 2. a Jewish religious holiday, observed about seven weeks after the Passover, celebrating the harvest and also the giving of the law to Moses. [< L *pentecoste* < Gk. *pentekoste (hemera)* fiftieth (day)]

**pen ur y** (pen′yər ē), *n.* great poverty. [< L *penuria*]

**per cap i ta** (pər kap′ə tə), for each person: *$40 for eight men is $5 per capita.* [< L]

**pe ren ni al** (pə ren′ē əl), *adj.* 1. lasting through the whole year: *a perennial stream.* 2. lasting for a very long time; enduring: *the perennial beauty of the hills.* [< L *perennis* lasting < *per-* through + *annus* year] —**per en′ni al ly,** *adv.*

**per force** (pər fôrs′ or pər fōrs′), *adv.* by necessity; necessarily. [< F *par* by + *force*]

**per jured** (pėr′jərd), *adj.* guilty of perjury.

**per jur y** (pėr′jər ē), *n., pl.* **-ries.** act of swearing that something is true which one knows to be false. [< AF *perjurie* < L *perjurium* < *perjurare*]

**per me ate** (pėr′mē āt), *v.,* **-at ed, -at ing.** 1. spread through the whole of; pass through; soak through: *Smoke permeated the house.* 2. penetrate: *Water will easily permeate a cotton dress.* [< L *permeare* < *per-* through + *meare* to pass]

**per ni cious** (pər nish′əs), *adj.* 1. that will destroy or ruin; causing great harm or damage: *Gambling is a pernicious habit.* 2. fatal: *perniciosus,* ult. < *per-* + *nex* death] —**per ni′cious ly,** *adv.* —**Syn.** 1. injurious, noxious.

**pe rox ide** (pe rok′sid), *v.,* **-id ed, -id ing.** bleach (hair) by applying hydrogen peroxide.

**per pe trate** (pėr′pə trāt), *v.,* **-trat ed, -trat ing.** do or commit (crime, fraud, trick, or anything bad or foolish). [< L *perpetrare* < *per-* (intensive) + *patrare* perform] —**per′pe tra′tion,** *n.* —**per′pe tra′tor,** *n.*

**per plex** (pər pleks′), *v.* 1. trouble with doubt; puzzle; bewilder. 2. make difficult to understand or settle; confuse. [originally adj., < L *perplexus* confused < *per-* completely + *plectere* intertwine] —**per plex′ing ly,** *adv.*

**per qui site** (pėr′kwə zit), *n.* anything received for work besides the regular pay:

*The maid had the old dresses of her mistress as a perquisite.* [< Med.L *perquisitum* (thing) gained, ult. < L *per-* carefully + *quaerere* seek]

**pe ruse** (pə rüz′), *v.,* **-rused, -rus ing.** 1. read through carefully. 2. read. [originally, use up < L *per-* to the end + E *use*]

**per verse** (pər vèrs′), *adj.* 1. contrary and willful; stubborn: *The perverse child did just what we told him not to do.* 2. persistent in wrong. 3. wicked. —**perverse′ly,** *adv.*

**per ver si ty** (pər vèr′sə tē), *n., pl.* **-ties.** 1. quality of being perverse. 2. perverse character or conduct.

**pes ti lence** (pes′tə ləns), *n.* disease that spreads rapidly, causing many deaths. Smallpox, yellow fever, and the plague are pestilences. —**Syn.** epidemic, pest.

**pet u lant** (pech′ə lənt), *adj.* peevish; subject to little fits of bad temper; irritable over trifles. [< L *petulans, -antis,* ult. < *petere* seek, aim at] —**pet′u lant ly,** *adv.*

**pha lanx** (fā′langks or fal′angks), *n., pl.* **pha lanx es, pha lan ges** (fə lan′jēz). 1. in ancient Greece, a special battle formation of infantry fighting in close ranks with their shields joined and long spears overlapping each other. 2. a compact or closely massed body of persons, animals, or things. 3. number of persons united for a common purpose. [< L < Gk.]

**phan tas ma go ri a** (fan taz′mə gô′rē ə or fan taz′mə gō′rē ə), *n.* 1. a shifting scene of real things, illusions, imaginary fancies, deceptions, and the like: *the phantasmagoria of a dream.* 2. show of optical illusions in which figures increase or decrease in size, fade away, and pass into each other. —**phan tas′ma go′ric,** *adj.* [< Gk. *phantasma* image + ? *agora* assembly]

**phi lan thro pist** (fə lan′thrə pist), *n.* person who shows his love for mankind by practical kindness and helpfulness to humanity.

**phlox** (floks), *n.* 1. plant with clusters of showy flowers in various colors. 2. the flower. [< L < Gk. *phlox,* a kind of plant literally, flame]

**phys ics** (fiz′iks), *n.* science that deals with matter and energy and their interrelationship in the studies of mechanics, heat, light, sound, and electricity. [pl. of *physic* (= *ta physika* the natural things)]

**pi az za** (pē az′ə), *n.* 1. *U.S.* a large porch along one or more sides of a house. 2. an open public square in Italian towns. [< Ital. *piazza* < L < Gk. *plateia (hodos)* broad (way)]

**pi e ty** (pī′ə tē), *n., pl.* **-ties.** being pious; reverence for God; devotion to religion. [< OF *piete* < L *pietas* < *pius* pious]

**pig Latin,** an English slang in which the first consonant or combination of consonants is deleted from the beginning of each word and added to its end with an additional *ay,* thus forming a new syllable: *Eadray the ueblay ookbay irstfay* means *read the blue book first.*

**pike** (pīk), *n.* a long wooden shaft with a sharp-pointed metal head; spear. Foot soldiers used to carry pikes. [< F *pique* < *piquer* pierce < *pic* a pick < Gmc.]

**pil grim age** (pil′grə mij), *n.* 1. a pilgrim's journey; journey to some sacred place as an act of religious devotion. 2. a long journey. 3. life thought of as a journey.

**pil lage** (pil′ij), *v.,* **-laged, -lag ing,** *n.* —*v.* rob with violence; plunder: *Pirates pillaged the towns along the coast.* —*n.* plunder; robbery.

**pimp** (pimp), *n.* person who helps other people indulge low desires, passions, or vices. —*v.* act as a pimp; supply material or opportunity for vices.

**pince-nez** (pans′nā′ or pins′nā′), *n.* eyeglasses kept in place by a spring that pinches the nose. [< F *pince-nez* pinch-nose]

**pine** (pīn), *v.,* **pined, pin ing.** 1. long eagerly; yearn. 2. waste away with pain, hunger, grief, or desire. [OE *pīnian* < *pīn,* *n.,* torture < L *poena* penalty < Gk. *poine*]

**pin na cle** (pin′ə kl), *n.* 1. a high peak or point of rock. 2. the highest point: *at the pinnacle of his fame.* 3. a slender tower or spire. [< OF < L *pinnaculum,* dim. of *pinna* wing, point]

**pi ous** (pī′əs), *adj.* 1. having or showing reverence for God; religious. 2. done or used from real or pretended religious motives. 3. *Archaic.* dutiful to parents. [< L *pius*] —**pi′ous ly,** *adv.*

**pit e ous** (pit′ē əs), *adj.* to be pitied; moving the heart; deserving pity. [< OF *pitos* < Med.L *pietosus* pitiful < L *pietas* pity; influenced in form by ME *pite* pity] —**pit′e ous ly,** *adv.*

**pi ton** (pē′ton, pē′tōn, or *esp. Fr.* pē tôN′), *n.* a metal spike, with an eye through which a rope may be passed, used for mountain climbing.

**plac ard** (plak′ärd), *n.* notice to be posted in a public place; poster. [< F *placard* < *plaque* plaque]

**plac er** (plas′ər), *n.* place where gold or other minerals can be washed out of loose sand or gravel. [Am.E; < Am. Sp. *placer* sandbank]

**plac id** (plas′id), *adj.* calm; peaceful; quiet: *a placid lake.* [< L *placidus* < *placere* please] —**plac′id ly,** *adv.*

**plait** (plāt or plat), *n., v.* braid. [< OF *pleit,* ult. < L *plicare* to fold]

**pla teau** (pla tō′), *n., pl.* **-teaus** or **-teaux** (-tōz′). 1. plain in the mountains or at a height above the sea; large, high plain. 2. a stable level of progress, population, ability, etc. [< F < OF *platel,* dim. of *plat* flat < VL *plattus*]

**plow share** (plou′shar′ or plou′ sher′), *n.* blade of a plow, the part that cuts the soil. Also, **ploughshare.**

**plum duff,** a flour pudding with raisins or currants in it, boiled in a cloth bag.

**poise** (poiz), *v.,* **poised, pois ing.** 1. balance: *Poise yourself on your toes.* 2. hold or carry evenly or steadily: *The athlete poised the weight in the air before throwing it.* [< OF *peser* weigh < L *pensare,* intensive of *pendere* weigh]

**Pol y ne sia** (pol′ə nē′zhə or pol′ə-nē′shə), *n.* group of many small islands in the Pacific, east of Australia and the Philippines. [< Gk. *polys* many + *nesos* island]

**po made** (pə mād′ or pə mäd′), *n.* a perfumed ointment for the scalp and hair. [< F < Ital. *pomata* < L *pomum* fruit]

**pom pous** (pom′pəs), *adj.* 1. trying to seem magnificent; fond of display; acting proudly; self-important: *The leader of the band bowed in a pompous manner.* 2. splendid; magnificent; stately. —**pom′pous ly,** *adv.*

**pon der ous** (pon′dər əs), *adj.* 1. very heavy. 2. heavy and clumsy. 3. dull; tiresome: *The speaker talked in a ponderous way.* [< L *ponderosus* < *pondus* weight] —**pon′der ous ly,** *adv.*

**por ten tous** (pôr ten′təs or pōr ten′təs), *adj.* 1. indicating evil to come; ominous; threatening. 2. amazing; extraordinary.

**port fo li o** (pôrt fō′lē ō or pōrt fō′lē ō), *n., pl.* **-li os.** briefcase; portable case for loose papers, drawings, etc. [< Ital. *portafoglio,* ult. < L *portare* carry + *folium* sheet, leaf]

**pos ter i ty** (pos ter′ə tē), *n.* 1. generations of the future: *If we burn up all the coal in the world, what will posterity do?* 2. all of a person's descendants.

**po tent** (pōt′nt), *adj.* 1. powerful; having great power: *a potent remedy for a disease.* 2. exercising great moral influence. [< L *potens, -entis,* ppr. of unrecorded OL *potere* be powerful] —**po′tent ly,** *adv.* —**Syn.** 1. mighty, strong.

**poult** (pōlt), *n.* a young chicken, turkey, pheasant, grouse, or other fowl. [< ME *pulte* young fowl < *polet* young chicken, young fowl]

**poul tice** (pōl′tis), *n.* a soft, moist mass of mustard, herbs, etc., applied to the body as a medicine. [ult. < L *pultes,* pl. of *puls* mush]

**powder horn,** powder flask made of an animal's horn.

**pre car i ous** (pri kar′ē əs or pri ker′ē-əs), *adj.* not safe or secure; uncertain; dangerous; risky: *A soldier leads a precarious life.* [< L *precarius,* originally, obtainable by entreaty, ult. < *prex* prayer] —**pre car′i ous ly,** *adv.*

**pred a to ry** (pred′ə tô′rē or pred′ə-tō′rē), *adj.* 1. of or inclined to plundering or robbery: *Predatory tramps infested the highways.* 2. preying upon other animals. Hawks and owls are predatory birds. [< L *praedatorius,* ult. < *praeda* prey]

**pred e ces sor** (pred′ə ses′ər), *n.* 1. person holding a position or office before another: *John Adams was Jefferson's predecessor as President.* 2. thing that came before another. 3. ancestor; forefather. [< LL *praedecessor,* ult. < *prae-* before + *decedere* retire < *de-* from + *cedere* withdraw]

**pre dom i nant** (pri dom′ə nənt), *adj.* 1. having more power, authority, or influence than others; superior. 2. prevailing; most noticeable. —**pre dom′i nant ly,** *adv.*

**pre med i tate** (prē med′ə tāt), *v.,* **-tated, -tat ing.** consider or plan beforehand: *The murder was premeditated.* [< L praemeditari < prae- before + meditari meditate]

**pre rog a tive** (pri rog′ə tiv), *n.* right or privilege that nobody else has: *The government has the prerogative of coining money.* —*adj.* having or exercising a prerogative. [< L *praerogativa*, originally fem. adj., asked to vote first, ult. < *prae-* before + *rogare* ask]

**pres age** (pri sāj′), *v.*, **pre saged**, **pre sag ing.** 1. give warning of; predict: *Some people think that a circle around the moon presages a storm.* 2. have or give a prophetic impression (of). [< L *praesagium*, ult. < *prae-* before + *sagus* prophetic]

**pres tige** (pres tēzh′ or pres′tij), *n.* reputation, influence, or distinction based on what is known of one's abilities, achievements, opportunities, associations, etc. [< F *prestige* magic spell, ult. < L *praestigiae* tricks]

**pre sump tion** (pri zump′shən), *n.* 1. thing taken for granted: *Since he had the stolen jewels, the presumption was that he was the thief.* 2. cause or reason for presuming; probability. 3. unpleasant boldness: *It is presumption to go to a party when one has not been invited.*

**pre sump tu ous** (pri zump′chü əs), *adj.* acting without permission or right; too bold; forward. —**pre sump′tu ous ly,** *adv.* —**Syn.** overbold, impudent, arrogant.

**pro cure** (prə kyùr′), *v.*,**-cured, -cur ing.** 1. obtain by care or effort; get: *A friend procured a position in the bank for my big brother.* 2. bring about; cause: *procure a person's death.* [< L *procurare* manage, ult. < *pro-* before + *cura* care]

**pro di gious** (prə dij′əs), *adj.* 1. very great; huge; vast: *The ocean contains a prodigious amount of water.* 2. wonderful; marvelous. [< L *prodigiosus* < *prodigium* prodigy, omen] —**pro di′gious ly,** *adv.*

**pro fane** (prə fān′), *v.*, **-faned, -fan ing.** 1. treat (holy things) with contempt or disregard: *Soldiers profaned the church when they stabled their horses in it.* 2. put to wrong or unworthy use. [< F < L *profanus* not sacred < *pro-* in front (outside) of + *fanum* shrine] —**pro fane′ly,** *adv.*

**pro found** (prə found′), *adj.* 1. very deep: *a profound sigh, a profound sleep.* 2. deeply felt; very great: *profound despair, profound sympathy.* 3. going far deeper than what is easily understood; having or showing great knowledge or understanding: *a profound book, a profound thinker, a profound thought.* 4. low; carried far down; going far down: *a profound bow.* [< OF < L *profundus* < *pro-* at some distance + *fundus* bottom] —**pro found′ly,** *adv.* —**pro found′ness,** *n.*

**pro hi bi tion** (prō′ə bish′ən), *n.* 1. act of prohibiting or forbidding. 2. law or order that prohibits.

**pro logue** or **pro log** (prō′lôg or prō′log), *n.* 1. speech or poem addressed to the audience by one of the actors at the beginning of a play. 2. introduction to a novel, poem, or other literary work. 3. any introductory act or event. [< L < Gk. *prologos* < *pro-* before + *logos* speech]

**prom i nent** (prom′ə nənt), *adj.*
1. well-known; important: *a prominent citizen.* 2. standing out; projecting; easy to see: *Some insects have prominent eyes.* [< L *prominens, -entis,* ppr. of *prominere* project < *pro-* forward + *men-* jut] —**prom′i nent ly,** *adv.*

**prop,** proprietor.

**prop a gate** (prop′ə gāt), *v.*, **-gat ed, -gat ing.** 1. produce offspring. 2. reproduce. 3. increase in number. 4. spread (news, knowledge, etc.): *Don't propagate unkind reports.* —**prop′a ga′tor,** *n.* —**Syn.** 3. multiply. 4. extend, diffuse.

**pro pen si ty** (prə pen′sə tē), *n., pl.* **-ties.** a natural inclination or bent; inclination: *Most boys have a propensity for playing with machinery.* [< L *propensus* inclined < *pro-* forward + *pendere* hang]

**pro pri e tor** (prə prī′ə tər), *n.* owner.

**pros pect** (pros′pekt), *n.* 1. thing expected or looked forward to. 2. act of looking forward; expectation: *The prospect of a vacation is pleasant.* 3. outlook for the future. [< L *prospectus,* ult. < *pro-* forward + *specere* to look] —**Syn.** 2. anticipation.

**pros trate** (pros′trāt), *v.*, **-trat ed, -trat ing.** 1. lay down flat; cast down. 2. make very weak or helpless; exhaust: *Sickness often prostrates people.* —*adj.* 1. lying flat with face downward. 2. lying flat. 3. overcome; helpless: *a prostrate enemy.* [< L *prostratus,* pp. of *prosternere* < *pro-* forth + *sternere* strew]

**pro tract** (prō trakt′), *v.* 1. draw out; lengthen in time: *protract a visit.* 2. slide out; thrust out; extend. [< L *protractus,* pp. of *protrahere* < *pro-* forward + *trahere* drag]

**prov i dence** (prov′ə dəns), *n.* 1. God's care and help. 2. instance of God's care and help. 3. **Providence.** God.

**prov i den tial** (prov′ə den′shəl), *adj.* 1. fortunate: *Our delay seemed providential, for the train we had planned to take was wrecked.* 2. of or proceeding from divine power or influence. —**prov′i den′tial ly,** *adv.*

**prow** (prou), *n.* the pointed front part of a ship or boat; bow.

**prow ess** (prou′is), *n.* 1. bravery; daring. 2. brave or daring acts. 3. unusual skill or ability. [< OF *proece* < *prod* valiant] —**Syn.** 1. courage, valor.

**pru dence** (prüd′ns), *n.* 1. wise thought before acting; good judgment. 2. good management; economy.

**pru dent** (prüd′nt), *adj.* planning carefully ahead of time; sensible; discreet: *A prudent man saves part of his wages.* —**pru′dent ly,** *adv.* —**Syn.** judicious, wise, cautious.

**pseu do** (sü′dō), *adj.* 1. false; sham; pretended. 2. having only the appearance of. [< Gk. *pseudes* false]

**psy chic** (sī′kik), *adj.* 1. of the soul or mind; mental: *illness due to psychic causes.* 2. outside the known laws of physics; supernatural. A psychic force or influence is believed by spiritualists to explain second sight, telepathy, table moving, tappings, etc. [< Gk. *psychikos* < *psyche* soul, mind]

hat, āge, fär; let, ēqual, tėrm; it, īce; hot, ōpen, ôrder; oil, out; cup, pùt, rüle; ch, child; ng, long; sh, she; th, thin; ŦH, then; zh, measure;

ə represents *a* in about, *e* in taken, *i* in pencil, *o* in lemon, *u* in circus.

< = from, derived from, taken from.

**psy chi cal** (sī′kə kl), *adj.* psychic.

**pul let** (pùl′it), *n.* a young hen, usually less than a year old. [< OF *poulette,* dim. of *poule* hen < VL *pulla,* fem. to L *pullus* young fowl]

**pum ice** (pum′is), *n.* a light, spongy stone thrown up from volcanoes, used for cleaning, smoothing, and polishing.

**pur ga to ry** (pėr′gə tô′rē or pėr′gə tō′rē), *n., pl.* **-ries.** 1. in the belief of the Roman Catholics, a temporary condition or place in which the souls of those who have died penitent are purified from venial sin or the effects of sin by punishment. 2. any condition or place of temporary suffering or punishment. [< Med.L *purgatorium,* originally neut. adj., purging < L *purgare.* See PURGE.]

**purge** (pėrj), *v.*, **purged, purg ing.** 1. wash away all that is not clean from; make clean. 2. become clean. 3. clear of any undesired thing or person, such as air in a water pipe or opponents in a nation. 4. empty (the bowels). [< OF < L *purgare* cleanse, ult. < *purus* pure + *agere* drive]

**pu tre fac tion** (pyü′trə fak′shən), *n.* decay; rotting.

**py ri tes** (pī rī′tēz, pə rī′tēz, or pī′rīts), *n.* iron pyrites, a mineral which has a yellow color and glitters so that it suggests gold; fool's gold. [< L < Gk. *pyrites* flint < *pyr* fire]

**quail** (kwāl), *v.* be afraid; lose courage; shrink back in fear: *The slave quailed at his master's look.* —**Syn.** quake, cower, flinch.

**quar ry**[1] (kwôr′ē or kwor′ē), *n., pl.* **-ries,** *v.,* **-ried, -ry ing.** —*n.* place where stone is dug, cut, or blasted out for use in building. —*v.* obtain from a quarry.

**quar ry**[2] (kwôr′ē or kwor′ē), *n., pl.* **-ries.** 1. animal chased in a hunt; game; prey. 2. anything hunted or eagerly pursued.

**quell** (kwel), *v.* 1. put down (disorder, rebellion, etc.): *quell a riot.* 2. put an end to; overcome: *quell one's fears.* [OE *cwellan* kill]

**quid** (kwid), *n., pl.* **quid.** *Brit. Slang.* one pound, or 20 shillings (about $2.60, as of 1972).

**quince** (kwins), *n.* 1. a hard, yellowish acid fruit, used for preserves. 2. tree it grows on.

**quip** (kwip), *n.* 1. a clever or witty saying. 2. a sharp, cutting remark. 3. something odd or strange. [for earlier *quippy* < L *quippe* indeed!, I dare say]

**quiv er** (kwiv′ər), *n.* case to hold arrows. [< AF *quiveir* probably < Gmc.]

**ram part** (ram′pärt), *n.* 1. a wide bank of earth, often with a wall on top, built around a fort to help defend it. 2. anything that defends; defense; protection. [< F *rempart* < *remparer* fortify, ult. < L *re-* back + *ante* before + *parare* prepare]

**ran cid** (ran′sid), *adj.* 1. stale; spoiled: *rancid fat.* 2. tasting or smelling like stale fat or butter. [< L *rancidus* < *rancere* be rank]

**ran cor** (rang′kər), *n.* bitter resentment or ill will; extreme hatred or spite. [< OF < LL *rancor* rankness < L *rancere* be rank] —**Syn.** malice, animosity.

**rank** (rangk), *adj.* 1. large and coarse: *rank grass.* 2. growing richly. 3. producing a dense but coarse growth: *rank swamp land.* 4. having a strong, bad smell or taste: *rank meat, rank tobacco.* [OE *ranc* proud] —**rank′ly,** *adv.*

**ra pi er** (rā′pē ər), *n.* a light sword used for thrusting.

**rap tor** (rap′tər), *n.* a bird of prey.

**ra tion al** (rash′ən l or rash′nəl), *adj.* 1. sensible; reasonable; reasoned out: *When very angry, people seldom act in a rational way.* 2. able to think and reason clearly. 3. of reason; based on reasoning. —*n.* quality of being rational; sense; reason. —**ra′tion al ly,** *adv.*

**rav age** (rav′ij), *v.,* **-aged, -ag ing.** lay waste; damage greatly; destroy: *The forest fire ravaged many miles of country.* [< F *ravager* < *ravir* ravish]

**re ac tion ar y** (rē ak′shən er′ē), *adj., n., pl.* **-ar ies.** —*adj.* having to do with, marked by, or favoring reaction. —*n.* person who favors reaction, especially in politics.

**re al ist** (rē′əl ist), *n.* 1. person interested in what is real and practical rather than what is imaginary or theoretical. 2. writer or artist who represents things as they are in real life.

**re buke** (ri byūk′), *v.,* **-buked, -buk ing.** express disapproval of; reprove. [< AF *rebuker.* Cf. OF *rebuchier* < *re-* back + *buchier* to strike] —**re buk′ing ly,** *adv.* —**Syn.** reprimand, censure.

**re cede** (ri sēd′), *v.,* **-ced ed, -ced ing.** 1. go backward; move backward. 2. slope backward: *He has a chin that recedes.* 3. withdraw: *He receded from the agreement.* [< L *recedere* < *re-* back + *cedere* go] —**Syn.** 1. retreat, retire.

**rec on cile** (rek′ən sil), *v.,* **-ciled, -cil ing.** 1. make friends again. 2. settle (a quarrel, disagreement, etc.). 3. make agree; bring into harmony: *It is impossible to reconcile his story with the facts.* 4. make satisfied; make no longer opposed: *It is hard to reconcile oneself to being sick a long time.* [< L *reconciliare,* ult. < *re-* back + *concilium* bond of union]

**reel** (rēl), *n.* 1. a lively dance. Two kinds

are the Highland reel and the Virginia reel. 2. music for it.

**re fec to ry** (ri fek′tər ē), *n., pl.* **-ries.** 1. a room for meals, especially in a monastery, convent, or school. 2. **refectory table,** a long narrow table with heavy legs. [< LL *refectorium,* ult. < L *reficere* refresh < *re-* again + *facere* make]

**ref er ent** (ref′ər ənt), *n.* what is referred to; the object referred to by a term.

**re gale** (ri gāl′), *v.,* **-galed, -gal ing.** 1. entertain agreeably; delight with something pleasing: *The old sailor regaled the boys with sea stories.* 2. entertain with a choice repast; feast. [< F *régaler,* ult. < MDutch *wale* wealth] —**re gale′ment,** *n.*

**re it e rate** (rē it′ə rāt′), *v.,* **-at ed, -at ing.** say or do several times; repeat (an action, demand, etc.) again and again. [< L *reiterare,* ult. < *re-* again + *iterum* again]

**re nas cence** (ri nas′ns or ri nā′sns), *n.* 1. revival; new birth; renewal. 2. **the Renascence,** the Renaissance.

**re past** (ri past′ or ri päst′), *n.* meal; attractive meal; food. [< OF *repast,* ult. < L *re-* again + *pascere* feed]

**re pose** (ri pōz′), *n.* 1. rest; sleep: *Do not disturb her repose.* 2. quietness; ease: *She has repose of manner.* 3. peace; calmness. [< F *repos < reposer < LL repausare* cause to rest < *re-* again + *pausare* to pause]

**re prove** (ri prüv′), *v.,* **-proved, -prov ing.** find fault with; blame: *Reprove the boy for teasing the cat.*

**re sign** (ri zīn′), *v.* 1. give up a job, position, etc. 2. give up. 3. **resign oneself,** submit quietly; adapt oneself without complaint. [< OF < L *resignare* unseal, ult. < *re-* back + *signum* seal]

**res o nant** (rez′ə nənt), *adj.* 1. resounding; continuing to sound; echoing. 2. tending to increase or prolong sounds. [< L *resonans, -antis,* ppr. of *resonare,* ult. < *re-* back + *sonus* sound] —**res′o nant ly,** *adv.*

**res pite** (res′pit), *n., v.,* **-pit ed, -pit ing.** —*n.* 1. time of relief and rest; lull: *A thick cloud brought a respite from the glare of the sun.* 2. a putting off; delay, especially, in carrying out a sentence of death; reprieve. —*v.* give a respite to. [< OF < VL *respectus* delay < LL *respectus* expectation < L *respectare* wait for]

**res tive** (res′tiv), *adj.* 1. restless; uneasy. 2. hard to manage. 3. refusing to go ahead; balky.

**re straint** (ri strānt′), *n.* 1. a holding back or being held back. 2. tendency to hold back natural feeling; reserve. 3. freedom from exaggeration or extravagance.

**ret i na** (ret′n ə), *n., pl.* **-nas, -nae** (-n ē) layer of cells at the back of the eyeball that is sensitive to light and receives the images of things looked at. [< Med.L *retina* < L *retinacula,* pl., band, reins < *retinere* retain]

**re tort** (ri tôrt′), *v.* 1. reply quickly or sharply. 2. return in kind; turn back on: *retort insult for insult or blow for blow.* —*n.* a sharp or witty reply. [< L *retortus,* pp. of *retorquere* throw back < *re-* back + *torquere* twist]

**rev el** (rev′l), *v.,* **-eled, -el ing** or *esp. Brit.*

**-elled, -el ling,** *n.* —*v.* 1. take great pleasure (*in*): *The children revel in country life.* 2. make merry. —*n.* a noisy good time; merrymaking. [< OF *reveler* be disorderly, make merry < L *rebellare*]

**rib ald** (rib′ld), *adj.* offensive in speech; coarsely mocking; irreverent; indecent; obscene. [< OF *ribauld,* ult. < MDutch *ribe* prostitute] —**Syn.** indelicate, gross.

**rig,** a carriage with its horses.

**rig or** (rig′ər), *n.* 1. strictness; severity; harshness: *the rigor of a long, cold winter.* 2. stiffness; rigidity. 3. chill caused by illness. [< OF < L *rigor* < *rigere* be stiff]

**rill** (ril), *n.* a tiny stream; little brook. [cf. Dutch *ril* groove, furrow]

**rod** (rod), *n.* a measure of length; 5¹⁄₂ yards or 16¹⁄₂ feet. A square rod is 30¹⁄₄ square yards or 272¹⁄₄ square feet.

**ro guish** (rō′gish), *adj.* 1. dishonest; rascally; having to do with or like rogues. 2. playfully mischievous. —**Syn.** 1. knavish, tricky, fraudulent. 2. waggish, sportive.

**rose beetle,** a copper-colored, hard-shelled beetle which lives in and destroys rosebushes. —**rose-beetle,** *adj.*

**rotgut,** *n. Slang.* bad liquor.

**rout** (rout), *n.* 1. flight of a defeated army in disorder. 2. a complete defeat. 3. *Archaic.* crowd; band. [< OF *route* detachment, ult. < L *rumpere* to break]

**row** (rou), *n.* 1. a noisy quarrel; disturbance; clamor. 2. *Informal.* squabble.

**rub ber neck** (rub′ər nek′), *U.S. Slang.* —*n.* person who wants to see everything and stretches his neck or turns his head to look at things. —*v.* stare. [Am.E]

**ru ble** (rü′bl), *n.* a silver coin of the Soviet Union equal to about $1.11 (1972). A ruble was equal to about $.50 in Chekhov's time.

**rude** (rüd), *adj.,* **rud er, rud est.** 1. impolite; not courteous. 2. roughly made or done; without finish or polish; coarse: *rude tools, a rude cabin.* 3. rough in manner or behavior; violent; harsh. [< L *rudis*] —**rude′ly,** *adv.* —**Syn.** 2. raw, crude.

**rue** (rü), *v.,* **rued, ru ing.** 1. be sorry for; regret. 2. *Archaic.* feel sorrow. [OE *hrēowan*]

**rue ful** (rü′fəl), *adj.* 1. sorrowful; unhappy; mournful: *a rueful expression.* 2. causing sorrow or pity: *a rueful sight.* —**rue′ful ly,** *adv.*

**rumble seat,** an extra, open seat in the back of an automobile.

**sac ri lege** (sak′rə lij), *n.* an intentional injury to anything sacred; disrespectful treatment of anyone or anything sacred: *Robbing the church was a sacrilege.* [< OF < L *sacrilegium* temple robbery < *sacrum* sacred object + *legere* pick up]

**sac ro sanct** (sak′rō sangkt), *adj.* 1. very holy; very sacred. 2. set apart as sacred; consecrated.

**sa dism** (sā′diz əm or sad′iz əm), *n.* 1. kind of insanity in which a person enjoys hurting someone else. 2. an unnatural love of cruelty. [< F; from the Count (or Marquis) de *Sade,* who wrote of it]

**sa dist** (sā′dist or sad′ist), *n.* one affected with sadism.

**saf fron** (saf′rən), *n.* 1. an orange yellow coloring matter obtained from a kind of crocus. Saffron is used to color and flavor candy, drinks, etc. 2. an autumn crocus with purple flowers having orange yellow stigmas. 3. an orange yellow. —*adj.* orange yellow. [OE *salo*]

**sage** (sāj), *adj.*, **sag er, sag est.** 1. wise: *a sage adviser.* 2. showing wisdom or good judgment: *a sage reply.* 3. wise-looking; grave; solemn: *Owls are sage birds.* [< OF *sage,* ult. < L *sapere* be wise] —**Syn.** 1, 2. judicious, prudent.

**sal low** (sal′ō), *adj.* having a sickly, yellowish color or complexion. [OE *salo*]

**sal u ta tion** (sal′yə tā′shən), *n.* 1. a greeting; saluting. 2. something uttered, written, or done to salute. You begin a letter with a salutation, such as "Dear Sir" or "My Dear Mrs. Jones."

**Sa mos** (sā′mos), *n.* a Greek island off W Turkey. 60,000 pop.; 181 sq. mi.

**sanc tu ar y** (sangk′chù er′ē), *n.*, *pl.* **-ar ies.** 1. a sacred place. 2. part of a church around the altar. 3. place of refuge or protection. [< L *sanctuarium,* ult. < *sanctus* holy]

**sanc tum** (sangk′təm), *n.*, *pl.* **-tums,** (*Rare*) **-ta** (-tə). 1. a sacred place. 2. a private room where a person can be undisturbed. [< L *sanctum,* originally neut. adj., holy]

**sar cas tic** (sär kas′tik), *adj.* using sarcasm; sneering; cutting: *"Don't hurry!" was his sarcastic comment as I began to dress at my usual slow rate.* —**sar cas′ti cal ly,** *adv.* —**Syn.** ironical, satirical, taunting, caustic.

**Sar dis** (sär′dis), *n.* ancient capital of Lydia.

**sar don ic** (sär don′ik), *adj.* bitter; sarcastic; scornful; mocking: *a fiend's sardonic laugh.* [< F < L < Gk. *Sardonios,* a supposed Sardinian plant that produced hysterical convulsions] —**sar don′i cal ly,** *adv.*

**sa rong** (sə rông′ or sə rong′), *n.* a rectangular piece of cloth, usually a brightly colored printed material, worn as a skirt by men and women in the Malay Archipelago, East Indies, etc. [< Malay *sārung*]

**sar to ri al** (sär tô′rē əl or sär tō′rē əl), *adj.* of tailors or their work. [< L *sartorius* of a tailor, ult. < *sarcire* to patch]

**satch el** (sach′əl), *n.* a small bag for carrying clothes, books, etc.; handbag.

**sat u rate** (sach′ə rāt), *v.*, **-rat ed, -rat ing.** soak thoroughly; fill full: *During the fog, the air was saturated with moisture.* [< L *saturare* glut < *satur* full] —**Syn.** steep, drench, imbue.

**saun ter** (sôn′tər or sän′tər), *v.* walk along slowly and happily; stroll: *saunter through the park.*

**scal a wag** (skal′ə wag), *n. Informal.* a good-for-nothing person; scamp; rascal.

**scoff** (skôf or skof), *v.* make fun to show one does not believe something; mock. —*n.* 1. mocking words or acts. 2. something ridiculed or mocked. [< Scand. (Danish) *skuffe* deceive] —**scoff′ing ly,** *adv.*

**score** (skôr or skōr), *n.* group or set of twenty; twenty.

**scourge** (skėrj), *n.* 1. a whip. 2. any means of punishment. 3. some thing or person that causes great trouble or misfortune. In olden times, an outbreak of disease was called a scourge.

**scroll** (skrōl), *n.* 1. roll of parchment or paper, especially one with writing on it: *He slowly unrolled the scroll as he read from it.* 2. ornament resembling a partly unrolled sheet of paper, or having a spiral or coiled form. —*v.* 1. to inscribe on or as if on a scroll. 2. to form into or adorn with scrolls. [alteration of *scrow* (influenced by *roll*), ult. < OF *escroe* scrap < Gmc.]

**scru ple** (skrü′pl), *n.* 1. a feeling of doubt about what one ought to do. 2. a feeling of uneasiness that keeps a person from doing something: *She has scruples about playing cards for money.* [< L *scrupulus* a feeling of uneasiness, originally dim. of *scrupus* sharp stone, figuratively, uneasiness, anxiety]

**scru ti nize** (skrüt′n īz), *v.*, **-nized, -niz ing.** examine closely; inspect carefully: *The jeweler scrutinized the diamond for flaws.*

**scru ti ny** (skrüt′n ē), *n.*, *pl.* **-nies.** close examination; careful inspection. [< LL *scrutinium* < L *scrutari* ransack]

**scuff** (skuf), *v.* 1. walk without lifting the feet; shuffle. 2. wear or injure the surface of by hard use: *scuff one's shoes.* —*n.* a scuffing. [var. of *scuffle*] —**scuffed,** *adj.*

**scur vy** (skėr′vē), *adj.*, **-vi er, -vi est.** low; mean; contemptible: *a scurvy fellow, a scurvy trick.* [< *scurf*]

**scut** (skut), *n.* a short tail, especially that of a rabbit or deer. [< Scand. *skutr* stern]

**sear** (sir), *adj.* dried up; withered. [OE *sēar,* adj.]

**sect** (sekt), *n.* 1. group of people having the same principles, beliefs, or opinions: *Each religious sect in the town had its own church.* 2. a religious group separated from an established church. [< L *secta* party, school, probably < *sectari* keep following, intensive of *sequi* follow]

**se duc tive** (si duk′tiv), *adj.* alluring; captivating; charming. —**se duc′tive ly,** *adv.*

**seed y** (sēd′ē), *adj.*, **seed i er, seed i est.** *Informal.* shabby; no longer fresh or new: *seedy clothes.*

**seethe** (sēᴛн), *v.*, **seethed, seeth ing.** 1. be excited; be disturbed: *The pirate crew was seething with discontent and ready for open rebellion.* 2. bubble and foam: *Water seethed under the falls.* 3. boil.

**self-immolation,** act of immolating oneself; sacrificing oneself.

**sem blance** (sem′bləns), *n.* 1. outward appearance: *His story had the semblance of truth, but was really false.* 2. likeness: *These clouds have the semblance of a huge head.* [< OF *semblance* < *sembler* seem, ult. < L *similis* similar]

**sen su ous** (sen′shù əs), *adj.* 1. of or derived from the senses; having an effect on the senses; perceived by the senses: *the sensuous thrill of a warm bath, a sensuous love of color.* 2. enjoying the pleasures of the senses.

**sen ti nel** (sen′tə nl), *n.* 1. one stationed to keep watch and guard against surprises. 2. **stand sentinel,** act as a sentinel; keep watch. [< F < Ital. *sentinella* < LL *sentinare* avoid danger wisely < L *sentire* feel]

**sen try** (sen′trē), *n.*, *pl.* **-tries.** 1. sentinel. 2. watch; guard: *We stood sentry over the sleepers.* [? abbreviation of *centrinel,* var. of *sentinel*]

**sep ul cher** (sep′l kər), *n.* place of burial; tomb; grave. —*v.* bury (a dead body) in a sepulcher. [< OF < L *sepulcrum* < *sepelire* bury]

**se pul chral** (sə pul′krəl), *adj.* 1. of sepulchers or tombs. 2. of burial: *sepulchral ceremonies.* 3. deep and gloomy; dismal; suggesting a tomb. —**se pul′chral ly,** *adv.*

**sere** (sir), *adj.* sear. [var. of *sear*]

**se rene** (sə rēn′), *adj.* 1. peaceful; calm: *a serene smile.* 2. clear; bright; not cloudy: *a serene sky.* [< L *serenus*] —**se rene′ly,** *adv.* —**Syn.** 1. tranquil, placid.

**ser i al** (sir′ē əl), *n.* story published, broadcast, or televised one part at a time in a magazine or newspaper or on the radio or television. [< NL *serialis* < L *series*]

**shak o** (shak′ō), *n.*, *pl.* **shak os.** a high, stiff military hat with a plume or other ornament. [< Hungarian *csákó* peaked (cap) < G *Zacke(n)* point, spike]

**shel lac** (shə lak′), *n.*, *v.*, **-lacked, -lack ing.** —*n.* liquid that gives a smooth, shiny appearance to wood, metal, etc. —*v.* 1. put shellac on; cover or fasten with shellac. 2. *Informal.* defeat completely. [< *shell* + *lac;* translation of F *laque en écailles* lac in thin plates]

**shil ling** (shil′ing), *n.* a former British monetary unit worth about $.18 when O'Connor wrote "The Idealist."

**Shin to** (shin′tō), *n.* 1. the native religion of Japan, primarily a system of nature worship and ancestor worship. 2. adherent of this religion. —*adj.* of or having to do with Shinto. [< Japanese < Chinese *shin tao* way of the gods]

**shrive** (shrīv), *v.*, **shrove** or **shrived, shriv en** or **shrived, shriv ing.** *Archaic.* 1. hear the confession of, impose penance on, and grant absolution to. 2. make confession. 3. **shrive oneself,** confess to a priest and do penance. [OE *scrifan* < L *scribere* write]

**shroud** (shroud), *n.* 1. cloth or garment in which a dead person is wrapped for burial. 2. something that covers, conceals, or veils: *The fog was a shroud over the city.* [OE *scrūd*]

**si dle** (sī′dl), *v.*, **-dled, -dling.** 1. move

sideways. 2. move sideways slowly so as not to attract attention: *The little boy shyly sidled up to the visitor.* [< *sideling* sidelong]

**siege** (sēj), *n.* 1. the surrounding of a fortified place by an army trying to capture it; a besieging or being besieged. 2. any long or persistent effort to overcome resistance; any long-continued attack: *a siege of illness.* [< OF *siege*, ult. < L *sedere* sit]

**si er ra** (sē er′ə), *n.* chain of hills or mountains with jagged peaks. [Am.E; < Sp. *sierra*, literally, a saw < L *serra*]

**si es ta** (sē es′tə), *n.* a nap or rest taken at noon or in the afternoon. [< Sp. < L *sexta (hora)* sixth (hour); noon]

**sight** (sīt), *n.* 1. device on a gun, surveying instrument, etc., to assist in taking aim or observing. 2. observation taken with a telescope or other instrument; aim with a gun, etc. [OE *(ge)siht*]

**sim per** (sim′pər), *v.* 1. smile in a silly, affected way. 2. express by a simper; say with a simper. —*n.* a silly, affected smile. [cf. G *zimper* affected, coy]

**sin ew** (sin′yü), *n.* 1. a tough, strong band or cord that joins muscle to bone; tendon: *You can see the sinews in a cooked chicken leg.* 2. means of strength; source of power. *Men and money are the sinews of war.* [OE *sionu*]

**singe** (sinj), *v.,* **singed, singe ing.** 1. burn a little: *The cook singed the chicken to remove the fine hairs.* 2. burn the ends or edges of. 3. injure slightly; harm: *Scandal singed the mayor's reputation.* —*n.* a slight burn. [OE *sengan*]

**sin gu lar** (sing′gyə lər), *adj.* 1. extraordinary; unusual: *"Treasure Island" is a story of singular interest to boys.* 2. strange; queer; peculiar: *The detectives were greatly puzzled by the singular nature of the crime.* 3. being the only one of its kind: *an event singular in history.* [< L *singularis* < *singulus* single] —**sin′gu lar ly,** *adv.*

**sire** (sīr), *n.* 1. a male ancestor; father. 2. title of respect used formerly to a great noble and now to a king. [< OF < VL *seior* < L *senior,* nominative, older]

**skep ti cal** (skep′tə kl), *adj.* 1. of or like a skeptic; inclined to doubt; not believing easily. 2. questioning the truth of theories or apparent facts. Also, **sceptical.** —**skep′ti cal ly,** *adv.* —**Syn.** 1. doubting, incredulous, disbelieving, distrustful.

**skep ti cism** (skep′tə siz əm), *n.* 1. skeptical attitude; doubt; unbelief. 2. doctrine that nothing can be proved absolutely. Also, **scepticism.**

**slag** (slag), *n.* 1. the rough, hard waste left after metal is separated from ore by melting. 2. a light, spongy lava. [< MLG *slagge*]

**slake** (slāk), *v.,* **slaked, slak ing.** 1. satisfy (thirst, revenge, wrath, etc.). 2. cause to be less active, intense, etc. 3. put out (a fire). [OE *slacian* < *slæc* slack]

**slan der** (slan′dər or slän′dər), *n.* 1. a false statement meant to do harm. 2. the spreading of false reports. —*v.* 1. talk

falsely about. 2. speak or spread slander. [< OF *esclandre* scandal < L *scandalum*] —**slan′der er,** *n.*

**slay** (slā), *v.,* **slew, slain, slay ing.** kill with violence. [OE *slēan*] —**slay′er,** *n.*

**slew** (slü), *v.* pt. of **slay.**

**sloop** (slüp), *n.* sailboat having one mast, a mainsail, a jib, and sometimes other sails. [< Dutch *sloep,* earlier *sloepe*]

**slug** (slug), *n.* 1. a slow-moving animal like a snail, without a shell or with only a very small shell. 2. caterpillar or larva that looks like a slug. [? < Scand. (dialectal Swedish) *slogga* be sluggish]

**smite** (smīt), *v.,* **smote, smit ten** or **smit, smit ing.** 1. strike; strike hard; hit hard. 2. come with force (upon): *The sound of a blacksmith's hammer smote upon their ears.* 3. affect with a sudden pain, disease, etc.: *The thief's conscience smote him.* 4. strike down; punish severly; destroy. [OE *smitan*]

**smith** (smith), *n.* 1. man who makes or shapes things out of metal. 2. blacksmith. [OE]

**smith e reens** (smiŦH′ə rēnz′), *n.pl.* Informal. small pieces; bits. [var. of dialectal *smithers* (of unknown origin) + Irish dim. suffix *-een*]

**smith y** (smith′ē or smiŦH′ē), *n., pl.* **smith ies.** workshop of a smith, especially a blacksmith.

**smote** (smōt), *v.* a pt. of **smite.**

**snuf fle** (snuf′l), *v.,* **-fled, -fling.** 1. breathe noisily through a partly clogged nose. 2. smell; sniff.

**sod den** (sod′n), *adj.* 1. soaked through: *The boy's clothing was sodden with rain.* 2. heavy and moist: *This bread is sodden because it was not baked well.* [old pp. of *seethe*]

**so journ** (*v.* sō jėrn′ or sō′jėrn; *n.* sō′jėrn), *v.* stay for a time: *The Israelites sojourned in the land of Egypt.* —*n.* a brief stay. [< OF *sojorner,* ult. < L *sub* under + *diurnus* of the day]

**sol ace** (sol′is), *v.,* **-aced, -ac ing.** comfort; relieve: *He solaced himself with a book.* [< OF < L *solacium* < *solari* console]

**sol der** (sod′ər), *v.* 1. fasten, mend, or join with solder. 2. unite firmly; join closely. 3. mend; repair; patch. [< OF *soldure,* ult. < L *solidus* solid]

**so lic it ous** (sə lis′ə təs), *adj.* 1. showing care or concern; anxious; concerned: *Parents are solicitous for their children's progress.* 2. desirous; eager: *solicitous to please.* —**so lic′it ous ly,** *adv.*

**so lic i tude** (sə lis′ə tüd or sə lis′ə tyüd), *n.* anxious care; anxiety; concern.

**som ber** (som′bər), *adj.* 1. dark; gloomy: *A cloudy winter day is somber.* 2. melancholy; dismal: *His losses made him very somber.* —**som′ber ly,** *adv.* —**Syn.** 1. cloudy, murky. 2. depressing, sad.

**sor did** (sôr′did), *adj.* 1. dirty; filthy: *The poor family lived in a sordid hut.* 2. caring too much for money; meanly selfish; mean; low; base. [< L *sordidus* dirty < *sordere* be dirty < *sordes* dirt] —**sor′did ly,** *adv.*

**sor rel** (sôr′əl or sor′əl), *adj.* reddish brown. —*n.* a reddish brown horse with

mane and tail of the same or a lighter color. [< OF *sorel* < *sor* yellowish brown]

**sou** (sü), *n.* 1. a former French coin, worth 5 centimes or 1/20 of a franc. 2. anything of little value. [< F *sou,* ult. < L *solidus,* a Roman coin]

**Sou sa** (sü′zə), *n.* **John Philip,** 1854-1932, American musical conductor and composer.

**span** (span), *n.* pair of horses or other animals harnessed and driven together. [Am.E; < Dutch or LG *span* < *spannen* stretch, yoke]

**sparse** (spärs), *adj.,* **spars er, spars est.** 1. thinly scattered; occurring here and there: *a sparse population, sparse hair.* 2. scanty; meager. [< L *sparsus,* pp. of *spargere* scatter] —**sparse′ly,** *adv.*

**spec ter** (spek′tər), *n.* 1. ghost. 2. thing causing terror or dread. [< L *spectrum* appearance]

**spew** (spyü), *v.* throw out; cast forth; vomit. [OE *spiwan*]

**spiel** (spēl), *U.S. Slang.* —*n.* talk; speech; harangue, especially one of a cheap, noisy nature. [Am.E; < dialectal G *Spiel* play]

**spire** (spīr), *n.* 1. the top part of a tower or steeple that narrows to a point. 2. anything tapering and pointed: *The sunset shone on the rocky spires of the mountains.* [OE *spir*]

**spright ly** (sprīt′lē), *adj.,* **-li er, -li est.** lively; gay. [< *spright,* var. of *sprite*] —**Syn.** spirited, animated, vivacious.

**sprite** (sprīt), *n.* elf; fairy; goblin. [< OF *esprit* spirit < L *spiritus*]

**sprock et** (sprok′it), *n.* 1. one of a set of projections on the rim of a wheel, arranged so as to fit into the links of a chain. The sprockets keep the chain from slipping. 2. wheel made with sprockets.

**squee gee** (skwē′jē), *n., v.,* **-geed, -gee ing.** —*n.* device with a roller for pressing water from photographic prints, etc. —*v.* sweep, scrape, or press with a squeegee. [? < *squeege,* var. of *squeeze*]

**stac ca to** (stə kä′tō), *adj.* with breaks between the successive tones; disconnected; abrupt. —*adv.* in a staccato manner. [< Ital. *staccato,* literally, detached]

**stanch** (stänch or stanch), *adj.* 1. firm; strong: *stanch walls, a stanch defense.* 2. loyal; steadfast: *a stanch friend, a stanch supporter of the law.* Also, **staunch.** —**stanch′ly,** *adv.*

**stat ic** (stat′ik), *adj.* 1. at rest; standing still: *Civilization does not remain static, but changes constantly.* 2. having to do with bodies at rest or with forces that balance each other. 3. acting by weight without producing motion: *static pressure.* [< Gk. *statikos* causing to stand, ult. < *stenai* stand]

**sta tus** (stā′təs or stat′əs), *n.* 1. condition; state: *Diplomats are interested in the status of world affairs.* 2. social or professional standing; position; rank: *his status as a doctor.* [< L *status* < *stare* stand]

**staunch** (stônch or stänch), *adj.* stanch.

**ste ril i ty** (stə ril′ə tē), *n., pl.* **-ties.** barrennness; sterile condition or character; a quality of being deprived of a power or function; being ineffective.

**sti let to** (stə let′ō), *n., pl.* **-tos** or **-toes.** a dagger with a narrow blade. [< Ital. *stiletto*, ult. < L *stilus* pointed instrument]

**still** (stil), *n.* **1.** apparatus for distilling liquids. A still is used in making alcohol. **2.** place where alcoholic liquors are distilled; distillery. [*n.* use of *still*, short form of *distill*]

**strick en** (strik′ən), *adj.* **1.** affected by (wounds, diseases, trouble, sorrows, etc.): *Help was rushed to the firestricken city.* **2. stricken in years,** old.

**strobe** (strōb), *n.* stroboscopic lamp, a lamp capable of producing an extremely short, brilliant burst of light, to be used with a camera having a high shutter speed, in order to photograph a rapidly moving object making it appear to stand still.

**stu por** (stü′pər or styü′pər), *n.* **1.** a dazed condition; loss or lessening of the power to feel: *The man lay in a stupor, unable to tell what had happened to him.* **2.** intellectual or moral numbness. [< L *stupor* < *stupere* be dazed] —**Syn. 1.** lethargy, torpor.

**sub jec tive** (səb jek′tiv), *adj.* existing in the mind; belonging to the person thinking rather than to the object thought of: *Base your subjective opinions on objective facts.* —**sub jec′tive ly,** *adv.*

**sub tle** (sut′l), *adj.* **1.** delicate; thin; fine: *a subtle odor of perfume.* **2.** faint; mysterious: *a subtle smile.* **3.** having a keen, quick mind; discerning; acute. **4.** sly; crafty; tricky. **5.** skillful; clever; expert. [< OF *soutil* < L *subtilis*, originally, woven underneath]

**sub tle ty** (sut′l tē), *n., pl.* **-ties. 1.** subtle quality. **2.** something subtle.

**sub tly** (sut′lē), *adv.* in a subtle manner; with subtlety.

**suc cumb** (sə kum′), *v.* **1.** give way; yield: *He succumbed to temptation and stole the money.* **2.** die. [< L *succumbere* < *sub-* down + *-cumbere* lie]

**sulk y** (sul′kē), *adj.,* **sulk i er, sulk i est.** silent and bad-humored because of resentment; sullen: *Spoiled children become sulky if they cannot have their own way.* [cf. OE *āsolcen* lazy] —**sulk′i ly,** *adv.*

**sul len** (sul′ən), *adj.* **1.** silent because of bad humor or anger: *The sullen child refused to answer my question.* **2.** showing bad humor or anger. **3.** gloomy; dismal: *The sullen skies threatened rain.* [< OF *solain,* ult. < L *solus* alone] —**sul′len ly,** *adv.*

**sul try** (sul′trē), *adj.,* **-tri er, -tri est. 1.** hot, close, and moist: *We expect sultry weather during July.* **2.** hot.

**sump** (sump), *n.* **1.** pit or reservoir for collecting water, oil, etc. **2.** pool at the bottom of a mine, where water collects and from which it is pumped. [< MDutch *somp* or MLG *sump* swamp]

**sun der** (sun′dər), *v.* separate; part; sever; split. [OE *sundrian* < *sundor* apart] —**Syn.** divide, disjoin, disconnect.

**sun dry** (sun′drē), *adj.* several; various: *From sundry hints, he guessed he was to be given a bicycle for his birthday.* [OE *syndrig* separate < *sundor* apart]

**su per fi cial** (sü′pər fish′əl), *adj.* concerned with or understanding only what is on the surface; not thorough; shallow:

*Girls used to receive only a superficial education.* [< L *superficialis* < *superficies* surface < *super-* above + *facies* form]

**sup plant** (sə plant′ or sə plänt′), *v.* take the place of; displace or set aside: *Machinery has supplanted hand labor in making shoes.* [< L *supplantare* trip up < *sub-* under + *planta* sole of the foot]

**sup pli ant** (sup′lē ənt), *n.* person who asks humbly and earnestly: *She knelt as a suppliant at the altar.*

**sup press** (sə pres′), *v.* **1.** put an end to; stop by force; put down: *The troops suppressed the rebellion by firing on the mob.* **2.** keep in; hold back; keep from appearing: *She suppressed a yawn.* **3.** check the flow of; stop: *suppress bleeding.* [< L *suppressus,* pp. of *supprimere* < *sub-* down + *premere* press] —**Syn. 1.** subdue, quell, crush. **2.** restrain, repress.

**su pra na tion al** (sü′prə nash′ən l or sü′prə nash′ nəl), *adj.* above a nation or state, as in authority; more important than any one nation or state.

**surge** (sèrj), *v.,* **surged, surg ing.** rise and fall; move like waves: *A great wave surged over us. The crowd surged through the streets.* [ult. (probably through OF *surgeon* a spring) < L *surgere* rise < *sub-* up + *regere* reach]

**sur ly** (sèr′lē), *adj.,* **-li er, -li est.** bad-tempered and unfriendly; rude; gruff: *They got a surly answer from the grouchy old man.* [ult. < *sir,* in sense of "lord"]

**sus tain** (səs tān′), *v.* **1.** keep up; keep going: *Hope sustains him in his misery.* **2.** supply with food, provisions, etc.: *sustain an army.* **3.** agree with; confirm: *The facts sustain his theory.* [< OF < L *sustinere* < *sub-* up + *tenere* hold] —**Syn. 1.** aid, assist, comfort.

**swarth y** (swôr′ᵺē or swôr′thē), *adj.,* **swarth i er, swarth i est.** having a dark skin. [earlier *swarfy* < *swarf* grit, OE *geswearf*]

**sweet meats** (swēt′mēts′), *n. pl.* **1.** candy; candied fruits; sugar-covered nuts; bonbons. **2.** preserves.

**swine herd** (swīn′hèrd′), *n.* one who tends pigs or hogs.

**syn chro nize** (sing′krə nīz), *v.,* **-nized, -niz ing. 1.** occur at the same time; agree in time. **2.** move or take place at the same rate and exactly together. **3.** make agree in time: *synchronize all the clocks in a building.* —**syn′chro ni za′tion,** *n.*

**Ta bas co** (tə bas′kō), *n. Trademark.* a kind of peppery sauce, used on fish, meat, etc., prepared from the fruit of a variety of capsicum. [Am.E; from *Tabasco,* state in Mexico]

**ta boo** (tə bü′), *n., pl.* **-boos. 1.** a prohibition; ban. **2.** system or act of setting things apart as sacred or cursed.

**tack** (tak), *v.* sail in a zigzag course against the wind. [< dialectal OF *taque* nail < Gmc.]

**taint** (tānt), *n.* stain or spot; trace of decay, corruption, or disgrace. —*v.* **1.** give a taint to; spoil: *His mind was tainted from read-*

**tempestuous**

hat, āge, fär; let, ēqual, tèrm;
it, īce; hot, ōpen, ôrder;
oil, out; cup, pùt, rüle;
ch, child; ng, long; sh, she;
th, thin; ᵺ, then; zh, measure;

ə represents *a* in about, *e* in taken,
*i* in pencil, *o* in lemon, *u* in circus.

< = from, derived from, taken from.

*ing bad books.* **2.** become tainted; decay. [partly var. of *attaint;* partly < OF *teint,* pp. of *teindre* dye < L *tingere*] —**Syn.** *n.* blemish.

**tal ent** (tal′ənt), *n.* **1.** a special natural ability; ability: *a talent for music.* **2.** an ancient unit of weight or money, varying with time and place.

**tan gi ble** (tan′jə bl), *adj.* **1.** capable of being touched or felt by touch: *A chair is a tangible object.* **2.** real; actual; definite. [< LL *tangibilis* < *tangere* touch]

**Ta no** (tä′nō), *n.* **1.** a group of former pueblos lying south of Santa Fe, New Mexico. **2.** an Indian of any of the Tano pueblos. —**Ta no′an,** *adj.*

**tan ta lize** (tan′tl īz), *v.,* **-lized, -liz ing.** torment or tease by keeping something desired in sight but out of reach, or by holding out hopes that are repeatedly disappointed. [< *Tantalus*] —**tan′ta li za′tion,** *n.* —**Syn.** plague, vex.

**tap es try** (tap′is trē), *n., pl.* **-tries.** heavy fabric with pictures or designs woven in it, used to hang on walls, cover furniture, etc. [< F *tapisserie,* ult. < *tapis* < Gk. *tapetion,* dim. of *tapes* carpet, covering]

**taunt** (tônt or tänt), *v.* **1.** jeer at; mock; reproach. **2.** get or drive by taunts: *They taunted him into taking the dare.* —*n.* a bitter or insulting remark; mocking; jeering. —**Syn.** *v.* **1.** deride, ridicule, flout.

**te di ous** (tē′dē əs or tē′jəs), *adj.* long and tiring: *A long talk that you cannot understand is tedious.* [< LL *taediosus* < L *taedium* tedium] —**Syn.** wearisome.

**tem per** (tem′pər), *n.* **1.** the hardness, toughness, etc., of a mixture given by tempering: *The temper of the clay was right for shaping.* **2.** substance added to something to modify its properties or qualities. [< v.] —*v.* **1.** moderate; soften: *Temper justice with mercy.* **2.** bring or be brought to a proper or desired condition by mixing or preparing. A painter tempers his colors by mixing them with oil. Steel is tempered by heating it and working it till it has the proper degree of hardness and toughness. [OE *temprian* < L *temperare,* originally, observe due measure < *tempus* time, interval]

**tem per a ment** (tem′pər ə mənt or tem′prə mənt), *n.* a person's nature or disposition: *a nervous temperament.*

**tem pest** (tem′pist), *n.* **1.** a violent storm with much wind. **2.** a violent disturbance. [< OF *tempest(e)* < var. of L *tempestas* < *tempus* time, season]

**tem pes tu ous** (tem pes′chù əs), *adj.*

1. stormy: *a tempestuous night.* 2. violent: *a tempestuous argument.*

**ten ta tive** (ten′tə tiv), *adj.* done as a trial or experiment; experimental: *a tentative plan.* [< Med.L *tentativus* < L *tentare* try out, intensive of *tendere* stretch, aim; associated in L with *temptare* feel out] —**ten′ta tive ly,** *adv.*

**ten ure** (ten′yər), *n.* 1. a holding; possessing. 2. length of time of holding or possessing: *The tenure of office of the president of our club is one year.* [< OF *tenure,* ult. < L *tenere* hold]

**ter rain** (te rān′ or ter′ān), *n.* land; tract of land, especially considered as to its extent and natural features in relation to its use in warfare. [< F *terrain,* ult. < L *terra* land]

**teth er** (teᴛʜ′ər), *n.* rope or chain for fastening an animal so that it can graze only within certain limits. —*v.* fasten with a tether.

**Te wa** (tā′wə or tē′wə), *n., pl.* **Te wa** or **Te was.** 1. any of several Tanoan peoples of northeastern Arizona and New Mexico. 2. a member of any such peoples. 3. a language of the Tewa peoples.

**thence** (ᴛʜens), *adv.* 1. from that place; from there: *A few miles thence is a river.* 2. for that reason; therefore: *You didn't work, thence no pay.* 3. from that time; from then: *a few years thence.* [ME *thennes* < OE *thanan(e)*]

**the o ret i cal** (thē′ə ret′ə kl), *adj.* 1. planned or worked out in the mind, not from experience; based on theory, not on fact; limited to theory. 2. dealing with theory only; not practical.

**the o ret i cal ly** (thē′ə ret′ik lē), *adv.* in theory; according to theory; in a theoretical manner.

**the o re ti cian** (thē′ər ə tish′ən), *n.* person who knows much about the theory of an art, science, etc.

**ther mal** (thèr′məl), *adj.* 1. of or having to do with heat. 2. warm; hot. [< Gk. *therme* heat]

**the sis** (thē′sis), *n., pl.* **-ses** (-sēz). proposition or statement to be proved or to be maintained against objections.

**thick et** (thik′it), *n.* shrubs, bushes, or small trees growing close together. [OE *thiccet* < *thicce* thick]

**third dimension,** 1. a quality that bestows reality or lifelikeness. 2. thickness or depth. —**third′ di men′sion al,** *adj.*

**thith er** (thiᴛʜ′ər or ᴛʜiᴛʜ′ər), *adv.* to that place; toward that place; there. —*adj.* on that side; farther. [OE *thider*]

**tho rax** (thô′raks or thō′raks), *n., pl.* **-rax es, -ra ces** (-rə sēz). part of the body between the neck and the abdomen. A man's chest is his thorax. [< L < Gk.]

**Thrace** (thrās), *n.* region in the E part of the Balkan Peninsula. In ancient times it was first an independent country and later a Roman province. Today most of the region is in Bulgaria, and the rest of it in Greece.

**Thra cian** (thrā′shən), *adj.* of or having to do with ancient Thrace or its people.

—*n.* native or inhabitant of ancient Thrace.

**thrive** (thrīv), *v.,* **throve** or **thrived, thrived** or **thriv en, thriv ing.** be successful; grow rich; grow strong; prosper: *Flowers will not thrive without sunshine.* [< Scand. *thrifa* (sk)] —**Syn.** flourish.

**thwart** (thwôrt), *v.* oppose and defeat; keep from doing something.

**Ti bet** (ti bet′), *n.* a former country of central Asia, now claimed by China as the **Tibetan Autonomous Region.** 1,275,000 pop.; 470,000 sq. mi. Also, **Thibet.**

**tic** (tik), *n.* a habitual, involuntary twitching of the muscles, especially those of the face. [< F]

**till** (til), *v.* cultivate (land); plow: *Farmers till the land.* [OE *tilian*]

**tim or ous** (tim′ər əs), *adj.* easily frightened; timid. [< Med.L *timorosus* < L *timor* fear] —**tim′or ous ly,** *adv.*

**tinge** (tinj), *n.* 1. a slight coloring or tint. 2. a very small amount; trace. [< L *tingere*]

**tin-pan alley,** district frequented by musicians, song writers, and song publishers.

**toad y** (tōd′ē), *v.* fawn upon; flatter.

**toilet water,** a fragrant liquid not so strong as perfume.

**top hat,** a tall, black silk hat worn by men in formal clothes.

**tou ché** (tü shā′), *interj.* acknowledgment of the success of an argument, the accuracy of an accusation, or a hit in fencing. —*n.* 1. a hit in fencing. 2. a telling remark or home thrust in argument. [< F ppr. of *toucher* to touch]

**touch stone** (tuch′stōn′), *n.* 1. a black stone used to test the purity of gold or silver by the color of the streak made on the stone by rubbing it with the metal. 2. any means of testing; a test.

**tram** (tram), *n. Esp. Brit.* streetcar. [< MDutch or MLG *trame* beam]

**tran quil li ty** or **tran quil i ty** (trang kwil′ə tē), *n.* calmness; peacefulness; quiet.

**tran scend** (tran send′), *v.* 1. go beyond the limits or powers of; exceed; be above: *The grandeur of Niagara Falls transcends description.* 2. be higher or greater than; surpass; excel. 3. be superior or extraordinary. [< L *transcendere* < *trans-* beyond + *scandere* climb]

**trans gress** (trans gres′ or tranz-gres′), *v.* 1. break a law, command, etc.; sin. 2. go contrary to; sin against. [< L *transgressus,* pp. of *transgredi* go beyond < *trans-* across + *gradi* to step]

**trans gres sion** (trans gresh′ən or tranz-gresh′ən), *n.* a transgressing; breaking a law, command, etc.; sin. [< L *transgressio, -onis,* originally, a going over < *transgredi* ] —**Syn.** violation, offense, fault, misdeed.

**tran sient** (tran′shənt), *adj.* 1. passing soon; fleeting; not lasting. 2. passing through and not staying long: *a transient guest in a hotel.* —*n.* visitor or boarder who stays for a short time. [< L *transiens, -entis,* ppr. of *transire* pass through < *trans-* through + *ire* go]

**trau mat ic** (trô mat′ik or trou mat′ik), *adj.* 1. of, having to do with, or produced by a wound or injury. 2. of, having the nature of, or resulting from an emotional experience or shock which has a lasting psychic effect.

**trem u lous** (trem′yə ləs), *adj.* 1. trembling; quivering. 2. timid; fearful. [< L *tremulus* < *tremere* tremble] —**trem′u lous ly,** *adv.* —**Syn.** 1. shaking, vibrating.

**trib u tar y** (trib′yə ter′ē), *adj.* 1. flowing into a larger stream or body of water. 2. paying tribute; required to pay tribute. 3. paid as tribute; of the nature of tribute. 4. contributing; helping.

**triv i al** (triv′ē əl), *adj.* 1. not important; trifling; insignificant. 2. *Archaic.* not new or interesting; ordinary. —*n.* something which is trivial.

**truc u lent** (truk′yə lənt or trü′kyə lənt), *adj.* savagely threatening or bullying; fierce and cruel. [< L *truculentus* < *trux* fierce] —**truc′u lent ly,** *adv.*

**tu mul tu ous** (tü mul′chü əs or tyü-mul′chü əs), *adj.* 1. characterized by tumult; very noisy or disorderly; violent. 2. greatly disturbed. 3. rough; stormy: *Tumultuous waves beat upon the rocks.* —**Syn.** 1. boisterous, turbulent.

**tur ban** (tèr′bən), *n.* 1. a scarf wound around the head or around a cap, worn by men in some Oriental countries. 2. headdress like this; big handkerchief tied around the head. 3. a small hat with little or no brim, worn by women and children.

**turn coat** (tèrn′kōt′), *n.* person who changes his party or principles; renegade.

**twain** (twān), *n., adj. Archaic* or *Poetic.* two. [OE *twēgen*]

**twoscore,** see score.

**tyr an nous** (tir′ə nəs), *adj.* acting like a tyrant; cruel or unjust; arbitrary; tyrannical. —**tyr′an nous ly,** *adv.*

**un al ter a ble** (un ôl′tər ə bl), *adj.* that cannot be altered; not changeable.

**un bi assed** or **un bi assed** (un bī′-əst), *adj.* not prejudiced; impartial; fair.

**unc tu ous** (ungk′chü əs), *adj.* 1. like an oil or ointment; oily; greasy. 2. soothing, sympathetic, and persuasive. 3. too smooth and oily: *the salesman's unctuous manner.* [< Med.L *unctuosus,* ult. < L *unguere* anoint]

**un du lant** (un′jə lənt or un′dyə lənt), *adj.* waving; wavy.

**un ob tru sive** (un′əb trü′siv), *adj.* not inclined to obtrude. —**un ob tru′sive ly,** *adv.*

**un or tho dox** (un ôr′thə doks), *adj.* not orthodox.

**un re lent ing** (un′ri len′ting), *adj.* 1. not yielding to feelings of kindness or compassion; merciless. 2. not slackening or relaxing in severity or determination. —**un′re lent′ing ly,** *adv.* —**Syn.** 1. unyielding, relentless.

**un sa vor y** (un sā′vər ē or un sāv′rē), *adj.* 1. tasteless. 2. unpleasant in taste or smell. 3. morally unpleasant; offensive.

**un scathed** (un skāᴛʜd′), *adj.* not harmed; uninjured.

**up braid** (up brād′), *v.* find fault with;

blame; reprove: *The captain upbraided his men for falling asleep.* [OE *upbregdan* < *upp* up + *bregdan* weave, braid] —**Syn.** reproach.

**urn** (ėrn), *n.* 1. vase with a foot or pedestal. Urns were used in Greece and Rome to hold the ashes of the dead. 2. place of burial; grave; tomb. [< L *urna*]

**u surp** (yü zėrp′ or yü sėrp′), *v.* seize and hold (power, position, authority, etc.) by force or without right: *The king's brother tried to usurp the throne.* [< L *usurpare*, ult. < *usu* through use + *rapere* seize]

**u ti li za tion** (yü′tl ə zā′shən), *n.* a making use of; act of putting to practical use.

**vague** (vāg), *adj.,* **va guer, va guest.** 1. not definitely or precisely expressed: *a vague statement.* 2. indefinite; indistinct: *a vague feeling.* 3. indistinctly seen or perceived; obscure; hazy: *In a fog everything looks vague.* 4. lacking clarity or precision: *a vague personality.* [< OF < L *vagus* wandering] —**vague′ly,** *adv.* —**vague′ness,** *n.*

**vain glo ri ous** (vān′glô′rē əs or vān′glō′rē əs), *adj.* excessively proud or boastful; extremely vain.

**val e dic tor y** (val′ə dik′tər ē), *n., pl.* **-ries.** a farewell address, especially at the graduating exercises of a school or college. —*adj.* bidding farewell.

**va lise** (və lēs′), *n.* a traveling bag to hold clothes, etc. [< F < Ital. *valigia*]

**val or** (val′ər), *n.* bravery; courage. [< LL *valor* < L *valere* be strong]

**vam pire** (vam′pīr), *n.* 1. corpse supposed to come to life at night and suck the blood of people while they sleep. 2. person who preys ruthlessly on others. 3. woman who flirts with men to get money or to please her vanity. 4. vampire bat. [< F < G *Vampir;* of Slavic origin]

**van tage** (van′tij or vän′tij), *n.* a better position or condition; advantage. [short for ME *advantage* advantage]

**vap id** (vap′id), *adj.* without much life or flavor; dull. [< L *vapidus*]

**var i a tion** (ver′ē ā′shən, var′ē ā′shən), *n.* 1. a varying in condition, degree, etc.; change. 2. amount of change. 3. a varied or changed form. 4. (in music) a tune or theme repeated with changes in rhythm, harmony, etc.

**vault** (vôlt), *n.* 1. an arched roof or ceiling; series of arches. 2. something like an arched roof. **The vault of heaven** means the sky. 3. place for storing valuable things and keeping them safe. [< OF *vaulte,* ult. < L *volvere* roll]

**vault ed** (vôl′tid), *adj.* 1. in the form of a vault; arched. 2. built or covered with a vault: *a vaulted room.*

**ve he ment** (vē′ə mənt), *adj.* 1. having or showing strong feeling; caused by strong feeling; eager; passionate. 2. forceful; violent. [< L *vehemens, -entis* < *vehere* carry] —**ve′he ment ly,** *adv.* —**Syn.** 1. ardent, fervid.

**ver mil ion** (vər mil′yən), *adj.* bright red.

**ver sa tile** (vėr′sə tl), *adj.* 1. able to do many things well: *Theodore Roosevelt was a versatile man; he was successful as a statesman, soldier, sportsman, explorer, and author.* 2. fickle; inconstant. [< L *versatilis* turning, ult. < *vertere* turn] —**Syn.** 1. many-sided.

**ver sion** (vėr′zhən), *n.* 1. a translation from one language to another: *a version of the Bible.* 2. one particular statement, account, or description: *Each of the three girls had her own version of the quarrel.* 3. a special form or variant of something: *a Scottish version of the Christmas tree.* [< L *versionem,* originally, a turning < *vertere* to turn]

**verve** (vėrv), *n.* enthusiasm; energy; vigor; spirit; liveliness. [< F < VL *verva* < L *verba* words]

**ves ti bule** (ves′tə byül), *n.* passage or hall between the outer door and the inside of a building.

**vex** (veks), *v.* 1. anger by trifles; annoy; provoke. 2. disturb; trouble. [< L *vexare*]

**vi al** (vī′əl), *n.* a small glass bottle for holding medicines or the like; bottle.

**vice** (vīs), *n.* 1. an evil habit or tendency: *Lying and cruelty are vices.* 2. evil; wickedness. 3. an undesirable habit; fault; defect. [< OF < L *vitium*] —**Syn.** 2. sin.

**vict ual** (vit′l), *n.* Usually, **victuals,** *pl.* Informal or Dialect. food. [< OF *vitaille* < L *victualia,* pl., ult. < *vivere* live]

**vig il** (vij′əl), *n.* 1. a staying awake for some purpose; a watching; watch: *All night the mother kept vigil over the sick child.* 2. a night spent in prayer. 3. **vigils,** *pl.* devotions, prayers, services, etc., on the night before a religious festival. 4. the day and night before a solemn religious festival. [< L *vigilia* < *vigil* watchful]

**vig or ous** (vig′ər əs), *adj.* full of vigor; strong and active; energetic; forceful: *wage a vigorous war against disease.* —**vig′or ous ly,** *adv.* —**vig′or ous ness,** *n.*

**vile** (vīl), *adj.,* **vil er, vil est.** 1. very bad: *vile weather.* 2. foul; disgusting; obnoxious: *a vile smell.* 3. evil; low; immoral: *vile language.* 4. poor; mean; lowly: *the vile tasks of the kitchen.* [< OF < L *vilis* cheap]

**vil la** (vil′ə), *n.* a house in the country or suburbs, sometimes at the seashore. A villa is usually a large or elegant residence. [< Ital. < L]

**vi o la tion** (vī′ə lā′shən), *n.* 1. use of force; violence. 2. a breaking (of a law, rule, agreement, promise, etc.); infringement. 3. interruption or disturbance. 4. treatment (of a holy thing) with disrespect or contempt.

**vi per** (vī′pər), *n.* 1. a thick-bodied, poisonous snake with a pair of large perforated fangs. 2. a spiteful, treacherous person. [< L *vipera* < *vivus* alive + *parere* bring forth]

**vir tu al ly** (vėr′chü əl ē), *adv.* in effect, though not in name; actually; really.

**vis age** (viz′ij), *n.* 1. face. 2. appearance. [< OF *visage* < *vis* face < L *visus* a look < *videre* see]

**vis cer a** (vis′ər ə), *n. pl. of* **vis cus** (vis′kəs). the soft inside parts of the body.

hat, āge, fär; let, ēqual, tėrm;
it, īce; hot, ōpen, ôrder;
oil, out; cup, put, rüle;
ch, child; ng, long; sh, she;
th, thin; ᴛʜ, then; zh, measure;

ə represents *a* in about, *e* in taken,
*i* in pencil, *o* in lemon, *u* in circus.

< = from, derived from, taken from.

The heart, stomach, liver, intestines, kidneys, etc., are viscera.

**vise** (vīs), *n.* 1. tool having two jaws moved by a screw, used to hold an object firmly while work is being done on it. 2. anything used as a vise to grip or hold. Also, *esp. Brit.* **vice.** [< OF *vis* screw < VL *vitium* < L *vitis* vine]

**vis ta** (vis′tə), *n.* 1. view seen through a narrow opening or passage. 2. a mental view: *Education should open up new vistas.* [< Ital. *vista,* ult. < L *videre* see]

**vol can ic** (vol kan′ik), *adj.* 1. of or caused by a volcano; having to do with volcanoes: *a volcanic eruption.* 2. characterized by the presence of volcanoes: *volcanic country.* 3. like a volcano; liable to break out violently: *a volcanic temper.* —**vol can′i cal ly,** *adv.*

**vo lu mi nous** (və lü′mə nəs), *adj.* of great size; very bulky; large: *A voluminous cloak covered him from head to foot.* —**vo lu′mi nous ly,** *adv.*

**voo doo** (vü′dü), *n., pl.* **-doos.** 1. mysterious rites, including magic and conjuration. Voodoo came from Africa; belief in it still prevails among some Negroes of the West Indies and southern United States. 2. person who practices such magic. [Am. E; of African origin]

**vo ra cious** (və rā′shəs), *adj.* 1. eating much; greedy in eating; ravenous. 2. very eager; unable to be satisfied. [< L *vorax, -acis* greedy] —**vo ra′cious ly,** *adv.*

**vor tex** (vôr′teks), *n., pl.* **-tex es** or **-ti ces.** 1. a whirling mass of water, air, etc., that sucks in everything near it; whirlpool; whirlwind. 2. whirl of activity or other situation from which it is hard to escape: *The two nations were unwillingly drawn into the vortex of war.*

**vul ner a ble** (vul′nər ə bl), *adj.* 1. capable of being wounded or injured; open to attack. 2. sensitive to criticism, temptations, influences, etc.: *Most people are vulnerable to ridicule.* [< LL *vulnerabilis* wounding, ult. < *vulnus* wound] —**vul′ner a bly,** *adv.*

**wail** (wāl), *v.i.* 1. cry loud and long because of grief or pain: *The baby wailed.* 2. make a mournful or shrill sound: *The wind wailed around the old house.* 3. lament; mourn. —*v.t.* 1. grieve for or because of; bewail. 2. utter (a wailing cry, bad news, etc.). —*n.* 1. a long cry of grief or pain. 2. a sound like such a cry: *the wail of a hungry coyote, the wail of a siren.* [< Scand. (Old Icelandic) *vǣla*] —**wail'er**, *n.*

**wan** (won), *adj.*, **wan ner, wan nest.** 1. pale; lacking natural color: *Her face looked wan after her long illness.* 2. looking worn or tired; faint; weak: *The sick boy gave the doctor a wan smile.* [OE *wann* dark]

**wane** (wān), *v.*, **waned, wan ing.** 1. become smaller; become smaller gradually. 2. decline in power, influence, importance, etc. 3. decline in strength, intensity, etc.: *The light of day wanes in the evening.* 4. draw to a close: *Summer wanes as autumn approaches.* —*n.* a waning. [OE *wanian*]

**wan ton** (won'tən), *adj.* 1. reckless; heartless: *That bad boy hurts animals from wanton cruelty.* 2. without reason or excuse: *a wanton attack, wanton mischief.* 3. not moral; not chaste: *a wanton woman.* 4. *Poetic.* frolicsome; playful: *a wanton breeze, a wanton child.* —*n.* a wanton person or thing. —**wan'ton ly**, *adv.*

**warp** (wôrp), *n.* the threads running lengthwise in a fabric. The warp is crossed by the weft. [OE *weorpan* throw]

**war rant** (wôr'ənt or wor'ənt), *v.* 1. authorize: *The law warrants his arrest.* 2. justify: *Nothing can warrant such rudeness.* 3. give one's word for; guarantee; promise: *The storekeeper warranted the quality of the coffee.* 4. *Informal.* declare positively; certify. [< OF *warant* < Gmc.] —**Syn.** 3. assure. 4. affirm, attest.

**wax** (waks), *n. esp. Brit.* a fit of anger; a rage.

**weal** (wēl), *n. Archaic.* well-being; prosperity; happiness: *Good citizens act for the public weal.* [OE *wela*]

**wean** (wēn), *v.* accustom (a child or young animal) to food other than its mother's milk. [OE *wenian*]

**weft** (weft), *n.* the threads running from side to side across a fabric; the woof. [OE *weft* < *wefan* weave]

**wench** (wench), *n.* 1. girl or young woman. 2. a woman servant.

**wheel** (hwēl), —*v.i.* 1. turn: *She wheeled around suddenly.* 2. turn or revolve about an axis or center; rotate. 3. move or perform in a curved or circular direction; circle: *gulls wheeling about.*

**where as** (hwer az', hwar az'), *conj.* 1. on the contrary; but; while: *Some children like school, whereas others do not.* 2. considering that; since: *"Whereas the people of the colonies have been grieved and burdened with taxes."*

**where fore** (hwar'fôr, hwer'fôr, hwar'fōr, or hwer'fōr), *adv.* 1. for what reason? why? 2. for which reason; therefore; so. —*conj.* for what reason; why. —*n.* reason. [< *where* + *for* prep.]

**where with al** (hwar'wiᴛʜ ôl or hwer'wiᴛʜ ôl), *n.* means, supplies, or money needed: *Has she the wherewithal to pay for the trip?*

**whet** (hwet), *v.*, **whet ted, whet ting.** 1. sharpen by rubbing: *whet a knife.* 2. make keen or eager; stimulate: *The smell of food whetted my appetite.* [OE *hwettan*]

**whey** (hwā), *n.* the watery part of milk that separates from the curd when milk sours and becomes coagulated or when cheese is made. [OE *hwǣg*]

**whim** (hwim), *n.* a sudden fancy or notion; freakish or capricious idea or desire: *Her whim for gardening won't last long.* [probably < Scand. Cf. Icelandic *hvim* unsteady look.]

**whim si cal** (hwim'zə kəl), *adj.* 1. full of whims; having many odd notions or fancies; capricious: *a whimsical person.* 2. of or like a whim or whims; odd; fanciful: *a whimsical expression.* —**whim'si cal ly,** *adv.* —**whim'si cal ness.** *n.*

**wick et** (wik'it), *n.* 1. in croquet, a wire arch stuck in the ground to knock the ball through. 2. in cricket: **a.** either of the two sets of sticks that one side tries to hit with the ball. **b.** the level space between these.

**wield** (wēld), *v.* hold and use; manage; control: *A soldier wields the sword. The people wield the power in a democracy.* [OE *wieldan*]

**wind break** (wind'brāk'), *n.* shelter from the wind. [Am.E]

**window-jamb,** see **jamb.**

**wing-toed,** *adj.* having to do with a kind of shoe in which the portion covering the toe, often in a perforated pattern, comes to a point in the center and extends backward along each side of the shoe.

**with al** (wiᴛʜ ôl' or with ôl'), *Archaic.* —*adv.* with it all; as well; besides; also: *The lady is rich and fair and wise withal.* —*prep.* with. [< *with* + *all*]

**with y** (wiᴛʜ'ē or with'ē), *n., pl.* **with ies.** willow or osier; any tough, easily bent twig suitable for binding things together. —*adj.* tough and flexible as a withy; made of withy. [OE *wiᴛʜig*]

**woe be gone** (wō'bi gôn' or wō'bi gon'), *adj.* looking sad, sorrowful, or wretched. Also, **wobegone.**

**wont** (wunt or wōnt), *adj.* accustomed: *He was wont to read the paper at breakfast.* [originally pp., ult. < OE *wunian* be accustomed]

**wrath** (rath or räth), *n.* very great anger; rage. [OE *wrǣththu*] —**Syn.** ire, fury, indignation, resentment.

**wreak** (rēk), *v.* 1. give expression to; work off (feelings, desires, etc.): *The cruel boy wreaked his bad temper on his dog.* 2. inflict (vengeance, punishment, etc.). 3. *Archaic.* avenge. [OE *wrecan*]

**writhe** (rīᴛʜ), *v.*, **writhed, writhed** or (*Obs. except Poetic*) **with en** (riᴛʜ'ən), **writh ing.** 1. twist and turn; twist: *The snake writhed along the branch. The wounded man writhed in agony.* 2. suffer mentally; be very uncomfortable.

**wrought** (rôt), *v.* a pt. and a pp. of **work.** —*adj.* 1. made: *The gate was wrought with great skill.* 2. formed with care; not rough or crude.

**yoke** (yōk), *n.* 1. a wooden frame to fasten two work animals together. 2. pair fastened together by a yoke: *The plow was drawn by a yoke of oxen.* 3. any frame connecting two other parts. [OE *geoc*]

**Yo ko ha ma** (yō'kə hä'mə), *n.* seaport in SE Japan. 1,375,000.

**zeal ous** (zel'əs), *adj.* full of zeal; eager; earnest; enthusiastic: *The children made zealous efforts to clean up the house for the party.* [< Med.L *zelosus* < L *zelus* zeal < Gk. *zelos*]

**ze nith** (zē'nith), *n.* 1. the point in the heavens directly overhead. 2. the highest point: *At the zenith of its power Rome ruled all of civilized Europe.* [< OF or Med.L *senit* < Arabic *samt (ar-rās)* the way (over the head)]

# Index of Authors and Titles

ANONYMOUS; *The Housewife's Lament*, 242
*Antigone*, 406
*Aphrodite Metropolis*, 218
ARCHILOCHOS; *The Fox and the Hedgehog*, 400; *The Good-Natured*, 401; *I Do Despise a Tall General*, 400; *May He Lose His Way*, 223; *Some Saian Mountaineer*, 400; *There's Nothing Now*, 401; *When You Upbraid Me*, 401
ARGENTARIUS, MARCUS; *Hesiod, Fortunate Deliverance From*, 398
ASIMOV, ISAAC; *My Planet 'Tis of Thee*, 186
*At the Theatre*, 225
*Bargain*, 47
*Barrio Boy*, from, 468
*Bean Eaters, The*, 238
BENÉT, STEPHEN VINCENT; *By the Waters of Babylon*, 134; *Melora Vilas*, 236
BENÉT, WILLIAM ROSE; *The Skater of Ghost Lake*, 258
*Between the Dark and the Daylight*, 454
*Birthday in the House of the Poor*, 247
*Black Elk Speaks*, from, 168
BOURKE-WHITE, MARGARET; from *Portrait of Myself*, 146
BROOKS, GWENDOLYN; *The Bean Eaters*, 238
BROUN, HEYWOOD; *The Fifty-first Dragon*, 128
*By Morning*, 220
*By the Waters of Babylon*, 134
CATULLUS; *Lesbia Is Always Talking Scandal About Me*, 402; *Living, Dear Lesbia, Is Useless Without Loving*, 402; *My Woman Says There Is No One She Would Rather Marry*, 402; *Suffenus, Varus, Whom You Know So Well*, 402
CHAYEFSKY, PADDY; *The Mother*, 516
CHEKHOV, ANTON; *The Lottery Ticket*, 78
*Claudine's Book*, 23
CLIFTON, LUCILLE; *Miss Rosie*, 235
COLERIDGE, SAMUEL TAYLOR; *The Rime of the Ancient Mariner*, 262
CONNELL, RICHARD; *The Most Dangerous Game*, 9
*Conquerors, The*, 228
*Conscientious Objector*, 227
*Courage That My Mother Had, The*, 234
CUMMINGS, E. E.; *dying is fine)but Death*, 461
DALEY, ROBERT; *The Risk Takers*, 198
*Daybreak in Alabama*, 459
*Death of Socrates, The*, 396
*Dedication of a Mirror*, 398
*Dog That Bit People, The*, 194
DOUGLASS, FREDERICK; from *Narrative of the Life of Frederick Douglass*, 161
DURRELL, GERALD; *The Rose-Beetle Man*, 179
*Dust of Snow*, 214
*dying is fine)but Death*, 461
*Earth Dweller*, 215
*El Momento más Grave de la Vida*, 251
*Endless Streetcar Ride into the Night and the Tinfoil Noose, The*, 55
*Epitaph for Slain Spartans*, 398

*Exposure*, 261
FEARING, KENNETH; *Aphrodite Metropolis*, 218; *Thirteen O'Clock*, 260
FEINBERG, LEONARD; *Fire Walking in Ceylon*, 492
*Fifty-first Dragon, The*, 128
*Fire Walking in Ceylon*, 492
*Flight of Aeneas, The*, 381
*Fog*, 219
*Forbidden Fries*, 449
*Fox and the Hedgehog, The*, 400
*freddy the rat perishes*, 460
FROST, ROBERT; *Dust of Snow*, 214; *Wild Grapes*, 464
GAINES, ERNEST; *The Sky Is Gray*, 61
GALARZA, ERNESTO; from *Barrio Boy*, 468
GIBBS, WOLCOTT; *Outwitting the Lightning*, 489
*Good-Natured, The*, 401
*Grass*, 232
GRAVES, ROBERT; *Traveller's Curse After Misdirection*, 222
GREEN, ROGER LANCELYN; *Odysseus in Ithaca*, 389
GUARESCHI, GIOVANNI; *Forbidden Fries*, 449
GUTHRIE, A. B.; *Bargain*, 47
HALE, NANCY; *Between the Dark and the Daylight*, 454
HAN-SHAN; *I Used to Be Fairly Poor*, 241
*Haunted*, 256
HAY, SARA HENDERSON; *Portrait of a Certain Gentleman*, 239; *The Witch*, 257
HAYDEN, ROBERT; *The Whipping*, 243
HERBERT, SIR A. P.; *At the Theatre*, 225
*Here Dead Lie We*, 226
*Hesiod, Fortunate Deliverance From*, 398
*Highland Boy, The*, 442
*Housewife's Lament, The*, 242
HOUSMAN, A. E.; *Here Dead Lie We*, 226; *Yonder See the Morning Blink*, 244
*How Everything Happens*, 252
HUGHES, LANGSTON; *Daybreak in Alabama*, 459
HURST, JAMES; *The Scarlet Ibis*, 111
*Idealist, The*, 82
*I Do Despise a Tall General*, 400
IKEDA, PATRICIA Y.; *Insomniac*, 245
*Inscription for the Tomb of Timon*, 398
*Insomniac*, 245
*Item*, 253
*I Used to Be Fairly Poor*, 241
JONAS, GERALD; *Lessons*, 248
JONES, LEROI; *Ka'Ba*, 255
JONES, RICHARD M.; *Trouble in Mind*, 240
*Ka'Ba*, 255
*Lesbia Is Always Talking Scandal About Me*, 402
*Lessons*, 248
*Living, Dear Lesbia, Is Useless Without Loving*, 402
LOEWINSOHN, RON; *Lots of Lakes*, 217
*Lots of Lakes*, 217
*Lottery Ticket, The*, 78
LOWELL, AMY; *Haunted*, 256
LUCILIUS; *On a Fortune-Teller*, 399

Luther, 37
Manoeuvre, The, 221
MARCUS ARGENTARIUS; *Hesiod Fortunate Deliverance From*, 398
MARQUIS, DON; *freddy the rat perishes*, 460
MARSHALL, PAULE; *To Da-duh, in Memoriam*, 120
MASEFIELD, JOHN; *The Surprise*, 376
*May He Lose His Way*, 223
McGINLEY, PHYLLIS; *The Conquerors*, 228
*Melora Vilas*, 236
MILLAY, EDNA ST. VINCENT; *Conscientious Objector*, 227; *The Courage That My Mother Had*, 234
MIMNERMUS OF COLOPHON; *The Warrior of the Past*, 399
*Miss Rosie*, 235
*Most Dangerous Game, The*, 9
*Most Perilous Moment in Life, The*, 250
*Mother, The*, 230
*Mother, The* (play), 516
*My Enemy Was Dreaming*, 231
*My Planet 'Tis of Thee*, 186
*My Woman Says There Is No One She Would Rather Marry*, 402
*Narrative of the Life of Frederick Douglass*, from, 161
NEIHARDT, JOHN G.; from *Black Elk Speaks*, 168
NEMEROV, HOWARD; *Item*, 253
NEUGEBOREN, JAY; *Luther*, 37
NICHOLS, JEANNETTE; *Birthday in the House of the Poor*, 247
*Nine Charms Against the Hunter*, 224
NORRIS, LESLIE; *The Highland Boy*, 442
O'CONNOR, FRANK; *The Idealist*, 82
*Odysseus in Ithaca*, 389
*On a Fortune-Teller*, 399
*On Mauros the Rhetor*, 399
*Outwitting the Lightning*, 489
OVID; *The Story of Cadmus*, 371; *The Story of Daedalus and Icarus*, 369
PALLADAS; *On Mauros the Rhetor*, 399
PEARSE, PADRAIC; *The Mother*, 230
*Peter Two*, 2
PLATO; *The Death of Socrates*, 396; *Dedication of a Mirror*, 398; *The Prophecy of Socrates*, 394
*Portrait of a Certain Gentleman*, 239
*Portrait of Myself*, from, 146
*Prophecy of Socrates, The*, 394
PTOLEMAIOS THE ASTRONOMER; *Inscription for the Tomb of Timon*, 398
*Rain on Tanyard Hollow*, 89
*Reading Problem, A*, 97
*Rime of the Ancient Mariner, The*, 262
*Risk Takers, The*, 198
*Romeo and Juliet*, 282
*Rose-Beetle Man, The*, 179

*Running*, 458
RUSSELL, NORMAN; *My Enemy Was Dreaming*, 231
SANDBURG, CARL; *Fog*, 219; *Grass*, 232
*Scarlet Ibis, The*, 111
SHAKESPEARE, WILLIAM; *Romeo and Juliet*, 282
SHAW, IRWIN; *Peter Two*, 2
SHEPHERD, JEAN; *The Endless Streetcar Ride into the Night and the Tinfoil Noose*, 55
SIMONIDES OF CEOS; *Epitaph for Slain Spartans*, 398
*Skater of Ghost Lake, The*, 258
*Sky Is Gray, The*, 61
*Some Saian Mountaineer*, 400
*Song of the Sky Loom*, 216
SOPHOCLES; *Antigone*, 406
STAFFORD, JEAN· *A Reading Problem*, 97
STAFFORD, WILLIAM; *Earth Dweller*, 215
STEWART, JOHN D.; *Vulture Country*, 483
*Story of Cadmus, The*, 371
*Story of Daedalus and Icarus, The*, 369
STUART, JESSE; *Rain on Tanyard Hollow*, 89
*Suffenus, Varus, Whom You Know So Well*, 402
*Surprise, The*, 376
SWADOS, HARVEY; *Claudine's Book*, 23
SWENSON, MAY; *By Morning*, 220; *How Everything Happens*, 252
TEASDALE, SARA; *There Will Come Soft Rains*, 233
TEWA INDIAN; *Song of the Sky Loom*, 216
*There's Nothing Now*, 401
*There Will Come Soft Rains*, 233
*Thirteen O'Clock*, 260
THURBER, JAMES; *The Dog That Bit People*, 194
*To Da-duh, in Memoriam*, 120
*Traveller's Curse After Misdirection*, 222
*Trouble in Mind*, 240
UPDIKE, JOHN; *Exposure*, 261
*Vale from Carthage*, 463
VALLEJO, CÉSAR; *El Momento más Grave de la Vida*, 251; *The Most Perilous Moment in Life*, 250
VIDAL, GORE; *Visit to a Small Planet*, 498
VIERECK, PETER; *Vale from Carthage*, 463
VIRGIL; *The Flight of Aeneas*, 381
*Visit to a Small Planet*, 498
*Vulture Country*, 483
WAGONER, DAVID; *Nine Charms Against the Hunter*, 224
*Warrior of the Past, The*, 399
*When You Upbraid Me*, 401
*Whipping, The*, 243
WILBUR, RICHARD; *Running*, 458
*Wild Grapes*, 464
WILLIAMS, WILLIAM CARLOS; *The Manoeuvre*, 221
*Witch, The*, 257
*Yonder See the Morning Blink*, 244

# Art and Photography